A Practical Introduction
to Environmental Law

A Practical Introduction to Environmental Law

Joel A. Mintz
Professor of Law
Nova Southeastern University Shepard Broad College of Law

John C. Dernbach
Commonwealth Professor of Environmental Law and Sustainability
Widener University Commonwealth Law School

Steve C. Gold
Professor of Law and Judge Raymond J. Dearie Scholar
Rutgers Law School

Kalyani Robbins
Associate Professor of Law
Florida International University College of Law

Clifford Villa
Assistant Professor of Law
University of New Mexico School of Law

Wendy Wagner
Contributing Author
Joe A. Worsham Centennial Professor in Law
University of Texas School of Law

CAROLINA ACADEMIC PRESS
Durham, North Carolina

LCCN: 2017947250
ISBN: 978-1-5221-0413-1
eISBN: 978-0-76989-128-6

Carolina Academic Press, LLC
700 Kent Street
Durham, North Carolina 27701
Telephone (919) 489-7486
Fax (919) 493-5668
www.cap-press.com

Printed in the United States of America

For my grandsons, Sam and Karl, and future generations.
J.A.M.

For Becky, Tess, and Ethan, and all who will inherit this world.
J.C.D.

To the memory of Jack and Annette, who made sure that their children received the education that they themselves were denied, and for Jenny, in gratitude for her constant love and support.
S.C.G.

For Skyler, Max, and the planet they will one day share with their children.
K.R.

For Olivia and Julian, as always; *para Angelica, el comienzo…*
C.V.

Contents

Standing
Overton Park
Chevron

2

Table of Principal Cases

Preface

For many people Environmental Law is a difficult subject to learn—and to teach—yet fascinating, engaging, and satisfying to practice. This book is intended to make the subject accessible for the beginning student, and less burdensome for the instructor, while providing a fair sampling of the practical challenges faced by environmental attorneys. Its five co-authors and contributing author have all had significant experience in environmental practice as well as in teaching the subject. We have included practice problems throughout the book that reflect our own practice and classroom teaching experiences and those of others. That emphasis is obviously reflected in the title of the book. It is, indeed, a "practical" introduction.

In some respects, this book includes basic topics covered by other casebooks in the field. After providing an introduction grounded in a varied set of the philosophies and perspectives that undergird the field, the book considers some administrative law doctrines particularly relevant to Environmental Law. It then surveys a number of the statutes, regulations, and judicial opinions widely seen as the "canon" of the field. Thus, it focuses in turn on such fundamental legislative enactments as the National Environmental Policy Act, the Endangered Species Act, the Clean Air Act, the Clean Water Act, the Resource Conservation and Recovery Act, CERCLA (or Superfund), the Federal Insecticide, Fungicide and Rodenticide Act, and the Toxic Substances Control Act, and a selection of the key judicial opinions and regulations those major statutes have spawned.

At the same time, however, this book differs from other casebooks in important respects. Beyond its practice problem orientation, we have included substantive coverage of environmental permitting—a facet of practice often engaged in by environmental lawyers. We have also included considerable material on the immense global challenges of climate change resulting from human emissions of greenhouse gasses, for which there is a striking and regrettable paucity of federal law. We focus therefore on various scientific and policy aspects of the issue, which we believe is in urgent need of both mitigation and adaptation. This book also pays more attention than most other textbooks to enforcement, a crucial aspect of environmental regulation; and it treats the most crucial components of the important amendments to the Toxic Substances Control Act passed by Congress in 2016.

An explanation of the editing conventions we have employed seems in order. Nearly all of the judicial opinions, passages from books and articles, and other materials included in this work have been edited for the sake of brevity and clarity. Although some dissenting and concurring judicial opinions have been included in part or whole, others have been entirely omitted. We have also edited out selected language and citations from published decisions and other materials. Where materials in original texts were not included we have indicated this by adding ellipses immediately before the excised materials. We also sometimes added words, phrases or brief summaries of extended passages that otherwise were omitted. These editor—added materials are surrounded in the text by brackets.

As this book goes to press, Environmental Law has entered a period of tumult and potential change. The precise nature and full extent of that change cannot now be predicted. We plan to carefully follow any and all significant changes in the field and to supplement this book as frequently as necessary to reflect them.

The co-authors have enjoyed working together to produce this book and we have learned much from one another in the process. We believe that competent environmental lawyers are now needed more than ever. We earnestly hope that this book will provide a valuable tool for effective instruction, and a useful foundation for the training of ethical, knowledgeable, and effective environmental lawyers. Much will be at stake in their professional efforts.

Joel A. Mintz
John C. Dernbach
Steve C. Gold
Kalyani Robbins
Clifford Villa
Wendy Wagner (contributing author)

Acknowledgments

The authors wish to thank the following individuals and institutions for their help in the preparation of this book.

Nova Southeastern University law librarian Becka Rich provided persistent, invaluable help in securing the consent of copyright holders to republish excerpts of their writings. Librarian Judith Simms of Rutgers Law School also went beyond the call of duty to assist with permissions and research.

Seattle University School of Law graduate Tyler Stewart provided stellar research support for the chapter on the Clean Water Act. University of New Mexico School of Law graduate Benjamin Guevara provided thorough editing and proofreading for the same. Rutgers Law School student Kylie Huff assisted immeasurably with the design, planning, and case selection for several chapters. Rutgers Law School students Jaimee Glinn, Christina Stripp, and Christopher Taillefer provided vital research assistance, cite checking and proofreading. Sylviane Gold brought her formidable editorial skills to bear at several critical junctures. Jennifer Aley carefully read and re-read portions of the manuscript, making improvements with each reading. Karen Rose, faculty assistant at Nova Southeastern University provided prompt and skillful typing and proofreading assistance.

Though he passed away before this book was written, Professor Emeritus Frank Grad of Columbia Law School selected some of the cases that form parts of chapter two of this book. His life's work was a guide and inspiration to generations of public interest environmental lawyers and we honor his memory.

The drafting of some practice problems was materially assisted by some members of the American Bar Association Section on Environment, Energy and Natural Resources—active environmental law practitioners who graciously responded to an online request for their own practice-based problems. In particular, we thank the following environmental lawyers for their thoughtful contributions: Scott Badenoch (who contributed the Drinking Water problem described in note 2 on pages 513 and 514), Ghislaine Bruner (Steptoe and Johnson), Pamela Elkow (Carmody, Torrance, Sandak, and Hennessey) and Sorrell Negro (Robinson and Cole).

We also acknowledge, with gratitude, the following permissions to republish segments from the works of other authors:

Fiona Harvey, "Paris Climate Change Agreement: The World's Greatest Diplomatic Success," *The Guardian*, December 14, 2015, reprinted with permission.

Alexandra Klass, "Federalism at Work: Recent Developments in Public Trust Lawsuits to Limit Greenhouse Gas Emissions," reprinted with permission.

William Easterling, III, Brian H. Hurd and Joel B. Smith, "Coping with Global Climate Change: The Role Of Adaptation in the United States," 2004, reprinted with permission by courtesy of Center for Climate and Energy Solutions (formerly the Pew Center on Global Climate Change).

National Research Council, "Limiting the Magnitude of Future Climate Change," the National Academies Press, 2010, reprinted with permission.

Michelle Leighton, "Climate Change and Migration: Key Issues for Legal Protection of Migrants and Displaced Persons," (2010), reprinted with permission of the German Marshall Fund of the United States.

Michael Specter, "The Climate Fixers: Is There a Technological Solution to Global Warming," *The New Yorker,* reprinted with permission.

Naomi Klein, "Geoengineering: Testing the Waters," *The New York Times*, October 27, 2012, reprinted with permission.

Jonathan S. Adams, Bruce A. Stein, and Lynn S. Kutner, "Precious Heritage" The Status of Biodiversity in the United States," in Bruce A. Stein, Lynn S. Kutner and Jonathan S. Adams, eds. *Biodiversity: Our Precious Heritage* (Oxford University Press, 2000), reprinted with permission.

R. Edward Grumbine, "What is Ecosystem Management?" 8 *Conservation Biology* 27 (1994), John Wiley and Sons, Inc., reprinted with permission.

James Salzman, "Valuing Ecosystem Services," 24 *Ecology L.Q.* 887 (1994), reprinted with permission.

Aldo Leopold, *A Sand County Almanac* (Oxford University Press, 2014), reprinted with permission.

R. T. Pierrehumbert, "Climate Change: A Catastrophe in Slow Motion," 6 *Chi. J. Int'l. L.* 573 (2006), reprinted with permission.

Alejandro E. Camacho, "Adapting Governance to Climate Change: Managing Uncertainty Through a Learning Infrastructure," 59 *Emory L.J.* (2009), reprinted with permission.

International Institute for Sustainable Development (IISD), "Summary of the United Nations Conference on Sustainable Development," 27 *Earth Negotiations Bulletin* No. 51 1 (June 25, 2012), reprinted with permission.

Robert Stavins, "Paris Agreement—A Good Foundation for Meaningful Progress," December 12, 2015, reprinted with permission.

Ahmed Djoglaf, "Climate Change and Biodiversity in Polar Regions," 8 *Sust. Dev. L. and Pol.* 14 (2008), reprinted with permission.

UNFCCC, United Nations, "Framework Convention on Climate Change," reprinted with permission.

Michael R. Greenberg, "The Environmental Impact Statement after Two Generations: Managing Environmental Power," (Routledge/Taylor and Francis Group, 2012), reprinted with permission.

United Nations, "Climate Change 2014 Synthesis Report," from *Climate Change 2014, Synthesis Report of Working Groups I, II, and III to the Fifth Assessment Report of the Intergovernmental Panel on Climate Change* (Core Writing Team, Pachauri, R.K. and Meyer, L. eds), IPCC, Geneva, Switzerland, 2014, reprinted with permission.

United Nations, "Convention on Biological Diversity," 1992, reprinted with permission.

Garrett Hardin, "The Tragedy of the Commons," 162 *Science* 1243 (1968), reprinted with permission.

Rachel Carson, *Silent Spring* (Houghton Mifflin, 1962 and subsequently), reprinted with permission.

Terry L. Anderson and Donald R. Leal, *Free Market Environmentalism* (Palgrave, 2001), reprinted with permission.

Frank Ackerman and Lisa Heinzerling, *Priceless* (The New Press, 2004), reprinted with permission.

Goldie Blumenstyk, "The Price of Research," *Chronicle of Higher Education*, October 31, 2003, reprinted with permission.

Joel A. Mintz, "Taking Congress's Words Seriously: Towards a Sound Construction of NEPA's Long Overlooked Interpretation Mandate," 38 *Envtl. L.* 1031 (2008), reprinted with permission.

Olga L. Moya and Andrew L. Fono, Federal Environmental Law: The User's Guide (West Academic, 3d ed. 2011), reprinted by permission of West Academic. Michael R. Greenberg, The Environmental Impact Statement after Two Generations (Routledge, 2012), reprinted with permission.

Randolph L. Hill, "An Overview of RCRA: The 'Mind-Numbing' Provisions of the Most Complicated Environmental Statute," 21 Envtl. L. Rep. 10,254 (May 1991), Copyright© 1991, Environmental Law Institute®, Washington, DC, reprinted with permission from ELI®.

Robert W. Adler, "In Defense of NEPA: The Case of the Legacy Parkway," 26 J. Land Resources & Envtl. L. 297 (2006), reprinted with permission.

Richard G. Stoll, *Coping with the RCRA Hazardous Waste System: A Few Practical Points for Fun and Profit*, C414 ALI-ABA (1989), reprinted with permission from American Law Institute CLE, www.alicle.org.

Michael Robinson-Dorn, "The Trail Smelter: Is What's Past Prologue?, EPA Blazes a New Trail for CERCLA," 14 *N.Y.U. Envtl. L.J.* 233 (2006), reprinted with permission.

A Practical Introduction
to Environmental Law

Chapter 1

Approaching Environmental Law: Some Theories and Perspectives

What is Environmental Law? We might say that say Environmental Law includes all legal regimes that shape the way human beings interact with their environment. That definition would be inclusive enough, but what would it leave out? *Every* human activity affects the environment *somehow*. As the nineteenth-century conservationist John Muir observed, "When we try to pick up anything in the universe, we find that it is hitched to everything else." So in some sense all law is environmental law; but Environmental Law cannot be all law.

The precise boundaries of Environmental Law—as a law school subject, a body of law, or a field of practice—are somewhat uncertain. But we can say that recognition of Environmental Law as a distinct entity began with the environmental movement of the 1970s and the burst of federal legislation enacted in response to that movement. Today, the concerns addressed by that body of statutes are widely recognized to constitute the core of Environmental Law, although no two professors, courses, or coursebooks are apt to include or exclude exactly the same material in their teaching. We have chosen to include in this book a range of Environmental Law topics that are important and timely, and that will allow you to synthesize general principles that you can apply to new Environmental Law challenges as they arise in your law practice—or simply in your life as a concerned citizen of Earth.

As a field of practice, Environmental Law is challenging, exciting, and varied. Environmental lawyers practice in every imaginable setting—large firms, small firms, government agencies, non-profit advocacy or legal services groups, trade associations, and in the legal departments of businesses. The subject matter of their work may be highly specialized or as broad as the scope of Environmental Law itself. They may engage in any of the activities that mark the practice of law—client counseling, litigation, negotiation and alternative dispute resolution, and structuring transactions.

Moreover, no environmental lawyer is only an environmental lawyer. As will become apparent throughout this book, Environmental Law touches and is affected by many other bodies of law that you may study in different law school courses—constitutional law, property law, tort law, land use regulation, civil procedure, and administrative law, to name a few of the major ones. Your detailed study of Environmental Law will enhance your understanding of many of these intersecting fields.

Conversely, many lawyers who do not specialize in Environmental Law nevertheless find that environmental law affects their practices and their clients. No significant real estate transaction, corporate merger or acquisition, construction project, securities disclosure, or business operation can (or should) proceed without consideration of the implications of Environmental Law on that undertaking. In such settings, specialists will likely be responsible for the Environmental Law issues, but the others on the legal team will need to be able to understand the Environmental Law issues well enough at least to assess their significance to the overall effort.

The chapters that follow focus on many of the key doctrines of Environmental Law — legal precepts drawn from statutes, judicial decisions, and agency regulations, all within the context of legal regulation of human activities that affect the natural environment and human health. Interspersed within those materials is a realistic set of practical problems — drawn from the "real world" experiences of experienced practicing attorneys — that reveal the kinds of challenges faced by environmental attorneys in their representation of clients.

This chapter, by contrast, will introduce you to some writings that exemplify or provide the theoretical underpinnings that helped Environmental Law develop, as well as of contentions advanced in criticism of existing Environmental Law. It includes examples of traditional economic analysis, competing economic perspectives, and approaches that fundamentally differ from the prescriptions and observations of economists. It also focuses on Environmental Justice, a dynamic and relatively new facet of the field.

I. Some Sources Informing Environmental Laws and Policies

A. Ethical Perspectives

Aldo Leopold, A Sand County Almanac

(Oxford University Press, 1989) (first published 1949)

The Ethical Sequence

The first ethics dealt with the relation between individuals; the Mosaic Decalogue is an example. Later accretions dealt with the relation between the individual and society. The Golden Rule tries to integrate the individual to society; democracy to integrate social organization to the individual.

There is as yet no ethic dealing with man's relation to land and to the animals and plants which grow upon it. Land . . . is still property. The land-relation is still strictly economic, entailing privileges but not obligations.

The extension of ethics to this third element in human environment is, if I read the evidence correctly, an evolutionary possibility and an ecological necessity. It is the third step in a sequence. The first two have already been taken. Individual thinkers since the days of Ezekiel and Isaiah have asserted that the despoliation of land is not only inexpedient but wrong. Society, however, has not yet affirmed their belief. I regard the present conservation movement as the embryo of such an affirmation.

An ethic may be regarded as a mode of guidance for meeting ecological situations so new or intricate, or involving such deferred reactions, that the path of social expediency is not discernible to the average individual. Animal instincts are modes of guidance for the individual in meeting such situations. Ethics are possibly a kind of community instinct in-the-making.

The Community Concept

All ethics so far evolved rest upon a single premise: that the individual is a member of a community of interdependent parts. His instincts prompt him to compete for his place in that community, but his ethics prompt him also to co-operate (perhaps in order that there may be a place to compete for).

The land ethic simply enlarges the boundaries of the community to include soils, waters, plants, and animals, or collectively: the land.

This sounds simple: do we not already sing our love for and obligation to the land of the free and the home of the brave? Yes, but just what and whom do we love? Certainly not the soil, which we are sending helter-skelter downriver. Certainly not the waters, which we assume have no function except to turn turbines, float barges, and carry off sewage. Certainly not the plants, of which we exterminate whole communities without batting an eye. Certainly not the animals, of which we have already extirpated many of the largest and most beautiful species. A land ethic of course cannot prevent the alteration, management, and use of these "resources," but it does affirm their right to continued existence, and, at least in spots, their continued existence in a natural state.

In short, a land ethic changes the role of *Homo sapiens* from conqueror of the land-community to plain member and citizen of it. It implies respect for his fellow-members, and also respect for the community as such.

In human history, we have learned (I hope) that the conqueror role is eventually self-defeating. Why? Because it is implicit in such a role that the conqueror knows, *ex cathedra,* just what makes the community clock tick, and just what and who is valuable, and what and who is worthless, in community life. It always turns out that he knows neither, and this is why his conquests eventually defeat themselves.

In the biotic community, a parallel situation exists. Abraham knew exactly what the land was for: it was to drip milk and honey into Abraham's mouth. At the present moment, the assurance with which we regard this assumption is inverse to the degree of our education.

The ordinary citizen today assumes that science knows what makes the community clock tick; the scientist is equally sure that he does not. He knows that the biotic mechanism is so complex that its workings may never be fully understood.

The Ecological Consequence

Conservation is a state of harmony between men and land. Despite nearly a century of propaganda, conservation still proceeds at a snail's pace; progress still consists largely of letterhead pieties and convention oratory. On the back forty we still slip two steps backward for each forward stride.

No important change in ethics was ever accomplished without an internal change in our intellectual emphasis, loyalties, affections, and convictions. The proof that conservation has not yet touched these foundations of conduct lies in the fact that philosophy and religion have not yet heard of it. In our attempt to make conservation easy, we have made it trivial.

Substitutes for a Land Ethic

When the logic of history hungers for bread and we hand out a stone, we are at pains to explain how much the stone resembles bread. I now describe some of the stones which serve in lieu of a land ethic.

One basic weakness in a conservation system based wholly on economic motives is that most members of the land community have no economic value. Wildflowers and songbirds are examples. Of the 22,000 higher plants and animals native to Wisconsin, it is doubtful whether more than 5 per cent can be sold, fed, eaten, or otherwise put to economic use. Yet these creatures are members of the biotic community, and if (as I believe) its stability depends on its integrity, they are entitled to continuance.

When one of these non-economic categories is threatened, and if we happen to love it, we invent subterfuges to give it economic importance. At the beginning of the century songbirds were supposed to be disappearing. Ornithologists jumped to the rescue with some distinctly shaky evidence to the effect that insects would eat us up if birds failed to control them. The evidence had to be economic in order to be valid . . . .

Lack of economic value is sometimes a character not only of species or groups, but of entire biotic communities: marshes, bogs, dunes, and "deserts" are examples. Our formula in such cases is to relegate their conservation to government as refuges, monuments, or parks. The difficulty is that these communities are usually interspersed with more valuable private lands; the government cannot possibly own or control such scattered parcels. The net effect is that we have relegated some of them to ultimate extinction over large areas. If the private owner were ecologically minded, he would be proud to be the custodian of a reasonable proportion of such areas, which add diversity and beauty to his farm and his community . . . .

There is a clear tendency in American conservation to relegate to government all necessary jobs that private landowners fail to perform. Government ownership, operation, subsidy, or regulation is now widely prevalent in forestry, range management, soil and watershed management, park and wilderness conservation, fisheries management, and migratory bird management, with more to come. Most of this growth in governmental conservation is proper and logical, some of it is inevitable. That I imply no disapproval of it is implicit in the fact that I have spent most of my life working for it. Nevertheless the question arises: What is the ultimate magnitude of the enterprise? Will the tax base carry its eventual ramifications? At what point will governmental conservation, like the mastodon, become handicapped by its own dimensions? The answer, if there is any, seems to be in a land ethic, or some other force which assigns more obligation to the private landowner . . . .

To sum up: a system of conservation based solely on economic self-interest is hopelessly lopsided. It tends to ignore, and thus eventually to eliminate, many elements in the land community that lack commercial value, but that are (as far as we know) essential to its healthy functioning. It assumes, falsely, I think, that the economic parts of the biotic clock will function without the uneconomic parts. It tends to relegate to government many functions eventually too large, too complex, or too widely dispersed to be performed by government.

An ethical obligation on the part of the private owner is the only visible remedy for these situations.

The Land Pyramid

An ethic to supplement and guide the economic relation to land presupposes the existence of some mental image of land as a biotic mechanism. We can be ethical only in relation to something we can see, feel, understand, love, or otherwise have faith in.

The image commonly employed in conservation education is "the balance of nature." For reasons too lengthy to detail here, this figure of speech fails to describe accurately what little we know about the land mechanism. A much truer image is that one employed in ecology: the biotic pyramid. I shall first sketch the pyramid as a symbol of land, and later develop some of its implications in terms of land-use.

Plants absorb energy from the sun. This energy flows through a circuit called the biota, which may be represented by a pyramid consisting of layers. The bottom layer is the soil. A plant layer rests on the soil, an insect layer on the plants, a bird and rodent layer on the insects, and so on up through various animal groups to the apex layer, which consists of the larger carnivores.

The species of a layer are alike not in where they came from, or in what they look like, but rather in what they eat. Each successive layer depends on those below it for food and often for other services, and each in turn furnishes food and services to those above. Proceeding upward, each successive layer decreases in numerical abundance. Thus, for every carnivore there are hundreds of his prey, thousands of their prey, millions of insects, uncountable plants. The pyramidal form of the system reflects this numerical progression from apex to base. Man shares an intermediate layer with the bears, raccoons, and squirrels which eat both meat and vegetables.

The lines of dependency for food and other services are called food chains. Thus soil-oak-deer-Indian is a chain that has now been largely converted to soil-corn-cow-farmer. Each species, including ourselves, is a link in many chains. The deer eats a hundred plants other than oak, and the cow a hundred plants other than corn. Both, then, are links in a hundred chains. The pyramid is a tangle of chains so complex as to seem disorderly, yet the stability of the system proves it to be a highly organized structure. Its functioning depends on the co-operation and competition of its diverse parts.

Land, then, is not merely soil; it is a fountain of energy flowing through a circuit of soils, plants, and animals. Food chains are the living channels which conduct energy upwards; death and decay return it to the soil. The circuit is not closed; some energy is dissipated in decay, some is added by absorption from the air, some is stored in soils, peats, and long-lived forests; but it is a sustained circuit, like a slowly augmented revolving fund of life. There is always a net loss by downhill wash, but this is normally small and offset by the decay of rocks. It is deposited in the ocean and, in the course of geological time, raised to form new lands and new pyramids.

The velocity and character of the upward flow of energy depend on the complex structure of the plant and animal community, much as the upward flow of sap in a tree depends on its complex cellular organization. Without this complexity, normal circulation would presumably not occur. Structure means the characteristic numbers, as well as the characteristic kinds and functions, of the component species. This interdependence between the complex structure of the land and its smooth functioning as an energy unit is one of its basic attributes.

When a change occurs in one part of the circuit, many other parts must adjust themselves to it. Change does not necessarily obstruct or divert the flow of energy; evolution is a long series of self-induced changes, the net result of which has been to elaborate the flow mechanism and to lengthen the circuit. Evolutionary changes, however, are usually slow and local. Man's invention of tools has enabled him to make changes of unprecedented violence, rapidity, and scope . . . .

The combined evidence of history and ecology seems to support one general deduction: the less violent the man-made changes, the greater the probability of successful readjustment in the pyramid . . . .

A land ethic, then, reflects the existence of an ecological conscience, and this in turn reflects a conviction of individual responsibility for the health of the land. Health is the capacity of the land for self-renewal. Conservation is our effort to understand and preserve this capacity . . . .

The Outlook

It is inconceivable to me that an ethical relation to land can exist without love, respect, and admiration for land, and a high regard for its value. By value, I of course mean something far broader than mere economic value; I mean value in the philosophical sense.

Perhaps the most serious obstacle impeding the evolution of a land ethic is the fact that our educational and economic system is headed away from, rather than toward, an intense consciousness of land. Your true modern is separated from the land by many middlemen, and by innumerable physical gadgets. He has no vital relation to it; to him it is the space between cities on which crops grow. Turn him loose for a day on the land, and if the spot does not happen to be a golf links or a "scenic" area, he is bored stiff . . . .

The "key-log" which must be moved to release the evolutionary process for an ethic is simply this: quit thinking about decent land-use as solely an economic problem. Examine each question in terms of what is ethically and esthetically right, as well as what is economically expedient. A thing is right when it tends to preserve the integrity, stability, and beauty of the of the biotic community. It is wrong when it tends otherwise.

It of course goes without saying that economic feasibility limits the tether of what can or cannot be done for land. It always has and it always will. The fallacy the economic determinists have tied around our collective neck, and which we now need to cast off, is the belief that economics determines *all* land-use. This is simply not true. An innumerable host of actions and attitudes, comprising perhaps the bulk of all land relations, is determined by "the land-users" tastes and predilections, rather than by his purse. The bulk of all land relations hinges on investments of time, forethought, skill, and faith rather than on investments of cash. As a land-user thinketh, so is he . . . .

The evolution of a land ethic is an intellectual as well as emotional process. Conservation is paved with good intentions which prove to be futile, or even dangerous, because they are devoid of critical understanding either of the land, or of economic land-use. I think it is a truism that as the ethical frontier advances from the individual to the community, its intellectual content increases.

The mechanism of operation is the same for any ethic: social approbation for right actions: social disapproval for wrong actions.

By and large, our present problem is one of attitudes and implements. We are remodeling the Alhambra with a steam-shovel, and we are proud of our yardage. We shall hardly relinquish the shovel, which after all has many good points, but we are in need of gentler and more objective criteria for its successful use.

RACHEL CARSON
SILENT SPRING
(Houghton, Mifflin, 1962)

For the first time in the history of the world, every human being is now subjected to contact with dangerous chemicals, from the moment of conception until death. In the less than two decades of their use, the synthetic pesticides have been so thoroughly distributed throughout the animate and inanimate world that they occur virtually everywhere. They have been recovered from most of the major river systems and even from streams of groundwater flowing unseen through the earth. Residues of these chemicals linger in soil to which they may have been applied a dozen years before. They have entered and lodged in the bodies of fish, birds, reptiles, and domestic and wild animals so universally that scientists carrying on animal experiments find it almost impossible to locate subjects free from such contamination. They have been found in fish in remote mountain lakes, in earthworms burrowing in soil, in the eggs of birds—and in man himself. For these chemicals are now stored in the bodies of the vast majority of human beings, regardless of age. They occur in the mother's milk, and probably in the tissues of the unborn child.

All this has come about because of the sudden rise and prodigious growth of an industry for the production of man-made or synthetic chemicals with insecticidal properties. This industry is a child of the Second World War. In the course of developing agents of chemical warfare, some of the chemicals created in the laboratory were found to be lethal to insects. The discovery did not come by chance: insects were widely used to test chemicals as agents of death for man.

The result has been a seemingly endless stream of synthetic insecticides. . . . What sets the new synthetic insecticides apart is their enormous biological potency. They have immense power not merely to poison but to enter into the most vital processes of the body and change them in sinister and often deadly ways. Thus, as we shall see, they destroy the very enzymes whose function is to protect the body from harm, they block the oxidation processes from which the body receives its energy, they prevent the normal functioning of various organs, and they may initiate in certain cells the slow and irreversible change that leads to malignancy.

Yet new and more deadly chemicals are added to the list each year and new uses are devised so that contact with these materials has become practically worldwide.

As man proceeds toward his announced goal of the conquest of nature, he has written a depressing record of destruction, directed not only against the earth he inhabits but against the life that shares it with him. The history of the recent centuries has its black passages—the slaughter of the buffalo on the western plains, the massacre of the shorebirds by the market gunners, the near-extermination of the egrets for their plumage. Now, to these and others like them, we are adding a new chapter and a new kind of havoc—the direct killing of birds, mammals, fishes, and indeed practically every form of wildlife by chemical insecticides indiscriminately sprayed on the land . . . .

B. Conflicting Economic Approaches

Scholars and other knowledgeable writers have provided a broad range of theories to justify, explain, or influence environmental law and policy. This note—and the excerpts that follow it—describe some traditional economic concepts that relate to environmental protection.

One key economic theory concerns "negative externalities." These are costs incurred in producing goods or services that are neither borne by the producer nor paid by the consumer. Environmental pollution is often described as a negative externality. Some economists argue that government regulation—or legally compelled compensation for pollution victims—is needed to "internalize the externalities" imposed by polluters on third parties. They contend that the absence of regulation and mechanisms for compensation result in an "underpricing" of such public resources as air and water that creates incentives for damage to or destruction of these resources.

By way of illustration, where a factory releases toxic chemicals that contaminate a reservoir used to store drinking water, external costs will be imposed. These costs may include the expense of diverting the contaminants away from the water supply, cleaning up the water supply after it has been contaminated, or even a complete loss of potable water. Absent some form of government intervention, some economists argue, those costs will typically be borne by those who drink the water, not by those who sell or buy the product that the factory produces.

A competing economic view is far more skeptical of the desirability of government regulation of pollution. Instead, it is theorized, environmental improvements are likely to result from the operation of a "free market" in goods and services, unfettered by governmental interventions. Adherents of this approach find some support in the writings of Ronald Coase, whose seminal article, *The Problem of Social Cost*, 3 J. L. AND ECON. 1 (1960), argued that problems of environmental harm stem from competition between and among parties that wish to make incompatible uses of the same resources. In Coase's view, these competing parties are likely to negotiate an efficient, socially beneficial allocation of resources if there are no "transaction costs" involved, i.e., costs that are incurred in overcoming such market imperfections as the unavailability of relevant information, costs of negotiation, legal fees, etc. Coase conceded that transaction costs will always exist in the marketplace. Nonetheless, he contends, the inevitability of such costs, and the presence of negative externalities, does not automatically justify government regulation.

While the details of Coase's theories remain controversial, his skepticism about the role of government intervention is consistent with the views of a number of free-market economists who see government regulation of the environment as a "dead hand" that impedes both economic growth and environmental protection.

Another economic approach that is sometimes used to oppose government environmental regulation — yet in some instances to justify it — is "cost-benefit analysis." This technique requires a formal comparison of the costs and benefits of proposed public policies or actions to determine whether they will result in greater economic efficiency. As some of the readings in this chapter illustrate, cost-benefit analysis has been subject to sharp criticism from scholars who have questioned the entire conceptual or theoretical validity of this economic tool, and oppose its use as a means of setting regulatory policy.

Cost-benefit analysis should not be confused with cost-effectiveness. The latter notion is not concerned with whether or not there should be environmental regulation or, if so, how stringent that regulation should be. Instead, its proponents argue that once it has been decided to regulate in a particular area, and an appropriately protective level of pollution control (or pollution cleanup) has been determined, the needed level of protection should be determined using the least costly approach that is effective to meet the needed environmental goal.

Mark Sagoff, *We Have Met the Enemy and He Is Us or Conflict and Contradiction in Environmental Law*
12 ENVTL. L. 283, 283–308 (1982)

In a course I teach on environmental ethics, I ask students to read the Supreme Court opinion in *Sierra Club v. Morton* [405 U.S. 727 (1972)]. In that case environmentalists challenged a decision by the Forest Service to lease the Mineral King

Valley, a wilderness area in the middle of Sequoia National Park, to Walt Disney Enterprises, to develop a ski resort. But let the Court describe the facts:

> The final Disney plan, approved by the Forest Service in January 1969, outlines a $35 million complex of motels, restaurants, swimming pools, parking lots, and other structures designed to accommodate 14,000 visitors daily. . . . Other facilities, including ski lifts, ski trails, a cog-assisted railway, and utility installations, are to be constructed on the mountain slopes and in other parts of the valley. . . . To provide access to the resort, the State of California proposes to construct a highway 20 miles in length. A section of this road would traverse Sequoia National Park, as would a proposed high-voltage power line . . . .

I asked how many of the students had visited the wilderness at Mineral King or thought they would visit it as long as it remains a wilderness. No one raised a hand. Why not? Too many mosquitoes, someone said. Not enough movies, said another. Another offered to explain in technical detail the difference between chilblain and trench foot . . . .

Then I asked how many students would like to visit the Mineral King Valley if it were developed in the way Disney planned. Every hand went up . . . .

I brought the students to order by asking if they thought the government did the right thing in giving Disney Enterprises a lease to develop Mineral King. I asked them, in other words, whether they thought that environmental policy, at least in this instance, should be based on the principle of maximizing the satisfaction of consumer demand. Was there a connection between what the students as individuals wanted for themselves and what they thought we should do, collectively, as a nation?

The response was unanimous, visceral, and grim. All of the students believed that the Disney plan was loathsome and despicable; that the Forest Service had violated a public trust by approving it; and that the values for which we stand as a nation compel us to preserve the little wilderness we have for its own sake and as an historic heritage for future generations.

The consumer interests or preferences of my students are typical of those of Americans in general. Most Americans like a warm bed better than a pile of wet leaves. They would rather have their meals prepared in a kitchen than to cook them over a camp stove. Disney's market analysis knew all this. They found that the resort would attract over 14,000 tourists a day, in summer and winter alike, which is a lot more people than now hike into Mineral King . . . .

You might suppose that most Americans approved of the Disney proposal; after all, it would service their consumer demands . . . .

Yet the public's response to the Disney project was like that of my students — visceral and grim. Public opinion was so unfavorable that Congress acted in 1978 to prohibit the project, by making the Mineral King Valley a part of Sequoia National Park . . . .

Economists have given us a sophisticated array of tools for measuring the costs and benefits associated with various public works projects. These techniques generally help us determine "consumer surplus"—that is, the amount that consumers are willing to pay for a project less the amount that the project will cost. The idea behind these techniques seems to be this: the use of resources that generates the greatest consumer surplus over the long run is the use that ought to be made of them. One such use I believe, would be the development of a Disney resort at Mineral King.

One problem with economic techniques of "cost-benefit analysis," however, is that they may fail to register ideological or ethical convictions citizens entertain about the very things that interest them as consumers . . . .

The things we cherish, admire, or respect are not always the things we are willing to pay for. Indeed they may be cheapened by being associated with money. It is fair to say that the worth of the things we love is better measured by our *unwillingness* to pay for them. Consider love itself. A civilized person may climb the highest mountain, swim the deepest sea, or cross the hottest desert for love, sweet love. He might do anything, indeed, except be willing to pay for it.

The things we are unwilling to pay for are not worthless to us. We simply think we ought not to pay for them. Love is not worthless. We would make all kinds of sacrifices for it. Yet a market in love—or in anything we consider "sacred"—is totally inappropriate. These things have a *dignity* rather than a *price*. The things that have a dignity, I believe, are in general the things that help us to define our relationship with one another. The environment we share has such a dignity. The way we use and the way we preserve our common natural heritage helps to define our relation or association with each other. It also helps to define our association with generations in the future and in the past.

Garrett Hardin, *The Tragedy of the Commons*
162 SCIENCE 1243, 1243–1248 (1968)

The tragedy of the commons develops in this way. Picture a pasture open to all. It is to be expected that each herdsman will try to keep as many cattle as possible on the commons. Such an arrangement may work reasonably satisfactorily for centuries because tribal wars, poaching, and disease keep the numbers of both man and beast well below the carrying capacity of the land. Finally, however, comes the day of reckoning, that is, the day when the long-desired goal of social stability becomes a reality. At this point, the inherent logic of the commons remorselessly generates tragedy.

As a rational being, each herdsman seeks to maximize his gain. Explicitly or implicitly, more or less consciously, he asks, "What is the utility *to me* of adding one more animal to my herd?" This utility has one negative and one positive component.

1. The positive component is a function of the increment of one animal. Since the herdsman receives all the proceeds from the sale of the additional animal, the positive utility is nearly +1.

2. The negative component is a function of the additional overgrazing created by one more animal. Since, however, the effects of overgrazing are shared by all the herdsmen, the negative utility for any particular decision-making herdsman is only a fraction of that.

Adding together the component partial utilities, the rational herdsman concludes that the only sensible course for his to pursue is to add another animal to his herd. And another; and another . . . . But this is the conclusion reached by each and every rational herdsman sharing a commons. Therein is the tragedy. Each man is locked into a system that compels him to increase his herd without limit — in a world that is limited. Ruin is the destination toward which all men rush, each pursuing his own best interest in a society that believes in the freedom of the commons. Freedom in a commons brings ruin to all . . . .

In an approximate way, the logic of the commons has been understood for a long time, perhaps since the discovery of agriculture or the invention of private property in real estate. But it is understood mostly only in special cases which are not sufficiently generalized. Even at this late date, cattlemen leasing national land on the western ranges demonstrate no more than an ambivalent understanding, in constantly pressuring federal authorities to increase the head count to the point where overgrazing produces erosion and weed-dominance. Likewise, the oceans of the world continue to suffer from the survival of the philosophy of the commons. Maritime nations still respond automatically to the shibboleth of the "freedom of the seas." Professing to believe in the "inexhaustible resources of the oceans," they bring species after species of fish and whales close to extinction.

The National Parks present another instance of the working out of the tragedy of the commons. At present, they are open to all, without limit. The parks themselves are limited in extent — there is only one Yosemite Valley — whereas population seems to grow without limit. The values that visitors seek in the parks are steadily eroded. Plainly, we must soon cease to treat the parks as commons or they will be of no value to anyone.

What shall we do? We have several options. We might sell them off as private property. We might keep them as public property, but allocate the right to enter them. The allocation might be on the basis of wealth, by the use of an auction system. It might be on the basis of merit, as defined by some agreed-upon standards. It might be by lottery. Or it might be on a first-come, first-serve basis, administered to long queues. These, I think, are all the reasonable possibilities. They are all objectionable. But we must choose — or acquiesce in the destruction of the commons that we call our National Parks.

In a reverse way, the tragedy of the commons reappears in problems of pollution. Here it is not a question of taking something out of the commons, but of putting something in — sewage, or chemical, radioactive, and heat wastes into water; noxious and dangerous fumes into the air; and distracting and unpleasant advertising signs into the line of sight. The calculations of utility are much the same as before. The rational man finds that his share of the cost of the wastes he discharges into the commons is less than the cost of purifying his wastes before releasing them. Since this is true for everyone, we are locked into a system of "fouling our own nest," so long as we behave only as independent, rational, free-enterprisers.

The tragedy of the commons as a food basket is averted by private property, or something formally like it. But the air and waters surrounding us cannot be readily be fenced, and so the tragedy of the commons as a cesspool must be prevented by different means, by coercive laws or taxing devices that make it cheaper for the polluter to treat his pollutants than to discharge them untreated. We have not progressed as far with the solution of this problem as we have with the first. Indeed, our particular concept of private property, which deters us from exhausting the positive resources of the earth, favors pollution. The owner of a factory on the bank of a stream—whose property extends to the middle of the stream—often has difficulty seeing why it is not his natural right to muddy the waters flowing past his door. The law, always behind the times, requires elaborate stitching and fitting to adapt it to this newly perceived aspect of the commons.

Frank Ackerman and Lisa Heinzerling
Priceless: On Knowing the Price of Everything
and the Value of Nothing 14–18; 39
(The New Press, 2004)

The simple economic ideas that figure so prominently in today's public policy discussions flow from an abstract academic vision of the marketplace—a vision that is scarcely recognizable as a portrait of a modern market economy. Surprisingly, political debates seem to turn on a chapter straight out of a college textbook—and not the liveliest one on campus, either.

For those who have avoided or forgotten the textbook, economic theory maintains that competitive markets lead to "optimal" results; that is, they are as efficient as possible. In the imaginary, idealized market economy, competition among buyers ensures that every resource ends up in its highest valued use; competition among employers implies that every worker finds the highest paid available job. Whatever you're looking for, you can have it your way.

Better yet, you can have it for exactly the cost of producing it in the most efficient possible manner. The price of a car necessarily includes the full cost of producing the steel, aluminum, plastics, and other materials in the car, because the automaker had to pay those costs to its suppliers. But in the ideal world, competition ensures that you are not charged any more than the bare minimum of costs for the capital, labor, and materials used in production.

This story about the benefits of competition offers an interesting insight, though hardly a universal explanation of economic life. Nor is it particularly new; it can be traced back at least to Adam Smith, who wrote more than 200 years ago. Smith originated, almost in passing, the metaphor of the market as an invisible hand, coordinating private producers to meet consumer demand. In the centuries since Smith, this image has repeatedly been adopted by conservatives who see any government policy as an unnecessary and inefficient interference with the market. Launched again with great fanfare in the latter part of the twentieth century as a new political insight, it may be the oldest new idea in public life.

Markets that perfectly fit the textbook description would indeed be efficient, for the reason that economists have explained. But that perfection is impossible to achieve; real markets do not even come close. Take away any one or more of the standard assumptions, and the efficiency of the unregulated market vanishes. When markets fall short of perfection, as inevitably happens, economic theory cannot prove that competition is always efficient, or that government intervention will always make things worse.

Monopoly power, for example, interferes with the efficiency of markets. . . .

Health and environmental problems present yet another form of market failure. Even idealized markets can be efficient only if everything of value has a price. The price of a new car includes the cost of the steel used in the car, because the automaker had to buy it from a steel company. Does the price of a car also include the cost of protecting workers' health in the auto plant where it was made, and the cost of preventing pollution from the iron mine that supplied the raw material for the car? Only if the auto company or steel company is forced to pay those costs by union contracts or government regulations. It is not that companies want to pollute; no one actually likes pollution, or wants to create more of it. But avoiding pollution can be troublesome and expensive, and many people and firms won't go to this trouble and expense unless they are required to do so.

It is not personal desires for pollution, but rather impersonal market forces and opportunities that create threats to health and nature. A competitive market economy allows and encourages all manner of individual initiatives. One way to succeed in the market is to find a profitable activity that no one else is engaged in. Since countless people and businesses are continually searching for market opportunities, *anything profitable that is not prohibited by law is likely to occur.* When laws allowed slavery, the United States had an active market in human beings. In countries that permit child labor, children make toys for other children. And when laws allow damage to human health and the natural environment, the result is dirty air and foul water. Cleaner, safer production processes are, unfortunately, often more expensive than the quick and dirty alternatives.

The problem goes even deeper. The efficiency of the market results, in theory, from the efforts of firms competing to sell exactly the same goods and services that consumers are willing to pay for. It is possible to talk about the efficient balance between cars and the clothing; consumer spending on these goods provides guidance about how much of each to produce. But what would be the efficient balance between producing cars and preventing cancer? Or between making clothing and mitigating climate change? For the market to answer these questions, consumers would have to buy, and producers would have to sell, prevention of cancer and mitigation of climate change. The market, in other words, would need prices for preventing the loss of life due to cancer and for protecting the environment for future generations. . . .

[T]he market has no answer, *because there are no such prices*. Life and nature are priceless. This does not mean that we can or should spent limitless amounts on protecting human lives and the environment, but it does mean that there is no natural or useful way to measure these values in dollars; we need a better way of thinking and deciding about them. There are resource constraints and painful choices in health and environmental policy, but the market cannot make our choices for us.

Despite these problems, the cost side is the easy part of cost-benefit analysis. In principle, one could correct for the potential sources of bias in estimating the costs of regulations and other public policies. No such correction is possible in assessing the benefits of regulation, because the benefits are, literally, priceless. Herein lies the fatal flaw of cost-benefit analysis: to compare costs and benefits in its rigid framework, they must be expressed in common units. Cancer deaths avoided, wilderness and whales saved, illnesses and anxieties prevented — all these and many other benefits must be reduced to dollar values to ensure that we are spending just enough on them, but not too much. . . . [M]uch of what we think is important about human life, health, and the environment is lost in this translation. By monetizing the things we hold most dear, economic analysis ends up cheapening and belittling them . . . .

Terry L. Anderson and Donald R. Leal
Free Market Environmentalism 1, 3–4
(Revised Edition, 2001).

For most people, markets are the cause of environmental problems, not the solution. The very notion of free market environmentalism is an oxymoron. Even conservative thinkers who support free enterprise and free trade find themselves uncomfortable with the idea of letting unfettered markets determine how and when natural resources are used. Markets may work fine to produce shoes or software, but the environment is somehow different and is too precious to be thrown to bulls and bears on Wall Street.

The feeling that markets and the environment do not mix is buttressed by the perception that resource exploitation and environmental degradation are inextricably linked to economic growth. This view, which first emerged with industrialization, builds on fears that we are running out of resources. After all, if resources are finite and production to meet material needs uses up some of those finite resources, the world's natural endowment must be getting more scarce. During the Industrial Revolution in England, the Reverend Thomas Malthus articulated this view, hypothesizing that exponential population growth would eventually overwhelm productivity growth and result in famine and pestilence. At the heart of Malthus' logic: population and growing consumption must eventually run into the wall of finite natural resources. . . .

The reason that Malthusian hypotheses are continually refuted is that they fail to take into account how human ingenuity stimulated by market forces finds ways to cope with natural resource constraints. As the late Julian Simon observed, the "ultimate resource" is the human mind, which has allowed us to avoid Malthusian cycles. Human ingenuity is switched on by market prices that signal increasing scarcity and provide rewards for those who mitigate resource constraints by reducing consumption, finding substitutes, and improving productivity. . . .

[We] challenge the perception that free market environmentalism is an oxymoron and indeed argue that if we are to continue improving environmental quality in the twenty-first century, we must harness market forces. We offer an alternative way of thinking about natural resource and environmental concerns that contrasts information and incentives generated by markets and politics. In general, free market environmentalism emphasizes the positive incentives associated with prices, profits, and entrepreneurship, as opposed to political environmentalism, which emphasizes negative incentives associated with regulation and taxes.

At the heart of free market environmentalism is a system of well-specified property rights to natural and environmental resources. Whether these rights are held by individuals, corporations, nonprofit environmental groups, or communal groups, a discipline is imposed on resource users because the wealth of the property owner is at stake if bad decisions are made. Moreover, if private owners can sell their rights to use resources, the owners must not only consider their own values, they must also consider what others are willing to pay. In the market setting, it is the potential for gains from trade that encourages cooperation. Both the discipline of private ownership and the potential for gains from trade stand in sharp contrast to the political setting. When resources are controlled politically, the costs of misuse are more diffused and the potential for cooperation is minimized because the rights are essentially up for grabs. . . .

Free market environmentalism emphasizes the importance of market processes in getting more human value from any given stock of resources. Only when rights are well defined, enforced, and transferable will self-interested individuals confront the tradeoffs inherent in a world of scarcity. As entrepreneurs move to fill profit niches, prices will reflect the values we place on resources and the environment. Mistakes will surely be made, but in the process a niche will be created and profit opportunities will attract resource managers with better ideas. Even externalities offer profit niches to the environmental entrepreneur who can better define and enforce property rights to the unowned resource and charge the free rider. In cases in which definition and enforcement costs are insurmountable, political solutions may be called for. Unfortunately, however, those kinds of solutions often become entrenched and stand in the way of innovative market processes that promote fiscal responsibility, efficient resource use, and individual freedom. . . .

Notes and Questions

1. Rachel Carson's book, SILENT SPRING, is a classic of the early environmental movement. Ms. Carson's sharp and eloquent criticisms of the pesticide industry and its products drew angry protests from spokespeople for the industry, which attacked the author's character as well as her research, professional credentials, and character.

Despite this, Ms. Carson persisted in her criticism. Her book attracted widespread public attention and support and it helped spark the environmental movement. Eventually, SILENT SPRING led to the banning of DDT and other harmful pesticides in the United States.

2. How persuasive did you find Anderson and Leal's advocacy of a free market approach to environmental protection? Do you agree with their contention that the free market imposes a "discipline" on the resource users "because the wealth of the property owner is at stake if bad decisions are made?" Can you think of any examples of this? Counter-examples?

3. How effectively do Hardin's ideas rebut those of Anderson and Leal?

4. Hardin's description of the tragedy of the commons has been the subject of intense academic scrutiny. A number of scholars have criticized Hardin's thesis by noting that, empirically, many pastoral societies avoided the destruction of their commons by developing social mechanisms to constrain overexploitation of the limited resource. Did Hardin anticipate this objection? Does this observation undermine Hardin's claim regarding the need for pollution control laws?

5. Compare and contrast the excerpt from Anderson and Leal's book with the alternative economic approaches of Ackerman and Heinzerling, Sagoff, and Hardin. What are the major points of similarity and difference? Of the various analyses presented, which theories struck you as the most viable and realistic?

6. Not all justifications for Environmental Law are framed by economic principles. The writings reproduced in the following section present a variety of alternatives to an economics-based approach to defending and evaluating environmental laws.

C. Alternative Approaches: Science, Pragmatism, and Sustainability

A. Dan Tarlock, *Environmental Law: Ethics or Science?*
7 DUKE ENVT'L. L. & POL'Y F. 193, 194–95, 221–223 (1996)

The principal argument of this article is that environmental law and management should derive their primary political power and legitimacy from science, not ethics. This is a deliberately provocative statement because it runs counter to the pluralistic justification for environmental law, which posits that environmentalism can be sustained from multiple sources of legitimacy all of which are equal. . . .

Ethics are not a substitute for scientific analysis, and thus environmental law and environmentalism are more contingent than many would prefer them to be. Any principles derived from science remain subject to revision in light of new evidence. Ethics can legitimately, however, bridge the gap between scientific uncertainty and the risks of inaction pending further research through the adoption of the cautionary principle. Environmentalism does represent a profound shift in our world-view of our physical surroundings. Through science we have increasingly come to see natural processes as phenomena to be respected rather than manipulated. This new-found respect can support laws, enacted in advance of conclusive scientific evidence, which recognize the value of new resource functions. . . . However, as long as we value rationality (an open question with respect to some strains of modern environmentalism), science will continue to serve an important checking function. The need for some scientific justification, however probabilistic, for environmental regulation is necessary to constrain the potential arbitrariness and unfairness that can result from the substitution of intuition for verification. . . .

The central project of environmental law has been to marry wonder to power. Environmentalism's central insight has been to demonstrate the need to supplant the Enlightenment view that humans are sovereign over nature with one which appreciates the many instrumental as well as intrinsic values of nature. In short, nature is both a commodity and a source of delight and wonder to be valued by different standards from the past. Environmental law's mission has been to counter the traditional bias in favor of the early and rapid exploitation of nature by using principles and procedures which try to sustain biodiversity over time. To many environmentalists this seems a modest if not incorrect objective, but it is Herculean in light of the continued dominance of the view that nature is a commodity for present consumption. . . . Biodiversity management can be informed by values which reflect the heightened appreciation of the functions that natural systems perform, but the management choices that are made must be grounded in science and recognized as contingent. Modification of management strategies and adjustment to new information, not the recognition of the rights of nature, will characterize the future of environmental law.

Joel A. Mintz, *Some Thoughts on the Merits of Pragmatism as a Guide to Environmental Protection*
31 B.C. ENV. AFF. L. REV. 1 (2004)

Pragmatism, a philosophy that emphasizes action, experimentation, and a concern with what "works" in human experience, has undergone a revival in recent years. First conceived in the final decade of the nineteenth century, philosophic pragmatism was initially intended to provide an alternative to foundationalism, i.e., the view that there are innate and indubitable beliefs upon which knowledge must be based. Traditional pragmatists, such as William James, Charles Pierce, John Dewey, Josiah Royce, and George Herbert Mead, viewed all human understanding as intrinsically fallible; they saw knowing as an open-ended quest for greater certainty, grounded in practical experience, and motivated by a desire for successful actions . . . .

Philosophical pragmatism, as initially articulated by William James and other early twentieth century academics, is, in one sense, an attitude or method of thought. It emphasizes a focus on facts and consequences, as opposed to theories and principles. As James explained it, pragmatism:

> Stands for no particular results. It has no dogmas, and no doctrines save for its method. . . . [I]t lies in the midst of our theories, like a corridor in a hotel. Innumerable chambers open out of it. In one you may find a man writing an

atheistic volume; in the next someone on his knees praying for faith and strength; in a third a chemist investigating a body's properties. In a fourth a system of idealistic metaphysics is being excogitated; in a fifth the impossibility of metaphysics is being shown. But they all own the corridor, and all must pass through it if they want a practicable way of getting into or out of their respective rooms.

In addition to being a method of thought — with sufficient flexibility to appeal to individuals who have divergent views in many respects, as noted above — philosophical pragmatism is also distinguished by its experiential, provisional, and pluralistic notion of truth. In Williams James's words:

> Pragmatism . . . asks its usual question. "Grant an idea or belief to be true," it says, "what concrete difference will its being true make in any one's actual life? How will the truth be realized? What experiences will be different from those which would obtain if the belief were false? What, in short, is the truth's cash-value in experiential terms?" The moment pragmatism asks this question, it seeks the answer: True ideas are those that we can assimilate, validate, corroborate, and verify. False ideas are those that we cannot. That is the practical difference it makes to us to have true ideas; that, therefore, is the meaning of truth, for it is all that truth is known as.

To this observer, pragmatism — and more specifically the method and attitudes of pragmatic thought — has a good deal to recommend as a theoretical underpinning for public environmental decision making. As much as any problems that arise in the arena of public policy environmental problems tend to be factually complex. They often involve technically complicated issues of science and engineering, multiplicity of institutional actors and commitments, rapid-paced changes in technologies and knowledge regarding their consequences, and far-reaching economic, social, and political consequences. In the face of this, pragmatism's insistent focus on particular facts, consequences and workable solutions, along with its skepticism as to grand theories and fixed, dogmatic notions, appears to be a good environmental fit . . . .

Another potential environmental benefit of pragmatism — with its insistence on social justice and the accomplishment of social ends — is that judicial adherence to its methods appears likely to increase the likelihood that environmental statutes will be afforded pro-environmental interpretations in the courts. Oliver Wendell Holmes, Jr.'s legal pragmatic idea of the judge as interstitial legislator, shaping the law consistent with prevalent moral and political theories, is certainly consistent with this interpretative possibility; as is Benjamin Cardozo's notion of the judge as the guardian of morality, reason, good conscience, and social justice. Richard Posner's staunch insistence on the superiority of practical reasoning over the rigidity of legal formalism also appears to have this same benefit for environmental proponents.

Moreover, pragmatism places a high value on experimentation and innovative problem solving. In view of the inherent complexity of environmental problems, as well as the legislative "gridlock" that has characterized environmental law since the early 1990s — particularly at the federal level — these aspects of pragmatic theory seem especially well suited to contemporary environmental policymaking. Although environmental law contains notable examples of bold, large-scale innovations — from technology-forcing requirements to emissions trading regimes — it is relatively devoid of small-scale pilot projects carefully designed to test the efficacy of particular technologies or regulatory techniques under controlled conditions. Those relatively inexpensive experiments, which hold the promise of eventual environmental improvements on a broader scale, are very much consistent with the pragmatic method.

Finally, one of the clear lessons of the past several decades of environmental policymaking is that a great many environmental problems tend to be long-lasting and persistent. There is a genuine need for the solutions to those dilemmas — and the institutions that foster and accomplish such solutions — to be equally stubborn and long-lasting.

John C. Dernbach
Acting as If Tomorrow Matters 3
(Environmental Law Institute, 2012)

We use the term "sustainability" and "sustainable development" more now than we did two decades ago. Still, it is far from clear that most of us understand what sustainability and sustainable development mean. For many, perhaps most, these are just vague words in the "green" vocabulary. For more than a few others, sustainability means something negative, like tree hugging. Yet sustainability is distinctive — and positive — in at least seven ways.

First, sustainability provides a framework for humans to live and prosper in harmony with nature rather than, as we have tended to do for centuries, at nature's expense. It is about finding ways to make our goals for environmental protection, economic growth, peace and security, and social well-being mutually reinforcing — rather than treating environmental degradation as the necessary price of progress. It is about quality of life and well-being. Although the terms *sustainability* and *sustainable development* were first used in an environmental context, they are not about the environment alone or the environment before everything else. [E]nvironmental, social, and economic goals. . . . are sometimes also called the three pillars of sustainability. Corporate sustainability efforts are often described in terms of a triple bottom line of, for example, "profit, people, and planet."

The three pillars and triple bottom line are used so often that a fourth dimension — peace and security — is often omitted. Yet most activities are difficult or impossible in the absence of peace and security. As the Rio Declaration states, "Peace, development and environmental protection are interdependent and indivisible." Some sustainability issues more obviously involve security than others. The use of petroleum for transportation, for instance, involves foreign oil supplies, and thus has national security implications . . . .

[T]he object of sustainability is to maximize the positive contribution of human activities to the environment, the economy, and society at the same time. The reuse and recycling of materials provides an example. If we buy things and then throw them out, we contribute to economic growth and job creation but the environmental impact is negative. If nearly everything is recycled or reused, on the other hand, we not only contribute to economic growth but also create more jobs than if materials were simply landfilled, save energy used to make and refine those materials that would otherwise be lost, and have almost no negative environmental impact. If we mined existing disposal facilities for metal and other materials, and converted the land to park or other use, we would have a positive environmental impact. Sustainability is not just about minimizing environmental damage; it is also about the restoration of environmental quality.

Sustainability is thus about *integrating* environmental protection and restoration into economic, social, and national security decisions and goals. If the risks of environmental degradation are accounted for, sustainability will be more efficient and less costly than making a development decision first and then figuring out what to do about the environment afterward, or addressing the environment as a costly add-on to a development project or manufacturing process. In principle, a dollar spent on sustainability will yield more benefits—and a greater variety of benefits—than a dollar spent only on economic development or the environment. In fact, sustainability is consistent with the fiscal discipline that current economic circumstances require. And for energy efficiency and conservation in particular, sustainability can, and usually does, also mean lower economic costs.

Second, sustainability focuses on both the short-term and long-term effects of decisions. The most widely accepted definition of sustainable development—"development that meets the needs of the present without compromising the ability of future generations to meet their own needs"—captures this point precisely. It is reinforced by one of the principles in the Rio Declaration—intergenerational equity. It is also consistent with much American political rhetoric that focuses on protecting the interests of our children and grandchildren. Sustainability is inconsistent with decisions that lead to long-term debts or problems that can only be resolved, if at all, by future generations—such as the federal budget deficit, climate change, overpopulation, depletion of resources, destruction of biodiversity, and the global accommodation of toxic materials.

Third, sustainability is about exercising precaution and making commonsense decisions in the face of known or likely risks. Sustainable development is not based on what we want to believe or not believe; it is anchored in reality and risk. Because sustainability is premised in part on avoiding or limiting risks, it does not require complete certainty before we act. That is how we ordinarily behave, and we should treat risks related to sustainability in the same way.

Fourth, sustainability is also a moral, ethical, and even a religious issue, not just a matter of policy or law. Environmental quality and the availability of natural resources directly affect human well-being, environmental damage hurts individuals, forcing them to breathe unhealthy air, drink filthy water, or ingest toxic chemicals. Environmental degradation also damages the vast ecological commons on which life depends.

To address this problem, the Rio Declaration mirrors a basic principle of U.S. environmental law, stating that "the polluter should, in principle, bear the cost of pollution," rather than imposing that cost on others or the environment. For those who recognize the existence of God, or another deity or force larger than themselves, environmental degradation also can be an offense against God, creation, or the natural order.

Fifth, sustainability is not directed just to government or industry, but to all parts of society, all ages, and all economic sectors. The Rio Declaration identifies public participation, access to information, and access to justice — key principles of American governance — as essential to sustainability. It is also directed to individuals, not simply as participants in the development of government policy but also as consumers and users of goods and services. The problems are so large, and the opportunities so many, that virtually every individual, organization, institution, corporation, and government needs to contribute to a more-sustainable world.

Sixth, sustainability requires considerable innovation in all spheres of public and private life. Many of the legal, policy, and other tools we need to achieve sustainability do not yet exist, are only now being attempted, or have only been tried for a short time. Sustainability is an effort to change the environmental habits, scripts, and patterns that have dominated the American landscape over the past several decades, and even longer. Day after day, at home, at work, and in school, most of us act in many ways that are not environmentally sustainable. We will need to change those habits, either through the use of new technologies, new options for doing things, new or different infrastructure, new or modified laws, or changes in personal habits.

Seventh, sustainability's objectives are human freedom, opportunity, and quality of life in a world in which the environment is protected and restored and in which natural resources are readily available. The objectives of sustainable development are in many ways the same as those of conventional development. It is easy to forget that sustainable development is, after all, a form of development. In *Our Common Future*, a landmark report on sustainable development, the World Commission on Environment and Development stated: "The satisfaction of human needs and aspirations is the major objective of development." International lawyer Rumu Sarkar explains that, "for most practitioners and theorists, the overall objectives of alleviating poverty and human suffering and of improving the human condition more generally are the desired end product of the development process." She adds that, "development aims at enlarging the opportunities people have in their lives." Amartya Sen, a professor of economics and philosophy at Harvard who has won the Nobel Prize in economics, describes development as a process that enlarges individual freedom.

Notes and Questions

1. Compare the excerpts from Leopold and Tarlock. To what extent do they conflict? In your view, are science and ethics mutually exclusive bases for defending environmental requirements? Beyond Tarlock's invocation of the "cautionary

principle" — the notion that where there is scientific uncertainty as to whether a human activity is causing harm, the prudent course is to regulate or prohibit that activity — is there a way that ethical precepts and scientific findings can be combined to justify environmental laws?

2. Recent public opinion polls have detected substantial public distrust of science (and of scientists). To what extent do you think that the results of those polls undercut Tarlock's argument? In his article, Tarlock notes that "scientific principles are subject to revision in light of new evidence." Moreover, conflicts between or among experts are quite common, both in disputes regarding governmental policies and in individual cases. In view of this, do you agree with Tarlock's claim that environmental law and management should "derive their primary political power from science"?

3. Tarlock describes science and science-based environmental policy as "contingent." Mintz describes pragmatism and pragmatism-based environmental policy as "provisional." How are these concepts similar or different? In what way is science contingent? In what way is pragmatism provisional? Are these desirable traits in environmental policy? Why?

4. The excerpt from Joel Mintz's article argues that pragmatism should play a significant role in the establishment of environmental laws and policies. Do you agree? Can a pragmatic approach be harmonized with defenses of environmental laws that are based on ethics and/or science? Can pragmatism, as the William James quote in the Mintz excerpt suggests, generate consensus on environmental policy among persons or interest groups with very different perspectives? In the context of a concrete environmental dispute — for example, whether to build a ski resort in the Mineral King Valley — would using the philosophy of pragmatism produce a policy decision that would satisfy Leopold, Sagoff, Ackerman and Heinzerling, and Anderson and Leal?

5. To your mind, how useful is the notion of sustainability, as described above by John Dernbach, one of its most distinguished theorists, as a guide to how environmental law should develop and be interpreted?

6. Are the objectives set forth in the Dernbach excerpt above practical and feasible? If sustainability includes social and economic maximization, profits for private companies, economic development, and human freedom, opportunity, and quality of life, why hasn't the free market resulted in sustainable resource use?

7. Do you agree with Prof. Dernbach that integrating environmental protection into economic, social, and national security decisions and goals is useful and important? To what extent, if any, do you think that this has already occurred? The Department of Defense and Central Intelligence Agency routinely assess the risks to peace and security that may result from environmental disruption across the globe.

8. To what extent do you find Rachel Carson's writing consistent with the notions of ethics, science, pragmatism, and sustainability advocated in the other excerpted writings that appear above?

II. Seeking Environmental Justice through the Law

Although its roots can be traced back to the common law doctrines of trespass and nuisance, much of the body of contemporary Environmental Law had its beginnings in the late 1960s and early 1970s, during a period that saw extraordinary manifestations of public outrage and concern about environmental pollution. Although the "environmental movement" continues to the present time, it received new impetus in the 1980s and 1990s when the disparate impact of environmental problems on poor people and minority groups came to the fore. This trend, generally referred to as the Environmental Justice movement, has taken many forms and focused on a variety of environmental problems and issues — from the location of polluting factories in low-income areas to the poisoning of drinking water in the mostly-minority city of Flint, Michigan.

The following excerpt is taken from a widely cited law review article by Professor Robert Kuehn that discusses how Environmental Justice is best defined and analyzed. Kuehn's piece provides an overview of some earlier definitions, along with a proposal for a "taxonomy" of the normative concepts that motivate (and justify) the quest for fairness and equity in environmental protection.

Following the Kuehn article is an edited version of a 1994 Executive Order by President Bill Clinton that represents an early governmental response to environmental inequities. As you read the Order, please consider whether it is an adequate response to the problems it addresses and how, if at all, it might be strengthened or superseded by new legislation.

Robert R. Kuehn, *A Taxonomy of Environmental Justice*
30 Envt'l. L. Rptr. 10681 (2000)

"Environmental justice" means many things to many people. To local communities feeling overburdened by environmental hazards and left out of the decision making process, it captures their sense of the unfairness of the development, implementation, and enforcement of environmental laws and policies. To regulated entities facing allegations that they have created or contributed to injustices, environmental justice is an amorphous term that wrongly suggests racial-based or class-based animus or, at the very least, indifference to the public health and welfare of distressed communities. The company may believe it did not even create, or at most only plays a small role in causing or solving, the community's problems. To government officials often the target of environmental justice activists' ire, the term may imply that they are executing their responsibilities in a biased or callous manner. Caught in the middle between local residents and industry, the call for environmental justice may pressure agency officials to move from a well-established, technocratic decision making approach to a largely undefined, populist approach that encompasses issues beyond the comfortable domain of the agency.

Efforts to understand environmental justice are further complicated by the term's international, national, and local scope; by its broad definition of the environment—where one lives, works, plays, and goes to school; and by its broad range of concerns—such as public health, natural resource conservation, and worker safety in both urban and rural environs. Disputes at the international level include allegations that governments and multinational corporations are exploiting indigenous peoples and the impoverished conditions of developing nations. At the national level, although an overwhelming number of studies show differences by race and income in exposures to environmental hazards, debate continues about the strength of that evidence and the appropriate political and legal response to such disparities. At the local level, many people of color and lower income communities believe that they have not been treated fairly regarding the distribution of the environmental benefits and burdens.

Over the past decade, during which communities, academics, regulated firms, and government officials have struggled with issues of the relationship of environmental quality to race and class, the quest to explain the essence of the problems underlying environmental justice disputes has been manifested in the varying terminology and definitions used to refer to such disputes. This Article contends that such efforts have largely failed to capture the essence and breadth of the different type of environmental justice concerns alleged at the international, national, and local levels. The Article instead proposes a four-part categorization of the environmental justice issues: (1) distributive justice; (2) procedural justice; (3) corrective justice; (4) social justice. This taxonomic approach, which moves beyond definitions and expands upon the earlier works of Dr. Robert Bullard and others, offers a method of collapsing the seemingly broad scope of environmental justice and identifying common causes of and solutions to environmental injustice. At its heart, this taxonomy seeks to identify the "justice" embodied in the concept of environmental justice.

Shifting Perspectives and Uses of Terms

The U.S. Environmental Protection Agency (EPA) initially used the term "environmental equity," as defined as the equitable distribution of environmental risks across population groups, to refer to the environmental justice phenomenon. Because this term implies the redistribution of risk across racial and economic groups rather than risk reduction and avoidance, it is no longer used by EPA, though it is still used by some states.

In some instances, the phrase "environmental racism," defined as "any policy, practice or directive that differentially affects or disadvantages (whether intended or unintended) individuals, groups, or communities based on race or color, is used to explain the differential treatment of populations on environmental issues. Commentators disagree over the proper usage of this term, particularly over whether action having an unequal distributive outcome across racial groups would in itself be a sufficient basis to label an action environmental racism or whether the action must be the result of intentional racism animus. Today, many environmental justice advocates and scholars avoid the term "environmental racism," though the phrase continues to be employed and is useful in identifying the institutional causes of some environmental injustices. This shift is attributable to a desire to focus on solutions rather than mere identification of problems, as well as a desire to encompass class concerns and not to be limited by issues of intentional conduct.

In 1994, President Clinton issued Executive Order No. 12898, "Federal Actions to Address Environmental Justice in Minority Populations and Low-Income Populations," and adopted the phrase "environmental justice" to refer to "disproportionately high and adverse human health or environmental effects . . . on minority populations and low-income populations." Rather than explicitly defining the phrase, the Executive Order elaborated on its meaning by requiring each federal agency to develop strategies to achieve environmental justice by, at a minimum: (1) identifying and addressing disproportionately high and adverse human health or environmental effects of agency programs, policies, and activities on minority populations and low-income populations; (2) promoting enforcement of all health and environmental statutes in areas with minority or low-income populations; (3) ensuring greater public participation; (4) improving research and data collection relating to the health and environment of minority and low-income populations; and (5) identifying differential patterns of consumption of natural resources among minority and low-income populations.

The Executive Order's use of the term "environmental justice" is significant in at least three respects. First, the Executive Order focuses not only on the disproportionate burdens addressed by the term environmental equity, but also on issues of enforcement of environmental laws and opportunities for public participation. Second, the Executive Order identifies not just minorities but also low-income populations as the groups who have been subject to, and entitled to relief from, unfair or unequal treatment. Finally, the Executive Order, and in particular the accompanying memorandum, refers to environmental justice as a goal or aspiration to be achieved, rather than as a problem or cause.

In 1998, EPA's Office of Environmental Justice set forth the Agency's "standard definition" of environmental justice:

> The fair treatment of people of all races, cultures, incomes, and educational levels with respect to the development and enforcement of environmental laws, regulations, and policies. Fair treatment implies that no population should be forced to shoulder a disproportionate share of exposure to the negative effects of pollution due to lack of political or economic strength.

Going beyond the issues of disproportionate exposures and participation in the development and enforcement of laws and policies, EPA further elaborated that environmental justice:

> is based on the premise that: 1) it is a basic right of all Americans to live and work in "safe, healthful, productive, and aesthetically and culturally pleasing surroundings"; 2) it is not only an environmental issue but a public health issue; 3) it is forward-looking and goal-oriented; and 4) it is also inclusive since it is based on the concept of fundamental fairness, which includes the concept of economic prejudices as well as racial prejudices.

Professor Bunyan Bryant defines environmental justice as referring "to those cultural norms and values, rules, regulations, behaviors, policies, and decisions to support sustainable communities, where people can interact with confidence that their environment is safe, nurturing, and protective." Some critiques of environmental justice by government agencies and environmental justice advocates are so broad and aspirational as not to state clearly the ends of environmental justice.

An alternative approach to defining environmental justice that does state its desired ends, albeit very ambitious ones, was developed by environmental justice leaders during the 1991 First People of Color Environmental Leadership Summit. Its "Principles of Environmental Justice" sets forth a 17-point paradigm that includes, *inter alia*, a call for cessation of the production of all toxins, hazardous wastes, and radioactive materials; recognizes the fundamental right to political, economic, cultural, and environmental self-determination of all peoples; holds all producers of waste strictly accountable for damages and protects the right of victims of environmental injustice to receive full compensation and reparations; demands the right to participate as equal partners at every level of decisionmaking; affirms the right of all workers to a safe and healthy work environment; and recognizes the special legal and natural relationship of native peoples to the U.S. government.

Dr. Robert Bullard has distilled the principles of environmental justice into a framework of five basic characteristics: (1) protect all persons from environmental degradation; (2) adopt a public health prevention of harm approach; (3) place the burden of proof on those who seek to pollute; (4) obviate the requirement to prove intent to discriminate; and (5) redress existing inequities by targeting action and resources. In his view, environmental justice seeks to make environmental protection more democratic and asks the fundamental ethical and political questions of "who gets what, why and how much."

Though these definitions and principles are essential to understanding the environmental justice phenomenon, my experience in teaching the subject suggests that neither fully informs the audience of the similarity of themes and concerns that arise in environmental justice disputes. Students and lawyers are often left without an understanding of unifying themes or common political, legal, or economic approaches to addressing allegations of injustice. The classification method set forth in this Article seeks to overcome this shortcoming and to advance the understanding of environmental justice by disassembling the term into the four traditional notions of "justice" that are implicated by allegations of environmental injustice . . . .

Federal Actions to Address Environmental Justice in Minority Populations and Low-Income Populations
Exec. Order No. 12898, 59 Fed. Reg. 7629 (February 11, 1994)

By the authority vested in me as President by the Constitution and the laws of the United States of America, it is hereby ordered as follows:

Section 1-1. *Implementation.*

1-101. *Agency Responsibilities.* To the greatest extent practicable and permitted by law, and consistent with the principles set forth in the report on the National Performance Review, each Federal agency shall make achieving environmental justice part of its mission by identifying and addressing, as appropriate, disproportionately high and adverse human health or environmental effects of its programs, policies, and activities on minority populations and low-income populations in the United States and its territories and possessions, the District of Columbia, the Commonwealth of Puerto Rico, and the Commonwealth of the [Northern] Mariana Islands.

[Note: at Section 1-102 (a), the Order creates an "Interagency Working Group on Environmental Justice," to be chaired by the Administrator of EPA or the Administrator's designee, and composed of the heads of the thirteen specifically named federal agencies and departments.]

(b) The Working Group shall: (1) provide guidance to Federal agencies on criteria for identifying disproportionately high and adverse human health or environmental effects on minority populations and low-income populations;

(2) coordinate with, provide guidance to, and serve as a clearinghouse for, each Federal agency as it develops an environmental justice strategy as required by section 1-103 of this order, in order to ensure that the administration, interpretation and enforcement of programs, activities and policies are undertaken in a consistent manner . . .

1-103. *Development of Agency Strategies.* (a) Except as provided in section 6-605 of this order, each Federal agency shall develop an agency-wide environmental justice strategy, as set forth in subsections (b)-(e) of this section, that identifies and addresses disproportionately high and adverse human health or environmental effects of its programs, policies, and activities on minority populations and low-income populations. The environmental justice strategy shall list programs, policies, planning and public participation processes, enforcement, and/or rulemakings related to human health or the environment that should be revised to, at minimum: (1) promote enforcement of all health and environmental statutes in areas with minority populations and low-income populations; (2) ensure greater public participation: (3) improve research and data collection relating to the health of minority populations and low-income populations; and (4) identify differential patterns of consumption of natural resources among minority populations and low-income populations. In addition, the environmental justice strategy shall include, where appropriate, a timetable for undertaking identified revisions and consideration of economic and social implications of the revisions.

(b) Within 4 months of the date of this order, each Federal agency shall identify an internal administrative process for developing its environmental justice strategy, and shall inform the Working Group of the process.

(c) Within 6 months of the date of this order, each Federal agency shall provide the Working Group with an outline of its proposed environmental justice strategy.

(d) Within 10 months of the date of this order, each Federal agency shall provide the Working Group with its proposed environmental justice strategy.

(e) Within 12 months of the date of this order, each Federal agency shall finalize its environmental justice strategy and provide a copy and written description of its description of its strategy to the Working Group. During the 12-month period from the fate of this order, each Federal agency, as part of its environmental justice strategy, shall identify several specific projects that can be promptly undertaken to address particular concerns identified during the development of the proposed environmental strategy, and a schedule for implementing those projects.

(f) Within 24 months of the date of this order, each Federal agency shall report to the Working Group on its progress in implementing its agency-wide environmental justice strategy.

(g) Federal agencies shall provide additional periodic reports to the Working Group as requested by the Working Group.

1-104. *Reports to the President.* Within 14 months of the date of this order, the Working Group shall submit to the President, through the Office of the Deputy Assistant to the President for Environmental Policy and the Office of the Assistant to the President for Domestic Policy, a report that describes the implementation of this order, and includes the final environmental strategies described in section 1-103(e) of this order.

Sec. 2-2. *Federal Agency Responsibilities for Federal Programs.* Each Federal agency shall conduct its programs, policies, and activities that substantially affect human health or the environment, in a manner that ensures that such programs, policies, and activities do not have the effect of excluding persons (including populations) from participation in, denying persons (including populations) the benefits of, or subjecting persons (including populations) to discrimination under, such programs, policies, and activities, because of their race, color, or national origin . . .

Sec. 5-5. *Public Participation and Access to Information.*

(a) The public may submit recommendations to Federal agencies relating to the incorporation of environmental justice principles into Federal agency programs or policies. Each Federal agency shall convey such recommendations to the Working Group.

(b) Each Federal agency may, whenever practicable and appropriate, translate crucial public documents, notices, and hearings relating to human health of the environment for limited English speaking populations.

(c) Each Federal agency shall work to ensure that public documents, notices, and hearings relating to human health or the environment are concise, understandable, and readily accessible to the public.

(d) The Working Group shall hold public meetings, as appropriate, for the purpose of fact-finding, receiving public comments, and conducting inquiries concerning environmental justice. The Working Group shall prepare for public review a summary of the comments and recommendations discussed at the public meetings.

Sec. 6-6. *General Provisions.*

6-601. *Responsibility for Agency Implementation.* The head of each Federal agency shall be responsible for ensuring compliance with this order. Each Federal agency shall conduct internal reviews and take such other steps as may be necessary to monitor compliance with this order . . .

6-609. *Judicial Review.* This order is intended only to improve the internal management of the executive branch and is not intended to, nor does it create any right, benefit, or trust responsibility, substantive or procedural, enforceable at law or equity by a party against the United States, its agencies, its officers, or any person. This order shall not be construed to create any right to judicial review involving the compliance or noncompliance of the United States, its agencies, its officers, or any other person with this order.

William J. Clinton

THE WHITE HOUSE,

February 11, 1994.

Notes and Questions

1. Consider the direction of Executive Order 12898 that "*each* Federal agency shall make achieving environmental justice part of its mission . . . ." Sec. 1-101 (emphasis added). What do you imagine it might mean substantively for the U.S. Navy, the Federal Emergency Management Agency, or the Securities and Exchange Commission to make "achieving environmental justice" part of their respective missions? One place to start might be to review the individual EJ strategies that the Executive Order required each agency to develop. Most of these strategies have been updated periodically since 1994 and are available online at www.epa.gov/environmentaljustice (last visited July 29, 2016).

2. As Professor Kuehn notes, the terms and understandings surrounding environmental justice have evolved as perspectives have shifted and broadened. Reflecting this evolution, the "standard definition" of environmental justice that Professor Kuehn quoted from 1998 has been revised by EPA over time to reach the following official EPA articulation:

> [Environmental justice means] the fair treatment and meaningful involvement of all people regardless of race, color, national origin or income with respect to the development, implementation, and enforcement of environmental laws, regulations and policies.

EPA, *EJ 2020 Action Agenda* (May 2016) at 1. How precisely does this current definition differ from the 1998 version? What policy changes or understandings might these differences reflect?

3. What is the *law* of environmental justice? As yet, there is no federal statute that expressly requires agencies or other parties to achieve "environmental justice." However, students and advocates of environmental justice may find sources of legal authority inherent in due process, equal protection, and other constitutional constructs. Additional authorities may be found in the Civil Rights Act, including Title VI, and other federal statutes, as well as state law, local codes, implementing regulations, and relevant case law. As you proceed through the chapters that follow, consider how each federal environmental statute examined in this book may be applied to achieve the goals of environmental justice.

III. Setting Environmental Policy: A Practical Problem

The Plastic Bag Problem

When we make a purchase at almost any type of store, the items we buy are placed, frequently, in one or more plastic bags. These bags are lightweight, well-suited to their purpose, and inexpensive for the stores to buy. The low price of plastic bags keeps product prices low by saving retailers money, relative to alternatives like paper bags. Of course, retailers could save even more money if consumers brought their own reusable bags to the store—and retailers could even make money by selling reusable bags to consumers.

Regardless of retailers' possible incentive to encourage consumers to buy and use reusable bags, many billions of plastic bags are used in the United States annually. Although many plastic bags (and paper bags) are now made in China or other foreign countries, plastic bag manufacturing (and paper bag manufacturing) continue to employ some thousands of Americans. The trade association for plastic bag manufacturers states that plastic bag manufacturing and recycling (about which more will be said below) support 30,000 American jobs.

Plastic bags are made, ultimately, from petroleum or natural gas, which are both non-renewable resources. Manufacturing the bags entails considerable energy use, thus also producing pollution, including greenhouse gas emissions to the air and some water pollution. Paper bags, by contrast, are made from trees, a renewable resource. However, producing paper bags requires harvesting trees, which drastically alters and simplifies forest ecosystems. Moreover, the manufacture of paper bags also requires considerable energy, causing greenhouse gas emissions. Further, paper bags are heavier than plastic bags, so shipping them to their point of use consumes more diesel fuel than shipping plastic bags, which again increases greenhouse gas emissions as well as potentially unhealthful pollution from diesel engines. Making paper also results in significant discharges of pollution to water bodies. On the other hand, paper bags are generally larger and stronger than plastic bags, so consumers use fewer of them. Scientific studies of the relative environmental impacts of making paper bags versus making plastic bags indicate that there is no clear advantage to either type; both have impacts, but the impacts are different.

Reusable bags are generally made either of polypropylene or of cloth. Polypropylene is a durable plastic, much thicker and heavier than the type of plastic used for the bags that stores give away. Polypropylene is made from petroleum. Some polypropylene bags, particularly those manufactured in foreign countries, may be contaminated with various other substances, including lead, which can be extremely dangerous to human health and to the environment if it somehow leaches out of the bag and is consumed by humans or other organisms. Cloth bags may be made of various plant fibers, notably cotton. Growing cotton consumes vast amounts of fresh water, a theoretically renewable but locally scarce resource in the parts of the world where cotton is grown. Cotton growers also use large quantities of potentially dangerous pesticides on their crops. And, because of the energy needed to produce both polypropylene and cotton bags, the bags must be used many times in order to have a "carbon footprint" smaller than that of ordinary plastic bags.

The use of ordinary plastic bags raises other concerns, however. Almost all of the many billions of bags distributed in the United States each year are used only once. The vast majority of consumers simply dispose of them, sometimes by putting them in their household trash, sometimes by dropping them off for recycling, and sometimes by littering. Only a very small percentage of plastic bags, and a slightly higher percentage of paper bags, are recycled.

Because of their shape and low weight, plastic bags in the environment easily catch the wind and are blown away. They can go quite high in the air and can travel many miles. You have probably seen plastic bags caught in tree branches along the highways, flapping in the wind. Some of these bags were litter, but many were disposed of properly yet blew away from trash bins, trash trucks, or landfills. Cloth and polypropylene bags are too heavy to blow very far. Paper bags may blow away, but they do not travel as well as plastic bags and they disintegrate relatively quickly in most environments because of the effects of water and microorganisms. Plastic bags are sometimes physically torn apart (for instance, robins sometimes shred plastic bags and use the pieces in their nests), but the plastic, and very often the entire bag, persists in the environment essentially forever.

Municipal solid waste managers are concerned about the cost of dealing with billions of single-use plastic bags in landfills or waste incinerators. Many citizens are concerned about the visual blight that results from plastic bags blowing along roads or caught in vegetation. Biologists are concerned about plastic bags because millions of the bags end up floating in the oceans. Sea turtles cannot distinguish between a puffy floating plastic bag and the bells of jellyfish, which are one of sea turtles' favorite foods. Many sea turtles end up eating plastic bags, which can block a turtle's esophagus or fill up a turtle's stomach, making it impossible for the turtle to eat real food, with fatal results. Plastic bags in the ocean can also harm or kill sea turtles (and other marine and freshwater animals) by entangling them. Most species of sea turtles are in imminent danger of extinction.

Notes and Questions

1. Are plastic bags an issue that should be addressed by collective action, i.e., legislation? If so, how should the issue be addressed, i.e., what should the legislation provide?

2. Based on the excerpts from their writings you have read, what positions would Aldo Leopold, Mark Sagoff, Garrett Hardin, Terry Anderson and Donald Leal, Dan Tarlock, Joel Mintz, and John Dernbach be likely to take regarding the above-mentioned questions? Why? In your view, which of these writings, if any, provides the strongest support for your own views on these questions?

Chapter 2

Environmental Agencies and the Courts: Pertinent Principles of Administrative Law and Remedies

I. Introduction

Because environmental law often involves heated controversies, with much at stake for all concerned, environmental organizations and other non-governmental organizations (NGOs), regulated entities, government agencies, and individual citizens often resort to litigation in hopes of obtaining results they desire through the courts. Environmental litigation reflects great variety. It sometimes consists of lawsuits intended to halt or modify construction projects—undertaken by government agencies or private developers—that will or may destroy the natural environment or threaten public health. The substantive basis for this litigation is frequently the federal legislation under which the agency is proceeding, or the federal statute under which the agency grants a permit to a private developer to proceed.

One recurring aspect of this kind of litigation is that the plaintiff typically moves promptly for a preliminary injunction. Such a motion is intended to protect the environmental resources at issue from destruction or irredeemable damage before the legal issues can be adequately dealt with. Preliminary injunctions are not granted lightly. As set forth in Rule 65 of the Federal Rules of Civil Procedure, plaintiffs who seek this sort of equitable relief must demonstrate that: (1) they will be irreparably damaged, or lack an adequate remedy at law, if an injunction is not issued, (2) the threatened injury to the plaintiff outweighs the harm that an injunction may inflict on the defendant, (3) the plaintiff has at least a reasonable chance of success on the merits, and (4) granting a preliminary injunction will serve the public interest.

Another common type of environmental litigation—and one that will receive much emphasis in this chapter—is a lawsuit seeking judicial review of agency rulemaking. Most of the federal pollution control statutes provide for review of agency actions to promulgate emission, effluent, or other standards. This is typically referred to as "pre-enforcement review" or "statutory review." The usual pattern is to allow for judicial review of the challenged standards by a U.S. Circuit Court of Appeals within a certain period, and to prohibit the raising of any issues relating to the standards as a defense in an enforcement action, where those issues could have been raised during the judicial review period.

In contrast, "non-statutory review" is judicial review under the Administrative Procedure Act (APA), usually in a U.S. District Court. Most often, this review is based upon the "arbitrary and capricious . . . or otherwise not in accordance with the law" standard of the APA. The federal courts vary, however, in the strictness of their reviews of agency rulemakings under this standard. As we shall see, some courts apply "hard look review," a demanding approach that requires agencies to show that they have considered all relevant facts and factors, and avoided clear errors of judgment, before taking the action under challenge. Other courts are far more deferential to agency decisions, accepting final agency actions in nearly all instances.

varying approach to facts

In the environmental context, one of the most common forms of non-statutory review is a lawsuit against a federal agency to enforce the National Environmental Policy Act (NEPA). As is treated more fully in Chapter 3, NEPA requires federal agencies and departments to prepare a detailed Environmental Impact Statement (EIS) for every "major federal action significantly affecting the quality of the human environment." Review of agency compliance with NEPA is subject to APA review because NEPA does not expressly provide for judicial review of the agency obligation to prepare an EIS.

NEPA + EIS

NEPA litigation may focus on whether particular agency actions are sufficiently federal or major — or have enough of a "significant" environmental impact — to require the preparation of an EIS. They may also consider whether an agency's preliminary or final EIS is sufficiently detailed and comprehensive to satisfy the mandate of NEPA, whether the agency is correctly following the procedural requirements for EIS preparation, consideration, and distribution called for by NEPA, and whether a court may stop an agency action from proceeding because the court deems the environmental costs of the action, as revealed by the EIS, to be too high.

In this chapter — and throughout this book — we will consider some challenges to environmentally harmful projects. We will also examine judicial review of agency decisions. Lawsuits based upon NEPA will be a focus of Chapter 3; and an additional type of environmental litigation, lawsuits by government officials and private citizens to enforce federal environmental standards, will be examined in Chapter 11.

II. Judicial Review of Agency Action

Scenic Hudson Preservation Conference v. Federal Power Commission

354 F.2d 608 (2d Cir. 1965)

Judge HAYS:

In this proceeding the petitioners are the Scenic Hudson Preservation Conference, an unincorporated association consisting of a number of non-profit, conservationist organizations, and the Towns of Cortland, Putnam Valley and Yorktown. Petitioners ask us, pursuant to Section 313(b) of the Federal Power Act, to set aside three orders of the respondent, the Federal Power Commission:

a. An order of March 9, 1965 granting a license to the intervener, the Consolidated Edison Company of New York, Inc., to construct a pumped storage hydroelectric project on the west side of the Hudson River at Storm King Mountain in Cornwall, New York;

b. An order of May 6, 1965 denying petitioners' application for a rehearing of the March 9 order, and for the reopening of the proceeding to permit the introduction of additional evidence;

c. An order of May 6, 1965 denying joint motions filed by the petitioners to expand the scope of supplemental hearings to include consideration of the practicality and cost of underground transmission lines, and of the feasibility of *any* type of fish protection device.

A pumped storage plant generates electric energy for use during peak load periods, using hydroelectric units driven by water from a head-water pool or reservoir. The contemplated Storm King project would be the largest of its kind in the world. Consolidated Edison has estimated its cost, including transmission facilities, at $162,000,000. The project would consist of three major components, a storage reservoir, a powerhouse, and transmission lines. The [240 acre] storage reservoir, located over a thousand feet above the powerhouse, is to be connected to the powerhouse, located on the river front, by a tunnel 40 feet in diameter. The powerhouse, which is both a pumping and generating station, would be 800 feet long and contain eight pump generators.

Transmission lines would run under the Hudson to the east bank and then underground for 1.6 miles to a switching station which Consolidated Edison would build at Nelsonville in the Town of Philipstown. Thereafter, overhead transmission lines would be placed on towers 100 to 150 feet high and these would require a path up to 125 feet wide through Westchester and Putnam Counties for a distance of some 25 miles until they reached Consolidated Edison's main connections with New York City.

During slack periods Consolidated Edison's conventional steam plants in New York City would provide electric power for the pumps at Storm King to force water up the mountain, through the tunnel, and into the upper reservoir. In peak periods water would be released to rush down the mountain and power the generators. Three kilowatts of power generated in New York City would be necessary to obtain two kilowatts from the Cornwall installation. When pumping the powerhouse would draw approximately 1,080,000 cubic feet of water per minute from the Hudson, and when generating would discharge up to 1,620,000 cubic feet of water per minute into the river. The installation would have a capacity of 2,000,000 kilowatts, but would be so constructed as to be capable of enlargement to a total of 3,000,000 kilowatts . . . .

The Storm King project has aroused grave concern among conservationist groups, adversely affected municipalities and various state and federal legislative units and administrative agencies.

To be licensed by the Commission a prospective project must meet the statutory test of being "best adapted to a comprehensive plan for improving or developing a waterway, Federal Power Act Section 10(a). In framing the issue before it, the Federal Power Commission properly noted:

> "[W]e must compare the Cornwall project with any alternatives that are available. If on this record Con Edison has available an alternative source for meeting its power needs which is better adapted to the development of the Hudson River for all beneficial uses, including scenic beauty, this application should be denied."

If the Commission is properly to discharge its duty in this regard, the record on which it bases its determination must be complete. The petitioners and the public at large have a right to demand this completeness. It is our view, and we find, that the Commission has failed to compile a record which is sufficient to support its decision. The Commission has ignored certain relevant factors and failed to make a thorough study of possible alternatives to the Storm King project. While the courts have no authority to concern themselves with the policies of the Commission, it is their duty to see that the Commission's decisions receive that careful consideration which the statute contemplates. . . . Petitioners' application, pursuant to Section 313(b) to adduce additional evidence is granted. We set aside the three orders of the Commission to which the petition is addressed and remand the case for further proceedings in accordance with this opinion.

The Storm King project is to be located in an area of unique beauty and major historical significance. The highlands and gorge of the Hudson offer one of the finest pieces of river scenery in the world. The great German traveler Baedeker called it "finer than the Rhine." Petitioners' contention that the Commission must take these factors into consideration in evaluating the Storm King project is justified by the history of the Federal Power Act . . . .

Congress gave the Federal Power Commission sweeping authority and a specific planning responsibility.

Section 10(a) of the Federal Power Act reads:

"' 803. Conditions of license generally.

All licenses issued . . . shall be on the following conditions:

. . . .

(a) That the project adopted, . . . shall be such as in the judgment of the Commission *will be best adapted to a comprehensive plan for improving or developing a waterway or waterways for the use or benefit of interstate or foreign commerce, for the improvement and utilization of water-power development, and for other beneficial public uses, including recreational purposes;* and if necessary in order to secure such plan the Commission shall have authority to require the modification of any project and of the plans and specifications of the project works before approval."(Emphasis added.)

"Recreational purposes" are expressly included among the beneficial public uses to which the statute refers. The phrase undoubtedly encompasses the conservation of natural resources, the maintenance of natural beauty, and the preservation of historic sites. All of these "beneficial uses," the Supreme Court has observed, "while unregulated, might well be contradictory rather than harmonious." In licensing a project, it is the duty of the Federal Power Commission properly to weigh each factor . . . .

In recent years the Commission has placed increasing emphasis on the right of the public to "out-door recreational resources." The Commission has recognized generally that members of the public have rights in our recreational, historic and scenic resources under the Federal Power Act. *Namekagon Hydro Co.*, 12 F.P.C. 203, 206 (1954) ("the Commission realizes that in many cases where unique and most special types of recreation are encountered a dollar evaluation is inadequate as the public interest must be considered and it cannot be evaluated adequately only in dollars and cents"). In affirming *Namekagon* the Seventh Circuit upheld the Commission's denial of a license, to an otherwise economically feasible project, because fishing, canoeing and the scenic attraction of a "beautiful stretch of water" were threatened. *Namekagon Hydro Co. v. Federal Power Comm.*, 216 F.2d 509, 511–512 (7th Cir. 1954).

Respondent argues that "petitioners do not have standing to obtain review" because they "make no claim of any personal economic injury resulting from the Commission's action."

Section 313(b) of the Federal Power Act reads:

> "(b) Any party to a proceeding under this chapter aggrieved by an order issued by the Commission in such proceeding may obtain a review of such order in the United States Court of Appeals for any circuit wherein the licensee or public utility to which the order relates is located . . . ."

[handwritten margin note: Court's decision that Scenic Hudson Preservation Conference was an "aggrieved party"]

The Commission takes a narrow view of the meaning of "aggrieved party" under the Act. The Supreme Court has observed that the law of standing is a "complicated specialty of federal jurisdiction, the solution of whose problems is in any event more or less determined by the specific circumstances of individual sections." Although a "case" or "controversy" which is otherwise lacking cannot be created by statute, a statute may create new interests or rights and thus give standing to one who would otherwise be barred by the lack of a "case" or "controversy." The "case" or "controversy" requirement of Article III, Section 2 of the Constitution does not require that an "aggrieved" or "adversely affected" party have a personal economic interest . . . .

At an earlier point in these proceedings the Commission apparently accepted this view. Consolidated Edison strongly objected to the petitioners' standing, but the Commission did not deny their right to file an application for a rehearing under Section 313 (a) of the Act which also speaks in terms of "aggrieved parties."

Moreover, petitioners have sufficient economic interest to establish their standing. The New York-New Jersey Trail Conference, one of the two conservation groups that organized Scenic Hudson, has some seventeen miles of trailways in the area of Storm

[handwritten footer note: Adduce : Cite as evidence]

King Mountain. Portions of these trails would be inundated by the construction of the project's reservoir.

The primary transmission lines are an integral part of the Storm King project. *See* Federal Power Act Section 3(11). The towns that are co-petitioners with Scenic Hudson have standing because the transmission lines would cause a decrease in the proprietary value of publicly held land, reduce tax revenues collected from privately held land, and significantly interfere with long-range community planning. Yorktown, for example, fears that the transmission lines would run over municipal land selected for a school site, greatly decreasing its value and interfering with school construction . . . .

We see no justification for the Commission's fear that our determination will encourage "literally thousands" to intervene and seek review in future proceedings . . . Our experience with public actions confirms the view that the expense and vexation of legal proceedings is not lightly undertaken.

[Under] the Federal Power Act . . . the Commission has ample authority reasonably to limit those eligible to intervene or to seek review. Representation of common interests by an organization such as Scenic Hudson serves to limit the number of those who might otherwise apply for intervention and serves to expedite the administrative process.

The Federal Power Act, § 313(b) reads in part:

> "(b) If any party shall apply to the court for leave to adduce additional evidence, and shall show to the satisfaction of the court that such additional evidence is material and that there were reasonable grounds for failure to adduce such evidence in the proceedings before the Commission, the court may order such additional evidence to be taken before the Commission and to be adduced upon the hearing in such manner and upon such terms and conditions as to the court may seem proper."

The Commission in its opinion recognized that in connection with granting a license to Consolidated Edison it "must compare the Cornwall Project with any alternatives that are available." There is no doubt that the Commission is under a statutory duty to give full consideration to alternative plans . . . .

In the present case, the Commission heard oral argument on November 17, 1964, on the various exceptions to the Examiner's report. On January 7, 1965 the testimony of Mr. Alexander Lurkis, as to the feasibility of an alternative to the project, the use of gas turbines, was offered to the Commission by Hilltop Cooperative of Queens, a taxpayer and consumer group. The petition to intervene and present this new evidence was rejected on January 13, 1965, as not "timely." It was more than two months after the offer of this testimony, on March 9, 1965, that the Commission issued a license to Consolidated Edison . . . . [We] have found in the record no meaningful evidence which contradicts the proffered testimony supporting the gas turbine alternative.

Mr. Lurkis is a consulting engineer of thirty-nine years' experience. He has served as Chief Engineer of the New York City Bureau of Gas and Electric, in charge of a staff of 400, and as Senior Engineer of the New York City Transit Authority, where he supervised the design and construction of power plants. The New York Joint Legislative Committee on Natural Resources, after holding hearings on the Storm King project on November 19 and 20, 1964, summarized Mr. Lurkis's testimony as follows:

> "Mr. Alexander Lurkis . . . presented a detailed proposal for using gas turbines. This, he claimed, would meet the alleged peaking need of Con Ed and result in a saving for its customers of $132,000,000. The Committee has learned that similar gas turbine installations are now in use or proposed for use by a number of progressive electric utilities throughout the nation. In addition to meeting the alleged peak power needs and saving money for the ratepayer, the gas turbines proposed by Mr. Lurkis would have the following advantages:
>
> 1) Permit the company greater flexibility in meeting the power needs of its service area . . . . Small installations can be added as needed to meet demand. This, in contrast to a single, giant, permanent installation such as Con Ed proposes at Storm King Mountain, which would tie the technology and investment of one company to a method of power production that might be obsolete in a few years.
>
> 2) Keep the power production facilities within New York City. This would not only avoid the desecration of the Hudson Gorge and Highlands, but, also, would eliminate the great swathe of destruction down through Putnam and Westchester Counties and their beautiful suburban communities." Preliminary Report at 6.

The Committee report, issued on February 16, 1965, three weeks before the license to Consolidated Edison was granted, concluded:

> "[T]he whole situation involved in the Consolidated Edison Storm King Mountain project, and the protection of the Hudson River and its shores, requires further and extensive study and investigation. . . . .
>
> This Committee goes on record as opposing Con Ed's application until there has been adequate study of the points indicated in this report." Preliminary Report at 8 . . . .

Aside from self-serving general statements by officials of Consolidated Edison, the only testimony in the record bearing on the gas turbine alternative was offered by Ellery R. Fosdick. Fosdick's hastily prepared presentation considered turbines driven by steam and liquid fuel as well as gas; his direct testimony occupied less than ten pages of the record. Fosdick's testimony was too scanty to meet the requirement of a full consideration of alternatives. Indeed, under the circumstances, we must conclude that there was no significant attempt to develop evidence as to the gas turbine alternative; at least, there is no such evidence in the record.

The Commission argues that petitioners made "no attempt to secure additional testimony." Yet the record indicates that more than two months before the license was granted the Commission summarily rejected the offer of Mr. Lurkis's testimony.

It is not our present function to evaluate this evidence. Our focus is upon the action of the Commission . . . .

Especially in a case of this type, where public interest and concern is so great, the Commission's refusal to receive the Lurkis testimony, as well as proffered information on fish protection devices and underground transmission facilities, exhibits a disregard of the statute and of judicial mandates instructing the Commission to probe all feasible alternatives.

[As] we have pointed out, Congress gave the Federal Power Commission a specific planning responsibility. *See* Federal Power Act Section 10(a). The totality of a project's immediate and long-term range effects, and not merely the engineering and navigation aspects, are to be considered in a licensing proceeding . . .

In this case, as in many others, the Commission has claimed to be the representative of the public interest. This role does not permit it to act as an umpire blandly calling balls and strikes for adversaries appearing before it; the right of the public must receive active and affirmative protection at the hands of the Commission.

This Court cannot and should not attempt to substitute its judgment for that of the Commission. But we must decide whether the Commission has correctly discharged its duties, including the proper fulfillment of its planning function in deciding that the "licensing of the project would be in the overall public interest." The Commission must see to it that the record is complete. The Commission has an affirmative duty to inquire into and consider all relevant facts.

In addition to the Commission's failure to receive or develop evidence concerning the gas turbine alternative, there are other instances where the Commission should have acted affirmatively in order to make a complete record.

The Commission neither investigated the use of interconnected power as a possible alternative to the Storm King project, nor required Consolidated Edison to supply such information. The record sets forth Consolidated Edison's interconnection with a vast network of other utilities, but the Commission dismissed this alternative by noting that "Con Edison is relying fully upon such interconnections in estimating its future available capacity." However, only ten pages later in its opinion the Commission conceded:

> "Of significant importance, in our opinion, is the absence in the record, or the inadequacy, of information in regard to Con Edison's future interconnection plans; its plans, if any, for upgrading existing transmission lines to higher voltages; and of its existing transmission line grid in this general area and its future plans."

Moreover, in its October 4, 1965 order, the Commission in explaining how Consolidated Edison would be able to send "substantial amounts" of Storm King power to upstate New York and New England power companies, each December, said:

> ". . . even at time of the greatest diversion of Cornwall power, Con Edison would have other power sources immediately available to it for its peak requirements."

If interconnecting power can replace the Storm King project in December, why was it not considered as a permanent alternative? . . .

Issue

There is no evidence in the record to indicate that either the Commission or Consolidated Edison ever seriously considered this alternative. Nor is there any evidence that a combination of devices, for example gas turbine and interconnections, were considered. Indeed, the Commission stated in its brief that it is "of doubtful relevance to the present case whether there are practical alternatives to an appropriate use of water power by which Con Ed could meet its anticipated needs for peaking power with generally comparable economy." The failure of the Commission to inform itself of these alternatives cannot be reconciled with its planning responsibility under the Federal Power Act.

Lack of evidence that alternatives were considered

In its March 9 opinion the Commission postponed a decision on the transmission routes to be chosen until the May 1965 hearings were completed. Inquiry into the cost of putting lines underground was precluded because the May hearings were limited to the question of overhead transmission routes. The petitioners' April 26, 1965 motion to enlarge the scope of the May hearing was denied. The Commission insisted that the question of underground costs had been "extensively considered." We find almost nothing in the record to support this statement . . . .

Consolidated Edison witnesses testified that the Storm King project would result in annual savings of $12,000,000 over a steam plant of equivalent capacity. Given these savings, the Commission should at least have inquired into the capital and annual cost of running segments of the transmission line underground in those areas where the overhead structures would cause the most serious scenic damage. We find no indication that the Commission seriously weighed the aesthetic advantages of underground transmission lines against the economic disadvantages . . . .

Just after the Commission closed its proceedings in November the hearings held by the New York State Legislative Committee on Natural Resources alerted many fisherman groups to the threat posed by the Storm King project. On December 24 and 30, January 8, and February 3 each of four groups, concerned with fishing, petitioned for the right to intervene and present evidence [of possible harm to fisheries because of the location of water intake for the project, contradicting the testimony of Consolidated Edison's expert, Dr. Perlmutter.] . . . The Commission rejected all these petitions as "untimely," and seemingly placing great reliance on the testimony of Dr. Perlmutter, concluded:

> "The project will not adversely affect the fish resources of the Hudson River provided adequate protective facilities are installed."

Although an opportunity was made available at the May hearings for petitioners to submit evidence on protective designs, the question of the adequacy of *any* protective design was inexplicably excluded by the Commission . . . .

On remand, the Commission should take the whole fisheries question into consideration before deciding whether the Storm King project is to be licensed.

(4) Commission failed to consider fish habitats

The Commission should reexamine all questions on which we have found the record insufficient and all related matters. The Commission's renewed proceedings must include as a basic concern the preservation of natural beauty and of national historic shrines, keeping in mind that, in our affluent society, the cost of a project is only one of several factors to be considered. The record as it comes to us fails markedly to make out a case for the Storm King project on, among other matters, costs, public convenience and necessity, and absence of reasonable alternatives. Of course, the Commission should make every effort to expedite the new proceedings.

Petitioners' application, pursuant to Federal Power Act Section 313(b), to adduce additional evidence concerning alternatives to the Storm King project and the cost and practicality of underground transmission facilities is granted.

The licensing order of March 9 and the two orders of May 6 are set aside, and the case remanded for further proceedings.

Decision:
Remand for further hearings by Federal Power Commission

Notes and Questions

1. After nearly two decades of controversy and litigation, representatives of 11 environmental, governmental and utility groups agreed to: (1) halt construction at Storm King and dedicate the 500-acre site to Cornwall, N.Y. for park use; (2) reduce destruction of fish and other aquatic life at six other generators on the Hudson by minimizing water withdrawal and partially closing the plants during spawning season, when pumps suck fish and eggs into their pipelines; (3) build a hatchery to stock the Hudson River with striped bass; (4) propose and build power plants on selected areas of the Hudson only if closed-cycle cooling systems can eliminate the environmental and fish life damage caused by cooling water uptake; (5) forgive the plants of any obligation to build cooling towers at selected sites, if partial closings are insufficient to prevent fish damage; (6) endow a new foundation to fund independent research on ways to lessen the impact on fish by power plants; and (7) drop all lawsuits and administrative proceedings among the parties. The settlement saved the utilities and their customers more than $240 million in cooling-tower construction costs and $90 million per year in operating and carrying charges. Consolidated Edison estimated that the settlement cost the utilities less than one-tenth of that amount. *See* Temple, *Peace at Storm King,* 7 EPA JOURNAL 28 (1981).

equitable conclusion

2. *Scenic Hudson* was a classic environmental law case. The Scenic Hudson Preservation Conference was a forerunner of the Natural Resources Defense Council, now one of the leading national conservation organizations. One of the plaintiffs' attorneys, the late David Sive, went on to become a celebrated environmental lawyer. Mr. Sive, who has been referred to as the "father of environmental law," is the individual who coined the term "environmental law" to describe this then-newly emerging field in the late 1960s.

3. Notice the court's broad reading of the doctrine of standing-to-sue in this case — a view that, as we shall see, presaged similar handling of the standing question by the U.S. Supreme Court in the 1970s. How persuasive is the *Scenic Hudson* court's opinion on this point?

4. One critical aspect of the *Scenic Hudson* decision is the extent to which the Second Circuit required the Federal Power Commission to consider less environmentally harmful alternatives to the proposed hydroelectric project that was before it. Is that appropriate? Notably, this portion of the *Scenic Hudson* decision was a harbinger of the approach to the consideration of alternatives adopted by Congress in the National Environmental Policy Act of 1969.

Citizens to Preserve Overton Park v. Volpe
401 U.S. 402 (1971)

Justice MARSHALL:

The growing public concern about the quality of our natural environment has prompted Congress in recent years to enact legislation designed to curb the accelerating destruction of our country's natural beauty. We are concerned in this case with Section 4(f) of the Department of Transportation Act of 1966 and Section 138 of the Federal-Aid Highway Act of 1968. These statutes prohibit the Secretary of Transportation from authorizing the use of federal funds to finance the construction of highways through public parks if a "feasible and prudent" alternative route exists. If no such route is available, the statutes allow him to approve construction through parks only if there has been "all possible planning to minimize harm" to the park.

Petitioners, private citizens as well as local and national conservation organizations, contend that the Secretary has violated these statutes by authorizing the expenditure of federal funds for the construction of a six-lane interstate highway through a public park in Memphis Tennessee. Their claim was rejected by the District Court, which granted the Secretary's motion for summary judgment, and the Court of Appeals for the Sixth Circuit affirmed. After oral argument, the Court granted a stay that halted construction and, treating the application for the stay as a petition for certiorari, granted review. We now reverse the judgment below and remand for further proceedings in the District Court.

Overton Park is a 342-acre city park located near the center of Memphis. The park contains a zoo, a nine-hole municipal golf course, an outdoor theater, nature trails, a bridle path, an art academy, picnic areas, and 170 acres of forest. The proposed highway, which is to be a six-lane, high-speed, expressway, will sever the zoo from the rest of the park. Although the roadway will be depressed below ground level except where it crosses a small creek, 26 acres of the park will be destroyed. The highway is to be a segment of Interstate Highway No. I-40, part of the National System of Interstate and Defense Highways. I-40 will provide Memphis with a major east-west expressway that will allow easier access to downtown Memphis from the residential areas on the eastern edge of the city.

Although the route through the park was approved by the Bureau of Public Roads in 1956 and by the Federal Highway Administrator in 1966, the enactment of Section 4(f) of the Department of Transportation Act prevented distribution of federal funds for the section of the highway designated to go through Overton Park until the Secretary of Transportation determined whether the requirements of Section 4(f) had been met. Federal funding for the rest of the project was, however, available; and the state acquired right-of-way on both sides of the park.

Summary judgment: request for court decision based on oral arguments only, without facts

Petition for certiorari: Document which a losing party files w/ Supreme Court asking for a review of the decision of a lower court

In April 1968, the Secretary announced that he concurred in the judgment of local officials that I-40 should be built through the park. And in September 1969 the State acquired the right-of-way inside Overton Park from the city. Final approval for the project—the route as well as the design—was not announced until November 1969, after Congress had reiterated in Section 138 of the Federal-Aid Highway Act that highway construction through public parks was to be restricted. Neither announcement approving the route and design of I-40 was accompanied by a statement of the Secretary's factual findings. He did not indicate why he believed there were no feasible and prudent alternative routes or why design changes could not be made to reduce the harm to the park.

Petitioners contend that the Secretary's action is invalid without such formal findings and that the Secretary did not make an independent determination but merely relied on the judgment of the Memphis City Council. They also contend that it would be "feasible and prudent" to route I-40 around Overton Park either to the north or to the south. And they argue that if these alternative routes are not "feasible and prudent," the present plan does not include "all possible" methods for reducing harm to the park. Petitioners claim that I-40 could be built under the park by using either of two possible tunneling methods, and they claim that, at a minimum, by using advanced drainage techniques the expressway could be depressed below ground level along the entire route through the park including the section that crosses the small creek . . . .

In the District Court, respondents introduced affidavits, prepared specifically for this litigation, which indicated that the Secretary had made the decision and that the decision was supportable. These affidavits were contradicted by affidavits introduced by petitioners, who also sought to take the deposition of a former federal highway administrator who had participated in the decision to route I-40 through Overton Park.

The District Court and the Court of Appeals found that formal findings by the Secretary were not necessary and refused to order the deposition of the former Federal Highway Administrator because those courts believed that probing of the mental processes of an administrative decision maker was prohibited. And, believing that the Secretary's authority was wide and reviewing courts' authority narrow in the approval of highway routes, the lower courts held that the affidavits contained no basis for a determination that the Secretary had exceeded his authority.

We agree that formal findings were not required. But we do not believe that in this case judicial review based solely on litigation affidavits was adequate.

A threshold question—whether petitioners are entitled to any judicial review—is easily answered. Section 701 of the Administrative Procedure Act [] provides that the action of "each authority of the Government of the United States," which includes the Department of Transportation, is subject to judicial review [aside from certain exceptions not applicable to this case].

Section 4(f) of the Department of Transportation Act and Section 138 of the Federal-Aid Highway Act are clear and specific directives. Both the Department of

Transportation Act and the Federal-Aid Highway Act provide that the Secretary "shall not approve any program or project" that requires the use of any public parkland "unless (1) there is no feasible and prudent alternative to the use of such land, and (2) such program includes all possible planning to minimize harm to such park ". . . . This language is a plain and explicit bar to the use of federal funds for construction of highways through parks—only the most unusual situations are exempted.

Despite the clarity of the statutory language, respondents argue that the Secretary has wide discretion. They recognize that the requirement that there be no "feasible" alternative route admits of little administrative discretion. For this exemption to apply the Secretary must find that as a matter of sound engineering it would not be feasible to build the highway along any other route. Respondents argue, however, that the requirement that there be no other "prudent" route requires the Secretary to engage in a wide-ranging balancing of competing interests. They contend that the Secretary should weigh the detriment resulting from the destruction of parkland against the cost of other routes, safety considerations, and other factors, and determine on the basis of the importance that he attaches to these other factors whether, on balance, alternative feasible routes would be "prudent."

But no such wide-ranging endeavor was intended. It is obvious that in most cases considerations of cost, directness of routes, and community disruption will indicate the parkland should be used for highway construction whenever possible. Although it may be necessary to transfer funds from one jurisdiction to another, there will always be a smaller outlay required from the public purse when parkland is used since the public already owns the land and there will be no need to pay for right-of-way. And since people do not live or work in parks, if a highway is built on parkland no one will have to leave his home or give up his business. Such factors are common to substantially all highway construction. Thus if Congress intended these factors to be on an equal footing with preservation of parkland there would have been no need for the statutes.

Congress clearly did not intend that cost and disruption of the community were to be ignored by the Secretary. But the very existence of the statute indicates that protection of parkland was to be given paramount importance. The few green havens that are public parks were not to be lost unless there were truly unusual factors present in a particular case or the cost or community disruption resulting from alternative routes reached extraordinary magnitudes. If the statutes are to have any meaning, the Secretary cannot approve the destruction of parkland unless he finds that alternative routes present unique problems . . . .

But the existence of judicial review is only the start: the standards for review must also be determined. For that we must look to Section 706 of the Administrative Procedure Act which provides that a "reviewing court shall . . . hold unlawful and set aside agency action, findings and conclusions found" not to meet six separate standards. In all cases agency action must be set aside if the action was "arbitrary, capricious, an abuse of discretion, or otherwise not in accordance with law" or if the action failed to meet statutory, procedural, or constitutional requirements.

Inquiry ①

. . . . The court is first required to decide whether the Secretary acted within the scope of his authority. This determination naturally begins with a delineation of the scope of the Secretary's authority and discretion. As has been shown, Congress has specified only a small range of choices that the Secretary can make. Also involved in this initial inquiry is a determination of whether on the facts the Secretary's decision can reasonably be said to be within that range. The reviewing court must consider whether the Secretary properly constructed his authority to approve the use of parkland as limited to situations where there are no feasible alternative routes or where feasible alternative routes involve uniquely difficult problems. And the reviewing court must be able to find that the Secretary could have reasonably believed that in this case there are no feasible alternatives or that alternatives do involve unique problems.

Inquiry ②

Scrutiny of the facts does not end, however, with the determination that the Secretary has acted within the scope of his statutory authority. § 706(2)(A) requires a finding that the actual choice made was not "arbitrary, capricious, an abuse of discretion, or otherwise not in accordance with law." To make this finding the court must consider whether the decision was based on a consideration of the relevant factors and whether there has been a clear error of judgment . . . .

Although this inquiry into the facts is to be searching and careful, the ultimate standard of review is a narrow one. The court is not empowered to substitute its judgment for that of the agency.

Inquiry ③

The final inquiry is whether the Secretary's action followed the necessary procedural requirements. Here the only procedural error alleged is the failure of the Secretary to make formal findings and state his reason for allowing the highway to be built through the park.

Undoubtedly, review of the Secretary's action is hampered by his failure to make such findings, but the absence of formal findings does not necessarily require that the case be remanded to the Secretary. Neither the Department of Transportation Act nor the Federal-Aid Highway Act requires such formal findings. . . .

The lower courts based their review on the litigation affidavits that were presented. These affidavits were merely "*post hoc*" rationalizations which have traditionally been found to be an inadequate basis for review. And they clearly do not constitute the "whole record" compiled by the agency: the basis for review required by Section 706 of the Administrative Procedure Act. . . .

Justice Marshall Decision →

Thus it is necessary to remand this case to the District Court for plenary review of the Secretary's decision. That review is to be based on the full administrative record that was before the Secretary at the time he made his decision.

But since the bare record may not disclose the factors that were considered or the Secretary's construction of the evidence it may be necessary for the District Court to require some explanation in order to determine if the Secretary acted within the scope of his authority and if the Secretary's action was justifiable under the applicable standard. . . .

Reversed and remanded.

Separate opinion of Justice BLACK:

I agree with the Court that the judgment of the Court of Appeals is wrong and that its action should be reversed. I do not agree that the whole matter should be remanded to the District Court. I think the case should be sent back to the Secretary of Transportation. It is apparent from the Court's opinion today that the Secretary of Transportation completely failed to comply with the duty imposed upon him by Congress not to permit a federally-financed public highway to run through a public park "unless (1) there is no feasible and prudent alternative to the use of such land, and (2) such program includes all possible planning to minimize harm to such park . . . ." That congressional command should not be taken lightly by the Secretary or by this Court . . . . The Act of Congress in connection with other Federal Highway Aid legislation, it seems to me, calls for hearings, hearings that a court can review, hearings that demonstrate more than mere arbitrary defiance by the Secretary . . . . I regret that I am compelled to conclude for myself that, except for some too-late formulations, apparently coming from the Solicitor General's Office, this record contains not one word to indicate that the Secretary raised even a finger to comply with the command of Congress. It is our duty, I believe, to remand this whole matter back to the Secretary of Transportation for him to give this mater the hearing it deserves in full good-faith obedience to the Act of Congress. That Act was obviously passed to protect our public parks from forays by road builders except in the most extraordinary and imperative circumstances . . . . I dissent from the Court's failure to send the case back to the Secretary, whose duty has not yet been performed.

Notes and Questions

1. *Overton Park* has been an influential decision, widely cited by lower federal courts. Among other things, it stands for the principle that federal agencies must compile a written administrative record in informal "notice and comment" rulemaking proceedings. This has led many agencies, on the advice of their lawyers, to compile extensive decisional files that form a reviewable record in such proceedings.

One scholarly critic of this trend contends that it has resulted in an "ossification" of complex agency rulemaking:

> Because the agencies perceive that the reviewing courts are inconsistent in the degree to which they are deferential [to agency decisions], they are constrained to prepare for the worst-case scenario on judicial review. This can be extremely resource-intensive and time-consuming. Moreover, since the criteria for substantive judicial review are the same for repealing old rules as for promulgating new rules, the agencies are equally chary of revisiting old rules, even in the name of flexibility. McGarity, *Some Thoughts On "Deossifying" the Rulemaking Process*, 41 DUKE L.J. 1419, 1420 (1992).

2. For provocative critiques of the result in *Overton Park,* see Strauss, *Considering Political Alternatives to "Hard Look" Review,* 1989 DUKE L.J. 538, 544–547 and Strauss, *Revisiting* Overton Park: *Political and Judicial Controls Over Administrative Actions Affecting the Community*, 39 UCLA L. REV. 1251 (1992).

3. On remand, following a 25-day trial, the U.S. District Court reversed the Secretary of Transportation's decision and remanded the case to the Department. The Secretary then declined to find that there was no feasible or prudent alternative to building I-40 through Overton Park. That decision was subsequently upheld, on judicial review, and the road through the park was not built. *See Citizens to Preserve Overton Park v. Brinegar,* 357 F. Supp. 846 (W.D. Tenn. 1973), *rev'd,* 494 F.2d 1212 (6th Cir. 1974), *cert. denied,* 421 U.S. 991 (1975).

4. The Supreme Court's *Overton Park* decision is frequently viewed as an example of "hard look" review, a term coined by Judge Harold Leventhal of the D.C. Circuit in *Greater Boston Television Corp. v. FCC,* 444 F.2d 841, 850 (D.C. Cir. 1970), *cert. denied* 403 U.S. 923 (1971) ("Its supervisory function calls on the court to intervene . . . if the court becomes aware, especially from a combination of danger signals, that the agency has not really taken a hard look at the salient problems, and has not genuinely engaged in reasoned decision-making.").

5. In light of *Overton Park,* may the federal courts require federal agencies to adopt rulemaking procedures that go beyond the straightforward notice and comment procedures prescribed by the Administrative Procedure Act? The U.S. Supreme Court resolved that question in the negative in *Vermont Yankee Nuclear Power Corp. v. Natural Resources Defense Council, Inc.,* 435 U.S. 519, 98 S. Ct. 1197, 55 L. Ed. 2d 460 (1978). Rejecting an attempt by the D.C. Circuit to impose "hybrid rulemaking" procedures on the Nuclear Regulatory Commission (in licensing proceedings regarding proposed nuclear power plants), the Court stated that where a court reviews administrative agency decisions that are accompanied by contemporaneous explanations, the court must not "stray beyond the judicial province to explore the procedural format or to impose upon the agency its own notion of which procedures are 'best' or most likely to further some vague, undefined public good."

Chevron U.S.A. v. Natural Resource Defense Council
467 U.S. 839 (1984)

Justice STEVENS:

In the Clean Air Act Amendments of 1977, Congress enacted certain requirements applicable to States that had not achieved the national air quality standards. . . . The amended Clean Air Act required these "nonattainment" States to establish a permit program regulating "new or modified major stationary sources" of air pollution. Generally, a permit may not be issued for a new or modified major stationary source unless several stringent conditions are met. The EPA regulation promulgated to implement this permit requirement allows a State to adopt a plant wide definition of the term "stationary source." Under this definition, an existing plant that contains several pollution-emitting devices may install or modify one piece of equipment without meeting the permit conditions if the alteration will not increase the total emissions from the plant. The question presented by these cases is whether EPA's decision to allow States to treat all of the pollution-emitting devices within the same industrial grouping as though they were encased within a single "bubble" is based on a reasonable construction of the statutory term "stationary source."

The EPA regulations containing the plant wide definition of the term stationary source were promulgated on October 14, 1981. Respondents filed a timely petition for review in the United States Court of Appeals for the District of Columbia Circuit. The Court of Appeals set aside the regulations. . . .

The court observed that the relevant part of the amended Clean Air Act "does not explicitly define what Congress envisioned as a 'stationary source,' to which the permit program . . . should apply," and further stated that the precise issue was not "squarely addressed in the legislative history." . . . Based on two of its precedents concerning the applicability of the bubble concept to certain Clean Air Act programs, the court stated that the bubble concept was "mandatory" in programs designed merely to maintain existing air quality [PSD programs], but held that it was "inappropriate" in programs enacted to improve air quality. Since the purpose of the [non-attainment area] permit program—its *"raison d'etre"* in the court's view—was to improve air quality, the court held that the bubble concept was inapplicable in these cases under its prior precedents. It therefore set aside the regulations embodying the bubble concept as contrary to law. We granted certiorari to review that judgment . . . , and we now reverse.

The basic legal error of the Court of Appeals was to adopt a static judicial definition of the term "stationary source" when it had decided that Congress itself had not commanded that definition. Respondents do not defend the legal reasoning of the Court of Appeals. Nevertheless, since this Court reviews judgments, not opinions, we must determine whether the Court of Appeals' legal error resulted in an erroneous judgment . . .

When a court reviews an agency's construction of the statute which it administers, it is confronted with two questions. First, always, is the question whether Congress has directly spoken to the precise question at issue. If the intent of Congress is clear, that is the end of the matter; for the court, as well as the agency, must give effect to the unambiguously expressed intent of Congress.

If, however, the court determines Congress has not directly addressed the precise question at issue, the court does not simply impose its own construction on the statute, as would be necessary in the absence of an administrative interpretation. Rather, if the statute is silent or ambiguous with respect to the specific issue, the question for the court is whether the agency's answer is based on a permissible construction of the statute.

"The power of an administrative agency to administer a congressionally created . . . program necessarily requires the formulation of policy and the making of rules to fill any gap left, implicitly or explicitly, by Congress." If Congress has explicitly left a gap for the agency to fill, there is an express delegation of authority to the agency to elucidate a specific provision of the statute by regulation. Such legislative regulations are given controlling weight unless they are arbitrary, capricious, or manifestly contrary to the statute. Sometimes the legislative delegation to an agency on a particular question is implicit rather than explicit. In such a case, a court may not substitute its own construction of a statutory provision for a reasonable interpretation made by the administrator of an agency.

We have long recognized that considerable weight should be accorded to an executive department's construction of a statutory scheme it is entrusted to administer, and the principle of deference to administrative interpretations

> has been consistently followed by this Court whenever a decision as to the meaning or reach of a statute has involved reconciling conflicting policies, and a full understanding of the force of the statutory policy in the given situation has depended upon more than ordinary knowledge respecting the matters subjected to agency regulations . . . .

> . . . If this choice represents a reasonable accommodation of conflicting policies that were committed to the agency's care by the statute, we should not disturb it unless it appears from the statute or its legislative history that the accommodation is not one that Congress would have sanctioned. *United States v. Shimer,* 367 U.S. 374, 382 383 (1961). . . .

In light of these well-settled principles it is clear that the Court of Appeals misconceived the nature of its role in reviewing the regulations at issue. Once it determined, after its own examination of the legislation, that Congress did not actually have an intent regarding the applicability of the bubble concept to the permit program, the question before it was not whether in its view the concept is "inappropriate" in the general context of a program designed to improve air quality, but whether the Administrator's view that it is appropriate in the context of this particular program is a reasonable one. Based on the examination of the legislation and its history which follows, we agree with the Court of Appeals that Congress did not have a specific intention on the applicability of the bubble concept in these cases, and conclude that the EPA's use of that concept here is a reasonable policy choice for the agency to make.

Section 111 (a) defined the terms that are to be used in setting and enforcing standards of performance for new stationary sources. It provided:

> For purposes of this section:

> (3) The term "stationary source" means any building, structure, facility, or installation which emits or may emit any air pollutant.

In the 1970 Amendments that definition was not only applicable to the NSPS program required by Section 111, but also was made applicable to a requirement of Section 110 that each state implementation plan contain a procedure for reviewing the location of any proposed new source and preventing its construction if it would preclude the attainment or maintenance of national air quality standards.

In due course, the EPA promulgated NAAQS's, approved SIP's, and adopted detailed regulations governing NSPS's for various categories of equipment. In one of its programs, the EPA used a plant wide definition of the term "stationary source." . . .

The 1970 legislation provided for the attainment of primary NAAQS's by 1975. In many areas of the country, particularly the most industrialized States, the statutory goals were not attained . . . .

The Clean Air Act Amendments of 1977 are a lengthy, detailed, technical, complex, and comprehensive response to a major social issue. A small portion of the statute expressly deals with nonattainment areas. The focal point of this controversy is one phrase in that portion of the Amendments. . . .

Most significantly for our purposes, the statute provided that each plan shall

"(6) require permits for the construction and operation of new or modified major stationary sources in accordance with Section 173."

The 1977 Amendments contain no specific reference to the "bubble concept." Nor do they contain a specific definition of the term "stationary source," though they did not disturb the definition of "stationary source" contained in Section 111 (a) (3), applicable by the terms of the Act to the NSPS program . . . .

The legislative history of the portion of the 1977 Amendments dealing with nonattainment areas does not contain any specific comment on the "bubble concept" or the question whether a plant wide definition of a stationary source is permissible under the permit program. It does, however, plainly disclose that in the permit program Congress sought to accommodate the conflict between the economic interest in permitting capital improvements to continue and the environmental interest in improving air quality. . . . .

As previously noted, prior to the 1977 Amendments, the EPA had adhered to a plant wide definition of the term "source" under a NSPS program . . . .

In 1981 a new administration took office and initiated a "Government-wide reexamination of regulatory burdens and complexities." In the context of that review, the EPA reevaluated the various arguments that had been advanced in connection with the proper definition of the term "source" and concluded that the term should be given the same definition in both nonattainment areas and PSD areas.

In explaining its conclusions, the EPA first noted that the definitional issue was not squarely addressed in either the statute or its legislative history and therefore that the issue involved an agency "judgment as how to best carry out the Act." It then set forth several reasons for concluding that the plant wide definition was more appropriate . . . .

Based on our examination of the legislative history, we agree with the Court of Appeals that it is unilluminating. . . . We find that the legislative history as a whole is silent on the precise issue before us. It is, however, consistent with the view that the EPA should have broad discretion in implementing the policies of the 1977 Amendments.

More importantly, that history plainly identifies the policy concerns that motivated the enactment; the plant wide definition is fully consistent with one of those concerns — the allowance of reasonable economic growth — and, whether or not we believe it most effectively implements the other, we must recognize that the EPA has advanced a reasonable explanation for its conclusion that the regulations serve the environmental objectives as well. . . .

Our review of the EPA's varying interpretations of the word "source"—both before and after the 1977 Amendments—convinces us that the agency primarily responsible for administering this important legislation has consistently interpreted it flexibly—not in a sterile textual vacuum, but in the context of implementing policy decisions in a technical and complex arena. The fact that the agency has from time to time changed its interpretation of the term "source" does not, as respondents argue, lead us to conclude that no deference should be accorded the agency's interpretation of the statute. An initial agency interpretation is not instantly carved in stone. On the contrary, the agency, to engage in informed rulemaking, must consider varying interpretations and the wisdom of its policy on a continuing basis. Moreover, the fact that the agency has adopted different definitions in different contexts adds force to the argument that the definition itself is flexible, particularly since Congress has never indicated any disapproval of a flexible reading of the statute . . . .

Reasoning

The arguments over policy that are advanced in the parties' briefs create the impression that respondents are now waging in a judicial forum a specific policy battle which they ultimately lost in the agency and in the 32 jurisdictions opting for the "bubble concept," but one which was never waged in Congress. Such policy arguments are more properly addressed to legislators or administrators, not to judges.

[T]he Administrator's interpretation represents a reasonable accommodation of manifestly competing interests and is entitled to deference: the regulatory scheme is technical and complex, the agency considered the matter in a detailed and reasoned fashion, and the decision involves reconciling conflicting policies. Congress intended to accommodate both interests, but did not do so itself on the level of specificity presented by these cases. Perhaps that body consciously desired the Administrator to strike that balance at this level, thinking that those with great expertise and charged with responsibility for administering the provision would be in a better position to do so; perhaps it simply did not consider the question at this level; and perhaps Congress was unable to forge a coalition on either side of the question, and those on each side decided to take their chances with the scheme devised by the agency. For judicial purposes, it matters not which of these things occurred.

Judges are not experts in the field, and are not part of either political branch of the Government. Courts must, in some cases, reconcile competing political interests, but not on the basis of the judges' personal policy preferences. In contrast, an agency to which Congress has delegated policymaking may, within the limits of that delegation, properly rely upon the incumbent administration's views of wise policy to inform its judgments. While agencies are not directly accountable to the people, the Chief Executive is, and it is entirely appropriate for this political branch of the Government to make such policy choices—resolving the competing interests which

Congress itself either inadvertently did not resolve, or intentionally left to be resolved by the agency charged with the administration of the statute in light of everyday realities.

When a challenge to an agency construction of a statutory provision, fairly conceptualized, really centers on the wisdom of the agency's policy, rather than whether it is a reasonable choice within a gap left open by Congress, the challenge must fail. In such a case, federal judges—who have no constituency—have a duty to respect legitimate policy choices made by those who do. The responsibilities for assessing the wisdom of such policy choices and resolving the struggle between competing views of the public interest are not judicial ones: "Our Constitution vests such responsibilities in the political branches." *TVA v. Hill,* 437 U.S. 153, 195 (1978).

We hold that the EPA's definition of the term "source" is a permissible construction of the statute which seeks to accommodate progress in reducing air pollution with economic growth . . . .

Decision

The judgment of the Court of Appeals is reversed.

Notes and Questions

1. Was the Supreme Court correct in determining that courts should give conclusive weight to "permissible" statutory interpretations of administrative agencies with regard to ambiguous statutory provisions? Are agencies necessarily better situated than courts to perform that function? Is the Court's view in *Chevron* consistent with the Administrative Procedure Act? (That statute provides, in part, that reviewing courts are to "decide all relevant questions of law, interpret constitutional and statutory provisions, and determine the meaning or applicability of the terms of an agency action." *See* 5 U.S.C. § 706).

2. The *Chevron* decision has been subject to scholarly and judicial criticism. In the view of one commentator: "Administrative agencies are constrained by statute, that is, law, and the mere fact that the statute is ambiguous shouldn't give the agency, of all people, the authority to decide on the meaning of the limitation. The cute way in which it's sometimes put is that foxes shouldn't guard henhouses. If *Chevron* is taken to mean that agencies judge the scope of their own authority, then one has precisely that problem." Sunstein, *Judicial Review of Administrative Action in a Conservative Era,* 39 Admin. L. Rev. 353, 362 (1987). Is this a fair evaluation of the *Chevron* doctrine? *See also* Breyer, *Judicial Review of Questions of Law and Policy,* 38 Admin. L. Rev. 363 (1986) (The *Chevron* doctrine is "seriously overbroad, counter-productive and sometimes useless.").

3. The *Chevron* decision has been widely cited by lower federal courts as a basis for deferring to agency decisions. Nonetheless, there is evidence that the case has often been ignored by the U.S. Supreme Court itself in its subsequent decisions. *See* Merrill, *Judicial Deference to Executive Precedent,* 101 Yale L. J. 969 (1992) and Merrill, *Textualism and the Future of the* Chevron *Doctrine,* 72 Wash. U. L. Q. 351 (1994).

III. Standing-to-Sue in Environmental Lawsuits

Sierra Club v. Morton
405 U.S. 727 (1972)

Justice STEWART:

FACTS

[Petitioners were seeking to enjoin the U.S. Forest Service from proceeding with a plan to turn Mineral King, an environmentally valuable area of great natural beauty in the Sierra Nevada Mountains adjacent to Sequoia National Park, into a major recreational development complex of motels, restaurants, swimming pools, parking lots and other structures designed to accommodate 14,000 visitors daily. Other facilities were to include ski lifts, ski trails, cog assisted railways and utility installations. To provide access to the resort, the construction of a 20-mile highway was proposed which would traverse Sequoia National Park, as would a proposed high voltage power line needed to provide electricity for the recreational complex.]

Can Sierra Club "stand to sue"?

The first question presented is whether the Sierra Club has alleged facts that entitle it to obtain judicial review of the challenged action. Whether a party has a sufficient stake in an otherwise justiciable controversy to obtain judicial resolution of that controversy is what has traditionally been referred to as the question of standing to sue. . . .

The Sierra Club relies upon Section 10 of the Administrative Procedure Act (APA) which provides:

> "A person suffering legal wrong because of agency action, or adversely affected or aggrieved by agency action within the meaning of a relevant statute, is entitled to judicial review thereof . . . ."

Q.

[T]he question, which has arisen with increasing frequency in federal courts in recent years, as to what must be alleged by persons who claim injury of a noneconomic nature to interests that are widely shared . . . . is presented in this case.

S-t-S req. #1: "injury in fact"

The injury alleged by the Sierra Club will be incurred entirely by reason of the change in the uses to which Mineral King will be put, and the attendant change in the aesthetics and ecology of the area. Thus, in referring to the road to be built through Sequoia National Park, the complaint alleged that the development "would destroy or otherwise affect the scenery, natural and historic objects and wildlife of the park and would impair the enjoyment of the park for future generations." We do not question that this type of harm may amount to an "injury in fact" sufficient to lay the basis for standing under Section 10 of the APA. Aesthetic and environmental well-being, like economic well-being, are important ingredients of the quality of life in our society, and the fact that particular environmental interests are shared by the many rather than the few does not make them less deserving of legal protection through the judicial process. But the "injury in fact" test requires more than an injury to a cognizable interest. It requires that the party seeking review be himself among the injured.

The impact of the proposed changes in the environment of Mineral King will not fall indiscriminately upon every citizen. The alleged injury will be felt directly only by those who use Mineral King and Sequoia National Park, and for whom the aesthetic and recreational values of the area will be lessened by the highway and ski resort. The Sierra Club failed to allege that it or its members would be affected in any of their activities or pastimes by the Disney development. Nowhere in the pleadings or affidavits did the Club state that its members use Mineral King for any purpose, much less that they use it in any way that would be significantly affected by the proposed actions of the respondents.

The Club apparently regarded any allegations of individualized injury as superfluous, on the theory that this was a "public" action involving questions as to the use of natural resources, and that the Club's longstanding concern with and expertise in such matters were sufficient to give it standing as "representative of the public." This theory reflects a misunderstanding of our cases involving so-called "public actions" in the area of administrative law . . . .

The trend of cases arising under the APA and other statutes authorizing judicial review of federal agency action has been towards recognizing that injuries other than economic harm are sufficient to bring a person within the meaning of the statutory language, and towards discarding the notion that an injury that is widely shared is *ipso facto* not an injury sufficient to provide the basis for judicial review. We noted this development with approval in saying that the interest alleged to have been injured "may reflect 'aesthetic, conservational, and recreational' as well as economic values." But broadening the categories of injury that may be alleged in support of standing is a different matter from abandoning the requirement that the party seeking review must have himself suffered an injury.

Some courts have indicated a willingness to take this latter step by conferring standing upon organizations that have demonstrated "an organizational interest in the problem" of environmental or consumer protection. It is clear that an organization whose members are injured may represent those members in a proceeding for judicial review. But a mere "interest in a problem," no matter how longstanding the interest and no matter how qualified the organization is in evaluating the problem, is not sufficient by itself to render the organization "adversely affected" or "aggrieved" within the meaning of the APA. The Sierra Club is a large and long-established organization, with an historic commitment to the cause of protecting our Nation's natural heritage from man's depredations. But if a "special interest" in this subject were enough to entitle the Sierra Club to commence this litigation, there would appear to be no objective basis upon which to disallow a suit by any other bona fide "special interest" organization however small or short-lived. And if any group with a bona fide "special interest" could initiate such litigation, it is difficult to perceive why any individual citizen with the same bona fide special interest would not also be entitled to do so.

The requirement that a party seeking review must allege facts showing that he is himself adversely affected does not insulate executive action from judicial review, nor does it prevent any public interests from being protected through the judicial

reg 3
injury likely
to be redressed
by court

Decision

process. It does serve as at least a rough attempt to put the decision as to whether review will be sought in the hands of those who have a direct stake in the outcome. That goal would be undermined were we to construe the APA to authorize judicial review at the behest of organizations or individuals who seek to do no more than vindicate their own value preferences through the judicial process. The principle that the Sierra Club would have us establish in this case would do just that.

As we conclude that the Court of Appeals was correct in its holding that the Sierra Club lacked standing to maintain this action, we do not reach any other questions presented in the petition, and we intimate no view on the merits of the complaint. The judgment is affirmed.

Justice POWELL and Justice REHNQUIST took no part in the consideration or decision of this case.

Justice DOUGLAS, dissenting:

I share the views of my Brother BLACKMUN and would reverse the judgment below.

The critical question of "standing" would be simplified and also put neatly in focus if we fashioned a federal rule that allowed environmental issues to be litigated before federal agencies or federal courts in the name of the inanimate object about to be despoiled, defaced, or invaded by roads and bulldozers and where injury is the subject of public outrage. Contemporary public concern for protecting nature's ecological equilibrium should lead to the conferral of standing upon environmental objects to sue for their own preservation. . . .

Inanimate objects are sometimes parties in litigation. A ship has a legal personality, a fiction found useful for maritime purposes. The corporation sole—a creature of ecclesiastical law—is an acceptable adversary and large fortunes ride on its cases. The ordinary corporation is a "person" for purposes of the adjudicatory processes, whether it represents proprietary, spiritual, aesthetic, or charitable causes.

So it should be as respects valleys, alpine meadows, rivers, lakes, estuaries, beaches, ridges, groves of trees, swampland, or even air that feels the destructive pressures of modern technology and modern life. The river, for example, is the living symbol of all the life it sustains or nourishes—fish, aquatic insects, water ouzels, otter, fisher, deer, elk, bear, and all other animals, including man, who are dependent on it or who enjoy it for its sight, its sound, or its life. The river as plaintiff speaks for the ecological unit of life that is part of it. Those people who have a meaningful relation to that body of water—whether it be a fisherman, a canoeist, a zoologist, or a logger—must be able to speak for the values which the river represents and which are threatened with destruction.

The voice of the inanimate object, therefore, should not be stilled. That does not mean that the judiciary takes over the managerial functions from the federal agency. It merely means that before these priceless bits of Americana (such as a valley, an alpine meadow, a river, or a lake) are forever lost or are so transformed as to be reduced to the eventual rubble of our urban environment, the voice of the existing beneficiaries of these environmental wonders should be heard . . . .

Those inarticulate members of the ecological group cannot speak. But those people who have so frequented the place as to know its values and wonders will be able to speak for the entire ecological community. . . .

That, as I see it, is the issue of "standing" in the present case and controversy.

Justice BLACKMUN, dissenting

. . . The ultimate result of the Court's decision today, I fear, and sadly so, is that the 35.3 million-dollar-complex, over 10 times greater than the Forest Service's suggested minimum, will now hastily proceed to completion; that serious opposition to it will recede in discouragement; and that Mineral King, the "area of great natural beauty nestled in the Sierra Nevada Mountains," to use the Court's words, will become defaced, at least in part, and, like so many other areas, will cease to be "uncluttered by the products of civilization."

Rather than pursue the course the Court has chosen to take by its affirmance of the judgment of the Court of Appeals, I would adopt one of two alternatives:

1. I would reverse that judgment and, instead, approve the judgment of the District Court which recognized standing in the Sierra Club and granted preliminary relief. I would be willing to do this on condition that the Sierra Club forthwith amend its complaint to meet the specifications the Court prescribes for standing. If Sierra Club fails or refuses to take that step, so be it; the case will then collapse. But if it does amend, the merits will be before the trial court once again. . . .

2. Alternatively, I would permit an imaginative expansion of our traditional concepts of standing in order to enable an organization such as the Sierra Club, possessed, as it is, of pertinent, bona fide and well-recognized attributes and purposes in the area of environment, to litigate environmental issues. This incursion upon tradition need not be very extensive. Certainly, it should be no cause for alarm . . . . It need only recognize the interest of one who has a provable, sincere, dedicated, and established status. We need not fear that Pandora's box will be opened or that there will be no limit to the number of those who desire to participate in an environmental litigation. The courts will exercise appropriate restraints just as they have exercised them in the past . . . . And Mr. Justice DOUGLAS, in his eloquent opinion, has imaginatively suggested another means and one, in its own way, with obvious, appropriate and self-imposed limitations as to standing. As I read what he has written, he makes only one addition to the customary criteria (the existence of a genuine dispute; the assurance of adversariness; and a conviction that the party whose standing is challenged will adequately represent the interests he asserts), that is, that the litigant be one who speaks knowingly for the environmental values he asserts. . . .

Notes and Questions

1. Was the Supreme Court correct in making some use of controverted resources, by an environmental organization's members, a key factor in determining whether that organization should have standing to sue?

2. Should other factors be given more weight? Might natural resources have value for persons who are never physically present on or near them?

3. How do you evaluate the suggestion of Justice Douglas, in dissent, that standing to sue in environmental suits should be granted to persons who know the "values and wonders" of a place and who bring suit in the name of a threatened natural resource or inanimate object? Could "public interest organizations" that represent the perspective of business interests have standing to sue under that approach? Should they? In fact, Douglas' dissent contains a legal inaccuracy. Inanimate objects have never actually been the plaintiff in any litigation. In admiralty, and in other areas, such objects were made defendants (as opposed to plaintiffs) because the real defendant (i.e., the owner of the object) was beyond the reach of the jurisdiction. To what extent does this mistake undercut the persuasiveness of Douglas' opinion?

4. In his dissenting opinion, Justice Blackmun suggested that the court might have granted standing to the Sierra Club, in this case, based upon its "provable, sincere, dedicated and established status" as an environmental organization. Would Blackmun's suggestion rule out standing to sue for smaller, newer environmental groups and/or for *ad hoc* committees of neighbors who join together in opposition to what they perceive as an environmentally unsound project? Is such a distinction justifiable?

5. In a footnote to its opinion in *Sierra Club v. Morton,* the Supreme Court indicated that, when the case returned to the U.S. District Court, the Sierra Club was to be permitted to amend its complaint. On remand the Club did so, alleging that some of its individual members used the Mineral King area, and also adding a new claim based upon the National Environmental Policy Act. Following some further litigation — and the preparation of an environmental impact statement — the proposal to build a ski resort was abandoned and, in 1978, Mineral King was made part of the Sequoia National Park.

6. To what extent should courts evaluate the motivations of individuals who make use of environmentally sensitive resources? *See Regional Ass'n. of Concerned Environmentalists v. U.S. Dep't of Agriculture,* 765 F. Supp. 502 (S.D. Ill. 1990), in which the court denied standing to an individual who had previously made a dozen visits to a forested area on the basis that those visits were in pursuit of an "ongoing crusade of environmental activism," rather than being for recreational purposes. Is this a sound result?

Lujan v. Defenders of Wildlife

504 U.S. 555 (1992)

Justice SCALIA:

[This case involves a challenge to a rule promulgated by the federal government interpreting Section 7 of the Endangered Species Act (ESA). The ESA requires each federal agency to insure that any action authorized, funded, or carried out by such agency will not jeopardize the continued existence of any endangered species or threatened species or result in the destruction or adverse modification of habitat. In 1986, the Interior Department promulgated a regulation stating that Section 7 is not applicable to actions taken in foreign nations. Respondents filed suit seeking to invalidate the regulation.]

Over the years, our cases have established that the irreducible constitutional minimum of standing contains three elements. First, the plaintiff must have suffered an "injury in fact"—an invasion of a legally protected interest which is (a) concrete and particularized . . . and (b) "actual or imminent, not 'conjectural' or 'hypothetical.'" Second, there must be a causal connection between the injury and the conduct complained of—the injury has to be "fairly . . . traceable to the challenged action of the defendant, and not . . . the result of the independent action of some third party not before the court." Third, it must be "likely," as opposed to merely "speculative," that the injury will be "redressed by a favorable decision."

The party invoking federal jurisdiction bears the burden of establishing [the elements necessary to demonstrate standing]. . . . When the suit is one challenging the legality of government action or inaction, the nature and extent of facts that must be averred (at the summary judgment stage) or proved (at the trial stage) in order to establish standing depends considerably upon whether the plaintiff is himself an object of the action (or forgone action) at issue. If he is, there is ordinarily little question that the action or inaction has caused him injury, and that a judgment preventing or requiring the action will redress it. When, however, as in this case, a plaintiff's asserted injury arises from the government's allegedly unlawful regulation (or lack of regulation) of *someone else,* much more is needed. In that circumstance, causation and redressability ordinarily hinge on the response of the regulated (or regulable) third party to the government action or inaction—and perhaps on the response of others as well. The existence of one or more of the essential elements of standing "depends on the unfettered choices made by independent actors not before the courts and whose exercise of broad and legitimate discretion the courts cannot presume either to control or to predict;" and it becomes the burden of the plaintiff to adduce facts showing that those choices have been or will be made in such manner as to produce causation and permit redressability of injury. Thus, when the plaintiff is not himself the object of the government action or inaction he challenges, standing is not precluded, but it is ordinarily "substantially more difficult" to establish. . . .

Respondents' claim to injury is that the lack of consultation with respect to certain [federal agency] funded activities abroad "increas[es] the rate of extinction of endangered and threatened species." Of course, the desire to use or observe an animal species, even for purely esthetic purposes, is undeniably a cognizable interest for purpose of standing. See, *e.g., Sierra Club v. Morton,* 405 U.S. [727], 734 [1972]. "But the 'injury in fact' test requires more than an injury to a cognizable interest. It requires that the party seeking review be himself among the injured." *Id.* at 734–735. To survive the Secretary's summary judgment motion, respondents had to submit affidavits or other evidence showing, through specific facts, not only that listed species were in fact being threatened by funded activities abroad, but also that one or more of respondents' members would thereby be "directly" affected apart from their "'special interest' in the subject:" *Id.* at 735, 739.

With respect to this aspect of the case, the Court of Appeals focused on the affidavits of two Defenders' members—Joyce Kelly and Amy Skilbred. Ms. Kelly stated that she traveled to Egypt in 1986 and "observed the traditional habitat of the endangered Nile crocodile there and intend[s] to do so again, and hope[s] to observe the crocodile directly," and that she "will suffer harm in fact as the result of [the] American . . . role . . . in overseeing the rehabilitation of the Aswan High Dam on the Nile . . . and [in] developing . . . Egypt's . . . Master Water Plan." Ms. Skilbred averred that she traveled to Sri Lanka in 1981 and "observed th[e] habitat" of "endangered species such as the Asian elephant and the leopard" at what is now the site of the Mahaweli project funded by the Agency for International Development (AID), although she "was unable to see any of the endangered species"; "this development project," she continued, "will seriously reduce endangered, threatened, and endemic species habitat including areas that I visited . . . [, which] may severely shorten the future of these species"; that threat, she concluded, harmed her because she "intend[s] to return to Sri Lanka in the future and hope[s] to be more fortunate in spotting at least the endangered elephant and leopard." When Ms. Skilbred was asked at a subsequent deposition if and when she had any plans to return to Sri Lanka, she reiterated that "I intend to go back to Sri Lanka," but confessed that she had no current plans: "I don't know [when]. There is a civil war going on right now. I don't know. Not next year, I will say. In the future."

We shall assume for the sake of argument that these affidavits contain facts showing that certain agency-funded projects threaten listed species—though that is questionable. They plainly contain no facts, however, showing how damage to the species will produce "imminent" injury to Mses. Kelly and Skilbred. That the women "had visited" the areas of the projects before the projects commenced proves nothing. As we have said in a related context, "'Past exposure to illegal conduct does not in itself show a present case or controversy regarding injunctive relief . . . if unaccompanied by any continuing, present adverse effects.'" And the affiants' profession of an "inten[t]" to return to the places they had visited before—where they will presumably, this time, be deprived of the opportunity to observe animals of the endangered species—is simply not enough. Such "some day" intentions—without any description of concrete plans, or indeed even any specification of *when* the some day will be—do not support a finding of the "actual or imminent" injury that our cases require.

Besides relying upon the Kelly and Skilbred affidavits, respondents propose a series of novel standing theories. The first, inelegantly styled "ecosystem nexus," proposes that any person who uses *any part* of a "contiguous ecosystem" adversely affected by a funded activity has standing even if the activity is located a great distance away. This approach, as the Court of Appeals correctly observed, is inconsistent with our opinion in *Lujan v. National Wildlife Federation,* which held that a plaintiff claiming injury from environmental damage must use the area affected by the challenged activity and not an area roughly "in the vicinity" of it. 497 U.S. at 887–889. It makes no difference that the general-purpose section of the ESA states that the Act was intended in part "to provide a means whereby the ecosystems upon which endangered species and threatened species depend may be conserved," 16 U.S.C. § 1531(b). To say that the Act protects ecosystems is not to say that the Act creates (if it were possible) rights of action in persons who have not been injured in fact, that is, persons who use portions of an ecosystem not perceptibly affected by the unlawful action in question.

Respondents' other theories are called, alas, the "animal nexus" approach, whereby anyone who has an interest in studying or seeing the endangered animals anywhere on the globe has standing; and the "vocational nexus" approach, under which anyone with a professional interest in such animals can sue. Under these theories, anyone who goes to see Asian elephants in the Bronx Zoo, and anyone who is a keeper of Asian elephants in the Bronx Zoo, has standing to sue because the Director of the Agency for International Development (AID) did not consult with the Secretary regarding the AID-funded project in Sri Lanka. This is beyond all reason. Standing is not "an ingenious academic exercise in the conceivable," *United States v. Students Challenging Regulatory Agency Procedures,* 412 U.S. 669, 688 (1973), but as we have said requires, at the summary judgment stage, a factual showing of perceptible harm. It is clear that the person who observes or works with a particular animal threatened by a federal decision is facing perceptible harm, since the very subject of his interest will no longer exist. It is even plausible — though it goes to the outermost limit of plausibility — to think that a person who observes or works with animals of a particular species in the very area of the world where that species is threatened by a federal decision is facing such harm, since some animals that might have been the subject of his interest will no longer exist. *See Japan Whaling Assn. v. American Cetacean Society,* 478 U.S. 221, 231 n. 4 (1986). It goes beyond the limit, however, and into pure speculation and fantasy, to say that anyone who observes or works with an endangered species, anywhere in the world, is appreciably harmed by a single project affecting some portion of that species with which he has no more specific connection.

Besides failing to show injury, respondents failed to demonstrate redressability. Instead of attacking the separate decisions to fund particular projects allegedly causing them harm, respondents chose to challenge a more generalized level of Government action (rules regarding consultation), the invalidation of which would affect all overseas projects. This programmatic approach has obvious practical advantages, but also obvious difficulties insofar as proof of causation or redressability is concerned. As we have said in another context, "suits challenging, not specifically identifiable Government violations of law, but the particular programs agencies establish to carry out their legal obligations . . . [are], even when premised on allegations of several instances of violations of law . . . rarely if ever appropriate for federal-court adjudication."

The most obvious problem in the present case is redressability. Since the agencies funding the projects were not parties to the case, the District Court could accord relief only against the [Secretary of Interior]: He could be ordered to revise his regulation to require consultation for foreign projects. But this would not remedy respondents' alleged injury unless the funding agencies were bound by the Secretary's regulation, which is very much an open question. . . .

A further impediment to redressability is the fact that the [U.S. federal] agencies generally supply only a fraction of the funding for a foreign project. AID, for example, has provided less than 10% of the funding for the Mahaweli project. Respondents have produced nothing to indicate that the projects they have named will either be suspended, or do less harm to listed species, if that fraction is eliminated. As in *Simon* [*v. Eastern Kentucky Welfare Rights Organization*], 426 U.S. [26], 43–44 [1976], it is entirely conjectural whether the non-agency activity that affects respondents will be altered or affected by the agency activity they seek to achieve. . . .

Notes and Questions

1. Was the Court correct in concluding that the plaintiffs suffered no injury in fact in this case? Should it have adopted one of the novel legal theories of standing to sue that the plaintiffs espoused? Is this case truly consistent with *Sierra Club v. Morton*?

2. What is your reaction to the portion of the *Lujan* decision that concerns redressability?

Bennett v. Spear

520 U.S. 154 (1997)

Justice SCALIA:

This is a challenge to a biological opinion issued by the Fish and Wildlife Service in accordance with the Endangered Species Act of 1973 (ESA) concerning the operation of the Klamath Irrigation Project by the Bureau of Reclamation, and the project's impact on two varieties of endangered fish. The question for decision is whether the petitioners, who have competing economic and other interests in Klamath Project water, have standing to seek judicial review of the biological opinion under the citizen-suit provision of the ESA and the Administrative Procedure Act (APA) . . . .

The Klamath Project, one of the oldest federal reclamation schemes, is a series of lakes, rivers, dams and irrigation canals in northern California and southern Oregon. The project was undertaken by the Secretary of the Interior pursuant to the Reclamation Act of 1902 and the Act of Feb. 9, 1905 and is administered by the Bureau of Reclamation, which is under the Secretary's jurisdiction. In 1992, the Bureau notified the Service that operation of the project might affect the Lost River Sucker . . . and Shortnose Sucker . . . species of fish that were listed as endangered in 1988. After formal consultation with the Bureau . . . the Service issued a Biological Opinion which concluded the "'long-term operation of the Klamath Project was likely to jeopardize the continued existence of the Lost River and shortnose suckers." The Biological Opinion identified "reasonable and prudent alternatives" the Service believed would avoid jeopardy, which included the maintenance of minimum water levels on Clear Lake and Gerber reservoirs. The Bureau later notified the Service that it intended to operate the project in compliance with the Biological Opinion.

Petitioners, two Oregon irrigation districts that receive Klamath Project water and the operators of two ranches within those districts, filed the present action against the director and regional director of the Service and the Secretary of the Interior . . . . The complaint asserts that the Bureau "has been following essentially the same procedures for storing and releasing water from Clear Lake and Gerber reservoirs throughout the twentieth century," that "there is no scientifically or commercially available evidence indicating that the populations of endangered suckers in Clear Lake and Gerber reservoirs have declined, are declining, or will decline as a result" of the Bureau's operation of the Klamath Project; that "there is no commercially or scientifically available evidence indicating that the restrictions on lake levels imposed in the Biological Opinion will have any beneficial effect on the . . . populations of suckers in the Clear Lake and Gerber reservoirs"; and that the Bureau nonetheless "will abide by the restrictions imposed by the Biological Opinion." . . .

Petitioner's Complaint

Petitioners' complaint . . . asserts that petitioners' use of the reservoirs and related waterways for "recreational, aesthetic and commercial purposes, as well as for their primary sources of irrigation water" will be "irreparably damaged" by the actions complained of, and that the restrictions on water delivery "recommended" by the Biological Opinion "adversely affect plaintiffs by substantially reducing the quantity of available irrigation water." In essence, petitioners claim a competing interest in the water the Biological Opinion declares necessary for the preservation of the suckers.

The District Court dismissed the complaint for lack of jurisdiction. It concluded that petitioners did not have standing because their "recreational, aesthetic, and commercial interests . . . do not fall within the zone of interest sought to be protected by ESA." The Court of Appeals for the Ninth Circuit affirmed. It held that the "zone of interests" test limits the class of persons who may obtain judicial review not only under the APA, but also under the citizen-suit provision of the ESA and that "only plaintiffs who allege an interest in the preservation of endangered species fall within the zone of interests protected by the ESA." We granted certiorari.

In this Court, petitioners raise two questions: first, whether the prudential standing rule known as the "zone of interests" test applies to claims brought under the citizen-suit provision of the ESA; and second, if so, whether petitioners have standing under that test notwithstanding that the interests they seek to vindicate are economic rather than environmental . . . .

*2 Issues
"Zone of interests"
&*

We first turn to the question the Court of Appeals found dispositive: whether petitioners lack standing by virtue of the zone-of-interests test . . . .

The question of standing "involves both constitutional limitations on federal-court jurisdiction and prudential limitations on its exercise." To satisfy the "case" or "controversy" requirement of Article III, which is the "irreducible constitutional minimum" of standing, a plaintiff must, generally speaking, demonstrate that he has suffered "injury in fact," that the injury is "fairly traceable" to the actions of the defendant, and that the injury will likely be redressed by a favorable decision. In addition to the immutable requirements of Article III, "the federal judiciary has also adhered to a set of prudential principles that bear on the question of standing." Like their constitutional

Requirements of standing to sue

counterparts, these "judicially self-imposed limits on the exercise of federal jurisdiction," are "founded in concern about the proper—properly limited—role of the courts in a democratic society"; but unlike their constitutional counterparts, they can be modified or abrogated by Congress. Numbered among these prudential requirements is the doctrine of particular concern in this case: that a plaintiff's grievance must arguably fall within the zone of interests protected or regulated by the statutory provision or constitutional guarantee involved in the suit . . . .

The first question in the present case is whether the ESA's citizen-suit provision negates the zone-of-interests test (or, perhaps more accurately, expands the zone of interests). We think it does. The first operative portion of the provision says that "any person may commence a civil suit"—an authorization of remarkable breadth when compared with the language Congress ordinarily uses. Even in some other environmental statutes, Congress has used more restrictive formulations . . . .

Our readiness to take the term "any person" at face value is greatly augmented by two interrelated considerations: that the overall subject matter of this legislation is the environment (a matter in which it is common to think all persons have an interest) and that the obvious purpose of the particular provision in question is to encourage enforcement by so-called "private attorneys general . . . ."

It is true that the plaintiffs here are seeking to prevent application of environmental restrictions rather than to implement them. But the "any person" formulation applies to all the causes of action authorized by Section 1540 (g)—not only to actions against private violators of environmental restrictions, and not only to actions against the Secretary asserting under-enforcement restrictions under Section 1533 but also to actions against the Secretary asserting over-enforcement under Section 1533. As we shall discuss below, the citizen-suit provision does favor environmentalists in that it covers all private violations of the Act but not all failures of the Secretary to meet his administrative responsibilities; but there is no textual basis for saying that its expansion of standing requirements applies to environmentalists alone. The Court of Appeals therefore erred in concluding that petitioners lacked standing under the zone-of-interests test to bring their claims under the ESA's citizen-suit provision.

. . . The Government's first contention is that petitioners' complaint fails to satisfy the standing requirements imposed by the "case" or "controversy" provision of Article III. This "irreducible constitutional minimum" of standing requires: (1) that the plaintiff have suffered an "injury in fact"—an invasion of a judicially cognizable interest which is (a) concrete and particularized and (b) actual or imminent, not conjectural or hypothetical; (2) that there be a causal connection between the injury and the conduct complained of—the injury must be fairly traceable to the challenged action of the defendant, and not the result of the independent action of some third party not before the court; and (3) that it be likely, as opposed to merely speculative, that the injury will be redressed by a favorable decision . . . .

The Government contends, first, that [petitioners'] allegations fail to satisfy the "injury in fact" element of Article III standing because they demonstrate only a diminution in the aggregate amount of available water, and do not necessarily establish (absent information concerning the Bureau's water allocation practices) that the petitioners will receive less water. [But] . . . while a plaintiff must "set forth" by affidavit or other evidence "specific facts," to survive a motion for summary judgment, Fed. Rule Civ. Proc. 56(e), and must ultimately support any contested facts with evidence adduced at trial, "at the pleading stage, general factual allegations of injury resulting from the defendant's conduct may suffice, for on a motion to dismiss we 'presume that general allegations embrace those specific facts that are necessary to support the claim.'" Given petitioners' allegation that the amount of available water will be reduced and that they will be adversely affected thereby, it is easy to presume specific facts under which petitioners will be injured — for example, the Bureau's distribution of the reduction *pro rata* among its customers. The complaint alleges the requisite injury in fact.

The Government also contests compliance with the second and third Article III standing requirements, contending that any injury suffered by petitioners is neither "fairly traceable" to the Service's Biological Opinion, nor "redressable" by a favorable judicial ruling, because the "action agency" (the Bureau) retains ultimate responsibility for determining whether and how a proposed action shall go forward . . . . This wrongly equates injury "fairly traceable" to the defendant with injury as to which the defendant's actions are the very last step in the chain of causation . . . .

By the Government's own account, while the Services Biological Opinion theoretically serves an "advisory function," in reality it has a powerful coercive effect on the action agency . . . . The action agency is technically free to disregard the Biological Opinion and proceed with its proposed action, but it does so at its own peril (and that of its employees), for "any person" who knowingly "takes" an endangered or threatened species is subject to substantial civil and criminal penalties, including imprisonment.

The Service itself is, to put it mildly, keenly aware of the virtually determinative effect of its biological opinions . . . .[I]t is not difficult to conclude that petitioners have met their burden — which is relatively modest at this stage of the litigation — of alleging that their injury is "fairly traceable" to the Service's Biological Opinion and that it will "likely" be redressed — *i.e.,* the Bureau will not impose such water level restrictions — if the Biological Opinion is set aside . . . .

In determining whether the petitioners have standing under the zone-of-interests test to bring their APA claims, we look not to the terms of the ESA's citizen-suit provision, but to the substantive provisions of the ESA, the alleged violations of which serve as the gravamen of the complaint. The classic formulation of the zone-of-interests test is . . . "whether the interest sought to be protected by the complainant is arguably within the zone of interests to be protected or regulated by the statute or constitutional guarantee in question." The Court of Appeals concluded that this test was not met here, since petitioners are neither directly regulated by the ESA nor seek to vindicate its overarching purpose of species preservation. That conclusion was error. . . .

In the claims that we have found not to be covered by the ESA's citizen suit provision, petitioners allege a violation of Section 7 of the ESA which requires, *inter alia,* that each agency "use the best scientific and commercial data available." Petitioners contend that the available scientific and commercial data show that the continued operation of the Klamath Project will not have a detrimental impact on the endangered suckers, that the imposition of minimum lake levels is not necessary to protect the fish, and that by issuing a Biological Opinion which makes unsubstantiated findings to the contrary the defendants have acted arbitrarily and in violation of Section 1536(a)(2). The obvious purpose of the requirement that each agency "use the best scientific and commercial data available" is to ensure that the ESA not be implemented haphazardly, on the basis of speculation or surmise. While this no doubt serves to advance the ESA's overall goal of species preservation, we think it readily apparent that another objective (if not indeed the primary one) is to avoid needless economic dislocation produced by agency officials zealously but unintelligently pursuing their environmental objectives. That economic consequences are an explicit concern of the Act is evidenced by Section 1536(h), which provides exemption from Section 1536(a)(2)'s no-jeopardy mandate where there are no reasonable and prudent alternatives to the agency action and the benefits of the agency action clearly outweigh the benefits of any alternatives. We believe the "best scientific and commercial data" provision is similarly intended, at least in part, to prevent uneconomic (because erroneous) jeopardy determinations. Petitioners' claim that they are victims of such a mistake is plainly within the zone of interests that the provision protects. . . .

Notes and Questions

1. Were you persuaded by the Supreme Court's interpretation of the purpose of the Endangered Species Act provision requiring use of "the best available scientific and commercial data available?" To what extent was a "primary goal" of that provision the avoidance of economic dislocation produced by zealous but unintelligent agency officials?

2. Does *Bennett v. Spear* strengthen the position of environmental organizations when they assert standing to sue under the citizen suit provision of the Endangered Species Act and/or the citizen suit sections of other statutes?

Friends of the Earth v. Laidlaw Environmental Services (TOC)

528 U.S. 167 (2000)

Justice GINSBURG:

· This case presents an important question concerning the operation of the citizen-suit provisions of the Clean Water Act. Congress authorized the federal district courts to entertain Clean Water Act suits initiated by "a person or persons having an interest which is or may be adversely affected." 33 U.S.C. § 1365(a), (g). To impel future compliance with the Act, a district court may prescribe injunctive relief in such a suit; additionally or alternatively, the court may impose civil penalties payable to the United States Treasury. § 1365(a). In the Clean Water Act citizen suit now before us, the District Court determined that injunctive relief was inappropriate because the defendant, after the institution of the litigation, achieved substantial compliance with the terms of its discharge permit. The court did, however, assess a civil penalty of $405,800.

The "total deterrent effect" of the penalty would be adequate to forestall future violations, the court reasoned, taking into account that the defendant "will be required to reimburse plaintiffs for a significant amount of legal fees and has, itself, incurred significant legal expenses."

The Court of Appeals vacated the District Court's order. The case became moot, the appellate court declared, once the defendant fully complied with the terms of its permit and the plaintiff failed to appeal the denial of equitable relief. "[C]ivil penalties payable to the government," the Court of Appeals stated, "would not redress any injury Plaintiffs have suffered." . . .

— Case has already been resolved by a court of law

We reverse the judgment of the Court of Appeals. The appellate court erred in concluding that a citizen suitor's claim for civil penalties must be dismissed as moot when the defendant, albeit after commencement of the litigation, has come into compliance. In directing dismissal of the suit on grounds of mootness, the Court of Appeals incorrectly conflated our case law on initial standing to bring suit, with our case law on post-commencement mootness. A defendant's voluntary cessation of allegedly unlawful conduct ordinarily does not suffice to moot a case. The Court of Appeals also misperceived the remedial potential of civil penalties. Such penalties may serve, as an alternative to an injunction, to deter further violations and thereby redress the injuries that prompted a citizen suitor to commence litigation . . . .

In 1986, defendant-respondent Laidlaw Environmental Services (TOC), Inc., bought a hazardous waste incinerator facility in Roebuck, South Carolina, that included a wastewater treatment plant. (The company has since changed its name to Safety-Kleen (Roebuck), Inc., but for simplicity we will refer to it as "Laidlaw" throughout.) Shortly after Laidlaw acquired the facility, the South Carolina Department of Health and Environmental Control (DHEC), acting under 33 U.S.C. § 1342(a)(1), granted Laidlaw an NPDES permit authorizing the company to discharge treated water into the North Tyger River. The permit, which became effective on January 1, 1987, placed limits on Laidlaw's discharge of several pollutants into the river, including — of particular relevance to this case — mercury, an extremely toxic pollutant. The permit also regulated the flow, temperature, toxicity, and pH of the effluent from the facility, and imposed monitoring and reporting obligations.

Once it received its permit, Laidlaw began to discharge various pollutants into the waterway; repeatedly, Laidlaw's discharges exceeded the limits set by the permit. In particular, despite experimenting with several technological fixes, Laidlaw consistently failed to meet the permit's stringent 1.3 ppb (parts per billion) daily average limit on mercury discharges. The District Court later found that Laidlaw had violated the mercury limits on 489 occasions between 1987 and 1995.

On April 10, 1992, plaintiff-petitioners Friends of the Earth (FOE) and Citizens Local Environmental Action Network, Inc. (CLEAN) (referred to collectively in this opinion, together with later joined plaintiff-petitioner, Sierra Club, as "FOE") took the preliminary step necessary to the institution of litigation. They sent a letter to Laidlaw notifying the company of their intention to file a citizen suit against it under § 505(a) of the Act after the expiration of the requisite 60-day notice period, i.e., on

Citizen suit: lawsuit by a private citizen to enforce a statute

or after June 10, 1992. Laidlaw's lawyer then contacted DHEC to ask whether DHEC would consider filing a lawsuit against Laidlaw. The District Court later found that Laidlaw's reason for requesting that DHEC file a lawsuit against it was to bar FOE's proposed citizen suit through the operation of 33 U.S.C. ' 1365 (b) (1) (B). DHEC agreed to file a lawsuit against Laidlaw; the company's lawyer then drafted the complaint for DHEC and paid the filing fee. On June 9, 1992, the last day before FOE's 60-day notice period expired, DHEC and Laidlaw reached a settlement requiring Laidlaw to pay $100,000 in civil penalties and to make "'every effort'" to comply with its permit obligations.

On June 12, 1992, FOE filed this citizen suit against Laidlaw under § 505(a) of the Act, alleging noncompliance with the NPDES permit and seeking declaratory and injunctive relief and an award of civil penalties. Laidlaw moved for summary judgment on the ground that FOE had failed to present evidence demonstrating injury in fact, and therefore lacked Article III standing to bring the lawsuit. In opposition to this motion, FOE submitted affidavits and deposition testimony from members of the plaintiff organizations. The record before the District Court also included affidavits from the organizations' members submitted by FOE in support of an earlier motion for preliminary injunctive relief. After examining this evidence, the District Court denied Laidlaw's summary judgment motion, finding—albeit "by the very slimmest of margins"—that FOE had standing to bring the suit.

Laidlaw also moved to dismiss the action on the ground that the citizen suit was barred under 33 U.S.C. § 1365(b)(1)(B) by DHEC's prior action against the company. The United States, appearing as *amicus curiae*, joined FOE in opposing the motion. After an extensive analysis of the Laidlaw-DHEC settlement and the circumstances under which it was reached, the District Court held that DHEC's action against Laidlaw had not been "diligently prosecuted;" consequently, the court allowed FOE's citizen suit to proceed. The record indicates that after FOE initiated the suit, but before the District Court rendered judgment, Laidlaw violated the mercury discharge limitation in its permit 13 times. The District Court also found that Laidlaw had committed 13 monitoring and 10 reporting violations during this period. The last recorded mercury discharge violation occurred in January, 1995, long after the complaint was filed but about two years before judgment was rendered.

On January 22, 1997, the District Court issued its judgment. It found that Laidlaw had gained a total economic benefit of $1,092,581 as a result of its extended period of noncompliance with the mercury discharge limit in its permit. The court concluded, however, that a civil penalty of $405,800 was adequate . . . In particular, the District Court stated that the lesser penalty was appropriate taking into account the judgment's "total deterrent effect." In reaching this determination, the court "considered that Laidlaw will be required to reimburse plaintiffs for a significant amount of legal fees." The court declined to grant FOE's request for injunctive relief, stating that an injunction was inappropriate because "Laidlaw has been in substantial compliance with all parameters in its NPDES permit since at least August 1992."

FOE appealed the District Court's civil penalty judgment, arguing that the penalty was inadequate, but did not appeal the denial of declaratory or injunctive relief. Laidlaw cross-appealed, arguing, among other things, that FOE lacked standing to bring the suit and that DHEC's action qualified as a diligent prosecution precluding FOE's litigation. The United States continued to participate as *amicus curiae* in support of FOE.

On July 16, 1998, the Court of Appeals for the Fourth Circuit issued its judgment. The Court of Appeals assumed without deciding that FOE initially had standing to bring the action, but went on to hold that the case had become moot. The appellate court stated, first, that the elements of Article III standing—injury, causation, and redressability—must persist at every stage of review, or else the action becomes moot. . . . [T]he Court of Appeals reasoned that the case had become moot because "the only remedy currently available to [FOE]—civil penalties payable to the government—would not redress any injury [FOE has] suffered." . . .

According to Laidlaw, after the Court of Appeals issued its decision but before this Court granted *certiorari*, the entire incinerator facility in Roebuck was permanently closed, dismantled, and put up for sale, and all discharges from the facility permanently ceased.

We granted *certiorari*, 525 U.S. 1176 (1999), to resolve the inconsistency between the Fourth Circuit's decision in this case and the decisions of several other Courts of Appeals, which have held that a defendant's compliance with its permit after the commencement of litigation does not moot claims for civil penalties under the Act.

The Constitution's case-or-controversy limitation on federal judicial authority, Art. III, § 2, underpins both our standing and our mootness jurisprudence, but the two inquiries differ in respects critical to the proper resolution of this case, so we address them separately. Because the Court of Appeals was persuaded that the case had become moot and so held, it simply assumed without deciding that FOE had initial standing. But because we hold that the Court of Appeals erred in declaring the case moot, we have an obligation to assure ourselves that FOE had Article III standing at the outset of the litigation. We therefore address the question of standing before turning to mootness . . . .

Laidlaw contends first that FOE lacked standing from the outset even to seek injunctive relief, because the plaintiff organizations failed to show that any of their members had sustained or faced the threat of any "injury in fact" from Laidlaw's activities. In support of this contention Laidlaw points to the District Court's finding, made in the course of setting the penalty amount, that there had been "no demonstrated proof of harm to the environment" for Laidlaw's mercury discharge violations . . . .

The relevant showing for purposes of Article III standing, however, is not injury to the environment but injury to the plaintiff. To insist upon the former rather than the latter as part of the standing inquiry (as the dissent in essence does) is to raise the standing hurdle higher than the necessary showing for success on the merits in an action alleging noncompliance with an NPDES permit. Focusing properly on injury to the plaintiff, the District Court found that FOE had demonstrated sufficient injury to establish standing. For example, FOE member Kenneth Lee Curtis averred in affidavits that he lived a half-mile from Laidlaw's facility; that he occasionally drove over the North Tyger River, and that it looked and smelled polluted; and that he would like to fish, camp, swim, and picnic in and near the river between 3 and 15 miles downstream from the facility, as he did when he was a teenager, but would not do so because he was concerned that the water was polluted by Laidlaw's discharges. Curtis reaffirmed these statements in extensive deposition testimony. For example, he testified that he would like to fish in the river at a specific spot he used as a boy, but that he would not do so now because of his concerns about Laidlaw's discharges.

Other members presented evidence to similar effect. [For example,] Gail Lee attested that her home, which is near Laidlaw's facility, had a lower value than similar homes located farther from the facility, and that she believed the pollutant discharges accounted for some of that discrepancy.

These sworn testimonies, as the District Court determined, adequately documented injury in fact. We have held that environmental plaintiffs adequately allege injury in fact when they aver that they use the affected area and are persons "for whom the aesthetic and recreational values of the area will be lessened" by the challenged activity. *Sierra Club v. Morton*, 405 U.S. 727, 735 (1972). . . .

[T]he affidavits and testimony presented by FOE in this case assert that Laidlaw's discharges, and the affiant members' reasonable concerns about the effects of those discharges, directly affected those affiants' recreational, aesthetic, and economic interests. These submissions present dispositively more than the mere "general averments" and "conclusory allegations" found inadequate in *National Wildlife Federation*. Nor can the affiants' conditional statements—that they would use the nearby North Tyger River for recreation if Laidlaw were not discharging pollutants into it—be equated with the speculative "'some day' intentions" to visit endangered species halfway around the world that we held insufficient to show injury in fact in *Defenders of Wildlife*. 504 U.S., at 564 . . . .

Laidlaw argues next that even if FOE had standing to seek injunctive relief, it lacked standing to seek civil penalties. Here the asserted defect is not injury but redressability. Civil penalties offer no redress to private plaintiffs, Laidlaw argues, because they are paid to the government, and therefore a citizen plaintiff can never have standing to seek them.

Laidlaw is right to insist that a plaintiff must demonstrate standing separately for each form of relief sought. But it is wrong to maintain that citizen plaintiffs facing ongoing violations never have standing to seek civil penalties.

We have recognized on numerous occasions that "all civil penalties have some deterrent effect." More specifically, Congress has found that civil penalties in Clean Water Act cases do more than promote immediate compliance by limiting the defendant's economic incentive to delay its attainment of permit limits; they also deter future violations. This congressional determination warrants judicial attention and respect . . . .

It can scarcely be doubted that, for a plaintiff who is injured or faces the threat of future injury due to illegal conduct ongoing at the time of suit, a sanction that

Supreme Court:
Redressability?
Yes

effectively abates that conduct and prevents its recurrence provides a form of redress. Civil penalties can fit that description. To the extent that they encourage defendants to discontinue current violations and deter them from committing future ones, they afford redress to citizen plaintiffs who are injured or threatened with injury as a consequence of ongoing unlawful conduct . . . .

In this case we need not explore the outer limits of the principle that civil penalties provide sufficient deterrence to support redressability. Here, the civil penalties sought by FOE carried with them a deterrent effect that made it likely, as opposed to merely speculative, that the penalties would redress FOE's injuries by abating current violations and preventing future ones — as the District Court reasonably found when it assessed a penalty of $405,800 . . . .

Satisfied that FOE had standing under Article III to bring this action, we turn to the question of mootness.

The only conceivable basis for a finding of mootness in this case is Laidlaw's voluntary conduct — either its achievement by August 1992 of substantial compliance with its NPDES permit or its more recent shutdown of the Roebuck facility. It is well settled that "a defendant's voluntary cessation of a challenged practice does not deprive a federal court of its power to determine the legality of the practice." "[I]f it did, the courts would be compelled to leave '[t]he defendant . . . free to return to his old ways.'" In accordance with this principle, the standard we have announced for determining whether a case has been mooted by the defendant's voluntary conduct is stringent: "A case might become moot if subsequent events made it absolutely clear that the allegedly wrongful behavior could not reasonably be expected to recur." The "heavy burden of persua[ding]" the court that the challenged conduct cannot reasonably be expected to start up again lies with the party asserting mootness. . . .

Standing doctrine functions to ensure, among other things, that the scarce resources of the federal courts are devoted to those disputes in which the parties have a concrete stake. In contrast, by the time mootness is an issue, the case has been brought and litigated, often (as here) for years. To abandon the case at an advanced stage may prove more wasteful than frugal. This argument from sunk costs does not license courts to retain jurisdiction over cases in which one or both of the parties plainly lacks a continuing interest, as when the parties have settled or a plaintiff pursuing a nonsurviving claim has died. . . .

Supreme Court:
mootness?
NO

Laidlaw also asserts, in a supplemental suggestion of mootness, that the closure of its Roebuck facility, which took place after the Court of Appeals issued its decision, mooted the case. The facility closure, like Laidlaw's earlier achievement of substantial compliance with its permit requirements, might moot the case, but — we once more reiterate — only if one or the other of these events made it absolutely clear that Laidlaw's permit violations could not reasonably be expected to recur. The effect of both Laidlaw's compliance and the facility closure on the prospect of future violations is a disputed factual matter. FOE points out, for example — and Laidlaw does not appear to contest — that Laidlaw retains its NPDES permit. These issues have not been aired in the lower courts; they remain open for consideration on remand . . . .

Notes and Questions

1. Were you persuaded by the majority's reasoning in this case?

2. Justice Stevens wrote a separate concurring opinion in *Laidlaw*. In his view, no post-judgment conduct of the respondent would warrant a vacation of the civil penalty that the District Court had assessed against the defendant. Thus, the case could not be moot—even if it were absolutely clear that the respondent posed no threat of future permit violations.

3. Justice Kennedy also concurred. Kennedy opined that "difficult and fundamental questions" are raised as to whether exactions of public fines by private litigants constitute a permissible delegation of executive power. In his view, however, those issues are "best reserved for a later case." To what extent does this represent a valid concern? Under what kinds of factual circumstances might defendants in citizen suits seek to raise a non-delegation defense?

4. Justices Scalia and Thomas dissented in the *Laidlaw* case. They reasoned that the plaintiff's affidavits were too "short on specific facts" to satisfy the plaintiff's burden of demonstrating injury-in-fact. Moreover, they opined, a plaintiff's desire to benefit from the deterrent effect of a public penalty for a polluter's past misconduct can never suffice to establish a "case or controversy" for purposes of standing-to-sue. The Court's discussion of that point, in their view, "promulgated a revolutionary new doctrine of standing that will permit the entire body of public civil penalties to be handed over to enforcement by private interests."

5. Why do you think that the United States filed an *amicus curiae* brief in support of the Friends of the Earth's position in this case? Was such a brief appropriate in your view?

6. The excerpt below includes the U.S. Supreme Court's treatment of the standing to sue of individual states in this challenge to an EPA finding that greenhouse gases do not create an endangerment that requires regulatory action. Another excerpt from this case will be included in Chapter 6 at page 428.

Massachusetts v. Environmental Protection Agency

549 U.S. 497 (2007)

Justice STEVENS:

Article III of the Constitution limits federal court jurisdiction to "Cases" and "Controversies." Those two words confine "the business of the federal courts to questions presented in an adversary context and in a form historically viewed as capable of resolution through the judicial process." . . . .

The parties' dispute turns on the proper construction of a congressional statute, a question eminently suitable to resolution in federal court. Congress has moreover authorized this type of challenge to EPA action. . . .   That authorization is of critical importance to the standing inquiry: "Congress has the power to define injuries and articulate chains of causation that will give rise to a case or controversy where none existed before . . . . "In exercising this power, however, Congress must at the very least identify the injury it seeks to vindicate and relate the injury to the class of persons entitled to bring suit." . . . . We will not, therefore, "entertain citizen suits to vindicate the public's nonconcrete interest in the proper administration of the laws." . . .

EPA maintains that because greenhouse gas emissions inflict widespread harm, the doctrine of standing presents an insuperable jurisdictional obstacle. We do not agree. ← *Supreme Court* At bottom, "the gist of the question of standing" is whether petitioners have "such a personal stake in the outcome of the controversy as to assure that concrete adverseness which sharpens the presentation of issues upon which the court so largely depends for illumination." *Baker v. Carr*, 369 U.S. 186, 204 (1982). As JUSTICE KENNEDY explained in his *Lujan* concurrence:

> "While it does not matter how many persons have been injured by the challenged action, the party brining suit must show that the action injures him in a concrete and personal way. This requirement is not just an empty formality. It preserves the vitality of the adversarial process by assuring both that the parties before the court have an actual, as opposed to professed, stake in the outcome, and that the legal questions presented . . . will be resolved, not in the rarified atmosphere of a debating society, but in a concrete factual context conducive to a realistic appreciation of the consequences of judicial action." 504 U.S. at 581 (internal quotation marks omitted).

To ensure the proper adversarial presentation, *Lujan* holds that a litigant must demonstrate that it has suffered a concrete and particularized injury that is either actual or imminent, that the injury is fairly traceable to the defendant, and that it is likely that a favorable decision will redress that injury . . . . However, a litigant to whom Congress has "accorded a procedural right to protect his concrete interests," . . . here, the right to challenge agency action unlawfully withheld . . . "can assert that right without meeting all the normal standards for redressability and immediacy." . . . When a litigant is vested with a procedural right, that litigant has standing if there is some possibility that the requested relief will prompt the injury-causing party to reconsider the decision that allegedly harmed the litigant . . . .

Only one of the petitioners needs to have standing to permit us to consider the petition for review . . . . We stress here, as did Judge Tatel below, the special position and interest of Massachusetts. It is of considerable relevance that the party seeking review here is a sovereign State and not, as it was in *Lujan*, a private individual.

Well before the creation of the modern administrative state, we recognized that States are not normal litigants for the purposes of invoking federal jurisdiction. As Justice Holmes explained in *Georgia v. Tennessee Copper Co.*, 206 U.S. 2340, 237 (1907), a case in which Georgia sought to protect its citizens from air pollution originating outside its borders:

> "The case has been argued largely as if it were one between two private parties; but it is not. The very elements that would be relied upon in a suit between fellow-citizens as a ground for equitable relief are wanting here. The State owns very little of the territory alleged to be affected, and the damage to it capable of estimate in money, possibly, at least, is small. This is a suit by a State for an

injury to it in its capacity of *quasi*-sovereign. In that capacity the State has an interest independent of and behind the titles of its citizens, in all the earth and air within its domain. It has the last word as to whether its mountains shall be stripped of their forests and its inhabitants shall breathe pure air."

Just as Georgia's "independent interest . . . in all the earth and air within its domain" supported federal jurisdiction a century ago, so too does Massachusetts' well-founded desire to preserve its sovereign territory today. Cf. *Alden v. Maine*, 527 U.S. 706, 715 (1999) (observing that in the federal system, the States "are not relegated to the role of mere provinces or political corporations, but retain the dignity, though not the full authority, of sovereignty"). That Massachusetts does in fact own a great deal of the "territory alleged to be affected" only reinforces the conclusion that its stake in the outcome of this case is sufficiently concrete to warrant the exercise of federal judicial power.

When a State enters the Union, it surrenders certain sovereign prerogatives. Massachusetts cannot invade Rhode Island to force reductions in greenhouse gas emissions, it cannot negotiate an emissions treaty with China or India, and in some circumstances the exercise of its police powers to reduce in-state motor-vehicle emissions might well be preempted . . . .

These sovereign prerogatives are now lodged in the Federal Government, and Congress has ordered EPA to protect Massachusetts (among others) by prescribing standards applicable to the "emission of any air pollutant from any class or classes of new motor vehicle engines, which in [the Administrator's] judgment cause, or contribute to, air pollution which may reasonably be anticipated to endanger public health or welfare." 42 U.S.C. § 7521(a)(1). Congress has moreover recognized a concomitant procedural right to challenge the rejection of its rulemaking petition as arbitrary and capricious . . . .Given that procedural right and Massachusetts' stake in protecting its quasi-sovereign interests, the Commonwealth is entitled to special solicitude in our standing analysis.

With that in mind, it is clear that petitioners' submissions as they pertain to Massachusetts have satisfied the most demanding standards of the adversarial process. EPA's steadfast refusal to regulate greenhouse gas emissions presents a risk of harm to Massachusetts that is both "actual" and "imminent." . . . . There is, moreover, a "substantial likelihood that the judicial relief requested" will prompt EPA to take steps to reduce that risk . . . .

IV. Attorneys' Fees in Environmental Litigation

Ruckelshaus v. Sierra Club
463 U.S. 680 (1983)

Justice REHNQUIST:

In 1979, following a year of study and public comment, the Environmental Protection Agency (EPA) promulgated standards limiting the emission of sulfur dioxide by coal-burning power plants. Both respondents in this case—the Environmental Defense Fund (EDF) and the Sierra Club—filed petitions for review of the agency's action in the United States Court of Appeals for the District of Columbia Circuit. EDF argued that the standards promulgated by the EPA were tainted by the agency's *ex parte* contacts with representatives of private industry, while the Sierra Club contended that EPA lacked authority under the Clean Air Act to issue the type of standards that it did. In a lengthy opinion, the Court of Appeals rejected all the claims of both EDF and the Sierra Club.

Notwithstanding their lack of success on the merits, EDF and the Sierra Club filed a request for attorney's fees incurred in the Sierra Club action. They relied on Section 307(f) of the Clean Air Act, which permits the award of attorney's fees in certain proceedings "whenever [the court] determines that such award is appropriate." Respondents argued that, despite their failure to obtain any of the relief they requested, it was "appropriate" for them to receive fees for their contributions to the goals of the Clean Air Act. The Court of Appeals agreed with respondents, ultimately awarding some $45,000 to the Sierra Club and some $46,000 to the EDF. We granted certiorari, to consider the important question decided by the Court of Appeals.

[margin note: Respondent's Argument]

The question presented by this case is whether it is "appropriate," within the meaning of Section 307(f) of the Clean Air Act, to award attorney's fees to a party that achieved no success on the merits of its claims. We conclude that the language of the section, read in the light of the historic principles of fee-shifting in this and other countries, requires the conclusion that some success on the merits be obtained before a party becomes eligible for a fee award under Section 307(f).

[margin note: Issue]

[margin note: Decision of Supreme Court]

Section 307(f) provides only that:

> "In any judicial proceeding under this section, the court may award costs of litigation (including reasonable attorney and expert witness fees) *whenever it determines that such award is appropriate.*" (emphasis added).

It is difficult to draw any meaningful guidance from Section 307(f)'s use of the word "appropriate," which means only "specially suitable: fit, proper." Webster's Third New International Dictionary 106 (1976). Obviously, in order to decide when fees should be awarded under Section 307(f), a court first must decide *what* the award should be "specially suitable," "fit," or "proper" *for.* Section 307(f) alone does not begin to answer this question, and application of the provision thus requires reference to other sources, including fee-shifting rules developed in different contexts. As demonstrated below, inquiry into these sources shows that requiring a defendant, completely successful on all issues, to pay the unsuccessful plaintiff's legal fees would be a radical departure from long-standing fee-shifting principles adhered to in a wide variety of contexts.

[margin note: Rationale]

Our basic point of reference is the "American Rule," under which even "the *prevailing* litigant is ordinarily not entitled to collect a reasonable attorneys' fee from the *loser.*" It is clear that generations of American judges, lawyers, and legislators, with this rule as the point of departure, would regard it as quite "inappropriate" to award the "loser" an attorney's fee from the prevailing party. Similarly, when Congress has chosen to depart from the American Rule by statute, virtually every one of the more than 150 existing federal fee-shifting provisions predicates fee awards on *some* success by the claimant; while these statutes contain varying standards as to the precise degree of success necessary for an award of fees — such as whether the fee claimant was the "prevailing party," the "substantially prevailing" party, or "successful"— the consistent rule is that complete failure will not justify shifting fees from the losing party to the winning party. . . . [Moreover], English courts have awarded counsel fees to *successful* litigants for 750 years, but they have never gone so far as to force a vindicated defendant to pay the plaintiff's legal expenses.

While the foregoing treatments of fee-shifting differ in many respects, they reflect one consistent, established rule: a successful party need not pay its unsuccessful adversary's fees. The uniform acceptance of this rule reflects, at least in part, intuitive notions of fairness to litigants . . . .

Also relevant in deciding whether to accept the reading of "appropriate" urged by respondents is the fact that Section 307(f) affects fee awards against the United States, as well as against private individuals. Except to the extent it has waived its immunity, the Government is immune from claims for attorney's fees. Waivers of immunity must be "construed strictly in favor of the sovereign," and not "enlarge[d] . . . beyond what the language requires." . . .

Given all the foregoing, we fail to find in Section 307(f) the requisite indication that Congress meant to abandon historic fee-shifting principles and intuitive notions of fairness when it enacted the section. Instead, we believe that the term "appropriate" modifies but does not completely reject the traditional rule that a fee claimant must "prevail" before it may recover attorney's fees. This result is the most reasonable interpretation of congressional intent . . . .

Respondent' arguments rest primarily on the following excerpt from the 1977 House Report on Section 307(f):

> "The committee bill also contains express authority for the courts to award attorneys' fees and expert witness fees . . . when the court determines such award is appropriate . . . . *The committee did not intend that the court's discretion to award fees under this provision should be restricted to cases in which the party seeking fees was the 'prevailing party.'* In fact, such an amendment was expressly rejected by the committee . . . ." (emphasis added).

[The Court read this legislative history against the "rather narrow" history of "prevailing party that prevailed in 1977, and concluded:]

Congress intended to eliminate both the restrictive readings of "prevailing party" adopted in some of the cases cited above and the necessity for case-by-case scrutiny by federal courts into whether plaintiffs prevailed "essentially" on "central issues." . . .

Section 304 suits may be brought against private businesses by any private citizen. Such suits frequently involve novel legal theories, theories that the EPA has rejected. After protracted litigation requiring payment of expensive legal fees and associated costs in both money and manpower, the private defendant may well succeed in refuting each charge against it—proving it was in complete compliance with every detail of the Clean Air Act. Yet, under respondents' view of the Act, the defendant's reward could be a second lawyer's bill—this one payable to those who wrongly accused it of violating the law. We simply do not believe that Congress would have intended such a result without clearly saying so. . . .

Hence, we hold that, absent some degree of success on the merits by the claimant, it is not "appropriate" for a federal court to award attorney's fees under Section 307(f). Accordingly, the judgment of the Court of Appeals is reversed.

Decision

Notes and Questions

1. To what extent might the Supreme Court's opinion in *Ruckelshaus* create practical barriers to the funding of environmental public interest litigation? How persuaded were you by the Court's invocation of the common law "American Rule" as to attorney's fees? Should it have mattered that, in § 307(f) of the Clean Air Act, Congress employed the phrase "whenever appropriate," rather than adopting the "prevailing or substantially prevailing party" standard that is used in the fee awards provision of other environmental statutes?

2. In a dissenting opinion in *Ruckelshaus,* Justice Stevens, joined by three other Justices, noted that the Sierra Club had been the only party in the case to brief and argue a critically important issue, and that its participation may well have made a difference in the outcome of the litigation. After examining the legislative history of the Clean Air Act in some detail, he concluded that § 307(f) of that Act had been intended to be broader than a prevailing party standard, and that reviewing courts are bound to defer to the determinations of trial courts in these matters.

3. In the aftermath of the *Ruckelshaus* decision, Congress has generally adopted the "prevailing or substantially prevailing party" standard in fashioning the attorney's fee award sections of other environmental litigation. *See, e.g.,* Resource Conservation and Recovery Act § 7002(e), 42 U.S.C. § 6972(e); Clean Water Act § 505(d), 33 U.S.C. § 1365(d); and Comprehensive Environmental Response, Compensation and Liability Act § 310(f), 42 U.S.C. § 9659(f).

City of Burlington v. Dague
505 U.S. 557 (1992)

Justice SCALIA:

This case presents the question whether a court, in determining an award of reasonable attorney's fees under Section 7002(e) of the Solid Waste Disposal Act (SWDA), or Section 505(d) of the Federal Water Pollution Control Act may enhance the fee award above the "lodestar" amount in order to reflect the fact that the party's attorneys were retained on a contingent-fee basis and thus assumed the risk of receiving no payment at all for their services. . . .

Issue

Respondent Dague (whom we will refer to in place of all the respondents) owns land in Vermont adjacent to a landfill that was owned and operated by petitioner City of Burlington. Represented by attorneys retained on a contingent-fee basis, he sued Burlington over its operation of the landfill. The District Court ruled, *inter alia,* that Burlington had violated provisions of the SWDA and the CWA, and ordered Burlington to close the landfill by January 1, 1990. It also determined that Dague was a "substantially prevailing party" entitled to an award of attorney's fees under the Acts.

In calculating the attorney's fees award, the District Court first found reasonable the figures advanced by Dague for his attorneys' hourly rates and for the number of hours expended by them, producing a resulting "lodestar" attorney's fee of $198,027.50. (What our cases have termed the "lodestar" is "the product of reasonable hours times a reasonable rate.") Addressing Dague's request for a contingency enhancement, the court looked to Circuit precedent, which provided that "the rationale that should guide the court's discretion is whether "without the possibility of a fee enhancement . . . competent counsel might refuse to represent [environmental] clients thereby denying them effective access to the courts." [On this basis, the District Court increased the attorney's fee by 25%. The Court of Appeals affirmed.] . . . .

Section 7002(e) of the SWDA and Section 505(d) of the CWA authorize a court to "award costs of litigation (including *reasonable attorney . . . fees)*" to a "prevailing or substantially prevailing party." (emphasis added). This language is similar to that of many other federal fee-shifting statutes; our case law construing what is a "reasonable" fee applies uniformly to all of them.

The "lodestar" figure has, as its name suggests, become the guiding light of our fee-shifting jurisprudence. We have established a "strong presumption" that the lodestar represents the "reasonable" fee, and have placed upon the fee applicant who seeks more than that the burden of showing that "such an adjustment is necessary to the determination of a reasonable fee." . . .

We note at the outset that an enhancement for contingency would likely duplicate in substantial part factors already subsumed in the lodestar. The risk of loss in a particular case (and, therefore, the attorney's contingent risk) is the product of two factors: (1) the legal and factual merits of the claim, and (2) the difficulty of establishing those merits. The second factor, however, is ordinarily reflected in the lodestar — either in the higher number of hours expended to overcome the difficulty, or in the higher hourly rate of the attorney skilled and experienced enough to do so. Taking account of it again through lodestar enhancement amounts to double-counting.

The first factor (relative merits of the claim) is not reflected in the lodestar, but there are good reasons why it should play no part in the calculation of the award. It is, of course, a factor that *always* exists (no claim has a 100% chance of success), so that computation of the lodestar would never end the court's inquiry in contingent-fee cases. Moreover, the consequence of awarding contingency enhancement to take account of this "merits" factor would be to provide attorneys with the same incentive to bring relatively meritless claims as relatively meritorious ones . . . .

[W]e see a number of reasons for concluding that no contingency enhancement whatever is compatible with the fee-shifting statutes at issue. First, just as the statutory language limiting fees to prevailing (or substantially prevailing) parties bars a prevailing plaintiff from recovering fees relating to claims on which he lost, so should it bar a prevailing plaintiff from recovering for the risk of loss. An attorney operating on a contingency-fee basis pools the risks presented by his various cases: cases that turn out to be successful pay for the time he gambled on those that did not. To award a contingency enhancement under a fee-shifting statute would in effect pay for the attorney's time (or anticipated time) in cases where his client does *not* prevail.

Second ... "we have generally turned away from the contingent-fee model"— which would make the fee award a percentage of the value of the relief awarded in the primary action—"to the lodestar model." We have done so, it must be noted, even though the lodestar model often (perhaps, generally) results in a larger fee award than the contingent-fee model. . . .

And finally, the interest in ready administrability that has underlain our adoption of the lodestar approach, and the related interest in avoiding burdensome satellite litigation, counsel strongly against adoption of contingency enhancement. Contingency enhancement would make the setting of fees more complex and arbitrary, hence more unpredictable, and hence more litigable. It is neither necessary nor even possible for application of the fee-shifting statutes to mimic the intricacies of the fee-paying market in every respect . . . .

[W]e hold that enhancement for contingency is not permitted under the fee-shifting statutes at issue. We reverse the Court of Appeals' judgment insofar as it affirmed the 25% enhancement of the lodestar.

V. Injunctive Relief in Environmental Law Suits

In *TVA v. Hill,* a 1978 decision that is excerpted below, in Chapter 4 at page 249, the U.S. Supreme Court enjoined the completion of a mostly built federal dam project on the basis that the Endangered Species Act contains an absolute prohibition on federal agency actions that will threaten the continued viability of listed endangered species. In the case below, however, the Court reversed the Court of Appeals and reinstated a U.S. District Court decision declining to enjoin weapons training and testing activities of the U.S. Navy near an island close to Puerto Rico that had not been authorized under a Clean Water Act NPDES permit. As you read this case, please consider whether the Court's decision was consistent with its opinion in *Hill,* and whether it establishes a sound judicial precedent.

Weinberger v. Romero-Barcelo
456 U.S. 305 (1982)

Justice WHITE:

The issue in this case is whether the Federal Water Pollution Control Act (FWPCA or the Act) requires a district court to enjoin immediately all discharges of pollutants that do not comply with the Act's permit requirements or whether the district court retains discretion to order other relief to achieve compliance. The Court of Appeals

Decision

for the First Circuit held that the Act withdrew the courts' equitable discretion. We reverse.

For many years, the Navy has used Vieques Island, a small island off the Puerto Rico coast, for weapons training. Currently all Atlantic Fleet vessels assigned to the Mediterranean and the Indian Ocean are required to complete their training at Vieques because it permits a full range of exercises under conditions similar to combat. During air-to-ground training, however, pilots sometimes miss land-based targets, and ordnance falls into the sea. That is, accidental bombings of the navigable waters and, occasionally, intentional bombings of water targets occur. The District Court found that these discharges have not harmed the quality of the water.

Facts

In 1978, respondents, who include the Governor of Puerto Rico and residents of the island, sued to enjoin the Navy's operations on the island. Their complaint alleged violations of numerous federal environmental statutes and various other acts. After an extensive hearing, the District Court found that under the explicit terms of the Act, the Navy had violated the Act by discharging ordnance into the waters surrounding the island without first obtaining a permit from the Environmental Protection Agency (EPA).

Under the FWPCA, the "discharge of any pollutant" requires a National Pollutant Discharge Elimination System (NPDES) permit. The term "discharge of any pollutant" is defined as: ". . . any addition of any *pollutant* to the waters of the contiguous zone or the ocean from any *point source* other than a vessel or other floating craft." (emphasis added). Pollutant, in turn, means, ". . . dredged spoil, solid wastes, incinerator residue, sewage, garbage, sewage sludge, *munitions,* chemical wastes, biological materials, radioactive materials, heat, wrecked or discarded equipment, rock, sand, cellar dirt and industrial, municipal and agricultural waste discharged into water. . . ." (emphasis added).

And, under the Act, a "point source" is "any discernible, confined and discrete *conveyance,* including but not limited to any pipe, ditch, channel, tunnel, conduit, well, discrete fissure, container rolling stock, concentrated animal feeding operation, or *vessel* or other *floating craft from which pollutants are or may be discharged. . . ."* (emphasis added). Under the FWPCA, the EPA may not issue an NPDES without state certification that the permit conforms to state water quality standards. A state has the authority to deny certification of the permit application or attach conditions to the final permit.

USDC ruling

As the District Court construed the FWPCA, the release of ordnance from aircraft or from ships into navigable waters is a discharge of pollutants, even though the Environmental Protection Agency, which administers the Act, had not promulgated any regulations setting effluent levels or providing for the issuance of a NPDES permit for this category of pollutants. Recognizing that violations of the Act "must be cured," the District Court ordered the Navy to apply for a NPDES permit. It refused, however, to enjoin Navy operations pending consideration of the permit application. It explained that the Navy's "technical violations" were not causing any "appreciable harm" to the environment. "Moreover, because of the importance of the island as a training center, the granting of the injunctive relief sought would cause grievous, and perhaps irreparable harm, not only to Defendant Navy, but to the general welfare of this Nation." The District Court concluded that an injunction was not necessary to ensure suitably prompt compliance by the Navy. To support this conclusion, it emphasized an equity court's traditionally broad discretion in deciding appropriate relief . . . .

The Court of Appeals for the First Circuit vacated the District Court's order and remanded with instructions that the court order the Navy to cease the violation until it obtained a permit. Relying on *TVA v. Hill,* in which this Court held that an imminent violation of the Endangered Species Act required injunctive relief, the Court of Appeals concluded that the District Court erred in undertaking a traditional balancing of the parties' competing interests. "Whether or not the Navy's activities in fact harm the coastal waters, it has an absolute statutory obligation to stop any discharges of pollutant until the permit procedure has been followed and the Administrator of the Environmental Protection Agency, upon review of the evidence, has granted a permit." The court suggested that if the order would interfere significantly with military preparedness, the Navy should request that the President grant it an exemption from the requirements in the interest of national security.

Because this case posed an important question regarding the power of the federal courts to grant or withhold equitable relief for violations of the FWPCA, we granted certiorari. We now reverse.

It goes without saying that an injunction is an equitable remedy. It "is not a remedy which issues as of course," or "to restrain an act the injurious consequences of which are merely trifling." An injunction should issue only where the intervention of a court of equity "is essential in order effectually to protect property rights against injuries otherwise irremediable." The Court has repeatedly held that the basis for injunctive relief in the federal courts has always been irreparable injury and the inadequacy of legal remedies.

Where plaintiff and defendant present competing claims of injury, the traditional function of equity has been to arrive at a "nice adjustment and reconciliation" between the competing claims. In such cases, the court "balances the conveniences of the parties and possible injuries to them according as they may be affected by the granting or withholding of the injunction." The essence of equity has been the power of the chancellor to do equity and to mold each decree to the necessities of the particular case. Flexibility rather than rigidity has distinguished it.

In exercising their sound discretion, courts of equity should pay particular regard for the public consequences in employing the extraordinary remedy of injunction. Thus, the Court has noted that "the award of an interlocutory injunction by courts of equity has never been regarded as strictly a matter of right, even though irreparable injury may otherwise result to the plaintiff," and that "where an injunction is asked which will adversely affect a public interest for whose impairment, even temporarily, an injunction bond cannot compensate, the court may in the public interest withhold relief until a final determination of the rights of the parties, though postponement may be burdensome to the plaintiff." The grant of jurisdiction to insure compliance with a statute hardly suggests an absolute duty to do so under any and all circumstances, and a federal judge sitting as chancellor is not mechanically obligated to grant an injunction for every violation of law . . . .

Of course, Congress may intervene and guide or control the exercise of the court's discretion, but we do not lightly assume that Congress has intended to depart from established principles. . . .

In *TVA v. Hill*, we held that Congress had foreclosed the exercise of the usual discretion possessed by a court of equity. There, we thought that "one would be hard pressed to find a statutory provision whose terms were any plainer" than that before us. The statute involved, the Endangered Species Act, required the district court to enjoin completion of the Tellico Dam in order to preserve the snail darter, a species of perch. The purpose and language of the statute under consideration in *Hill*, not the bare fact of a statutory violation, compelled that conclusion. Section 1536 of the Act requires federal agencies to "insure that actions authorized, funded, or carried out by them do not jeopardize the continued existence of [any] endangered species . . . or result in the destruction or habitat of such species which is determined . . . to be critical." The statute thus contains a flat ban on the destruction of critical habitats.

It was conceded in *Hill* that completion of the dam would eliminate an endangered species by destroying its critical habitat. Refusal to enjoin the action would have ignored the "explicit provisions of the Endangered Species Act." Congress, it appeared to us, had chosen the snail darter over the dam. The purpose and language of the statute limited the remedies available to the district court; only an injunction could vindicate the objectives of the Act.

That is not the case here. An injunction is not the only means of ensuring compliance. The FWPCA itself, for example, provides for fines and criminal penalties. Respondents suggest that failure to enjoin the Navy will undermine the integrity of the permit process by allowing the statutory violation to continue. The integrity of the nation's waters, however, not the permit process, is the purpose of the FWPCA. As Congress explained, the objective of the FWPCA is to "restore and maintain the chemical, physical and biological integrity of the Nation's waters."

This purpose is to be achieved by compliance with the Act, including compliance with the permit requirements. Here, however, the discharge of ordnance had not polluted the waters, and, although the District Court declined to enjoin the discharges, it neither ignored the statutory violation nor undercut the purpose and function of the permit system. The court ordered the Navy to apply for a permit. It temporarily, not permanently, allowed the Navy to continue its activities without a permit . . . .

The prohibition of the FWPCA against discharge of pollutants, in contrast, can be overcome by the very permit the Navy was ordered to seek. The Senate Report to the 1972 Amendments explains that it was enacting the Permit program because "the Committee recognizes the impracticality of any effort to halt all pollution immediately." That the scheme as a whole contemplates exercise of discretion and balancing of equities militates against the conclusion that Congress intended to deny courts their traditional equitable discretion in enforcing the statute . . . .

The FWPCA directs the Administrator of the EPA to seek an injunction to restrain immediately discharges of pollutants he finds to be presenting "an imminent and substantial endangerment of the health of persons or to the welfare of persons." This rule of immediate cessation, however, is limited to the indicated class of violations. For other kinds of violations, the FWPCA authorizes the Administrator of the EPA "to commence a civil action for appropriate relief, including a permanent or temporary injunction, for any violation for which he is authorized to issue a compliance order . . . ." The provision makes clear that Congress did not anticipate that all discharges would be immediately enjoined. Consistent with this view, the administrative practice has not been to request immediate cessation orders. "Rather, enforcement actions typically result, by consent or otherwise, in a remedial order setting out a detailed schedule of compliance designed to cure the identified violation of the Act." Brief for United States 17. . . .

Enforcement Action

This Court explained in *Hecht v. Bowles,* 321 U.S. 321 (1944), that a major departure from the long tradition of equity practice should not be lightly implied. As we did there, we construe the statute at issue "in favor of that interpretation which affords a full opportunity for equity courts to treat enforcement proceedings . . . in accordance with their traditional practices, as conditioned by the necessities of the public interest which Congress has sought to protect." We do not read the FWPCA as foreclosing completely the exercise of the court's discretion. Rather than requiring a District Court to issue an injunction for any and all statutory violations, the FWPCA permits the District Court to order that relief it considers necessary to secure prompt compliance with the Act. That relief can include, but is not limited to, an order of immediate cessation.

injunctive relief — gov't has discretion

The exercise of equitable discretion, which must include the ability to deny as well as grant injunctive relief, can fully protect the range of public interests at issue at this stage in the proceedings. The District Court did not face a situation in which a permit would very likely not issue and the requirements and objective of the statute could therefore not be vindicated if discharges were permitted to continue. Should it become clear that no permit will be issued and that compliance with the FWPCA will not be forthcoming, the statutory scheme and purpose would require the court to reconsider the balance it has struck.

Because Congress, in enacting the FWPCA, has not foreclosed the exercise of equitable discretion, the proper standard for appellate review is whether the district court abused its discretion in denying an immediate cessation order while the Navy applied for a permit. We reverse and remand to Court of Appeals for proceedings consistent with this opinion.

Justice STEVENS, dissenting:

The appropriate remedy for the violation of a federal statute depends primarily on the terms of the statute and the character of the violation. Unless Congress specifically commands a particular form of relief, the question of remedy remains subject to a court's equitable discretion. Because the Federal Water Pollution Control Act does not specifically command the federal courts to issue an injunction every time an unpermitted discharge of a pollutant occurs, the Court today is obviously correct in asserting that such injunctions should not issue "automatically" or "mechanically" in every case. It is nevertheless equally clear that by enacting the 1972 amendments to the FWPCA Congress channeled the discretion of the federal judiciary much more narrowly than the Court's rather glib opinion suggests. Indeed, although there may well be situations in which the failure to obtain an NPDES permit would not require immediate cessation of all discharges, I am convinced that Congress has circumscribed the district courts' discretion on the question of remedy so narrowly that a general rule of immediate cessation must be applied in all but a narrow category of cases. The Court of Appeals was quite correct in holding that this case does not present the kind of exceptional situation that justifies a departure from the general rule.

The Court's mischaracterization of the Court of Appeals' holding is the premise for its essay on equitable discretion. This essay is analytically flawed because it overlooks the limitations on equitable discretion that apply in cases in which public interests are implicated and the defendant's violation of the law is ongoing. Of greater importance, the Court's opinion grants an open-ended license to federal judges to carve gaping holes in a reticulated statutory scheme designed by Congress to protect a precious natural resource from the consequences of *ad hoc* judgments about specific discharges of pollutants.

Contrary to the impression created by the Court's opinion, the Court of Appeals did not hold that the District Court was under an absolute duty to require compliance with the FWPCA "under any and all circumstances," or that it was "mechanically obligated to grant an injunction for every violation of law." The only "absolute duty" that the Court of Appeals mentioned was the Navy's duty to obtain a permit before discharging pollutants into the waters off Vieques Island. In light of the Court's opinion the point is worth repeating — the Navy, like anyone else, must obey the law.

The Court of Appeals did not hold that the District Court had no discretion in formulating remedies for statutory violations. It merely "conclude[d] that the district court erred in undertaking a traditional balancing of the parties' competing interests." The District Court was not free to disregard the "congressional ordering of priorities" and "the judiciary's 'responsibility to protect the integrity of the ... process mandated by Congress.'" The Court of Appeals distinguished a statutory violation that could be deemed merely "technical" from the Navy's "utter [disregard of] the statutory mandate." It then pointed out that an order prohibiting any discharge of ordnance into the coastal waters off Vieques until an NPDES permit was obtained would not significantly affect the Navy's training operations because most, if not all, of the Navy's targets were land based. Finally, it noted that the statute authorized the Navy to obtain an exemption from the President if an injunction would have a significant effect on national security . . . .

The Court of Appeals' reasoning was correct in all respects. It recognized that the statute categorically prohibits discharges of pollutants without a permit. Unlike the Court it recognized that the requested injunction was the only remedy that would bring the Navy into compliance with the statute on Congress' timetable. It then demonstrated that none of the reasons offered by the District Court for refusing injunctive relief was consistent with the statute or was compelling under the circumstances. The position of the Court of Appeals in effect was that the federal courts' equitable discretion is constrained by a strong presumption in favor of enforcing the law as Congress has written it. By reversing the Court casts doubt on the validity of that position. This doubt is especially dangerous in the environmental area, where the temptations to delay compliance are already substantial.

Our cases concerning equitable remedies have repeatedly identified two critical distinctions that the Court simply ignores today. The first is the distinction between cases in which only private interests are involved and those in which a requested injunction will implicate a public interest. Second, within the category of public interest cases, those cases in which there is no danger that a past violation of law will recur have always been treated differently from those in which an existing violation is certain to continue . . . .

[T]oday the Court pays mere lip service to the statutory mandate and attaches no weight to the fact that the Navy's violation of law has not been corrected. The Court cites no precedent for its holding that an ongoing deliberate violation of a federal statute should be treated like any garden-variety private nuisance action in which the chancellor has the widest discretion in fashioning relief. . . .

The Court distinguishes *TVA v. Hill* on the ground that the Endangered Species Act contained a "flat ban" on the destruction of critical habitats. But the statute involved in this case also contains a flat ban against discharges of pollutants into coastal waters without a permit. Surely the congressional directive to protect the Nation's waters from gradual but possibly irreversible contamination is no less clear than the command to protect the snail darter. To assume that Congress has placed a greater value on the protection of vanishing forms of animal life than on the protection of our water resources is to ignore the text, the legislative history, and the previously consistent interpretation of this statute.

It is true that in *TVA v. Hill* there was no room for compromise between the federal project and the statutory objective to preserve an endangered species; either the snail darter or the completion of the Tellico Dam had to be sacrificed. In the FWPCA, the Court tells us, the congressional objective is to protect the integrity of the Nation's waters, not to protect the integrity of the permit process. Therefore, the Court continues, a federal court may compromise the process chosen by Congress to protect our waters as long as the court is content that the waters are not actually being harmed by the particular discharge of pollutants.

On analysis, however, this reasoning does not distinguish the two cases. Courts are in no better position to decide whether the permit process is necessary to achieve the objectives of the FWPCA than they are to decide whether the destruction of the snail darter is an acceptable cost of completing the Tellico Dam. Congress has made both decisions, and there is nothing in the respective statutes or legislative histories to suggest that Congress invited the federal courts to second-guess the former decision any more than the latter.

A disregard of the respective roles of the three branches of government also tarnishes the Court's other principal argument in favor of expansive equitable discretion in this area . . . . By requiring each discharger to obtain a permit *before* continuing its discharges of pollutants, Congress demonstrated an intolerance for delay in compliance with the statute. It is also obvious that the "exercise of discretion and balancing of equities" were tasks delegated by Congress to expert agencies, not to federal courts, yet the Court simply ignores the difference.

The decision in *TVA v. Hill* did not depend on any peculiar or unique statutory language. Nor did it rest on any special interest in snail darters. The decision reflected a profound respect for the law and the proper allocation of lawmaking responsibilities in our government. There we refused to sit as a committee of review. Today the Court authorizes free thinking federal judges to do just that. Instead of requiring adherence to carefully integrated statutory procedures that assign to nonjudicial decisionmakers the responsibilities for evaluating potential harm to our water supply as well as potential harm to our national security, the Court unnecessarily and casually substitutes the chancellor's clumsy foot for the rule of law.

I respectfully dissent.

Notes and Questions

1. Following the *Weinberger* decision, to what extent do trial courts now have discretion to permanently excuse compliance with requirements of environmental statutes? For a trenchant discussion of *Weinberger* and its implications, see Plater, *Statutory Violations and Equitable Discretion,* 70 Cal. L. Rev. 524 (1984). *See also* Farber, *Equitable Discretion, Legal Duties and Environmental Injunctions,* 45 U. Pitt. L. Rev. 513 (1984); and Note, *Injunctions for NEPA Violations: Balancing the Equities,* 59 U. Chi. L. Rev. 1263 (1992).

2. In *Amoco Production Co. v. Village of Gambell, Alaska,* 480 U.S. 531 (1987), the U.S. Supreme Court affirmed a lower court's denial of a motion by Alaska native villages for a preliminary injunction halting the Secretary of Interior's sale of oil and gas leases on federally owned lands in the outer continental shelf. Relying on *Weinberger,* the Court refused to accept the plaintiffs' contention that violations of procedural safeguards contained in the Alaska National Interest Lands Conservation Act constituted an irreparable injury that justified a preliminary injunction. Nonetheless, *in dicta,* the Court appeared to retreat from *Weinberger* to some extent, stating that "[e]nvironmental injury, by its nature, can seldom be adequately remedied by money damages and is often permanent or at least of long duration. If such injury is sufficiently likely, therefore, the balance of harms will usually favor the issuance of an injunction to protect the environment."

3. The U.S. Supreme Court revisited the question of the authority of U.S. District Courts to enjoin the actions of government agencies in *Monsanto Co. v. Geertson Seed Farms,* 130 S. Ct. 2743 (2010). In *Geertson Seed,* The Court reviewed a trial court decision to issue an injunction in a challenge by seed farms and environmental organizations to a decision by the Animal and Plant Health Inspection Service (APHIS) to deregulate a kind of alfalfa crop that had been genetically engineered to be tolerant of glyphosphate, the active ingredient in a herbicide, Roundup, produced by Monsanto. The Supreme Court accepted the District Court's conclusion that APHIS had been required to prepare an Environmental Impact Statement (EIS) under NEPA before fully deregulating the crop. Nonetheless, the Court rejected as overly broad what it described as a judicial decree ordering APHIS to rescind its decision to deregulate the crops in question, and enjoining all future planting of the genetically engineered alfalfa pending preparation of the EIS. Over a vigorous dissent by Justice Stevens, the Court applied the traditional test for the issuance of an injunction. It concluded that NEPA violations should not automatically result in the issuance of broad injunctions that prohibit all interim regulations; and because the factors that are traditionally required for the granting of permanent injunctive relief were not present, the District Court should have allowed APHIS to impose partial regulation on the crops in question while it complied with NEPA. Is this decision consistent with the Court's opinion in the *Weinberger* case or in *TVA v. Hill?*

Chapter 3

Taking the Environment into Account: The National Environmental Policy Act

I. Introduction

Rachel Carson's 1962 book, SILENT SPRING, made many Americans aware of the ecological interconnections of which Aldo Leopold had written more than a decade before. (See pp. 4, 9, above, for excerpts). Pesticides were hardly the only human activity causing collateral damage to the environment, however. In 1948, 20 people died when an atmospheric temperature inversion enveloped the steel town of Donora, Pennsylvania in its own air pollution—and this was not the only "killer smog." In 1952, oily pollution made the Cuyahoga River in Cleveland, Ohio, catch fire—for neither the first nor the last time, and not uniquely among American rivers. In 1963, the newly completed Glen Canyon Dam began impounding the Colorado River, generating water storage and electricity but flooding a scenic canyon and trapping the water and sediment flows essential to the ecology of the Grand Canyon and the rest of the river downstream. In 1969, an offshore oil well blew out off the coast of southern California, covering 800 square miles of ocean and 30 miles of beaches with oil. In countless other ways, human activities—industry, mining, logging, agriculture, wetland-draining, river-damming, landfilling, road-building, urban and suburban sprawl, and more—irrevocably altered ecological and social systems alike. By the late 1960s, the increasingly apparent consequences of pollution, resource exploitation, and waste disposal had begun to generate calls for some type of governmental response.

Against this backdrop, both the executive and legislative branches of the United States government began considering policies that would address the environment as a subject worthy of attention in its own right, rather than as a mere context for other activities and policies. The result was the National Environmental Policy Act of 1969, which passed both houses of Congress without significant opposition. President Nixon signed the bill on January 1, 1970, saying: "the 1970s absolutely must be the years when America pays its debt to the past by reclaiming the purity of its air, its waters, and our living environment. It is literally now or never." *Statement by the President upon Signing Bill Establishing the Council on Environmental Quality, Jan. 1, 1970*, 6 Weekly

Compilation of Presidential Documents 11 (reprinted in 2 National Environmental Policy Act of 1969 [Legislative History]).

II. The Nature of NEPA

NEPA begins with a ringing statement of the purposes of the statute:

The purposes of this Act ["Chapter," in the U.S. Code version] are: To declare a national policy which will encourage productive and enjoyable harmony between man and his environment; to promote efforts which will prevent or eliminate damage to the environment and biosphere and stimulate the health and welfare of man; to enrich the understanding of the ecological systems and natural resources important to the Nation; and to establish a Council on Environmental Quality.

42 U.S.C. § 4321 (NEPA § 2). These grand purposes are hardly self-executing (with the possible exception of establishing a Council on Environmental Quality). The very next subsection of NEPA declares the national policy that section 2 promises:

The Congress, recognizing the profound impact of man's activity on the inter-relations of all components of the natural environment, particularly the profound influences of population growth, high-density urbanization, indus-trial expansion, resource exploitation, and new and expanding technological advances and recognizing further the critical importance of restoring and maintaining environmental quality to the overall welfare and development of man, declares that it is the continuing policy of the Federal Government, in cooperation with State and local governments, and other concerned pub-lic and private organizations, to use all practicable means and measures, including financial and technical assistance, in a manner calculated to foster and promote the general welfare, to create and maintain conditions under which man and nature can exist in productive harmony, and fulfill the social, economic, and other requirements of present and future generations of Americans.

42 U.S.C. § 4331(a) (NEPA § 101(a)). The policy declaration, too, is long on rhetoric and short on direction. How should the policy be carried out? Subsequent provisions of NEPA provide some answers:

In order to carry out the policy set forth in this Act, it is the continuing respon-sibility of the Federal Government to use all practicable means, consistent with other essential considerations of national policy, to improve and coor-dinate Federal plans, functions, programs, and resources to the end that the Nation may—

(1) fulfill the responsibilities of each generation as trustee of the environment for succeeding generations;

(2) assure for all Americans safe, healthful, productive, and esthetically and culturally pleasing surroundings;

(3) attain the widest range of beneficial uses of the environment without degradation, risk to health or safety, or other undesirable and unintended consequences;

(4) preserve important historic, cultural, and natural aspects of our national heritage, and maintain, wherever possible, an environment which supports diversity and variety of individual choice;

(5) achieve a balance between population and resource use which will permit high standards of living and a wide sharing of life's amenities; and

(6) enhance the quality of renewable resources and approach the maximum attainable recycling of depletable resources.

NEPA § 101(b), 42 U.S.C. § 4331(b).

The Congress authorizes and directs that, to the fullest extent possible: (1) the policies, regulations, and public laws of the United States shall be interpreted and administered in accordance with the policies set forth in this Act, and (2) all agencies of the Federal Government shall —

(A) utilize a systematic, interdisciplinary approach which will insure the integrated use of the natural and social sciences and the environmental design arts in planning and in decision-making which may have an impact on man's environment;

(B) identify and develop methods and procedures, in consultation with the Council on Environmental Quality established by title II of this Act, which will insure that presently unquantified environmental amenities and values may be given appropriate consideration in decision-making along with economic and technical considerations;

(C) include in every recommendation or report on proposals for legislation and other major Federal actions significantly affecting the quality of the human environment, a detailed statement by the responsible official on —   *Environmental Impact Statement*

   (i) the environmental impact of the proposed action,

   (ii) any adverse environmental effects which cannot be avoided should the proposal be implemented,

   (iii) alternatives to the proposed action,

   (iv) the relationship between local short-term uses of man's environment and the maintenance and enhancement of long-term productivity, and

   (v) any irreversible and irretrievable commitments of resources which would be involved in the proposed action should it be implemented.

Prior to making any detailed statement, the responsible Federal official shall consult with and obtain the comments of any Federal agency which has jurisdiction by law or special expertise with respect to any environmental impact involved. Copies of such statement and the comments and views of the appropriate Federal, State, and local agencies, which are authorized to develop and enforce environmental standards, shall be made available to the President, the Council on Environmental Quality and to the public as provided by section 552 of title 5, United States Code, and shall accompany the proposal through the existing agency review processes;

. . .

(E) study, develop, and describe appropriate alternatives to recommended courses of action in any proposal which involves unresolved conflicts concerning alternative uses of available resources;

(F) recognize the worldwide and long-range character of environmental problems and, where consistent with the foreign policy of the United States, lend appropriate support to initiatives, resolutions, and programs designed to maximize international cooperation in anticipating and preventing a decline in the quality of mankind's world environment;

. . .

(H) initiate and utilize ecological information in the planning and development of resource-oriented projects . . . .

. . . .

NEPA § 102, 42 U.S.C. § 4332.

The sections you have just read are the key operative provisions of NEPA.

Notes and Questions

1. Environmental statutes, like most statutes, usually aim to modify the behavior of some identifiable class of actors by requiring, prohibiting, or attaching positive or negative consequences to certain actions. The "Superfund" statute, for example, made liable "persons" who have certain types of involvement with facilities from which hazardous substances are released, and defines "person" to include individuals, business entities of all types, and government agencies (see Chapter 9). Whose behavior was NEPA intended to modify? *Gov't Agencies*

2. Imagine it is January 1970. You have just begun working in the Office of General Counsel within the General Services Administration (GSA), the federal agency responsible for the construction, maintenance, and management of most federal government office buildings. The Administrator, who heads the agency and who just learned of NEPA's enactment, asks you to analyze the statute: "What does this law require our agency to do?" What advice would you give?

3. Section 103 of NEPA, 42 U.S.C. § 4333, required "all agencies of the Federal Government" to review their statutory authorities, regulations, policies, and procedures to determine whether they had "deficiencies or inconsistencies" making "full compliance with the purposes and provisions" of NEPA impossible, and to propose to the

[handwritten margin note: Super fund Statute — Federal gov's program to fund the cleanup of contaminated sites w/ hazardous pollutants and substances]

President "such measures as may be necessary to bring their authority and policies into conformity" with NEPA's "intent, purposes, and procedures." The statute gave agencies 18 months to complete this task. Section 105, 42 U.S.C. § 4335, describes NEPA's "policies and goals" as "supplementary" to the existing authorized purposes of federal agencies. Title II of NEPA, 42 U.S.C. §§ 4341–4347, established the Council on Environmental Quality. We will explain below the Council's role in NEPA implementation.

4. For a detailed description of NEPA's path through Congress, see RICHARD A. LIROFF, A NATIONAL POLICY FOR THE ENVIRONMENT 19–35 (1976).

A. Enforceability of NEPA

The enactment of NEPA portended a potentially revolutionary change in the federal government's approach to the environment. The new national environmental policy applied to "all federal agencies," though only a few agencies had missions that primarily or even tangentially involved environmental protection or resource conservation. It applied generally to agency "decision-making" that might have environmental impacts, though many agencies had traditionally ignored or given short shrift to environmental considerations.

Until NEPA's enactment, resource exploitation and economic development concerns, rather than environmental protection and conservation, had long dominated federal policy. By 1970, a host of federal agencies existed that were authorized by statute to take actions that, whatever their salutary intentions or results, also undeniably caused significant harm to the natural and human-built environment. By their decisions, federal agencies directly or indirectly cut forests, dammed rivers, and built highways, mines, oil and gas wells, and power plants. The cheapest and most direct route for a highway might run through a park or a vibrant neighborhood. Exploiting oil reserves might risk a spill that would devastate marine life and beaches. A dam might interrupt fish spawning runs, destroy a river's natural food web, and flood farms, woodlots, homes, or scenic canyons—including, in one famous but eventually abandoned proposal by the Bureau of Reclamation, parts of the Grand Canyon. *See* National Park Service, *Bureau of Reclamation Proposals*, in A SURVEY OF THE RECREATIONAL RESOURCES OF THE COLORADO RIVER BASIN (Chapter 7, *The Grand Canyon*) (1950), https://www.nps.gov/parkhistory/online_books/colorado/chap7.htm (last visited July 22, 2016); MARC REISNER, CADILLAC DESERT: THE AMERICAN WEST AND ITS DISAPPEARING WATER 272–90 (1986). To agencies intent on fulfilling their statutory mandate, these types of ancillary effects rarely, if ever, mattered. NEPA demanded their consideration.

Not surprisingly, many federal agencies did not embrace their new NEPA obligations with alacrity. Whether out of habit, a bureaucratic impulse to justify the continued growth of agency funding and staff, or a sincere belief that they were acting in the public interest, some agency officials interpreted and implemented NEPA in a crabbed fashion designed to minimize the statute's ability to disrupt "business as usual" in the pursuit of the agencies' primary missions.

At the same time, widespread dissatisfaction with the federal government's environmentally harmful actions—the same dissatisfaction that helped lead to NEPA's enactment—had spurred into action a fledgling group of public interest environmental lawyers. These lawyers—whether working in private law firms, long-established conservation organizations, or new non-profit environmental law firms—tried to use legal advocacy tools, especially litigation, to force federal agencies to make choices that would avoid or minimize environmental harm. They saw NEPA as a powerful tool to achieve their objectives. *See generally* A. Dan Tarlock, *The Story of* Calvert Cliffs: *A Court Construes the National Environmental Policy Act to Create a Powerful Cause of Action, in* ENVIRONMENTAL LAW STORIES 77, 99–100 n.81 (2005).

The development of the nuclear energy industry provided a stage for several early tests of NEPA's reach. After using nuclear weapons at the end of World War II, the United States government was determined to show that the power of the atom could also be harnessed for the benefit of humankind. The Atomic Energy Act of 1946 created the Atomic Energy Commission (AEC), which was tasked with both promoting and regulating the use of nuclear energy to generate electricity. Officials dreamed of electricity "too cheap to meter." The first privately financed nuclear electric generating plant opened in 1960. Several more had recently begun operating or were nearing final approval for construction or operation when NEPA was enacted in 1970. New orders for nuclear power plants peaked in 1973, shortly after the OPEC oil embargo. *See* www.nrc.gov/about-nrc/emerg-preparedness/history.html (last visited July 3, 2015). The development of nuclear power as a technologically and economically feasible source of electricity thus roughly coincided with the development of the environmental movement in the United States.

From its beginnings, nuclear power was controversial, in part because of the harms and risks that it presented to the environment from the beginning to the end of the "nuclear fuel cycle." Mining radioactive ore for nuclear fuel can spread low-level radioactive material, creating health and ecological risks in areas near the mines. Operating nuclear reactors can significantly harm fish and other river life because (at least in the design most often used in the United States) large amounts of water are needed to control the heat generated by the fission reactions that occur in reactors' fuel. Aquatic organisms may be killed at the intakes for cooling water, and may also be harmed by the discharge of warmed (although not radioactive) water that is released back into the river after passing through the power plant. Opponents of nuclear power also worried about the possibility that the cooling system might fail, leading to a meltdown of nuclear fuel, a breach of the containment walls, and a massive release of radioactive material: an event of low probability but catastrophic consequences. Opponents also pointed to the problem of nuclear waste, consisting of a mixture of radioisotopes created as a necessary by-product of reactor operation, some of which would emit deadly amounts of radiation for thousands of years. In the 1970s, no one knew how to dispose of such waste in a way that would be safe indefinitely, and even today the United States government has been unable to implement a disposal solution that is both socially acceptable and technologically likely to succeed.

To some environmental activists, to build and operate nuclear power plants despite the plants' environmental effects seemed inconsistent with the newly declared federal environmental policy of NEPA. The AEC's initial response to NEPA's enactment, however, did not suggest any great desire to allow consideration of "environmental amenities and values" to impede the mission of promoting development of a nuclear power industry in the United States. The conflicting visions reached the courts in the context of a dispute over a utility's application for a license to operate a nuclear plant on the scenic shores of the Chesapeake Bay.

Calvert Cliffs' Coordinating Committee, Inc. v. U.S. Atomic Energy Commission
449 F.2d 1109 (D.C. Cir. 1971)

Judge WRIGHT:

These cases are only the beginning of what promises to become a flood of new litigation—litigation seeking judicial assistance in protecting our natural environment. Several recently enacted statutes attest to the commitment of the Government to control, at long last, the destructive engine of material "progress." But it remains to be seen whether the promise of this legislation will become a reality. Therein lies the judicial role. In these cases, we must for the first time interpret the broadest and perhaps most important of the recent statutes: the National Environmental Policy Act of 1969 (NEPA). We must assess claims that one of the agencies charged with its administration has failed to live up to the congressional mandate. Our duty, in short, is to see that important legislative purposes, heralded in the halls of Congress, are not lost or misdirected in the vast hallways of the federal bureaucracy.

NEPA, like so much other reform legislation of the last 40 years, is cast in terms of a general mandate and broad delegation of authority to new and old administrative agencies. It takes the major step of requiring all federal agencies to consider values of environmental preservation in their spheres of activity, and it prescribes certain procedural measures to ensure that those values are in fact fully respected. Petitioners argue that rules recently adopted by the Atomic Energy Commission to govern consideration of environmental matters fail to satisfy the rigor demanded by NEPA. The Commission, on the other hand, contends that the vagueness of the NEPA mandate and delegation leaves much room for discretion and that the rules challenged by petitioners fall well within the broad scope of the Act. We find the policies embodied in NEPA to be a good deal clearer and more demanding than does the Commission. We conclude that the Commission's procedural rules do not comply with the congressional policy. Hence we remand these cases for further rule making . . . .

Arguments Presented

Decision

I.

We begin our analysis with an examination of NEPA's structure and approach and of the Atomic Energy Commission rules which are said to conflict with the requirements of the Act. The relevant portion of NEPA is Title I, consisting of five sections. Section 101 sets forth the Act's basic substantive policy: that the federal government "use all practicable means and measures" to protect environmental values. Congress did not establish environmental protection as an exclusive goal; rather, it desired a reordering of priorities, so that environmental costs and benefits will assume their proper place along with other considerations. In Section 101(b), imposing an explicit duty on federal officials, the Act provides that "it is the continuing responsibility of the Federal Government to use all practicable means, consistent with other essential considerations of national policy," to avoid environmental degradation, preserve "historic, cultural, and natural" resources, and promote "the widest range of beneficial uses of the environment without . . . undesirable and unintended consequences."

Thus the general substantive policy of the Act is a flexible one. It leaves room for a responsible exercise of discretion and may not require particular substantive results in particular problematic instances. However, the Act also contains very important "procedural" provisions — provisions which are designed to see that all federal agencies do in fact exercise the substantive discretion given them. These provisions are not highly flexible. Indeed, they establish a strict standard of compliance.

NEPA, first of all, makes environmental protection a part of the mandate of every federal agency and department. The Atomic Energy Commission, for example, had continually asserted, prior to NEPA, that it had no statutory authority to concern itself with the adverse environmental effects of its actions. Now, however, its hands are no longer tied. It is not only permitted, but compelled, to take environmental values into account. Perhaps the greatest importance of NEPA is to require the Atomic Energy Commission and other agencies to *consider* environmental issues just as they consider other matters within their mandates. This compulsion is most plainly stated in Section 102. There, "Congress authorizes and directs that, to the fullest extent possible: (1) the policies, regulations, and public laws of the United States shall be interpreted and administered in accordance with the policies set forth in this Act * * *." Congress also "authorizes and directs" that "(2) all agencies of the Federal Government shall" follow certain rigorous procedures in considering environmental values.[5]

The sort of consideration of environmental values which NEPA compels is clarified in Section 102(2)(A) and (B) . . . . In some instances environmental costs may outweigh economic and technical benefits and in other instances they may not. But NEPA mandates a rather finely tuned and "systematic" balancing analysis in each instance.

To ensure that the balancing analysis is carried out and given full effect, Section 102(2)(C) requires that responsible officials of all agencies prepare a "detailed statement" covering the impact of particular actions on the environment, the

---

5. Only once — in § 102(2)(B) — does the Act state, in terms, that federal agencies must give full "consideration" to environmental impact as part of their decision making processes. However, a requirement of consideration is clearly implicit in the substantive mandate of § 101, in the requirement of § 102(1) that all laws and regulations be "interpreted and administered" in accord with that mandate, and in the other specific procedural measures compelled by § 102(2) . . . . The requirements of § 102(2) must not be read so narrowly as to erase the general import of §§ 101, 102(1) and 102(2) (A) & (B).

environmental costs which might be avoided, and alternative measures which might alter the cost-benefit equation. The apparent purpose of the "detailed statement" is to aid in the agencies' own decision making process and to advise other interested agencies and the public of the environmental consequences of planned federal action. Beyond the "detailed statement," Section 102(2)[E] requires all agencies specifically to "study, develop, and describe appropriate alternatives to recommended courses of action in any proposal which involves unresolved conflicts concerning alternative uses of available resources." This requirement, like the "detailed statement" requirement, seeks to ensure that each agency decision maker has before him and takes into proper account all possible approaches to a particular project (including total abandonment of the project) which would alter the environmental impact and the cost-benefit balance. Only in that fashion is it likely that the most intelligent, optimally beneficial decision will ultimately be made. Moreover, by compelling a formal "detailed statement" and a description of alternatives, NEPA provides evidence that the mandated decision making process has in fact taken place and, most importantly, allows those removed from the initial process to evaluate and balance the factors on their own.

Of course, all of these Section 102 duties are qualified by the phrase "to the fullest extent possible." We must stress as forcefully as possible that this language does not provide an escape hatch for footdragging agencies; it does not make NEPA's procedural requirements somehow "discretionary." Congress did not intend the Act to be such a paper tiger. Indeed, the requirement of environmental consideration "to the fullest extent possible" sets a high standard for the agencies, a standard which must be rigorously enforced by the reviewing courts.

Unlike the substantive duties of Section 101(b), which require agencies to "use all practicable means consistent with other essential considerations," the procedural duties of Section 102 must be fulfilled to the "fullest extent possible." This contrast, in itself, is revealing . . . .

. . . .

Thus the Section 102 duties are not inherently flexible. They must be complied with to the fullest extent, unless there is a clear conflict of *statutory* authority. Considerations of administrative difficulty, delay or economic cost will not suffice to strip the section of its fundamental importance.

We conclude, then, that Section 102 of NEPA mandates a particular sort of careful and informed decisionmaking process and creates judicially enforceable duties. The reviewing courts probably cannot reverse a substantive decision on its merits, under Section 101, unless it be shown that the actual balance of costs and benefits that was struck was arbitrary or clearly gave insufficient weight to environmental values. But if the decision was reached procedurally without individualized consideration and balancing of environmental factors—conducted fully and in good faith—it is the responsibility of the courts to reverse. As one District Court has said of Section 102 requirements: "It is hard to imagine a clearer or stronger mandate to the Courts."

In the cases before us now, we do not have to review a particular decision by the Atomic Energy Commission granting a construction permit or an operating license.

Rather, we must review the Commission's recently promulgated rules which govern consideration of environmental values in all such individual decisions. The rules were devised strictly in order to comply with the NEPA procedural requirements — but petitioners argue that they fall far short of the congressional mandate.

. . . .

Order of events to enforce NEPA

The procedure for environmental study and consideration set up by the rules is as follows: Each applicant for an initial construction permit must submit to the Commission his own "environmental report," presenting his assessment of the environmental impact of the planned facility and possible alternatives which would alter the impact. When construction is completed and the applicant applies for a license to operate the new facility, he must again submit an "environmental report" noting any factors which have changed since the original report. At each stage, the Commission's regulatory staff must take the applicant's report and prepare its own "detailed statement" of environmental costs, benefits and alternatives. The statement will then be circulated to other interested and responsible agencies and made available to the public. After comments are received from those sources, the staff must prepare a final "detailed statement" and make a final recommendation on the application for a construction permit or operating license. [After the staff makes its final recommendation, the decision whether to issue the construction permit or license is made by a three-member "atomic safety licensing board" after an adjudicatory-style hearing, at which evidence is taken and opponents of the application may be heard.]

. . . . [Petitioners] attack four . . . specific parts of the rules which, they say, violate the requirements of Section 102 of NEPA. Each . . . in some way limits full consideration and individualized balancing of environmental values in the Commission's decision making process. (1) Although environmental factors must be considered by the agency's regulatory staff under the rules, such factors need not be considered by the hearing board conducting an independent review of staff recommendations, unless affirmatively raised by outside parties or staff members. (2) Another part of the procedural rules prohibits any such party from raising nonradiological environmental issues at any hearing if the notice for that hearing appeared in the Federal Register before March 4, 1971. (3) Moreover, the hearing board is prohibited from conducting an independent evaluation and balancing of certain environmental factors if other responsible agencies have already certified that their own environmental standards are satisfied by the proposed federal action. (4) Finally, the Commission's rules provide that when a construction permit for a facility has been issued before NEPA compliance was required and when an operating license has yet to be issued, the agency will not formally consider environmental factors or require modifications in the proposed facility until the time of the issuance of the operating license . . . .

II.

NEPA makes only one specific reference to consideration of environmental values in agency review processes. Section 102(2)(C) provides that copies of the staff's "detailed statement" and comments thereon "shall accompany the proposal through the existing agency review processes." The Atomic Energy Commission's rules may seem in technical compliance with the letter of that provision. They state:

> "12. If any party to a proceeding . . . raises any [environmental] issue . . . the Applicant's Environmental Report and the Detailed Statement will be offered in evidence. The atomic safety and licensing board will make findings of fact on, and resolve, the matters in controversy among the parties with regard to those issues. Depending on the resolution of those issues, the permit or license may be granted, denied, or appropriately conditioned to protect environmental values.

> "13. When no party to a proceeding . . . raises any [environmental] issue . . . such issues will not be considered by the atomic safety and licensing board. Under such circumstances, although the Applicant's Environmental Report, comments thereon, and the Detailed Statement will accompany the application through the Commission's review processes, they will not be received in evidence, and the Commission's responsibilities under the National Environmental Policy Act of 1969 will be carried out in toto outside the hearing process."

The question here is whether the Commission is correct in thinking that its NEPA responsibilities may "be carried out in toto outside the hearing process"—whether it is enough that environmental data and evaluation merely "accompany" an application through the review process, but receive no consideration whatever from the hearing board.

Issue 1

We believe that the Commission's crabbed interpretation of NEPA makes a mockery of the Act. What possible purpose could there be in the Section 102(2)(C) requirement (that the "detailed statement" accompany proposals through agency review processes) if "accompany" means no more than physical proximity—mandating no more than the physical act of passing certain folders and papers, unopened, to reviewing officials along with other folders and papers? What possible purpose could there be in requiring the "detailed statement" to be before hearing boards, if the boards are free to ignore entirely the contents of the statement? NEPA was meant to do more than regulate the flow of papers in the federal bureaucracy. The word "accompany" in Section 102(2)(C) must not be read so narrowly as to make the Act ludicrous. It must, rather, be read to indicate a congressional intent that environmental factors, as compiled in the "detailed statement," be *considered* through agency review processes.

Reasoning

Beyond Section 102(2)(C), NEPA requires that agencies consider the environmental impact of their actions "to the fullest extent possible." The Act is addressed to agencies as a whole, not only to their professional staffs. Compliance to the "*fullest*" possible extent would seem to demand that environmental issues be considered at every important stage in the decision making process concerning a particular action— at every stage where an overall balancing of environmental and nonenvironmental factors is appropriate and where alterations might be made in the proposed action to minimize environmental costs . . . .

. . . .

. . . . NEPA established environmental protection as an integral part of the Atomic Energy Commission's basic mandate. The primary responsibility for fulfilling that mandate lies with the Commission. Its responsibility is not simply to sit back, like an umpire, and resolve adversary contentions at the hearing stage. Rather, it must itself take the initiative of considering environmental values at every distinctive and comprehensive stage of the process beyond the staff's evaluation and recommendation.

III.

Congress passed the final version of NEPA in late 1969, and the Act went into full effect on January 1, 1970. Yet the Atomic Energy Commission's rules prohibit any consideration of environmental issues by its hearing boards at proceedings officially noted before March 4, 1971. This is 14 months after the effective date of NEPA. And the hearings affected may go on for as much as a year longer until final action is taken. The result is that major federal actions having a significant environmental impact may be taken by the Commission, without full NEPA compliance, more than two years after the Act's effective date. . . .

. . . .

. . . [T]he Commission's approach . . . seems to reveal a rather thoroughgoing reluctance to meet the NEPA procedural obligations in the agency review process, the stage at which deliberation is most open to public examination and subject to the participation of public intervenors . . . . Every federal court having faced the issues has held that the procedural requirements of NEPA must be met in order to uphold federal action taken after January 1, 1970 . . . .

. . . .

. . . . It seems an unfortunate affliction of large organizations to resist new procedures and to envision massive roadblocks to their adoption. Hence the Commission's talk of the need for an "orderly transition" to the NEPA procedures . . . . [T]he obvious sense of urgency on the part of Congress should make clear that a transition, however "orderly," must proceed at a pace faster than a funeral procession . . . .

IV.

The sweep of NEPA is extraordinarily broad, compelling consideration of any and all types of environmental impact of federal action. However, the Atomic Energy Commission's rules specifically exclude from full consideration a wide variety of environmental issues. First, they provide that no party may raise and the Commission may not independently examine any problem of water quality—perhaps the most significant impact of nuclear power plants. Rather, the Commission indicates that it will defer totally to water quality standards devised and administered by state agencies and approved by the federal government under the Federal Water Pollution Control Act. Secondly, the rules provide for similar abdication of NEPA authority to the standards of other agencies:

> "With respect to those aspects of environmental quality for which environmental quality standards and requirements have been established by authorized Federal, State, and regional agencies, proof that the applicant is equipped

to observe and agrees to observe such standards and requirements will be considered a satisfactory showing that there will not be a significant, adverse effect on the environment. Certification by the appropriate agency that there is reasonable assurance that the applicant for the permit or license will observe such standards and requirements will be considered dispositive for this purpose."

. . . .

We believe the Commission's rule is in fundamental conflict with the basic purpose of the Act. NEPA mandates a case-by-case balancing judgment on the part of federal agencies. In each individual case, the particular economic and technical benefits of planned action must be assessed and then weighed against the environmental costs; alternatives must be considered which would affect the balance of values. . . . Much will depend on the particular magnitudes involved in particular cases. In some cases, the benefits will be great enough to justify a certain quantum of environmental costs; in other cases, they will not be so great and the proposed action may have to be abandoned or significantly altered so as to bring the benefits and costs into a proper balance. The point of the individualized balancing analysis is to ensure that, with possible alterations, the optimally beneficial action is finally taken.

Certification by another agency that its own environmental standards are satisfied involves an entirely different kind of judgment. Such agencies, without overall responsibility for the particular federal action in question, attend only to one aspect of the problem: the magnitude of certain environmental costs. They simply determine whether those costs exceed an allowable amount. Their certification does not mean that they found no environmental damage whatever. In fact, there may be significant environmental damage (*e.g.*, water pollution), but not quite enough to violate applicable (*e.g.*, water quality) standards. Certifying agencies do not attempt to weigh that damage against the opposing benefits. Thus the balancing analysis remains to be done. It may be that the environmental costs, though passing prescribed standards, are nonetheless great enough to outweigh the particular economic and technical benefits involved in the planned action. The only agency in a position to make such a judgment is the agency with overall responsibility for the proposed federal action — the agency to which NEPA is specifically directed. *[handwritten: Rationale]*

The Atomic Energy Commission, abdicating entirely to other agencies' certifications, neglects the mandated balancing analysis . . . . *[handwritten: decision]*

V.

Petitioners' final attack is on the Commission's rules governing . . . nuclear facilities . . . for which construction permits were granted without consideration of environmental issues, but for which operating licenses have yet to be issued. These facilities, still in varying stages of construction, include . . . the Calvert Cliffs nuclear power plant on Chesapeake Bay in Maryland. *[handwritten: Issue 4]*

. . . . In cases where environmental costs were not considered in granting a construction permit, it is very likely that the planned facility will include some features which do significant damage to the environment and which could not have survived a rigorous balancing of costs and benefits. At the later operating license proceedings, this environmental damage will have to be fully considered. But by that time the situation will have changed radically. Once a facility has been completely constructed, the economic cost of any alteration may be very great. In the language of NEPA, there is likely to be an "irreversible and irretrievable commitment of resources," which will inevitably restrict the Commission's options. Either the licensee will have to undergo a major expense in making alterations in a completed facility or the environmental harm will have to be tolerated. It is all too probable that the latter result would come to pass.

By refusing to consider requirement of alterations until construction is completed, the Commission may effectively foreclose the environmental protection desired by Congress. It may also foreclose rigorous consideration of environmental factors at the eventual operating license proceedings. If "irreversible and irretrievable commitment[s] of resources" have already been made, the license hearing (and any public intervention therein) may become a hollow exercise. This hardly amounts to consideration of environmental values "to the fullest extent possible."

. . . .

decision

Thus we conclude that the Commission must go farther than it has in its present rules. It must consider action, as well as file reports and papers, at the pre-operating license stage. . . . All we demand is that the environmental review be as full and fruitful as possible.

VI.

Final Decision

We hold that, in the four respects detailed above, the Commission must revise its rules governing consideration of environmental issues. We do not impose a harsh burden on the Commission. For we require only an exercise of substantive discretion which will protect the environment "to the fullest extent possible." No less is required if the grand congressional purposes underlying NEPA are to become a reality.

Remanded for proceedings consistent with this opinion.

Notes and Questions

1. The "detailed statement" required by NEPA § 102(2)(C) is now universally known as an "Environmental Impact Statement" (often referred to by its acronym "EIS"), a phrase that does not appear in the statute. Guidelines, and later regulations, issued by the Council on Environmental Quality used the EIS nomenclature, which has become ubiquitous in case law and public discourse. *See generally* 43 Fed. Reg. 25230 (June 9, 1978) (announcing proposed regulations and comparing them to existing guidelines); 40 C.F.R. Part 1502 (setting requirements for EIS's).

2. In statutes and other controlling legal texts, minor drafting details can matter. The *Calvert Cliffs'* court relied heavily on NEPA's provision requiring federal agencies to undertake *all* of their statutory obligations under § 102 "to the fullest extent possible." In an earlier version of the bill that became NEPA, the phrase "to the fullest extent possible" modified only a small portion of § 102. It was moved to the beginning of the section as part of a legislative compromise. It is likely that some members of Congress thought that the phrase would be interpreted to limit the extent of agencies' NEPA obligations rather than to expand them. The *Calvert Cliffs'* court used portions of the legislative history (not included in the excerpt above) to support its expansive reading of the phrase. The legislative maneuvering is described briefly in A. Dan Tarlock, *The Story of* Calvert Cliffs: *A Court Construes the National Environmental Policy Act to Create a Powerful Cause of Action, in* ENVIRONMENTAL LAW STORIES 77, 99–100 n.81 (2005), and in more detail in Richard A. Liroff, A NATIONAL POLICY FOR THE ENVIRONMENT 26–31 (1976).

3. What provision of NEPA granted to a party like the Calvert Cliffs' Coordinating Committee a right to sue to enforce a federal agency's compliance with the statute? What did the D.C. Circuit identify as the source of that right? How did the case come before the court of appeals? What was being appealed?

Subsequent NEPA jurisprudence has emphasized that because NEPA does not expressly create a right of action, claims that an agency violated NEPA must be brought pursuant to the general judicial review provisions of the Administrative Procedure Act, 5 U.S.C. §§ 701–706. Among other limitations, those provisions allow courts to review only "final agency action" (unless a statute otherwise provides, which NEPA does not). *Id.* § 704. Thus, plaintiffs must wait until an agency acts before they can allege in court that the agency violated NEPA. *See, e.g., Public Citizen v. U.S. Trade Representative*, 5 F.3d 549, 551 (D.C. Cir. 1993) (holding that with respect to the North American Free Trade Agreement, final agency action is presidential submission of the treaty to Congress, and therefore plaintiff could not bring a claim alleging that negotiation of the treaty without preparation of an EIS violated NEPA). Did the *Calvert Cliffs'* petitioners challenge a final agency action of the Atomic Energy Commission? If so, what was it?

Calvert Cliffs' is an early example of the intersection of environmental law with administrative law. This intersection occurs frequently because environmental law is strongly dominated by statutes and by regulations that executive agencies promulgate pursuant to statutory grants of authority. Therefore many environmental law disputes present as challenges (by environmental groups, regulated industries, states, and others) to federal administrative actions. In Chapter 2, above, we explored some administrative law principles that are important to environmental law. Cases involving judicial review of administrative action often raise issues quite distinct from issues raised in other types of cases, such as enforcement actions seeking relief from alleged violators of pollution standards. When reading a court decision on environmental law, therefore, you should be alert to the context in which the case arose.

4. The only agency Congress established in NEPA is the Council on Environmental Quality. Why, then, was it appropriate for the Atomic Energy Commission (AEC) to promulgate the regulations that were challenged in *Calvert Cliffs'*? Federal agencies have a vast array of missions, but all must comply with NEPA in carrying out those missions. Would it be realistic to have the Council on Environmental Quality learn the processes of the AEC and dictate in detail how the AEC should implement NEPA in the context of those processes? And then repeat that for every federal agency?

Instead, the CEQ has taken the approach of setting broadly applicable standards for NEPA compliance and relying on each agency to craft its own procedures to implement those standards. *See* 40 C.F.R. § 1500.6. Agencies have done so using varying degrees of formality, ranging from internal handbooks to codified regulations. The CEQ maintains a list of links to the agencies' NEPA implementing procedures at https://ceq.doe.gov/nepa_contacts/Federal_Agency_NEPA_%20Implementing_Procedures_15July2013.pdf (last visited Sept. 15, 2016).

5. The *Calvert Cliffs'* decision required the AEC to rewrite its rules for compliance with NEPA's procedural requirements. As a result, no nuclear plants were licensed for 18 months. The Calvert Cliffs plant itself eventually received an operating license after the applicant completed an environmental impact statement. Tarlock, *supra*, at 101.

6. The D.C. Circuit contrasted the "flexible" substantive policy expressed in § 101 of NEPA with the more exacting procedural requirements of § 102. In *Calvert Cliffs'*, only procedural compliance was at issue. The petitioners did not challenge a decision to grant a license to the Calvert Cliffs plant, but rather challenged the AEC's rules that would limit consideration of environmental impacts in the hearing at which that decision would be made.

What if the petitioners *had* challenged a specific licensing decision on substantive grounds, arguing that a particular plant's environmental impacts were so harmful that it should not have been licensed? Would such a challenge have been possible, according to *Calvert Cliffs'*? If so, how would the more "flexible" nature of NEPA's substantive provision have affected the challenge, according to the D.C. Circuit?

7. As noted above, the initial decision to grant an application for a permit to construct or a license to operate a nuclear power plant is made by a three-member administrative body, the Atomic Safety and Licensing Board, after an adjudicatory hearing. A party dissatisfied with the decision may appeal to higher administrative bodies. After agency review of the decision is exhausted, an unhappy party's next recourse is to the courts, via a petition for review of the licensing decision filed with a federal court of appeals. Two such petitions for review led to the Supreme Court opinion that begins the next subsection of this chapter.

B. Substance versus Procedure in NEPA Compliance

Vermont Yankee Nuclear Power Corp. v. Natural Resources Defense Council, Inc.

435 U.S. 519 (1978)

Justice REHNQUIST:

I

A

Under the Atomic Energy Act of 1954. . . . a utility seeking to construct and operate a nuclear power plant must obtain [from the Atomic Energy Commission (AEC)] a separate permit or license at both the construction and the operation stage of the project . . . .

These cases arise from two separate decisions of the Court of Appeals for the District of Columbia Circuit. In the first, the court remanded a decision of the Commission to grant a license to petitioner Vermont Yankee Nuclear Power Corp. to operate a nuclear power plant. In the second, the court remanded a decision of that same agency to grant a permit to petitioner Consumers Power Co. to construct two pressurized water nuclear reactors to generate electricity and steam.

FACTS

B

[After obtaining a construction permit and building a nuclear power plant, Vermont Yankee applied for an operating license. The Natural Resources Defense Council (NRDC) objected, which triggered a hearing before a licensing board. The licensing board refused to hear evidence related to the environmental effects of the "back end" of the nuclear fuel cycle—fuel reprocessing and waste disposal. The AEC's Appeals Board affirmed that decision.

The AEC then began rulemaking proceedings to address "the question of consideration of environmental effects associated with the uranium fuel cycle in the individual cost-benefit analyses for light water cooled nuclear power reactors." Rather than use the "notice-and-comment" rulemaking procedures ordinarily allowed by the Administrative Procedure Act, the AEC held evidentiary hearings before promulgating its final rule. NRDC and other groups participated in the hearing. The AEC made available to all parties the documents on which the AEC intended to rely, allowed written comments as well as some oral statements at the hearing, and allowed thirty days to file additional written comments after circulating a transcript of the hearing, but did not allow discovery before the hearing or cross-examination at the hearing. After the hearing, the AEC issued a rule which provided that the environmental costs of the back end of the fuel cycle would be quantified in a table of values to be used in calculating the overall cost-benefit balance for each operating license.]

Respondents appealed from both the Commission's adoption of the rule and its decision to grant Vermont Yankee's license to the Court of Appeals for the District of Columbia Circuit.

C

[In January 1969, Consumers Power Co. applied for a construction permit for two nuclear reactors. As part of the application process, the Advisory Committee on Reactor Safeguards (ACRS) issued reports that "discussed specific problems and recommended solutions" and "made reference to 'other problems' of a more generic nature and suggested that efforts should be made to resolve them with respect to these as well as all other projects."

A group called Saginaw opposed the application. The licensing board held hearings on health and safety issues but refused to consider most environmental issues. On the last day of the hearings, however, the D.C. Circuit issued its *Calvert Cliffs'* opinion. Because of that decision, the AEC's staff prepared a draft environmental impact statement for the Consumers Power construction permit. In response, "Saginaw submitted 119 environmental contentions. . . ." The final EIS was issued in March, 1972. The licensing board then held further hearings, but Saginaw did not participate in them.

"At issue now are 17 of those 119 contentions which are claimed to raise questions of 'energy conservation.'" The licensing board declined to consider energy conservation as an alternative way to satisfy the demand for electricity that the nuclear plants were intended to meet. The AEC granted the construction permit. Saginaw then moved the AEC to reopen the proceedings in light of newly-promulgated CEQ regulations that required agencies to consider energy conservation in EIS's. The "Commission declined to reopen the proceedings."]

Respondents then challenged the granting of the construction permit in the Court of Appeals for the District of Columbia Circuit.

D

With respect to the challenge of Vermont Yankee's license, the court first ruled that in the absence of effective rulemaking proceedings, the Commission must deal with the environmental impact of fuel reprocessing and disposal in individual licensing proceedings. The court then examined the rulemaking proceedings and . . . overturned the rule. Accordingly, the Commission's determination with respect to Vermont Yankee's license was also remanded for further proceedings.

With respect to the permit to Consumers Power, the court first held that the environmental impact statement for construction of the . . . reactors was fatally defective for failure to examine energy conservation as an alternative to a plant of this size. The court also thought the report by ACRS was inadequate . . . .

II

. . . .

[T]he majority of the Court of Appeals struck down the [fuel cycle] rule because of the perceived inadequacies of the procedures employed in the rulemaking proceedings . . .

. . . .

. . . . Absent constitutional constraints or extremely compelling circumstances the "administrative agencies 'should be free to fashion their own rules of procedure and to pursue methods of inquiry capable of permitting them to discharge their multitudinous duties.'" . . .

. . . .

In short, nothing . . . permitted the court to review and overturn the rulemaking proceeding on the basis of the procedural devices employed (or not employed) by the Commission so long as the Commission employed at least the statutory *minima*, a matter about which there is no doubt in this case.

. . . .

III

A

We now turn to the Court of Appeals' holding "that rejection of energy conservation [. . .] was capricious and arbitrary." . . .

. . . .

. . . [U]nder the Atomic Energy Act of 1954, state public utility commissions . . . are empowered to make the initial decision regarding the need for power . . . . And it is clear that the need, as that term is conventionally used, for the power was thoroughly explored in the hearings. . . .

NEPA, of course, has altered slightly the statutory balance, requiring "a detailed statement by the responsible official on . . . alternatives to the proposed action." But, as should be obvious even upon a moment's reflection, the term "alternatives" is not self-defining. To make an impact statement something more than an exercise in frivolous boilerplate the concept of alternatives must be bounded by some notion of feasibility . . . .

. . . .

With these principles in mind we now turn to the notion of "energy conservation," an alternative the omission of which was thought by the Court of Appeals to have been "forcefully pointed out by Saginaw in its comments on the draft EIS." . . . [A]s a practical matter, it is hard to dispute the observation that it is largely the events of recent years that have emphasized not only the need but also a large variety of alternatives for energy conservation. Prior to the drastic oil shortages incurred by the United States in 1973, there was little serious thought in most Government circles of energy conservation alternatives. Indeed, the Council on Environmental Quality did not promulgate regulations which even remotely suggested the need to consider energy conservation in impact statements until August 1, 1973. . . . All this occurred over a year and a half after the draft environmental statement . . . had been prepared, and over a year after the final environmental statement had been prepared and the hearings completed.

We think these facts amply demonstrate that the concept of "alternatives" is an evolving one, requiring the agency to explore more or fewer alternatives as they become better known and understood. This was well understood by the Commission, which, unlike the Court of Appeals, recognized that the Licensing Board's decision had to be judged by the information then available to it. And judged in that light we have little doubt the Board's actions were well within the proper bounds of its statutory authority . . . .

. . . .

. . . [T]o characterize the actions of the Commission as "arbitrary or capricious" in light of the facts then available to it . . . is to deprive those words of any meaning. . . .

. . . .

"Neither the statute nor its legislative history contemplates that a court should substitute its judgment for that of the agency as to the environmental consequences of its actions."

We think the Court of Appeals has forgotten that injunction here and accordingly its judgment in this respect must also be reversed.

B

Finally, we turn to the Court of Appeals' holding that the Licensing Board should have returned the ACRS report to ACRS for further elaboration, understandable to a layman, of the reference to other problems.

. . . .

Again the Court of Appeals has unjustifiably intruded into the administrative process. . . .

. . . .

We . . . find absolutely nothing in the relevant statutes to justify what the court did here. . . .

All this leads us to make one further observation of some relevance to this case. To say that the Court of Appeals' final reason for remanding is insubstantial at best is a gross understatement. Consumers Power first applied in 1969 for a construction permit—not even an operating license, just a construction permit. The proposed plant underwent an incredibly extensive review. The reports filed and reviewed literally fill books. The proceedings took years, and the actual hearings themselves over two weeks. To then nullify that effort seven years later because one report refers to other problems, which problems admittedly have been discussed at length in other reports available to the public, borders on the Kafkaesque. Nuclear energy may some day be a cheap, safe source of power or it may not. But Congress has made a choice to at least try nuclear energy, establishing a reasonable review process in which courts are to play only a limited role. The fundamental policy questions appropriately resolved in Congress and in the state legislatures are not subject to reexamination in the federal courts under the guise of judicial review of agency action. Time may prove wrong the decision to develop nuclear energy, but it is Congress or the States within their appropriate agencies which must eventually make that judgment. In the meantime courts should perform their appointed function. NEPA does set forth significant substantive goals for the Nation, but its mandate to the agencies is essentially procedural. It is to insure a fully informed and well-considered decision, not necessarily a decision the judges of the Court of Appeals or of this Court would have reached had they been members of the decisionmaking unit of the agency. Administrative decisions should be set aside in this context, as in every other, only for substantial procedural or substantive reasons as mandated by statute, not simply because the court is unhappy with the result reached. And a single alleged oversight on a peripheral issue, urged by parties who never fully cooperated or indeed raised the issue below, must not be made the basis for overturning a decision properly made after an otherwise exhaustive proceeding.

Notes and Questions

1. The AEC prepared an Environmental Impact Statement for each of the two licenses challenged in *Vermont Yankee*; the challengers alleged that these EISs, however, did not fulfill NEPA's "detailed statement" requirement. What were the specific alleged shortcomings of each EIS that the Supreme Court addressed? How did the Court's holdings resolve each of these allegations? We will consider the legal standards for challenges to the adequacy of an EIS in more detail in Section IV, p. 170, below.

2. What relevance might consideration of energy conservation have had to the issue of whether to grant a construction license for the Midland nuclear power plant?

3. In assessing the environmental impacts of granting an operating license to the Vermont Yankee plant, the AEC decided not to consider the "back end" of the nuclear fuel cycle with respect to that plant specifically. Instead, the AEC initiated a rulemaking proceeding that resulted in a general determination that the environmental effects of nuclear waste would not be significant. Why do you think the AEC adopted this approach? Why do you think NRDC made such an issue of the AEC's procedural choices, such as the refusal to allow cross-examination at the rulemaking hearing?

4. Long-term disposal of spent fuel and high-level radioactive waste from nuclear power plants has proven to be an intractable issue. The AEC rule discussed in *Vermont Yankee* basically willed the issue away—the Commission concluded that a technical solution would eventually be found and the waste could be safely managed in the meantime. The Nuclear Waste Policy Act of 1982, 42 U.S.C. § 10101 *et seq.*, authorized the Department of Energy (DOE) to find a site to build a geologic repository to store high-level nuclear waste. DOE identified remote Yucca Mountain, in Nevada, as the best location. DOE completed an Environmental Impact Statement that concluded, among other things, that the repository could prevent human and environmental exposures to the highly radioactive waste for one million years. U.S. Dept. of Energy, *Final Environmental Impact Statement for a Geologic Repository for the Disposal of Spent Nuclear Fuel and High-Level Radioactive Waste at Yucca Mountain, Nye County, Nevada* S-43 (Feb. 2002), http://www.energy.gov/sites/prod/files/EIS-0250-FEIS_Summary -2002.pdf. That technical assessment, however, even if correct, has not sufficed to overcome the considerable opposition to the repository.

In July 2002, President George W. Bush signed a congressional joint resolution designating Yucca Mountain as the repository site. In 2008, DOE, as required by statute, applied to the Nuclear Regulatory Commission (NRC) for a construction license for the repository. The Obama Administration, however, concluded that Yucca Mountain "is not a workable option," and Congress cut the project's funding. U.S. Nuclear Regulatory Comm'n, *Supplement to the U.S. Department of Energy's Environmental Impact Statement for a Geologic Repository for the Disposal of Spent Nuclear Fuel and High-Level Radioactive Waste at Yucca Mountain, Nye County, Nevada* § 1.1 (May, 2016), http://www.nrc.gov/reading-rm/doc-collections/nuregs/staff/sr2184/. Despite a court order directing the NRC to resume some related activities, as of May 2016, the licensing proceeding remained suspended. *Id.* Among other issues that dog the possible repository, the State of Nevada (which opposes the repository) has refused to appropriate to DOE water rights that DOE needs to support the project. Eureka County, Nevada Nuclear Waste Office, FAQs, http://www.yuccamountain.org/faq .htm#why_yucca (last visited July 25, 2016). Thus, the status of the Yucca Mountain repository remains unresolved, and spent nuclear fuel and high-level nuclear waste remain in supposedly temporary storage locations across the nation.

5. *Vermont Yankee* stated that "Congress has made a choice to at least try nuclear energy. . . ." Is it not also true, as *Calvert Cliffs'* stated, that Congress had made a choice to "make[ ] environmental protection a part of the mandate of every federal agency and department"? Did the Supreme Court harmonize these statutory choices or did the Court treat the statutes as incompatible and privilege one over the other? If one statute must be subordinated, what principles might be used to decide which one?

After *Vermont Yankee*, the Supreme Court revisited the nature of agencies' NEPA obligations in the cases that follow.

Strycker's Bay Neighborhood Council, Inc. v. Karlen
444 U.S. 223 (1980)

PER CURIAM.

[As part of an "urban renewal" project, the United States Department of Housing and Urban Development (HUD) approved a plan by the New York City Planning Commission to construct a high-rise apartment building consisting entirely of low-income housing at a site on the Upper West Side of Manhattan. The plaintiffs, alleging that HUD had approved the plan without fulfilling its NEPA obligations, sued in federal district court for an injunction prohibiting construction of the project. The district judge held that HUD had not violated NEPA and dismissed the suit, but that judgment was reversed on appeal and the case remanded.]

On remand, HUD prepared a lengthy report entitled Special Environmental Clearance (1977). After marshaling the data, the report asserted that, "while the choice of Site 30 for development as a 100 percent low-income project has raised valid questions about the potential social environmental impacts involved, the problems associated with the impact on social fabric and community structures are not considered so serious as to require that this component be rated as unacceptable." The last portion of the report incorporated a study wherein the Commission evaluated nine alternative locations for the project and found none of them acceptable. While HUD's report conceded that this study may not have considered all possible alternatives, it credited the Commission's conclusion that any relocation of the units would entail an unacceptable delay of two years or more. According to HUD, "[m]easured against the environmental costs associated with the minimum two-year delay, the benefits seem insufficient to justify a mandated substitution of sites."

. . . [T]he District Court again entered judgment in favor of petitioners. The court was "impressed with [HUD's analysis] as being thorough and exhaustive," and found that "HUD's consideration of the alternatives was neither arbitrary nor capricious"; on the contrary, "[i]t was done in good faith and in full accordance with the law."

On appeal, the Second Circuit vacated and remanded again. The appellate court focused upon that part of HUD's report where the agency considered and rejected alternative sites, and in particular upon HUD's reliance on the delay such a relocation would entail. The Court of Appeals purported to recognize that its role in reviewing HUD's decision was defined by the Administrative Procedure Act (APA), 5 U.S.C. § 706(2)(A), which provides that agency actions should be set aside if found to be "arbitrary, capricious, an abuse of discretion, or otherwise not in accordance with law. . . ." Additionally, however, the Court of Appeals looked to "[t]he provisions of NEPA" for "the substantive standards necessary to review the merits of agency decisions. . . ." The Court of Appeals conceded that HUD had "given 'consideration' to alternatives" to redesignating the site. Nevertheless, the court believed that "'consideration' is not an end in itself." Concentrating on HUD's finding that development of an alternative location would entail an unacceptable delay, the appellate court held that such delay could not be "an overriding factor" in HUD's decision to proceed with the development. According to the court, when HUD considers such projects, "environmental factors, such as crowding low-income housing into a concentrated area, should be given determinative weight." The Court of Appeals therefore remanded the case to the District Court, instructing HUD to attack the shortage of low-income housing in a manner that would avoid the "concentration" of such housing on Site 30.

[handwritten margin note: Court of Appeals decision: remanded back to District Court]

In *Vermont Yankee Nuclear Power Corp. v. NRDC*, we stated that NEPA, while establishing "significant substantive goals for the Nation," imposes upon agencies duties that are "essentially procedural." As we stressed in that case, NEPA was designed "to insure a fully informed and well-considered decision," but not necessarily "a decision the judges of the Court of Appeals or of this Court would have reached had they been members of the decisionmaking unit of the agency." *Vermont Yankee* cuts sharply against the Court of Appeals' conclusion that an agency, in selecting a course of action, must elevate environmental concerns over other appropriate considerations. On the contrary, once an agency has made a decision subject to NEPA's procedural requirements, the only role for a court is to insure that the agency has considered the environmental consequences; it cannot "'interject itself within the area of discretion of the executive as to the choice of the action to be taken.'"[2]

[handwritten margin note: Reasoning]

In the present litigation there is no doubt that HUD considered the environmental consequences of its decision to redesignate the proposed site for low-income housing. NEPA requires no more. The petitions for certiorari are granted, and the judgment of the Court of Appeals is therefore

[handwritten margin note: Decision]

Reversed.

---

2. If we could agree with the dissent that the Court of Appeals held that HUD had acted "arbitrarily" in redesignating the site for low-income housing, we might also agree that plenary review is warranted. But the District Court expressly concluded that HUD had not acted arbitrarily or capriciously and our reading of the opinion of the Court of Appeals satisfies us that it did not overturn that finding. Instead, the appellate court required HUD to elevate environmental concerns over other, admittedly legitimate, considerations. Neither NEPA nor the APA provides any support for such a reordering of priorities by a reviewing court.

Justice MARSHALL, dissenting.

The issue raised by these cases is far more difficult than the *per curiam* opinion suggests. The Court of Appeals held that the Secretary of Housing and Urban Development (HUD) had acted arbitrarily in concluding that prevention of a delay in the construction process justified the selection of a housing site which could produce adverse social environmental effects, including racial and economic concentration. Today the majority responds that "once an agency has made a decision subject to NEPA's procedural requirements, the only role for a court is to insure that the agency has considered the environmental consequences," and that in this case "there is no doubt that HUD considered the environmental consequences of its decision to redesignate the proposed site for low-income housing. NEPA requires no more." The majority finds support for this conclusion in the closing paragraph of our decision in *Vermont Yankee Nuclear Power Corp. v. NRDC.*

Vermont Yankee does not stand for the broad proposition that the majority advances today. The relevant passage in that opinion was meant to be only a "further observation of some relevance to this case." That "observation" was a response to this Court's perception that the Court of Appeals in that case was attempting "under the guise of judicial review of agency action" to assert its own policy judgment as to the desirability of developing nuclear energy as an energy source for this Nation, a judgment which is properly left to Congress. The Court of Appeals had remanded the case to the agency because of "a single alleged oversight on a peripheral issue, urged by parties who never fully cooperated or indeed raised the issue below." It was in this context that the Court remarked that "NEPA does set forth significant substantive goals for the Nation, but its mandate to the agencies is *essentially* procedural." (emphasis supplied). Accordingly, "[a]dministrative decisions should be set aside in this context, *as in every other*, only for substantial procedural *or substantive* reasons as mandated by statute," (emphasis supplied). Thus *Vermont Yankee* does not stand for the proposition that a court reviewing agency action under NEPA is limited solely to the factual issue of whether the agency "considered" environmental consequences. The agency's decision must still be set aside if it is "arbitrary, capricious, an abuse of discretion, or otherwise not in accordance with law," 5 U.S.C. § 706(2)(A), and the reviewing court must still insure that the agency "has taken a 'hard look' at environmental consequences."

In the present case, the Court of Appeals did not "substitute its judgment for that of the agency as to the environmental consequences of its actions," for HUD in its Special Environmental Clearance Report acknowledged the adverse environmental consequences of its proposed action: "the choice of Site 30 for development as a 100 percent low-income project has raised valid questions about the potential social environmental impacts involved." These valid questions arise from the fact that 68% of all public housing units would be sited on only one crosstown axis in this area of New York City. As the Court of Appeals observed, the resulting high concentration of low-income housing would hardly further racial and economic integration. The environmental "impact . . . on social fabric and community structures" was given a B rating in the report, indicating that from this perspective the project is "questionable" and ameliorative measures are "mandated." The report lists 10 ameliorative measures necessary to make the project acceptable. The report also discusses two alternatives, Sites 9 and 41, both of which are the appropriate size for the project and require "only minimal" amounts of relocation and clearance. Concerning Site 9 the report explicitly concludes that "[f]rom the standpoint of social environmental impact, this location would be superior to Site 30 for the development of low-rent public housing." The sole reason for rejecting the environmentally superior site was the fact that if the location were shifted to Site 9, there would be a projected delay of two years in the construction of the housing.

The issue before the Court of Appeals, therefore, was whether HUD was free under NEPA to reject an alternative acknowledged to be environmentally preferable solely on the ground that any change in sites would cause delay. This was hardly a "peripheral issue" in the case. Whether NEPA, which sets forth "significant substantive goals," *Vermont Yankee*, permits a projected two-year time difference to be controlling over environmental superiority is by no means clear. Resolution of the issue, however, is certainly within the normal scope of review of agency action to determine if it is arbitrary, capricious, or an abuse of discretion.* The question whether HUD can make delay the paramount concern over environmental superiority is essentially a restatement of the question whether HUD in considering the environmental consequences of its proposed action gave those consequences a "hard look," which is exactly the proper question for the reviewing court to ask.

[margin handwritten note:] hierarchy of concerns to be addressed

The issue of whether the Secretary's decision was arbitrary or capricious is sufficiently difficult and important to merit plenary consideration in this Court. Further, I do not subscribe to the Court's apparent suggestion that *Vermont Yankee* limits the reviewing court to the essentially mindless task of determining whether an agency "considered" environmental factors even if that agency may have effectively decided to ignore those factors in reaching its conclusion. Indeed, I cannot believe that the Court would adhere to that position in a different factual setting. Our cases establish that the arbitrary-or-capricious standard prescribes a "searching and careful" judicial inquiry designed to ensure that the agency has not exercised its discretion in an unreasonable manner. Believing that today's summary reversal represents a departure from that principle, I respectfully dissent. . . .

Notes and Questions

1. Compare *Strycker's Bay* to *Calvert Cliffs'*. Is there a difference between the decisions with respect to the distinction between procedural and substantive NEPA challenges? If there is a difference, what is it?

---

* The Secretary concedes that if an agency gave little or no weight to environmental values its decision might be arbitrary or capricious.

Robertson v. Methow Valley Citizens Council

490 U.S. 332 (1989)

Justice STEVENS:

FACTS :

[The United States Forest Service manages the national forests for diverse purposes, one of which is outdoor recreation. Methow Recreation, Inc. applied to the United States Forest Service for a "special use permit" to build a ski area and hotel within the Okanogan National Forest, on a pristine mountain called Sandy Butte overlooking the scenic, sparsely populated Methow Valley. While considering the application, the Forest Service prepared an Environmental Impact Statement as required by NEPA. The EIS concluded that building a resort would encourage significant population and building growth in the vicinity, which could harm wildlife (because development would disrupt a migration path for an important herd of mule deer) and reduce air quality (because newly-built homes and businesses would burn wood for heating). The EIS identified ways to mitigate these adverse effects by land use planning and air quality regulations, but because most of these steps would apply to land outside the national forest, the Forest Service could not require them. Nevertheless, the Regional Forester decided to issue a special use permit for a ski area that could accommodate up to 8,200 skiers at a time. Four organizations opposed to the resort appealed to the Chief of the Forest Service (Robertson), who affirmed the Regional Forester's decision. The organizations filed a civil action in federal district court alleging that the EIS did not satisfy NEPA's requirements. The district court ruled in the Forest Service's favor, but the Ninth Circuit reversed. The Court of Appeals held that in the circumstances of the case, NEPA required the Forest Service to ensure that effective measures would be implemented to mitigate environmental impacts. The Supreme Court granted the Forest Service's petition for *certiorari.*]

Decision

Section 101 of NEPA declares a broad national commitment to protecting and promoting environmental quality. To ensure that this commitment is "infused into the ongoing programs and actions of the Federal Government, the act also establishes some important 'action-forcing' procedures." . . .

NEPA

The statutory requirement that a federal agency contemplating a major action prepare such an environmental impact statement serves NEPA's "action-forcing" purpose in two important respects. It ensures that the agency, in reaching its decision, will have available and will carefully consider detailed information concerning significant environmental impacts; it also guarantees that the relevant information will be made available to the larger audience that may also play a role in both the decision making process and the implementation of that decision.

. . . .

The sweeping policy goals announced in § 101 of NEPA are thus realized through a set of "action-forcing" procedures that require that agencies take a "'hard look' at environmental consequences," and that provide for broad dissemination of relevant environmental information. Although these procedures are almost certain to affect the agency's substantive decision, it is now well settled that NEPA itself does not

Substantive v. procedural (See p. 123)

mandate particular results, but simply prescribes the necessary process. [The Court cited *Strycker's Bay* and *Vermont Yankee*.] If the adverse environmental effects of the proposed action are adequately identified and evaluated, the agency is not constrained by NEPA from deciding that other values outweigh the environmental costs. In this case, for example, it would not have violated NEPA if the Forest Service, after complying with the Act's procedural prerequisites, had decided that the benefits to be derived from downhill skiing at Sandy Butte justified the issuance of a special use permit, notwithstanding the loss of 15 percent, 50 percent, or even 100 percent of the mule deer herd. Other statutes may impose substantive environmental obligations on federal agencies, but NEPA merely prohibits uninformed — rather than unwise — agency action.

Substantive hierarchy to be considered in a case

. . . .

There is a fundamental distinction . . . between a requirement that mitigation be discussed in sufficient detail to ensure that environmental consequences have been fairly evaluated, on the one hand, and a substantive requirement that a complete mitigation plan be actually formulated and adopted, on the other . . . . [I]t would be inconsistent with NEPA's reliance on procedural mechanisms — as opposed to substantive, result-based standards — to demand the presence of a fully developed plan that will mitigate environmental harm before an agency can act.

gov't can mess up environment, but doesn't have to mitigate

We thus conclude that the Court of Appeals erred, first, in assuming that "NEPA requires that 'action be taken to mitigate the adverse effects of major federal actions,'" and, second, in finding that this substantive requirement entails the further duty to include in every EIS "a detailed explanation of specific measures which *will* be employed to mitigate the adverse impacts of a proposed action."

Decision

. . . The judgment of the Court of Appeals is accordingly reversed and the case is remanded for further proceedings consistent with this opinion.

mitigation would have to be in surrounding areas that was out of the area they had control over.

Notes and Questions

1. The *Methow Valley* decision contended that even if NEPA imposed only procedural requirements, following those procedures would likely affect federal agencies' substantive decisions. Is the Court's reasoning persuasive?

2. In light of the *Methow Valley* decision, you might be surprised that the resort the Forest Service decided to permit was never built. Continued opposition (including suits brought under state law) and the changing economics of the ski industry combined to prevent it. Eventually the Trust for Public Land, an organization that acquires land for conservation purposes, bought the privately owned property that would have been an essential part of the resort.

↓ nepa is only procedural

3. Compare the *Methow Valley* opinion to the majority and dissenting opinions in *Strycker's Bay* and to the *Calvert Cliffs'* opinion, with respect to the distinction between procedural and substantive NEPA challenges. Then review the text of NEPA §§ 101 and 102 (pp. 94–96, above). Which judicial view does the text of NEPA better support?

A number of scholars have argued that various provisions of NEPA, properly understood, accomplished considerably more than the Supreme Court has given them credit for. The following excerpt is an example.

Joel A. Mintz, *Taking Congress's Words Seriously: Towards a Sound Construction of NEPA's Long Overlooked Interpretation Mandate*
38 ENVTL. L. 1031 (2008)

. . . .

[handwritten margin note: intended to apply to all gov't but some states refuse]

The interpretation provision of NEPA is notable for its brevity. Subsection 102(1) simply states that "the Congress authorizes and directs that, to the fullest extent possible[,] the policies, regulations, and public laws of the United States shall be interpreted and administered in accordance with the policies set forth in this chapter."

On a careful reading of this sentence, several of its aspects are immediately apparent. First, the subsection is unmistakably mandatory. In clear terms, Congress has not merely urged or suggested that the interpretation and administration of the laws referred to in the provision be consistent with NEPA's policies, it has required that to occur. The subsection employs the verb "shall," as opposed to "may" to describe what must occur, traditionally an indication of an intended command as opposed to a mere aspiration . . . .

Second, the subsection makes plain that what is to be construed and administered in accordance with NEPA's policies are "the policies, regulations, and public laws of the United States." . . . By its terms, the subsection appears to encompass, without limitation, all federal legal authorities that may be described as policies, regulations, or public laws.

Third, NEPA's interpretation mandate plainly directs that the required legal interpretation and administration it refers to must take place "to the fullest extent possible." . . . .[E]ven a cursory reading of that phrase makes it evident that in subsection 102(1) Congress was requiring a wholehearted and vigorous application of the policies set forth in NEPA. Partial and/or conditional implementation of NEPA's policies, or a failure or refusal to apply them to some particular subset of national policies, regulations, or public laws, seems far less than the statute demands.

Notwithstanding these self-explanatory features, however, the plain language of subsection 102(1) standing alone leaves certain questions unresolved. It is unclear from the provision itself precisely which policies "set forth in this chapter" are to provide the basis for interpreting and administering federal policies, regulations, and public laws. Moreover, NEPA's interpretation directive does not indicate, at least in so many words, to whom the provision applies. Finally, the phrase "to the fullest extent possible" is not squarely defined, either in subsection 102(1) or elsewhere in the statute.

The legislative history of NEPA sheds little light on these questions. . . .

. . . .

Although subsection 102(1) does not itself define the "policies set forth in the chapter" to which the interpretation mandate applies, it seems plain that those policies were fully expressed in sections 2 and 101 of NEPA, the portions of the statute to which that phrase obviously refers.

. . . .

As we have seen, subsection 102(1) directs that interpretation of the public laws of the United States, along with the nation's policies and regulations, is to be in accordance with NEPA's policies. The language of this subsection contrasts sharply with that of subsection 102(2), NEPA's EIS provision, which contains a specific set of mandates that are made expressly applicable to "all agencies of the Federal Government." The omission of any reference to "all agencies of the Federal Government" in subsection 102(1) appears highly significant. Had Congress wished to limit the applicability of the interpretation mandate to federal agencies, it could surely have drafted the subsection to declare that "all agencies of the Federal Government shall interpret and administer the policies, regulations, and public laws of the United States in accordance with the policies set forth in this chapter." Its refusal to do so carries an unmistakable implication: subsection 102(1) applies to all governmental entities in all branches of the federal government that are responsible for the interpretation as well as the administration of our nation's policies, regulations, and public laws.

In a common law system, it is axiomatic that one of the responsibilities of judges is to interpret the meaning of statutes. Federal agencies, of course, have an important role to play in the administration of federal laws; and (at least in some circumstances) courts will defer to the interpretations that those agencies make of federal statutes that the agencies have been directed to implement. Nevertheless, courts have construed legislative enactments since the earliest days of the Republic, a fact that Congress was undoubtedly aware of at the time that NEPA was passed into law. In view of this, it seems logical to read the nonspecific language of subsection 102(1) as a broad instruction — to courts and agencies alike — that they are to interpret federal statutes in accordance with NEPA's stated policies.

To date, no . . . reported case has yet addressed the question of whether the interpretation mandate applies to the federal judiciary . . . .

Nonetheless, upon a close reading of all judicial cases that refer to subsection 102(1), it seems fair to conclude that the words of that provision alone provide the best (and only) indication of whether its mandate extends to federal judges as well as Executive Branch officials. As discussed above, it appears that it does.

. . . .

As we have observed, section 102 of NEPA requires that both the interpretation and administration of federal laws and policies and the EIS requirement imposed on all federal agencies be carried out in accord with NEPA's policies "to the fullest extent possible." Thus far that phrase has not been judicially construed as it pertains specifically to subsection 102(1). Nonetheless, federal courts have addressed the meaning of "to the fullest extent possible" as those words apply to the duty of federal agencies to prepare and consider EISs. Those decisions appear to give some guidance—indirect and imprecise though it may be—for the future application of subsection 102(1).

The most influential interpretation of "to the fullest extent possible" was made soon after NEPA's enactment by Judge Skelly Wright in *Calvert Cliffs' Coordinating Committee, Inc. v. United States Atomic Energy Commission (Calvert Cliffs)*.

. . . .

. . . *Calvert Cliffs* does contain a firm indication that "to the fullest extent possible" is statutory language of considerable significance. It is a phrase that federal courts and agencies should not (and must not) ignore as they interpret NEPA.

In a decision handed down five years later, *Flint Ridge Development Co. v. Scenic Rivers Ass'n of Oklahoma (Flint Ridge)*, the U.S. Supreme Court accepted *Calvert Cliffs's* overall interpretation of "to the fullest extent possible" while adding a significant caveat. *Flint Ridge* concerned the question of whether the United States Department of Housing and Urban Development (HUD) was required to prepare an EIS whenever it receives a "statement of record" from a potential land developer pursuant to the Interstate Land Sales Full Disclosures Act. Such a statement—which must contain various information needed by potential purchasers to prevent false and deceptive practices in the interstate sale of undeveloped tracts of land—will become automatically effective under that Act on the thirtieth day after filing, unless HUD determines that it is incomplete or materially inaccurate.

The Court held that under these circumstances HUD was not required to prepare an EIS. Citing NEPA's legislative history, the Court implicitly accepted *Calvert Cliffs's* notion that the "to the fullest extent possible" language of section 102 reflected a congressional mandate that had to be implemented in a serious and resolute manner:

> NEPA's instruction that all federal agencies comply with the impact statement requirement—and with all the other requirements of § 102—"to the fullest extent possible" . . . is neither accidental nor hyperbolic. Rather, the phrase is a deliberate command that the duty NEPA imposes upon the agencies to consider environmental factors not be shunted aside in the bureaucratic shuffle.

At the same time, however, the Court concluded that NEPA must give way where there is a "clear and unavoidable statutory conflict." The Court reasoned that such a conflict existed in *Flint Ridge* since (as a practical matter) HUD could not actually comply with its statutory duty to allow statements of record to go into effect within thirty days of filing, absent inaccurate or incomplete disclosure, and simultaneously prepare EISs on proposed developments.

. . . .

Certainly *Calvert Cliffs* and the NEPA EIS cases that followed, along with the Supreme Court's opinion in *Flint Ridge*, make clear that the words "to the fullest extent possible" are far from empty rhetoric. They are, as the *Flint Ridge* Court opined, a "deliberate command" that is "neither accidental nor hyperbolic." At the same time, however, "to the fullest extent possible" appears to mean something less than "under all circumstances and notwithstanding all other considerations." Where another statute imposes a conflicting duty that makes it simply impossible to implement NEPA's policies without effectively voiding that other statute's mandate, the other statute must take precedence. Presumably, such situations will arise infrequently. Nonetheless, in circumstances where a statutory conflict is "clear and unavoidable," NEPA must give way.

. . . .

Subsection 102(1) of NEPA is indeed the "forgotten man" of that important environmental statute. Despite the emphatic clarity of its language, this brief subsection has been ignored by lawyers and federal judges in countless disputes in which it could have been — and arguably should have been — invoked, interpreted, and applied.

Nonetheless, the NEPA interpretation mandate may not be overlooked forever. . . . In a time when the United States is faced with serious and pressing environmental challenges — some of them entirely domestic and others shared with the world at large — the forgotten directive of NEPA's interpretation mandate may yet take its rightful place among the most influential precepts of U.S. environmental law.

Notes and Questions

1. Does the excerpt persuade you that subsection 102(1) of NEPA was intended to guide judicial interpretation of "policies, regulations, and public laws" other than NEPA? Does the excerpted article's argument raise separation-of-powers issues?

2. What would be the effect of applying subsection 102(1) as suggested by the excerpt?

III. Triggering the Requirement to Prepare an Environmental Impact Statement

NEPA's one universally acknowledged command to federal agencies — the only one courts have been willing to enforce as a binding obligation — is the requirement that every federal agency "include in every recommendation or report on proposals for legislation and other major Federal actions significantly affecting the quality of the human environment, a detailed statement" of, among other things, the environmental impact of the proposed action. NEPA § 102(2)(C), 42 U.S.C. § 4332(2)(C). Plaintiffs challenging agency decisions or actions frequently allege that an agency violated NEPA by failing to prepare a required "Environmental Impact Statement" or "EIS." Not every idea conceived by a federal agency, however, requires the agency to prepare an EIS. The NEPA "trigger" that requires preparation of an EIS has several components. Can you see that each component is potentially ambiguous and subject to interpretation?

The onus of interpreting NEPA's trigger fell initially on the agencies that had to decide in each circumstance whether to prepare an EIS, and then on the federal courts that were called upon to decide whether the agencies had decided correctly. To to provide some uniformity in NEPA's application across the federal government, President Nixon, by executive order, directed the CEQ (newly created by NEPA) to produce "guidelines" for federal agencies. *See* Exec. Order 11,514, 35 Fed. Reg. 4,247 (Mar. 7, 1970). These guidelines partly reflected and partly shaped the emerging NEPA case law; you will see them referred to in many early judicial decisions interpreting NEPA. In 1977, President Carter ordered the CEQ to promulgate regulations setting forth NEPA procedures that would be binding on all federal agencies. *See* Exec. Order 11,991, 42 Fed. Reg. 26,967 (May 25, 1977). These regulations are codified at 40 C.F.R. Parts 1500 through 1508. They provide a starting point for most judicial interpretation of NEPA today.

The most basic element of NEPA's trigger is that EISs are required only for "proposals" — either proposed legislation or proposed "other major federal actions significantly affecting the quality of the human environment." Proposals for legislation ordinarily originate in the legislative branch, but Congress has not prepared EISs, presumably because Congress does not consider itself an "agenc[y] of the Federal Government" to which the EIS requirement applies. *Cf.* 5 U.S.C. §551(1)(A) (excluding Congress from the Administrative Procedure Act's definition of "agency"). Executive branch agencies themselves rarely make proposals for legislation that require EISs. But federal agencies take "other major federal actions" all the time. When, in the course of agency deliberations, does an idea ripen into a proposal that could trigger the EIS requirement? The CEQ regulations provide that a

> *Proposal* exists at that stage in the development of an action when an agency subject to the Act has a goal and is actively preparing to make a decision on one or more alternative means of accomplishing that goal and the effects can be meaningfully evaluated. Preparation of an environmental impact statement on a proposal should be timed . . . so that the final statement may be completed in time for the statement to be included in any recommendation or report on the proposal . . . .

40 C.F.R. §1508.23.

Courts have occasionally held that an agency's thinking about a challenged project or policy is too preliminary or too inchoate to constitute a "proposal" that might require an EIS. In *Kleppe v. Sierra Club*, 427 U.S. 390 (1976), the Supreme Court rejected a claim that the Department of the Interior was required to prepare an EIS that considered the effects of leasing federal lands for coal mining in the "Northern Great Plains region." The Department had studied the coal resources of the region but denied that any decision-making would occur at the regional level; instead, the Interior Department prepared an EIS for its nationwide coal leasing program and also prepared an EIS for each individual lease. The Court stated that even if the Department "contemplated" a regional-scale coal leasing program, "the contemplation of a project and the accompanying study thereof do not necessarily result in a proposal for major federal action." *Id.* at 406. The only "proposals" were for the national policy and the individual, local-scale leases, the Court held, and therefore NEPA did not require a regional-scale EIS.

On the other hand, once a proposal exists, an agency must fulfill its NEPA obligations while there is still a pending proposal, and not after a final decision has been made. If an EIS is required,

> An agency shall commence preparation [of the EIS] as close as possible to the time the agency is developing or is presented with a proposal . . . so that preparation can be completed in time for the final statement to be included in any recommendation or report on the proposal. The statement shall be prepared early enough so that it can serve practically as an important contribution to the decisionmaking process and will not be used to rationalize or justify decisions already made . . . .

40 C.F.R. § 1502.5. Thus, the Ninth Circuit held that the National Marine Fisheries Service and other federal agencies violated NEPA when the agencies promised the Makah Indian Tribe that they would support the Tribe's request to the International Whaling Commission for permission to take up to five gray whales per year — and only afterward considered whether that decision triggered NEPA's EIS requirement. *See Metcalf v. Daley*, 214 F.3d 1135 (9th Cir. 2000).

Assuming that a federal agency has a proposal to consider, the next threshold questions are: whether the proposal is for a "major federal action" and whether that major federal action is one "significantly affecting the quality of the human environment." If the answer to both questions is yes, NEPA requires that an EIS be completed by the time a report or recommendation on the proposal is finished. *See Aberdeen & Rockfish R.R. Co. v. Students Challenging Regulatory Agency Procedures*, 422 U.S. 289 (1975). We consider these threshold questions one at a time.

A. Major Federal Action

Some actions are obviously federal: when the Bureau of Reclamation built the Glen Canyon Dam on the Colorado River upstream of the Grand Canyon, when the Army Corps of Engineers built the Mississippi River Gulf Outlet downstream from New Orleans, and when the Federal Aviation Administration redesigned the routes commercial airliners fly in the airspace above the New York and Philadelphia metropolitan areas, these were projects undertaken by federal agencies using appropriated federal funds. The EIS requirement may apply also to a project that would be undertaken by private entities or by agencies of state or local government, if a federal agency's approval is essential to the project. We have already seen, for example, that an action is "federal," thus potentially triggering the EIS requirement, when the NRC licenses a nuclear power plant, when HUD approves an urban renewal project, or when the Forest Service permits a ski resort. But what if federal approval is needed only for a small portion of a much larger nonfederal project? Or if the federal government's only role in a project is to provide grant funding, perhaps for only a portion of the project's total cost? Or if a federal agency merely acquiesces in a nonfederal action that the federal agency need not approve, but could in its discretion prevent? In such circumstances, determining the scope of "federal" action for NEPA purposes can be tricky.

Southwest Williamson County Community Ass'n, Inc. v. Slater

243 F.3d 270 (6th Cir. 2001)

Judge MOORE:

Plaintiff-Appellant Southwest Williamson County Community Association ("Association") appeals the district court's denial of its application for a preliminary injunction to halt construction on Route 840 South, a 77-mile length of highway . . . .

I. FACTS

. . . . The Association, a non-profit corporation comprised of members who live and work in Williamson County, first brought suit in federal district court against federal and state defendants seeking declaratory and injunctive relief to halt construction of Route 840 South. The highway, designed to provide an alternative route around Nashville, begins at I-40 West, runs south of the city through several counties including Williamson County, and crosses two federal interstates, I-65 South and I-24, before terminating at I-40 East. The Association's suit alleged that defendants were violating the National Environmental Policy Act . . . .

    . . . .

. . . . [T]he district court denied the Association's motion for a preliminary injunction. The district court first assessed the Association's likelihood of success on the merits of its claims, the first prong of the relevant analysis for a preliminary injunction. Analyzing the relevant statutory language and associated regulations, the district court noted that "most circuit courts look to whether a federal agency has the ability to influence or control the non-federal activity" when assessing whether such activity constitutes a "major Federal action[ ]" under NEPA. After evaluating the numerous federal actions which the Association alleges constitute proof of the federalization of the highway, the district court determined that the actions in aggregate did not "give FHWA authority to control the 840 South Highway Project and thereby turn it into a 'major federal action.'" . . .[6]

    . . . .

---

6. The district court considered the following federal actions as alleged by the Association:
    (1) Federal approval of the design, construction, location and alignment of 840 South with existing interstate highways . . . [The interchange approvals];
    (2) FHWA consultation with TDOT [Tennessee Department of Transportation] and the National Park Service to determine where 840 South will cross the federally-protected Natchez Trace Parkway;
    (3) The Secretary of the Interior's permission, control and approval of a right-of-way across the federally-protected Natchez Trace Parkway . . . pursuant to Section 106 of the National Historic Preservation Act and mitigation and consultation to protect the Eggert sunflower pursuant to the Endangered Species Act . . .
    (4) Secretary of the Army's review, approval and permitting three separate crossings of waters of the United States including filling wetlands . . . ;
    (5) FHWA approval of the Nashville Long Range Transportation Plan Conformity Redetermination required by the Clean Air Act . . . ;
    (6) The FHWA funding of a study resulting in the Air Quality Conformity Redetermination mentioned above [and of planning studies] which included three traffic capacity analysis [sic] for [840 South] interchanges . . . ; and

V. ANALYSIS

.... Although it does not dispute the fact that Route 840 South has been exclusively funded by the state, the Association argues that the federal government has failed to fulfill its obligation under NEPA to assess comprehensively the environmental consequences of constructing a four-lane highway through a largely rural area of middle Tennessee. Pointing to thirty-one separate instances of alleged federal control and decision-making which serve to "federalize" the entire highway project, including the four federal interchange approvals by the FHWA, the Association strongly argues that there is "massive and pervasive federal control and influence over nearly every aspect of the planning and construction of the Route 840 South corridor including the FHWA's continuing responsibility to ensure the interstate interchanges comply with federal regulation." Federal defendants argue, in response, that Route 840 South was designed, constructed, and funded by the state [and] that they lack jurisdiction under the relevant statute over the state's construction of the highway corridor ....

Plaintiff argument

Defendants argument in response

A. Application of NEPA

....

Typically, a project is considered a major federal action when it is funded with federal money. This case, however, requires us to determine at what point a state-funded project is transformed into a major federal action by virtue of multiple federal agencies' involvement in the project ....

Issue

B. Major Federal Actions May Arise From A Non-Federal Project

Federal defendants may be bound by NEPA to perform additional environmental review of Route 840 South, notwithstanding the fact that the project is not federally funded. According to the regulations promulgated by the CEQ, major federal actions "include[ ] actions with effects that may be major and which are potentially subject to Federal control and responsibility." 40 C.F.R. § 1508.18. These actions may be "assisted, conducted, regulated, or approved by federal agencies." Id. § 1508.18(a). The regulation goes on to provide:

> Federal actions tend to fall within one of the following categories:
>
> Approval of specific projects, such as construction or management activities located in a defined geographic area. Projects include actions approved by permit or other regulatory decision as well as federal and federally assisted activities.

---

(7) The formal application by the State Defendant to the Federal Defendant in November, 1991, for federal interstate status, subsequently withdrawn for two principal reasons: 1) The State did not want to comply with NEPA; and 2) The State can build 840 South, then apply for interstate status at a later time, which would be granted after only a simple inspection to determine whether or not the road was built according to geometric designs.

Id. § 1508.18(b)(4). These regulations are due substantial deference from reviewing courts. The regulations clearly indicate that major federal actions need not be federally funded to invoke NEPA requirements. . . .

In addition, it is apparent that a non-federally funded project may become a major federal action by virtue of the aggregate of federal involvement from numerous federal agencies, even if one agency's role in the project may not be sufficient to create major federal action in and of itself. See 40 C.F.R. §§ 1508.25; 1508.27(b) (noting that "more than one agency may make decisions about partial aspects of a major [Federal] action"). Thus, the federal defendants' argument that they were only involved in one aspect of the highway's design and approval process, namely the four interchanges, does not necessarily serve to defeat the Association's claim that the pervasiveness of federal activity required to complete the highway converts the project into a major federal action.

C. Standard for Evaluating When a Non-Federal Project Becomes a Major Federal Action

Although this circuit has never enunciated a standard for evaluating whether non-federal projects rise to the level of "major Federal action," our sister circuits have undertaken such an examination. In [*Maryland Conservation Council, Inc. v.*] *Gilchrist*, [808 F.2d 1039 (4th Cir. 1986)], the Fourth Circuit decision on which the Association urges us to rely, the court determined that a county-funded highway was a major federal action because construction of the highway would likely require multiple federal agencies' approval before completion. [Federal agency approvals were required because the proposed road would cross a park and wetlands protected by federal law.] Determining that "[a] non-federal project is considered a 'federal action' if it cannot begin or continue without prior approval of a federal agency," the court held that "[b]ecause of the inevitability of the need for at least one federal approval, we think that the construction of the highway will constitute a major federal action." . . .

Clearly animating the court's analysis was the fact that the state had already begun to build the portions of the highway that entered and exited the park without having obtained the requisite federal approvals to build the middle section. According to the court, the applicable agencies "would inevitably be influenced if the County were allowed to construct major segments of the highway before issuance of a final EIS." . . .

. . . . [A]s the court noted, the CEQ regulations [40 C.F.R. § 1506.1] sought to avoid a situation where the non-federal actor presents the federal agency with a fait accompli which significantly limits the federal agency's ability to reject the proposal . . . .

. . . . In *North Carolina v. City of Virginia Beach*, 951 F.2d 596 (4th Cir.1991), ... plaintiffs sought an injunction against the construction of a city pipeline connecting Lake Gaston, which sits in North Carolina and Virginia, with the City of Virginia Beach . . . .

The Fourth Circuit reversed the district court's grant of an injunction forbidding any construction on the pipeline because it found that FERC [the Federal Energy

Regulatory Commission] would not be unduly pressured by the city's desire to work on a small part of the pipeline falling outside of the FERC's jurisdiction . . . . Ultimately concluding that "construction which lies beyond the boundaries of FERC's jurisdiction can be enjoined only when it has a direct and substantial probability of influencing FERC's decision," the court determined that Virginia Beach [which sought to proceed "on only two small areas of the pipeline"] had failed to meet that standard.

In *Macht v. Skinner*, 916 F.2d 13, 19 (D.C.Cir.1990), the . . . issue . . . was whether a state-funded light-rail project was sufficiently federalized by federal agency involvement such that the state was required to follow NEPA procedures. Plaintiffs in this case sought an injunction on construction, alleging that state and federal officials failed to comply with NEPA. First, the D.C. Circuit aptly noted that NEPA applies only to federal agencies, not to the state or private parties. Therefore, the court declined to find the state in violation of NEPA and to issue an injunction against it . . . . Instead, the court characterized the question before it as "whether state or private action on an entire project should be enjoined until the federal agencies that must approve particular portions of the project have complied with NEPA." Noting that "there is no allegation that the Army Corps has failed to comply with NEPA" and that "the Army Corps has discretion over only a negligible portion of the entire project," the court found that the federal involvement in the state project was insufficient to "federalize" it.

[handwritten: Example]

With the CEQ regulations and case law in mind, we conclude that there are two alternative bases for finding that a non-federal project constitutes a "major Federal action" such that NEPA requirements apply: (1) when the non-federal project restricts or limits the statutorily prescribed federal decision-makers' choice of reasonable alternatives; or (2) when the federal decision-makers have authority to exercise sufficient control or responsibility over the non-federal project so as to influence the outcome of the project.[7]

[handwritten: "Major Federal Action" requirements under NEPA]

If either test is satisfied, the non-federal project must be considered a major federal action. Both tests require a situation-specific and fact-intensive analysis . . . .

[handwritten: TEST #1] 1. Restricting Choice of Reasonable Alternatives

Employing our first test, we evaluate whether the state's actions restricted or limited the federal decision-makers' choice of reasonable alternatives when granting federal approvals for the highway construction . . . . The first segment of the highway is not at issue in this case. Construction on the second segment of the highway, from I-24 to I-65 South, did not begin until 1995. Work on the third section, from I-65 South to I-40 W, began in late 1997 and is still substantially incomplete. Actual construction and paving of the third section has not, according to the record before us, even begun . . . . [W]e conclude that the FHWA was afforded ample time and opportunity to respond to the state's proposal before action by the state which would harm

7. We distinguish our alternative tests from the single ["authority-to-control"] test employed by the district court . . . . We believe that the "authority-to-control" standard will not always adequately encompass the concerns of the CEQ regulations, to which we defer.

the environment or limit the agency's choice of reasonable alternatives, the concerns enunciated by the CEQ regulations.

The other federal agency approvals required for construction of the highway involve the second and third sections of Route 840 South. In response to the state's requests, the Army Corps of Engineers issued several . . . permits allowing the state to cross several streams and fill almost four acres of wetlands. . . . The Association does not allege that the Secretary of the Army was pressured to render its decision or that its choice of action was limited by the state's construction.

[The state also asked the Secretary of the Interior to approve] a right-of-way to cross the federally-protected Natchez Trace Parkway . . . . While we are concerned that the state began building Route 840 South prior to receiving final approval from the Secretary of the Interior, we note that the Association concedes that there has been extensive contact, beginning as early as 1990, between the state and the [National Park Service] . . . regarding where the highway should cross the Parkway. We also observe that the Association does not seek to enjoin construction of the highway in order to allow the Secretary of the Interior time to respond . . . . [U]nder our first test, we conclude that the state's work on Route 840 South did not restrict the federal decision-makers' choice of reasonable alternatives.

TEST #2   2. Agency Control or Responsibility for Outcome

Pursuant to our second test, which we use as an alternative basis of analysis, we evaluate whether the FHWA and other federal agencies have sufficient control or responsibility over the construction of Route 840 South to influence the outcome of the project . . . . FHWA clearly has jurisdiction over the four interchanges where Route 840 South intersects with federal highways[, and a federal statute provides that FHWA approval is required before a state may construct interchanges with a federal highway] . . . .

Moreover, it is clear that agency approval of the interchanges must conform with NEPA procedures . . . . On a plain reading of the [FHWA's NEPA] regulations, agency review of . . . interchanges . . . invokes NEPA procedures; interchange construction must therefore be a major federal action . . . .

No part of the [Federal-Aid Highway Act] confers jurisdiction on the FHWA, however, to oversee the construction of the highway corridor that runs between the interchanges unless the state attempts to comply with federal regulations in order to seek federal reimbursement for construction costs. Importantly, the Association no longer claims that the state is seeking federal funding for Route 840 South. Indeed, should the state seek federal funding in the future, absent a change in the federal [FHWA] regulations, its failure to comply with NEPA would make it ineligible to receive such funding. Thus, there is no statutory basis to establish FHWA authority over the highway corridor.

. . . .

Because no federal agency has jurisdiction over the non-federal project, we must conclude that . . . the federal defendants lack sufficient control or responsibility over the state highway to influence the project's outcome . . . .

. . . . This case would be different if the Association sought an injunction because FHWA . . . or the Army Corps of Engineers had not yet [satisfied their NEPA obligations with respect to the interchange approvals and the wetland filling permits, respectively]. As the district court found, however, all applicable federal agencies fulfilled or were fulfilling their duty, pursuant to their respective statutory jurisdictions, to issue the appropriate environmental documentation. Instead, the Association seeks to enjoin the state and halt construction of the entire non-federal project so that the FHWA can review the environmental impact of the project, despite the fact that the federal agency lacks jurisdiction over the highway corridor . . . . No court has ever approved the kind of injunction the Association requests.[17] Because we conclude, pursuant to our second test, that the relevant federal decision-makers do not have authority to exercise sufficient control or responsibility over Route 840 South so as to influence the outcome of the project, we agree no preliminary injunction should issue.

Analysis

. . . .

Notes and Questions

Not a federal action subject to NEPA

1. What, exactly, did the plaintiff allege was a "major federal action" that triggered the EIS requirement in *Southwest Williamson County Community Association*? In the *Gilchrist*, *Virginia Beach*, and *Macht* cases the opinion discusses?

2. The D.C. Circuit backed away from the idea that federal agencies' involvement could "federalize" for NEPA purposes a project undertaken by a state or local government. *See Karst Envtl. Educ. & Protection, Inc. v. EPA*, 475 F.3d 1291, 1297 (D.C. Cir. 2007) ("the federalization theory . . . lacks vitality today given our decisions . . . reiterating the requirement that NEPA claims be brought under the APA and allege final agency action").

→ we don't want this to happen

3. When NEPA was enacted, the federal government was in the midst of the largest highway-building endeavor in the nation's history. President Eisenhower, famously motivated by a slow and arduous cross-country trip during his army service shortly after World War I, signed the Federal-Aid Highway Act of 1956, authorizing long-term funding for construction of the Interstate Highway System. *See* David A. Pfeiffer, *Ike's Interstates at 50: Anniversary of the Highway System Recalls Eisenhower's Role as Catalyst*, Prologue Mag. (vol. 38, No. 2, Summer, 2006). http://www.archives.gov/publications/prologue/2006/summer/interstates.html. By 1970, more than 30,000 miles of interstate highways were open to traffic, but more than another 10,000 miles were still planned or under construction. Engineering, rather than environmental, considerations had dominated decision-making about highway planning and

---

17. Under the authority-to-control test, courts have found "major Federal actions" despite a federal agency's lack of jurisdiction over the non-federal project when the court determines either (1) that the state was improperly attempting to "segment" its project into discrete sections in order to circumvent NEPA requirements or (2) that the state was improperly attempting to "de-segment" a major federal action to permit construction of one segment without complying with NEPA. However, as the district court noted, the Association dropped its segmentation claim in its amended complaint, and the Association never pursued a "de-segmentation" theory.

routing. Opponents became increasingly concerned about the destruction of parks, rural landscapes, and urban communities for the construction of highways and about the sprawling, auto-dependent land-use patterns that interstates and other roads encouraged. The 1973 OPEC oil embargo (and later, the increasingly obvious effects of greenhouse gas emissions on global climate) focused concern on the energy requirements of an automobile-centered transportation network. NEPA, which required federal agencies to consider such issues, understandably became a focal point for many organizations opposed to specific highway projects. Transportation projects are heavily represented in NEPA judicial decisions.

4. As the Sixth Circuit implied, the factual scenario of *Southwest Williamson County Community Association* is a recurring one. If no state or local statute requires environmental impact assessment, states and other project proponents sometimes work hard to avoid subjecting a project to NEPA requirements. Severing those parts of a larger project that do not require federal agency involvement is a frequently used technique. Whether the technique succeeds has varied with the law of the relevant circuit and the facts of the particular case. For some examples in addition to those discussed above, see *Rattlesnake Coalition v. U.S. Environmental Protection Agency*, 509 F.3d 1095 (9th Cir. 2007) (holding that the state-funded portion of a multi-year sewer and wastewater treatment project was not federal action); *Coalition for Underground Expansion v. Mineta*, 333 F.3d 193 (D.C. Cir. 2003) (holding that the locally funded segments of a rail transportation system were not federal actions despite federal funding for connecting parts of the system); *Ross v. Federal Highway Admin.*, 162 F.3d 1046 (10th Cir. 1998) (holding that a road segment to be built with non-federal funds was a federal project where the segment had been separated from a larger project partly built with federal funds); *Save Barton Creek Ass'n v. Federal Highway Admin.*, 950 F.2d 1129 (5th Cir. 1992) (holding that highway segments to be built without federal funding were not federal actions even though segmentation of the highway was designed to preserve federal funding availability for other segments); *Scottsdale Mall v. Indiana*, 549 F.2d 484 (7th Cir. 1977) (holding that the last segment of a highway project, withdrawn from the federal aid program after federal funds were used to build the other segments, was a federal action).

5. Aside from segmentation issues, disputes also arise over whether specific types and amounts of federal involvement suffice to make a project a federal action. Again, the resolutions of such disputes reflect applications of somewhat varying legal standards to highly disparate facts. For some examples, see *New Jersey Dept. of Environmental Protection and Energy v. Long Island Power Auth.*, 30 F.3d 403 (3d Cir. 1994) (holding that shipment of radioactive material by a private shipper was not major federal action, despite Coast Guard approval of the shipper's voluntarily submitted operations plan, where Coast Guard approval of the plan was not legally required); *Sierra Club v. Hodel*, 848 F.2d 1068 (10th Cir. 1988) (holding that a proposed county road construction project passing through environmentally sensitive lands was a federal action where the United States Department of the Interior was legally obligated to prevent unnecessary destruction of wilderness areas in changes to rights-of-way); *Atlanta Coalition on the Transportation Crisis, Inc. v. Atlanta Regional Comm'n*, 559 F.2d 1333 (5th

Cir. 1979) (holding that federal funding assistance for the local planning process was not major federal action where state and local agencies were responsible for all planning decisions).

6. Our discussion of NEPA's EIS trigger has focused on whether an action is "federal," but disputes also sometimes arise over the "action" part of "major federal action," particularly when an agency decides *not* to do something that it has the authority to do. Must an agency analyze the environmental impacts of its failure to take affirmative action to protect the environment? We describe two cases that reached opposite results.

The first case involved commercial salmon fishing. Under the Fishery Conservation and Management Act, a non-federal entity called a Fishery Management Council is responsible for preparing and submitting to the U.S. Department of Commerce a management plan to govern fishing for a particular species in a given geographic area. The plan does not require government approval to go into effect, but the Secretary of Commerce may disapprove the plan and thereby prevent it from becoming effective. In *Ramsey v. Kantor*, 96 F.3d 434 (9th Cir. 1996), the court held that the Commerce Department's failure to disapprove a fishery management plan for North Pacific salmon was a major federal action under NEPA.

The second case involved a shipment of vitrified high-level nuclear waste from France to Japan. The vessel carrying the waste notified the U.S. Coast Guard that it would travel past the coast of Puerto Rico, outside U.S. territorial waters but within the United States' Exclusive Economic Zone (EEZ) — international waters where customary international law nevertheless allows coastal states limited authority. The ship did not need the United States' permission to traverse the EEZ. The Coast Guard did nothing to stop or to assure the safety of the vessel's travel through the EEZ. In *Mayaguezanos por la Salud y el Ambiente v. United States*, 198 F.3d 297 (1st Cir. 1999), the court held that the government's failure to do anything about the shipment was not a major federal action under NEPA.

[handwritten margin note: economic zone is 200mi offshore]

Can you see the distinction between the two cases? Assess whether the agency's failure to act in each case fits within the regulatory definition of "major federal action" quoted immediately below.

[handwritten margin mark: ✗]

7. In its NEPA regulations, 40 C.F.R. § 1508.18, the Council on Environmental Quality defined "major federal action" as follows:

> "Major Federal action" includes actions with effects that may be major and which are potentially subject to federal control and responsibility. Major reinforces but does not have a meaning independent of significantly (§ 1508.27). Actions include the circumstance where the responsible officials fail to act and that failure to act is reviewable by courts or administrative tribunals under the Administrative Procedure Act or other applicable law as agency action.
>
> (a) Actions include new and continuing activities, including projects and programs entirely or partly financed, assisted, conducted, regulated, or approved by federal agencies; new or revised agency rules, regulations, plans, policies, or procedures; and legislative proposals. Actions do not include funding

assistance solely in the form of general revenue sharing funds . . . with no federal agency control over the subsequent use of such funds. Actions do not include bringing judicial or administrative civil or criminal enforcement actions.

(b) Federal actions tend to fall within one of the following categories:

(1) Adoption of official policy, such as rules, regulations, and interpretations adopted pursuant to the Administrative Procedure Act; treaties and international conventions or agreements; formal documents establishing an agency's policies which will result in or substantially alter agency programs.

(2) Adoption of formal plans, such as official documents prepared or approved by federal agencies which guide or prescribe alternative uses of federal resources, upon which future agency actions will be based.

(3) Adoption of programs, such as a group of concerted actions to implement a specific policy or plan; systematic and connected agency decisions allocating agency resources to implement a specific statutory program or executive directive.

(4) Approval of specific projects, such as construction or management activities located in a defined geographic area. Projects include actions approved by permit or other regulatory decision as well as federal and federally assisted activities.

8. Whether a federal action is "major" rarely becomes an issue in NEPA litigation because, as you just read, the CEQ equates a "major" action with one that "significantly" affects the quality of the human environment—which brings us to the second part of the EIS trigger.

B. Significantly Affecting the Quality of the Human Environment

The purpose of an Environmental Impact Statement is to provide information about a proposed major federal action's anticipated effects on the quality of the human environment. Yet NEPA requires an EIS only for proposals for major federal actions "significantly affecting the quality of the human environment." Presumably some major federal actions do not have significant environmental effects—and therefore do not require preparation of an EIS. But how can an agency know that without preparing an Environmental Impact Statement to find out what the environmental impacts are?

Hanly v. Kleindienst ("Hanly II")
471 F.2d 823 (2d Cir. 1972)

[The United States Department of Justice wanted to build a jail for pre-trial detainees as an annex to the federal court building in lower Manhattan. Nearby residents, organized as the Chatham Square Civic Committee for a Planned Community, opposed the plan. After NEPA was enacted, the General Services Administration

(GSA)—the federal agency that builds and manages most United States government buildings—concluded that the project would have no adverse environmental impact. Hanly and other members of the Civic Committee sued. The district judge denied the plaintiffs' motion for a preliminary injunction. The plaintiffs appealed. In *Hanly v. Mitchell*, 460 F.2d 640 (2d Cir. 1972) ("*Hanly I*"), the Court of Appeals described the GSA's first attempt at NEPA compliance as follows:

> GSA's entire determination regarding the Courthouse Annex—including both office building and jail—is found principally in a memorandum dated February 23, 1971, of George M. Paduano, who was then Regional Director of the Public Buildings Service of GSA, and, according to defendants, the proper official to make such a decision under GSA's regulations. Since the memorandum is short and crucial to the decision on this appeal, we quote it in full:

> Application of the National Environmental Policy Act of 1969 Relative to Foley Square Courthouse Annex-Project No. 31-0323

> *Environmental Statement:*

> In accordance with GSA Order PBS 1095.1 dated December 11, 1970 and in response to telephone request from your office on February 16, 1971 the following information is furnished in connection with the subject project:

> The impact of the proposed action will have no adverse effects on the environment, including ecological systems, population distribution, transportation, water or air pollution, nor will it be any threat to health or life systems or urban congestion. These points are further amplified as follows:

> 1. It is our intention to connect with the existing New York utility services, including water supply, sewage disposal, solid waste disposal, storm water drainage, etc.

> 2. It is planned that the heating will be by purchase steam from Con Edison Company of New York (same as 26 Federal Plaza).

> 3. Trash removal will be by commercial contract.

> 4. There will be no relocation of people involved as the proposed project is adjacent to the Foley Square Courthouse and only a short additional traveling distance by public transportation from the present Bureau of Prisons location at 427 West Street.

> 5. There will be no material impact at all on public transportation.

> 6. Number of people to be housed in the Bureau of Prisons operation is given as 405.

> 7. Zoning—C6-1.

> 8. We intend to follow the existing zoning regulations.

> (Signed) G. M. PADUANO

[handwritten margin note: EIS was new, so this was how short first ones were]

The Court of Appeals concluded that this memo, which failed to consider the effects that a jail and an associated drug treatment program would have on the neighborhood—particularly with respect to noise, crime, and possible prison disturbances and riots—did not satisfy NEPA's requirements. The Court of Appeals held that the plaintiffs were entitled to a preliminary injunction unless and until GSA considered these effects and either concluded that they were not significant (and therefore no EIS was required) or concluded that they were significant and prepared an EIS. After remand and further environmental impact assessment as described below, the district court again denied plaintiffs' motion for preliminary injunction. The plaintiffs appealed again.]

Court of Appeals decision

↓

→ remand back to District Court which denied preliminary injunction, 2nd time

Judge MANSFIELD:

. . . . Following the district court's denial for the second time of a preliminary injunction against construction of a jail and other facilities known as the Metropolitan Correction Center ("MCC") we are called upon to decide whether a redetermination by the General Services Administration ("GSA") that the MCC is not a facility "significantly affecting the quality of the human environment," made pursuant to this Court's decision remanding the case after the earlier appeal (herein "*Hanly I*"), satisfies the requirements of NEPA and thus renders it unnecessary for GSA to [prepare an] environmental impact statement. In view of the failure of the GSA, upon redetermination, to make findings with respect to certain relevant factors and to furnish an opportunity to appellants to submit relevant evidence, the case is again remanded.

Issue

Supreme Court decision

. . . .

The MCC will serve as the detention center for approximately 449 persons awaiting trial or convicted of short term federal offenses and will be large enough to provide space not only for incarceration but for diagnostic services, and medical, recreational and administrative facilities. A new program will provide service for out-patient non-residents. The MCC will be serviced by approximately 130 employees, only 90 of whom will be present on the premises at any one time.

. . . .

Following the remand [*in Hanly I*], a new threshold determination in the form of a 25-page "Assessment of the Environmental Impact" ("Assessment" herein) was made by the GSA and submitted to the district court on June 15, 1972. This document reflects a detailed consideration of numerous relevant factors. Among other things, it analyzes the size, exact location, and proposed use of the MCC; its design features, construction, and aesthetic relationship to its surroundings; the extent to which its occupants and activities conducted in it will be visible by the community; the estimated effects of its operation upon traffic, public transit and parking facilities; its approximate population, including detainees and employees; its effect on the level of noise, smoke, dirt, obnoxious odors, sewage and solid waste removal; and its energy demands. It also sets forth possible alternatives, concluding that there is none that is satisfactory. Upon the basis of this Assessment the Acting Commissioner of the

Public Building Service Division of the GSA, who is the responsible official in charge, concluded on June 7, 1972, that the MCC was not an action significantly affecting the quality of the human environment.

On August 2, 1972, appellants renewed their application to Judge Tenney for a preliminary injunction, arguing that the Assessment failed to comply with this Court's direction in *Hanly I*, that it amounted to nothing more than a rewrite of the earlier statement that had been found inadequate, and that some of its findings were incorrect or insufficient. On August 8, 1972, Judge Tenney, in a careful opinion, denied appellants' motions.

Discussion

At the outset we accept . . . that the agency in charge of a proposed federal action (in this case the GSA) is the party authorized to make the threshold determination whether an action is one "significantly affecting the quality of the human environment" as that phrase is used in § 102(2)(C) . . . .

We are next confronted with a question that was deferred in *Hanly I*—the standard of review that must be applied by us in reviewing GSA's action. The action involves both a question of law—the meaning of the word "significantly" in the statutory phrase "significantly affecting the quality of the human environment"—and a question of fact—whether the MCC will have a "significantly" adverse environmental impact. Strictly speaking, our function as a reviewing court is to determine *de novo* "all relevant questions of law," and, with respect to GSA's factual determinations, to abide by the Administrative Procedure Act, which limits us in matters not involving an agency's rule-making or adjudicatory function to determining whether its findings are "arbitrary, capricious, an abuse of discretion, or otherwise not in accordance with law" or "without observance of procedure required by law," APA § 10(e), 5 U.S.C. § 706(2)(A) and (D).

Where the court's interpretation of statutory language requires some appraisal of facts, a neat delineation of the legal issues for the purpose of substituted judicial analysis has sometimes proven to be impossible or, at least, inadvisable . . . .

. . . . [W]e believe that the appropriate criterion in the present case is the "arbitrary, capricious" standard established by the Administrative Procedure Act, . . . since the APA standard permits effective judicial scrutiny of agency action and concommitantly permits the agencies to have some leeway in applying the law to factual contexts in which they possess expertise . . . .

Upon attempting, according to the foregoing standard, to interpret the amorphous term "significantly," as it is used in § 102(2)(C), we are faced with the fact that almost every major federal action, no matter how limited in scope, has *some* adverse effect on the human environment. Congress could have decided that every major federal action must therefore be the subject of a detailed impact statement prepared according to the procedure prescribed by § 102(2)(C). By adding the word "significantly," however, it demonstrated that before the agency in charge triggered that procedure, it should conclude that a greater environmental impact would result than from "any major federal action." Yet the limits of the key term have not been adequately defined by Congress or by guidelines issued by the CEQ and other responsible federal agencies vested with broad discretionary powers under NEPA . . . .

[This case was decided before CEQ promulgated the now-codified definition of "significantly," 40 C.F.R. § 1508.27. The court discussed how to define "significantly," with the majority adopting an approach that, the majority claimed, would encourage agencies to prepare EIS's in cases in the "'grey areas.'" This issue is further addressed in the dissenting opinion.]

[Regarding the proposed jail, n]ow that the GSA has made and submitted its redetermination in the form of a 25-page "Assessment," our task is to determine (1) whether it satisfies the foregoing tests as to environmental significance, and (2) whether GSA, in making its assessment and determination, has observed "procedure required by law" as that term is used in § 10 of the APA, 5 U.S.C. § 706(2)(D).   *Issue*

The Assessment closely parallels in form a detailed impact statement. The GSA's finding that the MCC would harmonize architecturally with existing buildings in the area, and even enhance the appearance of the neighborhood, is supported by details of the proposed building, architectural renditions, and photographs of the area. The windows, which will be glazed with unbreakable polycarbonate plastic shatter-proof sheets will be recessed and will be of a dark gray color designed to insulate the community from visual contact with the detainees. Moreover, there will be no fortress walls or unsightly steel-barred windows . . . .

The Assessment further describes efforts that will be made to minimize any contact between detainees and members of the community . . . . [A]ll prisoners will enter the building through an entrance . . . located on the side opposite from and out of view of neighborhood residential apartments. Although there will be a roof-top recreational area for detainees, a 20-foot wall will minimize their visibility from the apartments.

The Assessment further notes that any increase in traffic from MCC will be extremely slight . . . .

. . . . The GSA Assessment projected on the basis of past experience that approximately 130 visitors will arrive per day with no more than 20 on the premises at any one time. This would not impose any excessive burden on mass transportation [or parking] facilities . . . . There will be only four truck deliveries of supplies per day to the premises.

The windows of the MCC are designed to minimize any noise from within the premises, in addition to which detainees will be under constant supervision when outside on the roof-top for recreational purposes. During the past five years there have been only two small inside disturbances at the present detention facility at West Street, Manhattan, and three outside disturbances, the latter confined to non-violent picketing, marching and the like, incidents which have been common occurrence in the Foley Square area during the same period.

The Assessment makes clear that the MCC will not produce any unusual or excessive amounts of smoke, dirt, obnoxious odors, solid waste, or other forms of pollution. The utilities required to heat and air-condition the building are readily available and the MCC is designed to incorporate energy-saving features, so that no excessive power demands are posed. The GSA further represents that the building will conform to all local codes, use and zoning . . . .

. . . . A comparison of the 25-page detailed Assessment with the earlier statement [that the Second Circuit rejected in *Hanly I*] reveals that the former is far more than a "rewrite" and that it furnishes detailed findings with respect to most of the relevant factors unmentioned in the earlier statement. . . . Judged by the comparative uses in the area and according to its quantitative environmental effects, the MCC should not have a significant effect upon the human environment.

Appellants offer little or no evidence to contradict the detailed facts found by the GSA. For the most part their opposition is based upon a psychological distaste for having a jail located so close to residential apartments, which is understandable enough. It is doubtful whether psychological and sociological effects upon neighbors constitute the type of factors that may be considered in making such a determination since they do not lend themselves to measurement. However we need not decide that issue because these apartments were constructed within two or three blocks of another existing jail, The Manhattan House of Detention for Men, which is much larger than the proposed MCC . . . .

Despite the GSA's scrupulous efforts the appellants do present one or two factual issues that merit further consideration and findings by the GSA. One bears on the possibility that the MCC will substantially increase the risk of crime in the immediate area, a relevant factor as to which the Assessment fails to make an outright finding despite the direction to do so in *Hanly I*. Appellants urge that the Community Treatment Program and the program for observation and study of non-resident out-patients will endanger the health and safety of the immediate area by exposing neighbors and passersby to drug addicts visiting the MCC for drug maintenance and to drug pushers and hangers-on who would inevitably frequent the vicinity of a drug maintenance center. If the MCC were to be used as a drug treatment center, the potential increase in crime might tip the scales in favor of a mandatory detailed impact statement. The Government has assured us by post-argument letter addressed to the Court that:

> "Neither the anticipated nonresident pre-sentence study program nor any program to be conducted within the Metropolitan Correction Center will include drug maintenance."

While we do not question the Government's good faith, a finding in the matter by GSA is essential, since the Assessment is ambiguous as to the scope of the non-resident out-patient observation program and makes no finding on the subject of whether the MCC will increase the risk of crime in the community.[15] . . .

_____

15. If the Government should later change the use of the premises to include a drug treatment center, or any other change that might significantly affect the quality of the human environment, then a detailed § 102(C) impact statement would be required at that time.

. . . .

Decision

. . . . [W]e remand the case for the purpose of requiring the GSA to make a further investigation of these issues, with directions to accept from appellants and other concerned citizens such further evidence as they may proffer within a reasonable period, to make supplemental findings with respect to these issues, and to redetermine whether the MCC "significantly affects the quality of the human environment". If, as a result of such further investigation, the GSA concludes that a detailed environmental impact statement is required, a preliminary injunction will be granted restraining further construction of the MCC until the agency has complied with the procedures required by § 102(2)(C) of NEPA. In the event that the GSA reaffirms its initial determination, the district court will determine, should a further request be made, whether preliminary injunctive relief is warranted.

With the aid of hindsight we recognize, as does the dissent, that a further Assessment, when added to the time and expense already incurred, will prolong the final determination far beyond the time that would have been required if the energies of the GSA had been directed initially toward the preparation of an impact statement. However, important issues have been presented and there is no suggestion of bad faith or deliberate delay on the part of anyone . . . .

The case is remanded for further proceedings not inconsistent with this opinion . . . .

Judge FRIENDLY, dissenting:

The learned opinion of my brother MANSFIELD gives these plaintiffs, and environmental advocates in future cases, both too little and too much. It gives too little because it raises the floor of what constitutes "major Federal actions significantly affecting the quality of the human environment," higher than I believe Congress intended. It gives too much because it requires that before making a threshold determination that no impact statement is demanded, the agency must go through procedures which I think are needed only when an impact statement must be made. The upshot is that a threshold determination that a proposal does not constitute major Federal action significantly affecting the quality of the human environment becomes a kind of mini-impact statement. The preparation of such a statement under the conditions laid down by the majority is unduly burdensome when the action is truly minor or insignificant. On the other hand, there is a danger that if the threshold determination is this elaborate, it may come to replace the impact statement in the grey area between actions which, though "major" in a monetary sense, are obviously insignificant (such as the construction of the proposed office building) and actions that are obviously significant (such as the construction of an atomic power plant). We would better serve the purposes of Congress by keeping the threshold low enough to insure that impact statements are prepared for actions in this grey area and thus to permit the determination that no statement is required to be made quite informally in cases of true insignificance . . . .

. . . .

The energies my brothers would require GSA to devote to still a third assessment designed to show that an impact statement is not needed would better be devoted to making one.

I would reverse and direct the issuance of an injunction until a reasonable period after the making of an impact statement.

Notes and Questions

1. In response to *Hanly II*, the plaintiffs unsuccessfully petitioned the Supreme Court for *certiorari*, after which the case returned to the district court on remand. The district court again denied plaintiffs' request for an injunction. The Second Circuit affirmed, 484 F.2d 448 (2d Cir. 1973), and the Supreme Court again denied *certiorari*, finally ending the lawsuit. The government built the jail, which is still in use today.

2. At the time of the *Hanly* litigation, federal agencies had little experience with NEPA. One almost senses, from GSA's first attempt at NEPA compliance with respect to the proposed jail, that Mr. Paduano was surprised to be asked to prepare an "Environmental Statement" about a project that undoubtedly already had been in the planning stages for some time. Similarly, federal courts at the time had little experience reviewing agencies' compliance with NEPA. Among the novel issues the Second Circuit confronted was the appropriate standard of review to apply to the agency's action. The court's choice — the "arbitrary and capricious" standard of the Administrative Procedure Act — was later adopted by the Supreme Court in *Marsh v. Oregon Natural Resources Council*, 490 U.S. 360, 377 (1989).

3. Footnote 15 of the *Hanly II* opinion foreshadows an issue to which we will return: what if something about a proposed major federal action changes after an agency has concluded the action will not have a significant environmental impact and therefore does not require an EIS? Or, for that matter, what if something changes after an agency has completed an EIS? *Hanly II* confidently predicted that an EIS would be required if a drug treatment center were later added to the planned jail, based in part on an early CEQ guideline encouraging agencies to evaluate the environmental impact of "further" major federal actions even if those further actions arose from a project or program initiated before NEPA's enactment. Since *Hanly II*, CEQ regulations, as well as the Supreme Court in *Marsh v. Oregon Natural Resources Council*, p. 190 below, have addressed more fully how changing circumstances affect an agency's NEPA obligations.

[handwritten marginalia: If there's a change after F-EIS, they can require supplemental EIS]

4. Judge Friendly agreed with the majority that GSA's determination that the jail would have no significant environmental impact was legally deficient. He also agreed that the proposal to build the jail was in a "grey area" between major federal actions that obviously would significantly affect the environment and those that obviously would not do so. Why, then, did he dissent? For actions in the "grey area," Judge Friendly would have directed preparation of an EIS, rather than provide repeat opportunities for an agency to assess whether the "significantly affecting" threshold was crossed. The CEQ's regulations later incorporated the tripartite classification of major federal actions and prescribed an approach to the "grey area."

Regulations of the Council on Environmental Quality

Code of Federal Regulations, Title 40 (2015)

§ 1501.4 Whether to prepare an environmental impact statement.

In determining whether to prepare an environmental impact statement the Federal agency shall:

(a) Determine under its procedures supplementing these regulations (described in § 1507.3) whether the proposal is one which:

(1) Normally requires an environmental impact statement, or

(2) Normally does not require either an environmental impact statement or an environmental assessment (categorical exclusion).

(b) If the proposed action is not covered by paragraph (a) of this section, prepare an environmental assessment (§ 1508.9). The agency shall involve environmental agencies, applicants, and the public, to the extent practicable, in preparing assessments required by § 1508.9(a)(1).

(c) Based on the environmental assessment make its determination whether to prepare an environmental impact statement.

(d) Commence the scoping process (§ 1507.7), if the agency will prepare an environmental impact statement.

(e) Prepare a finding of no significant impact (§ 1508.13), if the agency determines on the basis of the environmental assessment not to prepare a statement.

(1) The agency shall make the finding of no significant impact available to the affected public as specified in § 1506.6.

(2) In certain limited circumstances, which the agency may cover in its procedures under § 1507.3, the agency shall make the finding of no significant impact available for public review (including State and area-wide clearinghouses) for 30 days before the agency makes its final determination whether to prepare an environmental impact statement and before the action may begin. The circumstances are:

(i) The proposed action is, or is closely similar to, one which normally requires the preparation of an environmental impact statement under the procedures adopted by the agency pursuant to § 1507.3, or

(ii) The nature of the proposed action is one without precedent.

§ 1508.4 Categorical exclusion.

Categorical exclusion means a category of actions which do not individually or cumulatively have a significant effect on the human environment and which have been found to have no such effect in procedures adopted by a Federal agency in implementation of these regulations (§ 1507.3) and for which, therefore, neither an environmental assessment nor an environmental impact statement is required. An agency may decide in its procedures or otherwise, to prepare environmental assessments for the reasons stated in § 1508.9 even though it is not required to do so. Any procedures under this section shall provide for extraordinary circumstances in which a normally excluded action may have a significant environmental effect.

§ 1508.9 Environmental assessment.

Environmental assessment:

(a) Means a concise public document for which a Federal agency is responsible that serves to:

(1) Briefly provide sufficient evidence and analysis for determining whether to prepare an environmental impact statement or a finding of no significant impact.

(2) Aid an agency's compliance with the Act when no environmental impact statement is necessary.

(3) Facilitate preparation of a statement when one is necessary.

(b) Shall include brief discussions of the need for the proposal, of alternatives as required by section 102(2)(E), of the environmental impacts of the proposed action and alternatives, and a listing of agencies and persons consulted.

§ 1508.13 Finding of no significant impact.

Finding of no significant impact means a document by a Federal agency briefly presenting the reasons why an action, not otherwise excluded (§ 1508.4), will not have a significant effect on the human environment and for which an environmental impact statement therefore will not be prepared. It shall include the environmental assessment or a summary of it and shall note any other environmental documents related to it (§ 1501.7(a)(5)). If the assessment is included, the finding need not repeat any of the discussion in the assessment but may incorporate it by reference.

§ 1508.27 Significantly. "major federal action"

Significantly as used in NEPA requires considerations of both context and intensity:

(a) *Context*. This means that the significance of an action must be analyzed in several contexts such as society as a whole (human, national), the affected region, the affected interests, and the locality. Significance varies with the setting of the proposed action. For instance, in the case of a site-specific action, significance would usually depend upon the effects in the locale rather than in the world as a whole. Both short- and long-term effects are relevant.

(b) *Intensity*. This refers to the severity of impact. Responsible officials must bear in mind that more than one agency may make decisions about partial aspects of a major action. The following should be considered in evaluating intensity:

(1) Impacts that may be both beneficial and adverse. A significant effect may exist even if the Federal agency believes that on balance the effect will be beneficial.

(2) The degree to which the proposed action affects public health or safety.

(3) Unique characteristics of the geographic area such as proximity to historic or cultural resources, park lands, prime farmlands, wetlands, wild and scenic rivers, or ecologically critical areas.

(4) The degree to which the effects on the quality of the human environment are likely to be highly controversial.

(5) The degree to which the possible effects on the human environment are highly uncertain or involve unique or unknown risks.

(6) The degree to which the action may establish a precedent for future actions with significant effects or represents a decision in principle about a future consideration.

(7) Whether the action is related to other actions with individually insignificant but cumulatively significant impact. Significance exists if it is reasonable to anticipate a cumulatively significant impact on the environment. Significance cannot be avoided by terming an action temporary or by breaking it down into small component parts.

(8) The degree to which the action may adversely affect districts, sites, highways, structures, or objects listed in or eligible for listing in the National Register of Historic Places or may cause loss or destruction of significant scientific, cultural, or historical resources.

(9) The degree to which the action may adversely affect an endangered or threatened species or its habitat that has been determined to be critical under the Endangered Species Act of 1973.

(10) Whether the action threatens a violation of Federal, State, or local law or requirements imposed for the protection of the environment.

§ 1508.3 Affecting.

Affecting means will or may have an effect on.

§ 1508.8 Effects.

Effects include:

(a) Direct effects, which are caused by the action and occur at the same time and place.

(b) Indirect effects, which are caused by the action and are later in time or farther removed in distance, but are still reasonably foreseeable . . . .

Effects includes ecological . . . , aesthetic, historic, cultural, economic, social, or health, whether direct, indirect, or cumulative . . . .

§ 1508.14 Human environment.

Human environment shall be interpreted comprehensively to include the natural and physical environment and the relationship of people with that environment . . . . This means that economic or social effects are not intended by themselves to require preparation of an environmental impact statement. When an environmental impact statement is prepared and economic or social and natural or physical environmental effects are interrelated, then the environmental impact statement will discuss all of these effects on the human environment.

Notes and Questions

1. How do the CEQ regulations quoted above help a federal agency decide whether the agency must complete an EIS before deciding to undertake a particular proposed federal action? The regulations divide major federal actions into three categories. What are they? How must an agency proceed with respect to actions in the "grey area" described in *Hanly II*? In effect, the NEPA regulations prescribe a decision tree for agencies, which can be diagrammed as follows:

Figure 3-1. NEPA Decision Tree, from Proposal to Action

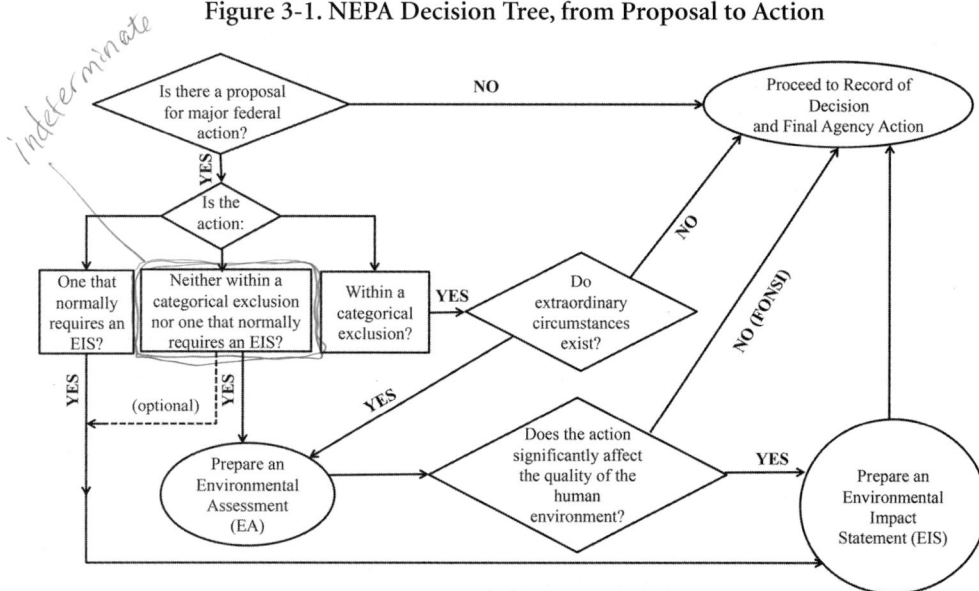

As Figure 3-1 shows, the CEQ rules divide proposals for major federal actions into three basic categories: those that normally require an EIS, those that normally don't require an EIS, and those that normally may or may not require an EIS. The solution to the indeterminate category is the production of an Environmental Assessment (EA), which leads either to preparation of an EIS or to a Finding of No Significant Impact (FONSI). Agencies are always free to produce more environmental impact analysis than is required by a proposed action's category—but that does not happen much.

2. To whom do the CEQ regulations assign the responsibility for placing an agency's proposed actions into the appropriate NEPA category? Does this allocation of responsibility make sense?

3. Consider the regulatory definitions of the key words in the statutory phrase "significantly affecting the quality of the human environment." How helpful would these regulations be to an agency trying to decide whether a particular proposed action required an EIS?

4. Recall that in *Hanly II* the plaintiffs argued that an EIS was required to evaluate the proposed jail's "psychological and sociological effects upon neighbors" and the possibility that the jail would "increase the risk of crime in the immediate area." When you contemplate whether a proposed major federal action will significantly affect the quality of the human environment, are these the types of effects that come to mind? The aftermath of a serious nuclear accident afforded the Supreme Court an opportunity to consider the types of effects that could trigger an EIS.

Metropolitan Edison Co. v. People Against Nuclear Energy
460 U.S. 766 (1983)

Justice REHNQUIST:

The issue in these cases is whether petitioner Nuclear Regulatory Commission (NRC) complied with the National Environmental Policy Act of 1969 when it considered whether to permit petitioner Metropolitan Edison Co. to resume operation of the Three Mile Island Unit 1 nuclear power plant (TMI-1). . . .

Metropolitan owns two nuclear power plants at Three Mile Island near Harrisburg, Pa. Both of these plants were licensed by the NRC after extensive proceedings, which included preparation of Environmental Impact Statements (EIS's). On March 28, 1979, TMI-1 was not operating; it had been shut down for refueling. TMI-2 was operating, and it suffered a serious accident that damaged the reactor. Although, as it turned out, no dangerous radiation was released, the accident caused widespread concern. The Governor of Pennsylvania recommended an evacuation of all pregnant women and small children, and many area residents did leave their homes for several days.

After the accident, the NRC ordered Metropolitan to keep TMI-1 shut down until it had an opportunity to determine whether the plant could be operated safely. The NRC then published a notice of hearing specifying several safety-related issues for consideration. The notice stated that the Commission had not determined whether to consider psychological harm or other indirect effects of the accident or of renewed operation of TMI-1. It invited interested parties to submit briefs on this issue.

Respondent People Against Nuclear Energy (PANE) intervened and responded to this invitation. PANE is an association of residents of the Harrisburg area who are opposed to further operation of either TMI reactor. PANE contended that restarting TMI-1 would cause both severe psychological health damage to persons living in the vicinity, and serious damage to the stability, cohesiveness, and well-being of the neighboring communities.

The NRC decided not to take evidence concerning PANE's contentions. PANE filed a petition for review in the Court of Appeals. . . . Metropolitan intervened on the side of the NRC. [While the petition was pending, the NRC finalized an Environmental Assessment and concluded that no EIS was required before permitting TMI-1 to resume operating.]

The Court of Appeals concluded that . . . NEPA requires the NRC to evaluate "the potential psychological health effects of operating" TMI-1 which have arisen since the original EIS was prepared. It also held that, if the NRC finds that significant new circumstances or information exist on this subject, it shall prepare a "supplemental [EIS] which considers not only the effects on psychological health but also effects on the well-being of the communities surrounding Three Mile Island." We granted certiorari.

← Supreme Court decision

All the parties agree that effects on human health can be cognizable under NEPA, and that human health may include psychological health. The Court of Appeals thought these propositions were enough to complete a syllogism that disposes of the case: NEPA requires agencies to consider effects on health. An effect on psychological health is an effect on health. Therefore, NEPA requires agencies to consider the effects on psychological health asserted by PANE. PANE, using similar reasoning, contends that because the psychological health damage to its members would be caused by a change in the environment (renewed operation of TMI-1), NEPA requires the NRC to consider that damage. Although these arguments are appealing at first glance, we believe they skip over an essential step in the analysis. They do not consider the closeness of the relationship between the change in the environment and the "effect" at issue.

Rationale

. . . .

To paraphrase the statutory language in light of the facts of this case, where an agency action significantly affects the quality of the human environment, the agency must evaluate the "environmental impact" and any unavoidable adverse environmental effects of its proposal. The theme of § 102 is sounded by the adjective "environmental": NEPA does not require the agency to assess *every* impact or effect of its proposed action, but only the impact or effect on the environment. If we were to seize the word "environmental" out of its context and give it the broadest possible definition, the words "adverse environmental effects" might embrace virtually any consequence of a governmental action that someone thought "adverse." But we think the context of the statute shows that Congress was talking about the physical environment — the world around us, so to speak. NEPA was designed to promote human welfare by alerting governmental actors to the effect of their proposed actions on the physical environment.

. . . .

Thus, although NEPA states its goals in sweeping terms of human health and welfare, these goals are *ends* that Congress has chosen to pursue by *means* of protecting the physical environment.

To determine whether § 102 requires consideration of a particular effect, we must look at the relationship between that effect and the change in the physical environment caused by the major federal action at issue . . . .

Some effects that are "caused by" a change in the physical environment in the sense of "but for" causation, will nonetheless not fall within § 102 because the causal chain is too attenuated. For example, residents of the Harrisburg area have relatives in other parts of the country. Renewed operation of TMI-1 may well cause psychological health problems for these people. They may suffer "anxiety, tension and fear, a sense of helplessness," and accompanying physical disorders, because of the risk that their relatives may be harmed in a nuclear accident. However, this harm is simply too remote from the physical environment to justify requiring the NRC to evaluate the psychological health damage to these people that may be caused by renewed operation of TMI-1.

Our understanding of the congressional concerns that led to the enactment of NEPA suggests that the terms "environmental effect" and "environmental impact" in § 102 be read to include a requirement of a reasonably close causal relationship between a change in the physical environment and the effect at issue. This requirement is like the familiar doctrine of proximate cause from tort law.[7] The issue before us, then, is how to give content to this requirement. . . .

The federal action that affects the environment in this case is permitting renewed operation of TMI-1. The direct effects on the environment of this action include release of low-level radiation, increased fog in the Harrisburg area (caused by operation of the plant's cooling towers), and the release of warm water into the Susquehanna River. The NRC has considered each of these effects in its EIS, and again in the EIA. Another effect of renewed operation is a risk of a nuclear accident. The NRC has also considered this effect.[9]

PANE argues that the psychological health damage it alleges "will flow directly from the risk of [a nuclear] accident." But a *risk* of an accident is not an effect on the physical environment. A risk is, by definition, unrealized in the physical world. In a causal chain from renewed operation of TMI-1 to psychological health damage, the element of risk and its perception by PANE's members are necessary middle links. We believe that the element of risk lengthens the causal chain beyond the reach of NEPA.

Risk is a pervasive element of modern life; to say more would belabor the obvious. Many of the risks we face are generated by modern technology, which brings both the possibility of major accidents and opportunities for tremendous achievements. Medical experts apparently agree that risk can generate stress in human beings, which in turn may rise to the level of serious health damage. For this reason, among many others, the question whether the gains from any technological advance are worth its attendant risks may be an important public policy issue. Nonetheless, it is quite

---

7. In drawing this analogy, we do not mean to suggest that any cause-effect relation too attenuated to merit damages in a tort suit would also be too attenuated to merit notice in an EIS; nor do we mean to suggest the converse. In the context of both tort law and NEPA, courts must look to the underlying policies or legislative intent in order to draw a manageable line between those causal changes that may make an actor responsible for an effect and those that do not.

9. The NRC concluded that the risk of an accident had not changed significantly since the EIS for TMI-1 was prepared in 1972.

We emphasize that in this case we are considering effects caused by the risk of an accident. The situation where an agency is asked to consider effects that will occur if a risk is realized, for example, if an accident occurs at TMI-1, is an entirely different case. The NRC considered, in the original EIS and in the most recent EIA for TMI-1, the possible effects of a number of accidents that might occur at TMI-1.

different from the question whether the same gains are worth a given level of alteration of our physical environment or depletion of our natural resources. The latter question rather than the former is the central concern of NEPA.

Time and resources are simply too limited for us to believe that Congress intended to extend NEPA as far as the Court of Appeals has taken it. The scope of the agency's inquiries must remain manageable if NEPA's goal of "[insuring] a fully informed and well-considered decision," is to be accomplished.

. . . .

The Court of Appeals thought that . . . PANE raised an issue of health damage . . . [rather than] of fear or policy disagreement. We do not believe this line is so easily drawn. Anyone who fears or dislikes a project may find himself suffering from "anxiety, tension[,] fear, [and] a sense of helplessness." Neither the language nor the history of NEPA suggests that it was intended to give citizens a general opportunity to air their policy objections to proposed federal actions. The political process, and not NEPA, provides the appropriate forum in which to air policy disagreements.

We do not mean to denigrate the fears of PANE's members, or to suggest that the psychological health damage they fear could not, in fact, occur. Nonetheless, it is difficult for us to see the differences between someone who dislikes a government decision so much that he suffers anxiety and stress, someone who fears the effects of that decision so much that he suffers similar anxiety and stress, and someone who suffers anxiety and stress that "flow directly" from the risks associated with the same decision. It would be extraordinarily difficult for agencies to differentiate between "genuine" claims of psychological health damage and claims that are grounded solely in disagreement with a democratically adopted policy. Until Congress provides a more explicit statutory instruction than NEPA now contains, we do not think agencies are obliged to undertake the inquiry.

. . . .

For these reasons, we hold that the NRC need not consider PANE's contentions. NEPA does not require agencies to evaluate the effects of risk *qua* risk. The judgment of the Court of Appeals is reversed, and the case is remanded with instructions to dismiss the petition for review.

Supreme Court decision

Notes and Questions

1. What was the consequence, with respect to NEPA's procedural requirements and the NRC's decision-making process, of the NRC's refusal to take evidence about PANE's allegations of psychological health damage?

2. Why, exactly, did the Supreme Court uphold the NRC's refusal to receive PANE's proffered evidence? Did the court hold that harm to mental health is not an effect on the human environment? That restarting TMI-1 would not affect the psychological well-being of PANE's members? That restarting TMI-1 might affect the psychological well-being of PANE's members, but would not be the proximate cause of that harm? That any mental health harms would not result from a change in the physical

environment? That the claim of psychological injury was only a pretext for a policy disagreement?

3. Do you agree that some boundary must be drawn to limit the scope of effects an agency must think about when deciding whether a proposed action will significantly affect the quality of the human environment? If so, who should decide where that boundary lies? Who drew the boundary in *Metropolitan Edison v. PANE*? Who must draw the boundary *after* the *Metropolitan Edison* decision?

4. The Supreme Court concluded that to merit consideration under NEPA, an effect of a major federal action must have a "reasonably close causal relationship . . . like . . . proximate cause" to a change in the physical environment. According to the Court, what is the source of that requirement? What interpretive tools did the Court use to reach its conclusion?

5. The Court distinguished between the effects of a "risk *qua* risk" and the effects of a risk that came to pass, holding that only the latter must be considered under NEPA. How persuasive is this distinction? The NRC acknowledged that re-starting TMI-1 posed a risk (however small) of a nuclear accident. If creating that risk required NRC to consider the effects that *might* occur as a result, why did it not require NRC to consider the psychological effects that (according to PANE's proffered evidence) *would* occur as a result?

6. In *Metropolitan Edison*, the Supreme Court stated that "NEPA does not require the agency to assess *every* impact . . . of its proposed action, but only the impact . . . on the environment." Did the Court thereby imply that a major federal action's effects on society are outside NEPA's scope? In a passage not excerpted above, the Court cited three cases in which a court of appeals rejected a plaintiff's argument that an EIS was required to analyze the risk of crime resulting from proposed construction of a public facility, even though the plaintiffs could have alleged (though they did not actually allege) that the fear of crime would harm their psychological health. The Court did not cite *Hanly II*.

Did *Metropolitan Edison* undermine the reasoning of *Hanly II*? The Eighth Circuit seemed to think so. In *Olmsted Citizens for a Better Community v. United States*, 793 F.2d 201, 205 (8th Cir. 1986), the court affirmed a summary judgment against plaintiffs who alleged that an EIS was required before the Bureau of Prisons approved a proposal to convert a former state psychiatric hospital into a federal prison hospital, holding that the alleged significant environmental impacts "follow not from any physical changes connected with the conversion but from the social changes reflected in the nature of the use of the facility and in the types of people that will be present." By contrast, the Seventh Circuit—in one of the opinions the Supreme Court cited in *Metropolitan Edison*—stated that "NEPA must be construed to include protection of the quality of life for city residents," including socioeconomic issues that interact with environmental issues, even though the court of appeals upheld the agency's finding of no significant impact. *First Natl. Bank of Chicago v. Richardson*, 484 F.2d 1369, 1377 (7th Cir. 1973) (affirming district court judgment that no EIS was required before building a jail near the federal courthouse in Chicago).

The CEQ's regulations state that social or economic effects alone are insufficient to trigger the EIS requirement, but if an EIS is required because a major federal action will or may have significant environmental impacts, the EIS must examine social and economic effects related to the environmental effects. 40 C.F.R. § 1508.14. For an analysis of the issues involved in applying NEPA to the interwoven environmental and socioeconomic impacts of land use decisions in urban areas, see Hope Babcock, *The National Environmental Policy Act in the Urban Environment: Oxymoron or a Useful Tool to Combat the Destruction of Neighborhoods and Urban Sprawl*, 23 J. Envtl. L. & Litig. 1 (2008).

7. The plaintiffs in *Metropolitan Edison* argued that the NRC's decision not to prepare a supplemental EIS was unlawful because, in concluding that restarting TMI-1 would not significantly affect the quality of the human environment, the NRC failed to consider a particular type of impact. Much more commonly, an agency's Environmental Assessment (EA) does consider the environmental impact(s) of concern to a plaintiff, but the plaintiff disagrees with the agency's conclusion that the impact(s) will not be "significant." The case that follows presents one variation of such a dispute.

Thomas v. Peterson
753 F.2d 754 (9th Cir. 1985)

Judge SNEED:

Plaintiffs sought to enjoin construction of a timber road in a former National Forest roadless area. The District Court granted summary judgment in favor of defendant R. Max Peterson, Chief of the Forest Service, and plaintiffs appealed. We affirm in part, reverse in part, and remand for further proceedings consistent with this opinion.

[handwritten: Supreme Court Decision]

We conclude that . . . The National Environmental Policy Act (NEPA) requires the Forest Service to prepare an Environmental Impact Statement (EIS) that analyzes the combined environmental impacts of the road and the timber sales that the road is designed to facilitate.

I.

. . . .

[handwritten: FACTS]

Plaintiffs—landowners, ranchers, outfitters, miners, hunters, fishermen, recreational users, and conservation and recreation organizations—challenge actions of the United States Forest Service in planning and approving a timber road in the Jersey Jack area of the Nezperce National Forest in Idaho. The area is adjacent to the Salmon River, a congressionally-designated Wild and Scenic River, and is bounded on the west by the designated Gospel Hump Wilderness and on the east by the River of No Return Wilderness. The area lies in a "recovery corridor" identified by the U.S. Fish & Wildlife Service for the Rocky Mountain Gray Wolf, an endangered species.

The Jersey Jack area was originally part of the larger Gospel Hump roadless area, but when Congress created the Gospel Hump Wilderness in 1978, it did not include the Jersey Jack area . . . . In 1980, Congress passed the Central Idaho Wilderness Act, which created the River of No Return Wilderness to the east of the Jersey Jack area, but left the Jersey Jack area as non-wilderness. The Act stated as one of its purposes to assure that "adjacent lands better suited for multiple uses other than wilderness will be managed by the Forest Service under existing laws and applicable land management plans."

. . .

 . . . . In November, 1980, the Forest Service solicited public comments and held a public hearing on a proposed gravel road [in Jersey Jack] that would provide access to timber to be sold. The Forest Service prepared an environmental assessment (EA) to determine whether an EIS would be required for the road. Based on the EA, the Forest Service concluded that no EIS was required, and issued a Finding of No Significant Impact (FONSI). The FONSI and the notice of the Forest Supervisor's decision to go ahead with the road were issued in a single document on February 9, 1981 . . . .

The EA for the road discussed only the environmental impacts of the road itself; it did not consider the impacts of the timber sales that the road was designed to facilitate. Subsequently, on November 23, 1981, and on June 30, 1982, the Forest Service issued EA's for, and approved, two of the timber sales. An EA for a third timber sale was also issued prior to the commencement of this action in district court. Each EA covered only the effects of a single timber sale; none discussed cumulative impacts of the sales or of the sales and the road. Each EA resulted in a FONSI, and therefore no environmental impact statements were prepared.

The plaintiffs appealed the Forest Supervisor's decision on the road to the Regional Forester, who affirmed the decision on May 26, 1981. The Regional Forester's decision was then appealed to the Chief of the Forest Service, who affirmed the decision on November 24, 1981.

The plaintiffs filed this action, challenging the Chief's decision, on June 30, 1982. [They allege that] . . . NEPA, and regulations issued by the Council on Environmental Quality (CEQ), require the Forest Service to prepare an EIS that analyzes the combined effects of the proposed road and the timber sales that the road is designed to facilitate. . . .

 . . . [T]he district court granted summary judgment for the Forest Service [and held] . . . . that the court was "unable to find that the decision to build the road in question is anything more than a decision to build a forest road" and that an EIS covering both the road and the timber sales "would require needless speculation."

II.

The NEPA Claim

The central question that plaintiffs' NEPA claim presents is whether the road and the timber sales are sufficiently related so as to require combined treatment in a single EIS that covers the cumulative effects of the road and the sales. If so, the Forest Service has proceeded improperly. An EIS must be prepared and considered by the

Forest Service before the road can be approved. If not, the Forest Service may go ahead with the road, and later consider the environmental impacts of the timber sales.

Section 102(2)(C) of NEPA requires an EIS for "major Federal actions significantly affecting the quality of the human environment." While it is true that administrative agencies must be given considerable discretion in defining the scope of environmental impact statements, there are situations in which an agency is required to consider several related actions in a single EIS. Not to require this would permit dividing a project into multiple "actions," each of which individually has an insignificant environmental impact, but which collectively have a substantial impact. . . . [T]he Council on Environmental Quality (CEQ) has issued regulations that define the circumstances under which multiple related actions must be covered by a single EIS. The CEQ regulations and this court's precedents both require the Forest Service to prepare an EIS analyzing the combined environmental impacts of the road and the timber sales.

A. *CEQ Regulations*

1. *Connected actions*

The CEQ regulations require "connected actions" to be considered together in a single EIS. *See* 40 C.F.R. § 1508.25(a)(1) (1984). "Connected actions" are defined, in a somewhat redundant fashion, as actions that

"(i) Automatically trigger other actions which may require environmental impact statements.

(ii) Cannot or will not proceed unless other actions are taken previously or simultaneously.

(iii) Are interdependent parts of a larger action and depend on the larger action for their justification." *Id.*

The construction of the road and the sale of the timber in the Jersey Jack area meet the second and third, as well as perhaps the first,[2] of these criteria. It is clear that the timber sales cannot proceed without the road, and the road would not be built but for the contemplated timber sales. This much is revealed by the Forest Service's characterization of the road as a "logging road," and by the first page of the environmental assessment for the road, which states that "[t]he need for a transportation route in the assessment area is to access the timber lands to be developed over the next twenty years." Moreover, the environmental assessment for the road rejected a "no action" alternative because that alternative would not provide the needed timber access. The Forest Service's cost-benefit analysis of the road considered the timber to be the benefit of the road, and while the Service has stated that

---

2. Because, by the time this action was filed in district court, . . . at least two of the sales had been approved, at that time the Jersey Jack road arguably had come to meet the first of the three criteria, that is, that construction of the road would "automatically trigger" the timber sales. Forest Service documents in the record indicate that the two approved sales were awaiting only the approval and construction of the road before going forward.

the road will yield other benefits, it does not claim that such other benefits would justify the road in the absence of the timber sales. Finally, . . . an August 1981 letter in the record from the Regional Forester to the Forest Supervisor . . . . states, "We understand that sales in the immediate future will be dependent on the early completion of portions of the Jersey Jack Road. It would be advisable to divide the road into segments and establish separate completion dates for those portions to be used for those sales."

We conclude, therefore, that the road construction and the contemplated timber sales are inextricably intertwined, and that they are "connected actions" within the meaning of the CEQ regulations.

2. *Cumulative Actions*

The CEQ regulations also require that "cumulative actions" be considered together in a single EIS. 40 C.F.R. § 1508.25(a)(2). "Cumulative actions" are defined as actions "which when viewed with other proposed actions have cumulatively significant impacts." The record in this case contains considerable evidence to suggest that the road and the timber sales will have cumulatively significant impacts. The U.S. Fish & Wildlife Service, the Environmental Protection Agency, and the Idaho Department of Fish & Game have asserted that the road and the timber sales will have significant cumulative effects that should be considered in an EIS. The primary cumulative effects, according to these agencies, are the deposit of sediments in the Salmon River to the detriment of that river's population of salmon and steelhead trout, and the destruction of critical habitat for the endangered Rocky Mountain Gray Wolf. These agencies have criticized the Forest Service for not producing an EIS that considers the cumulative impacts of the Jersey Jack road and the timber sales. For example, the Fish & Wildlife Service has written, "Separate documentation of related and cumulative potential impacts may be leading to aquatic habitat degradation unaccounted for in individual EA's (i.e., undocumented cumulative effects). . . . Lack of an overall effort to document cumulative impacts could be having present and future detrimental effects on wolf recovery potential." These comments are sufficient to raise "substantial questions" as to whether the road and the timber sales will have significant cumulative environmental effects. Therefore, on this basis also, the Forest Service is required to prepare an EIS analyzing such effects.

B. *Ninth Circuit Precedents*

. . . . In *Trout Unlimited v. Morton*, we addressed the issue of when subsequent phases of development must be covered in an environmental impact statement on the first phase. We stated that an EIS must cover subsequent stages when "[t]he dependency is such that it would be irrational, or at least unwise, to undertake the first phase if subsequent phases were not also undertaken." The dependency of the road on the timber sales meets this standard; it would be irrational to build the road and then not sell the timber to which the road was built to provide access. . . . The Forest Service has not alleged that the Jersey Jack road has sufficient utility independent from the timber sales to justify its construction. Severance of the road from the timber sales for purposes of NEPA, therefore, is not permissible.

C. *Timing of the EIS*

The Forest Service argues that the cumulative environmental effects of the road and the timber sales will be adequately analyzed and considered in the EA's and/or EIS's that it will prepare on the individual timber sales. The EA or EIS on each action, it contends, will document the cumulative impacts of that action and all previous actions.

We believe that consideration of cumulative impacts after the road has already been approved is insufficient to fulfill the mandate of NEPA. A central purpose of an EIS is to force the consideration of environmental impacts in the decisionmaking process. That purpose requires that the NEPA process be integrated with agency planning "at the earliest possible time," 40 C.F.R. § 1501.2, and the purpose cannot be fully served if consideration of the cumulative effects of successive, interdependent steps is delayed until the first step has already been taken.

The location, the timing, or other aspects of the timber sales, or even the decision whether to sell any timber at all affects the location, routing, construction techniques, and other aspects of the road, or even the need for its construction. But the consideration of cumulative impacts will serve little purpose if the road has already been built. Building the road swings the balance decidedly in favor of timber sales even if such sales would have been disfavored had road and sales been considered together before the road was built. Only by selling timber can the bulk of the expense of building the road be recovered. Not to sell timber after building the road constitutes the "irrational" result that *Trout Unlimited's* standard is intended to avoid. Therefore, the cumulative environmental impacts of the road and the timber sales must be assessed before the road is approved.

The Forest Service argues that the sales are too uncertain and too far in the future for their impacts to be analyzed along with that of the road. This comes close to saying that building the road now is itself irrational. We decline to accept that conclusion. Rather, we believe that if the sales are sufficiently certain to justify construction of the road, then they are sufficiently certain for their environmental impacts to be analyzed along with those of the road . . . .

Moreover, the record contains substantial evidence that the timber sales were in fact at an advanced stage of planning by the time that the decision to build the road was made. The Forest Service issued EA's for, and approved, two of the timber sales nine and sixteen months after it issued the road EA, and it had issued an EA for a third sale by the time that this action was filed. In fact, one of the Forest Service's own affidavits shows that the Service was preparing the EA on at least one of the sales at the same time that it was preparing the EA on the road. The record plainly establishes that the Forest Service, in accordance with good administrative practices, was planning contemporaneously the timber sales and the building of the road. Either without the other was impractical. The Forest Service knew this and cannot insist otherwise to avoid compliance with NEPA.

We therefore reverse the district court on the NEPA issue and hold that, before deciding whether to approve the proposed road, the Forest Service is required to

Decision

prepare and consider an environmental impact statement that analyzes the combined impacts of the road and the timber sales that the road is designed to facilitate.

. . .

. . . [F]or the purpose of fashioning an appropriate remedy for the Service's failure to comply with NEPA, we remand this case to the district court for proceedings consistent with this opinion.

Notes and Questions

1. In *Thomas v. Peterson*, what "proposal for major federal action" did the Forest Service assess for significant environmental impact? What potentially significant impacts did the Forest Service assess? According to the plaintiffs, how did the Forest Service violate NEPA?

2. The Ninth Circuit quoted a CEQ regulation, 40 C.F.R. § 1508.25, that defines "connected actions" and "cumulative actions." That regulation concerns the "scope" of *an EIS*—"the range of actions, alternatives, and impacts to be considered in an environmental impact statement." *Id.* How did the Ninth Circuit use the regulation? Was this use appropriate? Look back at the CEQ regulations excerpted at pp. 142–145, above. Can you construct an alternative rationale to support the Ninth Circuit's conclusion that the Jersey Jack road and the anticipated timber sales should have been assessed as a single "proposal for major federal action" that might "significantly affect[ ] the quality of the human environment"?

3. What standard of review did the Ninth Circuit apply to the Forest Service's FONSI?

4. Having concluded that the Forest Service violated NEPA, what remedy did the Ninth Circuit order? Is the court's choice of remedy justified? Could the court have chosen a different remedy? *See, e.g., Center for Biological Diversity v. Nat'l Highway Traffic Safety Admin.*, 538 F.3d 1172, 1225–27 (9th Cir. 2008) (explaining that the appropriate remedy for a violation of NEPA at the EA stage depends on the nature of the violation).

5. Considering the sprawling reach of the federal government's activities, and the centrality of the environmental impact statement to NEPA's statutory scheme, one might think that federal agencies prepare a very large number of EISs. In fact, however, the annual number of EISs prepared was highest soon after NEPA's enactment and then fell steadily through the 1970s and 1980s before leveling off in the range of 200 to 300 final EISs per year since the 1990s. Council on Environment Quality, *Environmental Impact Statements Filed Through 2012*, https://ceq.doe.gov/nepa/EISs_by_Year_1970_to_2012.pdf (last visited Sept. 28, 2016). Precise data are hard to come by, but it is clear that Environmental Assessments followed by FONSIs far outnumber EISs. CEQ estimates the annual number of EAs as "tens of thousands." CEQ, *NEPA Litigation*, https://ceq.doe.gov/legal_corner/litigation.html (last visited Oct. 24, 2016).

The sheer number of EAs that are not followed by EISs might suggest that ample opportunities exist for project opponents to challenge agencies' FONSIs. Such judicial challenges occur regularly, but the available data suggest that only a small percentage of EAs and FONSIs — on the order of a few dozens per year — generate litigation. According to CEQ's annual summaries of NEPA litigation, the government prevailed in 62 percent of 383 claims of unlawful EAs and FONSIs that were decided on the merits from 2001 through 2013.

6. The so-called "mitigated FONSI" is one device federal agencies use to avoid preparing an EIS. In a mitigated FONSI, the EA identifies one or more environmental impacts of the proposed project that would be "significant," but also identifies mitigation measures that will reduce those impacts below the threshold of significance. The agency then chooses an alternative that includes implementation of the mitigation measures, and issues a finding of no significant impact based on the assumption or commitment that the mitigation measures will be implemented.

The CEQ regulations do not expressly authorize federal agencies to produce mitigated FONSIs, but most courts have upheld the practice. *See* Albert I. Herson, *Project Mitigation Revisited: Most Courts Approve Findings of No Significant Impact Justified by Mitigation*, 13 Ecology L.Q. 51, 54–63 & n.29 (1986) (reviewing case law showing that the Fourth, Fifth, Ninth, and D.C. Circuits had approved mitigated FONSIs in principle, but the First Circuit had rejected use of mitigated FONSIs); Peter J. Eglick & Henryk J. Hiller, *The Myth of Mitigation Under NEPA and SEPA*, 20 Envtl. L. 773, 778 n.15 (1990) (adding Eleventh Circuit to the list of courts approving mitigated FONSIs); *see also National Audubon Soc. v. Hoffman*, 132 F.3d 7, 17 (2d Cir. 1997) (approving use of mitigated FONSIs in principle). Does allowing agencies to use mitigated FONSIs advance or hinder the achievement of NEPA's statutory objectives?

The fact that a court accepts the use of mitigated FONSIs as a general proposition, however, does not assure that any mitigated FONSI will be approved. In *National Audubon Society v. Hoffman*, the Second Circuit rejected the mitigated FONSI for a road in a National Forest because the record lacked substantial evidence that measures to mitigate impacts on bird and bear habitat would be implemented and would be effective. 132 F.3d at 17. In *Hill v. Boy*, 144 F.3d 1446, 1451 (11th Cir. 1998), the court remanded to the Army Corps of Engineers a FONSI for a permit to construct a dam and reservoir, holding that the record did not support the Corps' acceptance of the permit applicant's representation that a petroleum pipeline would be moved from its current location under the site of the proposed reservoir. In *O'Reilly v. U.S. Army Corps of Engineers*, 477 F.3d 225, 234 (5th Cir. 2007), the court affirmed a district court's conclusion that the EA for a permit to fill wetlands "fail[ed] to sufficiently demonstrate that the mitigation measures adequately address and remediate the adverse impacts so that they will not significantly affect the environment."

Overall, courts reviewing mitigated FONSIs have exhibited somewhat varying degrees of insistence on record evidence showing that the mitigation measures will be implemented, will achieve their intended results, and will push a proposed action's environmental impacts below the significance threshold. As the sample of cases shows, agencies' EAs also vary in this regard. If the major federal action in question is an agency project, of course, the agency can build the mitigation measures into its choice of alternative and its record of decision. If the major federal action is the grant of a permit to a non-federal permittee, the agency can condition the permit on performance of the mitigation measures. Some federal agencies, at least formally, require that a mitigated FONSI ensure implementation of the mitigation measures. *E.g.*, 39 C.F.R. §775.9(a)(2) (Postal Service regulation providing that "use of a mitigated FONSI is conditioned upon the implementation of the identified mitigation measures in the EA"). What if an agency issues a mitigated FONSI and then fails to follow through on its own commitment to implement mitigation or fails to enforce a permit condition requiring mitigation?

You can condition funding to ensure mitigation measures will take place.

What types of measures to mitigate environmental impacts ought to justify a mitigated FONSI? In *Ohio Valley Envtl. Coalition v. Hurst*, 556 F.3d 177 (4th Cir. 2009), the plaintiffs challenged the Corps of Engineers' use of mitigated FONSIs for four permits for "mountaintop removal" coal mining that would cause large amounts of soil and rock to obliterate streams in the valleys below. Recognizing that the streams below the mountaintop mines could not be protected from burial, the Corps conditioned the permits on "compensatory restoration"— requiring the permittees to enhance or create stream habitat at other locations. The district court held that the Corps had violated NEPA, issued an injunction rescinding the permits, and remanded to the Corps. A divided court of appeals reversed, holding that the mitigated FONSI was not arbitrary and capricious. Is this decision consistent with NEPA? With the CEQ's regulation, 40 C.F.R. § 1508.20, defining "mitigation"?

7. As noted above, agencies prepare a far greater number of Environmental Assessments than Environmental Impact Statements. But agencies undertake the vast majority of major federal actions without preparing either an EA or an EIS, by invoking the third category described in the CEQ regulations—the Categorical Exclusion. We turn to this category next.

California v. Norton

311 F.3d 1162 (9th Cir. 2002)

Judge D.W. NELSON:

Appellants:
Federal agencies
"United States"

Appellants ([the Secretary of the Interior and other federal agencies and officials, collectively referred to as the] "United States") granted "suspensions" of thirty-six oil leases offshore of central California pursuant to 43 U.S.C. § 1334(a)(1). The purpose of the lease suspensions was to extend the lives of the leases and to allow the lessees to "facilitate proper development of the lease[s]." Without the suspensions, the leases would have expired and the lessees would have lost all production rights because the lessees had not begun production in paying quantities and the term of the leases had elapsed.

Appellee:
state agencies
"California"

Appellee ([a number of state agencies and officials collectively referred to as] "California") ... objected to the lease suspensions on grounds that the United States failed to perform an environmental review of the lease suspensions pursuant to the National Environmental Policy Act ("NEPA") .... The United States ... asserted that the lease suspensions were categorically excluded from environmental review pursuant to NEPA.

California filed suit in federal district court seeking to . . . force the United States to prepare an Environmental Impact Statement ("EIS") before approving the lease suspensions. Ten environmental groups [and two California counties] intervened as plaintiffs with California . . . . The lessees [the "Oil Companies"] intervened as defendants with the United States . . . .

The district court held that . . . the United States did not adequately document its reliance on the claimed categorical exclusion pursuant to NEPA and ordered the United States to provide an explanation for the applicability of the categorical exclusion to these lease suspensions. The United States and the Oil Companies timely appealed.

We have jurisdiction pursuant to 28 U.S.C. § 1291, and we affirm.

I. Background

. . . .

B. Statutory Background

. . . .

4. The National Environmental Policy Act

. . . . An agency must prepare NEPA documents before any irreversible and irretrievable commitment of resources is made. Generally, the agency is required to prepare an EIS or an Environmental Assessment ("EA") before committing resources to an action. A federal agency may adopt a "categorical exclusion" for a "category of actions which do not individually or cumulatively have a significant effect on the human environment." 40 C.F.R. 1508.4 (2001). Generally, if an action falls within an adopted categorical exclusion the agency is not required to prepare an EIS or an EA. *Id.* However, an agency adopting a categorical exclusion must "provide for extraordinary circumstances in which a normally excluded action may have a significant environmental effect." *Id.* In such extraordinary circumstances, a categorically excluded action would nevertheless trigger preparation of an EIS or an EA.

C. The 36 Leases at Issue

The thirty-six leases that are the subject of this litigation were issued between 1968 and 1984. They have not yet begun producing paying quantities of oil or gas and would have expired but for previous suspensions. The latest round of suspensions, which are challenged in this lawsuit, were issued to prevent the leases from expiring in 1999. Within the boundaries of the leaseholds at issue, there have been thirty-eight exploratory wells drilled resulting in seventeen discoveries. The most recent well was drilled in 1989. The oil companies paid the United States approximately $1.25 billion for the leases. The leaseholds are located between the Channel Islands National Marine Sanctuary and the Monterey Bay National Marine Sanctuary, which contain many species that are particularly sensitive to the impacts of spilled oil . . . .

In May of 1999, the lessees submitted requests for suspensions of all thirty-six leases .... [T]he United States granted the suspension requests for the thirty-six leases ....

....

II. District Court Proceedings

....

B. NEPA Claim

In the district court, California sought to force the United States to prepare an EIS or an EA before approving any lease suspensions. California argued that environmental documentation was required because circumstances had changed since the original leases had been granted and since earlier environmental documentation had been prepared assessing the expected impacts of exploration and drilling activity on the leaseholds. Among the changed circumstances cited by California was the expansion of the territory of the threatened sea otter towards the lease area.

California also argued that the United States improperly relied upon the categorical exclusion for lease suspensions. The parties do not dispute that the United States properly adopted a categorical exclusion from the requirement for environmental documentation for lease suspensions pursuant to 40 C.F.R. § 1508.4. However, 40 C.F.R. § 1508.4 requires that an agency adopting a categorical exclusion "provide for extraordinary circumstances in which a normally excluded action may have a significant environmental effect." When extraordinary circumstances are present, the agency must prepare environmental documentation despite the fact that the activity in question falls within a categorical exclusion.

The district court held that the United States failed to provide a reasoned explanation for its reliance on the categorical exclusion and failed to explain the inapplicability of the extraordinary circumstances exceptions to the lease suspensions. The district court held that the United States could not rely on the categorical exclusion without providing these explanations and ordered the United States to provide both of these explanations. It held that the United States was not required to prepare an EIS or an EA "at this time."

....

IV. Discussion

....

B. National Environmental Policy Act Claims

....

The United States has adopted a categorical exclusion for lease suspensions. National Environmental Policy Act; Implementing Procedures for Minerals Management Service, 51 Fed.Reg. 1855, 1857 (Jan. 15, 1986). The United States has also adopted a list of ten exceptions to the categorical exclusion for lease suspensions. National

Environmental Policy Act; Revised Implementing Procedures, 49 Fed.Reg. 21437, 21439 (May 21, 1984).

The United States did not prepare environmental documentation regarding its decision to approve the lease suspensions. The United States argues that no environmental documentation was required because lease suspensions are categorically excluded and none of the exceptions to the exclusion apply in this case.

The Environmental Groups argue that the United States cannot rely on the categorical exclusion because the United States did not make a categorical exclusion determination at the time it granted the lease suspensions. The implication is that the United States is using the categorical exclusion as a post hoc rationalization when in fact it simply failed entirely to consider the potential environmental consequences of its decision at the time the decision was made. This would frustrate the fundamental purpose of NEPA, which is to ensure that federal agencies take a "hard look" at the environmental consequences of their actions early enough so that it can serve as an important contribution to the decision making process.

The United States does not point to any documentation in the record that would suggest that it made a categorical exclusion determination at the time the lease suspensions were approved. Instead it argues that the lease suspensions are indeed categorically exempt and that none of the exceptions applies. The United States argues that this Court can rely on the existing record to determine that the lease suspensions are categorically exempt because it is evident from the record that the duly-promulgated categorical exclusion for lease suspensions applies here . . . .

. . . .

. . . . "An agency satisfies NEPA if it applies its categorical exclusions and determines that neither an EA nor an EIS is required, so long as the application of the exclusions to the facts of the particular action is not arbitrary and capricious." It is difficult for a reviewing court to determine if the application of an exclusion is arbitrary and capricious where there is no contemporaneous documentation to show that the agency considered the environmental consequences of its action and decided to apply a categorical exclusion to the facts of a particular decision. Post hoc invocation of a categorical exclusion does not provide assurance that the agency actually considered the environmental effects of its action before the decision was made . . . .

In many instances, a brief statement that a categorical exclusion is being invoked will suffice. Here, concern for adequate justification of the categorical exclusion is heightened because there is substantial evidence in the record that exceptions to the categorical exclusion are applicable. Exception 2.8 disallows use of the categorical exclusion where the agency action may "[h]ave adverse effects on species listed or proposed to be listed on the list of Endangered or Threatened Species, or have effects on designated Critical Habitat for these species." 49 Fed.Reg. at 21439. The Chair of the California Coastal Commission wrote to the United States expressing concern over the effects of the lease suspensions on the threatened southern sea otter. Exception 2.2 disallows use of the categorical exclusion where the agency action may have adverse effects on "ecologically significant or critical areas." The Chair of the California Coastal Commission also expressed concern that the approval of the lease suspensions could impact the Monterey Bay National Marine Sanctuary and the Channel Islands National Marine Sanctuary. Both of California's United States Senators also wrote expressing concern about impacts on the marine sanctuaries.

Exception 2.3 disallows use of categorical exclusions for actions which may "[h]ave highly controversial environmental effects." The environmental effects of the leases are the subject not only of scientific, but also of public controversy. California Governor Gray Davis and United States Senator Dianne Feinstein both wrote on behalf of the people of California to express strong opposition to suspension of the leases because of concern over environmental effects . . . .

. . . .

Rationale

At the very least there is substantial evidence in the record that exceptions to the categorical exclusion *may* apply, and the fact that the exceptions may apply is all that is required to prohibit use of the categorical exclusion. 49 Fed.Reg. at 21439.

Where there is substantial evidence in the record that exceptions to the categorical exclusion may apply, the agency must at the very least explain why the action does not fall within one of the exceptions . . . .

Although California, the Counties, and the Environmental Groups argue that the categorical exclusion cannot be applied to these lease suspensions and an EIS is required, they do not ask us to modify the decision of the district court, but rather urge that we affirm in all respects. The district court held that the United States must provide a reasoned explanation for its reliance on the categorical exclusion, including an explanation of why the exceptions do not apply. The district court left open the possibility of requiring an Environmental Impact Statement if the United States fails to provide an adequate explanation. We affirm the decision of the district court with respect to the NEPA claim, and leave it to the district court to determine in due course what, if any, further NEPA documentation is required.

Decision

Notes and Questions

1. What was the proposed federal action that, according to California, required an EA or EIS? Why do you suppose California sued over it?

California v. Norton is a chapter in a decades-long (though intermittent) dispute between the State of California and the federal government, with their respective allies, concerning the Interior Department's efforts to lease offshore oil drilling rights in the Outer Continental Shelf adjacent to parts of the California coast. As the Ninth Circuit described at length in an omitted portion of the opinion, the dispute dates back at least to 1969, when a blowout during drilling of a well off the coast of Santa Barbara caused a massive oil spill that contaminated a vast swath of ocean and beaches. The spill was one of the catalysts for NEPA's enactment. For a description of it, see Keith C. Clarke & Jeffrey J. Hemphill, *The Santa Barbara Oil Spill: A Retrospective*, in Proc. 64th Annual Meeting Ass'n Pacific Coast Geographers (2001), http://www2.bren.ucsb.edu/%7Edhardy/1969_Santa_Barbara_Oil_Spill/Essays.html (last visited Oct. 4, 2016).

Nearly 50 years later, the environmental risks associated with extraction and transport of offshore oil continue to make that activity controversial in southern California. In 2015, a rupture in an onshore pipeline transporting oil from offshore wells caused a much smaller oil spill that again fouled beaches near Santa Barbara. *See* National Oceanic and Atmospheric Administration, *Refugio State Beach Oil Spill Near Santa Barbara, California*, available at response.restoration.noaa.gov/oil-and-chemical -spills/significant-incidents/refugio-state-beach-oil-spill-near-santa-barbara-calif (last visited Oct. 4, 2016).

The 1969 Santa Barbara spill stood as the largest release of oil from a United States offshore well until the deadly explosion and vastly larger release at the Deepwater Horizon drilling rig in the Gulf of Mexico in 2010. BP's exploration activity at Deepwater Horizon, interestingly enough, also proceeded pursuant to a categorical exclusion, albeit after the responsible federal agency, the Minerals Management Service, completed a "programmatic" EIS for offshore drilling in the Gulf of Mexico in general. *See* Oliver A. Houck, *Worst Case and the Deepwater Horizon Blowout: There Ought to Be a Law*, 40 Envtl. L. Rep. 11033, 11035–36 (Nov. 2010) (criticizing the programmatic EIS for downplaying the environmental risks of an offshore well blowout and describing the subsequent use of categorical exclusions).

2. Refer to the definition of "Categorical Exclusion" in CEQ's NEPA regulations, 40 C.F.R. § 1508.4, p. 142, above. Courts have observed that despite the lack of either an EA or an EIS, an agency's proper "[a]pplication of a categorical exclusion is not an exemption from NEPA; rather, it is a form of NEPA compliance." *Center for Biological Diversity v. Salazar*, 706 F.3d 1085, 1096 (9th Cir. 2013). What, then, was the basis for the plaintiffs' claim, in *California v. Norton*, that the Interior Department had violated NEPA? Can you think of other arguments that a plaintiff, unhappy with an agency's invocation of a categorical exclusion, might make?

3. The purpose of categorical exclusions, of course, is to help agencies avoid spending time, money, staff effort, and other resources on the unnecessary environmental assessment of agency actions that predictably will be found to have no significant environmental impact. Agencies can use the resources thus saved to do better EAs and EISs—or to pursue their non-environmental missions. *See* 40 C.F.R. §§ 1500.4, 1500.5 (requiring use of categorical exclusions to reduce paperwork and delay); Council on Environmental Quality, Final Guidance for Federal Departments and Agencies on Establishing, Applying, and Revising Categorical Exclusions Under the National Environmental Policy Act, 75 Fed. Reg. 75628 (Dec. 6, 2010) (hereafter "Categorical Exclusion Guidance"). At the same time, the "extraordinary circumstances" requirement is designed to ensure that agency action does not elude environmental assessment in "situations or circumstances that may warrant additional analysis and documentation." Categorical Exclusion Guidance, 75 Fed. Reg. at 75630.

How hard must an agency look for extraordinary circumstances? The question has important implications, because (according to CEQ) agencies invoke categorical exclusions hundreds of thousands of times a year. CEQ, *NEPA Litigation*, https://ceq .doe.gov/legal_corner/litigation.html (last visited Oct. 24, 2016). In *California v. Norton*, the Ninth Circuit tried to walk a fine line, understanding that to require too much would undermine the purpose of categorical exclusions, while requiring too little would undermine the extraordinary circumstances exception. How well do you think the Ninth Circuit did?

4. In *California v. Norton*, the Ninth Circuit held that "[w]here there is substantial evidence in the record that exceptions to the categorical exclusion may apply, the agency must at the very least explain why the action does not fall within one of the exceptions." How is the "record" the court referred to generated?

5. In *Utah Environmental Congress v. Bosworth*, 443 F.3d 732 (10th Cir. 2006), the court rejected an "extraordinary circumstances" challenge to an agency's use of a categorical exclusion. The United States Forest Service approved a timber-thinning project on 123 acres of the Fishlake National Forest that were infested with the spruce beetle. Relying on a categorical exclusion for "sanitation harvest of trees to control insects" in areas 250 acres or less, the Forest Service did not prepare an EA or EIS. The plaintiff contended that the possible presence of an endangered woodpecker in the project area constituted an extraordinary circumstance. The court, however, agreed with the Forest Service that only a "potentially significant" environmental impact would "trigger a finding of extraordinary circumstances" and held that the record supported the Forest Service's conclusion that any effect on the woodpecker would not be significant.

6. As we have seen, in extraordinary circumstances a proposed major federal action may require an EA or EIS even if it fits within a categorical exclusion. In some cases, however, the issue is not whether extraordinary circumstances exist, but whether the proposed major federal action fits the category that is excluded from the EIS requirement. The Forest Service Handbook, for example, includes a categorical exclusion for "[r]ules, regulations, or policies to establish Service-wide administrative procedures, program processes, or instructions." *California* ex rel. *Lockyer v. U.S. Dept. of Agriculture*, 575 F.3d 999, 1017 (9th Cir. 2009) (quoting Forest Service Handbook 1909.15 § 31.1b., ¶ 2). The Forest Service argued that this exclusion covered a rule promulgated during the George W. Bush Administration to replace a Clinton Administration rule governing the management of roadless areas in National Forests. *Id*. at 1009–10. The Ninth Circuit held that even though the replacement rule did not directly change the Forest Service's management of any particular roadless tract in a National Forest, it worked a substantive change in Forest Service policy and therefore was outside the bounds of a categorical exclusion previously applied only to "routine and rather mundane matters." *Id*. at 1017; *see id*. at 1016–18. The court concluded that the Forest Service violated NEPA by promulgating the new rule without conducting any environmental impact analysis, and therefore affirmed the district court's judgment that enjoined the replacement rule and reinstated the Clinton Administration rule.

7. Who makes the decision that a particular category of major federal actions should be excluded from NEPA's EIS requirement? How is that decision put into effect? What if that decision is inconsistent with the definition of a categorical exclusion set forth in the CEQ regulations?

In some cases, the issue is not whether a proposed major federal action is within the ambit of a categorical exclusion, but whether the categorical exclusion is appropriate in the first place. Again, our example involves the Forest Service during the George W. Bush Administration. "President Bush established the Healthy Forests Initiative . . . to improve regulatory processes to ensure more timely decisions, greater efficiency, and better results in reducing the risk of catastrophic wildfires by restoring forest health." U.S. Dept. of Agriculture & U.S. Dept. of the Interior, National Environmental Policy Act Documentation Needed for Fire Management Activities; Categorical Exclusions, 68 Fed. Reg. 33814 (June 5, 2003). Pursuant to this direction, the Forest Service promulgated a categorical exclusion covering certain "hazardous fuels reduction activities." One way to reduce the fuel available to burn in a forest fire is to cut down trees. Some environmentalists suspected that the categorical exclusion would shortcut environmental impact assessment for timber harvesting not genuinely needed for reducing fire risks. *See id.* at 33816 (describing and responding to public comment). In the context of a challenge to several fuels reduction projects for which the Forest Service invoked the categorical exclusion, the Ninth Circuit held that the promulgation of the categorical exclusion violated NEPA because the record did not adequately explain the basis for the agencies' conclusion that the excluded fuels reduction projects would not individually or cumulatively have a significant effect on the quality of the human environment. *Sierra Club v. Bosworth*, 510 F.3d 1016, 1026–33 (9th Cir. 2007).

8. Even if an agency can be confident that each individual action within a categorical exclusion will not significantly affect the quality of the human environment, how can an agency determine whether these actions cumulatively have a significant environmental impact, as required by the CEQ regulations? Some plaintiffs have argued that agencies must undertake a cumulative impacts assessment before deciding whether to apply a categorical exclusion to a particular agency action. The courts, reasoning that generally imposing such a requirement would undermine the purpose of categorical exclusions and that exceptional cases can be addressed as "extraordinary circumstances," have been unsympathetic. *See Utah Environmental Congress v. Bosworth*, 443 F.3d 732, 740–41 (10th Cir. 2006); *accord, Center for Biological Diversity v. Salazar*, 706 F.3d 1085, 1096–98 (9th Cir. 2013).

9. The Categorical Exclusion Guidance published by the Obama Administration CEQ was "designed to afford Federal agencies flexibility in developing and implementing categorical exclusions, while ensuring that categorical exclusions are administered to further the purposes of NEPA and the CEQ Regulations." 75 Fed. Reg. 75631. Much like *California v. Norton*, the Categorical Exclusion Guidance stated that little or no documentation is required for some applications of categorical exclusions, while in other situations agencies should develop additional documentation "tailored to the type of action involved, the potential for extraordinary circumstances and environmental effects." *Id.* at 75636. CEQ implied that, in some situations, instead of producing a lengthy justification for use of a categorical exclusion, an agency might prefer to go ahead and produce an Environmental Assessment. *Id.* ("If lengthy documentation is needed . . . an agency should consider whether it is appropriate to apply the categorical exclusion in that particular situation.").

Note on Additional Exceptions to the EIS Requirement

Section 102(2)(C) of NEPA requires inclusion of an EIS in "*every* recommendation or report on proposals for . . . major federal actions significantly affecting the quality of the human environment," without exception. 42 U.S.C. § 4332(2)(C) (emphasis added). All three branches of government, however, have carved out limited exceptions to this requirement for certain federal agency actions that otherwise would trigger an EIS.

The easiest exceptions to understand and apply are statutory. NEPA is, after all, a legislative enactment, and Congress may by legislation limit its reach. Rather than do this by amending NEPA, however, Congress has inserted into other statutes provisions exempting agency actions from the EIS requirement.

Thus, for example, the Energy Supply and Coordination Act of 1974, P.L. 93-319, in response to the OPEC oil embargo, temporarily authorized the Federal Energy Administrator to issue orders prohibiting specified industrial facilities from burning petroleum or natural gas if those facilities were also capable of burning coal and other conditions were satisfied. P.L. 93-319 § 2. The statute further provided that, for a limited period, such orders would not be deemed major federal actions significantly affecting the quality of the human environment within the meaning of NEPA, although a NEPA-like analysis would still be required before or soon after issuance of the order. *Id.* § 6(c). Much more broadly, the statute also provided that "[n]o action taken under the Clean Air Act [(see Chapter 5)] . . . shall be deemed a major federal action significantly affecting the quality of the human environment," *id.* § 6(b), a provision still on the books and operational. 15 U.S.C. § 793(C)(1). Similarly, in the 1972 enactment of the modern Clean Water Act (see Chapter 7), Congress exempted from the EIS requirement all actions the Environmental Protection Agency (EPA) takes under that statute, other than providing grants for construction of sewage treatment plants and issuing permits for new sources of water pollution. 33 U.S.C. § 1371(c)(1). Congress may not have thought it necessary or desirable for environmental impact assessment to delay implementation of environmental protection legislation that would require EPA to consider the environmental effects of its decisions as a matter of course.

A few other federal statutes exclude specific agency actions from the class of "major federal actions significantly affecting the quality of the human environment." In some cases the motive for the exclusion appears to be congressional desire to allow the agency to act as quickly as possible. *See, e.g.,* 42 U.S.C. § 5159 (excluding from the EIS requirement the provision of federal disaster assistance that restores a facility substantially to its pre-disaster condition). In other cases, Congress apparently concluded that other mandatory procedures required agencies to undertake environmental analyses sufficient to substitute for an EIS. *See, e.g.,* 16 U.S.C. § 1536(k) (excluding from the EIS requirement decisions of the Endangered Species Committee on exemption requests under the Endangered Species Act, see p. 258, below).

Federal courts have also crafted similar exceptions to the EIS requirement for certain agency actions undertaken pursuant to other environmental statutes. In the leading case, *Portland Cement Ass'n v. Ruckelshaus*, 486 F.2d 375 (D.C. Cir. 1973), an industry trade group argued that EPA was required to prepare an EIS before promulgating New Source Performance Standards (see p. 346, below) limiting the industry's air pollution emissions. The D.C. Circuit, noting the irony of using NEPA to challenge an anti-pollution regulation, concluded that the provision of the Clean Air Act under which EPA acted required EPA to perform an analysis that was "the functional equivalent of a NEPA impact statement" and, therefore, that issuance of this type of regulation did not require an EIS. *Id.* at 384.

The *Portland Cement* holding became a moot point when Congress enacted the statutory EIS exemption for actions taken under the Clean Air Act, described above. Courts have applied the "functional equivalent" reasoning, however, in other contexts. *See, e.g., Alabama* ex rel. *Siegelman v. Environmental Protection Agency*, 911 F.2d 499 (11th Cir. 1990) (upholding EPA's position, *see* 40 C.F.R. § 124.9(b)(6), that no EIS is required before granting a permit under the Resource Conservation and Recovery Act to a facility that will treat, store, or dispose of hazardous waste (see p. 704, below)); *Merrell v. Thomas*, 807 F.2d 776 (9th Cir. 1986) (holding, as did several other circuits, that no EIS is required before EPA approves or cancels the registration of a pesticide under the Federal Insecticide, Fungicide, and Rodenticide Act (see p. 880, below)). But agencies have not always persuaded courts that other statutory procedures may substitute for an EIS. *Compare Douglas County v. Babbitt*, 48 F.3d 1495 (9th Cir. 1995) (holding that no EIS is required before the Fish and Wildlife Service designates critical habitat for a listed species under the Endangered Species Act (see p. 229, below)) *with Catron County Bd. of Comm'rs v. U.S. Fish and Wildlife Service*, 75 F.3d 1429 (10th Cir. 1996) (holding that an EIS is required before critical habitat designation); *see also Texas Comm. on Natural Resources v. Bergland*, 573 F.2d 201 (5th Cir. 1978) (holding that although the National Forest Management Act required the Forest Service to take account of environmental as well as economic considerations in forest planning, the agency remained obligated to comply with NEPA's EIS requirement).

Courts have also exempted an agency's performance of a mandatory duty prescribed by another statute in terms that make NEPA compliance impossible or meaningless. For example, the Supreme Court held that because the Department of Housing and Urban Development could not simultaneously comply with the EIS requirement and an obligation to approve or disapprove certain documents within 30 days, the approval decision did not require an EIS. *Flint Ridge Development Co. v. Scenic Rivers Ass'n of Oklahoma*, 426 U.S. 776 (1976) (see p. 122, above). Another example, *Citizens Against Rails-to-Trails v. Surface Transportation Board*, 267 F.3d 1144 (D.C. Cir. 2001), involved a statutory requirement that the Surface Transportation Board "shall" approve an application to use a former railroad right-of-way as a walking or biking trail, provided the applicant agrees to accept responsibility for maintaining the rail-trail. The court reasoned that because the statute allowed the Board no discretion to deny a satisfactory application, "the information that NEPA provides can have no affect [sic] on the agency's actions, and therefore NEPA is inapplicable." *Id.* at 1151.

The executive branch has created an exception to the EIS requirement as well. CEQ's regulations allow agencies to make "alternative arrangements" in lieu of an EIS or even an EA if "emergency circumstances make it necessary to take an action with significant environmental impact without observing" required NEPA procedures. 40 C.F.R. § 1506.11. Alternative arrangements were used, for example, when the Coast Guard decided to redeploy resources to the Gulf of Mexico while responding to the Deepwater Horizon oil well blowout and oil spill, reducing the government's ability to clean up promptly any oil discharges that might occur elsewhere in the nation. *See* https://www.dhs.gov/sites/default/files/publications/mgmt-nepa-alternative -arrangements-2010-07-12_0.pdf (last visited Oct. 4, 2016). The CEQ maintains a list of agency requests for alternative arrangements at https://ceq.doe.gov/nepa/eis /Alternative_Arrangements_Chart_091815.pdf (last visited Oct. 4, 2016).

Practice Problems: Triggering the EIS Requirement

Practice Problem 1:

In Zavala City, in the southwestern United States, much of the economy depends on the presence of nearby Zavala Air Force Base, where the United States military has stationed aircraft since World War II. Recently, the United States Air Force announced plans to close Zavala Air Force Base because of budgetary constraints.

The mayor of Zavala City knows that the Air Force, after it stops using the base for military purposes, will clean up widespread contamination of soil and groundwater that resulted from decades of improvident handling of solvents used at the base for aircraft maintenance. The mayor—hoping to provide some construction jobs, to generate some revenue, and to ensure that the cleanup workers will spend as much time and money as possible in Zavala City—develops a plan to build and operate a large incinerator that, the mayor believes, the Air Force will need in order to treat the contaminated soils and groundwater.

Construction of the incinerator is estimated to cost at least $350 million. Zavala City plans to finance construction of the incinerator through a combination of sources, including federal loans. It then plans to charge the Air Force a premium price for use of the incinerator during the years of cleanup work on the closed base.

At a public meeting hosted by the mayor to discuss the incinerator proposal, someone asks whether an Environmental Impact Statement will be prepared to evaluate alternatives to the incinerator. The mayor, knowing something about NEPA, quickly answers, "No, because the feds will neither own nor operate the incinerator."

As the city attorney, do you agree with the mayor's response? Why or why not? What additional information would you like in order to be sure of your answer?

Practice Problem 2:

Can you determine whether an EIS is required in the following two scenarios?

Scenario A:

The Atomic Energy Commission (now called the Nuclear Regulatory Commission or NRC) granted a license to Public Electricity Providers, Inc. (PEPI) to operate a newly constructed nuclear power plant. Before granting the license, the Atomic Energy Commission performed an exhaustive analysis and prepared a thorough environmental impact statement that analyzed all of the radiation and non-radiation environmental impacts expected to result from operation of the plant. The license authorized PEPI to operate its nuclear plant at full power for a term of 40 years. The license expires soon.

Recently, PEPI applied to the NRC for renewal of the plant's operating license. PEPI does not seek to change any of the operating parameters of the plant or the basic nuclear technology of the plant, but wants a license to continue operating the same plant in the same way for an additional 20 years.

The chair of the NRC is concerned about NEPA compliance and seeks the advice of the NRC's general counsel. You are an attorney in the NRC's General Counsel's office. What advice do you give? Does the proposed renewal of the plant's operating license require an Environmental Impact Statement, an Environmental Assessment, or neither?

Scenario B:

Honeybees pollinate more than 100 crops that are worth about $15 billion a year and that constitute more than one-third of the nation's diet. To protect honeybees, Congress passed the Honeybee Act, 7 U.S.C. § 281, which authorizes the Secretary of Agriculture "to prohibit or restrict the importation ... of honeybees ... into ... the United States." The Secretary of Agriculture delegated this authority to the Animal and Plant Health Inspection Service (APHIS), a subagency within the Department of Agriculture. Pursuant to this authority, APHIS issued regulations that prohibit importation of adult honeybees unless accompanied by a permit issued by APHIS that authorizes the specific shipment (except for imports from Australia, Canada, and New Zealand, which are allowed without a permit). To receive a permit, an applicant must satisfy many requirements, including the requirement that the so-called "restricted organisms" must be shipped to an apiary or containment facility that APHIS has inspected and approved.

Honeybees in the United States have been in decline for about 40 years. Since 2006, especially, beekeepers, scientists, and crop growers have been deeply concerned about "colony collapse disorder" (CCD) — the sudden death of many honeybee colonies. Despite much research, scientists have not determined the cause of CCD nor found any way to prevent it.

On an expedition to Turkey, Dr. A.P. Ismel found a new subspecies of honeybee, currently found nowhere else in the world, that may be genetically resistant to colony collapse disorder. Dr. Ismel would like to conduct further research on the new subspecies at her university laboratory in the United States, in the hope that eventually this non-indigenous subspecies could be bred with domestic bees to form new hives resistant to CCD. Dr. Ismel's laboratory has a containment facility that APHIS has already inspected and approved.

Dr. Ismel applied for a permit to import some honeybees of the new subspecies from Turkey to the United States. The permit application stated that the Turkish bees would be shipped directly to the containment facility at Dr. Ismel's laboratory. APHIS approved the permit request without preparing any environmental impact assessment document.

Dr. Ismel's university publicized the discovery and planned importation of the Turkish honeybee subspecies on the university's social media platforms. The executive director of the Institute for Bee Protection (IBP), an organization whose members raise and observe honeybees, took note of Dr. Ismel's plans. IBP opposes importation of honeybees because it believes that despite containment measures imported honeybees might escape and cause harm to American hives.

IBP asked the Green American Lawyers Alliance (GALA) to file a lawsuit alleging that the permit is illegal and seeking a temporary restraining order against the planned honeybee importation. You are a GALA staff attorney. Your supervisor asks you to figure out whether IBP could bring a successful NEPA claim against APHIS. What do you conclude? Did the permit APHIS granted Dr. Ismel require an Environmental Impact Statement, an Environmental Assessment, or neither?

IV. Adequacy of the Environmental Impact Statement

Thus far we have considered the circumstances in which NEPA does or does not require an agency to prepare an Environmental Impact Statement. Now we consider a different issue: If a proposal for major federal action significantly affecting the quality of the human environment does trigger the EIS requirement, what must the action agency do to satisfy that requirement?

The Council on Environmental Quality has prescribed both procedural steps for completing an EIS and substantive minima that an EIS must meet. *See generally* 40 C.F.R. Part 1502. An agency must begin preparing an EIS "early enough so that it can serve practically as an important contribution to the decision-making process" rather than as justification for a decision already made. 40 C.F.R. § 1502.5. Once an agency decides to prepare an EIS, its first task is "scoping"—deciding the range of actions, alternatives, and impacts that the EIS will consider. *See id.* §§ 1501.7 (describing the scoping process), 1508.25 (defining "scope" of an EIS). Can you see why decisions made at the scoping stage are critically important?

Because scoping is so important, the CEQ regulations require agencies at this early stage in the process to solicit the participation of others: affected federal, state, local, and tribal government agencies, the proponent of the action, other interested persons (specifically including those who might object to the proposed action because of its environmental impact), and the general public. 40 C.F.R. §§ 1501.7 (requiring

Notice of Intent

Scoping

publication in the Federal Register of a notice of intent to prepare an EIS), 1508.22 (describing notice of intent), 1501.7(a)(1) (identifying parties to receive notice of scoping process), 1506.6 (describing acceptable notice procedures). The notice regulations were written in an era of print media and mail delivery; although notices of intent are still published in the Federal Register, many agencies today use web sites or social media to inform the public of pending environmental impact statements.

Once the scope of an EIS is decided, the agency begins the hard work of preparing the EIS—documenting the reasons for the proposed action, describing the nature of the proposed action and alternatives to it, gathering information to allow assessment of the significant environmental impacts of the proposed action and alternatives, and identifying ways to mitigate those impacts. Federal agencies often contract with consultants who perform these tasks. If the proposed major federal action is granting a non-federal applicant's request for a federal permit or funding, the agency may require the applicant to provide environmental information. But the federal agency remains ultimately responsible for its EIS, and is supposed to independently evaluate information received from a contractor or applicant. 40 C.F.R. § 1506.5.

An agency must first produce a draft environmental impact statement (DEIS) and then a final environmental impact statement (FEIS). 40 C.F.R. § 1502.9. The agency must make a DEIS available to and request comment from the public, the project applicant if any, other interested persons, other federal agencies with jurisdiction over or expertise regarding any environmental impact involved, and appropriate environmental agencies at any level of government. *Id.* §§ 1502.19 (requiring circulation of DEIS), 1503.1 (requiring solicitation of comments). A federal agency with jurisdiction or expertise has an obligation to reply to the request for comments, even if the only reply is to say that the agency has no comment. 42 U.S.C. § 4332(2)(C) (requiring action agency to "consult with and obtain the comments of any Federal agency which has jurisdiction . . . or special expertise"); 40 C.F.R. §§ 1503.1 (echoing the statutory provision), 1503.2 (requiring agencies with jurisdiction or expertise to respond). EPA must comment on every EIS and rate the environmental effects of each action studied in an EIS, as required not by NEPA itself, but by a provision of the Clean Air Act, which was enacted less than a year after NEPA. *See* 42 U.S.C. § 7609 (Clean Air Act § 309).

After receiving comments, the agency responsible for the EIS must then prepare, circulate, 40 C.F.R. § 1502.19, make available to the public, *id.* § 1506.6, and file with EPA, *id.* § 1506.9, a final EIS that includes the agency's response to comments received. *Id.* §§ 1502.9(b), 1503.4. An agency may invite further comment about the pending proposal for major federal action even after the FEIS is filed, *id.* § 1503.1(b), but in general, 30 days after publishing notice of the completed FEIS, an agency is free to make its decision regarding the proposal for major federal action, *id.* § 1506.10(b)(2). The agency informs the public of the agency's choice in a "record of decision," (ROD), *id.* § 1505.2, and then may proceed to implement the chosen major federal action. *Until* the agency makes its final decision, however, the agency is forbidden from taking action on the proposal that would have an adverse environmental effect or would limit the choice of reasonable alternatives. *Id.* § 1506.1. Can you see why this prohibition is important?

Under certain circumstances, an agency may be required to produce a supplemental environmental impact statement (SEIS) even after completing the FEIS, after issuing the Record of Decision, or indeed after beginning to implement the major federal action. (Recall that the plaintiff in *Metropolitan Edison v. PANE*, p. 146, above, alleged that the NRC was required to supplement the original EIS for the TMI-1 operating license.) The Supreme Court considered what circumstances require an SEIS in *Marsh v. Oregon Natural Resources Council*, p. 190, below.

Figure 3-2 illustrates the EIS process as prescribed by the CEQ's regulations, beginning with the Notice of Intent to prepare an EIS and continuing through implementation of the action and supplementation of the EIS if necessary. Solid arrows indicate procedural steps the agency must take, dashed arrows indicate procedural steps the agency may take (or must take only under certain conditions), and open arrows indicate opportunities for comment by other agencies and the public.

Figure 3-2. The EIS Process, from Notice of Intent to Action Implementation

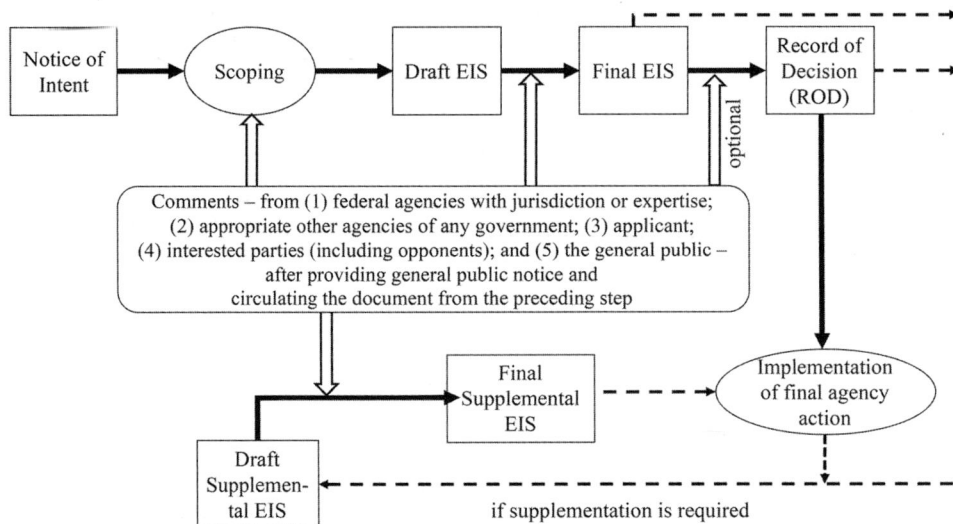

Notice of Intent → Scoping → Draft EIS → Final EIS → Record of Decision (ROD)

Comments – from (1) federal agencies with jurisdiction or expertise; (2) appropriate other agencies of any government; (3) applicant; (4) interested parties (including opponents); and (5) the general public – after providing general public notice and circulating the document from the preceding step

optional

Draft Supplemental EIS → Final Supplemental EIS

Implementation of final agency action

if supplementation is required

In addition to prescribing the procedural steps an agency must take when preparing an EIS, the CEQ regulations specify the material that an EIS must cover. As a decision-making tool, an environmental impact statement is fundamentally a comparison of alternative courses of action. 42 U.S.C. § 4332(2)(C)(iii) (requiring detailed statement on "alternatives to the proposed action); 40 C.F.R. § 1502.14 (comparison of alternatives' environmental impacts "is the heart of" an EIS). To facilitate this comparison, an EIS must explain "the underlying purpose and need to which the agency is responding in proposing the alternatives including the proposed action." 40 C.F.R. § 1502.13. For each alternative considered, the EIS must describe the affected environment and the environmental consequences. *Id.* §§ 1502.15, 1502.16.

If comparing alternatives is the heart of an EIS, the choice of alternatives to compare is obviously critical. We have already seen, in *Vermont Yankee*, p. 108, above, that an agency's decision to exclude certain alternatives from consideration can be controversial. The CEQ regulations specify that an agency must consider the proposed action, a "no action" alternative, and "[o]ther reasonable courses of action," and ways to mitigate the environmental impacts of the alternatives. 40 C.F.R. § 1508.25(b); *see id.* § 1402.14 (requiring comparison of alternatives including the proposed action and no action). As we saw in *Thomas v. Peterson*, p. 151, above, the agency must consider the proposed action and certain types of related actions—"connected," "cumulative," and "similar" actions—together in an EIS, rather than in isolation. *Id.* § 1508.25(a)(1), (a)(2). And the EIS must evaluate the direct, indirect, and cumulative impacts of the alternatives considered. *Id.* § 1508.25.

What if an agency goes through all of the required procedural steps to produce an EIS, but leaves out one of the required elements of the EIS? Or what if an agency prepares an EIS that includes all of the required elements but fails to discuss a reasonable alternative or a significant environmental impact? Or prepares an EIS that is formally complete but includes analysis that is perfunctory or simply wrong? Since *Calvert Cliffs'*, p. 99 above, courts have accepted the proposition that plaintiffs with standing to sue may seek judicial review of the "adequacy" of an EIS prepared for a reviewable final agency action. The following decision canvasses many of the issues that frequently arise in such cases.

Utahns for Better Transportation v. U.S. Department of Transportation

305 F.3d 1152 (10th Cir. 2002)

Judge KELLY:

This appeal arises from the district court's order denying the Appellants' request that the Records of Decision issued by the Federal Highway Administration and the U.S. Army Corps of Engineers (collectively the "Agencies") concerning the Legacy Parkway project be vacated and that the Legacy Parkway Final Environmental Impact Statement be remanded for further agency action . . . . We affirm in part, reverse in part, and remand.

Background

The Great Salt Lake ("GSL") and the wetlands surrounding its shoreline serve as an important habitat for a variety of birds, reptiles, amphibians, and mammals, some of which are endangered. The wetlands of the GSL account for 75 percent of all wetlands in the State of Utah, whose total land area consists of only 1.5 percent wetlands. The shores of the GSL are internationally important because they are a link of the Pacific Flyway for migratory waterfowl and a link of the Western Hemisphere Shorebird Reserve Network ("WHSRN"). Some two to five million birds use the GSL yearly and 90 percent of that use is concentrated in the eastern shore.

By the year 2020, population and travel demand in the five counties along the eastern shore of the GSL is anticipated to increase by 60 percent and 69 percent, respectively. To prepare the transportation infrastructure to meet this future demand, Utah's state, local, and regional officials have developed a three-part plan collectively called

"Shared Solution." The plan calls for improving and expanding Interstate 15, expanding transit, and constructing the Legacy Parkway. The Legacy Parkway is to be a four-lane, divided, limited access, state-funded highway. As currently proposed, it is to be 330 feet wide consisting of four lanes, a 65.6-foot median, a 59-foot berm and utility corridor, and a 13.1-foot pedestrian/equestrian/bike trail. It is to start near Salt Lake City ("SLC"), run north along the eastern portion of the GSL, and end fourteen miles later by connecting with US 89.

Because the Legacy Parkway will connect to the interstate highway system and will require filling in 114 acres of wetland, it must receive approval from the Federal Highway Administration ("FHWA") and a [Clean Water Act] § 404(b) permit from the U.S. Army Corps of Engineers ("COE"). Because both the approval and the permit qualify as major federal actions, an Environmental Impact Statement ("EIS") is required. The Utah Department of Transportation ("UDOT") and its private contractors began preparing a Draft Environmental Impact Statement ("DEIS") shortly after plans for a new highway were announced by Utah's governor in July 1996. The FHWA and the COE adopted UDOT's DEIS and issued it for public comment in September 1998. The Final Environmental Impact Statement ("FEIS") was released for public comment in June 2000. In December 2000, UDOT awarded the contract for construction of the Legacy Parkway. On January 9, 2001, the COE released its Record of Decision ("ROD") issuing the § 404(b) permit to UDOT; and, on October 31, 2000, the FHWA issued its ROD approving UDOT's request for additions and modifications of access points to the interstate highway system.

The Appellants, whose complaints were consolidated by the district court, filed an appeal pursuant to the APA from the RODs as final agency actions. The Appellants asked the district court to vacate the FHWA's and COE's RODs that approved construction of the Legacy Parkway, and to order the preparation of a new EIS for the Legacy Parkway. The district court denied the Appellants' request. After the district court decision was certified as an appealable order, the Appellants appealed to this court and sought an Emergency Motion for Injunction Pending Appeal. On a preliminary record, we granted the motion requiring a $ 50,000.00 bond.

.... Appellants contend that ... NEPA [was] violated when various project impacts were not evaluated correctly and other NEPA requirements were ignored. The Appellants summarize their argument as urging the court to order the Agencies to prepare a new or supplemental EIS ... that adequately addresses the following factors: (1) mass transit alternatives, (2) alternative land use scenarios, (3) land use and growth impacts, (4) impacts on Salt Lake City, (5) wetlands and wildlife impacts, and (6) air quality impacts.

Statutory Overview

.... We apply a rule of reason standard (essentially an abuse of discretion standard) in deciding whether claimed deficiencies in a FEIS are merely flyspecks, or are significant enough to defeat the goals of informed decisionmaking and informed public comment. ...

....

Analysis

I. NEPA

A. D&RG Alignment

The Appellants contend that at least three practicable alternatives to the Legacy Parkway exist including (i) a different highway alignment, (ii) a narrower highway configuration, and (iii) a mass transit alternative. They urge that these alternatives are far less environmentally damaging and would have reduced significantly the wetlands impact from the project.

We begin with the argument that NEPA was violated by the elimination of the Denver & Rio Grande (D&RG) Regional Alignment as an alternative in the FEIS. The FEIS's chapter on alternatives states that the D&RG Regional Alignment was not selected for further study because of its high cost and high impact on existing development relative to the GSL Regional Alignment [that was eventually chosen for the Legacy Parkway] . . .

The Appellants contend that the D&RG Regional Alignment was eliminated in violation of NEPA because the Agencies failed to verify the cost estimates supplied by the Applicant UDOT and failed to respond to comments filed by the Appellants raising this issue. Both NEPA and the COE regulations for implementing NEPA require that the agency verify the accuracy of information supplied by an applicant, 40 C.F.R. § 1506.5(a); 33 C.F.R. Part 325, and respond to substantive issues raised in comments, 40 C.F.R. § 1503.4(a) . . . . The record does not reveal, and the Appellees do not assert, that they either verified the cost estimates supplied by the Applicant or responded to the comments submitted by the Appellants on this issue. The Agencies, therefore, failed to follow their own regulations. Agencies are under an obligation to follow their own regulations, procedures, and precedents, or provide a rational explanation for their departure. No rational explanation has been given.

This is more than a technical requirement when it comes to the cost of the project and alternatives. The FEIS rejected the D&RG Regional Alignment in part on the basis of comparative costs—a $ 300 million estimate for the Legacy Parkway and a $ 460 million estimate for the D&RG Regional Alignment. Appellants suggest that shortly after the COE permit decision, the estimated cost for the Legacy Parkway was $ 451 million, significantly closer to the initial $ 460 million estimate for the DR&G Regional Alignment. They suggest that the COE also relied upon the outdated cost estimates. Appellees counter that had the D&RG Regional Alignment cost estimate been updated, there would have been a proportional increase, and thus, the relative cost relationships would have remained the same. This is pure speculation because there is no cost methodology applicable to the D&RG Regional Alignment contained in the record. It also demonstrates why the FEIS is inadequate to meet the NEPA goals of informed decisionmaking and public comment . . . .

. . . .

B. Narrower Right of Way

The Appellants claim that NEPA was violated by the Agencies' failure to consider a narrower right of way ("ROW") for the Legacy Parkway as a reasonable alternative in the FEIS. While the Legacy's ROW could have been as narrow as 110 feet, the Legacy ROW, at almost 330 feet, will be the widest four lane highway in Utah. The median is to be 65.6 feet wide . . . .

NEPA requires that the Agencies "rigorously explore and objectively evaluate all reasonable alternatives, and for alternatives which were eliminated from detailed study, briefly discuss the reasons for their having been eliminated." 40 C.F.R. § 1502.14(a). The range of alternatives that the agency must consider is not infinite, of course, but it does include all reasonable alternatives to the proposed action. The APA's reasonableness standard applies both to which alternatives the agency discusses and the extent to which it discusses them.

1. Median Width

The Appellants argue that the Applicant chose the wide median so that the Legacy Parkway could be expanded in the future from four to six lanes, and that the Agencies have failed to consider whether a narrower median is a reasonable alternative in the FEIS. While acknowledging that there is "ample space" for two additional lanes within the current median, the Appellees insist that the 65.6-foot median is necessary for both water quality and safety. While the safety justification does not appear to be discussed in the FEIS, the water quality justification is elaborated on as follows:

> The median . . . would serve as a vegetated buffer to filter runoff and minimize concentrated discharges. These vegetated medians would have to be maintained to satisfy water quality certification requirements. If replacing these vegetated medians with additional highway lanes is ever proposed, environmental clearances would be necessary and replacement of the water quality functions of the vegetated medians would be required.

Although none of the cited materials explain exactly how large a vegetated median must be necessary to filter pollutants out of the runoff, the FEIS demonstrates that the Agencies concluded that a narrower median would require a substitute water quality control facility. We hold that the Agencies gave a reasonable explanation for selecting the median width and, therefore, satisfied the requirements of NEPA's 40 C.F.R. § 1502.14(a). . .

. . . .

C. "Maximum Transit" Alternative

Appellants assert that the Agencies violated NEPA by inadequately evaluating whether mass transit was a reasonable alternative to the Legacy Parkway. Appellants have raised a host of contentions under this issue.

1. Failure to Respond to Recommendations and Criticism of an FHWA Headquarter's [sic] Expert that No Alternative Analysis had been done on Aggressive Transit

Appellants protest that the FHWA approved the Legacy Parkway without responding to the recommendations and stinging criticism of the transit analysis from a leading expert from headquarters. The Appellants identify this headquarters expert as Dr. Bruce Spear, and point out that the Appellees have cited to nothing in the record indicating that they made any effort to undertake Dr. Spear's recommendations or to explain why they rejected them. The Appellants conclude that "[a] decision is arbitrary and capricious if an agency ignores the uncontradicted advice of any expert, let alone its own." To support their argument, the Appellants cite to a five-page document entitled "Comments on the Sierra Club Critique of the Travel Demand Models for the Legacy Parkway FEIS and WFRC Response." No date or name appears on the document. . . . Consequently, the Appellants have established only that the author of the "Comments" document had a difference of opinion on whether aggressive transit had been adequately considered as a reasonable alternative. The author's opinion was clearly not "uncontradicted." Even assuming that the author of the "Comments" document was an expert, it is well established that agencies are entitled to rely on their own experts so long as their decisions are not arbitrary and capricious. Therefore, the Appellants have failed to establish a violation of NEPA as to this document.

2. Unexplained Failure of Agencies to Perform a More Complete Alternative Transit Analysis

Appellants assert that the Agencies violated NEPA by not requiring the more complete alternative transit analysis recommended by the Applicant's contractor. NEPA requires that an agency "rigorously explore and objectively evaluate all reasonable alternatives." 40 C.F.R. § 1502.14(a). However, there is nothing in NEPA to suggest that the transit alternative could not be rigorously explored and objectively evaluated absent the alternative transit analysis recommended by an Applicant's contractor. The FEIS contains four independent methods of analysis to determine what contribution transit could make in serving transportation demand. The Appellants have failed to establish that the Agencies acted improperly in not performing the analysis recommended by the contractor . . . .

. . . .

6. Failure to Consider Alternative Sequencing of the "Shared Solution"

The Appellants claim that an alternative sequencing of the "Shared Solution," such that public transit is expanded before the Legacy Parkway is built, is a reasonable alternative and the FEIS is inadequate under NEPA because it failed to explore rigorously and evaluate objectively this alternative. The Shared Solution includes: (1) improving and expanding I-15, (2) an extraordinary expansion of the public transit system, and (3) constructing the Legacy Parkway. Appendix G of the FEIS contains a detailed discussion of why the Legacy Parkway should be built before I-15 is improved and expanded. However, no mention is made in Appendix G as to when the "extraordinary expansion of the public transit system" should occur relative to the Legacy and I-15 projects. The Appellants have provided expert opinion and comments submitted to the Agencies on the importance of expanding public transit prior to constructing new roads.

The Appellees respond that the implementation of rail transit is five to fifteen years behind the Legacy Parkway, and argue that Utah has not begun to meet the requirements for federal rail funding. They conclude that "regional transit choices that may be made in the future are not reasonable alternatives to off-set [sic] the need for new roadway construction now."

There are three problems with Appellees' response. First, the expansion of public transit under consideration is broader than just rail transit. Second, the regional transit choices that are at issue here are not ones "that may be made in the future," but are being made. The FEIS is relying on public transit to meet 12 percent of the 2020 demand and maybe the additional 10 percent of demand that will not be met under the Shared Solution. A . . . study [by a regional planning agency] on the best modes of mass transit was expected to be completed in 2001. There is no question as to whether a regional transit choice will be made. Third, while the project may address a "need for new road construction now," the decided focus of the FEIS and its evaluation of alternatives "is to provide a solution to meet the 2020 transportation needs of the North Corridor." The estimated time to construct the Legacy Parkway and reconstruct I-15 is seven years. Delaying the Legacy Parkway and I-15 project until after all or part of the public transit expansion is in place is an alternative that could be reasonable and one the Agencies did not include in the FEIS, thus rendering it inadequate . . . .

. . . .

7. Failure to Consider Integration of the Legacy Parkway and Transit

In an argument closely related to an alternative sequencing, the Appellants assert that NEPA was violated by a failure to consider integrating the construction of the Legacy Parkway with the expansion of public transit as a reasonable alternative . . . . [N]o mention is made in Appendix G of when public transit should be expanded relative to the Legacy Project. Appellants have cited comments by the [Federal Transit Administration, part of the U.S. Department of Transportation] and comments submitted to the Agencies discussing the significant savings to be gained by building the Legacy Parkway and expanding public transit simultaneously. Appellees' only response is to cite to comments in the COE's ROD, COE . . . and FHWA comments made after the FEIS, and a January 2001 letter from the COE to the EPA. All of these came after the June 2000 FEIS; none of them demonstrate that integration was considered; and none of them explain why integrating the Legacy Parkway with the expansion of public transit is not a reasonable alternative. We, therefore, conclude that omitting integration as a reasonable alternative in the FEIS renders it inadequate . . . .

. . . .

9. Failure to Give Basis for Financial Constraints Estimates on Transit Expansion

Appellants suggest that NEPA was violated because the FEIS limited the amount of transit capacity that could be developed based on assumptions of the likely future financial resources of the Utah Transit Authority ("UTA") without setting forth those assumptions in either the FEIS or the record. . . . However, ... the FEIS states and the record supports that the information used in the FEIS for projecting UTA's future financial resources was developed by the Agencies "in consultation with the UTA," not merely supplied by the UTA without verification by the Agencies. The fact that Appellants disagree with the financial projections that UTA and the Agencies made does not by itself make those projections inadequate.

The Appellants also charge that "the Federal Agencies failed to anticipate the hundreds of millions of dollars of additional revenue from the sales tax for transit projects passed by referendum in November 2000." However, Appellants have failed to explain how a FEIS from June 2000 violated NEPA by not anticipating a sales tax that was passed in November 2000, especially when voters had previously rejected a tax increase to support transit.

D. Reducing Travel Demand and Alternative Land Use Scenario Alternative

The Appellants contend that NEPA was violated by the FEIS's failure to consider reducing travel demand through alternative land use scenarios in combination with mass transit as a reasonable alternative. . . . The Agencies argue that reducing travel demand through alternative land use scenarios alone or in combination with mass transit was not a reasonable alternative. To be a reasonable alternative, it must be non-speculative and bounded by some notion of feasibility. In finding that a FEIS adequately considered energy conservation as an alternative, the Supreme Court [in *Vermont Yankee*] noted that

> There is reason for concluding that NEPA was not meant to require detailed discussion of the environmental effects of "alternatives" put forward in comments when these effects cannot be readily ascertained and the alternatives are deemed only remote and speculative possibilities, in view of basic changes required in statutes and policies of other agencies—making them available, if at all, only after protracted debate and litigation not meaningfully compatible with the time-frame of the needs to which the underlying proposal is addressed.

> . . . .

Land use is a local and regional matter. . . . There are . . . a number of local and regional governmental entities whose cooperation would be necessary to make an alternative land use scenario a reality. The Appellees replied to comments made after the FEIS that "to date, [the state, regional and local entities with responsibility for land use planning] have resoundingly declined to alter their plans based upon such comments." We, therefore, conclude that the Agencies' treatment of the alternative land use was adequate.

E. Cumulative Effects of Six Lanes

The Appellants allege that NEPA was violated by the FEIS's failure to consider the cumulative impact of a future expansion of the Legacy Parkway from four lanes to six. "An environmental impact statement must analyze not only the direct impacts of a proposed action, but also the indirect and cumulative impacts." Cumulative impact is defined as:

the impact on the environment which results from the incremental impact of the action when added to other past, present, and reasonably foreseeable future actions regardless of what agency (Federal or non-Federal) or person undertakes such other actions. Cumulative impacts can result from individually minor but collectively significant actions taking place over a period of time.

40 C.F.R. § 1508.7. The Tenth Circuit has "expressed the test for whether particular actions could be considered cumulative impacts of the proposed action as whether the actions were so interdependent that it would be unwise or irrational to complete one without the others." *Airport Neighbors Alliance, Inc. v. United States*, 90 F.3d 426, 430 (10th Cir. 1996) . . . .

In this case, the Appellants assert that it is reasonably foreseeable that the Legacy Parkway will be expanded to six lanes because of the "Note" in the Evaluation Report that the wide median is necessary for the possible addition of two lanes, the fact that the FEIS points out that there is ample room in the median for two additional lanes, the suggestion that the Legacy Parkway be expanded to six lanes by 2015 in [a separate study called the Western Transportation Corridor Major Investment Study (WTC MIS)], and the fact that the Shared Solutions Plan will only meet 90 percent of the demand projected for the year 2020. The Agencies argue that they reasonably concluded that the FEIS did not need to consider the potential impacts of an expansion to six lanes because the Legacy Parkway has been defined as a four-lane highway in the FEIS. The only place that six lanes were proposed was in the [WTC MIS]. Additionally, the record shows that the Agencies considered whether the cumulative impacts of adding two lanes needed to be included in the FEIS and determined that it did not.

Under the arbitrary and capricious standard of review, this court must give the Agencies' decision substantial deference. . . . [W]e conclude that the Legacy Parkway as currently planned and the possible addition of two lanes are not so interdependent that it would be unwise or irrational to complete one without the other. Therefore, it was unnecessary to include the cumulative impact of any potential expansion to six lanes in the EIS.

F. Failure to Consider Land Use Impacts

An EIS must analyze not only the direct impacts of a proposed action, but also the indirect impacts of past, present, and reasonably foreseeable future actions regardless of what agency or person undertakes such other actions. Indirect impacts are defined by the NEPA regulations as being "caused by the action and are later in time or farther removed in distance, but are still reasonably foreseeable. . . . [They] may include growth inducing effects . . . ." 40 C.F.R. § 1508.8(b). Appellants consider the FEIS to be inadequate under NEPA because it does not consider the land use impacts that the Legacy Parkway will have on the North Corridor. "In reviewing the adequacy of a final environmental impact statement we merely examine whether there is a reasonable, good faith, objective presentation of the topics [NEPA] requires an [EIS] to cover."

The FEIS states that:

> Consultations with local planners indicate that ultimate growth patterns and planned land uses would not change as a result of building the Legacy Parkway. However, the type of development that would occur around the area of the Legacy Parkway interchanges (at 500 South and at Parrish Lane) would likely be different than the type of development that would occur without the Parkway. . . . Therefore, the development would occur sooner with the Parkway than without it.

The Appellants argue that the FEIS's conclusion that there would be no land use impacts attributable to the Legacy Parkway is circular and illogical "because municipal planners had already modified their land use plans to accommodate the sprawl development that will be caused by construction of the Legacy Parkway." The Legacy Parkway has been under consideration in some form or another since 1996 and most if not all of the local governments in the North Corridor have revised their land use plans in the intervening six years.

We reject Appellants' challenge. First, there is some authority for allowing agencies to rely on local planning documents in an EIS to establish that a proposed highway will not result in further growth. Such reliance may readily show that land use impacts may be nil because the surrounding land at issue is already developed or is otherwise committed to uses that were not contingent on the project under consideration. Second, the FEIS states that the Agencies consulted with local planners, not local plans. Appellees' citations to local plans that reflect the Legacy Parkway does not prove that the local planners were not able to advise the Agencies of what land use would occur without the Legacy Parkway.

Appellants additionally note that the FEIS's finding of no land use impacts was criticized by other agencies. However, NEPA requires agencies preparing an EIS to consider and respond to the comments of other agencies, not to agree with them. The record indicates that the Agencies considered and responded to the comments of other agencies. Many of the criticisms cited by the Appellants in their brief were made early in the NEPA process and do not reflect the agencies' final positions on this issue. The FEIS's conclusion that the Legacy Parkway would not impact land use does not render the EIS inadequate.

G. Failure to Consider Impacts to SLC [Salt Lake City]

Appellants assert that the FEIS is inadequate under NEPA because it did not consider the impact construction of the Legacy Parkway will have on SLC. . . . The Agencies responded on at least one occasion to comments expressing concern about impacts on SLC from the construction of the Legacy Parkway by stating that the purpose of the Legacy Parkway was not to bring more cars to SLC. As the Appellants point out in their brief, purpose and intent respecting a project's impacts are irrelevant. Agencies must evaluate all reasonably foreseeable project impacts regardless of whether they are intentional.

. . . .

2. Impact Increased Auto Congestion will have on SLC

Appellants assert that the FEIS failed to discuss the impact increased auto congestion caused by construction of the Legacy Parkway will have on parking, arterial and side streets, and pedestrian and bicycle safety in SLC. The Agencies only have a duty to discuss in the FEIS impacts that are reasonably foreseeable. Even as to impacts that are sufficiently likely to occur such that they are reasonably foreseeable and merit inclusion, the FEIS need only furnish such information as appears to be reasonably necessary under the circumstances for evaluation of the project.

Both the Agencies' comments and the FEIS note that with or without the Legacy Parkway there will be a substantial increase in travel demand in SLC by 2020. The FEIS calculated the percentage of the total demand in 2020 that will be caused by the construction of the Legacy Parkway at 3.3 percent or less. The 3.3 percent estimate includes all traffic in both directions. When adjusted for the directional split, the fact is that while a portion of the traffic is headed in the peak direction, the other portion is traveling in the off-peak direction, and only 1.98 percent of the travel demand going to SLC in 2020 will be caused by the construction of the Legacy Parkway. While the Appellants still consider this to be a significant amount, the Agencies reasonably concluded that this amount was too small for its inclusion in the FEIS to be reasonably necessary under the circumstances for evaluation of the project . . . .

. . . .

I. Impacts to Wetlands

. . . . The Appellants allege that the Agencies violated NEPA by their inadequate analysis of impacts on wetlands. After reviewing the FEIS . . . we find that the indirect impact on wetlands analysis is not inadequate to the point of being arbitrary and capricious.

. . . .

J. Failure to Consider Impacts to Wildlife

The Appellants charge that the FEIS is inadequate and violates NEPA regulations because: (1) only wildlife impacts within 1000 feet of the ROW [right of way] were considered, (2) the FEIS contains inadequate wildlife impact analysis; (3) the Agencies failed to adequately consider noise impacts on wildlife; and (4) wildlife impact and success of mitigation were not considered in light of the dynamic cycle of the GSL. Because we find that the wildlife impact analysis is inadequate under NEPA because the 1000-foot radius excluded consideration of impacts on migratory birds, it is not necessary to reach (2)-(4).

1. Only considered impacts to wildlife within 1000 feet of project

Appellants contend that the FEIS violated NEPA by only considering impacts on wildlife habitat within an arbitrary 1000-foot distance from the right of way. This was done even though the FWS presented evidence to the Federal Agencies that roads can cause significant adverse effects to bird populations as far as 1.24 miles from roadways, especially in open terrain like that adjacent to the proposed Legacy Parkway.

In response to a comment that was submitted alleging that the 1000-foot distance was chosen arbitrarily, the Federal Agencies made the following response:

> The HGM [hydrogeomorphic methodology] model used 1000 feet because the data we collected for land use (which extended to 1 mile from the edge of the wetland) did not result in any statistical difference from the data collected at 1000 feet.

However, by only evaluating impacts to habitat structure within 1000 feet of the roadway, the Applicant and Agencies effectively limited any assessment of wildlife use and value to smaller, less mobile species and ignored the primary concern of many public and private entities: impacts to the GSL ecosystem and its ability to continue as a nationally and internationally significant wildlife use area, particularly for migratory birds. The record repeatedly and without contradiction indicates that the 1000-foot limit used in the FEIS does not allow for consideration of impacts on migratory birds. While we recognize that the failure "to employ a particular method of analysis" in an EIS does not render it inadequate, here the FEIS simply is inadequate to address the impact on migratory birds.

The Appellees respond that they fully explained the rationale for their decision to study indirect wildlife impacts in a 1000-foot zone on each side of the Parkway right-of-way. However, their only citation in support of this statement is a response to a comment from October 2000 that does not address their own admission that birds were beyond the scope of the HGM. Further, this response regarding statistical differences in "land use" is so unclear as to make us question whether it even relates to the effects on wildlife. The Appellees also reply that 317 acres of land preservation were added to the mitigation package because of the criticisms. Increasing the mitigation package, however, does not resolve the inadequacy of the FEIS's wildlife impact analysis. Given that some two to five million birds use the GSL each year, a large portion of which are migratory birds, we find that limiting the wildlife impact analysis so that migratory birds are beyond its scope renders the FEIS inadequate.

K. Air Quality Impacts

In response to comments on the DEIS, the FEIS increased by two million its estimate of Vehicle Miles Traveled ("VMT") per day in 2020 under both the no-build and build scenarios . . . . Appellants assert that the FEIS is inadequate because the air pollution analysis was not adjusted to reflect the increase in VMT . . . .

The FEIS did not recalculate the impact on air pollution. This was because of the addition of a fourth county to the revised model, was explained in the FEIS, and does not make the FEIS inadequate. . . .

. . . .

O. Segmentation of Transportation Projects

. . . . The Legacy Parkway will provide a portion of the transportation facilities needed as one element of the "Shared Solution" transportation plan. The Shared Solution also includes reconstruction and expansion of I-15 to ten lanes, and expansion of the public transit system. According to the FEIS, the I-15 project "is being proposed concurrently with the Legacy Parkway," but the results of this evaluation are being reported in a separate EIS. The FEIS for the I-15 project was scheduled to be completed by mid-2000 with construction to begin in 2008 after completion of the Legacy Parkway . . . .

NEPA instructs that significant cumulative impacts are not to be made to appear insignificant by breaking a project down into small component parts. 40 C.F.R. §1508.27(b)(7). NEPA's description of the proper scope of an EIS in 40 C.F.R. §1508.25 instructs that (1) connected actions should be discussed in the same EIS, and (2) similar actions should be discussed in the same EIS when the best way to assess adequately the combined impacts of the similar actions or reasonable alternatives to such actions is to treat them in a single impact statement . . . .

. . . .

"Generally [under NEPA], segmentation of highway projects is improper for the purpose of preparing environmental documentation." However, the rule against segmentation is not required to be applied in every situation. To determine the appropriate scope for an EIS, courts have considered such factors as whether the proposed segment

(1) has logical termini,
(2) has substantial independent utility,
(3) does not foreclose the opportunity to consider alternatives, and
(4) does not irretrievably commit federal funds for closely related projects . . . .

. . . .

The Appellants assert that NEPA requires that a single EIS be prepared for the Legacy Parkway, the I-15 project, and the expansion of the public transit. They characterize all three projects as connected and similar actions and as interdependent parts such that the "best way" to assess adequately the combined impacts of the three components and reasonable alternatives both to and among the components is "without doubt" a single EIS.

Appellants rely upon the FEIS:

> It is not reasonable to include construction of I-15 North in the No-Build Alternative because of the unlikely chance that any advantages whatsoever would develop compared to the extreme cost to travelers. In fact, the entire cost of Legacy Parkway is economically justified, based on its value as an alternative route during reconstruction of I-15.

> The Legacy Parkway is part of the Shared Solution of transportation systems management, transit, and roadways proposed for the North Corridor. The 2020 capacity needs in the North Corridor would not be met without both the Legacy Parkway and the I-15 North Improvements, even with aggressively enhanced transit. Moreover, the North Corridor transportation needs for safety and an alternate north-south route, as well as engineering and construction constraints, compel a reasonable sequencing of construction

under which the I-15 North Improvements would occur after completion of the Legacy Parkway.

What this tells us is that the I-15 reconstruction will not proceed without the Legacy Parkway, and that Legacy Parkway's utility as an alternate route during that reconstruction alone would justify the Legacy Parkway's cost.

Applying the test contained in the regulation, [40 C.F.R. § 1508.25(a)(1)(i),] the Legacy Parkway does not "automatically trigger" the reconstruction of I-15, or the transit expansion. The Legacy Parkway may proceed without the reconstruction of I-15; the regulation views actions as connected if they "cannot or will not proceed unless other actions are taken previously or simultaneously." [40 C.F.R. § 1508.25(a)(1)(ii)]. Here, the I-15 project will occur, if at all, subsequently.

The Appellants argue that the three components of the Shared Solution require a single EIS. The FEIS estimates that the Legacy Parkway will facilitate 16 percent of the 2020 demand, the expansion to I-15 will facilitate 8 percent, and the expanded transit will facilitate 12 percent. Each component can serve its transportation purpose whether or not the other projects are built. The components, although interrelated as part of an overall transportation plan, should individually contribute to alleviation of the traffic problems in the Northern Corridor, and are therefore not improperly segmented as separate projects. Additionally, the FEIS does not state that the I-15 project lacks independent utility from the Legacy Project. It merely points out that, without the Legacy Parkway as an alternative route, large scale reconstruction and expansion of I-15 would impede traffic to the point that the short-term costs of the project would outweigh the long-term benefits. Moreover, there is some evidence of coordination insofar as preparation of the EIS is concerned. Given our deferential standard of review, we cannot conclude that the FEIS is deficient because the three aspects of the Shared Solution were not evaluated in a single EIS . . .

. . . .

Conclusion

We affirm in part and reverse and remand in part. We find that the FEIS was inadequate on the following grounds: elimination of the D&RG as an alternative based upon inadequate cost estimates, failure to consider alternative sequencing of the Shared Solution, failure to consider integration of the Legacy Parkway and transit, and failure to consider impacts to wildlife. . . .

decision

On remand, our injunction shall remain but the bond shall be exonerated.

Notes and Questions

1. The plaintiffs in *Utahns* sought judicial review of federal agency action. Can you identify the action(s) that the court reviewed? What standard of review did the Tenth Circuit apply?

2. Why did NEPA require preparation of an EIS for construction of the Legacy Parkway? How did the proposals for major federal actions significantly affecting the quality of the human environment fit into the Legacy Parkway project? How much

did the plaintiffs' objections to the EIS relate to the specifics of the proposed major federal actions?

3. The CEQ has emphasized that "[u]ltimately . . . it is not better documents but better decisions that count." What decision(s) did the *Utahns* plaintiffs seek to improve?

4. Did the federal action agencies involved in *Utahns* appropriately follow the prescribed procedures for preparing an EIS? Who actually prepared the EIS for the Legacy Parkway? How much time elapsed between (a) the proposal to build the Legacy Parkway and completion of the draft EIS, (b) completion of the draft EIS and completion of the final EIS, (c) completion of the final EIS and issuance of the federal agencies' RODs?

5. The Utah Department of Transportation (UDOT) awarded the contract for construction of the Legacy Parkway after the FEIS was issued but before the U.S. Army Corps of Engineers had issued a Record of Decision. Was doing so consistent with NEPA?

6. What was the significance of the Tenth Circuit's order granting an injunction pending appeal?

7. The plaintiffs alleged that the Legacy Parkway EIS was inadequate in numerous ways (some of which the Tenth Circuit addressed in portions of its opinion not included in the foregoing excerpt). Can you link each challenge discussed in the excerpt to a provision in NEPA or the CEQ's NEPA regulations? Do you agree with the court's disposition of each alleged inadequacy of the EIS?

8. Was the plaintiffs' approach good litigation strategy? Did it serve the purposes for which NEPA was enacted? On how many of their challenges did plaintiffs prevail? What relief did the plaintiffs obtain? Did the number of successful challenges affect the relief granted? Why do you think the court spent the time (and pages) to discuss all of the numerous plaintiffs' challenges that the court rejected?

9. Law professor Robert W. Adler, who represented one of the plaintiffs in *Utahns*, chronicled how the Legacy Parkway decision-making process unfolded after the Tenth Circuit decided the appeal. The court of appeals enjoined work on the parkway and remanded the case to the district court, which in turn remanded the RODs and EIS to the federal agencies as required by the appellate court's mandate. To address the inadequacies found in the FEIS, the agencies undertook to prepare a supplemental EIS (SEIS), starting with a new scoping process. A little more than two years later, the agencies issued a draft SEIS. In response, the plaintiffs submitted comments suggesting an alternative location and design for the road. The parties then negotiated a settlement agreement under which the road would be built along the originally proposed route but with more protection of wetlands and with many design changes to reduce the harm to wetland habitats and the migratory birds dependent on them. The settlement also provided for funding to initiate environmental impact analysis of expanding mass transit. The State of Utah enacted legislation ratifying the settlement agreement and the Tenth Circuit, at the parties' joint request, dissolved the injunction. Robert W. Adler, *In Defense of NEPA: The Case of the Legacy Parkway*, 26

J. Land Resources & Envtl. L. 297, 306–07 (2006). The Legacy Parkway opened to the public in September 2008. Joseph M. Dougherty, *The Legacy Parkway Is Done and It's Open to Commuters*, Deseret News (Sept. 14, 2008), http://www.deseretnews .com/article/700258693/The-Legacy-Parkway-is-done — and-its-open-to-commut ers.html?pg=all.

10. Suppose that, on remand, the federal agencies had issued a new EIS stating that the D&RG alignment was a reasonable alternative, that the Legacy Parkway project could be resequenced and integrated with mass transit, and that the Legacy Parkway as proposed would have severe impacts on wildlife more than 1,000 feet from the road — but that they had nevertheless decided to approve the proposed highway interchanges and to grant the required wetland-filling permit. What would be the result of a suit under NEPA challenging those decisions?

11. Some elected officials, including the then-governor of Utah (but not the then-mayor of Salt Lake City, who was a plaintiff in *Utahns*), strongly supported the original proposal for the Legacy Parkway. Adler, *supra*, at 302–03. For another example of a court enjoining a politically popular road project because of an inadequate EIS, see *Sierra Club v. U.S. Army Corps of Engineers*, 701 F.2d 1011 (2d Cir. 1983) (affirming injunction that voided a permit for filling in part of the Hudson River adjacent to Manhattan to build the proposed "Westway" superhighway). The entire saga of Westway — which was never built — is described in William W. Buzbee, Fighting Westway (2014).

12. The plaintiffs in *Utahns* alleged that one reason the EIS was inadequate was its failure to analyze the "cumulative impacts" of an eventual expansion of the Legacy Parkway to six lanes, in addition to analyzing the environmental impacts of the original proposal for a four-lane highway. The court acknowledged that the CEQ regulations require consideration of cumulative impacts, but concluded that it was not arbitrary and capricious for the U.S. Department of Transportation and the Army Corps of Engineers to omit this particular cumulative impacts analysis. Why did the court reach that conclusion? Did the court apply the correct test, in light of the CEQ's definition of cumulative impacts (40 C.F.R. § 1508.7, quoted in the excerpt, p. 180, above)?

The need for some type of cumulative impacts analysis to protect the integrity of the NEPA process is readily apparent: without consideration of cumulative impacts, the environment might suffer "death by a thousand cuts," with each incremental effect evading analysis because of its individual "insignificance." *See* 40 C.F.R. § 1508.7 (noting possible impacts of "individually minor but collectively significant actions"). It also makes sense that such analysis should not be limited to the effects of multiple *federal* actions, because federal and nonfederal actions could combine to have significant environmental effects. For example, the environmental impacts of a federal agency decision to destroy a small amount of federally owned tallgrass prairie or old-growth forest might be magnified if the agency considered that all similar habitats in private ownership were likely to be plowed under or clearcut. In the Legacy Parkway case, if the road had been built with the original design, it might have been possible for the Utah Department of Transportation to add two travel lanes without any further federal involvement (and therefore without further NEPA analysis). Thus the NEPA regulations, *id.*, call for analysis of the cumulative impacts of the proposed major federal action when added to other actions, even if a private person or a nonfederal agency undertakes those other actions.

On the other hand, absent some limiting principle, to require cumulative impacts analysis could mean (theoretically) that each EIS must situate the analyzed proposal for major federal action in the context of all anthropogenic modification of the environment, consistent with the ecological truism that "everything is connected to everything else." In practice, of course, nothing of the sort occurs. At least three limiting principles serve to keep the requirement for cumulative impacts analysis within reasonable bounds: the significance threshold (42 U.S.C. § 4332(2)(C); 40 C.F.R. 1508.27), the scoping process (42 U.S.C. § 1508.25), and the definition of cumulative impacts that requires consideration of future actions only if they are "reasonably foreseeable" (40 C.F.R. § 1508.7). In *Utahns*, when the original FEIS was prepared, was expansion of the Legacy Parkway to six lanes reasonably foreseeable?

Environmental impacts that by their very nature result from the incremental contributions of many actions present particularly difficult challenges for cumulative impacts analysis. Disruption of the global climate by emissions of greenhouse gases (see Chapter 6) is a paradigmatic example.

Increased global temperature is a function of worldwide concentration of greenhouse gases that enter the atmosphere in huge quantity and from innumerable sources. With the possible exception of regulatory actions directly affecting emissions from important sectors of the economy such as electricity generation or transportation (see p. 402, below), no single action of a United States government agency by itself is likely to significantly alter the trajectory of the changing climate. On the other hand, the United States emits more greenhouse gases than any other nation except China. In the aggregate, federal agency policies and projects surely can have a significant effect on climate even if almost no individual agency action does so. In light of the magnitude of the potential consequences of climate disruption, it is hard to imagine an effect on the human environment for which a cumulative impacts analysis would be more important. But then again, the fate of the climate depends on the decisions and actions of governments and people around the world. It is hard to imagine analyzing all these "past, present, and reasonably foreseeable future actions," 40 C.F.R. § 1508.7, in an EIS for, say, a permit to fill wetlands to build a new bridge. How, if at all, should agencies apply NEPA to the climate change impacts of their proposed actions?

In 2006, the National Highway Transportation Safety Administration (NHTSA) took one approach when it promulgated a rule setting corporate average fuel economy (CAFE) standards for light trucks. NHTSA issued a FONSI after preparing an Environmental Assessment that noted that the new rule would have a very small effect on total United States emissions of greenhouse gases. On a challenge by a coalition of environmental organizations and states, the Ninth Circuit held:

that the EA's cumulative impacts analysis is inadequate. . . . The impact of greenhouse gas emissions on climate change is precisely the kind of cumulative impacts analysis that NEPA requires agencies to conduct. Any given rule setting a CAFE standard might have an 'individually minor' effect on the environment, but these rules are 'collectively significant actions taking place over a period of time.'"

Center for Biological Diversity v. NHTSA, 538 F.3d 1172, 1216–17 (9th Cir. 2008). The court ordered a remand to NHTSA so the agency could prepare a revised EA and, if necessary, an EIS. *Id.* at 1227.

After President Obama took office, the CEQ devoted considerable attention to the problem of how to address climate disruption in NEPA analyses. After inviting and considering public comments on two draft documents, just a few months before the end of the Obama Administration the CEQ issued a Final Guidance "to assist Federal agencies in their consideration of the effects of greenhouse gas (GHG) emissions and climate change when evaluating proposed Federal actions in accordance with" NEPA. Memorandum from Christina Goldfuss, Council on Environmental Quality, *Final Guidance for Federal Departments and Agencies on Consideration of Greenhouse Gas Emissions and the Effects of Climate Change in National Environmental Policy Act Reviews* 1 (Aug. 1, 2016) (hereafter "*NEPA Climate Guidance*"). Like other "guidance documents," the NEPA Climate Guidance disclaimed any enforceable or binding regulatory effect, offering "recommendations" instead. *Id.* at 1–2 n.3.

CEQ recommended that agencies consider the effects that a proposed action may have on GHG emissions (and therefore on climate) as well as the effects that a changing climate may have on a proposed action and its environmental impact. *NEPA Climate Guidance* at 4. If possible, agencies should use quantitative estimates of the proposed action's effects on GHG emissions in assessing the proposed action's effect on climate. *Id.* CEQ continued:

> This guidance does not establish any particular quantity of GHG emissions as "significantly" affecting the quality of the human environment . . . . Climate change results from the incremental addition of GHG emissions from millions of individual sources, which collectively have a large impact on a global scale . . . . Therefore, a statement that emissions from a proposed Federal action represent only a small fraction of global emissions is essentially a statement about the nature of the climate change challenge, and is not an appropriate basis for deciding whether or to what extent to consider climate change impacts under NEPA . . . . When considering GHG emissions and their significance, agencies should use appropriate tools and methodologies for quantifying GHG emissions and comparing GHG emissions across alternative scenarios . . . . The agency should focus on significant potential effects and conduct an analysis that is proportionate to the environmental consequences of the proposed action. Agencies can rely on basic NEPA principles to determine and explain the reasonable parameters of their analyses in order

to disclose the reasonably foreseeable effects that may result from their proposed action . . . .

All GHG emissions contribute to cumulative climate change impacts. However, for most Federal agency actions CEQ does not expect that an EIS would be required based *solely* on the global significance of cumulative impacts of GHG emissions, as it would not be consistent with the rule of reason to require the preparation of an EIS for every Federal action that may cause GHG emissions regardless of the magnitude of those emissions . . . .

[T]he analysis of the effects of GHG emissions is essentially a cumulative effects analysis that is subsumed within the general analysis and discussion of climate change impacts. Therefore, direct and indirect effects analysis for GHG emissions will adequately address the cumulative impacts for climate change from the proposed action and its alternatives and a separate cumulative effects analysis for GHG emissions is not needed.

NEPA Climate Guidance at 9–11, 14, 17. Did the NEPA Climate Guidance embody a sound solution to the problem? Would the approach that NHTSA took in the EA for its 2006 CAFE regulations have been consistent with the NEPA Climate Guidance?

Despite the disclaimer of any binding effect, agencies probably would have endeavored to follow the recommendations of the NEPA Climate Guidance, and courts probably would have accorded those recommendations considerable weight — had that document remained in effect. At the beginning of the Trump Administration, however, CEQ was ordered to rescind the NEPA Climate Guidance. Exec. Order 13,783, 82 Fed. Reg. 16,093 (Mar. 28, 2017). With the NEPA Climate Guidance rescinded, how should agencies address climate change impacts in their EAs and EISs? How should courts assess whether the agencies' chosen approaches comply with NEPA?

13. At the end of the NEPA Climate Guidance, the CEQ clarified that it did "not expect agencies to apply this guidance to concluded NEPA reviews and actions." *NEPA Climate Guidance* at 33. Recall, however, that the CEQ regulations require an agency to supplement a completed EIS under certain circumstances. In *Utahns*, the agencies completed a supplemental EIS (SEIS) to comply with the Ninth Circuit's judgment. But aside from such a circumstance, when must an agency prepare an SEIS, and when may an agency let a finished EIS and ROD stay finished without supplementation? The CEQ regulations and the Supreme Court have provided an answer.

Marsh v. Oregon Natural Resources Council
490 U.S. 360 (1989)

Justice STEVENS:

This case . . . arises out of a controversial decision to construct a dam at Elk Creek in the Rogue River Basin in southwest Oregon . . . . [I]t presents the question whether information developed after the completion of the EIS requires that a supplemental EIS be prepared before construction of the dam may continue.

I

In the 1930's in response to recurring floods in the Rogue River Basin, federal and state agencies began planning a major project to control the water supply in the Basin. In 1961 a multiagency study recommended the construction of three large dams: the Lost Creek Dam on the Rogue River, the Applegate Dam on the Applegate River, and the Elk Creek Dam on the Elk Creek near its confluence with the Rogue River. The following year, Congress authorized the Army Corps of Engineers (Corps) to construct the project in accordance with the recommendations of the 1961 study. The Lost Creek Dam was completed in 1977, and the Applegate Dam was completed in 1981.

. . . .

In 1971, the Corps completed its EIS for the Elk Creek portion of the three-dam project and began development by acquiring 26,000 acres of land and relocating residents, a county road, and utilities. Acknowledging incomplete information, the EIS recommended that further studies concerning the project's likely effect on turbidity be developed. The results of these studies were discussed in a draft supplemental EIS completed in 1975. However, at the request of the Governor of Oregon, further work on the project was suspended, and the supplemental EIS was not filed to make it possible to analyze the actual consequences of the construction of the Lost Creek Dam, which was nearing completion, before continuing with the Elk Creek project. Following that analysis and the receipt of a statement from the Governor that he was "extremely interested in pursuing construction of the Elk Creek Dam," the Corps completed and released its final Environmental Impact Statement, Supplement No. 1 (FEISS), in December 1980.

Because the Rogue River is one of the Nation's premier fishing grounds, the FEISS paid special heed to the effects the dam might have on water quality, fish production, and angling . . . . Using computer simulation models, the 1974 study predicted that the Elk Creek Dam might, at times, increase the temperature of the Rogue River by one to two degrees Fahrenheit and its turbidity by one to three JTU's [Jackson Turbidity Units]. The 1979 study took a second look at the potential effect of the Elk Creek Dam on turbidity and, by comparing the 1974 study's predictions concerning the effects of the Lost Creek Dam with actual measurements taken after that dam became operational, it "increased technical confidence in the mathematical model predictions . . . and reinforced the conclusions of the 1974 [study]." Based on these studies, the FEISS predicted that changes in the "turbidity regime" would not have any major effect on fish production, but that the combined effect of the Lost Creek and Elk Creek Dams on the turbidity of the Rogue River might, on occasion, impair fishing . . . .

. . . .

On February 19, 1982, after reviewing the FEISS, the Corps' Division Engineer made a formal decision to proceed with construction of the Elk Creek Dam, "subject to the approval of funds by the United States Congress." . . . In August 1985, Congress appropriated the necessary funds. The dam is now about one-third completed and the creek has been rechanneled through the dam.

II

In October 1985, four Oregon nonprofit corporations filed this action in the United States District Court for the District of Oregon seeking to enjoin construction of the Elk Creek Dam. [They claimed] . . . that the Corps violated NEPA by failing . . . to prepare a second supplemental EIS to review information developed after 1980.

After conducting a hearing on respondents' motion for a preliminary injunction, the District Judge denied relief . . . .

The new information relied upon by respondents is found in two documents. The first, an internal memorandum prepared by two Oregon Department of Fish and Wildlife (ODFW) biologists based upon a draft ODFW study, suggested that the dam will adversely affect downstream fishing, and the second, a soil survey prepared by the United States Soil Conservation Service (SCS), contained information that might be taken to indicate greater downstream turbidity than did the FEISS. As to both documents, the District Judge concluded that the Corps acted reasonably in relying on the opinions of independent and Corps experts discounting the significance of the new information . . . .

The Court of Appeals reversed . . . . With regard to the failure to prepare a second supplemental EIS, the Court of Appeals concluded that the ODFW and SCS documents brought to light "significant new information" . . . and that the Corps' experts failed to evaluate the new information with sufficient care. The court thus concluded that a second supplemental EIS should have been prepared . . . .

III

The subject of postdecision supplemental environmental impact statements is not expressly addressed in NEPA. Preparation of such statements, however, is at times necessary to satisfy the Act's "action-forcing" purpose. NEPA does not work by mandating that agencies achieve particular substantive environmental results. Rather, NEPA promotes its sweeping commitment to "prevent or eliminate damage to the environment and biosphere" by focusing Government and public attention on the environmental effects of proposed agency action. By so focusing agency attention, NEPA ensures that the agency will not act on incomplete information, only to regret its decision after it is too late to correct. Similarly, the broad dissemination of information mandated by NEPA permits the public and other government agencies to react to the effects of a proposed action at a meaningful time. It would be incongruous with this approach to environmental protection, and with the Act's manifest concern with preventing uninformed action, for the blinders to adverse environmental effects, once unequivocally removed, to be restored prior to the completion of agency action simply because the relevant proposal has received initial approval . . . . [A]lthough "it would make sense to hold NEPA inapplicable at some point in the life of a project, because the agency would no longer have a meaningful opportunity to *weigh* the benefits of the project versus the detrimental effects on the environment," up to that point, "NEPA cases have generally required agencies to file environmental impact statements when the remaining governmental action would be environmentally 'significant.'"

This reading of the statute is supported by Council on Environmental Quality (CEQ) and Corps regulations, both of which make plain that at times supplementation is required. The CEQ regulations, which we have held are entitled to substantial deference, impose a duty on all federal agencies to prepare supplements to either draft or final EIS's if there "are significant new circumstances or information relevant to environmental concerns and bearing on the proposed action or its impacts." [40 C.F.R. § 1502.9(c) (1987)]. Similarly, the Corps' own NEPA implementing regulations require the preparation of a supplemental EIS if "new significant impact information, criteria or circumstances relevant to environmental considerations impact on the recommended plan or proposed action." [33 C.F.R. § 230.11(b) (1987)].

The parties are in essential agreement concerning the standard that governs an agency's decision whether to prepare a supplemental EIS. They agree that an agency should apply a "rule of reason," and the cases . . . make clear that an agency need not supplement an EIS every time new information comes to light after the EIS is finalized. To require otherwise would render agency decisionmaking intractable, always awaiting updated information only to find the new information outdated by the time a decision is made. On the other hand, and as the petitioners concede, NEPA does require that agencies take a "hard look" at the environmental effects of their planned action, even after a proposal has received initial approval. Application of the "rule of reason" thus turns on the value of the new information to the still pending decision-making process. In this respect the decision whether to prepare a supplemental EIS is similar to the decision whether to prepare an EIS in the first instance: If there remains "major Federal actio[n]" to occur, and if the new information is sufficient to show that the remaining action will "affec[t] the quality of the human environment" in a significant manner or to a significant extent not already considered, a supplemental EIS must be prepared.

[The court held that judicial review of an agency's decision not to prepare a supplemental EIS is governed by the "arbitrary and capricious" standard of the Administrative Procedure Act, 5 U.S.C. § 706(2)(A).] . . . Accordingly, as long as the Corps' decision not to supplement the FEISS was not "arbitrary or capricious," it should not be set aside.

. . . . When specialists express conflicting views, an agency must have discretion to rely on the reasonable opinions of its own qualified experts even if, as an original matter, a court might find contrary views more persuasive. On the other hand, in the context of reviewing a decision not to supplement an EIS, courts should not automatically defer to the agency's express reliance on an interest in finality without carefully reviewing the record and satisfying themselves that the agency has made a reasoned decision based on its evaluation of the significance—or lack of significance—of the new information. A contrary approach would not simply render judicial review generally meaningless, but would be contrary to the demand that courts ensure that agency decisions are founded on a reasoned evaluation "of the relevant factors."

IV

Respondents' argument that significant new information required the preparation of a second supplemental EIS rests on two written documents. The first of the documents is the so-called "Cramer Memorandum," an intraoffice memorandum prepared on February 21, 1985, by two scientists employed by ODFW. The Cramer Memorandum, in turn, relied on a draft ODFW study describing the effects of the Lost Creek Dam on fish production. The second document is actually a series of maps prepared in 1982 by SCS to illustrate the composition of soil near the Elk Creek shoreline. The information was provided to the Corps for use in managing the project . . . . The Corps responded to the claim that these documents demonstrate the need for supplementation of the FEISS by preparing a formal Supplemental Information Report [SIR], dated January 10, 1986. The SIR explained: "While it is clear based upon our review that this information does not require additional NEPA documentation, Corps regulations provide that a Supplemental Information Report can be used to disseminate information on points of concern regarding environmental impacts set forth in the EIS."

The significance of the Cramer Memorandum and the SCS survey is subject to some doubt. Before respondents commenced this litigation in October 1985, no one had suggested that either document constituted the kind of new information that made it necessary or appropriate to supplement the FEISS . . . . Yet, even if both documents had given rise to prompt expressions of concern, there are good reasons for concluding that they did not convey significant new information requiring supplementation of the FEISS.

. . . .

. . . [T]he Cramer Memorandum reported that the authors of the draft ODFW study had found that warming of the Rogue River caused by the Lost Creek Dam had reduced the survival of spring chinook fry; however, the extent of that reduction was not stated, nor did the memorandum estimate the extent of warming to be expected due to closure of the Elk Creek Dam . . . . The authors of the memorandum concluded that because the Elk Creek Dam is likely to increase the temperature of the Rogue River, further evaluation of this effect should be completed "before ODFW sets its final position on this project."

The Corps' response to this concern in its SIR acknowledged that the "biological reasoning is sound and has been recognized for some time," but then explained why the concern was exaggerated . . . .

. . . .

In . . . concluding that the Cramer Memorandum did not present significant new information requiring supplementation of the FEISS, the Corps carefully scrutinized the proffered information. Moreover, in disputing the accuracy and significance of this information, the Corps did not simply rely on its own experts. Rather, two independent experts hired by the Corps to evaluate the ODFW study on which the Cramer Memorandum was premised found significant fault in the methodology and conclusions of the study . . . .

The Court of Appeals also expressed concern that the SCS survey, by demonstrating that the soil content in the Elk Creek watershed is different than assumed in the FEISS, suggested a greater turbidity potential than indicated in the FEISS . . . . Although the SIR did not expressly comment on the SCS survey, in light of the in-depth 1974 and 1979 studies, its conclusion that "the turbidity effects are not expected to differ from those described in the 1980 EISS" surely provided a legitimate reason for not preparing a supplemental FEISS to discuss the subject of turbidity.

There is little doubt that if all of the information contained in the Cramer Memorandum and SCS survey was both new and accurate, the Corps would have been required to prepare a second supplemental EIS. It is also clear that, regardless of its eventual assessment of the significance of this information, the Corps had a duty to take a hard look at the proffered evidence. However, having done so and having determined based on careful scientific analysis that the new information was of exaggerated importance, the Corps acted within the dictates of NEPA in concluding that supplementation was unnecessary. Even if another decisionmaker might have reached a contrary result, it was surely not "a clear error of judgment" for the Corps to have found that the new and accurate information contained in the documents was not significant and that the significant information was not new and accurate. As the SIR demonstrates, the Corps conducted a reasoned evaluation of the relevant information and reached a decision that, although perhaps disputable, was not "arbitrary or capricious."

. . . .

Judicial deference

Notes and Questions

1. In *Marsh*, the Supreme Court articulated two different types of judicial deference to administrative agencies. First, the Court gave deference to the NEPA implementing regulations promulgated by the CEQ and the Corps. Second, in applying the arbitrary and capricious standard, the Court gave deference to the Corps' decision not to prepare a second supplemental EIS. Which of these two forms of deference was more significant to the outcome in *Marsh*? Which would be more significant in later cases in which *Marsh* was applied as precedent?

2. The Supreme Court's standard for mandatory supplementation of an EIS is easy enough to restate, but can be troublesome to apply. In March 2014, the Federal Transit Administration (FTA) issued a ROD approving (and facilitating federal funding for) a controversial light rail project, the Purple Line, to be built by the State of Maryland in the suburbs of Washington, D.C. In August 2016, just days before the planned award of a $900 million federal grant for the project, a federal district judge ordered vacatur of the ROD. The Purple Line was designed in part to connect several radial spokes in Washington's downtown-to-suburbs subway system; the FEIS projected that more than a quarter of Purple Line riders would transfer between the light rail line and the subway. The court held that a series of highly publicized safety problems on the subway system, and declining subway ridership for several years in a row after completion of the studies on which the FEIS was based, undermined the

ridership projection and required an SEIS. *Friends of the Capital Crescent Trail v. Federal Transit Admin.*, 200 F. Supp. 3d 248, 253–54 (D.D.C. 2016). Why would a decrease in projected ridership require an SEIS? Did the court correctly apply the *Marsh* standard?

The State of Maryland, arguing that vacating the ROD would greatly increase the cost of the light rail line and could jeopardize the federal grant and therefore the entire project, asked the court to modify its judgment to allow the ROD to remain in effect while the FTA considered *whether* an SEIS was needed. The court agreed that the FTA, rather than the court, should make the initial decision about the need for an SEIS. The court therefore ordered the FTA to prepare, "as expeditiously as possible," what amounted to a supplemental environmental assessment, and set a schedule for further briefing in the event FTA were to decide against preparing an SEIS. *Friends of the Capital Crescent Trail v. Federal Transit Admin.*, 218 F. Supp. 3d 53, 59 (D.D.C. 2016). But the court refused to reinstate the FTA's prior ROD pending the outcome of the additional environmental assessment. The court reasoned that, even though vacating the ROD could disrupt the project, it would be even more harmful if work on the Purple Line were to proceed, "only to have the agency determine as a result of the required analysis that some other alternative is now preferable . . . . Vacatur ensures that the project will proceed only with the benefit of a fully fleshed-out consideration of the issues required by NEPA." *Id.*

3. Environmental impact analysis is, fundamentally, an exercise in prediction. What if an agency made a decision after a fully adequate EIS, but during implementation of the decision it became apparent that the EIS's prediction of environmental impacts and analysis of alternatives was incorrect — perhaps because the real environmental impacts were much worse than predicted, because the project's benefits were much smaller than predicted, or because the project's environmental impacts were not bad enough to justify the amount of mitigation that the agency decided to require? Would NEPA provide a remedy in such circumstances?

4. Similar questions may arise with respect to mitigation measures that an agency relies on to justify a decision to undertake an action that otherwise might cause unacceptable environmental impacts. Recall that an EIS must discuss mitigation measures. 40 C.F.R. § 1508.25(b)(3). Mitigation includes, as you might expect, avoiding or minimizing the impact by not taking or by reducing the magnitude of all or parts of a proposed action. Mitigation can also include measures taken after an action causes environmental impact, such as restoring a damaged environment or replacing or providing a substitute for a damaged or destroyed resource. *Id.* § 1508.20 (defining mitigation). In *Utahns*, for example, the original ROD, to mitigate the loss of wetlands caused by construction of the Legacy Parkway, called for preserving other wetland areas where building might otherwise occur in the future.

The Supreme Court held in *Methow Valley* (p. 118, above) that although an EIS must analyze mitigation options, NEPA does not require an agency to develop a plan for implementing mitigation measures or to include mitigation in the agency's final decision. Often, however, agencies do include mitigation measures in their chosen agency actions or as conditions of permits or grants to non-federal actors. The CEQ regulations provide that "[m]itigation and other conditions . . . committed as part of the decision shall be implemented . . . ." 40 C.F.R. § 1505.3. Suppose a federal agency commits to specific mitigation actions in its ROD but then (for whatever reason) does not follow through, or fails to enforce a mitigation requirement against a permittee or grantee who does not comply with one. Would NEPA provide a remedy?

V. Remedies for NEPA Violations

Many types of litigation present courts with difficult choices about what relief to order for a prevailing plaintiff. In environmental litigation, even for common-law claims for environmental harm, the choice may be particularly stark: can a plaintiff who wins a nuisance claim against an industrial polluter of plaintiff's property win an injunction to stop the pollution, or only money damages to compensate for the harm? *Compare Madison v. Ducktown Sulphur, Copper & Iron Co.*, 83 S.W. 658 (Tenn. 1904) (limiting farmers whose lands were ruined by emissions from nearby smelters to damages as a remedy) *with Georgia v. Tennessee Copper Co.*, 206 U.S. 230 (1907) (holding that the State of Georgia, having established a claim for public nuisance, would be entitled to an injunction if smelters failed to abate the nuisance). As you saw in Chapter 2, the appropriateness of injunctive relief can also be controversial for claims brought under modern environmental statutes.

The Supreme Court's interpretation that NEPA's mandate is purely procedural further sharpens the focus on the appropriate relief to grant a prevailing plaintiff. A NEPA plaintiff necessarily alleges procedural defects in an agency's decision-making process. The plaintiff would have little incentive to sue to vindicate NEPA's procedural requirements, however, unless the plaintiff also disagreed with the agency's actual decision — the substantive outcome of the decision-making process. But because NEPA does not direct substantive outcomes, the typical remedy for a NEPA procedural default is more procedure: prepare an EA to correct an improper use of a categorical exclusion, prepare a new EA to correct an EA that did not adequately justify a FONSI, prepare an EIS to correct an unsupportable FONSI, or prepare a new EIS or SEIS to correct an inadequate first EIS.

Sometimes added procedure suffices to stop or change implementation of the agency's decision, because circumstances change, or because the agency reconsiders, or because public or political pressure forces the agency to reconsider. But sometimes an agency is certain of the correctness of its decision and determined to proceed. A plaintiff confronting such an agency — or that believes it is confronting such an agency — typically seeks an injunction prohibiting the agency from implementing its decision until mandatory NEPA analyses are correctly completed. In *Utahns*, for example (p. 173, above), the Tenth Circuit did not simply order the federal agencies to prepare a new EIS; the court also enjoined construction of the Legacy Parkway until NEPA procedures had been properly followed.

usual remedy is more procedure

Moreover, even before the *Utahns* plaintiffs obtained that permanent injunction, they sought and obtained a temporary injunction to maintain the *status quo* while the appeal was pending. Such preliminary relief can be critically important, because implementation of the challenged agency decision can render a NEPA claim moot. *See, e.g., Bayou Liberty Ass'n, Inc. v. U.S. Army Corps of Engineers*, 217 F.3d 393 (5th Cir. 2000) (directing district court to dismiss, as moot, a NEPA claim challenging the Corps' FONSI for issuance of a permit to fill and build upon wetlands, because the wetlands were filled and construction completed during the pendency of plaintiff's appeal from the district court's denial of plaintiff's motion for a preliminary injunction).

In the decision that follows, the Supreme Court considered the standards for injunctive relief to remedy NEPA violations. The injunction reviewed was a permanent injunction after a judgment on the merits, but note the important role played by the plaintiffs' failure to obtain early, temporary injunctive relief.

Monsanto Co. v. Geertson Seed Farms
561 U.S. 139 (2010)

Justice ALITO:

   . . . .

The Plant Protection Act (PPA) provides that the Secretary of the Department of Agriculture (USDA) may issue regulations "to prevent the introduction of plant pests into the United States or the dissemination of plant pests within the United States." The Secretary has delegated that authority to APHIS, a division of the USDA . . . . APHIS has promulgated regulations . . . [under which] certain genetically engineered plants are presumed to be "plant pests"—and thus "regulated articles" under the PPA—until APHIS determines otherwise. However, any person may petition APHIS for a determination that a regulated article does not present a plant pest risk and therefore should not be subject to the applicable regulations . . . .

   . . . .

This case involves Roundup Ready Alfalfa (RRA), a kind of alfalfa crop that has been genetically engineered to be tolerant of glyphosate, the active ingredient of the herbicide Roundup. Petitioner Monsanto Company (Monsanto) owns the intellectual property rights to RRA . . . .

   . . . .

APHIS initially classified RRA as a regulated article, but in 2004 petitioners sought nonregulated status for two strains of RRA. In response, APHIS prepared a draft EA assessing the likely environmental impact of the requested deregulation. It then published a notice in the Federal Register advising the public of the deregulation petition and soliciting public comments on its draft EA. After considering the hundreds of public comments that it received, APHIS issued a Finding of No Significant Impact and decided to deregulate RRA unconditionally and without preparing an EIS . . . .

Approximately eight months after APHIS granted RRA nonregulated status, respondents (two conventional alfalfa seed farms and environmental groups concerned with food safety) filed this action against the Secretary of Agriculture and certain other officials in Federal District Court, challenging APHIS's decision to completely deregulate RRA . . . . Respondents did not seek preliminary injunctive relief pending resolution of those claims. Hence, RRA enjoyed nonregulated status for approximately two years. During that period, more than 3,000 farmers in 48 States planted an estimated 220,000 acres of RRA.

. . . . [T]he District Court held that APHIS violated NEPA by deregulating RRA without first preparing an EIS. In particular, the court found that APHIS's EA failed to answer substantial questions concerning two broad consequences of its proposed action: first, the extent to which complete deregulation would lead to the transmission of the gene conferring glyphosate tolerance from RRA to organic and conventional alfalfa; and, second, the extent to which the introduction of RRA would contribute to the development of Roundup-resistant weeds . . . .

. . . . The court then asked the parties to submit proposed judgments embodying their preferred means of remedying the NEPA violation. APHIS's proposed judgment would have ordered the agency to prepare an EIS, vacated the agency's deregulation decision, and replaced that decision with the terms of the judgment itself[, which] would have permitted the continued planting of RRA pending completion of the EIS, subject to [certain] restrictions . . . .

The District Court rejected APHIS's proposed judgment. In its preliminary injunction, the District Court prohibited almost all future planting of RRA pending APHIS's completion of the required EIS. But in order to minimize the harm to farmers who had relied on APHIS's deregulation decision, the court expressly allowed those who had already purchased RRA to plant their seeds until March 30, 2007. [The District Court then entered a permanent injunction and judgment, described below.] . . . .

[Petitioners] appealed, challenging the scope of the relief granted but not disputing the existence of a NEPA violation. A divided panel of the Court of Appeals for the Ninth Circuit affirmed . . . .

. . . .

We granted certiorari . . . .

The District Court sought to remedy APHIS's NEPA violation in three ways: First, it vacated the agency's decision completely deregulating RRA; second, it enjoined APHIS from deregulating RRA, in whole or in part, pending completion of the mandated EIS; and third, it entered a nationwide injunction prohibiting almost all future planting of RRA. Because petitioners and the Government do not argue otherwise, we assume without deciding that the District Court acted lawfully in vacating the deregulation decision. We therefore address only the latter two aspects of the District Court's judgment . . . .

"[A] plaintiff seeking a permanent injunction must satisfy a four-factor test before a court may grant such relief. A plaintiff must demonstrate: (1) that it has suffered an irreparable injury; (2) that remedies available at law, such as monetary damages, are inadequate to compensate for that injury; (3) that, considering the balance of hardships between the plaintiff and defendant, a remedy in equity is warranted; and (4) that the public interest would not be disserved by a permanent injunction." The traditional four-factor test applies when a plaintiff seeks a permanent injunction to remedy a NEPA violation.

. . . .

. . . . It is not enough for a court considering a request for injunctive relief to ask whether there is a good reason why an injunction should *not* issue; rather, a court must determine that an injunction *should* issue under the traditional four-factor test set out above.

. . . .

We first consider whether the District Court erred in enjoining APHIS from partially deregulating RRA during the pendency of the EIS process.

The relevant part of the District Court's judgment states that, "[b]efore granting Monsanto's deregulation petition, *even in part,* the federal defendants shall prepare an environmental impact statement." . . .

In our view, none of the traditional four factors governing the entry of permanent injunctive relief supports the District Court's injunction prohibiting partial deregulation . . . .

Respondents in this case brought suit under the APA to challenge a particular agency order: APHIS's decision to *completely* deregulate RRA. The District Court held that the order in question was procedurally defective, and APHIS decided not to appeal that determination. At that point, it was for the agency to decide whether and to what extent it would pursue a *partial* deregulation. If the agency found, on the basis of a new EA, that a limited and temporary deregulation satisfied applicable statutory and regulatory requirements, it could proceed with such a deregulation even if it had not yet finished the onerous EIS required for complete deregulation. If and when the agency were to issue a partial deregulation order, any party aggrieved by that order could bring a separate suit under the Administrative Procedure Act to challenge the particular deregulation attempted.

In this case, APHIS apparently sought to "streamline" the proceedings by asking the District Court to craft a remedy that, in effect, would have partially deregulated RRA until such time as the agency had finalized the EIS needed for a complete deregulation . . . .

The District Court may well have acted within its discretion in refusing to craft a judicial remedy that would have *authorized* the continued planting and harvesting of RRA while the EIS is being prepared. It does not follow, however, that the District Court was within its rights in *enjoining* APHIS from allowing such planting and harvesting pursuant to the authority vested in the agency by law . . . .

. . . .

. . . [I]t is clear that the order enjoining any deregulation whatsoever does not satisfy the traditional four-factor test for granting permanent injunctive relief. Most importantly, respondents cannot show that they will suffer irreparable injury if APHIS is allowed to proceed with any partial deregulation, for at least two independent reasons.

First, if and when APHIS pursues a partial deregulation that arguably runs afoul of NEPA, respondents may file a new suit challenging such action and seeking appropriate preliminary relief. Accordingly, a permanent injunction is not now needed to guard against any present or imminent risk of likely irreparable harm.

Second, a partial deregulation need not cause respondents any injury at all, much less irreparable injury; if the scope of the partial deregulation is sufficiently limited, the risk of gene flow to their crops could be virtually nonexistent. For example, suppose that APHIS deregulates RRA only in a remote part of the country in which respondents neither grow nor intend to grow non-genetically-engineered alfalfa, and in which no conventional alfalfa farms are currently located. Suppose further that APHIS issues an accompanying administrative order mandating isolation distances so great as to eliminate any appreciable risk of gene flow to the crops of conventional farmers who might someday choose to plant in the surrounding area. Finally, suppose that APHIS concludes in a new EA that its limited deregulation would not pose a significant risk of gene flow or harmful weed development, and that the agency adopts a plan to police vigorously compliance with its administrative order in the limited geographic area in question. It is hard to see how respondents could show that such a limited deregulation would cause them likely irreparable injury . . . . In any case, the District Court's order prohibiting *any* partial deregulation improperly relieves respondents of their burden to make the requisite evidentiary showing.

. . . .

We now turn to petitioners' claim that the District Court erred in entering a nationwide injunction against planting RRA . . . . We agree that the District Court's injunction against planting went too far . . . .

First, the impropriety of the District Court's broad injunction against planting flows from the impropriety of its injunction against partial deregulation. If APHIS may partially deregulate RRA before preparing a full-blown EIS—a question that we need not and do not decide here—farmers should be able to grow and sell RRA in accordance with that agency determination. Because it was inappropriate for the District Court to foreclose even the possibility of a partial and temporary deregulation, it necessarily follows that it was likewise inappropriate to enjoin any and all parties from acting in accordance with the terms of such a deregulation decision.

Second, respondents have represented to this Court that the District Court's injunction against planting does not have any meaningful practical effect independent of its vacatur. An injunction is a drastic and extraordinary remedy, which should not be granted as a matter of course. If a less drastic remedy (such as partial or complete vacatur of APHIS's deregulation decision) was sufficient to redress respondents' injury, no recourse to the additional and extraordinary relief of an injunction was warranted . . . .

In sum, the District Court abused its discretion in enjoining APHIS from effecting a partial deregulation and in prohibiting the possibility of planting in accordance with the terms of such a deregulation. Given those errors, this Court need not express any view on whether injunctive relief of some kind was available to respondents on the record before us . . . .

Justice STEVENS, dissenting:

The Court does not dispute the District Court's critical findings of fact: First, Roundup Ready Alfalfa (RRA) can contaminate other plants. Second, even planting in a controlled setting had led to contamination in some instances. Third, the Animal and Plant Health Inspection Service (APHIS) has limited ability to monitor or enforce limitations on planting. And fourth, genetic contamination from RRA could decimate farmers' livelihoods and the American alfalfa market for years to come. Instead, the majority faults the District Court for "enjoining APHIS from partially deregulating RRA."

In my view, the District Court may not have actually ordered such relief, and we should not so readily assume that it did. Regardless, the District Court did not abuse its discretion when . . . it issued the order now before us . . . .

. . . .

Despite substantial evidence that RRA genes could transfer to other plants, APHIS issued a Finding of No Significant Impact and agreed to deregulate RRA "unconditionally." With no EIS to wait for and no regulation blocking its path, petitioners began selling RRA. Farmers and environmental groups swiftly brought this lawsuit to challenge APHIS's decision to deregulate, raising claims under NEPA and other statutes.

The District Court carefully reviewed a long record and found that "APHIS's reasons for concluding" that the risks of genetic contamination are low were "not 'convincing.'" . . . In light of the "acknowledged" risk of RRA gene transmission and the potential "impact on the development of Roundup resistant weeds," the court concluded that there was a significant possibility of serious environmental harm, and granted summary judgment for the plaintiffs.

At this point, the question of remedy arose . . . .

While the District Court considered the [parties' and intervenors'] proposed judgments, it issued a preliminary injunction. Ordinarily, the court explained, the remedy for failure to conduct an EIS is to vacate the permit that was unlawfully given — the result of which, in this case, would be to prohibit any use of RRA. But this case presented a special difficulty: Following APHIS's unlawful deregulation order, some farmers had begun planting genetically modified RRA. In its preliminary injunction, the District Court ordered that no new RRA could be planted until APHIS completed the EIS or the court determined that some other relief was appropriate. But, so as to protect these farmers, the court declined to prohibit them from "harvesting, using, or selling" any crops they had already planted. And "to minimize the harm to those growers who intend to imminently plant Roundup Ready alfalfa," the court permitted "[t]hose growers who intend to plant [RRA] in the next three weeks and have already purchased the seed" to go ahead and plant. Essentially, the court grandfathered in those farmers who had relied, in good faith, on APHIS's actions.

. . . . The parties submitted "competing proposals for permanent injunctive relief." The plaintiffs requested that no one—not even the grandfathered-in farmers—be allowed to plant, grow, or harvest RRA until the full EIS had been prepared. APHIS and the intervenors instead sought a remedy that would "facilitat[e] the continued and dramatic growth" of RRA: a "partial deregulation" order that would permit planting subject to certain conditions, such as specified minimum distances between RRA and conventional alfalfa and special cleaning requirements for equipment used on the genetically modified crop.

The court adopted a compromise. First, it declined to adopt the APHIS—Monsanto proposal . . . . The "partial deregulation" proposed by petitioners, the court noted, was really "deregulation with certain conditions," which, for the same reasons given in the court's earlier order, requires an EIS . . . .

Next, the court rejected the plaintiffs' proposed remedy of "enjoin[ing] the harvesting and sale of already planted" RRA. Although any planting or harvesting of RRA poses a contamination risk, the court reasoned that the equities were different for those farmers who had already invested time and money planting RRA in good-faith reliance on APHIS's deregulation order . . . .

As to all other RRA, however, the court sided with the plaintiffs and enjoined planting during the pendency of the EIS. Balancing the equities, the court explained that the risk of harm was great. "[C]ontamination cannot be undone; it will destroy the crops of those farmers who do not sell genetically modified alfalfa." And because those crops "cannot be replanted for two to four years," that loss will be even greater. On the other side of the balance, the court recognized that some farmers may wish to switch to genetically modified alfalfa immediately, and some companies like Monsanto want to start selling it to them just as fast. But, the court noted, RRA is a small percentage of those companies' overall business; unsold seed can be stored; and the companies "'have [no] cause to claim surprise'" as to any loss of anticipated revenue, as they "were aware of plaintiffs' lawsuit" and "nonetheless chose to market" RRA.

. . . .

Even assuming that the majority has correctly interpreted the District Court's judgment, I do not agree that we should reverse the District Court.

At the outset, it is important to observe that when a district court is faced with an unlawful agency action, a set of parties who have relied on that action, and a prayer for relief to avoid irreparable harm, the court is operating under its powers of equity. In such a case, a court's function is "to do equity and to mould each decree to the necessities of the particular case." "Flexibility" and "practicality" are the touchstones of these remedial determinations, as "the public interest," "private needs," and "competing private claims" must all be weighed and reconciled against the background of the court's own limitations and its particular familiarity with the case.

When a district court takes on the equitable role of adjusting legal obligations, we review the remedy it crafts for abuse of discretion . . . . And historically, courts have had particularly broad equitable power — and thus particularly broad discretion — to remedy public nuisances and other "'purprestures upon public rights and properties,'" which include environmental harms.

In my view, . . . the District Court's judgment can be understood as either of two reasonable exercises of its equitable powers. . . .

First, the District Court's decision can be understood as an equitable application of administrative law. Faced with two different deregulation proposals, the District Court appears to have vacated the deregulation that had already occurred, made clear that NEPA requires an EIS for any future deregulation of RRA, and partially stayed the vacatur to the extent it affects farmers who had already planted RRA.

. . . . In light of . . . evidence [presented to the District Court], the court may well have concluded that any deregulation of RRA, even in a "limited . . . geographic area" with "stringent . . . regulations governing harvesting and distribution," requires an EIS under NEPA. Indeed, it appears that any deregulation of a genetically modified, herbicide-resistant crop that can transfer its genes to other organisms and cannot effectively be monitored easily fits the criteria for when an EIS is required . . . .

Moreover, given that APHIS had already been ordered to conduct an EIS on deregulation of RRA, the court could have reasonably feared that partial deregulation would undermine the agency's eventual decision. Courts confronted with NEPA violations regularly adopt interim measures to maintain the status quo, particularly if allowing agency action to go forward risks foreclosing alternative courses of action that the agency might have adopted following completion of an EIS. The applicable regulations, to which the District Court owed deference, provide that during the preparation of an EIS, "no action concerning the [agency's] proposal shall be taken which would . . . [h]ave an adverse environmental impact" or "[l]imit the choice of reasonable alternatives." 40 CFR § 1506.1(a) (2009). As exemplified by the problem of what to do with farmers who had already purchased or planted RRA prior to the District Court's judgment, even minimal deregulation can limit future regulatory options. "Courts must remember that in many cases allowing an agency to proceed makes a mockery of the EIS process, converting it from analysis to rationalization."

. . . . Exercising its equitable discretion to balance the interests of the parties and the public, the District Court would have been well within its rights to find that NEPA requires an EIS before the agency grants "Monsanto's deregulation petition, even in part," yet also to find that a partial stay of the vacatur was appropriate to protect the interests of those farmers who had already acted in good-faith reliance on APHIS.

. . . .

Second, the District Court's judgment can be understood as a reasonable response to the nature of the risks posed by RRA. Separate and apart from NEPA's requirement of an EIS, these risks were sufficiently serious, in my view, that the court's injunction was a permissible exercise of its equitable authority.

. . . .

. . . . It was clear to the court that APHIS had only limited capacity to monitor planted RRA, and some RRA had already been planted. The marginal threat posed by additional planting was therefore significant . . . . Under these circumstances, it was not unreasonable for the court to conclude that the most equitable solution was to allocate the limited amount of potentially safe RRA to the farmers who had already planted that crop.

. . . .

. . . . APHIS and petitioners argued to the District Court that partial deregulation could be safely implemented, they submitted evidence intended to show that planting restrictions would prevent the spread of the newly engineered gene, and they contested "virtually every factual issue relating to possible environmental harm." But lacking "the benefit of the development of all the relevant data," the District Court did not find APHIS's and petitioners' assertions to be convincing. I cannot say that I would have found otherwise. It was reasonable for the court to conclude that planting could not go forward until more complete study, presented in an EIS, showed that the known problem of gene flow could, in reality, be prevented.

The District Court's decision that more study was needed to assess whether limits on deregulation could prevent environmental damage is further reinforced by the statutory context in which the issue arose . . . . Congress recognized in NEPA that complex environmental cases often require exceptionally sophisticated scientific determinations, and that agency decisions should not be made on the basis of "incomplete information." Congress also recognized that agencies cannot fully weigh the consequences of these decisions without obtaining public comments through an EIS. While a court may not presume that a NEPA violation requires an injunction, it may take into account the principles embodied in the statute in considering whether an injunction would be appropriate . . . . In enjoining partial deregulation until it had the benefit of an EIS to help parse the evidence, the court acted with exactly the sort of caution that Congress endorsed in NEPA . . . .

. . . .

. . . . In my view, the District Court was well within its discretion to order the remedy that the Court now reverses. Accordingly, I respectfully dissent.

Notes and Questions

1. Why was the plaintiffs' failure to obtain preliminary injunctive relief important to the ultimate outcome of *Monsanto*?

2. Arguably since *Strycker's Bay* (p. 114, above), and certainly since *Methow Valley* (p. 118 above), the Supreme Court has unequivocally held that NEPA imposes purely procedural obligations on federal agencies. In the ultimate source of this construction of NEPA, *Vermont Yankee* (p. 108, above), the Court expressed concern that courts not engage in policy-making "under the guise of judicial review of agency action." In *Monsanto*, the court held that even after finding that an agency violated

NEPA, before enjoining the agency's substantive decision, a court must consider the "balance of hardships" and "the public interest." Do these factors allow the courts to indulge their own policy preferences in the guise of the exercise of equitable discretion?

3. If a court finds that the agency decision-making process did not comply with NEPA, but refuses to enjoin the agency's decision to implement a major federal action, how could the court remedy the procedural violation? Did *Monsanto* effectively hold that agencies may—at least sometimes—violate NEPA with impunity?

4. Consider the relief granted to plaintiffs in several cases excerpted or described earlier in this Chapter: *Thomas v. Peterson*, p. 151; *California* ex rel. *Lockyer v. U.S. Dept. of Agriculture*, p. 164; *Utahns for Better Transportation v. U.S. Dept. of Transportation*, p. 173; *Sierra Club v. U.S. Army Corps of Engineers*, p. 187; and *Friends of the Capital Crescent Trail v. Federal Transit Admin.*, p. 196. Was the relief granted in each case appropriate, under the standard announced in *Monsanto*?

5. Neither the majority nor the dissenting opinion in *Monsanto* mentioned *Tennessee Valley Auth. v. Hill*, a case under the Endangered Species Act that involved what may be the most famous injunction ever issued in an environmental law case. See p. 249, below. Are the two opinions consistent with one another? Can they be distinguished from one another?

VI. Evaluating NEPA

The National Environmental Policy Act has been the law of the land for nearly half a century. The statute's boldly stated purpose was "to promote efforts which will prevent or eliminate damage to the environment and biosphere and stimulate the health and welfare of" humanity. The main mechanism for achieving that purpose has been the statute's requirement that federal agencies study in detail the anticipated significant environmental impacts of their proposed actions before taking those actions. The theory, as the Supreme Court described it in *Methow Valley*, is that forcing agencies to consider environmental values will induce agencies to make decisions more consonant with NEPA's environmental protection policy. After nearly 50 years it is fair to ask: has it worked?

Michael R. Greenberg
The Environmental Impact Statement after
Two Generations
(Routledge 2012)

NEPA and its state and local progeny have had four decades of field trials. This section summarizes the major strengths and then weaknesses of the EIS process.

Beginning with strengths, one important accomplishment of this process at the federal, state, and local levels has been its widespread use as a substitute for planning.

The EIS has become in practice an explicit assertion that development requires early planning to avoid degrading the quality of the environment . . . .

NEPA is often viewed as a conscious[ness]-raising statement . . . . The law rejects the idea of economic growth without consideration of environmental, public health, and social consequences, and without reflection . . . .

. . . .

Part of NEPA's appeal is the widespread assertion that it has changed practice by federal agencies, which has led to better decisions. NEPA, say its proponents, has been instrumental in the cancellation or postponement of highways, dams, airports, nuclear waste disposal programs, outer continental shelf leases, and other proposals. More often, the scoping, preparation, and presentation of the results have caused changes in locations, designs, and other changes to mitigate undesirable environmental effects. Doubtless, there are many such instances, and it would be fruitful to have these documented systematically.

. . . . NEPA clearly encourages multi-disciplinary agency and community participation, including obtaining input and requiring carrying through comments from multiple parties through the process . . . .

. . . .

The criticisms of NEPA probably exceed the praise, at least as this author measures them by volume of pages collected. Some have charged that the EIS process has been less effective than it could be . . . . The law creates the opportunity for considering environmental factors in government actions. Yet Section 102(2)(c) is a procedural requirement. If the procedure is followed correctly, the federal agency can make a decision that many think severely degrades the environment . . . .

. . . . In other words, an excellent document may make no difference . . . .

. . . .

. . . . Some contend that many actions with environmentally significant impacts are not accompanied by an EIS because agencies decide that the actions are not "major" or "significant," or do not constitute an agency "proposal" or "action." In addition, to avoid preparation of an EIS, or to makes sure that one is not vulnerable to legal opposition, documents are infused with as much information as possible to protect the agency's position . . . .

Yet another criticism focuses on scientific evaluation of impacts. No matter how detailed or comprehensive the document may be . . . there is no way of ensuring that all impacts considered by all parties will be included . . . .

. . . .

Two further concerns related to science are measuring and weighing impacts . . . . Overall, the limits inherent in estimating environmental impacts are an unending source of criticism of the EIS.

. . . .

The most widely publicized criticisms from both proponents and opponents are economic. Some argue that government has made little investment in the EIS process . . . .

In contrast, the loudest voices during the past fifteen years have focused on the economic costs associated with the EIS process. Representatives of the business community contend that the EIS process is a slow-growth policy, and in some cases a no-growth policy, that hurts the economy. They point to time involved in preparing and reviewing EISs and the inflationary impact on costs. This inflationary impact is further increased when delays result from NEPA litigation and potential injunctions . . . .

. . . .

I have heard NEPA referred to as a toothless tiger, which it is not because it has teeth if the decision-maker does not muzzle them. I have heard it referred to as a predator feasting on government and business dollars and of little value to decision-makers, which is hard to justify with published data. And I have called it a chameleon capable of blending into agencies' façades. It has been used both as a scientific façade to support decisions that government seemingly was determined to make, and as the rare or only tool available to bring attention to an environmental issue . . . .

Notes and Questions

1. As the excerpt explains, NEPA has been criticized both for doing too little to protect the environment (because NEPA does not prevent agencies from making informed but "unwise" decisions that opponents view as too environmentally destructive) and too much (because NEPA compliance and NEPA litigation can lead to the delay or cancellation of actions that proponents view as socially beneficial). Both of these criticisms are rooted in the complete emphasis that NEPA (as construed by the Supreme Court) places on the procedural mechanism of the EIS requirement—which one author described as "both [NEPA's] singular genius and its fatal flaw." Bradley C. Karkkainen, *Toward a Smarter NEPA: Monitoring and Managing Government's Environmental Performance*, 102 COLUM. L. REV. 903, 904 (2002). In defense of the statute, a participant in the Legacy Parkway dispute (see *Utahns*, p. 173, above) questioned the dichotomous worldview of NEPA's critics:

> The NEPA debate is often waged on an inappropriately win-lose, pass-fail basis. Because the Supreme Court has ruled so clearly that NEPA imposes purely procedural requirements, . . . it works or does not work depending on the integrity of the process itself. That integrity can be abused by either side in the yes-no, "build it or stop it" spectrum. Detractors argue that irresponsible plaintiffs can abuse NEPA simply to delay a project long enough that it falls of its own weight, either financially or politically. On the other side, NEPA cynics claim that agencies have learned to game the NEPA process so that results are typically decided at the outset, and simply ratified by a well-oiled EIS factory in which the right issues are addressed, and the right words are magically invoked to survive any judicial review. Having practiced and taught NEPA law for many years, I have no doubt that there is some truth to both claims.

In the middle, however, are a large number of projects, perhaps the vast majority, which have been made more environmentally sound by routine NEPA compliance. Moreover, where citizens seek judicial redress to bad NEPA processes, judicial review can stimulate an improved process, and an improved result. The point I want to make most urgently, then, is that Legacy highlights the perils of debating the merits of information-based approaches to environmental matters based solely on extreme cases, in which projects either are stopped altogether due to litigation delay, or in which . . . shallow impact statements result in rubber stamp ratification of projects without legitimate attention to environmental matters. The Legacy saga shows NEPA can work, because it ultimately brought the parties together to forge a project combining the best aspects of the state's original proposal with the best ideas from members of the affected public.

Robert W. Adler, *In Defense of NEPA: The Case of the Legacy Parkway*, 26 J. LAND RESOURCES & ENVTL L. 297, 300–01 (2006).

2. Arguments about NEPA — whether in favor of the statute's effectiveness, against the statute as ineffective, or against the statute as overeffective — often rely on impressionistic and anecdotal evidence. Empirical data about NEPA's overall effect are hard to come by, partly because NEPA implementation goes on in a milieu of innumerable other influences on environmental quality and partly because it is usually impossible to know how any particular decision regarding a proposal for major federal action (or even the nature and existence of the proposal itself) would have been different if NEPA had never been enacted. In 2014, in response to a request by some members of Congress for information on "issues related to costs, time frames, and litigation associated with completing NEPA analyses," the General Accountability Office concluded that:

> Little information exists on the costs and benefits of completing NEPA analyses. Agencies do not routinely track the cost of completing NEPA analyses . . . . Information on the benefits of completing NEPA analyses is largely qualitative. According to studies and agency officials, some of the qualitative benefits of NEPA include its role in encouraging public participation and in discovering and addressing project design problems that could be more costly in the long run. Complicating the determination of costs and benefits, agency activities under NEPA are hard to separate from other required environmental analyses . . . .

General Accountability Office, *National Environmental Policy Act: Little Information Exists on NEPA Analyses*, GAO 14-369 Highlights, April 2014. For a description of the vast scholarly literature evaluating NEPA, including some empirical analysis of NEPA's effects on agency decision-making, see Daniel R. Mandelker et al., NEPA LAW AND LITIGATION §§ 11.1–11.7 (2d ed. July, 2016 update).

3. Commentators on NEPA frequently observe that both the statute itself and assessments of its performance have little to say about the post-decisional phase. Are categorically excluded actions not having a significant effect, individually and cumulatively, on the quality of the human environment? Do EAs and FONSIs correctly predict that the selected federal action will have no significant effect on the quality of the human environment? Do EISs accurately predict the significant environmental impacts of major federal actions? Are mitigation measures included in EISs and RODs actually implemented, and do they mitigate environmental impacts as predicted? *See* Karkkainen, *supra*, at 927 (noting that "the agency conducting the EA or EIS ordinarily has no obligation to follow up on its predictions to determine their accuracy"); Michael B. Gerrard, *The Effect of NEPA Outside the Courtroom*, 39 ENVTL. L. REP. 10615, 10616–17 (July 2009) (noting that existing research suggests that NEPA analyses are not grossly inaccurate, but that research is limited because "very little post-EIS auditing of the results" exists); *see also* Oliver A. Houck, *Worst Case and the Deepwater Horizon Blowout: There Ought to Be a Law*, 40 ENVTL. L. REP. 11033, 11035-36 (Nov. 2010) (criticizing "on paper" compliance with NEPA that failed to predict the catastrophic consequences that could ensue from a blowout but suggesting that NEPA, if properly implemented, could be effective). If NEPA's information-gathering requirements were found to result in predictions of environmental impact that are to some degree incomplete or inaccurate, would that justify abandoning the information-gathering effort?

4. Regardless of NEPA's pros and cons, similar laws requiring environmental impact analysis have been adopted by many state and local governments, as well as by national governments around the world. *See* Karkkainen, *supra*, 905–06. Moreover, the theory of NEPA — that careful consideration of previously underemphasized impacts can affect decision-making — has been applied to numerous other contexts, often by critics of environmental regulation. President Reagan, for example, introduced the "Regulatory Impact Analysis" as a way "to reduce the burdens of existing and future regulations." Exec. Order. 12291 (Feb. 17, 1981); *see also* 5 U.S.C. §§ 603–604 (requiring NEPA-like analysis of the effect of proposed regulations on small businesses). President George W. Bush required agencies to prepare a "Statement of Energy Effects" for "significant energy actions." Exec. Order 13211 (May 18, 2001) (using language parallel to NEPA provisions). In a very different vein, a law professor suggested applying a NEPA-like process to protect privacy in an era of mass surveillance. A. Michael Froomkin, *Regulating Mass Surveillance as Privacy Pollution: Learning from Environmental Impact Statements*, 2015 U. ILL. L. REV. 1713 (2015).

5. The available data on NEPA litigation show that challenges to EISs and SEISs (or to the lack of an SEIS) are more common than challenges to FONSIs or categorical exclusions, but still affect only a relatively small fraction of actions for which EISs are prepared. For the period 2001–2013, CEQ reported an average of about 47 decisions per year on challenges to EISs and SEISs. According to CEQ, the government prevailed in 57 percent of those decisions. CEQ, *NEPA Litigation*, https://ceq.doe.gov /legal_corner/litigation.html (last visited Oct. 24, 2016).

6. The view that NEPA causes undesirable delay has been reflected in a number of federal statutes that, without entirely exempting any proposals for major federal actions from NEPA's requirements, nevertheless constrain the NEPA process with respect to certain types of federal actions in an attempt to speed the implementation of such actions. Among other provisions, these statutes typically impose time limits on various aspects of the NEPA process (such as the time for preparing an EIS or the time for an expert agency or the public to provide comments on a draft EIS). Some statutes limit in various ways the opportunity for interested parties to seek judicial relief for alleged NEPA violations.

One such statute is the Fixing America's Surface Transportation (FAST) Act, P.L. 114-94 (2015). For projects covered by the pertinent provisions of the statute, the FAST Act authorizes the lead federal agency to set a permitting timetable, thus allowing the federal sponsor of the permit or project to limit the time available to other federal agencies with expertise or jurisdiction to review NEPA documents. 42 U.S.C. § 4370m-2(c). The statute also sets a 180-day deadline for completion of any document required under NEPA "after the date on which all information needed to complete" the document "is in the possession of the agency." *Id.* § 4370m-1(c)(1)(C)(ii)(II)(cc). In addition, the FAST Act imposes new limits on lawsuits alleging NEPA violations with respect to covered projects: a shorter statute of limitations, a requirement that the plaintiff alert the agency to the issue in suit by filing detailed public comments, and an apparently stricter standard for issuance of a preliminary injunction. *Id.* § 4370m-6. A "covered project" is one that is likely to cost more than $200 million and involves construction for "energy production, electricity transmission, surface transportation, aviation, ports and waterways, water resource projects, broadband, pipelines, manufacturing, or any other sector as determined by a majority vote" of the Federal Permitting Improvement Council created by the statute, *id.* § 4370m(6) — in other words, depending on one's perspective, the biggest and most urgently needed projects, or the biggest and most environmentally destructive projects. The practical effect of the FAST Act on the behavior of federal agencies and courts remains to be seen.

7. NEPA's forward-looking approach to evaluating environmental impacts can produce information not only about the aggregate environmental effects of a proposed major federal action, but also about the geographic and social distribution of those effects. NEPA analyses thus provide federal agencies with excellent opportunities to take heed of environmental justice concerns as required by Executive Order No. 12898, see p. 29, above. Consideration of cumulative impacts at both the EA and EIS stage can be particularly valuable in addressing environmental justice, as the concentration of polluting facilities and other environmental harms in low-income and minority communities can have major effects even if the marginal effect of a particular proposal may be relatively small. *See, e.g., South Camden Citizens in Action v. N.J. Dept. of Environmental Protection*, 145 F. Supp. 2d 446 (D.N.J. 2001), *modified*, 145 F. Supp. 2d 505 (D.N.J. 2001), *rev'd*, 274 F.3d 771 (3d Cir. 2001). The role that NEPA could play in rectifying environmental injustice was not lost on the CEQ, which issued the following guidance to federal agencies.

COUNCIL ON ENVIRONMENTAL QUALITY
ENVIRONMENTAL JUSTICE: GUIDANCE UNDER THE
NATIONAL ENVIRONMENTAL POLICY ACT

(Dec. 10, 1997)

Environmental justice issues may arise at any step of the NEPA process and agencies should consider these issues at each and every step of the process, as appropriate. Environmental justice issues encompass a broad range of impacts covered by NEPA, including impacts on the natural or physical environment and interrelated social, cultural and economic effects . . . . Environmental justice concerns may arise from impacts on the natural and physical environment, such as human health or ecological impacts on minority populations, low-income populations, and Indian tribes, or from related social or economic impacts . . . .

Agencies should recognize that the question of whether agency action raises environmental justice issues is highly sensitive to the history or circumstances of a particular community or population, the particular type of environmental or human health impact, and the nature of the proposed action itself. There is not a standard formula for how environmental justice issues should be identified or addressed . . . .

      . . . .

The Executive Order [No. 12898] does not change the prevailing legal thresholds and statutory interpretations under NEPA and existing case law . . . .

Under NEPA, the identification of a disproportionately high and adverse human health or environmental effect on a low-income population, minority population, or Indian tribe does not preclude a proposed agency action from going forward, nor does it necessarily compel a conclusion that a proposed action is environmentally unsatisfactory . . . .

      . . . .

1. Scoping   — community impacts

During the scoping process, an agency should preliminarily determine whether an area potentially affected by a proposed agency action may include low-income populations, minority populations, or Indian tribes, and seek input accordingly. When the scoping process is used to develop an EIS or EA, an agency should seek input from low income populations, minority populations, or Indian tribes as early in the process as information becomes available . . . .

If an agency identifies any potentially affected minority populations, low-income populations, or Indian tribes, the agency should develop a strategy for effective public involvement in the agency's determination of the scope of the NEPA analysis . . . .

The participation of diverse groups in the scoping process is necessary for full consideration of the potential environmental impacts of a proposed agency action and any alternatives . . . . For this participation to be meaningful, the public should have access to enough information so that it is well informed and can provide constructive input . . . .

. . . .

2. Public Participation

. . . . Participation of low-income populations, minority populations, or tribal populations may require adaptive or innovative approaches to overcome linguistic, institutional, cultural, economic, historical, or other potential barriers to effective participation in the decision-making processes of Federal agencies under customary NEPA procedures . . . .

3. Determining the Affected Environment

In order to determine whether a proposed action is likely to have disproportionately high and adverse human health or environmental effects on low-income populations, minority populations, or Indian tribes, agencies should identify a geographic scale for which they will obtain demographic information on the potential impact area . . . .

Agencies should recognize that the impacts within minority populations, low-income populations, or Indian tribes may be different from impacts on the general population due to a community's distinct cultural practices. For example, data on different patterns of living, such as subsistence fish, vegetation, or wildlife consumption and the use of well water in rural communities may be relevant to the analysis . . . .

4. Analysis

When a disproportionately high and adverse human health or environmental effect on a low-income population, minority population, or Indian tribe has been identified, agencies should analyze how environmental and health effects are distributed within the affected community . . . .

Where a potential environmental justice issue has been identified by an agency, the agency should state clearly in the EIS or EA whether, in light of all of the facts and circumstances, a disproportionately high and adverse human health or environmental impact on minority populations, low-income populations, or Indian tribe is likely to result from the proposed action and any alternatives. This statement should be supported by sufficient information for the public to understand the rationale for the conclusion . . . .

5. Alternatives

Agencies should encourage the members of the communities that may suffer a disproportionately high and adverse human health or environmental effect from a proposed agency action to help develop and comment on possible alternatives to the proposed agency action as early as possible in the process.

Where an EIS is prepared, CEQ regulations require agencies to identify an environmentally preferable alternative in the record of decision (ROD). When the agency has identified a disproportionately high and adverse human health or environmental effect on low-income populations, minority populations, or Indian tribes from either the proposed action or alternatives, the distribution as well as the magnitude of the disproportionate impacts in these communities should be a factor in determining the environmentally preferable alternative. In weighing this factor, the agency should consider the views it has received from the affected communities, and the magnitude of environmental impacts associated with alternatives that have a less disproportionate and adverse effect on low-income populations, minority populations, or Indian tribes.

6. Record of Decision

When an agency reaches a decision on an action for which an EIS was prepared, a public record of decision (ROD) must be prepared that provides information on the alternatives considered and the factors weighed in the decision-making process. Disproportionately high and adverse human health or environmental effects on a low-income population, minority population, or Indian tribe should be among those factors explicitly discussed in the ROD, and should also be addressed in any discussion of whether all practicable means to avoid or minimize environmental and other interrelated effects were adopted. Where relevant, the agency should discuss how these issues are addressed in any monitoring and enforcement program summarized in the ROD.

Dissemination of the information in the ROD may provide an effective means to inform the public of the extent to which environmental justice concerns were considered in the decision-making process, and where appropriate, whether the agency intends to mitigate any disproportionately high and adverse human health or environmental effects . . . .

7. Mitigation

Throughout the process of public participation, agencies should elicit the views of the affected populations on measures to mitigate a disproportionately high and adverse human health or environmental effect on a low-income population, minority population, or Indian tribe and should carefully consider community views in developing and implementing mitigation strategies. Mitigation measures identified in an EIS or developed as part of a FONSI should reflect the needs and preferences of affected low-income populations, minority populations, or Indian tribes to the extent practicable.

. . . .

In circumstances in which an EIS or EA will not be prepared [*e.g.*, statutory exemption, categorical exclusion or functional equivalent] and a disproportionately high and adverse human health or environmental impact on low-income populations, minority populations, or Indian tribes may exist, agencies should augment their procedures as appropriate to ensure that the otherwise applicable process or procedure for a federal action addresses environmental justice concerns. Agencies should ensure that the goals for public participation . . . are satisfied to the fullest extent possible.

Agencies also should fully develop and consider alternatives to the proposed action whenever possible, as would be required by NEPA.

Notes and Questions

1. The potential of NEPA to reduce disparate environmental impacts of major federal actions is clear. Has that potential been realized? The evidence is sparse, even though CEQ's environmental justice guidance has been in effect for nearly 20 years and Executive Order No. 12898 (p. 29, above) for longer than that.

A group of researchers reviewed all draft EISs prepared from the date President Clinton issued the executive order on environmental justice through 2001. The authors found that fewer than half of the draft EISs explicitly discussed environmental justice issues, although the percentage increased over time to roughly two-thirds of draft EISs produced in 2000 and 2001. According to the researchers, of the EISs they reviewed, none recommended rejecting a proposal because of environmental justice impacts. Linda Rose et al., *Environmental Justice Analysis: How Has It Been Implemented in Draft Environmental Impact Statements*, 7 ENVTL. PRAC. 235, 235 (2005).

2. In recent years, some NEPA plaintiffs have challenged the adequacy of the environmental justice analysis in EAs/FONSIs or EISs. Courts, deciding these claims using the same standards applied to other NEPA claims, have generally ruled in favor of the government. *See, e.g., Latin Americans for Social & Economic Development v. Federal Highway Admin.*, 756 F.3d 447 (6th Cir. 2014) (holding that FHWA adequately considered environmental justice impacts of bridge site selection and was not required to select the alternative that would least harm the affected community); *Communities Against Runway Expansion, Inc. v. Federal Aviation Admin.*, 355 F.3d 678 (D.C. Cir. 2004) (holding that FAA's selection of the "comparison population" for environmental justice analysis was not arbitrary and capricious); *Mid States Coalition for Progress v. Surface Transportation Board*, 345 F.3d 520 (8th Cir. 2003) (holding that agency's method for identifying communities with environmental justice concerns was not arbitrary and capricious); *Saint Paul Branch NAACP v. U.S. Dept. of Transportation*, 764 F. Supp. 2d 1092 (D. Minn. 2011) (holding that FEIS for light rail project adequately analyzed project's gentrification impact on a predominantly African-American neighborhood).

3. During the Obama Administration, the CEQ and other federal agencies heavily involved in NEPA implementation made environmental justice a more visible priority. In 2011 the Administration formed an interagency working group on environmental justice. That group surveyed the approaches and techniques various agencies were using to incorporate environmental justice analyses into NEPA implementation. The result was a set of recommendations, ranging from the general to the highly specific, of "promising practices" for agencies to consider adopting. *See* Federal Interagency Working Group on Environmental Justice & NEPA Committee, *Promising Practices for EJ Methodologies in NEPA Reviews* (March 2016), https://www.epa.gov/sites/production/files/2016-08/documents/nepa_promising_practices_ document_2016.pdf (last visited Oct. 24, 2016).

Chapter 4

Preventing Species and Ecosystem Loss: Biodiversity Law and Policy

Biodiversity, a term that refers to the diversity of animal and plant life on Earth, is inescapably intertwined with human behavior. We are the species that has had the greatest capability of any in history to alter the conditions on the planet we all inhabit. In addition to our ability to destroy or sustain nature's diversity, we are also dependent upon it for our own existence, to an extent well beyond what most people have considered. Nature, and the biodiversity that it requires, is often seen as an amenity for those who are personally drawn to its aesthetic qualities and economically capable of having such a luxurious priority. Sadly, this misguided attitude has impacted the manner in which modern civilization developed, resulting in a disastrous decline in biodiversity worldwide.

Biodiversity loss became apparent throughout the twentieth century, typically in relation to specific charismatic species that either went extinct or were in very serious trouble. Eventually protective laws developed in response to these trends. Unlike the problems of air, water, and land pollution covered in other chapters of this text, the impacts on biodiversity go well beyond commercial industrial action, resulting in far greater regulation of individual citizens in the use of their private land. This diffuse nature makes biodiversity protection especially challenging, and it is often the goal of evolving policy approaches to address this feature of the problem. Add to this the fact that our scientific understanding of ecological functioning is always increasing but never complete, and you have a recipe for even greater complexity and policy disagreement.

This chapter begins by introducing the concept of biodiversity and providing for a basic understanding of the subject. This is followed by some background on the development of biodiversity law in the United States. The majority of the chapter is focused on the Endangered Species Act, which is the primary U.S. law governing species protection. Finally, we will review some key components of international biodiversity law before concluding with a look to the future of biodiversity protection.

I. Introduction to Biodiversity

Jonathan S. Adams, Bruce A. Stein & Lynn S. Kutner, *Biodiversity: Our Precious Heritage*

PRECIOUS HERITAGE: THE STATUS OF BIODIVERSITY IN THE UNITED STATES 7–10

(Bruce A. Stein, Lynn S. Kutner & Jonathan S. Adams eds., 2000)

From the Devils Hole pupfish to the delicate spring ecosystems at Ash Meadows to the Mohave Desert, from genes to species to ecosystems to landscapes: Each is part of the fabric of life. Each is a component of biodiversity. But what is biodiversity? Although the term is now common, many people are bewildered by it. Still others use it in an all-encompassing way to refer to any and all nature.

Biodiversity is, in essence, the full array of life on Earth. The most tangible manifestations of this concept are the species of plants, animals, and microorganisms that surround us. Yet biodiversity is more than just the number and diversity of species, as immense as that might be. It also includes the genetic material that makes up those species. And at a higher level, it includes the natural communities, ecosystems, and landscapes of which species are a part. The concept of biodiversity includes both the variety of these things and the variability found within and among them. Biodiversity also encompasses the processes — both ecological and evolutionary — that allow life on Earth to continue adapting and evolving.

While the term *biodiversity* was coined and popularized only recently, the concept is as old as the human desire to know and name all the creatures of the earth. Nature's daunting complexity demands some method of differentiating among its various components. Four of the principal levels of biological organization are genes, species, ecosystems, and landscapes.

Genetic diversity refers to the unique combinations of genes found within and among organisms. Genes, composed of DNA sequences, are the fundamental building blocks of life. The complexes of genes found within individual organisms, and their frequencies of occurrence within a population, are the basic levels at which evolution occurs. Genetic variability is an important trait in assuring the long-term survival of most species, since it allows them to respond to unpredictable changes in their environment.

Species diversity encompasses the variety of living organisms inhabiting an area. This is most commonly gauged by the number of different of organisms — for instance, the number of different birds or plants in a state, country, or ecosystem. While species are the most widely understood aspect of biodiversity, it is actually the individual populations that together make up a species that are the focus of on-the-ground conservation efforts.

Ecological diversity refers to the higher-level organization of different species into natural communities, and the interplay between these communities and the physical environment that forms ecosystems. Interactions are key to ecological diversity. This includes interactions among different species—predators and prey, for instance, or pollinators and flowers—as well as interaction among these species and the physical processes, such as nutrient cycling or periodic fires, that are essential to maintain ecosystem functioning.

Landscape diversity refers to the geography of different ecosystems across a large area and the connection among them. Natural communities and ecosystems change across the landscape in response to environmental gradients such as climate, soils, or altitude and form characteristic mosaics. Understanding the patterns among these natural ecosystems and how they relate to other landscape features, such as farms, cities, and roads, is key to maintaining such regional diversity.

Conservation of biodiversity requires attention to each of these levels, because all contribute to the persistence of life on Earth. More than most people realize, humans rely on wild biological resources for food and shelter. Genes from wild plants, for instance, allow plant breeders to develop disease-resistant crops or increase crop yields, passing along the benefits of biodiversity to farmers and ultimately consumers. Similarly, medicines derived from plants, animals, and especially microbes are an established part of the Western pharmacy and include such widely used medications as aspirin, penicillin, and digitalis. The emerging biotechnology industry, perhaps more than any other, depends on such wild genetic resources. Indeed, a crucial piece of the technology that enables scientists and industry to easily multiply strands of DNA—and thereby create useful commercial products—derives from the bacterium *Thermus aquaticus*, first discovered in a hot spring in Yellowstone National Park.

The value of these biodiversity goods is enormous, but even so it is just a fraction of the value of the ecosystem services on which human life depends, such as waste assimilation, climate regulation, water supply and regulation, erosion control and sediment retention, soil formation, waste treatment, and pollination. Ecosystem services, however, are largely outside the financial markets and therefore are ignored or undervalued. By one rough estimate the value of ecosystem services for the entire biosphere is $33 trillion, nearly double the global gross national product.

When most people think about biodiversity, however, they think not about ecosystems and their services but rather about species. Yet scientists still don't know how many species share the planet with us. Estimates vary by an order of magnitude. A conservative guess is roughly 14 million species, only one-eighth supports far more species than previously believed, from tremendous numbers of beetles living in the canopy of tropical trees to bacteria inhabiting rocks more than a mile beneath the earth's surface.

Individual species, like the pupfishes of the desert Southwest, form threads in the lustrous ecological tapestry of the United States. Further examination reveals a dense weave of thousands of species, many found nowhere else. Together these threads spell out superlatives: tallest, largest, oldest. Topping out at more than 360 feet in height, northern California's redwoods (*Sequoia sempervivens*) are the tallest trees in the world. Their close relatives the giant sequoias (*Sequoiadendron giganteum*) rank among the most massive living things on Earth, and bristlecone pines (*Pinus longaeva*), overlooking the Owens Valley near the summit of eastern California's White Mountains, are the world's oldest living trees, some dating back nearly 5,000 years.

The difference between two species can be visually obvious, as with the Devils Hole and Owens pupfish, or so subtle that only sophisticated molecular techniques can reveal the distinctions. Nonetheless, scientists have documented more than 200,000 species from the United States, and the true number of species living here is probably at least double this figure. By any measure, the United States is home to an exceptionally diverse flora and fauna. On a global scale the nation is particularly noteworthy for certain groups of organisms, including salamanders, coniferous plants, and freshwater fishes, turtles, mussels, snails, and crayfishes. The United States harbors nearly 16,000 species of vascular plants, about 9% of the world's total mammal species, and about 10% of known freshwater fishes worldwide.

This wealth of life owes a great deal to the nation's size and location. While covering only about 6% of the earth's total land area, the United States spans nearly a third of the globe, extending more than 120 degrees of longitude from eastern Maine to the tip of the Aleutian chain, and 50 degrees in latitude from Point Barrow above the Arctic Circle to the southern tip of Hawaii below the tropic of Cancer. Together with this expanse of terrain comes a variety of topographic features and climates, from Death Valley to Mt. McKinley. This range of climates has given rise to a wide array of ecological types, from tundra and subarctic conifer forests called taiga, to deserts, prairie, boreal forest, deciduous forests, temperate rain forest, and even tropical rain forests.

While still far from complete, the process of documenting the nation's ecological diversity suggests that the United States is also extraordinary from an ecological perspective. For example, of the 14 biome types worldwide that represent major ecosystem groups, the United States contains 12, more than any other country. Three biomes—temperate broadleaf forests, temperate grasslands, and mixed mountain systems—are particularly well represented: At least 10% of their area occurs in the United States. Around the world and on a more detailed scale within the United States, ecologists have also identified relatively large areas, known as ecoregions, that in ecological terms function more or less as a unit. With 21 of 28 globally defined ecoregions, the United States is also the most diverse country in the world from an ecoregional perspective.

II. History of U.S. Wildlife Law

The Endangered Species Act, while far from perfect, was the result of an evolution of wildlife statutes that were either ineffective or very narrow in application. It was the first comprehensive species-protection statute in the United States that provided meaningful prohibitions and potential for enforcement of those provisions. Before we get into the details of how the statute functions, it is helpful to consider the history of U.S. wildlife law that preceded it.

Kalyani Robbins, *Coordinating the Overlapping Regulation of Biodiversity and Ecosystem Management*

THE LAW AND POLICY OF ENVIRONMENTAL FEDERALISM: A COMPARATIVE ANALYSIS

(Edward Elgar Publishing, Kalyani Robbins ed., 2016)

I. A review of our historical relationship with wildlife and the development of powers to regulate it

Regulation of wildlife has evolved along two completely separate tracks at the state and national levels, nearly to the point of each system operating in a vacuum. It is no surprise, then, that we see substantial regulatory overlap and little cooperation. [T]his overlap can be beneficial to vulnerable species and ecosystems, but creates regulatory inefficiencies as well. . . .

A. The states

For most of U.S. history wildlife has been regulated by the states. Our relationship with wildlife, and attitude toward it, evolved substantially over that time. Early common law, especially through the 19th century, held that wildlife was state property. While this philosophy still exists somewhat, it has eroded over time, beginning with the Supreme Court's 1896 holding in *Geer v. Connecticut*, 161 U.S. 519 (1896). Although the *Geer* court upheld the states' special right to wildlife, it noted that wildlife in a state of nature cannot truly be owned at all, and that to the limited extent that the state was capable of owning it, it was for the benefit of all the people in common. State ownership of wildlife formally expired in 1979 when the Supreme Court overruled *Geer* in *Hughes v. Oklahoma*, 441 U.S. 322 (1979), holding that states do not have an ownership interest in wildlife that would trump Commerce Clause authority, but rather the same regulatory interest in wildlife as they do in other natural resources.

After the initial property-based power, the next phase of state wildlife regulation turned the focus to more traditional police powers. While *Geer* conceded limited state ownership of wildlife, it refocused the source of regulatory power as flowing from the general police powers within the state. *Geer* then limited this power for the first time, stating that it was subject to federal preemption, even though there were no federal wildlife statutes at the time. This tentative and prospective limitation was necessitated by the shift from a proprietary role to a police power focus. The Court's discussion of preservation for the common good was a precursor to the concept of trust duty in relation to wildlife. That said, it appears that the primary purpose of this shift into police power was to set up the future potential for federal preemption, and as such, *Geer* arguably represents the dawn of wildlife federalism.

Around the same time as this shift was pushed forward by *Geer*, the public trust doctrine was taking shape in other contexts, and would ultimately play a role in wildlife regulation. In 1892, just four years before *Geer*, the U.S. Supreme Court had established in *Illinois Central Railroad v. Illinois*, 146 U.S. 387 (1892), that the public trust doctrine applies to the states, though in that case the focus was on land and

Public Trust Doctrine:

waterways. This doctrine holds that certain natural resources belong to the public to enjoy or use, and that the state government has an affirmative duty to preserve these inalienable resources for the public, effectively serving in the role of a trustee. *Geer* began the process of extending this doctrine to wildlife, though somewhat vaguely and via dicta. By the late 20th century, court opinions routinely hinged on application of the doctrine to wildlife values. In *National Audubon Society v. Superior Court*, 33 Cal.3d 419 (1983), the famous 1983 Mono Lake case, the California Supreme Court ruled Mono Lake a public trust resource, holding that the doctrine extends to the value of the land or water *to wildlife*. A 1980 Washington case, *Washington Department of Fisheries v. Gillette*, 621 P.2d 764 (1980), held that the state's trust duty over the fish in the state *obligated* it to seek damages against a private party damaging that resource.

Biodiversity values developed slowly. Initially state fish and game management was entirely focused on commercial value: increasing supply and controlling demand via game restrictions. Part of the problem was that state fish and game commissions tend to be dominated by hunters, farmers, and commercial fishers. Court challenges by organizations with non-consumptive interest in wildlife failed to change this council structure. Thankfully in recent decades we have seen an explosion of state endangered species acts, so the legislatures have stepped in to fill the void often observed at the local level. All but a few states now have such statutes and list their own endangered species for protection, which demonstrates an evolution of state priorities, and perhaps a response to the development of public trust doctrine in relation to wildlife. It is worth noting, in relation to some of the points to come, that the federal Endangered Species Act (ESA) was designed as it was in a world without state ESAs.

Separation of State & Federal ESA statutes ⊗

B. *The federal government*

1. The Lacey Act of 1900

The 19th century saw serious wildlife depletion, due largely to our consumptive focus and state under-enforcement of game restrictions. Responding to this problem, the Lacey Act made violations of state game laws a federal crime if the illegal game was to be transported across state lines. This allows the federal government to prosecute state offenses in some cases, which represents the beginning of our current system of overlapping federalism. The Lacey Act also seeks to prevent the introduction of non-native species into new ecosystems, making it a first small step in science-based federal regulation of wildlife, which would eventually become the norm. It may not seem like much, but it was the first federal law protecting wildlife, which is, in itself, a big move.

2. The Migratory Bird Treaty Act of 1918

Well into the 20th century, states continued to cling to the view that their control over wildlife was more proprietary than regulatory. The Migratory Bird Treaty Act, which implemented several international treaties to protect migratory birds, was immediately challenged in *Missouri v. Holland* under the 10th Amendment. Missouri argued that birds were under exclusive state control. The Supreme Court rejected this notion and upheld the Act under the federal treaty power, securing its place as the next major federal statute protecting wildlife. Because states had bird hunting restrictions already, this was also another step in the development of overlapping authority over wildlife. In spite of *Geer*'s dicta, Congress had still not exercised its prerogative of preempting state law.

3. The Federal Aid in Wildlife Restoration Act of 1937

The next method Congress used to address wildlife protection came in the form of federal aid. Commonly known as the Pittman-Robertson Act, this was the first federal effort to get states to do more to conserve wildlife and habitat. The federal government had thus far asserted so little authority to regulate wildlife that it had to pay the states to conserve and restore habitat. Before this, state agencies were entirely funded by taxes and fees on hunters and fishers, who consequently had great influence. The Act introduced the first conservation-driven funding of state wildlife agency administration, which in turn led to a greater balancing of interests in state and local wildlife management. This is why conservation-based funding is essential. ✳

4. The Wild Free-Roaming Horses and Burros Act of 1971

After using the Commerce Clause, the treaty power, and then the funding approach, Congress next made use of the Property clause. Slowly inching forward in terms of overall protective coverage, the next step was to protect wild horses and burros on federal land. What makes this step especially interesting for the purpose of this chapter is the impact it had on wholly *intrastate* wildlife and state actors. In *Kleppe v. New Mexico* the Supreme Court upheld the statute's application to prohibit the New Mexico Livestock Board from taking wild burros, under the federal property power. This is a significant step, given the early tradition of state ownership of all wildlife within the state, which did not formally come to an end until three years later in *Hughes v. Oklahoma*. The federal government was able to prohibit state actors from accessing wildlife within the state.

5. The Marine Mammal Protection Act of 1972

The first meaningful precursor to the ESA, albeit still extremely limited in scope (compared with what would follow), was the Marine Mammal Protection Act (MMPA). Not only was it a clear and unprecedentedly broad assertion of federal power in the realm of wildlife conservation, making use of the Commerce Clause power, but it also ushered in several key statutory innovations for the field. First, it had a scientific focus, expecting the use of science in its implementation as well as taking into account populations and ecosystems. Second, it preempted all state laws, as had been previously avoided, resulting in a strong assertion of federal power. Finally, the MMPA represented an effort to address competing political interests: on the one hand it shifted the focus to populations and away from yield, but on the other hand it still maintained a management focus rather than one of complete protection.

6. The Endangered Species Act of 1973

Finally, the ESA was passed and biodiversity was serious federal business. The ESA was enacted in 1973 as the first comprehensive U.S. effort to preserve biodiversity.

Tennessee Valley Authority v. Hill, 437 U.S. 153 (1978), the most famous ESA case, told us that the Act was intended "to halt and reverse the trend toward species extinction, whatever the cost." The ESA requires the listing of threatened and endangered species for protection, as well as the designation of their critical habitat, also to be protected. It prohibits "take" of individual members of a listed species by any person, and requires all federal agencies to ensure that their actions (including permitting or funding private actions) neither jeopardize the continued existence of a listed species nor destroy or adversely modify its designated critical habitat. It was the biggest and boldest step Congress ever took to federalize conservation, and had amazing potential. Unfortunately, due largely to lack of funding and partly to political pressures, the ESA is not even close to being fully implemented. In spite of an inability to administer the statute federally, there has been little effort to involve the states, other than some assistance with recovery plan management.

Setbacks

Notes and Questions

1. The above excerpt notes that state fish and game commissions tend to be dominated by hunters, farmers, and commercial fishers, and that efforts to include members with non-consumptive interests in wildlife were unsuccessful. An important case that closed the door on this effort in one state was *Humane Soc. of U.S., New Jersey Branch, Inc. v. New Jersey State Fish and Game Council*, 70 N.J. 565 (1976), which reversed a lower court's holding that limiting the council to sportsmen, farmers, and commercial fishers was unconstitutional.

2. There were two federal statutes for wildlife protection that closely preceded the MMPA, which were the embryonic stages of ESA development, but neither had any teeth. They were at best warnings of the movement toward the meaningful protections provided in the ESA. First was the Endangered Species Preservation Act of 1966, which was the first species-listing statute, but it had no enforcement potential. Next was the Endangered Species Conservation Act of 1969, which increased protections for invertebrate species and restrictions on interstate commerce in listed species, but still did not provide for external enforcement. For further discussion of these pre-ESA developments, see Kalyani Robbins, *Strength in Numbers: Setting Quantitative Criteria for Listing Species under the Endangered Species Act*, 27 UCLA J. Envtl L. & Pol. 1, 5–7 (2009).

3. The Migratory Bird Treaty Act, 16 U.S.C. § 703, was originally passed by Congress in 1918 to confirm treaty commitments with Great Britain (on behalf of Canada) to protect migratory birds in North America, particularly from the devastation of commercial hunting. The statute was quickly challenged by states, arguing violation of the Tenth Amendment, but was upheld by the Supreme Court as a valid exercise of the treaty-making power of Congress. *See Missouri v. Holland*, 252 U.S. 416 (1920). In reaching this conclusion, Justice Oliver Wendell Holmes, for the majority, found that, "Here, a national interest of very nearly the first magnitude is involved. . . . But for the treaty and the statute, there soon might be no birds for any powers to deal with." *Id.* at 435.

Since that time, the Migratory Bird Treaty Act (MBTA), while often overshadowed by the Endangered Species Act and momentous cases such as *TVA v. Hill*, has proven a durable statute for protecting biodiversity, with potentially a much broader reach than the ESA. In significant part, the MBTA provides as follows:

> Unless and except as permitted . . . , it shall be unlawful . . . to pursue, hunt, take, capture, kill, attempt to take, capture, or kill, possess, ship, export, import, . . . transport or cause to be transported . . . , any migratory bird, any part, nest, or eggs of any such bird, or any product, whether or not manufactured, which consists, or is composed in whole or part, of any such bird or any part, nest, or egg thereof.

Notably, a bird species does not have to be endangered or threatened in any legal or lay sense in order to receive protection under the MBTA. A bird species simply must be included on the List of Migratory Birds maintained by the U.S. Fish and Wildlife Service. This list includes not only rare species of birds, but practically all of the most common native species as well, such as the American crow, American robin, Mallard duck, Song sparrow, and the Canada goose. *See* 50 C.F.R. § 10.13. Given the blanket prohibition of harming any individual migratory bird, or possessing "any part, nest, or eggs of any such birds," without a permit, combined with all the diverse habitats, including all urban as well as rural environments, where birds may be found, do you see why the reach of the MBTA may be broader than that of the ESA? Do you think this potential breadth was intended by Congress when the original MBTA statute was passed in 1918? If you were an environmental group concerned with protecting unique habitats, how might you apply the MBTA in order to achieve your goals?

III. The Endangered Species Act

The Endangered Species Act (ESA) is the first and only comprehensive U.S. statute governing the protection of imperiled species. Although it mentions the protection of ecosystems in its statement of purpose, it is almost entirely focused on individual species. Indeed, the Act does not even treat species differently based on their ecological value, nor on their charismatic value to people. It was drafted with the goal (however unrealistic) of saving them all. There is little guidance in the Act regarding how to triage species when this proves impossible, though it does provide the implementing agencies with some limited authority to do so.

The Endangered Species Act is one of several environmental statutes that contain citizen suit provisions. A citizen suit provision allows anyone to sue over a violation of the statute, thereby providing an additional enforcement mechanism. This is explained in further detail in the judicial review chapter. Of course, nothing Congress places into a statute can override the requirement that one have constitutional standing to bring a case to the courts. Thus, a plaintiff must still show the essential trio of injury, causation, and redressability.

A. The Species Listing Process

The Endangered Species Act provides a process for listing vulnerable species and then protects them via prohibitions on both government and private behavior. The Act's protections apply only to listed species, so getting at-risk species listed is extremely important. Nonetheless, it can be quite challenging to do so. Both political clashes and resource scarcity prevent many species of concern from making their way into the ESA's entry gates.

Kalyani Robbins, *Strength in Numbers: Setting Quantitative Criteria for Listing Species under the Endangered Species Act*
27 UCLA J. Envtl L. & Pol. 1 (2009)

II. An Overview of the ESA and Listing Species

A. In the Beginning: The Evolution of U.S. Endangered Species Legislation and Listing Priorities

The first U.S. endangered species legislation, the Endangered Species Preservation Act of 1966, was the result of the Department of Interior's effort to obtain funding for an endangered species program after failed attempts to get that funding absent a preservation statute. The 1966 Act required the Secretary of the Interior to list species that were threatened with extinction, in consultation "with various scientific groups having expertise in this field." The Departments of Interior, Agriculture, and Defense were all charged with protecting these species and their habitats.

Next came the Endangered Species Conservation Act of 1969, which increased protections for invertebrate species and restrictions on interstate commerce in listed species. The 1969 Act included listing language still in use today, requiring the decisions be based on "the best scientific and commercial data available." The term "commercial data" refers only to data that goes to a species' vulnerability—such as threats from overutilization in commerce—and not to the consideration of economic factors, as Congress later clarified. While the legislative history does not elucidate the meaning of "best scientific data available," a "plausible explanation is that Congress intended through this language to continue the 1966 Act's requirement that Interior seek the input of independent biologists before making listing decisions." If this explanation is true, we must take into account an obvious goal behind this requirement, which was to increase objectivity and consistency in the listing process.

In 1973, the ESA, which was made possible by the enormous political support for environmental ideals at the time, became "the most comprehensive legislation for the preservation of endangered species ever enacted by any nation." Among the numerous improvements (from the preservation perspective) were the inclusion of species not yet on the brink of the abyss, protection for plant species, prohibitions of private actions on private land, and a requirement that federal agencies must not jeopardize the continued existence of a protected species. The ESA's 1982 amendments also made a key change to the listing process, adding the word "solely" before the existing language of listing "on the basis of the best scientific and commercial data available," thus creating the somewhat controversial "strictly science mandate." The purpose of this change was to do away with the irrelevant economic impact analyses being conducted by the Reagan administration and require listing determinations to be purely about a species' biological condition.

At several points in the evolution of the ESA, Congress has made it clear that the listing process was intended to move forward as quickly and efficiently as possible. First, in explaining why the 1969 Act did not require the formal Administrative Procedure Act procedures to be followed, Congress stated that "[i]f the full right of hearing and judicial review is granted, the publication of the final list may be delayed for many months—months which may be crucial in determining whether a given species or subspecies will be able to survive." In 1979, concerned with the slow pace of listing that had resulted in only a tiny percentage of listings out of thousands of candidates, Congress established a priority system for considering species for listing. By 1988, the problem of delay had gotten out of control, with over 3000 candidate species, including nearly 1000 already deemed eligible but not yet listed, and only about 50 species being listed per year. Congress expressed concern that this rate would result in many species becoming extinct while they waited. Accordingly, they directed the Secretary to monitor all candidate species and "make prompt use" of the emergency listing process to prevent such loss.

B. The ESA Listing Process

The power to list endangered and threatened species belongs to the Secretary of the Interior and the Secretary of Commerce, who have delegated that power to the Fish and Wildlife Service (FWS) and National Marine Fisheries Service (NMFS), respectively (collectively "the Services"). The majority of species—terrestrial species and freshwater fish—are the responsibility of FWS, whereas NMFS is generally charged with the protection of marine species and anadromous fish, such as salmonids.

A species is endangered if it "is in danger of extinction throughout all or a significant portion of its range," and it is threatened if it "is likely to become an endangered species within the foreseeable future throughout all or a significant portion of its range." In determining whether a species fits into one of these two categories, the Services must consider five factors:

(A) the present or threatened destruction, modification, or curtailment of its habitat or range;

(B) overutilization for commercial, recreational, scientific, or educational purposes;

(C) disease or predation;

(D) the inadequacy of existing regulatory mechanisms; or

(E) other natural or manmade factors affecting its continued existence.

While these factors do constitute "criteria" to consider in determining a species' listing status, these criteria are highly generalized. They offer factors to subjectively consider, but no formulae to follow.

Citizens may petition the Secretary to list, uplist, downlist, or delist a species, and the Secretary must acknowledge the petition within thirty days. The Secretary has ninety days to determine whether the petition "presents substantial scientific or commercial information indicating that the petitioned action may be warranted." Substantial information means "that amount of information that would lead a reasonable person to believe that the measure proposed in the petition may be warranted." If the petition passes this bar, the Secretary must then commence a status review of the species, and is required within twelve months to determine whether the listing is warranted, not warranted, or warranted but precluded by competing demands.

The final category—warranted but precluded—was the brainchild of the Reagan Administration, putatively to allow those species in greatest need to be addressed first. It was never intended "to allow the Secretary to delay commencing the rulemaking process for any reason other than the existence of pending or imminent proposals to list species subject to a greater degree of threat." In reality, however, it has become a major source of additional discretion, leading to politically-based decisions rather than prioritization on the basis of threat. The category is an ER waiting room strewn with the corpses of those species who were forced to wait too long.

The status review is to be conducted in the same manner for citizen petitions as it is for those initiated by the agency. The Services have issued policy statements regarding the information standards for the status review process. Some of the requirements thus created are: (1) biologists must evaluate all information used, (2) these biologists must prefer primary sources wherever possible, (3) they must also seek out and objectively evaluate data that conflicts with the agency's position on the advisability of the listing and (4) the agency must obtain peer review by "three appropriate and independent specialists" for all listing proposals. Although these procedures generally coincide with those of the scientific method, it is worth noting that the agencies have not relinquished any discretion here. The scientists are either agency biologists or, in the case of the three mandatory peer reviews, specialists hand-selected by the agency. In addition to selecting the peer reviewers, the agency is also free to choose not to follow their advice, though it does have to include a summary of their views in the final rule.

As noted above, the status review results in one of three possible findings. A negative finding—either not warranted or warranted but precluded—is subject to immediate judicial review. A warranted finding leads to the administrative rulemaking process before listing, and is thus not a final agency action subject to review. Finally, if the agency does not take action within the required time limits, citizens can sue to compel agency action.

Once an action is deemed warranted, a final proposed listing regulation is published, and citizens have forty-five days to request a hearing. The public has sixty days to comment on the proposed listing, and the final published rule includes a review of these comments, summaries and explanations of any data used, and "a summary of factors affecting the species." The listing is to take effect no less than thirty days after the publication of the final rule, and no less than ninety days after it was formally proposed.

C. Lock, Stock, and Barrel: The Benefits of Getting Past the Velvet Rope

Although the listing process is somewhat broken, in the event that a species is lucky enough to make it through, the ESA has much to offer. It is because of the extensive protections offered these species that the ESA is so often called the "pit bull" of environmental legislation. This view, of course, ignores the fact that these generous protections are exceedingly difficult to come by, resulting in a statute with far duller teeth. In any event, the protective portion of the ESA is quite powerful, which is why the listing process is so incredibly important.

The first thing the agency must do upon listing a species is to designate critical habitat to allow that species some living space. The listing then "triggers the duty to prepare a recovery plan; the duty to conserve the species; the duty to consult; the duty to ensure that federal action is not likely to 'jeopardize' listed species or adversely modify critical habitat; and a prohibition on 'taking' listed species." The following is a slightly more detailed description of the two most key protective sections of the ESA: the section 7 consultation requirement and the section 9 take prohibition.

Section 7 requires all federal agencies to ensure that the actions they carry out, fund or authorize (such as by granting permits to private individuals) are not likely to jeopardize the continued existence of any listed species or adversely modify any designated critical habitat. The action agency accomplishes this via formal consultation with the wildlife agency responsible for the listed species at issue, which includes any species that may be affected by the agency action. The Secretary must then issue a formal biological opinion determining whether the action is or is not likely to jeopardize the species or adversely modify the critical habitat. The action agency holds the ultimate responsibility for compliance with the section and is not bound by the biological opinion in determining how to proceed.

Section 7

Section 9 prohibits any person, public or private, from "taking" a listed species of fish or wildlife. "Take" is a term of art—and a relatively broad one—encompassing both direct harm to the animals and indirect harm through habitat alterations that injure the animals. "Section 9 imposes extraordinarily broad liability, particularly in comparison to the laws that preceded it." The ESA directly entitles endangered species to this protection, while threatened species can only obtain section 9 protection via regulations. All threatened species (with limited exceptions) governed by FWS have this coverage, and NMFS provides it case-by-case to individual species.

Section 9

* * *

Notes and Questions

1. The excerpt refers to the National Marine Fisheries Service (NMFS) for its role listing marine mammals, salt water fish, and anadromous fish. NMFS is within the National Oceanic & Atmospheric Administration (NOAA), and is now more frequently referred to as NOAA Fisheries. However, you will often see the NMFS

acronym in older cases and writings, and it is still accurate and even used on the NOAA Fisheries website (such as when referring to which species are under NMFS's jurisdiction)

2. Anadromous fish are the sole exception to the division of species between FWS and NMFS being cleanly determined by whether the species is a marine species (of fish or mammal) covered by NMFS or a terrestrial species (including freshwater fish and avian species) covered by FWS. Anadromous fish cannot be categorized as either for one simple reason: they are technically both. Anadromous fish, such as salmon, are born in freshwater and travel to the ocean, where their physiology actually changes to allow them to be temporarily a marine species. They feed and grow to full adulthood in salt water and then return to their original freshwater homes to spawn the next generation, again requiring physiological changes to adapt to the changed environment. Species vary with regard to whether they can do this cycle multiple times or die after returning to spawn once. While tagging studies have demonstrated that the vast majority of anadromous fish return to their own precise birthplace to spawn, it is unknown how they achieve this remarkable feat.

3. The Act's original definition for the species it set out to protect included "any subspecies of fish or wildlife or plants and any other group of fish or wildlife of the same species or smaller taxa in common spatial arrangement that interbreed when mature." This meant that it was only possible to list an entire species or subspecies, even if its strength varied in different geographic areas. Congress amended the ESA to include distinct population segments (DPS) in 1978. The definition of species has since included "any subspecies of fish or wildlife or plants, and any distinct population segment of any species of vertebrate fish or wildlife which interbreeds when mature." However, it was not until 1996 that the wildlife agencies published their policy regarding how to determine whether a population qualified as a DPS. The Policy contains three evaluative steps, each one serving as a prerequisite to consideration of the next.

First, the Services will consider the "[d]iscreteness of the population segment in relation to the remainder of the species to which it belongs." Discreteness of a population may be based on its being either "markedly separated from other populations of the same taxon as a consequence of physical, physiological, ecological, or behavioral factors;" or "delimited by international governmental boundaries" where there are significantly different regulatory protections.

Next, and only if the Services have determined a population to be discrete, they will evaluate "[t]he significance of the population segment to the species to which it belongs." Significance is determined based upon the following four criteria: (1) Persistence of the discrete population segment in an ecological setting unusual or unique for the taxon, (2) Evidence that loss of the discrete population segment would result in a significant gap in the range of a taxon, (3) Evidence that the discrete population segment represents the only surviving natural occurrence of a taxon that may be more abundant elsewhere as an introduced population outside its historic range, or (4) Evidence that the discrete population segment differs markedly from other populations of the species in its genetic characteristics.

It is only then, once a DPS has been found to be both discrete and significant, that the Services move on to the third step and consider the population's conservation status under the ESA, in the same manner as with species in general. In other words, they will next consider the five factors noted above for listing species as threatened or endangered, as applied to the population at issue.

4. The ESA is a well-known nemesis of the land development and logging industries. Because of its ability to interfere with substantial projects on which many depend for their livelihoods, it is a constant source of controversy. The following cases should provide you with a sense of this problem.

Northern Spotted Owl v. Hodel

716 F. Supp. 479 (W.D. Wash. 1988)

Judge ZILLY:

A number of environmental organizations bring this action against the United States Fish & Wildlife Service ("Service") and others, alleging that the Service's decision not to list the northern spotted owl as endangered or threatened under the Endangered Species Act of 1973, as amended, 16 U.S.C. § 1531 *et seq.* ("ESA" or "the Act"), was arbitrary and capricious or contrary to law.

Since the 1970s the northern spotted owl has received much scientific attention, beginning with comprehensive studies of its natural history by Dr. Eric Forsman, whose most significant discovery was the close association between spotted owls and old-growth forests. This discovery raised concerns because the majority of remaining old-growth owl habitat is on public land available for harvest.

In January 1987, plaintiff Greenworld, pursuant to Sec. 4(b)(3) of the ESA, petitioned the Service to list the northern spotted owl as endangered. In August 1987, 29 conservation organizations filed a second petition to list the owl as endangered both in the Olympic Peninsula in Washington and in the Oregon Coast Range, and as threatened throughout the rest of its range.

The ESA directs the Secretary of the Interior to determine whether any species have become endangered or threatened due to habitat destruction, overutilization, disease or predation, or other natural or manmade factors. 16 U.S.C. § 1533(a)(1). The Act was amended in 1982 to ensure that the decision whether to list a species as endangered or threatened was based solely on an evaluation of the biological risks faced by the species, to the exclusion of all other factors. *See* Conf. Report 97-835, 97th Cong. 2d Sess. (Sept. 17, 1982) at 19, *reprinted in* 1982 U.S. Code Cong. & Admin. News 2860.

The Service's role in deciding whether to list the northern spotted owl as endangered or threatened is to assess the technical and scientific data in the administrative record against the relevant listing criteria in section 4(a)(1) and then to exercise its own expert discretion in reaching its decision.

In July 1987, the Service announced that it would initiate a status review of the spotted owl and requested public comment. The Service assembled a group of Service biologists, including Dr. Mark Shaffer, its staff expert on population viability, to conduct the review. The Service charged Dr. Shaffer with analyzing current scientific information on the owl. Dr. Shaffer concluded that:

the most reasonable interpretation of current data and knowledge indicate continued old growth harvesting is likely to lead to the extinction of the subspecies in the foreseeable future which argues strongly for listing the subspecies as threatened or endangered at this time.

The Service invited a peer review of Dr. Shaffer's analysis by a number of U.S. experts on population viability, all of whom agreed with Dr. Shaffer's prognosis for the owl, although each had some criticisms of his work.

The Service's decision is contained in its 1987 Status Review of the owl ("Status Review") and summarized in its Finding on Greenworld's petition ("Finding"). The Status Review was completed on December 14, 1987, and on December 17 the Service announced that listing the owl as endangered under the Act was not warranted at that time.[5] 52 Fed. Reg. 48552, 48554 (Dec. 23, 1987). This suit followed. Both sides now move for summary judgment on the administrative record before the Court. . . .

This Court reviews the Service's action under the "arbitrary and capricious" standard of the Administrative Procedure Act ("APA"). This standard is narrow and presumes the agency action is valid, but it does not shield agency action from a "thorough, probing, in-depth review." Courts must not "rubber-stamp the agency decision as correct."

Rather, the reviewing court must assure itself that the agency decision was "based on a consideration of the relevant factors. . . ." Moreover, it must engage in a "substantial inquiry" into the facts, one that is "searching and careful." This is particularly true in highly technical cases. . . .

Agency action is arbitrary and capricious where the agency has failed to "articulate a satisfactory explanation for its action including a 'rational connection between the facts found and the choice made.'"

The Status Review and the Finding to the listing petition offer little insight into how the Service found that the owl currently has a viable population. Although the Status Review cites extensive empirical data and lists various conclusions, it fails to provide any analysis. The Service asserts that it is entitled to make its own decision, yet it provides no explanation for its findings. An agency must set forth clearly the grounds on which it acted. Judicial deference to agency expertise is proper, but the Court will not do so blindly. The Court finds that the Service has not set forth the grounds for its decision against listing the owl.

---

5. The Service's Finding provides as follows:

A finding is made that a proposed listing of the northern spotted owl is not warranted at this time. Due to the need for population trend information and other biological data, priority given by the Service to this species for further research and monitoring will continue to be high. Interagency agreements and Service initiatives support continued conservation efforts.

The Service's documents also lack any expert analysis supporting its conclusion. Rather, the expert opinion is entirely to the contrary. The only reference in the Status Review to an actual opinion that the owl does not face a significant likelihood of extinction is a mischaracterization of a conclusion of Dr. Mark Boyce:

Boyce in his analysis of the draft preferred alternative conclusions that there is a low probability that the spotted owls will go extinct. He does point out that population fragmentation appears to impose the greatest risks to extinction. . . .

Dr. Boyce responded to the Service:

I did not conclude that the Spotted Owl enjoys a low probability of extinction, and I would be very disappointed if efforts to preserve the Spotted Owl were in any way thwarted by a misinterpretation of something I wrote.

Numerous other experts on population viability contributed to or reviewed drafts of the Status Review, or otherwise assessed spotted owl viability. Some were employed by the Service; others were independent. None concluded that the northern spotted owl is not at risk of extinction. For example, as noted above, Dr. Shaffer evaluated the current data and knowledge and determined that continued logging of old growth likely would lead to the extinction of the owl in the foreseeable future. This risk, he concluded, argued strongly for immediate listing of the subspecies as threatened or endangered.

The Service invited a peer review of Dr. Shaffer's analysis. Drs. Michael Soule, Bruce Wilcox, and Daniel Goodman, three leading U.S. experts on population viability, reviewed and agreed completely with Dr. Shaffer's prognosis for the owl.

For example, Dr. Soule, the acknowledged founder of the discipline of "conservation biology" (the study of species extinction), concluded:

I completely concur with your conclusions, and the methods by which you reached them. The more one hears about *Strix occidentalis caurina*, the more concern one feels. Problems with the data base and in the models notwithstanding, and politics notwithstanding, I just can't see how a responsible biologist could reach any other conclusion than yours.

The Court will reject conclusory assertions of agency "expertise" where the agency spurns unrebutted expert opinions without itself offering a credible alternative explanation. Here, the Service disregarded all the expert opinion on population viability, including that of its own expert, that the owl is facing extinction, and instead merely asserted its expertise in support of its conclusions.

The Service has failed to provide its own or other expert analysis supporting its conclusions. Such analysis is necessary to establish a rational connection between the evidence presented and the Service's decision. Accordingly, the United States Fish and Wildlife Service's decision not to list at this time the northern spotted owl as endangered or threatened under the Endangered Species Act was arbitrary and capricious and contrary to law.

The Court further finds that it is not possible from the record to determine that the Service considered the related issue of whether the northern spotted owl is a threatened species. This failure of the Service to review and make an express finding on the issue of threatened status is also arbitrary and capricious and contrary to law.

Decision: Remanded

In deference to the Service's expertise and its role under the Endangered Species Act, the Court remands this matter to the Service, which has 90 days from the date of this order to provide an analysis for its decision that listing the northern spotted owl as threatened or endangered is not currently warranted. Further, the Service is ordered to supplement its Status Review and petition Finding consistent with this Court's ruling.

Notes and Questions

1. This case shows how politically fraught listing decisions can be. Judges will only rarely find agency action to be arbitrary and capricious, which is a very low bar for the agency to overcome, but here the facts clearly did not support the agency's decision. Why do you think the agency might not list a species in spite of its qualification for listing? *Political, logging business agenda*

2. Regardless of political motivations, the demands of implementing the Endangered Species Act have always stretched the U.S. Fish & Wildlife Service's resources thin. The resulting backlog of species in need of listing (the only way to receive the full protections provided by the ESA) has led to regular litigation with biodiversity advocacy groups. In May and July of 2011, plaintiffs WildEarth Guardians and the Center for Biological Diversity (CBD) entered into major settlement agreements with FWS. The settlements set a schedule for FWS to resolve the backlog of candidate species, requiring that a determination be made for every species on the 2010 candidate list by the end of fiscal year 2017. At the time of this writing, the resulting multi-year work plan is well underway but not on schedule for the original goals. The following is a portion of the text on the FWS webpage for the plan's implementation schedule, which was updated on June 27, 2016:

> As the MDL agreement nears its end, the Service anticipates updating the workplan to include future actions out through FY2023.

> While this workplan is subject to revision due to unanticipated work demands or changes in the availability of funds or staffing during this planning timeframe, it is our intention to minimize changes to the dates for individual listing actions so as to maximize predictability for other agencies and the public. We will update this workplan periodically to reflect additions or other changes.

Western Watersheds Project v. U.S. Fish & Wildlife Service
2012 U.S. Dist. LEXIS 13771 (D. Idaho 2012)

Judge WINMILL:

Facts

The sage grouse is being squeezed. Its western range is consumed by wildfires; its eastern range is trampled by oil and gas drilling. The resulting fragmented habitat isolates and weakens populations, causing a dramatic decline in the species.

Alarmed by these trends, the Fish and Wildlife Service (FWS) decided that listing of the sage grouse was warranted under the Endangered Species Act. At the same time, however, the FWS declined to begin drafting rules to protect the birds because the agency has a limited budget and many other species were in worse condition.

This toothless finding—declaring that the sage grouse deserves protection but doing nothing about it—is known as a "warranted-but-precluded" finding. Critics claim that the agency has used this category as a dumping ground for politically-charged species, calling it "an ER waiting room strewn with the corpses of those species who were forced to wait too long." Kalyani Robbins, *Strength in Numbers: Setting Quantitative Criteria for Listing Species Under the Endangered Species Act*, 27 UCLA J. Envtl. L. & Pol'y 1 (2009).

Indeed, the backlog at the agency was challenged by environmental groups. Some of those groups reached a settlement with the FWS, committing the agency to a timetable to reduce the backlog. Specifically with regard to the sage grouse, the FWS agreed to remove the bird from its "warranted-but-precluded" limbo by 2015.

Plaintiff WWP, however, did not enter into that settlement, and continues to litigate here, seeking a faster resolution for the sage grouse. For reasons explained below, the Court rejects arguments that WWP is barred from proceeding with this lawsuit because it is somehow bound by a settlement that it did not sign.

WWP asks the Court to reverse the FWS's warranted-but-precluded decision for the sage grouse, and to order the agency to prepare listing rules for the sage grouse within 90 days. WWP is challenging the "precluded" portion of the "warranted-but-precluded" decision, focusing on a key finding by the Director of the FWS that the threats to the sage grouse were merely "moderate" rather than "high". This finding, which WWP alleges was based on politics rather than science, essentially guaranteed that the listing would be "precluded." *[WWP Argument]*

Before making this finding, the FWS Director had received a recommendation from FWS Regional Director Steve Guertin that the listing be "warranted-but-precluded." Guertin's recommendation ignored his agency's own guidelines, contained no scientific analysis, and featured off-hand comments about the various political interests at play in the case. Given that political meddling has already resulted in one reversal in this case, the Court was frankly astonished at Guertin's cavalier recommendation.

It was not until after Guertin made his recommendation that the agency's scientists supplied the necessary scientific analysis to the Director. This sequence of events raises a red flag of warning: Did the agency scientists "bend" the science to justify Guertin's recommendation? To answer this question, the Court engaged in an especially thorough review of the record. It contains evidence that (1) sage grouse populations in some areas are stable, (2) substantial habitat exists in many parts of the range, and (3) 96% of all populations will remain above effective population sizes over the next 30 years. All of this supports the finding of the Director that the threat level is moderate. *[Issue]*

However, the record also contains substantial contrary evidence which indicates that the threats to the sage grouse are high and immediate. The science is thus not conclusive on the threat level — it does not lead inevitably to a threat level finding that fits precisely within the bureaucratic designations of "high" or "moderate." Given this, the Director had to exercise his discretion to make a difficult decision. In reviewing that decision, the Court is prohibited by law from substituting its own judgment for that of the Director, but must instead defer to that decision so long as it is not arbitrary or capricious.

Decision

The initial recommendation of Regional Director Guertin was clearly arbitrary and capricious, since it was offered before receiving any scientific input. But the subsequent decision of the Director was based on sound science and cured the significant deficiencies of the recommendation. The Court therefore upholds the Director's decision that the threat level to the sage grouse falls into the moderate category.

"Warranted-but-precluded" Criticism

The Director also had to certify that the FWS is making expeditious progress on its ESA duties in order to place the sage grouse in the warranted-but-precluded category. Congress originally intended that this category be used sparingly and that it not become a bottomless pit where controversial species are dumped and forgotten. There are now over 250 species in this category, and the average time spent there is about 19 years. Species have gone extinct while waiting for listing rules. By no common sense measure of the word "expeditious" has the FWS made expeditious progress in its ESA duties. While the FWS blames these delays on a lack of funding by Congress, some of the agency's financial woes are self-inflicted. In the past, the FWS's parent agency — the Interior Department — has refused to seek sufficient funds from Congress and has actively sought caps on ESA spending.

Nevertheless, as discussed above, the FWS has recently committed to reducing the backlog, and has made specific commitments regarding the sage grouse. These commitments are the only reason the Court will uphold the agency's certification that it is making expeditious progress. If those commitments prove unreliable, the Court will quickly revisit its findings here upon prompting from any party.

Decision

Despite troubling aspects of the FWS decision process, the Court ultimately finds that the Director's decision to place the sage grouse in the warranted-but-precluded category is not arbitrary or capricious.

B. Critical Habitat Designation

When a species is listed as endangered or threatened under the ESA, the listing agency is usually required to simultaneously designate the geographic areas that are critical habitat for that species. Critical habitat is habitat deemed essential to the recovery of the species. Getting to that understanding of the term was no easy task, however, and there is an evolution we can observe leading up to it. That evolution begins with substantial controversy over the value of critical habitat.

Kalyani Robbins, *Recovery of an Endangered Provision: Untangling and Reviving Critical Habitat under the Endangered Species Act*

58 Buff. L. Rev. 1095 (2010)

I. The Fundamentals of Critical Habitat

* * *

[handwritten margin note: ① every species needs a place to live ↳ for recovery, it includes where species is suitable to live (expansion)]

A. Designation

The ESA requires that critical habitat be designated "concurrently" with listing a species as threatened or endangered, at least "to the maximum extent prudent and determinable." The "prudent and determinable" language has been used as a source of discretion by the Services, forcing the courts to define and limit the terms. One of the factors to consider in designating critical habitat is the economic impact of doing so, though this factor is strictly forbidden in making decisions regarding the listing of species in the first place. This distinction is important . . . .

Critical habitat is defined as habitat which is "essential to the conservation of the species." [T]he ESA defines "conservation" as synonymous with recovery, so the combination of these two definitions makes clear that critical habitat is that habitat which the species needs in order to recover to the point of no longer being identifiable as threatened or endangered. Although these two definitions make it abundantly clear that the goal of critical habitat is to recover the species to health, Congress took it a step further and provided for the designation of critical habitat that is no longer occupied by the species, but which is also deemed "essential for the conservation of the species." The only conceivable reason to designate habitat not currently occupied by the species as critical habitat is in the hope that the species may use that habitat in order to expand its occupation to what it once was (i.e., recovery).

So, in a nutshell, what we see thus far is that the ESA requires the Services to list species as threatened or endangered, and then adds to that listing the designation of critical habitat. Listing and designation are the essential labeling provisions that set the scene for later provisions with actual teeth. The listings and designations are tools to work with later in the Act, and Congress must have sought to achieve something beyond what it could by working with listing alone. The statutory definition of critical habitat indicates that this something was recovery.

B. Consultation

[F]ederal agencies are not to take action "likely to jeopardize the continued existence of any endangered species or threatened species or result in the destruction or adverse modification" of its critical habitat. This requirement is referred to as the "consultation requirement" because action agencies must consult first with one of the Services. The prohibition against jeopardy is provided to a species simply because it is listed. Because the very first factor considered in the decision to list a species is "the present or threatened destruction, modification, or curtailment of its habitat or range," it is clear that a listed species can be jeopardized via harm to its habitat. Indeed, harm to habitat is frequently at issue in cases involving jeopardy.

Nonetheless, Congress saw fit to set aside certain habitats to be protected from any destruction or adverse modification at all, not just that which rises to the level of jeopardizing the continued existence of the species. Clearly, something more was at stake here, or it would be superfluous. Species were to be listed and protected from actions, including habitat modification, which placed their very existence in jeopardy. On top of that, certain habitat was to be identified for the conservation (i.e., recovery) of these species, and that habitat was to be more heavily protected in order to be available for that purpose. In other words, agencies cannot damage critical habitat, even if it would not jeopardize the continued existence of the species, as that habitat is there to promote conservation. Clearly, this adds value for the species above listing alone.

Jeopardy standard [margin note]

* * *

C. Importance

The Supreme Court has recognized that "[t]he plain intent of Congress in enacting [the ESA] was to halt and reverse the trend toward species extinction, whatever the cost." Recovery of struggling species is the goal, not merely protecting the status quo. As a practical matter, however, there is only one provision in the ESA that lends itself to any significant potential for recovery, and that is critical habitat. The prohibition against "take" protects individuals of a listed species from harm, which is more about survival. Likewise, the jeopardy standard, albeit not purely about survival . . . , is primarily focused on "continued existence," which does not necessarily require full recovery to the point of delisting. The only place in the ESA where the express goal of a specific provision (as opposed to the general purposes stated for the Act) is recovery to this point is critical habitat. It is thus arguably the most important piece of the entire puzzle.

Destruction and/or adverse modification of habitat is the leading danger to species in North America. Even with the protection of critical habitat as weak as it has been under the Services' regulations, species with designated critical habitat are more than twice as likely to improve their status and less than half as likely to decline in status. If the inadequately protected critical habitat can make this much of a difference, it is not difficult to see how significant the improvement could be with stronger protection for critical habitat that focuses on recovery. Species with designated critical habitat are also more likely to have recovery plans created for them than the far more numerous species without designated critical habitat. Also, of all species with recovery plans, those with designated critical habitat have greater task implementation than the rest. Moreover, public awareness of critical habitat areas tends to result in greater general care efforts in these areas.

A road realignment proposal in Hawaii provided an excellent example of how differently a species can be treated simply because it has critical habitat. The project was to take place within the critical habitat designated for the Palila, leading the U.S. Army and the federal Department of Transportation to propose $14 million in mitigation projects. However, there were more than a dozen other listed species in the project area, none of which had critical habitat designations. No mitigation measures were considered for these other listed species.

Finally, a key advantage to critical habitat designation is that it is the only provision in the entire ESA that provides any protection for unoccupied habitat. It stands to reason that a species that has diminished to the point of listing under the ESA is going to occupy a smaller habitat than it did when it was doing well. Naturally, if our goal is to recover the species to its prior condition, it will be necessary to protect some of its former habitat as well as that which it currently occupies. That Congress acknowledged this need is evident from the fact that it provided for designation of unoccupied critical habitat. The majority of species still do not have designated critical habitat, and as such, nothing is being done to prevent the complete development of their former habitat, which could make it too late for recovery once the Services are eventually forced to designate critical habitat for all.

Natural Resources Defense Council v. U.S. Department of the Interior

113 F.3d 1121 (9th Cir. 1997)

Judge PREGERSON:

This case presents the question whether the defendants violated the Endangered Species Act by failing to designate critical habitat for the coastal California gnatcatcher. . . . The coastal California gnatcatcher is a songbird unique to coastal southern California and northern Baja California. The gnatcatcher's survival depends upon certain subassociations of coastal sage scrub, a type of habitat that has been severely depleted by agricultural and urban development. Approximately 2500 pairs of gnatcatchers survive in southern California today.

On March 30, 1993, the U.S. Fish and Wildlife Service listed the gnatcatcher under the Endangered Species Act as a "threatened species." Under section 4 of the Act, the listing of a threatened species must be accompanied by the concurrent designation of critical habitat for that species "to the maximum extent prudent and determinable." The designation of critical habitat in turn triggers the protections of section 7 of the Act. Section 7 requires that federal agencies consult with the Secretary of the Interior (the "Secretary") to ensure that actions authorized, funded, or carried out by federal agencies do not harm critical habitat.

At the time of the gnatcatcher's listing as a threatened species, the Service found that coastal sage scrub habitat loss posed "a significant threat to the continued existence of the coastal California gnatcatcher." Nevertheless, the Service concluded that critical habitat designation would not be "prudent" within the meaning of section 4 for two reasons. First, the Service claimed that the public identification of critical habitat would increase the risk that landowners might deliberately destroy gnatcatcher habitat. Second, the Service claimed that critical habitat designation "would not appreciably benefit" the gnatcatcher because most gnatcatcher habitat is found on private lands to which section 7's consultation requirement does not apply. . . .

The Service's Failure to Designate Critical Habitat

Section 4 of the Act requires that the gnatcatcher's listing as a threatened species be accompanied by concurrent designation of critical habitat "*to the maximum extent prudent* and determinable":

> The Secretary, by regulation promulgated in accordance with subsection (b) of this section and *to the maximum extent prudent* and determinable—
>
> (A) shall, concurrently with making a determination under paragraph
>
> (1) that a species is an endangered species or a threatened species, designate any habitat of such species which is then considered to be critical habitat; and
>
> (B) may, from time-to-time thereafter as appropriate, revise such designation.

16 U.S.C. § 1533(a)(3) (emphasis added).

The Act itself does not define the term "prudent." The Service has defined what would *not* be prudent, however, in the regulations promulgated under the Act. According to the regulations, critical habitat designation is not prudent "when one or both of the following situations exist":

> (i) The species is threatened by taking or other human activity, and identification of critical habitat can be expected to *increase the degree of such threat to the species,* or
>
> (ii) Such designation of critical habitat *would not be beneficial to the species.*

50 C.F.R. § 424.12(a)(1)(I)-(ii) (1995) (emphasis added).

When the Service published the gnatcatcher's final listing as a threatened species, the Service stated that critical habitat designation would not be prudent under either prong of the regulatory definition. The final listing fails to show, however, that the Service adequately "considered the relevant factors and articulated a rational connection between the facts found and the choice made". . . .

A. Increased Threat to the Species

The Service's first reason for declining to designate critical habitat was that designation would increase the degree of threat to the gnatcatcher. The final listing referred to eleven cases in which landowners or developers had destroyed gnatcatcher sites; in two of these cases, habitat was destroyed after the Service notified local authorities that gnatcatchers were present at a proposed development site. On the basis of this history, the Service concluded that because the publication of critical habitat descriptions and maps would enable more landowners to identify gnatcatcher sites, designating critical habitat "would likely make the species more vulnerable to [prohibited takings] activities."

This "increased threat" rationale fails to balance the pros and cons of designation as Congress expressly required under section 4 of the Act. Section 4(b)(2) states that the Secretary may only exclude portions of habitat from critical habitat designation "if he determines that the benefits of such exclusion *outweigh the benefits* of specifying such area as part of the critical habitat." 16 U.S.C. § 1533(b)(2) (emphasis added). In addition, the Service itself has said that it will forgo habitat designation as a matter of prudence only "in those cases in which the possible adverse consequences would *outweigh the benefits* of designation." 49 Fed. Reg. 38900, 38903 (1984) (emphasis added).

In this case, the Service never weighed the benefits of designation against the risks of designation. The final listing decision cited only eleven cases of habitat destruction, out of 400,000 acres of gnatcatcher habitat. The listing did not explain how such evidence shows that designation would cause more landowners to destroy, rather than protect, gnatcatcher sites. The absence of such an explanation is particularly troubling given that the record shows these areas had already been surveyed extensively in other gnatcatcher or coastal sage scrub studies published prior to the date of final listing.

By failing to balance the relative threat of coastal sage scrub takings both with and without critical habitat designation, the Service failed to consider all relevant factors. . . . The Service's reliance on the "increased threat" exception to section 4 designation was therefore improper.

B. No Benefit to the Species

The Service's second reason for declining to designate habitat was that designation "would not appreciably benefit the species." According to the Service's final listing decision, most populations of gnatcatchers are found on private lands to which section 7's consultation requirement would not apply. The final listing decision suggests that designation may only be deemed "beneficial to the species" and therefore "prudent" if it would result in the application of section 7 to "the *majority* of land-use activities occurring within critical habitat."

By rewriting its "beneficial to the species" test for prudence into a "beneficial to *most* of the species" requirement, the Service expands the narrow statutory exception for imprudent designations into a broad exemption for imperfect designations. This expansive construction of the "no benefit" prong to the imprudence exception is inconsistent with clear congressional intent.

The fact that Congress intended the imprudence exception to be a narrow one is clear from the legislative history, which reads in part:

The committee intends that in most situations the Secretary will . . . designate critical habitat at the same time that a species is listed as either endangered or threatened. *It is only in rare circumstances where the specification of critical habitat concurrently with the listing would not be beneficial to the species.*

H.R. Rep. No. 95-1625 at 17 (1978), *reprinted in* 1978 U.S.C.C.A.N. 9453, 9467 (emphasis added). *See also* Enos v. Marsh, 769 F.2d 1363, 1371 (9th Cir.1985) (holding that the Secretary "may only fail to designate critical habitat under *rare* circumstances") (emphasis added); Northern Spotted Owl v. Lujan, 758 F. Supp. 621, 626 (W.D.Wash.1991) ("This legislative history leaves little room for doubt regarding the intent of Congress: The designation of critical habitat is to coincide with the final listing decision absent *extraordinary* circumstances") (emphasis added).

By expanding the imprudence exception to encompass all cases in which designation would fail to control "*the majority* of land-use activities occurring within critical habitat," the Service contravenes the clear congressional intent that the imprudence exception be a rare exception. Since "the court, as well as the agency, must give effect to the unambiguously expressed intent of Congress," we reject the Service's suggestion that designation is only necessary where it would protect the majority of species habitat.

In the present case, the Service found that of approximately 400,000 acres of gnatcatcher habitat, over 80,000 acres were publicly-owned and therefore subject to section 7 requirements. Other privately-owned lands would also be subject to section 7 requirements if their use involved any form of federal agency authorization or action.

The Service does not explain why a designation that would benefit such a large portion of critical habitat is not "beneficial to the species" within the plain meaning of the regulations and "prudent" within the clear meaning of the statute. Accordingly, we conclude that the Service's "no benefit" argument fails to "articulate[ ] a rational connection between the facts found and the choice made".... The Service's reliance on the "no benefit" exception to section 4 designation was therefore improper.

C. Less Benefit to the Species

In addition to the above two rationales which were stated in the final listing, the defendants now offer a third argument in defense of the Service's failure to designate critical habitat. The defendants contend that a "far superior" means of protecting gnatcatcher habitat is provided by the state-run "comprehensive habitat management program" created under California's Natural Communities Conservation Program ("NCCP"). The Service has endorsed the NCCP as a "special rule" for gnatcatcher protection under section 4(d) of the Act, 16 U.S.C. § 1533(d).

Regulations under the Act provide that "the reasons for not designating critical habitat will be stated in the publication of proposed and final rules listing a species." 50 C.F.R. § 424.12(a). The NCCP alternative was not identified in the Service's proposed or final listings as a reason not to designate critical habitat. Therefore, this argument is not properly before us for consideration.

Even if we were to consider the NCCP alternative, however, the existence of such an alternative would not justify the Service's failure to designate critical habitat. The Act provides that designation of critical habitat is necessary except when designation would not be "prudent" or "determinable." The Service's regulations define "*not* prudent" as "increasing the degree of [takings] threat to the species" or "*not* . . . beneficial to the species." 50 C.F.R. § 424.12(a)(1)(I)-(ii) (emphasis added). Neither the Act nor the implementing regulations sanctions nondesignation of habitat when designation would be merely less beneficial to the species than another type of protection.

In any event, the NCCP alternative cannot be viewed as a functional substitute for critical habitat designation. Critical habitat designation triggers mandatory consultation requirements for federal agency actions involving critical habitat. The NCCP alternative, in contrast, is a purely voluntary program that applies only to non-federal land-use activities. The Service itself recognized at the time of its final listing decision that "no substantive protection of the coastal California gnatcatcher is currently provided by city/county enrollments [in the NCCP]." Accordingly, we reject the defendants' post hoc invocation of the NCCP to justify the Service's failure to designate critical habitat. . . .

Dissent

Judge O'SCANNLAIN, dissenting:

. . . The majority states that a determination of whether a designation would be prudent must include weighing the benefits of designation against its risks. Our cases do not support this conclusion, however; they generally require only that the agency follow a rational decision-making process. . . . That point aside, however, I believe that a fair reading of the Service's decision reveals that it did in fact conduct precisely the balancing test called for by the majority when it concluded that designation may cause the intentional destruction of habitat by private landowners, but would produce little benefit since most of the habitat is not on publicly-owned land. It is worth quoting the Service at length:

[S]ome landowners or project developers have brushed or graded sites occupied by gnatcatchers prior to regulatory agency review or the issuance of a grading permit. In some instances, gnatcatcher habitat was destroyed shortly after the Service notified a local regulatory agency that a draft environmental review document for a proposed housing development failed to disclose the presence of gnatcatchers onsite. On the basis of these kinds of activities, *the Service finds that publication of critical habitat descriptions and maps would likely make the species more vulnerable* to [prohibited] activities. . . .

Most populations of the coastal California gnatcatcher in the United States are found on private lands where Federal involvement in land-use activities does not generally occur. Additional protection resulting from critical habitat designation is achieved through the section 7 consultation process. *Since section 7 would not apply to the majority of land-use activities occurring within critical habitat, its designation would not appreciably benefit the species.*

58 Fed. Reg. 16742, 16756 (1993) (emphasis added). In my view, applying the majority's balancing requirement, the Service indeed weighed the benefits and risks of designation and came to a rational, defensible conclusion that designation was not prudent. . . .

opinion

The second situation in which designation would not be prudent exists when "such designation of critical habitat would not be beneficial to the species." 50 C.F.R. §424.12(a)(1)(ii) (1996). . . . In my view, the majority takes too narrow a view of the phrase "beneficial to the species." The question should not be whether any member of the species would be better off by a slender margin, but whether the species as a whole would benefit from the designation. Even though the gnatcatchers in most of the habitat would not benefit, reasons the majority, some of the gnatcatchers would benefit, and hence designation would be beneficial for the species. The problem with this argument is that it overlooks the Service's expert opinion, to which we are required to defer, that designation may harm the gnatcatchers when landowners intentionally destroy the habitat. Even though individual pockets of gnatcatchers may benefit, the species as a whole may not.

Notes and Questions

1. As the dissent points out, likely harm to the species, such as by attracting poachers to it, is indeed a permissible basis for an agency finding that critical habitat designation is not prudent. Do you think that the majority held otherwise, or did the facts of this case fit better with a typical listed species entitled to critical habitat? How do these facts differ from those of concern for purposes of the "not prudent" exception? How does the danger described in the dissent differ from that of any critical habitat designation? Is there a black market for gnatcatcher products?

Gifford Pinchot Task Force v. U.S. Fish & Wildlife Service
378 F.3d 1059 (9th Cir. 2004)

Judge GOULD:

This is a record review case in which the Appellants, an assortment of environmental organizations, challenge six biological opinions (BiOps) issued by the United States Fish and Wildlife Service (USFWS or FWS) pursuant to the Endangered Species Act (ESA). The BiOps in question allowed for timber harvests in specified Northwest forests and also authorized incidental "takes" of the Northern spotted owl (spotted owl), a threatened species under the ESA. . . .

[T]he federal government adopted a comprehensive forest management plan for the entire range of the spotted owl known as the "Northwest Forest Plan." The NFP survived litigation, *see Seattle Audubon Soc'y v. Moseley*, 80 F.3d 1401 (9th Cir. 1996), and currently controls the use of the forests at the heart of this challenge. Relevant to this appeal, the NFP allocated the forests into "late successional reserves" (LSRs), "matrix" lands, and "adaptive management areas," with different harvesting rules applied to each area. The LSR allows less harvesting than matrix lands. An interagency analysis of the NFP found that it would provide for stable and well-distributed owl populations, though owl populations were projected to decline in the short-term. The NFP was subject to a Section 7 consultation and the resulting BiOp concerning this broad forest plan found no jeopardy or adverse modification. Because the NFP covered such a wide area, from Northern Washington to Northern California, involving virtually all of the federal government's forested land in this expansive area, the NFP BiOp explicitly declined to address the unique impacts of any particular action or implementation of the NFP. The NFP BiOp did not authorize incidental takes, deferring such consideration instead to future BiOps that would address specific projects.

Since the government approval of the NFP, the FWS has issued at least 298 BiOps and incidental take statements for spotted owls in the lands covered by the NFP. A total of 1080 incidental takes of spotted owls have been authorized, and 82,000 acres of spotted owl habitat have been removed, downgraded, or degraded. Six representative

BiOps are the subject of this litigation. [The district court granted summary judgment for the FWS]. . . .

We . . . turn to the critical habitat portion of the challenged BiOps. It is here that the picture is complicated by error and, on our analysis, becomes less rosy for the FWS.

1

Appellants first argue that the FWS's interpretation of "adverse modification" is unlawful. ESA Section 7 consultations require that in every biological opinion, the consulting agency (here the FWS) ensure that the proposed action "is not likely to jeopardize the continued existence of" an endangered or threatened species and that the federal action will not result in the "destruction or adverse modification" of the designated "critical habitat" of the listed species.

Section 7 Analysis

The FWS, in turn, defined "destruction or adverse modification" as:

> [A] direct or indirect alteration that appreciably diminishes the value of critical habitat for both the survival and recovery of a listed species. Such alterations include, but are not limited to, alterations adversely modifying any of those physical or biological features that were the basis for determining the habitat to be critical.

50 C.F.R. § 402.02. This regulation requires a close reading to grasp its import. Appellants argue that the regulatory definition sets the bar too high because the adverse modification threshold is not triggered by a proposed action until there is an appreciable diminishment of the value of critical habitat for both survival and recovery.[6]

We agree. Here, the FWS has interpreted "destruction or adverse modification" as changes to the critical habitat "that appreciably diminish[] the value of critical habitat for *both* the survival *and* recovery of a listed species." 50 C.F.R. § 402.02 (emphases added). This regulatory definition explicitly requires appreciable diminishment of the critical habitat necessary for survival before the "destruction or adverse modification" standard could ever be met. Because it is logical and inevitable that a species requires more critical habitat for recovery than is necessary for the species survival, the regulation's singular focus becomes "survival." Given this literal understanding of the regulation's express definition of "adverse modification," we consider whether that definition is a permissible interpretation of the ESA.

"Survival" vs. "recovery"

To answer that question, there is no need to go beyond *Chevron*'s first step in analyzing the permissibility of the regulation; the regulatory definition of "adverse modification" contradicts Congress's express command. As the Fifth and Tenth Circuits have already recognized, the regulatory definition reads the "recovery" goal out of the adverse modification inquiry; a proposed action "adversely modifies" critical habitat if, and only if, the value of the critical habitat for *survival* is appreciably diminished. The FWS could authorize the complete elimination of critical habitat necessary only for recovery, and so long as the smaller amount of critical habitat necessary for

---

6. This claim, which challenges the FWS regulation, is reviewed under the familiar *Chevron U.S.A., Inc. v. Natural Resources Defense Council, Inc.*, 467 U.S. 837 (1984), framework.

survival is not appreciably diminished, then no "destruction or adverse modification," as defined by the regulation, has taken place. This cannot be right. If the FWS follows its own regulation, then it is obligated to be indifferent to, if not to ignore, the recovery goal of critical habitat.

The agency's controlling regulation on critical habitat thus offends the ESA because the ESA was enacted not merely to forestall the extinction of species (i.e., promote a species survival), but to allow a species to recover to the point where it may be delisted. *See* 16 U.S.C. § 1532(3) (defining conservation as all methods that can be employed to "bring any endangered species or threatened species to the point at which the measures provided pursuant to this [Act] are no longer necessary"). The ESA also defines critical habitat as including "the specific areas . . . occupied by the species . . . which are . . . essential to the *conservation* of the species" and the "specific areas outside the geographical area occupied by the species . . . that . . . are essential for the *conservation* of the species. . . ." 16 U.S.C. § 1532(5)(A) (emphases added). By these definitions, it is clear that Congress intended that conservation and survival be two different (though complementary) goals of the ESA. *See* 16 U.S.C. § 1533(f)(1) ("The Secretary shall develop and implement plans . . . for the *conservation* and *survival* of endangered species and threatened species.") (emphasis added). Clearly, then, the purpose of establishing "critical habitat" is for the government to carve out territory that is not only necessary for the species' survival but also essential for the species' recovery.

Congress, by its own language, viewed conservation and survival as distinct, though complementary, goals, and the requirement to preserve critical habitat is designed to promote both conservation and survival. Congress said that "destruction or adverse modification" could occur when sufficient critical habitat is lost so as to threaten a species' recovery even if there remains sufficient critical habitat for the species' survival. The regulation, by contrast, finds that adverse modification to critical habitat can only occur when there is so much critical habitat lost that a species' very survival is threatened. The agency's interpretation would drastically narrow the scope of protection commanded by Congress under the ESA. To define "destruction or adverse modification" of critical habitat to occur only when there is appreciable diminishment of the value of the critical habitat for both survival *and* conservation fails to provide protection of habitat when necessary only for species' recovery. The narrowing construction implemented by the regulation is regrettably, but blatantly, contradictory to Congress' express command. Where Congress in its statutory language required "or," the agency in its regulatory definition substituted "and." This is not merely a technical glitch, but rather a failure of the regulation to implement Congressional will. . . .

That the agency was operating under a regulation that we now hold was impermissible has an inescapable bearing on the requisite showing of whether the FWS considered recovery in its critical habitat inquiry. Here, the Supreme Court demands that we afford the agency a presumption of regularity. In other words, the FWS must be presumed to have followed the adverse modification regulation. Thus, when analyzing the BiOps' critical habitat analysis, we must presume, unless rebutted by evidence in the record, that the FWS followed its definition of adverse modification and thereby ignored the evaluation of whether adequate critical habitat would remain to ensure species recovery. . . .

[The court reviewed each of the BiOps and concluded that the role of critical habitat in facilitating the recovery of the owls was either neglected or cursory, so the flaws in the agency's regulation did not constitute a harmless error].

2

. . . . Appellants claim that the critical habitat analysis relies, in part, on alternative habitat in the LSRs and that such reliance on the LSR to compensate for a loss of critical habitat is unlawful. The FWS responds that the LSR is not used as a substitute, but as a mutually overlapping regime. The rule that designated the critical habitat for the spotted owl specifically provided that adverse modification analysis should take into account consistency with other conservation plans.

There is little doubt that there is overlap and complementation between critical habitat areas and LSRs. In our view, however, Appellants have the better of the argument as to why LSRs cannot stand in for critical habitat within the meaning of the ESA. First, the plain language of the ESA requires that the adverse modification inquiry examine a given project's effect on critical habitat, that is, the land specifically designated by the Secretary of Interior for that purpose. The purpose of designating "critical habitat" is to set aside certain areas as "essential" for the survival and recovery of the threatened species. To create critical habitat, there is extensive study, detailed analysis, and ultimately notice and comment rule-making. Once designated, critical habitat receives its legal protection because it is subject to the exact Section 7 consultations at issue in this case. If we allow the survival and recovery benefits derived from a parallel habitat conservation project (the NFP and its LSRs) that is not designated critical habitat to stand in for the loss of designated critical habitat in the adverse modification analysis, we would impair Congress' unmistakable aim that critical habitat analysis focus on the actual critical habitat. We would also be approving a transition away from ESA protections to mere compliance with the broader but perhaps less rigorous NFP. Compliance with the NFP, as important as it is, does not in itself generate the same protection for habitat as Section 7 compliance. Congressional intent is clear, and existing or potential conservation measures outside of the critical habitat cannot properly be a substitute for the maintenance of critical habitat that is required by Section 7.

This conclusion, which is borne out by analysis of the ESA, is mandated by the Supreme Court. *See TVA v. Hill*, 437 U.S. 153, 171–72 (1978) (holding that the potential to transplant the endangered snail darter to suitable habitat does not circumvent the ESA's bar on destruction of critical habitat). Suitable alternative habitat, here LSRs, is no substitute for designated critical habitat. If it were, then the Court in *TVA* would have allowed the completion of the Tellico Dam and simply required that the snail darter be moved to the suitable alternative habitat. However, the Court held that the ESA's plain language precluded such a result. In our case, the result is the same: That the spotted owl has suitable alternative habitat (e.g., non-critical habitat

LSRs) has, strictly speaking, no bearing on whether there is adverse modification of critical habitat.

decision

If the FWS wants to change the boundaries of the critical habitat, it might do so if permitted by law after notice and comment procedures. But it cannot rely on a conservation program that has the same goal as critical habitat to change the boundaries of the spotted owl's critical habitat. Congress told the FWS to designate critical habitat and ensure that the designated critical habitat is not adversely modified. It matters not if there is worthwhile and possibly suitable habitat outside of the designated "critical habitat;" what mattered to Congress, and what must matter to the agency, is to protect against loss or degradation of the designated "critical habitat" itself. We hold that the agency's finding that loss of critical habitat was not an "adverse modification" because of the existence of suitable external habitat is arbitrary and capricious and is contrary to law. . . .

Notes and Questions

1. This 2004 case invalidated the regulation defining adverse modification of critical habitat, as it did not adequately protect against harms that impact recovery of the species. It was more than a decade before the FWS bothered to replace this regulation. It was eventually published in 2016. That said, the administration noted that the 2016 regulation merely codifies the approach in use ever since this 2004 invalidation of the former rule. The new regulatory definition is as follows:

> *Destruction or adverse modification* means a direct or indirect alteration that appreciably diminishes the value of critical habitat for the conservation of a listed species. Such alterations may include, but are not limited to, those that alter the physical or biological features essential to the conservation of a species or that preclude or significantly delay development of such features.

2. Although the new definition sticks with the term "conservation," as noted above that term has been defined in reference to recovery. In the FWS press release on the new definition, they also refer to recovery:

> [The new definition] retains the current focus of the Services' review of federal actions on how those actions affect the "physical or biological features essential to the conservation of a listed species," and the ability of that habitat to support the species throughout its life cycle, and to meet the species' recovery needs.

C. Consultation Requirement

Now that a species has been listed and may or may not have some designated critical habitat, we can begin to review the resulting protections it now enjoys. The first of the two main sections of the ESA providing for protection of listed species is Section 7, which requires all federal agencies (of any kind) to ensure, via consultation with the relevant wildlife agency, that their actions will neither jeopardize the continued existence of a listed species nor adversely modify its critical habitat. Although this is referred to as the consultation section, it is actually more substantive than procedural, because the ultimate responsibility to avoid jeopardy or adverse modification lies with the action agency. It must follow the consultation procedures, but regardless of how that process goes, it must ultimately refrain from causing either of these harms (this applies to actions taken, funded, or authorized by the agency).

The most famous ESA case of all time is a jeopardy/consultation case, *Tennessee Valley Authority v. Hill*, though it is primarily known for its emphasis on the statute's ability to trump all other considerations, even at the expense of hundreds of millions of dollars. It was the first case to uncover the inflexible nature of the statute's drafting, and the once-popular bipartisan project has never been the same since. While everyone had agreed on it in theory, it suddenly became clear that many had not very carefully thought through its potential impact in practice.

Tennessee Valley Authority v. Hill
437 U.S. 153 (1978)

Justice BURGER:

The questions presented in this case are (a) whether the Endangered Species Act of 1973 requires a court to enjoin the operation of a virtually completed federal dam—which had been authorized prior to 1973—when, pursuant to authority vested in him by Congress, the Secretary of the Interior has determined that operation of the dam would eradicate an endangered species; and (b) whether continued congressional appropriations for the dam after 1973 constituted an implied repeal of the Endangered Species Act, at least as to the particular dam.

I

The Little Tennessee River originates in the mountains of northern Georgia and flows through the national forest lands of North Carolina into Tennessee, where it converges with the Big Tennessee River near Knoxville. The lower 33 miles of the Little Tennessee takes the river's clear, free-flowing waters through an area of great natural beauty. Among other environmental amenities, this stretch of river is said to contain abundant trout. Considerable historical importance attaches to the areas immediately adjacent to this portion of the Little Tennessee's banks. To the south of the river's edge lies Fort Loudon, established in 1756 as England's southwestern outpost in the French and Indian War. Nearby are also the ancient sites of several native American villages, the archeological stores of which are to a large extent unexplored. These include the Cherokee towns of Echota and Tennase, the former being the sacred capital of the Cherokee Nation as early as the 16th century and the latter providing the linguistic basis from which the State of Tennessee derives its name.

In this area of the Little Tennessee River the Tennessee Valley Authority, a wholly owned public corporation of the United States, began constructing the Tellico Dam and Reservoir Project in 1967, shortly after Congress appropriated initial funds for its development. Tellico is a multi-purpose regional development project designed principally to stimulate shoreline development, generate sufficient electric current to heat 20,000 homes, and provide flatwater recreation and flood control, as well as improve economic conditions in "an area characterized by underutilization of human resources and outmigration of young people." Of particular relevance to this case is one aspect of the project, a dam which TVA determined to place on the Little Tennessee, a short distance from where the river's waters meet with the Big Tennessee. When fully operational, the dam would impound water covering some 16,500 acres — much of which represents valuable and productive farmland — thereby converting the river's shallow, fast-flowing waters into a deep reservoir over 30 miles in length.

The Tellico Dam has never opened, however, despite the fact that construction has been virtually completed and the dam is essentially ready for operation. Although Congress has appropriated monies for Tellico every year since 1967, progress was delayed, and ultimately stopped, by a tangle of lawsuits and administrative proceedings. After unsuccessfully urging TVA to consider alternatives to damming the Little Tennessee, local citizens and national conservation groups brought suit in the District Court, claiming that the project did not conform to the requirements of the National Environmental Policy Act of 1969 (NEPA). After finding TVA to be in violation of NEPA, the District Court enjoined the dam's completion pending the filing of an appropriate environmental impact statement. The injunction remained in effect until late 1973, when the District Court concluded that TVA's final environmental impact statement for Tellico was in compliance with the law.

A few months prior to the District Court's decision dissolving the NEPA injunction, a discovery was made in the waters of the Little Tennessee which would profoundly affect the Tellico Project. Exploring the area around Coytee Springs, which is about seven miles from the mouth of the river, a University of Tennessee ichthyologist, Dr. David A. Etnier, found a previously unknown species of perch, the snail darter, or Percina (Imostoma) tanasi. This three-inch, tannish-colored fish, whose numbers are estimated to be in the range of 10,000 to 15,000, would soon engage the attention of environmentalists, the TVA, the Department of the Interior, the Congress of the United States, and ultimately the federal courts, as a new and additional basis to halt construction of the dam.

Until recently the finding of a new species of animal life would hardly generate a cause celebre. This is particularly so in the case of darters, of which there are approximately 130 known species, 8 to 10 of these having been identified only in the last five years.[7] The moving force behind the snail darter's sudden fame came some four months after its discovery, when the Congress passed the Endangered Species Act of 1973 (Act). This legislation, among other things, authorizes the Secretary of the Interior to declare species of animal life "endangered" and to identify the "critical habitat" of these creatures. When a species or its habitat is so listed, the following portion of the Act — relevant here — becomes effective:

---

7. In Tennessee alone there are 85 to 90 species of darters, of which upward to 45 live in the Tennessee River system. New species of darters are being constantly discovered and classified — at the rate of about one per year. This is a difficult task for even trained ichthyologists since species of darters are often hard to differentiate from one another.

"The Secretary [of the Interior] shall review other programs administered by him and utilize such programs in furtherance of the purposes of this chapter. All other Federal departments and agencies shall, in consultation with and with the assistance of the Secretary, utilize their authorities in furtherance of the purposes of this chapter by carrying out programs for the conservation of endangered species and threatened species listed pursuant to section 1533 of this title and *by taking such action necessary to insure that actions authorized, funded, or carried out by them do not jeopardize the continued existence of such endangered species and threatened species or result in the destruction or modification of habitat of such species* which is determined by the Secretary, after consultation as appropriate with the affected States, to be critical." 16 U.S.C. § 1536 (1976 ed.) (emphasis added).

In January 1975, the respondents in this case and others petitioned the Secretary of the Interior to list the snail darter as an endangered species. After receiving comments from various interested parties, including TVA and the State of Tennessee, the Secretary formally listed the snail darter as an endangered species on October 8, 1975. In so acting, it was noted that "the snail darter is a living entity which is genetically distinct and reproductively isolated from other fishes." More important for the purposes of this case, the Secretary determined that the snail darter apparently lives only in that portion of the Little Tennessee River which would be completely inundated by the reservoir created as a consequence of the Tellico Dam's completion.[12] The Secretary went on to explain the significance of the dam to the habitat of the snail darter:

"[The] snail darter occurs only in the swifter portions of shoals over clean gravel substrate in cool, low-turbidity water. Food of the snail darter is almost exclusively snails which require a clean gravel substrate for their survival. *The proposed impoundment of water behind the proposed Tellico Dam would result in total destruction of the snail darter's habitat.*" (emphasis added).

Subsequent to this determination, the Secretary declared the area of the Little Tennessee which would be affected by the Tellico Dam to be the "critical habitat" of the snail darter. Using these determinations as a predicate, and notwithstanding the near completion of the dam, the Secretary declared that pursuant to §7 of the Act, "all Federal agencies must take such action as is necessary to insure that actions authorized, funded, or carried out by them do not result in the destruction or modification of this critical habitat area." 41 Fed.Reg. 13928 (1976) (to be codified as 50 CFR § 17.81(b)). This notice, of course, was pointedly directed at TVA and clearly aimed at halting completion or operation of the dam.

* * *

12. Searches by TVA in more than 60 watercourses have failed to find other populations of snail darters. The Secretary has noted that "more than 1,000 collections in recent years and additional earlier collections from central and east Tennessee have not revealed the presence of the snail darter outside the Little Tennessee River." It is estimated, however, that the snail darter's range once extended throughout the upper main Tennessee River and the lower portions of its major tributaries above Chattanooga—all of which are now the sites of dam impoundments.

II

We begin with the premise that operation of the Tellico Dam will either eradicate the known population of snail darters or destroy their critical habitat. Petitioner does not now seriously dispute this fact. In any event, under § 4 (a)(1) of the Act, the Secretary of the Interior is vested with exclusive authority to determine whether a species such as the snail darter is "endangered" or "threatened" and to ascertain the factors which have led to such a precarious existence. By § 4(d) Congress has authorized — indeed commanded — the Secretary to "issue such regulations as he deems necessary and advisable to provide for the conservation of such species." As we have seen, the Secretary promulgated regulations which declared the snail darter an endangered species whose critical habitat would be destroyed by creation of the Tellico Reservoir. Doubtless petitioner would prefer not to have these regulations on the books, but there is no suggestion that the Secretary exceeded his authority or abused his discretion in issuing the regulations. Indeed, no judicial review of the Secretary's determinations has ever been sought and hence the validity of his actions are not open to review in this Court.

Starting from the above premise, two questions are presented: (a) Would TVA be in violation of the Act if it completed and operated the Tellico Dam as planned? (b) If TVA's actions would offend the Act, is an injunction the appropriate remedy for the violation? For the reasons stated hereinafter, we hold that both questions must be answered in the affirmative.

(A)

It may seem curious to some that the survival of a relatively small number of three-inch fish among all the countless millions of species extant would require the permanent halting of a virtually completed dam for which Congress has expended more than $100 million. The paradox is not minimized by the fact that Congress continued to appropriate large sums of public money for the project, even after congressional Appropriations Committees were apprised of its apparent impact upon the survival of the snail darter. We conclude, however, that the explicit provisions of the Endangered Species Act require precisely that result.

One would be hard pressed to find a statutory provision whose terms were any plainer than those in § 7 of the Endangered Species Act. Its very words affirmatively command all federal agencies "to *insure* that actions *authorized, funded, or carried out* by them do not *jeopardize* the continued existence" of an endangered species or "*result in the destruction or modification of habitat of such species....*" 16 U. S. C. § 1536 (1976 ed.). (Emphasis added.) This language admits of no exception. Nonetheless, petitioner urges, as do the dissenters, that the Act cannot reasonably be interpreted as applying to a federal project which was well under way when Congress passed the Endangered Species Act of 1973. To sustain that position, however, we would be forced to ignore the ordinary meaning of plain language. It has not been shown, for example, how TVA can close the gates of the Tellico Dam without "carrying out" an action that has been "authorized" and "funded" by a federal agency. Nor can we understand how such action will "*insure*" that the snail darter's habitat is not disrupted.

Reasoning

Accepting the Secretary's determinations, as we must, it is clear that TVA's proposed operation of the dam will have precisely the opposite effect, namely the eradication of an endangered species.

Concededly, this view of the Act will produce results requiring the sacrifice of the anticipated benefits of the project and of many millions of dollars in public funds. But examination of the language, history, and structure of the legislation under review here indicates beyond doubt that Congress intended endangered species to be afforded the highest of priorities. . . .

The legislative proceedings in 1973 are, in fact, replete with expressions of concern over the risk that might lie in the loss of any endangered species. . . . Congress was concerned about the unknown uses that endangered species might have and about the unforeseeable place such creatures may have in the chain of life on this planet.

In shaping legislation to deal with the problem thus presented, Congress started from the finding that "[the] two major causes of extinction are hunting and destruction of natural habitat." Of these twin threats, Congress was informed that the greatest was destruction of natural habitats. Witnesses recommended, among other things, that Congress require all land-managing agencies "to avoid damaging critical habitat for endangered species and to take positive steps to improve such habitat." Virtually every bill introduced in Congress during the 1973 session responded to this concern by incorporating language similar, if not identical, to that found in the present §7 of the Act. These provisions were designed, in the words of an administration witness, "for the first time [to] *prohibit* [a] federal agency from taking action which does jeopardize the status of endangered species," furthermore, the proposed bills would "[direct] all . . . Federal agencies to utilize their authorities for carrying out programs for the protection of endangered animals." (Emphasis added.)

As it was finally passed, the Endangered Species Act of 1973 represented the most comprehensive legislation for the preservation of endangered species ever enacted by any nation. Its stated purposes were "to provide a means whereby the ecosystems upon which endangered species and threatened species depend may be conserved," and "to provide a program for the conservation of such . . . species. . . ." In furtherance of these goals, Congress expressly stated in §2 (c) that "all Federal departments and agencies *shall* seek *to conserve endangered species* and threatened species. . . ." (Emphasis added.) Lest there be any ambiguity as to the meaning of this statutory directive, the Act specifically defined "conserve" as meaning "to use and the use of *all methods and procedures which are necessary* to bring *any endangered species* or threatened species to the point at which the measures provided pursuant to this chapter are no longer necessary." (Emphasis added.) Aside from §7, other provisions indicated the seriousness with which Congress viewed this issue: Virtually all dealings with endangered species, including taking, possession, transportation, and sale, were prohibited, except in extremely narrow circumstances. The Secretary was also given extensive power to develop regulations and programs for the preservation of endangered and threatened species. Citizen involvement was encouraged by the Act, with provisions allowing interested persons to petition the Secretary to list a species as endangered or threatened, and bring civil suits in United States district courts to force compliance with any provision of the Act.

Section 7 of the Act, which of course is relied upon by respondents in this case, provides a particularly good gauge of congressional intent. As we have seen, this provision had its genesis in the Endangered Species Act of 1966, but that legislation qualified the obligation of federal agencies by stating that they should seek to preserve endangered species only *"insofar as is practicable and consistent with [their] primary purposes. . . ."* Likewise, every bill introduced in 1973 contained a qualification similar to that found in the earlier statutes. Exemplary of these was the administration bill, H. R. 4758, which in § 2(b) would direct federal agencies to use their authorities to further the ends of the Act *"insofar as is practicable and consistent with [their] primary purposes. . . ."* (Emphasis added.) Explaining the idea behind this language, an administration spokesman told Congress that it "would further signal to all . . . agencies of the Government that this is the *first priority, consistent with their primary objectives."* (Emphasis added.) This type of language did not go unnoticed by those advocating strong endangered species legislation. A representative of the Sierra Club, for example, attacked the use of the phrase "consistent with the primary purpose" in proposed H. R. 4758, cautioning that the qualification "could be construed to be a declaration of congressional policy that other agency purposes are necessarily more important than protection of endangered species and would always prevail if conflict were to occur."

What is very significant in this sequence is that the final version of the 1973 Act carefully omitted all of the reservations described above. . . . It is against this legislative background that we must measure TVA's claim that the Act was not intended to stop operation of a project which, like Tellico Dam, was near completion when an endangered species was discovered in its path. While there is no discussion in the legislative history of precisely this problem, the totality of congressional action makes it abundantly clear that the result we reach today is wholly in accord with both the words of the statute and the intent of Congress. The plain intent of Congress in enacting this statute was to halt and reverse the trend toward species extinction, whatever the cost. This is reflected not only in the stated policies of the Act, but in literally every section of the statute. All persons, including federal agencies, are specifically instructed not to "take" endangered species, meaning that no one is "to harass, harm, pursue, hunt, shoot, wound, kill, trap, capture, or collect" such life forms. Agencies in particular are directed by §§ 2(c) and 3(2) of the Act to "use . . . *all methods* and procedures which are necessary" to preserve endangered species. (emphasis added). In addition, the legislative history undergirding § 7 reveals an explicit congressional decision to require agencies to afford first priority to the declared national policy of saving endangered species. The pointed omission of the type of qualifying language previously included in endangered species legislation reveals a conscious decision by Congress to give endangered species priority over the "primary missions" of federal agencies.

It is not for us to speculate, much less act, on whether Congress would have altered its stance had the specific events of this case been anticipated. In any event, we discern no hint in the deliberations of Congress relating to the 1973 Act that would compel a different result than we reach here. Indeed, the repeated expressions of congressional concern over what it saw as the potentially enormous danger presented by the eradication of any endangered species suggest how the balance would have been struck had the issue been presented to Congress in 1973.

Furthermore, it is clear Congress foresaw that §7 would, on occasion, require agencies to alter ongoing projects in order to fulfill the goals of the Act. Congressman Dingell's discussion of Air Force practice bombing, for instance, obviously pinpoints a particular activity—intimately related to the national defense—which a major federal department would be obliged to alter in deference to the strictures of §7.... One might dispute the applicability of these examples to the Tellico Dam by saying that in this case the burden on the public through the loss of millions of unrecoverable dollars would greatly outweigh the loss of the snail darter. But neither the Endangered Species Act nor Art. III of the Constitution provides federal courts with authority to make such fine utilitarian calculations. On the contrary, the plain language of the Act, buttressed by its legislative history, shows clearly that Congress viewed the value of endangered species as "incalculable." Quite obviously, it would be difficult for a court to balance the loss of a sum certain—even $100 million—against a congressionally declared "incalculable" value, even assuming we had the power to engage in such a weighing process, which we emphatically do not....

Notwithstanding Congress' expression of intent in 1973, we are urged to find that the continuing appropriations for Tellico Dam constitute an implied repeal of the 1973 Act, at least insofar as it applies to the Tellico Project. In support of this view, TVA points to the statements found in various House and Senate Appropriations Committees' Reports; as described in Part I, *supra*, those Reports generally reflected the attitude of the *Committees* either that the Act did not apply to Tellico or that the dam should be completed regardless of the provisions of the Act. Since we are unwilling to assume that these latter Committee statements constituted advice to ignore the provisions of a duly enacted law, we assume that these Committees believed that the Act simply was not applicable in this situation. But even under this interpretation of the Committees' actions, we are unable to conclude that the Act has been in any respect amended or repealed. There is nothing in the appropriations measures, as passed, which states that the Tellico Project was to be completed irrespective of the requirements of the Endangered Species Act. These appropriations, in fact, represented relatively minor components of the lump-sum amounts for the entire TVA budget. To find a repeal of the Endangered Species Act under these circumstances would surely do violence to the "'cardinal rule ... that repeals by implication are not favored.'" ... The doctrine disfavoring repeals by implication "applies with full vigor when ... the subsequent legislation is an appropriations measure." ... Perhaps mindful of the fact that it is "swimming upstream" against a strong current of well-established precedent, TVA argues for an exception to the rule against implied repealers in a circumstance where, as here, Appropriations Committees have expressly stated their "understanding" that the earlier legislation would not prohibit the proposed expenditure. We cannot accept such a proposition. Expressions of committees dealing with requests for appropriations cannot be equated with statutes enacted by Congress, particularly not in the circumstances presented by this case. First, the Appropriations Committees had no jurisdiction over the subject of endangered species, much less did they conduct the type of extensive hearings which preceded passage of the earlier Endangered Species Acts, especially the 1973 Act. . . . Second, there is no indication that Congress as a whole was aware of TVA's position, although the Appropriations Committees apparently agreed with petitioner's views.

(B)

Having determined that there is an irreconcilable conflict between operation of the Tellico Dam and the explicit provisions of § 7 of the Endangered Species Act, we must now consider what remedy, if any, is appropriate. It is correct, of course, that a federal judge sitting as a chancellor is not mechanically obligated to grant an injunction for every violation of law. . . . As a general matter it may be said that "[since] all or almost all equitable remedies are discretionary, the balancing of equities and hardships is appropriate in almost any case as a guide to the chancellor's discretion." . . . But these principles take a court only so far. Our system of government is, after all, a tripartite one, with each branch having certain defined functions delegated to it by the Constitution. While "[it] is emphatically the province and duty of the judicial department to say what the law is," Marbury v. Madison, 1 Cranch 137, 177 (1803), it is equally—and emphatically—the exclusive province of the Congress not only to formulate legislative policies and mandate programs and projects, but also to establish their relative priority for the Nation. Once Congress, exercising its delegated powers, has decided the order of priorities in a given area, it is for the Executive to administer the laws and for the courts to enforce them when enforcement is sought. Here we are urged to view the Endangered Species Act "reasonably," and hence shape a remedy "that accords with some modicum of common sense and the public weal." But is that our function? We have no expert knowledge on the subject of endangered species, much less do we have a mandate from the people to strike a balance of equities on the side of the Tellico Dam. Congress has spoken in the plainest of words, making it abundantly clear that the balance has been struck in favor of affording endangered species the highest of priorities, thereby adopting a policy which it described as "institutionalized caution." Our individual appraisal of the wisdom or unwisdom of a particular course consciously selected by the Congress is to be put aside in the process of interpreting a statute. Once the meaning of an enactment is discerned and its constitutionality determined, the judicial process comes to an end. We do not sit as a committee of review, nor are we vested with the power of veto. The lines ascribed to Sir Thomas More by Robert Bolt are not without relevance here:

> "The law, Roper, the law. I know what's legal, not what's right. And I'll stick to what's legal. . . . I'm not God. The currents and eddies of right and wrong, which you find such plain-sailing, I can't navigate, I'm no voyager. But in the thickets of the law, oh there I'm a forester. . . . What would you do? Cut a great

road through the law to get after the Devil? . . . And when the last law was
down, and the Devil turned round on you—where would you hide, Roper,
the laws all being flat? . . . This country's planted thick with laws from coast to
coast—Man's laws, not God's—and if you cut them down . . . d'you really
think you could stand upright in the winds that would below then? . . . Yes,
I'd give the Devil benefit of law, for my own safety's sake." R. Bolt, A Man for
All Seasons, Act 1, p. 147 (Three Plays, Heinemann ed. 1967).

We agree with the Court of Appeals that in our constitutional system the commitment to the separation of powers is too fundamental for us to pre-empt congressional
action by judicially decreeing what accords with "common sense and the public weal."
Our Constitution vests such responsibilities in the political branches.

Justice POWELL, with whom Justice BLACKMUN joins, dissenting.

Dissent

The Court today holds that §7 of the Endangered Species Act requires a federal
court, for the purpose of protecting an endangered species or its habitat, to enjoin
permanently the operation of any federal project, whether completed or substantially
completed. This decision casts a long shadow over the operation of even the most
important projects, serving vital needs of society and national defense, whenever it is
determined that continued operation would threaten extinction of an endangered species or its habitat. This result is said to be required by the "plain intent of Congress"
as well as by the language of the statute.

In my view §7 cannot reasonably be interpreted as applying to a project that is completed or substantially completed when its threat to an endangered species is discovered. Nor can I believe that Congress could have intended this Act to produce the
"absurd result"—in the words of the District Court—of this case. If it were clear from
the language of the Act and its legislative history that Congress intended to authorize
this result, this Court would be compelled to enforce it. It is not our province to rectify
policy or political judgments by the Legislative Branch, however egregiously they
may disserve the public interest. But where the statutory language and legislative history, as in this case, need not be construed to reach such a result, I view it as the duty
of this Court to adopt a permissible construction that accords with some modicum
of common sense and the public weal.

. . . I have little doubt that Congress will amend the Endangered Species Act to prevent the grave consequences made possible by today's decision. Few, if any, Members
of that body will wish to defend an interpretation of the Act that requires the waste
of at least $53 million, and denies the people of the Tennessee Valley area the benefits
of the reservoir that Congress intended to confer. There will be little sentiment to leave
this dam standing before an empty reservoir, serving no purpose other than a conversation piece for incredulous tourists.

But more far reaching than the adverse effect on the people of this economically
depressed area is the continuing threat to the operation of every federal project, no
matter how important to the Nation. If Congress acts expeditiously, as may be

anticipated, the Court's decision probably will have no lasting adverse consequences. But I had not thought it to be the province of this Court to force Congress into otherwise unnecessary action by interpreting a statute to produce a result no one intended.

Notes and Questions

1. Many viewed the outcome in *TVA v. Hill* as disastrous, and, indeed, it did not take long for Congress to take action, both in relation to the case itself and the unveiled dangers of the ESA. To allow the Tellico Dam to proceed, Congress passed a bill exempting it from the ESA's reach. To prepare for future such emergencies, the ESA itself was amended to create a special Endangered Species Committee with the power to send a species to extinction if the circumstances were dire enough to make such a hard choice. Because of this ability, the committee is colloquially referred to as "the God Squad." This title also makes sense in relation to the membership, which is made up of several high-level cabinet members. The God Squad is composed of seven members: the Secretary of Agriculture, Secretary of the Army, Chairman of the Council of Economic Advisors, Administrator of the Environmental Protection Agency, Secretary of the Interior, Administrator of the National Oceanic and Atmospheric Administration, and one individual from the affected state, as determined by the Secretary of the Interior and appointed by the President. The Committee is empowered to grant an exemption to the Section 7 prohibition on jeopardy or adverse modification caused by federal agency action. *See* ESA § 7(e), 16 U.S.C. § 1536(e).

D. The Take Prohibition — Section 9

The other primary protective provision for listed species is the § 9 prohibition against "take" of endangered species. Take is defined as "harass, harm, pursue, hunt, shoot, wound, kill, trap, capture, or collect, or to attempt to engage in any such conduct." Section 9 differs from § 7 in several important ways, besides the obvious functional difference: (1) It only applies to species listed as endangered, though threatened species can receive the same protections by agency regulation, and most do; (2) It only applies to wildlife, and excludes plants; and (3) It applies to all people, public or private, rather than just to federal agencies. The two wildlife agencies each take a different approach to applying the take prohibition to threatened species. The FWS created a blanket rule extending it to all threatened species within its jurisdiction, subject to exceptions created by individual-species rules as needed. The NMFS does it the harder way, creating an individual rule for each threatened species it lists (called a 4(d) rule, in reference to the statutory section authorizing it), applying the take prohibition one listing at a time. Species of threatened fish or wildlife without take protection are very rare and generally reflect special circumstances, as we will see with the controversial polar bear. As you read about and discuss the § 9 take prohibition, contemplate the exclusion of listed flora. Can you think of a good reason for this?

Babbitt v. Sweet Home Chapter of Communities for a Great Oregon

515 U.S. 687 (1995)

Justice STEVENS:

The Endangered Species Act of 1973 (ESA or Act), contains a variety of protections designed to save from extinction species that the Secretary of the Interior designates as endangered or threatened. Section 9 of the Act makes it unlawful for any person to "take" any endangered or threatened species. The Secretary has promulgated a regulation that defines the statute's prohibition on takings to include "significant habitat modification or degradation where it actually kills or injures wildlife." This case presents the question whether the Secretary exceeded his authority under the Act by promulgating that regulation.

I

Section 9(a)(1) of the Endangered Species Act provides the following protection for endangered species:

Except as provided in sections 1535(g)(2) and 1539 of this title, with respect to any endangered species of fish or wildlife listed pursuant to section 1533 of this title it is unlawful for any person subject to the jurisdiction of the United States to . . . (B) take any such species within the United States or the territorial sea of the United States[.]

Section 3(19) of the Act defines the statutory term "take": "The term 'take' means to harass, harm, pursue, hunt, shoot, wound, kill, trap, capture, or collect, or to attempt to engage in any such conduct." The Act does not further define the terms it uses to define "take." The Interior Department regulations that implement the statute, however, define the statutory term "harm": "Harm in the definition of 'take' in the Act means an act which actually kills or injures wildlife. Such act may include significant habitat modification or degradation where it actually kills or injures wildlife by significantly impairing essential behavioral patterns, including breeding, feeding, or sheltering." This regulation has been in place since 1975.[2]

A limitation on the §9 "take" prohibition appears in §10(a)(1)(B) of the Act, which Congress added by amendment in 1982. That section authorizes the Secretary to grant a permit for any taking otherwise prohibited by §9(a)(1)(B) "if such taking is incidental to, and not the purpose of, the carrying out of an otherwise lawful activity."

. . . Respondents in this action are small landowners, logging companies, and families dependent on the forest products industries in the Pacific Northwest and in the Southeast, and organizations that represent their interests. They brought this declaratory judgment action against petitioners, the Secretary of the Interior and the Director of the Fish and Wildlife Service, in the United States District Court for

---

2. The Secretary, through the Director of the Fish and Wildlife Service, originally promulgated the regulation in 1975 and amended it in 1981 to emphasize that actual death or injury of a protected animal is necessary for a violation.

the District of Columbia to challenge the statutory validity of the Secretary's regulation defining "harm," particularly the inclusion of habitat modification and degradation in the definition. Respondents challenged the regulation on its face. Their complaint alleged that application of the "harm" regulation to the red-cockaded woodpecker, an endangered species, and the northern spotted owl, a threatened species, had injured them economically.

Respondents advanced three arguments to support their submission that Congress did not intend the word "take" in § 9 to include habitat modification, as the Secretary's "harm" regulation provides. First, they correctly noted that language in the Senate's original version of the ESA would have defined "take" to include "destruction, modification, or curtailment of [the] habitat or range" of fish or wildlife, but the Senate deleted that language from the bill before enacting it. Second, respondents argued that Congress intended the Act's express authorization for the Federal Government to buy private land in order to prevent habitat degradation in § 5 to be the exclusive check against habitat modification on private property. Third, because the Senate added the term "harm" to the definition of "take" in a floor amendment without debate, respondents argued that the court should not interpret the term so expansively as to include habitat modification.

[The District Court upheld the regulation. On appeal, the D.C. Circuit first upheld the regulation 2–1, but on rehearing the court struck down the regulation 2–1 after Judge Williams changed his mind.]

II

Because this case was decided on motions for summary judgment, we may appropriately make certain factual assumptions in order to frame the legal issue. First, we assume respondents have no desire to harm either the red-cockaded woodpecker or the spotted owl; they merely wish to continue logging activities that would be entirely proper if not prohibited by the ESA. On the other hand, we must assume arguendo that those activities will have the effect, even though unintended, of detrimentally changing the natural habitat of both listed species and that, as a consequence, members of those species will be killed or injured. Under respondents' view of the law, the Secretary's only means of forestalling that grave result—even when the actor knows it is certain to occur—is to use his § 5 authority to purchase the lands on which the survival of the species depends. The Secretary, on the other hand, submits that the § 9 prohibition on takings, which Congress defined to include "harm," places on respondents a duty to avoid harm that habitat alteration will cause the birds unless respondents first obtain a permit pursuant to § 10.

The text of the Act provides three reasons for concluding that the Secretary's interpretation is reasonable. First, an ordinary understanding of the word "harm" supports it. The dictionary definition of the verb form of "harm" is "to cause hurt or damage to: injure." In the context of the ESA, that definition naturally encompasses habitat modification that results in actual injury or death to members of an endangered or threatened species.

Respondents argue that the Secretary should have limited the purview of "harm" to direct applications of force against protected species, but the dictionary definition does not include the word "directly" or suggest in any way that only direct or willful action that leads to injury constitutes "harm."[10] Moreover, unless the statutory term "harm" encompasses indirect as well as direct injuries, the word has no meaning that does not duplicate the meaning of other words that §3 uses to define "take." A reluctance to treat statutory terms as surplusage supports the reasonableness of the Secretary's interpretation.[11]

Second, the broad purpose of the ESA supports the Secretary's decision to extend protection against activities that cause the precise harms Congress enacted the statute to avoid. In *TVA v. Hill*, 437 U.S. 153 (1978), we described the Act as "the most comprehensive legislation for the preservation of endangered species ever enacted by any nation." Whereas predecessor statutes enacted in 1966 and 1969 had not contained any sweeping prohibition against the taking of endangered species except on federal lands, the 1973 Act applied to all land in the United States and to the Nation's territorial seas. As stated in §2 of the Act, among its central purposes is "to provide a means whereby the ecosystems upon which endangered species and threatened species depend may be conserved. . . ."

Respondents advance strong arguments that activities that cause minimal or unforeseeable harm will not violate the Act as construed in the "harm" regulation. Respondents, however, present a facial challenge to the regulation. Thus, they ask us to invalidate the Secretary's understanding of "harm" in every circumstance, even when an actor knows that an activity, such as draining a pond, would actually result in the extinction of a listed species by destroying its habitat. Given Congress' clear expression of the ESA's broad purpose to protect endangered and threatened wildlife, the Secretary's definition of "harm" is reasonable.

---

10. Respondents and the dissent emphasize what they portray as the "established meaning" of "take" in the sense of a "wildlife take," a meaning respondents argue extends only to "the effort to exercise dominion over some creature, and the concrete effect of [sic] that creature." This limitation ill serves the statutory text, which forbids not taking "some creature" but "tak[ing] any [endangered] species"—a formidable task for even the most rapacious feudal lord. More importantly, Congress explicitly defined the operative term "take" in the ESA, no matter how much the dissent wishes otherwise, thereby obviating the need for us to probe its meaning as we must probe the meaning of the undefined subsidiary term "harm." Finally, Congress' definition of "take" includes several words—most obviously "harass," "pursue," and "wound," in addition to "harm" itself—that fit respondents' and the dissent's definition of "take" no better than does "significant habitat modification or degradation."

11. In contrast, if the statutory term "harm" encompasses such indirect means of killing and injuring wildlife as habitat modification, the other terms listed in §3—"harass," "pursue," "hunt," "shoot," "wound," "kill," "trap," "capture," and "collect"—generally retain independent meanings. Most of those terms refer to deliberate actions more frequently than does "harm," and they therefore do not duplicate the sense of indirect causation that "harm" adds to the statute. In addition, most of the other words in the definition describe either actions from which habitat modification does not usually result (e.g., "pursue," "harass") or effects to which activities that modify habitat do not usually lead (e.g., "trap," "collect"). To the extent the Secretary's definition of "harm" may have applications that overlap with other words in the definition, that overlap reflects the broad purpose of the Act.

Third, the fact that Congress in 1982 authorized the Secretary to issue permits for takings that § 9(a)(1)(B) would otherwise prohibit, "if such taking is incidental to, and not the purpose of, the carrying out of an otherwise lawful activity," strongly suggests that Congress understood § 9(a)(1)(B) to prohibit indirect as well as deliberate takings. The permit process requires the applicant to prepare a "conservation plan" that specifies how he intends to "minimize and mitigate" the "impact" of his activity on endangered and threatened species, making clear that Congress had in mind foreseeable rather than merely accidental effects on listed species. No one could seriously request an "incidental" take permit to avert § 9 liability for direct, deliberate action against a member of an endangered or threatened species, but respondents would read "harm" so narrowly that the permit procedure would have little more than that absurd purpose. "When Congress acts to amend a statute, we presume it intends its amendment to have real and substantial effect." Congress' addition of the § 10 permit provision supports the Secretary's conclusion that activities not intended to harm an endangered species, such as habitat modification, may constitute unlawful takings under the ESA unless the Secretary permits them.

The Court of Appeals made three errors in asserting that "harm" must refer to a direct application of force because the words around it do.[15] First, the court's premise was flawed. Several of the words that accompany "harm" in the § 3 definition of "take," especially "harass," "pursue," "wound," and "kill," refer to actions or effects that do not require direct applications of force. Second, to the extent the court read a requirement of intent or purpose into the words used to define "take," it ignored § 9's express provision that a "knowing" action is enough to violate the Act. Third, the court employed *noscitur a sociis* to give "harm" essentially the same function as other words in the definition, thereby denying it independent meaning. The canon, to the contrary, counsels that a word "gathers meaning from the words around it." The statutory context of "harm" suggests that Congress meant that term to serve a particular function in the ESA, consistent with but distinct from the functions of the other verbs used to define "take." The Secretary's interpretation of "harm" to include indirectly injuring endangered animals through habitat modification permissibly interprets "harm" to have "a character of its own not to be submerged by its association."

Nor does the Act's inclusion of the § 5 land acquisition authority and the § 7 directive to federal agencies to avoid destruction or adverse modification of critical habitat alter our conclusion. Respondents' argument that the Government lacks any incentive to purchase land under § 5 when it can simply prohibit takings under § 9 ignores the

---

15. The dissent makes no effort to defend the Court of Appeals' reading of the statutory definition as requiring a direct application of force. Instead, it tries to impose on § 9 a limitation of liability to "affirmative conduct intentionally directed against a particular animal or animals." Under the dissent's interpretation of the Act, a developer could drain a pond, knowing that the act would extinguish an endangered species of turtles, without even proposing a conservation plan or applying for a permit under § 9(a)(1)(B); unless the developer was motivated by a desire "to get at a turtle," no statutory taking could occur. Because such conduct would not constitute a taking at common law, the dissent would shield it from § 9 liability, even though the words "kill" and "harm" in the statutory definition could apply to such deliberate conduct....

practical considerations that attend enforcement of the ESA. Purchasing habitat lands may well cost the Government less in many circumstances than pursuing civil or criminal penalties. In addition, the § 5 procedure allows for protection of habitat before the seller's activity has harmed any endangered animal, whereas the Government cannot enforce the § 9 prohibition until an animal has actually been killed or injured. The Secretary may also find the § 5 authority useful for preventing modification of land that is not yet but may in the future become habitat for an endangered or threatened species. The § 7 directive applies only to the Federal Government, whereas the § 9 prohibition applies to "any person." Section 7 imposes a broad, affirmative duty to avoid adverse habitat modifications that § 9 does not replicate, and § 7 does not limit its admonition to habitat modification that "actually kills or injures wildlife." Conversely, § 7 contains limitations that § 9 does not, applying only to actions "likely to jeopardize the continued existence of any endangered species or threatened species," and to modifications of habitat that has been designated "critical" pursuant to § 4. Any overlap that § 5 or § 7 may have with § 9 in particular cases is unexceptional, and simply reflects the broad purpose of the Act set out in § 2 and acknowledged in *TVA v. Hill.*

We need not decide whether the statutory definition of "take" compels the Secretary's interpretation of "harm," because our conclusions that Congress did not unambiguously manifest its intent to adopt respondents' view and that the Secretary's interpretation is reasonable suffice to decide this case. [*Chevron*] The latitude the ESA gives the Secretary in enforcing the statute, together with the degree of regulatory expertise necessary to its enforcement, establishes that we owe some degree of deference to the Secretary's reasonable interpretation.

III

Our conclusion that the Secretary's definition of "harm" rests on a permissible construction of the ESA gains further support from the legislative history of the statute. . . . The Senate Report stressed that "'[t]ake' is defined . . . in the broadest possible manner to include every conceivable way in which a person can 'take' or attempt to 'take' any fish or wildlife." The House Report stated that "the broadest possible terms" were used to define restrictions on takings . . . [By contrast, the fact that a proposed endangered species bill included "the destruction, modification, or curtailment of [the] habitat or range of fish and wildlife" does not indicate the take prohibition that was ultimately adopted excludes habitat protection. Additionally, "the history of the 1982 amendment that gave the Secretary authority to grant permits for 'incidental' takings provides further support for his reading of the Act. The House Report expressly states that '[b]y use of the word "incidental" the Committee intends to cover situations in which it is known that a taking will occur if the other activity is engaged in but such taking is incidental to, and not the purpose of, the activity.'"]

IV

When it enacted the ESA, Congress delegated broad administrative and interpretive power to the Secretary. The task of defining and listing endangered and threatened species requires an expertise and attention to detail that exceeds the normal province of Congress. Fashioning appropriate standards for issuing permits under § 10 for takings that would otherwise violate § 9 necessarily requires the exercise of broad discretion. The proper interpretation of a term such as "harm" involves a complex policy choice. When Congress has entrusted the Secretary with broad discretion, we are especially reluctant to substitute our views of wise policy for his. [*Chevron*] In this case, that reluctance accords with our conclusion, based on the text, structure, and legislative history of the ESA, that the Secretary reasonably construed the intent of Congress when he defined "harm" to include "significant habitat modification or degradation that actually kills or injures wildlife."

In the elaboration and enforcement of the ESA, the Secretary and all persons who must comply with the law will confront difficult questions of proximity and degree; for, as all recognize, the Act encompasses a vast range of economic and social enterprises and endeavors. These questions must be addressed in the usual course of the law, through case-by-case resolution and adjudication.

Concur

Justice O'CONNOR, concurring:

My agreement with the Court is founded on two understandings. First, the challenged regulation is limited to significant habitat modification that causes actual, as opposed to hypothetical or speculative, death or injury to identifiable protected animals. Second, even setting aside difficult questions of scienter, the regulation's application is limited by ordinary principles of proximate causation, which introduce notions of foreseeability. These limitations, in my view, call into question *Palila v. Hawaii Dept. of Land and Natural Resources*, 852 F.2d 1106 (C.A.9 1988) (*Palila II*), and with it, many of the applications derided by the dissent. Because there is no need to strike a regulation on a facial challenge out of concern that it is susceptible of erroneous application, however, and because there are many habitat-related circumstances in which the regulation might validly apply, I join the opinion of the Court....

Dissent

Justice SCALIA, with whom The Chief Justice and Justice THOMAS join, dissenting:

I think it unmistakably clear that the legislation at issue here (1) forbade the hunting and killing of endangered animals, and (2) provided federal lands and federal funds for the acquisition of private lands, to preserve the habitat of endangered animals. The Court's holding that the hunting and killing prohibition incidentally preserves habitat on private lands imposes unfairness to the point of financial ruin — not just upon the rich, but upon the simplest farmer who finds his land conscripted to national zoological use. I respectfully dissent.

I

... The regulation has three features which ... do not comport with the statute. First, it interprets the statute to prohibit habitat modification that is no more than the cause-in-fact of death or injury to wildlife. Any "significant habitat modification" that in fact produces that result by "impairing essential behavioral patterns" is made unlawful, regardless of whether that result is intended or even foreseeable, and no matter how long the chain of causality between modification and injury. *See, e.g., Palila v. Hawaii Dept. of Land and Natural Resources (Palila II)*, 852 F.2d 1106, 1108–1109

(9th Cir. 1988) (sheep grazing constituted "taking" of palila birds, since although sheep do not destroy full-grown mamane trees, they do destroy mamane seedlings, which will not grow to full-grown trees, on which the palila feeds and nests).

Second, the regulation does not require an "act": the Secretary's officially stated position is that an omission will do. . . . The third and most important unlawful feature of the regulation is that it encompasses injury inflicted, not only upon individual animals, but upon populations of the protected species. "Injury" in the regulation includes "significantly impairing essential behavioral patterns, including breeding." Impairment of breeding does not "injure" living creatures; it prevents them from propagating, thus "injuring" a population of animals which would otherwise have maintained or increased its numbers. What the face of the regulation shows, the Secretary's official pronouncements confirm. The Final Redefinition of "Harm" accompanying publication of the regulation said that "harm" is not limited to "direct physical injury to an individual member of the wildlife species," and refers to "injury to a population." . . .

II

The Court [argues that] "the broad purpose of the [Act] supports the Secretary's decision to extend protection against activities that cause the precise harms Congress enacted the statute to avoid." I thought we had renounced the vice of "simplistically . . . assum[ing] that whatever furthers the statute's primary objective must be the law." . . . Second, the Court maintains that the legislative history of the 1973 Act supports the Secretary's definition. Even if legislative history were a legitimate and reliable tool of interpretation (which I shall assume in order to rebut the Court's claim); and even if it could appropriately be resorted to when the enacted text is as clear as this, here it shows quite the opposite of what the Court says. I shall not pause to discuss the Court's reliance on such statements in the Committee Reports as "'[t]ake' is defined . . . in the broadest possible manner to include every conceivable way in which a person can 'take' or attempt to 'take' any fish or wildlife." This sort of empty flourish—to the effect that "this statute means what it means all the way"—counts for little even when enacted into the law itself. . . . Both the Senate and House floor managers of the bill explained it in terms which leave no doubt that the problem of habitat destruction on private lands was to be solved principally by the land acquisition program of § 1534, while § 1538 solved a different problem altogether—the problem of takings . . . Habitat modification and takings, in other words, were viewed as different problems, addressed by different provisions of the Act. . . .

III

In response to the points made in this dissent, the Court's opinion stresses two points, neither of which is supported by the regulation, and so cannot validly be used to uphold it. First, the Court and the concurrence suggest that the regulation should be read to contain a requirement of proximate causation or foreseeability, principally because the statute does—and "[n]othing in the regulation purports to weaken those requirements [of the statute]." I quite agree that the statute contains such a limitation, because the verbs of purpose in § 1538(a)(1)(B) denote action directed at animals. But the Court has rejected that reading. The critical premise on which it has upheld the regulation is that, despite the weight of the other words in § 1538(a)(1)(B), "the statutory term 'harm' encompasses indirect as well as direct injuries." Consequently, unless there is some strange category of causation that is indirect and yet also proximate, the Court has already rejected its own basis for finding a proximate-cause limitation in the regulation. In fact "proximate" causation simply means "direct" causation.

. . . The regulation says (it is worth repeating) that "harm" means (1) an act which (2) actually kills or injures wildlife. If that does not dispense with a proximate-cause requirement, I do not know what language would. And changing the regulation by judicial invention, even to achieve compliance with the statute, is not permissible.

The second point the Court stresses in its response seems to me a belated mending of its hold. It apparently concedes that the statute requires injury to particular animals rather than merely to populations of animals. The Court then rejects my contention that the regulation ignores this requirement, since, it says, "every term in the regulation's definition of 'harm' is subservient to the phrase 'an act which actually kills or injures wildlife.'" As I have pointed out, this reading is incompatible with the regulation's specification of impairment of "breeding" as one of the modes of "kill[ing] or injur[ing] wildlife."[5]

---

5. JUSTICE O'CONNOR supposes that an "impairment of breeding" intrinsically injures an animal because "[t]o make it impossible for an animal to reproduce is to impair its most essential physical functions and to render that animal, and its genetic material, biologically obsolete." This imaginative construction does achieve the result of extending "impairment of breeding" to individual animals; but only at the expense of also expanding "injury" to include elements beyond physical harm to individual animals. For surely the only harm to the individual animal from impairment of that "essential function" is not the failure of issue (which harms only the issue), but the psychic harm of perceiving that it will leave this world with no issue (assuming, of course, that the animal in question, perhaps an endangered species of slug, is capable of such painful sentiments). If it includes that psychic harm, then why not the psychic harm of not being able to frolic about—so that the draining of a pond used for an endangered animal's recreation, but in no way essential to its survival, would be prohibited by the Act? That the concurrence is driven to such a dubious redoubt is an argument for, not against, the proposition that "injury" in the regulation includes injury to populations of animals. Even more so with the concurrence's alternative explanation: that "impairment of breeding" refers to nothing more than concrete injuries inflicted by the habitat modification on the animal who does the breeding, such as "physical complications [suffered] during gestation." Quite obviously, if "impairment of breeding" meant such physical harm to an individual animal, it would not have had to be mentioned. The concurrence entangles itself in a dilemma while attempting to explain the Secretary's commentary to the harm regulation, which stated that "harm" is not limited to "direct physical injury to an individual member of the wildlife species." The concurrence denies that this means that the regulation does not require injury to particular animals, because "one could just as easily emphasize the word 'direct' in this sentence as the word 'individual.'" One could; but if the concurrence does, it thereby refutes its separate attempt to exclude indirect causation from the regulation's coverage. The regulation, after emerging from the concurrence's analysis, has acquired both a proximate-cause limitation and a particular-animals limitation—precisely the one meaning that the Secretary's quoted declaration will not allow, whichever part of it is emphasized.

... The Endangered Species Act is a carefully considered piece of legislation that forbids all persons to hunt or harm endangered animals, but places upon the public at large, rather than upon fortuitously accountable individual landowners, the cost of preserving the habitat of endangered species. There is neither textual support for, nor even evidence of congressional consideration of, the radically different disposition contained in the regulation that the Court sustains. For these reasons, I respectfully dissent.

Notes and Questions

1. Section 10 of the ESA makes it possible for landowners to engage in actions, such as land development, that may incidentally take some members of a listed species. Without this provision it would be impossible to use a huge percentage of the privately owned land throughout the country. While that may sound great for protecting biodiversity, as a practical and political matter, the ESA could not survive. That said, § 10 incidental take permits are not simply handed out upon request. The applicant must plan and commit to conservation measures to mitigate the harm caused. For more on incidental take under the Endangered Species Act, see Chapter 8, Endangered Species Act Incidental Take Permit.

2. Private parties wishing to gain permission for any amount of take (which is common in land development) must submit a habitat conservation plan (HCP) for that species, containing mitigation planning that is directly tied to the species take that will occur. The wildlife agencies then have the option to approve the plan along with the expected take. Traditionally this was done individually by parties seeking permission for their own projects, but in recent years HCPs have been consolidating into larger regional jointly filed HCPs.

> Both the number of HCPs and the size and complexity of the areas they cover have increased. More than 430 HCPs have been approved, with many more in the planning stage. Most of the earlier HCPs approved were for planning areas of less than 1,000 acres; now 10 exceed 500,000 acres, with several larger than 1,000,000 acres. In some cases, there are more than one incidental take permit associated with a HCP. For example, the Central Coastal Orange County HCP was developed as an overall plan under which each individual participating entity received a separate incidental take permit. This suggests that HCPs are evolving from a process adopted primarily to address single projects to broad-based, landscape-level planning, utilized to achieve long-term biological and regulatory goals.

U.S. Fish & Wildlife *Service Fact Sheet on Habitat Conservation Plans*, available at https://www.fws.gov/midwest/endangered/permits/hcp/hcp_wofactsheet.html

3. An Incidental Take Statement (ITS) is similar to an HCP, but applies to federal agencies engaging in (or authorizing or funding) projects that have survived the § 7 consultation process. Within the Biological Opinion that concludes that the project will not jeopardize the listed species, and only if there is the potential for some take of listed species, there will be an ITS allowing but limiting that take.

Problem

The Okiedokie Swamp in the State of Florgia is home to a tremendously diverse ecosystem, including hundreds of species of birds, reptiles, and mammals. To help residents and tourists enjoy this biodiversity wonderland, private developers, with the support of the State of Florgia, plan to construct a destination resort in the very heart of the Okiedokie Swamp. The resort itself will require filling of approximately 430 acres of wetlands, plus additional acreage for construction of access roads and other tourist amenities. Recognizing obligations under the Clean Water Act, the developers begin the process of applying for a § 404 permit from the U.S. Army Corps of Engineers.

The biggest tourist draw to the Okiedokie Swamp is the chance to see the elusive Purple panther (*Panthera purpura*), the rarest subspecies of cat in North America. The Okiedokie Swamp is designated critical habitat for the purple panther, which is listed as endangered under the Endangered Species Act.

1. The resort developers are aware of the ESA listing for the purple panther. However, they declare that no consultation under ESA § 7 is necessary in this case because § 7 only applies to federal agencies, and no federal agencies are involved in the proposed resort development. You are an attorney for the Regional Solicitor's office of the U.S. Department of the Interior. Do you agree or disagree with the developer's conclusion regarding § 7 in this case? Explain.

2. As the attorney for the developers, you are aware that ESA § 9 may apply to private parties. Advise your developer clients of their potential obligations in this matter under § 9 and how they might meet those obligations most efficiently.

3. If the purple panther is removed from ESA listing and no other species found in the Okiedokie Swamp are listed as either endangered or threatened, are there any other protections under ESA or other statutes that might be available to help ensure the continued survival of species in the Okiedokie Swamp?

E. Recovery Planning

In addition to the ESA's relatively powerful provisions (the jeopardy and take prohibitions, and especially their lack of flexibility, have led to the common reference to the ESA as the "pit bull" of environmental law), there are also some provisions with potential but no teeth, due to their lack of mandatory language. One more obscure example of this is a requirement that all federal agencies proactively take measures to conserve listed species — absent a timeline or any context this is almost entirely unenforced (with rare exceptions). Its value lies in its provision of authority to take conservation into account when doing so is not otherwise in an agency's mandate.

A better known example is recovery planning, which is equally unenforceable as a mandate but actually gets some regular use (likely because it falls in the laps of the actual wildlife agencies rather than all federal agencies). Section 4(f) of the ESA states

"The Secretary shall develop and implement plans (hereinafter in this subsection referred to as "recovery plans") for the conservation and survival of endangered species and threatened species listed pursuant to this section." In spite of the "shall" language, there is no deadline, so the requirement is not enforceable. That said, there are clear substantive requirements for recovery plans, so once an agency creates one, it becomes subject to judicial review for its sufficiency. The agency must:

incorporate in each plan —

  (i) a description of such site-specific management actions as may be necessary to achieve the plan's goal for the conservation and survival of the species;

  (ii) objective, measurable criteria which, when met, would result in a determination, in accordance with the provisions of this section, that the species be removed from the list; and

  (iii) estimates of the time required and the cost to carry out those measures needed to achieve the plan's goal and to achieve intermediate steps toward that goal.

Each of the substantive requirements of recovery planning has been the subject of court challenges to recovery plans. The following case is one example of such a challenge.

Strahan v. Linnon

967 F. Supp. 581 (D. Mass. 1997)

Judge WOODLOCK:

[Plaintiff Max Strahan was an activist concerned about several whale species as well as other endangered marine mammals that live in the Atlantic Ocean off the coast of New England, some of which have been killed by Coast Guard vessels operating in the area. Strahan filed a citizen suit alleging that NMFS had failed to prepare recovery plans for some of the resident species and had created recovery plans for other species that were not compliant with the ESA's substantive requirements.] *Facts*

The plaintiff . . . alleges that NMFS has violated § 4(f) of the ESA because it has not "developed and implemented plans for the conservation and survival of endangered species and threatened species. . . ." 16 U.S.C. § 1533(f). Plaintiff makes two separate arguments with respect to NMFS's recovery plans. First, he contends that *2 Plaintiff arguments* NMFS has violated the ESA because it has not developed any recovery plans for the Blue, Sei, Fin, or Minke whales, but only the Right and Humpback whales. The plaintiff then alleges that the existing Right whale recovery plan is insufficient because it does not "incorporate implementable site-specific management actions necessary to achieve the plan's goal" and because it does not "establish a realistic recovery goal." The Amended Complaint further alleges that the existing plan has not been revised.

With respect to the claim that NMFS has violated §4(f) because it has not developed recovery plans for federally protected whales other than Right and Humpback whales, the defendants respond that the there are no time limits in §4(f) within which the Secretary must develop, implement, or revise a recovery plan. I am persuaded by the defendants' argument. *See Oregon Natural Resource Council v. Turner*, 863 F. Supp. 1277, 1282–83 (D.Or.1994). The court observed:

> Congress recognized that the development of recovery plans for listed species would take significant time and resources. It therefore provided in the ESA that the Secretary could establish a priority system for developing and implementing such plans. This priority system allows the Secretary broad discretion to allocate scare resources to those species that he or she determines would most likely benefit from development of a recovery plan. Unlike other requirements under the ESA, such as the designation of critical habitat, the statute places no time constraints on the development of recovery plans.[18]

decision

Accordingly, the Secretary has developed a priority system for developing such recovery plans. I find, therefore, that the fact that NMFS has not issued recovery plans for Sei, Blue, and Fin whales[19] does not constitute a violation of §4(f).

The plaintiff also asserts that the recovery plans that do exist, are deficient and thus violative of the statute. He claims that "as a general matter, [the recovery plan] does not contain objective, scientific, measurable criteria." More specifically, the plaintiff contends that the plan "fails to include . . . an annual census, a population viability analysis, modeling of ship-whale interactions, risk analysis, and interim numerical goals." The defendants assert that the discretionary nature of a recovery plan also applies to the plan's content and that "it is not necessary for a recovery plan to be an exhaustively detailed document."

Case law instructs that the defendants are correct in their assertion that the content of recovery plans is discretionary. For example, in *Fund for Animals, Inc. v. Rice*, 85 F.3d 535 (11th Cir.1996), the plaintiffs' argument relied on the assumption that "Recovery Plan[s] [are] document[s] with the force of law." *Id.* at 547. The court rejected that characterization stating that "section 4(f) makes it plain that recovery

---

18. I am also persuaded, therefore, that there are no stringent time requirements for revising a recovery plan. The plaintiff argues, nevertheless, that NMFS itself determined that the Recovery Plan should be revised every three years for the first fifteen years and every five years thereafter. At oral argument, plaintiff argued that such revision was, therefore, nondiscretionary. The relevant language in the Recovery Plan states that "three-year intervals [for updating the Plan] are recommended." This is clearly the language of discretion. Moreover, inasmuch as 16 U.S.C. §1533(f) requires NMFS to report to Congress "on the status of efforts to develop and implement recovery plans," the defendants represented at oral argument that the 1996 report was forthcoming. Considering these factors, I find the plaintiff's allegation with respect to revision to be meritless.

19. The plaintiff includes Minke whales in his list. Minke whales, however, are not listed as an endangered or threatened species under the ESA.

plans are for guidance purposes only." *Id.* Similarly, the court in *Morrill v. Lujan*, 802 F. Supp. 424, 433 (S.D.Ala.1992), found that "the contents of [recovery] plans are discretionary." While it is true that § 4(f) "does not permit an agency unbridled discretion," and "imposes a clear duty on the agency to fulfill the statutory command to the extent that it is feasible or possible," *Fund for Animals v. Babbitt*, 903 F. Supp. 96, 107 (D.D.C.1995), the requirement does not mean that the agency can be forced to include specific measures in its recovery plan. In fact, all that is required in a recovery plan is "the identification of management actions necessary to achieve the Plan's goals for the conservation and survival of the species." *Id.* at 108.

In any event, the evidence does not support that the measures suggested by the plaintiff are "necessary to achieve the plan's goal for the conservation and survival of the species." 16 U.S.C. § 1533(f)(B)(ii). And in fact, some of the measures advocated by the plaintiff are currently being implemented by NMFS [such as a population study]. Experts in the field plainly have different opinions as to what measures should be taken most effectively to promote conservation efforts for Right whales. It is also plain, however . . . that NMFS has considered the alternatives suggested by the plaintiff. The fact that NMFS did not adopt precisely the recommended measures in its recovery plan, does not make that plan deficient. Indeed, especially when expert, scientific judgments are involved, the court must afford the agency's decision a great deal of deference.

Last, I find that the recovery plan does contain "objective, measurable criteria," § 4(f)(1)(B)(ii), and "a description of site-specific management actions," § 4(f)(1)(B)(i). In terms of "objective, measurable criteria," the recovery plan states that the recovery goal is 7000 animals. The plaintiff argues that this goal is unrealistic and meaningless without a provision for interim goals. I find nothing in § 4(f) that mandates such interim goals. I also find that the Recovery Plan satisfies the "site-specific" requirement. The term "site-specific" has been interpreted to refer to geographical areas, requiring that the agency "in designing management actions, consider the distinct needs of separate ecosystems or recovery zones occupied by a threatened or endangered species." *Fund for Animals,* 903 F. Supp. at 106. The Recovery Plan meets this requirement because it considers the separate needs of the northern Atlantic population and the northern Pacific population. Additionally, the plan also addresses the different habitats of Northern Right whales at different times of year and contains measures specifically directed at each habitat. I find that the Recovery Plan is not arbitrary and capricious.

The plaintiff argues that even if the Recovery Plan is not arbitrary and capricious, NMFS has still violated the ESA because it has not implemented the plan. To support this contention, the plaintiff lists certain goals limned in the Recovery Plan that are not yet in effect. While it appears that some of the Recovery Plan's goals have not been implemented, *e.g.*, "appropriate seasonal or geographic regulations for the use of certain fishing gear in" the Bay of Fundy and the Southern Nova Scotia Shelf, I find plaintiff's allegations to be largely unfounded and needlessly technical. For example, the plaintiff states that no regulations on whale-watch vessels exist today. In February,

1997, however, NMFS issued a rule restricting all vessels and aircraft from approaching Right whales at a distance closer than 500 yards. Moreover, while the plaintiff asserts that "NMFS still has not located the unknown wintering area it alleges exists," [a government expert] avers that the research enabling NMFS to "find the unknown summer nursery and wintering grounds" is ongoing. After considering these efforts, I find that NMFS is taking steps to implement its Recovery Plan and that no ESA violation exists. . . .

Notes and Questions

1. On appeal, the First Circuit affirmed in an unpublished opinion and rejected the challenges to the recovery plan "essentially for the reasons stated by the district court." *See Strahan v. Linnon*, 187 F.3d 623 (1st Cir.1998).

2. Another interesting case responding to substantive challenges to a recovery plan, in this case for the grizzly bear, was *Fund for Animals v. Babbitt*, 903 F. Supp. 96 (D.D.C. 1995), in which the court held that the FWS violated §4 of the ESA by failing to incorporate objective, measurable recovery criteria into its recovery plan for the threatened grizzly bear (it did not tie the recovery goals to the five listing criteria), but that it satisfied the requirement that it incorporate site-specific management actions into the plan (the plaintiff had complained that the prescribed actions were not site-specific because the FWS used the same plan for different ecosystems).

F. Applying the ESA Abroad

How does the ESA apply to species located abroad? The following case addresses this issue. However, as you can see from the Supreme Court's later treatment of this case, which is included in Chapter 2, the Eighth Circuit's decision was reversed on the different ground of lack of standing to sue. Our highest court never addressed this question. The following opinion may still provide some insight, albeit imperfect, into how the question might ultimately be resolved.

Defenders of Wildlife v. Lujan
911 F.2d 117 (8th Cir. 1990)

Judge GIBSON:

[In 1978, the Fish and Wildlife Service and the National Marine Fisheries Service promulgated a joint regulation extending the Section 7 consultation requirement (and its corresponding substantive prohibitions) to federal agency actions taking place in foreign countries. The agencies changed their position in 1986 and issued a new regulation limiting the scope of the consultation duties to federal agency actions within the United States or on the high seas. Environmentalists sued to overturn the 1986 regulation and to require, for example, the Agency for International Development to engage in a section 7 consultation before funding development projects that could jeopardize the habitat of endangered crocodiles, elephants, and leopards in Africa.]

. . . It cannot be denied that Congress has chosen expansive language which admits to no exceptions. Reduced to its simplest form, the statute clearly states that each federal agency must consult with the Secretary regarding any action to insure that such action is not likely to jeopardize the existence of any endangered species. We recognize, however, that the use of all-inclusive language in this particular section of the Act is not determinative of the issue. We must search the Act further for clear expression of congressional intent.

The Supreme Court extensively discussed the Act's ambitious purpose in *Tennessee Valley Authority v. Hill.* "The plain intent of Congress in enacting this statute was to halt and reverse the trend toward species extinction, whatever the cost. This is reflected not only in the stated policies of the Act, but in literally every section of the statute." The Court described the Act as "the most comprehensive legislation for the preservation of endangered species ever enacted by any nation."

In the Act, Congress declared that "the United States has pledged itself as a sovereign state in the international community to conserve to the extent practicable the various species of fish or wildlife and plants facing extinction." The Act lists various international agreements which guide this pledge. Congress also committed itself to meeting the international commitments of the United States to existing conservation programs. The Act further declares one of its purposes is to take the appropriate steps to achieve the purposes of the international treaties and conventions just mentioned.

The Act defines "endangered species" broadly and without geographic limitations. Furthermore, the Act sets out a detailed procedure for determining whether a species is endangered. This section states that the Secretary shall determine whether a species is endangered or threatened after taking into account "those efforts, if any, being made by any State or foreign nation . . . to protect such species." The Secretary is instructed to give consideration to species which have been designated as requiring protection from unrestricted commerce by any foreign nation, or pursuant to any international agreement, and species identified as in danger of extinction by any State agency or by any agency of a foreign nation. Moreover, the Secretary is required to give actual notice to and invite comment from each foreign nation in which species proposed for listing as endangered are found.

The Secretary is instructed to publish a list of all species found to be threatened. Defenders asserts, and the Secretary does not contest, that "[a]s of May 1989, of 1,046 species listed as endangered or threatened, 507 were species whose range is outside the United States. In addition, there are 71 listed species whose range includes both United States and foreign territory." The listing process does not distinguish between domestic and foreign species.

The Act contains a section entitled "International Cooperation" which declares that the United States' commitment to worldwide protection of endangered species will be backed by financial assistance, personnel assignments, investigations, and by encouraging foreign nations to develop their own conservation programs. While the Secretary argues that this section and section 1538, dealing with imports and exports of wildlife, embody Congress' complete response to the international problem of endangered species, we are persuaded that this provision cannot be so neatly excised from the larger statutory scheme. Rather, we believe that the Act, viewed as a whole, clearly demonstrates congressional commitment to worldwide conservation efforts. To limit the consultation duty in a manner which protects only domestic endangered species runs contrary to such a commitment.

Based upon the foregoing examination of the Act as a whole, we are convinced that congressional intent can be gleaned from the plain language of the Act. Accordingly, we owe no deference to the Secretary's construction of the Act. *See Chevron*, 467 U.S. at 842–43. Furthermore, "[t]he judiciary is the final authority on issues of statutory construction and must reject administrative constructions which are contrary to clear congressional intent."

We believe that the answer to the extraterritorial issue can be found in the plain words of the statute. Our examination of the statute's legislative history, however, also reinforces our conclusion.

The original Environmental Species Act was enacted in 1973. Soon thereafter, the Secretary initiated a rulemaking process in order to implement the Act. In regard to the consultation requirement at issue here, the Secretary solicited comment from various agencies. Several agencies, including the Army Corps of Engineers, the State Department, and the Defense Department, expressed opposition to extraterritorial application. The Council on Environmental Quality, the Interior Department Solicitor's Office, and the General Counsel's Office of the National Oceanic and Atmospheric Administration, however, took the position that the consultation duty extended to foreign countries. After considering the extensive commentary, the Secretary concluded that Congress intended the duty to extend beyond the United States, and published a final rule on January 4, 1978, providing that: Section 7 . . . requires every Federal agency to insure that its activities or programs in the United States, upon the high seas, and in foreign countries, will not jeopardize the continued existence of a listed species. At that time, the Secretary justified the extraterritorial application by stressing the Act's broad, inclusive language; its legislative history; and its policy implications.

After these regulations were issued, Congress amended the consultation section of the Act to reflect its present version. The amendment was essentially a reorganization to allow additions to the rest of the section. The conference report to these 1978 amendments indicates that no substantive changes were intended. . . . In light of the fact that the "existing law" at the time of the 1978 amendments included the prior regulation requiring consultation on foreign projects, we believe that the above language provides strong evidence of the conference committee's tacit approval of the prior regulation. . . .

Despite this evidence of congressional intent, in 1983, the Secretary issued a notice of proposed rulemaking to revise the regulation. The proposed regulation eliminated the need for consultation on foreign projects and defined "action" to exclude foreign activities. The Secretary attributed its radical shift on extraterritorial application to "the apparent domestic orientation of the consultation and exemption processes resulting from the [1978] Amendments, and because of the potential for interference with the sovereignty of foreign nations."

We are compelled to reject this justification. We recognize that "[a]n administrative agency is not disqualified from changing its mind," and that "substantial deference is nonetheless appropriate if there appears to be have been good reason for the change." In this situation, however, the reasons offered for the change fall far short when examined in the context of the Act's language and legislative history previously discussed.

The Secretary places great emphasis upon the Act's treatment of the critical habitat clause, as support for its position. According to the Secretary, Congress could not have intended that the critical habitat provisions apply only to domestic projects while the consultation requirement extends to foreign projects. We are not persuaded. The Act reveals an intent to separately address the concerns raised by critical habitats and endangered species. The designation of critical habitat is governed by different procedures and standards than the listing of endangered species. Furthermore, we observe that the Secretary was not troubled by this alleged inconsistency when it promulgated its earlier regulation permitting differing geographic scopes of the two concerns. The evidence reveals that the consultation requirement and the critical habitat designation have been viewed as severable as to their geographical scope.

The Secretary claims that the domestic orientation of the consultation requirement is shown by the exemption provision added by the 1978 amendments. Specifically, the Secretary points out that exemptions are granted only if "the action is of regional or national significance," and require the weighing of public interests, which would be a gross intrusion upon the sovereignty of foreign nations. Again, we are unpersuaded. The exemption clauses provide that "the Governor of the State in which an agency action will occur, if any, . . . may apply to the Secretary for an exemption." This language, when considered with the substantive and persuasive evidence previously discussed, leads us to conclude that the exemption provisions do not limit the consultation requirement geographically. The Secretary also identifies other provisions of the Act which purportedly limit the consultation duty. We have carefully considered these arguments and believe that they do not compel a different result here. They merit no further discussion.

To support its construction of the Act, the Secretary relies heavily upon the canon of statutory construction that statutes are presumed to have domestic scope only. To overcome the presumption that the statute was not intended to have extraterritorial application, there must be clear expression of such congressional intent. We are convinced that evidence of such intent is found both in the words of the Act and in its legislative history as previously set forth. This evidence leaves us with the belief that Congress intended for the consultation obligation to extend to all agency actions affecting endangered species, whether within the United States or abroad.

The Secretary also expresses concerns about the impact on foreign relations stemming from extraterritorial application of the consultation duty. It urges that such a construction would be viewed as an intrusion upon the sovereign right of foreign nations to strike their own balance between development of natural resources and protection of endangered species. We note initially that the Act is directed at the actions of federal agencies, and not at the actions of sovereign nations. Congress may decide that its concern for foreign relations outweighs its concern for foreign wildlife; we, however, will not make such a decision on its behalf.

Notes and Questions

1. Although the Supreme Court reversed on the basis of standing, Justice Stevens merely concurred in the judgment. He would have held that the plaintiffs did have standing, but he disagreed with the Eighth Circuit on the merits and would have held that the ESA does not apply extraterritorially. The issue remains unresolved by the Supreme Court. What do you think the current court would do with the question?

IV. International Law

Biodiversity loss is a global crisis. Along with climate disruption, it is one of the two most serious problems facing the planet. Both phenomena are existential threats to life on earth. Humankind has become increasingly aware of our dependence on ecosystem services in order to survive, which services are provided by healthy and biodiverse ecosystems. We need not feel compassion for wildlife nor enjoy its presence to make wildlife conservation a priority. We need only the desire to survive ourselves.

Many other countries, like the United States, have their own legislation to protect biodiversity. That material is well beyond the scope of this book. This portion of the chapter will provide two important sources of international biodiversity law. First, the Convention on International Trade in Endangered Species of Wild Fauna and Flora (CITES), which is a treaty prohibiting international trade in species whose country of origin has listed them for legal protection domestically. The United States ratified CITES and uses the ESA for enforcement, as discussed in the case below. Second, the Convention on Biological Diversity, which was drafted by a United Nations Environment Programme (UNEP) working group and opened up for signature at the 1992 United Nations Conference on Environment and Development (the Rio "Earth Summit"). It has been ratified by 168 countries (notably, not the United States, see notes following the text), and has three main objectives: "1. The conservation of biological diversity, 2. The sustainable use of the components of biological diversity, 3. The fair and equitable sharing of the benefits arising out of the utilization of genetic resources."

Castlewood Products, L.L.C. v. Norton
365 F.3d 1076 (D.C. Cir. 2004)

Judge EDWARDS:

This case concerns the United States' detention of several shipments of bigleaf mahogany from Brazil. The United States and Brazil are both signatories to the Convention on International Trade in Endangered Species of Wild Fauna and Flora

("CITES" or "Convention"). The Convention governs trade in endangered species that are listed in its appendices. Article V provides that an export permit for species included in Appendix III can be granted by the exporting country only when, *inter alia*, the designated Management Authority of the exporting country is satisfied that the specimen was not obtained in contravention of its laws. Brazil has included bigleaf mahogany in Appendix III. In the United States, the Endangered Species Act, 16 U.S.C. §§ 1531–44 (2000) ("ESA"), prohibits trade in violation of the Convention and authorizes the Secretary of the Interior and the Secretary of Agriculture to enforce the ESA.

This case arose when the Animal and Plant Health Inspection Service ("APHIS") of the United States Department of Agriculture ("USDA") refused entry at U.S. ports to certain shipments of bigleaf mahogany after Brazil's Management Authority gave information to the United States Department of the Interior's Fish and Wildlife Service ("FWS") suggesting that the specimens in the shipments were not legally obtained. On July 23, 2002, Castlewood Products, L.L.C., Interforest Corp., M. Bohlke Veneer Corp., Marwood, Inc., United Veneer, L.L.C., Veneer Technologies, Inc., and Aljoma Lumber, Inc., the U.S. corporate consignees of the disputed shipments, brought this action in the United States District Court for the District of Columbia to compel delivery of the shipments. The plaintiffs claimed that, because the export permits accompanying the shipments were signed and issued by Brazil's Management Authority, APHIS's detention of the shipments was arbitrary and capricious. The District Court denied the plaintiffs' motion for summary judgment and granted summary judgment to the Government, holding that the decision to detain the shipments was authorized by treaty, statute, and regulation. Interforest, Marwood, Veneer Technologies, and Aljoma Lumber appealed and we now affirm the judgment of the District Court.

I. Background

A. Regulatory Background

The Convention governs the import and export of certain species of endangered fauna and flora that are listed in its appendices. This case concerns bigleaf mahogany, which Brazil has included in Appendix III. Article V of CITES provides that the export of any species listed in Appendix III requires "the prior grant and presentation of an export permit." That article provides:

An export permit shall only be granted when the following conditions have been met:

(a) a Management Authority of the State of export is satisfied that the specimen was not obtained in contravention of the laws of that State for the protection of fauna and flora;

(b) a Management Authority of the State of export is satisfied that any living specimen will be so prepared and shipped as to minimize the risk of injury, damage to health or cruel treatment.

A Management Authority is designated by each state to "grant permits or certificates on behalf of that Party." The United States has designated the Secretary of the Interior as the CITES Management Authority, and the Secretary's functions in this capacity are carried out through FWS. In Brazil, the Instituto Brasileiro do Meio Ambiente e dos Recursos Naturais Renovaveis or the Brazilian Institute of the Environment and Renewable Natural Resources (also known as "IBAMA") is the Management Authority under CITES.

Article VIII of the Convention provides:

(1) The Parties shall take appropriate measures to enforce the provisions of the present Convention and to prohibit trade in specimens in violation thereof. These shall include measures:

(a) to penalize trade in, or possession of, such specimens, or both; and

(b) to provide for the confiscation or return to the State of export of such specimens.

Article XIV makes it clear that the Convention does not purport to limit the right of the Parties to adopt "stricter domestic measures regarding the conditions for trade, taking possession or transport of specimens of species included in Appendices I, II, and III, or complete prohibition thereof. . . ."

Article XI provides for regular meetings of the Parties to the Convention, at which they may, inter alia, "make recommendations for improving the effectiveness of the present Convention." These recommendations, adopted through resolutions, are intended to give guidance to the Parties in implementing the Convention. Since ratification, the Parties have adopted two resolutions recommending specific measures to strengthen enforcement of the Convention. One, Resolution 11.3, recommends that,

(c) if an importing country has reason to believe that an Appendix-II or -III species is traded in contravention of the laws of any country involved in the transaction, it:

(i) immediately inform the country whose laws were thought to have been violated and, to the extent possible, provide that country with copies of all documentation relating to the transaction; and

(ii) where possible, apply stricter domestic measures to that transaction as provided for in Article XIV of the Convention.

The other, Resolution 12.3, recommends that "the Parties refuse to accept any permit or certificate that is invalid, including authentic documents that do not contain all the required information . . . or that contain information that brings into question the validity of the permit or certificate."

Congress implemented the Convention into U.S. law in the Endangered Species Act of 1973. The ESA makes it unlawful to "engage in any trade in any specimens contrary to the provisions of the Convention." It provides that any fish, wildlife or plants possessed or transferred in violation of the ESA or its regulations "shall be subject to forfeiture to the United States." The Secretary of the Interior is authorized to promulgate regulations as may be appropriate to enforce the ESA. The statute also provides for the coordination of the administration of the ESA between the Secretary of

Agriculture and the Secretary of the Interior. FWS and APHIS work together to enforce the provisions of CITES.

The Department of the Interior has promulgated regulations to implement the ESA. One regulation provides: "In order to import into the United States any wildlife or plant listed in appendix III from a foreign country that has listed such animal or plant in appendix III, a valid foreign export permit or re-export certificate issued by such country must be obtained prior to such importation." Another regulation states: "Only export permits, re-export certificates, certificates of origin, or other certificates issued and signed by a management authority will be accepted as a valid foreign document from a country that is a party to the Convention."

B. Factual Background

The facts are largely undisputed. In the fall of 2001, FWS and APHIS learned that the Brazilian government had imposed a moratorium on the logging, transport, and export of bigleaf mahogany timber. In February 2002, APHIS placed holds on shipments of bigleaf mahogany from Brazil. FWS sent a letter to IBAMA, noting that "none of the permits accompanying the shipments were endorsed . . . by the export inspection authorities in Brazil," and stating that USDA was detaining the shipments until officials in the United States could gain "verification of the validity of accompanying CITES permits." IBAMA informed FWS that recent shipments of bigleaf mahogany arriving in the United States from Brazil were accompanied by export permits that IBAMA had issued pursuant to preliminary judicial injunctions. IBAMA stated that its issuance of these permits did not reflect its independent judgment that the mahogany had been obtained lawfully.

[Due to pending litigation, there were impediments to providing unequivocal information to the U.S. regarding the legality of this harvest. APHIS did release 5 of the shipments, however, based on evidence that those portions had been lawfully obtained.]

On July 23, 2002, the plaintiffs commenced this action in the United States District Court for the District of Columbia to compel the delivery of the mahogany shipments that were still being detained. They filed a complaint for injunctive and declaratory relief against APHIS, FWS, Gale A. Norton, in her official capacity as the Secretary of the Interior, Steven A. Williams, in his official capacity as the Director of FWS, Ann M. Veneman, in her official capacity as the Secretary of Agriculture, and Craig A. Reed, in his official capacity as Administrator of APHIS. The plaintiffs argued that, pursuant to the ESA and its implementing regulations, APHIS is required to validate a shipment for import upon presentment of all documentation required by the implementing regulations, and that a valid foreign export permit is the only document from the exporting country that is required under the Convention.

On January 23, 2003, APHIS entered a Memorandum for the Record "to document the decision of the U.S. Department of Agriculture (USDA) to refuse entry into the United States of certain shipments of bigleaf mahogany lumber and veneers that the Convention on International Trade in Endangered Species (CITES) management authority of Brazil (known as IBAMA) has been unable to confirm originated from legal sources." The memorandum stated:

> IBAMA confirmed that although it had issued the CITES export permits for the shipments, it had done so under court injunctions which it was appealing. IBAMA indicated it had not determined whether the mahogany had been legally acquired, which is a prerequisite to the issuance of a CITES export permit for this species. For that reason, APHIS has held those and subsequent mahogany shipments imported into the United States in order to determine from IBAMA if the mahogany was legally acquired.

The memorandum explained APHIS's position that, since it had the express authority to seize and forfeit articles traded in violation of the CITES treaty, it also had the discretion to choose a less drastic action, such as to refuse entry to a commodity. It pointed out that its action complied with CITES Resolution 10.2 § II(h), which recommended that the signatories "not authorize the import of any specimen if they have reason to believe that it was not legally acquired in the country of origin."

The parties then filed cross-motions for summary judgment in the District Court. The District Court determined that the decision to seize, detain, and confiscate contraband specimens under the ESA was within the agency's clear statutory and regulatory authority. Based on the record before it, the District Court found that APHIS and Brazilian officials had agreed to adopt a "chronological approach," under which the United States would allow the release of shipments in chronological order of shipping, until the total amount released equaled the amount calculated by IBAMA to be of legal origin. It noted that, "in every instance in which IBAMA has confirmed the legality of a shipment, APHIS has released that shipment." The District Court concluded that "the defendants' actions were in all respects authorized by treaty, statute, and regulation, and that the government did not act arbitrarily, capriciously, nor did it abuse its discretion in the matter." It therefore granted the Government's motion for summary judgment.

Four of the plaintiffs now appeal the District Court's judgment denying their motion for summary judgment and awarding summary judgment to the Government.

II. Analysis

A. Standard of Review

We review de novo the District Court's grant of summary judgment, which means that we review the agency's decision on our own. [The court then applied an arbitrary and capricious standard.]

B. The Requirement of a "Valid Foreign Export Permit"

1

Appellants challenge the decision by FWS and APHIS to detain the mahogany shipments as arbitrary and capricious, claiming that it rests on impermissible interpretations of 50 C.F.R. §§ 23.12(a) and 23.14(a). We find no merit in this challenge.

Section 23.12(a)(3)(i) provides:

> In order to import into the United States any wildlife or plant listed in appendix III from a foreign country that has listed such animal or plan in appendix III, a valid foreign export permit or re-export certificate issued by such country must be obtained prior to such importation.

APHIS detained the mahogany shipments at issue here, because, in its representations to FWS, "IBAMA indicated it had not determined whether the mahogany had been legally acquired, which is a prerequisite to the issuance of a CITES export permit for this species." This application of the regulation reflects the Government's position that a foreign export permit cannot be "valid" under CITES absent an assurance from the exporting country "that the specimen was not obtained in contravention of the laws of that State."

Appellants argue that the Government's interpretation of § 23.12(a)(3)(i) is at odds with the plain text of § 23.14(a), which states:

> Only export permits, re-export certificates, certificates of origin, or other certificates issued and signed by a management authority will be accepted as a valid foreign document from a country that is a party to the Convention.

Appellants contend that, under § 23.14(a), once the Management Authority of the exporting state has issued an export permit, the permit must be accepted as "valid" by authorities in the United States. In other words, according to appellants, the plain language of § 23.14(a) precludes United States agencies from imposing other conditions precedent to the import of Appendix III species. This "plain language" argument is plainly wrong.

Section 23.12(a)(3)(i) merely requires a valid foreign export permit, but it does not specify the conditions that a foreign export permit must meet in order for U.S. officials to regard the permit as valid, i.e., to conclude that the exporting Management Authority was "satisfied that the specimen was not obtained in contravention of the laws of that State." Section 23.14(a) requires that an export permit be issued and signed by the foreign Management Authority in order be accepted, but it does not say that these requirements are the only conditions that an agency may lawfully require before accepting a permit. Therefore, the language of the regulations is ambiguous as to whether U.S. officials may "look behind" a lawfully signed and issued export permit to determine whether the substantive requirements of CITES (i.e., that the Management Authority was satisfied that the specimen was not obtained unlawfully) had actually been met.

The Supreme Court has held that, "[i]n situations in which 'the meaning of [regulatory] language is not free from doubt,' the reviewing court should give effect to the agency's interpretation so long as it is 'reasonable.'" *Martin v. OSHRC*, 499 U.S. 144, 150–51, 111 S.Ct. 1171, 1176, 113 L.Ed.2d 117 (1991) (quoting *Ehlert v. United States*, 402 U.S. 99, 105, 91 S.Ct. 1319, 1323, 28 L.Ed.2d 625 (1971)). Here, FWS and APHIS read § 23.12(a)(3)(i) as allowing U.S. officials to require more than facial satisfaction of § 23.14(a), at least in cases where the United States has reason to doubt whether the export permits in question were issued in compliance with CITES. The regulations were promulgated pursuant to the Secretary of the Interior's clear statutory authority under the ESA to "promulgate such regulations as may be appropriate to enforce" the ESA. The ESA makes it "unlawful for any person subject to the jurisdiction of the United States to engage in any trade in any specimens contrary to the provisions of the Convention, or to possess any specimens traded contrary to the provisions of the Convention." And, the stated purpose of the regulations at 50 C.F.R. pt. 23 is to "implement the Convention on International Trade in Endangered Species of Wild Fauna and Flora."

In light of these statutory and regulatory provisions, the Government acted reasonably in requiring more than facial satisfaction of § 23.14(a) when determining whether an export permit is "valid" (i.e., issued in compliance with CITES) under § 23.12(a)(3)(i). The regulations were promulgated to implement the ESA, which was itself passed, in part, to implement the Convention. The ESA specifically prohibits trade contrary to the provisions of the Convention, and provides that any specimens that are imported in violation of the ESA are subject to forfeiture to the United States. The Convention requires that an export permit for an Appendix III species shall only be granted when "a Management Authority of the State of export is satisfied that the specimen was not obtained in contravention of the laws of that State for the protection of fauna and flora."

Furthermore, Article XI provides for regular meetings of the Parties to the Convention, at which they may, inter alia, "make recommendations for improving the effectiveness of the present Convention." These recommendations, adopted through resolutions, are intended to give guidance to the Parties in implementing the Convention. Resolution 11.3 recommends that, "if an importing country has reason to believe that an Appendix . . . III species is traded in contravention of the laws of any country involved in the transaction, it . . . immediately inform the country whose laws were thought to have been violated." And Resolution 12.3 recommends that "the Parties refuse to accept any permit or certificate that is invalid, including authentic documents that do not contain all the required information . . . or that contain information that brings into question the validity of the permit or certificate."

These provisions, taken together, make it clear that the agencies' interpretation of the applicable regulations is perfectly reasonable. It is also clear here that, to date, there are no "valid" export permits for the disputed shipments. There is no dispute that Brazil's Management Authority questioned whether the goods in the disputed shipments were obtained legally. The United States thus had a reasonable basis for inquiring further and detaining the shipments until a finding of legal acquisition could be made.

Appellants argue, and the Government does not dispute, that the CITES resolutions are merely recommendations to the Parties and, therefore, they are not binding on the United States. This does not render the resolutions meaningless, however. There would be no point in the contracting states agreeing on resolutions only to then completely ignore them. Therefore, while not binding, it was surely reasonable for FWS and APHIS to look to the CITES resolutions for guidance in interpreting the regulations implementing CITES.

Furthermore, appellants' claim that they did not have notice of the Government's interpretation is meritless. It is clear from the text of the Convention that signatories may only issue export permits for Appendix III goods upon determining that they were legally obtained, so appellants can claim no surprise or confusion over this.

2

We also reject appellants' argument that the decision by a Brazilian federal court in *Bianchini E Serafim LTDA v. IBAMA*, Writ of Mandamus No.2002.001437-0 (10th Fed. Dist. Ct. of Curitiba, June 28, 2002), J.A. 262-65 (trans. Berlitz GlobalNet, J.A. 253-61), compels reversal in this case. The decision in *Bianchini* has no bearing on the shipments at issue in this case.

The Government acknowledges that the United States will release detained shipments when judicial review in a foreign state concludes that the goods were legally obtained, regardless of whether the foreign Management Authority disagrees with the judicial decision. There is no serious dispute over this point. Indeed, the Government followed this precept in this case in response to the *Bianchini* decision. . . .

. . . That holding applied only to the wood in the specific shipment at issue in that case. The United States then released that particular shipment, even though IBAMA appealed the decision. And, while the appeal was pending, IBAMA acknowledged that the final judicial determination that the wood was legally acquired meant the wood had to be released. Therefore, neither the parties nor IBAMA dispute that a final judicial determination that the goods in a shipment were legally obtained, upon review of a Management Authority's decision to the contrary, amounts to a finding of legal acquisition as required by CITES.

It is undisputed that *Bianchini* involved a different shipment than those at issue here. In contrast to *Bianchini*, there was no final judicial disposition as to the legal acquisition of the wood in the shipments at issue in this case. For the shipments at issue here, the Brazilian court had issued ex parte orders requiring IBAMA to issue the export permits. These preliminary injunctions did not purport to find that the mahogany in the shipments at issue here was legally obtained. Therefore, APHIS reasonably detained the shipments for want of assurance, either from IBAMA or pursuant to judicial decree, that the wood in the disputed shipments was legally obtained. In the absence of a valid export permit for these shipments, the Government had the authority to detain them.

decision

Notes and Questions

1. The International Union for the Conservation of Nature (IUCN) is an international nongovernmental organization whose mission is to provide scientific expertise free of political influence to aid conservation programs worldwide. It initially formed in 1948 and released its first Red Data Book (listing species by degree of vulnerability) in 1960. The IUCN's most current "Red List Categories and Criteria," which sets out

clear quantitative criteria for identifying varying threat levels, were created over the course of more than a decade of collaboration and revision by scientists from around the world. The IUCN criteria have become widely recognized internationally, and are currently applied by numerous governmental and non-governmental organizations. Perhaps most notable is the 1994 adoption of IUCN-devised criteria for use in the primary international treaty to protect endangered species, CITES. The new CITES criteria have been described as the most objective standards in endangered species listing being used in the world, and after the adoption of these criteria for use in CITES, the process of listing species became clearer and firmer. We still do not have anything approaching this kind of consistently applied criteria for listing species in the U.S.

United Nations Conference on Environment and Development Convention on Biological Diversity

June 5, 1992

Preamble

The Contracting Parties,

Conscious of the intrinsic value of biological diversity and of the ecological, genetic, social, economic, scientific, educational, cultural, recreational and aesthetic values of biological diversity and its components,

Conscious also of the importance of biological diversity for evolution and for maintaining life sustaining systems of the biosphere,

Affirming that the conservation of biological diversity is a common concern of humankind,

Reaffirming that States have sovereign rights over their own biological resources,

Reaffirming also that States are responsible for conserving their biological diversity and for using their biological resources in a sustainable manner,

Concerned that biological diversity is being significantly reduced by certain human activities,

Aware of the general lack of information and knowledge regarding biological diversity and of the urgent need to develop scientific, technical and institutional capacities to provide the basic understanding upon which to plan and implement appropriate measures.

Noting that it is vital to anticipate, prevent and attack the causes of significant reduction or loss of biological diversity at source.

Noting also that where there is a threat of significant reduction or loss of biological diversity, lack of full scientific certainty should not be used as a reason for postponing measures to avoid or minimize such a threat,

Noting further that the fundamental requirement for the conservation of biological diversity is the in-situ conservation of ecosystems and natural habitats and the maintenance and recovery of viable populations of species in their natural surroundings,

Noting further that ex-situ measures, preferably in the country of origin, also have an important role to play,

Recognizing the close and traditional dependence of many indigenous and local communities embodying traditional lifestyles on biological resources, and the desirability of sharing equitably benefits arising from the use of traditional knowledge, innovations and practices relevant to the conservation of biological diversity and the sustainable use of its components,

Recognizing also the vital role that women play in the conservation and sustainable use of biological diversity and affirming the need for the full participation of women at all levels of policy-making and implementation for biological diversity conservation,

Stressing the importance of, and the need to promote, international, regional and global cooperation among States and intergovernmental organizations and the non-governmental sector for the conservation of biological diversity and the sustainable use of its components,

Acknowledging that the provision of new and additional financial resources and appropriate access to relevant technologies can be expected to make a substantial difference in the world's ability to address the loss of biological diversity,

Acknowledging further that special provision is required to meet the needs of developing countries, including the provision of new and additional financial resources and appropriate access to relevant technologies,

Noting in this regard the special conditions of the least developed countries and small island States,

Acknowledging that substantial investments are required to conserve biological diversity and that there is the expectation of a broad range of environmental, economic and social benefits from those investments,

Recognizing that economic and social development and poverty eradication are the first and overriding priorities of developing countries,

Aware that conservation and sustainable use of biological diversity is of critical importance for meeting the food, health and other needs of the growing world population, for which purpose access to and sharing of both genetic resources and technologies are essential,

Noting that, ultimately, the conservation and sustainable use of biological diversity will strengthen friendly relations among States and contribute to peace for humankind,

Desiring to enhance and complement existing international arrangements for the conservation of biological diversity and sustainable use of its components, and

Determined to conserve and sustainably use biological diversity for the benefit of present and future generations,

Have agreed as follows:

Article 1. Objectives

The objectives of this Convention, to be pursued in accordance with its relevant provisions, are the conservation of biological diversity, the sustainable use of its components and the air and equitable sharing of the benefits arising out of the utilization of genetic resources, including by appropriate access to genetic resources and by appropriate transfer of relevant technologies, taking into account all rights over those resources and to technologies, and by appropriate funding.

Article 2. Use of Terms

For the purposes of this Convention:

"Biological diversity" means the variability among living organisms from all sources including, inter alia, terrestrial, marine and other aquatic ecosystems and the ecological complexes of which they are part; this includes diversity within species, between species and of ecosystems.

"Biological resources" includes genetic resources, organisms or parts thereof, populations, or any other biotic component of ecosystems with actual or potential use or value for humanity.

"Biotechnology" means any technological application that uses biological systems, living organisms, or derivatives thereof, to make or modify products or processes for specific use.

"Country of origin of genetic resources" means the country which possesses those genetic resources in in-situ conditions.

"Country providing genetic resources" means the country supplying genetic resources collected from in-situ sources, including populations of both wild and domesticated species, or taken from ex-situ sources, which may or may not have originated in that country.

"Domesticated or cultivated species" means species in which the evolutionary process has been influenced by humans to meet their needs.

"Ecosystem" means a dynamic complex of plant, animal and microorganism communities and their non-living environment interacting as a functional unit.

"Ex-situ conservation" means the conservation of components of biological diversity outside their natural habitats.

"Genetic material" means any material of plant, animal, microbial or other origin containing functional units of heredity.

"Genetic resources" means genetic material of actual or potential value.

"Habitat" means the place or type of site where an organism or population naturally occurs.

"In-situ conditions" means conditions where genetic resources exist within eco-systems and natural habitats, and, in the case of domesticated or cultivated species, in the surroundings where they have developed their distinctive properties.

"In-situ conservation" means the conservation of ecosystems and natural habitats and the maintenance and recovery of viable populations of species in their natural surroundings and, in the case of domesticated or cultivated species, in the surroundings where they have developed their distinctive properties.

"Protected area" means a geographically defined area which is designated or regulated and managed to achieve specific conservation objectives.

"Regional economic integration organization" means an organization constituted by sovereign States of a given region, to which its member States have transferred competence in respect of matters governed by this Convention and which has been duly authorized, in accordance with its internal procedures, to sign, ratify, accept, approve or accede to it.

"Sustainable use" means the use of components of biological diversity in a way and at a rate that does not lead to the long-term decline of biological diversity, thereby maintaining its potential to meet the needs and aspirations of present and future generations.

"Technology" includes biotechnology.

Article 3. Principle

States have, in accordance with the Charter of the United Nations and the principles of international law, the sovereign right to exploit their own resources pursuant to their own environmental policies, and the responsibility to ensure that activities within their jurisdiction or control do not cause damage to the environment of other States or of areas beyond the limits of national jurisdiction.

The nation is the sovereign

Article 4. Jurisdictional Scope

Subject to the rights of other States, and except as otherwise expressly provided in this Convention, the provisions of this Convention apply, in relation to each Contracting Party:

(a) In the case of components of biological diversity, in areas within the limits of its national jurisdiction; and

(b) In the case of processes and activities, regardless of where their effects occur, carried out under its jurisdiction or control, within the area of its national jurisdiction or beyond the limits of national jurisdiction.

Article 5. Cooperation

Each Contracting Party shall, as far as possible and as appropriate, cooperate with other Contracting Parties, directly or, where appropriate, through competent international organizations, in respect of areas beyond national jurisdiction and on other matters of mutual interest, for the conservation and sustainable use of biological diversity.

— identification & monitoring
— maintaining data

Article 6. General Measures for Conservation and Sustainable Use Each Contracting Party shall, in accordance with its particular conditions and capabilities:

(a) Develop national strategies, plans or programmes for the conservation and sustainable use of biological diversity or adapt for this purpose existing strategies, plans or programmes which shall reflect, inter alia, the measures set out in this Convention relevant to the Contracting Party concerned; and

(b) Integrate, as far as possible and as appropriate, the conservation and sustainable use of biological diversity into relevant sectoral or cross-sectoral plans, programmes and policies.

Article 7. Identification and Monitoring

Each Contracting Party shall, as far as possible and as appropriate, in particular for the purposes of Articles 8 to 10:

(a) Identify components of biological diversity important for its conservation and sustainable use having regard to the indicative list of categories set down in Annex I;

(b) Monitor, through sampling and other techniques, the components of biological diversity identified pursuant to subparagraph (a) above, paying particular attention to those requiring urgent conservation measures and those which offer the greatest potential for sustainable use;

(c) Identify processes and categories of activities which have or are likely to have significant adverse impacts on the conservation and sustainable use of biological diversity, and monitor their effects through sampling and other techniques; and

(d) Maintain and organize, by any mechanism data, derived from identification and monitoring activities pursuant to subparagraphs (a), (b) and (c) above.

Article 8. In-situ Conservation

Each Contracting Party shall, as far as possible and as appropriate:

(a) Establish a system of protected areas or areas where special measures need to be taken to conserve biological diversity;

(b) Develop, where necessary, guidelines for the selection, establishment and management of protected areas or areas where special measures need to be taken to conserve biological diversity;

(c) Regulate or manage biological resources important for the conservation of biological diversity whether within or outside protected areas, with a view to ensuring their conservation and sustainable use;

(d) Promote the protection of ecosystems, natural habitats and the maintenance of viable populations of species in natural surroundings;

(e) Promote environmentally sound and sustainable development in areas adjacent to protected areas with a view to furthering protection of these areas;

(f) Rehabilitate and restore degraded ecosystems and promote the recovery of threatened species, inter alia, through the development and implementation of plans or other management strategies;

(g) Establish or maintain means to regulate, manage or control the risks associated with the use and release of living modified organisms resulting from biotechnology which are likely to have adverse environmental impacts that could affect the conservation and sustainable use of biological diversity, taking also into account the risks to human health;

(h) Prevent the introduction of, control or eradicate those alien species which threaten ecosystems, habitats or species;

(i) Endeavour to provide the conditions needed for compatibility between present uses and the conservation of biological diversity and the sustainable use of its components;

(j) Subject to its national legislation, respect, preserve and maintain knowledge, innovations and practices of indigenous and local communities embodying traditional lifestyles relevant for the conservation and sustainable use of biological diversity and promote their wider application with the approval and involvement of the holders of such knowledge, innovations and practices and encourage the equitable sharing of the benefits arising from the utilization of such knowledge, innovations and practices;

(k) Develop or maintain necessary legislation and/or other regulatory provisions for the protection of threatened species and populations;

(l) Where a significant adverse effect on biological diversity has been determined pursuant to Article 7, regulate or manage the relevant processes and categories of activities; and

(m) Cooperate in providing financial and other support for in-situ conservation outlined in subparagraphs (a) to (l) above, particularly to developing countries.

Article 9. Ex-situ Conservation

Each Contracting Party shall, as far as possible and as appropriate, and predominantly for the purpose of complementing in-situ measures:

(a) Adopt measures for the ex-situ conservation of components of biological diversity, preferably in the country of origin of such components;

(b) Establish and maintain facilities for ex-situ conservation of and research on plants, animals and micro-organisms, preferably in the country of origin of genetic resources;

(c) Adopt measures for the recovery and rehabilitation of threatened species and for their reintroduction into their natural habitats under appropriate conditions;

(d) Regulate and manage collection of biological resources from natural habitats for ex-situ conservation purposes so as not to threaten ecosystems and in-situ populations of species, except where special temporary ex-situ measures are required under subparagraph (c) above; and

(e) Cooperate in providing financial and other support for ex-situ conservation outlined in subparagraphs (a) to (d) above and in the establishment and maintenance of ex-situ conservation facilities in developing countries.

Article 10. Sustainable Use of Components of Biological Diversity

Each Contracting Party shall, as far as possible and as appropriate:

(a) Integrate consideration of the conservation and sustainable use of biological resources into national decision-making;

(b) Adopt measures relating to the use of biological resources to avoid or minimize adverse impacts on biological diversity;

(c) Protect and encourage customary use of biological resources in accordance with traditional cultural practices that are compatible with conservation or sustainable use requirements;

(d) Support local populations to develop and implement remedial action in degraded areas where biological diversity has been reduced; and

(e) Encourage cooperation between its governmental authorities and its private sector in developing methods for sustainable use of biological resources.

Article 11. Incentive Measures

Each Contracting Party shall, as far as possible and as appropriate, adopt economically and socially sound measures that act as incentives for the conservation and sustainable use of components of biological diversity.

Article 12. Research and Training

The Contracting Parties, taking into account the special needs of developing countries, shall:

(a) Establish and maintain programmes for scientific and technical education and training in measures for the identification, conservation and sustainable use of biological diversity and its components and provide support for such education and training for the specific needs of developing countries;

(b) Promote and encourage research which contributes to the conservation and sustainable use of biological diversity, particularly in developing countries, inter alia, in accordance with decisions of the Conference of the Parties taken in consequence of recommendations of the Subsidiary Body on Scientific, Technical and Technological Advice; and

(c) In keeping with the provisions of Articles 16, 18 and 20, promote and cooperate in the use of scientific advances in biological diversity research in developing methods for conservation and sustainable use of biological resources.

Article 13. Public Education and Awareness

The Contracting Parties shall:

(a) Promote and encourage understanding of the importance of, and the measures required for, the conservation of biological diversity, as well as its propagation through media, and the inclusion of these topics in educational programmes; and

(b) Cooperate, as appropriate, with other States and international organizations in developing educational and public awareness programmes, with respect to conservation and sustainable use of biological diversity.

Article 14. Impact Assessment and Minimizing Adverse Impacts

1. Each Contracting Party, as far as possible and as appropriate, shall:

(a) Introduce appropriate procedures requiring environmental impact assessment of its proposed projects that are likely to have significant adverse effects on biological diversity with a view to avoiding or minimizing such effects and, where appropriate, allow for public participation in such procedures;

(b) Introduce appropriate arrangements to ensure that the environmental consequences of its programmes and policies that are likely to have significant adverse impacts on biological diversity are duly taken into account;

(c) Promote, on the basis of reciprocity, notification, exchange of information and consultation on activities under their jurisdiction or control which are likely to significantly affect adversely the biological diversity of other States or areas beyond the limits of national jurisdiction, by encouraging the conclusion of bilateral, regional or multilateral arrangements, as appropriate;

(d) In the case of imminent or grave danger or damage, originating under its jurisdiction or control, to biological diversity within the area under jurisdiction of other States or in areas beyond the limits of national jurisdiction, notify immediately the potentially affected States of such danger or damage, as well as initiate action to prevent or minimize such danger or damage; and

(e) Promote national arrangements for emergency responses to activities or events, whether caused naturally or otherwise, which present a grave and imminent danger to biological diversity and encourage international cooperation to supplement such national efforts and, where appropriate and agreed by the States or regional economic integration organizations concerned, to establish joint contingency plans.

2. The Conference of the Parties shall examine, on the basis of studies to be carried out, the issue of liability and redress, including restoration and compensation, for damage to biological diversity, except where such liability is a purely internal matter.

Article 15. Access to Genetic Resources

1. Recognizing the sovereign rights of States over their natural resources, the authority to determine access to genetic resources rests with the national governments and is subject to national legislation.

2. Each Contracting Party shall endeavour to create conditions to facilitate access to genetic resources for environmentally sound uses by other Contracting Parties and not to impose restrictions that run counter to the objectives of this Convention.

3. For the purpose of this Convention, the genetic resources being provided by a Contracting Party, as referred to in this Article and Articles 16 and 19, are only those that are provided by Contracting Parties that are countries of origin of such resources or by the Parties that have acquired the genetic resources in accordance with this Convention.

4. Access, where granted, shall be on mutually agreed terms and subject to the provisions of this Article.

5. Access to genetic resources shall be subject to prior informed consent of the Contracting Party providing such resources, unless otherwise determined by that Party.

6. Each Contracting Party shall endeavour to develop and carry out scientific research based on genetic resources provided by other Contracting Parties with the full participation of, and where possible in, such Contracting Parties.

7. Each Contracting Party shall take legislative, administrative or policy measures, as appropriate, and in accordance with Articles 16 and 19 and, where necessary, through the financial mechanism established by Articles 20 and 21 with the aim of sharing in a fair and equitable way the results of research and development and the benefits arising from the commercial and other utilization of genetic resources with the Contracting Party providing such resources. Such sharing shall be upon mutually agreed terms.

Article 16. Access to and Transfer of Technology

1. Each Contracting Party, recognizing that technology includes biotechnology, and that both access to and transfer of technology among Contracting Parties are essential elements for the attainment of the objectives of this Convention, undertakes subject to the provisions of this Article to provide and/or facilitate access for and transfer to other Contracting Parties of technologies that are relevant to the conservation and sustainable use of biological diversity or make use of genetic resources and do not cause significant damage to the environment.

2. Access to and transfer of technology referred to in paragraph 1 above to developing countries shall be provided and/or facilitated under fair and most favourable terms, including on concessional and preferential terms where mutually agreed, and, where necessary, in accordance with the financial mechanism established by Articles 20 and 21. In the case of technology subject to patents and other intellectual property rights, such access and transfer shall be provided on terms which recognize and are consistent with the adequate and effective protection of intellectual property rights.

. . .

[Some of the remaining provisions address matters such as financing of compliance and relationships between developed and developing countries for this purpose. The remainder of the Convention can be viewed online.]

Notes and Questions

1. Parties to the Convention are presently operating under the Strategic Plan for Biodiversity 2011–2020, drafted at the 10th meeting of the Conference of the Parties, which includes the Aichi Biodiversity Targets. These targets are important and thus fully reproduced below. There are 20 in all, which are structured under five strategic goals.

Aichi Biodiversity Targets

Strategic Goal A: Address the underlying causes of biodiversity loss by mainstreaming biodiversity across government and society

Target 1

By 2020, at the latest, people are aware of the values of biodiversity and the steps they can take to conserve and use it sustainably.

Target 2

By 2020, at the latest, biodiversity values have been integrated into national and local development and poverty reduction strategies and planning processes and are being incorporated into national accounting, as appropriate, and reporting systems.

Target 3

By 2020, at the latest, incentives, including subsidies, harmful to biodiversity are eliminated, phased out or reformed in order to minimize or avoid negative impacts, and positive incentives for the conservation and sustainable use of biodiversity are developed and applied, consistent and in harmony with the Convention and other relevant international obligations, taking into account national socio economic conditions.

Target 4

By 2020, at the latest, Governments, business and stakeholders at all levels have taken steps to achieve or have implemented plans for sustainable production and consumption and have kept the impacts of use of natural resources well within safe ecological limits.

Strategic Goal B: Reduce the direct pressures on biodiversity and promote sustainable use

Target 5

By 2020, the rate of loss of all natural habitats, including forests, is at least halved and where feasible brought close to zero, and degradation and fragmentation is significantly reduced.

Target 6

By 2020 all fish and invertebrate stocks and aquatic plants are managed and harvested sustainably, legally and applying ecosystem based approaches, so that overfishing is avoided, recovery plans and measures are in place for all depleted species, fisheries have no significant adverse impacts on threatened species and vulnerable ecosystems and the impacts of fisheries on stocks, species and ecosystems are within safe ecological limits.

Target 7

By 2020 areas under agriculture, aquaculture and forestry are managed sustainably, ensuring conservation of biodiversity.

Target 8

By 2020, pollution, including from excess nutrients, has been brought to levels that are not detrimental to ecosystem function and biodiversity.

Target 9

By 2020, invasive alien species and pathways are identified and prioritized, priority species are controlled or eradicated, and measures are in place to manage pathways to prevent their introduction and establishment.

Target 10

By 2015, the multiple anthropogenic pressures on coral reefs, and other vulnerable ecosystems impacted by climate change or ocean acidification are minimized, so as to maintain their integrity and functioning.

Strategic Goal C: To improve the status of biodiversity by safeguarding ecosystems, species and genetic diversity

Target 11

By 2020, at least 17 per cent of terrestrial and inland water, and 10 per cent of coastal and marine areas, especially areas of particular importance for biodiversity and ecosystem services, are conserved through effectively and equitably managed, ecologically representative and well connected systems of protected areas and other effective area-based conservation measures, and integrated into the wider landscapes and seascapes.

Target 12

By 2020 the extinction of known threatened species has been prevented and their conservation status, particularly of those most in decline, has been improved and sustained.

Target 13

By 2020, the genetic diversity of cultivated plants and farmed and domesticated animals and of wild relatives, including other socio-economically as well as culturally valuable species, is maintained, and strategies have been developed and implemented for minimizing genetic erosion and safeguarding their genetic diversity.

Strategic Goal D: Enhance the benefits to all from biodiversity and ecosystem services

Target 14

By 2020, ecosystems that provide essential services, including services related to water, and contribute to health, livelihoods and well-being, are restored and safeguarded, taking into account the needs of women, indigenous and local communities, and the poor and vulnerable.

Target 15

By 2020, ecosystem resilience and the contribution of biodiversity to carbon stocks has been enhanced, through conservation and restoration, including restoration of at least 15 per cent of degraded ecosystems, thereby contributing to climate change mitigation and adaptation and to combating desertification.

Target 16

By 2015, the Nagoya Protocol on Access to Genetic Resources and the Fair and Equitable Sharing of Benefits Arising from their Utilization is in force and operational, consistent with national legislation.

Strategic Goal E: Enhance implementation through participatory planning, knowledge management and capacity building

Target 17

By 2015 each Party has developed, adopted as a policy instrument, and has commenced implementing an effective, participatory and updated national biodiversity strategy and action plan.

Target 18

By 2020, the traditional knowledge, innovations and practices of indigenous and local communities relevant for the conservation and sustainable use of biodiversity, and their customary use of biological resources, are respected, subject to national legislation and relevant international obligations, and fully integrated and reflected in the implementation of the Convention with the full and effective participation of indigenous and local communities, at all relevant levels.

Target 19

By 2020, knowledge, the science base and technologies relating to biodiversity, its values, functioning, status and trends, and the consequences of its loss, are improved, widely shared and transferred, and applied.

Target 20

By 2020, at the latest, the mobilization of financial resources for effectively implementing the Strategic Plan for Biodiversity 2011–2020 from all sources, and in accordance with the consolidated and agreed process in the Strategy for Resource

Mobilization, should increase substantially from the current levels. This target will be subject to changes contingent to resource needs assessments to be developed and reported by Parties.

V. The Future of Biodiversity

The future of biodiversity likely lies in our development of a more holistic mind-set, a trend that is already thankfully underway. The future of biodiversity requires greater attention to ecosystems rather than individual species. It is also extremely important to find a balance between ecosystem integrity and human uses of resources, as the latter is unavoidable. These considerations played important roles in the development of the 2005 Millennium Ecosystem Assessment Synthesis Report (MEA), a five-year UN project involving numerous scientists and policy experts from around the world. The MEA reached the following four principal findings in relation to ecosystems and human well-being:

1. Over the past 50 years, humans have changed ecosystems more rapidly and extensively than in any comparable period in human history, largely to meet rapidly growing demands for food, fresh water, timber, fiber and fuel. This has resulted in a substantial and largely irreversible loss in the diversity of life on Earth.

2. The changes that have been made to ecosystems have contributed to substantial net gains in human well-being and economic development, but these gains have been achieved at growing costs in the form of the degradation of many ecosystem services, increased risks of nonlinear changes, and the exacerbation of poverty for some groups of people. These problems, unless addressed, will substantially diminish the benefits that future generations obtain from ecosystems.

3. The degradation of ecosystem services could grow significantly worse during the first half of this century and is a barrier to achieving the Millennium Development Goals.

4. The challenge of reversing the degradation of ecosystems while meeting increasing demands for their services can be partially met under some scenarios that the MEA has considered but these involve significant changes in policies, institutions and practices, that are not currently under way. Many options exist to conserve or enhance specific ecosystem services in ways that reduce negative tradeoffs or that provide positive synergies with other ecosystem services.

MILLENNIUM ECOSYSTEM ASSESSMENT, ECOSYSTEMS AND HUMAN WELL-BEING: SYNTHESIS 1 (2005).

Because of the increasing importance of focusing policy efforts on ecosystems, we may well see a good deal of new law, both domestic legislation and international agreement, relating to how we manage ecosystems. Ecosystem concerns are already a part of many species-focused laws, including the ESA, which states its purpose as being "to provide a means whereby the ecosystems upon which endangered species and threatened species depend may be conserved." To date, though, the United States has little in the way of major comprehensive laws for ecosystem management. This is due, in part, to the fact that this is still a relatively new concept, and in part to the fact that ecosystem management takes place at the local level and thus varies from place to place. Nonetheless, scholars have argued for some time for comprehensive laws leading to more ecosystem management projects and providing substantive guidance for them, even if the details may vary from place to place. The following is the seminal paper defining the nascent field of ecosystem management. More than two decades following its publication, consider whether it is time for additional policy work in this field.

R. Edward Grumbine, *What Is Ecosystem Management?*
8 Conservation Biology 27 (1994)

Introduction

Deep in a mixed conifer forest on the east side of the Washington Cascades, a U.S. Forest Service silviculturalist, responding to a college student's query, suggests that ecosystem management means snag retention and management of coarse woody debris on clear cut units.

In northern Florida on a US. Department of Defense reservation, a team of biologists and managers struggles with the design of a fire management plan in longleaf pine (Pinus palustris) forests that mimics natural disturbance regimes while minimizing the risk of burning adjacent private lands.

To avert what he calls "national train wrecks," Interior Secretary Bruce Babbitt announces that the Clinton Administration plans to shift federal policy away from a single species approach to one that looks "at entire ecosystems."

Commenting on a draft federal framework for the Greater Yellowstone Ecosystem that proposes increased interagency cooperation, a lawyer claims that "Congress does not intend that national forests should be managed like national parks" and that there exists no need to create ecosystem management.

Other observers in the Greater Yellowstone region contend that an ecosystem approach could provide just the holistic management necessary for sustaining resources in a complex ecological/political landscape.

What is ecosystem management?

The above vignettes portray but a few of the various interpretations of ecosystem management that can be found in the conservation biology, resource management, and popular literature. Since the ecosystem approach is relatively new, and still unformed, this is not surprising. As any concept evolves, debates over definition, fundamental principles, and policy implications proceed apace. Yet the discussion surrounding ecosystem management is not merely academic. Nor is it limited to those scientists, resources professionals, and policymakers who work directly with federal management issues. The debate is raising profound questions for most people who are concerned with the continuing loss of biodiversity at all scales and across many administrative boundaries and ownerships. Along with defining the ecosystem management approach as a new policy framework there appears to be a parallel process of redefining the fundamental role of humans in nature.

Dominant Themes of Ecosystem Management

Ecosystem management has not been uniformly defined or consistently applied by federal or state management agencies. Yet consensus is developing, at least within the academic literature. Using standard keyword search techniques focused on "ecosystem management," "ecosystem health," "biodiversity" "management," "adaptive management," etc., I surveyed papers published on ecosystem management in peer reviewed journals (Conservation Biology, Environmental Management, Ecological Applications, Society and Natural Resources etc.) up through June 1993 to determine where agreement exists on the subject. Articles came from a broad spectrum of disciplines including conservation biology, resource management, and public policy. I also reviewed books with substantive accounts of ecosystem management, lay environmental publications, and several federal and state-level documents that discuss ecosystem level policymaking.

Ten dominant themes of ecosystem management emerged from my review. Dominant themes were those attributes that authors identified explicitly as critical to the definition, implementation, or overall comprehension of ecosystem management. The ten dominant themes emerged repeatedly throughout the literature. I believe the following themes faithfully represent areas of agreement.

1. **Hierarchical Context.** A focus on any one level of the biodiversity hierarchy (genes, species, populations, ecosystems, landscapes) is not sufficient. When working on a problem at any one level or scale, managers must seek the connections between all levels. This is often described as a "systems" perspective.

2. **Ecological Boundaries.** Management requires working across administrative/political boundaries (i.e., national forests, national parks) and defining ecological boundaries at appropriate scales.

3. **Ecological Integrity**. Norton defines managing for ecological integrity as protecting total native diversity (species, populations, ecosystems) and the ecological patterns and processes that maintain that diversity. Most authors discuss this as conservation of viable populations of native species, maintaining natural disturbance regimes, reintroduction of native, extirpated species, representation of ecosystems across natural ranges of variation, etc.

4. **Data Collection.** Ecosystem management requires more research and data collection (i.e., habitat inventory/classification, disturbance regime dynamics, baseline species and population assessment) as well as better management and use of existing data.

5. **Monitoring.** Managers must track the results of their actions so that success or failure may be evaluated quantitatively. Monitoring creates an ongoing feedback loop of useful information.

6. **Adaptive Management.** Adaptive management assumes that scientific knowledge is provisional and focuses on management as a learning process or continuous

experiment where incorporating the results of previous actions allows managers to remain flexible and adapt to uncertainty.

7. **Interagency Cooperation.** Using ecological boundaries requires cooperation between federal, state, and local management agencies as well as private parties. Managers must team to work together and integrate conflicting legal mandates and management goals.

8. **Organizational Change.** Implementing ecosystem management requires changes in the structure of land management agencies and the way they operate. These may range from the simple (forming an interagency committee) to the complex (changing professional norms, altering power relationships).

9. **Humans Embedded In Nature.** People cannot be separated from nature. Humans are fundamental influences on ecological patterns and processes and are in turn affected by them.

10. **Values.** Regardless of the role of scientific knowledge, human values play a dominant role in ecosystem management goals.

These ten dominant themes form the basis of a working definition: *Ecosystem management integrates scientific knowledge of ecological relationships within a complex sociopolitical and values framework toward the general goal of protecting native ecosystem integrity over the long term.*

Ecosystem Management Goals

Most of the authors cited in this review agree that setting clear goals is crucial to the success of ecosystem management. Within the overall goal of sustaining ecological integrity, five specific goals were frequently endorsed:

1. Maintain viable populations of all native species in situ.

2. Represent, within protected areas, all native ecosystem types across their natural range of variation.

3. Maintain evolutionary and ecological processes (i.e., disturbance regimes, hydrological processes, nutrient cycles, etc.)..

4. Manage over periods of time long enough to maintain the evolutionary potential of species and ecosystems.

5. Accommodate human use and occupancy within these constraints.

The first four of these goals are value statements derived from current scientific knowledge that aim to reduce (and eventually eliminate) the biodiversity crisis. The fifth goal acknowledges the vital (if problematic) role that people have to play in all aspects of the ecosystem management debate.

These fundamental goals provide a striking contrast to the goals of traditional resource management. Though different agencies operate under a variety of federal and state mandates, current resource management in the U.S. is based on maximizing production of goods and services, whether these involve number of board feet (commodities) or wilderness recreational visitor days (amenities). Managers and lawmakers have always been careful to speak of "balance" and "sustained yield" but this language is obfuscatory—balance has never been defined in any U.S. environmental law and sustained yield has often been confused with sustainability.

If ecosystem management is to take hold and flourish, the relationship between the new goal of protecting ecological integrity and the old standard of providing goods and services for humans must be reconciled. Much of the oft-complained "fuzziness" or lack of precision surrounding ecosystem management derives from alternative views on this point. Kessler et al., for example, suggest that ecosystem management represents a further evolution of multiple use, sustained yield policy where managers "must not diminish the importance of products and services, but instead treat them within a broader ecological and social context." These authors envision ecosystem-level management as an expansion of focus from particular resource outputs to the ecosystem as "life support system [for humans]." Kessler et al. fail to see that expanding the scale of concern by itself does not address the fact that there are certain ecological limits in any system which constrain human use. Ecological integrity as expressed by the five specific goals explicitly considers all resource use as a managerial artifact that may flow sustainably from natural systems only if basic ecosystem patterns and processes are maintained.

Echoing Kessler et al., the most detailed Forest Service working definition of ecosystem management exemplifies lack of clarity over the key policy problem of defining ecosystem management goals. The report defines the philosophy of ecosystem management as sustaining "the patterns and processes of ecosystems for the benefit of future generations, while providing goods and services for each generation." The study characterizes the main limiting factors to ecosystem management as defining societal expectations, integrating these expectations with the sustainable capabilities of ecosystems, and filling information gaps in baseline data describing historical ecosystem variability and disturbance regimes. The Forest Service prescribes adaptive management as a process to blend ecosystem sustainability and human concerns. Specific solutions offered, however, are problematic. If societal goals conflict with ecosystem sustainability, cost/benefit analyses are offered as the standard for solutions. Adaptive management is described as an ongoing experiment yet "landscapes can be restored," managers are said to already be capable of mimicking natural disturbance regimes successfully, and there is speculation that future experiments may reveal new sustainable ecosystem states that may differ from evolutionary and historical states. In short, the Forest Service defines the goals of ecosystem management narrowly within the old resource management paradigm ("for the benefit of future generations") and seeks to operationalize this goal within a positivistic scientific framework. These characterizations of ecosystem management are also found in the other government policy documents in this review.

As several analysts point out, however, it takes more than scientific knowledge to reframe successfully complex policy problems. Knowledge of organizational structure and behavior as well as the policy process itself are equally important. Yet none of the five government treatments of the ecosystem management concept reviewed here mention substantive organizational change, nor do they discuss the policy process as it is defined by policy scientists. This emphasis on science is an artifact of the training and professional norms of the major group writing about ecosystem management—scientists. But defining ecosystem management goals is also a political process; those authors advocating a new vision of ecological integrity are more often employed independently or in academia. Authors affiliated with government agencies tend to support the Forest Service version of ecosystem management. As policy analyst Tim Clark (personal communication) has pointed out, "'the ecosystem management debate' is really a complex, competitive, conflictual social process about whose values will dominate, it is not about science."

Management goals are statements of values—certain outcomes are selected over others. Choosing the management goal of maintaining ecological integrity along with the five specific goals may be debated, but in the academic and popular literature there is general agreement that maintaining ecosystem integrity should take precedence over any other management goal. This may be due partially to the fact that, given the rate and scale of environmental deterioration along with our profound scientific ignorance of ecological patterns and processes, we are in no position to make judgments about what ecosystem elements to favor in our management efforts. An increasing number of people also believe that humans do not have any privileged ethical standing from which to arbitrate these types of questions.

Conclusion

History tells us that change does not always come easily, peacefully, or in a planned manner. Implementing the short-term scientific aspects of ecosystem management is daunting enough. For the moment, however, ecosystem management provides our best opportunity to describe, understand, and fit in with nature. We know that the risk of extinction increases under certain conditions, that wildfires cannot long be suppressed without significant successional consequences, that political power must somehow become less centralized, that whales and spiders must also be allowed to vote. We are also coming to realize that resourcism has for so long prevented us from putting our ecological knowledge to work that we are facing the limits of life on Earth for many species. Where once we thought endangered species were the problem, we now face the loss of entire ecosystems.

Ecosystem management, at root, is an invitation, a call to restorative action that promises a healthy future for the entire biotic enterprise. The choice is ours—a world where the gap between people and nature grows to an incomprehensible chasm, or a world of damaged but recoverable ecological integrity where the operative word is hope.

Notes and Questions

1. Recall the various authors of the excerpts included in Chapter 1: Rachel Carson, Aldo Leopold, Mark Sagoff, Garrett Hardin, Dan Tarlock, Terry Anderson and Donald Leal, Frank Ackerman and Lisa Heinzerling, and casebook authors Mintz and Dernbach. How do you imagine each would respond to Grumbine's ideas?

2. We stand the best chance of developing greater ecosystem management law and policy if more people understand their own reliance on ecosystems better. One avenue to getting this message across is by economically valuing the ecosystem services upon which we depend. But is doing so realistically possible?

James Salzman, *Valuing Ecosystem Services*

24 Ecology L.Q. 887 (1997)

(Book review of Gretchen Daily, Nature's Services: Societal Dependence on Natural Ecosystems, Island Press 1997)

INTRODUCTION

Beneath the Arizona desert sun on September 26, 1991, amid reporters and flashing cameras, eight men and women entered a huge glass-enclosed structure and sealed shut the outer door. Their 3.15 acre miniature world, called Biosphere II, was designed to re-create the conditions of the earth (modestly named Biosphere I). Built at a cost of over $200 million, Biosphere II boasted a self-sustaining environment complete with rain forest, ocean, marsh, savanna, and desert habitats. The eight "Bionauts" intended to remain inside for two years. Within sixteen months, however, oxygen levels had plummeted thirty-three percent, nitrous oxide levels had increased 160-fold, ants and vines had overrun the vegetation, and nineteen of the twenty-five vertebrate species and all the pollinators had gone extinct. Eden did not last long.

What went wrong? With a multimillion dollar budget, the designers of Biosphere II had sought to recreate the level of basic services that support life itself—services such as purification of air and water, pest control, renewal of soil fertility, climate regulation, pollination of crops and vegetation, and waste detoxification and decomposition. Together, these are known as "ecosystem services," taken for granted yet absolutely essential to our existence, as the inhabitants of Biosphere II ruefully learned. Created by the interactions of living organisms with their environment, ecosystem services provide both the conditions and processes that sustain human life. Despite their obvious importance to our wellbeing, recognition of ecosystem services and the roles they play rarely enters policy debates or public discussion.

The general ignorance of ecosystem services is partly the result of modern society's dissociation between computers, cars and clothing on the one hand and biodiversity, nutrient cycling, and pollination on the other. It is perhaps not surprising that many children, when asked where milk comes from will reply without hesitation, "from the grocery store." The primary reason that ecosystem services are taken for granted, however, is that they are free. We explicitly value and place dollar figures on "ecosystem goods" such as timber and fish. Yet the services underpinning these goods generally have no market value—not because they are worthless, but rather because there is no market to capture and express their value directly.

Perhaps the most fundamental policy challenge facing ecosystem protection is that of valuation—how to translate an ecosystem's value into common units for assessment of development alternatives. The tough decisions revolve not around whether protecting ecosystems is a good thing but, rather, how much we should protect and at what cost. For example, how would the flood control and water purification services of a particular forest be diminished by the clearcutting or selective logging of 10%, 20% or 30% of its area? At what point does the ecosystem's net value to humans diminish, and by how much? Can the degradation of these services (in addition to ecosystem goods) be accurately measured? And, if so, how can partial loss of these services be balanced against benefits provided by development or pollution?

One might argue that ecosystem services cannot be evaluated, but this is clearly incorrect. We implicitly assess the value of these services every time we choose to protect or degrade the environment. The fundamental question is whether our implicit valuation of ecosystem services is accurate, and if not, what should be done about it. Indeed, studies such as Nature's Services indicate that our valuations are grossly and systematically understated. This essay explores the importance—and the challenges— of integrating ecosystem services research with the law. The potential is exciting, for a focus on ecosystem services would significantly change the way we understand and apply environmental law.

I. ECOSYSTEM SERVICES

Nature's Services addresses two basic questions: what services do natural ecosystems provide society, and what is a first approximation of their monetary value? Separate chapters describe the range of services and physical benefits provided by climate, biodiversity, soil, pollinators, pest control, the major biomes (oceans, freshwater, forests, and grasslands), and offer case studies of ecosystem services whose values are particularly well-known. The authors do not attempt to measure non-use values such as aesthetic or existence values, arguing that such work has already been done elsewhere. Instead, the authors determine lower-bound estimates of monetary value, using replacement costs where possible. Such information, it is hoped, will provide a basis for better incorporation of ecosystem services in decisionmaking.

The chapter on soil provides a useful example of the book's specific findings. More than a clump of dirt, soil is a complex matrix of organic and inorganic constituents transformed by numerous tiny organisms. The level of biological activity within soil is staggering. Under a square meter of pasture soil in Denmark, scientists identified over 50,000 worms, 48,000 small insects, and ten million nematodes. This living soil provides six ecosystem services: buffering and moderation of the hydrological cycle (so precipitation may be soaked up and metered out rather than rushing off the land in flash floods); physical support for plants; retention and delivery of nutrients to plants; disposal of wastes and dead organic matter; renewal of soil fertility; and regulation of the major element cycles. What are these services worth in the aggregate?

Take, for example, soil's service of providing nitrogen to plants. Nitrogen is supplied to plants through both nitrogen-fixing organisms and recycling of nutrients in the soil. As mentioned above, the authors rely primarily on replacement costs to estimate the value of ecosystem services. If nitrogen were provided by commercial fertilizer rather than natural processes, the lowest-cost estimate for its use on crops in the U.S. would be $45 billion, the figure for all land plants $320 billion. Most of the services identified in the book, however, such as breaking down dead organic material, are not valued in dollars because no technical substitutes are available.

Overall, Nature's Services reaches four conclusions. First, the services that ecosystems provide are both wide-ranging and critical. The question, "where would we be without ecosystem services?" is nonsensical, for we simply would not exist without them. Second, as Biosphere II's failure showed, the substitute technologies for most ecosystem services are either prohibitively expensive or nonexistent. Massive hydroponic gardening in the absence of soil is at least conceivable, if unfeasible. Substitutes for climate regulation are neither conceivable nor feasible. Third, our overall understanding of ecosystem services—the contributions of individual species, threshold effects, synergies, etc.—is poor. Finally, even taking into account the inevitable imprecision of such valuation exercises, ecosystem services have extraordinarily high values. A recent study in the journal Nature estimated their aggregate value at between $16–54 trillion per year. The global GNP is $18 trillion.

Whether such a total estimate is precisely accurate is beside the point. The sheer magnitude of their dollar figures dictates that ecosystem services cannot be treated as merely add-on considerations. Nor can they be shunted aside as soft numbers (as often occurs with scenic beauty or existence value) when assessing the impacts of development or pollution. Tastes may differ over beauty, but they are in universal accord over fertile soil. If the goal of ecologists is to wake people up with big numbers, Nature's Services delivers. But are these numbers a convertible currency?

The greatest shortcoming of Nature's Services, one openly admitted by its authors, is the macro-scale of the analysis. The fact that pollinators annually provide Americans up to $1.6 billion of service or that soil fertility is worth $45 billion is important to know for general policy direction, but that fact does not help to inform specific land-use or pollution permitting decisions. One cannot divide the $45 billion value of soil fertility by the nation's total agricultural acreage to determine the value of the services of five acres of land threatened by development. Thus, the greatest need for ecosystem service valuation is at the margins. Few policy decisions, thankfully, will involve obliterating an ecosystem service. Rather, policy decisions tend to be incremental. What is the extent of degradation to these services at various points along a continuum of impacts? Given the complexity of ecosystem services, the responses are almost certainly nonlinear.

This problem, the assessment and valuation of services at the margin, is at once the most useful and most difficult challenge for economists and ecologists. Nature's Services establishes the range of ecosystem services and their great significance. The next step is to pick up where the book leaves off and identify how ecosystem services should be explicitly considered in real-life decisions, for ecosystem services are rarely, if ever, considered in current agency cost-benefit analyses.

. . .

Chapter 5

Protecting the Air We Breathe:
The Clean Air Act

I. Introduction

Air pollution adversely affects human health and our natural environment in many ways. These impacts increased dramatically over the course of the twentieth century, until public concern regarding air pollution reached the point in the latter half of the 20th century that it was adequate to support congressional action on the issue. Common air pollutants have been linked to chronic respiratory ailments, such as asthma, bronchitis, and emphysema, as well as cancer and heart disease. Acute episodes of pollution in urban areas have been marked by large increases in death and illness rates, especially among the elderly, infants, and people with preexisting cardiac or respiratory conditions. Air pollution also inflicts costly, extensive damage on buildings and materials, dims visibility (both in cities and in rural areas) and harms plant life, including food crops. Moreover, as we will explore further in Chapter 6, the emission of carbon dioxide, methane, and other gases is now known to contribute to an exacerbated greenhouse effect that is causing a profound disruption of the Earth's climate.

This chapter considers the American legal response to the risks and challenges posed by air pollution, with particular attention to the Clean Air Act. This major, comprehensive piece of federal legislation was crafted in its modern formulation in 1970 and subsequently amended by Congress in 1977 and 1990. After a brief examination of private common law rights to a healthful atmosphere — which form the legal backdrop for the now prevailing law — we will examine key components of the Clean Air Act's approach to preventing and reducing any pollution. These will include the Act's scheme for regulating the most common, harmful air pollutants — so-called "criteria pollutants" — through the establishment of National Ambient Air Quality Standards ("NAAQS"), which will protect public health and welfare, the identification of areas that do and do not attain the levels of air purity reflected in the NAAQS, and the adoption of State Implementation Plans (SIPs) that contain enforceable emissions limitations to assure the implementation and maintenance of NAAQS. We will also consider other important Clean Air Act provisions, including the Act's requirements regarding the Prevention of Significant Deterioration in clean air "attainment areas," the control of toxic air pollutants, and the limitations placed on newly constructed sources of air pollution. Finally, we'll examine—somewhat more briefly—the regulation of air pollution from motor vehicles.

II. Common Law Approaches to Air Pollution Control

Although much of the law of air pollution control today is public law, the common-law doctrines of nuisance and trespass, along with local smoke abatement ordinances, form the legal foundations on which the modern public law stands. These doctrines and enactments, which provided the earliest relief from air pollution, have ancient roots. Private common law actions date back to early English common law, and the earliest abatement ordinance was passed in London in the thirteenth century.

The case that follows illustrates the potential for continued utilization of nuisance actions as a means of resolving air pollution problems, as well as the inherent limitations that exist on controlling air pollution problems through common-law suits.

Boomer v. Atlantic Cement Co.
257 N.E.2d 870 (2 N.Y. 2d 219 (1970))

Judge BERGAN:

Defendant operates a large cement plant near Albany. These are actions for injunction and damages by neighboring land owners alleging injury to property from dirt, smoke and vibration emanating from the plant. . . .

The public concern with air pollution arising from many sources in industry and in transportation is currently accorded ever wider recognition accompanied by a growing sense of responsibility in State and Federal Governments to control it. Cement plants are obvious sources of air pollution in the neighborhoods where they operate.

But there is now before the court private litigation in which individual property owners have sought specific relief from a single plant operation. The threshold question raised by the division of view on this appeal is whether the court should resolve the litigation between the parties now before it as equitably as seems possible, or whether, seeking promotion of the general public welfare, it should channel private litigation into broad public objectives.

A court performs its essential function when it decides the rights of parties before it. Its decision of private controversies may sometimes greatly affect public issues. Large questions of law are often resolved by the manner in which private litigation is decided. But this is normally an incident to the court's main function to settle controversy. It is a rare exercise of judicial power to use a decision in private litigation as a purposeful mechanism to achieve direct public objectives greatly beyond the rights and interests before this court.

Effective control of air pollution is a problem presently far from solution even with the full public and financial powers of government. In large measure adequate technical procedures are yet to be developed and some that appear possible may be economically impracticable.

It seems apparent that the amelioration of air pollution will depend on technical research in great depth; on a carefully balanced consideration of the economic impact of close regulation, and of the actual effect on public health. It is likely to require massive public expenditure and to demand more than any local community can accomplish and to depend on regional and interstate controls.

A court should not try to do this on its own as a by-product of private litigation, and it seems manifest that the judicial establishment is neither equipped in the limited nature of any judgment it can pronounce nor prepared to lay down and implement an effective policy for the elimination of air pollution. This is an area beyond the circumference of one private lawsuit. It is a direct responsibility for government and should not thus be undertaken as an incident to solving a dispute between property owners and a single cement plant — one of many — in the Hudson River valley.

The cement making operations of defendant have been found by the court at Special Term to have damaged the nearby properties of plaintiffs in these two actions. That court, as it has been noted, accordingly found defendant maintained a nuisance, and this has been affirmed at the Appellate Division. The total damage to plaintiffs' properties is, however, relatively small in comparison with the value of defendant's operation and with the consequences of the injunction which plaintiffs seek.

The ground for the denial of injunction, notwithstanding the finding both that there is a nuisance and that plaintiffs have been damaged substantially, is the large disparity in economic consequences of the nuisance and of the injunction. This theory cannot, however, be sustained without overruling a doctrine which has been consistently reaffirmed in several leading cases in this court and which has never been disavowed here, namely that where a nuisance has been found and where there has been any substantial damage shown by the party complaining an injunction will be granted.

[handwritten: reference to common law]

The rule in New York has been that such a nuisance will be enjoined although marked disparity be shown in economic consequence between the effect of the injunction and the effect of the nuisance. . . .

Although the court at Special Term and the Appellate Division held that injunction should be denied, it was found that plaintiffs had been damaged in various specific amounts up to the time of the trial and damages to the respective plaintiffs was awarded for those amounts. The effect of this was, injunction having been denied, plaintiffs could maintain successive actions at law for damages thereafter as further damage was incurred.

The court at Special Term also found the amount of permanent damage attributable to each plaintiff, for the guidance of the parties in the event both sides stipulated to the payment and acceptance of such permanent damage as a settlement of all the controversies among the parties. The total of permanent damages to all plaintiffs thus found was $185,000. This basis of adjustment has not resulted in any stipulation by the parties.

This result at Special Term and at the Appellate Division is a departure from a rule that has become settled; but to follow the rule literally in these cases would be to close down the plant at once. This court is fully agreed to avoid that immediately drastic remedy; the difference in view is how best to avoid it.

decision

One alternative is to grant the injunction but postpone its effect to a specified future date to give opportunity for technical advances to permit defendant to eliminate the nuisance; another is to grant the injunction conditioned on the payment of permanent damages to plaintiffs which would compensate them for the total economic loss to their property present and future caused by defendant's operations. For reasons which will be developed the court chooses the latter alternative.

If the injunction were to be granted unless within a short period, *e.g.* 18 months, the nuisance [would be] be abated by improved methods, there would be no assurance that any significant technical improvement would occur. *no incentive to defendant*

The parties could settle this private litigation at any time if defendant paid enough money and the imminent threat of closing the plant would build up the pressure on defendant. If there were no improved techniques found, there would inevitably be applications to the court at Special Term for extensions of time to perform on showing of good faith efforts to find such techniques.

Moreover, techniques to eliminate dust and other annoying by-products of cement making are unlikely to be developed by any research the defendant can undertake within any short period, but will depend on the total resources of the cement industry nation-wide and throughout the world. The problem is universal wherever cement is made.

For obvious reasons the rate of the research is beyond control of defendant. If at the end of eighteen months the whole industry has not found a technical solution a court would be hard put to close down this one cement plant if due regard be given to equitable principles.

On the other hand, to grant the injunction unless defendant pays plaintiff such permanent damages as may be fixed by the court seems to do justice between the contending parties. All of the attributions of economic loss to the properties on which plaintiffs' complaints are based will have been redressed.

The nuisance complained of by these plaintiffs may have other public or private consequences, but these particular parties are the only ones who have sought remedies and the judgment proposed will fully redress them. The limitation of relief granted is a limitation only within the four corners of these actions and does not foreclose public health or other public agencies from seeking proper relief in a proper court.

It seems reasonable to think that the risk of being required to pay permanent damages to injured property owners by cement plant owners would itself be a reasonably effective spur to research for improved techniques to minimize nuisance.

The power of the court to condition on equitable grounds the continuance of an injunction on the payment of permanent damages seems undoubted . . . .

Thus it seems fair to both sides to grant permanent damages to plaintiffs which will terminate this private litigation. The theory of damage is the "servitude on land" of plaintiffs imposed by defendant's nuisance. . . .

The judgment, by allowance of permanent damages imposing a servitude on land, which is the basis of the actions, would preclude future recovery by plaintiffs or their grantees.

This should be placed beyond debate by a provision of the judgment that the payment by defendant and the acceptance by plaintiffs of permanent damages found by the court shall be in compensation for a servitude on the land. . . .

The orders should be reversed, without costs, and the cases remitted to Special Term to grant an injunction which shall be vacated upon payment by defendant of such amounts of permanent damage to the respective plaintiffs as shall for this purpose be determined by the court.

dissent

Judge JASEN (dissenting): I agree with the majority that a reversal is required here, but I do not subscribe to the newly enunciated doctrine of assessment of permanent damages, in lieu of an injunction, where substantial property rights have been impaired by the creation of a nuisance.

common law

It has long been the rule in this state, as the majority acknowledges, that a nuisance which results in substantial continuing damage to neighbors must be enjoined. To now change the rule to permit the cement company to continue polluting the air indefinitely upon the payment of permanent damages is, in my opinion, compounding the magnitude of a very serious problem in our state and nation today. . . .

The harmful nature and widespread occurrence of air pollution have been extensively documented. Congressional hearings have revealed that air pollution causes substantial property damage, as well as being a contributing factor to a rising incidence of lung cancer, emphysema, bronchitis and asthma.

The specific problem faced here is known as particulate contamination because of the fine dust particles emanating from defendant's cement plant. The particular type of nuisance is not new, having appeared in many cases for at least the past sixty years. It is interesting to note that cement production has recently been identified as a significant source of particulate contamination in the Hudson Valley. This type of pollution, wherein very small particles escape and stay in the atmosphere, has been denominated as the type of air pollution which produces the greatest hazard to human health. We have thus a nuisance which not only is damaging to the plaintiffs, but also is decidedly harmful to the general public.

I see grave dangers in overruling our long-established rule of granting an injunction where a nuisance results in substantial continuing damage. In permitting the injunction to become inoperative upon the payment of permanent damages, the majority is, in effect, licensing a continuing wrong. It is the same as saying to the cement company, you may continue to do harm to your neighbors so long as you pay a fee for it. Furthermore, once such permanent damages are assessed and paid, the incentive to alleviate the wrong would be eliminated, thereby continuing air pollution of an area without abatement. . . .

This kind of inverse condemnation may not be invoked by a private person or corporation for private gain or advantage. Inverse condemnation should only be permitted when the public is primarily served in the taking or impairment of property. The promotion of the interests of the polluting cement company has, in my opinion, no public use or benefit.

I would enjoin the defendant cement company from continuing the discharge of dust particles upon its neighbors' properties unless, within 18 months, the cement company abated this nuisance . . . .

Notes and Questions

1. There was more to the concern for the cement company's hardship than meets the eye based on the appellate opinion. A significant concern at the trial stage was the importance of the plant to the local economy. Closing the plant would have destroyed the town at every level—schools, property values, etc. The trial court chose not to risk granting a permanent injunction without certainty that it could be settled for damages between the parties. It calculated decline in value and added a $35,000 penalty to that. Why did the court impose a penalty when calculating the total damage award? Was the court imposing punitive damages?

2. What would have happened if the court had granted a permanent injunction? Would the plant have shut down? Consider the possible alternative outcomes, and how they might be achieved. Suppose, for example, that the parties were to settle for a mutually agreed-upon damage amount—would such a process reach a more economically appropriate figure than the court could come up with on its own, or less so? If such an approach were taken, what might be some impediments to its successful resolution?

3. A legal dispute similar to the one that led to the *Boomer* decision arose in the late nineteenth century. The case, which involved pollution of some nearby farms by air pollutants from a copper smelter, gave rise to both private and public nuisance suits. In the private nuisance action, the Tennessee Supreme Court balanced the economic importance of the smelter against the damage done to the dirt farmers and refused to grant an injunction, instead leaving the remedy to damages. *See Madison v. Ducktown Sulphur, Copper and Iron Co.*, 83 S.W. 658 (1904). In the public nuisance action, however, the U.S. Supreme Court took a remedial approach somewhat more aggressive than the one implemented by the New York Court of Appeals in *Boomer*. The Court granted the plaintiffs an injunction, but gave the defendant smelting company time to abate its emissions. Eventually a technological solution to the smelter emissions problem was found. However, the research that led to that solution was slow and frustrating. In the meanwhile, rather than close the plant, the Court established a claims process, and most of the injured farmers settled for relatively small amounts of damages. *See Georgia v. Tennessee Copper Co.*, 237 U.S. 474 (1915).

4. This case was brought as a private nuisance case, but in some cases it can be advantageous to sue for public nuisance. This is especially true where members of the affected community arrived after the nuisance was already in place, as most states do not permit damage recovery under private nuisance where a plaintiff has "come to the nuisance." This issue came up, but with an interesting twist, in *Spur Industries, Inc. v. Del E. Webb Development Co.*, 494 P.2d 700 (Ariz. 1972), when a large retirement community in Arizona was suffering from the stench of a nearby cattle feedlot. The feedlot, however, had been there before the community. Had the community grown up around the feedlot, one residence on a small lot at a time, this would have been a pure public nuisance case, and Spur (the feedlot) might well have been out of luck and out of business. Had one individual plunked down next to Spur and brought a private nuisance claim, it would have failed as a result of coming to the nuisance. In this case, Del Webb, a private developer in the business of designing retirement communities and selling them from a distance, had built the community here and sold off the units to unsuspecting seniors, resulting in somewhat of a hybrid situation. Following public nuisance policy (with such a large affected community), it was necessary to move or close Spur, but following private nuisance principles as well (because Spur was way out in agricultural land without residential development before Del Webb came along), the court had Del Webb reimburse Spur for the expense of moving or closing.

5. Given the availability of nuisance actions for air pollution problems, why do we need the Clean Air Act? Before getting into the details of the statute, what do you find lacking in the common law option? Does the retroactivity of such actions concern you? What gaps might you want to fill if you were involved in the transition from common law cases to legislative control over air pollution?

6. While state common law claims remain available for air pollution, federal common law claims have been displaced by the Clean Air Act. This is true regardless of whether the plaintiffs are interested in damages, *Native Village of Kivalina v. Exxon-Mobil Corp.*, 696 F.3d 849 (9th Cir. 2012), or injunctive relief, *American Elec. Power Co., Inc. v. Connecticut*, 564 U.S. 410, 131 S. Ct. 2527 (2011). Incidentally, these two cases involved lawsuits over greenhouse gas emissions contributing to climate disruption, a topic covered in greater detail in Chapter 6.

III. National Ambient Air Quality Standards and State Implementation Plans

The Clean Air Act provides for the establishment of several distinct yet complimentary sets of requirements for the control of air pollution emissions from stationary and mobile sources. While many of these requirements are meant to be created directly by the U.S. Environmental Protection Agency (EPA), the statute also affords a significant regulatory role to the states.

A critical aspect of the Act is its scheme for the regulation of so-called "criteria pollutants," air pollutants from numerous or diverse sources that, in the EPA's judgment, may reasonably be anticipated to endanger public health or welfare. Clean Air Act § 108, 42 U.S.C. § 7408. Under the Act, the EPA Administrator was initially required to list such pollutants in the Federal Register and then, as to each of them, prepare "air quality criteria" documents that identify effects on public health or welfare, as well as the techniques that are available to prevent or control their emissions. Clean Air Act § 108(a)(2), 42 U.S.C. § 7408(a)(2). This has been done for six pollutants: sulfur dioxide (SO2), nitrogen dioxide (NO2), ozone, carbon monoxide (CO), suspended particulate matter, and lead.

Following its identification of "criteria pollutants," the EPA was compelled to establish National Ambient Air Quality Standards (NAAQS) as to each listed criteria pollutant. Clean Air Act § 109; 42 U.S.C. § 7409. These standards were to reflect the EPA's determination of the limit on ambient air pollution that is necessary to protect the public health and the public welfare. Health-based standards are referred to in the Act as "primary standards." Welfare-protective NAAQS, on the other hand, are known as "secondary standards." Which do you think would lead to a more stringent air quality standard: protection of public health or protection of public welfare?

The Clean Air Act directs EPA to set all primary standards with an "adequate margin of safety." As we shall see in *American Trucking Associations v. United States Environmental Protection Agency*, p. 318 below, that language has been interpreted by the United States Supreme Court as not permitting the Agency to consider implementation costs when it establishes such standards.

Once NAAQS are established for criteria pollutants, each individual state is required to identify and designate those air quality control regions within the state that do and do not meet the standards, as well as those that cannot be classified. Clean Air Act § 110, 42 U.S.C. § 7410. Regions that meet the NAAQS for particular pollutants are deemed "attainment areas." Those that do not are termed "nonattainment areas."

SIPs

Each of the states is then responsible for adopting a State Implementation Plan (SIP) that contains enforceable limitations that will assure the implementation and maintenance of NAAQS in all air quality control regions throughout the state. Clean Air Act § 110, 42 U.S.C. § 7410. SIPs contain many of the specific detailed substantive requirements that govern the type and amount of air pollution that air pollution sources are legally permitted to emit. They are the source of many of the requirements that are incorporated into individual permits issued to facilities that emit air pollutants.

State Implementation Plans must be prepared following "a satisfactory process of consultation" with general-purpose local governments and designated organizations of elected local officials. They must meet a detailed list of requirements set forth in the statute. They must also be the subject of a public hearing prior to adoption. Clean Air Act § 110(a)(2), 42 U.S.C. § 7410(a)(2).

Once an SIP has been adopted, it must be submitted to the EPA for whole or partial approval, conditional approval, or disapproval. Where a state fails to adopt a plan, or the EPA determines that a state's plan is inconsistent with the Act's mandates, the EPA is authorized to adopt a plan for the state, commonly referred to as a Federal

Implementation Plan (or FIP). After EPA approval—or federal promulgation—a SIP or FIP is legally binding under both federal and state law, and it may be enforced by the EPA, state officials, or private citizens (under the Act's citizen suit provision). *See* Clean Air Act §§ 110(a)(1), 110(c)(1), and 304, 42 U.S.C. §§ 7410(a)(1), 7410(c)(1), and 7604.

When states prepare SIPs, they must require stationary sources of air pollution in non-attainment areas to adhere to standards established by EPA. Among other things, states must require already-existing stationary sources in these dirty air areas to apply "reasonably available control technology" (often referred to as "RACT"). Clean Air Act § 172(c)(1); 42 U.S.C. § 7502(c)1). This requirement is generally defined by the states in their SIPs through the application of "Control Techniques Guidelines," (CTGs) issued by the EPA for particular types of sources on an informal basis. The Guidelines describe reasonably available air pollution control methods and the levels of control those methods can be expected to achieve. In fact, EPA has promulgated a number of Control Technique Guidelines. These documents are often lengthy and complex. For a sampling of them, *see* https://www.epa.gov/sites/production/files/2016-10/documents/2016-ctg-oil-and-gas. pdf (CTG for the oil and gas industry); http://epa.gov/staitonary-sources-air-pollution/fact-sheet-control-techniques-guidelines-ctg-shipbuilding-and-ship (CTG for Shipbuilding and Ship Repair Surface Coating Operations); and http://epa.gov/ozone-pollution/contol-tcchniques-guidelines-and-alternativr-techniques-documents-reducing (CTG for Reducing Ozone-Causing Emissions).

In addition, nonattainment area SIPs must contain control measures for existing sources that will lead to "reasonable further progress towards the attainment of NAAQS." They must include other means or techniques (including economic incentives such as fees, marketable permits, and auctions of emission rights) that may be necessary to provide NAAQS attainment. And they must be accompanied by a state-prepared inventory of actual emissions from all sources of criteria pollutants in the nonattainment area, which must be comprehensive, accurate, and current. *See* Clean Air Act §§ 172(c)(1), (2), and (3); 42 U.S.C. §§ 7502(c)(1), (2), and (3).

A. What Must a State Implementation Plan Contain?

While a state's SIP must be capable of achieving the NAAQS, it was important also to determine just how far the states could go. Could they push regulated entities beyond what was immediately feasible? The next case resolved this issue.

Union Electric Co. v. EPA
427 U.S. 246 (1976)

Justice MARSHALL:

After the Administrator of the Environmental Protection Agency (EPA) approves a state implementation plan under the Clean Air Act, the plan may be challenged in a court of appeals within 30 days, or after 30 days have run if newly discovered or available information justifies subsequent review. We must decide whether the operator of a regulated emission source, in a petition for review of an EPA-approved state plan filed after the original 30-day appeal period, can raise the claim that it is economically or technologically infeasible to comply with the plan.

We have addressed the history and provisions of the Clean Air Act Amendments of 1970 in detail . . . and will not repeat that discussion here. Suffice it to say that the Amendments reflect congressional dissatisfaction with the progress of existing air pollution programs and a determination to "tak[e] a stick to the States in order to guarantee the prompt attainment and maintenance of specified air quality standards." The heart of the Amendments is the requirement that each State formulate, subject to EPA approval, an implementation plan designed to achieve national primary ambient air quality standards—those necessary to protect the public health—"as expeditiously as practicable but . . . in no case later than three years from the date of approval of such plan." Section 110(a)(2)(A) of the Clean Air Act. The plan must also provide for the attainment of national secondary ambient air quality standards—those necessary to protect the public welfare—within a "reasonable time." Each State is given wide discretion in formulating its plan, and the Act provides that the Administrator "shall approve" the proposed plan if it has been adopted after public notice and hearing and if it meets eight specified criteria. Section 110(a)(2).

On April 30, 1971, the Administrator promulgated national primary and secondary standards for six air pollutants he found to have an adverse effect on the public health and welfare. Included among them was sulfur dioxide, at issue here. After the promulgation of the national standards, the State of Missouri formulated its implementation plan and submitted it for approval. . . . The Administrator approved the plan on May 31, 1972.

Petitioner is an electric utility company servicing the St. Louis metropolitan area, large portions of Missouri, and parts of Illinois and Iowa. Its three coal-fired generating plants in the metropolitan St. Louis area are subject to the sulfur dioxide restrictions in the Missouri implementation plan. Petitioner did not seek review of the Administrator's approval of the plan within 30 days, as it was entitled to do under Section 307(b)(1) of the Act . . . but rather applied to the appropriate state and county agencies for variances from the emission limitations affecting its three plants. Petitioner received one-year variances, which could be extended upon reapplication. The variances on two of petitioner's three plants had expired and petitioner was applying for extensions when, on May 31, 1974, the Administrator notified petitioner that sulfur dioxide emissions from its plants violated the emission limitations contained in the Missouri plan. Shortly thereafter petitioner filed a petition in the Court of Appeals for the Eighth Circuit for review of the Administrator's 1972 approval of the Missouri implementation plan.

Section 307(b)(1) allows petitions for review to be filed in an appropriate court of appeals more than 30 days after the Administrator's approval of an implementation plan only if the petition is "based solely on grounds arising after such 30th day."

Petitioner claimed to meet this requirement by asserting, *inter alia*, that various economic and technological difficulties had arisen more than 30 days after the Administrator's approval and that these difficulties made compliance with the emission limitations impossible.

Since a reviewing court—regardless of when the petition for review is filed—may consider claims of economic and technological infeasibility only if the Administrator may consider such claims in approving or rejecting a state implementation plan, we must address ourselves to the scope of the Administrator's responsibility. The Administrator's position is that he has no power whatsoever to reject a state implementation plan on the ground that it is economically or technologically infeasible, and we have previously accorded great deference to the Administrator's construction of the Clean Air Act. After surveying the relevant provisions of the Clean Air Act Amendments of 1970 and their legislative history, we agree that Congress intended claims of economic and technological infeasibility to be wholly foreign to the Administrator's consideration of a state implementation plan.

As we have previously recognized, the 1970 Amendments to the Clean Air Act were a drastic remedy to what was perceived as a serious and otherwise uncheckable problem of air pollution. The Amendments place the primary responsibility for formulating pollution control strategies on the States, but nonetheless subject the States to strict minimum compliance requirements. These requirements are of a "technology-forcing character," and are expressly designed to force regulated sources to develop pollution control devices that might at the time appear to be economically or technologically infeasible.

The approach is apparent on the face of Section 110(a)(2). The provision sets out eight criteria that an implementation plan must satisfy, and provides that if these criteria are met and if the plan was adopted after reasonable notice and hearing, the Administrator "shall approve" the proposed state plan. The mandatory "shall" makes it quite clear that the Administrator is not to be concerned with factors other than those specified and none of the eight factors appears to permit consideration of technological or economic infeasibility. . . .

Amici . . . argue that the Amendments do not give such broad power to the States. They claim that the States are precluded from submitting implementation plans more stringent than federal law demands by Section 110(a)(2)'s second criterion—that the plan contain such control devices "as may be necessary" to achieve the primary and secondary air quality standards. Section 110(a)(2)(B). The contention is that an overly restrictive plan is not "necessary" for attainment of the national standards and so must be rejected by the Administrator.

Amici's principal support for this theory lies in the fact that while the House and Senate versions of Section 110(a)(2) both expressly provided that the States could submit for the Administrator's approval plans that were stricter than the national standards required the section as enacted contains no such express language. Amici argue that the Conference Committee must have decided to require state implementation simply—and precisely—to meet the national standards. Amici's argument proves too much. A Conference Committee lacks power to make substantive changes on matters about which both Houses agree. . . . And while the final language of Section 110(a)(2)(B) may be less explicit than the versions originally approved by the House and the Senate, the most natural reading of the "as may be necessary" phrase in context is simply that the Administrator must assure that the minimal, or "necessary," requirements are met, not that he detect and reject any state plan more demanding than federal law requires. . . .

We read the "as may be necessary" requirement of Section 110(a)(2)(B) to demand only that the implementation plan submitted by the State meet the "minimum conditions" of the Amendments. . . . Beyond that, if a State makes the legislative determination that it desires a particular air quality by a certain date and that it is willing to force technology to attain it — or lose a certain industry if attainment is not possible — such a determination is fully consistent with the structure and purpose of the Amendments, and Section 110(a)(2)(B) provides no basis for the EPA Administrator to object to the determination on the ground of infeasibility. . . .

[T]he language of Section 110(a)(2)(A) provides no basis for the Administrator ever to reject a state implementation plan on the ground that it is economically or technologically infeasible. Accordingly, a court of appeals reviewing an approved plan under Section 307(b)(1) cannot set it aside on those grounds, no matter when they are raised. . . .

In short, the Amendments offer ample opportunity for consideration of claims of technological and economic infeasibility. Always, however, care is taken that consideration of such claims will not interfere substantially with the primary goal of prompt attainment of the national standards. Allowing such claims to be raised by appealing the Administrator's approval of an implementation plan, as petitioner suggests, would frustrate congressional intent. It would permit a proposed plan to be struck down as infeasible before it is given a chance to work, even though Congress clearly contemplated that some plans would be infeasible when proposed. And it would permit the Administrator or a federal court to reject a State's legislative choices in regulating air pollution, even though Congress plainly left with the States, so long as the national standards were met, the power to determine which sources would be burdened by regulation and to what extent. Technology forcing is a concept somewhat new to our national experience and it necessarily entails certain risks. But Congress considered those risks in passing the 1970 Amendments and decided that the dangers posed by uncontrolled air pollution made them worth taking. Petitioner's theory would render that considered legislative judgment a nullity, and that is a result we refuse to reach.

Notes and Questions

1. This case highlights the "technology forcing" nature of the Clean Air Act, a feature it shares with other statutes from this decade of environmental legislation. It may be hard to imagine such congressional choices if you were born in the 1990s, but keep in mind that when this all began the country was choking on pollution, experiencing disturbing cancer clusters, and watching rivers burn. There was an urgency to the

problem that required a technological response beyond what had already been achieved — innovation was essential to our survival. The quickest way to make such innovation happen was to make it economically necessary to entire industries, or at least to subsets of them. Technology forcing regulation creates that economic urgency and thus results in better and faster pollution control than working with what is presently feasible.

2. Compare the technology-forcing approach Congress took in crafting the Clean Air Act with the approach of the New York Court of Appeals in *Boomer v. Atlantic Cement Company*. Which reflects better pollution control policy in your view? Why?

3. If petitioners found themselves in a bind, what other avenues might they have taken to get some relief, at least temporarily?

4. Congress left the myriad implementation policy choices to the states, including where to place the burdens. They could be evenly distributed or more heavily forced on a particular industry. Why do you think the states were given such broad policy power within this federal program?

5. In spite of the substantial implementation discretion granted to the states, there are some limits on what a state can do. It cannot, for example, venture too far into the EPA's role, at least not without EPA authority to determine the reasonableness of such choices. *See Alaska Dep't of Envtl. Conservation v. EPA*, 540 U.S. 461 (2004) (allowing EPA to halt mine construction on the basis of its determination that state's permit contained unreasonable definition of Best Available Control Technology or BACT).

6. When setting the NAAQS, what should the EPA take into account? In line with the feasibility (or lack thereof) discussion above, do you think that economic feasibility would be a factor in this process? Or even a standard cost-benefit analysis? The next case excerpt addresses this question.

Practice Problem

You are an attorney who represents Wartco, a large investor-owner electric utility company in the State of Coriander. To turn the turbines that generate electricity, Wartco burns a variety of fuels in its boilers at different times. These fuels include coal, oil, natural gas, and biofuels. In response to a call from the EPA to revise its State Implementation Plan (SIP), the Coriander Department of Environmental Quality (CDEQ) has proposed an SIP revision. Under Coriander law, CDEQ is required to hold a public hearing on its new SIP proposal and take written comments from all interested parties. It must then submit its final SIP proposal to the Coriander legislature for approval.

The draft proposal from the CDEQ would require Wartco to phase out its combustion of coal and oil within 18 months of legislative approval of the new regulation, to eliminate all use of natural gas within a 30-month period, and to burn only biofuels in its boilers thereafter. Your client's engineers believe that the deadlines included in the proposed SIP are unrealistic and, that, as a practical matter, they are impossible for the company to meet. They have also told you that, if it goes into effect, the proposed SIP will require Wartco to spend very large sums of money to comply, only a fraction of which can be passed along to the utility's customers in the form of higher electric bills. Given these facts, what strategy (or strategies) would you choose to pursue to protect your client's interest? Why?

B. Setting National Ambient Air Quality Standards

Whitman v. American Trucking Association, Inc.
531 U.S. 457 (2001)

Justice SCALIA:

These cases present the following questions: (1) Whether § 109(b)(1) of the Clean Air Act (CAA) delegates legislative power to [EPA]. (2) Whether the [EPA] Administrator may consider the costs of implementation in setting national ambient air quality standards (NAAQS) under § 109(b)(1).

In *Lead Industries Association, Inc. v. EPA*, 647 F. 2d 1130 (D.C. Cir. 1980), the [D.C.] Circuit held that "economic considerations [may] play no part in the promulgation of ambient air quality standards under Section 109 of the CAA." In the present cases, the court adhered to that holding, as it had done on many other occasions. Respondents argue that these decisions are incorrect. We disagree, however, and since the first step in assessing whether a statute delegates legislative power is to determine what authority the statute confers, we address that issue of interpretation first. . . .

Section 109(b)(1) instructs the EPA to set primary ambient air quality standards "the attainment and maintenance of which . . . are requisite to protect the public health" with "an adequate margin of safety." 42 U.S.C. § 7409(b)(1). Were it not for the hundreds of pages of briefing respondents have submitted on the issue, one would have thought it fairly clear that this text does not permit the EPA to consider costs in setting the standards. The language, as one scholar has noted, "is absolute." The EPA, "based on" the information about health effects contained in the technical "criteria" documents compiled under § 108(a)(2), is to identify the maximum airborne concentration of a pollutant that the public health can tolerate, decrease the concentration to provide an "absolute" margin of safety, and set the standard at that level. Nowhere are the costs of achieving such a standard made part of that initial calculation. . . .

[T]o prevail in their present challenge, respondents must show a textual commitment of authority to the EPA to consider costs in setting NAAQS under § 109(b)(1). And because § 109(b)(1) and the NAAQS for which it provides are the engine that drives nearly all of Title I of the CAA, 42 U.S.C. §§ 7401–7515, that textual commitment must be a clear one. Congress, as we have held, does not alter the fundamental details of a regulatory scheme in vague terms or ancillary provisions—it does not, one might say, hide elephants in mouse holes. Respondents' textual arguments ultimately founder upon this principle.

Their first claim is that § 109(b)(1)'s terms "adequate margin" and "requisite" *Argument 1* leave room to pad health effects with cost concerns. . . . [W]e find it implausible *SC decision* that Congress would give to the EPA through these modest words the power to determine whether implementation costs should moderate national air quality standards.

The same defect inheres in respondents' next two arguments: that while the Admin- *Arguments 2 + 3* istrator's judgment about what is requisite to protect the public health must be "based on [the] criteria" documents developed under § 108(a)(2), *see* § 109(b)(1), it need not be based *solely* on those criteria; and that those criteria themselves, while they must include "effects on public health or welfare which may be expected from the presence of such pollutant in the ambient air," are not necessarily *limited* to those effects. Even if we were to concede those premises, we still would not conclude that one of the unenumerated factors that the agency can consider in developing and applying the criteria is cost of implementation. That factor is *both* so indirectly related *SC decision* to public health and so full of potential for canceling the conclusions drawn from direct health effects that it would surely have been expressly mentioned in §§ 108 and 109 had Congress meant it to be considered. Yet while those provisions describe in detail how the health effects of pollutants in the ambient air are to be calculated and given effect, *see* § 108(a)(2), they say not a word about costs.

Respondents point, finally, to a number of provisions in the CAA that do require attainment cost data to be generated. Section 108(b)(1), for example, instructs the Administrator to "issue to the States," simultaneously with the criteria documents, "information on air pollution control techniques, which information shall include data relating to the cost of installation and operation." And § 109(d)(2)(C)(iv) requires the Clean Air Scientific Advisory Committee to "advise the Administrator of any adverse public health, welfare, social, economic, or energy effects which may result from various strategies for attainment and maintenance" of NAAQS. Respondents argue that these provisions make no sense unless costs are to be considered in setting the NAAQS. This is not so. These provisions enable to Administrator to assist the States in carrying out their statutory role as primary *implementers* of the NAAQS. It is to the States that the Act assigns initial and primary responsibility for deciding what emissions reductions will be required from which sources. See 42 U.S.C. §§ 7407(a), 7410 (giving States the duty of developing implementation plans). It would be impossible to perform that task intelligently without considering which abatement techniques are most efficient, and most economically feasible — which is why we have said that "the most important forum for consideration of claims of economic and technological infeasibility is before the state agency formulating the implementation plan," *Union Elec. Co. v. EPA*, 427 U.S., at 266. Thus, federal clean air legislation has, from the very beginning, directed federal agencies to develop and transmit implementation data, including cost data, to the States. That Congress chose to carry forward this research program to assist States in choosing the means through which they would implement the standards is perfectly sensible, and has no bearing upon whether cost considerations are to be taken into account in formulating the standards . . . .

The text of § 109(b), interpreted in its statutory and historical context and with appreciation for its importance to the CAA as a whole, unambiguously bars cost considerations from the NAAQS-setting process. . . . We therefore affirm the judgment of the Court of Appeals on that point.

Notes and Questions

1. The Court notes that Congress does not "hide elephants in mouseholes." What would be the elephant and the mousehole in this case?   *cited on p 328*

2. Determining when it is appropriate to consider costs is not as complicated as it might appear. When looking at any stage of administrative process, it is generally helpful to ask first whether the step relates to risk assessment or risk management. Risk assessment is an informational endeavor. It is, at least in theory, a scientific question (in theory because in the implementation of environmental laws every question is a policy question). *See* Wendy Wagner, *The Science Charade*, 95 Colum. L. Rev. 1613 (1995). Risk assessment is a determination of how vulnerable something is (as with listing species under the Endangered Species Act) or how dangerous something is (as with setting the NAAQS), so the relevant statutes tend to phrase such inquiries in terms of applying science. Of course, it is a subjective matter how thin we are comfortable letting a species' population get or how much risk we are willing to take with public health, but under no circumstances does cost play a formal role in the simple question of what is safe. Risk management, on the other hand, is where we decide what to do about those risks we've assessed, which is an unclosed policy question. What are you willing to sacrifice to save that species or to reach that clean air goal sooner? This is the stage when costs are generally considered. Such decisions tend to rely on cost-benefit analyses.

3. As discussed above on page 312, EPA is required to establish National Ambient Air Quality Standards that protect public health and the public welfare for each criteria pollutant it has identified. Should the EPA list greenhouse gases that contribute to global climate change as criteria pollutants? What reasons support such a move and what might be the hurdles? This is exactly what the Center for Biological Diversity and 350.org petitioned the EPA to do in December 2009. The full petition can be found at http://www.biologicaldiversity.org/programs/climate_law_institute/global_warming _litigation/clean_air_act/pdfs/Petition_GHG_pollution_cap_12-2-2009.pdf. In 2015 the EPA unveiled its approach to GHGs, the Clean Power Plan. These and other materials relating to regulating GHGs under the Clean Air Act will be discussed in greater detail in Chapter 6.   *Considered pollutants, but not criteria pollutants.*

[margin notes: ① Assess risk ② Decide what to do w/ risk. held that cost could not be a factor in setting NAAQS]

Lead Industries Association, Inc. v. EPA

647 F.2d 1130 (D.C. Cir. 1980)

Judge WRIGHT:

. . . In the present consolidated cases we are asked to review EPA regulations establishing national ambient air quality standards for lead. These air quality standards prescribe the maximum concentrations of lead that will be permitted in the air of our country. We must decide whether EPA's Administrator acted within the scope of his *Issue* statutory authority in promulgating these regulations and, if so, whether the evidence adduced at the rulemaking proceeding supports his final determinations. In addition, we must examine the petitioners' claims that infirmities in the procedures employed by EPA in this rulemaking warrant remand of the regulations to the Agency. Petitioners are the Lead Industry Association, Inc. (LIA), a nonprofit trade association whose 78 members include most of the country's producers and commercial consumers of lead and St. Joe Minerals Corporation (St. Joe).

Man's ability to alter his environment to achieve perceived goals has undoubtedly made an enormous contribution to his economic and social well-being. This undertaking is not, however, without attendant costs. One of these costs is the toll that these alterations may exact on the environment itself and, in turn, the dangers that this may pose for the public health and welfare. Unfortunately, man's ability to alter the environment often far outstrips his ability to foresee with any degree of certainty what untoward effects these changes may bring. The issues presented by these cases illustrate this sad fact.

Lead's environmental significance is a consequence of both its abundance and its utility. The relative abundance of lead in the earth's crust makes it unique among the toxic heavy metals. And centuries of mining and smelting, and the use of lead in a variety of human activities, have increased the natural background concentration of lead in the environment. But it is only since the industrial age and the use of lead as a gasoline additive that lead has become pervasive. Today lead is ubiquitous. It is found in almost every medium with which we come into contact-food, water, air, soil, dust, and paint, each of which represents a potential pathway for human lead exposure through ingestion or inhalation. The widespread presence of this toxic metal in the environment poses a significant health risk. Lead is a poison which has no known beneficial function in the body, but when present in the body in sufficient concentrations lead attacks the blood, kidneys, and central nervous and other systems and can cause anemia, kidney damage, severe brain damage, and death. . . .

[The court summarized at length the detailed description of the health effects of lead that was included in EPA's criteria document for lead.]

Simultaneously with the publication of the Lead Criteria Document . . . the Administrator proposed a national primary ambient air quality standard for lead of 1.5 µg Pb/m^3 monthly average. He also proposed that the secondary air quality standard be set at the same level as the primary standard because the welfare effects associated with lead exposure did not warrant imposition of a stricter standard. . . .

The Administrator [accepted public comments] and promulgated the final air quality standards on October 5, 1978, prescribing national primary and secondary ambient air quality standards for lead of 1.5 µg Pb/m^3, averaged over a calendar quarter. . . .

On December 8, 1978 LIA petitioned EPA for reconsideration and a stay of the lead standards. The Administrator denied the petition on February 2, 1979. These petitions for review of the lead standards regulations followed. Before examining the petitioners' challenges to the regulations, we consider the limits of our reviewing function. . . .

[The Court applied the "arbitrary, capricious, etc." standard under Section 307(d) of the CAA, citing particularly the reference to setting aside any action found "without observance of procedure required by law" under Section 307(d)(8), and relying also on the *Overton Park* standard, including an inquiry into the consideration of "relevant factors" and an examination into the "rational basis" for every decision.]

Petitioner's argument

The petitioners' first claim is that the Administrator exceeded his authority under the statute by promulgating a primary air quality standard for lead, which is more stringent than is necessary to protect the public health because it is designed to protect the public against "sub-clinical" effects which are not harmful to health. According to petitioners, Congress only authorized the Administrator to set primary air quality standards that are aimed at protecting the public against health effects which are known to be *clearly harmful* They argue that Congress so limited the Administrator's authority because it was concerned that excessively stringent air quality standards could cause massive economic dislocation.

In developing this argument St. Joe contends that EPA erred by refusing to consider the issues of economic and technological feasibility in setting the air quality standards for lead. St. Joe's claim that the Administrator should have considered these issues is based on the statutory provision directing him to allow an "adequate margin of safety" in setting primary air quality standards. In St. Joe's view, the Administrator must consider the economic impact of the proposed standard on industry and the technological feasibility of compliance by emission sources in determining the appropriate allowance for a margin of safety. St. Joe argues that the Administrator abused his discretion by refusing to consider these factors in determining the appropriate margin of safety for the lead standards, and maintains that the lead air quality standards will have a disastrous economic impact on industrial sources of lead emissions.

This argument is totally without merit. St. Joe is unable to point to anything in either the language of the Act or its legislative history that offers any support for its claim that Congress, by specifying that the Administrator is to allow an "adequate margin of safety" in setting primary air quality standards, thereby required the Administrator to consider economic or technological feasibility. To the contrary, the statute and its legislative history make clear that economic considerations play no part in the promulgation of ambient air quality standards under Section 109. . . .

Furthermore, we agree with the Administrator that requiring EPA to wait until it can conclusively demonstrate that a particular effect is adverse to health before it acts is inconsistent with both the Act's precautionary and preventive orientation and the nature of the Administrator's statutory responsibilities. Congress provided that the Administrator is to use his judgment in setting air quality standards precisely to permit him to act in the face of uncertainty. And as we read the statutory provisions and the legislative history, Congress directed the Administrator to err on the side of caution in making the necessary decisions. We see no reason why this court should put a gloss on Congress' scheme by requiring the Administrator to show that there is a medical consensus that the effects on which the lead standards were based are *"clearly harmful to health."* All that is required by the statutory scheme is evidence in the record which substantiates his conclusions about the health effects on which the standards were based.

Accordingly, we reject LIA's claim that the Administrator exceeded his statutory authority and turn to LIA's challenge to the evidentiary basis for the Administrator's decisions. . . .

[The Court next reviewed the standards and the supporting data in considerable detail, and concluded that the standards were based on sound decisions concerning health effects, and did not exceed the adequate margin of safety required by the statute. The Court concluded that in its judgment and choice of methods, the Administrative standard-setting had not been arbitrary or capricious. The Court also rejected LIA's contention that the Administrator had no authority to adopt the secondary standard without making findings showing that the standard was necessary to protect the public welfare, accepting EPA's conclusion that the welfare effects of lead exposure did not justify promulgation of a secondary standard for lead more stringent than the primary standard.]

We have accorded these cases the most careful consideration, combining as we must careful scrutiny of the evidence in the record with deference to the Administrator's judgments. We conclude that in this rulemaking proceeding the Administrator complied with the substantive and procedural requirements of the Act, and that his decisions are both adequately explained and amply supported by evidence in the record. Accordingly, we reject petitioners' claims of error. The regulations under review herein are affirmed.

Notes and Questions

1. Air quality standards are set by a notice and comment rulemaking procedure in which the EPA publishes its findings (the criteria document) and proposed rule, collects input from interested parties, then publishes its final rule along with responses to that input. EPA's Lead Criteria Document laid out, step-by-step, the available scientific knowledge about lead. First, EPA described the devastating health effects of lead in the body. Then, EPA attempted to identify the "threshold concentrations" for those health effects; that is, the levels of lead in human blood below which health effects will not occur. Finally, EPA tried to determine the "air lead to blood lead ratio": how the concentration of lead in the outside air—which is what EPA is authorized to regulate—translates to the level of lead in people's blood. The latter is what causes the health effects that EPA is supposed to protect against.

Such determinations are accorded great deference in part due to their characterization as science-based. However, while science gives us facts, policy gives us our degree of risk tolerance. How would you characterize the EPA's standards: science, policy, or a blend of the two? How does this characterization impact your views on agency deference? What might happen as administrations change?

2. EPA considered two major issues in establishing the final rule. First, what is a safe blood-lead level for children? Second, what proportion of the target population should be kept below this level? These related determinations resulted in the ultimate standard. In thinking about the questions in Note 1 above, would you define these considerations as more science-based or policy-based?

3. The EPA is required to review the NAAQS for each pollutant every five years, updating each NAAQS if new information indicates the need to do so. Lawsuits for failure to revise the NAAQS tend to fail in courts so long as there is any evidence that the EPA has at least reconsidered the standards in that time. Of course, sometimes the review does lead to revision, as recently happened when EPA tightened the ground-level ozone standards, stating:

> On October 1, 2015, EPA strengthened the National Ambient Air Quality Standards (NAAQS) for ground-level ozone to 70 parts per billion (ppb), based on extensive scientific evidence about ozone's effects on public health and welfare. The updated standards will improve public health protection, particularly for at-risk groups including children, older adults, people of all ages who have lung diseases such as asthma, and people who are active outdoors, especially outdoor workers. They also will improve the health of trees, plants and ecosystems.

See https://www3.epa.gov/airquality/ozonepollution/actions.html#current.

4. Notwithstanding the reality that risk tolerance is a largely subjective policy matter, scientific research renders the health consequences of lead abundantly clear as a factual matter. Scientific uncertainty generally leads to inadequate regulation, not overregulation, and that is exactly what happened here. In the decades that followed this case, research proved that the EPA's "conservative" standard was actually far too risky and harmful. Subsequent neuroscientific research on the effects of the phase-down in airborne lead levels that followed the *Lead Industries* decision vindicated EPA's belief that that reducing lead in the air would reduce lead levels in the blood of children. This proved to be the case notwithstanding the fact that some children are poisoned by lead when they ingest lead paint. In 2008 the EPA published these findings and dramatically strengthened the lead standard—by a full tenfold. Thus, for the current standard, all you need to do is take the standard above and move the decimal point one place to the left. In fact, today many neuroscientists believe that there is no safe level of human exposure to lead—particularly for children. What does this say about the standards in general? About the line-drawing chosen throughout environmental law? About the practice of cost-benefit analysis in environmental decision-making?

5. Air pollution does not respect political boundaries. It often crosses state lines, creating difficult problems of allocating responsibility for pollution control and abatement between and among states. The next case considers how Congress, EPA, and the federal courts have grappled with this complex regulatory challenge.

[handwritten margin note: There is no safe amount of lead in your blood]

Environmental Protection Agency v. EME Homer Generation
134 S. Ct. 1584 (2014)

Justice GINSBURG:

These cases concern the efforts of Congress and the Environmental Protection Agency (EPA or Agency) to cope with a complex problem: air pollution emitted in one State, but causing harm in other States. Left unregulated, the emitting or upwind State reaps the benefits of the economic activity causing the pollution without bearing all the costs. Conversely, downwind States to which the pollution travels are unable to achieve clean air because of the influx of out-of-state pollution they lack authority to control. To tackle the problem, Congress included a Good Neighbor Provision in the Clean Air Act (Act or CAA). That provision, in its current phrasing, instructs States to prohibit in-state sources "from emitting any air pollutant in amounts which will . . . contribute significantly" to downwind States' "nonattainment . . . or interfere with maintenance," of any EPA-promulgated national air quality standard. 42 U.S.C. §7410(a)(2)(D)(i).

Interpreting the Good Neighbor Provision, EPA adopted the Cross-State Air Pollution Rule (commonly and hereinafter called the Transport Rule). The rule calls for consideration of costs, among other factors, when determining the emission reductions an upwind State must make to improve air quality in polluted downwind areas. The Court of Appeals for the D.C. Circuit vacated the rule in its entirety. It held, 2 to 1, that the Good Neighbor Provision requires EPA to consider only such upwind State's physically proportionate responsibility for each downwind State's air quality problem. That reading is demanded, according to the D.C. Circuit, so that no State will be required to decrease its emission by more than its ratable share of downwind-state pollution. . . .

In 2005, EPA issued the Clean Air Interstate Rule, or CAIR . . . . The D.C. Circuit initially vacated CAIR as arbitrary and capricious. On rehearing, the court decided to leave the rule in place, while encouraging EPA to act with dispatch in dealing with problems the court had identified.

The rule challenged here . . . is EPA's response to the D.C. Circuit's decision. Finalized in August 2011, the Transport Rule curtails NO_x and SO_2 emissions of 27 upwind States to achieve downwind attainment of three different NAAQS: the two 1997 NAAQS previously addressed by CAIR, and the 2006 NAAQS for PM2.5 levels measured on a daily basis.

Under the Transport Rule, EPA employed a "two-step approach" to determine when upwind States "contribute[d] significantly to nonattainment," and therefore in "amounts" that had to be eliminated. At step one, called the "screening" analysis, the Agency excluded as de minimis any upwind State that contributed less than one percent of the three NAAQS to any downwind State "receptor," a location at which EPA measures air quality. If all of an upwind State's contributions fell below the one-percent threshold, that State would be considered not to have "contribute[d] significantly" to the nonattainment of any downwind State. States in that category were screened out and exempted from regulation under the rule.

The remaining States were subjected to a second inquiry, which EPA called the "control" analysis. At this stage, the Agency sought to generate a cost-effective allocation of emission reductions among those upwind States "screened in" at step one . . .

[U]nder the Transport Rule, an upwind State "contribute[d] significantly" to downwind nonattainment to the extent its exported pollution both (1) produced one percent or more of a NAAQS in at least one downwind State (step one) and (2) could be eliminated cost-effectively, as determined by EPA (step two). Upwind States would be obliged to eliminate all and only emissions meeting both of these criteria.

For each State regulated by the Transport Rule, EPA contemporaneously promulgated a FIP [i.e. a Federal Implementation Plan] allocating the State's emission budget among its in-state sources. For each of these States, EPA had determined that the State had failed to submit a SIP adequate for compliance with the Good Neighbor Provision. . . .

If EPA determines a SIP to be inadequate . . . the Agency has a statutory duty to issue a FIP "at any time" within two years (unless the State first "corrects the deficiency," which no one contends occurred here) . . . .

Nothing in the Act differentiates the Good Neighbor Provision from the several other matters a State must address in its SIP. Rather, the statute speaks without reservation: Once a NAAQS has been issued, a State "shall" propose a SIP within three years, § 7410 (a) (1), and that SIP "shall" include, among other components, provisions adequate to satisfy the Good Neighbor Provision, § 7410 (a) (2).

Nor does the Act condition the duty to promulgate a FIP on EPA's having first quantified an upwind State's good neighbor obligations . . . . The Act empowers the Agency to promulgate a FIP "at any time" within the two-year limit . . . .

The practical difficulties cited by the Court of Appeals do not justify departure from the Act's plain text . . . . When Congress elected to make EPA's input a prerequisite to state action under the Act, it did so expressly . . . A State's obligation to adopt a SIP, moreover, arises only after EPA has first set the NAAQS the State must meet. § 7410(a)(1). Had Congress intended similarly to defer States' discharge of their obligations under the Good Neighbor Provision, Congress, we take it, would have included a similar direction in that section . . . .

The statute requires States to eliminate those "amounts" of pollution that "contribute significantly to *maintenance*" in downwind States. 42 U.S.C. § 7410(a)(2)(D)(i) (emphasis added). Thus, EPA's task is to reduce upwind pollution, but only in "amounts" that push a downwind State's pollution concentrations above the relevant NAAQS. As noted earlier, however, the nonattainment of downwind States results from the collective and interwoven contributions of multiple upwind States. The statute therefore calls upon the Agency to address a theory causation problem: How should EPA allocate among multiple contributing upwind States responsibility for a downwind State's excess pollution? . . .

[T]he Court of Appeals believes that the Act speaks clearly, requiring EPA to allocate responsibility for reducing emissions in "a manner proportional to" each State's "contribution" to the problem. Nothing in the text of the Good Neighbor Provision propels EPA down this path. Understandably so, for as EPA notes, the D.C. Circuit's proportionality approach could scarcely be satisfied in practice.

The dissent, for its part, strains to give meaning to the D.C. Circuit's proportionality constraint as applied to a world in which multiple upwind States contribute emissions to multiple downwind locations. . . . The dissent's formulation, however, does not account for the combined and cumulative effect of each upwind State's reductions on attainment in multiple downwind locations. . . .

In the dissent's view, upwind States must eliminate emissions by "whatever minimum amount reduces" their share of the overage in each and every one of the downwind States to which they are linked. In practical terms, this means each upwind State will be required to reduce emissions by the amount necessary to eliminate that State's largest downwind contribution. The dissent's formulation, however, does not account for the combined and cumulative effort of each upwind State's reductions on attainment in multiple downwind locations: "Under a proportional-reduction approach, State X would be required to eliminate emissions of that pollutant by whatever minimum amount reduces *both* State A's level by 0.2 unit and State B's by 0.7 unit." (emphasis added). The result would be costly overregulation unnecessary to, indeed in conflict with, the Good Neighbor Provisions' goal of attainment . . . .

Persuaded that the Good Neighbor Provision does not dictate the particular allocation of emissions among contributing States advanced by the D.C. Circuit, we must next decide whether the allocation method chosen by EPA is a "permissible construction of the statute." *Chevron*, 467 U.S. 837, at 843 . . . .

Using costs in the Transport Rule calculus, we agree with EPA, also makes good sense. Eliminating those amounts that can cost-effectively be reduced is an efficient and equitable solution to the allocation problem the Good Neighbor Provision requires the Agency to address. Efficient because EPA can achieve the levels of attainment, *i.e.,* of emission reductions, the proportional approach aims to achieve, but at a much lower overall cost. Equitable because, by imposing uniform cost thresholds on regulated States, EPA's rule subjects to stricter regulation those States that have done relatively less in the past to control their pollution. Upwind States that have not yet implemented pollution controls of the same stringency as their neighbors will be stopped from free riding on their neighbors' efforts to reduce pollution. They will have to bring down their emissions by installing devices of the kind in which neighboring States have already invested . . . .

Lacking a dispositive statutory instruction to guide it, EPA's decision, we conclude, is a "reasonable" way of filling the "gap left open by Congress." *Chevron*, 467 U.S., at 866.

We agree with the Court of Appeals to this extent: EPA cannot require a State to reduce its output of pollution by more than is necessary to achieve attainment in every downwind State or at odds with the one-percent threshold the Agency has set. If EPA requires an upwind State to reduce emissions by more than the amount necessary to achieve attainment in *every* downwind State to which it is linked, the Agency will have overstepped its authority, under the Good Neighbor Provision, to eliminate those "amounts [that] contribute ... to nonattainment." Nor can EPA demand reductions that would drive an upwind State's contribution to every downwind State to which it is linked below one percent of the relevant NAAQS. Doing so would be counter to step one of the Agency's interpretation of the Good Neighbor Provision. ...

Justice SCALIA, with whom Justice THOMAS joins, dissenting:

I would affirm the judgment of the D.C. Circuit that EPA violated the law both in crafting the Transport Rule and in implementing it ....

As described in the Government's briefing:

> "[T]he term 'significantly' ... is ambiguous, and ... EPA may permissibly determine the amount of a State's 'significant' contribution by reference to the amount of emissions reductions achievable through application of highly cost-effective controls."

But of course the statute does not focus on whether the upwind State has "achieved significantly;" it asks whether the State has "contributed significantly" to downwind pollution .... [I]t does not matter whether the phrase "amounts which ... contribute significantly [to downwind NAAQS nonattainment]" is ambiguous when EPA has interpreted it to mean "amounts which are inexpensive to eliminate."

It would be extraordinary for Congress, by use of the single word "significantly," to transmogrify a statute that assigns responsibility on the basis of amounts of pollutants emitted into a statute authorizing EPA to reduce interstate pollution in the manner that it believes most efficient. We have repeatedly said that Congress "does not alter the fundamental details of a regulatory scheme in vague terms or ancillary provisions ... it does not, one might say, hide elephants in mouseholes." *Whitman v. American Trucking Assn., Inc.*, 531 U.S. 457, 468 ....

The Good Neighbor Provision is one of the requirements with which SIPs must comply. § 7410 (a) (2) (D) (i) (I). The statutory structure [of the *Clean Air Act*] ... plainly demands that EPA afford States a meaningful opportunity to allocate reduction responsibilities among the sources within their borders. But the majority holds that EPA may in effect force the States to guess at what those responsibilities might be by requiring them to submit SIPs before learning what the Agency regards as a "significan[t]" contribution — with the consequence of losing their regulatory primacy if they guess wrong ....

The majority attempts to place the blame for hollowing out the core of the Clean Air Act on "the Act's plain text." The first textual element to which it refers is § 7410(c)'s requirement that after EPA has disapproved of a SIP, it "shall promulgate a [FIP] at any time within 2 years." That is to say, the Agency has discretion whether to act at once or to defer action until some later point during the 2-year period. But it also has discretion to work within the prescribed timetable to respect the rightful role of States in the statutory scheme by delaying the issuance or enforcement of FIPs pending the resubmission and approval of SIPs—as EPA's conduct surrounding CAIR clearly demonstrates. And all of this assumes that the Agency insists on disapproving SIPs before promulgating the applicable good-neighbor standards—though in fact EPA has discretion to publicize those metrics before the window to submit SIPs closes in the first place.

Notes and Questions

1. As you read in the excerpt, EPA's initial attempt to deal with interstate movement of air pollutants, The Clean Air Interstate Rule (CAIR), a regional emissions trading program, was struck down but remained in effect pending the long battle over the rule at issue in this case. In July 2011 the EPA finalized and began to implement the Cross-State Air Pollution Rule, aka the Transport Rule, but a few months later the D.C. Circuit stayed the new rule pending judicial review. As a result, in January 2012 the EPA reinstated CAIR, so the applicable rule was bouncing back and forth. After the Supreme Court's decision upholding the Transport Rule in this case, the Transport Rule finally went into effect in 2015.

2. *American Trucking* held that cost could not be a factor in setting the NAAQS. How would you distinguish this case, in which costs may be considered? What role does the stage of decision-making (standard setting being risk assessment and the Transport Rule being an approach to risk management) play in your analysis?

IV. Hazardous Air Pollutant Standards

The Clean Air Act Amendments of 1990 established a fresh, comprehensive approach to the regulation of hazardous air pollutants (HAPs, also known as air toxics) that are not criteria pollutants. This approach reflected congressional concern that the risk-based strategy regarding those pollutants contained in previous versions of the Act was dilatory and unworkable, and that unregulated toxic air pollution poses a significant public health problem. Indeed, the pollutants regulated under this program are the most dangerous—causing cancers, birth defects, etc.—even in relatively small concentrations. Unlike criteria pollutants, for which the states implement their own implementation programs to attain the EPA-set NAAQS, HAP controls are directly enforced by the EPA.

To avoid partial, piecemeal regulation, the legislation includes a list of 189 specific toxic substances that are presumed to require stringent control. This list must be reviewed by EPA periodically and, where appropriate, added to, when an unlisted pollutant is found to present a threat of adverse effects on human health or the environment. In addition, "any person" is permitted to petition the agency for the addition (or deletion) of particular hazardous substances from the statutory list, on the ground that those substances do (or do not) cause adverse effects. In the first quarter-century of the program the EPA has made four amendments to the list—three deletions and one addition, resulting in a present list of 187 HAPs.

The statute directs the EPA to publish a list of all categories and subcategories of "major sources" of the toxic substances that were specifically identified in the statute. Major sources are defined as sources that are within a contiguous area, under common control, and that emit (or have the potential to emit, in the aggregate) at least 10 tons per year of any hazardous pollutant or 25 tons per year or more of any combination of hazardous air pollutants. Sources too small to meet this definition are referred to as "area sources."

Major sources

The agency also must list all categories and subcategories of area sources of hazardous substances. These sources—which must include 90 percent of the area source emissions of the 30 hazardous area pollutants presenting the greatest threat to public health in urban areas—are subject to emission standards less stringent than the standards that apply to major sources. However, EPA has the discretion to apply the same standard to area sources if it chooses to do so.

Area Sources

Once the EPA has listed categories and subcategories of sources of toxic pollutants, the agency is responsible for establishing technology-based emissions standards for each such category or subcategory, with respect to both new and existing sources. The standards are to be based upon the maximum achievable control technology (MACT) for major sources, although the EPA has discretion to be more stringent. With respect to new sources, they must reflect the emission control that is achieved in practice by the best controlled similar sources. And where a new major source of hazardous pollutants is modified, constructed, or reconstructed before EPA has issued a relevant MACT standard, the permitting authority for the state in which the source is located must determine MACT for the facility on a case-by-case basis. The EPA may choose to apply MACT to all or may allow area sources to use "generally available control technologies" (GACT).

Focus on emissions standards, doesn't cite specific technology to use] gives industry flexibility in developing their own methods to reduce emissions

The Act establishes a timetable, spread over a 10-year period, that the EPA had to adhere to in establishing MACT standards for the categories and subcategories of sources it has identified. These standards may provide for control measures that include the pretreatment of industrial, commercial, and residential discharges that cause emissions of hazardous air pollutants. They may also include process or product substitutions or limitations that may be effective in reducing such emissions, as well as uniform sampling, modeling, and risk assessment methods.

Once a MACT standard has been established by the EPA with respect to a new source, no person or entity may operate such a source in violation of that standard. Existing sources, in contrast, must comply with MACT standard compliance schedules, to be established by the EPA. Those schedules must provide for compliance "as expeditiously as practicable, but in no event later than three years after the effective date of such standard." In addition, the statute provides that where the agency has failed to promulgate a MACT standard in a timely manner, with respect to a hazardous air pollutant subject to regulation, the EPA, or the state, must determine MACT or its equivalent, on a case-by-case basis, when it issues a permit for the emission of the pollutant in question.

MACT standards are at the crux of the Clean Air Act's regulatory scheme for controlling hazardous air pollutants. However, the legislation does not rely entirely on those technology-based limitations. It also requires the EPA to study, and report to Congress, within six years, on any public health risks that will remain once MACT standards have been implemented, and on "technologically and commercially available methods and costs of reducing such risks." Moreover, if Congress chooses not to act on any recommendation for legislation contained in the EPA's report, the agency is authorized to set additional standards for major sources that will protect the public health with "an ample margin of safety." If promulgated, those standards must reduce lifetime excess cancer risks, to the individual most exposed to the hazardous pollutants in question, to less than one in one million.

Finally, to implement its various emission requirements and other standards regarding hazardous air pollutants, the Act permits each state to develop a program and submit it to the EPA for approval. The agency may approve such a program, and delegate its responsibility for regulating hazardous air pollutants to the state, where certain statutory requirements are satisfied. However, when and where such a delegation is made, the agency will retain its independent authority to enforce hazardous air pollutant standards and requirements.

Notably, the current Clean Air Act approach to the control of hazardous air pollutants was preceded by a set of health-based standards, established for individual pollutants from specific sources, that were referred to as National Emissions Standards for Hazardous Air Pollutants (NESHAPS). *See generally* 40 CFR part 61. A number of these NESHAPS regulations have retained their importance and are actively enforced. For example, violations of the national emission standard for asbestos demolition and renovation—which requires that that asbestos be handled using specific workplace techniques—have been the basis for numerous criminal enforcement cases brought by EPA and the U.S. Department of Justice. *See* 40 CFR § 61.145(c)(2).

National Mining Association v. United States Environmental Protection Agency
59 F.3d 1351 (D.C. Cir. 1995)

PER CURIAM:

This is a petition for review of an order of the Environmental Protection Agency implementing the 1990 amendments to § 112 of the Clean Air Act. Petitioners are General Electric Company and four trade associations: (1) National Mining Association, which represents companies that produce metal, coal, and minerals, and that manufacture mining equipment; (2) American Forest and Paper Association, which represents companies that make pulp, paper, paperboard, and solid wood; (3) Chemical Manufacturers Association, which represents companies that manufacture industrial chemicals; and (4) American Petroleum Institute, which represents companies engaged in the petroleum industry. . . .

In 1990, as part of its comprehensive overhaul of the Clean Air Act, Congress revised § 112 of the Act, which regulates emissions of hazardous air pollutants. Dissatisfied with EPA's health-based regulation of hazardous air pollutants under the 1970 program, Congress replaced this approach with a detailed, technology-based regulatory scheme. The 1990 amendments to § 112 establish an initial list, which EPA may periodically revise, of 189 hazardous air pollutants. EPA must publish a list of "categories and subcategories" of "major sources" and certain "area sources" that emit these pollutants. For each listed "category or subcategory of major sources and area sources" of hazardous air pollutants, § 112(d) of the Act directs EPA to promulgate emission standards.

Under the Act, "major sources" of hazardous air pollutants are potentially subject to stricter regulatory control than are "area sources." For example, major sources must comply with the technology-based emission standards requiring the maximum degree of reduction in emissions EPA deems achievable, often referred to as "maximum achievable control technology" or MACT standards. In order to obtain an operating permit under title V of the Act, major sources must comply with extensive monitoring, reporting and record-keeping requirements. Further, § 112(g) generally conditions the modification, construction or reconstruction of a major source on the source's meeting MACT emission limitations.

"Area sources" of hazardous air pollutants are not necessarily subject to such stringent regulation. EPA need not list all "categories and subcategories" of area sources, and it does not have to establish emission standards for unlisted area sources. For listed area sources, EPA may choose to promulgate emission standards requiring only "generally available control technologies or management policies." These standards can be less rigorous than those required for major sources. . . . Area sources are not subject to title V permitting requirements or to § 112(g)'s restrictions on modification, construction and reconstruction of their facilities.

In July 1992, pursuant to § 112(c)(1), EPA published an initial list of categories of sources that emit hazardous air pollutants, and almost seventeen months later, it published a schedule for promulgation of emission standards for these listed source categories, as required by § 112(c). In August 1993, in order to "eliminate the need to repeat general information and requirements within each [emission] standard," EPA proposed a rule codifying the "procedures and criteria needed to implement" emission standards for hazardous air pollutants. It promulgated a final rule, which is the subject of this dispute, adopting these general provisions on March 16, 1994.

Among other things, the general provisions rule implements § 112(a)(1)'s definition of "major source." The rule defines "major source" in terms nearly identical to those in § 112(a)(1) of the Clean Air Act:

> Major source means any stationary source or group of stationary sources located within a contiguous area and under common control that emits or has the potential to emit considering controls, in the aggregate, 10 tons per year or more of any hazardous air pollutant or 25 tons per year or more of any combination of hazardous air pollutants, unless the Administrator

establishes a lesser quantity, or in the case of radionuclides, different criteria from those specified in this sentence . . . .

General Electric and National Mining Association. . . . maintain that EPA may not, in determining whether a site is a major source, include emissions from all facilities on a contiguous plant site under common control. These petitioners assert that, for purposes of major source determinations, EPA may aggregate emissions from different facilities on a contiguous plant site under common control only when the facilities fall within a similar industrial classification. . . .

In the preamble to the final rule, EPA made clear that in determining whether a source is major, emissions from all sources of hazardous air pollutants within a plant site must be aggregated, so long as the sources are geographically adjacent and under common control. As a result, if the total annual emissions of hazardous air pollutants from a plant site exceed the designated thresholds, each source emitting pollutants at the site must comply with the stricter MACT emission standards applicable to sources under § 112(d)(2), and with other requirements applicable to major sources. . . .

Under petitioners' theories, it is possible that only some of a site's sources would have to comply with the regulatory requirements applicable to major sources, including the stricter emission limitations of § 112(d)(2). Other sources of hazardous air pollutants would be regarded as area sources, possibly subject to less stringent emission standards or to none at all. 42 U.S.C. § 7412(c)(5) . . . .

EPA rejected petitioners' methods of implementing "major source." With respect to General Electric's source category definition, EPA acknowledged that "[m]ore than one source category on the EPA's source category list may be represented within a plant that is a major source" of hazardous air pollutants, as is the case for a large chemical manufacturing complex. Congress intended, according to EPA, "that all portions of a major source be subject to MACT [emission standards] regardless of the number of source categories into which the facility is divided." "Thus, the EPA will set one or more MACT standards for a major source, and sources within that major source will be covered by the standard(s), regardless of whether, when standing alone, each one of those regulated sources would be major." . . .

If § 112(a)(1) is viewed in isolation, EPA's reading of the provision is not simply consistent with the provision; it is nearly compelled by the statutory language. Section 112(a)(1) states that a "group of stationary sources" need meet only three conditions to be termed a "major source": (1) sources within the group must be "located within a contiguous area"; (2) they must be "under common control"; and (3) in the aggregate, they must emit, or, considering controls, have the potential to emit 10 or more tons per year of a single hazardous air pollutant or 25 or more tons per year of any combination of hazardous air pollutants. Section 112(a)(1) says nothing about combining emissions only from sources within the same source categories or SIC Codes. In this respect, EPA's definition of "major source," set forth in the preamble to the final rule, is faithful to the language of § 112(a)(1). . . .

[I]n determining whether a source is to be categorized as a "major source" of emissions (or by default, an "area" source), EPA was directed by Congress to calculate the amount of hazardous air pollutants a stationary source "emits or has the potential to emit *considering controls*." Clean Air Act § 112(a)(1). In its final rule, EPA defined a source's "potential to emit" as its "maximum capacity . . . to emit a pollutant under its physical and operational design." To comply with the statutory directive to "consider controls" while determining emissions capacities, the rule also provides:

> Any physical or operational limitation on the capacity of the stationary source to emit a pollutant, including air pollution control equipment and restrictions on hours of operations or on the type or amount or material combusted, stored, or processed, shall be treated as part of its design *if the limitation or the effect it would have on emissions is federally enforceable.* (emphasis added).

Under the rule, a control is deemed to be "federally enforceable" if it is "enforceable by the Administrator and citizens under the Act or . . . under other statutes administered by the Administrator."

Petitioner Chemical Manufacturers Association argues that this restrictive definition—which disregards emissions limitations imposed by state or local regulations not deemed "federally enforceable"—is contrary to the language of § 112(a)(1) of the Act. The government contends that since the word "controls" is not defined in the statute, it was open to EPA under *Chevron* to define the term, and it has done so reasonably. *See Chevron U.S. Inc. v. Natural Resources Defense Council, Inc.* According to petitioners, even if *Chevron* Step II is to be reached—because the statute does not reveal a specific congressional intent—we should conclude that EPA's construction of "controls" is impermissible. . . .

[I]t is certainly permissible for EPA to have refused to take into account ineffective controls (indeed, it is likely that a contrary interpretation would be impermissible). But is it also open to EPA under the statute to refuse to consider controls on grounds other than their lack of effectiveness? To qualify as "federally enforceable," (as best we can determine) controls are required, in addition to being effective as a practical matter, to have been approved by EPA and integrated into the state implementation plan, or SIP, drawn up by each state to enforce substantive restrictions under the Clean Air Act and submitted to the Administrator for approval under § 110. Once included within the SIP, a state control becomes enforceable not only by the state which is its primary regulating authority, but also by the Administrator under § 113 of Act, and, in certain settings, by private citizens, who can bring suit for noncompliance with federal pollution control programs under § 304.

EPA has identified several state and local regulatory approaches through which states can impose restraints and have them deemed "federally enforceable." Constraints imposed upon a source under a state operating permit, for example, will be deemed "federally enforceable" if the state program has been approved as a "federally enforceable state operating permit program," or FESOPP, by EPA. A state permitting program cannot stand alone: it must be incorporated into the SIP, must impose upon sources a legal obligation to observe the permit constraints, must be enforceable as a practical matter — *i.e.*, must be "effective" — must not be inconsistent with other requirements under the SIP or federal law, and must be issued pursuant to a public hearing process." . . .

EPA has proposed conditions for achieving "federal enforceability" that go beyond the mere effectiveness of particular constraint as a practical matter. Inclusion in the SIP, for example, is required in each instance even though EPA's own approach suggests that it is a consideration independent of and in addition to the need that a constraint be effective for it to count towards reductions. There may, moreover, be regulatory techniques in addition to those that EPA deems susceptible to "federal enforceability" that are equally effective, and yet which are foreclosed as mechanisms for reducing a source's capacity to emit as a result of EPA's approach.

What EPA has not explained is how its refusal to consider limitations other than those that are "federally enforceable" serves the statute's directive to "consider controls" when it results in a refusal to credit controls imposed by a state or locality even if they are unquestionably effective. Under EPA's regime, even a state program of unassailable effectiveness would not qualify in computing a source's capacity to emit unless it has been submitted not only for EPA approval, but also for inclusion in the SIP. In so doing, EPA would sacrifice a statutory objective in pursuit of ends that, at least as presented in argument to us, have not been justified, either in terms of § 112 or other provisions of the Act. EPA has not explained why it is essential that a control be included within a SIP. It is not apparent why a state's or locality's controls, when demonstrably effective, should not be credited in determining whether a source subject to those controls should be classified as a major or area source. . . .

In sum, EPA's definition of "major source" without respect to source categories or two-digit SIC codes is reasonable, as is its requirement that fugitive emissions be included in a source's aggregate emissions in determining whether the source is major. We therefore deny the petition for review with respect to these issues, advanced here by petitioners General Electric, National Mining Association and American Forest and Paper Association. However, EPA has not explained why the criteria for federal approval and the consequences of that approval are related to ensuring the practical effectiveness of state controls such that the set of controls considered under § 112 should be limited in that fashion. We therefore grant the petition for review with respect to the challenge raised by Chemical Manufacturers' Association and American Petroleum Institute.

Notes and Questions

1. National Mining is a good example of the many cases in the field of environmental law that deal with definitions generally, and who meets them specifically. Definitions and categories are extremely consequential. What would have happened if the court had ruled the other way in this case?

2. If you are wondering what all this means for your own health and safety, the EPA maintains a useful website titled National Air Toxics Assessment, or NATA. It provides up-to-date emissions data and related health risks by geographic area, focusing on 33 pollutants that pose the greatest risk to public health both due to their toxicity and due to population density where they are prevalent. *See* https://www.epa.gov /national-air-toxics-assessment.

3. The determination in *National Mining* that the EPA may determine whether a source is major based on its overall emissions, regardless of how many source categories it falls into, is frankly the most practical and sensible approach, even if it hadn't been so clear from the statute. Categorization of sources and categorization as major or not are based on two completely different implementation concerns. Source categorization is all about determining the appropriate technological standard to apply — it is entirely about the technological makeup of the source. The distinction between major and area sources, in contrast, is all about the quantity of emissions going into the air. These categorizations are thus unrelated.

Michigan v. Environmental Protection Agency
135 S. Ct. 2699 (2015)

Justice SCALIA:

The Clean Air Act directs the Environmental Protection Agency to regulate emissions of hazardous air pollutants from power plants if the Agency finds regulation "appropriate and necessary." We must decide whether it was reasonable for EPA to refuse to consider cost when making this finding.

The Clean Air Act establishes a series of regulatory programs to control air pollution from stationary sources (such as refineries and factories) and moving sources (such as cars and airplanes). One of these is the National Emissions Standards for Hazardous Air Pollutants Program — the hazardous-air-pollutants program, for short. . . .

Congress established a unique procedure to determine the applicability of the program to fossil-fuel-fired power plants. The Act refers to these plants as electric utility steam generating units, but we will simply call them power plants. Quite apart from the hazardous-air-pollutants program, the Clean Air Act Amendments of 1990 subjected power plants to various regulatory requirements. The parties agree that these requirements were expected to have the collateral effect of reducing power plants' emissions of hazardous air pollutants, although the extent of the reduction was unclear. Congress directed the Agency to "perform a study of the hazards to public health reasonably anticipated to occur as a result of emissions by [power plants] of [hazardous air pollutants] after imposition of the requirements of this chapter." § 7412(n)(1)(A). If the Agency "finds . . . regulation is appropriate and necessary after considering the results of the study," it "shall regulate [power plants] under [§ 7412]." . . .

EPA must first divide sources covered by the program into categories and subcategories in accordance with statutory criteria. § 7412(c)(1). For each category or subcategory, the Agency must promulgate certain minimum emission regulations, known as floor standards. § 7412(d)(1)(3). The statute generally calibrates the floor standards to reflect the emissions limitations already achieved by the best-performing 12% of sources within the category or subcategory. § 7412(d)(3). In some circumstances, the Agency may also impose more stringent emissions regulations, known as beyond-the-floor standards. The statute expressly requires the Agency to consider cost (alongside other specified factors) when imposing beyond-the-floor standards. § 7412(d)(2).

EPA . . . concluded that regulation of coal-and oil-fired power plants was "appropriate and necessary" in 2000. In 2012, it reaffirmed the appropriate-and-necessary finding, divided power plants into subcategories, and promulgated floor standards. The Agency found regulation "appropriate" because (1) power plants' emissions of mercury and other hazardous air pollutants posed risks to human health and the environment and (2) controls were available to reduce these emissions. It found regulation "necessary" because the imposition of the Act's other requirements did not eliminate these risks. EPA concluded that "costs should not be considered" when deciding whether power plants should be regulated under § 7412.

In accordance with Executive Order, the Agency issued a "Regulatory Impact Analysis" alongside its regulation. This analysis estimated that the regulation would force power plants to bear costs of $9.6 billion per year. The Agency could not fully quantify the benefits of reducing power plants' emissions of hazardous air pollutants; to the extent it could, it estimated that these benefits were worth $4 to $6 million per year. The costs to power plants were thus between 1,600 and 2,400 times as great as the quantifiable benefits from reduced emissions of hazardous air pollutants. The Agency continued that its regulation would have ancillary benefits—including cutting power plants' emissions of particulate matter and sulfur dioxide, substances that are not covered by the hazardous-air-pollutants program. Although the Agency's appropriate-and-necessary finding did not rest on these ancillary effects, the regulatory impact analysis took them into account, increasing the Agency's estimate of the quantifiable benefits of its regulation to $37 to $90 billion per year. EPA concedes that the regulatory impact analysis "played no role" in its appropriate-and-necessary finding.

Petitioners (who include 23 States) sought review of EPA's rule in the Court of Appeals for the D.C. Circuit. As relevant here, they challenged the Agency's refusal to consider cost when deciding whether to regulate power plants. The Court of Appeals upheld the Agency's decision not to consider cost, with Judge Kavanaugh concurring in part and dissenting in part.

Federal administrative agencies are required to engage in "reasoned decision making." Not only must an agency's decreed result be within the scope of its lawful authority, but the process by which it reaches that result must be "logical and rational." It follows that agency action is lawful only if it rests "on a consideration of the relevant factors."

EPA's decision to regulate power plants under § 7412 allowed the Agency to reduce power plants' emissions of hazardous air pollutants and thus to improve public health and the environment. But the decision also ultimately cost power plants, according to the Agency's own estimate, nearly $10 billion a year. EPA refused to consider whether

Cost to industry outweigh benefits to health & environment

the costs of its decision outweighed the benefits. The Agency gave cost no thought *at all*, because it considered cost irrelevant to its initial decision to regulate.

EPA's disregard of cost rested on its interpretation of §7412(n)(1)(A), which, to repeat, directs the Agency to regulate power plants if it "finds such regulation is appropriate and necessary." The Agency accepts that it *could* have interpreted this provision to mean that cost is relevant to the decision to add power plants to the program. But it chose to read the statute to mean that cost makes no difference to the initial decision to regulate.

We review this interpretation under the standard set out in *Chevron U.S.A. Inc. v. Natural Resources Defense Council, Inc. Chevron* directs courts to accept an agency's reasonable resolution of an ambiguity in a statute that the agency administers. Even under this deferential standard, however, "agencies must operate within the bounds of reasonable interpretation." EPA strayed far beyond these bounds when it read §7412 (n)(1) to mean that it could ignore cost when deciding whether to regulate power plants.

The Clean Air Act treats power plants differently from other sources for purposes of the hazardous-air-pollutants program. Elsewhere in §7412, Congress established cabined criteria for EPA to apply when deciding whether to include sources in the program. It required the Agency to regulate sources whose emissions exceed specified numerical thresholds (major sources). It also required the Agency to regulate sources whose emissions fall short of these thresholds (area sources) if they "presen[t] a threat of adverse effects to human health or the environment . . . warranting regulation." §7412(c)(3). In stark contrast, Congress instructed EPA to add power plants to the program If (but only if) the Agency finds regulation "appropriate and necessary." §7412(n)(1)(A). One does not need to open up a dictionary in order to realize the capaciousness of this phrase. In particular "appropriate" is "the classic broad and all-encompassing term that naturally and traditionally includes consideration of all the relevant factors." Although this term leaves agencies with flexibility, an agency may not "entirely fai[l] to consider an important aspect of the problem" when deciding whether regulation is appropriate.

Read naturally in the present context, the phrase "appropriate and necessary" requires at least some attention to cost. One would not say that it is even rational, never mind "appropriate," to impose billions of dollars in economic costs in return for a few dollars in health or environmental benefits. In addition, "cost" includes more than the expense of complying with regulations; any disadvantage could be termed a cost. EPA's interpretation precludes the Agency from considering *any* type of cost—including, for instance, harms that regulation might do to human health or the environment. The Government concedes that if the Agency were to find that emissions from power plants do damage to human health, but that the technologies needed to eliminate these emissions do even more damage to human health, it would *still* deem regulation appropriate. No regulation is "appropriate" if it does significantly more harm than good.

There are undoubtedly settings in which the phrase "appropriate and necessary" does not encompass cost. But this is not one of them. Section 7412(n)(1)(A) directs

EPA to determine whether "*regulation* is appropriate and necessary." (Emphasis added.) Agencies have long treated cost as a centrally relevant factor when deciding whether to regulate. Consideration of cost reflects the understanding that reasonable regulation ordinarily requires paying attention to the advantages and the disadvantages of agency decisions. It also reflects the reality that "too much wasteful expenditure devoted to one problem may well mean considerably fewer resources available to deal effectively with other (perhaps more serious) problems." Against the backdrop of this established administrative practice, it is unreasonable to read an instruction to an administrative agency to determine whether "regulation is appropriate and necessary" as an invitation to ignore cost. . . .

EPA identifies a handful of reasons to interpret § 7412(n)(1)(A) to mean that cost is irrelevant to the initial decision to regulate. We find those reasons unpersuasive.

EPA points out that other parts of the Clean Air Act expressly mention cost, while § 7412(n)(1)(A) does not. But this observation shows only that § 7412(n)(1)(A)'s broad reference to appropriateness encompasses *multiple* relevant factors (which include but are not limited to cost); other provisions' specific references to cost encompass just cost. It is unreasonable to infer that, by expressly making cost relevant to other decisions, the Act implicitly makes cost irrelevant to the appropriateness of regulating power plants. . . .

Along similar lines, EPA seeks support in this Court's decision in *Whitman v. American Trucking Assns, Inc.* There, the Court addressed a provision of the Clean Air Act requiring EPA to set ambient air quality standards at levels "requisite to protect the public health" with an "adequate margin of safety." 42 U.S.C. § 7904(b). Read naturally, that discrete criterion does not encompass cost; it encompasses health and safety. The Court refused to read that provision as carrying with it an implicit authorization to consider cost, in part because authority to consider cost had "elsewhere, and so often, been expressly granted." *American Trucking* thus establishes the modest principle that where the Clean Air Act expressly directs EPA to regulate on the basis of a factor that on its face does not include cost, the Act normally should not be read as implicitly allowing the Agency to consider cost anyway. That principle has no application here. "Appropriate and necessary" is a far more comprehensive criterion than "requisite to protect the public health;" read fairly and in context, as we have explained, the term plainly subsumes consideration of cost.

Turning to the mechanics of the hazardous-air-pollutants program, EPA argues that it need not consider cost when first deciding *whether* to regulate power plants because it can consider cost later when deciding *how much* to regulate them. The question before us, however, is the meaning of the "appropriate and necessary" standard that governs the initial decision to regulate. And as we have discussed, context establishes that this expansive standard encompasses cost. Cost may become relevant again at a later stage of the regulatory process, but that possibility does not establish its irrelevance at *this* stage. . . .

EPA argues that the Clean Air Act makes cost irrelevant to the initial decision to regulate sources other than power plants. The Agency claims that it is reasonable to interpret § 7412(n)(1)(A) in a way that "harmonizes" the program's treatment of power plants with its treatment of other sources. This line of reasoning overlooks the whole point of having a separate provision about power plants: treating power plants *differently* from other stationary sources. Congress crafted narrow standards for EPA to apply when deciding whether to regulate other sources; in general, these standards concern the volume of pollution emitted by the source, § 7412(c)(1), and the threat posed by the source "to human health or the environment." § 7412(c)(3). But Congress wrote the provision before us more expansively, directing the Agency to regulate power plants if "appropriate and necessary." That congressional election settles this case. [The Agency's] preference for symmetry cannot trump an asymmetrical statute." . . .

[F]or what it is worth, the dissent vastly overstates the influence of cost at later stages of the regulatory process. . . . All in all, the dissent has at most shown that some elements of the regulatory scheme mitigate cost in limited ways; it has not shown that these elements ensure cost-effectiveness . . . .

Our reasoning so far establishes that it was unreasonable for EPA to read § 7412(n)(1)(A) to mean that cost is irrelevant to the initial decision to regulate power plants. The Agency must consider cost—including, most importantly, cost of compliance—before deciding whether regulation is appropriate and necessary. We need not and do not hold that the law unambiguously required the Agency, when making this preliminary estimate, to conduct a formal cost-benefit analysis in which each advantage and disadvantage is assigned a monetary value. It will be up to the Agency to decide (as always, within the limits of reasonable interpretation) how to account for cost. . . .

We hold that EPA interpreted § 7412(n)(1)(A) unreasonably when it deemed cost irrelevant to the decision to regulate power plants. . . .

Justice THOMAS, concurring:

The Environmental Protection Agency (EPA) asks the Court to defer to its interpretation of the phrase "appropriate and necessary" in § 112(n)(1)(A) of the Clean Air Act, 42 U.S.C. § 7412. Justice Scalia's opinion for the Court demonstrates why EPA's interpretation deserves no deference under our precedents. I write separately to note that its request for deference raises serious questions about the constitutionality of our broader practice of deferring to agency interpretations of federal statutes. *See Chevron U.S.A. Inc. v. Natural Resources Defense Council, Inc.*, 467 U.S. 837 (1984). . . .

As I have explained elsewhere, "[T]he judicial power, as originally understood, requires a court to exercise its independent judgment in interpreting and expounding upon the laws." Interpreting federal statutes—including ambiguous ones administered by an agency—"calls for that exercise of independent judgment." *Chevron* deference precludes judges from exercising that judgment, forcing them to abandon what they believe is "the best reading of an ambiguous statute" in favor of an agency's construction. It thus wrests from Courts the ultimate interpretative authority to "say what the law is," *Marbury v. Madison*, and hands it over to the Executive. . . .

In reality, as the Court illustrates in the course of dismantling EPA's interpretation of §112(n)(1)(A), agencies "interpreting" ambiguous statutes typically are not engaged in acts of interpretation at all. Instead, as *Chevron* itself acknowledged, they are engaged in the "formulation of policy." Statutory ambiguity thus becomes an implicit delegation of rule-making authority, and that authority is used not to find the best meaning of the text, but to formulate legally binding rules to fill in gaps based on policy judgments made by the agency rather than Congress. . . .

Justice KAGAN, dissenting:

The Environmental Protection Agency placed emissions limits on coal and oil power plants following a lengthy regulatory process during which the Agency carefully considered costs. At the outset, EPA determined that regulating plants' emissions of hazardous air pollutants is "appropriate and necessary" given the harm they cause, and explained that it would take costs into account in developing suitable emissions standards. Next, EPA divided power plants into groups based on technological and other characteristics bearing significantly on their cost structures. It required plants in each group to match the emissions levels already achieved by the best-performing reflecting those plants' own cost analyses. EPA then adopted a host of measures designed to make compliance with its proposed emissions limits less costly for plants that needed to catch up with their cleaner peers. And with only one narrow exception, EPA decided not to impose any more stringent standards (beyond what some plants had already achieved on their own) because it found that doing so would not be cost-effective. After all that, EPA conducted a formal cost-benefit study which found that the quantifiable benefits of its regulation would exceed the costs up to nine times over — by as much as $80 billion each year. Those benefits include as many as 11,000 fewer premature deaths annually, along with a far greater number of avoided illnesses.

Despite that exhaustive consideration of costs, the Court strikes down EPA's rule on the ground that the Agency "unreasonably . . . deemed cost irrelevant." On the majority's theory, the rule is invalid because EPA did not explicitly analyze costs at the very first stage of the regulatory process, when making its "appropriate and necessary" finding. And that is so even though EPA later took costs into account again and again and . . . so on. The majority thinks entirely immaterial, and so entirely ignores, all the subsequent times and ways EPA considered costs in deciding what any regulation would look like.

That is a peculiarly blinkered way for a court to assess the lawfulness of an agency's rulemaking. I agree with the majority — let there be no doubt about this — that EPA's power plant regulation would be unreasonable if "[t]he Agency gave cost no thought *at all*." But that is just not what happened here. Over more than a decade, EPA took costs into account at multiple stages and through multiple means as it set emissions limits for power plants. And when making its initial "appropriate and necessary" finding, EPA knew it would do exactly that — knew it would thoroughly consider the cost-effectiveness of emissions standards later on. That context matters. The Agency acted well within its authority in declining to consider costs at the opening bell of the regulatory process given that it would do so in every round thereafter—and given that the emissions limits finally issued would depend crucially on those accountings. Indeed, EPA could not have measured costs at the process's initial stage with any accuracy. And the regulatory path EPA chose parallels the one it has trod in setting emissions limits, at Congress's explicit direction, for every other source of hazardous air pollutants over two decades. The majority's decision that EPA cannot take the same approach here—its micromanagement of EPA's rulemaking, based on little more than the word "appropriate"—runs counter to Congress's allocation of authority between the Agency and the courts. Because EPA reasonably found that it was "appropriate" to decline to analyze costs at a single stage of a regulatory proceeding otherwise imbued with cost concerns, I respectfully dissent. . . .

Cost is almost always a relevant—and usually, a highly important—factor in regulation. Unless Congress provides otherwise, an agency acts unreasonably in establishing "a standard-setting process that ignore[s] economic considerations." . . . Absent contrary indication from Congress an agency must take into account in some manner before imposing significant regulatory burdens.

That proposition, however, does not decide the issue before us because the "appropriate and necessary" finding was only the beginning. At that stage, EPA knew that a lengthy rulemaking process lay ahead of it; the determination of emissions limits was still years away. And the Agency, in making its kick-off finding, explicitly noted that consideration of costs would follow: "As a part of developing a regulation" that would impose those limits, "the effectiveness and costs of controls will be examined." Likewise, EPA explained that, in the course of writing its regulation, it would explore regulatory approaches "allowing for least-cost solutions." That means the Agency, when making its "appropriate and necessary" finding, did not decline to consider costs as part of the regulatory process. Rather, it declined to consider costs at a single stage of that process, knowing that they would come in later on.

The only issue in these cases, then, is whether EPA acted reasonably in structuring its regulatory process in that way—in making its "appropriate and necessary finding" based on pollution's harmful effects and channeling cost considerations to phases of the rulemaking in which emission levels are actually set. Said otherwise, the question is not whether EPA can reasonably find it "appropriate" to regulate without thinking about costs, full stop. It cannot, and it did not. Rather, the question is whether EPA can reasonably find it "appropriate" to trigger the regulatory process based on harms (and technological feasibility) alone, given that costs will come into play, in multiple ways and at multiple stages, before any emission limit goes into effect.

In considering that question, the very nature of the word "appropriate" matters. "[T]e word 'appropriate,'" this Court has recognized, "is inherently context-dependent." Giving it context requires paying attention to the surrounding circumstances. . . . The statutory language, in other words, is a directive to remove one's blinders and view things whole—to consider what it is fitting to do at the threshold stage, given what will happen at every other.

And that instruction is primarily given to EPA, not to courts: Judges may interfere only if the Agency's way of ordering its regulatory process is unreasonable—i.e., something Congress would never have allowed. The question here, as in our seminal case directing courts to defer to agency interpretations of their own statutes, arises "not in a sterile textual vacuum, but in the context of implementing policy decisions in a technical and complex arena." *Chevron U.S.A. Inc. v. Natural Resources Defense Council, Inc.* EPA's experience and expertise in that arena—and courts' lack of those attributes—demand that judicial review proceed with caution and care. The majority actually phrases this principle well, though honors it only in the breach. . . .

[O]ur decision here properly rests on something the majority thinks irrelevant: an understanding of the full regulatory process relating to power plants and of EPA's reasons for considering costs only after making its initial "appropriate and necessary" finding. . . .

In the years after its "appropriate and necessary" finding, EPA made good on its promise to account for costs "[a]s a part of developing a regulation." For more than a decade, as EPA deliberated on and then set emissions limits, costs came into the calculus at nearly every turn. Reflecting that consideration, EPA's final role noted that steps taken during the regulatory process had focused on "flexib[ility] and cost-effective[ness]" and had succeeded in making "the rule less costly and compliance more readily manageable." And the regulation concluded that "the benefits of th[e] rule" to public health and the environment "far outweigh the costs." . . .

Costs matter in regulation. But when Congress does not say how to take costs into account, agencies have broad discretion to make that judgment. . . . Far more than courts, agencies have the expertise and experience necessary to design regulatory processes suited to "a technical and complex arena." *Chevron*, 467 U.S., at 863. And in any event, Congress has entrusted such matters to them, not to us.

EPA exercised that authority reasonably and responsibly in setting emissions standards for power plants. The Agency treated those plants just as it had more than 100 other industrial sources of hazardous air pollutants, at Congress's direction and with significant success. . . . That approach is wholly consistent with the statutory scheme. Its adoption was "up to the Agency to decide."

The majority arrives at a different conclusion only by disregarding most of EPA's regulatory process. It insists that EPA must consider costs—when EPA did just that, over and over and over again. It concedes the importance of "context" in determining what the "appropriate and necessary" standard mean—and then ignores every aspect of the rulemaking context in which that standard play a part. The result is a decision that deprives the Agency of the latitude Congress gave it to design an emissions-setting process sensibly accounting for costs and benefits alike. And the result is a decision that deprives the American public of the pollution control measures that the responsible Agency, acting well within its delegated authority, found would save many, many lives. I respectfully dissent.

Notes and Questions

1. *Michigan v. EPA* is still a relatively new case, so its broader ramifications have yet to become clear, Nonetheless, one can see a step back in deference more substantial than usual. What might this analysis mean for *Chevron* deference? Note that the Court finds ambiguity in the statute, so the case is decided at *Chevron* step two, meaning that the EPA's interpretation of its discretion is not reasonable. While the majority and dissent agree on the idea that costs should be considered at some point, the majority delves into the weeds, finding fault with *when* and *how* the EPA does so — fault great enough to fail *Chevron* step two reasonableness. This is not a routine outcome. Does this case signal a scaling back of *Chevron* deference? If so, what are some of the impacts this might have on agency functioning?

2. Is *Michigan v. EPA* consistent with *American Trucking*? How do this question and analysis differ from the comparison between *American Trucking* and *EME Homer*?

3. The holding in *Michigan v. EPA*, while certainly having doctrinal impact, had little practical impact on the matter at hand. A few months later the EPA issued a "supplemental finding," stating that it had considered costs and doing so did not alter its decision to regulate toxic air pollution from power plants. The EPA weighed the costs of compliance (including the impact on consumer prices) against the devastating health effects of the poison emissions and corresponding healthcare costs.

V. Requirements that Apply to New Air Pollution Sources

Stationary sources of air pollutants are potentially subject to several sets of emissions standards. They must meet applicable New Source Performance Standards (NSPS). Moreover, major sources of criteria pollutants in designated non-attainment areas must satisfy New Source Review (NSR) requirements. And air pollution sources in attainment areas are obligated to comply with Prevention of Significant Deterioration (PSD) standards — a topic we will consider separately *infra*.

The Clean Air Act directs EPA to publish (and from time to time revise) a list of categories of stationary sources that cause, or contribute significantly to, air pollution that may reasonably be anticipated to endanger public health or welfare. Following that, the agency must propose and promulgate "standards of performance" for listed source categories that reflect "the degree of emission limitation achievable through the application of the best system of emission reduction which (taking into account the cost of achieving such reduction and any non-air quality health or environmental impact and energy requirements) the [EPA] Administrator determines has been adequately demonstrated."

In establishing these NSPS, the EPA was required to comply with a six-year timetable set forth in the 1990 Clean Air Act Amendments. It was authorized to distinguish among classes, types, and sizes within categories of new sources, for standard-setting purposes. In addition, the agency was allowed to promulgate design, equipment, work practice, or operational standards, of equivalent stringency, where it concluded that standards of performance could not feasibly be prescribed or enforced. The agency has carried out the statute's mandate by publishing, in the *Federal Register*, specific standards that apply only to certain stationary source categories (such as pulp and paper mills, electroplating facilities, municipal waste incinerators, and the like).

New and modified sources of criteria pollutants in nonattainment areas are subject to another, more stringent, set of limitations, often referred to as "new source review." To the extent that such sources are "major stationary sources," as defined by the statute, they must satisfy the technology-based standards that reflect the "lowest achievable emission rate" (LAER). This is defined in the Act as the most stringent achievable emission limit contained in the implementation plan of any state for the class or category of source in question, or any more stringent emission limitation that is achieved in practice for that source class or category.

New major stationary sources in nonattainment areas must also comply with "emission offset" requirements. These are legally enforceable reductions in emissions from other sources in the same nonattainment area, above and beyond any reductions that would otherwise be mandated for those other sources. Offsets can result from the shutdown of those other sources or from the use of very advanced control techniques to mitigate emissions from them.

Owners or operators of proposed new or modified sources in nonattainment areas must demonstrate that all major stationary sources that they own or operate within the same state are in compliance, or on a schedule for compliance, with all applicable Clean Air Act emission limitations. Finally, they must perform an analysis of the proposed source, and of alternative sites, sizes, production processes, and environmental control techniques, which must show that "the benefits of the proposed source significantly outweigh the environmental and social costs imposed as a result of its location, construction, or modification."

Given the more stringent standards applicable to new or modified sources, defining the class is extremely important. Definitions are controversial throughout environmental law, as they so frequently determine whether and how each entity will be regulated. How to determine whether a source is "new or modified" is an excellent example of this phenomenon, and is demonstrated nicely in the following cases.

ASARCO, Inc. v. EPA

578 F.2d 319 (D.C. Cir 1978)

Judge WRIGHT:

These cases involve challenges by ASARCO Incorporated, Newmont Mining Corporation, and Magma Copper Company (hereinafter referred to collectively as ASARCO) and the Sierra Club (Sierra) to regulations issued by the Environmental Protection Agency (EPA). The challenged provisions modify previous regulations implementing § 111 of the Clean Air Act, which mandates national emission standards for new stationary sources of air pollution, by introducing a limited form of what the parties call the "bubble concept." . . .

The New Source Performance Standards (NSPSs) established under § 111 are designed to force new sources to employ the best demonstrated systems of emission reduction. Since the NSPSs are likely to be stricter than emission standards under State Implementation Plans, plant operators have an incentive to avoid application of the NSPSs.

The basic controversy in the cases before us concerns the determination of the units to which the NSPSs apply. Under the Act the NSPSs apply to "new sources." A "new source" is defined as "any stationary source, the construction or modification of which" begins after the NSPS covering that type of source is published. § 111(a)(2). Further statutory definitions explain the terms used in this [provision]. A "stationary source" means any building, structure, facility, or installation which emits or may emit any air pollutant." § 111(a)(3). A "modification" means "any physical change in, or change in the method of operation of, a stationary source which increases the amount of any air pollutant emitted by such source or which results in the emission of any air pollutant not previously emitted." § 111(a)(4). The statute thus directs that the NSPSs are to apply to any building, structure, facility, or installation which emits or may emit any air pollutant and which is either (1) newly constructed or (2) physically or operationally changed in such a way that *its* emission of any air pollutant increases.

The "bubble concept" is based on defining a *stationary source* as a *combination* of facilities, such as an *entire plant,* and applying the NSPSs only when a new *plant* is constructed or when an existing *plant* is physically or operationally changed in such a way that *net* emissions of any pollutant form the *entire plant* increase. If applied consistently, the bubble concept would allow the operator of an existing plant to avoid application of the strict NSPSs by offsetting any increase in pollution caused by a change in the plant (*e.g.*, modification or replacement of an existing facility, or even addition of a new facility) against a decrease in pollution from other units within the plant as a whole. . . .

EPA's original regulations interpreting § 111, promulgated in 1971, repeated the statutory definitions of "stationary source" and "modification" almost word for word and did not contain any version of the "bubble concept." . . .

The new regulations would classify an entire plant as a single stationary source by embellishing the statutory definition of a stationary source as follows:

"Stationary source" means any building, structure, facility, or installation which emits or may emit any air pollutant *and which contains any one or combination of the following:*

(1)   Affected facilities.

(2)   Existing facilities.

(3)   Facilities of the type for which no standards have been promulgated in this part.

The italicized language is not included in the statutory definition of "stationary source' ("any building, structure, facility, or installation which emits or may emit any air pollutant"), nor was it included in the prior regulations. Thus the present regulations, instead of limiting the definition of "stationary source" to one "facility" as the statute does, make it cover "any one or combination of" facilities. The preamble to the new regulations makes it clear that the purpose of this change is to define a statutory source as an entire plant.

Relying on this new definition of a statutory source, EPA applies the bubble concept to allow a plant operator who alters an existing facility in a way that increases its emissions to avoid application of the NSPSs by decreasing emissions from other facilities within the plant. The regulations provide that "[a] modification shall not be deemed to occur" unless the change in an existing facility results in a net increase in the emission of a pollutant from the whole "source." ...

[T]he new regulations do not consistently apply the bubble concept to treat an entire plant as a single stationary source. EPA continues to apply NSPSs to all *newly constructed* facilities, even when the emission increases from the new facilities are off-set by emission decreases from other facilities in the same plant. Newly constructed facilities are thus treated as independent stationary sources. In order to draw a line defining when the bubble concept will be applied, the regulations classify any changes in existing facilities that cost more than a fixed percentage of the value of the changed facility as "reconstruction." "Reconstructed" facilities, like new facilities, are subject to NSPSs regardless of whether emissions from the plant of which they are a part increase.

In its petition for review ASARCO argues that the bubble concept must be applied to allow emission increases from reconstruction and new construction to be offset. Sierra [Club] argues that the Act defines a "source" as an *individual* facility, as distinguished from a combination of facilities such as a plant, and that the bubble concept must therefore be rejected *in toto*. For the reasons stated below we agree with Sierra and remand to EPA for further proceedings consistent with this opinion.

The Sierra Club's basic contention is that the new regulations are inconsistent with the plain language of Section 111. The statute defines a *stationary source* as "any building, structure, *facility*, or installation which emits or may emit any air pollutant." § 111(a)(3) (emphasis added). In contrast, the new regulations define stationary source to include "any ... *combination* of ... facilities. ..." (emphasis added).

This change in the definition of a stationary source is essential to EPA's adoption of the bubble concept. By treating a combination of facilities as a single source, the regulations allow a facility whose emissions are increased by alterations to avoid complying with the applicable NSPS as long as emission decreases from other facilities within the same "source" cancel out the increase from the altered facility. Sierra argues forcefully that this result is incompatible with the statute's mandate that NSPSs should be applied to "*any* structure, building, facility, or installation" that undergoes "any physical change ... or ... change in the method of operation ... which increases the amount of any air pollutant emitted by such [structure, building, facility, or installation]."

EPA responds that the "broad" statutory definition of *stationary source* gives it "discretion" to define a *stationary source* as either a single facility or a combination of facilities. We find this response unpersuasive. The regulations plainly indicate that EPA has attempted to change the basic unit to which the NSPSs apply from a *single* building, structure, facility, or installation—the unit prescribed in the statute—to a *combination* of such units. The agency has no authority to rewrite the statute in this fashion.

Our conclusion that the regulations incorporating the bubble concept must be rejected as inconsistent with the language of the Act is reinforced when we consider the purpose of the Clean Air Act and § 111, the confusion generated by the present regulations, and the weakness of EPA's arguments in favor of the bubble concept.

"[T]he goal of the Clean Air Act," as EPA admits in its brief, "is to *enhance* air quality and not merely to *maintain* it." § 111's provisions mandating New Source Performance Standards were passed because Congress feared that the system of state plans designed to keep air pollution below nationally determined levels, was insufficient by itself to achieve the goal of protecting and *improving* air quality. The New Source Performance Standards are designed to enhance air quality by forcing all newly constructed *or modified* buildings, structures, facilities, or installations to employ pollution control systems that will limit emissions to the level "achievable through application of the best technological system of continuous emission reduction which . . . the Administrator determines has been adequately demonstrated." The bubble concept in the challenged regulations would undercut § 111 by allowing operators to avoid installing the best pollution control technology on an altered facility as long as the emissions from the entire plant do not increase. For example, under the bubble concept an operator who alters one of its facilities so that its emission of some pollutant increases might avoid application of the NSPS by simultaneously equipping other plant facilities with additional, but inferior, pollution control technology or merely reducing their production. Applying the bubble concept thus postpones the time when the best technology must be employed and at best maintains the present level of emissions. . . .

EPA's main argument in support of its regulations is that its version of the bubble concept is necessary to provide flexibility in applying the NSPSs to modified facilities because the cost of bringing *existing* facilities into compliance with NSPSs is allegedly much greater than the cost of bringing *new* facilities into compliance. This argument does not survive analysis. . . . The record does not indicate why more flexibility than this is necessary or even appropriate. Even if flexibility were a problem, the statute itself allows for cost considerations to be taken into account in setting NSPSs. . . .

We therefore agree with the Sierra Club that EPA's regulations incorporating the bubble concept are inconsistent with the language and purpose of the statute and cannot be justified by any alleged need for flexibility. . . .

Notes and Questions

1. Why do you think Congress chose to regulate new sources differently from existing sources? If you think about it in terms of new sources creating new pollution, it is easier to understand the position held by the industry side in *ASARCO*. And, of course, this is an important factor, as well as one that is targeted by the offset requirements discussed in *CARE v. EPA* below. However, when looking at the more stringent technology requirements, it is easy to see another reason to apply these only to new sources: because during construction is when it is most economical to do so. It is far easier to ask that new construction utilize the best design than to ask existing plants to redo their design. Of course, that does happen even with the less challenging tech standards for existing sources, but is less onerous than LAER, as well as resulting in fewer total plants having to make changes. When thinking of it this way, the bubbling approach becomes less palatable — one would expect anyone engaged in new construction at any level within their plant to use the best technology in doing so.

2. A couple of years after this decision was handed down, Ronald Reagan was elected president and quickly opted to switch gears on this issue of the bubble policy for plants in nonattainment areas. The EPA issued new regulations permitting this approach, and the Natural Resources Defense Council immediately challenged it, based on concern that it was not appropriate to allow plants in nonattainment areas to upgrade their equipment without simultaneously bringing it up to date with regard to emissions-reducing technology. It was this challenge that resulted in the most famous Administrative Law opinion in Supreme Court history, *Chevron U.S.A., Inc. v. Natural Resources Defense Council*, 467 U.S. 837 (1984). *See* Chapter 2 at page 52.

Environmental Defense v. Duke Energy Corporation
549 U.S. 561 (2007)

Justice SOUTER:

In the 1970s, Congress added two air pollution control schemes to the Clean Air Act: New Source Performance Standards (NSPS) and Prevention of Significant Deterioration (PSD), each of them covering modified, as well as new, stationary sources of air pollution. The NSPS provisions define the term "modification," 42 U.S.C. § 7411(a)(4), while the PSD provisions use that word "as defined in" NSPS, § 7479(2)(C). The Court of Appeals concluded that the statute requires the Environmental Protection Agency (EPA) to conform its PSD regulations on "modification" to their NSPS counterparts, and that EPA's 1980 PSD regulations can be given this conforming construction . . . .

The Clean Air Amendments of 1970 broadened federal authority to combat air pollution, *see Chevron U.S.A., Inc. v. Natural Resources Defense Council, Inc.*, 467 U.S. 837, 845–846 (1984), and directed EPA to devise National Ambient Air Quality Standards

(NAAQS) limiting various pollutants, which the States were obliged to implement and enforce. The amendments dealing with NSPS authorized EPA to require operators of stationary sources of air pollutants to use the best technology for limiting pollution, both in newly constructed sources and those undergoing "modification." § 111(a) of the 1970 amendments defined this term within the NSPS scheme as "any physical change in, or change in the method of operation of, a stationary source which increases the amount of any air pollutant emitted by such source or which results in the emission of any air pollutant not previously emitted."

EPA's 1975 regulations implementing NSPS provided generally that "any physical or operational change to an existing facility which results in an increase in the emission rate to the atmosphere of any pollutant to which a standard applies shall be considered a modification within the meaning of § 111." (Especially significant here is the identification of an NSPS "modification" as a change that "increase(s) . . . the emission rate," which "shall be expressed as kg/hr of any pollutant discharged into the atmosphere."

NSPS, however, did too little to "achiev(e) the ambitious goals of the 1970 Amendments" and the Clean Air Act Amendments of 1977 included the PSD provisions, which aimed at giving added protection to air quality in certain parts of the country "notwithstanding attainment and maintenance of" the NAAQS. The 1977 amendments required a PSD permit before a "major emitting facility" could be "constructed" in an area covered by the scheme. As originally enacted, PSD applied only to newly constructed sources, but soon a technical amendment added the following subparagraph: "The term 'construction' when used in connection with any source or facility, includes the modification (as defined in § 111(a)) of any source or facility." 42 U.S.C. § 7479(2)(C). In other words, the "construction" requiring a PSD permit under the statute was made to include (though it was not limited to) a "modification" as defined in the statutory NSPS provisions.

In 1980, EPA issued PSD regulations, which "limited the application of [PSD] review" of modified sources to instances of "'major' modification[n]," defined as "any physical change in or change in the method of operation of a major stationary source that would result in a significant net emissions increase of any pollution subject to regulation under the Act." Further regulations in turn addressed various elements of this definition, three of which are to the point here. First, the regulations specified that an operational change consisting merely of "[a]n increase in the hours of operation or in the production rate" would not generally constitute a "physical change or change in the method of operation." For purposes of a PSD permit, that is, such an operational change would not amount to a "modification" as the Act defines it. Second, the PSD regulations defined a "net emissions increase" as "[a]ny increase in actual emissions from a particular physical change or change in the method of operation," net of other contemporaneous "increases and decreases in actual emissions at the source." "Actual emissions" were defined to "equal the average rate, in tons per year, at which the unit actually emitted the pollutant during a two-year period which precedes the particular date and which is representative of normal source operation."

"[A]ctual emissions" were to be "calculated using the unit's actual operating hours [and] production rates." Third, the term "significant" was defined as "a rate of emissions that would equal or exceed" one or another enumerated threshold, each expressed in "tons per year."

It would be bold to try to synthesize these statutory and regulatory provisions in a concise paragraph, but three points are relatively clear about the regime that covers this case:

(a) The Act defines modification of a stationary source of a pollutant as a physical change to it, or a change in the method of the operation, that increases the amount of a pollutant discharged or emits a new one.

(b) EPA's NSPS regulations require a source to use the best available pollution-limiting technology only when a modification would increase the rate of discharge of pollutants measured in kilograms per hour.

(c) EPA's 1980 PSD regulations require a permit for a modification (with the same statutory definition) only when a modification would increase the actual annual emission of a pollutant above the actual average for the two prior years.

The Court of Appeals held that Congress's provision defining a PSD modification by reference to an NSPS modification caught not only the statutory NSPS definition, but also whatever regulatory gloss EPA puts on that definition of any given time (for the purpose of the best technology requirement). When, therefore, EPA's PSD regulations specify the "change" that amounts to a "major modification" requiring a PSD permit, they must measure an increase in "the amount of any air pollutant emitted," in terms of the hourly rate of discharge, just the way NSPS regulations do. Petitioners and the United States say, on the contrary, that when EPA addresses the object of the PSD scheme it is free to put a different regulatory interpretation on the common statutory core of "modification," by the actual, annual discharge of a pollutant that will follow the modification, regardless of rate per hour. This disagreement is the nub of the case.

Respondent Duke Energy Corporation runs 30 coal-fired electric generating units at eight plans in North and South Carolina. The units were placed in service between 1940 and 1975, and each includes a boiler containing thousands of steel tubes arranged in sets. Between 1988 and 2000, Duke replaced or redesigned 29 tube assemblies in order to extend the life of the units and allow them to run longer each day.

The United States filed this action in 2000, claiming, among other things, that Duke violated the PSD provisions by doing this work without permits. Environmental Defense, North Carolina Sierra Club, and North Carolina Public Interest Research Group Citizen Lobby/Education Fund intervened as plaintiffs and filed a complaint charging similar violations.

Duke moved for summary judgment, one of the positions being that none of the projects was a "major modification" requiring a PSD permit because none increased hourly rates of emissions. The District Court agreed with Duke's reading of the 1980 PSD regulations . . . .

The Court of Appeals for the Fourth Circuit affirmed, "albeit for somewhat different reasons." "[T]he language and various interpretations of the PSD regulations . . . are largely irrelevant to the proper analysis of the case," reasoned the Court of Appeals, "because Congress' decision to create identical statutory definitions of the term 'modification'" in the NSPS and PSD provisions of the Clean Air Act "has affirmatively mandated that this term be interpreted identically" in the regulations promulgated under those provisions . . . .

Supreme Court decision

We granted the petition for certiorari brought by intervenor-plaintiffs, and now vacate . . . .

In applying the 1980 PSD regulations to Duke's conduct, the Court of Appeals thought that, by defining the term "modification" identically in its NSPS and PSD provisions, the Act required EPA to conform its PSD interpretation of that definition to any such interpretation it reasonably adhered to under NSPS. But principles of statutory construction are not so rigid. Although we presume that the same term has the same meaning when it occurs here and there in a single statute, the Court of Appeals mischaracterized that presumption as "effectively irrebuttable." We also understand that "[m]ost words have different shades of meaning and consequently may be variously construed, not only when they occur in different statutes, but when used more than once in the same statute or even in the same section." Thus, the "natural presumption that identical words used in different parts of the same act are intended to have the same meaning . . . is not rigid and readily yields whenever there is such variation in the connection in which the words are used as reasonably to warrant the conclusion that they were employed in different parts of the act with different intent." A given term in the same statute may take on distinct characters from association with distinct statutory objects calling for different implementation strategies . . . .

It is true that the Clean Air Act did not merely repeat the term "modification" or the same definition of that word in its NSPS and PSD sections; the PSD language referred back to the section defining "modification" for NSPS purposes, 42 U.S.C. §7479(2)(C). However, nothing to the text or the legislative history of the technical amendment that added the cross-reference to NSPS suggests that Congress had details of regulatory implementation in mind when it imposed PSD requirements on modified sources; the cross-reference alone is certainly no unambiguous congressional code for eliminating the customary agency discretion to resolve questions about a statutory definition by looking to the surroundings of the defined term, where it occurs. Absent any iron rule to ignore the reasons for regulating PSD and NSPS "modifications" differently, EPA's construction need do no more than fall within the limits of what is reasonable, as set by the Act's common definition.

The Court of Appeals' reasoning that the PSD regulations must conform to their NSPS counterparts led the court to read those PSD regulations in a way that seems to us too far a stretch for the language used. The 1980 PSD regulations on "modification" simply cannot be taken to track the agency's regulatory definition under the NSPS . . . .

We think (the Court of Appeals') understanding of the 1980 PSD regulations makes the mistake of overlooking the difference between the two separate components of the regulatory definition of "major modification": [1] any physical change in or change in the method of operation of a major stationary source that [2] would result in a significant net emissions increase of any pollutant subject to regulation under the Act.

The exclusion of "increase in . . . hours . . . or . . . production rate," speaks to the first of these components ("physical change . . . or change in . . . method," but not to the second ("significant net emissions increase.") As the preamble to the 1980 PSD regulations explains, forcing companies to obtain a PSD permit before they could simply adjust operating hours "would severely and unduly hamper the ability of any company to take advantage of favorable market conditions." In other words, a mere increase in the hours of operation, standing alone, is not a "physical change or change in the method of operation."

In sum, the text of the 1980 PSD regulations on "modification" doomed the Court of Appeals' attempt to equate those regulations with their NSPS counterpart. . . .

Justice THOMAS, concurring in part:

. . . I write separately to note my disagreement with the dicta in that portion of the opinion, which states that the statutory cross-reference does not mandate a singular regulatory construction.

The Prevention of Significant Deterioration (PSD) statute explicitly links the definition of the term "modification" to that term's definition in the New Source Performance Standards (NSPS) statute:

> "The term 'construction' when used in connection with any source or facility, includes the modification (as defined in section 7411(a) of this title) of any source or facility."

Section 7411(a) contains the NSPS definition of "modification," which the parties agree is the relevant statutory definition of the term for both PSD and NSPS. Because of the cross-reference, the definitions of "modification" in PSD and NSPS are one and the same. The term "modification" therefore has the same meaning despite contextual variations in the two admittedly different statutory schemes. Congress' explicit linkage of PSD's definition of "modification" to NSPS' prevents the Environmental Protection Agency (EPA) from adopting differing regulatory definitions of "modification" for PSD and NSPS.

Even if the cross-reference were merely the equivalent of repeating the words of the definition, we must still apply our usual presumption that the same words repeated in different parts of the same statute have the same meaning. That presumption has not been overcome here. While the broadly stated regulatory goals of PSD and NSPS differ, these contextual differences do not compel different definitions of "modification." . . . EPA demonstrated as much when it recently proposed regulations that would unify the regulatory definitions of "modification."

The majority opinion does little to overcome the presumption that the same words, when repeated, carry the same meaning. Instead, it explains that this Court's cases do not compel identical language to be interpreted identically in all situations. Granting that point, the majority still has the burden of stating why our general presumption does not control the outcome here. It has not done so.

Notes and Questions

1. Why should the EPA treat this issue differently in the context of PSD areas than it does in nonattainment areas? Do you agree with this approach? If you would prefer a single approach, would it be hourly or annual?

2. This was a unanimous Supreme Court decision, which means it had the support of both conservative and liberal justices. Many cases dealing with environmental laws have split the court. What do you think made this case different, substantively speaking? Note that the lower courts had both gone the other way.

3. The *Duke Energy* case represents a lengthy saga stretching from an initial complaint filed in 2000 to a consent decree entered in September 2015. As a result, most of the violating plants have been shut down permanently. The settlement saves 51,000 tons per year in emissions, as that was the amount emitted in 2000 by the 13 plants in the settlement, which are now emitting zero. The deal also required Duke to spend at least $4.4 million on environmental mitigation projects, in a range of areas, including Forest Service, National Parks, and funding of projects supporting development of electric vehicles, energy efficiency, and clean energy. To top it all off, Duke Energy paid civil penalties totaling $975,000. Violating EPA regulations should not be undertaken lightly.

[handwritten margin note: EPA was correct]

Citizens Against the Refinery's Effects, Inc. v. United States Environmental Protection Agency

643 F.2d 183 (4th Cir. 1981)

Judge HALL:

Citizens Against the Refinery's Effects (CARE) appeals from a final ruling by the Administrator of the Environmental Protection Agency (EPA) approving the Virginia State Implementation Plan (SIP) for reducing hydrocarbon pollutants. The plan requires the Virginia Highway Department to decrease usage of a certain type of asphalt, thereby reducing hydrocarbon pollution by more than enough to offset expected pollution from the Hampton Roads Energy Company's (HREC) proposed refinery. We affirm the action of the administration in approving the state plan. *[handwritten: decision]*

The Clean Air Act established National Ambient Air Quality Standards (NAAQS) for five major air pollutants. The EPA has divided each state into Air Quality Control Regions (AQCRs) and monitors each region to assure that the national standard for each pollutant is met. Where the standard has not been attained for a certain pollutant, the state must develop a State Implementation Plan designed to bring the area

[handwritten margin note: VA SIP]

into attainment within a certain period. In addition, no new source of that pollutant may be constructed until the standard is attained.

The Clean Air Act created a no-growth environment in areas where the clean air requirements had not been attained. EPA recognized the need to develop a program that encouraged the need to develop a program that encouraged attainment of clean air standards without discouraging economic growth. Thus the agency proposed an Interpretive Ruling in 1976 which allowed the states to develop an "offset program" within the State Implementation Plans. The offset program, later codified by Congress in the 1977 Amendments to the Clean Air Act, permits the states to develop plans which allow construction of new pollution sources where accompanied by a corresponding reduction in an existing pollution source. In effect, a new emitting facility can be built if an existing pollution source decreases its emissions or ceases operations as long as a positive net air quality benefit occurs.

If the proposed factory will emit carbon monoxide, sulfur dioxide, or particulates, the EPA requires that the offsetting pollution source be within the immediate vicinity of the new plant. The other two pollutants, hydrocarbons and nitrogen oxide are less "site-specific," and thus the ruling permits the offsetting source to locate anywhere within a broad vicinity of the new source.

The offset program has two other important requirements. First, a base time period must be determined in which to calculate how much reduction is needed in existing pollutants to offset the new source. This base period is defined as the first year of the SIP or, where the state has not yet developed a SIP, as the year in which a construction permit application is filed. Second, the offset program requires that the new source adopt the Lowest Achievable Emissions Rate (LAER) using the most modern technology available in the industry.

HREC proposes to build a petroleum refinery and offloading facility in Portsmouth, Virginia. Portsmouth has been unable to reduce air pollution enough to attain the national standard for one pollutant, photochemical oxidants, which is created when hydrocarbons are released into the atmosphere and react with other substances. Since a refinery is a major source of hydrocarbons, the Clean Air Act prevents construction of the HREC plant until the area attains the national standard.

In 1975, HREC applied to the Virginia State Air Pollution Control Board (VSAPCB) for a refinery construction permit. The permit was issued . . . . The VSAPCB, in an effort to help HERC meet the clean air requirements, proposed to use the offset ruling to comply with the Clean Air Act.

On November 28, 1977, the VSAPCB submitted a State Implementation Plan to EPA which included the HREC permit. The Virginia Board proposed to offset the new HREC hydrocarbon pollution by reducing the amount of cutback asphalt used for road paving operations in three highway districts by the Virginia Department of Highways. By switching from "cutback" to "emulsified" asphalt, the state can reduce hydrocarbon pollutants by the amount necessary to offset the pollutants from the proposed refinery.

The EPA administrator . . . approved the Virginia offset plan on January 31, 1980.

Arguments/Issues

CARE raised four issues regarding the state plan. First, they argue that the geographic area used as the base for the offset was arbitrarily determined and that ① the area as defined violates the regulations. Second, CARE contends that EPA ② should have used 1975 instead of 1977 as the base year to compare usage of cutback asphalt. Third, CARE insists that the offset plan should have been disapproved since the ③ state is voluntarily reducing usage of cutback asphalt anyway. Fourth, CARE questions the approval of the plan without definite Lowest Achievable Emission Rates (LAER) as required by the statute. We reject the CARE challenges

Decision → to the state plan. *Supreme court rejects all 4 arguments*

[T]he standard of review here is whether the agency action was arbitrary, capricious, an abuse of discretion, or otherwise not in accordance with law.

Reasoning:

CARE contends that the state plan should not have been approved by EPA since the three highway-district area where cutback usage will be reduced to offset refinery emissions was artificially developed by the state. The ruling permits a broad area (usually within one AQCR) to be used as the offset basis. The ruling does not specify how *(R1)* to determine the area, nor provide a standard procedure for defining the geographic area . . . .

The agency action in approving the use of three highway districts was neither arbitrary, capricious, nor outside the statute. First, Congress intended that the states and the EPA be given flexibility in designing and implementing SIPs. Such flexibility allows the states to make reasoned choices as to which areas may be used to offset new pollution and how the plan is to be implemented. Second, the offset program was initiated to encourage economic growth in the state. Thus a state plan designed to reduce highway department pollution in order to attract another industry is a reasonable contribution to economic growth without a corresponding increase in pollution. Third, to be sensibly administered the offset plan had to be divided into districts which could be monitored by the highway department. Use of any areas other than highway districts would be unwieldy and difficult to administer. Fourth, the scientific understanding of ozone pollution is not advanced to the point where exact air transport may be predicted. Designation of the broad area in which hydrocarbons may be transported is well within the discretion and expertise of the agency.

Asphalt consumption varies greatly from year to year, depending upon weather and road conditions. Yet EPA must accurately determine the volume of hydrocarbon emissions from cutback asphalt. Only then can the agency determine whether the reduction in cutback usage will result in an offset great enough to account for the new refinery pollution. To calculate consumption of a material where it constantly varies, a base year must be selected. In this case, EPA's Interpretive Ruling established the base year as the year in which the permit application is made. EPA decided that 1977 was an acceptable base year. CARE argues that EPA illegally chose 1977 instead of 1975.

Considering all of the circumstances, including the unusually high asphalt consumption in 1977, the selection by EPA of that as the base year was within the discretion of the agency. Since the EPA Interpretive Ruling allowing the offset was not issued until 1976, 1977 was the first year after the offset ruling and the logical base year in which to calculate the offset. Also, the permit issued by the VSAPCB was reissued in 1977 with extensive additions and revisions after a full hearing. Under these circumstances, 1977 appears to be a logical choice of a base year.

For several years, Virginia has pursued a policy of shifting from cutback asphalt to the less expensive emulsified asphalt in road-paving operations. The policy was initiated in an effort to save money, and was totally unrelated to a State Implementation Plan. Because of this policy, CARE argues that hydrocarbon emissions were decreasing independent of this SIP and therefore are not a proper offset against the refinery. They argue that there is not, in effect, an actual reduction in pollution.

The Virginia voluntary plan is not enforceable and therefore is not in compliance with the 1976 Interpretive Ruling which requires that the offset program be enforceable. The EPA, in approving the state plan, obtained a letter from the Deputy Attorney General of Virginia in which he stated that the requisites had been satisfied for establishing and enforcing the plan with the Department of Highways. Without such authority, no decrease in asphalt-produced pollution is guaranteed. In contrast to the voluntary plan, the offset plan guarantees a reduction in pollution resulting from road-paving operations.

Finally, CARE argues that the Offset Plan does not provide adequate Lowest Achievable Emission Rates (LAER) as required by the 1976 Interpretive Ruling because the plan contains only a 90% vapor recovery requirement, places an excessive 176.5 ton limitation on hydrocarbon emissions, and does not require specific removal techniques at the terminal. EPA takes the position that the best technique available for marine terminals provides only a 90% recovery and that the 176.5 ton limit may be reduced by the agency after the final product mix at the terminal is determined.

Since the record shows no evidence of arbitrary or capricious action in approving the HREC emissions equipment, the agency determination of these technical matters must be upheld. . . .

In approving the state plan, EPA thoroughly examined the data, requested changes in the plan, and approved the plan only after the changes were made. There is no indication that the agency acted in an arbitrary or capricious manner or that it stepped beyond the bounds of the Clean Air Act. We affirm the decision of the administrator in approving the state plan.

Notes and Questions

1. *CARE v. EPA* reveals some of the potential pitfalls of designing an offset program. How might you do so? What issues might you need to plan ahead for? Take a moment to think about how you would draft offset regulations if it were up to you. Would you specify a distance limit, or use some other method of geographic outlining? How else would you limit what would qualify as an offset?

2. In *CARE v. EPA,* a state SIP is the source of controversy. The EPA was deferential to the state, and the court was deferential to the EPA, so the SIP survived in spite of the weaknesses CARE pointed out. The Clean Air Act is the classic example of cooperative federalism, in which Congress divides authority for implementing its legislation between the states and a federal agency, in this case the EPA. In this model, the states are encouraged to design implementation programs for the statute, following certain parameters and meeting certain standards. The federal agency is given both a broad oversight role (which includes design of standards the states must implement with their programs) and some programs to implement itself directly with the regulated entities (such as programs that lend themselves well to universal regulation approaches or those relating to interstate problems). Although states are often in a better position to determine which approaches to implementation will work best for their communities, there are also downsides to giving too much deference to states — downsides that ideally cooperative federalism would minimize via that federal oversight. States have many concerns to consider other than those that the statute is designed to address, which results in some scholars questioning the value of the SIP system, or at least of giving too much deference to SIPs. *See, e.g.,* Arnold W. Reitze, Jr., *Air Quality Protection Using State Implementation Plans — Thirty-Seven Years of Increasing Complexity,* 15 Vill. Envtl. L.J. 209 (2004).

Practice Problem

The City of Zavala, in southern New Lilliput, plans to construct a large incinerator in order to treat contaminated soils and groundwater from the neighboring Carson Air Force Base, which is scheduled to be closed next year. Engineering evaluations indicate that the incinerator has the potential to emit up to 165 tons of pollutants per year. However, that estimate assumes the incinerator will be operated 24 hours per day, 365 days per year — something the city mayor, in response to public concerns, promised would not happen. Pollutants that are expected to be emitted from incineration of the contaminated soils and groundwater include mercury, benzene, and trichloroethylene, in varying amounts.

In a rush toward construction of the incinerator, the City has been less than forthcoming with additional information about the incinerator project. Concerned citizens have heard something about a "Clean Air Act" and wonder if this law applies to this project. They thus engage you, hometown attorney with training in environmental law, to help them answer some important questions.

a.   Based upon the information provided above, does it appear that the incinerator construction requires a permit under the Clean Air Act? If so, what kind of permit, and who would be responsible for issuing this permit?

b.   If a permit is required under the Clean Air Act, what standards for technology would apply to the proposed incinerator?

VI. The Control of New Sources of Air Pollution in Clean Air Areas

Major new or modified sources of criteria pollutants in attainment areas—where existing air quality is better than the National Ambient Air Quality Standards (NAAQS)—are required to meet the involved requirements set forth in Part C of the Clean Air Act, regarding the prevention of significant deterioration of air quality (PSD). In general, these requirements are intended to protect public health and prevent any adverse effects that may occur from the introduction of air pollution notwithstanding the attainment and maintenance of NAAQS. They have several other expressed purposes, as well. Those include the preservation of air quality in national parks and other areas of natural or scenic value, and the promotion of economic growth in a manner consistent with preserving existing clean air resources. PSD standards apply mainly in rural areas where air quality exceeds the NAAQS.

In order to ascertain whether proposed or modified state or local air pollution sources in attainment areas are subject to PSD requirements, attorneys and officials must ascertain, from engineering estimates, the levels of criteria pollutants that these sources will theoretically have the potential to emit, if they are operated at full capacity without pollution controls. The Act defines "major emitting facilities," which are subject to PSD requirements, as stationary sources that appear on a list of types of sources contained in the statute, and that emit or have the potential to emit 100 tons per year or more of any pollutant. The term also includes any other (non-listed) sources with the potential to emit 250 tons per year or more of any air pollutant.

The Clean Air Act requires that the states classify their attainment areas into Classes I, II, or III. These are defined according to how pristine they are, in other words how far below the NAAQS their air quality falls, and are also referred to as PSD increments. These classifications differ with regard to the maximum amounts of increases in outdoor pollution that will be permitted, with Class I areas (the cleanest) receiving the most stringent protection and Class III areas allowing the greatest increases in air pollutant emissions over "baseline levels."

Facilities that plan to construct new (or modified) major emitting facilities in attainment areas must apply for "preconstruction permits" from EPA (or state) officials. Before beginning facility construction, or modification, they must also do the following:

1. Demonstrate that emissions from the construction or operation of the proposed new or modified facility will not cause or contribute to air pollution in excess of the NAAQS or any maximum allowable pollutant concentration for an area subject to PSD regulation (defined by increment);

2. Analyze the "air quality impact" of any growth that will be associated with the proposed facility;

3. Show that the facility will utilize the "best available control technology" (BACT) for each regulated pollutant it will emit; and

4. Agree to conduct whatever emissions self-monitoring as may be necessary to determine the effect of the facility's emissions on air quality.

Alaska Department of Environmental Conservation v. Environmental Protection Agency

540 U.S. 461 (2004)

Justice GINSBURG:

This case concerns the authority of the Environmental Protection Agency (EPA or Agency) to enforce the provisions of the Clean Air Act's (CAA or Act) Prevention of Significant Deterioration (PSD) program. Under that program, no major air pollutant emitting facility may be constructed unless the facility is equipped with "the best available control technology" (BACT). BACT, as defined in the CAA, means, for any major air pollutant emitting facility, "an emission limitation based on the maximum degree of [pollutant] reduction ... which the permitting authority, on a case-by-case basis, taking into account energy, environmental, and economic impacts and other costs, determines is achievable for [the] facility ...."

For Attainment Areas [handwritten margin note]

In the case before us, "the permitting authority" ... is the State of Alaska, acting through Alaska's Department of Environmental Conservation (ADEC). The question presented is what role EPA has with respect to ADEC's BACT determinations. Specifically, may EPA act to block construction of a new major pollutant emitting facility permitted by ADEC when EPA finds ADEC's BACT determination unreasonable in light of the guides [the statute] prescribes? We hold that the Act confers that checking authority on EPA ....

The PSD requirements, enacted as part of 1977 amendments to the Act ... "are designed to ensure that the air quality in attainment areas or areas that are already 'clean' will not degrade." ...

Northwest Alaska, the region this case concerns, is classified as an attainment or unclassifiable area for nitrogen dioxide. [T]herefore, the PSD program applies to emissions of that pollutant in the region.

Section 165 of the Act, installs a permitting requirement for any "major emitting facility," defined to include any source emitting more than 250 tons of nitrogen oxides per year. No such facility may be constructed or modified unless a permit prescribing emission limitations has been issued for the facility.... Modifications to major emitting facilities that increase nitrogen oxide emissions in excess of 40 tons per year require a PSD permit.

The Act sets out preconditions for the issuance of PSD permits. *Inter alia*, no PSD permit may issue unless "the proposed facility is subject to the best available control technology for each pollutant subject to [CAA] regulation ... emitted from ... [the] facility." As described in the Act's definitional provisions, "best available control technology" (BACT) means:

[A]n emission limitation based on the maximum degree of reduction of each pollutant subject to regulation under this chapter emitted from or which results from any major emitting facility, which the permitting authority, on a case-by-case basis, taking into account energy, environmental, and economic impacts and other costs, determines is achievable for such facility through application of production processes and available methods, systems, and techniques. . . . In no event shall application of 'best available control technology' result in emissions of any pollutants which will extend the emissions allowed by any applicable standard established pursuant to section 7411 or 7412 of this title [emission standards for new and existing stationary sources]. . . .

Alaska's SIP contains provisions that track the statutory BACT requirement and definition . . .

CAA also provides that a PSD permit may issue only if a source "will not cause, or contribute to, air pollution in excess of any . . . maximum allowable increase or maximum allowable concentration for any pollutant" or any NAAQS. . . .

Among measures EPA may take to ensure compliance with the PSD program, two have special relevance here. The first prescription, provides that "[w]henever, on the basis of any available information, [EPA] finds that a State is not acting in compliance with any requirement or prohibition of the chapter relating to the construction of new sources or the modification of existing sources," EPA may "issue an order prohibiting the construction or modification of any major stationary source in any area to which such requirement applies." The second measure, § 167 of the Act, trains on enforcement of the PSD program; it requires EPA to "take such measures, including issuance of an order, or seeking injunctive relief, as necessary to prevent the construction or modification of a major emitting facility which does not conform to the [PSD] requirements." . . .

Cominco Alaska, Inc. (Cominco), operates a zinc concentrate mine, the Red Dog Mine, in northwest Alaska approximately 100 miles north of the Arctic Circle and close to the native Alaskan villages of Kivalina and Noatak. The mine is the region's largest private employer. It supplies a quarter of the area's wage base. . . .

In 1988, Cominco obtained authorization to operate the mine, a "major emitting facility" under the Act and Alaska's SIP. The mine's PSD permit authorized five 5,000 kilowatt Wartsila diesel electric generators, MG-1 through MG-5, subject to operating restrictions; two of the five generators were permitted to operate only in standby status. Petitioner Alaska Department of Environmental Conservation (ADEC) issued a second PSD permit in 1994 allowing addition of a sixth full-time generator (MG-6), removing standby status from MG-2, and imposing a new operational cap that allowed all but one generator to run full time.

In 1996, Cominco initiated a project, with funding from the State, to expand zinc production by 40%. Anticipating that the project would increase nitrogen oxide emissions by more than 40 tons per year, Cominco applied to ADEC for a PSD permit to allow, *inter alia*, increased electricity generation by its standby generator, MG-5. On

March 3, 1999, ADEC preliminarily proposed as BACT for MG-5 the emission control technology known as selective catalyst reduction (SCR), which reduces nitrogen oxide emissions by 90%. In response, Cominco amended its application to add a seventh generator, MG-17, and to propose as BACT an alternative control technology—Low NOx—that achieves a 30% reduction in nitrogen oxide pollutants. . . .

Despite its staff's clear view "that SCR (the most effective individual technology) [was] technologically, environmentally, and economically feasible for the Red Dog power plant engines," ADEC endorsed the alternative proffered by Cominco. . . .

On the final day of the public comment period, July 2, 1999, the United States Department of the Interior, National Parks Service (NPS), submitted comments to ADEC. NPS objected to the projected offset of new emissions from MG-5 and MG-17 against emissions from other existing generators that were not subject to BACT. . . .

Following NPS's lead, EPA wrote to ADEC on July 29, 1999, commenting: "Although ADEC states in its analysis that [SCR], the most stringent level of control, is economically and technologically feasible, ADEC did not propose to require SCR. . . . [O]nce it is determined that an emission unit is subject to BACT, the PSD program does not allow the imposition of a limit that is less stringent than BACT." A permitting authority, EPA agreed with NPS, could not offset new emissions "by imposing new controls on other emission units" that were not subject to BACT. New emissions could be offset only against reduced emissions from sources covered by the same BACT authorization. EPA further agreed with NPS that, based on the existing information, BACT would be required for MG-1, MG-3, MG-4, and MG-5.

After receiving EPA comments, ADEC issued a second draft PSD permit and technical analysis report on September 1, 1998, again finding Low NOx to be BACT for MG-17. . . .

ADEC conceded that, lacking data from Cominco, it had made "no judgment . . . as to the impact of . . . . [SCR] on the operation, profitability, and competitiveness of the Red Dog Mine." Contradicting the May 1999 conclusion that SCR was "technically and economically feasible," ADEC found in September 1999 that SCR imposed "a disproportionate cost" on the mine. ADEC concluded, on a "cursory review," that requiring SCR for a rural Alaska utility would lead to a 20% price increase, and that in comparison with other BACT technologies, SCR came at a "significantly higher" cost. No economic basis for a comparison between the mine and a rural utility appeared in ADEC's technical analysis.

EPA protested the revised permit. . . .

On December 10, 1999, ADEC issued the final permit and technical analysis report. Once again, ADEC approved low NOx as BACT for MG-17 "[t]o support Cominco's Red Dog Mine Production Rate Increase Project, and its contribution to the region." . . .

The same day, December 10, 1999, EPA issued an order to ADEC, under §§ 113(a)(5) and 167 of the Act, 42 U.S.C. §§ 7413(a)(5) and 7477, prohibiting ADEC from issuing a PSD permit to Cominco "unless ADEC satisfactorily documents why SCR is not BACT for the Wartsila diesel generator [MG-17]." In the letter accompanying the order, the Agency stated that "ADEC's own analysis supports the determination that BACT is [SCR], and that ADEC's decision in the proposed permit therefore is both arbitrary and erroneous."

On February 8, 2000, EPA, again invoking its authority under §§ 113(a)(5) and 167 of the Act, issued a second order, this time prohibiting Cominco from beginning "construction or modification activities at the Red Dog Mine." A third order, issued on March 7, 2000, superseding and vacating the February 8 order, generally prohibited Cominco from acting on ADEC's December 10 PSD order but allowed limited summer construction. On April 25, 2000, EPA withdraw its December 10 order. Once ADEC issued the permit, EPA explained, that order lacked utility. On July 16, 2003, ADEC granted Cominco a PSD permit to construct MG-17 with SCR as BACT. Under the July 16, 2003 permit, SCR ceases to be BACT "if and when the case currently pending before the Supreme Court of the United States of America is decided in favor of the State of Alaska."

The day EPA issued its first order against Cominco, February 8, 2000, ADEC and Cominco petitioned the Court of Appeals for the Ninth Circuit for review of EPA's orders. . . . EPA had properly exercised its discretion in issuing the three orders, the Ninth Circuit ultimately determined, because (1) Cominco failed to "demonstrate[e] that SCR was economically infeasible," and (2) "ADEC failed to provide a reasoned justification for its elimination of SCR as a control option." We granted certiorari to resolve an important question of federal law, *i.e.*, the scope of EPA's authority under §§ 113(a)(5) and 167, and now affirm the Ninth Circuit's judgment.

Centrally at issue in this case is the question whether EPA's oversight role, described by Congress in CAA §§ 113(a)(5) and 167, extends to ensuring that a state permitting authority's BACT determination is reasonable in light of the statutory guides. Sections 113(a)(5) and 167 lodge in the Agency encompassing supervisory responsibility over the construction and modification of pollutant emitting facilities in areas covered by the PSD program. In notably capacious terms, Congress armed EPA with authority to issue orders stopping construction when "a State is not acting in compliance with any [CAA] requirement or prohibition . . . relating to the construction of new sources or the modification of existing sources," or when "construction or modification of a major emitting facility . . . does not conform to the requirements of [the PSD program]." . . .

All parties agree that one of the "many requirements in the PSD provisions that the EPA may enforce" is "that a [PSD] permit contain a BACT limitation." It is therefore undisputed that the Agency may issue an order to stop a facility's construction if a PSD permit contains no BACT designation.

EPA reads the Act's definition of BACT, together with CAA's explicit listing of BACT as a "[p]reconstruction requiremen[t]," to mandate not simply a BACT designation, but a determination of BACT faithful to the statute's definition. In keeping with the broad oversight role §§ 113(a)(5) and 167 vest in EPA, the Agency maintains, it may review permits to ensure that a State's BACT determination is reasonably moored to the Act's provisions. We hold, as elaborated below, that the Agency has rationally construed the Act's text and that EPA's construction warrants our respect and approbation.

BACT's statutory definition requires selection of an emission control technology that results in the "maximum" reduction of a pollutant "achievable for [a] facility" in view of "energy, environmental, and economic impacts, and other costs." This instruction, EPA submits, cabins state permitting authorities' discretion by granting only "authority to make *reasonable* BACT determinations," *i.e.*, decisions made with fidelity to the Act's purpose "to insure that economic growth will occur in a manner consistent with the preservation of existing clean air resources." Noting that state permitting authorities' statutory discretion is constrained by CAA's strong, normative terms "maximum" and "achievable," EPA reads §§ 113(a)(5) and 167 to empower the federal Agency to check a state agency's unreasonably lax BACT designation.

EPA stresses Congress' reason for enacting the PSD program — to prevent significant deterioration of air quality in clean-air areas within a State and in neighboring States. That aim, EPA urges, is unlikely to be realized absent an EPA surveillance role that extends to BACT determinations. . . .

Understandably, Congress entrusted state permitting authorities with initial responsibility to make BACT determinations "case-by-case." A state agency, no doubt, is best positioned to adjust for local differences in raw materials or plant configurations, differences that might make a technology "unavailable" in a particular area. But the fact that the relevant statutory guides — "maximum" pollution reduction, considerations of energy, environmental, and economic impacts — may not yield a "single, objectively 'correct' BACT determination," surely does not signify that there can be no *unreasonable* determinations. Nor does Congress' sensitivity to site-specific factors necessarily imply a design to preclude in this context meaningful EPA oversight under §§ 113(a)(5) and 167. EPA claims no prerogative to designate the correct BACT; the Agency asserts only the authority to guard against unreasonable designations. . . .

In sum, EPA interprets the Act to allow substantive federal Agency surveillance of state permitting authorities' BACT determinations subject to federal court review. We credit EPA's longstanding construction of the Act and confirm EPA's authority, pursuant to §§ 113(a)(5) and 167, to rule on the reasonableness of BACT decisions by state permitting authorities.

We turn finally, and more particularly, to the reasons why we conclude that EPA properly exercised its authority in this case. . . . Treating the case-specific issue as embraced within the sole question presented, we are satisfied that EPA did not act arbitrarily in finding that ADEC furnished no tenable accounting for its determination that Low NOx was BACT for MG-17.

Because the Act itself does not specify a standard for judicial review in this instance, we apply the familiar default standard of the Administrative Procedure Act, and ask whether the Agency's action was "arbitrary, capricious, an abuse of discretion, or otherwise not in accordance with law." Even when an agency explains its decision with "less than ideal clarity," a reviewing court will not upset the decision on that account "if the agency's path may reasonably be discerned." EPA's three skeletal orders to ADEC and Cominco surely are not composed with ideal clarity. These orders, however, are properly read together with accompanying explanatory correspondence from EPA; so read, the Agency's comments and orders adequately ground the determination that ADEC's acceptance of Low NOx for MG-17 was unreasonable given the facts ADEC found. . . .

We do not see how ADEC, having acknowledged that no determination "[could] be made as to the impact of [SCR's] cost on the operation . . . and competitiveness of the [mine]," could simultaneously proffer threats to the mine's operation or competitiveness as reasons for declaring SCR economically infeasible. ADEC, indeed, forthrightly explained why it was disarmed from reaching any judgment on whether, or to what extent, implementation of SCR would adversely affect the mine's operation or profitability: Cominco had declined to provide the relevant financial data, disputing the need for such information and citing "confidentiality" concerns[.] No record evidence suggests that the mine, were it to use SCR for its new generator, would be obliged to cut personnel, or raise zinc prizes. Absent evidence of that order, ADEC lacked cause for selecting Low NOx as BACT based on the more stringent control's impact on the mine's operation or competitiveness. . . .

Nor has ADEC otherwise justified its choice of Low NOx. . . .

In sum, we conclude that EPA has supervisory authority over the reasonableness of state permitting authorities' BACT determinations and may issue a stop construction order, under §§ 113(a)(5) and 167, if a BACT selection is not reasonable. We further conclude that, in exercising that authority, the Agency did not act arbitrarily or capriciously in finding that ADEC's BACT decision in this instance lacked evidentiary support. EPA's orders, therefore, were neither arbitrary nor capricious.

Justice KENNEDY dissenting:

The majority, in my respectful view, rests its holding on mistaken premises, for its reasoning conflicts with the express language of the Clean Air Act (CAA or Act), with sound rules of administrative law, and with principles that preserve the integrity of States in our federal system. The State of Alaska had in place procedures that were in full compliance with the governing statute and accompanying regulations promulgated by the Environmental Protection Agency (EPA). As I understand the opinion of the Court and the parties' submissions, there is no disagreement on this point. Alaska followed these procedures to determine the best available control technology (BACT). EPA, however, sought to overturn the State's decision, not by the process of judicial review, but by administrative fiat. The Court errs, in my judgment, by failing to hold that EPA, based on nothing more than its substantive disagreement with the State's discretionary judgment, exceeded its powers in setting aside Alaska's BACT determination.

The majority holds that, under the CAA, state agencies are vested with "initial responsibility for identifying BACT in line with the Act's definition of that term" and that EPA has a "broad oversight role" to ensure that a State's BACT determination is "reasonably moored to the Act's provisions." The statute, however, contemplates no such arrangement. It directs the "permitting authority"—here, the Alaska Department of Environmental Conservation (ADEC)—to "determine" what constitutes BACT. To "determine" is not simply to make an initial recommendation that can later be overturned. It is "[t]o decide or settle... conclusively and authoritatively." American Heritage Dictionary 495 (4th ed. 2000). Cf. 5 U. S. C. § 554 ("to be determined on the record after opportunity for an agency hearing") . . . .

When the statute is read as a whole, it is clear that the CAA commits BACT determinations to the discretion of the relevant permitting authorities. Unless an objecting party, including EPA, prevails on judicial review, the determinations are conclusive.

When Congress intends to give EPA general supervisory authority, it says so in clear terms. In addition to requiring EPA's advance approval of BACT determinations in some instances the statute grants EPA powers to block the construction or operation of polluting sources in circumstances not at issue here. Outside the context of the CAA, Congress likewise knows how to establish federal oversight in unambiguous language.42 U. S. C. § 1396a(a)(13)(A) (1994 ed.) No analogous language is used in the statutory definition of BACT.

EPA insists it needs oversight authority to prevent a "race to the bottom," where jurisdictions compete with each other to lower environmental standards to attract new industries and keep existing businesses within their borders. Whatever the merits of these arguments as a general matter, EPA's distrust of state agencies is inconsistent with the Act's clear mandate that States bear the primary role in controlling pollution and, here, the exclusive role in making BACT determinations. In "cho[osing] not to dictate a Federal response to balancing sometimes conflicting goals" at the expense of "[m]aximum flexibility and State discretion," Congress made the overriding judgment that States are more responsive to local conditions and can strike the right balance between preserving environmental quality and advancing competing objectives. By assigning certain functions to the States, Congress assumed they would have a stake in implementing the environmental objectives of the Act. At the same time, Congress charged EPA with setting ambient standards and enforcing emission limits, to ensure that the Nation takes the necessary steps to reduce air pollution.

There is a final deficiency in the scheme the majority finds in the statute. Nothing in the Court's analysis prevents EPA from issuing an order setting aside a BACT determination months, or even years, later. Congress cannot have intended this result. After all, when Congress provides for EPA's involvement, it directs the agency to act sooner rather than later by establishing a pre-authorization procedure. The majority misses the point when it faults ADEC for "overlook[ing] the obvious difference between a statutory requirement... and a statutory authorization." Ante, at 25 (emphasis deleted). ADEC does not overlook the difference between approval before the fact and oversight after the fact. Rather, ADEC, unlike the majority, recognizes that the Act's explicit provision for a preauthorization process underscores the need for finality in state permitting decisions, making implausible an interpretation of the statute that would allow a post hoc veto procedure that upsets the same reliance and expectation interests.

The majority's initial response that "[t]his case threatens no such development [because] [i]t involves preconstruction orders issued by EPA . . . , not post construction federal Agency directives," provides no assurance that the logic of its reasoning would not in the future allow EPA's belated interventions. When the majority confronts the problem, it concludes that "EPA, we are confident, could not indulge in the inequitable conduct ADEC and the dissent hypothesize while the federal courts sit to review EPA's actions." . . . The authority it cites for this proposition, however, consists of nothing more than a religious exemption case that is far removed from the issues presented here and a dissent from a case that has been overruled in part. State agencies rely on this dictum at their own risk . . . .

Regulated persons and entities should be able to consult an agency staff with certainty and confidence, giving due consideration to agency recommendations and guidance. After today's decision, however, a state agency can no longer represent itself as the real governing body. No matter how much time was spent in consultation and negotiation, a single federal administrator can in the end set all aside by a unilateral order. This is a great step backward in Congress' design to grant States a significant stake in developing and enforcing national environmental objectives.

If EPA were to announce that permit applications subject to BACT review must be submitted to it in the first instance and can be forwarded to the State only with EPA's advance approval, I should assume even the majority would find the basic structure of the BACT provisions undercut. In practical terms, however, the majority displaces state agencies, and degrades their role, in much the same way. In the case before us the applicant made elaborate submissions to ADEC. For over a year and a half, there ensued the constructive discourse that is the very object of the agency process, with both the ADEC staff and the applicant believing the State's decision would be dispositive. EPA did not participate in the administrative process, but waited until after the record was closed to intervene by issuing an order setting aside the BACT determination.

In the end EPA appears to realize the weakness of its arguments and asks us simply to defer to its expertise in light of the purported statutory ambiguity. To its credit, the majority holds Chevron deference inapplicable. Deference is inappropriate for all the reasons the majority recites, plus one more: The statute is not in any way ambiguous. As a result, our inquiry should proceed no further.

Actions, however, speak louder than words, and the majority ends up giving EPA the very Chevron deference—and more—it says should be denied. The Court's opinion is chock full of Chevron-like language . . . . So deficient are its statutory arguments that the majority must hide behind Chevron's vocabulary, despite its explicit holding that Chevron does not apply. In applying Chevron de facto under these circumstances, however, the majority undermines the well-established distinction our precedents draw between Chevron and less deferential forms of judicial review.

For these reasons, and with all respect, I dissent from the opinion and the judgment of the Court.

Notes and Questions

1. The dissenting opinion in *Alaska DEC v. EPA* describes the CAA as providing a "clear mandate that States bear the primary role in controlling pollution." Based on what you have learned about the statute thus far, was this your impression? Did you envision that the EPA or the states had the "primary role" at all, or simply that they had different roles? This hits right at the heart of the federalism issues raised by a cooperative federalism model. Indeed, seeking a "primary" player at all may well be at odds with this model.

2. *Alaska DEC v. EPA* raises other questions regarding the cooperative federalism approach. The majority views the EPA as having an oversight role in the implementation of the CAA, while the dissent limits the EPA's role to "setting ambient standards and enforcing emission limits." Each has textual arguments relating to the statute, but which comports with the theoretical underpinnings of the cooperative federalism model? Cooperative federalism was designed at least in part to simultaneously take advantage of state and local insights while retaining central oversight to prevent states from prioritizing their economic concerns about the goals of the statute. The oversight role is arguably as essential to the model as the standard-setting role. Can you think of additional reasons why federal oversight might be essential to effective implementation of a cooperative federalism statute?

3. The dissent in *Alaska DEC v. EPA* also raises a practical concern: if we follow the majority's reasoning, where does this leave state agency authority over regulated entities, and how can such entities rely on the state administrative process? The majority, of course, seeing a clear oversight role for the EPA, need not concern itself with resulting practical issues. That said, how would you respond to this? How does the state permitting process apply going forward?

Practice Problem

You are a staff attorney in the Office of General Counsel of the Alaska Department of Environmental Conservation (ADEC). Green Cat Mine, Inc., has applied for a PSD permit to operate a new zinc mine in northwest Alaska, not far from the Red Dog Mine at issue in *Alaska DEC v. EPA*. The proposed facility will generate NO_x from three new diesel generators that it will install. A majority of the ADEC's engineers who have examined Green Cat's permit application agree with the company's assertion that there are enough technical differences between the proposed Green Cat Mine and the Red Dog Mine that the Green Cat facility can make use of Low NO_x control technology to satisfy the BACT requirement called for under the PSD program. However, one of the ADEC's staff engineers disagrees with that assessment and the engineers are uncertain whether EPA will agree with the opinion of most of the ADEC engineering staff. In light of the U.S. Supreme Court's decision in *Alaska DEC v. EPA*, how will you recommend that the ADEC proceed in this matter? Why?

VII. Controls on Air Pollution from Motor Vehicles

For decades, motor vehicles have been a significant contributor to air pollution around the world. In the United States, they emit a substantial proportion of three designated criteria pollutants: carbon monoxide, nitrogen oxide (NOx), and ground-level ozone—a photochemical oxidant (often referred to as smog) that is formed from a combination of hydrocarbons and NO_x in the presence of sunlight. In recognition of the hazards posed to human health and the environment from motor vehicle pollution, the Clean Air Act has established standards limiting motor vehicle tailpipe emissions and governing the contents of vehicle fuels and fuel additives.

Under § 202(a)(1) of the Act, EPA was directed to prescribe standards "applicable to the emission of any class or classes of new motor vehicles or new motor vehicle engines which, in the [EPA] Administrator's judgment, cause or contribute to air pollution which may reasonably be anticipated to endanger public health or welfare." These new vehicle standards must reflect "the greatest degree of emission reduction achievable through the application of [available] technology . . . giving appropriate consideration to cost, energy and safety factors," Clean Air Act § 202(a)(3)(A)(i), and they must be applied during the entire "useful life" of the vehicle, which is generally defined under the Act as 10 years or 100,000 miles. Consistent with this congressional mandate, EPA promulgated separate sets of emissions standards for light-duty passenger vehicles, light-duty trucks, motorcycles, and heavy-duty vehicles. *See* 40 CFR part 86.

Although the Clean Air Act preempts state regulation of motor vehicle emissions as a general matter, Congress created a special exception for the State of California. In addition, other states may decide to adopt California's standards as long as the standards they adopt are precisely identical to California's. To establish their own set of requirements, California—and states that decide to adhere to California's vehicle emission standards—must adopt their statewide standards at least two years before the start of the model year that those requirements will apply to. Clean Air Act § 177.

At the federal level, EPA conducts a testing program on samples of new model cars that must be provided by the manufacturer. EPA's tests are conducted in a laboratory in Ann Arbor, Michigan, on dynamometer equipment, to determine whether new vehicle models comply with applicable emission standards. Vehicles that pass the Agency's testing receive a "certificate of conformity" from EPA, the issuance of which is legally required before any motor vehicle can be sold in the United States. Clean Air Act §§ 206(a)(1) and (2). Penalties of up to $10,000 per individual vehicle may be imposed for vehicles sold without the requisite certificate. Clean Air Act § 205.

While EPA's vehicle testing program has generally been successful in uncovering noncompliance with vehicle emission standards, recent events have demonstrated that the program is not without flaws and vulnerabilities. Beginning in 2009, Volkswagen (VW) illegally installed "defeat device" software on the emission control systems of more than 11 million of its new diesel engine vehicles. This software was designed to activate pollution control technology when a diesel-powered VW was undergoing an emissions test and then switch off the control technology in order to boost vehicle performance when the same car was operating in real-world driving conditions. As a result of this deception, VW's diesel vehicles emitted NO_x in quantities up to 40 times greater than EPA standards allow.

VW's transgression was detected during independent testing performed in May 2014 by an NGO, the International Council on Green Transportation, and the University of West Virginia—and later substantiated in vehicle tests carried out by the California Air Resources Board. VW was subsequently made the target of an enforcement action by EPA and the U.S. Department of Justice that resulted in substantial penalties and remedial commitments by VW; and, at this writing, the Agency was investigating ways to upgrade its vehicle emissions testing to detect (and prevent) future cheating by automakers.

Chapter 6

The Race to Mitigate and Adapt: Climate Change Law and Policy

I. Anthropogenic Climate Change

The terminology of climate change is always evolving: initially we used "global warming," which was a potentially misleading oversimplification, so we shifted to the broader and presently most common "climate change." Many scholars now use the arguably even more accurate "climate disruption." Whatever you call it (we'll use "climate change" in this edition, because it matches the sources reproduced in this chapter), "'climate change' means a change of climate which is attributed directly or indirectly to human activity that alters the composition of the global atmosphere and that is in addition to natural climate variability observed over comparable time periods." United Nations Framework Convention on Climate Change (UNFCCC), Article I.

Global climate change is rapidly becoming the greatest worldwide problem since the dawn of humanity. While there would presently be some gradual warming of the atmosphere anyway, as part of a grand-scale climate cycle, human activity has accelerated this warming. We have dramatically increased, to an unnatural level, an otherwise natural occurrence known as greenhouse gases. This term well describes the phenomenon. Under normal atmospheric conditions, energy from the sun enters the atmosphere, after which some of it is absorbed and some (quite a bit) is sent back into space. How the energy is divided between these two potential outcomes determines the atmospheric temperature. The more it is sent into space, of course, the cooler the atmosphere, and vice versa. Greenhouse gases absorb and re-emit infra-red radiation, standing in the way of some of the energy-reflection from the earth. When the energy is re-emitted, some of it goes into space and some back toward the earth. Because this creates a net increase in retained solar radiation, more greenhouse gases in the atmosphere result in warmer average temperatures within the earth's atmosphere. There are natural greenhouse gases for which we cannot take the blame (and that are not blameworthy anyway, as without them the earth's atmosphere would be inhospitably cold), but when we emit certain chemicals into the air, particularly carbon dioxide, methane, nitrous oxide, and sulphur hexafluoride, they collect in the atmosphere in unnatural quantities and contribute to the excessive greenhouse effect.

The results of these phenomena, for our purposes, include destructive changes in our climate and hydrological cycles, impacting agriculture and increasing the frequency of natural disasters, as well as sea level rise that places many highly populated communities at risk. While scientists had already been concerned about it for decades, former Vice President Al Gore popularized this concern and made the data more accessible in his 2006 documentary, *An Inconvenient Truth*. Since then, increased public awareness of the issue has placed even greater pressure on governments to work more quickly toward our globally shared goal of delaying the catastrophic consequences that are beginning to appear inevitable at some point in time.

The climate problem is not, however, a novel concern for the U.S. Congress. Indeed, it has passed climate change legislation on several occasions, all well before there was a surge in public attention. First enacted was the National Climate Program Act of 1978, which had the "purpose of ... establish[ing] a national climate program that will assist the Nation and the world to understand and respond to natural and man-induced climate processes and their implications." 15 U.S.C. § 2902. In 1990 Congress passed the Global Climate Change Prevention Act, which directs the Secretary of Agriculture to research climate change in relation to agricultural and Forest Service activity. Two other pieces of climate-related legislation were enacted in 1990: the Global Change Research Act of 1990, and a 1990 amendment to the Clean Air Act titled Stratospheric Ozone Protection. That said, the world continues to await more comprehensive U.S. climate change legislation. For an analysis of how we should go about drafting such legislation, see Richard J. Lazarus, *Super Wicked Problems and Climate Change: Restraining the Present to Liberate the Future*, 94 CORNELL L. REV. 1153 (2009). In the meantime, states have been stepping up to fill the void with their own climate laws. A useful discussion of such state programs can be found in Robert B. McKinstry Jr. & Thomas D. Peterson, *The Implications of the New "Old" Federalism in Climate-Change Legislation: How to Function in a Global Marketplace When States Take the Lead*, 20 PAC. MCGEORGE GLOBAL BUS. & DEV. L.J. 61 (2007).

About a decade before Al Gore mainstreamed climate awareness, world leaders were working together to reduce greenhouse gases in the atmosphere and thereby slow the progression of anthropogenic (human-caused) climate change. The Kyoto Protocol, in which certain ratifying countries agreed to reduce their GHG emissions, was adopted in 1997. The stated purpose of the Protocol was "stabilization of greenhouse gas concentrations in the atmosphere at a level that would prevent dangerous anthropogenic interference with the climate system. Such a level should be achieved within a time-frame sufficient to allow ecosystems to adapt naturally to climate change, to ensure that food production is not threatened and to enable economic development to proceed in a sustainable manner."

Environmental policy choices typically require trade-offs between the cost of restraining economic activity and the benefit to the environment, taking into account its value to public health and welfare. Although such benefits tend to be difficult to quantify for use in a cost-benefit analysis, there are usually at least somewhat immediate consequences at stake. Climate change creates a bit of a policy analysis time warp, however, in that the economic sacrifices made in one year will have benefits many years later. The next excerpt provides a vivid picture of the stretched-out time frame we are working with when we regulate in this area.

R.T. Pierrehumbert, *Climate Change: A Catastrophe in Slow Motion*

6 Chi. J. Int. L. 573 (2006).

The word catastrophe usually brings to mind phenomena like tsunamis, earthquakes, mudslides, or asteroid impacts—disasters that are over in an instant and have immediately evident dire consequences. The changes in Earth's climate wrought by industrial carbon dioxide emissions do not at first glance seem to fit this mold since they take a century or more for their consequences to fully manifest. However, viewed from the perspective of geological time, human-induced climate change, known more familiarly as "global warming," is a catastrophe equal to nearly any other in our planet's history. Seen by a geologist a million years from now, the era of global warming will probably not seem as consequential as the asteroid impact that killed the dinosaurs. It will, however, appear in the geological record as an event comparable to such major events as the onset or termination of an ice age or the transition to the hot, relatively ice-free climates that prevailed seventy million years ago when dinosaurs roamed the Earth. It will be all the more cataclysmic for having taken place in the span of one or a few centuries, rather than millennia or millions of years.

Humans have become a major geological force with the power to commit future millennia to practically irreversible changes in global conditions. This is what Bill McKibben refers to as "The End of Nature." As an example of the impact life has on global climate, the imminent global warming caused by humans does not stand out as unique or even unusually impressive. When oxygen-generating photosynthetic algae evolved between one and two-and-one-half billion years ago, they changed the composition of one-fifth of the atmosphere, poisoned much of the previous ecosystem, and more or less terminated the dominant role of methane as a greenhouse gas (oxygenation also, to be fair, set the stage for evolution of multi-celled organisms—the animals and plants we know and love). And when plants colonized land half a billion years ago, they vastly increased the rate at which atmospheric carbon dioxide is converted to limestone in the soil, leading to severe global cooling. One hardly wants to contemplate the kind of environmental impact statement that would have to be filed for either of these innovations.

What makes global warming unique in the four billion year history of the planet is that the causative agents—humans—are sentient. We can foresee the consequences of our actions, albeit imperfectly, and we have the power, if not necessarily the will, to change our behavior so as to effectuate a different future. The conjuncture of foresight and unprecedented willful power over the global future thrusts the matter onto the stage where notions of responsibility, culpability, and ethics come into play. The philosopher Hans Jonas finds in this "imperative of responsibility" a need for a fundamentally new formulation of ethics—one that takes greater cognizance of future generations and of the biosphere at large. It is against this backdrop that the foundation of international institutions capable of dealing with the catastrophe of global warming must be seen.

II. Unique Physical Aspects of the Climate Change Problem: Imposing Our Will on the Next 5000 Generations

In this section I will review the basic physical features that make global warming fundamentally different from all other pollution problems faced by humans. The problem of ozone destruction by chlorofluorocarbons (the "ozone hole" problem) was a small warm-up act sharing some characteristics with the global warming problem. But because the ozone hole problem was somewhat more limited in scope, and abatement of chlorofluorocarbons did not force society to confront any really difficult economic decisions, it is in a qualitatively different class. Human-induced emissions of several gases other than carbon dioxide also contribute to global warming, but in the long run, carbon dioxide is by far the biggest player and the most embedded in economic activity. I will thus restrict my discussion to this gas alone.

Carbon dioxide is present only in very low concentrations in the atmosphere. Immediately before the beginning of the industrial era, you would have needed to sift through a million molecules of air to find 280 molecules of carbon dioxide. If all of the carbon dioxide in the atmosphere were gathered together into a layer near the ground, the layer would be about two meters deep. Most of us would have to stand on a chair to breathe. It is because there is relatively little carbon dioxide in the atmosphere that human economic activity has the prospect of doubling its concentration within the twenty-first century, with greater increases in sight thereafter. It would be much harder for anything we do to significantly change the atmosphere's oxygen content, which makes up about a fifth of the atmosphere. Despite its low concentration, carbon dioxide plays a key role in determining the Earth's climate because this gas greatly retards the efficiency with which the planet loses energy to space by infrared (heat) radiation. The major constituents of the atmosphere are essentially transparent to infrared radiation. Carbon dioxide warms the Earth in the same way a sleeping bag or down comforter warms a person — by reducing the rate of heat loss. For the Earth, this additional blanketing allows the planet to maintain a higher temperature than would otherwise be possible, given the rate of solar energy input from the Sun.

Water vapor is the other major player in the Earth's energy budget, but its concentration in the atmosphere is buffered on a time scale of weeks by the huge oceanic reservoir of water, which can rapidly evaporate into the atmosphere and equally rapidly rain out. Water vapor thus adjusts in response to other changes in climate (principally temperature); rather than being a prime mover, it is a feedback amplifying other causes of climate change, including carbon dioxide increase. This is why water vapor, though an important greenhouse gas, is not regulated under the Kyoto Protocol or under proposed California state-level climate control regulations.

Carbon dioxide, in contrast, has a very long lifetime in the atmosphere and very weak natural sources; therefore, changes in the rate at which carbon dioxide is put into the atmosphere have great leverage over the atmosphere's carbon dioxide content. Carbon dioxide is implicated in virtually all of the great climate shifts in Earth's history, including the coming and going of the Ice Ages; the eons of warm ice-free states that the dinosaurs lived in some seventy million years ago; the collapse of the Earth into a globally frozen state in the Neoproterozoic era some six hundred million years ago; and the maintenance of conditions favorable to life on the very young Earth, when the Sun was much fainter than it is today. We know from Earth's history that carbon dioxide has an enormous impact on the habitability of our planet, but history also humbles us by revealing major gaps in our understanding of the nature and severity of the impact. For a geologist, the idea of doubling the atmosphere's carbon dioxide concentration is outright terrifying, akin to closing one's eyes and spinning a thermostat dial that has not been touched in a long time, and without even the benefit of knowing quite whether it is a gas furnace or a hydrogen bomb at the nether end of the thermostat's wires.

The unique character of the challenge posed by carbon dioxide pollution derives from a triad of properties. First, human-induced emissions of carbon dioxide constitute a huge disturbance of the natural carbon cycle, causing changes in the atmosphere's carbon dioxide concentration that are large and of unprecedented speed in the annals of geological history. In the absence of fossil fuel burning, the natural carbon dioxide level is maintained by volcanic activity, specifically an escape of about five hundred million metric tons of carbon per year into the atmosphere from the Earth's interior. Fossil fuel burning currently puts about fifteen times this amount into the atmosphere annually, and the rate is increasing exponentially. As a result, the atmospheric carbon dioxide level has already increased from its pre-industrial value of 280 molecules per million to a present value of 370 molecules per million, and this level is expected to reach twice the pre-industrial value before the end of the current century. By way of comparison, carbon dioxide concentration during the two million years prior to the industrial era, encompassing the entire history of the human species, had fluctuated between a low of 180 molecules per million during the Ice Ages and a high of about 300 molecules per million during the inter-glacial periods. One has to go back perhaps ten million years to find another time when the carbon dioxide concentration was as high as we will make it during the next century. Looking a little further into the future, fossil fuel burning could quadruple the pre-industrial concentration within four hundred years under a business-as-usual scenario. This is comparable to the values that climate modelers use to reproduce the steamy, ice-free climate of the Cretaceous that existed some seventy million years ago. To turn back the climate clock seventy million years in the course of a few centuries is not a thing to be undertaken lightly.

Second, the expected changes in temperature caused by the increase of carbon dioxide are of a direction and magnitude unprecedented in the past two million years. During that time, the climate has fluctuated from a maximum global mean warmth approximating values prevailing around 1950 to temperatures about six degrees colder during the major Ice Ages. Simulations of global mean warming associated with a doubling of carbon dioxide lie in the range of two to four degrees Centigrade, with no guarantee that the higher figure truly represents the worst possible case. At the high end of this range, we are talking about a climate change two-thirds as big as the transition to an ice age but with this important difference: the expected warming would be added on top of the maximum temperatures experienced in the past two million years. Therefore, we have no natural analogues to tell us how the complex web of physical and biological interactions would respond to such a drastic climate change. We are driving into unknown territory, and, given the present imperfect state of physical and especially ecological simulations, with a windshield heavily encrusted with mud.

Third, and most significant, the excess carbon dioxide we put in the atmosphere today is removed exceedingly slowly, meaning that the carbon dioxide we emit in the next half-century will alter the climate for millennia to come; even if we wholly ceased using fossil fuels after fifty years, the harm could not be undone. The lifetime of carbon dioxide in the atmosphere is often mistakenly quoted as being on the order of a hundred years; this figure is actually the result of a fallacious and largely meaningless method of aggregating the many physical processes that operate on widely differing time scales into a single number which is supposed to represent the amount of time some extra added carbon dioxide will stay in the atmosphere. The fact is that for each kilogram of carbon dioxide put into the atmosphere today, only a small portion will be rapidly absorbed into the ocean. After five hundred to one thousand years of slow uptake by the ocean, fully one-quarter of that kilogram will remain in the atmosphere. A portion of that will be taken up by the ocean over the next ten thousand years by slow processes related to ocean sediments, but fully 7 percent of our initial kilogram will stick around for hundreds of thousands of years. It has been estimated that fossil fuel exploitation could eliminate the natural ice age cycle for the next half-million years, with presently unforeseeable consequences for the storing and catastrophic release of exotic methane-bearing ices in the ocean. The long reach of our actions over the eons gives us unprecedented power over the future, and with that power comes unprecedented responsibility.

An innocuous-sounding two to four degree Centigrade increase in average global temperature carries along with it much larger regional changes in temperature and precipitation, which can in turn have profound consequences. Polar regions warm more than the average, and already, at the present early stage of warming, one-fifth of Arctic summer sea ice has disappeared. Arctic summer ice may be gone in fifty years, which will have dire consequences for polar bears and other marine mammals. The opening of arctic ports and shipping routes may well prove to be a boon for the market economy (as well as a source of political conflict and territorial disputes), but the increasingly intensive exploitation of the area is hardly likely to be good for natural ecosystems. We are learning, too, that land ice can respond more rapidly to climate than previously thought. The Greenland summer melt zone has expanded dramatically and many of the Greenland glaciers are surging into the ocean. At the opposite pole, the Larsen B ice shelf in the Antarctic has collapsed for the first time in ten millennia. The success of the documentary film March of the Penguins, a straightforward account of a year in the life of the Antarctic's emperor penguins, is a testament to the deep affinity people feel for these brave creatures. Emperor penguins adapted over millions of years to life on the ice. Their life cycle is intimately tied up with the long inland march along sea ice and shelf ice, undertaken to protect their newborns from oceanic predators. The penguins would struggle mightily to undo ten million years of evolution in a century.

In the tropics, temperature changes little in the normal course of the year. How will the Amazon ecosystem respond to the extensive warming and drying predicted by some models? Warm water holds less oxygen than cold water. Throughout the world, then, global warming will stress sensitive freshwater fish living in shallow streams; coastal saltwater shellfish will likely also be affected by the heat. Agricultural diseases, human diseases, and parasite infestations (including potato blight, bark beetles, West Nile, and malaria) can expand their range with warming. Summer heat waves will become more severe, placing particular stress on places that are already barely tolerable during the summer. Some regions will experience extensive droughts, and if the monsoons should cease, the results will be catastrophic for countries such as India. Also, hurricanes draw their energy from warm water, so the intensity (and perhaps also the number) of hurricanes is likely to increase in the future. There are indications that the expected increase in the destructive power of hurricanes is already underway. The impact in low-lying coastal regions may be exacerbated by a sea level rise even greater than currently forecast, if glaciers should prove more responsive to temperature increases than conventionally thought.

Major ocean circulations are also likely to change, with uncertain consequences for the Earth's climate and its oceanic ecosystems. Carbon dioxide becomes an acid when it dissolves in water; the resulting acidification of the ocean will make it harder for coral to form their skeletons. While carbon dioxide in the air acts as a fertilizer for many kinds of plants, meaning that an increase in its concentration could have limited beneficial effects on agricultural plants, this increase could also have adverse and unexpected consequences for land ecosystems (just as dumping phosphate and nitrate fertilizer into the Gulf of Mexico has not proved beneficial for the environment).

In addition, historical evidence shows that the climate system has abrupt switches built into it, and that climate changes in fits and starts rather than along a smooth, gentle curve. Notwithstanding the movie The Day After Tomorrow, this does not mean that global warming risks bringing on an ice age. Rather, what we risk is a switch to a climate that has much more dramatic swings in it from one decade to the next, making adaptation much more difficult. The last ten thousand years, which embrace the entire history of civilization, have had an unusually steady climate, and we are uncertain about what it would take to disrupt this happy state of affairs.

Many of the above impacts are in the realm of the possible rather than the probable, and it is presently difficult to say how large such impacts would be, or even how probable they are. However, a cogent case has been made that one should pay more attention to low-risk but potentially catastrophic events, as opposed to the current focus on the "most probable" case. Those who would sneer that such an application of the "precautionary principle" would lead to paralysis are relying on an extreme caricature of the principle that has little resemblance to the way it is used in practice. For example, if one is thinking about driving down a mountain road at night and has faulty headlights, knows that the ravine ahead has a rickety bridge over it, and has heard that there has been a storm that may have washed the bridge away, one would be quite justified in driving slowly or perhaps even postponing the trip, even if it was not known for certain that the bridge had been swept away. No doubt, those who disdain the "precautionary principle" would be quite happy to load their whole family in the car and put the pedal to the floor.

The global nature of the climate change problem has some novel policy implications and also creates some opportunities. The atmosphere is well-mixed with regard to carbon dioxide. From the standpoint of climate change, carbon dioxide released in Sydney, Australia is in every regard interchangeable with carbon dioxide released in Beijing, China or Edmonton, Canada. The atmosphere truly is a global commons with respect to carbon dioxide, making emissions trading schemes far more benign than would be the case for pollutants, such as mercury, which have locally lethal impacts. The harm caused by the emission of carbon dioxide in Edmonton is not felt primarily, if at all, in Edmonton. This scenario means that one is confronted with an especially severe form of the free rider problem. A particularly unstable situation is created when a major emitter like the United States perceives (foolishly) that it will suffer minimal harm from the impacts of climate change and perceives (also foolishly) that actions taken to reduce emissions will derail its economy.

Because of the extremely long-term impact of each additional year's carbon dioxide emissions, the calculus of delay is completely changed as compared to other pollution problems. Ordinarily, in the face of uncertainty, a certain amount of delay could be justified; technology improves so as to make abatement cheaper, and one could wait to get a peek at the growing impacts to see just how deleterious they actually are. For many kinds of pollution, bad decisions are, to some extent, reversible. For example, suppose that at some point society has decided that it can no longer afford stringent restrictions on particulate emissions by power plants. It holds to this decision despite the possibility that a rather modest rollback in tax cuts for the wealthy could easily cover the costs. Such a society, in essence, places a higher value on the ability of wealthy individuals to afford new Hummers than it does on the health of children and other vulnerable populations. A future generation with different values may ultimately have to live with the guilt of a large number of preventable deaths of children from asthma and other respiratory ailments. However, a feeling of guilt is all that future generations are burdened with since the adverse impacts will disappear within a few years of action taken by more enlightened leaders. We do not have even this dubious luxury with respect to global warming. If we wait forty or fifty years before taking serious action, the die will have been cast and a thousand generations of our descendants will have to live with the consequences of the climate we bequeathed them.

The problem of long-term consequences is compounded by the long lead time for developing new energy infrastructure and technology and by the long capital life—well over a half-century—of newly built electric power plants. Investments being made today, investments that the coming generation will be reluctant to write down, are committing the world economy to another half-century of runaway carbon dioxide emissions. We are, in fact, rapidly running out of time to act.

Notes and Questions

1. Although we are already beginning to experience some of the consequences of climate change, and can expect to see them get worse within most of our lifetimes, the worst will likely fall on future generations. Today's economic restraint is an investment in a future that policy-makers will not themselves see. How might this temporal distance impact our choices? We are also paying a price today for the actions of our ancestors over the last two centuries (much of the industrial revolution took place in the nineteenth century). Are we now to be the sandwich generation, paying for both the mistakes of the past and the survival of the future? What duty does our generation owe to future generations? Recent litigation focusing on the atmosphere as a public trust resource to be protected for future generations — commonly referred to as "atmospheric trust litigation" — attempts to address this question, and is covered in more detail later in this chapter.

2. The use of cost-benefit analysis is common in making policy decisions, as well as implementation choices. When the benefit is to accrue in the future, it is common to "discount" that benefit, using mathematical formulae similar to compounding interest, only in the reverse direction. The result of such processes is that, just as a dollar today may be worth two dollars in 10 years, we also determine that two dollars in 10 years is worth only a dollar today. When we evaluate environmental benefits in the future, and apply such discounting methods to them, they can be worth very little in today's cost-benefit analysis. For an excellent discussion (and criticism) of the justifications underlying intergenerational discounting in the climate change context, see Richard L. Revesz & Matthew R. Shahabiand, *Climate Change and Future Generations*, 84 S. Cal. L. Rev. 1097 (2011). For an enlightening analysis of the impact of discounting on policy, see Daniel A. Farber, *From Here to Eternity: Environmental Law and Future Generations*, 2003 U. Ill. L. Rev. 289 (2003).

Of course, we can always count on Cass Sunstein to provide an original perspective. He and Arden Rowell propose that we are looking at the problem in the wrong way:

> There is an elaborate debate over the practice of "discounting" regulatory benefits, such as environmental improvements and decreased risks to health and life, when those benefits will not be enjoyed until some future date. Economists tend to think that, as a general rule, such benefits should be discounted in the same way as money; many philosophers and lawyers doubt that conclusion on empirical and normative grounds. Both sides frequently neglect a simple point: if regulators are interested in how people currently value risks that will not come to fruition for a significant time, they can use people's current willingness to pay to reduce those risks. And if the question involves people's willingness to pay in the future, what is being discounted is merely money, not regulatory benefits as such. No one seeks to discount health and life as such — only the money that might be used to reduce threats to these goods. If willingness to pay to reduce risk is the appropriate metric for allocating regulatory resources, discounting merely adjusts that metric to make

expenditures comparable through time. To be sure, cost-benefit analysis with discounting can produce serious problems of intergenerational equity; but those problems, involving the obligations of the present to the future, require an independent analysis. Failing to discount will often hurt, rather than help, future generations, and solutions to the problem of intergenerational equity should not be conflated with the question of whether to discount.

Cass R. Sunstein & Arden Rowell, *On Discounting Regulatory Benefits: Risk, Money, and Intergenerational Equity*, 74 U. Chi. L. Rev. 171 (2007).

3. Might our obligation to mitigate climate change go beyond such economic analyses entirely? Might it go beyond our duty to future generations of human beings? What would Aldo Leopold say? As you may have observed in Chapter 1 of this text, he argued for an ethical duty to the natural world itself, called a land ethic, which resulted in a very simple (yet tough to follow) command: "A thing is right when it tends to preserve the integrity, stability, and beauty of the biotic community. It is wrong when it tends otherwise." Aldo Leopold, A Sand County Almanac and Sketches Here and There 262 (1949).

4. Is it possible that some people and businesses will actually benefit from climate change? Considering the changes taking place and how they vary from one region to the next, which areas might see the greatest short-term benefits from advancing climate change? How might these temporary advantages be harnessed? Could doing so jeopardize the movement to mitigate climate change? For a discussion of these issues see J.B. Ruhl, *The Political Economy of Climate Change Winners*, 97 Minn. L. Rev. 206 (2012).

5. We are not all on the same page when it comes to the existence of climate change, at least not in the layperson community. Even today there remains a significant percentage of Americans who seriously doubt that these changes are taking place, or at least that humans have caused them. This phenomenon betrays different views of science, economics, ethics, media, and ultimate values, as explored in great depth in Mike Hulme, Why We Disagree About Climate Change: Understanding Controversy, Inaction and Opportunity (2009).

II. Global Efforts to Address Climate Change

Climate change is about as global an issue as possible, in relation to both causation and impact, so international cooperation is key to addressing it. This section provides the highlights of this incredibly vast and complex area of international law and policy.

A. The Science

In 1988 the United Nations Environment Programme (UNEP) and the World Meteorological Association (WMO) established an international working group of leading climate scientists called the Intergovernmental Panel on Climate Change (IPCC), which is now the preeminent authority for assessing climate change. There are, at present, 195 countries with IPCC membership, which means that they have representatives in the group and approval authority for its reports. The work of the IPCC is intended to be purely scientific, with experts assessing the current state of scientific knowledge and reporting it for use in setting policy, but without prescribing policy actions themselves. That said, as you read the following IPCC report, think about how the political influence of such a large international membership might play a role in its content.

Climate Change 2014 Synthesis Report
Summary for Policymakers
Intergovernmental Panel on Climate Change, 2014

https://www.ipcc.ch/report/ar5/syr/

Introduction

This Synthesis Report is based on the reports of the three Working Groups of the Intergovernmental Panel on Climate Change (IPCC), including relevant Special Reports. It provides an integrated view of climate change as the final part of the IPCC's Fifth Assessment Report (AR5).

This summary follows the structure of the longer report which addresses the following topics: Observed changes and their causes; Future climate change, risks and impacts; Future pathways for adaptation, mitigation and sustainable development; Adaptation and mitigation.

In the Synthesis Report, the certainty in key assessment findings is communicated as in the Working Group Reports and Special Reports. It is based on the author teams' evaluations of underlying scientific understanding and is expressed as a qualitative level of confidence (from *very low* to *very high*) and, when possible, probabilistically with a quantified likelihood (from *exceptionally unlikely* to *virtually certain*). Where appropriate, findings are also formulated as statements of fact without using uncertainty qualifiers.

SPM 1. Observed Changes and their Causes

Human influence on the climate system is clear, and recent anthropogenic emissions of greenhouse gases are the highest in history. Recent climate changes have had widespread impacts on human and natural systems.

SPM 1.1 Observed changes in the climate system

Warming of the climate system is unequivocal, and since the 1950s, many of the observed changes are unprecedented over decades to millennia. The atmosphere and ocean have warmed, the amounts of snow and ice have diminished, and sea level has risen.

Each of the last three decades has been successively warmer at the Earth's surface than any preceding decade since 1850. The period from 1983 to 2012 was *likely* the warmest 30-year period of the last 1400 years in the Northern Hemisphere, where such assessment is possible (*medium confidence*). The globally averaged combined land and ocean surface temperature data as calculated by a linear trend show a warming of 0.85 [0.65 to 1.06] °C over the period 1880 to 2012, when multiple independently produced datasets exist.

In addition to robust multidecadal warming, the globally averaged surface temperature exhibits substantial decadal and interannual variability. Due to this natural variability, trends based on short records are very sensitive to the beginning and end dates and do not in general reflect long-term climate trends. As one example, the rate of warming over the past 15 years (1998–2012; 0.05 [0.05 to 0.15] °C per decade), which begins with a strong El Niño, is smaller than the rate calculated since 1951 (1951–2012; 0.12 [0.08 to 0.14] °C per decade).

Ocean warming dominates the increase in energy stored in the climate system, accounting for more than 90% of the energy accumulated between 1971 and 2010 (*high confidence*), with only about 1% stored in the atmosphere. On a global scale, the ocean warming is largest near the surface, and the upper 75 m warmed by 0.11 [0.09 to 0.13] °C per decade over the period 1971 to 2010. It is *virtually certain* that the upper ocean (0–700 m) warmed from 1971 to 2010, and it *likely* warmed between the 1870s and 1971.

Averaged over the mid-latitude land areas of the Northern Hemisphere, precipitation has increased since 1901 (*medium confidence* before and *high confidence* after 1951). For other latitudes, area-averaged long-term positive or negative trends have *low confidence*. Observations of changes in ocean surface salinity also provide indirect evidence for changes in the global water cycle over the ocean (*medium confidence*). It is *very likely* that regions of high salinity, where evaporation dominates, have become more saline, while regions of low salinity, where precipitation dominates, have become fresher since the 1950s.

Since the beginning of the industrial era, oceanic uptake of CO2 has resulted in acidification of the ocean; the pH of ocean surface water has decreased by 0.1 (*high confidence*), corresponding to a 26% increase in acidity, measured as hydrogen ion concentration.

Over the period 1992 to 2011, the Greenland and Antarctic ice sheets have been losing mass (*high confidence*), *likely* at a larger rate over 2002 to 2011. Glaciers have continued to shrink almost worldwide (*high confidence*). Northern Hemisphere spring snow cover has continued to decrease in extent (*high confidence*). There is *high confidence* that permafrost temperatures have increased in most regions since the early 1980s in response to increased surface temperature and changing snow cover.

The annual mean Arctic sea-ice extent decreased over the period 1979 to 2012, with a rate that was *very likely* in the range of 3.5 to 4.1% per decade. Arctic sea-ice extent has decreased in every season and in every successive decade since 1979, with the most rapid decrease in decadal mean extent in summer (*high confidence*). It is *very likely* that the annual mean Antarctic sea-ice extent increased in the range of 1.2 to 1.8%

per decade between 1979 and 2012. However, there is *high confidence* that there are strong regional differences in Antarctica, with extent increasing in some regions and decreasing in others.

Over the period 1901 to 2010, global mean sea level rose by 0.19 [0.17 to 0.21] m. The rate of sea level rise since the mid-19th century has been larger than the mean rate during the previous two millennia (*high confidence*).

SPM 1.2 Causes of climate change

Anthropogenic greenhouse gas emissions have increased since the pre-industrial era, driven largely by economic and population growth, and are now higher than ever. This has led to atmospheric concentrations of carbon dioxide, methane and nitrous oxide that are unprecedented in at least the last 800,000 years. Their effects, together with those of other anthropogenic drivers, have been detected throughout the climate system and are *extremely likely* to have been the dominant cause of the observed warming since the mid-20th century.

Anthropogenic greenhouse gas (GHG) emissions since the pre-industrial era have driven large increases in the atmospheric concentrations of carbon dioxide (CO_2), methane (CH_4) and nitrous oxide (N_2O). Between 1750 and 2011, cumulative anthropogenic CO_2 emissions to the atmosphere were 2040 ± 310 $GtCO_2$. About 40% of these emissions have remained in the atmosphere (880 ± 35 $GtCO_2$); the rest was removed from the atmosphere and stored on land (in plants and soils) and in the ocean. The ocean has absorbed about 30% of the emitted anthropogenic CO_2, causing ocean acidification. About half of the anthropogenic CO_2 emissions between 1750 and 2011 have occurred in the last 40 years (*high confidence*).

Total anthropogenic GHG emissions have continued to increase over 1970 to 2010 with larger absolute increases between 2000 and 2010, despite a growing number of climate change mitigation policies. Anthropogenic GHG emissions in 2010 have reached 49 ± 4.5 $GtCO_2$-eq/yr. Emissions of CO_2 from fossil fuel combustion and industrial processes contributed about 78% of the total GHG emissions increase from 1970 to 2010, with a similar percentage contribution for the increase during the period 2000 to 2010 (*high confidence*). Globally, economic and population growth continued to be the most important drivers of increases in CO_2 emissions from fossil fuel combustion. The contribution of population growth between 2000 and 2010 remained roughly identical to the previous three decades, while the contribution of economic growth has risen sharply. Increased use of coal has reversed the long-standing trend of gradual decarbonization (i.e., reducing the carbon intensity of energy) of the world's energy supply (*high confidence*).

The evidence for human influence on the climate system has grown since the IPCC Fourth Assessment Report (AR4). It is *extremely likely* that more than half of the observed increase in global average surface temperature from 1951 to 2010 was caused by the anthropogenic increase in GHG concentrations and other anthropogenic forcings together. The best estimate of the human-induced contribution to warming is similar to the observed warming over this period. Anthropogenic forcings have *likely* made a substantial contribution to surface temperature increases since the mid-20th century over every continental region except Antarctica. Anthropogenic influences have *likely* affected the global water cycle since 1960 and contributed to the retreat of glaciers since the 1960s and to the increased surface melting of the Greenland ice sheet since 1993. Anthropogenic influences have *very likely* contributed to Arctic sea-ice loss since 1979 and have *very likely* made a substantial contribution to increases in global upper ocean heat content (0—700 m) and to global mean sea level rise observed since the 1970s.

SPM 1.3 Impacts of climate change

In recent decades, changes in climate have caused impacts on natural and human systems on all continents and across the oceans. Impacts are due to observed climate change, irrespective of its cause, indicating the sensitivity of natural and human systems to changing climate.

Evidence of observed climate change impacts is strongest and most comprehensive for natural systems. In many regions, changing precipitation or melting snow and ice are altering hydrological systems, affecting water resources in terms of quantity and quality (*medium confidence*). Many terrestrial, freshwater and marine species have shifted their geographic ranges, seasonal activities, migration patterns, abundances and species interactions in response to ongoing climate change (*high confidence*). Some impacts on human systems have also been attributed to climate change, with a major or minor contribution of climate change distinguishable from other influences. Assessment of many studies covering a wide range of regions and crops shows that negative impacts of climate change on crop yields have been more common than positive impacts (*high confidence*). Some impacts of ocean acidification on marine organisms have been attributed to human influence (*medium confidence*).

SPM 1.4 Extreme events

Changes in many extreme weather and climate events have been observed since about 1950. Some of these changes have been linked to human influences, including a decrease in cold temperature extremes, an increase in warm temperature extremes, an increase in extreme high sea levels and an increase in the number of heavy precipitation events in a number of regions.

It is *very likely* that the number of cold days and nights has decreased and the number of warm days and nights has increased on the global scale. It is *likely* that the frequency of heat waves has increased in large parts of Europe, Asia and Australia. It is *very likely* that human influence has contributed to the observed global scale changes in the frequency and intensity of daily temperature extremes since the mid-20th century. It is *likely* that human influence has more than doubled the probability of occurrence of heat waves in some locations. There is *medium confidence* that the observed warming has increased heat-related human mortality and decreased cold-related human mortality in some regions.

There are *likely* more land regions where the number of heavy precipitation events has increased than where it has decreased. Recent detection of increasing trends in extreme precipitation and discharge in some catchments implies greater risks of flooding at regional scale (*medium confidence*). It is *likely* that extreme sea levels (for example, as experienced in storm surges) have increased since 1970, being mainly a result of rising mean sea level.

Impacts from recent climate-related extremes, such as heat waves, droughts, floods, cyclones and wildfires, reveal significant vulnerability and exposure of some ecosystems and many human systems to current climate variability (*very high confidence*).

SPM 2. Future Climate Changes, Risks and Impacts

Continued emission of greenhouse gases will cause further warming and long-lasting changes in all components of the climate system, increasing the likelihood of severe, pervasive and irreversible impacts for people and ecosystems. Limiting climate change would require substantial and sustained reductions in greenhouse gas emissions which, together with adaptation, can limit climate change risks.

SPM 2.1 Key drivers of future climate

Cumulative emissions of CO2 largely determine global mean surface warming by the late 21st century and beyond. Projections of greenhouse gas emissions vary over a wide range, depending on both socio-economic development and climate policy.

Anthropogenic GHG emissions are mainly driven by population size, economic activity, lifestyle, energy use, land use patterns, technology and climate policy. . . .

Multiple lines of evidence indicate a strong, consistent, almost linear relationship between cumulative CO2 emissions and projected global temperature change to the year 2100 . . .

SPM 2.2 Projected changes in the climate system

Surface temperature is projected to rise over the 21st century under all assessed emission scenarios. It is *very likely* that heat waves will occur more often and last longer, and that extreme precipitation events will become more intense and frequent in many regions. The ocean will continue to warm and acidify, and global mean sea level to rise.

Future climate will depend on committed warming caused by past anthropogenic emissions, as well as future anthropogenic emissions and natural climate variability. The global mean surface temperature change for the period 2016—2035 relative to 1986—2005 . . . will likely be in the range 0.3°C to 0.7°C (*medium confidence*). This assumes that there will be no major volcanic eruptions or changes in some natural sources (e.g., CH4 and N2O), or unexpected changes in total solar irradiance. By mid-21st century, the magnitude of the projected climate change is substantially affected by the choice of emissions scenario. . . .

It is *virtually certain* that there will be more frequent hot and fewer cold temperature extremes over most land areas on daily and seasonal timescales, as global mean surface temperature increases. It is *very likely* that heat waves will occur with a higher frequency and longer duration. Occasional cold winter extremes will continue to occur. . . .

The global ocean will continue to warm during the 21st century, with the strongest warming projected for the surface in tropical and Northern Hemisphere subtropical regions.

Earth System Models project a global increase in ocean acidification for all [mitigation modeling] scenarios by the end of the 21st century . . .

Year-round reductions in Arctic sea ice are projected for all [mitigation modeling] scenarios. . . .

It is *virtually certain* that near-surface permafrost extent at high northern latitudes will be reduced as global mean surface temperature increases, with the area of permafrost near the surface (upper 3.5 m) projected to decrease by 37% to 81% for the multi-model average (*medium confidence*). . . .

There has been significant improvement in understanding and projection of sea level change since the [fourth assessment report]. Global mean sea level rise will continue during the 21st century, *very likely* at a faster rate than observed from 1971 to 2010. . . .

SPM 2.3 Future risks and impacts caused by a changing climate

Climate change will amplify existing risks and create new risks for natural and human systems. Risks are unevenly distributed and are generally greater for disadvantaged people and communities in countries at all levels of development.

Risk of climate-related impacts results from the interaction of climate-related hazards (including hazardous events and trends) with the vulnerability and exposure of human and natural systems, including their ability to adapt. Rising rates and magnitudes of warming and other changes in the climate system, accompanied by ocean acidification, increase the risk of severe, pervasive and in some cases irreversible detrimental impacts. Some risks are particularly relevant for individual regions, while others are global. The overall risks of future climate change impacts can be reduced by limiting the rate and magnitude of climate change, including ocean acidification. The precise levels of climate change sufficient to trigger abrupt and irreversible change remain uncertain, but the risk associated with crossing such thresholds increases with rising temperature (*medium confidence*). For risk assessment, it is important to evaluate the widest possible range of impacts, including low-probability outcomes with large consequences.

A large fraction of species faces increased extinction risk due to climate change during and beyond the 21st century, especially as climate change interacts with other stressors (*high confidence*). Most plant species cannot naturally shift their geographical ranges sufficiently fast to keep up with current and high projected rates of climate change in most landscapes; most small mammals and freshwater molluscs will not be able to keep up at the rates projected under [one of the mitigation models] and above in flat landscapes in this century (*high confidence*). Future risk is indicated to be high by the observation that natural global climate change at rates lower than current anthropogenic climate change caused significant ecosystem shifts and species extinctions during the past millions of years. Marine organisms will face progressively lower oxygen levels and high rates and magnitudes of ocean acidification (*high confidence*), with associated risks exacerbated by rising ocean temperature extremes (*medium confidence*). Coral reefs and polar ecosystems are highly vulnerable. Coastal systems and low-lying areas are at risk from sea level rise, which will continue for centuries even if the global mean temperature is stabilized (*high confidence*). . . .

Until mid-century, projected climate change will impact human health mainly by exacerbating health problems that already exist (*very high confidence*). Throughout the 21st century, climate change is expected to lead to increases in ill-health in many regions and especially in developing countries with low income, as compared to a baseline without climate change (*high confidence*). By 2100 for [one of the mitigation models], the combination of high temperature and humidity in some areas for parts of the year is expected to compromise common human activities, including growing food and working outdoors (*high confidence*).

In urban areas climate change is projected to increase risks for people, assets, economies and ecosystems, including risks from heat stress, storms and extreme precipitation, inland and coastal flooding, landslides, air pollution, drought, water scarcity, sea level rise and storm surges (*very high confidence*). These risks are amplified for those lacking essential infrastructure and services or living in exposed areas.

Rural areas are expected to experience major impacts on water availability and supply, food security, infrastructure and agricultural incomes, including shifts in the production areas of food and non-food crops around the world (*high confidence*). . . .

Climate change is projected to increase displacement of people (*medium evidence, high agreement*). Populations that lack the resources for planned migration experience higher exposure to extreme weather events, particularly in developing countries with low income. Climate change can indirectly increase risks of violent conflicts by amplifying well-documented drivers of these conflicts such as poverty and economic shocks (*medium confidence*).

SPM 3. Future Pathways for Adaptation, Mitigation and Sustainable Development

Adaptation and mitigation are complementary strategies for reducing and managing the risks of climate change. Substantial emissions reductions over the next few decades can reduce climate risks in the 21st century and beyond, increase prospects for effective adaptation, reduce the costs and challenges of mitigation in the longer term and contribute to climate-resilient pathways for sustainable development.

. . .

SPM 3.2 Climate change risks reduced by mitigation and adaptation

Without additional mitigation efforts beyond those in place today, and even with adaptation, warming by the end of the 21st century will lead to high to very high risk of severe, widespread and irreversible impacts globally (*high confidence*). Mitigation involves some level of co-benefits and of risks due to adverse side effects, but these risks do not involve the same possibility of severe, widespread and irreversible impacts as risks from climate change, increasing the benefits from near-term mitigation efforts.

. . .

SPM 3.3 Characteristics of adaptation pathways

Adaptation can reduce the risks of climate change impacts, but there are limits to its effectiveness, especially with greater magnitudes and rates of climate change. Taking a longer-term perspective, in the context of sustainable development, increases the likelihood that more immediate adaptation actions will also enhance future options and preparedness.

Adaptation can contribute to the well-being of populations, the security of assets and the maintenance of ecosystem goods, functions and services now and in the future. Adaptation is place- and context-specific (*high confidence*). A first step towards adaptation to future climate change is reducing vulnerability and exposure to present climate variability (*high confidence*). Integration of adaptation into planning, including policy design, and decision-making can promote synergies with development and disaster risk reduction. . . .

SPM 3.4 Characteristics of mitigation pathways

There are multiple mitigation pathways that are *likely* to limit warming to below 2°C relative to pre-industrial levels. These pathways would require substantial emissions reductions over the next few decades and near zero emissions of $CO2$ and other long-lived greenhouse gases by the end of the century. Implementing such reductions poses substantial technological, economic, social and institutional challenges, which increase with delays in additional mitigation and if key technologies are not available. Limiting warming to lower or higher levels involves similar challenges but on different timescales.

. . .

SPM 4. Adaptation and Mitigation

Many adaptation and mitigation options can help address climate change, but no single option is sufficient by itself. Effective implementation depends on policies and cooperation at all scales and can be enhanced through integrated responses that link adaptation and mitigation with other societal objectives.

. . .

SPM 4.4 Policy approaches for adaptation and mitigation, technology and finance

Effective adaptation and mitigation responses will depend on policies and measures across multiple scales: international, regional, national and sub-national. Policies across all scales supporting technology development, diffusion and transfer, as well as finance for responses to climate change, can complement and enhance the effectiveness of policies that directly promote adaptation and mitigation.

International cooperation is critical for effective mitigation, even though mitigation can also have local co-benefits. Adaptation focuses primarily on local to national scale outcomes, but its effectiveness can be enhanced through coordination across governance scales, including international cooperation:

- The United Nations Framework Convention on Climate Change (UNFCCC) is the main multilateral forum focused on addressing climate change, with nearly universal participation. Other institutions organized at different levels of governance have resulted in diversifying international climate change cooperation.

- The Kyoto Protocol offers lessons towards achieving the ultimate objective of the UNFCCC, particularly with respect to participation, implementation, flexibility mechanisms and environmental effectiveness (*medium evidence, low agreement*).

- Policy linkages among regional, national and sub-national climate policies offer potential climate change mitigation benefits (*medium evidence, medium agreement*). Potential advantages include lower mitigation costs, decreased emission leakage and increased market liquidity.

- International cooperation for supporting adaptation planning and implementation has received less attention historically than mitigation but is increasing and has assisted in the creation of adaptation strategies, plans and actions at the national, sub-national and local level (*high confidence*).

There has been a considerable increase in national and sub-national plans and strategies on both adaptation and mitigation since the [fourth assessment report], with an increased focus on policies designed to integrate multiple objectives, increase co-benefits and reduce adverse side effects (*high confidence*):

- National governments play key roles in adaptation planning and implementation (*robust evidence, high agreement*) through coordinating actions and providing frameworks and support. While local government and the private sector have different functions, which vary regionally, they are increasingly recognized as critical to progress in adaptation, given their roles in scaling up adaptation of communities, households and civil society and in managing risk information and financing (*medium evidence, high agreement*).

- Institutional dimensions of adaptation governance, including the integration of adaptation into planning and decision-making, play a key role in promoting the transition from planning to implementation of adaptation (*robust evidence, high agreement*). Examples of institutional approaches to adaptation involving multiple actors include economic options (e.g., insurance, public-private partnerships), laws and regulations (e.g., land-zoning laws) and national and government policies and programmes (e.g., economic diversification).

- In principle, mechanisms that set a carbon price, including cap and trade systems and carbon taxes, can achieve mitigation in a cost-effective way but have been implemented with diverse effects due in part to national circumstances as well as policy design. The short-run effects of cap and trade systems have been limited as a result of loose caps or caps that have not proved to be constraining (*limited evidence, medium agreement*). In some countries, tax-based policies specifically aimed at reducing GHG emissions—alongside technology and other policies—have helped to weaken the link between GHG emissions and GDP (*high confidence*). In addition, in a large group of countries, fuel taxes (although not necessarily designed for the purpose of mitigation) have had effects that are akin to sectoral carbon taxes.

- Regulatory approaches and information measures are widely used and are often environmentally effective (*medium evidence, medium agreement*). Examples of regulatory approaches include energy efficiency standards; examples of information programmes include labelling programmes that can help consumers make better-informed decisions.

- Sector-specific mitigation policies have been more widely used than economy-wide policies (*medium evidence, high agreement*). Sector-specific policies may be better suited to address sector-specific barriers or market failures and may be bundled in packages of complementary policies. Although theoretically more cost-effective, administrative and political barriers may make economy-wide policies harder to implement. Interactions between or among mitigation policies may be synergistic or may have no additive effect on reducing emissions.

- Economic instruments in the form of subsidies may be applied across sectors, and include a variety of policy designs, such as tax rebates or exemptions, grants, loans and credit lines. An increasing number and variety of renewable energy (RE) policies including subsidies—motivated by many factors—have driven escalated growth of RE technologies in recent years. At the same time, reducing subsidies for GHG-related activities in various sectors can achieve emission reductions, depending on the social and economic context (*high confidence*).

Co-benefits and adverse side effects of mitigation could affect achievement of other objectives such as those related to human health, food security, biodiversity, local environmental quality, energy access, livelihoods and equitable sustainable development. . . .

Notes and Questions

1. While the assessment in this report may strike you as dire, it should be noted that it is actually quite conservative. Even at the time it was drafted it was necessarily restrained in tone and substance, due to the rigorous process required for its drafting. Not only are there several draft stages for expert and governmental review, but each member state has to provide *line-by-line approval* for the Executive Summary and Summary for Policy Makers. That said, although consensus is required for each line, there is a back-up plan for tough situations, allowing for a dissenting view to be noted. Because of the IPCC's highly politicized process, the resulting product is generally going to be relatively conservative.

2. Not only was the report conservative in representing the predictions at the time, but in the couple of years since we have already learned that the situation is worse than we thought then. *See, e.g., Global Warming Set to Pass 2C Threshold in 2050: Report*, Phys.org September 29, 2016 (quoting the IPCC chair as having stated that "Climate change is happening now and much faster than anticipated."); Eric Holthaus, *Our*

Planet's Temperature Just Reached a Terrifying Milestone, SLATE, March 12, 2016 (reporting on a period then occurring, in which the temperature was already 2C above normal).

3. Most likely you noticed the italicized uncertainty terms (*very likely, unlikely, high confidence*, etc.) as you read the report. Do you think that you and your classmates may interpret these differently? Well, if this bothered you at all, perhaps this was for good reason. A recent study on how people interpret these terms demonstrated that there was wide variation, which not surprisingly related to the reader's individual political beliefs. The study found that coupling such terms with numerical assessments had significantly greater success in achieving a consensus of understanding. The researchers concluded "that using a dual (verbal-numerical) scale would be superior to the current mode of communication as it (a) increases the level of differentiation between the various terms, (b) increases the consistency of interpretation of these terms, and (c) increases the level of consistency with the IPCC guidelines. Most importantly, these positive effects are independent of the respondents' ideological and environmental views." David V. Budescu et al., *Effective Communication of Uncertainty in the IPCC Reports*, 113 CLIMATIC CHANGE 181–200 (2012).

B. Precursors to the Paris Agreement: A Little History

Two years before the most recent IPCC report excerpted above, the United Nations Conference on Sustainable Development, also known as Rio+20, had just taken place in Rio de Janeiro, 20 years after the historic 1992 United Nations Conference on Environment and Development (UNCED) was held in the same location (hence the name Rio+20). This meeting resulted in a 49-page vision document titled *The Future We Want*. By most accounts, little was actually accomplished at this meeting, apart from committing to future efforts at progress, though a good deal of that was achieved. The following short excerpt summarizes the more recent Rio+20.

Summary of the United Nations Conference on Sustainable Development

EARTH NEGOTIATIONS BULLETIN, Vol. 27, No. 51, 25 June 2012, pp. 1–2

available at http://www.iisd.ca/download/pdf/enb2751e.pdf

The agreement adopted in Rio calls for the UN General Assembly (UNGA), at its next session, to take decisions on, *inter alia*: designating a body to operationalize the 10-year framework of programmes on sustainable consumption and production; determining the modalities for the third international conference on small island developing states, which is to convene in 2014; identifying the format and organizational aspects of the high-level forum, which is to replace the Commission on Sustainable Development; strengthening the UN Environment Programme (UNEP); constituting a working group to develop global sustainable development goals (SDGs) to be agreed by UNGA; establishing an intergovernmental process under UNGA to prepare a report proposing options on an effective sustainable development financing strategy; and considering a set of recommendations from the Secretary-General for a facilitation mechanism that promotes the development, transfer and dissemination of clean and environmentally sound technologies.

In addition, the UNGA is called on to take a decision in two years on the development of an international instrument under the UN Convention on the Law of the Sea (UNCLOS) regarding marine biodiversity in areas beyond national jurisdiction. Furthermore, the UN Statistical Commission is called on to launch a programme of work on broader measures to complement gross domestic product, and the UN system is encouraged, as appropriate, to support industry, interested governments and relevant stakeholders in developing models for best practice and facilitate action for the integration of sustainability reporting. The text also includes text on trade-distorting subsidies, fisheries and fossil fuel subsidies.

While many had held out hope that Rio+20 would launch new processes and significantly alter the international framework—from establishing a new High Commissioner for Future Generations, to upgrading the UN Environment Programme to the status of a specialized agency, to identifying significant means of implementation, to establishing concrete targets and a "roadmap" for the green economy—the UNCSD outcome document was much more modest. But while some criticized the document for "kicking the can" down the road and missing an opportunity to boldly redirect sustainable development actions, others focused on the upcoming opportunities within the UNGA and other fora to shape the true Rio+20 legacy.

Notes and Questions

1. For a brief description of the original Rio meeting and resulting United Nations Framework Convention on Climate Change (UNFCCC), see Ruth Gordon, *Climate Change and the Poorest Nations: Further Reflections on Global Inequality*, 78 U. Colo. L. Rev. 1559, 1582–5 (2007).

2. An important agreement quickly arose out of the UNFCC. The Kyoto Protocol, which was the primary international agreement for mitigating greenhouse gases for nearly two decades prior to the Paris Agreement (albeit in effect for just over a decade), was infamously never ratified by the United States. For the full text, see http://unfccc.int/essential_background/kyoto_protocol/items/1678.php The following excerpt is a summary from the UNFCCC website.

A Summary of the Kyoto Protocol   1997

United Nations Framework Convention on Climate Change

http://unfccc.int/kyoto_protocol/background/items/2879.php

* It took all of one year for the member countries of the Framework Convention on Climate Change to decide that **the Convention had to be augmented by an agreement with stricter demands for reducing greenhouse-gas emissions.** The Convention took effect in 1994, and by 1995 governments had begun negotiations on a protocol—an international agreement linked to the existing treaty, but standing on its own. The text of the Kyoto Protocol was adopted unanimously in 1997; it entered into force on 16 February 2005.

* The Protocol's major feature is that it has **mandatory targets on greenhouse-gas emissions for the world's leading economies which have accepted it.** These targets range from −8 per cent to +10 per cent of the countries' individual 1990 emissions levels "with a view to reducing their overall emissions of such gases by at least 5 per cent below existing 1990 levels in the commitment period 2008 to 2012." In almost all cases — even those set at +10 per cent of 1990 levels — the limits call for significant reductions in currently projected emissions. Future mandatory targets are expected to be established for "commitment periods" after 2012. These are to be negotiated well in advance of the periods concerned.

* **Commitments under the Protocol vary from nation to nation.** The overall 5 per cent target for developed countries is to be met through cuts (from 1990 levels) of 8 per cent in the European Union (EU[15]), Switzerland, and most Central and East European states; 6 per cent in Canada; 7 per cent in the United States (although the US has since withdrawn its support for the Protocol); and 6 per cent in Hungary, Japan, and Poland. New Zealand, Russia, and Ukraine are to stabilize their emissions, while Norway may increase emissions by up to 1 per cent, Australia by up to 8 per cent (subsequently withdrew its support for the Protocol), and Iceland by 10 per cent. The EU has made its own internal agreement to meet its 8 per cent target by distributing different rates to its member states. These targets range from a 28 per cent reduction by Luxembourg and 21 per cent cuts by Denmark and Germany to a 25 per cent increase by Greece and a 27 per cent increase by Portugal.

* To compensate for the sting of "binding targets," as they are called, the agreement offers **flexibility in how countries may meet their targets.** For example, they may partially compensate for their emissions by increasing "sinks" — forests, which remove carbon dioxide from the atmosphere. That may be accomplished either on their own territories or in other countries. Or they may pay for foreign projects that result in greenhouse-gas cuts. Several mechanisms have been set up for this purpose. (See the sub-chapters on "emissions trading," the "clean development mechanism," and "joint implementation.")

* The Kyoto Protocol is a complicated agreement that has been slow in coming — there are reasons for this. **The Protocol not only has to be effective against a complicated worldwide problem — it also has to be politically acceptable.** As a result, panels and committees have multiplied to monitor and referee its various programmes, and even after the agreement was approved in 1997, further negotiations were deemed necessary to hammer out instructions on how to "operate" it. These rules, adopted in 2001, are called the "Marrakesh Accords."

* There is a **delicate balance** to international treaties. Those appealing enough to gain widespread support often aren't strong enough to solve the problems they focus on. (Because the Framework Convention was judged to have this weakness, despite its many valuable provisions, the Protocol was created to supplement it.) Yet treaties with real "teeth" may have difficulty attracting enough widespread support to be effective.

* **Some mechanisms of the Protocol had enough support that they were set up in advance of the Protocol's entry into force.** The Clean Development Mechanism, for example—through which industrialized countries can partly meet their binding emissions targets through "credits" earned by sponsoring greenhouse-gas-reducing projects in developing countries—already had an executive board before the Kyoto Protocol entered into force on 16 February 2005.

C. The Paris Agreement

In December 2015, nearly every country on earth reached a historic agreement to mitigate greenhouse gases and slow climate change. Meetings in preparation of this agreement took place in Paris, France, resulting in its being known as the Paris Agreement. While the agreement falls short of reducing emissions to the degree recommended by the IPCC, it is by far the most ambitious and inclusive agreement yet, with the greatest potential so far to make a meaningful difference. The full text of the agreement can be found here: https://unfccc.int/files/meetings/paris_nov_2015/applica tion/pdf/paris_agreement_english_.pdf. This text instead provides two easily digestible sources: a recounting of the agreement process, and expert commentary (from the Harvard Project on Climate Agreements) regarding the agreement.

Fiona Harvey, *Paris Climate Change Agreement: The World's Greatest Diplomatic Success*

THE GUARDIAN, December 14, 2015

With all 196 nations having a say, the UN climate deal, with all its frustrations and drama, has proven that compromise works for the planet

In the final meeting of the Paris talks on climate change on Saturday night, the debating chamber was full and the atmosphere tense. Ministers from 196 countries sat behind their country nameplates, aides flocking them, with observers packed into the overflowing hall.

John Kerry, the US secretary of state, talked animatedly with his officials, while China's foreign minister Xie Zhenhua wore a troubled look. They had been waiting in this hall for nearly two hours. The French hosts had trooped in to take their seats on the stage, ready to applaud on schedule at 5.30pm—but it was now after 7pm, and the platform was deserted.

After two weeks of fraught negotiations, was something going badly wrong?

Then at 7.16pm, the French foreign minister, Laurent Fabius, returned abruptly to the stage, flanked by high-ranking UN officials. The last-minute compromises had been resolved, he said. And suddenly they were all on their feet. Fabius brought down the green-topped gavel, a symbol of UN talks, and announced that a Paris agreement had been signed. The delegates were clapping, cheering and whistling wildly, embracing and weeping. Even the normally reserved economist Lord Stern was whooping.

Outside the hall, a "Mexican wave" of standing ovations rippled across the conference centre as news reached participants gathered around screens outside for the translation into their own language. The 50,000 people who attended the summit had been waiting for this moment, through marathon negotiating sessions and sleepless nights.

The contrast with the last global attempt to resolve climate change, at Copenhagen in 2009, which collapsed into chaos and recriminations, could not have been greater. In a city recently hit by terrorist attacks that left 130 dead and scores more critically injured, collective will had prevailed.

Paris produced an agreement hailed as "historic, durable and ambitious". Developed and developing countries alike are required to limit their emissions to relatively safe levels, of 2C with an aspiration of 1.5C, with regular reviews to ensure these commitments can be increased in line with scientific advice. Finance will be provided to poor nations to help them cut emissions and cope with the effects of extreme weather. Countries affected by climate-related disasters will gain urgent aid.

Like any international compromise, it is not perfect: the caps on emissions are still too loose, likely to lead to warming of 2.7 to 3C above pre-industrial levels, breaching the 2C threshold that scientists say is the limit of safety, beyond which the effects—droughts, floods, heatwaves and sea level rises—are likely to become catastrophic and irreversible. Poor countries are also concerned that the money provided to them will not be nearly enough to protect them. Not all of the agreement is legally binding, so future governments of the signatory countries could yet renege on their commitments.

These flaws may shadow the future of climate change action, but on Saturday night they took second place. As the news spread through the world, the reaction from civil society groups, governments and businesses, was overwhelmingly positive.

Kumi Naidoo, executive director of Greenpeace International, summed up the mood: "It sometimes seems that the countries of the UN can unite on nothing, but nearly 200 countries have come together and agreed a deal. Today, the human race has joined in a common cause. The Paris agreement is only one step on a long road and there are parts of it that frustrate, that disappoint me, but it is progress. The deal alone won't dig us out of the hole that we're in, but it makes the sides less steep."

Even as delegates celebrated at the conference's end, there was a palpable sense of relief from the exhausted French hosts. At many points in this fortnight of marathon negotiating sessions, it looked as if a deal might be beyond reach. That it ended in success was a tribute in part to their diligence and efficiency and the efforts of the UN.

"France has brought openness and experience in diplomacy, and mutual respect to these talks," said Stern, one of the world's leading climate economists. "They have taken great care to make everyone listened to, that they were consulted. There was a great sense of openness, of professional diplomacy, and skill."

Saturday night was the culmination not only of a fortnight of talks, but of more than 23 years of international attempts under the UN to forge collective action on this global problem. Since 1992, all of the world's governments had been pledging to take measures that would avoid dangerous warming. Those efforts were marked by discord and failure, the refusal of the biggest emitters to take part, ineffective agreements and ignored treaties.

For these reasons, the Paris talks were widely seen as make-or-break for the UN process. If they failed, collective global efforts would be at an end and the world would be left without a just and robust means of tackling climate change.

The threat was catastrophic and the stakes could scarcely be higher. Without urgent action, warming was predicted to reach unprecedented levels, of as much as 5C above current temperatures—a level that would see large swathes of the globe rendered virtually uninhabitable. What is more, infrastructure built today—coal-fired power plants, transport networks, buildings—that entail high carbon emissions will still be operating decades into the future, giving the world a narrow window in which to change the direction of our economies.

"This was the last chance," said Miguel Arias Canete, Europe's climate chief. "And we took it."

The terrorist attacks on Paris raised questions about whether the talks would go ahead at all but François Hollande, the French president, insisted that they must and, in a show of unity, more than 150 heads of state landed in the French capital for the opening day. Barack Obama hailed the conference as "an act of defiance" in the face of terrorism.

Immediately after the attacks, the first concern was for security. A planned march through central Paris by protesters was cancelled, though a version of it did go ahead as the talks opened and was marred by clashes with police and a small number of protesters, and arrests. Security for the conference was stepped up, with police and army patrolling the immediate area and transport routes nearby shut down for two days.

This was the biggest ever gathering of world leaders, whose presence was needed to empower their negotiators to move out of positions entrenched for more than 20 years. When they arrived, a series of key meetings were held, with Obama seeing Xi Jinping of China, Narendra Modi of India and representatives from the least developed countries. Hollande concentrated on forging links with the developing world. Angela Merkel, in a private meeting with Vladimir Putin, secured his pledge that Russia would not stand in the way of a deal.

Behind the conference centre gates, French delegates were marshalling their diplomatic forces. They had carefully arranged the conference centre so that their part of the compound—behind barriers staffed by UN guards and secret service officers, unlike the rest of the delegations which were open to access—was directly above the UN's offices.

Fabius, from his office, could be with Christiana Figueres, the UN climate change chief, for a face-to-face chat within seconds. His fellow minister, Ségolène Royal, was just along the corridor, flanked with the offices of ambassadors and high-ranking officials. Within the buzzing control room, screens relayed pictures of what was happening in each of the conference rooms scattered around the compound and 24 hour news from French and international channels.

About 60 French officials were there. In preparation for the all-night sessions that began almost immediately the conference started, a room with 20 cubicled beds was waiting for exhausted officials to refresh themselves with a few snatched moments of sleep.

Procedurally, the French took great care. They instituted a series of talks known as "confessionals". These were intended as confidential places where delegates could, in the words of one French official, "speak from the heart" to listening French diplomats, with no holds barred and an assurance of privacy.

There were also the absurdly named "informal informals", in which a small group of delegates from various countries were charged with tackling a small piece of disputed text often as little as a paragraph at a time. Their task was to try to remove the infamous "square brackets" denoting areas of disagreement on the text and they met in small huddles around the conference centre, squatting on the floor in corridors or standing around a smart phone.

After these measures were still not producing enough progress, Fabius turned to "indabas"—by Zulu tradition, these are groups of elders convened to try to discuss disputes in communities. They were first tried out at the Durban climate talks in South Africa, in 2011, and under France's plan they consisted of groups of up to 80 delegates at a time gathered to thrash out the remaining disagreements.

While the French could draft in experienced diplomats on every side, some of the smallest countries had difficulty in keeping up with the meetings—many happened in parallel and they did not have the personnel to attend them all.

One way of getting around that was the formation of a "coalition of high ambition", which was announced with three days to Friday's deadline. Forged by small island states—a key figure was Tony de Brum of the Marshall Islands—and the EU, it was joined by many of the least developed countries, adding up to more than 100 nations. They could then negotiate together, with an agreed common interest. Before the end, this coalition had been joined by the US, Canada and Australia. It was hailed by Europe's climate and energy commissioner Miguel Cañete as a key factor in the end agreement.

And yet with three days of the conference to go, it looked as if all of these efforts might yet come to nothing. On the second Wednesday of the talks, the French produced a second iteration of the core text, reducing the number of brackets from more than 300 to fewer than 40. They were hopeful that this could be almost the end— and it needed to be in order to have the legal "scrubbers" and linguistic experts assess the text and ensure it was in line with international law and accurate in all languages.

But it soon became apparent that things were not going to plan. As countries examined the draft agreement, ministers started raising concerns. On Wednesday afternoon, leading delegations trooped one by one into Fabius' personal office: Edna

Molewa of South Africa, Xie Zhenhua of China, John Kerry of the US, Julie Bishop of Australia.

For South Africa, issues over "loss and damage" emerged—for developed countries, this meant the question of whether developing countries should be entitled to special aid in the event of climate-related disasters; for the developing, it meant compensation and liability, which the US would never agree to. For China, a key sticking point was differentiation—the concept that developing countries have less responsibility for climate change. For the US, some parts of the deal could not be legally binding in order to pass Congress.

Fabius sought to allay their concerns and find a compromise. At 8pm, he convened a new plenary session, at which all countries were able to speak. It carried on through the night.

At this point, it was clear that further efforts were needed. There followed a rapid round of telephone diplomacy. Obama spoke personally to the Chinese leader. Hollande picked up the phone to as many of his counterparts across the world as he could manage.

Finally, after two more days of fraught negotiation, a consensus emerged. None of the major countries wanted to be seen as wrecking a deal that had come so close. All could agree that they wanted an agreement and all made compromises. The EU backed down on having the intended emissions cuts, agreed at a national level, to be legally binding; the US accepted language on "loss and damage"; China and India agreed that an aspiration of holding warming to 1.5C could be included.

For the diplomats involved, the efforts were exhausting. The talks took a personal toll. In the months before the conference, Laurence Tubiana, appointed as special ambassador on climate change, played a key role in liaising with developing and developed countries. Then disaster struck. A week before the COP was scheduled to begin, she suffered a sudden sharp pain. It was acute appendicitis, necessitating emergency surgery. Within days, however, she had resumed her key role. When the deal was signed, she was on the podium, receiving hugs from Ban Ki-moon, Figueres, Fabius and Hollande, a recognition of the sacrifices she had made.

All of these efforts came to a head in the final crucial days. On Saturday morning, a new draft text was prepared. Fabius assembled the delegates and told them to have lunch while they waited for it to be translated. That afternoon, they examined the text and nearly all agreed that, with minor reservations, they could accept it. The final meeting was scheduled for 5.30pm. As for the last-minute hitch that kept delegates waiting in the hall for two hours? A matter of minor aspects of wording, including the translation of a few terms and the placement of a comma. It was rectified, apologies given, and the jubilation could begin.

It is easy to forget what an extraordinary event these UN talks were. The UNFCCC is one of the last remaining forums in the world where every country, however small, is represented on the same basis and has equal say with the biggest economies. Most modern diplomacy carries on in small, self-selected groups dominated by richer countries—the G7, the G20, the OECD, OPEC—but all 196 states have a seat and a say at the UNFCCC. Agreement can only be accepted by consensus.

If this makes for an unwieldy and frustrating process, it is also a fair one. The poorest countries of the world, so often left out of international consideration, are those which have done least to create climate change, but will suffer the most from it. Only at the UN are they heard.

Robert Stavins, *Paris Agreement—A Good Foundation for Meaningful Progress*

December 12, 2015, http://www.robertstavinsblog.org/2015/12/12 /paris-agreement-a-good-foundation-for-meaningful-progress/

The Paris Agreement, a truly landmark climate accord, which was gaveled through today, December 12, 2015, at 7:26 pm (Paris time) at the Twenty-First Conference of the Parties (COP-21), checks all the boxes in my five-point scorecard for a potentially effective Paris Agreement, described in my November 17th blog essay, Paris Can Be a Key Step. The Agreement provides a broad foundation for meaningful progress on climate change, and represents a dramatic departure from the Kyoto Protocol and the past 20 years of climate negotiations.

Essential Background

Anyone who has read this blog over the past several years, or—even more so— my academic writing over the past twenty years on international climate change policy architecture, knows that I have viewed the dichotomous distinction between Annex I and non-Annex I countries as the major stumbling block to progress. That distinction was first introduced in the climate negotiations at COP-1 in Berlin in 1995. That was, in my view, an unfortunate and narrow interpretation of the sound equity principle in the United Nations Framework Convention on Climate Change (UNFCCC, 1992)—"common but differentiated responsibilities and respective capabilities." It was codified two years later in the Kyoto Protocol.

The Kyoto Protocol, which has been the primary international agreement to reduce the greenhouse-gas emissions that cause global climate change, included mandatory emissions-reduction obligations only for developed countries. Developing countries had no emissions-reduction commitments. The dichotomous distinction between the developed and developing countries in the Kyoto Protocol has made progress on climate change impossible, because growth in emissions since the Protocol came into force in 2005 is entirely in the large developing countries—China, India, Brazil, Korea, South Africa, Mexico, and Indonesia. The big break came at the annual UNFCCC negotiating session in Durban, South Africa in 2011, where a decision was adopted by member countries to "develop [by December 2015, in Paris] a protocol, another legal instrument or an agreed outcome with legal force under the Convention *applicable to all Parties*." This "Durban Platform for Enhanced Action" broke with the Kyoto Protocol and signaled a new opening for innovative thinking (which we, at the Harvard Project on Climate Agreements, took to heart).

The Paris Agreement is a Departure from the Past

Today, in Paris, representatives of 195 countries adopted a new hybrid international climate policy architecture that includes: bottom-up elements in the form of "Intended Nationally Determined Contributions" (INDCs), which are national targets and actions that arise from national policies; and top-down elements for oversight, guidance, and coordination. Now, all countries will be involved in taking actions to reduce emissions.

Remarkably, 186 of the 195 members of the UNFCCC submitted INDCs by the end of the Paris talks, representing some 96% of global emissions. Contrast that with the Kyoto Protocol, which now covers countries (Europe and New Zealand) accounting for no more than 14% of global emissions (and 0% of global emissions growth).

This broad scope of participation under the new Paris Agreement is a necessary condition for meaningful action, but, of course, it is not a sufficient condition. Also required is adequate ambition of the individual contributions. But this is only the first step with this new approach. The INDCs will be assessed and revised every five years, with their collective ambition ratcheted up over time. That said, even this initial set of contributions could cut anticipated temperature increases this century to about 3.5 degrees Centigrade, more than the frequently-discussed aspirational goal of limiting temperature increases to 2 degrees C (or the new aspirational target from Paris of 1.5 degrees C), but much less than the 5–6 degrees C increase that would be expected without this action. (An amendment to the Montreal Protocol to address hydrofluorocarbons (HFCs) is likely to shave an addition 0.5 C of warming.)

The problem has not been solved, and it will not be for years to come, but the new approach brought about by the Paris Agreement can be a key step toward reducing the threat of global climate change.

The new climate agreement, despite being path-breaking and the result of what Coral Davenport writing in The New York Times rightly called "an extraordinary effort at international diplomacy," is only a foundation for moving forward, but it is a sufficiently broad and sensible foundation to make increased ambition over time feasible for the first time. Whether the Agreement is truly successful, whether this foundation for progress is effectively exploited over the years ahead by the Parties to the Agreement, is something we will know only ten, twenty, or more years from now.

What is key in the Agreement is the following: the centrality of the INDC structure (through which 186 countries representing 96% of global emissions have made submissions); the most balanced transparency requirements ever promulgated; provision for heterogeneous linkage, including international carbon markets (through "internationally transferred mitigation outcomes"—ITMOs); explicit clarification in a decision that agreement on "loss and damage" does not provide a basis for liability of compensation; and 5-year periods for stocktaking and improvement of the INDCs.

The Key Elements of the Paris Agreement

Here are some of the highlights of what stands out to me in the Paris Agreement.

Article 2 of the Agreement reaffirms the *goal* of limiting the global average temperature increase above the pre-industrial level to 2 degrees C, and adds 1.5 degrees C as something even more aspirational. In my opinion, these aspirational goals — which come not from science (although endorsed by most scientists) nor economics, and may not even be feasible — are much less important than the critical components of the agreement: the scope of participation through the INDC structure, and the mechanisms for implementation (see below).

Article 3 makes it clear that the *INDC structure* is central and universal for all parties, although Article 4 blurs this a bit with references to the circumstances of developing country Parties. But throughout the Agreement, it is abundantly clear that the firewall from the 1995 Berlin Mandate has finally been breached. In addition, *five-year periods for the submission of revised INDCs* (and global stocktaking of the impact of the Paris Agreement) are included in Article 14. The first stocktaking review will be in 2018, with the start date for new INDCs set for 2020.

Article 4 importantly describes *transparency requirements* (domestic monitoring, reporting, and verification). This is crucial, and represents a striking compromise between the U.S. and Europe, on the one hand, and China and India, on the other hand. All countries must eventually face the same monitoring and reporting requirements, regardless of their status as developed or developing.

Article 6 provides for *international policy linkage*, and is thereby *exceptionally important* for the successful exploitation of the foundation provided by the Paris Agreement. The necessary language for heterogeneous international policy linkage (not only international carbon markets, but international linkage of other national policy instruments) is included. I have written about this key issue many times over the past ten years. It can bring down compliance costs greatly, and thereby facilitate greater ambition over time. . . . The Paris Agreement accomplishes this through provision for "internationally transferred mitigation outcomes." With this provision, we have a new climate policy acronym — ITMOs . . .

There is considerable discussion of "finance" in Article 9, but the numbers do not appear in the Agreement, only in the accompanying Decision, where item 54 states that by 2025, the Parties will revisit the total quantity of funding, using the current $100 billion target as a "floor."

Finally, the Agreement's Article 8 on Loss and Damage was necessary from the point of view of the most vulnerable countries, but the most contentious issue is settled in Decision 52, where the Parties agree that this "does not involve or provide a basis for any liability of compensation." That decision was absolutely essential from the perspective of the largest emitters.

Anticipated Impacts of the Paris Agreement

Before I turn to my assessment of the Agreement, I should comment briefly on a topic that seems to be of considerable interest to many people (based on the questions I received from the press during my 10 days in Paris), namely what effect will the Agreement have on business, what signals will it send to the private sector?

My answer is that impacts on businesses will come largely not directly from the Paris Agreement, but from the policy actions that the various Parties undertake domestically in their respective jurisdictions to comply with the Paris Agreement. I am again referring to the 186 countries which submitted Intended Nationally Determined Contributions—INDCs—under the Agreement.

So, in the case of the United States, for example, those policies that will enable the country to achieve its submitted INDC are: the Clean Power Plan (which will accelerate the shift in many states from coal to natural gas for electricity generation, as well as provide incentives in some states for renewable electricity generation); CAFE (motor vehicle fuel efficiency) standards increasing over time (as already enacted by Congress); appliance efficiency standards moving up over time (as also already enacted by Congress); California's very aggressive climate policy (AB-32); and the northeast states' Regional Greenhouse Gas Initiative.

These various policies are credible, and they will send price signals that affect business decisions (but not across the board nor with ideal efficiency, as would a national carbon tax or a national carbon cap-and-trade system). In terms of impacts on specific companies, impacts will continue to vary greatly. But a useful generalization is that a major effect of most climate policies is to raise energy costs, which tends to be good news for producers of energy-consuming durable goods (for example, the Boeing Company) and bad news for consumers of those same energy-consuming durable goods (for example, United Airlines).

An Assessment with my Paris Scorecard

Lastly, here is my November 17th scorecard and my assessment of the five key elements I said would constitute a successful 21st Conference of the Parties:

1. **Include approximately 90% of global emissions** in the set of INDCs that are submitted and part of the Paris Agreement (compared with 14% in the current commitment period of the Kyoto Protocol). This was obviously **achieved**, with total coverage reaching 96% of global emissions.

2. **Establish credible reporting and transparency** requirements. This was **achieved**, through long negotiations between China and India, on the one hand, and Europe and the United States, on the other.

3. **Move forward with finance for climate adaptation (and mitigation)** B the famous $100 billion commitment. This was **achieved**.

4. **Agree to return to negotiations periodically, such as every 5 years**, to revisit the ambition and structure of the INDCs. This was **achieved**.

5. **Put aside unproductive disagreements**, such as on so-called "loss and damage," which appears to rich countries like unlimited liability for bad *weather* events in developing countries, and the insistence by some parties that the INDCs themselves be binding under international law. This would have

required Senate ratification of the Agreement in the United States, which would have meant that the United States would *not* be a party to the Agreement. There was **success** on both of these.

Final Words

*So, my fundamental assessment of the Paris climate talks is that they were a great **success**.* Unfortunately, as I have said before, some advocates and some members of the press will likely characterize the outcome as a "failure," because the 2 degree C target has not been achieved immediately.

Let me conclude where I started. The Paris Agreement provides an important new foundation for meaningful progress on climate change, and represents a dramatic departure from the past 20 years of international climate negotiations. Of course, the problem has not been solved, and it will not be for many years to come. But the new approach brought about by the Paris Agreement can be a key step toward reducing the threat of global climate change. In truth, only time will tell.

Notes and Questions

1. During the first couple of years following the agreement, the member countries ratified it one by one. On October 5, 2016, the threshold was met for the agreement to go into effect, in that it was ratified by at least 55 Parties to the Convention, accounting for a combined total of at least 55 percent of the total global greenhouse gas emissions. The Paris Agreement entered into force on 4 November 2016, 30 days later.

2. The ratification process following the Paris Agreement reflected unprecedented international cooperation, motivated by the scientific evidence of global danger. UN Secretary-General Ban Ki-moon said: "Strong international support for the Paris Agreement entering into force is testament to the urgency for action, and reflects the consensus of governments that robust global cooperation is essential to meet the climate challenge."

3. Reflecting on this period of rapid agreement two to four years later, how might other developments in international relations impact this historic tone of cooperation?

4. While the Paris Agreement may be the most exciting step toward mitigation of climate change observed yet, an important consideration is enforceability. As with international agreements generally, this has always been a concern for addressing climate change effectively. *See* Scott Barrett, *Climate Treaties and the Imperative of Enforcement*, 24 Oxford Rev. Econ. Pol. 239 (2008). While there are impediments to direct enforcement of agreements among sovereign countries, there is optimism that the Paris Agreement's approach of frequent monitoring and reporting will serve as a form of peer-pressure enforcement. *See Ban Ki-Moon on Enforcing the Paris Agreement: U.N. Secretary-General Discusses Why He Thinks Countries Will Honor Their Commitments*, Wall Street Journal, April 12, 2016. Time, of course, will tell.

III. United States Climate Change Law and Policy

In 2008 the U.S. Congress commissioned the National Academy of Sciences to "investigate and study the serious and sweeping issues relating to global climate change and make recommendations regarding the steps that must be taken and what strategies must be adopted in response to global climate change." The resulting work, whose summary follows, jump-started the previously nonexistent U.S. climate policy agenda. In the years since, many agencies have provided guidance regarding the consideration of climate change in the implementation of their existing programs, citizens have developed creative litigation strategies to take these efforts even further, and the EPA has fought a long battle to determine how the Clean Air Act may be used to address greenhouse gas emissions.

NATIONAL RESEARCH COUNCIL
LIMITING THE MAGNITUDE OF FUTURE CLIMATE CHANGE

(The National Academies Press, 2010)

Summary

In the legislation calling for an assessment of America's climate choices, Congress directed the National Research Council (NRC) to "investigate and study the serious and sweeping issues relating to global climate change and make recommendations regarding the steps that must be taken and what strategies must be adopted in response to global climate change." As part of the response to this request, the America's Climate Choices Panel on Limiting the Magnitude of Future Climate Change was charged to "describe, analyze, and assess strategies for reducing the net future human influence on climate, including both technology and policy options, focusing on actions to reduce domestic greenhouse gas (GHG) emissions and other human drivers of climate change, but also considering the international dimensions of climate stabilization"

Our panel responded to this charge by evaluating the choices available for the United States to contribute to the global effort of limiting future climate change. More specifically, the panel focused on strategies to reduce concentrations of GHGs in the atmosphere, including strategies that are technically and economically feasible in the near term, as well as strategies that could potentially play an important role in the longer term.

Because policy that limits climate change is highly complex and involves a wide array of political and ethical considerations, scientific analysis does not always point to unequivocal answers. We offer specific recommendations in cases where research clearly shows that certain strategies and policy options are particularly effective; but in other cases, we simply discuss the range of possible choices available to decision makers. On the broadest level, we conclude that the United States needs the following:

- *Prompt and sustained strategies to reduce GHG emissions.* There is a need for policy responses to promote the technological and behavioral changes necessary for making substantial near-term GHG emission reductions. There is also a need to aggressively promote research, development, and deployment of new technologies, both to enhance our chances of making the needed emissions reductions and to reduce the costs of doing so.

- An inclusive *national framework for instituting response strategies and policies.* National policies for limiting climate change are implemented through the actions of private industry, governments at all levels, and millions of households and individuals. The essential role of the federal government is to put in place an overarching, national policy framework designed to ensure that all of these actors are furthering the shared national goal of emissions reductions. In addition, a national policy framework that both generates and is underpinned by international cooperation is crucial if the risks of global climate change are to be substantially curtailed.

- *Adaptable means for managing policy responses.* It is inevitable that policies put in place now will need to be modified in the future as new scientific information emerges, providing new insights and understanding of the climate problem. Even well-conceived policies may experience unanticipated difficulties, while others may yield unexpectedly high levels of success. Moreover, the degree, rate, and direction of technological innovation will alter the array of response options available and the costs of emissions abatement. Quickly and nimbly responding to new scientific information, the state of technology, and evidence of policy effectiveness will be essential to successfully managing climate risks over the course of decades.

While recognizing that there is ongoing debate about the goals for international efforts to limit climate change, for this analysis we have focused on a range of global atmospheric GHG concentrations between 450 and 550 parts per million (ppm) CO_2-equivalent (eq), a range that has been extensively analyzed by the scientific and economic communities and is a focus of international climate policy discussions. In evaluating U.S. climate policy choices, it useful to set goals that are consistent with those in widespread international use, both for policy development and for making quantitative assessments of alternative strategies.

Global temperature and GHG concentration targets are needed to help guide long-term global action. Domestic policy, however, requires goals that are more directly linked to outcomes that can be measured and affected by domestic action. The panel thus recommends that the U.S. policy goal be stated as a quantitative limit on domestic GHG emissions over a specified time period—in other words, a GHG emissions budget.

The panel does not attempt to recommend a specific budget number, because there are many political and ethical judgments involved in determining an "appropriate" U.S. share of global emissions. As a basis for developing and assessing domestic strategies, however, the panel used recent integrated assessment modeling studies to suggest that a reasonable "representative" range for a domestic emissions budget would be 170 to 200 gigatons (Gt) of CO_2-eq for the period 2012 through 2050. This corresponds roughly to a reduction of emissions from 1990 levels by 80 to 50 percent, respectively. We note that this budget range is based on "global least cost" economic efficiency criteria for allocating global emissions among countries. Using other criteria, different budget numbers could be suggested. (For instance, some argue that, based on global "fairness" concerns, a more aggressive U.S. emission-reduction effort is warranted.)

As illustrated in Figure S.1, meeting an emissions budget in the range suggested above, especially the more stringent budget of 170 Gt CO_2-eq, will require a major departure from business-as-usual emission trends (in which U.S. emissions have been rising at a rate of ~1 percent per year for the past three decades). The main drivers of GHG emissions are population growth and economic activity, coupled with energy use per capita and per unit of economic output ("energy intensity"). Although the energy intensity of the U.S. economy has been improving for the past two decades, total emissions will continue to rise without a significant change from business as usual. Our analyses thus indicate that, without prompt action, the current rate of GHG emissions from the energy sector would consume the domestic emissions budget well before 2050.

Figure S.1. Illustration of the representative U.S. cumulative GHG emissions budget targets: 170 and 200 Gt CO_2-eq (for Kyoto gases) (Gt, gigatons, or billion tons; Mt, megatons, or million tons). The exact value of the reference budget is uncertain, but nonetheless illustrates a clear need for a major departure from business as usual.

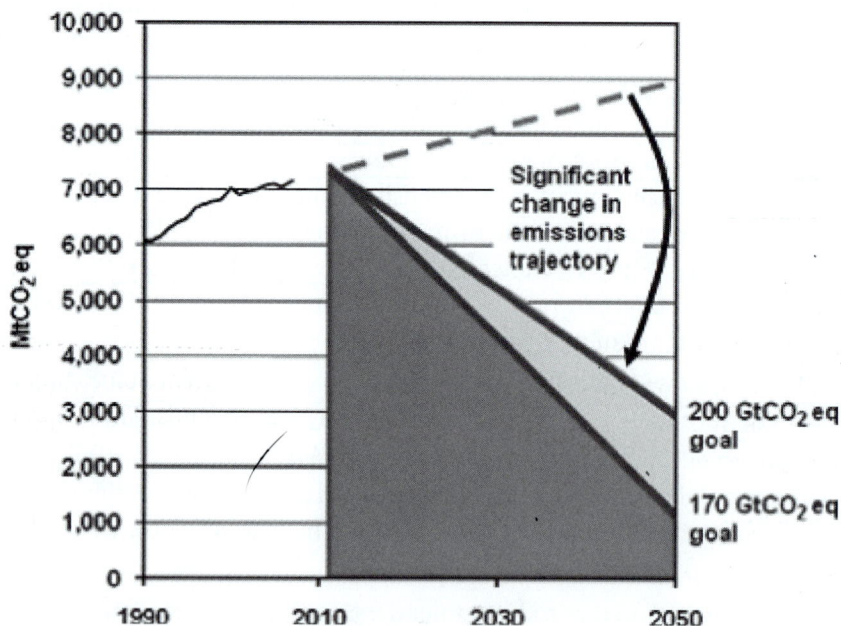

More than 80 percent of U.S. GHG emissions are in the form of CO_2 from combustion of fossil fuels. As illustrated in Figure S.2, there is a range of different opportunities to reduce emissions from the energy system, including reducing demand for goods and services requiring energy, improving the efficiency with which the energy is used to provide these goods and services, and reducing the carbon intensity of this energy supply (e.g., replacing fossil fuels with renewables or nuclear power, or employing carbon capture and storage).

Figure S.2. The chain of factors that determine how much CO_2 accumulates in the atmosphere. The blue boxes represent factors that can potentially be influenced to affect the outcomes in the purple circles.

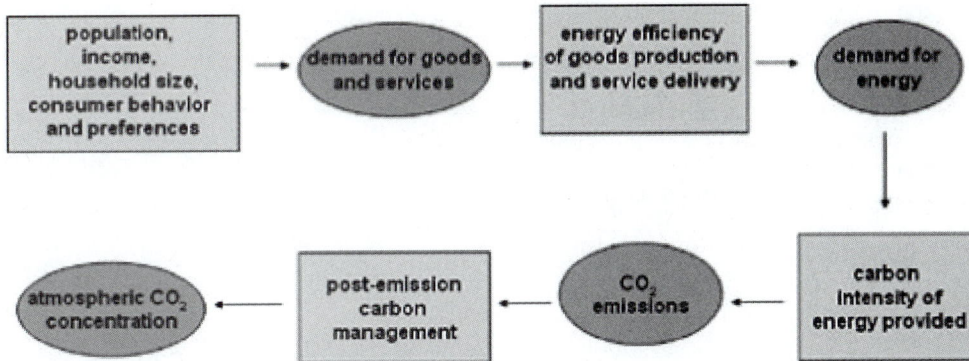

To evaluate the magnitude and feasibility of needed changes in all of these areas, we examined the results of a recent NRC study, *America's Energy Future*, which estimated the technical potential for aggressive near-term (i.e., for 2020 and 2035) deployment of key technologies for energy efficiency and low-carbon energy production. We compared this to estimates of the technology deployment levels that might be needed to meet the representative emissions budget. This analysis suggests that limiting domestic GHG emissions to 170 Gt CO_2-eq by 2050 by relying only on these near-term opportunities may be technically possible but will be very difficult. Meeting the 200-Gt CO_2-eq goal will be somewhat less difficult but also very demanding. In either case, however, falling short of the full technical potential for technology deployment is likely, as it would require overcoming many existing barriers (e.g., social resistance and institutional and regulatory concerns).

Some important opportunities exist to control non-CO_2 GHGs (such as methane, nitrous oxide, and the long-lived fluorinated gases) and to enhance biological uptake of CO_2 through afforestation and tillage change on suitable lands. These opportunities are worth pursuing, especially as a near-term strategy, but they are not large enough to make up the needed emissions reductions if the United States falls short in reducing CO_2 emissions from energy sources.

Acting to reduce GHG emissions in any of these areas will entail costs as well as benefits, but it is difficult to estimate overall economic impacts over time frames spanning decades. While different model projections suggest a range of possible impacts, all recent studies indicate that gross domestic product (GDP) continues to increase substantially over time. Studies also clearly indicate that the ultimate cost of GHG emission reduction efforts depends upon successful technology innovation (Figure S.3).

Figure S.3. A model projection of the future price of CO_2 emissions under two scenarios: a "reference" case that assumes continuation of historical rates of technological improvements and an "advanced" case with more rapid technological change. The absolute costs are highly uncertain, but studies clearly indicate that costs are reduced dramatically when advanced technologies are available. Source: Adapted from Kyle et al. (2009).
These recommendations are each discussed in greater detail below.

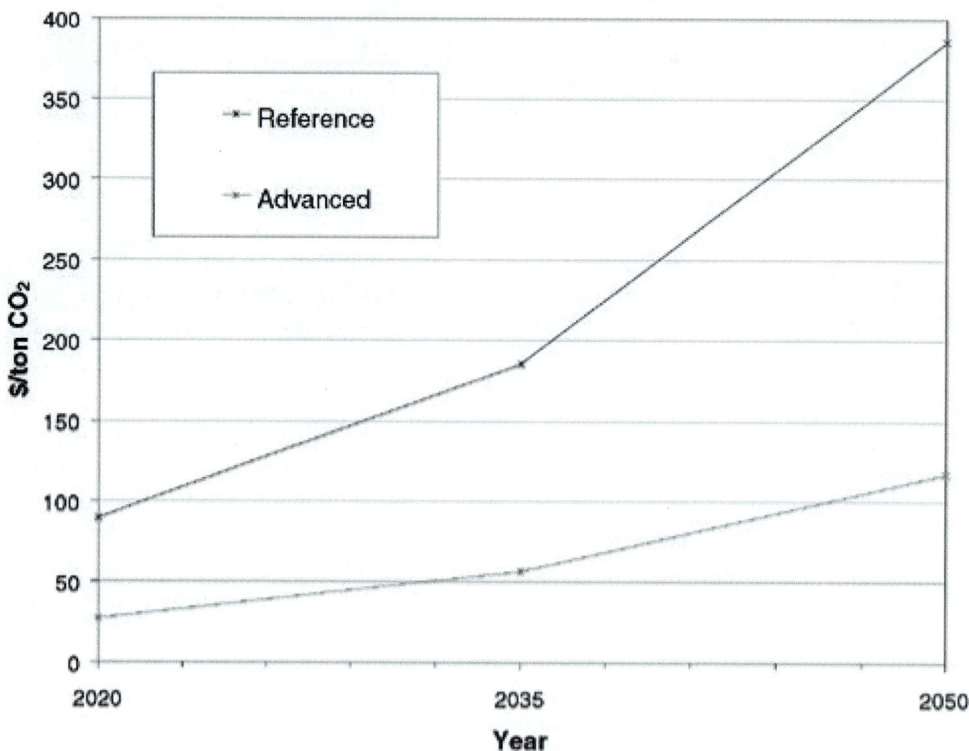

We thus conclude that there is an urgent need for U.S. action to reduce GHG emissions. In response to this need for action, we recommend the following core strategies to U.S. policy makers:

- Adopt a mechanism for setting an economy-wide carbon-pricing system.
- Complement the carbon price with a portfolio of policies to
  - realize the practical potential for near-term emissions reductions through energy efficiency and low-emission energy sources in the electric and transportation sectors;
  - establish the technical and economic feasibility of carbon capture and storage and new-generation nuclear technologies; and
  - accelerate the retirement, retrofitting, or replacement of GHG emission-intensive infrastructure.
- Create new technology choices by investing heavily in research and crafting policies to stimulate innovation.

- Consider potential equity implications when designing and implementing climate change limiting policies, with special attention to disadvantaged populations.

- Establish the United States as a leader to stimulate other countries to adopt GHG reduction targets.

- Enable flexibility and experimentation with policies to reduce GHG emissions at regional, state, and local levels.

- Design policies that balance durability and consistency with flexibility and capacity for modification as we learn from experience.

Adopt a mechanism for setting an economy-wide carbon pricing system.

A carbon pricing strategy is a critical foundation of the policy portfolio for limiting future climate change. It creates incentives for cost-effective reduction of GHGs and provides the basis for innovation and a sustainable market for renewable resources. An economy-wide carbon-pricing policy would provide the most cost-effective reduction opportunities, would lower the likelihood of significant emissions leakage, and could be designed with a capacity to adapt in response to new knowledge. [Emissions leakage refers to the phenomenon whereby controlling emissions within one region or sector causes activity and resulting emissions to shift to another, uncontrolled region or sector.]

Incentives for emissions reduction can be generated either by a taxation system or a cap-and-trade system. Taxation sets prices on emissions and lets quantities of emissions vary; cap-and-trade systems set quantity limits on emissions and let prices vary. There are also options for hybrid approaches that integrate elements of both taxation and cap-and-trade systems.

Any such systems face common design challenges. On the question of how to allocate the financial burden, research strongly suggests that economic efficiency is best served by avoiding free allowances (in cap-and-trade) or tax exemptions. On the question of how to use the revenues created by tax receipts or allowance sales, revenue recycling could play a number of important roles—for instance, by supporting complementary efforts such as research and development (R&D) and energy efficiency programs, by funding domestic or international climate change adaptation efforts, or by reducing the financial burden of a carbon-pricing system on low-income groups.

In concept, both tax and cap-and-trade mechanisms offer unique advantages and could provide effective incentives for emission reductions. In the United States and other countries, however, cap-and-trade has received the greatest attention, and we see no strong reason to argue that this approach should be abandoned in favor of a taxation system. In addition, the cap-and-trade system has features that are particularly compatible with other of our recommendations. For instance, it is easily compatible with the concept of an emissions budget and more transparent with regard to monitoring progress toward budget goals. It is also likely to be more durable over time, since those receiving emissions allowances have a valued asset that they will likely seek to retain.

High-quality domestic and international GHG offsets can play a useful role in lowering the overall costs of achieving a specific emissions reduction, both by expanding the scope of a pricing program to include uncovered emission sources and by offering a financing mechanism for emissions reduction in developing countries (although only for cases where adequate certification, monitoring, and verification are possible, including a demonstration that the reductions are real and additional). Note, however, that using international offsets as a way to meet the domestic GHG emissions budget could ultimately create a more onerous emissions-reduction burden for the countries selling the offsets; absent some form of compensation to ease this burden, seller countries may resist the use of offsets that are counted against their own emission budget.

Complement the carbon-pricing system with policies to help realize the practical potential of near-term technologies; to accelerate the retrofit, replacement, or retirement of emission-intensive infrastructure; and to create new technology choices.

Pricing GHGs is a crucial but insufficient component of the effort to limit future climate change. Because many market barriers exist and a national carbon pricing system will take time to develop and mature, a strategic, cost-effective portfolio of complementary policies is necessary to encourage early actions that increase the likelihood of meeting the 2050 emissions budget. This policy portfolio should have three major objectives, listed below.

1. Realize the practical potential for near-term emission reductions.

End-use energy demand and the technologies used for electricity generation and transportation drive the majority of U.S. CO_2 emissions. Key near-term opportunities for emission reductions in these areas include the following:

- *Increase energy efficiency.* Enhancing efficiency in the production and use of electricity and fuels offers some of the largest near-term opportunities for GHG reductions. These opportunities can be realized at a relatively low marginal cost, thus leading to an overall lowering of the cost of meeting the 2050 emissions budget. Furthermore, achieving greater energy efficiency in the near term can help defer new power plant construction while low-GHG technologies are being developed.

- *Increase the use of low-GHG-emitting electricity generation options, including the following:*

  - *Accelerate the use of renewable energy sources.* Renewable energy sources offer both near-term opportunities for GHG emissions reduction and potential long-term opportunities to meet global energy demand. Some renewable technologies are at and others are approaching economic parity with conventional power sources (even without a carbon-pricing system in place), but continued policy impetus is needed to encourage their development and adoption. This includes, for instance, advancing the development of needed transmission infrastructure, offering long-term stability in financial incentives, and encouraging the mobilization of private capital support for research, development, and deployment.

○ *Address and resolve key barriers to the full-scale testing and commercial-scale demonstration of new-generation nuclear power.* Improvements in nuclear technology are commercially available, but power plants using this technology have not yet been built in the United States. Although such plants have a large potential to reduce GHG emissions, the risks of nuclear power such as waste disposal and security and proliferation issues remain significant concerns and must be successfully resolved.

○ *Develop and demonstrate power plants equipped with carbon capture and storage technology.* Carbon capture and storage could be a critically important option for our future energy system. It needs to be commercially demonstrated in a variety of full-scale power plant applications to better understand the costs involved and the technological, social, and regulatory barriers that may arise and require resolution.

• *Advance low-GHG-emitting transportation options.* Near-term opportunities exist to reduce GHGs from the transportation sector through increasing vehicle efficiency, supporting shifts to energy-efficient modes of passenger and freight transport, and advancing low-GHG fuels (such as cellulosic ethanol).

2. Accelerate the retirement, retrofitting, or replacement of emissions-intensive infrastructure.

Transitioning to a low-carbon energy system requires clear and credible policies that enable not only the deployment of new technologies but also the retrofitting, retiring, or replacement of existing emissions-intensive infrastructure. However, the turnover of the existing capital stock of the energy system may be very slow. Without immediate action to encourage retirements, retrofitting, or replacement, the existing emissions-intensive capital stock will rapidly consume the U.S. emissions budget.

3. Create new technology choices.

The United States currently has a wide range of policies available to facilitate technological innovation, but many of these policies need to be strengthened, and in some cases additional measures enacted, to accelerate the needed technology advances. The magnitude of U.S. government spending for (nondefense) energy-related R&D has declined substantially since its peak nearly three decades ago. The United States also lags behind many other leading industrialized countries in the rate of government spending for energy-related R&D as a share of national GDP. While recommendations for desired levels and priorities for federal energy R&D spending are outside the scope of this study, we do find that the level and stability of current spending do not appear to be consistent with the magnitude of R&D resources needed to address the challenges of limiting climate change. In the private sector as well, compared to other U.S. industries, the U.S. energy sector spends very little on R&D relative to income or sales profits.

Research is a necessary first step in developing many new technologies, but bringing innovations to market requires more than basic research. Policies are also needed to establish and expand markets for low-GHG technologies, to more rapidly bring new technologies to commercial scale (especially support for large-scale demonstrations), to foster workforce development and training, and more generally to improve our understanding of how social and behavioral dynamics interact with technology and how technological changes interact with the broader societal goals of sustainable development.

Consider potential equity implications when designing and implementing policies to limit climate change, with special attention to disadvantaged populations.

Low-income groups consume less energy per capita and therefore contribute less to energy-related GHG emissions. Yet, low-income and some disadvantaged minority groups are likely to suffer disproportionately from adverse impacts of climate change and may also be adversely affected by policies to limit climate change. For instance, energy-related goods make up a larger share of expenditures in poor households, so raising the price of energy for consumers may impose the greatest burden on these households. Likewise, limited discretionary income may preclude these households from participating in many energy-efficiency incentives. Because these impacts are likely but not well understood, it will be important to monitor the impacts of climate change limiting policies on poor or disadvantaged communities and to adapt policies in response to unforeseen adverse impacts. Some key strategies to consider include the following:

- structuring policies to offset adverse impacts to low-income and other disadvantaged households (for instance, structuring carbon pricing policies to provide relief from higher energy prices to low-income households);

- designing incentive-based climate change limiting policies to be accessible to poor households (such as graduated subsidies for home heating or insulation improvements);

- ensuring that efforts to reduce energy consumption in the transport sector avoid disadvantaging those with already limited mobility; and

- actively and consistently engaging representatives of poor and minority communities in policy planning efforts.

Major changes to our nation's energy system will inevitably result in shifting employment opportunities, with job gains in some sectors and regions but losses in others (i.e., energy-intensive industries and regions most dependent on fossil fuel production). Policy makers could help smooth this transition for the populations that are most vulnerable to job losses through additional, targeted support for educational, training, and retraining programs.

Establish the United States as a leader to stimulate other countries to adopt GHG emissions reduction targets.

Even substantial U.S. emissions reductions will not, by themselves, substantially alter the rate of climate change. Although the United States is responsible for the largest share of historic contributions to global GHG concentrations, all major emitters must ultimately reduce emissions substantially. However, the *indirect* effects of U.S. action or inaction are likely to be very large. That is, what this nation does about its own GHG emissions will have a major impact on how other countries respond to the climate change challenge, and without domestic climate change limiting policies that are credible to the rest of the world, no U.S. strategy to achieve global cooperation is likely to succeed. Continuing efforts to inform the U.S. public of the dangers of climate change and to devise cost-effective response options will therefore be essential for global cooperation as well as for effective, sustained national action.

The U.S. international climate change strategy will need to operate at multiple levels. Continuing attempts to negotiate a comprehensive climate agreement under the United Nations Climate Change Convention are essential to establish good faith and to maximize the legitimacy of policy. At the same time, intensive negotiations must continue with the European Union, Japan, and other Organisation for Economic Cooperation and Development (i.e., high-income) countries and with low- and middle-income countries that are major emitters of, or sinks for, GHGs (especially China, India, Brazil, and countries of the former Soviet Union). These multiple tracks need to be pursued in ways that reinforce rather than undermine one another. It may be worth-while to negotiate sectoral as well as country-wide agreements, and GHGs other than CO_2 should be subjects for international consideration. In such negotiations, the United States should press for institutional arrangements that provide credible assessment and verification of national policies around the world and that help the low- and middle-income countries attain their broader goals of sustainable development.

Competition among countries to take the lead in advancing green technology will play an important role in stimulating emissions-reduction efforts, but strong cooperative efforts will be needed as well. Sustaining large, direct governmental financial transfers to low-income countries may pose substantial challenges of political feasibility; however, large financial transfers via the private sector could be facilitated via a carbon pricing system that allows purchases of allowances or offsets. There is a clear need for support of innovative scientific and technical efforts to help low- and middle-income countries limit their emissions. To provide leadership in these efforts, the United States needs to develop and share technologies that not only reduce GHG emissions but also help advance economic development and reduce local environmental stresses.

Enable flexibility and experimentation with emissions-reduction policies at regional, state, and local levels.

State and local action on climate change has already been significant and wide-ranging. For instance, states are operating cap-and-trade programs, imposing performance standards on utilities and auto manufacturers, running renewable portfolio standard programs, and supporting and mandating energy efficiency. Cities across the United States are developing and implementing climate change action plans. Many federal policies to limit climate change will need ongoing cooperation of states and localities in order to be successfully implemented—including, for example, energy-efficiency programs, which are run by localities or state-level programs, and energy-efficiency building standards, which are sometimes enacted statewide and implemented by local authorities. Moreover, states have regulatory capacity (for example, in regulating energy supply and implementing building standards) that may be needed for implementing new federal initiatives.

Subnational programs will thus need to continue playing a major role in meeting U.S. climate change goals. In addition, since climate change limiting policies will continue to evolve, policy experimentation at subnational levels will provide useful experience for national policy makers to draw upon. On the other hand, subnational regulation can pose costs, such as the fact that businesses operating in multiple jurisdictions may face multiple state regulatory programs and therefore increased compliance burdens. Overlap with state cap-and-trade programs can make a federal program less effective by limiting the freedom of the market to distribute reductions efficiently. These costs, however, may be worth the benefits gained from state and local regulatory innovation; regardless, they illustrate the trade-offs Congress will have to consider when deciding whether to preempt state action.

Thus, a balance must be struck to preserve the strengths and dynamism of state and local actions, while tough choices are made about the extent to which national policies should prevail. In some instances, it may be appropriate to limit state and local authority and instead mandate compliance with minimum national standards. But Congress could promote regulatory flexibility and innovation across jurisdictional boundaries when this is consistent with effective and efficient national policy. To this end, we suggest that Congress avoid punishing or disadvantaging states (or entities within the states) that have taken early action to limit GHG emissions, avoid preempting state and local authority to regulate GHG emissions more stringently than federal law without a strong policy justification, and ensure that subnational jurisdictions have sufficient resources to implement and enforce programs mandated by Congress.

Design policies that balance durability and consistency with flexibility and capacity for modification as we learn from experience.

The strategies and policies outlined above are complex efforts with extensive implications for other domestic issues and for international relations. It is therefore crucial that policies be properly implemented and enforced and be designed in ways that are durable and resistant to distortion or undercutting by subsequent pressures. At the same time, policies must be sufficiently flexible to allow for modification as we gain experience and understanding (as discussed earlier in this Summary). Transparent, predictable mechanisms for policy evolution will be needed.

There are inherent tensions between these goals of durability and adaptability, and it will be an ongoing challenge to find a balance between them. Informing such efforts requires processes for ensuring that policy makers regularly receive timely information about scientific, economic, technological, and other relevant developments. One possible mechanism for this process is a periodic (e.g., biennial) collection and analysis of key information related to our nation's climate change response efforts. This effort could take the form of a "Climate Report of the President" that would provide a focal point for analysis, discussion, and public attention and, ideally, would include requirements for responsible implementing agencies to act upon pertinent new information gained through this reporting mechanism.

A. Federal Agency Policy Guidance Relating to Climate Change

Most federal agencies whose mission is in any way impacted by climate change have issued guidance documents to address that relationship. The broadest and most general of these documents is former President Barack Obama's Climate Action Plan, an excerpt of which appears below.

President Obama's Climate Action Plan
(June 2013)

https://www.whitehouse.gov/sites/default/files/image
/president27sclimateactionplan.pdf

"We, the people, still believe that our obligations as Americans are not just to ourselves, but to all posterity. We will respond to the threat of climate change, knowing that the failure to do so would betray our children and future generations. Some may still deny the overwhelming judgment of science, but none can avoid the devastating impact of raging fires and crippling drought and more powerful storms.

The path towards sustainable energy sources will be long and sometimes difficult. But America cannot resist this transition, we must lead it. We cannot cede to other nations the technology that will power new jobs and new industries, we must claim its promise. That's how we will maintain our economic vitality and our national treasure—our forests and waterways, our croplands and snow-capped peaks. That is how we will preserve our planet, commanded to our care by God.

That's what will lend meaning to the creed our fathers once declared."

—*President Obama, Second Inaugural Address, January 2013*

THE CASE FOR ACTION

While no single step can reverse the effects of climate change, we have a moral obligation to future generations to leave them a planet that is not polluted and damaged. Through steady, responsible action to cut carbon pollution, we can protect our children's health and begin to slow the effects of climate change so that we leave behind a cleaner, more stable environment.

In 2009, President Obama made a pledge that by 2020, America would reduce its greenhouse gas emissions in the range of 17 percent below 2005 levels if all other major economies agreed to limit their emissions as well. Today, the President remains firmly committed to that goal and to building on the progress of his first term to help put us and the world on a sustainable long-term trajectory. Thanks in part to the

Administration's success in doubling America's use of wind, solar, and geothermal energy and in establishing the toughest fuel economy standards in our history, we are creating new jobs, building new industries, and reducing dangerous carbon pollution which contributes to climate change. In fact, last year, carbon emissions from the energy sector fell to the lowest level in two decades. At the same time, while there is more work to do, we are more energy secure than at any time in recent history. In 2012, America's net oil imports fell to the lowest level in 20 years and we have become the world's leading producer of natural gas—the cleanest-burning fossil fuel.

While this progress is encouraging, climate change is no longer a distant threat—we are already feeling its impacts across the country and the world. Last year was the warmest year ever in the contiguous United States and about one-third of all Americans experienced 10 days or more of 100-degree heat. The 12 hottest years on record have all come in the last 15 years. Asthma rates have doubled in the past 30 years and our children will suffer more asthma attacks as air pollution gets worse. And increasing floods, heat waves, and droughts have put farmers out of business, which is already raising food prices dramatically.

These changes come with far-reaching consequences and real economic costs. Last year alone, there were 11 different weather and climate disaster events with estimated losses exceeding $1 billion each across the United States. Taken together, these 11 events resulted in over $110 billion in estimated damages, which would make it the second-costliest year on record.

In short, America stands at a critical juncture. Today, President Obama is putting forward a broad-based plan to cut the carbon pollution that causes climate change and affects public health. Cutting carbon pollution will help spark business innovation to modernize our power plants, resulting in cleaner forms of American-made energy that will create good jobs and cut our dependence on foreign oil. Combined with the Administration's other actions to increase the efficiency of our cars and household appliances, the President's plan will reduce the amount of energy consumed by American families, cutting down on their gas and utility bills. The plan, which consists of a wide variety of executive actions, has three key pillars:

1) **Cut Carbon Pollution in America:** In 2012, U.S. carbon emissions fell to the lowest level in two decades even as the economy continued to grow. To build on this progress, the Obama Administration is putting in place tough new rules to cut carbon pollution—just like we have for other toxins like mercury and arsenic—so we protect the health of our children and move our economy toward American-made clean energy sources that will create good jobs and lower home energy bills.

2) **Prepare the United States for the Impacts of Climate Change:** Even as we take new steps to reduce carbon pollution, we must also prepare for the impacts of a changing climate that are already being felt across the country. Moving forward, the Obama Administration will help state and local governments strengthen our roads, bridges, and shorelines so we can better protect people's homes, businesses and way of life from severe weather.

3) **Lead International Efforts to Combat Global Climate Change and Prepare for its Impacts:** Just as no country is immune from the impacts of climate change, no country can meet this challenge alone. That is why it is imperative for the United States to couple action at home with leadership internationally. America must help forge a truly global solution to this global challenge by galvanizing international action to significantly reduce emissions (particularly among the major emitting countries), prepare for climate impacts, and drive progress through the international negotiations.

Climate change represents one of our greatest challenges of our time, but it is a challenge uniquely suited to America's strengths. Our scientists will design new fuels, and our farmers will grow them. Our engineers to devise new sources of energy, our workers will build them, and our businesses will sell them. All of us will need to do our part. If we embrace this challenge, we will not just create new jobs and new industries and keep America on the cutting edge; we will save lives, protect and preserve our treasured natural resources, cities, and coastlines for future generations.

What follows is a blueprint for steady, responsible national and international action to slow the effects of climate change so we leave a cleaner, more stable environment for future generations. It highlights progress already set in motion by the Obama Administration to advance these goals and sets forth new steps to achieve them.

Notes and Questions

1. The remainder of the Climate Action Plan, too lengthy for full inclusion here, may be viewed at https://www.whitehouse.gov/sites/default/files/image/president27sclimate-actionplan.pdf

2. As you can see from the internal block quote at the beginning of the document, President Obama had indicated his interest in tackling climate change, even if unilaterally, during his second inaugural speech. Following that speech, and months ahead of the formal Plan, Cass Sunstein published a brief argument in favor of unilateral U.S. action. *See* Cass Sunstein, *U.S. Should Act Unilaterally on Climate Change*, BLOOMBERG VIEW, January 23, 2013.

3. The Council on Environmental Quality (CEQ) has issued guidance, broadly applicable to federal agencies as they implement their NEPA obligations, requiring federal agencies to think about climate change as they assess whether proposals for major federal actions will significantly affect the quality of the human environment and also when they prepare environmental impact statements. We should mention that this assessment includes consideration of both "how will the proposed federal action and alternatives to it affect the climate?" and "how does climate change affect the merits of the proposed federal action?" We should also mention that the CEQ eschews "climate change is so big, and my action is so little relative to it, that I don't need to think about it" reasoning. More information and a brief excerpt of the guidance may be found in Chapter 3.

4. The Securities and Exchange Commission (SEC), which regulates the information that publicly traded companies must disclose to investors and the public, has recognized that climate change may have sufficient impact on corporations' earnings, prospects, and values to require consideration in corporate disclosure reports. Specifically, SEC guidance directs corporations to consider the impact of climate legislation and regulation, international accords related to climate, indirect economic consequences of climate change (such as strengthening or weakening particular sectors of the economy), and physical consequences of climate change (such as the effect of rising sea levels and increased flooding on an oil company with refineries located in low-lying coastal areas). These disclosure requirements may serve to make the private sector more aware of the impacts of climate change.

5. Other agencies with missions beyond environmental regulation have also had reason to consider climate change in their policy choices and/or guidance. The disruption of the world's climate patterns impacts many areas of life. In addition to the examples above, what other agencies or departments do you think might want to concern themselves with climate impacts?

6. It should come as little surprise that another agency to have issued guidance addressing the relationship between climate change and its mission and implementation of that mission would be the U.S. Fish & Wildlife Service, tasked with protecting the resource that is arguably at greatest risk. The following is an excerpt from that guidance.

U.S. Fish & Wildlife Service
Rising to the Urgent Challenge: Strategic Plan for Responding to Accelerating Climate Change
(2010)
http://www.fws.gov/home/climatechange/pdf/CCStrategicPlan.pdf

Over the 21st century, the U.S. Fish and Wildlife Service and the Department of the Interior envision a North American continent continuing to be altered by accelerating climate change, but managed to sustain diverse, distributed, and abundant populations of fish and wildlife through conservation of healthy habitats in a network of interconnected, ecologically functioning landscapes.

While many species will continue to thrive, we also envision that some populations and species may decline or be lost, and some will only survive in the wild through our direct and continuous intervention. We will be especially challenged to conserve species and habitats that are particularly vulnerable to climate-driven changes, but we will dedicate our absolute best efforts and expertise to the task, understanding fully that we must continue to meet our obligations for conserving trust species. We will need to make choices and set priorities and, working with our partners, apply ourselves where we can make the greatest difference.

We see climate change as an issue that will unite the conservation community like no other issue has since the early 1960s, when Rachel Carson sounded an alarm about pesticides. We envision a new era of collaborative conservation in which members of the conservation community work interdependently, building knowledge, sharing expertise, and pooling resources as we craft explicit landscape-scale goals and pursue these goals together. We foresee unparalleled opportunities to engage with, and enlist the involvement of, private citizens, businesses and industry, nongovernmental organizations, and national and international governments at all levels to conserve fish and wildlife in the face of climate change.

Climate change is an immense, serious, and sobering challenge — one that will affect fish and wildlife profoundly. At the same time, climate change is galvanizing the conservation community in ways we have not seen since a half-century ago, when Silent Spring alerted the world to the hazards of overuse of pesticides and launched a worldwide environmental movement.

. . .

Across the Service, our employees have initiated action to address climate change. Some employees are monitoring sea level rise and exploring ways of safeguarding our coastal National Wildlife Refuges and the trust resources they support. Others are working tirelessly with water managers to ensure fish and wildlife resources are considered meaningfully in water allocation decisions, particularly in the Southwest, where climate change is likely to exacerbate drought. Some are busy calculating the Service's carbon footprint and devising innovative ways to help the Service become carbon neutral. Still other employees are reaching out to our workforce and our external partners to help them better understand the direction and magnitude of climate change and its effects on fish and wildlife.

It remains for the Service to do two things: First, we must focus the talents, creativity and energy of our employees on a common set of strategies, goals, objectives and actions for addressing climate change impacts. Second, we must provide employees with additional support in terms of knowledge, technology, and resources to enable them to realize their full potential in conserving fish and wildlife in the face of climate change.

[Here the guidance summarized the IPCC Report's description of the likely dire impacts of climate change on biodiversity and ecosystems.]

Climate change has the potential to cause abrupt ecosystem changes and increased species extinctions. These changes will reduce the ability of natural systems to provide many societal goods and services — including the availability of clean water, our planet's lifeblood — which in turn will impact local, regional, and national economies and cultures. Clearly, we cannot delay in addressing climate change effects on fish and wildlife. They demand urgent attention and aggressive action . . . .

Climate change is the transformational conservation challenge of our time, not only because of its direct effects, but also because of its influence on the other stressors that have been and will continue to be major conservation priorities.

Many other issues, such as the spread and control of invasive species; the mounting pressures on limited water supplies; the need for robust fire management to help conserve natural systems; the harm to species from exposure to environmental contaminants; continued changes in land use, specifically habitat loss; and the impacts of all of these factors on biodiversity, have been and will continue to pose tremendous challenges to sustaining healthy, vibrant ecosystems.

Climate change does not replace these other threats or render them less important; they must remain priorities in the years ahead. It is, however, essential that we understand how climate change will exacerbate these threats and pose new ones. For example, climate change will allow the range of some invasive species to expand, perhaps markedly. Climate change will also make some regions drier, further complicating what are already very challenging efforts to capture water and deliver it to natural systems. These changes in precipitation patterns will also affect fire regimes. Our employees and partners will need to take this into account in their management activities so as to protect both the natural world and the places where people live.

In addition, climate change will have many unforeseen impacts on land use and development. For example, rising seas will result in immense pressure to build sea walls and other structures to protect coastal development. These actions will impact the fish and wildlife that rely upon nearby beaches, salt marshes and other natural habitats. Furthermore, climate change may divert development pressure from coastal areas to relatively higher ground as people seek to escape places threatened by rising seas. Together, all of these stressors will have impacts on species that are imperiled today, and they could cause others to become imperiled for the first time . . . .

Finally, unanticipated impacts of climate change have already occurred and are likely to occur in the future. These impacts are difficult to predict based on our current understanding of climate and ecological systems, adding further uncertainty to our ability to predict the future. We must account for this uncertainty as we design, implement and evaluate our plans in response to climate change and as we carry out our management, regulatory and monitoring programs. We must learn as we go, using new knowledge and results of focused research to reduce uncertainty. As we learn more about climate change, we will be better able to refine our planning, decisions, and management actions to reflect that greater understanding.

Notes and Questions

1. After the above assessment portion, the FWS climate change strategy document goes on to list "Seven Bold Commitments," and "Three Progressive Strategies: Adaptation, Mitigation, and Engagement." Six years later this is still the material FWS uses for its policy planning. https://www.fws.gov/home/climatechange/strategy.html

2. The Obama administration described climate change as "the single biggest threat to wildlife," but how realistic is the hope that it can make a difference without further legislation? Given all that you have learned from the earlier chapters in this casebook, what powers might the FWS have to address these problems? Which aspects of ESA implementation might create an opening to consider the impacts of climate change?

3. When the FWS lists a species as endangered or threatened, it must describe the threats to the species that led to its needing to be listed. Increasingly, climate change is turning up as a cause of the threat to species' survival. *See, e.g., Endangered and Threatened Wildlife and Plants; Emergency Listing of the Miami Blue Butterfly as Endangered, and Emergency Listing of the Cassius Blue, Ceraunus Blue, and Nickerbean Blue Butterflies as Threatened Due to Similarity of Appearance to the Miami Blue Butterfly*, 76 Fed. Reg. 49542 (2011); *Endangered and Threatened Wildlife and Plants; 12-Month Finding on a Petition to List the Nueces River and Plateau Shiners as Threatened or Endangered*, 76 Fed. Reg. 48777 (2011).

4. The following case provides one example of how climate change impacts are to be considered in the implementation of the ESA, at least in the § 7 consultation process. The resulting agency guidance immediately follows the case.

Natural Resources Defense Council v. Kempthorne

506 F. Supp. 2d 322 (E.D. Cal. 2007)

(See also p 487)

Judge WANGER:

I. INTRODUCTION

This case concerns the effect on a threatened species of fish, the Delta smelt (*Hypomesus transpacificus*), of the coordinated operation of the federally-managed Central Valley Project ("CVP") and the State of California's State Water Project ("SWP"), among the world's largest water diversion projects. Both projects divert large volumes of water from the California Bay (Sacramento—San Joaquin) Delta ("Delta") and use the Delta to store water.

For over thirty years, the projects have been operated pursuant to a series of cooperation agreements. In addition, the projects are subject to ever-evolving statutory, regulatory, contractual, and judicially-imposed requirements. The Long-Term Central Valley Project and State Water Project Operations Criteria and Plan ("2004 OCAP" or "OCAP") surveys how the projects are currently managed in light of these evolving circumstances. At issue in this case is a 2005 biological opinion ("BiOp"), issued by the United States Fish and Wildlife Service ("FWS" or "Service") pursuant to the Endangered Species Act ("ESA"), which concludes that current project operations described in the OCAP and certain planned future actions will not jeopardize the continued existence of the Delta smelt or adversely modify its critical habitat.

The Delta smelt is a small, slender-bodied fish endemic to the Delta. Historically, Delta smelt could be found throughout the Delta. Although abundance data on the smelt indicates that the population has fluctuated wildly in the past, it is undisputed that, overall, the population has declined significantly in recent years, to its lowest reported volume in fall 2004.

In this case, Plaintiffs, a coalition of environmental and sportfishing organizations, challenge the 2005 BiOp's no jeopardy and no adverse modification findings as arbitrary, capricious, and contrary to law under the Administrative Procedure Act, 5 U.S.C. §§ 702 et seq. Before the court for decision is Plaintiffs' motion for summary judgment. Among other things, Plaintiffs allege that the BiOp fails to consider the best available science, relies upon uncertain (and allegedly inadequate) adaptive management processes to monitor and mitigate the potential impacts of the OCAP, fails to meaningfully analyze whether the 2004 OCAP will jeopardize the continued existence of the Delta smelt, fails to consider the OCAP's impact upon previously designated critical habitat, and fails to address the impacts of the entire project . . . .

F. Relationship Between Smelt and "X2."

Smelt are euryhaline (tolerant of a wide range of salinities), but generally occur in water with less than 10–12 parts per thousand (ppt) salinity. For a large part of its life span, Delta smelt are thought to be associated with the "freshwater edge of the mixing zone," where the salinity is approximately 2 parts per thousand (often referred to as "X2"). The summer TNS index [the Tow Net Survey index, to determine abundance] increases dramatically whenever X2 is located between Chipps and Roe islands. Whenever the location of X2 shifts upstream of the confluence of the Sacramento and San Joaquin, either as a result of water diversions or natural conditions, smelt abundance decreases . . . .

3. Global Climate Change Evidence.

Plaintiffs next argue that the BiOp ignored data about Global Climate Change that will adversely affect the Delta smelt and its habitat. This is potentially significant because the BiOp's conclusions are based in part on the assumption that the hydrology of the water bodies affected by the OCAP will follow historical patterns for the next 20 years (explaining that CALSIM II modeling involved making "adjustments to historic water supplies . . . by imposing future level land use on historical meteorological and hydrologic conditions").

In a July 28, 2004 comment letter, Plaintiff NRDC directed FWS's attention to several studies on the potential effects of climate change on water supply reliability, urging that the issue be considered in the BiOp. The comment letter stated:

The best scientific data available today establishes that global climate change is occurring and will affect western hydrology. At least half a dozen models predict warming in the western United States of several degrees Celsius over the next 100 years. Such sophisticated regional climate models must be considered as part of the FWS' consideration of the best available scientific data.

Unfortunately, the Biological Assessment provided by the Bureau to FWS entirely ignores global climate change and existing climate change models. Instead, the BA projects future project impacts in explicit reliance on seventy-two years of historical records. In effect, the Biological Assessment assumes that neither climate nor hydrology will change. This assumption is not supportable.

In California, a significant percentage of annual precipitation falls as snow in the high Sierra Nevada mountains. Snowpack acts as a form of water storage by melting to release water later in the spring and early summer months. The effects of global climate change are expected to have a profound effect on this dynamic. *Among other things, more precipitation will occur as rain rather than snow, less water will be released slowly from snowpack "storage" during spring and summer months, and flooding is expected to increase. These developments will make it more difficult to fill the large*

reservoirs in most years, reducing reservoir yields and will magnify the effect of CVP oper-
ations on downstream fishes. These developments will also dramatically increase the cost
of surface storage relative to other water supply options, such as conservation.

While the precise magnitude of these changes remains uncertain, judgments about
the likely range of impacts can and have been made. The Service can and must evaluate how that range of likely impacts would affect CVP operations and impacts, including the Bureau's ability to provide water to contractors while complying with
environmental standards. We therefore request that the Service review and consider
the work cited above, as well as the background and Dettinger presentation at a recent
climate change conference held in Sacramento, June 9–11, 2004 and climate change
reports.

A second presentation by Michael Dettinger at a December 8–9, 2004 CALFED
meeting [The CALFED Bay-Delta Program is a collaboration of 25 state and federal
agencies working to protect the Bay Delta], attended by FWS staff, concluded that
"warming is already underway . . ."; that this would result in earlier flows, more
floods, and drier summers; and that "California water supplies/ecosystems are likely
to experience changes earliest and most intensely." Following Dettinger's presentation, members of CALFED noted "the need to reevaluate water storage policies and
ERP [Ecosystem Recovery Program] recovery strategies, all of which would be
affected by projected climate changes." The record reflects that extreme water temperatures can have dramatic impacts upon smelt abundance.

In addition to the specific studies and data cited by NRDC, FWS scientists recognized the issue of climate change warranted further consideration. At a June 2003 symposium entitled "Framing the issues for Environmental and Ecological Effects of
Proposed Changes in Water Operations: Science Symposium on the State of Knowledge," a number of questions regarding climate change were raised, including: "How
does the proposed operations plan account for the potential effects of climate change
(e.g., El Nino or La Nina, long term changes in precipitation and runoff patters, or
increases in water temperature)?"

Plaintiffs argue that, despite this evidence that climate change could seriously
impact the smelt by changing Delta hydrology and temperature, the BiOp "did not so
much as mention the probable effects of climate change on the delta smelt, its habitat, or the magnitude of impacts that could be expected from the 2004 OCAP operations, much less analyze those effects." Defendants and Defendant—Intervenors
respond by arguing (1) that the evidence before FWS at the time the BiOp was issued
was inconclusive about the impacts of climate change; and (2) that, far from ignoring climate change, the issue is built into the BiOp's analysis through the use of X2 as
a proxy for the location and distribution of Delta smelt.

a. Inconclusive Nature of Available Information Regarding the Impacts of Global Climate Change on Precipitation.

Federal Defendants and the State Water Contractors characterize Mr. Dettinger's
presentation, as reflecting "a great deal of uncertainty that climate change will impact
future precipitation." The presentation is entitled "Climate Change Uncertainties and

CALFED Planning." Dettinger acknowledges that, although current climate models "yield consistent warming scenarios for California", there is no similar consensus regarding the impact of warming on future precipitation. Federal Defendants suggest that FWS "responsibly refused to engage in sheer guesswork, and properly declined to speculate as to how global warming might affect delta smelt." But, the NRDC letter cited a number of studies in addition to Mr. Dettinger's presentations, all of which predict that anticipated climate change will adversely impact future water availability in the Western United States.

At the very least, these studies suggest that climate change will be an "important aspect of the problem" meriting analysis in the BiOp. *Pacific Coast Fed'n*, 265 F.3d at 1034. However, . . . the climate change issue was not meaningfully discussed in the biological opinion, making it impossible to determine whether the information was rationally discounted because of its inconclusive nature, or arbitrarily ignored.

Plaintiffs argue that "[r]egardless of the uncertainty involved in predicting the consequences of climate change, FWS had an obligation under the ESA to address the probable effects on Delta smelt." In response, the State Water Contractors quote the following passage from *Bennett v. Spear*, 520 U.S. 154, 176—177 (1997), in support of the proposition that the ESA intended to preclude exactly this kind of argument:

> The obvious purpose of the requirement that each agency "use the best scientific and commercial data available" is to ensure that the ESA not be implemented haphazardly, on the basis of speculation or surmise. While this no doubt serves to advance the ESA's overall goal of species preservation, we think it readily apparent that another objective (if not indeed the primary one) is to avoid needless economic dislocation produced by agency officials zealously but unintelligently pursuing their environmental objectives.

But, this passage from *Bennett* was part of a broader discussion holding that persons who are economically burdened by a decision made under the ESA fall within the zone of interests the statute protects for the purposes of standing. *Bennett* sheds little light on the current inquiry—whether and to what extent the data that was before the FWS regarding climate change should have been considered and addressed in the BiOp.

b. X2 as a Proxy for Climate Change.

The State Water Contractors argue that the approaches taken in the DSRAM [Delta Smelt Risk Assessment Matrix] are "more than adequate to deal with the projected impacts of climate change—assuming they occur." For example, Plaintiffs' suggestion that climate change will produce earlier flows, more floods, and drier summers is addressed by the DSRAM's X2 trigger. Flow level changes will be reflected in the position of X2. If climate change alters water temperatures, DSRAM also includes a temperature trigger, that monitors the temperature range within which successful Delta smelt spawning occurs.

The DSRAM offers no assurance that any mitigating fish protection actions will be implemented if the X2 criteria is triggered. That X2 indirectly monitors climate change does not assuage Plaintiffs' concerns that the BiOp has not adequately analyzed the potential impact of climate change on the smelt.

The BiOp does not gauge the potential effect of various climate change scenarios on Delta hydrology. Assuming, arguendo, a lawful adaptive management approach, there is no discussion when and how climate change impacts will be addressed, whether existing take limits will remain, and the probable impacts on CVP—SWP operations.

FWS acted arbitrarily and capriciously by failing to address the issue of climate change in the BiOp. This absence of any discussion in the BiOp of how to deal with any climate change is a failure to analyze a potentially "important aspect of the problem."

There is no basis to determine what weight FWS should ultimately give the climate change issue in its analysis.

Plaintiffs' motion for summary adjudication is GRANTED as to this claim.   *Decision*

Memorandum of May 14, 2008
U.S. Fish and Wildlife Service

To: Regional Directors, Regions 1–8

From: Director

Subject: Expectations for Consultations on Actions that Would Emit Greenhouse Gases

Recently, questions have been raised regarding compliance with section 7 of the Endangered Species Act concerning emissions of greenhouse gases (GHG), how these emissions contribute to global climate change, and any effects they may cause to listed species and designated critical habitats. These questions became evident as we analyzed the climate change information relevant to the polar bear listing determination. Based on our review of the information and issues considered during the analysis of the polar bear's status, I am writing to establish an analytical framework within which the Service will be able to assist Federal action agencies (including the Service itself when intra-Service consultation is appropriate) in achieving procedural and substantive compliance with the Act.

We recognize the primacy of a Federal action agency's role in determining how to conform its proposed actions to the requirements of section 7 and its responsibility to make the initial determination as to whether consultation is required on its action. As part of its ESA responsibilities, an action agency must examine the effects of its action in order to determine if consultation is necessary. Based on the attached memorandum to me from the Director of the U.S. Geological Survey, however, the Service does not anticipate that the mere fact that a Federal agency authorizes a project that is likely to emit GHG will require the initiation of section 7 consultation. Consultation is required for proposed Federal actions that may affect a listed species. The determination of whether consultation is triggered requires an examination of whether the direct and indirect effects of a particular action reach the regulatory threshold of "may affect". GHG that are projected to be emitted from a facility would not, in and of themselves trigger section 7 consultation for a particular action unless it is established that the emissions from the proposed action cause an indirect effect to listed species or critical habitat. To constitute an indirect effect, the impact to the species must be later in time, must be caused by the proposed action, and must be reasonably certain to occur. The best scientific data available today do not allow us to draw a causal connection between GHG emissions from a given facility and effects posed to listed species or their habitats, nor are there sufficient data to establish that such impacts are reasonably certain to occur. Without sufficient data to establish the required causal connection — to the level of reasonable certainty — between a new facility's GHG emissions and impacts to listed species or critical habitat, section 7 consultation would not be required to address impacts of a facility's GHG emissions.

A question has also been raised regarding the possible application of section 7 to effects that may arise from oil and gas development activities conducted within the habitat of listed species. It is clear that any direct effects of oil and gas development operations, such as drilling activities, vehicular traffic to and from drill sites, and other on-site operational support activities that pose adverse effects to listed species and their critical habitat would need to be evaluated through the section 7 consultation process. It is also clear that any indirect effects from oil and gas development activities, such as impacts from the spread of contaminants (accidental oil spills, or the unintentional release of other contaminants) that are caused by the oil and gas development activities under consultation and that are reasonably certain to occur, (e.g., that are outside of the footprint of the action and spread into habitat areas used by listed species) would also need to be evaluated through the section 7 consultation process.

However, the future effects of any emissions that may result from the consumption of petroleum products refined from crude oil pumped from a particular drilling site would not constitute indirect effects and therefore would not be considered during section 7 consultations. The best scientific data available to the Service today do not provide the degree of precision needed to draw a causal connection between the oil produced at a particular drilling site, the GHG emissions that may eventually result from the consumption of the refined petroleum product, and a particular impact to listed species or their habitats. At present there is a lack of scientific or technical knowledge to determine a relationship between oil and gas leasing, development, or production activity and the effects of the ultimate consumption of petroleum products (GHG emissions). There are discernible limits to the establishment of a causal connection, such as uncertainties regarding the amount of production from a field; whether any or all of that production will be refined for plastics or other products that will not be burned; what mix of vehicles or factories might use the product; and what mitigation measures might offset consumption. Furthermore, there is no traceable nexus between the ultimate consumption of the petroleum product and any particular effect to listed species or their habitats. In short, the emissions effects resulting from the consumption of petroleum derived from an oil field would not constitute an indirect effect of any Federal agency action to approve the development of that field.

As we move into and adapt to this new field of consultations, we must recognize the needs of our fellow agencies for assistance and consultation in the broadest sense. While the foregoing discussion describes our expectations with regard to certain types of Federal actions, you need to be prepared to respond to any Federal agency that believes it may have a compliance duty under section 7 for its programs or actions affecting the production of GHGs. As new information and knowledge about emissions and specific impacts to species and their habitats is developed, we will adapt our framework for consultations accordingly. This is particularly important as more regionally-based models are developed and refined to the level of specificity and reliability needed for the Service to execute its implementation of the Act's provisions ensuring consistency with the statute's best available information standard. Regional Directors are expected to brief the Director as these new models and sources of information ripen at the appropriate scale prior to incorporation into implementing the Act.

Notes and Questions

1. Do you agree with this approach? Would you do more?

2. On the same day that the FWS consultation memo was released, the Department of the Interior announced that it was listing the polar bear as threatened, as well as creating a special 4(d) rule applicable to the polar bear. This was the end result of a three-year process initiated by the Center for Biological Diversity, which had filed a petition in 2005 to list the polar bear as threatened due to climate-change-induced melting of its sea-ice habitat. Delays in responding to the petition led to litigation, which resulted in the final listing. However, because the Secretary felt pressured into this listing by "the legal standards under the ESA," he simultaneously issued a special rule "tailored to the conservation needs of the polar bear."

3. In a press conference announcement tied to the above actions, Secretary Kempthorne expressly noted that climate change is the reason for the polar bear listing, but then went on to say that the ESA will not protect the polar bear from this threat. The announced special 4(d) rule removes from take enforcement any actions that are not already violations of the Marine Mammal Protection Act. Ultimately, does this listing decision have any impact at all? If there is a traditional take of a polar bear, now both statutes can apply. Apart from having direct enforcement value (which is arguably lacking here), what are some of the other possible benefits to having the polar bear listed?

4. In the Omnibus Appropriations Act of 2009, Congress gave the Obama administration an opportunity to withdraw the special 4(d) rule, but after a period of consideration the new administration declined to do so. Secretary Salazar stated that polar bear recovery was a high priority for the administration, but that "the Endangered Species Act is not the proper mechanism for controlling our nation's carbon emissions." The new administration did, however, toss out another one of the Bush administration's lame duck regulations, which would have more broadly altered the § 7 consultation requirement, cutting back on the range of contexts that might be considered the proximate cause of jeopardy. Do you think this was a fair compromise? Would you have decided differently about whether to keep the polar bear rule? What might the consequences be of eliminating that rule?

5. What would have happened if the polar bear were listed as endangered? Recall from Chapter 4 that species listed as endangered receive their take protection from the ESA directly, whereas threatened species must be protected from take via regulation. If the polar bear had been listed as endangered, there would have been no potential for this special rule. Can you imagine how that might have played out? It will have to happen at some point (a species being listed as *endangered* because of climate change), so then what sort of litigation might we expect to see? Do you think that the choice to list the polar bear as threatened rather than endangered may have been outcome-driven?

B. The Clean Air Act and Climate Change

Whether and how to regulate greenhouse gases under the Clean Air Act has been the source of controversy for many years, but is finally beginning to take shape. The Supreme Court has played an important role in the development of climate policy under the CAA, beginning with the question of whether greenhouse gases even qualify as a pollutant under the Act, which generally focuses on air quality. The impacts of GHGs are both different and less local than the problem of dirty air. The first case in this section resolved this issue and paved a way for the series of rulemaking that followed. It was also an important standing to sue case. As you'll recall, that portion of the opinion was excerpted in Chapter 2.

Massachusetts v. Environmental Protection Agency
549 U.S. 497 (2007)

Justice STEVENS:

A well-documented rise in global temperatures has coincided with a significant increase in the concentration of carbon dioxide in the atmosphere. Respected scientists believe the two trends are related. For when carbon dioxide is released into the atmosphere, it acts like the ceiling of a greenhouse, trapping solar energy and retarding the escape of reflected heat. It is therefore a species—the most important species—of a "greenhouse gas."

Calling global warming "the most pressing environmental challenge of our time," a group of States, local governments, and private organizations alleged in a petition for certiorari that the Environmental Protection Agency (EPA) has abdicated its responsibility under the Clean Air Act to regulate the emissions of four greenhouse gases, including carbon dioxide. Specifically, petitioners asked us to answer two questions concerning the meaning of § 202(a)(1) of the Act: whether EPA has the statutory authority to regulate greenhouse gas emissions from new motor vehicles; and if so, whether its stated reasons for refusing to do so are consistent with the statute.

In response, EPA, supported by 10 intervening States and six trade associations, correctly argued that we may not address those two questions unless at least one petitioner has standing to invoke our jurisdiction under Article III of the Constitution. Notwithstanding the serious character of that jurisdictional argument and the absence of any conflicting decisions construing § 202(a)(1), the unusual importance of the underlying issue persuaded us to grant the writ.

EPA argument

Decision of Supreme Court

I

Section 202(a)(1) of the Clean Air Act provides:

> The [EPA] Administrator shall by regulation prescribe (and from time to time revise) in accordance with the provisions of this section, standards applicable to the emission of any air pollutant from any class or classes of new motor vehicles or new motor vehicle engines, which in his judgment cause, or contribute to, air pollution which may reasonably be anticipated to endanger public health or welfare. . . .

The Act defines "air pollutant" to include "any air pollution agent or combination of such agents, including any physical, chemical, biological, radioactive . . . substance or matter which is emitted into or otherwise enters the ambient air." "Welfare" is also defined broadly: among other things, it includes "effects on . . . weather . . . and climate."

When Congress enacted these provisions, the study of climate change was in its infancy. In 1959, shortly after the U.S. Weather Bureau began monitoring atmospheric carbon dioxide levels, an observatory in Mauna Loa, Hawaii, recorded a mean level of 316 parts per million. This was well above the highest carbon dioxide concentration — no more than 300 parts per million — revealed in the 420,000-year-old ice-core record. By the time Congress drafted § 202(a)(1) in 1970, carbon dioxide levels had reached 325 parts per million.

In the late 1970's, the Federal Government began devoting serious attention to the possibility that carbon dioxide emissions associated with human activity could provoke climate change. . . .

[Justice Stevens then summarized the history of U.S. legislation relating to climate change, which can be found early in this chapter, as well as a few points from the IPCC report, also above.]

Responding to the IPCC report, the United Nations convened the "Earth Summit" in 1992 in Rio de Janeiro. The first President Bush attended and signed the United Nations Framework Convention on Climate Change (UNFCCC), a nonbinding agreement among 154 nations to reduce atmospheric concentrations of carbon dioxide and other greenhouse gases for the purpose of "prevent[ing] dangerous anthropogenic [i.e., human-induced] interference with the [Earth's] climate system." The Senate unanimously ratified the treaty.

Rio Summit 1992

Some five years later — after the IPCC issued a second comprehensive report in 1995 concluding that "[t]he balance of evidence suggests there is a discernible human

Kyoto Protocol 1997

influence on global climate"—the UNFCCC signatories met in Kyoto, Japan, and adopted a protocol that assigned mandatory targets for industrialized nations to reduce greenhouse gas emissions. Because those targets did not apply to developing and heavily polluting nations such as China and India, the Senate unanimously passed a resolution expressing its sense that the United States should not enter into the Kyoto Protocol. President Clinton did not submit the protocol to the Senate for ratification.

II

On October 20, 1999, a group of 19 private organizations filed a rulemaking petition asking EPA to regulate "greenhouse gas emissions from new motor vehicles under §202 of the Clean Air Act." Petitioners maintained that 1998 was the "warmest year on record"; that carbon dioxide, methane, nitrous oxide, and hydrofluorocarbons are "heat trapping greenhouse gases"; that greenhouse gas emissions have significantly accelerated climate change; and that the IPCC's 1995 report warned that "carbon dioxide remains the most important contributor to [manmade] forcing of climate change." The petition further alleged that climate change will have serious adverse effects on human health and the environment....

VI

Issue #1

On the merits, the first question is whether §202(a)(1) of the Clean Air Act authorizes EPA to regulate greenhouse gas emissions from new motor vehicles in the event that it forms a "judgment" that such emissions contribute to climate change. We have little trouble concluding that it does. In relevant part, §202(a)(1) provides that EPA "shall by regulation prescribe ... standards applicable to the emission of any air pollutant from any class or classes of new motor vehicles or new motor vehicle engines, which in [the Administrator's] judgment cause, or contribute to, air pollution which may reasonably be anticipated to endanger public health or welfare." 42 U.S.C. §7521(a)(1). Because EPA believes that Congress did not intend it to regulate substances that contribute to climate change, the agency maintains that carbon dioxide is not an "air pollutant" within the meaning of the provision.

The statutory text forecloses EPA's reading. The Clean Air Act's sweeping definition of "air pollutant" includes "any air pollution agent or combination of such agents, including any physical, chemical ... substance or matter which is emitted into or otherwise enters the ambient air...." §7602(g) (emphasis added). On its face, the definition embraces all airborne compounds of whatever stripe, and underscores that intent through the repeated use of the word "any." Carbon dioxide, methane, nitrous oxide, and hydrofluorocarbons are without a doubt "physical [and] chemical ... substance [s] which [are] emitted into ... the ambient air." The statute is unambiguous.

Rather than relying on statutory text, EPA invokes postenactment congressional actions and deliberations it views as tantamount to a congressional command to refrain from regulating greenhouse gas emissions. Even if such postenactment legislative history could shed light on the meaning of an otherwise-unambiguous statute, EPA never identifies any action remotely suggesting that Congress meant to curtail its power to treat greenhouse gases as air pollutants. That subsequent Congresses have eschewed enacting binding emissions limitations to combat global warming tells us nothing about what Congress meant when it amended § 202(a)(1) in 1970 and 1977. And unlike EPA, we have no difficulty reconciling Congress' various efforts to promote interagency collaboration and research to better understand climate change with the Agency's pre-existing mandate to regulate "any air pollutant" that may endanger the public welfare. Collaboration and research do not conflict with any thoughtful regulatory effort; they complement it.

EPA's reliance on *Brown & Williamson Tobacco Corp.*, 529 U.S. 120, is similarly misplaced. In holding that tobacco products are not "drugs" or "devices" subject to Food and Drug Administration (FDA) regulation pursuant to the Food, Drug and Cosmetic Act (FDCA), we found critical at least two considerations that have no counterpart in this case.

First, we thought it unlikely that Congress meant to ban tobacco products, which the FDCA would have required had such products been classified as "drugs" or "devices." Here, in contrast, EPA jurisdiction would lead to no such extreme measures. EPA would only regulate emissions, and even then, it would have to delay any action "to permit the development and application of the requisite technology, giving appropriate consideration to the cost of compliance," § 7521(a)(2). However much a ban on tobacco products clashed with the "common sense" intuition that Congress never meant to remove those products from circulation, there is nothing counterintuitive to the notion that EPA can curtail the emission of substances that are putting the global climate out of kilter.

Second, in *Brown & Williamson* we pointed to an unbroken series of congressional enactments that made sense only if adopted "against the backdrop of the FDA's consistent and repeated statements that it lacked authority under the FDCA to regulate tobacco." Id., at 144. We can point to no such enactments here: EPA has not identified any congressional action that conflicts in any way with the regulation of greenhouse gases from new motor vehicles. Even if it had, Congress could not have acted against a regulatory "backdrop" of disclaimers of regulatory authority. Prior to the order that provoked this litigation, EPA had never disavowed the authority to regulate greenhouse gases, and in 1998 it in fact affirmed that it had such authority. There is no reason, much less a compelling reason, to accept EPA's invitation to read ambiguity into a clear statute.

EPA arguments:

① Not convenient to do it now

EPA finally argues that it cannot regulate carbon dioxide emissions from motor vehicles because doing so would require it to tighten mileage standards, a job (according to EPA) that Congress has assigned to DOT. But that DOT sets mileage standards in no way licenses EPA to shirk its environmental responsibilities. EPA has been charged with protecting the public's "health" and "welfare," a statutory obligation wholly independent of DOT's mandate to promote energy efficiency. The two obligations may overlap, but there is no reason to think the two agencies cannot both administer their obligations and yet avoid inconsistency.

② it's DOT's job

While the Congresses that drafted § 202(a)(1) might not have appreciated the possibility that burning fossil fuels could lead to global warming, they did understand that without regulatory flexibility, changing circumstances and scientific developments would soon render the Clean Air Act obsolete. The broad language of § 202(a)(1) reflects an intentional effort to confer the flexibility necessary to forestall such obsolescence. See *Pennsylvania Dept. of Corrections v. Yeskey*, 524 U.S. 206, 212 (1998) ("[T]he fact that a statute can be applied in situations not expressly anticipated by Congress does not demonstrate ambiguity. It demonstrates breadth" (internal quotation marks omitted)). Because greenhouse gases fit well within the Clean Air Act's capacious definition of "air pollutant," we hold that EPA has the statutory authority to regulate the emission of such gases from new motor vehicles.

VII

The alternative basis for EPA's decision—that even if it does have statutory authority to regulate greenhouse gases, it would be unwise to do so at this time—rests on reasoning divorced from the statutory text. While the statute does condition the exercise of EPA's authority on its formation of a "judgment," that judgment must relate to whether an air pollutant "cause[s], or contribute[s] to, air pollution which may reasonably be anticipated to endanger public health or welfare." Put another way, the use of the word "judgment" is not a roving license to ignore the statutory text. It is but a direction to exercise discretion within defined statutory limits.

If EPA makes a finding of endangerment, the Clean Air Act requires the Agency to regulate emissions of the deleterious pollutant from new motor vehicles. [CAA] (stating that "[EPA] shall by regulation prescribe . . . standards applicable to the emission of any air pollutant from any class or classes of new motor vehicles"). EPA no doubt has significant latitude as to the manner, timing, content, and coordination of its regulations with those of other agencies. But once EPA has responded to a petition for rulemaking, its reasons for action or inaction must conform to the authorizing statute. Under the clear terms of the Clean Air Act, EPA can avoid taking further action only if it determines that greenhouse gases do not contribute to climate change or if it provides some reasonable explanation as to why it cannot or will not exercise its discretion to determine whether they do. To the extent that this constrains agency discretion to pursue other priorities of the Administrator or the President, this is the congressional design.

EPA has refused to comply with this clear statutory command. Instead, it has offered a laundry list of reasons not to regulate. For example, EPA said that a number of voluntary Executive Branch programs already provide an effective response to the threat of global warming, that regulating greenhouse gases might impair the President's ability to negotiate with "key developing nations" to reduce emissions, and that curtailing motor-vehicle emissions would reflect "an inefficient, piecemeal approach to address the climate change issue."

Although we have neither the expertise nor the authority to evaluate these policy judgments, it is evident they have nothing to do with whether greenhouse gas emissions contribute to climate change. Still less do they amount to a reasoned justification for declining to form a scientific judgment. In particular, while the President has broad authority in foreign affairs, that authority does not extend to the refusal to execute domestic laws. In the Global Climate Protection Act of 1987, Congress authorized the State Department—not EPA—to formulate United States foreign policy with reference to environmental matters relating to climate. EPA has made no showing that it issued the ruling in question here after consultation with the State Department. Congress did direct EPA to consult with other agencies in the formulation of its policies and rules, but the State Department is absent from that list.

Nor can EPA avoid its statutory obligation by noting the uncertainty surrounding various features of climate change and concluding that it would therefore be better not to regulate at this time. If the scientific uncertainty is so profound that it precludes EPA from making a reasoned judgment as to whether greenhouse gases contribute to global warming, EPA must say so. That EPA would prefer not to regulate greenhouse gases because of some residual uncertainty—which, contrary to Justice Scalia's apparent belief, is in fact all that it said, see 68 Fed.Reg. 52929—52930 ("We do not believe . . . that it would be either effective or appropriate for EPA *to establish [greenhouse gas] standards for motor vehicles* at this time" (emphasis added))—is irrelevant. The statutory question is whether sufficient information exists to make an endangerment finding.

In short, EPA has offered no reasoned explanation for its refusal to decide whether greenhouse gases cause or contribute to climate change. Its action was therefore "arbitrary, capricious, . . . or otherwise not in accordance with law." We need not and do not reach the question whether on remand EPA must make an endangerment finding, or whether policy concerns can inform EPA's actions in the event that it makes such a finding. We hold only that EPA must ground its reasons for action or inaction in the statute.

VIII

The judgment of the Court of Appeals is reversed, and the case is remanded for further proceedings consistent with this opinion. DECISION

It is so ordered.

Justice SCALIA, with whom THE CHIEF JUSTICE, Justice THOMAS, and Justice ALITO join, dissenting. DISSENT

. . . As the Court recognizes, the statute "condition[s] the exercise of EPA's authority on its formation of a 'judgment.'" There is no dispute that the Administrator has made no such judgment in this case.

The question thus arises: Does anything require the Administrator to make a "judgment" whenever a petition for rulemaking is filed? Without citation of the statute or any other authority, the Court says yes. Why is that so? When Congress wishes to make private action force an agency's hand, it knows how to do so. Where does the CAA say that the EPA Administrator is required to come to a decision on this question whenever a rulemaking petition is filed? The Court points to no such provision because none exists.

Instead, the Court invents a multiple-choice question that the EPA Administrator must answer when a petition for rulemaking is filed. The Administrator must exercise his judgment in one of three ways: (a) by concluding that the pollutant does cause, or contribute to, air pollution that endangers public welfare (in which case EPA is required to regulate); (b) by concluding that the pollutant does not cause, or contribute to, air pollution that endangers public welfare (in which case EPA is not required to regulate); or (c) by "provid[ing] some reasonable explanation as to why it cannot or will not exercise its discretion to determine whether" greenhouse gases endanger public welfare (in which case EPA is not required to regulate).

I am willing to assume, for the sake of argument, that the Administrator's discretion in this regard is not entirely unbounded—that if he has no reasonable basis for deferring judgment he must grasp the nettle at once. The Court, however, with no basis in text or precedent, rejects all of EPA's stated "policy judgments" as not "amount[ing] to a reasoned justification," effectively narrowing the universe of potential reasonable bases to a single one: Judgment can be delayed only if the Administrator concludes that "the scientific uncertainty is [too] profound." The Administrator is precluded from concluding for other reasons "that it would . . . be better not to regulate at this time." Such other reasons—perfectly valid reasons—were set forth in the Agency's statement.

"We do not believe . . . that it would be either effective or appropriate for EPA to establish [greenhouse gas] standards for motor vehicles at this time. As described in detail below, the President has laid out a comprehensive approach to climate change that calls for near-term voluntary actions and incentives along with programs aimed at reducing scientific uncertainties and encouraging technological development so that the government may effectively and efficiently address the climate change issue over the long term.

. . . . .

"[E]stablishing [greenhouse gas] emission standards for U.S. motor vehicles at this time would . . . result in an inefficient, piecemeal approach to addressing the climate change issue. The U.S. motor vehicle fleet is one of many sources of [greenhouse gas] emissions both here and abroad, and different [greenhouse gas] emission sources face different technological and financial challenges in reducing emissions. A sensible regulatory scheme would require that all significant sources and sinks of [greenhouse gas] emissions be considered in deciding how best to achieve any needed emission reductions.

"Unilateral EPA regulation of motor vehicle [greenhouse gas] emissions could also weaken U.S. efforts to persuade developing countries to reduce the [greenhouse gas] intensity of their economies. Considering the large populations and growing economies of some developing countries, increases in their [greenhouse gas] emissions could quickly overwhelm the effects of [greenhouse gas] reduction measures in developed countries. Any potential benefit of EPA regulation could be lost to the extent other nations decided to let their emissions significantly increase in view of U.S. emissions reductions. Unavoidably, climate change raises important foreign policy issues, and it is the President's prerogative to address them."

The Court dismisses this analysis as "rest[ing] on reasoning divorced from the statutory text." "While the statute does condition the exercise of EPA's authority on its formation of a 'judgment,' . . . that judgment must relate to whether an air pollutant 'cause[s], or contribute[s] to, air pollution which may reasonably be anticipated to endanger public health or welfare.'" True but irrelevant. When the Administrator makes a judgment whether to regulate greenhouse gases, that judgment must relate to whether they are air pollutants that "cause, or contribute to, air pollution which may reasonably be anticipated to endanger public health or welfare." 42 U.S.C. § 7521(a)(1). But the statute says nothing at all about the reasons for which the Administrator may defer making a judgment — the permissible reasons for deciding not to grapple with the issue at the present time. Thus, the various "policy" rationales, that the Court criticizes are not "divorced from the statutory text," except in the sense that the statutory text is silent, as texts are often silent about permissible reasons for the exercise of agency discretion. The reasons EPA gave are surely considerations executive agencies regularly take into account (and ought to take into account) when deciding whether to consider entering a new field: the impact such entry would have on other Executive Branch programs and on foreign policy. There is no basis in law for the Court's imposed limitation.

EPA's interpretation of the discretion conferred by the statutory reference to "its judgment" is not only reasonable, it is the most natural reading of the text. The Court nowhere explains why this interpretation is incorrect, let alone why it is not entitled to deference under *Chevron U.S.A. Inc. v. Natural Resources Defense Council, Inc.*, 467 U.S. 837 (1984). As the Administrator acted within the law in declining to make a "judgment" for the policy reasons above set forth, I would uphold the decision to deny the rulemaking petition on that ground alone.

B

Even on the Court's own terms, however, the same conclusion follows. As mentioned above, the Court gives EPA the option of determining that the science is too uncertain to allow it to form a "judgment" as to whether greenhouse gases endanger public welfare. Attached to this option (on what basis is unclear) is an essay requirement: "If," the Court says, "the scientific uncertainty is so profound that it precludes EPA from making a reasoned judgment as to whether greenhouse gases contribute to global warming, EPA must say so." But EPA has said precisely that — and at great length, based on information contained in a 2001 report by the National Research Council (NRC) entitled Climate Change Science: An Analysis of Some Key Questions:

> "As the NRC noted in its report, concentrations of [greenhouse gases (GHGs)] are increasing in the atmosphere as a result of human activities (pp. 9 — 12). It also noted that '[a] diverse array of evidence points to a warming of global surface air temperatures' (p. 16). The report goes on to state, however, that '[b]ecause of the large and still uncertain level of natural variability inherent in the climate record and the uncertainties in the time histories of the various forcing agents (and particularly aerosols), a [causal] linkage between the buildup of [GHGs] in the atmosphere and the observed climate changes during the 20th century cannot be unequivocally established. The fact that the magnitude of the observed warming is large in comparison to natural

variability as simulated in climate models is suggestive of such a linkage, but it does not constitute proof of one because the model simulations could be deficient in natural variability on the decadal to century time scale'.

"The NRC also observed that 'there is considerable uncertainty in current understanding of how the climate system varies naturally and reacts to emissions of [GHGs] and aerosols'. As a result of that uncertainty, the NRC cautioned that 'current estimate of the magnitude of future warming should be regarded as tentative and subject to future adjustments (either upward or downward).' Id. It further advised that '[r]educing the wide range of uncertainty inherent in current model predictions of global climate change will require major advances in understanding and modeling of both (1) the factors that determine atmospheric concentrations of [GHGs] and aerosols and (2) the so-called "feedbacks" that determine the sensitivity of the climate system to a prescribed increase in [GHGs].' Id.

"The science of climate change is extraordinarily complex and still evolving. Although there have been substantial advances in climate change science, there continue to be important uncertainties in our understanding of the factors that may affect future climate change and how it should be addressed. As the NRC explained, predicting future climate change necessarily involves a complex web of economic and physical factors including: Our ability to predict future global anthropogenic emissions of GHGs and aerosols; the fate of these emissions once they enter the atmosphere (e.g., what percentage are absorbed by vegetation or are taken up by the oceans); the impact of those emissions that remain in the atmosphere on the radiative properties of the atmosphere; changes in critically important climate feedbacks (e.g., changes in cloud cover and ocean circulation); changes in temperature characteristics (e.g., average temperatures, shifts in daytime and evening temperatures); changes in other climatic parameters (e.g., shifts in precipitation, storms); and ultimately the impact of such changes on human health and welfare (e.g., increases or decreases in agricultural productivity, human health impacts). The NRC noted, in particular, that '[t]he understanding of the relationships between weather/climate and human health is in its infancy and therefore the health consequences of climate change are poorly understood' (p. 20). Substantial scientific uncertainties limit our ability to assess each of these factors and to separate out those changes resulting from natural variability from those that are directly the result of increases in anthropogenic GHGs.

"Reducing the wide range of uncertainty inherent in current model predictions will require major advances in understanding and modeling of the factors that determine atmospheric concentrations of [GHGs] and aerosols, and the processes that determine the sensitivity of the climate system." 68 Fed. Reg. 52930.

I simply cannot conceive of what else the Court would like EPA to say.

II

A

Even before reaching its discussion of the word "judgment," the Court makes another significant error when it concludes that "§ 202(a)(1) of the Clean Air Act authorizes EPA to regulate greenhouse gas emissions from new motor vehicles in the event that it forms a 'judgment' that such emissions contribute to climate change." For such authorization, the Court relies on what it calls "the Clean Air Act's capacious definition of 'air pollutant.'"

"Air pollutant" is defined by the Act as "any air pollution agent or combination of such agents, including any physical, chemical, . . . substance or matter which is emitted into or otherwise enters the ambient air." 42 U.S.C. § 7602(g). The Court is correct that "[c]arbon dioxide, methane, nitrous oxide, and hydrofluorocarbons," ante, at 1462, fit within the second half of that definition: They are "physical, chemical, . . . substance[s] or matter which [are] emitted into or otherwise ente[r] the ambient air." But the Court mistakenly believes this to be the end of the analysis. In order to be an "air pollutant" under the Act's definition, the "substance or matter [being] emitted into . . . the ambient air" must also meet the first half of the definition—namely, it must be an "air pollution agent or combination of such agents." The Court simply pretends this half of the definition does not exist.

The Court's analysis faithfully follows the argument advanced by petitioners, which focuses on the word "including" in the statutory definition of "air pollutant." As that argument goes, anything that follows the word "including" must necessarily be a subset of whatever precedes it. Thus, if greenhouse gases qualify under the phrase following the word "including," they must qualify under the phrase preceding it. Since greenhouse gases come within the capacious phrase "any physical, chemical, . . . substance or matter which is emitted into or otherwise enters the ambient air," they must also be "air pollution agent[s] or combination[s] of such agents," and therefore meet the definition of "air pollutant[s]."

That is certainly one possible interpretation of the statutory definition. The word "including" can indeed indicate that what follows will be an "illustrative" sampling of the general category that precedes the word. Often, however, the examples standing alone are broader than the general category, and must be viewed as limited in light of that category. The Government provides a helpful (and unanswered) example: "The phrase 'any American automobile, including any truck or minivan,' would not naturally be construed to encompass a foreign-manufactured [truck or] minivan." The general principle enunciated—that the speaker is talking about American automobiles—carries forward to the illustrative examples (trucks and minivans), and limits them accordingly, even though in isolation they are broader. Congress often uses the word "including" in this manner. In 28 U.S.C. § 1782(a), for example, it refers to "a proceeding in a foreign or international tribunal, including criminal investigations conducted before formal accusation." Certainly this provision would not encompass criminal investigations underway in a domestic tribunal.

In short, the word "including" does not require the Court's (or the petitioners') result. It is perfectly reasonable to view the definition of "air pollutant" in its entirety: An air pollutant can be "any physical, chemical, . . . substance or matter which is emitted into or otherwise enters the ambient air," but only if it retains the general characteristic of being an "air pollution agent or combination of such agents." This is precisely the conclusion EPA reached: "[A] substance does not meet the CAA definition of 'air pollutant' simply because it is a 'physical, chemical, . . . substance or matter which is emitted into or otherwise enters the ambient air.' It must also be an 'air pollution agent.'" 68 Fed.Reg. 52929, n. 3. See also id., at 52928 ("The root of the definition indicates that for a substance to be an 'air pollutant,' it must be an 'agent' of 'air pollution'").

Once again, in the face of textual ambiguity, the Court's application of Chevron deference to EPA's interpretation of the word "including" is nowhere to be found. Evidently, the Court defers only to those reasonable interpretations that it favors.

B

Using (as we ought to) EPA's interpretation of the definition of "air pollutant," we must next determine whether greenhouse gases are "agent[s]" of "air pollution." If so, the statute would authorize regulation; if not, EPA would lack authority.

Unlike "air pollutants," the term "air pollution" is not itself defined by the CAA; thus, once again we must accept EPA's interpretation of that ambiguous term, provided its interpretation is a "permissible construction of the statute." *Chevron*, 467 U.S., at 843. In this case, the petition for rulemaking asked EPA for "regulation of [greenhouse gas] emissions from motor vehicles to reduce the risk of global climate change." 68 Fed.Reg. 52925. Thus, in deciding whether it had authority to regulate, EPA had to determine whether the concentration of greenhouse gases assertedly responsible for "global climate change" qualifies as "air pollution." EPA began with the commonsense observation that the "[p]roblems associated with atmospheric concentrations of CO2," id., at 52927, bear little resemblance to what would naturally be termed "air pollution":

"EPA's prior use of the CAA's general regulatory provisions provides an important context. Since the inception of the Act, EPA has used these provisions to address air pollution problems that occur primarily at ground level or near the surface of the earth. For example, national ambient air quality standards (NAAQS) established under CAA section 109 address concentrations of substances in the ambient air and the related public health and welfare problems. This has meant setting NAAQS for concentrations of ozone, carbon monoxide, particulate matter and other substances in the air near the surface of the earth, not higher in the atmosphere . . . . CO2, by contrast, is fairly consistent in concentration throughout the world's atmosphere up to approximately the lower stratosphere." Id., at 52926—52927.

In other words, regulating the buildup of CO2 and other greenhouse gases in the upper reaches of the atmosphere, which is alleged to be causing global climate change, is not akin to regulating the concentration of some substance that is polluting the air.

We need look no further than the dictionary for confirmation that this interpretation of "air pollution" is eminently reasonable. The definition of "pollute," of course, is "[t]o make or render impure or unclean." Webster's New International Dictionary 1910 (2d ed.1949). And the first three definitions of "air" are as follows: (1) "[t]he invisible, odorless, and tasteless mixture of gases which surrounds the earth"; (2) "[t]he body of the earth's atmosphere; esp., the part of it near the earth, as distinguished from the upper rarefied part"; (3) "[a] portion of air or of the air considered with respect to physical characteristics or as affecting the senses." Id., at 54. EPA's conception of "air pollution"—focusing on impurities in the "ambient air" "at ground level or near the surface of the earth"—is perfectly consistent with the natural meaning of that term.

In the end, EPA concluded that since "CAA authorization to regulate is generally based on a finding that an air pollutant causes or contributes to air pollution," 68 Fed. Reg. 52928, the concentrations of CO2 and other greenhouse gases allegedly affecting the global climate are beyond the scope of CAA's authorization to regulate. "[T]he term 'air pollution' as used in the regulatory provisions cannot be interpreted to encompass global climate change." Ibid. Once again, the Court utterly fails to explain why this interpretation is incorrect, let alone so unreasonable as to be unworthy of Chevron deference . . . .

Notes and Questions

1. The EPA had to respond with a series of approaches to climate mitigation after *Massachusetts v. EPA*. The most immediately mandated step took place on December 7, 2009, when the EPA published a finding that six greenhouse gases constitute a threat to public health and welfare, and that motor vehicle emissions cause and contribute to the climate change problem.

2. On May 13, 2010, EPA set greenhouse gas emissions thresholds, determining the point at which CAA permits are required for new and existing industrial facilities (stationary sources). This final rule "tailored" these requirements to apply to only the largest greenhouse gas emitters: power plants, refineries, and cement production facilities. The next case in this section represents the Supreme Court's final say on that rule.

3. On March 27, 2012, EPA proposed a "Carbon Pollution Standard for New Power Plants" that would set national limits on the amount of carbon pollution that power plants are allowed to emit. This rule applies only to new fossil-fuel-fired electric utility generating units. Commonly referred to as the Clean Power Plan, the rule was finalized on August 3, 2015, and remains subject to ongoing litigation at this time.

Utility Air Regulatory Group v. EPA

134 S. Ct. 2427 (2014)

Justice SCALIA:

[Following *Massachusetts v. EPA*, EPA made its GHG endangerment finding and issued regulations for new vehicles. It then sought to regulate greenhouse gas emissions from stationary sources under the PSD and Title V provisions of the Clean Air

Act. These provisions require that BACT standards apply to any "major emitting facility," defined as any stationary source with the potential to emit 250 tons per year of "any air pollutant." It was not possible to regulate all sources that meet this threshold for GHGs, so EPA set a threshold of 75,000 tons per year before its tech standards would apply. The Court granted cert. to address the question: "Whether EPA permissibly determined that its regulation of greenhouse gas emissions from new motor vehicles triggered permitting requirements under the Clean Air Act for stationary sources that emit greenhouse gases."]

II. Analysis

This litigation presents two distinct challenges to EPA's stance on greenhouse-gas permitting for stationary sources. First, we must decide whether EPA permissibly determined that a source may be subject to the PSD and Title V permitting requirements on the sole basis of the source's potential to emit greenhouse gases. Second, we must decide whether EPA permissibly determined that a source already subject to the PSD program because of its emission of conventional pollutants (an "anyway" source) may be required to limit its greenhouse-gas emissions by employing the "best available control technology" for greenhouse gases. The Solicitor General joins issue on both points but evidently regards the second as more important; he informs us that "anyway" sources account for roughly 83% of American stationary-source greenhouse-gas emissions, compared to just 3% for the additional, non-"anyway" sources EPA sought to regulate at Steps 2 and 3 of the Tailoring Rule.

[The Court noted that it would apply *Chevron* deference.]

A. The PSD and Title V Triggers

We first decide whether EPA permissibly interpreted the statute to provide that a source may be required to obtain a PSD or Title V permit on the sole basis of its potential greenhouse-gas emissions.

1.

EPA thought its conclusion that a source's greenhouse-gas emissions may necessitate a PSD or Title V permit followed from the Act's unambiguous language. The Court of Appeals agreed and held that the statute "compelled" EPA's interpretation. We disagree. The statute compelled EPA's greenhouse-gas-inclusive interpretation with respect to neither the PSD program nor Title V.

The Court of Appeals reasoned by way of a flawed syllogism: Under *Massachusetts,* the general, Act-wide definition of "air pollutant" includes greenhouse gases; the Act requires permits for major emitters of "any air pollutant"; therefore, the Act requires permits for major emitters of greenhouse gases. The conclusion follows from the premises only if the air pollutants referred to in the permit-requiring provisions (the minor premise) are the same air pollutants encompassed by the Act-wide definition as interpreted in *Massachusetts* (the major premise). Yet no one—least of all EPA— endorses that proposition, and it is obviously untenable.

The Act-wide definition says that an air pollutant is "any air pollution agent or combination of such agents, including any physical, chemical, biological, [or] radioactive . . . substance or matter which is emitted into or otherwise enters the ambient air." § 7602(g). In *Massachusetts*, the Court held that the Act-wide definition includes greenhouse gases because it is all-encompassing; it "embraces all airborne compounds of whatever stripe." But where the term "air pollutant" appears in the Act's operative provisions, EPA has routinely given it a narrower, context-appropriate meaning.

That is certainly true of the provisions that require PSD and Title V permitting for major emitters of "any air pollutant." Since 1978, EPA's regulations have interpreted "air pollutant" in the PSD permitting trigger as limited to *regulated* air pollutants, . . .

Although these limitations are nowhere to be found in the Act-wide definition, in each instance EPA has concluded—as it has in the PSD and Title V context—that the statute is not using "air pollutant" in *Massachusetts* broad sense to mean any airborne substance whatsoever.

Massachusetts did not invalidate all these longstanding constructions. That case did not hold that EPA must always regulate greenhouse gases as an "air pollutant" everywhere that term appears in the statute, but only that EPA must "ground its reasons for action *or inaction* in the statute," rather than on "reasoning divorced from the statutory text." EPA's inaction with regard to Title II was not sufficiently grounded in the statute, the Court said, in part because nothing in the Act suggested that regulating greenhouse gases under that Title would conflict with the statutory design. Title II would not compel EPA to regulate in any way that would be "extreme," "counterintuitive," or contrary to "'common sense.'" At most, it would require EPA to take the modest step of adding greenhouse-gas standards to the roster of new-motor-vehicle emission regulations.

Massachusetts does not strip EPA of authority to exclude greenhouse gases from the class of regulable air pollutants under other parts of the Act where their inclusion would be inconsistent with the statutory scheme. The Act-wide definition to which the Court gave a "sweeping" and "capacious" interpretation is not a command to regulate, but a description of the universe of substances EPA may *consider* regulating under the Act's operative provisions. *Massachusetts* does not foreclose the Agency's use of statutory context to infer that certain of the Act's provisions use "air pollutant" to denote not every conceivable airborne substance, but only those that may sensibly be encompassed within the particular regulatory program. As certain *amici* felicitously put it, while *Massachusetts* "rejected EPA's categorical contention that greenhouse gases *could not* be 'air pollutants' for any purposes of the Act," it did not "embrace EPA's current, equally categorical position that greenhouse gases *must* be air pollutants for all purposes" regardless of the statutory context.

We need not, and do not, pass on the validity of all the limiting constructions EPA has given the term "air pollutant" throughout the Act. We merely observe that taken together, they belie EPA's rigid insistence that when interpreting the PSD and Title V permitting requirements it is bound by the Act-wide definition's inclusion of greenhouse gases, no matter how incompatible that inclusion is with those programs' regulatory structure.

In sum, there is no insuperable textual barrier to EPA's interpreting "any air pollutant" in the permitting triggers of PSD and Title V to encompass only pollutants emitted in quantities that enable them to be sensibly regulated at the statutory thresholds, and to exclude those atypical pollutants that, like greenhouse gases, are emitted in such vast quantities that their inclusion would radically transform those programs and render them unworkable as written.

2.

Having determined that EPA was mistaken in thinking the Act *compelled* a greenhouse-gas-inclusive interpretation of the PSD and Title V triggers, we next consider the Agency's alternative position that its interpretation was justified as an exercise of its "discretion" to adopt "a reasonable construction of the statute." We conclude that EPA's interpretation is not permissible.

Even under *Chevron*'s deferential framework, agencies must operate "within the bounds of reasonable interpretation." And reasonable statutory interpretation must account for both "the specific context in which ... language is used" and "the broader context of the statute as a whole." A statutory "provision that may seem ambiguous in isolation is often clarified by the remainder of the statutory scheme ... because only one of the permissible meanings produces a substantive effect that is compatible with the rest of the law." Thus, an agency interpretation that is "inconsisten[t] with the design and structure of the statute as a whole," does not merit deference.

EPA itself has repeatedly acknowledged that applying the PSD and Title V permitting requirements to greenhouse gases would be inconsistent with — in fact, would overthrow — the Act's structure and design. In the Tailoring Rule, EPA described the calamitous consequences of interpreting the Act in that way. Under the PSD program, annual permit applications would jump from about 800 to nearly 82,000; annual administrative costs would swell from $12 million to over $1.5 billion; and decade-long delays in issuing permits would become common, causing construction projects to grind to a halt nationwide. The picture under Title V was equally bleak ... EPA stated that these results would be so "contrary to congressional intent," and would so "severely undermine what Congress sought to accomplish," that they necessitated as much as a 1,000 — fold increase in the permitting thresholds set forth in the statute.

Like EPA, we think it beyond reasonable debate that requiring permits for sources based solely on their emission of greenhouse gases at the 100- and 250-tons-per-year levels set forth in the statute would be "incompatible" with "the substance of Congress' regulatory scheme." A brief review of the relevant statutory provisions leaves no doubt that the PSD program and Title V are designed to apply to, and cannot rationally be extended beyond, a relative handful of large sources capable of shouldering heavy substantive and procedural burdens ....

The fact that EPA's greenhouse-gas-inclusive interpretation of the PSD and Title V triggers would place plainly excessive demands on limited governmental resources is alone a good reason for rejecting it; but that is not the only reason. EPA's interpretation is also unreasonable because it would bring about an enormous and transformative expansion in EPA's regulatory authority without clear congressional authorization. When an agency claims to discover in a long-extant statute an unheralded power to regulate "a significant portion of the American economy," we typically greet its announcement with a measure of skepticism. We expect Congress to speak clearly if it wishes to assign to an agency decisions of vast "economic and political significance." The power to require permits for the construction and modification of tens of thousands, and the operation of millions, of small sources nationwide falls comfortably within the class of authorizations that we have been reluctant to read into ambiguous statutory text. Moreover, in EPA's assertion of that authority, we confront a singular situation: an agency laying claim to extravagant statutory power over the national economy while at the same time strenuously asserting that the authority claimed would render the statute "unrecognizable to the Congress that designed" it. Since, as we hold above, the statute does not compel EPA's interpretation, it would be patently unreasonable — not to say outrageous — for EPA to insist on seizing expansive power that it admits the statute is not designed to grant.

3.

EPA thought that despite the foregoing problems, it could make its interpretation reasonable by adjusting the levels at which a source's greenhouse-gas emissions would oblige it to undergo PSD and Title V permitting. Although the Act, in no uncertain terms, requires permits for sources with the potential to emit more than 100 or 250 tons per year of a relevant pollutant, EPA in its Tailoring Rule wrote a new threshold of *100,000* tons per year for greenhouse gases. Since the Court of Appeals thought the statute unambiguously made greenhouse gases capable of triggering PSD and Title V, it held that petitioners lacked Article III standing to challenge the Tailoring Rule because that rule did not injure petitioners but merely relaxed the pre-existing statutory requirements. Because we, however, hold that EPA's greenhouse-gas-inclusive interpretation of the triggers was *not* compelled, and because EPA has essentially admitted that its interpretation would be unreasonable without "tailoring," we consider the validity of the Tailoring Rule.

huge increase

We conclude that EPA's rewriting of the statutory thresholds was impermissible and therefore could not validate the Agency's interpretation of the triggering provisions. An agency has no power to "tailor" legislation to bureaucratic policy goals by rewriting unambiguous statutory terms. Agencies exercise discretion only in the interstices created by statutory silence or ambiguity; they must always "'give effect to the unambiguously expressed intent of Congress.'" It is hard to imagine a statutory term less ambiguous than the precise numerical thresholds at which the Act requires PSD and Title V permitting. When EPA replaced those numbers with others of its own choosing, it went well beyond the "bounds of its statutory authority."

The Solicitor General does not, and cannot, defend the Tailoring Rule as an exercise of EPA's enforcement discretion. The Tailoring Rule is not just an announcement of EPA's refusal to enforce the statutory permitting requirements; it purports to alter those requirements and to establish with the force of law that otherwise-prohibited conduct will not violate the Act. This alteration of the statutory requirements was crucial to EPA's "tailoring" efforts. Without it, small entities with the potential to emit greenhouse gases in amounts exceeding the statutory thresholds would have remained subject to citizen suits—authorized by the Act—to enjoin their construction, modification, or operation and to impose civil penalties of up to $37,500 per day of violation. EPA itself has recently affirmed that the "independent enforcement authority" furnished by the citizen-suit provision cannot be displaced by a permitting authority's decision not to pursue enforcement. The Solicitor General is therefore quite right to acknowledge that the availability of citizen suits made it necessary for EPA, in seeking to mitigate the unreasonableness of its greenhouse-gas-inclusive interpretation, to go beyond merely exercising its enforcement discretion . . . .

Were we to recognize the authority claimed by EPA in the Tailoring Rule, we would deal a severe blow to the Constitution's separation of powers. Under our system of government, Congress makes laws and the President, acting at times through agencies like EPA, "faithfully execute[s]" them. U.S. Const., Art. II, § 3. The power of executing the laws necessarily includes both authority and responsibility to resolve some questions left open by Congress that arise during the law's administration. But it does not include a power to revise clear statutory terms that turn out not to work in practice.

In the Tailoring Rule, EPA asserts newfound authority to regulate millions of small sources—including retail stores, offices, apartment buildings, shopping centers, schools, and churches—and to decide, on an ongoing basis and without regard for the thresholds prescribed by Congress, how many of those sources to regulate. We are not willing to stand on the dock and wave goodbye as EPA embarks on this multiyear voyage of discovery. We reaffirm the core administrative-law principle that an agency may not rewrite clear statutory terms to suit its own sense of how the statute should operate. EPA therefore lacked authority to "tailor" the Act's unambiguous numerical thresholds to accommodate its greenhouse-gas-inclusive interpretation of the permitting triggers. Instead, the need to rewrite clear provisions of the statute should have alerted EPA that it had taken a wrong interpretive turn. Agencies are not free to "adopt . . . unreasonable interpretations of statutory provisions and then edit other statutory provisions to mitigate the unreasonableness." Because the Tailoring Rule cannot save EPA's interpretation of the triggers, that interpretation was impermissible under *Chevron*.

B. BACT for "Anyway" Sources

For the reasons we have given, EPA overstepped its statutory authority when it decided that a source could become subject to PSD or Title V permitting by reason of its greenhouse-gas emissions. But what about "anyway" sources, those that would need permits based on their emissions of more conventional pollutants (such as particulate matter)? We now consider whether EPA reasonably interpreted the Act to require those sources to comply with "best available control technology" emission standards for greenhouse gases.

1.

To obtain a PSD permit, a source must be "subject to the best available control technology" for "each pollutant subject to regulation under [the Act]" that it emits. The Act defines BACT as "an emission limitation based on the maximum degree of reduction of each pollutant subject to regulation" that is "achievable . . . through application of production processes and available methods, systems, and techniques, including fuel cleaning, clean fuels, or treatment or innovative fuel combustion techniques." BACT is determined "on a case-by-case basis, taking into account energy, environmental, and economic impacts and other costs."

Some petitioners urge us to hold that EPA may never require BACT for greenhouse gases—even when a source must undergo PSD review based on its emissions of conventional pollutants—because BACT is fundamentally unsuited to greenhouse-gas regulation. BACT, they say, has traditionally been about end-of-stack controls "such as catalytic converters or particle collectors"; but applying it to greenhouse gases will make it more about regulating energy use, which will enable regulators to control "every aspect of a facility's operation and design," right down to the "light bulbs in the factory cafeteria."

EPA has published a guidance document that lends some credence to petitioners' fears. It states that at least initially, compulsory improvements in energy efficiency will be the "foundation" of greenhouse-gas BACT, with more traditional end-of-stack controls either not used or "added as they become more available." But EPA's guidance also states that BACT analysis should consider options *other than* energy efficiency, such as "carbon capture and storage." EPA argues that carbon capture is reasonably comparable to more traditional, end-of-stack BACT technologies, and petitioners do not dispute that.

Moreover, assuming without deciding that BACT may be used to force some improvements in energy efficiency, there are important limitations on BACT that may work to mitigate petitioners' concerns about "unbounded" regulatory authority. For one, BACT is based on "control technology" for the applicant's "proposed facility"; therefore, it has long been held that BACT cannot be used to order a fundamental redesign of the facility. For another, EPA has long interpreted BACT as required only for pollutants that the source itself emits; accordingly, EPA acknowledges that BACT may not be used to require "reductions in a facility's demand for energy from the electric grid." Finally, EPA's guidance suggests that BACT should not require every conceivable change that could result in minor improvements in energy efficiency, such as the aforementioned light bulbs. The guidance explains that permitting authorities should instead consider whether a proposed regulatory burden outweighs any reduction in emissions to be achieved, and should concentrate on the facility's equipment that uses the largest amounts of energy.

2.

The question before us is whether EPA's decision to require BACT for greenhouse gases emitted by sources otherwise subject to PSD review is, as a general matter, a permissible interpretation of the statute under *Chevron*. We conclude that it is.

The text of the BACT provision is far less open-ended than the text of the PSD and Title V permitting triggers. It states that BACT is required "for each pollutant subject to regulation under this chapter" (*i.e.,* the entire Act), a phrase that—as the D.C. Circuit wrote 35 years ago—"would not seem readily susceptible [of] misinterpretation." Whereas the dubious breadth of "any air pollutant" in the permitting triggers suggests a role for agency judgment in identifying the subset of pollutants covered by the particular regulatory program at issue, the more specific phrasing of the BACT provision suggests that the necessary judgment has already been made by Congress. The wider statutory context likewise does not suggest that the BACT provision can bear a narrowing construction: There is no indication that the Act elsewhere uses, or that EPA has interpreted, "each pollutant subject to regulation under this chapter" to mean anything other than what it says.

Even if the text were not clear, applying BACT to greenhouse gases is not so disastrously unworkable, and need not result in such a dramatic expansion of agency authority, as to convince us that EPA's interpretation is unreasonable. We are not talking about extending EPA jurisdiction over millions of previously unregulated entities, but about moderately increasing the demands EPA (or a state permitting authority) can make of entities already subject to its regulation. And it is not yet clear that EPA's demands will be of a significantly different character from those traditionally associated with PSD review. In short, the record before us does not establish that the BACT provision as written is incapable of being sensibly applied to greenhouse gases.

We acknowledge the potential for greenhouse-gas BACT to lead to an unreasonable and unanticipated degree of regulation, and our decision should not be taken as an endorsement of all aspects of EPA's current approach, nor as a free rein for any future regulatory application of BACT in this distinct context. Our narrow holding is that nothing in the statute categorically prohibits EPA from interpreting the BACT provision to apply to greenhouse gases emitted by "anyway" sources.

However, EPA may require an "anyway" source to comply with greenhouse-gas BACT only if the source emits more than a *de minimis* amount of greenhouse gases. As noted above, the Tailoring Rule applies BACT only if a source emits greenhouse gases in excess of 75,000 tons per year CO2e, but the Rule makes clear that EPA did not arrive at that number by identifying the *de minimis* level. EPA may establish an appropriate *de minimis* threshold below which BACT is not required for a source's greenhouse-gas emissions. We do not hold that 75,000 tons per year CO2e necessarily exceeds a true *de minimis* level, only that EPA must justify its selection on proper grounds.

To sum up: We hold that EPA exceeded its statutory authority when it interpreted the Clean Air Act to require PSD and Title V permitting for stationary sources based on their greenhouse-gas emissions. Specifically, the Agency may not treat greenhouse gases as a pollutant for purposes of defining a "major emitting facility" (or a "modification" thereof) in the PSD context or a "major source" in the Title V context. To the extent its regulations purport to do so, they are invalid. EPA may, however, continue to treat greenhouse gases as a "pollutant subject to regulation under this chapter" for purposes of requiring BACT for "anyway" sources. The judgment of the Court of Appeals is affirmed in part and reversed in part.

It is so ordered.

Justice BREYER, concurring in part and dissenting in part.

... The interpretive difficulty in these cases arises out of the definition's use of the phrase "two hundred fifty tons per year or more," which I will call the "250 tpy threshold." When applied to greenhouse gases, 250 tpy is far too low a threshold. As the Court explains, tens of thousands of stationary sources emit large quantities of one greenhouse gas, carbon dioxide. To apply the programs at issue here to all those sources would be extremely expensive and burdensome, counterproductive, and perhaps impossible; it would also contravene Congress's intent that the programs' coverage be limited to those large sources whose emissions are substantial enough to justify the regulatory burdens. The EPA recognized as much, and it addressed the problem by issuing a regulation — the Tailoring Rule — that purports to raise the coverage threshold for greenhouse gases from the statutory figure of 250 tpy to 100,000 tpy in order to keep the programs' coverage limited to "a relatively small number of large industrial sources."

The Tailoring Rule solves the practical problems that would have been caused by the 250 tpy threshold. But what are we to do about the statute's language? The statute specifies a definite number — 250, not 100,000 — and it says that facilities that are covered by that number must meet the program's requirements. The statute says nothing about agency discretion to change that number. What is to be done? How, given the statute's language, can the EPA exempt from regulation sources that emit more than 250 but less than 100,000 tpy of greenhouse gases (and that also do not emit other regulated pollutants at threshold levels)?

The Court answers by (1) pointing out that regulation at the 250 tpy threshold would produce absurd results, (2) refusing to read the statute as compelling such results, and (3) consequently interpreting the phrase "*any* air pollutant" as containing an implicit exception for greenhouse gases. (Emphasis added.) Put differently, the Court reads the statute as defining "major emitting facility" to mean "stationary sources that have the potential to emit two hundred fifty tons per year or more of any air pollutant *except for those air pollutants, such as carbon dioxide, with respect to which regulation at that threshold would be impractical or absurd or would sweep in smaller sources that Congress did not mean to cover.*"

I agree with the Court that the word "any," when used in a statute, does not normally mean "any in the universe." Rather, "[g]eneral terms as used on particular occasions often carry with them implied restrictions as to scope," and so courts must interpret the word "any," like all other words, in context. As Judge Learned Hand pointed out when interpreting another statute many years ago, "[w]e can best reach the meaning here, as always, by recourse to the underlying purpose, and, with that as a guide, by trying to project upon the specific occasion how we think persons, actuated by such a purpose, would have dealt with it, if it had been presented to them at the time." The pursuit of that underlying purpose may sometimes require us to "abandon" a "literal interpretation" of a word like "any." . . .

But I do not agree with the Court that the only way to avoid an absurd or otherwise impermissible result in these cases is to create an atextual greenhouse gas exception to the phrase "any air pollutant." After all, the word "any" makes an earlier appearance in the definitional provision, which defines "major emitting facility" to mean "*any* . . . source with the potential to emit two hundred and fifty tons per year or more of any air pollutant." As a linguistic matter, one can just as easily read an implicit exception for small-scale greenhouse gas emissions into the phrase "any source" as into the phrase "any air pollutant." And given the purposes of the PSD program and the Act as a whole, as well as the specific roles of the different parts of the statutory definition, finding flexibility in "any source" is far more sensible than the Court's route of finding it in "any air pollutant."

The implicit exception I propose reads almost word for word the same as the Court's, except that the location of the exception has shifted. To repeat, the Court reads the definition of "major emitting facility" as if it referred to "any source with the potential to emit two hundred fifty tons per year or more of any air pollutant *except for those air pollutants, such as carbon dioxide, with respect to which regulation at that threshold would be impractical or absurd or would sweep in smaller sources that Congress did not mean to cover.*" I would simply move the implicit exception, which I've italicized, so that it applies to "source" rather than "air pollutant": "any *source* with the potential to emit two hundred fifty tons per year or more of any air pollutant *except for those sources, such as those emitting unmanageably small amounts of greenhouse gases, with respect to which regulation at that threshold would be impractical or absurd or would sweep in smaller sources that Congress did not mean to cover.*"

From a legal, administrative, and functional perspective—that is, from a perspective that assumes that Congress was not merely trying to arrange words on paper but was seeking to achieve a real-world *purpose*—my way of reading the statute is the more sensible one. For one thing, my reading is consistent with the specific purpose underlying the 250 tpy threshold specified by the statute. The purpose of that number was not to prevent the regulation of dangerous air pollutants that cannot be sensibly regulated at that particular threshold, though that is the effect that the Court's reading gives the threshold. Rather, the purpose was to limit the PSD program's obligations to larger sources while exempting the many small sources whose emissions are low enough that imposing burdensome regulatory requirements on them would be senseless.

. . .

An implicit source-related exception would serve this statutory purpose while going no further. The implicit exception that the Court reads into the phrase "any air pollutant," by contrast, goes well beyond the limited congressional objective. Nothing in the statutory text, the legislative history, or common sense suggests that Congress, when it imposed the 250 tpy threshold, was trying to undermine its own deliberate decision to use the broad language "any air pollutant" by removing some substances (rather than some facilities) from the PSD program's coverage.

For another thing, a source-related exception serves the flexible nature of the Clean Air Act. We observed in *Massachusetts* that "[w]hile the Congresses that drafted" the Act "might not have appreciated the possibility that burning fossil fuels could lead to global warming, they did understand that without regulatory flexibility, changing circumstances and scientific developments would soon render the Clean Air Act obsolete." 549 U.S., at 532. We recognized that "[t]he broad language of" the Act-wide definition of "air pollutant" "reflects an intentional effort to confer the flexibility necessary to forestall such obsolescence." Ibid.

The Court's decision to read greenhouse gases out of the PSD program drains the Act of its flexibility and chips away at our decision in *Massachusetts*. What sense does it make to read the Act as generally granting the EPA the authority to regulate greenhouse gas emissions and then to read it as denying that power with respect to the programs for large stationary sources at issue here? . . .

C. United States Adaptation Policy

Although it is quite clear that we need to find a way to reduce our GHG emissions with the goal of slowing down (and eventually halting) our impact on global climate, we have also learned that climate change is already underway, that it operates with a multi-decade lag time, and that we are neither economically nor politically capable of immediate and/or complete cessation of GHG emissions. In other words, we will be stuck with climate change for at least a few decades, likely longer, and it is likely to get worse before it gets better. *See* T.M.L. Wigley, *The Climate Change Commitment*, 307 SCIENCE 1766 (2005). This subsection provides a brief introduction to climate adaptation issues and U.S. policies relating to them.

William E. Easterling III, Brian H. Hurd & Joel B. Smith, *Coping with Global Climate Change: The Role of Adaptation in the United States*

Pew Center on Global Climate Change, 2004
http://www.c2es.org/docUploads/Adaptation.pdf

Executive Summary

Climate change resulting from increased greenhouse gas concentrations has the potential to harm societies and ecosystems. In particular, agriculture, forestry, water resources, human health, coastal settlements, and natural ecosystems will need to adapt to a changing climate or face diminished functions. Reductions in emissions of greenhouse gases and their concentration in the atmosphere will tend to reduce the degree and likelihood that significantly adverse conditions will result. Consideration of actions—e.g., mitigation policy—that can reduce this likelihood is reasonable and prudent, and has generally been the primary focus of public attention and policy efforts on climate change. However, recognition is increasing that the combination of continued increases in emissions and the inertia of the climate system means that some degree of climate change is inevitable. Even if extreme measures could be instantly taken to curtail global emissions, the momentum of the earth's climate is such that warming cannot be completely avoided. Although essential for limiting the extent, and indeed the probability, of rapid and severe climate change, mitigation is not, and this paper argues, should not be, the only protective action in society's arsenal of responses.

Adaptation actions and strategies present a complementary approach to mitigation. While mitigation can be viewed as reducing the likelihood of adverse conditions, adaptation can be viewed as reducing the severity of many impacts if adverse conditions prevail. That is, adaptation reduces the level of damages that might have otherwise occurred. However, adaptation is a risk-management strategy that is not free of cost nor foolproof, and the worthiness of any specific actions must therefore carefully weigh the expected value of the avoided damages against the real costs of implementing the adaptation strategy.

Adaptation to environmental change is a fundamental human trait and is not a new concept. Throughout the ages, human societies have shown a strong capacity for adapting to different climates and environmental changes, although not always successfully. As evidenced by the widespread and climatically diverse location of human settlements throughout the world, humans have learned how to thrive in a wide variety of climate regimes, ranging from cold to hot and from humid to dry. The resilience and flexibility exhibited in the patterns of human settlements evidence an inherent desire and some measure of capacity to adapt.

For human systems, the success of adaptation depends critically on the availability of necessary resources, not only financial and natural resources, but also knowledge, technical capability, and institutional resources. The types and levels of required resources, in turn, depend fundamentally on the nature and abruptness of the actual or anticipated environmental change and the range of considered responses.

The processes of adaptation to climate change in both human and natural systems are highly complex and dynamic, often entailing many feedbacks and dependencies on existing local and temporal conditions. The uncertainties introduced by the complexity, scale, and limited experience with respect to anthropogenic climate change explain the limited level of applied research conducted thus far on adaptation, the reliance on mechanistic assumptions, and the widespread use of scenarios and historical analogues. In addition, many social, economic, technological and environmental trends will critically shape the future ability of societal systems to adapt to climate change. While such factors as increased population and wealth will likely increase the potential level of material assets that are exposed to the risks of climate change, greater wealth and improved technology also extend the resources and perhaps the capabilities to adapt to climate change. These trends must be taken into account when evaluating the nature and scale of future adaptive responses and the likelihood that they will succeed.

The implications of climate change are more dire for natural systems, because it will be difficult for many species to change behavior or migrate in response to climate change. While biological systems might accommodate minor (or slowly occurring) perturbations in a smooth continuous fashion, even minor changes in climate may be disruptive for many ecosystems and individual species. In addition, many of the world's species are currently stressed by a variety of factors including urban development, pollution, invasive species, and fractured (or isolated) habitats. Such conditions, coupled with the relatively rapid rate of anticipated climate change, are likely to challenge many species' resiliency and chances for successful adaptation.

Key insights and findings on adaptation and its potential for success are summarized below:

1) Adaptation and mitigation are necessary and complementary for a comprehensive and coordinated strategy that addresses the problem of global climate change. By lessening the severity of possible damages, adaptation is a key defensive measure. Adaptation is particularly important given the mounting evidence that some degree of climate change is inevitable. Recognizing a role for adaptation does not, however, diminish or detract from the importance of mitigation in reducing the rate and likelihood of significant climate change.

2) The literature indicates that U.S. society can on the whole adapt with either net gains or some costs if warming occurs at the lower end of the projected range of magnitude, assuming no change in climate variability and generally making optimistic assumptions about adaptation. However, with a much larger magnitude of warming, even making relatively optimistic assumptions about adaptation, many sectors would experience net losses and higher costs. The thresholds in terms of magnitudes or rates of change (including possible non-linear responses) in climate that will pose difficulty for adaptation are uncertain. In addition, it is uncertain how much of an increase in frequency, intensity, or persistence of extreme weather events the United States can tolerate.

3) To say that society as a whole "can adapt" does not mean that regions and peoples will not suffer losses. For example, while the agricultural sector as a whole may successfully adapt, some regions may gain and others may lose. Agriculture in many northern regions is expected to adapt to climate change by taking advantage of changing climatic conditions to expand production, but agriculture in many southern regions is expected to contract with warmer, drier temperatures. Individual farmers not benefiting from adaptation may lose their livelihoods. In addition, other individuals or populations in these and other regions can be at risk, because they could be adversely affected by climate change and lack the capacity to adapt. This is particularly true of relatively low-income individuals and groups whose livelihoods are dependent on resources at risk from climate change.

4) Adaptation is not likely to be a smooth process or free of costs. While studies and history show that society can on the whole adapt to a moderate amount of warming, it is reasonable to expect that mistakes will be made and costs will be incurred along the way. People are neither so foolish as to continue doing what they have always done in the face of climate change, nor so omniscient as to perfectly understand what will need to be done and to carry it out most efficiently. In reality, we are more likely to muddle through, taking adaptive actions as necessary, but often not doing what may be needed for optimal or ideal adaptation. Additionally, adaptation is an on-going process rather than a one-shot instantaneous occurrence. Compounding society's shortcomings, a more rapid, variable, or generally unpredictable climate change would add further challenges to adaptation.

5) Effects on ecosystems, and on species diversity in particular, are expected to be negative at all but perhaps the lowest magnitudes of climate change because of the limited ability of natural systems to adapt. Although biological systems have an inherent capacity to adapt to changes in environmental conditions, given the rapid rate of projected climate change, adaptive capacity is likely to be exceeded for many species. Furthermore, the ability of ecosystems to adapt to climate change is severely limited by the effects of urbanization, barriers to migration paths, and fragmentation of ecosystems, all of which have already critically stressed ecosystems independent of climate change itself.

6) Institutional design and structure can heighten or diminish society's exposure to climate risks. Long-standing institutions, such as disaster relief payments and insurance programs, affect adaptive capacity. Coastal zoning, land-use planning, and building codes are all examples of institutions that can contribute to (or detract from) the capacity to withstand climate changes in efficient and effective ways.

7) Proactive adaptation can reduce U.S. vulnerability to climate change. Proactive adaptation can improve capacities to cope with climate change by taking climate change into account in long-term decision-making, removing disincentives for changing behavior in response to climate change (such as removing subsidies for maladaptive activities), and introducing incentives to modify behavior in response to climate change (such as the use of market-based mechanisms to promote adaptive responses). Furthermore, improving and strengthening human capital through education, outreach, and extension services improves decision-making capacity at every level and increases the collective capacity to adapt.

Alejandro E. Camacho, *Adapting Governance to Climate Change: Managing Uncertainty through a Learning Infrastructure*

59 Emory L. J. 1 (2009)

II. Adapting to Climate Change

Exceptional uncertainty is the core challenge that natural resource governance faces from climate change. Ecologists and other scientists are being forced to reconsider long-held assumptions and methodologies for studying natural systems, and agencies are being pressed to prepare for problems they have never faced before. In short, adapting to climate change necessitates the coordination and mobilization of scientific and management information to a degree never attempted. To be sure, government institutions must develop a suite of strategies to both prevent further climatic change and foster suitable adaptations to its effects on natural and human systems. More importantly, natural resource governance must develop an infrastructure that enhances the capacity of public and private actors to assess and manage an uncertain regulatory environment.

A. The Need for Adaptation

Despite the sizeable uncertainty that accompanies any comprehensive effort to manage the effects of climate change, climate change adaptation is a vital complement to mitigation activities that seek to curb further climatic change. On the one hand, focusing more attention on adaptation should certainly not supplant vital efforts to abate greenhouse gas emissions. Extensive evidence compiled by thousands of independent scientists indicates that without swift, comprehensive efforts to substantially reduce emissions, the effects of climate change on natural systems will undoubtedly be more severe. . . . Emissions reduction through efforts, such as the currently pending Waxman-Markey American Clean Energy and Security Act of 2009, that seek a cap-and-trade or emission tax system to mitigate greenhouse gas emissions should not be merely an afterthought, but rather a vital part of any sensible response to climate change.

On the other hand, no amount of abatement, even if enacted tomorrow, is likely to diminish the effects of climate change for several decades. Evidence suggests that the effects of global warming are already being experienced in the United States, and climate change is likely to continue for decades, even in the event of significant reduction of emissions. Countless people and ecosystems are and will continue to be threatened by the effects of climate change, at least until abatement measures show results.

Climate change thus will increasingly place considerable stress on the perpetually limited resources allocated to manage natural resources. Government institutions must be tactical in trying to expand the capacity to address existing regulatory vulnerabilities while anticipating and averting severe climate change effects. Unfortunately, legislators and regulators in the United States and elsewhere have only begun to consider the role of adaptation in combating climate change.

B. A Typology of Government Adaptation Strategies

Greater attention must be given to reducing the existing and future adverse effects of climate change on natural resources. To advance this endeavor, this section proposes a framework for classifying government adaptation measures according to three particularly relevant parameters: (1) whether the adaptation primarily anticipates or reacts to effects from climate change; (2) whether the strategy focuses exclusively, partially, or only indirectly on projected climate change effects; and (3) whether the strategy is a "substantive" response to the direct effects of climate change, or an indirect "procedural" adaptation of a process for deciding among substantive adaptations. All of these government strategies likely have a role to play in any comprehensive approach to climate change adaptation. However, as detailed here, the uncertainty attributable to climate change, and the inevitable scarcity of resources allocated for natural resource governance, counsel for an emphasis on proactive, procedural strategies directed at addressing existing key regulatory vulnerabilities likely to be exacerbated by climate change. Such strategies can provide a basis for government regulators to manage uncertainty and reduce the risk of regulatory waste.

1. Proactive and Reactive Strategies

The timing of an adaptation's implementation is likely to have significant repercussions on the cost and success of the strategy. A proactive adaptation "takes place before impacts of climate change are observed." Such strategies seek to formulate long-term strategies for infrastructure, education, outreach, and improving collective capacities to adapt, as well as create incentives to change behaviors suited to the shifting climate. However, such strategies are susceptible to the considerable uncertainty inherent in predictive modeling. Therefore, to be successful, proactive strategies must be designed to adapt to a range of possible effects and must be nimble enough to respond to new information obtained during implementation.

In contrast, a reactive adaptation is "a deliberate response to a climatic shock or impact, in order to recover and prevent similar impacts in the future." Such strategies have the key inherent advantage of being subject to less uncertainty, as they are only implemented in response to actualized risks. However, various intrinsic problems exist with reactive approaches. Because they are only implemented after-the-fact, "a high degree of ecosystem and infrastructure damage is likely to occur before reactive measures are taken." Due to "inefficiencies in the response when it is needed, wasted investments made in ignorance of future conditions, or potentially even greater damages because precautionary actions were not taken," reactive adaptations may be more vulnerable to higher long-term administrative costs and damages. The limitations of reactive strategies are particularly problematic when addressing high-cost or irreversible impacts of long-term and expensive investments, or when otherwise important to prevent (and not merely respond to) climate effects. Unfortunately, such circumstances are quite common in the context of climate change, particularly in the context of threats to certain biological resources.

Thus, in adapting to the effects of climate change on ecological resources it is better to prevent negative consequences by employing proactive adaptations based on the precautionary principle. Reactive adaptations should be left to circumstances in which proactive strategies were unsuccessful in identifying and preventing a hazard from occurring. Establishing a systematic approach for cultivating successful proactive adaptations is thus crucial to developing effective adaptation strategies.

2. Exclusive, Co-benefit, or No-Regret Strategies

Another variable for distinguishing among adaptation strategies emphasizes the orientation of the adaptation in terms of the benefit provided. Exclusive adaptations are directed exclusively at reducing the effects of climate change. A co-benefit strategy is in part directed at reducing vulnerabilities related to climate change but is also expected to produce other public benefits. No-regrets adaptations are directed at providing net benefits irrespective of the effects of climate change.

Due to existing uncertainties about such effects, prudent regulators should seek to maximize the use of no-regrets adaptations. No-regrets strategies reduce the risks of regulatory waste from uncertainty because they are a net benefit to their particular natural and/or regulatory system regardless of whether (or to what extent) the projected effects of climate change occur. However, given the magnitude and speed of impacts anticipated by climate change, it is doubtful that reliance on no-regrets strategies alone could forestall all the heretofore unknown effects of climate change. Because the exact effects of climate change remain uncertain, regulators also should seek to adopt partial or co-benefit adaptations that maximize supplementary public benefits in order to minimize the risks from costly adaptations. Only as a precaution against particularly large or catastrophic risks should regulators consider employing exclusive adaptations that lack other public benefits.

3. Substantive and Procedural Strategies

In classifying potential adaptation strategies, perhaps the most important distinction is one that has not been identified in the scientific or legal literature: whether the adaptation is primarily a substantive or procedural strategy. This distinction considers whether the strategy principally seeks to address the direct effects of climate change (substantive), or to change a process for deciding among substantive adaptations (procedural).

a. Substantive Governmental Strategies

Most of the strategies mentioned by natural resource managers and discussed in the growing scholarly literature on climate change adaptation are substantive. For example, many proposed adaptations focus on altering the environment to minimize the direct effects of sea level rise and severe weather events such as storm intensity, floods, and droughts. These sorts of direct, discrete adaptations, such as physical removal of invasive species or construction of breakwaters, rock sills, levees, or dams, tend to be reactive.

Other substantive adaptations seek to alter the way private actors interact with the immediate environment to reduce the effect of climate change, often through the disclosure of information or changes to regulations that encourage or mandate particular private conduct. For example, regulatory adaptations that address increased risks to coastal resources could include (1) public information disclosure or education initiatives regarding flood risk; (2) early warning systems; (3) changes to government flood insurance; (4) subsidies or changes to zoning or building codes to increase the capacity of private property to withstand climate events; (5) modifications to permit programs to reduce coastal erosion, such as prohibitions on private seawalls; or (6) relocations of private structures from flood-prone areas through government acquisition.

On a larger scale, substantive adaptations also include agency management planning, varying from site-specific to program-wide plans. An example of a program-wide plan is EPA's new National Water Strategy, which seeks to modify EPA's water programs to address climate change effects. As adaptation strategies necessarily are specific to their application, the list of potential discrete or concrete strategies for any particular plan may be extensive. Management planning strategies being considered include the creation of additional protected areas, wildlife corridors, and replicate ecosystems; increased protection of vulnerable genotypes, species, and communities; ecosystem restoration; and "assisted migration" of species.

b. Procedural Governmental Strategies

Though most commenters have focused on substantive strategies that seek to minimize or reverse the adverse effects of climate change on natural systems, the most crucial adaptations may take the more indirect form of procedural governmental strategies. Rather than focusing on directly managing the effects of climate change—or the natural systems or human conduct that may exacerbate such effects—this category is intended to encompass strategies that manage the regulatory programs and processes that develop more direct strategies. Such approaches might seek to change the decision-making process officials use to select direct adaptation strategies. At their broadest level, such approaches might also seek a more fundamental transformation of the government institutions society relies on to manage natural resources. For example, procedural adaptation strategies should be created to flexibly manage the considerable uncertainty surrounding climate change to avert and minimize the harm from mistakes throughout the regulatory process.

The concept of "adaptive management" was originally proposed by scientists in the 1970s who sought a more effective approach to natural resource management in response to the significant uncertainty that regularly exists in ecosystems. This increasingly influential model seeks to address information gaps in management plans that surface during plan formation by including systematic monitoring procedures for obtaining more data to adjust the management strategies during implementation.

At the broadest level, procedural adaptation strategies may also include large-scale modifications to governance—that is, how regulators manage the programs that govern natural systems and how societies manage these regulators. Such approaches might include wholesale changes to existing statutory regimes or programs, the creation of new programs or agencies, or other fundamental changes to decision-making processes for regulating or managing natural resources. A few observers have discussed the need to make systemic or large-scale governance changes to respond to climate change. Yet, . . . few recognize the need to increase the adaptive capacity of natural resource programs and governance to manage the uncertainty that climate change brings.

C. The Value of Procedural Strategies

Though the value of direct substantive adaptations may be more apparent in comprehensive attempts to address the effects of climate change, a central assertion of this Article is that procedural strategies that transform existing approaches to natural resource governance are even more vital given the uncertainties that exist for addressing the impacts of a warming climate. For all the reasons that apply regarding the effects from climate change, substantive government adaptations—and in particular those seeking to regulate or manage ecosystems—are subject to the uncertainties of climate change as impact models are downscaled to specific locations. This uncertainty is compounded by the limited information that exists regarding the suitability and efficacy of possible adaptation strategies. For example, captive breeding and assisted migration strategies are less likely to work if climate change effects are rapid or substantial, yet the speed and magnitude of change are largely unknown for particular ecosystems. This uncertainty is again amplified because analyses of such strategies are rare, particularly in response to climate change, and protocols identifying when such strategies may be appropriate often do not exist. Additionally, some strategies are likely to conflict with other conservation methods or resource uses, and the optimal reconciliation of such conflicts is debatable.

However, uncertainty over the exact future consequences and optimal substantive strategies should not lead to the conclusion that regulators and the public can afford to neglect adaptation. As is often the case when inexorable uncertainty exists in assessing long-term environmental harms, the key question is not whether something should be done. Indeed, the United States is already investing enormously in climate change adaptation, though most of these costs are not counted as such because they are treated as facets of more conventional management activities, such as drought relief or storm damage recovery, and are aimed at problems such as water resource planning for which climate change is only one stressor. The key question is, based on the best available data, what strategies are likely to be most effective and cost efficient at averting or minimizing potential damage from climate change.

Procedural strategies can serve as the crucial bridge between uncertainty and the need for adaptation. Designed properly, such strategies are crucial for helping managers and regulators manage the substantial uncertainty about both the effects of climate change and the efficacy and side effects of substantive adaptation responses. Furthermore, larger-scale governance strategies can be cultivated that seek to create and disseminate information to regulatory actors, stakeholders, and the public to minimize uncertainty about climate change effects, substantive adaptations, and smaller-scale procedural adaptations. Procedural strategies can thus serve to strengthen the adaptability of existing processes and help avoid and adjust over- and under-regulation in response to climate change.

U.S. GLOBAL CHANGE RESEARCH PROGRAM (USGCRP)
PRELIMINARY REVIEW OF ADAPTATION OPTIONS FOR CLIMATE-SENSITIVE ECOSYSTEMS AND RESOURCES
U.S. Environmental Protection Agency (2008)

Executive Summary

Climate variables are key determinants of geographic distributions and biophysical characteristics of ecosystems, communities, and species. Climate *change*[1] is therefore affecting many species attributes, ecological interactions, and ecosystem processes.

---

1. Climate change refers to any change in climate over time, whether due to natural variability or as a result of human activity. This usage differs from that in the United Nations Framework Convention on Climate Change, which defines "climate change" as: "a change of climate which is attributed directly or indirectly to human activity that alters the composition of the global atmosphere and which is in addition to natural climate variability observed over comparable time periods."

Because changes in the climate system will continue into the future regardless of emissions mitigation, strategies for protecting climate-sensitive ecosystems through management will be increasingly important. While there will always be uncertainties associated with the future path of climate change, the response of ecosystems to climate impacts, and the effects of management, it is both possible and essential for adaptation to proceed using the best available science.

This report provides a preliminary review of adaptation options for climate-sensitive ecosystems and resources in the United States. The term "adaptation" in this document refers to adjustments in human social systems (*e.g.*, management) in response to climate stimuli and their effects. Since management always occurs in the context of desired ecosystem conditions or natural resource management goals, it is instructive to examine particular goals and processes used by different organizations to fulfill their objectives. Such an examination allows for discussion of specific adaptation options as well as potential barriers and opportunities for implementation. Using this approach, this report presents a series of chapters on the following selected management systems: National Forests, National Parks, National Wildlife Refuges, Wild and Scenic Rivers, National Estuaries, and Marine Protected Areas. For these chapters, the authors draw on the literature, their own expert opinion, and expert workshops composed of resource management scientists and representatives of managing agencies. The information drawn from across these chapters is then analyzed to develop the key synthetic messages presented below.

Many existing best management practices for "traditional" stressors of concern have the added benefit of reducing climate change exacerbations of those stressors. Changes in temperature, precipitation, sea level, and other climate-related factors can often exacerbate problems that are already of concern to managers. For example, increased intensity of precipitation events can further increase delivery of non-point source pollution and sediments to rivers, estuaries, and coasts. Fortunately, many management practices that exist to address such "traditional" stressors can also address climate change impacts. One such practice with multiple benefits is the construction of riparian buffer strips that (1) manage pollution loadings from agricultural lands into rivers today and (2) establish protective barriers against increases in both pollution and sediment loadings due to climate changes in the future. While multiple benefits may result from continuing with today's best practices, key adjustments in their application across space and time may be needed to ensure their continued effectiveness in light of climate change.

Seven "adaptation approaches" can be used for strategic adjustment of best management practices to maximize ecosystem resilience to climate change. As defined in this report, the goal of adaptation is to reduce the risk of adverse environmental outcomes through activities that increase the resilience of ecological systems to climate change. Here, resilience refers to the amount of change or disturbance that a system can absorb without undergoing a fundamental shift to a different set of processes and structures. Managers' past experiences with unpredictable and extreme events have already led to some existing approaches that can be adjusted for use in adapting to longer-term climate change. The specific "adaptation approaches" described below are derived from discussions of existing (and new) management practices to maintain or increase ecosystem resilience, drawn from across the chapters of this report.

Protecting key ecosystem features involves focusing management protections on structural characteristics, organisms, or areas that represent important "underpinnings" or "keystones" of the overall system. **Reducing anthropogenic stresses** is the approach of minimizing localized human stressors (*e.g.*, pollution, fragmentation) that hinder the ability of species or ecosystems to withstand climatic events. **Representation** refers to protecting a portfolio of variant forms of a species or ecosystem so that, regardless of the climatic changes that occur, there will be areas that survive and provide a source for recovery. **Replication** centers on maintaining more than one example of each ecosystem or population such that if one area is affected by a disturbance, replicates in another area provide insurance against extinction and a source for recolonization of affected areas. **Restoration** is the practice of rehabilitating ecosystems that have been lost or compromised. **Refugia** are areas that are less affected by climate change than other areas and can be used as sources of "seed" for recovery or as destinations for climate-sensitive migrants. **Relocation** refers to human-facilitated transplantation of organisms from one location to another in order to bypass a barrier (*e.g.*, urban area).

7
Adaptation
Approaches

Each of these adaptation approaches ultimately contributes to resilience, whether at the scale of individual protected area units, or at the scale of regional/national systems. The approaches above are not mutually exclusive and may be implemented jointly. The specific management activities that are selected under one or more approaches above should then be based on considerations such as: the ecosystem management goals, type and degree of climate effects, type and magnitude of ecosystem responses, spatial and temporal scales of ecological and management responses, and social and economic factors.

Levels of confidence in these adaptation approaches vary and are difficult to assess, yet are essential to consider in adaptation planning. . . .

One method for integrating confidence estimates into resource management given uncertainty is adaptive management. Adaptive management is a process that promotes flexible decision-making so that adjustments are made in decisions as outcomes from management actions and other events are better understood. This method supports managers in taking action today using the best available information while also providing the possibility of ongoing future refinements through an iterative learning process.

The success of adaptation strategies may depend on recognition of potential barriers to implementation and creation of opportunities for partnerships and leveraging. In many cases, perceived barriers associated with legal or social constraints, restrictive management procedures, limitations on human and financial capital, and gaps in information may be converted into opportunities. For example, there may be a possibility to address difficulties associated with information or capacity shortages through leveraging of human capital. Existing staff could receive training on addressing climate change issues within the context of their current job descriptions and management frameworks, but a critical requirement for success of this activity would be to ensure that employees feel both valued as "climate adaptation specialists" and empowered by their institutions to develop and implement innovative adaptive management approaches that might be perceived as "risky." As a second example, partnerships among managers, scientists, and educators can go a long way toward efficiently closing information gaps. With good communication and coordination, scientists can target their research to better inform management challenges, resource managers can share data and better design monitoring to test scientific hypotheses, and outreach specialists can better engage the public in understanding and supporting adaptation activities. Two additional categories of opportunities that are especially promising are highlighted below.

The Nation's adaptive capacity can be increased through expanded collaborations among ecosystem managers. When managers seize opportunities to link with other managers to coordinate adaptation planning, they are able to broaden the spatial and ecological scope of potential adaptation options with a shared vision for increasing adaptive capacity. For example, many management units are nested within or adjacent to other systems. Collaboration across systems allows individual units to be, in effect, extended beyond their official boundaries to encompass entire ecosystems or regions; the result is a larger array of options for responding to future climate change impacts. Collaboration may also enhance research capacity and offer opportunities to share data, models, and experiences. In addition to overcoming limiting factors such as inadequate resources and mismatches of management unit size with ecosystem extent, collaborations may also be used to create flexible boundaries that follow unanticipated changes in ecosystems or species in response to climate change. Exercising opportunities for collaboration has the advantage of reducing uncertainties associated with attaining management goals under climate change because (1) the increase in the geographic range over which resources can be managed and the associated increase in available adaptation options makes success more likely, and (2) the increase in the resource base, in research capabilities, and in the size of data sets through data sharing and coordinated monitoring reduces statistical uncertainties and increases the probability of success.

The Nation's adaptive capacity can be increased through creative re-examination of program goals and authorities. Anticipated climate-induced changes in ecosystems and species and the uncertain nature of some of those changes will necessitate dynamic management systems that can accommodate and address such changes. Existing management authorities may be malleable enough to allow for changing conditions and dynamic responses, and with creative re-examination of those authorities their full capabilities could be applied. For example, federal land and water managers may be able to strategically apply traditional legislative authorities in non-traditional ways to coordinate management outside of jurisdictional boundaries. Similarly, while management policies can sometimes be limiting, the iterative nature of management planning may allow priorities and plans to be revisited on a cyclical basis to allow for periodic adjustments. Greater agility in program planning can increase the probability of meeting management goals by overcoming implementation barriers associated with narrowly defined and interpreted authorities.

Establishing current baselines, identifying thresholds, and monitoring for changes will be essential elements of any adaptation approach. Climate changes may cause ecological thresholds to be exceeded, leading to abrupt shifts in the structure of ecosystems. Threshold changes in ecosystems have profound implications for management because such changes may be unexpected, large, and difficult to reverse. If these ecosystems cannot then be restored, actions to increase their resilience will no longer be viable. Understanding where thresholds have been exceeded in the past and where (and how likely) they may be exceeded in the future allows managers to plan accordingly and avoid tipping points where possible. . . .

Beyond "managing for resilience," the Nation's capability to adapt will ultimately depend on our ability to be flexible in setting priorities and "managing for change." Prioritizing actions and balancing competing management objectives at all scales of decision making is essential, especially in the midst of shifting budgets and rapidly changing ecosystems. Using a systematic framework for priority setting would help managers catalog information, design strategies, allocate resources, evaluate progress, and inform the public. This priority-setting could happen in an ongoing way to address changing ecological conditions and make use of new information. Over time, our ability to "manage for resilience" of current systems in the face of climate change will be limited as temperature thresholds are exceeded, climate impacts become severe and irreversible, and socioeconomic costs of maintaining existing ecosystem structures, functions, and services become excessive. At this point, it will be necessary to "manage for change," with a re-examination of priorities and a shift to adaptation options that incorporate information on projected ecosystem changes. Both "managing for resilience" and "managing for change" require more observation and experimentation to fill knowledge gaps on how to adapt to climate change. This report presents a preliminary review of existing adaptation knowledge to support managers in taking immediate actions to meet their management goals in the context of climate change. However, this is only a first step in better understanding this burgeoning area of research in adaptation science and management. It will be necessary to continuously refine and add to this body of knowledge in order to meet the challenge of preserving the Nation's lands and waters in a rapidly changing world.

Notes and Questions

1. Should governments focus their limited resources (both actual and political) more on mitigation or on adaptation? Is one more important—or urgent—than the other? In what ways do the two efforts relate to one another?

2. How effective do you believe existing mitigation efforts are likely to be? Is there hope for reining in the climate disruption problem before it exceeds our ability to adapt?

3. In considering the costs of adaptation, how much greater are they likely to become if climate change accelerates more rapidly? How do you think these higher adaptation costs would compare with the cost of mitigation? What factors would you consider in your cost-benefit analysis?

4. Reflecting on your response to Note 3, what impact does it have on your analysis if those bearing the cost of mitigation are not the same entities as those bearing the cost of adaptation? How, then, are we to engage in a proper cost-benefit analysis?

D. Creative Litigation Strategies to Address Climate Change

There is an intriguing new litigation trend, with the potential to be a game-changer if successful (it is underway at the time of this edition), described in this Center for Progressive Reform (CPR) blog post by Professor Klass. The most recent opinion in the ongoing litigation immediately follows.

Alexandra Klass, *Federalism at Work: Recent Developments in Public Trust Lawsuits to Limit Greenhouse Gas Emissions*

http://www.progressivereform.org/CPRBlog.cfm?idBlog=8092FA68-ADF9-7258
-98BF80BAC5FA4AA7

In a CPR Blog post in May 2011, I discussed the lawsuits filed on behalf of children against all 50 states and several federal agencies alleging that these governmental entities have violated the common law public trust doctrine by failing to limit greenhouse gas emissions that contribute to climate change. The suits were filed by Our Children's Trust, an Oregon-based nonprofit. The claims sought judicial declaration that states have a fiduciary duty to future generations with regard to an "atmospheric trust" and that states and the federal government must take immediate action to protect and preserve that trust. At the time, I opined that although these claims were novel and would likely have little, if any, immediate effect on state climate policy, they relied on what has proved to be a flexible and powerful common law doctrine in at least some states. As a result, I concluded there was likely to be significant variation in results between the states on creating opportunities for a new forum for consideration of climate change harms and potential legal responses. Now, just over a year later, some lower courts have issued decisions in the cases and, as expected, the results vary widely from state to state.

The public trust doctrine is a concept dating back to Roman law which holds that there are certain natural resources that are forever subject to government ownership and must be held in trust for the use and benefit of the public. In the United States, plaintiffs have used the public trust doctrine successfully to prevent states and other governmental entities from conveying public trust resources such as submerged lands or municipal harbors into private ownership, to create public beach access, and to otherwise ensure public access to water-based resources. Until the 1970s, however, the doctrine had little to do with environmental protection and instead was used almost exclusively to prevent the privatization of water-based resources or to preserve public access to fishing, boating, or commerce. Since that time, however, with the help of an influential law review article by Professor Joseph Sax, some states, like California, Louisiana, and Hawaii, have applied the common law doctrine to protect rivers, lakes, and other water-based resources as well as land-based resources such as birds and other wildlife. As I have discussed in my scholarly work on the public trust doctrine, other states have bolstered their common law public trust doctrine by relying on state constitutional provisions and state statutes mandating governmental protection of environmental resources. In this way, these states use the common law, state constitutions, and state statutes together to protect what I call generally "public trust principles." Despite these developments, however, there are still states that have a much more limited version of the common law public trust doctrine, with courts in those states limiting the doctrine's reach to ensuring continuing public ownership of water-based resources rather than using it for environmental protection purposes.

This brings us to the current lawsuits, which argue that the common law public trust doctrine is broad enough to encompass an "atmospheric trust" and that states have a duty to protect and preserve this trust resource for the benefit of present and future generations. As relief in the state court lawsuits, the plaintiffs sought a declaration that an atmospheric trust exists and that defendants have a duty to protect and preserve it. So how have courts responded? Not surprisingly, courts in several states, including Colorado, Oregon, Arizona, Washington, Arkansas, and Minnesota dismissed the cases early on, finding no basis for an "atmospheric trust" under state common law. Most of these states do not have a history of broad common law public trust doctrine protection for environmental resources, instead limiting the common law doctrine to its historic protection of submerged lands and access to navigable waters. In California, the plaintiffs voluntarily dismissed the case to pursue settlement talks. This too is not surprising because California has already been a leader in enacting statutes and regulations to reduce greenhouse gas emissions and is also one of the states most likely to recognize an atmospheric trust under common law doctrine. Thus, the ultimate goals of the plaintiffs and the State of California are much more aligned than in other states around the country.

Two victories for the petitioners, though, come from recent decisions in the New Mexico and Texas courts. In New Mexico, in January, on a motion to dismiss, the district court stated that the atmosphere could be recognized as within the public trust doctrine's protection and allowed the plaintiffs leave to amend their complaint to refine the relief they sought and to specify the government actions causing harm. Then, on Monday, a district court in Austin, Texas issued a ruling rejecting the Texas Commission on Environmental Quality's conclusion that the public trust doctrine is exclusively limited to the conservation of water in the state. Instead, the court held that the public trust doctrine is much broader, and includes all of the natural resources of the state, including air quality. In reaching this decision, the court expressly stated that the public trust doctrine "is not simply a common law doctrine" but is incorporated into the Texas Constitution, which (1) protects "the conservation and development of all the resources of the State," (2) declares conservation of those resources "public rights and duties," and (3) directs the

Legislature to pass appropriate laws to protect these resources. The court also relied upon the Texas Clean Air Act as an additional ground of Commission authority to act in this case "to protect against adverse effects, including global warming."

The decisions in the public trust cases to date highlight both the diversity of approaches to the public trust doctrine from state to state and the continuing ability of the doctrine to create new grounds for natural resource protection in the courts. As I noted in my post last year, it is unlikely these lawsuits will result in any quick decisions by courts to order their state agencies to set limits on greenhouse gas emissions. It is also unlikely that a majority of states will expressly recognize an atmospheric trust under state common law—the doctrine is simply not well-developed enough in most states to make such a jump. Nevertheless, the variety of approaches to this doctrine among the states in our federalist system means that some state courts may be able to shape the public trust doctrine based on their own state common law, statutes, and constitution to recognize the modern threat to natural resources caused by climate change. The decisions so far are a classic example of federalism at work as well as evidence of the continuing power and potential of the public trust doctrine to protect the natural resources when regulation fails to meet present-day environmental protection needs.

Juliana v. United States
2016 WL 6661146

Judge AIKEN:

Plaintiffs in this civil rights action are a group of young people between the ages of eight and nineteen ("youth plaintiffs"); Earth Guardians, an association of young environmental activists; and Dr. James Hansen, acting as guardian for future generations. Plaintiffs filed this action against defendants the United States, President Barack Obama, and numerous executive agencies. Plaintiffs allege defendants have known for more than fifty years that the carbon dioxide ("CO_2") produced by burning fossil fuels was destabilizing the climate system in a way that would "significantly endanger plaintiffs, with the damage persisting for millenia." Despite that knowledge, plaintiffs assert defendants, "[b]y their exercise of sovereign authority over our country's atmosphere and fossil fuel resources, . . . permitted, encouraged, and otherwise enabled continued exploitation, production, and combustion of fossil fuels, . . . deliberately allow[ing] atmospheric CO_2 concentrations to escalate to levels unprecedented in human history[.]" Although many different entities contribute to greenhouse gas emissions, plaintiffs aver defendants bear "a higher degree of responsibility than any other individual, entity, or country" for exposing plaintiffs to the dangers of climate change. Plaintiffs argue defendants' actions violate their substantive due process rights to life, liberty, and property, and that defendants have violated their obligation to hold certain natural resources in trust for the people and for future generations.

Plaintiffs assert there is a very short window in which defendants could act to phase out fossil fuel exploitation and avert environmental catastrophe. They seek (1) a declaration their constitutional and public trust rights have been violated and (2) an order

Plaintiff argument

enjoining defendants from violating those rights and directing defendants to develop a plan to reduce CO_2 emissions.

Defendants moved to dismiss this action for lack of subject matter jurisdiction and failure to state a claim. Intervenors the National Association of Manufacturers, the American Fuel & Petrochemical Manufacturers, and the American Petroleum Institute moved to dismiss on the same grounds. . . .

US argument

For the reasons set forth below, I [adopt a prior magistrate ruling and] deny the motions to dismiss.

Decision

BACKGROUND

This is no ordinary lawsuit. Plaintiffs challenge the policies, acts, and omissions of the President of the United States, the Council on Environmental Quality, the Office of Management and Budget, the Office of Science and Technology Policy, the Department of Energy, the Department of the Interior, the Department of Transportation ("DOT"), the Department of Agriculture, the Department of Commerce, the Department of Defense, the Department of State, and the Environmental Protection Agency ("EPA"). This lawsuit challenges decisions defendants have made across a vast set of topics—decisions like whether and to what extent to regulate CO_2 emissions from power plants and vehicles, whether to permit fossil fuel extraction and development to take place on federal lands, how much to charge for use of those lands, whether to give tax breaks to the fossil fuel industry, whether to subsidize or directly fund that industry, whether to fund the construction of fossil fuel infrastructure such as natural gas pipelines at home and abroad, whether to permit the export and import of fossil fuels from and to the United States, and whether to authorize new marine coal terminal projects. Plaintiffs assert defendants' decisions on these topics have substantially caused the planet to warm and the oceans to rise. They draw a direct causal line between defendants' policy choices and floods, food shortages, destruction of property, species extinction, and a host of other harms.

issues

This lawsuit is not about proving that climate change is happening or that human activity is driving it. For the purposes of this motion, those facts are undisputed. The questions before the Court are whether defendants are responsible for some of the harm caused by climate change, whether plaintiffs may challenge defendants' climate change policy in court, and whether this Court can direct defendants to change their policy without running afoul of the separation of powers doctrine.

issues

DISCUSSION

. . . Defendants and intervenors . . . contend plaintiffs' claims must be dismissed for lack of jurisdiction because the case presents non-justiciable political questions, plaintiffs lack standing to sue, and federal public trust claims cannot be asserted against the federal government. They further argue plaintiffs have failed to state a claim on which relief can be granted. I first address the threshold challenges to jurisdiction, and then proceed to address the viability of plaintiffs' due process and public trust claims.

defendant's arguments

I. *Political Question*

D. *Summary: This Case Does Not Raise a Nonjusticiable Political Question*

There is no need to step outside the core role of the judiciary to decide this case. At its heart, this lawsuit asks this Court to determine whether defendants have violated plaintiffs' constitutional rights. That question is squarely within the purview of the judiciary.

Should plaintiffs prevail on the merits, this Court would no doubt be compelled to exercise great care to avoid separation-of-powers problems in crafting a remedy. The separation of powers might, for example, permit the Court to direct defendants to ameliorate plaintiffs' injuries but limit its ability to specify precisely how to do so. . . . In any event, speculation about the difficulty of crafting a remedy could not support dismissal at this early stage. . . .

II. *Standing to Sue*

. . . To demonstrate standing, a plaintiff must show (1) she suffered an injury in fact that is concrete, particularized, and actual or imminent; (2) the injury is fairly traceable to the defendant's challenged conduct; and (3) the injury is likely to be redressed by a favorable court decision. . . .

A. *Injury in Fact*

In an environmental case, a plaintiff cannot demonstrate injury in fact merely by alleging injury to the environment; there must be an allegation that the challenged conduct is harming (or imminently will harm) the plaintiff. . . .

Plaintiffs adequately allege injury in fact. Lead plaintiff Kelsey Juliana alleges algae blooms harm the water she drinks, and low water levels caused by drought kill the wild salmon she eats. Plaintiff Xiuhtezcatl Roske-Martinez alleges increased wildfires and extreme flooding jeopardize his personal safety. Plaintiff Alexander Loznak alleges record-setting temperatures harm the health of the hazelnut orchard on his family farm, an important source of both revenue and food for him and his family. Plaintiff Jacob Lebel alleges drought conditions required his family to install an irrigation system at their farm. Plaintiff Zealand B. alleges he has been unable to ski during the winter as a result of decreased snowpack. Plaintiff Sahara V. alleges hot, dry conditions caused by forest fires aggravate her asthma.

The most recent allegations of injury appear in the supplemental declaration of plaintiff Jayden F., a thirteen-year-old resident of Rayne, Louisiana. Jayden alleges that at five o'clock the morning of August 13, 2016, her siblings woke her up. She stepped out of bed into ankle-deep water. By the end of the day,

> Flood waters were pouring into our home through every possible opening. We tried to stop it with towels, blankets, and boards. The water was flowing down the hallway, into my Mom's room and my sisters' room. The water drenched my living room and began to cover our kitchen floor. Our toilets, sinks, and bathtubs began to overflow with awful smelling sewage because

our town's sewer system also flooded. Soon the sewage was everywhere. We had a stream of sewage and water running through our house.

With no shelters available and nowhere else to go, the family remained in the flooded house for weeks. The floodwaters eventually receded, but the damage remains: the carpets are soaked with sewage water. The water-logged walls must be torn down to prevent the growth of black mold. The entire family sleeps together in the living room because the bedrooms are uninhabitable. Jayden alleges the storm that destroyed her home "ordinarily would happen once every 1,000 years, but is happening now as a result of climate change."

The government contends these injuries are not particular to plaintiffs because they are caused by climate change, which broadly affects the entire planet (and all people on it) in some way. According to the government, this renders plaintiffs' injuries non-justiciable generalized grievances.

The government misunderstands the generalized grievance rule. . . . Applying the correct formulation of the generalized grievance rule, plaintiffs' alleged injuries — harm to their personal, economic and aesthetic interests — are concrete and particularized, not abstract or indefinite.

B. *Causation*

The government contends plaintiffs have not adequately alleged causation, relying on the Ninth Circuit's decision in [*Washington Environmental Council v.*] *Bellon* [732 F.3d 1131 (2013)]. In that case, environmental advocacy groups sought to compel the Washington State Department of Ecology and other regional agencies "to regulate greenhouse gas emissions" ("GHGs") from five oil refineries. The court held plaintiffs lacked standing to sue because the causal link between the agencies' regulatory decisions and the plaintiffs' injuries was "too attenuated." The court explained the special challenge of showing causation with respect to the production of greenhouse gases:

> Greenhouse gases, once emitted from a specific source, quickly mix and disperse in the global atmosphere and have a long atmospheric lifetime. Current research on how greenhouse gases influence global climate change has focused on the cumulative environmental effects from aggregate regional or global sources. But there is limited scientific capability in assessing, detecting, or measuring the relationship between a certain GHG emission source and localized climate impacts in a given region.

The court noted that the five oil refineries at issue were responsible for just under six percent of total greenhouse gas emissions produced in the state of Washington, and quoted the state's expert's declaration that the effect of those emissions on global climate change was "scientifically indiscernible, given the emission levels, the dispersal of GHGs world-wide, and the absence of any meaningful nexus between Washington refinery emissions and global GHG concentrations now or as projected in the future." The court concluded the "causal chain [wa]s too tenuous to support standing."

. . . Here, by contrast, plaintiffs' chain of causation rests on the core allegation that defendants are responsible for a substantial share of worldwide greenhouse gas emissions. Plaintiffs allege that over the 263 years between 1751 and 2014, the United States produced more than twenty-five percent of global CO_2 emissions. Greenhouse gas emissions produced in the United States continue to increase. . . .

The causal chain alleged by plaintiffs here is conclusory, but that is because they have not yet had the opportunity to present evidence. And unlike in *Bellon*, plaintiffs' causation allegations are not vague. At oral argument, plaintiffs explained that their theory of causation has two components. The first relates to defendants' affirmative acts. Specifically, plaintiffs allege that fossil fuel combustion accounts for approximately ninety-four percent of United States CO_2 emissions. Defendants lease public lands for oil, gas, and coal production; undercharge royalties in connection with those leases; provide tax breaks to companies to encourage fossil fuel development; permit the import and export of fossil fuels; and incentivize the purchase of sport utility vehicles. Here, the chain of causation is: fossil fuel combustion accounts for the lion's share of greenhouse gas emissions produced in the United States; defendants have the power to increase or decrease those emissions; and defendants use that power to engage in a variety of activities that actively cause and promote higher levels of fossil fuel combustion.

The second component of plaintiffs' causation theory involves defendants' failure to act in areas where they have authority to do so. Plaintiffs allege that together, power plants and transportation produce nearly two-thirds of CO_2 emissions in the United States. Plaintiffs also allege DOT and EPA have broad power to set emissions standards in these sectors. So the chain of causation is: DOT and EPA have jurisdiction over sectors producing sixty-four percent of United States emissions, which in turn constitute roughly fourteen percent of emissions worldwide; they allow high emissions levels by failing to set demanding standards; high emissions levels cause climate change; and climate change causes plaintiffs' injuries.

C. *Redressability* — Does the gov't have the ability to fix/improve injury to plaintiffs

The final prong of the standing inquiry is redressability. . . .

The declaratory and injunctive relief plaintiffs request meets this standard. Most notably, plaintiffs ask this Court to "[o]rder Defendants to prepare and implement an enforceable national remedial plan to phase out fossil fuel emissions and draw down excess atmospheric CO_2[.]" If plaintiffs can show, as they have alleged, that defendants have control over a quarter of the planet's greenhouse gas emissions, and that a reduction in those emissions would reduce atmospheric CO_2 and slow climate change, then plaintiffs' requested relief would redress their injuries.

III. *Due Process Claims*

The Due Process Clause of the Fifth Amendment to the United States Constitution bars the federal government from depriving a person of "life, liberty, or property" without "due process of law." Plaintiffs allege defendants have violated their due process rights by "directly caus[ing] atmospheric CO_2 to rise to levels that dangerously interfere with a stable climate system required alike by our nation and Plaintiffs[,]"..."knowingly endanger[ing] Plaintiffs' health and welfare by approving and promoting fossil fuel development, including exploration, extraction, production, transportation, importation, exportation, and combustion," and, "[a]fter knowingly creating this dangerous situation for Plaintiffs, ... continu[ing] to knowingly enhance that danger by allowing fossil fuel production, consumption, and combustion at dangerous levels."

Defendants and intervenors challenge plaintiffs' due process claims on two grounds. First, they assert any challenge to defendants' affirmative actions (*i.e.* leasing land, issuing permits) cannot proceed because plaintiffs have failed to identify infringement of a fundamental right or discrimination against a suspect class of persons. Second, they argue plaintiffs cannot challenge defendants' inaction (*i.e.*, failure to prevent third parties from emitting CO_2 at dangerous levels) because defendants have no affirmative duty to protect plaintiffs from climate change.

A. *Infringement of a Fundamental Right*

When a plaintiff challenges affirmative government action under the due process clause, the threshold inquiry is the applicable level of judicial scrutiny. The default level of scrutiny is rational basis, which requires a reviewing court to uphold the challenged governmental action so long as it "implements a rational means of achieving a legitimate governmental end [.]" When the government infringes a "fundamental right," however, a reviewing court applies strict scrutiny. Substantive due process "forbids the government to infringe certain 'fundamental' liberty interests *at all*, no matter what process is provided, unless the infringement is narrowly tailored to serve a compelling state interest." It appears undisputed by plaintiffs, and in any event is clear to this Court, that defendants' affirmative actions would survive rational basis review. Resolution of this part of the motions to dismiss therefore hinges on whether plaintiffs have alleged infringement of a fundamental right.

Fundamental liberty rights include both rights enumerated elsewhere in the Constitution and rights and liberties which are either (1) "deeply rooted in this Nation's history and tradition" or (2) "fundamental to our scheme of ordered liberty[.]" ...

This does not mean that "new" fundamental rights are out of bounds, though. When the Supreme Court broke new legal ground by recognizing a constitutional right to same-sex marriage, Justice Kennedy wrote that

> The nature of injustice is that we may not always see it in our own times. The generations that wrote and ratified the Bill of Rights ... did not presume to know the extent of freedom in all its dimensions, and so they entrusted to future generations a charter protecting the right of all persons to enjoy liberty as we learn its meaning. When new insight reveals discord between the Constitution's central protections and a received legal stricture, a claim to liberty must be addressed.

Obergefell v. Hodges, 135 S.Ct. 2584, 2598 (2015). Thus, "[t]he identification and protection of fundamental rights is an enduring part of the judicial duty to interpret the Constitution ... [that] has not been reduced to any formula." In determining whether a right is fundamental, courts must exercise "reasoned judgment," keeping in mind that "[h]istory and tradition guide and discipline this inquiry but do not set its outer boundaries." The genius of the Constitution is that its text allows "future generations [to] protect ... the right of all persons to enjoy liberty as we learn its meaning."

Exercising my "reasoned judgment," I have no doubt that the right to a climate system capable of sustaining human life is fundamental to a free and ordered society. Just as marriage is the "foundation of the family," a stable climate system is quite literally the foundation "of society, without which there would be neither civilization nor progress."

Defendants and intervenors contend plaintiffs are asserting a right to be free from pollution or climate change, and that courts have consistently rejected attempts to define such rights as fundamental. Defendants and intervenors mischaracterize the right plaintiffs assert. Plaintiffs do not object to the government's role in producing *any* pollution or in causing *any* climate change; rather, they assert the government has caused pollution and climate change on a catastrophic level, and that if the government's actions continue unchecked, they will permanently and irreversibly damage plaintiffs' property, their economic livelihood, their recreational opportunities, their health, and ultimately their (and their children's) ability to live long, healthy lives. Echoing *Obergefell*'s reasoning, plaintiffs allege a stable climate system is a necessary condition to exercising other rights to life, liberty, and property.

In framing the fundamental right at issue as the right to a climate system capable of sustaining human life, I intend to strike a balance and to provide some protection against the constitutionalization of all environmental claims. On the one hand, the phrase "capable of sustaining human life" should not be read to require a plaintiff to allege that governmental action will result in the extinction of humans as a species. On the other hand, acknowledgment of this fundamental right does not transform any minor or even moderate act that contributes to the warming of the planet into a constitutional violation. In this opinion, this Court simply holds that where a complaint alleges governmental action is affirmatively and substantially damaging the climate system in a way that will cause human deaths, shorten human lifespans, result in widespread damage to property, threaten human food sources, and dramatically alter the planet's ecosystem, it states a claim for a due process violation. To hold otherwise would be to say that the Constitution affords no protection against a government's knowing decision to poison the air its citizens breathe or the water its citizens drink. Plaintiffs have adequately alleged infringement of a fundamental right.

B. *"Danger Creation" Challenge to Inaction*

With limited exceptions, the Due Process Clause does not impose on the government an affirmative obligation to act, even when "such aid may be necessary to secure life, liberty, or property interests of which the government itself may not deprive the individual." This rule is subject to two exceptions: "(1) the 'special relationship' exception; and (2) the 'danger creation' exception." The "special relationship" exception provides that when the government takes an individual into custody against his or her will, it assumes some responsibility to ensure that individual's safety. The "danger creation" exception permits a substantive due process claim when government conduct "places a person in peril in deliberate indifference to their safety[.]" Plaintiffs purport to challenge the government's failure to limit third-party CO_2 emissions pursuant to the danger creation exception.

In the Ninth Circuit, a plaintiff challenging government inaction on a danger creation theory must first show the "state actor create[d] or expose[d] an individual to a danger which he or she would not have otherwise faced." The state action must place the plaintiff "in a worse position than that in which he would have been had the state not acted at all." Second, the plaintiff must show the "state actor . . . recognize[d]" the unreasonable risks to the plaintiff and "actually intend[ed] to expose the plaintiff to such risks without regard to the consequences to the plaintiff." The defendant must have acted with "[d]eliberate indifference," which "requires a culpable mental state more than gross negligence."

Plaintiffs allege that "[a]cting with full appreciation of the consequences of their acts, Defendants knowingly caused, and continue to cause, dangerous interference with our atmosphere and climate system." They allege this danger stems, "in substantial part, [from] Defendants' historic and continuing permitting, authorizing, and subsidizing of fossil fuel extraction, production, transportation, and utilization." Plaintiffs allege defendants acted "with full appreciation" of the consequences of their acts, specifically "[harm to] Plaintiffs' dignity, including their capacity to provide for their basic human needs, safely raise families, practice their religious and spiritual beliefs, maintain their bodily integrity, and lead lives with access to clean air, water, shelter, and food." In the face of these risks, plaintiffs allege defendants "have had longstanding, actual knowledge of the serious risks of harm and have failed to take necessary steps to address and ameliorate the known, serious risk to which they have exposed Plaintiffs." In sum: plaintiffs allege defendants played a unique and central role in the creation of our current climate crisis; that they contributed to the crisis with full knowledge of the significant and unreasonable risks posed by climate change; and that the Due Process Clause therefore imposes a special duty on defendants to use their statutory and regulatory authority to reduce greenhouse gas emissions. Accepting the allegations of the complaint as true, plaintiffs have adequately alleged a danger creation claim.

[D]efendants contend application of the danger creation exception in this context would permit plaintiffs to "raise a substantive due process claim to challenge virtually any government program"—for example, to challenge foreign policy decisions that heighten or exacerbate international tensions, or to health and safety regulations the plaintiff deems insufficiently stringent. Defendants fail to recognize [the] rigorous proof requirements. A plaintiff asserting a danger-creation due process claim must show (1) the government's acts created the danger to the plaintiff; (2) the government *knew* its acts caused that danger; and (3) the government with *deliberate indifference* failed to act to prevent the alleged harm. These stringent standards are sufficient safeguards against the flood of litigation concerns raised by defendants—indeed, they pose a significant challenge for plaintiffs in this very lawsuit.

Questions about difficulty of proof, however, must be left for another day. At the motion to dismiss stage, I am bound to accept the factual allegations in the complaint as true. Plaintiffs have alleged that defendants played a significant role in creating the current climate crisis, that defendants acted with full knowledge of the consequences of their actions, and that defendants have failed to correct or mitigate the harms they helped create in deliberate indifference to the injuries caused by climate change. They may therefore proceed with their substantive due process challenge to defendants' failure to adequately regulate CO_2 emissions.

IV. *Public Trust Claims*

In its broadest sense, the term "public trust" refers to the fundamental understanding that no government can legitimately abdicate its core sovereign powers. The public trust doctrine rests on the fundamental principle that "[e]very succeeding legislature possesses the same jurisdiction and power with respect to [the public interest] as its predecessors." The doctrine conceives of certain powers and obligations—for example, the police power—as inherent aspects of sovereignty. Permitting the government to permanently give one of these powers to another entity runs afoul of the public trust doctrine because it diminishes the power of future legislatures to promote the general welfare.

Plaintiffs' public trust claims arise from the particular application of the public trust doctrine to essential natural resources. With respect to these core resources, the sovereign's public trust obligations prevent it from "depriving a future legislature of the natural resources necessary to provide for the well-being and survival of its citizens." Application of the public trust doctrine to natural resources predates the United States of America. Its roots are in the Institutes of Justinian, part of the Corpus Juris Civilis, the body of Roman law that is the "foundation for modern civil law systems." Timothy G. Kearley, *Justice Fred Blume and the Translation of Justinian's Code*, 99 Law Libr. J. 525, ¶ 1 (2007). The Institutes of Justinian declared "the following things are by natural law common to all—the air, running water, the sea, and consequently the seashore." J. Inst. 2.1.1 (J.B. Moyle trans.). The doctrine made its way to the United States through the English common law.

The first court in this country to address the applicability of the public trust doctrine to natural resources was the New Jersey Supreme Court, in 1821. The court explained that public trust assets were part of a taxonomy of property:

> Every thing susceptible of property is considered as belonging to the nation that possesses the country, as forming the entire mass of its wealth. But the nation does not possess all those things in the same manner. By very far the greater part of them are divided among the individuals of the nation, and become *private property*. Those things not divided among the individuals still belong to the nation, and are called *public property*. Of these, again, some are reserved for the necessities of the state, and are used for the public benefit,

and those are called "*the domain of the crown or of the republic*," others remain common to all the citizens, who take of them and use them, each according to his necessities, and according to the laws which regulate their use, and are called *common property*. Of this latter kind, according to the writers upon the law of nature and of nations, and upon the civil law, are the air, the running water, the sea, the fish, and the wild beasts.

Arnold v. Mundy, 6 N.J.L. 1, 71 (N.J. 1821) (emphasis in original).

The seminal United States Supreme Court case on the public trust is *Illinois Central Railroad Company v. Illinois*, 146 U.S. 387, 13 S.Ct. 110, 36 L.Ed. 1018 (1892). The Illinois legislature had conveyed to the Illinois Central Railroad Company title to part of the submerged lands beneath the harbor of Chicago, with the intent to give the company control over the waters above the submerged lands "against any future exercise of power over them by the state." The Supreme Court held the legislature's attempt to give up its title to lands submerged beneath navigable waters was either void on its face or always subject to revocation. "The state can no more abdicate its trust over property in which the whole people are interested, like navigable waters and soils under them . . . than it can abdicate its police powers in the administration of government and the preservation of the peace." In light of the "immense value" the harbor of Chicago carried for the people of Illinois, the "idea that its legislature can deprive the state of control over its bed and waters, and place the same in the hands of a private corporation" could not "be defended."

The natural resources trust operates according to basic trust principles, which impose upon the trustee a fiduciary duty to "protect the trust property against damage or destruction." The trustee owes this duty equally to both current and future beneficiaries of the trust. In natural resources cases, the trust property consists of a set of resources important enough to the people to warrant public trust protection. The government, as trustee, has a fiduciary duty to protect the trust assets from damage so that current and future trust beneficiaries will be able to enjoy the benefits of the trust. The public trust doctrine is generally thought to impose three types of restrictions on governmental authority:

> [F]irst, the property subject to the trust must not only be used for a public purpose, but it must be held available for use by the general public; second, the property may not be sold, even for a fair cash equivalent; and third, the property must be maintained for particular types of uses.

Joseph L. Sax, *The Public Trust Doctrine in Natural Resource Law: Effective Judicial Intervention*, 68 Mich. L. Rev. 471, 477 (1970).

This lawsuit is part of a wave of recent environmental cases asserting state and national governments have abdicated their responsibilities under the public trust doctrine. These lawsuits depart from the "traditional" public trust litigation model, which generally centers on the second restriction, the prohibition against alienation of a public trust asset. Instead, plaintiffs assert defendants have violated their duties as trustees by nominally retaining control over trust assets while actually allowing their depletion and destruction, effectively violating the first and third restrictions by excluding the public from use and enjoyment of public resources.

Defendants and intervenors argue the public trust doctrine has no application in this case. They advance four arguments: (1) the atmosphere, the central natural resource at issue in this lawsuit, is not a public trust asset; (2) the federal government, unlike the states, has no public trust obligations; (3) any common-law public trust claims have been displaced by federal statutes; and (4) even if there is a federal public trust, plaintiffs lack a right of action to enforce it. I address each contention in turn.

A. *Scope of Public Trust Assets*

The complaint alleges defendants violated their duties as trustees by failing to protect the atmosphere, water, seas, seashores, and wildlife. Defendants and intervenors argue plaintiffs' public trust claims fail because the complaint focuses on harm to the atmosphere, which is not a public trust asset. I conclude that it is not necessary at this stage to determine whether the atmosphere is a public trust asset because plaintiffs have alleged violations of the public trust doctrine in connection with the territorial sea.

The federal government holds title to the submerged lands between three and twelve miles from the coastlines of the United States. Time and again, the Supreme Court has held that the public trust doctrine applies to "lands beneath tidal waters." Because a number of plaintiffs' injuries relate to the effects of ocean acidification and rising ocean temperatures, they have adequately alleged harm to public trust assets.

[In subsection B, the court discussed a variety of arguments on both sides of the question whether the public trust duty applies to the federal government, concluding that it does.]

D. *Enforceability of Public Trust Obligations in Federal Court*

As a final challenge to plaintiffs' public trust claims, defendants contend that even if the public trust doctrine applies to the federal government, plaintiffs lack a cause of action to enforce the public trust obligations. Relatedly, defendants argue that creation of a right of action to permit plaintiffs to assert their claims in federal court would be an exercise in federal common law-making subject to the same statutory displacement arguments outlined above.

In order to evaluate the merits of these arguments, I must first locate the source of plaintiffs' public trust claims. I conclude plaintiffs' public trust rights both predated the Constitution and are secured by it.

The public trust doctrine defines inherent aspects of sovereignty. The Social Contract theory, which heavily influenced Thomas Jefferson and other Founding Fathers, provides that people possess certain inalienable lights and that governments were established by consent of the governed for the purpose of securing those rights. Accordingly, the Declaration of Independence and the Constitution did not *create* the rights to life, liberty, or the pursuit of happiness—the documents are, instead, vehicles for protecting and promoting those already-existing rights. Governments, in turn, possess certain powers that permit them to safeguard the rights of the people; these powers are inherent in the authority to govern and cannot be sold or bargained away. One example is the police power. Another is the status as trustee pursuant to the public trust doctrine.

Although the public trust predates the Constitution, plaintiffs' right of action to enforce the government's obligations as trustee arises from the Constitution. [P]laintiffs' public trust claims are properly categorized as substantive due process claims. As explained, the Due Process Clause's substantive component safeguards fundamental rights that are "implicit in the concept of ordered liberty" or "deeply rooted in this Nation's history and tradition." Plaintiffs' public trust rights, related as they are to inherent aspects of sovereignty and the consent of the governed from which the United States' authority derives, satisfy both tests. Because the public trust is not enumerated in the Constitution, substantive due process protection also derives from the Ninth Amendment. *See* U.S. Const. amend. IX ("The enumeration in the Constitution, of certain rights, shall not be construed to deny or disparage others retained by the people."). But it is the Fifth Amendment that provides the right of action.

Plaintiffs' claims rest "directly on the Due Process Clause of the Fifth Amendment." They may, therefore, be asserted in federal court.

CONCLUSION

Throughout their objections, defendants and intervenors attempt to subject a lawsuit alleging constitutional injuries to case law governing statutory and common-law environmental claims. They are correct that plaintiffs likely could not obtain the relief they seek through citizen suits brought under the Clean Air Act, the Clean Water Act, or other environmental laws. But that argument misses the point. This action is of a different order than the typical environmental case. It alleges that defendants' actions and inactions—whether or not they violate any specific statutory duty—have so profoundly damaged our home planet that they threaten plaintiffs' fundamental constitutional rights to life and liberty.

A deep resistance to change runs through defendants' and intervenors' arguments for dismissal: they contend a decision recognizing plaintiffs' standing to sue, deeming the controversy justiciable, and recognizing a federal public trust and a fundamental right to climate system capable of sustaining human life would be unprecedented, as though that alone requires its dismissal. This lawsuit may be groundbreaking, but that fact does not alter the legal standards governing the motions to dismiss. Indeed, the seriousness of plaintiffs' allegations underscores how vitally important it is for this Court to apply those standards carefully and correctly.

Federal courts too often have been cautious and overly deferential in the arena of environmental law, and the world has suffered for it. As Judge Goodwin recently wrote,

> The current state of affairs ... reveals a wholesale failure of the legal system to protect humanity from the collapse of finite natural resources by the uncontrolled pursuit of short-term profits.... [T]he modern judiciary has

enfeebled itself to the point that law enforcement can rarely be accomplished by taking environmental predators to court. . . .

The third branch can, and should, take another long and careful look at the barriers to litigation created by modern doctrines of subject-matter jurisdiction and deference to the legislative and administrative branches of government.

Alfred T. Goodwin, *A Wake-Up Call for Judges*, 2015 Wis. L. Rev. 785, 785 — 86, 788 (2015).

Judge Goodwin is no stranger to highly politicized legal disputes. Nearly fifty years ago, he authored the landmark opinion that secured Oregon's ocean beaches for public use. Private landowners wanted to construct fences and otherwise keep private the beaches in front of their properties; they brought suit to challenge an Oregon state law requiring public access to all dry sand beaches. Writing for five of the six members of the Oregon Supreme Court, then-Justice Goodwin rooted his determination the beaches were public property in a concept from English common law:

> Because so much of our law is the product of legislation, we sometimes lose sight of the importance of custom as a source of law in our society. It seems particularly appropriate in the case at bar to look to an ancient and accepted custom in this state as the source of a rule of law. The rule in this case, based upon custom, is salutary in confirming a public right, and at the same time it takes from no man anything which he has a legitimate reason to regard as exclusively his.

State ex rel. Thornton v. Hay, 254 Or. 584, 462 P.2d 671, 678 (1969).

In an argument with strong echoes in defendants' and intervenors' objections here, the plaintiff private property owner contended it was "constitutionally impermissible . . . to dredge up an inapplicable, ancient English doctrine that has been universally rejected in modern America." Kathryn A. Straten, *Oregon's Beaches: A Birthright Preserved* 65 (Or. State Parks & Recreation 1977). The Oregon Supreme Court was not persuaded by this call to judicial conservatism. Because of the application of an ancient doctrine, Oregon's beaches remain open to the public now and forever.

"A strong and independent judiciary is the cornerstone of our liberties." These words, spoken by Oregon Senator Mark O. Hatfield, are etched into the walls of the Portland United States courthouse for the District of Oregon. The words appear on the first floor, a daily reminder that it is "emphatically the province and duty of the judicial department to say what the law is." *Marbury*, 5 U.S. at 177. Even when a case implicates hotly contested political issues, the judiciary must not shrink from its role as a coequal branch of government.

DECISION :

Defendants' Motion to Dismiss and Intervenors' Motion to Dismiss are DENIED.

IT IS SO ORDERED.

IV. Existing Challenges Aggravated by Climate Change

Climate change is so pervasive and global that it overlaps with many, perhaps most, of the other issues we seek to address on an international scale. Below are just a few examples of such interrelated problems.

A. Human Rights

Michelle Leighton, *Climate Change and Migration: Key Issues for Legal Protection of Migrants and Displaced Persons*
German Marshall Fund of the United States (June 2010)

There are a number of scenarios in which people could be displaced or forced to migrate due to climate change and extreme weather events. Hurricanes and floods, generally rapid-onset events, may lead to temporary human displacement. Drought and desertification, slower-onset events, may not immediately threaten human life but can become serious environmental and human disasters over longer periods of time. Droughts already affect millions of people worldwide, threatening food security, sustainable development and human livelihoods. The competition over scarce water supplies, land and jobs that can result from prolonged drought could lead to social upheaval and an increased incidence of violence and ethnic tension, a situation that is already contributing to conflict in East Africa.

The movement of people in response to these climate-induced events implicates human rights and humanitarian law. Moreover, the potential impact from the implementation of disaster response strategies or climate adaptation programs may also raise human rights concerns, particularly if governments resettle large numbers of people. Notwithstanding that some standards exist for internally displaced persons, there are uncertainties in the law and gaps in the legal protection of climate-affected populations, including the extent to which persons migrating away from flood or drought disaster areas can legally cross international borders in search of jobs or to otherwise engage in labor migration as a means of survival. The lack of clear standards in this area leaves many climate victims unprotected and vulnerable to abuse. As future climate disasters multiply, so too will the number of migrants or displaced who are unprotected.

This paper provides a brief overview of the human rights and humanitarian norms related to migrant protection, recognizing that a much more comprehensive, in-depth analysis may be warranted as policymakers engage in further dialogue. The paper begins by providing a brief analysis of the general human rights principles relevant to people displaced or who migrate internally and across borders in response to disaster, and the relevant government obligations of assistance. It then highlights the areas in which the law is less clear in its application to climate change migrants or where standards are absent in existing law. The paper identifies the groups that are consequently unprotected and, in the final part, discusses the policy considerations being advanced by humanitarian agencies and others to provide greater protection for displacees and migrants.

International legal standards relevant to victims of climate disasters

Climate-induced displacement and migration implicate a number of human rights and humanitarian standards. The extent of the rights of victims and the corresponding obligations of states is dynamic and evolves as the international community gains more understanding and experience in addressing the needs of disaster victims. At present, the extent of government obligation and level of protection afforded victims depends on the context of the disaster and on whether victims are displaced temporarily, forced to migrate, or voluntarily move away from the disaster zone. It should be noted at the outset that widespread understanding of the impact of climate change is relatively recent and legal standards have not yet caught up with scientific predictions, leaving conclusions regarding the application of human rights law somewhat speculative.

In general, human rights norms are more protective of those who are displaced or who migrate within their country of origin than for those who migrate internationally. This is because governments have adopted certain baseline standards to protect the internally displaced, which govern the state's treatment of such persons in the course of natural disasters or armed conflict. However, governments have not adopted a similar set of standards for persons who migrate internationally in response to climate disasters, such as severe droughts. The rights of these persons and government obligations in this area have yet to be clarified.

This section first identifies the general government obligations with respect to disaster relief and cooperation. It then considers the situations of victims forced to migrate internationally and who are less protected, followed by a discussion of those displaced internally by disaster who would be entitled to greater protection by their country of origin. Both rapid-onset and slow-onset disasters are discussed within the context of international migration and internal displacement.

General obligations of states

International law is fundamentally concerned with the obligations that states owe to each other. The subset of human rights doctrine, however, comprises additional duties owed by states to individuals and groups. It also prescribes special responsibility for the protection of vulnerable populations and minorities, including women, children and indigenous groups.

Human rights law, as a general matter, obligates states to safeguard the life and property of those within a state's territory against threats of disaster and foreseeable harm. It requires states to mitigate the negative impacts of disaster when these occur, including through legal and administrative mechanisms, evacuation and possible temporary or permanent relocation of affected persons consonant with the right of freedom of movement. It further obligates governments to be particularly sensitive to the needs of vulnerable groups, such as women, children, minorities and indigenous peoples. These groups may be especially vulnerable to climate shocks if they are already suffering from poverty, discrimination or other adverse socio-economic and political impacts.

The legal framework governing international aid and assistance in times of disaster victims has emerged from a myriad set of multilateral instruments and has been distilled, in part, within the 2005 Hyogo Framework for Action. Under this Framework, governments recognize that developing countries are more vulnerable to disasters and need to undertake preventative measures to reduce vulnerability programs within disaster risk reduction programs, early warning systems, and public safety awareness and preparedness.

Specifically, governments are to adopt legal measures at the local and national levels to coordinate disaster response, and must ensure that programs for displaced persons do not increase risk and vulnerability to hazards. Though the government in whose territory disaster occurs has the primary obligation to protect its citizens, international agencies and the international community of nations share obligations of humanitarian assistance.

Though not express, the duty to cooperate among nations on disaster reduction and response could presumably include an obligation of receiving states to provide some level of assistance to victims of disasters that move into or remain in the state's territory after a disaster, at least on a temporary basis. The Framework emphasizes more strategic coordination among states. Its principles have been supported by the 2006 Operational Guidelines on Human Rights and Natural Disasters, adopted by the Inter-Agency Standing Committee of humanitarian agencies established by the United Nations to help countries coordinate disaster reduction and relief, and the International Committee of the Red Cross (ICRC) Guidelines for the Domestic Facilitation and Regulation of International Disaster Relief and Initial Recovery Assistance.

International human rights law reinforces the humanitarian obligation of states to cooperate and assist governments less able to fulfill and protect the human rights of those displaced by a disaster. For example, the treaty body established to monitor the implementation of the International Covenant on Economic, Social and Cultural Rights has stated that "States parties have a joint and individual responsibility, in accordance with the Charter of the United Nations and relevant resolutions of the United Nations General Assembly and of the World Health Assembly, to cooperate in providing disaster relief and humanitarian assistance in times of emergency, including assistance to refugees and internally displaced persons."

While international law relating to refugees is generally inapplicable to climate change, certain refugee related principles and humanitarian norms convey government obligations that are relevant. Moreover, some governments have adopted voluntary discretionary mechanisms that could apply temporarily to protect international migrants displaced by extreme weather events or by conflict related to such events. However, as will be discussed, longer-term legal protection is quite limited for international migrants.

Rights and obligations related to international migrants

As a general rule, people who move voluntarily or who are forced to move across an international border are entitled to all of their fundamental human rights guarantees that protect human dignity. These include civil, political, economic, social and cultural rights such as the right of freedom of movement; to choose their place of residence; to engage in religion or cultural practice; the right to life, privacy and to health; the right to seek employment; and the right not to be discriminated. With few exceptions, however, this does not include a right to enter another country, to work or remain there, or to receive the same legal protection as a refugee under international law.

This poses a serious concern for disaster victims who face little alternative to survival than to cross into another country because international migration may afford them greater human security. Many victims of slow-onset drought disasters view themselves in this light. A prolonged drought event may not appear as urgent as a tsunami or flood which attracts immediate international attention, but the need for protection, for a new survival strategy, for jobs outside the drought-affected area, e.g., via labor migration, may be just as compelling a humanitarian issue.

Humanitarian agencies are increasingly occupied with drought concerns in the Horn of Africa where, for example, a severe drought is entering its fifth year in the region. Millions of people are suffering food insecurity, water scarcity and loss of employment. This has led to increased migration throughout the region. The International Organization for Migration (IOM) recently reported that the border of Liboi into Kenya has become a major border crossing for drought-affected Somalis who are undocumented but searching for better livelihood or work in Kenya. The Norwegian Refugee Council also reported similar international border crossings during the 2004 drought in Burundi, where drought-affected migrants moved to Rwanda.

Slow-onset and drought related disaster and migrants

Yet, the protection of humanitarian law in the context of severe or prolonged droughts is uncertain. Refugee law is limited in large part because the legal definition of an international refugee under the 1951 Convention relating to the Status of Refugees does not include persons fleeing environmental harm. Governments are therefore not generally required to protect or provide special legal status to the victims entering their territory from climate events. In narrow circumstances a case could be made that some drought-affected victims are entitled to protection by the host country under the principle of non-refoulement recognized in the 1951 Convention. The principle would prevent a government's return of a person in their country, regardless of legal status, where the person's life or integrity are at risk, or where return would subject the person to the risk of cruel, unusual or degrading treatment. Whether a drought event would rise to this level of risk would have to be demonstrated on a case-by-case basis.

Under the 1969 OAU convention on Specific Aspects of Refugee Problems in Africa, the refugee definition includes those fleeing "events seriously disturbing public order in either part or the whole of his country of origin or nationality." A similar provision is contained in the Cartagena Declaration on Refugees. While the victims of natural disasters (tsunamis, earthquakes, floods) might arguably be included in this definition, it is much less certain whether victims of protracted droughts, like the one ongoing in East Africa, would be included. If a country affected by a severe drought declared a national emergency or formally identified the disaster as one disrupting public order, an argument could be made that international migrants from that country should receive temporary asylum or refuge in the host country and/or international assistance.

More significant humanitarian protection arises for those fleeing serious conflicts that erupt in the wake of environmental scarcity or drought. Normally, these persons should be protected under international refugee law due to the presence of violent or serious conflict. For example, drought, water scarcity and food insecurity are currently the most significant climate-related hazard contributing to conflict and mass displacement in the Horn of Africa. The competition for scarce land and water resources for pastoralists are increasing. Higher levels of cattle rustling incidents have been documented in the region recently as owners seek to restock herds badly affected by the prolonged drought that has swept across East Africa. Humanitarian agencies have reported that pastoralists living along the borders of Sudan, Kenya, Ethiopia, Tanzania and Uganda are losing their lives from increased cross-border resource-based armed conflicts.

A conflict refugee should receive the protection of a host government even if the cause of flight across the border was due to a combination of conflict and other causes, such as severe drought. The government's obligation to provide these persons with shelter, food, and security may not extend to the provision of employment or jobs. In this way, the designation of "refugee" status for those experiencing both conflict and drought may be of limited value for some victims. Depending on the level of conflict, those migrating due to combined conflict and environmental factors may cross an international border in search of both refuge and temporary employment. Since humanitarian law does not easily facilitate these mixed motives, conflict refugees may shun traditional host government protection in favor of seeking employment, even if it means they remain undocumented. For example, in East Africa the IOM has documented that many now crossing into Kenya due to the drought and resource conflicts are choosing not to seek status as "refugees" or to enter the refugee camps in Kenya because Kenyan law would prevent them from freely traveling or working. This has led to an increase in undocumented migrants. Without clarification and perhaps new standards, international refugee norms are of diminished utility in protecting persons forced to move because of combined humanitarian crises.

International agencies, such as the IOM and the Office for the Coordination of Humanitarian Affairs (OCHA), consider that effectively addressing these mixed humanitarian crises should include facilitating cross-border mobility for labor migration and access to water and pasturelands as a complement or alternative to traditional refugee camps or asylum. Yet, there are no international or cross-border agreements for this type of economic migration. Hence, the agencies have identified the need to establish a regional normative framework to facilitate this regularized mobility.

International migrants that have left drought or disaster areas are not otherwise wholly unprotected. As mentioned, each person carries fundamental human rights which governments must safeguard irrespective of their country of origin such as freedom from discrimination, freedom of thought and religion, and other rights related to the protection of human dignity.

These rights have been reinforced and clarified in the International Convention on the Protection of the Rights of All Migrant Workers and Members of their Families. Where governments have ratified the convention, it would generally apply to climate-related migrants who engage in international labor migration. The main concern with this treaty is that the United States and a number of other countries with high levels of immigration are not legal parties. Where the treaty codifies existing human rights norms and customary international law, such norms would be applicable. However, the treaty's mechanisms for accountability would not apply to non-party countries and international migrants would have limited recourse to remedies.

The European Convention on Migrant Workers contains similar provisions clarifying protection of labor migrants but includes that social and medical assistance to migrants be provided on a nondiscriminatory basis as other nationals. Its provisions would have broader reach among countries of Europe receiving migrants than the Migrant Workers Convention but similarly, the determination of immigrant status is largely discretionary. Each country is authorized to determine which international migrants will be provided legal status to enter, remain and work in their territories.

Rapid-onset disaster and migrants

The conditions facing rapid-onset disaster migrants and those confronted by slow-onset and drought-related disaster migrants are significantly different. Victims migrating from storms or floods most often seek to return home shortly after disasters occur or when it is safe to do so — as opposed to drought-related migrants who may seek to engage in international labor migration as a means of coping with longer-term or persistent drought situations. As such, rapid-onset disaster migrants have an immediate and temporary need for protection and, where return is delayed, may need to engage in short-term employment.

Rapid-onset disaster migrants who are forced to cross international borders are perhaps better protected under international law than drought victims. Major floods or storms, tsunamis and earthquakes related to climate change may cause serious disruptions to a country's infrastructure, housing, and food distribution systems and may disrupt public order. Such events could lead to mass displacement. Victims of these disasters may qualify as refugees and be entitled to asylum protection and government assistance under the 1969 OAU refugee convention referred to above or the

Cartagena Declaration on Refugees. In fact, general humanitarian assistance and temporary assistance has been provided to such victims crossing borders, as demonstrated by government action after the 2004 Asian tsunami.

For those not qualifying as refugees but who cannot return to their country of origin because of the impacts of a natural disaster, some countries provide for Temporary Protected Status (TPS). The United States Immigration Act of 1990 provides for discretionary grants of TPS in events such as earthquakes, floods, droughts, epidemics, other environmental disasters or disruptions to living conditions where the state of origin cannot adequately manage the return of its nationals. The status has been granted in a few circumstances when disasters occurred in Montserrat, Nicaragua and Honduras. It applies only to those in the United States at the time of disaster and allows for a six-month stay which can be extended to 18 months. During the stay, residents can work but cannot apply for admission of spouses or family members.

Countries in Europe have similar TPS exceptions, though criteria vary. The Finnish and Swedish Alien Acts provide for TPS when victims cannot return due to serious environmental disruption, and Denmark can provide even an expanded protection for victims and their families seeking humanitarian asylum from drought disaster. Much more narrowly, the Council of Europe adopted a directive on TPS for situations of a mass influx due to armed conflict and where the disruption prevents return to the country of origin or the persons would be subject to serious human rights violations and would not qualify otherwise under the 1951 Convention. In such cases, the Council of Europe may decide to convey temporary status up to one year, which can be extended.

Those who do not qualify for these narrow exceptions, such as slow-onset disaster migrants are not entitled to asylum or special status. As yet, there is no global migration agreement, nor known bi-national agreements that cover migration, voluntary or forced, due to environmental disasters. Each country determines the terms (e.g., visas) and the grounds for entry of migrants to enter and to work in its territory.

Sea-level rise and migrants

Of the various categories of climate change migrants, persons expected to cross borders due to sea-level rise inundating part or all of small-island nations are in a particularly unique position. These persons are covered by the same human rights principles pertaining to migrant workers but are not as yet viewed as "refugees." However these victims may become "stateless" persons and the provisions of various treaties and international instruments relevant to stateless persons may apply. International law in this area does not require states to provide permanent refuge. The principle of non-refoulement discussed above would seemingly prevent return if the victims would risk human life but beyond that, international law is unclear about providing a stateless person with a new state. The European Directive on Subsidiary Protection might be most pertinent as it would convey at least temporary status to third country nationals or stateless persons not otherwise qualifying as a refugee where return would risk "serious and individual threat to a civilian's life or person due to violent, armed conflict."

Rights and obligations related to internally displaced persons

International standards of law are clearer in the protection of those internally displaced by conflict or disaster. Human rights doctrine now includes a set of Guiding Principles for the protection of internally displaced persons (IDPs). These are "persons or groups of persons who have been forced or obliged to flee or to leave their homes or places of habitual residence, in particular as a result of or in order to avoid the effects of armed conflict, situations of generalized violence, violations of human rights or natural or human-made disasters, and who have not crossed an internationally recognized state border." Victims of immediate-onset disasters, such as hurricanes and floods, would be covered by such protection. If situations of drought and desertification (environmental changes which occur more slowly over time) are considered disasters, then victims who are forced to migrate inside their country of origin should be covered by IDP principles. This may occur when climate change produces serious or prolonged drought.

The IDP principles codify the state's human rights obligations towards those displaced in its territory, including the right to life, dignity and security of persons displaced. IDPs have the right to move to other parts of the country or to leave their country, to have their family members remain together or be reunited if separated. They have the right to an adequate standard of living, food, water, basic shelter and housing, property restitution, essential medical services and sanitation and they continue to enjoy the right to seek employment and participate in economic activities. The principles reiterate that governments are prohibited from discriminating against IDPs in the distribution of aid or other treatment and must adhere to human rights protections in the resettlement and reintegration of IDPs. Forced relocation is to be used only as a last resort to protect the health and safety of those affected and may not be arbitrary or discriminatory, nor harmful to the needs of indigenous or marginalized groups dependent or attached to their lands.

Most governments appear to accept these principles and have confirmed their importance. These principles are reflected in the United Nations General Assembly Outcome Document, adopted by consensus after the 2005 World Summit on Development (recognizing the principles as "an important international framework for the protection of internally displaced persons.") They have been incorporated by governments in domestic policy and law and in international agreements adopted by governments in various regions. Most recently, they served as the foundation for the African Union Convention for the Protection and Assistance of Internally Displaced Persons in Africa ("Kampala Convention"), concluded in November 2009. The Kampala Convention recognizes that climate change may cause internal displacement and provides a detailed description of government obligations, including reparations for failure to act, and encourages non-governmental and other assistance in the region for IDPs when a state affected by disaster is unable to provide full assistance.

Furthermore, governments may be held accountable if they fail to act according to their human rights obligations in preventing disasters or impacts where such harm is foreseeable. This principle has been reinforced by international human rights treaty bodies, including the Human Rights Committee (established to monitor implementation of the International Covenant on Civil and Political Rights), the Inter-American Commission and Court of Human Rights, and the European Court of Human Rights. These bodies have issued legal decisions regarding the state's positive obligation to take precautions against foreseeable harm, including environmental harm, and to support persons forced to move away from high risk zones. For example, after several storms led to devastating mudslides in the Central Caucuses region, the local government failed to repair infrastructure, prepare the public or take other public safety measures to prevent harm. The impact of storms subsequently led to death and harm to human life, and left many in the community displaced without homes. The European Court of Human Rights determined that Russia had violated its human rights obligations because it failed to take measures that could have reduced the damage to human life and property caused by the natural disasters.

Conclusions

The number of climate disasters is rising. It is now better understood that these climatic events will have, in some regions, very severe impact on human life, health and property. General human rights and humanitarian principles provide fundamental rights to all persons, and states have the duty to protect those in their territories from harm that is foreseeable. With the growing scientific evidence of more severe disasters to come, governments possibly have a more immediate obligation to take proactive, affirmative steps to identify and protect those most vulnerable, to help them adapt, and to cooperate with other states on assistance. This, in essence, requires precautionary measures to prevent further harm to communities where climate disasters are predicted to occur or likely to recur (e.g., storm surges, floods, and droughts).

The global community has yet to adopt specific standards related to climate change or to protect climate disaster victims. While some humanitarian standards exist for internally displaced persons, these are still largely voluntary. There are, moreover, great uncertainties in the law to protect persons migrating across an international border in response to climate disasters. Refugee laws provide little, if any, protection. Mixed climate and conflict crises may give rise to government obligations to provide temporary asylum to victims. However, drought victims are in a more precarious legal position, even if they view themselves as having little choice but to engage in labor migration as a means of future policy dialogue: (1) whether migrant movements that are forced or voluntary are to be treated differently in the climate context from other development-related migration; (2) whether the treatment of migrants responding to the effects of prolonged drought should differ from the treatment of migrants of rapid-onset disasters; and (3) whether and how policies would treat some forms of migration as an appropriate adaptation strategy in response to climate change.

Protecting victims displaced from sea-level rise presents yet a different challenge for governments. The likely inundation or loss of entire islands by the end of the century suggests that governments will need to clarify the international migration and resettlement policies applicable to island populations in the near-term, well before the eventual submergence of these island states. Human rights law would require that the affected populations participate in the negotiation of such measures that, quite literally, affect their fate as a community and a nation.

In sum, governments should begin to clarify the rights of affected climate migrants and the responsibilities of host countries and countries of origin in their treatment of both persons who move as an immediate response to natural disaster and persons who migrate in response to a prolonged drought disaster, where either movement is motivated by a need for basic survival. As policymakers seek to clarify existing human rights norms or to develop a new humanitarian framework, the important inquiry for international law should be whether persons who cross borders "have a need for international protection; and, if so, on what grounds this need may be considered an entitlement."

B. Biodiversity

Kalyani Robbins, *The Biodiversity Paradigm Shift: Adapting the Endangered Species Act to Climate Change*

27 Fordham Envtl. L. Rev. 57 (2016)

I. IMPACT: THE DRAMATIC AND PERMANENT ALTERATION OF THE EARTH'S ECOSYSTEMS

. . . Climate change is impacting biodiversity across the board. Indeed, biodiversity may well be the catastrophe's greatest victim. We have already seen relatively dramatic changes in habitat and species behavior, and it is very clear that what has taken place so far is only the tip of the iceberg. The following is a sampling of some of the major areas of concern.

A. Hydrology

While the hydrological cycle may not be the first thing people think of when wringing their hands over climate change, the impact in this area may be substantial, with serious consequences for both human populations and ecosystems. Research has found that the greenhouse effect "will alter the timing and magnitude of runoff and soil moisture, change lake levels, and affect water quality."

A warmer atmosphere increases the rate of evaporation, which speeds up the entire hydrologic cycle. This, along with greater pressures on air currents, is pushing storm activity further from the equator. The result is that wet areas are getting wetter and dry areas are getting drier. A greater proportion of precipitation falls as rain rather than snow, which reduces the capacity for water storage. Rivers and streams are maintained by the gradual melting of water previously stored as snow, and will lose volume during the lengthened dry seasons with the diminished quantity of snow melting more quickly and running out. This will cause water shortages for human communities as well as severe harm to aquatic and riparian ecosystems. In addition to regional changes, precipitation is becoming more temporally concentrated into heavy rainfall events separated by longer dry periods, which leads, paradoxically, to an increase in both droughts and floods. Both events cause problems for ecosystems and can kill off large populations of plant and tree species.

Hydrologic changes also create increased competition for the limited and fluctuating water resource between human populations and dwindling fish species. Because many of the impacted species are listed under the ESA, we have already begun to see courts requiring the wildlife agencies to consider climate change impacts on species in their decision-making. One example of this is the California delta smelt at issue in . . . *Natural Resources Defense Council v. Kempthorne*, [506 F. Supp. 2d 322 (E.D. Cal. 2007),] in which a biological opinion allowing for a water project that delivered water to much of southern California was struck down for failing to consider the impact of climate change on the delta smelt. The Fish & Wildlife Service (FWS) should have taken into account the likelihood of climate-change-caused decreases in water volume and increases in water temperature, both of which could be devastating to the fish. This ruling initially halted the water diversions to California's arid south. They were only partially resumed, and users were forced to manage on just forty percent of their expectations. One can imagine future scenarios in which the human cost is too great to bend to the dictates of the ESA, which could endanger the statute itself. The climate change context creates conflicts that go beyond the traditional economic sacrifices associated with the ESA.

B. Seasons

The shifting of seasons is one of the easiest changes for average people to observe in their everyday lives. The flowers are budding earlier, the fall colors come later, and the birds are migrating by at different times than one might recall from their youth.

In the United States, spring now arrives an average of 10 days to two weeks earlier than it did 20 years ago. The growing season is lengthening over much of the continental United States. Many migratory bird species are arriving earlier. For example, a study of northeastern birds that migrate long distances found that birds wintering in the southern United States now arrive back in the Northeast an average of 13 days earlier than they did during the first half of the last century. Birds wintering in South America arrive back in the Northeast an average of four days earlier.

While such shifts may not seem like cause for great alarm, and one might even find some positive spin (such as the increase in growing season for crops and recreational opportunities, though it also increases fire season for foresters), it serves as a canary in the planetary coalmine. Once you let it sink in—the timeframe in which this can be observed—it becomes quite ominous. Moreover, the shifting of seasons plays a role in the habitat selection patterns of those bird and land species that do migrate, resulting in the range alterations and jumbled ecosystems described next.

C. Species Geographic Range

We have begun to see shifts in the geographic ranges of many species, and expect to see such movement increase substantially if not impeded. Species are seeking out their historic climates, the conditions in which they evolved. With a warming atmosphere, one must keep moving in order to stay the same, whether northward or upward in altitude. While this can sound like a self-managed problem, it is rare that such migrations are successful. If they need to move northward, they run quickly into the upper boundaries of their conservation island, unable to cross large areas of human development (or even something as narrow as a road, for some species), even if there is any suitable habitat to the north of it (which there may not be in any case). If they are moving up in altitude, some may find short-term success, due to less human development on mountains than elsewhere, but there is a rather obvious endpoint: the mountaintop itself. Even if there is suitable habitat on a higher mountain nearby, there is no way to survive the trip through the valley in between, so the population is stranded. Finally, even where migration is not impeded, a population may be faced with leaving behind certain habitat needs or encountering a new predator. Ecosystems are complex interdependent webs, no more designed to be broken apart than the organs in your body. Studies show species populations at the southern end of the species' range going extinct in spite of the availability of suitable habitat to the north.

Further, species migration may harm other species, leading to cascading effects. As just one example, tree species face the same predicament as wildlife, also moving northward albeit a bit more slowly. When entire forests move, it not only alters the habitat they provide within, but also encroaches on non-forest habitat to the north. Caribou, for example, require open tundra habitat to the north of the tree line. As the tree line moves north, the southern border of caribou habitat moves north. The northern border, however, remains the same, so the result is a continuous shrinking of total caribou habitat.

D. Dispersal and Invasion

As mentioned above, some species will attempt to move northward or upward in altitude. Others, however, will not do so, or will do so on a later schedule, due to variation in sensitivity to both climate change and migration. This variation in movement will result in a breaking up of ecosystems, which carries the potential to be the greatest catastrophe for biodiversity, as well as for human enjoyment of ecosystem services. The results of such a phenomenon are difficult to predict, as it is unprecedented, but there is no question that many species will not survive the crumbling of their ecosystems.

Not only will this new tendency toward dispersal be harmful to the scattering ecosystem itself, but the pieces it sends out into the world may wreak havoc wherever they land. After habitat destruction, invasive species are the second leading cause of species extinctions. Most invasive species problems thus far have been introduced directly by human beings. Generally with innocent intentions, shortsighted individuals and governments have attempted to solve small problems by introducing new species that ultimately created large problems. Some infamous examples are kudzu ("the vine that ate the south"), Asian carp, and the zebra mussel. The break-up of eco-systems and migration of species will usher in a new era of invasive species: species that showed up in their new homes completely on their own, with no direct assistance from humans. Of course, these invasions are still human-caused (due to anthropogenic climate change), and still our responsibility to address.

Some climate-encouraged invasions have even more sinister impacts than simply destroying their host ecosystems, in that they can contribute directly to the greenhouse gas overload. Mountain pine beetles, like most insects, are heavily dependent on climate. Warmer temperatures speed up their life cycles and the expanding area of warm climate has substantially increased their geographic range. Shorter and less intense winters are especially valuable to the beetle, as cold winters are what traditionally kept their populations in check, even in those regions in which they could survive part of the year. The mountain pine beetle destroys pines in a rapid and widespread fashion, and has spread to nearly double its former range, pushing up into Canadian forests and causing great devastation there. These pine forests serve as carbon sinks, so not only does this cause loss of their potential to continue to absorb carbon, but worse, their destruction releases all that stored carbon into the atmosphere.

E. Ocean Acidification and Oxygen-Poor Dead Zones

What is likely the most devastating issue is unfortunately also the least commonly understood or even known. Perhaps because many never see the ocean, and we do not live there, it has received deceptively little play in the media. Or perhaps it is because even the scientific community waited so long to research the issue, such that we've only had information to access (or not access, as the case may be) for a couple of decades. We ignore this 70% of our planet at our peril, as the ocean is absorbing an entire third of all that excessive CO_2 we are emitting into the atmosphere. When this carbon dioxide dissolves in water it acidifies the water, resulting in poor conditions for coral species to form their skeletons. This is a problem not only for coral, but for shellfish as well. Researchers for the U.S. Global Change Research Program warned that "[i]f carbon dioxide concentrations continue to rise and the resulting acidification proceeds, eventually, corals and other ocean life that rely on calcium carbonate will not be able to build these skeletons and shells at all." If it gets to that, the entire food chain will be thrown off, resulting in widespread human suffering. The ocean, a living resource, will die.

Changes in ocean chemistry will probably affect marine life in three different ways: (1) decreased carbonate ion concentration could affect the calcification process for calcifying organisms (e.g., corals); (2) lowered pH could affect acid-base regulation, as well as a variety of other physiological processes; and (3) increased dissolved CO_2 could alter the ability of primary producers to photo-synthesize.

Speaking to the second point in this list, if you have ever tried to care for a home aquarium, you know that fish are extremely sensitive to even the slightest alterations in water temperature or chemistry. Given that climate change has a substantial impact on both of these characteristics of water bodies, it places a heavy burden on fisheries. It will become increasingly important to manage aquatic ecosystems for resilience.

Finally, when you combine a reduction in photosynthesis with the increase in fertilizer run-off that we already struggle with, you maximize the problem of oxygen-poor dead zones. These are areas in which the oxygen level drops so dramatically that everything there dies at once. Even the warming itself contributes to the problem, as warm water holds less oxygen than cold water. Such dead zones have been on the rise for years. While there is some public awareness of the hypoxic coastal dead zones caused by agricultural run-off, many do not realize that the deep ocean has become an oxygen-poor dead zone that is expanding upward due to warming temperatures and declining ocean circulation. "It leaves just a very thin lens on the top of the ocean where most organisms can live," according to Sarah Moffitt of the Bodega Marine Laboratory at the University of California, Davis, which in turn results in an increased risk for historically deep-water species of falling prey to surface predators or getting caught in long-lines from fishing boats.

F. Melting Sea Ice and Sea Level Rise

Some geographic areas are more sensitive than others, as well as more susceptible to catastrophic tipping points or even rapidly escalating feedback loops. The Arctic is an excellent example of all three weaknesses in one region. Because much of the Arctic habitat consists of sea ice, the habitat literally melts away, leaving its inhabitants stranded and homeless. In addition to being hypersensitive to warming temperatures due to ice-dependency, the Arctic also suffers from a relatively early tipping point. This is because it does not take very much warming, melting of ice, and reduction (in both range and duration) of snow cover to trigger a devastating feedback loop. To wit: there is an initial reduction of snow cover and melting of ice, thereby reducing the reflective surface area for deflecting the sun's radiation, causing more of it to be absorbed, resulting in additional warming and melting, and so on.

This places sea-ice-dependent species among those with the most urgent of circumstances, as they are rapidly losing their habitat. Their habitat is not merely undergoing gradual change; it is disappearing altogether.

Walruses, polar bears, seals, and other marine mammals that rely on sea ice for resting, feeding, hunting, and breeding are particularly threatened by climate change. For example, studies reveal that in 1980, the average weight of female polar bears in western Hudson Bay, Canada, was 650 pounds. While in 2004, their average weight was only 507 pounds. It is believed that the progressively earlier breakup of the Arctic sea ice is responsible for the decrease in the polar bears' average weight, as this ice loss reduces their hunting season and food intake.

In addition to the devastating loss of sea ice habitat, all this melting ice is resulting in sea level rise. Indeed, the Intergovernmental Panel on Climate Change ("IPCC") concluded that sea level rise was "inevitable" no matter what we do at this point. The causes of sea level rise include not only melting ice sheets and glaciers, but a substantial contribution comes from ocean expansion due to warming, with an estimated 2,000-year commitment to rising seas already underway. Rising seas are devastating to coastal ecosystems such as tidal marshland or mangroves. For this reason, creative efforts at adaptation assistance to such ecosystems will be essential.

. . .

Notes and Questions

1. The ocean is the world's largest habitat, covering more than 70 percent of the planet and containing more than half of all living species on earth. In spite of this, ocean acidification tends to get short shrift in the conversations about climate change, but it is a very serious problem.

> Changes in ocean chemistry will probably affect marine life in three differ-ent ways: (1) decreased carbonate ion concentration could affect the calcifi-cation process for calcifying organisms (e.g., corals); (2) lowered pH could affect acid-base regulation, as well as a variety of other physiological processes; and (3) increased dissolved CO_2 could alter the ability of primary producers to photo-synthesize.

Cheryl A. Logan, *A Review of Ocean Acidification and America's Response*, 60 Bio-Science 819 (2010) (recommended reading for a more in-depth analysis of these issues).

2. The National Oceanic and Atmospheric Administration has a program to mon-itor ocean acidification, but as yet we have engaged in little response to the problem. Other countries have begun to take action, however. A useful review of the harms caused by ocean acidification, as well as the governmental responses to the issue, can be found in Heidi R. Lamirande, *From Sea to Carbon Cesspool: Preventing the World's Marine Ecosystems from Falling Victim to Ocean Acidification*, 34 Suffolk Transnat'l L. Rev. 183 (2011).

3. While NOAA begins to look at ocean acidification, the broader issue of climate change impacts on biodiversity generally also requires attention. The U.S. agency tasked with such concerns is, as you may have gathered by now, the Fish & Wildlife Service. The FWS report on the problems created by climate change as well as the agen-cy's plan to address them was included in this chapter. How does the perspective there presented compare with what you read in this excerpt?

4. As students may have already been aware before taking this course, the Arctic regions are in especially dire circumstances. The following excerpt provides some brief insights into the concerns and the efforts to address those concerns.

Ahmed Djoghlafa, *Climate Change and Biodiversity in Polar Regions*

8 Sust. Dev. L. & Pol. 14 (2008).

INTRODUCTION

Polar ecosystems are home to an array of plants and animals that survive in some of the most extreme conditions in the world. For example, the seas surrounding the Antarctic are rich in plankton, which support a rich marine food chain, while the Arc-tic itself supports many mammals and plays an important role in the annual cycle of migratory birds. The scientific studies carried out at the occasion of the celebration of the International Polar Year have provided additional evidence of the rich, unique nature of the marine Arctic environment. Indeed the biodiversity of the Arctic is fun-damental to the livelihoods of Arctic peoples. However, the Millennium Ecosystem

Assessment, along with recent reports from the Intergovernmental Panel on Climate Change, have made us aware that climate change negatively impacts existing ecosystems and is one of the main drivers of biodiversity loss. Particular attention is now being paid to Polar Regions, where evidence of the impacts of climate change have been observed and widely reported. Indeed, Polar Regions are currently experiencing some of the most rapid and severe climate change on Earth, which will contribute to environmental and socio-economic changes, many of which have already begun. During the twentieth century, Arctic air temperatures increased by approximately five degrees Celsius, which is an increase that is ten times faster than the observed global-mean surface temperature. An additional warming of about four to seven degrees Celsius in the Arctic is predicted over the next hundred years. Moreover, Polar Regions are particularly threatened by climate change since Polar species and societies have developed very specialized adaptations to the harsh conditions found at the poles, thus making them extremely vulnerable to dramatic changes in these conditions.

OBSERVED AND PROJECTED IMPACTS

Walruses, polar bears, seals, and other marine mammals that rely on sea ice for resting, feeding, hunting, and breeding are particularly threatened by climate change. For example, studies reveal that in 1980, the average weight of female polar bears in western Hudson Bay, Canada, was 650 pounds. While in 2004, their average weight was only 507 pounds. It is believed that the progressively earlier breakup of the Arctic sea ice is responsible for the decrease in the polar bears' average weight, as this ice loss reduces their hunting season and food intake. Although for a different reason, reduced sea-ice extent is also believed to have caused a fifty percent decline in emperor penguin populations in Terre Adélie. Populations of krill and other small organisms may also decline as ice recedes. Due to the high importance of krill in various food chains, the entire marine food web could be adversely affected.

Climate change is already affecting the livelihood of indigenous peoples in the Arctic. Losses in biodiversity affect the traditional practices of indigenous people, particularly fishing and hunting. For example, the Saami people have observed changes in reindeer grazing pastures, while the Inuit people of Canada have observed reductions in the ringed seal population, their single most important source of food.

CLIMATE CHANGE AND INDIGENOUS AND LOCAL COMMUNITIES IN THE ARCTIC

Due to its unique nature, climate, and sensitivity to climate changes, the Arctic is an important early warning system as far as climate change is concerned. The findings of the Intergovernmental Panel on Climate Change show that eleven of the last twelve years (1995–2006) rank among the twelve warmest years in the instrumental record of global surface temperatures since 1850. In the past one hundred years, average temperatures in the Arctic increased by almost twice the global average rate. Consequently, the annual average Arctic sea ice extent has shrunk by 2.1 to 3.1 percent per decade. Further, temperatures at the top of the permafrost layer have generally increased up to three degrees Celsius since the 1980s. It is projected that higher temperatures will contribute to continuing snow contraction and widespread increases in thaw depth over permafrost regions. Also, the gradual melting of the Greenland ice sheet is projected to contribute to sea level rise, even beyond the year 2100.

The consequences of climate change are becoming more visible in the Arctic, and are greatly influencing the environment, animals, and living conditions of humans, especially the indigenous peoples who strongly depend on the Arctic ecosystem and natural resources. The Arctic indigenous peoples, their life, culture, and traditional knowledge, are adapted to and largely dependent on the cold and extreme physical conditions of the region. Over the years, they have adapted to the challenges brought about by the Arctic geography and climate. Although the Arctic climate has always undergone change, the ongoing changes in the climate are taking place at such an alarming speed that indigenous communities are having severe difficulties coping.

The Arctic Climate Impact Assessment ("ACIA"), commissioned by the Arctic Council, provides important insight into the impacts of climate change in the Arctic region. Over a period of five years, an international team of over three hundred scientists, others experts, and members of indigenous communities prepared this assessment. The ACIA Report identifies a range of climate change impacts including: rising temperatures in the Arctic with worldwide implications; shifts in Arctic vegetation zones; changes in animal species' diversity, ranges, and distribution; and increased exposure to storms by coastal communities.

The ACIA Report devotes a separate chapter to address matters concerning the changing Arctic from an indigenous perspective. Indigenous peoples have provided case studies addressing the situation in Kotzebue, the Aleutian and Pribilof Islands Region, the Yukon Territory, Denendeh, Nunavut, Greenland, Sápmi, and Kola. An important common theme or observation in the case studies is that the weather in the Arctic region has become more variable and less predictable by traditional means.

The Arctic Climate Impact Assessment recognizes that further research is required to understand environmental changes occurring in the Arctic, as well as the ways in which people view these changes. It states that in both cases, there is a growing, but still insufficient, body of research to draw on, in particular in those Arctic areas where few or no current records of indigenous observations are available. The assessment concludes that further research needs to detect and interpret climate change, and to determine appropriate response strategies.

V. Geoengineering

What if mitigation and adaptation aren't enough? What if it becomes necessary to do more to survive? These are scary thoughts, but most policymakers are not yet ready to take desperate measures. However, people are developing extreme methods of intentionally interfering with the earth's climate, and governments are watching with interest and/or funding such research and development. Alas, there is presently little to prevent a wealthy private party from taking action that only governments should be in a position to decide on. The following article provides some insight into the nascent field of geoengineering.

Michael Specter, *The Climate Fixers:*
Is There a Technological Solution to Global Warming?
The New Yorker, May 14, 2012

Late in the afternoon on April 2, 1991, Mt. Pinatubo, a volcano on the Philippine island of Luzon, began to rumble with a series of the powerful steam explosions that typically precede an eruption. Pinatubo had been dormant for more than four centuries, and in the volcanological world the mountain had become little more than a footnote. The tremors continued in a steady crescendo for the next two months, until June 15th, when the mountain exploded with enough force to expel molten lava at the speed of six hundred miles an hour. The lava flooded a two-hundred-and-fifty-square-mile area, requiring the evacuation of two hundred thousand people.

Within hours, the plume of gas and ash had penetrated the stratosphere, eventually reaching an altitude of twenty-one miles. Three weeks later, an aerosol cloud had encircled the earth, and it remained for nearly two years. Twenty million metric tons of sulfur dioxide mixed with droplets of water, creating a kind of gaseous mirror, which reflected solar rays back into the sky. Throughout 1992 and 1993, the amount of sunlight that reached the surface of the earth was reduced by more than ten per cent.

The heavy industrial activity of the previous hundred years had caused the earth's climate to warm by roughly three-quarters of a degree Celsius, helping to make the twentieth century the hottest in at least a thousand years. The eruption of Mt. Pinatubo, however, reduced global temperatures by nearly that much in a single year. It also disrupted patterns of precipitation throughout the planet. It is believed to have influenced events as varied as floods along the Mississippi River in 1993 and, later that year, the drought that devastated the African Sahel. Most people considered the eruption a calamity.

For geophysical scientists, though, Mt. Pinatubo provided the best model in at least a century to help us understand what might happen if humans attempted to ameliorate global warming by deliberately altering the climate of the earth.

For years, even to entertain the possibility of human intervention on such a scale—geoengineering, as the practice is known—has been denounced as hubris. Predicting long-term climatic behavior by using computer models has proved difficult, and the notion of fiddling with the planet's climate based on the results generated by those models worries even scientists who are fully engaged in the research. "There will be no easy victories, but at some point we are going to have to take the facts seriously," David Keith, a professor of engineering and public policy at Harvard and one of geoengineering's most thoughtful supporters, told me. "Nonetheless," he added, "it is hyperbolic to say this, but no less true: when you start to reflect light away from the planet, you can easily imagine a chain of events that would extinguish life on earth."

There is only one reason to consider deploying a scheme with even a tiny chance of causing such a catastrophe: if the risks of not deploying it were clearly higher. No one is yet prepared to make such a calculation, but researchers are moving in that direction. To offer guidance, the Intergovernmental Panel on Climate Change (I.P.C.C.) has developed a series of scenarios on global warming. The cheeriest assessment predicts that by the end of the century the earth's average temperature will rise between 1.1 and 2.9 degrees Celsius. A more pessimistic projection envisages a rise of between 2.4 and 6.4 degrees — far higher than at any time in recorded history. (There are nearly two degrees Fahrenheit in one degree Celsius. A rise of 2.4 to 6.4 degrees Celsius would equal 4.3 to 11.5 degrees Fahrenheit.) Until recently, climate scientists believed that a six-degree rise, the effects of which would be an undeniable disaster, was unlikely. But new data have changed the minds of many. Late last year, Fatih Birol, the chief economist for the International Energy Agency, said that current levels of consumption "put the world perfectly on track for a six-degree Celsius rise in temperature. . . . Everybody, even schoolchildren, knows this will have catastrophic implications for all of us."

Tens of thousands of wildfires have already been attributed to warming, as have melting glaciers and rising seas. (The warming of the oceans is particularly worrisome; as Arctic ice melts, water that was below the surface becomes exposed to the sun and absorbs more solar energy, which leads to warmer oceans — a loop that could rapidly spin out of control.) Even a two-degree climb in average global temperatures could cause crop failures in parts of the world that can least afford to lose the nourishment. The size of deserts would increase, along with the frequency and intensity of wildfires. Deliberately modifying the earth's atmosphere would be a desperate gamble with significant risks. Yet the more likely climate change is to cause devastation, the more attractive even the most perilous attempts to mitigate those changes will become.

[handwritten margin note: Arctic feedback loop]

"We don't know how bad this is going to be, and we don't know when it is going to get bad," Ken Caldeira, a climate scientist with the Carnegie Institution, told me. In 2007, Caldeira was a principal contributor to an I.P.C.C. team that won a Nobel Peace Prize. "There are wide variations within the models," he said. "But we had better get ready, because we are running rapidly toward a minefield. We just don't know where the minefield starts, or how long it will be before we find ourselves in the middle of it."

The Maldives, a string of islands off the coast of India whose highest point above sea level is eight feet, may be the first nation to drown. In Alaska, entire towns have begun to shift in the loosening permafrost. The Florida economy is highly dependent upon coastal weather patterns; the tide station at Miami Beach has registered an increase of seven inches since 1935, according to the National Oceanic and Atmospheric Administration. One Australian study, published this year in the journal *Nature Climate Change*, found that a two-degree Celsius rise in the earth's temperature would be accompanied by a significant spike in the number of lives lost just in Brisbane. Many climate scientists say their biggest fear is that warming could melt the Arctic permafrost — which stretches for thousands of miles across Alaska, Canada, and Siberia. There is twice as much CO_2 locked beneath the tundra as there is in the earth's atmosphere. Melting would release enormous stores of methane, a greenhouse gas nearly thirty times more potent than carbon dioxide. If that happens, as the hydrologist Jane C. S. Long told me when we met recently in her office at the Lawrence Livermore National Laboratory, "it's game over."

The Stratospheric Particle Injection for Climate Engineering project, or SPICE, is a British academic consortium that seeks to mimic the actions of volcanoes like Pinatubo by pumping particles of sulfur dioxide, or similar reflective chemicals, into the stratosphere through a twelve-mile-long pipe held aloft by a balloon at one end and tethered, at the other, to a boat anchored at sea.

The consortium consists of three groups. At Bristol University, researchers led by Matt Watson, a professor of geophysics, are trying to determine which particles would have the maximum desired impact with the smallest likelihood of unwanted side effects. Sulfur dioxide produces sulfuric acid, which destroys the ozone layer of the atmosphere; there are similar compounds that might work while proving less environmentally toxic—including synthetic particles that could be created specifically for this purpose. At Cambridge, Hugh Hunt and his team are trying to determine the best way to get those particles into the stratosphere. A third group, at Oxford, has been focusing on the effect such an intervention would likely have on the earth's climate.

Hunt and I spoke in Cambridge, at Trinity College, where he is a professor of engineering and the Keeper of the Trinity College clock, a renowned timepiece that gains or loses less than a second a month. In his office, dozens of boomerangs dangle from the wall. When I asked about them, he grabbed one and hurled it at my head. "I teach three-dimensional dynamics," he said, flicking his hand in the air to grab it as it returned. Hunt has devoted his intellectual life to the study of mechanical vibration. His Web page is filled with instructive videos about gyroscopes, rings wobbling down rods, and boomerangs.

"I like to demonstrate the way things spin," he said, as he put the boomerang down and picked up an inflated pink balloon attached to a string. "The principle is pretty simple." Holding the string, Hunt began to bobble the balloon as if it were being tossed by foul weather. "Everything is fine if it is sitting still," he continued, holding the balloon steady. Then he began to wave his arm erratically. "One of the problems is that nothing is going to be still up there. It is going to be moving around. And the question we've got is . . . this pipe"—the industrial hose that will convey the particles into the sky—"is going to be under huge stressors." He snapped the string connected to the balloon. "How do you know it's not going to break? We are really pushing things to the limit in terms of their strength, so it is essential that we get the dynamics of motion right."

Most scientists, even those with no interest in personal publicity, are vigorous advocates for their own work. Not this group. "I don't know how many times I have said this, but the last thing I would ever want is for the project I have been working on to be implemented," Hunt said. "If we have to use these tools, it means something on this planet has gone seriously wrong."

Last fall, the SPICE team decided to conduct a brief and uncontroversial pilot study. At least they thought it would be uncontroversial. To demonstrate how they would disperse the sulfur dioxide, they had planned to float a balloon over Norfolk, at an altitude of a kilometre, and send a hundred and fifty litres of water into the air through a hose. After the date and time of the test was announced, in the middle of September, more than fifty organizations signed a petition objecting to the experiment, in part because they fear that even to consider engineering the climate would provide politicians with an excuse for avoiding tough decisions on reducing greenhouse-gas emissions. Opponents of the water test pointed out the many uncertainties in the research (which is precisely why the team wanted to do the experiment). The British government decided to put it off for at least six months.

"When people say we shouldn't even explore this issue, it scares me," Hunt said. He pointed out that carbon emissions are heavy, and finding a place to deposit them will not be easy. "Roughly speaking, the CO_2 we generate weighs three or four times as much as the fuel it comes from." That means that a short round-trip journey — say, eight hundred miles — by car, using two tanks of gas, produces three hundred kilograms of CO_2. "This is ten heavy suitcases from one short trip," Hunt said. "And you have to store it where it can't evaporate.

"So I have three questions, Where are you going to put it? Who are you going to ask to dispose of this for you? And how much are you reasonably willing to pay them to do it?" he continued. "There is nobody on this planet who can answer any of those questions. There is no established place or technique, and nobody has any idea what it would cost. And we need the answers now."

Hunt stood up, walked slowly to the window, and gazed at the manicured Trinity College green. "I know this is all unpleasant," he said. "Nobody wants it, but nobody wants to put high doses of poisonous chemicals into their body, either. That is what chemotherapy is, though, and for people suffering from cancer those poisons are often their only hope. Every day, tens of thousands of people take them willingly — because they are very sick or dying. This is how I prefer to look at the possibility of engineering the climate. It isn't a cure for anything. But it could very well turn out to be the least bad option we are going to have."

The notion of modifying the weather dates back at least to the eighteen-thirties, when the American meteorologist James Pollard Espy became known as the Storm King, for his (prescient but widely ridiculed) proposals to stimulate rain by selectively burning forests. More recently, the U.S. government project Stormfury attempted for decades to lessen the force of hurricanes by seeding them with silver iodide. And in 2008 Chinese soldiers fired more than a thousand rockets filled with chemicals at clouds over Beijing to prevent them from raining on the Olympics. The relationship between carbon emissions and the earth's temperature has been clear for more than a century: in 1908, the Swedish scientist Svante Arrhenius suggested that burning fossil fuels might help prevent the coming ice age. In 1965, President Lyndon Johnson received a report from his Science Advisory Committee, titled "Restoring the Quality of Our Environment," that noted for the first time the potential need to balance increased greenhouse-gas emissions by "raising the albedo, or the reflectivity, of the earth." The report suggested that such a change could be achieved by spreading small reflective particles over large parts of the ocean.

While such tactics could clearly fail, perhaps the greater concern is what might happen if they succeeded in ways nobody had envisioned. Injecting sulfur dioxide, or particles that perform a similar function, would rapidly lower the temperature of the earth, at relatively little expense—most estimates put the cost at less than ten billion dollars a year. But it would do nothing to halt ocean acidification, which threatens to destroy coral reefs and wipe out an enormous number of aquatic species. The risks of reducing the amount of sunlight that reaches the atmosphere on that scale would be as obvious—and immediate—as the benefits. If such a program were suddenly to fall apart, the earth would be subjected to extremely rapid warming, with nothing to stop it. And while such an effort would cool the globe, it might do so in ways that disrupt the behavior of the Asian and African monsoons, which provide the water that billions of people need to drink and to grow their food.

"Geoengineering" actually refers to two distinct ideas about how to cool the planet. The first, solar-radiation management, focusses on reducing the impact of the sun. Whether by seeding clouds, spreading giant mirrors in the desert, or injecting sulfates into the stratosphere, most such plans seek to replicate the effects of eruptions like Mt. Pinatubo's. The other approach is less risky, and involves removing carbon directly from the atmosphere and burying it in vast ocean storage beds or deep inside the earth. But without a significant technological advance such projects will be expensive and may take many years to have any significant effect.

There are dozens of versions of each scheme, and they range from plausible to absurd. There have been proposals to send mirrors, sunshades, and parasols into space. Recently, the scientific entrepreneur Nathan Myhrvold, whose company Intellectual Ventures has invested in several geoengineering ideas, said that we could cool the earth by stirring the seas. He has proposed deploying a million plastic tubes, each about a hundred metres long, to roil the water, which would help it trap more CO_2. "The ocean is this giant heat sink," he told me. "But it is very cold. The bottom is nearly freezing. If you just stirred the ocean more, you could absorb the excess CO_2 and keep the planet cold." (This is not as crazy as it sounds. In the center of the ocean, wind-driven currents bring fresh water to the surface, so stirring the ocean could transform it into a well-organized storage depot. The new water would absorb more carbon while the old water carried the carbon it has already captured into the deep.)

The Harvard physicist Russell Seitz wants to create what amounts to a giant oceanic bubble bath: bubbles trap air, which brightens them enough to reflect sunlight away from the surface of the earth. Another tactic would require maintaining a fine spray of seawater—the world's biggest fountain—which would mix with salt to help clouds block sunlight.

The best solution, nearly all scientists agree, would be the simplest: stop burning fossil fuels, which would reduce the amount of carbon we dump into the atmosphere.

That fact has been emphasized in virtually every study that addresses the potential effect of climate change on the earth — and there have been many — but none have had a discernible impact on human behavior or government policy. Some climate scientists believe we can accommodate an atmosphere with concentrations of carbon dioxide that are twice the levels of the preindustrial era — about five hundred and fifty parts per million. Others have long claimed that global warming would become dangerous when atmospheric concentrations of carbon rose above three hundred and fifty parts per million. We passed that number years ago. After a decline in 2009, which coincided with the harsh global recession, carbon emissions soared by six per cent in 2010 — the largest increase ever recorded. On average, in the past decade, fossil-fuel emissions grew at about three times the rate of growth in the nineteen-nineties.

Although the I.P.C.C., along with scores of other scientific bodies, has declared that the warming of the earth is unequivocal, few countries have demonstrated the political will required to act — perhaps least of all the United States, which consumes more energy than any nation other than China, and, last year, more than it ever had before. The Obama Administration has failed to pass any meaningful climate legislation. Mitt Romney, the presumptive Republican nominee, has yet to settle on a clear position. Last year, he said he believed the world was getting warmer — and humans were a cause. By October, he had retreated. "My view is that we don't know what is causing climate change on this planet," he said, adding that spending huge sums to try to reduce CO_2 emissions "is not the right course for us." China, which became the world's largest emitter of greenhouse gases several years ago, constructs a new coal-burning power plant nearly every week. With each passing year, goals become exponentially harder to reach, and global reductions along the lines suggested by the I.P.C.C. seem more like a "pious wish," to use the words of the Dutch chemist Paul Crutzen, who in 1995 received a Nobel Prize for his work on ozone depletion.

"Most nations now recognize the need to shift to a low-carbon economy, and nothing should divert us from the main priority of reducing global greenhouse gas emissions," Lord Rees of Ludlow wrote in his 2009 forward to a highly influential report on geoengineering released by the Royal Society, Britain's national academy of sciences. "But if such reductions achieve too little, too late, there will surely be pressure to consider a 'plan B' — to seek ways to counteract climatic effects of green-house gas emissions."

While that pressure is building rapidly, some climate activists oppose even holding discussions about a possible Plan B, arguing, as the Norfolk protesters did in September, that it would be perceived as indirect permission to abandon serious efforts to cut emissions. Many people see geoengineering as a false solution to an existential crisis — akin to encouraging a heart-attack patient to avoid exercise and continue to gobble fatty food while simply doubling his dose of Lipitor. "The scientist's focus on tinkering with our entire planetary system is not a dynamic new technological and scientific frontier, but an expression of political despair," Doug Parr, the chief scientist at Greenpeace UK, has written.

During the 1974 Mideast oil crisis, the American engineer Hewitt Crane, then working at S.R.I. International, realized that standard measurements for sources of energy—barrels of oil, tons of coal, gallons of gas, British thermal units—were nearly impossible to compare. At a time when these commodities were being rationed, Crane wondered how people could conserve resources if they couldn't even measure them. The world was burning through twenty-three thousand gallons of oil every second. It was an astonishing figure, but one that Crane had trouble placing into any useful context.

Crane devised a new measure of energy consumption: a three-dimensional unit he called a cubic mile of oil. One cubic mile of oil would fill a pool that was a mile long, a mile wide, and a mile deep. Today, it takes three cubic miles' worth of fossil fuels to power the world for a year. That's a trillion gallons of gas. To replace just one of those cubic miles with a source of energy that will not add carbon dioxide to the atmosphere—nuclear power, for instance—would require the construction of a new atomic plant every week for fifty years; to switch to wind power would mean erecting thousands of windmills each month. It is hard to conceive of a way to replace that much energy with less dramatic alternatives. It is also impossible to talk seriously about climate change without talking about economic development. Climate experts have argued that we ought to stop emitting greenhouse gases within fifty years, but by then the demand for energy could easily be three times what it is today: nine cubic miles of oil.

The planet is getting richer as well as more crowded, and the pressure to produce more energy will become acute long before the end of the century. Predilections of the rich world—constant travel, industrial activity, increasing reliance on meat for protein—require enormous physical resources. Yet many people still hope to solve the problem of climate change just by eliminating greenhouse-gas emissions. "When people talk about bringing emissions to zero, they are talking about something that will never happen," Ken Caldeira told me. "Because that would require a complete alteration in the way humans are built."

Caldeira began researching geoengineering almost by accident. For much of his career, he has focussed on the implications of ocean acidification. During the nineteen-nineties, he spent a year in the Soviet Union, at the Leningrad lab of Mikhail Budyko, who is considered the founder of physical climatology. It was Budyko, in the nineteen-sixties, who first suggested cooling the earth by putting sulfur particles in the sky.

"In the nineteen-nineties, when I was working at Livermore, we had a meeting in Aspen to discuss the scale of the energy-system transformation needed in order to address the climate problem," Caldeira said. "Among the people who attended was Lowell Wood, a protégé of Edward Teller. Wood is a brilliant but sometimes erratic man . . . lots of ideas, some better than others." At Aspen, Wood delivered a talk on geoengineering. In the presentation, he explained, as he has many times since, that shielding the earth properly could deflect one or two per cent of the sunlight that reaches the atmosphere. That, he said, would be all it would take to counter the worst effects of warming.

David Keith was in the audience with Caldeira that day in Aspen. Keith now splits his time between Harvard and Calgary, where he runs Carbon Engineering, a company that is developing new technology to capture CO_2 from the atmosphere—at a cost that he believes would make it sensible to do so. At the time, though, both men considered Wood's idea ridiculous. "We said this will never happen," Caldeira recalled. "We were so certain Wood was nuts, because we assumed you can change the global mean temperature, but you will still get seasonal and regional patterns you can't correct. We were in the back of the room, and neither of us could believe it."

Caldeira decided to prove his point by running a computer simulation of Wood's approach. Scenarios for future climate change are almost always developed using powerful three-dimensional models of the earth and its atmosphere. They tend to be most accurate when estimating large numbers, like average global temperatures. Local and regional weather patterns are more difficult to predict, as anyone who has relied on a five-day weather forecast can understand. Still, in 1998 Caldeira tested the idea, and, "much to my surprise, it seemed to work and work well," he told me. It turned out that reducing sunlight offset the effect of CO_2 both regionally and seasonally. Since then, his results have been confirmed by several other groups.

Recently, Caldeira and colleagues at Carnegie and Stanford set out to examine whether the techniques of solar-radiation management would disrupt the sensitive agricultural balance on which the earth depends. Using two models, they simulated climates with carbon-dioxide levels similar to those which exist today. They then doubled those concentrations to reflect levels that would be likely in several decades if current trends continue unabated. Finally, in a third set of simulations, they doubled the CO_2 in the atmosphere, but added a layer of sulfate aerosols to the stratosphere, which would deflect about two per cent of incoming sunlight from the earth. The data were then applied to crop models that are commonly used to project future yields. Again, the results were unexpected.

Farm productivity, on average, went up. The models suggested that precipitation would increase in the northern and middle latitudes, and crop yields would grow. In the tropics, though, the results were significantly different. There heat stress would increase, and yields would decline. "Climate change is not so much a reduction in productivity as a redistribution," Caldeira said. "And it is one in which the poorest people on earth get hit the hardest and the rich world benefits"—a phenomenon, he added, that is not new.

"I have two perspectives on what this might mean," he said. "One says: humans are like rats or cockroaches. We are already living from the equator to the Arctic Circle. The weather has already become .7 degrees warmer, and barely anyone has noticed or cares. And, yes, the coral reefs might become extinct, and people from the Seychelles might go hungry. But they have gone hungry in the past, and nobody cared. So basically we will live in our gated communities, and we will have our TV shows and Chicken McNuggets, and we will be O.K. The people who would suffer are the people who always suffer.

"There is another way to look at this, though," he said. "And that is to compare it to the subprime-mortgage crisis, where you saw that a few million bad mortgages led to a five-per-cent drop in gross domestic product throughout the world. Something that was a relatively small knock to the financial system led to a global crisis. And that could certainly be the case with climate change. But five per cent is an interesting figure, because in the Stern Report"—an often cited review led by the British economist Nicholas Stern, which signalled the alarm about greenhouse-gas emissions by focussing on economics—"they estimated climate change would cost the world five per cent of its G.D.P. Most economists say that solving this problem is one or two per cent of G.D.P. The Clean Water and Clean Air Acts each cost about one per cent of G.D.P.," Caldeira continued. "We just had a much worse shock to our banking system. And it didn't even get us to reform the economy in any significant way. So why is the threat of a five-per-cent hit from climate change going to get us to transform the energy system?"

Solar-radiation management, which most reports have agreed is technologically feasible, would provide, at best, a temporary solution to rapid warming—a treatment but not a cure. There are only two ways to genuinely solve the problem: by drastically reducing emissions or by removing the CO_2 from the atmosphere. Trees do that every day. They "capture" carbon dioxide in their leaves, metabolize it in the branch system, and store it in their roots. But to do so on a global scale would require turning trillions of tons of greenhouse-gas emissions into a substance that could be stored cheaply and easily underground or in ocean beds.

Until recently, the costs of removing carbon from the atmosphere on that scale have been regarded by economists as prohibitive. CO_2 needs to be heated in order to be separated out; using current technology, the expense would rival that of creating an entirely new energy system. Typically, power plants release CO_2 into the atmosphere through exhaust systems referred to as flues. The most efficient way we have now to capture CO_2 is to remove it from flue gas as the emissions escape. Over the past five years, several research groups—one of which includes David Keith's company, Carbon Engineering, in Calgary—have developed new techniques to extract carbon from the atmosphere, at costs that may make it economically feasible on a larger scale.

Early this winter, I visited a demonstration project on the campus of S.R.I. International, the Menlo Park institution that is a combination think tank and technological incubator. The project, built by Global Thermostat, looked like a very high-tech elevator or an awfully expensive math problem. "When I called chemical engineers and said I want to do this on a planetary scale, they laughed," Peter Eisenberger, Global Thermostat's president, told me. In 1996, Eisenberger was appointed the founding director of the Earth Institute, at Columbia University, where he remains a professor of earth and environmental sciences. Before that, he spent a decade running the materials research institute at Princeton University, and nearly as much time at Exxon, in charge of research and development. He believes he has developed a system to capture CO_2 from the atmosphere at low heat and potentially at low cost.

The trial project is essentially a five-story brick edifice specially constructed to function like a honeycomb. Global Thermostat coats the bricks with chemicals called amines to draw CO_2 from the air and bind with it. The carbon dioxide is then separated with a proprietary method that uses low-temperature heat—something readily available for free, since it is a waste product of many power plants. "Using low-temperature heat changes the equation," Eisenberger said. He is an excitable man with the enthusiasm of a graduate student and the manic gestures of an orchestra conductor. He went on to explain that the amine coating on the bricks binds the CO_2 at the molecular level, and the amount it can capture depends on the surface area; honeycombs provide the most surface space possible per square metre.

There are two groups of honey-combs that sit on top of each other. As Eisenberger pointed out, "You can only absorb so much CO_2 at once, so when the honeycomb is full it drops into a lower section." Steam heats and releases the CO_2—and the honeycomb rises again. (Currently, carbon dioxide is used commercially in carbonated beverages, brewing, and pneumatic drying systems for packaged food. It is also used in welding. Eisenberger argues that, ideally, carbon waste would be recycled to create an industrial form of photosynthesis, which would help reduce our dependence on fossil fuels.)

Unlike some other scientists engaged in geoengineering, Eisenberger is not bothered by the notion of tinkering with nature. "We have devised a system that introduces no additional threats into the environment," he told me. "And the idea of interfering with benign nature is ridiculous. The Bambi view of nature is totally false. Nature is violent, amoral, and nihilistic. If you look at the history of this planet, you will see cycles of creation and destruction that would offend our morality as human beings. But somehow, because it's 'nature,' it's supposed to be fine." Eisenberger founded and runs Global Thermostat with Graciela Chichilnisky, an Argentine economist who wrote the plan, adopted in 2005, for the international carbon market that emerged from the Kyoto Climate talks. Edgar Bronfman, Jr., an heir to the Seagram fortune, is Global Thermostat's biggest investor. (The company is one of the finalists for Richard Branson's Virgin Earth Challenge prize. In 2007, Branson offered a cash prize of twenty-five million dollars to anyone who could devise a process that would drain large quantities of greenhouse gases from the atmosphere.)

"What is fascinating for me is the way the innovation process has changed," Eisenberger said. "In the past, somebody would make a discovery in a laboratory and say, 'What can I do with this?' And now we ask, 'What do we want to design?,' because we believe there is powerful enough knowledge to do it. That is what my partner and I did." The pilot, which began running last year, works on a very small scale, capturing about seven hundred tons of CO_2 a year. (By comparison, an automobile puts out about six tons a year.) Eisenberger says that it is important to remember that it took more than a century to assemble the current energy system: coal and gas plants, factories, and the worldwide transportation network that has been responsible for depositing trillions of tons of CO_2 into the atmosphere. "We are not going to get it all out of the atmosphere in twenty years," he said. "It will take at least thirty years to do this, but if we start now that is plenty of time. You would just need a source of low-temperature heat—factories anywhere in the world are ideal." He envisions a network of twenty thousand such devices scattered across the planet. Each would cost about a hundred million dollars—a two-trillion-dollar investment spread out over three decades.

"There is a strong history of the system refusing to accept something new," Eisenberger said. "People say I am nuts. But it would be surprising if people didn't call me crazy. Look at the history of innovation! If people don't call you nuts, then you are doing something wrong."

After leaving Eisenberger's demonstration project, I spoke with Curtis Carlson, who, for more than a decade, has been the chairman and chief executive officer of S.R.I. and a leading voice on the future of American innovation. "These geoengineering methods will not be implemented for decades—or ever," he said. Nonetheless, scientists worry that if methane emissions from the Arctic increase as rapidly as some of the data now suggest, climate intervention isn't going to be an option. It's going to be a requirement. "When and where do we have the serious discussion about how to intervene?" Carlson asked. "There are no agreed-upon rules or criteria. There isn't even a body that could create the rules."

Over the past three years, a series of increasingly urgent reports—from the Royal Society, in the U.K., the Washington-based Bipartisan Policy Center, and the Government Accountability Office, among other places—have practically begged decision-makers to begin planning for a world in which geoengineering might be their only recourse. As one recent study from the Wilson International Center for Scholars concluded, "At the very least, we need to learn what approaches to avoid even if desperate."

The most environmentally sound approach to geoengineering is the least palatable politically. "If it becomes necessary to ring the planet with sulfates, why would you do that all at once?" Ken Caldeira asked. "If the total amount of climate change that occurs could be neutralized by one Mt. Pinatubo, then doesn't it make sense to add one per cent this year, two per cent next year, and three per cent the year after that?" he said. "Ramp it up slowly, throughout the century, and that way we can monitor what is happening. If we see something at one per cent that seems dangerous, we can easily dial it back. But who is going to do that when we don't have a visible crisis? Which politician in which country?"

Unfortunately, the least risky approach politically is also the most dangerous: do nothing until the world is faced with a cataclysm and then slip into a frenzied crisis mode. The political implications of any such action would be impossible to overstate. What would happen, for example, if one country decided to embark on such a program without the agreement of other countries? Or if industrialized nations agreed to inject sulfur particles into the stratosphere and accidentally set off a climate emergency that caused drought in China, India, or Africa?

"Let's say the Chinese government decides their monsoon strength, upon which hundreds of millions of people rely for sustenance, is weakening," Caldeira said. "They have reason to believe that making clouds right near the ocean might help, and they started to do that, and the Indians found out and believed—justifiably or not—that it would make their monsoon worse. What happens then? Where do we go to discuss that? We have no mechanism to settle that dispute."

Most estimates suggest that it could cost a few billion dollars a year to scatter enough sulfur particles in the atmosphere to change the weather patterns of the planet. At that price, any country, most groups, and even some individuals could afford to do it. The technology is open and available—and that makes it more like the Internet than like a national weapons program. The basic principles are widely published; the intellectual property behind nearly every technique lies in the public domain. If the Maldives wanted to send airplanes into the stratosphere to scatter sulfates, who could stop them?

"The odd thing here is that this is a democratizing technology," Nathan Myhrvold told me. "Rich, powerful countries might have invented much of it, but it will be there for anyone to use. People get themselves all balled up into knots over whether this can be done unilaterally or by one group or one nation. Well, guess what. We decide to do much worse than this every day, and we decide unilaterally. We are polluting the earth unilaterally. Whether it's life-taking decisions, like wars, or something like a trade embargo, the world is about people taking action, not agreeing to take action. . . .

Notes and Questions

1. The concept of geoengineering is still reaching fresh ears, though many have been researching the options for years. As articles like those above appear in popular sources, awareness increases, and we see widely diverging opinions form. Some are excited about the prospect of taking control of the climate, potentially averting catastrophe. Others are very concerned about the danger of tinkering with something so massive as our entire planet, risking even more immediate catastrophe. Of course, the actions categorized as geoengineering vary widely in both risk and effectiveness, so one cannot view them all equally. Where do you stand? Should we proceed with certain forms of geoengineering, or table the concept entirely and focus on GHG mitigation instead? Does engaging in geoengineering also create the risk of reducing political pressure to reduce GHG emissions? Is it worth it?

2. Given the extreme risks and potential benefits of geoengineering, who should be in charge of it? Governments? What if private parties with enormous personal resources decide to engage in geoengineering projects? (This has actually happened.) Should they be allowed to do so? Are they as likely to take your interests into account as government policymakers? How should this potential be regulated? How can it be enforced?

Practice Problem

Friendbook, a social networking application with more than 750 million members worldwide, is looking for a site to construct the largest data center in the world. After considering a number of sites around the world, Friendbook settles upon the beautiful Olivia Valley in the State of Montarado, on the eastern slope of the Rocky

Mountains. Friendbook is attracted to Montarado by the abundant sunshine, low traffic, cheap land prices, and ready workforce. State officials in Montarado are delighted with being selected by Friendbook, as the data center promises to create up to 340 jobs upon opening, with possible expansions down the road.

Given the intended size of the data center, energy and water needs will be significant. Specifically, upon initial operation, the data center may require more than 140 megawatts and 1.8 million gallons of water daily. Energy needs in the Olivia Valley are currently met primarily by coal-fired power plants, with abundant coal resources available in the local area. Water for drinking, agriculture, and industrial uses is largely supplied by the Olivia River, which flows out of snow-capped peaks in the adjacent Rocky Mountains. Computer modeling indicates that the environment of the Olivia Valley will get hotter in the next 25 years, with possibly interrupted flows of water in the Olivia River due to lighter winter snows and thinner snowpack.

You are staff counsel to the Olivia Valley Planning Commission (OVPC). Under state law, the OVPC is charged with ensuring efficient and productive uses of the Olivia River water and with mediating disputes among water users.

1. As staff counsel to the OVPC, your job includes reviewing proposals for developments that may require new allocations of water from the Olivia River. One factor in reviewing proposals for new water allocation is whether and to what extent the proposal allows for adaptation to climate change over the next 25 years. Given the information above, identify questions you may want to ask Friendbook in order to determine whether the data center proposal appears well-adapted to the changing climate.

2. As staff counsel to the OVPC, in addition to water allocation, you are also concerned about energy uses that may contribute to climate change and the continued warming of this semi-arid environment. What questions may you want to ask Friendbook to address this issue?

Chapter 7

Protecting Our Nation's Waters:
The Clean Water Act

I. Introduction

The regulation of water pollution in the United States is largely subject to one federal statute commonly known as the Clean Water Act, 33 U.S.C. § 1251 *et seq.*, Pub. L. 92-500. Like other federal statutes we will explore in this book, the Clean Water Act adopts a framework of cooperative federalism, with states and other delegated authorities carrying out most water pollution control programs in the United States, subject to federal oversight.

This framework has resulted in a number of successes. In the decades leading up to passage of the modern Clean Water Act in 1972, water quality had become severely diminished in many places with the postwar expansion of urban and industrial development. After the passage and implementation of the Clean Water Act, water quality in most places around the country began to improve, in many cases dramatically. In the first 14 years after the Clean Water Act, pollutant discharges from municipal treatment plants dropped more than 90 percent. Within 40 years, the percentage of assessed U.S. water bodies meeting national standards for "fish/swimmable" water quality more than doubled, while at the same time the population of the U.S. grew by 52% and Gross Domestic Product per capita more than doubled. Today, rivers that once caught fire or resembled open sewers have become centerpieces of urban renewal and economic redevelopment. Even so, much work remains in order to maintain the gains achieved in water quality and to address some serious problems of water pollution that persist in the United States. As we will see, many of these problems today no longer involve direct discharges from industrial facilities, but runoff from croplands, construction sites, forestry operations, livestock areas, and urban streets. These continuing challenges imply continuing needs for regulation and innovation.

This chapter provides an introduction and overview of the Clean Water Act, its major programs and regulatory frameworks, in order to help students prepare for a law practice where impacts to waters of the United States may be implicated. Before diving into the Clean Water Act directly, however, we will first take a look at efforts to control water pollution that preceded the modern Clean Water Act, including applications of private litigation under common law.

II. Private Litigation

For almost the first two centuries of our nation's history, the waters of the United States were treated as convenient means for waste disposal. Agriculture, manufacturing, mining, municipalities, and other sectors withdrew water from rivers, lakes, and other water bodies, but also used those same water bodies to carry away their wastes. As a result, water pollution became pervasive in the United States, causing adverse impacts on lives and livelihoods and spawning claims for damages. Plaintiffs in these cases recorded some noted successes. *See, e.g., Springer v. Joseph Schlitz Brewing Company,* 510 F.2d 468 (4th Cir. 1975) (brewery not immune from liability to injured downstream riparian owner where brewery knew or should have known that discharges to city sewage treatment plant would exceed treatment plant capacity); *Landers v. East Texas Salt Water Disposal Co.,* 248 S.W.2d 731 (1952) (joint and several liability available against oil company and pipeline owner responsible for discharge of oil and salt water that polluted plaintiff's private lake and killed his fish); *Parker v. American Woolen Co.,* 195 Mass. 591 (1907) (upstream paper mill enjoined from discharging pollutants into a brook in order to protect plaintiff's downstream property); *Suffolk Gold Mining & Milling Co. v. San Miguel Mining & Milling Co.,* 9 Colo. App. 407 (1897) (upstream mining company must impound its polluted discharge to keep residual flow fit for desired uses of downstream plaintiffs). In other cases, however, courts allowed polluters to continue polluting. *See, e.g., Luama v. Bunker Hill & Sullivan Mining and Concentrating Co.,* 41 F.2d 358 (1930) (upstream mining company's pollution easement defeated claims by downstream farmer for injury to farmland and livestock).

As you read the following case, consider both the outcome obtained and the time and effort needed to achieve that outcome.

Middlesex County Sewerage Authority v. National Sea Clammers Ass'n

453 U.S. 1 (1981)

Justice POWELL:

In these cases, involving alleged damage to fishing grounds caused by discharges and ocean dumping of sewage and other waste, we are faced with questions concerning the availability of a damages remedy, based either on federal common law or on the provisions of two Acts—the Federal Water Pollution Control Act (FWPCA), 86 Stat. 816, as amended, 33 U.S.C. § 1251 *et seq.* [aka the Clean Water Act], and the Marine Protection, Research, and Sanctuaries Act of 1972 (MPRSA), 86 Stat. 1052, as amended, 33 U.S.C. § 1401 *et seq.*.

FACTS

Respondents are an organization whose members harvest fish and shellfish off the coast of New York and New Jersey, and one individual member of that organization. In 1977, they brought suit in the United States District Court for the District of New Jersey against petitioners—various governmental entities and officials from New York, New Jersey, and the Federal Government. Their complaint alleged that sewage, sewage "sludge," and other waste materials were being discharged into New York Harbor

Nat'l Sea
Clammers arguments—

and the Hudson River by some of the petitioners. In addition it complained of the dumping of such materials directly into the ocean from maritime vessels. The complaint alleged that, as a result of these activities, the Atlantic Ocean was becoming polluted, and it made special reference to a massive growth of algae said to have appeared offshore in 1976. It then stated that this pollution was causing the "collapse of the fishing, clamming and lobster industries which operate in the waters of the Atlantic Ocean."

Invoking a wide variety of legal theories, respondents sought injunctive and declaratory relief, $250 million in compensatory damages, and $250 million in punitive damages. The District Court granted summary judgment to petitioners on all counts of the complaint.

Nat'l Sea Clammers seek injunctive relief

In holdings relevant here, the District Court rejected respondents' nuisance claim under federal common law, see *Illinois v. Milwaukee*, 406 U.S. 91 (1972), on the ground that such a cause of action is not available to private parties. With respect to the claims based on alleged violations of the FWPCA, the court noted that respondents had failed to comply with the 60-day notice requirement of the "citizen suit" provision in § 505(b)(1)(A) of the Act. This provision allows suits under the Act by private citizens, but authorizes only prospective relief, and the citizen plaintiffs first must give notice to the EPA, the State, and any alleged violator. *Ibid.* Because respondents did not give the requisite notice, the court refused to allow them to proceed with a claim under the Act independent of the citizen-suit provision and based on the general jurisdictional grant in 28 U.S.C. § 1331. The court applied the same analysis to respondents' claims under the MPRSA, which contains similar citizen-suit and notice provisions. 33 U.S.C. § 1415(g). Finally, the court rejected a possible claim of maritime tort, both because respondents had failed to plead such claim explicitly and because they had failed to comply with the procedural requirements of the federal and state Tort Claims Acts.

USDC decision

The United States Court of Appeals for the Third Circuit reversed as to the claims based on the FWPCA, the MPRSA, the federal common law of nuisance, and maritime tort. With respect to the FWPCA, the court held that failure to comply with the 60-day notice provision in § 505(b)(1)(A), does not preclude suits under the Act in addition to the specific "citizen suits" authorized in § 505. It based this conclusion on the saving clause in § 505(e), preserving "any right which any person (or class of persons) may have under any statute or common law to seek enforcement of any effluent standard or limitation or to seek any other relief." The Court of Appeals then went on to apply our precedents in the area of implied statutory rights of action, and concluded that "Congress intended to permit the federal courts to entertain a private cause of action implied from the terms of the [FWPCA], preserved by the savings clause of the Act, on behalf of individuals or groups of individuals who have been or will be injured by pollution in violation of its terms."

Court of Appeals reversal of USDC

The court then applied this same analysis to the MPRSA, concluding again that the District Court had erred in dismissing respondents' claims under this Act. Although the court was not explicit on this question, it apparently concluded that suits for *damages*, as well as for injunctive relief, could be brought under the FWPCA and the MPRSA.

With respect to the federal common-law nuisance claims, the Court of Appeals rejected the District Court's conclusion that private parties may not bring such claims. It also held, applying common-law principles, that respondents "alleged sufficient individual damage to permit them to recover damages for this essentially public nuisance."

Petitions for a writ of certiorari raising a variety of arguments were filed in this Court. . . . We granted these petitions, limiting review to three questions: (i) whether FWPCA and MPRSA imply a private right of action independent of their citizen-suit provisions, (ii) whether all federal common-law nuisance actions concerning ocean pollution now are pre-empted by the legislative scheme contained in the FWPCA and the MPRSA, and (iii) if not, whether a private citizen has standing to sue for damages under the federal common law of nuisance. We hold that there is no implied right of action under these statutes and that the federal common law of nuisance has been fully pre-empted in the area of ocean pollution.

The Federal Water Pollution Control Act was first enacted in 1948. Act of June 30, 1948, 62 Stat. 1155. It emphasized state enforcement of water quality standards. When this legislation proved ineffective, Congress passed the Federal Water Pollution Control Act Amendments of 1972, Pub. L. 92–500, 86 Stat. 816, 33 U.S.C. § 1251 *et seq.* [aka Clean Water Act]. The Amendments shifted the emphasis to "direct restrictions on discharges," *EPA v. California ex rel. State Water Resources Control Board*, 426 U.S. 200, 204 (1976), and made it "unlawful for any person to discharge a pollutant without obtaining a permit and complying with its terms," *id.*, at 205. While still allowing for state administration and enforcement under federally approved state plans, §§ 402(b), (c), the Amendments created various federal minimum effluent standards, §§ 301–307.

The Marine Protection, Research, and Sanctuaries Act of 1972, Pub. L. 92–532, 86 Stat. 1052, sought to create comprehensive federal regulation of the dumping of materials into ocean waters near the United States coastline. Section 101(a) of the Act requires a permit for any dumping into ocean waters, when the material is transported from the United States or on an American vessel or aircraft. In addition, it requires a permit for the dumping of material transported from outside the United States into the territorial seas or in the zone extending 12 miles from the coastline, "to the extent that it may affect the territorial sea or the territory of the United States."

The exact nature of respondents' claims under these two Acts is not clear, but the claims appear to fall into two categories. The main contention is that the EPA and the Army Corps of Engineers have permitted the New Jersey and New York defendants to discharge and dump pollutants in amounts that are not permitted by the Acts. In addition, they seem to allege that the New York and New Jersey defendants have violated the terms of their permits. The question before us is whether respondents may raise either of these claims in a private suit for injunctive and monetary relief, where such a suit is not expressly authorized by either of these Acts . . . .

These Acts contain unusually elaborate enforcement provisions, conferring authority to sue for this purpose both on government officials and private citizens. The FWPCA, for example, authorizes the EPA Administrator to respond to violations of the Act with compliance orders and civil suits. § 309. He may seek a civil penalty of up to $10,000 per day, § 309(d), and criminal penalties also are available, § 309(c). States desiring to administer their own permit programs must demonstrate that state officials possess adequate authority to abate violations through civil or criminal penalties or other means of enforcement. § 402(b)(7). In addition, under § 509(b), "any interested person" may seek judicial review in the United States courts of appeals of various particular actions by the Administrator, including establishment of effluent standards and issuance of permits for discharge of pollutants. Where review could have been obtained under this provision, the action at issue may not be challenged in any subsequent civil or criminal proceeding for enforcement.

These enforcement mechanisms, most of which have their counterpart under the MPRSA, are supplemented by the express citizen-suit provisions in § 505(a) of the FWPCA, and § 105(g) of the MPRSA. These citizen-suit provisions authorize private persons to sue for injunctions to enforce these statutes. Plaintiffs invoking these provisions first must comply with specified procedures — which respondents here ignored — including in most cases 60 days' prior notice to potential defendants.

In view of these elaborate enforcement provisions it cannot be assumed that Congress intended to authorize by implication additional judicial remedies for private citizens suing under MPRSA and FWPCA. As we stated in *Transamerica Mortgage Advisors, supra,* "it is an elemental canon of statutory construction that where a statute expressly provides a particular remedy or remedies, a court must be chary of reading others into it." 444 U.S., at 19. In the absence of strong indicia of a contrary congressional intent, we are compelled to conclude that Congress provided precisely the remedies it considered appropriate.

As noted above, the Court of Appeals avoided this inference. Discussing the FWPCA, it held that the existence of a citizen-suit provision in § 505(a) does not rule out implied forms of private enforcement of the Act. It arrived at this conclusion by asserting that Congress intended in § 505(a) to create a limited cause of action for "private attorneys general" — "non-injured member[s] of the public" suing to promote the general welfare rather than to redress an injury to their own welfare. It went on to conclude:

> "A private party who is *injured* by the alleged violation, as these plaintiffs allege they were, has an alternate basis for suit under section 505(e), and the general federal question jurisdiction of the Judicial Code, 28 U.S.C. § 1331 (1976). Section 505(e) is a savings clause that preserves all rights to enforce the Act or seek relief against the Administrator. Coupled with the general federal question jurisdiction it permits this suit to be brought by these parties." *Ibid.* (footnotes omitted) (emphasis added).

There are at least three problems with this reasoning. First, the language of the saving clause on which the Court of Appeals relied, is quite ambiguous

SC disagrees w/ Court of Appeals for 3 reasons

concerning the intent of Congress to "preserve" remedies under the FWPCA itself. It merely states that nothing in the citizen-suit provision "shall restrict any right which any person . . . may have under any statute or common law to seek enforcement of any effluent standard or limitation or to seek any other relief." It is doubtful that the phrase "any statute" includes the very statute in which this statement was contained.

Moreover, the reasoning on which the Court of Appeals relied is flawed for another reason. It draws a distinction between "non-injured" plaintiffs who may bring citizen suits to enforce provisions of these Acts, and the "injured" plaintiffs in this litigation who claim a right to sue under the Acts, not by virtue of the citizen-suit provisions, but rather under the language of the saving clauses. In fact, it is clear that the citizen-suit provisions apply only to persons who can claim some sort of injury and there is, therefore, no reason to infer the existence of a separate right of action for "injured" plaintiffs . . . .

Finally, the Court of Appeals failed to take account of the rest of the enforcement scheme expressly provided by Congress—including the opportunity for "any interested person" to seek judicial review of a number of EPA actions within 90 days, § 509(b).

The Court of Appeals also applied its reasoning to the MPRSA. But here again we are persuaded that Congress evidenced no intent to authorize by implication private remedies under these Acts apart from the expressly authorized citizen suits . . . .

In *Cort v. Ash*, 422 U.S. 66, 78 (1975), the Court identified several factors that are relevant to the question of implied private remedies. These include the legislative history. See *ibid.* ("Second, is there any indication of legislative intent, explicit or implicit, either to create such a remedy or to deny one?") This history does not lead to a contrary conclusion with respect to implied remedies under either Act. Indeed, the Reports and debates provide affirmative support for the view that Congress intended the limitations imposed on citizen suits to apply to all private suits under these Acts. Thus, both the structure of the Acts and their legislative history lead us to conclude that Congress intended that private remedies in addition to those expressly provided should not be implied. Where, as here, Congress has made clear that implied private actions are not contemplated, the courts are not authorized to ignore this legislative judgment . . . .

We therefore must dismiss the federal common-law claims because their underlying legal basis is now pre-empted by statute. As discussed above, we also dismiss the claims under the MPRSA and the FWPCA because respondents lack a right of action under those statutes. We vacate the judgment below with respect to these two claims, and remand for further proceedings.

[The opinion of Justice STEVENS, concurring in the judgment in part and dissenting in part, has been omitted.]

Notes and Questions

1. After the Supreme Court's decision in *National Sea Clammers* (1981), what potential remedies remain available to private plaintiffs under common law? For one influential argument endorsing the continued use of common law claims in the era of citizen suits under the Clean Water Act and under statutes, see Michael D. Axline, *The Limits of Statutory Law and the Wisdom of Common Law*, 28 ENVTL. L. REP. NEWS & ANALYSIS 10268 (April 2008).

2. A Problem Concerning Drinking Water. The Clean Water Act, as you will see fully later in this chapter, seeks primarily to protect the quality of *surface* waters, such as lakes and rivers, making them suitable for such uses as fish habitat ("fishable") and recreation ("swimmable"). The Clean Water Act does *not* focus on making water safe for human consumption. This important concern is governed by a separate federal statute: the Safe Drinking Water Act (SDWA), 42 U.S.C. § 300f *et seq.*, which, among other requirements, call for EPA to establish national standards for contaminants that may cause adverse public health effects. *See* National Primary Drinking Water Regulations at 40 C.F.R. Part 141. In the recent health crisis in Flint, Michigan, where tens of thousands of residents were served drinking water with toxic levels of lead contamination caused by old pipes and corrosive water, Judge O'Meara of the Federal District Court, Eastern District of Michigan, dismissed for lack of subject matter jurisdiction a class action complaint filed by Flint residents seeking compensatory damages due to the consumption of toxic drinking water. *See Bolder v. Early,* Case No. 16-10323, E.D. Mich., South. Div., April 19, 2016. Several of their causes of action alleged violations of 42 U.S.C. § 1983, also known as the Civil Rights Act of 1871, for substantive due process violations of bodily integrity and property. Judge O'Meara used *Middlesex v. National Sea Clammers* to avoid ruling on the merits, stating that because the circumstances of the case fall under the Safe Drinking Water Act, all remedies must be sought within its "comprehensive" remedial scheme. *Id.* Unfortunately for the plaintiffs in Flint, the SDWA does not provide for compensatory damages in citizen suits, only injunctive relief, penalties paid to the U.S. Treasury, and attorney fees.

However, the SDWA, like other environmental statutes, includes a saving clause preserving causes of action outside of the code itself. 42 U.S.C. § 300j-8(e). In a dissenting opinion in *National Sea Clammers,* Justice Stevens points out that "express statutory language or clear references in the legislative history will rebut whatever presumption of exclusivity arises from comprehensive remedial provisions [. . . and here . . .] the statutory language and legislative history reveal [. . .] a clear congressional mandate to preserve all existing remedies, including a private right of action under § 1983." *National Sea Clammers* at 28. Compare the majority and dissenting opinions. Contrast *National Sea Clammers* with the Supreme Court rulings in *Exxon Shipping Co. v. Baker,* 554 U.S. 471 (2008) and *Fitzgerald v. Barnstable School Committee,* 555 U.S. 246 (2009). What arguments could be made by citizens of Flint to distinguish their case from *National Sea Clammers*? Given the potential broader implications of *National Sea Clammers* in areas such as climate change and environmental justice, consider other options for ensuring access to justice for the communities disproportionately impacted by water pollution.[1]

III. Evolution of the Clean Water Act

For the first century of U.S. history, water pollution was subject to little or no government regulation. One of the first pieces of federal legislation to address the problems of water pollution was the Rivers and Harbors Act of 1899, 33 U.S.C. § 403 *et seq.*, and in particular a section still known today as the Refuse Act, 33 U.S.C. § 407, which generally prohibits the dumping of any "refuse matter" into the waterways of the United States. However, the primary concern of the Rivers and Harbors Act was the protection of navigation from floating obstructions rather than the protection of water quality.

Threats to the purity of water, if considered at all, were regarded almost exclusively as matters for state or local authorities. This perspective was reflected in the Water Pollution Act of 1948, one of the federal government's first efforts to address the problems of water pollution nationwide, which provided, among other things, "[I]t is hereby declared to be a policy of Congress to recognize, preserve, and protect the primary responsibilities and rights of the states in controlling water pollution." Act of June 30, 1948, Ch. 758, 62 Stat. 1155 (1948). Consistent with this policy, Congress hoped that, with federal support, local programs would be able to handle pollution problems effectively. Thus, the 1948 Water Pollution Act allowed only a narrow federal role in enforcement, authorizing federal courts to grant relief from pollution after considering the feasibility of abatement. The 1948 statute, originally set to expire in five years, was reauthorized and extended through 1956, while at the same time, water pollution increased in the postwar industrial economy. In 1956, the Federal Water Pollution Control Act (FWPCA) reaffirmed the states' primary responsibility for water pollution control, authorizing grants to states and local agencies for purposes of water pollution research and training. The 1956 Act also authorized substantial annual appropriations to help states, cities, and other government agencies construct wastewater treatment systems.

The Water Quality Act of 1965 continued the construction grants program while maintaining the policy of Congress of deferring water pollution regulation to state and local agencies. The 1965 Act also required states to establish standards for water quality, subject to federal approval. However, many states were slow to establish these water quality standards; by 1972, only about one-third of states had adopted any such standards. Among the states that did adopt standards, there remained significant challenges and delays with enforcing them.

---

1. This problem was suggested by attorney Scott Badenoch, a member of the ABA Section of Environment, Energy, and Resources.

Perhaps the final momentum for comprehensive federal legislation to address water pollution came with the national attention captured when oil and industrial pollution fueled an infamous fire on the Cuyahoga River on June 22, 1969. In the next year, 1970, Congress passed the modern Clean Air Act and President Nixon by executive order created the United States Environmental Protection Agency (EPA). Two years later, in 1972, amendments to the Federal Water Pollution Control Act — later to become known universally as the Clean Water Act — established the fundamental framework for addressing water pollution in the United States that remains in place today. For a comprehensive history of efforts to promote water pollution control in the United States leading up to passage of the Clean Water Act in 1972, see William L. Andreen, *The Evolution of Water Pollution Control in the United States — State, Local, and Federal Efforts, 1792–1972: Part I*, 22 STANFORD ENVTL. L. J. 145 (2003), and *Part II*, 22 STANFORD ENVTL. L. J. 215 (2003).

The Clean Water Act in 1972 marked a significant departure in the water pollution control program in the United States. Whereas the early federal legislation implicitly allowed water pollution up to a standard of water quality set by states, the Clean Water Act in 1972 reversed the paradigm, presumptively banning the discharge of pollutants into surface waters, except as specifically authorized by permits from the government. *See* Clean Water Act § 301(a), 33 U.S.C. 1311(a). This paradigm shift supported ambitious goals for the Clean Water Act. In § 101 of the new statute, Congress declared it an objective to "restore and maintain the chemical, physical, and biological integrity of the Nation's waters." 33 U.S.C. § 1251(a). More specifically, Congress established a national "interim goal . . . for the protection and propagation of fish, shellfish, and wildlife and [providing] for recreation in and on the water be achieved by July 1, 1983." *Id.* § 1251(a)(2). Congress also declared rather ambitiously that "it is the national goal that the discharge of pollutants into the navigable waters be eliminated by 1985 . . . ." *Id.* § 1251(a)(1).

Needless to say, neither the "interim goal" for attaining the so-called "fishable/swimmable" standard by July 1, 1983, nor the "national goal" of eliminating the discharge of pollutants into the navigable waters by 1985, was achieved. This was probably not surprising to anyone, including the drafters of the statute, who at the same time as they expressed a goal of eliminating water pollution also created programs to allow water pollution. These permit programs include the ironically titled National Pollutant Discharge Elimination System (NPDES), established by CWA § 402, and the "dredge and fill" program, most often associated with wetlands protection, established by CWA § 404. Notwithstanding these programs for permitting water pollution, as noted above, substantial progress has been made toward meeting the ambitious goals of the Clean Water Act, and work toward these goals continues under programs established by the Clean Water Act, together with the CWA's subsequent amendments, implementing regulations, and delegated authorities.

Notes and Questions

1. Should zero discharge of pollutants into the navigable waters remain the "national goal" of the United States? What factors might argue for maintaining this national goal? What factors may legislate against it?

2. Note that the Clean Water Act, Safe Drinking Water Act, and Refuse Act each in some way place restrictions on water pollution. As you learn more in this chapter about water pollution control, consider the ways in which these three statutes may intersect, overlap, or complement each other. Is there also any way in which they may conflict?

3. Despite its title, the National Pollutant Discharge Elimination System (NPDES) specifically authorizes the continued discharge (not elimination) of pollutants. However, as we will see later in this chapter and Chapter 12 (Permitting), obtaining a permit to discharge pollutants under the NPDES program may or may not be a simple thing, as it may require years of sustained effort and trigger the application of other statutes, including NEPA and the Endangered Species Act.

4. Practice tip. Note that NPDES stands for the "National *Pollutant* Discharge Elimination System" (emphasis added). In your future law practice, note how often practicing attorneys (and even law professors) will erroneously identify NPDES as the "National *Pollution* Discharge Elimination System" (emphasis added). You will never make this amateur mistake now, will you?

IV. Clean Water Act Jurisdiction

At first glance, the basic elements for Clean Water Act jurisdiction appear fairly straightforward. The jurisdictional elements begin with CWA § 301(a), which provides, "Except as in compliance with this section and [other sections including §§ 402 and 404], the discharge of any pollutant by any person shall be unlawful." 33 U.S.C. § 1311(a). Section 502 then provides some key definitions. Most significantly, § 502 defines "discharge of a pollutant" to include "any addition of any pollutant to navigable waters from any point source . . . ." 33 U.S.C. § 1362(6). Pulling these provisions together gives us four key elements for CWA jurisdiction: (1) an *addition* (2) of a *pollutant* (3) from a *point source* (4) to *navigable waters*. After more than 40 years since passage of the Clean Water Act, and especially given definitions of *pollutant*, *point source*, and *navigable waters* provided in the statute itself, one might expect these four elements to be fairly resolved by now. Unfortunately, lawyers and judges continue to grapple with the meaning of these terms, with particular confusion over *navigable waters* engendered by relatively recent decisions of the U.S. Supreme Court. *See Solid Waste Agency of Northern Cook County v. United States Army Corps of Engineers*, 531 U.S. 159 (2001) ("*SWANCC*"); *Rapanos v. United States*, 547 U.S. 715 (2006). This section will attempt to clarify the meaning of these terms as much as possible, recognizing that the related law remains subject to continuing development.

A. Pollutant

To understand the meaning of "pollutant" under the Clean Water Act, we must begin, as usual, by reading the law, which provides the following statutory definition:

> The term "pollutant" means dredged spoil, solid waste, incinerator residue, sewage, garbage, sewage sludge, munitions, chemical wastes, biological materials, radioactive materials, heat, wrecked or discarded equipment, rock, sand, cellar dirt and industrial, municipal, and agricultural waste discharged into water. This term does not mean [exclusions related to sewage from vessels and well injections from oil and gas production].

CWA § 502(6), 33 U.S.C. § 1362(6). Including such broad terms as "rock," "garbage," and "chemical wastes," the definition of "pollutant" has been construed broadly by courts. *See, e.g., Sierra Club, Lone Star Chapter v. Cedar Point Oil Co.,* 73 F.3d 546, 565 (5th Cir. 1996), citing *Nat'l Wildlife Fed'n v. Gorsuch*, 693 F.2d 156, 173 n.52 (D.C. Cir. 1982) ("the breadth of many of the items in the list of 'pollutants' tends to eviscerate any restrictive effect"). However, the plain language of this definition is not always dispositive, as the following Supreme Court case determined soon after the CWA was passed in 1972.

Train v. Colorado Public Interest Research Group
426 U.S. 1 (1976)

Justice MARSHALL:

The issue in this case is whether the Environmental Protection Agency (EPA) has the authority under the Federal Water Pollution Control Act (FWPCA), as amended in 1972, to regulate the discharge into the Nation's waterways of nuclear waste materials subject to regulation by the Atomic Energy Commission (AEC) and its successors [now the Nuclear Regulatory Commission (NRC)] under the Atomic Energy Act of 1954 (AEA). 68 Stat. 919, as amended, 42 U.S.C. § 2011 et seq. In statutory terms, the question is whether these nuclear materials are "pollutants" within the meaning of the FWPCA.

Respondents are Colorado-based organizations and Colorado residents who claim potential harm from the discharge of radioactive effluents from two nuclear plants: the Fort St. Vrain Nuclear Generating Station and the Rocky Flats nuclear weapons components plant. These facilities are operated in conformity with radioactive effluent standards imposed by the AEC pursuant to the Atomic Energy Act. The dispute in this case arises because the EPA has disclaimed any authority under the FWPCA to set standards of its own to govern the discharge of radioactive materials subject to regulation under the AEA. Respondents, taking issue with the EPA's disclaimer of authority, brought this suit against petitioners, the EPA and its Administrator, under § 505 of the FWPCA, 33 U.S.C. § 1365, which authorizes "citizen suits" against the Administrator for failure to perform nondiscretionary duties under the FWPCA. They sought a declaration that the definition of a "pollutant" under the FWPCA encompasses all radioactive materials, including those regulated under the terms of the AEA of 1954, and an injunction directing the EPA and its Administrator to regulate the discharge of all such radioactive materials.

FACTS:

On cross-motions for summary judgment, the United States District Court for the District of Colorado held that the AEC had exclusive authority to regulate discharges of radioactive materials covered by the AEA. The Court of Appeals for the Tenth Circuit reversed, holding that the FWPCA requires the EPA to regulate discharges into the Nation's waters of all radioactive materials, including those covered by the AEA. Because of the importance of the issue involved in this case, we granted certiorari. We now reverse . . . .

The comprehensive regulatory scheme created by the AEA embraces the production, possession, and use of three types of radioactive materials: source material, special nuclear material, and byproduct material. In carrying out its regulatory duties under the AEA, the AEC is authorized to establish "such standards . . . as (it) may deem necessary or desirable . . . to protect health or to minimize danger to life or property." 42 U.S.C. § 2201(b). Pursuant to this authority, the AEC [NRC] has established by regulation maximum permissible releases of source, byproduct, and special nuclear materials into the environment by licensees. 10 CFR § 20.106 and App. B, Table II (1976). The regulations further provide that licensees should, in addition to complying with the established limits, "make every reasonable effort to maintain . . . releases of radioactive materials in effluents . . . as low as is reasonably achievable." 10 CFR § 20.1(c)(1976). Similarly, the regulations require that nuclear facilities be designed to keep levels of radioactive material in effluents "as low as is reasonably achievable." 10 CFR § 50.34a (1976).

The FWPCA established a regulatory program to control and abate water pollution, stating as its ultimate objective the elimination of all discharges of "pollutants" into the navigable waters by 1985. In furtherance of this objective, the FWPCA calls for the achievement of effluent limitations that require applications of the "best practicable control technology currently available" by July 1, 1977, and the "best available technology economically achievable" by July 1, 1983. 33 U.S.C. § 1311(b). These effluent limitations are enforced through a permit program. The discharge of "pollutants" into water is unlawful without a permit issued by the Administrator of the EPA or, if a State has developed a program that complies with the FWPCA, by the State.

The term "pollutant" is defined by the FWPCA to include, inter alia, "radioactive materials." But when the Administrator of the EPA adopted regulations governing the permit program, he specifically excluded source, byproduct, and special nuclear materials, those covered by the AEA, from the program upon his understanding of the relevant legislative history of the FWPCA:

> "The legislative history of the Act reflects that the term 'radioactive materials' as included within the definition of 'pollutant' in section 502 of the Act covers only radioactive materials which are not encompassed in the definition of source, byproduct, or special nuclear materials as defined by the Atomic Energy Act of 1954, as amended, and regulated pursuant to the latter Act. Examples of radioactive materials not covered by the Atomic Energy Act

and, therefore, included within the term 'pollutant' are radium and accelerator produced isotopes." 40 CFR § 125.1(y) (1975).

It was the Administrator's exclusion of source, byproduct, and special nuclear materials from the permit program, and consequent refusal to regulate them, that precipitated the instant lawsuit. The question we are presented with, then, is whether source, byproduct, and special nuclear materials are "pollutants" within the meaning of the FWPCA.

The Court of Appeals resolved the question exclusively by reference to the language of the statute. It observed that the FWPCA defines "pollution" as "the man-made or man-induced alteration of the chemical, physical, biological, and radiological integrity of water." And it noted that the reference to "radioactive materials" in the definition of "pollutant" was without express qualification or exception, despite the fact that the overall definition of "pollutant" does contain two explicit exceptions. The court concluded from this analysis of the language that by the reference to "radioactive materials" Congress meant all radioactive materials . . . .

To the extent that the Court of Appeals excluded reference to the legislative history of the FWPCA in discerning its meaning, the court was in error . . . .

The legislative history of the FWPCA speaks with force to the question whether source, byproduct, and special nuclear materials are "pollutants" subject to the Act's permit program. The House Committee Report was quite explicit on the subject:

> "The term 'pollutant' as defined in the bill includes 'radioactive materials.' These materials are those not encompassed in the definition of source, byproduct, or special nuclear materials as defined by the Atomic Energy Act of 1954, as amended, and regulated pursuant to that Act. 'Radioactive materials' encompassed by this bill are those beyond the jurisdiction of the Atomic Energy Commission. Examples of radioactive material not covered by the Atomic Energy Act, and, therefore, included within the term 'pollutant,' are radium and accelerator produced isotopes." H.R.Rep. No. 92-911, p. 131 (1972), 1 Leg.Hist. 818 (emphasis added).

The definition of "pollutant" in the House version of the bill contained the same broad reference to "radioactive materials" as did the definition in the Senate bill, and the bill ultimately enacted as the FWPCA . . . . Thus, the House Committee, describing the import of the precise statutory language with which we are concerned, cautioned that the definition of "pollutant" did not include those radioactive materials subject to regulation under the AEA.

Respondents claim to find in the Senate Committee Report an indication that the statutory definition of "pollutant" embraces radioactive materials subject to AEA regulation. Section 306 of the Senate bill required that the EPA Administrator establish "standards of performance" with respect to the discharge of pollutants from specified categories of sources, to be revised from time to time by the Administrator. The Senate Committee Report noted that nuclear fuels processing plants were not included, because the EPA did not then have "the technical capability to establish controls for such plants." The Report then observed that the Committee "expects that EPA will develop the capability," and continued: "The Bureau of Radiological Health, which was transferred to the Environmental Protection Agency, should have the capacity to determine those levels of control which can be achieved for nuclear fuel processing plants. If they do not, such a capability should be developed and this particular source should be added to the list of new sources as soon as possible." *Ibid.*

Petitioners assert that this statement by the Committee has no bearing on the question before the Court. The statement, petitioners suggest, reflects no more than a recognition, shared by them, that the plants referred to were not intended to be wholly excluded from the reach of the FWPCA: a recognition that in their view means that the EPA can control the discharge from such plants of polluting materials other than source, byproduct, and special nuclear materials. In short, petitioners contend that the statement sheds no light on the question whether source, byproduct, and special nuclear materials are pollutants under the FWPCA.

We agree with the petitioners that the Senate Committee statement is addressed to the inclusion of nuclear fuels processing plants in the category of sources subject to the EPA's control, not to the inclusion of any particular materials within the definition of "pollutant." [The Court then discussed other aspects of the Clean Water Act's legislative history, concluding that they provide additional support for the notion that "source, byproduct, and special nuclear materials" are beyond the reach of the Clean Water Act.]

If it was not clear at the outset, we think it abundantly clear after a review of the legislative materials that reliance on the "plain meaning" of the words "radioactive materials" contained in the definition of "pollutant" in the FWPCA contributes little to our understanding of whether Congress intended the Act to encompass the regulation of source, byproduct, and special nuclear materials. To have included these materials under the FWPCA would have marked a significant alteration of the pervasive regulatory scheme embodied in the AEA. Far from containing the clear indication of legislative intent that we might expect before recognizing such a change in policy, the legislative history reflects, on balance, an intention to preserve the pre-existing regulatory plan.

We conclude, therefore, that the "pollutants" subject to regulation under the FWPCA do not include source, byproduct, and special nuclear materials, and that the EPA Administrator has acted in accordance with his statutory mandate in declining to regulate the discharge of such materials. The judgment of the Court of Appeals is

Reversed.

Notes and Questions

1. The Supreme Court begins its opinion with the stated understanding that the two nuclear facilities at issue in this case, a private nuclear power plant and a nuclear weapons plant operated by the U.S. government, "are operated in conformity with radioactive effluent standards imposed by the [NRC] pursuant to the Atomic Energy

Act." If it was true that the two facilities were operating in conformance with NRC standards at the time, why did the petitioners want these facilities to be regulated by the Clean Water Act? Do you find any clues in this opinion that suggest differences between the two regulatory regimes?

2. Consider the EPA's position in this litigation. Do you find it curious that the EPA argued all the way to the U.S. Supreme Court for the right to *not* regulate a category of radioactive materials under the Clean Water Act? Why might EPA have taken that position in this case? For a more modern analogue, consider the EPA's position in *Massachusetts v. EPA*, 549 U.S. 497 (2007), where the EPA argued before the Supreme Court that it did not have authority to regulate greenhouse gases under the Clean Air Act. After losing *Massachusetts v. EPA*, the EPA embraced its authority to regulate greenhouse gases under the Clean Air Act, promulgating and proposing a number of rules that rely upon this authority. How would you explain this apparent change in attitude toward its own regulatory authority?

3. The *Train v. CoPIRG* decision appeared to rely heavily on the legislative history of the Clean Water Act, including statements by its primary sponsor, Senator Ed Muskie. Would this legislative history support the same outcome if *Train v. CoPIRG* were decided today instead of in 1976? While federal courts at least since *Chevron v. NRDC*, 467 U.S. 837 (1984), have accorded wide deference to federal agencies in the reasonable interpretation of laws they are charged with implementing, there has been a countervailing argument, led by the late Justice Antonin Scalia, emphasizing the supremacy of statutory text over interpretations relying upon external authorities such as legislative history. *See, e.g., City of Chicago v. Envtl. Def. Fund,* 511 U.S. 328, 337 (1994) (Justice Scalia delivering the opinion of the Court: "[I]t is the statute, and not the Committee Report, which is the authoritative expression of the law . . .").

4. If the EPA decided today that the NRC regulatory scheme for source, byproduct, or special nuclear materials was inadequate to protect human health and the environment, could the EPA amend its regulatory definition by eliminating the exception at issue in *Train v. CoPIRG*? If such action appeared legally or politically infeasible at this time, are there other legal authorities that the EPA might use to establish regulatory standards for these materials? In that context, consider 40 CFR Part 300, Table 302.4 (list of "hazardous substances" subject to CERCLA authority, explicitly including plutonium and other radionuclides).

5. Are *you* a "pollutant" under the Clean Water Act? Consider within the statutory definition of "pollutant" the sweeping term "biological materials." In one modern decision, *National Cotton Council of America v. U.S. EPA*, 553 F.3d 927 (6th Cir. 2009), the Sixth Circuit Court of Appeals had to decide whether "biological pesticides," which might include concentrations of viruses, bacteria, fungi, and plant matter, would constitute a "pollutant" when applied to waters for the purpose of controlling pests such as mosquito larvae or aquatic weeds. The court reasoned and concluded as follows:

> Continuing our review under *Chevron*, we must examine the "ordinary, contemporary, [and] common meaning" of "biological materials." Environmental Petitioners point out that *Webster's Third New International Dictionary*

(Gove ed. 1993) defines "material" as "of, relating to, or consisting of matter" and "the basic matter from which the whole or the great part of something is made." Id. at 1392. The *Oxford English Dictionary* provides that "material" is "that which constitutes the substance of a thing (physical or nonphysical); a physical substance; a material thing." The plain, unambiguous nature of this language compels this Court to find that matter of a biological nature, such as biological pesticides, qualifies as a biological material and falls under the [CWA] if it is "discharged into water." 33 U.S.C. § 1362(6).

The EPA points to Ninth Circuit case law that holds than "mussel shells and mussel byproduct are not pollutants" under the [CWA]. *Ass'n to Protect Hammersley, Eld & Totten Inlets v. Taylor*, 299 F.3d 1007, 1016 (9th Cir. 2002). The *Hammersley* court found the [CWA] to be "ambiguous on whether 'biological materials' means all biological matter regardless of quantum and nature." Id. While that case is distinguishable, we choose a more limited analysis. We see our obligation not as defining the outer-most bounds of "biological materials," but rather simply as deciding whether biological pesticides fit into the ordinary meaning of "biological materials."

The term "biological materials" cannot be read to exclude biological pesticides or their residuals. The EPA's Final Rule treats biological pesticides no differently from chemical pesticides, exempting both from NPDES permitting requirements in certain circumstances. We find this interpretation to be contrary to the plain meaning of the [CWA]. In 33 U.S.C. § 1362, Congress purposefully included the term "biological materials," rather than a more limited term such as "biological wastes." Congress easily could have drafted the list of pollutants in the [CWA] to include "chemical wastes" and "biological wastes." But, here, the word "waste" does not accompany "biological materials." Thus, if we are to give meaning to the word "waste," in "chemical waste," we must recognize Congress's intent to treat biological and chemical pesticides differently.

This interpretation is consistent with the precedent of this court and others. In *National Wildlife Federation v. Consumers Power Co.*, 862 F.2d 580 (6th Cir. 1988), we determined that "[m]illions of pounds of live fish, dead fish and fish remains annually discharged in Lake Michigan by [a] facility are pollutants within the meaning of the [CWA], since they are 'biological'" materials. Likewise, the District Court of Maine determined that "salmon feces and urine that exit the net pens and enter the waters are pollutants as they constitute 'biological materials' or 'agricultural wastes.'" *United States Pub. Interest Research Group v. Atl. Salmon of Maine*, 215 F.Supp.2d 239, 247 (D. Me. 2002). Biological pesticides similarly must be considered "biological materials."

National Cotton Council of America at 937–938. Given the breadth of the term "biological materials" as recognized by the Sixth Circuit and other courts, does it seem plausible now that you, jumping into a lake on a summer day, could be a "pollutant" under the Clean Water Act? Even so, and even if your act met all other jurisdictional elements of the Clean Water Act, we probably need not fear legal jeopardy because swimming in a lake, along with a world of other benign activities, is not likely to draw any enforcement response from any agency. But consider other cases that may be less innocuous. If we are not concerned with human bodies swimming in a lake, should we be concerned, for example, with human blood dumped into a river? *See U.S. v. Plaza Health Laboratories*, 3 F.3d 643 (2ᵈ Cir. 1993).

6. At a minimum, *Train v. CoPIRG* and other cases should remind students and practitioners of environmental law that terms defined by statutes may also be subject to definitions promulgated in agency rules. The Clean Water Act definition of "pollutant," for example, still includes "radioactive materials," but in practice the Clean Water Act doesn't regulate radioactive materials much at all due to the regulatory definition at 40 CFR 122.2, which still excludes source, byproduct, and special nuclear materials as challenged and upheld in *Train v. CoPIRG*. Of course, notwithstanding the remonstrations of adherents to strict statutory readings, students and practitioners might also do well to consult relevant agency guidance documents, legislative histories, case law, dictionaries, and other traditional methods for comprehending the meaning of terms in the complex scheme of environmental law.

B. Addition of Any Pollutant

As indicated above, the jurisdiction of the Clean Water Act depends upon the "discharge of a pollutant," which § 502 defines to include "any *addition* of any pollutant to navigable waters from any point source . . . ." 33 U.S.C. § 1362(6) (emphasis added). In most cases involving the Clean Water Act, the "addition" of a pollutant will be readily apparent: pollution leaked from a drum, discharged from a pipe, or dumped from a ship, for example. In some cases, however, the "addition" will not be so obvious, as where pollution in the water of one watershed is pumped to another watershed, or pollution accumulated in a river bed is released into the water above it. In this minority of cases, practitioners may need to pay particular attention to the facts of each case, as neither the statute nor its implementing regulations define "addition" for purposes of Clean Water Act jurisdiction and courts have decided cases both ways. For example, in *National Wildlife Federation v. Gorsuch*, 693 F.2d 156 (D.C. Cir. 1982), the D.C. Circuit Court of Appeals decided that water flowing over a dam, resulting in the supersaturation of gases below the dam, did not constitute the "addition" of a pollutant, even though it had an adverse effect on the quality of water below the dam. By contrast, in *Rybacheck v. U.S. Environmental Protection Agency*, 904 F.2d 1276 (9ᵗʰ Cir. 1990), the Ninth Circuit found that placer mining activities, which disturb streambed sediments in the search for valuable minerals, did indeed result in the "addition" of a pollutant where rock, sand, and minerals from the streambed were released into the water column.

One of the trickiest questions concerns the movement of contaminants through the transfer of water from one water body to another: does that constitute the "addition" of a pollutant for purposes of the Clean Water Act? The Supreme Court considered this question in *South Florida Water Management District v. Miccosukee*

Tribe of Indians (*Miccosukee I*), 541 U.S. 95 (2004). The case concerned the movement of water polluted with phosphates from fertilizers within the Florida Everglades ecosystem. The Miccosukee Tribe and environmental groups filed a citizen suit alleging that the pumping of water with phosphates from a canal to nearby wetlands without a permit constituted a violation of the Clean Water Act. In its defense, the Water District asserted that there was no Clean Water Act violation in this case because there was no "addition" of a pollutant, only perhaps the movement of one. The Southern District of Florida, rejecting this defense, granted summary judgment for the plaintiffs, and the Eleventh Circuit Court of Appeals affirmed. In considering this question, the Supreme Court declined to decide this question of water transfers directly, but remanded for factual findings on whether or not the canal and wetlands were distinct water bodies, such that the movement of water between them might constitute the "addition" of pollutants to the receiving water.

After the *Miccosukee I* decision, the district court eventually found that NPDES discharge permits are required for water transfers within the Everglades ecosystem. However, the Eleventh Circuit reversed, 570 F.3d 1210 (11ᵗʰ Cir. 2009), giving *Chevron* deference to a new rule, the Water Transfers Rule, promulgated by the EPA in 2008. See EPA Water Transfers Rule, 73 Fed. Reg. 33,697 (June 13, 2008), codified at 40 C.F.R. pt. 122). Under the Water Transfers Rule, EPA exempted water transfers from NPDES permitting requirements as long as the transfer simply conveyed or connected waters of the United States without subjecting the transferred water to any intervening industrial, municipal, or commercial use.

Underlying this rule was a concept known as the "unitary waters" theory, which the government asserted in the *Miccosukee* litigation. According to this theory, the phrase "any addition of any pollutant to navigable waters" means that once a pollutant is in any navigable water, the movement of pollutants from one water body to another cannot constitute an "addition to . . . navigable waters." The "unitary waters" theory did not receive specific consideration by the Supreme Court in *Miccosukee*, but it had, in effect, been rejected by other courts reviewing similar cases. *See, e.g., Dague v. City of Burlington*, 935 F.2d 1343, 1354–55 (2d Cir. 1991) (flow of landfill leachate from beaver pond through railroad culvert to marsh constitutes "addition" of pollutant), *rev'd in part on other grounds*, 505 U.S. 557 (1992); *Dubois v. U.S. Dept. of Agriculture*, 102 F.3d 1273 (1ˢᵗ Cir. 1996) (transfer of water from river to pristine pond for snowmaking purposes within White Mountain National Forest constitutes "addition" of pollutant); *Catskill Mountains Chapter of Trout Unlimited, Inc. v. City of New York*, 273 F.3d 481 (2d Cir. 2001) ("*Catskill I*") (pumping of turbid drinking water through tunnel into trout stream constitutes "addition" of pollutant); *Catskill Mountains Chapter of Trout Unlimited, Inc., v. City of New York*, 451 F.3d 77, 83084 (2d Cir. 2006) ("*Catskill II*") (affirming prior decision).

Upon promulgation of the Water Transfers Rule, the rule was immediately challenged by environmental groups, joined by a number of states and the Canadian province of Manitoba. The rule was invalidated by the trial court, which found that the Water Transfers Rule was neither reasoned nor consistent with purposes of the Clean Water Act. *Catskill Mountains Chapter of Trout Unlimited, Inc., et al., v. U.S.*

EPA, 8 F. Supp. 3d 500 (S.D.N.Y. 2014). However, in January 2017, the Second Circuit Court of Appeals reversed. 846 F.3d 492 (2d Cir. 2017) ("*Catskill III*"). In general, the Second Circuit found that under *Chevron* "step one" the Clean Water Act "did not speak directly to the precise question of whether NPDES permits are required for water transfers." Proceeding then to *Chevron* "step two," the court found that "the Water Transfers Rules's interpretation of the Clean Water Act is reasonable." Thus, unless the U.S. Supreme Court enters this fray again, it appears likely that the Water Transfers Rule will stand, presumptively exempting water transfers from NPDES permit requirements.

C. Point Source

To establish Clean Water Act jurisdiction for NPDES permitting requirements, the "addition of any pollutant" must be from a "*point source.*" CWA § 502, 33 U.S.C. § 1362(12) (emphasis added). The Clean Water Act defines "point source" broadly to mean "any discernible, confined and discrete conveyance, including but not limited to any pipe, ditch, channel, tunnel, conduit, well, discrete fissure, container, rolling stock, concentrated animals feeding operation, or vessel or other floating craft, from which pollutants are or may be discharged." CWA § 502(14), 33 U.S.C. § 1362(14). The statutory definition includes two exclusions: "agricultural stormwater discharges" and "return flows from irrigated agricultural." *Id.* However, the non-exclusive framing of the definition ("including but not limited to") signals congressional intent that "point source" be given an expansive reach, a breadth embraced in EPA's implementing regulations, see 40 C.F.R. § 122.2, and affirmed by most reviewing courts. *See, e.g., Dague v. City of Burlington,* 935 F.2d 1343, 1354–55 (2d Cir. 1991) (concept of "point source" was designed to "embrac[e] the broadest possible definition of any identifiable conveyance from which pollutants might enter waters of the United States"), rev'd in part on other grounds, 505 U.S. 557 (1992).

The Clean Water Act requirement for a "point source" divides water pollution into two broad categories: those where a "discrete conveyance" may be discerned (i.e., a "point source discharge") and those without any discrete conveyance (i.e., a "non-point source discharge"). In most cases involving Clean Water Act enforcement, given the expansive definition provided by Congress, the existence of a point source will be apparent. However, in more challenging cases, the existence of a point source may be vigorously contested by the defense. Consider whether a "point source" may include a bulldozer, an airplane, or *you,* as you read the following case.

United States v. Plaza Health Laboratories, Inc.
3 F.3d 643 (2d Cir. 1993)

Judge PRATT:

Defendant Geronimo Villegas appeals from a judgment entered in the United States District Court for the Eastern District of New York, convicting him of two counts of knowingly discharging pollutants into the Hudson River in violation of the Clean

Water Act ("CWA"). *See* 33 U.S.C. §§ 1311 and 1319(c)(2). The government cross-appeals, claiming the district court erred in its post-verdict grant of a judgment of acquittal on two counts of violating the knowing-endangerment provisions of the act. *See* 33 U.S.C. § 1319(c)(3).

FACTS

Villegas was co-owner and vice president of Plaza Health Laboratories, Inc., a blood-testing laboratory in Brooklyn, New York. On at least two occasions between April and September 1988, Villegas loaded containers of numerous vials of human blood generated from his business into his personal car, and drove to his residence at the Admirals Walk Condominium in Edgewater, New Jersey. Once at his condominium complex, Villegas removed the containers from his car and carried them to the edge of the Hudson River. On one occasion he carried two containers of the vials to the bulkhead that separates his condominium complex from the river, and placed them at low tide within a crevice in the bulkhead that was below the high-water line.

On May 26, 1988, a group of eighth graders on a field trip at the Alice Austin House in Staten Island, New York, discovered numerous glass vials containing human blood along the shore. Some of the vials had washed up on the shore; many were still in the water. Some were cracked, although most remained sealed with stoppers in solid-plastic containers or ziplock bags. Fortunately, no one was injured. That afternoon, New York City workers recovered approximately 70 vials from the area.

On September 25, 1988, a maintenance worker employed by the Admirals Walk Condominium discovered a plastic container holding blood vials wedged between rocks in the bulkhead. New Jersey authorities retrieved numerous blood vials from the bulkhead later that day.

Ten of the retrieved vials contained blood infected with the hepatitis-B virus. All of the vials recovered were eventually traced to Plaza Health Laboratories.

Based upon the May 1988 discovery of vials, Plaza Health Laboratories and Villegas were indicted on May 16, 1989, on two counts each of violating §§ 1319(c)(2) and (3) of the Clean Water Act. 33 U.S.C. §§ 1251 *et seq.* A superseding indictment charged both defendants with two additional CWA counts based upon the vials found in September 1988 . . . .

4 COUNTS Against defendant

Counts II and IV of the superseding indictment charged Villegas with knowingly discharging pollutants from a "point source" without a permit. *See* 33 U.S.C. §§ 1311(a), 1319(c)(2). Counts I and III alleged that Villegas had discharged pollutants, knowing that he placed others in "imminent danger of death or serious bodily injury". *See* 33 U.S.C. § 1319(c)(3). On January 31, 1991, following a trial before Judge Korman, the jury found Villegas guilty on all four counts . . . .

Defendant argument

Villegas contends that one element of the CWA crime, knowingly discharging pollutants from a "point source", was not established in his case. He argues that the definition of "point source", 33 U.S.C. § 1362(14), does not include discharges that result from the individual acts of human beings. Raising primarily questions of legislative intent and statutory construction, Villegas argues that at best, the term "point source" is ambiguous as applied to him, and that the rule of lenity should result in reversal of his convictions. The government has cross-appealed from the district court's post-verdict order acquitting Villegas on the two knowing-endangerment counts.

. . . During and after Villegas's trial, Judge Korman labored over how to define "point source" in this case. At one point he observed that the image of a human being is not "conjured up" by congress's definition of "point source". Ultimately, he never defined the "point source" element but he did charge the jury:

> Removing pollutants from a container, and a vehicle is a container, parked next to a navigable body of water and physically throwing the pollutant into the water constitutes a discharge from a point source.

In ruling on Villegas's rule 29 motion, however, Judge Korman held that the element "point source" may reasonably be read

> to include any discrete and identifiable conduit—*including a human being*—designated to collect or discharge pollutants produced in the course of a waste-generating activity. (emphasis added).

As the parties have presented the issue to us in their briefs and at oral argument, the question is "whether a human being can be a point source." Both sides focus on the district court's conclusion in its rule 29 memorandum that, among other things, the requisite "point source" here could be Villegas himself.   *Issue*

Significantly, the jury was never clearly instructed on this legal theory, and the instruction actually given bordered on an improper removal of the determination of an essential element of the crime from the jury's consideration. Serious problems might be presented by the government's attempt to justify Judge Korman's post-verdict definitional efforts as an alternate theory upon which to uphold Villegas's convictions. *Chiarella v. United States,* 445 U.S. 222, 236 (1980) (court may not affirm criminal conviction on basis of theory not presented to jury).

However, far more fundamental than any error in jury instructions is the problem highlighted by the district court's analytical struggle to find somewhere in the Villegas transaction a "discernible, confined and discrete conveyance". Simply put, that problem is that this statute was never designed to address the random, individual polluter like Villegas.

To determine the scope of the CWA's "point source" definition, we first consider the language and structure of the act itself. If the language is not plain, an excursion into legislative history and context may prove fruitful. Judicial interpretations of the term can be instructive as well, as may be interpretive statements by the agency in charge of implementing the statute. If we conclude after this analysis that the statute is ambiguous as applied to Villegas, then the rule of lenity may apply. *Moskal v. United States,* 498 U.S. 103, 107 (1990); *United States v. Concepcion,* 983 F.2d 369, 380 (2d Cir.1992).

Rule of Lenity: judicial doctrine requiring that those ambiguities in a criminal statute relating to prohibition & penalties be resolved in favor of the defendant if it is not contrary to legislative intent.

Human beings are not among the enumerated items that may be a "point source". Although by its terms the definition of "point source" is nonexclusive, the words used to define the term and the examples given ("pipe, ditch, channel, tunnel, conduit, well, discrete fissure", etc.) evoke images of physical structures and instrumentalities that systematically act as a means of conveying pollutants from an industrial source to navigable waterways.

In addition, if every discharge involving humans were to be considered a "discharge from a point source", the statute's lengthy definition of "point source" would have been unnecessary. It is elemental that congress does not add unnecessary words to statutes. Had congress intended to punish any human being who polluted navigational waters, it could readily have said: "any person who places pollutants in navigable waters without a permit is guilty of a crime."

The Clean Water Act generally targets industrial and municipal sources of pollutants, as is evident from a perusal of its many sections. Consistent with this focus, the term "point source" is used throughout the statute, but invariably in sentences referencing industrial or municipal discharges . . . .

This emphasis was sensible, as "[i]ndustrial and municipal point sources were the worst and most obvious offenders of surface water quality. They were also the easiest to address because their loadings emerge from a discrete point such as the end of a pipe." David Letson, *Point/Nonpoint Source Pollution Reduction Trading: An Interpretive Survey*, 32 Nat. Resources J. 219, 221 (1992).

Finally on this point, we assume that congress did not intend the awkward meaning that would result if we were to read "human being" into the definition of "point source." Section 1362(12)(A) defines "discharge of a pollutant" as "any addition of any pollutant to navigable waters from any point source". Enhanced by this definition, § 1311(a) reads in effect "the addition of any pollutant to navigable waters *from any point source by any person* shall be unlawful" (emphasis added). But were a human being to be included within the definition of "point source", the prohibition would then read: "the addition of any pollutant to navigable waters *from any person by any person* shall be unlawful", and this simply makes no sense. As the statute stands today, the term "point source" is comprehensible only if it is held to the context of industrial and municipal discharges.

. . . The legislative history of the CWA, while providing little insight into the meaning of "point source", confirms the act's focus on industrial polluters. Congress required NPDES permits of those who discharge from a "point source". The term "point source", introduced to the act in 1972, was intended to function as a means of identifying industrial polluters — generally a difficult task because pollutants quickly disperse throughout the subject waters . . . .

We find no suggestion either in the act itself or in the history of its passage that congress intended the CWA to impose criminal liability on an individual for the myriad, random acts of human waste disposal, for example, a passerby who flings a candy

Reasoning

wrapper into the Hudson River, or a urinating swimmer. Discussions during the passage of the 1972 amendments indicate that congress had bigger fish to fry . . . .

Our search for the meaning of "point source" brings us next to judicial constructions of the term . . . [T]he cases that have interpreted "point source" have done so in civil-penalty or licensing settings, where greater flexibility of interpretation to further remedial legislative purposes is permitted, and the rule of lenity does not protect a defendant against statutory ambiguities . . . . We cannot, however, make the further leap of writing "human being" into the statutory language without doing violence to the language and structure of the CWA . . . .

In sum, although congress had the ability to so provide, § 1362(14) of the CWA does not expressly recognize a human being as a "point source"; nor does the act make structural sense when one incorporates a human being into that definition. The legislative history of the act adds no light to the muddy depths of this issue, and cases urging a broad interpretation of the definition in the civil-penalty context do not persuade us to do so here, where congress has imposed heavy criminal sanctions. Adopting the government's suggested flexibility for the definition would effectively read the "point source" element of the crime out of the statute, and not even the EPA has extended the term "point source" as far as is urged here.

We accordingly conclude that the term "point source" as applied to a human being is at best ambiguous.

In criminal prosecutions the rule of lenity requires that ambiguities in the statute be resolved in the defendant's favor . . . . In other words, we cannot add to the statute what congress did not provide. "[B]efore a man can be punished as a criminal under the Federal law his case must be 'plainly and unmistakably' within the provisions of some statute." *United States v. Gradwell*, 243 U.S. 476, 485 (1917).

Since the government's reading of the statute in this case founders on our inability to discern the "obvious intention of the legislature" to include a human being as a "point source", we conclude that the criminal provisions of the CWA did not clearly proscribe Villegas's conduct and did not accord him fair warning of the sanctions the law placed on that conduct. Under the rule of lenity, therefore, the prosecutions against him must be dismissed . . . .

Decision

Judge OAKES, dissenting:

DISSENT

. . . I begin with the obvious, in hopes that it will illuminate the less obvious: the classic point source is something like a pipe. This is, at least in part, because pipes and similar conduits are needed to carry large quantities of waste water, which represents a large proportion of the point source pollution problem. Thus, devices designed to convey large quantities of waste water from a factory or municipal sewage treatment facility are readily classified as point sources. Because not all pollutants are liquids, however, the statute and the cases make clear that means of conveying solid wastes to be dumped in navigable waters are also point sources. *See, e.g.*, 33 U.S.C. § 1362(14) ("rolling stock," or railroad cars, listed as an example of a point source); *Avoyelles Sportsmen's League, Inc. v. Marsh,* 715 F.2d 897, 922 (5th Cir.1983) (backhoes and bulldozers used to gather fill and deposit it on wetlands are point sources).

What I take from this look at classic point sources is that, at the least, an organized means of channeling and conveying industrial waste in quantity to navigable waters is a "discernible, confined and discrete conveyance." The case law is in accord: courts have deemed a broad range of means of depositing pollutants in the country's navigable waters to be point sources . . . .

Further, the legislative history indicates that the Act was meant to control periodic, as well as continuous, discharges. S.Rep. No. 92-414, 92d Cong. 1st Sess. (1971).

In short, the term "point source" has been broadly construed to apply to a wide range of polluting techniques, so long as the pollutants involved are not just human-made, but reach the navigable waters by human effort or by leaking from a clear point at which waste water was collected by human effort. From these cases, the writers of one respected treatise have concluded that such a "man-induced gathering mechanism plainly is the essential characteristic of a point source" and that a point source, "[p]ut simply, . . . is an identifiable conveyance of pollutants." 5 Robert E. Beck, *Waters & Water Rights* § 53.01(b)(3) at 216–17 (1991), *citing Sierra Club v. Abston Constr. Co.,* 620 F.2d at 45 (miners channeled waters into sump pits which leaked after heavy rains) . . . .

Nonetheless, the term "point source" sets significant definitional limits on the reach of the Clean Water Act. Fifty percent or more of all water pollution is thought to come from nonpoint sources. S. Rep. 99-50, 99th Cong., 1st Sess. 8 (1985); William F. Pedersen, Jr., *Turning the Tide on Water Quality,* 15 Ecol. L. Q. 69, n. 10 (1988). So, to further refine the definition of "point source," I consider what it is that the Act does not cover: nonpoint source discharges.

Nonpoint source pollution is, generally, runoff: salt from roads, agricultural chemicals from farmlands, oil from parking lots, and other substances washed by rain, in diffuse patterns, over the land and into navigable waters. The sources are many, difficult to identify and difficult to control. Indeed, an effort to greatly reduce nonpoint source pollution could require radical changes in land use patterns which Congress evidently was unwilling to mandate without further study. The structure of the statute—which regulates point source pollution closely, while leaving nonpoint source regulation to the states under the Section 208 program—indicates that the term "point source" was included in the definition of discharge so as to ensure that nonpoint source pollution would *not* be covered. Instead, Congress chose to regulate first that which could easily be regulated: direct discharges by identifiable parties, or point sources.

This rationale for regulating point and nonpoint sources differently—that point sources may readily be controlled and are easily attributable to a particular source, while nonpoint sources are more difficult to control without radical change, and less easily attributable, once they reach water, to any particular responsible party—helps define what fits within each category. Thus, Professor Rodgers has suggested, "[t]he statutory 'discernible, confined and discrete conveyance' . . . can be understood as singling out those candidates suitable for control-at-the-source." 2 William H. Rodgers, Jr., *Environmental Law: Air and Water* § 4.10 at 150 (1986). And, as Professor Rodgers notes, "[c]ase law confirms the controllability theory, adding to it a responsibility component, so that 'point sources' are understood both as sources that can be cleaned up and as sources where fairness suggests the named parties should do the cleaning." *Id* . . . .

While Villegas' activities were not prototypical point source discharges—in part because he was disposing of waste that could have been disposed of on land, and so did not need a permit or a pipe—they much more closely resembled a point source discharge than a nonpoint source discharge. First, Villegas and his lab were perfectly capable of avoiding discharging their waste into water: they were, in Professor Rodgers' terms, a "controllable" source.

Furthermore, the discharge was directly into water, and came from an identifiable point, Villegas. Villegas did not dispose of the materials on land, where they could be washed into water as nonpoint source pollution. Rather, he carried them, from his firm's laboratory, in his car, to his apartment complex, where he placed them in a bulkhead below the high tide line. I do not think it is necessary to determine whether it was Mr. Villegas himself who was the point source, or whether it was his car, the vials, or the bulkhead: in a sense, the entire stream of Mr. Villegas' activity functioned as a "discrete conveyance" or point source. The point is that the source of the pollution was clear, and would have been easy to control. Indeed, Villegas was well aware that there were methods of controlling the discharge (and that the materials were too dangerous for casual disposal): his laboratory had hired a professional medical waste handler. He simply chose not to use an appropriate waste disposal mechanism.

Villegas' method may have been an unusual one for a corporate officer, but it would undermine the statute—which, after all, sets as its goal the elimination of discharges, 33 U.S.C. § 1311(a)—to regard as "ambiguous" a Congressional failure to list an unusual method of disposing of waste. I doubt that Congress would have regarded an army of men and women throwing industrial waste from trucks into a stream as exempt from the statute. Since the Act contains no exemption for de minimis violations—since, indeed, many Clean Water Act prosecutions are for a series of small discharges, each of which is treated as a single violation—I cannot see that one man throwing one day's worth of medical waste into the ocean differs (and indeed, with this type of pollution, it might be that only a few days' violations could be proven even if the laboratory regularly relied on Villegas to dispose of its waste by throwing it into the ocean). A different reading would encourage corporations perfectly capable of abiding by the Clean Water Act's requirements to ask their employees to stand between the company trucks and the sea, thereby transforming point source pollution (dumping from trucks) into nonpoint source pollution (dumping by hand). Such a method is controllable, easily identifiable, and inexcusable. To call it nonpoint source pollution is to read a technical exception into a statute which attempts to define in broad terms an activity which may be conducted in many different ways . . . .

Having resorted to the language and structure, legislative history and motivating policies of the Clean Water Act, I think it plain enough that Congress intended the statute to bar corporate officers from disposing of corporate waste into navigable waters by hand as well as by pipe. Further, I would note that this is not the sort of activity that Villegas could honestly have believed violated no statute, whether promulgated by federal, state, or local authorities. Thus, this is not a case in which the defendant had no fair warning that his actions were illegal. No compliance attorney here could have struggled with the difficulty of deciding whether this was activity for which a permit should be sought, as might be the case in a factory dealing with run-off that arguably was channeled and thereby transformed from nonpoint to point source pollution; rather, an attorney asked to advise Villegas whether his activity was permissible might say that there was as yet no case law indicating that such activity was point source pollution under the Clean Water Act, but that such a view was certainly consistent with the Act and that the behavior would almost certainly be proscribed by that Act or some other . . . .

Accordingly, I would affirm the rulings of the district court.

Notes and Questions

1. Whose understanding of "point source" do you find more persuasive in this case, Judge Pratt for the court or Judge Oakes for the dissent? If you find Judge Pratt's reasoning more persuasive, denying the existence of a point source where pollutants are discharged by hand, how do you respond to Judge Oakes's suggestion that this theory would create an end-run around NPDES permitting requirements if a load of wastes, for example, were simply hand-carried from a truck down to the water? If you find Judge Oakes' dissent more persuasive, on the other hand, are you completely convinced that the "entire stream of Mr. Villegas' activity," including his car, the vials, and the bulkhead, "functioned as a 'discrete conveyance' or point source"? Would this also mean that any road, bike trail, sidewalk, stairs, and skateboard could also be point sources if Mr. Villegas used them to transport his medical waste? Do you believe that view would be consistent with the meaning of a "discrete" conveyance?

2. Would the decision on "point source" in this criminal case have been different in a civil case to enforce the Clean Water Act? Note the emphasis that Judge Pratt places on the rule of lenity as a doctrine of criminal law. If Mr. Villegas were not indicted on criminal charges but instead assessed a civil penalty under the Clean Water Act for the same conduct, do you think the court would have agreed to the existence of a "point source" in that case?

3. What do think of Judge Pratt's conclusion that Congress could not have intended the Clean Water Act to impose criminal liability on "a passerby who flings a candy wrapper into the Hudson River, or a urinating swimmer"? Would it matter if the

passerby flings raw sewage into the river? *See, e.g., Mercury Skyline Yacht Charters v. Dave Matthews Band, Inc.,* 2005 WL 3159680 (N.D. Ill. 2005) (driver of tour bus for Dave Matthews Band charged with release of raw sewage from bus through bridge grate into Chicago River in August 2004). Would it matter if the river were polluted by 50,000 urinating swimmers? *See, e.g., U.S. Public Interest Research Group v. Atlantic Salmon of Maine, L.L.C.,* 215 F. Supp. 2d 239 (D. Maine 2002) (salmon feces and urine originating from offshore salmon pens constitutes discharge of a pollutant from a point source). Does the pollutant being discharged have any bearing on the means (or the "conveyance") for the discharge? As a practical matter, even if it were clear that a candy wrapper (or swimmer urine) originated from a classic point source, such as a pipe or ditch, how likely do you think it would be that a prosecutor would bring criminal charges for such action?

4. The dissenting opinion from Judge Oakes emphasizes the breadth of things that courts have recognized to constitute "point sources" under the Clean Water Act, either as a result of the express inclusion within the statutory definition or implementing rules, or within a fair application of the narrative description. As noted by Judge Oakes, recognized point sources include railroad cars, backhoes and bulldozers, tug boats, strip mines, and mushroom farm operations. Other courts have recognized "point source" to include Navy planes, *Weinberger v. Romero-Barcelo,* 456 U.S. 305 (1982); aerial pesticide applicators, *League of Wilderness Defenders v. Forsgren,* 309 F.3d 1181 (9th Cir. 2002); septic systems, *U.S. v. Lucas,* 516 F.3d 316 (5th Cir. 2008); a shooting range, *Stone v. Naperville Park Dist.,* 38 F. Supp. 2d 651 (N.D. Ill. 1999); cattle feedlots, *Carr v. Alta Verde Indus., Inc.,* 931 F.2d 1055 (5th Cir. 1991); and waste lagoons, *Fishel v. Westinghouse Elec. Corp.,* 640 F. Supp. 442 (M.D. Pa. 1986). If the human hand is *not* a point source, but a backhoe *is*, what about a wheelbarrow or a shovel? Where would you draw the line?

5. Given the broad scope of "point source," what is a "nonpoint source"? The Clean Water Act itself specifically excludes from the definition of point source "agricultural stormwater discharges and return flows from irrigated agriculture." Section 502(14). Given the substantial fraction of the land and economy in the United States dedicated to agriculture, this is obviously a significant exclusion from point source regulation. Nonpoint source discharges may also include atmospheric deposition and stormwater runoff from urbanization and impervious surfaces. However, note that the statutory exclusion does not include all sources of stormwater runoff. In fact, Congress clearly intended the Clean Water Act permit requirements to apply to some forms of stormwater discharges. *See, e.g.,* 33 U.S.C. § 1342(p) ("Municipal and industrial stormwater discharges"). Consistent with this statutory framework, stormwater runoff from mining sites, construction sites, and certain forestry operations (or "silvicultural activities") have all been found to be discharges from point sources. *See, e.g., Comm. to Save Mokelumne River v. East Bay Mun. Util. Dist.,* 13 F.3d 305 (9th Cir. 1993) (runoff from mine site); *Washington Wilderness Coalition v. Hecla Mining Co.,* 870 F.Supp.983 (E.D. Wash. 1994) (runoff from mine tailings pond); see also 40 C.F.R. pt. 122, subpt. B (permit requirements for "storm water point sources").

Nevertheless, what is and is not a point source for purposes of Clean Water Act regulation continues to be a frequently contested issue before the courts. *See, e.g., Decker v. Northwest Environmental Defense Center*, 568 U.S. __ (2013), 133 S. Ct. 1326 (2013) (upholding EPA's "Industrial Stormwater Rule" against challenge by environmental group that logging roads, which contribute sediment to nearby rivers and streams, must be regulated as point sources); *Ecological Rights Foundation v. Pacific Gas & Electric Co.*, 713 F.3d 502 (9th Cir. 2013) (stormwater runoff from utility poles does not constitute point source discharge); *Oregon Natural Desert Ass'n v. Dombeck*, 151 F.3d 945 (9th Cir. 1998) (cows in a creek are not a point source).

D. Navigable Waters

To establish Clean Water Act jurisdiction, the "addition of any pollutant" from a "point source" must be to "*navigable waters*." CWA § 502, 33 U.S.C. § 1362(12) (emphasis added). "Navigable waters," as a matter of federal law, is a term that considerably predates the Clean Water Act of 1972, appearing in both common law usage as well as early statutes such as the federal Rivers and Harbors Act of 1899, 33 U.S.C. § 401. Traditionally, "navigable waters" referred to waters that were "navigable in fact" or waters that were once navigable or could be made navigable through engineering efforts. *See, e.g.,* 33 C.F.R. § 321.2(a) (defining "navigable waters of the United States" as meaning "those waters . . . that are subject to the ebb and flow of the tide shoreward to the mean high water mark and/or are presently used, or have been used in the past, or may be susceptible to use to transport interstate or foreign commerce").

Despite this historic usage, when the modern Clean Water Act was passed in 1972, it is clear that Congress intended a broader meaning for "navigable waters." As explained in the House Report:

> One term that the Committee was reluctant to define was the term "navigable waters." The reluctance was based on the fear that any interpretation would be read narrowly. However, this is not the Committee's intent. The Committee fully intends that the term "navigable waters" be given the broadest possible constitutional interpretation, unencumbered by agency determinations which have been made or may be made for administrative purposes.

Similar views were expressed in both the House and Senate floor debates. Confirming the notion that Clean Water Act jurisdiction should extend above and beyond traditionally navigable waters, the Senate Public Works Committee observed, "Water moves in hydrologic cycles and it is essential that discharge of pollutants be controlled at the source." S. Rep. No. 92-414, at 77 (1977).

Consistent with these sentiments, § 502(7) of the Clean Water Act defines "navigable waters" more broadly than prior constructions, to mean "the waters of the United States, including the territorial seas." *Id.* § 1362(7). "Waters of the United States" includes most obvious water bodies, including major rivers, lakes, and bays in the United States. However, the full scope of "waters of the United States" leaves many questions unanswered. These questions have led, among other things, to substantial controversy and litigation over the last 20 years, as will be explored in the next section. For example, do "waters of the United States" include groundwater? Wetlands? Tundra? Prairie potholes? Private ponds? Swimming pools? Concrete ditches? Dusty arroyos in the Southwest that only carry water a few days or weeks per year?

V. Waters of the United States

As noted so far, jurisdiction under the Clean Water Act depends on a finding of "navigable waters," defined by the statute to mean "the waters of the United States." But what kind of "waters" does this include? If "waters of the United States" includes lakes and rivers, does it also include ponds and streams that sometimes go dry? Does it include wetlands? Groundwater? Concrete ditches? To help answer these questions, the U.S. EPA and the U.S. Army Corps of Engineers have promulgated rules and issued guidance to clarify the scope of "waters of the United States." Via rulemaking, EPA previously defined "waters of the United States" to mean:

(a) All waters which are currently used, were used in the past, or may be susceptible to use in interstate or foreign commerce, including all waters which are subject to the ebb and flow of the tide;

(b) All interstate waters, including interstate "wetlands;"

(c) All other waters such as intrastate lakes, rivers, streams (including intermittent streams), mudflats, sandflats, "wetlands," sloughs, prairie potholes, wet meadows, playa lakes, or natural ponds the use, degradation, or destruction of which would affect or could affect interstate or foreign commerce . . .

(d) All impoundments of waters otherwise defined as waters of the United States under this definition;

(e) Tributaries of waters identified in paragraphs (a) through (d) of this definition;

(f) The territorial sea; and

(g) "Wetlands" adjacent to waters (other than waters that are themselves wetlands) identified in paragraphs (a) through (d) of this definition.

40 C.F.R. § 122.2 (2014).

Parallel to this regulatory definition promulgated by the U.S. EPA, the Corps of Engineers has promulgated an equivalent rule at 33 C.F.R. § 328.3 for use in the context of dredge and fill permits under § 404 of the Clean Water Act. Naturally, the rules promulgated by the EPA and Corps of Engineers have been subject to legal challenges by parties who would prefer a different (often narrower) scope of "waters of the United States." In 1985, the U.S. Supreme Court upheld the Corps' definition of "waters of the United States" that included wetlands adjacent to navigable waters. See

United States v. Riverside Bayview Homes, Inc., 474 U.S. 121 (1985). In the year following *Riverside Bayview*, the Corps of Engineers attempted to clarify its regulatory definition by providing examples of cases where isolated, nonnavigable waters may still be subject to Clean Water Act jurisdiction. The clarification, which became known as the Migratory Bird Rule, was challenged and sustained in a number of cases until the Supreme Court took it under consideration in the following case.

[handwritten left margin: Migratory Bird Rule]

Solid Waste Agency of Northern Cook County v. U.S. Army Corps of Engineers

531 U.S. 159 (2001)

Chief Justice REHNQUIST:

Section 404(a) of the Clean Water Act (CWA or Act), 86 Stat. 884, as amended, 33 U.S.C. § 1344(a), regulates the discharge of dredged or fill material into "navigable waters." The United States Army Corps of Engineers (Corps) has interpreted § 404(a) to confer federal authority over an abandoned sand and gravel pit in northern Illinois which provides habitat for migratory birds. We are asked to decide whether the provisions of § 404(a) may be fairly extended to these waters, and, if so, whether Congress could exercise such authority consistent with the Commerce Clause, U.S. Const., Art. I, § 8, cl. 3. We answer the first question in the negative and therefore do not reach the second. *[handwritten: Decision]*

[handwritten right margin: Issue]

Petitioner, the Solid Waste Agency of Northern Cook County (SWANCC), is a consortium of 23 suburban Chicago cities and villages that united in an effort to locate and develop a disposal site for baled nonhazardous solid waste. The Chicago Gravel Company informed the municipalities of the availability of a 533-acre parcel, bestriding the Illinois counties Cook and Kane, which had been the site of a sand and gravel pit mining operation for three decades up until about 1960. Long since abandoned, the old mining site eventually gave way to a successional stage forest, with its remnant excavation trenches evolving into a scattering of permanent and seasonal ponds of varying size (from under one-tenth of an acre to several acres) and depth (from several inches to several feet).

The municipalities decided to purchase the site for disposal of their baled nonhazardous solid waste. By law, SWANCC was required to file for various permits from Cook County and the State of Illinois before it could begin operation of its balefill project. In addition, because the operation called for the filling of some of the permanent and seasonal ponds, SWANCC contacted federal respondents (hereinafter respondents), including the Corps, to determine if a federal landfill permit was required under § 404(a) of the CWA, 33 U.S.C. § 1344(a).

Section 404(a) grants the Corps authority to issue permits "for the discharge of dredged or fill material into the navigable waters at specified disposal sites." *Ibid.* The term "navigable waters" is defined under the Act as "the waters of the United States, including the territorial seas." § 1362(7). The Corps has issued regulations defining the term "waters of the United States" to include waters such as intrastate lakes, rivers, streams (including intermittent streams), mudflats, sandflats, wetlands, sloughs, prairie potholes, wet meadows, playa lakes, or natural ponds, the use, degradation or destruction of which could affect interstate or foreign commerce . . . . 33 CFR § 328.3(a)(3) (1999).

In 1986, in an attempt to "clarify" the reach of its jurisdiction, the Corps stated that § 404(a) extends to intrastate waters:

"a. Which are or would be used as habitat by birds protected by Migratory Bird Treaties; or

"b. Which are or would be used as habitat by other migratory birds which cross state lines; or

"c. Which are or would be used as habitat for endangered species; or

"d. Used to irrigate crops sold in interstate commerce." 51 Fed.Reg. 41217.

This last promulgation has been dubbed the "Migratory Bird Rule."

The Corps initially concluded that it had no jurisdiction over the site because it contained no "wetlands," or areas which support "vegetation typically adapted for life in saturated soil conditions," 33 CFR § 328.3(b) (1999). However, after the Illinois Nature Preserves Commission informed the Corps that a number of migratory bird species had been observed at the site, the Corps reconsidered and ultimately asserted jurisdiction over the balefill site pursuant to subpart (b) of the "Migratory Bird Rule." The Corps found that approximately 121 bird species had been observed at the site, including several known to depend upon aquatic environments for a significant portion of their life requirements. Thus, on November 16, 1987, the Corps formally "determined that the seasonally ponded, abandoned gravel mining depressions located on the project site, while not wetlands, did qualify as 'waters of the United States' . . . based upon the following criteria: (1) the proposed site had been abandoned as a gravel mining operation; (2) the water areas and spoil piles had developed a natural character; and (3) the water areas are used as habitat by migratory bird [sic] which cross state lines."

During the application process, SWANCC made several proposals to mitigate the likely displacement of the migratory birds and to preserve a great blue heron rookery located on the site. Its balefill project ultimately received the necessary local and state approval. By 1993, SWANCC had received a special use planned development permit from the Cook County Board of Appeals, a landfill development permit from the Illinois Environmental Protection Agency, and approval from the Illinois Department of Conservation.

Despite SWANCC's securing the required water quality certification from the Illinois Environmental Protection Agency, the Corps refused to issue a § 404(a) permit. The Corps found that SWANCC had not established that its proposal was the "least environmentally damaging, most practicable alternative" for disposal of nonhazardous solid waste; that SWANCC's failure to set aside sufficient funds to remediate leaks posed an "unacceptable risk to the public's drinking water supply"; and that the impact of the project upon area-sensitive species was "unmitigatable since a landfill surface cannot be redeveloped into a forested habitat."

Petitioner filed suit under the Administrative Procedure Act, 5 U.S.C. § 701 *et seq.,* in the Northern District of Illinois challenging both the Corps' jurisdiction over the site and the merits of its denial of the § 404(a) permit. The District Court granted summary judgment to respondents on the jurisdictional issue, and petitioner abandoned its challenge to the Corps' permit decision. On appeal to the Court of Appeals for the Seventh Circuit, petitioner renewed its attack on respondents' use of the "Migratory Bird Rule" to assert jurisdiction over the site. Petitioner argued that respondents had exceeded their statutory authority in interpreting the CWA to cover nonnavigable, isolated, intrastate waters based upon the presence of migratory birds and, in the alternative, that Congress lacked the power under the Commerce Clause to grant such regulatory jurisdiction.

USDC

Court of Appeals

The Court of Appeals began its analysis with the constitutional question, holding that Congress has the authority to regulate such waters based upon "the cumulative impact doctrine, under which a single activity that itself has no discernible effect on interstate commerce may still be regulated if the aggregate effect of that class of activity has a substantial impact on interstate commerce." 191 F.3d 845, 850 (C.A.7 1999). The aggregate effect of the "destruction of the natural habitat of migratory birds" on interstate commerce, the court held, was substantial because each year millions of Americans cross state lines and spend over a billion dollars to hunt and observe migratory birds. The Court of Appeals then turned to the regulatory question. The court held that the CWA reaches as many waters as the Commerce Clause allows and, given its earlier Commerce Clause ruling, it therefore followed that respondents' "Migratory Bird Rule" was a reasonable interpretation of the Act.

SC decision : We granted certiorari, and now reverse.

. . . In *United States v. Riverside Bayview Homes, Inc.,* 474 U.S. 121 (1985), we held that the Corps had § 404(a) jurisdiction over wetlands that actually abutted on a navigable waterway. In so doing, we noted that the term "navigable" is of "limited import" and that Congress evidenced its intent to "regulate at least some waters that would not be deemed 'navigable' under the classical understanding of that term." But our holding was based in large measure upon Congress' unequivocal acquiescence to, and approval of, the Corps' regulations interpreting the CWA to cover wetlands adjacent to navigable waters. We found that Congress' concern for the protection of water quality and aquatic ecosystems indicated its intent to regulate wetlands "inseparably bound up with the 'waters' of the United States."

It was the significant nexus between the wetlands and "navigable waters" that informed our reading of the CWA in *Riverside Bayview Homes.* Indeed, we did not "express any opinion" on the "question of the authority of the Corps to regulate discharges of fill material into wetlands that are not adjacent to bodies of open water. . . ." In order to rule for respondents here, we would have to hold that the jurisdiction of the Corps extends to ponds that are *not* adjacent to open water. But we conclude that the text of the statute will not allow this.

Indeed, the Corps' *original* interpretation of the CWA, promulgated two years after its enactment, is inconsistent with that which it espouses here. Its 1974 regulations defined § 404(a)'s "navigable waters" to mean "those waters of the United States which are subject to the ebb and flow of the tide, and/or are presently, or have been in the past, or may be in the future susceptible for use for purposes of interstate or foreign commerce." 33 CFR § 209.120(d)(1). The Corps emphasized that "[i]t is the water body's capability of use by the public for purposes of transportation or commerce which is the determinative factor." § 209.260(e)(1). Respondents put forward no persuasive evidence that the Corps mistook Congress' intent in 1974.

Respondents next contend that whatever its original aim in 1972, Congress charted a new course five years later when it approved the more expansive definition of "navigable waters" found in the Corps' 1977 regulations. In July 1977, the Corps formally adopted 33 CFR § 323.2(a)(5) (1978), which defined "waters of the United States" to include "isolated wetlands and lakes, intermittent streams, prairie potholes, and other waters that are not part of a tributary system to interstate waters or to navigable waters of the United States, the degradation or destruction of which could affect interstate commerce." Respondents argue that Congress was aware of this more expansive interpretation during its 1977 amendments to the CWA. Specifically, respondents point to a failed House bill, H.R. 3199, that would have defined "navigable waters" as "all waters which are presently used, or are susceptible to use in their natural condition or by reasonable improvement as a means to transport interstate or foreign commerce." 123 Cong. Rec. 10420, 10434 (1977) . . . .

Although we have recognized congressional acquiescence to administrative interpretations of a statute in some situations, we have done so with extreme care. A bill can be proposed for any number of reasons, and it can be rejected for just as many others . . . .

We conclude that respondents have failed to make the necessary showing that the failure of the 1977 House bill demonstrates Congress' acquiescence to the Corps' regulations or the "Migratory Bird Rule," which, of course, did not first appear until 1986 . . . .

We thus decline respondents' invitation to take what they see as the next ineluctable step after *Riverside Bayview Homes:* holding that isolated ponds, some only seasonal, wholly located within two Illinois counties, fall under § 404(a)'s definition of "navigable waters" because they serve as habitat for migratory birds. As counsel for respondents conceded at oral argument, such a ruling would assume that "the use of the word navigable in the statute . . . does not have any independent significance." We cannot agree that Congress' separate definitional use of the phrase "waters of the United States" constitutes a basis for reading the term "navigable waters" out of the statute. We said in *Riverside Bayview Homes* that the word "navigable" in the statute was of "limited import" 474 U.S., at 133, and went on to hold that § 404(a) extended to nonnavigable wetlands adjacent to open waters. But it is one thing to give a word limited effect and quite another to give it no effect whatever. The term "navigable" has at least the import of showing us what Congress had in mind as its authority for enacting the CWA: its traditional jurisdiction over waters that were or had been navigable in fact or which could reasonably be so made.

Respondents — relying upon all of the arguments addressed above — contend that, at the very least, it must be said that Congress did not address the precise question of § 404(a)'s scope with regard to nonnavigable, isolated, intrastate waters, and that, therefore, we should give deference to the "Migratory Bird Rule." *See, e.g., Chevron U.S.A. Inc. v. Natural Resources Defense Council, Inc.,* 467 U.S. 837 (1984). We find § 404(a) to be clear, but even were we to agree with respondents, we would not extend *Chevron* deference here.

Where an administrative interpretation of a statute invokes the outer limits of Congress' power, we expect a clear indication that Congress intended that result. This requirement stems from our prudential desire not to needlessly reach constitutional issues and our assumption that Congress does not casually authorize administrative agencies to interpret a statute to push the limit of congressional authority. This concern is heightened where the administrative interpretation alters the federal-state framework by permitting federal encroachment upon a traditional state power . . . .

Twice in the past six years we have reaffirmed the proposition that the grant of authority to Congress under the Commerce Clause, though broad, is not unlimited. See *United States v. Morrison,* 529 U.S. 598 (2000); *United States v. Lopez,* 514 U.S. 549 (1995). Respondents argue that the "Migratory Bird Rule" falls within Congress' power to regulate intrastate activities that "substantially affect" interstate commerce. They note that the protection of migratory birds is a "national interest of very nearly the first magnitude," *Missouri v. Holland,* 252 U.S. 416, 435 (1920), and that, as the Court of Appeals found, millions of people spend over a billion dollars annually on recreational pursuits relating to migratory birds. These arguments raise significant constitutional questions. For example, we would have to evaluate the precise object or activity that, in the aggregate, substantially affects interstate commerce. This is not clear, for although the Corps has claimed jurisdiction over petitioner's land because it contains water areas used as habitat by migratory birds, respondents now, *post litem motam,* focus upon the fact that the regulated activity is petitioner's municipal landfill, which is "plainly of a commercial nature." But this is a far cry, indeed, from the "navigable waters" and "waters of the United States" to which the statute by its terms extends.

These are significant constitutional questions raised by respondents' application of their regulations, and yet we find nothing approaching a clear statement from Congress that it intended § 404(a) to reach an abandoned sand and gravel pit such as we have here. Permitting respondents to claim federal jurisdiction over ponds and mudflats falling within the "Migratory Bird Rule" would result in a significant impingement of the States' traditional and primary power over land and water use. Rather than expressing a desire to readjust the federal-state balance in this manner, Congress chose to "recognize, preserve, and protect the primary responsibilities and rights of States . . . to plan the development and use . . . of land and water resources. . . ." 33 U.S.C. § 1251(b). We thus read the statute as written to avoid the significant constitutional and federalism questions raised by respondents' interpretation, and therefore reject the request for administrative deference.

We hold that 33 CFR § 328.3(a)(3) (1999), as clarified and applied to petitioner's balefill site pursuant to the "Migratory Bird Rule," 51 Fed. Reg. 41217 (1986), exceeds the authority granted to respondents under § 404(a) of the CWA. The judgment of the Court of Appeals for the Seventh Circuit is therefore

Reversed.

Justice STEVENS, with whom Justice SOUTER, Justice GINSBURG, and Justice BREYER join, dissenting:

In 1969, the Cuyahoga River in Cleveland, Ohio, coated with a slick of industrial waste, caught fire. Congress responded to that dramatic event, and to others like it, by enacting the Federal Water Pollution Control Act (FWPCA) Amendments of 1972, 86 Stat. 817, as amended, 33 U.S.C. § 1251 *et seq.*, commonly known as the Clean Water Act (Clean Water Act, CWA, or Act). The Act proclaimed the ambitious goal of ending water pollution by 1985. § 1251(a). The Court's past interpretations of the CWA have been fully consistent with that goal. Although Congress' vision of zero pollution remains unfulfilled, its pursuit has unquestionably retarded the destruction of the aquatic environment. Our Nation's waters no longer burn. Today, however, the Court takes an unfortunate step that needlessly weakens our principal safeguard against toxic water . . . .

The Court has previously held that the Corps' broadened jurisdiction under the CWA properly included an 80-acre parcel of low-lying marshy land that was not itself navigable, directly adjacent to navigable water, or even hydrologically connected to navigable water, but which was part of a larger area, characterized by poor drainage, that ultimately abutted a navigable creek. *United States v. Riverside Bayview Homes, Inc.*, 474 U.S. 121 (1985). Our broad finding in *Riverside Bayview* that the 1977 Congress had acquiesced in the Corps' understanding of its jurisdiction applies equally to the 410-acre parcel at issue here. Moreover, once Congress crossed the legal watershed that separates navigable streams of commerce from marshes and inland lakes, there is no principled reason for limiting the statute's protection to those waters or wetlands that happen to lie near a navigable stream.

In its decision today, the Court draws a new jurisdictional line, one that invalidates the 1986 migratory bird regulation as well as the Corps' assertion of jurisdiction over all waters except for actually navigable waters, their tributaries, and wetlands adjacent to each. Its holding rests on two equally untenable premises: (1) that when Congress passed the 1972 CWA, it did not intend "to exert anything more than its commerce power over navigation"; and (2) that in 1972 Congress drew the boundary defining the Corps' jurisdiction at the odd line on which the Court today settles.

[T]he text of the 1972 amendments affords no support for the Court's holding, and amendments Congress adopted in 1977 do support the Corps' present interpretation of its mission as extending to so-called "isolated" waters. Indeed, simple common sense cuts against the particular definition of the Corps' jurisdiction favored by the majority . . . .

Because of the statute's ambitious and comprehensive goals, it was, of course, necessary to expand its jurisdictional scope. Thus, although Congress opted to carry over the traditional jurisdictional term "navigable waters" from the [Rivers and Harbors Act of 1899] and prior versions of the FWPCA, it broadened the *definition* of that term to encompass all "waters of the United States." § 1362(7). Indeed, the 1972 conferees arrived at the final formulation by specifically deleting the word "navigable" from the definition that had originally appeared in the House version of the Act. The majority today undoes that deletion.

The Conference Report explained that the definition in § 502(7) was intended to "be given the broadest possible constitutional interpretation." S. Conf. Rep. No. 92-1236, p. 144 (1972). The Court dismisses this clear assertion of legislative intent with the back of its hand. The statement, it claims, "signifies that Congress intended to exert [nothing] more than its commerce power over navigation."

The majority's reading drains all meaning from the conference amendment. By 1972, Congress' Commerce Clause power over "navigation" had long since been established. *The Daniel Ball,* 10 Wall. 557 (1871); *Gilman v. Philadelphia,* 3 Wall. 713 (1866); *Gibbons v. Ogden,* 9 Wheat. 1 (1824). Why should Congress intend that its assertion of federal jurisdiction be given the "broadest possible constitutional interpretation" if it did not intend to reach beyond the very heartland of its commerce power? The activities regulated by the CWA have nothing to do with Congress' "commerce power over navigation." Indeed, the goals of the 1972 statute have nothing to do with *navigation* at all.

As we recognized in *Riverside Bayview,* the interests served by the statute embrace the protection of "'significant natural biological functions, including food chain production, general habitat, and nesting, spawning, rearing and resting sites'" for various species of aquatic wildlife. For wetlands and "isolated" inland lakes, that interest is equally powerful, regardless of the proximity of the swamp or the water to a navigable stream. Nothing in the text, the stated purposes, or the legislative history of the CWA supports the conclusion that in 1972 Congress contemplated—much less commanded—the odd jurisdictional line that the Court has drawn today.

The majority accuses respondents of reading the term "navigable" out of the statute. But that was accomplished by Congress when it deleted the word from the § 502(7) definition. After all, it is the *definition* that is the appropriate focus of our attention . . . . Viewed in light of the history of federal water regulation, the broad § 502(7) definition, and Congress' unambiguous instructions in the Conference Report, it is clear that the term "navigable waters" operates in the statute as a shorthand for "waters over which federal authority may properly be asserted." . . .

Although it might have appeared problematic on a "linguistic" level for the Corps to classify "lands" as "waters" in *Riverside Bayview,* 474 U.S., at 131–132, we squarely held that the agency's construction of the statute that it was charged with enforcing was entitled to deference under *Chevron U.S.A. Inc. v. Natural Resources Defense Council, Inc.,* 467 U.S. 837 (1984). Today, however, the majority refuses to extend such deference to the same agency's construction of the same statute. This refusal is unfaithful to both *Riverside Bayview* and *Chevron*. For it is the majority's reading, not the agency's, that does violence to the scheme Congress chose to put into place.

Contrary to the Court's suggestion, the Corps' interpretation of the statute does not "encroac[h]" upon "traditional state power" over land use. "Land use planning in essence chooses particular uses for the land; environmental regulation, at its core, does not mandate particular uses of the land but requires only that, however the land is used, damage to the environment is kept within prescribed limits." *California Coastal Comm'n v. Granite Rock Co.*, 480 U.S. 572, 587(1987). The CWA is not a land-use code; it is a paradigm of environmental regulation . . . .

After the Supreme Court's decision addressing isolated wetlands in *SWANNC*, the Supreme Court took up the question of adjacent wetlands five years later in a case that ultimately engendered at least as much confusion as clarity. As you read the following decision, consider what rules you are able to identify from the fractured opinions, and what questions remain.

Rapanos v. United States

547 U.S. 715 (2006)

Justice SCALIA announced the judgment of the Court and delivered and opinion, in which THE CHIEF JUSTICE, Justice THOMAS, and Justice ALITO join.

In April 1989, petitioner John A. Rapanos backfilled wetlands on a parcel of land in Michigan that he owned and sought to develop. This parcel included 54 acres of land with sometimes-saturated soil conditions. The nearest body of navigable water was 11 to 20 miles away. 339 F.3d 447, 449 (C.A.6 2003) *(Rapanos I)*. Regulators had informed Mr. Rapanos that his saturated fields were "waters of the United States," 33 U.S.C. § 1362(7), that could not be filled without a permit. Twelve years of criminal and civil litigation ensued . . . .

In these consolidated cases, we consider whether four Michigan wetlands, which lie near ditches or man-made drains that eventually empty into traditional navigable waters, constitute "waters of the United States" within the meaning of the Act. [T]he Rapanos and their affiliated businesses deposited fill material without a permit into wetlands on three sites near Midland, Michigan: the "Salzburg site," the "Hines Road site," and the "Pine River site." The wetlands at the Salzburg site are connected to a man-made drain, which drains into Hoppler Creek, which flows into the Kawkawlin River, which empties into Saginaw Bay and Lake Huron. The wetlands at the Hines Road site are connected to something called the "Rose Drain," which has a surface connection to the Tittabawassee River. And the wetlands at the Pine River site have a surface connection to the Pine River, which flows into Lake Huron. It is not clear whether the connections between these wetlands and the nearby drains and ditches are continuous or intermittent, or whether the nearby drains and ditches contain continuous or merely occasional flows of water.

The United States brought civil enforcement proceedings against the Rapanos petitioners. The District Court found that the three described wetlands were "within federal jurisdiction" because they were "'adjacent to other waters of the United States,'" and held petitioners liable for violations of the CWA at those sites. On appeal, the United States Court of Appeals for the Sixth Circuit affirmed, holding that there was federal jurisdiction over the wetlands at all three sites because "there were hydrological connections between all three sites and corresponding adjacent tributaries of navigable waters." . . .

The Rapanos petitioners contend that the terms "navigable waters" and "waters of the United States" in the Act must be limited to the traditional definition of *The Daniel Ball*, which required that the "waters" be navigable in fact, or susceptible of being rendered so. See 10 Wall., at 563. But this definition cannot be applied wholesale to the CWA. The Act uses the phrase "navigable waters" as a *defined* term, and the definition is simply "the waters of the United States." 33 U.S.C. § 1362(7). Moreover, the Act provides, in certain circumstances, for the substitution of state for federal jurisdiction over "navigable waters . . . *other than* those waters which are presently used, or are susceptible to use in their natural condition or by reasonable improvement as a means to transport interstate or foreign commerce . . . including wetlands adjacent thereto." § 1344(g)(1) (emphasis added). This provision shows that the Act's term "navigable waters" includes something more than traditional navigable waters. We have twice stated that the meaning of "navigable waters" in the Act is broader than the traditional understanding of that term, *SWANCC*, 531 U.S., at 167; *Riverside Bayview*. We have also emphasized, however, that the qualifier "navigable" is not devoid of significance, *SWANCC*.

We need not decide the precise extent to which the qualifiers "navigable" and "of the United States" restrict the coverage of the Act. Whatever the scope of these qualifiers, the CWA authorizes federal jurisdiction only over "waters." 33 U.S.C. § 1362(7). The only natural definition of the term "waters," our prior and subsequent judicial constructions of it, clear evidence from other provisions of the statute, and this Court's canons of construction all confirm that "the waters of the United States" in § 1362(7) cannot bear the expansive meaning that the Corps would give it.

The Corps' expansive approach might be arguable if the CWA defined "navigable waters" as "water of the United States." But "the waters of the United States" is something else. The use of the definite article ("the") and the plural number ("waters") shows plainly that § 1362(7) does not refer to water in general. In this form, "the waters" refers more narrowly to water "[a]s found in streams and bodies forming geographical features such as oceans, rivers, [and] lakes," or "the flowing or moving masses, as of waves or floods, making up such streams or bodies." Webster's New International Dictionary 2882 (2d ed.1954) (hereinafter Webster's Second). On this definition, "the waters of the United States" include only relatively permanent, standing or flowing bodies of water. The definition refers to water as found in "streams," "oceans," "rivers," "lakes," and "bodies" of water "forming geographical features." All of these terms connote continuously present, fixed bodies of water, as opposed to ordinarily dry channels through which water occasionally or intermittently flows. Even the least substantial of the definition's terms, namely, "streams," connotes a continuous flow of water in a permanent channel—especially when used in company with other terms such as "rivers," "lakes," and "oceans." None of these terms encompasses transitory puddles or ephemeral flows of water.

The restriction of "the waters of the United States" to exclude channels containing merely intermittent or ephemeral flow also accords with the commonsense understanding of the term. In applying the definition to "ephemeral streams," "wet meadows," storm sewers and culverts, "directional sheet flow during storm events," drain tiles, man-made drainage ditches, and dry arroyos in the middle of the desert, the Corps has stretched the term "waters of the United States" beyond parody. The plain language of the statute simply does not authorize this "Land Is Waters" approach to federal jurisdiction.

In addition, the Act's use of the traditional phrase "navigable waters" (the defined term) further confirms that it confers jurisdiction only over relatively *permanent* bodies of water .... As we noted in *SWANCC*, the traditional term "navigable waters"—even though defined as "the waters of the United States"—carries *some* of its original substance: "[I]t is one thing to give a word limited effect and quite another to give it no effect whatever." That limited effect includes, at bare minimum, the ordinary presence of water.

Our subsequent interpretation of the phrase "the waters of the United States" in the CWA likewise confirms this limitation of its scope. In *Riverside Bayview,* we stated that the phrase in the Act referred primarily to "rivers, streams, and other *hydrographic features more conventionally identifiable as 'waters'* " than the wetlands adjacent to such features. We thus echoed the dictionary definition of "waters" as referring to "streams and bodies *forming geographical features* such as oceans, rivers, [and] lakes." Webster's Second 2882 (emphasis added). Though we upheld in that case the inclusion of wetlands abutting such a "hydrographic featur[e]"—principally due to the difficulty of drawing any clear boundary between the two—nowhere did we suggest that "the waters of the United States" should be expanded to include, in their own right, entities other than "hydrographic features more conventionally identifiable as 'waters.'" Likewise, in both *Riverside Bayview* and *SWANCC*, we repeatedly described the "navigable waters" covered by the Act as "open water" and "open waters." . . . Under no rational interpretation are typically dry channels described as "*open* waters." . . .

Even if the phrase "the waters of the United States" were ambiguous as applied to intermittent flows, our own canons of construction would establish that the Corps' interpretation of the statute is impermissible. As we noted in *SWANCC*, the Government's expansive interpretation would "result in a significant impingement of the States' traditional and primary power over land and water use." Regulation of land use, as through the issuance of the development permits sought by petitioners in both of these cases, is a quintessential state and local power .... The extensive federal jurisdiction urged by the Government would authorize the Corps to function as a *de facto* regulator of immense stretches of intrastate land—an authority the agency has shown its willingness to exercise with the scope of discretion that would befit a local zoning board. See 33 CFR § 320.4(a)(1) (2004). We ordinarily expect a "clear and manifest" statement from Congress to authorize an unprecedented intrusion into traditional state authority . . . . The phrase "the waters of the United States" hardly qualifies.

Likewise, just as we noted in *SWANCC*, the Corps' interpretation stretches the outer limits of Congress's commerce power and raises difficult questions about the ultimate scope of that power . . . . Even if the term "the waters of the United States" were ambiguous as applied to channels that sometimes host ephemeral flows of water (which it is not), we would expect a clearer statement from Congress to authorize an agency theory of jurisdiction that presses the envelope of constitutional validity. . . .

Reasoning

In sum, on its only plausible interpretation, the phrase "the waters of the United States" includes only those relatively permanent, standing or continuously flowing bodies of water "forming geographic features" that are described in ordinary parlance as "streams[,] . . . oceans, rivers, [and] lakes." See Webster's Second 2882. The phrase does not include channels through which water flows intermittently or ephemerally, or channels that periodically provide drainage for rainfall. The Corps' expansive interpretation of the "the waters of the United States" is thus not "based on a permissible construction of the statute." *Chevron U.S.A. Inc. v. Natural Resources Defense Council, Inc.,* 467 U.S. 837, 843 (1984) . . . .

Therefore, *only* those wetlands with a continuous surface connection to bodies that are "waters of the United States" in their own right, so that there is no clear demarcation between "waters" and wetlands, are "adjacent to" such waters and covered by the Act. Wetlands with only an intermittent, physically remote hydrologic connection to "waters of the United States" do not implicate the boundary-drawing problem of *Riverside Bayview,* and thus lack the necessary connection to covered waters that we described as a "significant nexus" in *SWANCC*. Thus, establishing that wetlands such as those at the Rapanos and Carabell sites are covered by the Act requires two findings: first, that the adjacent channel contains a "wate[r] of the United States," (*i.e.,* a relatively permanent body of water connected to traditional interstate navigable waters); and second, that the wetland has a continuous surface connection with that water, making it difficult to determine where the "water" ends and the "wetland" begins . . . .

Chief Justice ROBERTS, concurring.

Five years ago, this Court rejected the position of the Army Corps of Engineers on the scope of its authority to regulate wetlands under the Clean Water Act. The Corps had taken the view that its authority was essentially limitless; this Court explained that such a boundless view was inconsistent with the limiting terms Congress had used in the Act.

In response to the *SWANCC* decision, the Corps and the Environmental Protection Agency (EPA) initiated a rulemaking to consider "issues associated with the scope of waters that are subject to the Clean Water Act (CWA), in light of the U.S. Supreme Court decision in *[SWANCC]*." 68 Fed. Reg.1991 (2003). The "goal of the agencies" was "to develop proposed regulations that will further the public interest by clarifying what waters are subject to CWA jurisdiction and affording full protection to these waters through an appropriate focus of Federal and State resources consistent with the CWA."

Agencies delegated rulemaking authority under a statute such as the Clean Water Act are afforded generous leeway by the courts in interpreting the statute they are entrusted to administer. See *Chevron U.S.A. Inc. v. Natural Resources Defense Council, Inc.*, 467 U.S. 837, 842–845 (1984). Given the broad, somewhat ambiguous, but nonetheless clearly limiting terms Congress employed in the Clean Water Act, the Corps and the EPA would have enjoyed plenty of room to operate in developing *some* notion of an outer bound to the reach of their authority.

The proposed rulemaking went nowhere. Rather than refining its view of its authority in light of our decision in *SWANCC*, and providing guidance meriting deference under our generous standards, the Corps chose to adhere to its essentially boundless view of the scope of its power. The upshot today is another defeat for the agency.

It is unfortunate that no opinion commands a majority of the Court on precisely how to read Congress' limits on the reach of the Clean Water Act. Lower courts and regulated entities will now have to feel their way on a case-by-case basis. This situation is certainly not unprecedented . . . . What is unusual in this instance, perhaps, is how readily the situation could have been avoided.

Justice KENNEDY, concurring in the judgment.

Twice before the Court has construed the term "navigable waters" in the Clean Water Act . . . .

Riverside Bayview and *SWANCC* establish the framework for the inquiry in the cases now before the Court: Do the Corps' regulations, as applied to the wetlands in *Carabell* and the three wetlands parcels in *Rapanos*, constitute a reasonable interpretation of "navigable waters" as in *Riverside Bayview* or an invalid construction as in *SWANCC?* Taken together these cases establish that in some instances, as exemplified by *Riverside Bayview*, the connection between a nonnavigable water or wetland and a navigable water may be so close, or potentially so close, that the Corps may deem the water or wetland a "navigable water" under the Act. In other instances, as exemplified by *SWANCC*, there may be little or no connection. Absent a significant nexus, jurisdiction under the Act is lacking. Because neither the plurality nor the dissent addresses the nexus requirement, this separate opinion, in my respectful view, is necessary.

The plurality's opinion begins from a correct premise. As the plurality points out, and as *Riverside Bayview* holds, in enacting the Clean Water Act Congress intended to regulate at least some waters that are not navigable in the traditional sense. This conclusion is supported by "the evident breadth of congressional concern for protection of water quality and aquatic ecosystems." . . . It is further compelled by statutory text, for the text is explicit in extending the coverage of the Act to some nonnavigable waters. . . .

From this reasonable beginning the plurality proceeds to impose two limitations on the Act; but these limitations, it is here submitted, are without support in the language and purposes of the Act or in our cases interpreting it . . . .

The plurality's first requirement — permanent standing water or continuous flow, at least for a period of "some months," makes little practical sense in a statute concerned with downstream water quality. The merest trickle, if continuous, would count as a "water" subject to federal regulation, while torrents thundering at irregular intervals through otherwise dry channels would not. Though the plurality seems to presume that such irregular flows are too insignificant to be of concern in a statute focused on "waters," that may not always be true. Areas in the western parts of the Nation provide some examples. The Los Angeles River, for instance, ordinarily carries only a trickle of water and often looks more like a dry roadway than a river. . . . Yet it periodically releases water volumes so powerful and destructive that it has been encased in concrete and steel over a length of some 50 miles . . . . Though this particular waterway might satisfy the plurality's test, it is illustrative of what often-dry watercourses can become when rain waters flow. . . .

To be sure, Congress could draw a line to exclude irregular waterways, but nothing in the statute suggests it has done so . . . .

The plurality's second limitation — exclusion of wetlands lacking a continuous surface connection to other jurisdictional waters — is also unpersuasive. To begin with, the plurality is wrong to suggest that wetlands are "*indistinguishable*" from waters to which they bear a surface connection. Even if the precise boundary may be imprecise, a bog or swamp is different from a river . . . .

While the plurality reads nonexistent requirements into the Act, the dissent reads a central requirement out — namely, the requirement that the word "navigable" in "navigable waters" be given some importance. Although the Court has held that the statute's language invokes Congress' traditional authority over waters navigable in fact or susceptible of being made so, the dissent would permit federal regulation whenever wetlands lie alongside a ditch or drain, however remote and insubstantial, that eventually may flow into traditional navigable waters. The deference owed to the Corps' interpretation of the statute does not extend so far.

Congress' choice of words creates difficulties, for the Act contemplates regulation of certain "navigable waters" that are not in fact navigable. Nevertheless, the word "navigable" in the Act must be given some effect. Thus, in *SWANCC* the Court rejected the Corps' assertion of jurisdiction over isolated ponds and mudflats bearing no evident connection to navigable-in-fact waters. And in *Riverside Bayview,* while the Court indicated that "the term 'navigable' as used in the Act is of limited import," . . . , it relied, in upholding jurisdiction, on the Corps' judgment that "wetlands adjacent to lakes, rivers, streams, and other bodies of water may function as integral parts of the aquatic environment even when the moisture creating the wetlands does not find its source in the adjacent bodies of water," . . . The implication, of course, was that wetlands' status as "integral parts of the aquatic environment"—that is, their significant nexus with navigable waters—was what established the Corps' jurisdiction over them as waters of the United States.

Consistent with *SWANCC* and *Riverside Bayview* and with the need to give the term "navigable" some meaning, the Corps' jurisdiction over wetlands depends upon the existence of a significant nexus between the wetlands in question and navigable waters in the traditional sense. The required nexus must be assessed in terms of the statute's goals and purposes. Congress enacted the law to "restore and maintain the chemical, physical, and biological integrity of the Nation's waters," 33 U.S.C. § 1251(a), and it pursued that objective by restricting dumping and filling in "navigable waters," §§ 1311(a), 1362(12). With respect to wetlands, the rationale for Clean Water Act regulation is, as the Corps has recognized, that wetlands can perform critical functions related to the integrity of other waters—functions such as pollutant trapping, flood control, and runoff storage. 33 CFR § 320.4(b)(2). Accordingly, wetlands possess the requisite nexus, and thus come within the statutory phrase "navigable waters," if the wetlands, either alone or in combination with similarly situated lands in the region, significantly affect the chemical, physical, and biological integrity of other covered waters more readily understood as "navigable." When, in contrast, wetlands' effects on water quality are speculative or insubstantial, they fall outside the zone fairly encompassed by the statutory term "navigable waters." . . .

When the Corps seeks to regulate wetlands adjacent to navigable-in-fact waters, it may rely on adjacency to establish its jurisdiction. Absent more specific regulations, however, the Corps must establish a significant nexus on a case-by-case basis when it seeks to regulate wetlands based on adjacency to nonnavigable tributaries. Given the potential overbreadth of the Corps' regulations, this showing is necessary to avoid unreasonable applications of the statute. Where an adequate nexus is established for a particular wetland, it may be permissible, as a matter of administrative convenience or necessity, to presume covered status for other comparable wetlands in the region. That issue, however, is neither raised by these facts nor addressed by any agency regulation that accommodates the nexus requirement outlined here.

This interpretation of the Act does not raise federalism or Commerce Clause concerns sufficient to support a presumption against its adoption. To be sure, the significant-nexus requirement may not align perfectly with the traditional extent of federal authority. Yet in most cases regulation of wetlands that are adjacent to tributaries and possess a significant nexus with navigable waters will raise no serious constitutional or federalism difficulty . . . . As explained earlier, moreover, and as exemplified by *SWANCC*, the significant-nexus test itself prevents problematic applications of the statute. The possibility of legitimate Commerce Clause and federalism concerns in some circumstances does not require the adoption of an interpretation that departs in all cases from the Act's text and structure . . . .

In both the consolidated cases before the Court the record contains evidence suggesting the possible existence of a significant nexus according to the principles outlined above. Thus the end result in these cases and many others to be considered by the Corps may be the same as that suggested by the dissent, namely, that the Corps' assertion of jurisdiction is valid. Given, however, that neither the agency nor the reviewing courts properly considered the issue, a remand is appropriate, in my view, for application of the controlling legal standard. . . .

DISSENT

Justice STEVENS, with whom Justice SOUTER, Justice GINSBURG, and Justice BREYER join, dissenting.

The narrow question presented in [*Rapanos*] is whether wetlands adjacent to tributaries of traditionally navigable waters are "waters of the United States" subject to the jurisdiction of the Army Corps; the question in [*Carabell*] is whether a manmade berm separating a wetland from the adjacent tributary makes a difference. The broader question is whether regulations that have protected the quality of our waters for decades, that were implicitly approved by Congress, and that have been repeatedly enforced in case after case, must now be revised in light of the creative criticisms voiced by the plurality and Justice KENNEDY today. Rejecting more than 30 years of practice by the Army Corps, the plurality disregards the nature of the congressional delegation to the agency and the technical and complex character of the issues at stake. Justice KENNEDY similarly fails to defer sufficiently to the Corps, though his approach is far more faithful to our precedents and to principles of statutory interpretation than is the plurality's.

In my view, the proper analysis is straightforward. The Army Corps has determined that wetlands adjacent to tributaries of traditionally navigable waters preserve the quality of our Nation's waters by, among other things, providing habitat for aquatic animals, keeping excessive sediment and toxic pollutants out of adjacent waters, and reducing downstream flooding by absorbing water at times of high flow. The Corps' resulting decision to treat these wetlands as encompassed within the term "waters of the United States" is a quintessential example of the Executive's reasonable interpretation of a statutory provision . . . .

Our unanimous opinion in *Riverside Bayview* squarely controls these cases . . . .

Contrary to the plurality's revisionist reading today . . . , *Riverside Bayview* nowhere implied that our approval of "adjacent" wetlands was contingent upon an understanding that "adjacent" means having a "continuous surface connection" between the wetland and its neighboring creek. Instead, we acknowledged that the Corps defined "adjacent" as including wetlands "'that form the border of or are in reasonable proximity to other waters'" and found that the Corps reasonably concluded that adjacent wetlands are part of the waters of the United States. Indeed, we explicitly acknowledged that the Corps' jurisdictional determination was reasonable . . . .

Disregarding the importance of *Riverside Bayview*, the plurality relies heavily on the Court's subsequent opinion in [*SWANCC*]. In stark contrast to *Riverside Bayview*, however, *SWANCC* had nothing to say about wetlands, let alone about wetlands adjacent to traditionally navigable waters or their tributaries. Instead, *SWANCC* dealt with a question specifically reserved by *Riverside Bayview*, namely, the Corps' jurisdiction over isolated waters—"'waters that are *not* part of a tributary system to interstate waters or to navigable waters of the United States, the degradation or destruction of which could affect interstate commerce.'" . . . .

Unlike *SWANCC* and like *Riverside Bayview*, the cases before us today concern wetlands that are adjacent to "navigable bodies of water [or] their tributaries." . . . Specifically, these wetlands abut tributaries of traditionally navigable waters. As we recognized in *Riverside Bayview*, the Corps has concluded that such wetlands play important roles in maintaining the quality of their adjacent waters . . . and consequently in the waters downstream . . . .

I would affirm the judgments in both cases, and respectfully dissent from the decision of five Members of this Court to vacate and remand. I close, however, by noting an unusual feature of the Court's judgments in these cases. It has been our practice in a case coming to us from a lower federal court to enter a judgment commanding that court to conduct any further proceedings pursuant to a specific mandate. That prior practice has, on occasion, made it necessary for Justices to join a judgment that did not conform to their own views. In these cases, however, while both the plurality and Justice KENNEDY agree that there must be a remand for further proceedings, their respective opinions define different tests to be applied on remand. Given that all four Justices who have joined this opinion would uphold the Corps' jurisdiction in both of these cases—and in all other cases in which either the plurality's or Justice KENNEDY's test is satisfied—on remand each of the judgments should be reinstated if *either* of those tests is met.

[The dissenting opinion of Justice BREYER has been omitted.]

After Rapanos: *The Clean Water Rule.*

As Chief Justice Roberts suggested in his concurrence, it was perhaps "unfortunate" that no opinion commanded a majority of the Court in *Rapanos*, as the 4-1-4 decision gave rise to extensive litigation and confusion among lower courts. Many courts responded by invoking the guidance from *Marks v. United States*, 430 U.S. 188 (1977): "[W]hen a fragmented Court decides a case and no single rationale explaining the result enjoys the assent of five justices, the holding of the Court may be viewed as that position taken by those Members who concurred in the judgment . . . on the narrowest grounds." *Marks*, 430 U.S. at 193 (internal quotations omitted). Determining the "narrowest grounds" of *Rapanos*, however, proved challenging for many lower courts. As the Chief Justice predicted in his *Rapanos* concurrence, many courts and regulated entities did indeed proceed to "feel their way on a case-by-case basis," often with conflicting results. Consistent with the rule expounded by Justice Stevens in his *Rapanos* dissent, many courts, including the First and Eight Circuits, found "navigable waters" where the subject waters met *either* Justice Scalia's "relatively permanent" or Justice Kennedy's "significant nexus" tests. *See, e.g., United States v. Johnson*, 467 F.3d 56, 66 (1ˢᵗ Cir. 2006), *cert. denied*, 552 U.S. 948 (2007); *United States v. Bailey*, 571 F.3d 791, 798–99 (8ᵗʰ Cir. 2009); *United States v. Evans*, 2006 WL 2221629 (M.D. Fla. 2006). On the other hand, some courts, including the Eleventh Circuit, held that only Justice Kennedy's "significant nexus" standard should be applied. *United States v. McWane*, 505 F.3d 1208 (11ᵗʰ Cir. 2007), *cert. denied*, 555 U.S. 1045 (2008). Still other courts, including the Seventh and Ninth Circuits, focused on Justice Kennedy's test while remaining open to Scalia's standard. *See, e.g., United States v. Gerke Excavating, Inc.*, 464 F.3d 723 (7ᵗʰ Cir. 2006); *Northern California River Watch v. City of Healdsburg*, 457 F.3d 1023 (9ᵗʰ Cir. 2006).

As an initial measure to address this disarray, the EPA and Corps of Engineers issued joint guidance in June 2007, with an additional clarification in December 2008, interpreting the scope of "waters of the United States." The joint guidance sought to help identify "waters of the United States" through a tiered analysis. First, traditional navigable waters (TNW) and the adjoining wetlands would be considered *per se* "waters of the United States." Second, "waters of the United States" would also include "relatively permanent" non-navigable tributaries of TNWs, plus wetlands that directly abut such tributaries. Third, "waters of the United States" would further include tributaries and adjacent wetlands that do not fall into the first two categories if they can be shown to have a "significant nexus" with a TNW, either individually or cumulatively. See *Rapanos* guidance (2008), available at: http://www.usace.army.mil/Portals/2/docs/civilworks/regulatory/cwa_guide/cwa_juris_2dec08.pdf

After issuing the *Rapanos* guidance with relative rapidity, the EPA and Corps of Engineers also embarked on a multi-year effort to promulgate a rule for determining "waters of the United States." The process resulted in the publication of the final "Clean Water Rule" on June 29, 2015. *See Clean Water Rule: Definition of "Waters of the United States,"* 80 Fed. Reg. 37,054 (June 29, 2015).

The Clean Water Rule attempted to resolve uncertainty regarding Clean Water Act jurisdiction by amending the regulatory definition of "waters of the United States" at 33 CFR Part 328 and conforming parts of 40 C.F.R. to clarify water bodies and other landscape features that the agencies would—or would *not*—consider "waters of the United States." The new rule specifically identified eight categories of water bodies and landscape features that would—or, on a case-by-case basis, could—be considered "waters of the United States." These eight categories are as follows:

1. All waters which are currently used, were used in the past, or may be susceptible to use in interstate or foreign commerce, including all waters subject to the ebb and flow of the tide;

2. All interstate waters, including interstate wetlands;

3. The territorial seas;

4. All impoundments of waters otherwise identified as waters of the United States under this section;

5. All tributaries, as defined in paragraph (c)(3) of this section, of waters identified in paragraphs (a)(1) through (3) of this section;

6. All waters adjacent to a water identified in paragraphs (a)(1) through (5) of this section, including wetlands, ponds, lakes, oxbows, impoundments, and similar waters;

new definitions of tributaries, adjacent waters + neighboring waters

7. All waters in paragraphs (a)(7)(i) through (v) of this section where they are determined, on a case-specific basis, to have a significant nexus to a water identified in paragraphs (a)(1) through (3) of this section . . . .

   i. *Prairie potholes* . . .

   ii. *Carolina bays and Delmarva bays* . . .

   iii. *Pocosins* . . .

   iv. *Western vernal pools* . . .

   v. *Texas coastal prairie wetlands* . . .

Justice Kennedy's nexus test

8. All waters located within the 100-year floodplain of a water identified in paragraphs (a)(1) through (3) of this section and all waters located within 4,000 feet of the high tide line or ordinary high water mark of a water identified in paragraphs (a)(1) through (5) of this section where they are determined on a case-specific basis to have a significant nexus to a water identified in paragraphs (a)(1) through (3) of this section . . . .

80 Fed. Reg. 37,104 — 37,105, to be codified at 33 C.F.R. § 328.3(a) and conforming regulations of 40 C.F.R.

The first four categories of waters preserve the Clean Water Act jurisdiction for "traditionally navigable waters" and thus should engender little controversy. Category 5 (tributaries) and Category 6 (adjacent waters) may engender more controversy, particularly due to new definitions of *tributaries*, § 328.3(c)(3); *adjacent waters*, § 328.3(c)(1); and *neighboring* waters, § 328.3(c)(2). Categories 7 and 8 invoke Justice Kennedy's significant nexus test from *Rapanos* for case-specific determinations of "waters of the United States." To clarify this test, the Clean Water Rule provides as follows:

> The term *significant nexus* means that a water, including wetlands, either alone or in combination with other similarly situated waters in the region, significantly affects the chemical, physical, or biological integrity of a water identified in paragraphs (a)(1) through (3) of this section. The term "in the region" means the watershed that drains to the nearest water identified in paragraphs (a)(1) through (3) of this section. For an effect to be significant, it must be more than speculative or insubstantial. Waters are similarly situated when they function alike and are sufficiently close to function together in affecting downstream waters . . . . *Id.* § 328.3(c)(5).

In addition to defining waters that would be included in "waters of the United States," the Clean Water Rule also identified waters that would *not* be included. These exclusions include:

Waters NOT included :

(1) Waste treatment systems, including treatment ponds or lagoons designed to meet the requirements of the Clean Water Act

(2) Prior converted cropland . . . .

(3) The following ditches:

　　(i) Ditches with ephemeral flow that are not a relocated tributary or excavated in a tributary.

　　(ii) Ditches with intermittent flow that are not a relocated tributary, excavated in a tributary, or drain wetlands.

　　(iii) Ditches that do not flow, either directly or through another water, into a water identified in paragraphs (a)(1) through (3) of this section.

(4) The following features:

　　(i) Artificially irrigated areas that would revert to dry land should application of water to that area cease;

　　(ii) Artificial, constructed lakes and ponds created in dry land such as farm and stock watering ponds, irrigation ponds, settling basins, fields flooded for rice growing, log cleaning ponds, or cooling ponds;

　　(iii) Artificial reflecting pools or swimming pools created in dry land;

　　(iv) Small ornamental waters created in dry land;

　　(v) Water-filled depressions created in dry land incidental to mining or construction activity, including pits excavated for obtaining fill, sand, or gravel that fill with water;

　　(vi) Erosional features, including gullies, rills, and other ephemeral features that do not meet the definition of tributary, non-wetland swales, and lawfully constructed grassed waterways; and

　　(vii) Puddles.

(5) Groundwater, including groundwater drained through subsurface drainage systems.

(6) Stormwater control features constructed to convey, treat, or store stormwater that are created in dry land.

(7) Wastewater recycling structures constructed in dry land; detention and retention basins built for wastewater recycling; groundwater recharge basins; percolation ponds built for wastewater recycling; and water distributary structures built for wastewater recycling.

Id. § 328.3(b).

Notes and Questions

1. The Scope of "Waters of the United States" in the Clean Water Rule. What do you think of the new definition of "waters of the United States" as defined in the Clean Water Rule? Is it overinclusive? Underinclusive? Both? Consider Category 8 in the regulatory definition of "waters of the United States," which includes all waters "located within the 100-year floodplain" of the first three categories of "waters of the United States" as well as all waters "located within 4,000 feet of the high tide line or ordinary high water mark" of the first five categories of "waters of the United States." Do you believe the "100-year floodplain" will allow accurate determinations of "waters of the United States" now and into the future marked by climate change? Do you believe that waters 3,999 feet within the ordinary high water mark of a river may have a "significant nexus" to the river, but that waters 4,005 feet from the ordinary high water mark of the river cannot have a significant nexus? If you suspect that the "4,000 feet" standard did not derive from precise scientific calculations, where do you suppose this number came from? More to the point, why do you believe EPA and the Corps chose to incorporate this numeric standard within the definition of "waters of the United States"? Do you suspect it will withstand judicial scrutiny?

2. Exclusions from "Waters of the United States." Consider the list of specific features, such as "swimming pools" and "puddles," excluded from the regulatory definition of "waters of the United States." Do you imagine anyone ever seriously suggested that swimming pools and puddles should be regulated under the Clean Water Act? If not, why do you think the agencies chose to make these exclusions explicit? Consider also the exclusion of three categories of "ditches," including ditches that "are not a relocated tributary or excavated in a tributary." How would one determine whether a ditch today is not a "relocated tributary" or was not "excavated in a tributary"? In the American Southwest, many "ditches" or *acequias* could be centuries old. Is there any relevant timeframe for making this determination about the origin of a ditch?

3. Groundwater. Note the exclusion of "groundwater" from the definition of "waters of the United States" in the Clean Water Rule. The discharge of pollutants into wells that may result in the contamination of groundwater is generally regulated through the Underground Injection Control program of the federal Safe Drinking Water Act, 42 U.S.C. §§ 300h. But what about the discharge of pollutants into groundwater that may result in the pollution of surface waters? Is that or should that be regulated under the Clean Water Act? For many years, federal courts have been split on this question. Some courts have denied that the Clean Water Act may regulate discharges to groundwater even if the groundwater is hydrologically connected to surface water. For example, in *Village of Oconomowoc Lake v. Dayton Hudson Corp.*, 24 F.3d 962 (7th Cir. 1994), *cert. denied*, 513 U.S. 930 (1994), the Seventh Circuit concluded that "[n]either the Clean Water Act nor the EPA's definition of [waters of the United States] asserts authority over ground waters, just because they may be hydrologically connected with surface waters." *Id.* at 965. In reaching this conclusion, the Seventh Circuit drew support from the legislative history of the Clean Water Act, observing that "[m]embers of Congress have proposed adding ground water to the scope of the Clean Water Act, but these proposals have been defeated . . . ." *Id.* A number of other courts have reached similar conclusions. *See, e.g., Town of Norfolk v. United States Army Corps of Engineers*, 968 F.2d 1438, 1451 (1st Cir. 1992); *Exxon Corp. v. Train*, 554 F.2d 1310, 1325–29 (5th Cir. 1977); *Umatilla Water Quality Protection Assn. v. Smith Frozen Foods, Inc.*, 962 F. Supp. 1312, 1318 (D. Or. 1997); *Kelley v. United States*, 618 F. Supp. 1103 (W.D. Mich. 1985).

On the other hand, some courts have found the opposite: that Clean Water Act jurisdiction can extend to discharges to groundwater that connect to surface waters. *See, e.g., Friends of Santa Fe County v. LAC Minerals, Inc.,* 892 F. Supp. 1333, 1357–58 (D.N.M. 1995); *Washington Wilderness Coalition v. Hecla Mining Co.,* 870 F. Supp. 983, 989–90 (E.D. Wash. 1994); *Sierra Club v. Colorado Refining Co.,* 838 F. Supp. 1428, 1434 (D.Colo. 1993); *McClellan Ecological Seepage Situation v. Weinberger,* 707 F. Supp. 1182, 1193–96 (E.D. Cal. 1988), *vacated on other grounds,* 47 F.3d 325 (9th Cir. 1995) *cert. denied,* 516 U.S. 807 (1995). Given this split among the federal courts, do you believe it is appropriate for EPA to resolve the differences via rulemaking? Or would this be better left to appellate courts? Or to Congress? Given the stay imposed by the Sixth Circuit and possible invalidation of the rule in further litigation, does this mean that groundwater may remain subject to Clean Water Act jurisdiction in at least some federal districts?

4. Legal Challenges to the Clean Water Rule. Upon promulgation of the final Clean Water Rule, it was challenged immediately by many states, industry groups, and other interested parties. Most of the challengers complained that the rule was too broad in scope, allowing EPA and the Corps to extend Clean Water Act jurisdiction beyond the bounds of either the statute or the Constitution. *See, e.g.,* Todd Gaziano and M. Reed Hopper, *Final "Waters of the U.S." Rule Is More Over-Reach by EPA,* Forbes (Aug. 3, 2015) (op-ed by attorneys for Pacific Legal Foundation). Other critics, however, complained that the Clean Water Rule was drawn too narrowly, excluding waters that could and should be regulated under the Clean Water Act. *See, e.g.,* Patrick Parenteau, *A Bright Line Mistake: How EPA Bungled the Clean Water Rule,* 46 Envtl. L. 379 (2016) (arguing that "bright line" rule excluding lakes, ponds, and wetlands lying more than 4,000 feet from the ordinary high water mark of jurisdictional waters is unlawful); Michael C. Blumm & Steven M. Thiel, *(Ground)Waters of the United States: Unlawfully Excluding Tributary Groundwaters from Clean Water Jurisdiction,* 46 Envtl. L. 333 (2016) (arguing that regulatory exclusion of all groundwaters is unlawful).

Petitions for judicial review were filed in multiple federal district courts and circuit courts. Responding to one group of 18 states, the Sixth Circuit Court of Appeals in October 2015 stayed implementation of the rule nationwide. *Ohio v. U.S. Army Corps of Engineers,* 803 F.3d 804 (6th Cir. 2015). In staying the rule, the Sixth Circuit concluded that the petitioners had a substantial likelihood of prevailing on the merits. Among other reasons, the Sixth Circuit questioned whether "the new rule's distance limitations are harmonious with" Justice Kennedy's "significant nexus" test in *Rapanos. Id.* at 807. The circuit court did, however, recognize "the need for a new Rule," given that "the definitions of 'navigable waters' and 'waters of the United States' have been clouded by uncertainty, in spite of (or exacerbated by) a series of Supreme Court decisions over the last thirty years." *Id.*

As this book goes to press, the Clean Water Rule remains in a state of flux. On January 13, 2017, the Supreme Court granted certiorari on the question of the Sixth Circuit's finding of its own original jurisdiction to hear the challenge to the Clean Water

Rule, contrary to the finding of other U.S. district courts, which also found original jurisdiction. *National Ass'n of Manufacturers v. Dept. of Defense*, No. 16-299 (Jan. 13, 2017). Outside the judicial branch, of course, the executive branch has experienced changes following the 2016 presidential election. On February 28, 2017, President Trump issued a "Presidential Executive Order on Restoring the Rule of Law, Federalism, and Economic Growth by Reviewing the 'Waters of the United States' Rule." Among other things, the order directed EPA and the Corps of Engineers to review the final Clean Water Rule and "publish for notice and comment a proposed rule rescinding or revising the rule, as appropriate and consistent with law." (Sec. 2) Consistent with that direction, the EPA under new EPA Administrator Scott Pruitt, promptly published a Notice of Intention to Review and Rescind or Revise the Clean Water Rule. 82 Fed. Reg. 12,532 (Mar. 6, 2017). Further rulemaking and litigation may be expected to continue, preserving for the indefinite future the confusion engendered by *Rapanos* in 2006.

VI. Clean Water Act Administration

Like the modern Clean Air Act passed in 1970, the Clean Water Act, enacted in 1972, adopts the model of cooperative federalism whereby implementation authorities are shared largely between the U.S. Environmental Protection Agency and delegated states and tribes. Unique to the Clean Water Act, implementation authority is also shared with the U.S. Army Corps of Engineers, reflecting the historic role of the Corps in protecting navigable waterways. This section will provide a brief outline of the respective duties of the federal, state, and tribal agencies under the Clean Water Act.

A. EPA and the Corps of Engineers

If the respective roles of the EPA and Corps of Engineers under the Clean Water Act appear confusing at first, most questions can be answered by the statute itself. Section 101 of the Clean Water Act designates EPA as the presumptive lead agency: "Except as otherwise expressly provided in this chapter [the Clean Water Act], the Administrator of the Environmental Protection Agency (hereinafter . . . called 'Administrator') shall administer this chapter." 33 U.S.C. § 1251(d). Consistent with this designation, the EPA Administrator (often delegating authority down to Regional Administrators or other EPA officials) is charged by the Clean Water Act with a number of specific duties, to include the following:

- Making grants to states and municipalities for construction of sewage treatment plants. CWA § 201(g).
- Setting standards for pollution control technologies. CWA § 301(b).
- Approving state standards for water quality. CWA § 303(c).
- Reviewing facility records and conducting inspections. CWA § 308(a).
- Taking enforcement actions in response to violations. CWA § 309.

- Issuing permits for the discharge of pollutants into waters of the United States. CWA §402(a).

The primary role for the Corps of Engineers is defined by the statute at §404 of the Clean Water Act. Section 404 provides that "The Secretary may issue permits, after notice and opportunity for public hearings for the discharge of dredged or fill material into the navigable waters...." 33 U.S.C. §1344(a). *See also* CWA §404(d): "The term 'Secretary' as used in this section means the Secretary of the Army, acting through the Chief of Engineers." 33 U.S.C. §1344(d). Consistent with this role established by CWA §404, the statute also charges the Corps of Engineers with limited enforcement actions in response to alleged violations of §404. *See* CWA §309(g)(1)(B), 33 U.S.C. §1319(g)(1)(B) (authorizing the Corps to assess administrative penalties in response to violations of §404); CWA §404(s), 33 U.S.C. §1344(s) (authorizing Corps to issue administrative orders or commence civil litigation in response to violation of permits issued under §404). The Corps also participates in rulemaking to implement its responsibilities under the Clean Water Act. *See, e.g., supra* Section V (joint EPA-Corps regulatory definition of "waters of the United States"). Further, the Corps carries out other related duties in cooperation with EPA. *See, e.g., infra* Section VIII (jurisdictional determinations performed by Corps).

Most of the time, the respective roles of the EPA and the Corps in administering the Clean Water Act inspire little controversy. However, that is not always true, as demonstrated by the following case, which went all the way to the U.S. Supreme Court on the seemingly simple question of which agency had the authority to issue a Clean Water Act permit for a proposed mine in Alaska. As you will see, even then, there were strong differences of opinion among the learned justices of the Supreme Court, with the majority opinion accompanied by a vigorous dissent.

Coeur Alaska, Inc. v. Southeast Alaska Conservation Council

557 U.S. 261 (2009)

Justice KENNEDY delivered the opinion of the Court.

These cases require us to address two questions under the Clean Water Act (CWA or Act). The first is whether the Act gives authority to the United States Army Corps of Engineers, or instead to the Environmental Protection Agency (EPA), to issue a permit for the discharge of mining waste, called slurry. The Corps of Engineers has issued a permit to petitioner Coeur Alaska, Inc. (Coeur Alaska), for a discharge of slurry into a lake in Southeast Alaska. The second question is whether, when the Corps issued that permit, the agency acted in accordance with law. We conclude that the Corps was the appropriate agency to issue the permit and that the permit is lawful.

With regard to the first question, §404(a) of the CWA grants the Corps the power to "issue permits ... for the discharge of ... fill material." 86 Stat. 884; 33 U.S.C. §1344(a). But the EPA also has authority to issue permits for the discharge of pollutants. Section 402 of the Act grants the EPA authority to "issue a permit for the discharge of any pollutant" "[e]xcept as provided in" §404. 33 U.S.C. §1342(a). We conclude that because the slurry Coeur Alaska wishes to discharge is defined by regulation as "fill material," 40 CFR § 232.2 (2008), Coeur Alaska properly obtained its permit from the Corps of Engineers, under § 404, rather than from the EPA, under § 402.

The second question is whether the Corps permit is lawful. Three environmental groups, respondents here, sued the Corps under the Administrative Procedure Act, arguing that the issuance of the permit by the Corps was "not in accordance with law." 5 U.S.C. § 706(2)(A). The environmental groups are Southeast Alaska Conservation Council, Sierra Club, and Lynn Canal Conservation (collectively, SEACC). The State of Alaska and Coeur Alaska are petitioners here.

SEACC argues that the permit from the Corps is unlawful because the discharge of slurry would violate an EPA regulation promulgated under § 306(b) of the CWA, 33 U.S.C. § 1316(b). The EPA regulation, which is called a "new source performance standard," forbids mines like Coeur Alaska's from discharging "process wastewater" into the navigable waters. 40 CFR § 440.104(b)(1). Coeur Alaska, the State of Alaska, and the federal agencies maintain that the Corps permit is lawful nonetheless because the EPA's performance standard does not apply to discharges of fill material.

Reversing the judgment of the District Court, the Court of Appeals held that the EPA's performance standard applies to this discharge so that the permit from the Corps is unlawful.

Petitioner Coeur Alaska plans to reopen the Kensington Gold Mine, located some 45 miles north of Juneau, Alaska. The mine has been closed since 1928, but Coeur Alaska seeks to make it profitable once more by using a technique known as "froth flotation." Coeur Alaska will churn the mine's crushed rock in tanks of frothing water. Chemicals in the water will cause gold-bearing minerals to float to the surface, where they will be skimmed off.

At issue is Coeur Alaska's plan to dispose of the mixture of crushed rock and water left behind in the tanks. This mixture is called slurry. Some 30 percent of the slurry's volume is crushed rock, resembling wet sand, which is called tailings. The rest is water.

The standard way to dispose of slurry is to pump it into a tailings pond. The slurry separates in the pond. Solid tailings sink to the bottom, and water on the surface returns to the mine to be used again.

Rather than build a tailings pond, Coeur Alaska proposes to use Lower Slate Lake, located some three miles from the mine in the Tongass National Forest. This lake is small—800 feet at its widest crossing, 2,000 feet at its longest, and 23 acres in area. Though small, the lake is 51 feet deep at its maximum. The parties agree the lake is a navigable water of the United States and so is subject to the CWA. They also agree there can be no discharge into the lake except as the CWA and any lawful permit allow.

Over the life of the mine, Coeur Alaska intends to put 4.5 million tons of tailings in the lake. This will raise the lakebed 50 feet—to what is now the lake's surface— and will increase the lake's area from 23 to about 60 acres. To contain this wider, shallower body of water, Coeur Alaska will dam the lake's downstream shore. The transformed lake will be isolated from other surface water. Creeks and stormwater runoff will detour around it. Ultimately, lakewater will be cleaned by purification systems and will flow from the lake to a stream and thence onward.

The CWA classifies crushed rock as a "pollutant." 33 U.S.C. § 1362(6). On the one hand, the Act forbids Coeur Alaska's discharge of crushed rock "[e]xcept as in compliance" with the Act. CWA § 301(a), 33 U.S.C. § 1311(a). Section 404(a) of the CWA, on the other hand, empowers the Corps to authorize the discharge of "dredged or fill material." 33 U.S.C. § 1344(a). The Corps and the EPA have together defined "fill material" to mean any "material [that] has the effect of . . . [c]hanging the bottom elevation" of water. 40 CFR § 232.2. The agencies have further defined the "discharge of fill material" to include "placement of . . . slurry, or tailings or similar mining-related materials."

[margin note: 2 conflicting sides]

In these cases the Corps and the EPA agree that the slurry meets their regulatory definition of "fill material." On that premise the Corps evaluated the mine's plan for a § 404 permit. After considering the environmental factors required by § 404(b), the Corp issued Coeur Alaska a permit to pump the slurry into Lower Slate Lake . . . .

The Corps determined that the environmental damage caused by placing slurry in the lake will be temporary. And during that temporary disruption, Coeur Alaska will divert waters around the lake through pipelines built for this purpose. Coeur Alaska will also treat water flowing from the lake into downstream waters, pursuant to strict EPA criteria. Though the slurry will at first destroy the lake's small population of common fish, that population may later be replaced. After mining operations are completed, Coeur Alaska will help "recla[im]" the lake by "[c]apping" the tailings with about 4 inches of "native material." The Corps concluded that

> "[t]he reclamation of the lake will result in more emergent wetlands/vegetated shallows with moderate values for fish habitat, nutrient recycling, carbon/detrital export and sediment/toxicant retention, and high values for wildlife habitat."

If the tailings did not go into the lake, they would be placed on nearby wetlands. The resulting pile would rise twice as high as the Pentagon and cover three times as many acres. If it were chosen, that alternative would destroy dozens of acres of wetlands—a permanent loss. On the premise that when the mining ends the lake will be at least as environmentally hospitable, if not more so, than now, the Corps concluded that placing the tailings in the lake will cause less damage to the environment than storing them above ground: The reclaimed lake will be "more valuable to the aquatic ecosystem than a permanently filled wetland . . . that has lost all aquatic functions and values."

The EPA had the statutory authority to veto the Corps permit, and prohibit the discharge, if it found the plan to have "an unacceptable adverse effect on municipal water supplies, shellfish beds and fishery areas . . . , wildlife, or recreational areas." CWA § 404(c), 33 U.S.C. § 1344(c). After considering the Corps findings, the EPA did not veto the Corps permit, even though, in its view, placing the tailings in the lake was not the "environmentally preferable" means of disposing of them. By declining to exercise its veto, the EPA in effect deferred to the judgment of the Corps on this point.

The EPA's involvement extended beyond the agency's veto consideration. The EPA also issued a permit of its own—not for the discharge from the mine into the lake but for the discharge from the lake into a downstream creek. Section 402 grants the EPA authority to "issue a permit for the discharge of any pollutant," "[e]xcept as provided in [CWA § 404]." 33 U.S.C. § 1342(a). The EPA's § 402 permit authorizes Coeur Alaska to discharge water from Lower Slate Lake into the downstream creek, subject to strict water-quality limits that Coeur Alaska must regularly monitor.

The EPA's authority to regulate this discharge comes from a regulation, termed a "new source performance standard," that it has promulgated under authority granted to it by § 306(b) of the CWA . . . .

Applying that standard to the discharge of water from Lower Slate Lake into the downstream creek, the EPA's § 402 permit sets strict limits on the amount of pollutants the water may contain. The permit requires Coeur Alaska to treat the water using "reverse osmosis" to remove aluminum, suspended solids, and other pollutants. Coeur Alaska must monitor the water flowing from the lake to be sure that the pollutants are kept to low, specified minimums.

SEACC brought suit against the Corps of Engineers and various of its officials in the United States District Court for the District of Alaska. The Corps permit was not in accordance with law, SEACC argued, for two reasons. First, in SEACC's view, the permit was issued by the wrong agency—Coeur Alaska ought to have sought a § 402 permit from the EPA, just as the company did for the discharge of water from the lake into the downstream creek. Second, SEACC contended that regardless of which agency issued the permit, the discharge itself is unlawful because it will violate the EPA new source performance standard for froth-flotation gold mines. (This is the same performance standard described above, which the EPA has already applied to the discharge of water from the lake into the downstream creek. See *ibid.*) SEACC argued that this performance standard also applies to the discharge of slurry into the lake.

The District Court granted summary judgment in favor of the defendants.

The Court of Appeals for the Ninth Circuit reversed and ordered the District Court to vacate the Corps of Engineers' permit. The court held that the EPA's new source performance standard "applies to discharges from the froth-flotation mill at Coeur Alaska's Kensington Gold Mine into Lower Slate Lake." . . .

The question of which agency has authority to consider whether to permit the slurry discharge is our beginning inquiry. We consider first the authority of the EPA and second the authority of the Corps. Our conclusion is that under the CWA the Corps had authority to determine whether Coeur Alaska was entitled to the permit governing this discharge.

Section 402 gives the EPA authority to issue "permit[s] for the discharge of any pollutant," with one important exception: The EPA may not issue permits for fill material that fall under the Corps' § 404 permitting authority . . . .

This is not to say the EPA has no role with respect to the environmental consequences of fill. The EPA's function is different, in regulating fill, from its function in regulating other pollutants, but the agency does exercise some authority. Section 404 assigns the EPA two tasks in regard to fill material. First, the EPA must write guidelines for the Corps to follow in determining whether to permit a discharge of fill material. CWA § 404(b); 33 U.S.C. § 1344(b). Second, the Act gives the EPA authority to "prohibit" any decision by the Corps to issue a permit for a particular disposal site. CWA § 404(c); 33 U.S.C. § 1344(c). We, and the parties, refer to this as the EPA's power to veto a permit.

The Act is best understood to provide that if the Corps has authority to issue a permit for a discharge under § 404, then the EPA lacks authority to do so under § 402.

Even if there were ambiguity on this point, the EPA's own regulations would resolve it. Those regulations provide that "[d]ischarges of dredged or fill material into waters of the United States which are regulated under section 404 of CWA" "do not require [§ 402] permits" from the EPA. 40 CFR § 122.3 . . . .

The agency's interpretation is not "plainly erroneous or inconsistent with the regulation"; and so we accept it as correct. *Auer v. Robbins,* 519 U.S. 452, 461 (1997) (internal quotation marks omitted).

The question whether the EPA is the proper agency to regulate the slurry discharge thus depends on whether the Corps of Engineers has authority to do so. If the Corps has authority to issue a permit, then the EPA may not do so. We turn to the Corps' authority under § 404.

Section 404(a) gives the Corps power to "issue permits . . . for the discharge of dredged or fill material." 33 U.S.C. § 1344(a). As all parties concede, the slurry meets the definition of fill material agreed upon by the agencies in a joint regulation promulgated in 2002. That regulation defines "fill material" to mean any "material [that] has the effect of . . . [c]hanging the bottom elevation" of water — a definition that includes "slurry, or tailings or similar mining-related materials." 40 CFR § 232.2.

SEACC concedes that the slurry to be discharged meets the regulation's definition of fill material . . . .

Rather than challenge the agencies' decision to define the slurry as fill, SEACC instead contends that § 404 contains an implicit exception. According to SEACC, § 404 does not authorize the Corps to permit a discharge of fill material if that material is subject to an EPA new source performance standard.

But § 404's text does not limit its grant of power in this way. Instead, § 404 refers to all "fill material" without qualification. Nor do the EPA regulations support SEACC's reading of § 404. The EPA has enacted guidelines, pursuant to § 404(b), to guide the Corps permitting decision. 40 CFR pt. 230. Those guidelines do not strip the Corps of power to issue permits for fill in cases where the fill is also subject to an EPA new source performance standard.

SEACC's reading of § 404 would create numerous difficulties for the regulated industry. As the regulatory regime stands now, a discharger must ask a simple question — is the substance to be discharged fill material or not? The fill regulation, 40 CFR § 232.2, offers a clear answer to that question; and under the agencies' view, that answer decides the matter — if the discharge is fill, the discharger must seek a § 404 permit from the Corps; if not, only then must the discharger consider whether any EPA performance standard applies, so that the discharger requires a § 402 permit from the EPA.

Under SEACC's interpretation, however, the discharger would face a more difficult problem. The discharger would have to ask — is the fill material also subject to one of the many hundreds of EPA performance standards, so that the permit must come from the EPA, not the Corps? The statute gives no indication that Congress intended to burden industry with that confusing division of permit authority.

The regulatory scheme discloses a defined, and workable, line for determining whether the Corps or the EPA has the permit authority. Under this framework, the Corps of Engineers, and not the EPA, has authority to permit Coeur Alaska's discharge of the slurry . . . .

Justice GINSBURG, with whom Justice STEVENS and Justice SOUTER join, dissenting. *DISSENT*

Petitioner Coeur Alaska, Inc. proposes to discharge 210,000 gallons per day of mining waste into Lower Slate Lake, a 23-acre subalpine lake in Tongass National Forest. The "tailings slurry" would contain concentrations of aluminum, copper, lead, and mercury. Over the life of the mine, roughly 4.5 million tons of solid tailings would enter the lake, raising the bottom elevation by 50 feet. It is undisputed that the discharge would kill all of the lake's fish and nearly all of its other aquatic life.

Coeur Alaska's proposal is prohibited by the Environmental Protection Agency (EPA) performance standard forbidding any discharge of process wastewater from new "froth-flotation" mills into waters of the United States. See 40 CFR § 440.104(b)(1) (2008). Section 306 of the Clean Water Act directs EPA to promulgate such performance standards, 33 U.S.C. § 1316(a), and declares it unlawful for any discharger to violate them, § 1316(e). Ordinarily, that would be the end of the inquiry.

Coeur Alaska contends, however, that its discharge is not subject to EPA's regulatory regime, but is governed, instead, by the mutually exclusive permitting authority of the Army Corps of Engineers. The Corps has authority, under § 404 of the Act, § 1344(a), to issue permits for discharges of "dredged or fill material." By regulation, a discharge that has the effect of raising a water body's bottom elevation qualifies as "fill material." See 33 CFR § 323.2(e) (2008). Discharges properly within the Corps' permitting authority, it is undisputed, are not subject to EPA performance standards.

The litigation before the Court thus presents a single question: Is a pollutant discharge prohibited under § 306 of the Act eligible for a § 404 permit as a discharge of fill material? In agreement with the Court of Appeals, I would answer no. The statute's text, structure, and purpose all mandate adherence to EPA pollution-control requirements. A discharge covered by a performance standard must be authorized, if at all, by EPA . . . .

Is a pollutant discharge prohibited under § 306(e) eligible to receive a § 404 permit as a discharge of fill material? All agree on preliminary matters. Only one agency, the Corps or EPA, can issue a permit for the discharge. Only EPA, through the NPDES program, issues permits that implement § 306. Further, § 306(e) and EPA's froth-flotation performance standard, unless inapplicable here, bar Coeur Alaska's proposed discharge.

No part of the statutory scheme, in my view, calls into question the governance of EPA's performance standard. The text of § 306(e) states a clear proscription: "[I]t shall be unlawful for any owner or operator of any new source to operate such source in violation of any standard of performance applicable to such source." 33 U.S.C. § 1316(e). Under the standard of performance relevant here, "there shall be no discharge of process wastewater to navigable waters from mills that use the froth-flotation process" for mining gold. 40 CFR § 440.104(b)(1). The Act imposes these requirements without qualification.

Section 404, stating that the Corps "may issue permits" for the discharge of "dredged or fill material," does not create an exception to § 306(e)'s plain command. 33 U.S.C. § 1344(a). Section 404 neither mentions § 306 nor states a contrary requirement. The Act can be home to both provisions, with no words added or omitted, so long as the category of "dredged or fill material" eligible for a § 404 permit is read in harmony with § 306. Doing so yields a simple rule: Discharges governed by EPA performance standards are subject to EPA's administration and receive permits under the NPDES, not § 404.

This reading accords with the Act's structure and objectives. It retains, through the NPDES, uniform application of the Act's core pollution-control requirements, and it respects Congress' special concern for new sources. Leaving pollution-related decisions to EPA, moreover, is consistent with Congress' delegation to that agency of primary responsibility to administer the Act. Most fundamental, adhering to § 306(e)'s instruction honors the overriding statutory goal of eliminating water pollution, and Congress' particular rejection of the use of navigable waters as waste disposal sites. See also 33 U.S.C. § 1324 (creating "clean lakes" program requiring States to identify and restore polluted lakes).

The Court's reading, in contrast, strains credulity. A discharge of a pollutant, otherwise prohibited by firm statutory command, becomes lawful if it contains sufficient solid matter to raise the bottom of a water body, transformed into a waste disposal facility. Whole categories of regulated industries can thereby gain immunity from a variety of pollution-control standards . . . .

In sum, it is neither necessary nor proper to read the statute as allowing mines to bypass EPA's zero-discharge standard by classifying slurry as "fill material." The use of waters of the United States as "settling ponds" for harmful mining waste, the Court of Appeals correctly held, is antithetical to the text, structure, and purpose of the Clean Water Act . . . .

For the reasons stated, I would affirm the judgment of the Ninth Circuit.

Notes and Questions

1. In his majority opinion, Justice Kennedy attempts to articulate the respective roles of EPA and the Corps of Engineers for implementing the Clean Water Act, focusing on the role of EPA under § 402 and the role of the Corps under § 404. Particularly after reading Justice Ginsburg's dissent, do you believe that Justice Kennedy gave sufficient consideration to the role of EPA under § 306 for defining new source performance standards? How did Justice Kennedy resolve the apparent conflict between EPA's performance standards forbidding any discharge of process wastewater from new "froth-flotation" mills into waters of the United States and the permit issued by the Corps that would specifically authorize that discharge?

2. While describing the lead role of the Corps of Engineers for § 404, Justice Kennedy acknowledges two important roles here for EPA. First, EPA is responsible under § 404(b)(1) for writing "guidelines" that the Corps must follow in issuing permits under § 404(a). Second, under § 404(c), EPA has the authority to "veto" any § 404 permits proposed by the Corps.

Consistent with § 404(b)(1), EPA has promulgated the "404(b)(1) Guidelines" as rules set forth in 40 C.F.R. Part 230. By its own rule, the Corps has declared that it will deny a 404 permit for any proposed activity that would be inconsistent with these guidelines. *See* 33 C.F.R. § 320.4(a)(1); *Fox Bay Partners v. U.S. Army Corps of Engineers*, 831 F. Supp. 605 (N.D. Ill. 1993). Substantive elements of the 404(b)(1) Guidelines will be considered *infra* in Section VII.C.

Under § 404(c), EPA "is authorized to . . . deny or restrict the use of any defined area . . . as a disposal site, whenever he determines, after notice and opportunity for public hearings, that the discharge of such materials into such area will have an unacceptable adverse effect on municipal water supplies, shellfish beds and fishery areas . . . , wildlife, or recreational areas." 33 U.S.C. § 1344(c). This is the so-called "veto" authority recognized by Justice Kennedy and all parties in *Coeur Alaska*. Without question, this veto authority provides EPA with significant leverage in any issue concerning the issuance of a 404 permit. However, EPA has also used this authority very sparingly. Out of the thousands of 404 permits that the Corps has issued every year for more than 40 years of the Clean Water Act, EPA has only used this veto authority 13 times. *See* https://www.epa.gov/bristolbay/bristol-bay-404c-process (last visited June 22, 2016).

Use of the 404(c) veto is a significant undertaking for EPA. Perhaps the most contentious use of the veto authority in recent history may be EPA's determination concerning the proposed Pebble Mine in Alaska, which sits at the headwaters of Bristol Bay, the world's largest sockeye salmon fishery, with important cultural and economic value to many Alaskans. Following years of scientific study and months of opportunity for public comments, EPA Region 10 proposed using the 404(c) authority to impose restrictions on any permit for the proposed Pebble Mine, which would be one of the largest open-pit copper mines in the world. *See generally, The Effects of Large Scale Mining on the Salmon Ecosystems of the Nushagak and Kvichak River* (EPA, 2014).

Not surprisingly, years of litigation ensued, with a preliminary injunction issued in November 2014 before EPA even made a final determination to exercise its 404(c) authority. *Pebble Limited Partnership v. U.S. Environmental Protection Agency*, No. 3:14-cv-0171-HRH (D. Alaska) (Nov. 25, 2014) (preliminary injunction).

Given the enormous resource demands associated with exercise of the 404(c) authority, coupled with the EPA's resource limitations, how convinced are you of Justice Kennedy's observation in *Coeur Alaska* that, "By declining to exercise its veto, the EPA in effect deferred to the judgment of the Corps"? Are there other reasons the EPA might have declined to exercise its veto authority in this case?

3. After the Supreme Court's 2009 decision in *Coeur Alaska*, affirming the authority of the Corps to issue a 404 permit for the Kensington Mine operation, what happened to Lower Slate Lake? In 2010, the Kensington Mine was indeed reopened and the mining company began to use Lower Slate Lake for disposal of the mine tailings. Now known as the "Tailings Treatment Facility," the former Lower Slate Lake is being filled with mine waste and subjected to monitoring by state and federal agencies to ensure compliance with permit conditions. Despite Justice Ginsburg's astute observation that filling a lake with mining pollution is "antithetical" to the express goals of the Clean Water Act, early assessment from fishery biologists indicates that the watershed downstream from the new "Tailings Treatment Facility" is *not* experiencing an ecological catastrophe. *See Benjamin P. Brewster, Aquatic Studies at Kensington Gold Mine, 2015*, Tech. Rpt. No. 16-03 (Feb. 2016) (report by fisheries biologist with Alaska Dept. of Fish and Game). Can you see why? After the Court's ruling in *Coeur Alaska*, what regulatory requirements under the Clean Water Act remain in place to protect the downstream ecology?

B. State Implementation

As mentioned, the Clean Water Act, like the Clean Air Act and other pollution control statutes, adopts the model of "cooperative federalism," with CWA programs intended to be implemented primarily by states, consistent with national standards. Clean Water Act § 101 makes this intent explicit: "It is the policy of the Congress to recognize, preserve, and protect the primary responsibilities and rights of States to prevent, reduce, and eliminate pollution . . . ." 33 U.S.C. § 1251(b). Consistent with this stated policy, Congress provided two principal means for engaging states—and also potentially tribes and U.S. territories—in implementation of the Clean Water Act. First, Congress authorized states to assume responsibility for the issuance and enforcement of discharge permits under § 402. 33 U.S.C. § 1342(b) ("State permit programs"). Second, Congress authorized states to establish water quality standards, subject to federal "floors." 33 U.S.C. § 1313. We will address the state role in water quality standards when we consider the process for establishing water quality standards later in this chapter. For now, however, we will consider the related questions of: (1) how states obtain authority to implement the CWA permit programs and (2) how state implementation remains subject to EPA oversight.

1. How States and Tribes Obtain Authority

As with other pollution control statutes, states have no obligation carry out CWA programs, but most of them do. As of 2015, only four states (Idaho, New Mexico, New Hampshire, Massachusetts) and the District of Columbia had no authorization to carry out the National Pollutant Discharge Elimination System (NPDES) permit program under § 402. See https://www.epa.gov/sites/production/files/2015-10/documents /state_npdes_program_status.pdf (last visited 6/23/16). In these four states and the District of Columbia, EPA retains principal responsibility for issuing and enforcing all NPDES permits. In a number of other states that are "partially authorized," EPA retains responsibility for issuing certain NPDES permits, such as permits issued to federal facilities. Moreover, EPA always retains authority for issuing NPDES on tribal lands, unless the tribal government itself is authorized to issue permits under the process known as Treatment as State. See CWA § 518(e), 33 U.S.C. § 1377(e).

The requirements for states seeking authorization to implement the NPDES permit program appear in CWA § 402(b) and implementing regulations at 40 C.F.R. Part 123. The process begins with a letter from the State's governor describing the capacity of the state to implement a program and a letter from the state's attorney certifying that the state has the state laws and other legal authority to carry out the proposed programs. At that point, EPA "shall approve" the state's program, unless EPA finds that the program does not meet certain criteria, to include the following:

- Permits issued by the state must ensure compliance with the same substantive standards as permits issued by EPA. 33 U.S.C. § 1342(b)(1).

- Permits issued by the state allow for monitoring and inspection of the permitted facility, consistent with § 308. 33 U.S.C. § 1342(b)(2).

- The public, any affected state, and EPA receive notice and opportunity to comment on a proposed permit. 33 U.S.C. § 1342(b)(3), (4).

- Violations of the permit or permit program are punishable by civil and criminal penalties. 33 U.S.C. § 1342(b)(7).

In addition to these requirements, in order for a tribe to receive authorization to carry out CWA authorities, they must be federally recognized, *see* 33 U.S.C. § 1377(h) (2) ("Indian tribe" means any Indian tribe, band, group, or community recognized by the Secretary of the Interior), and have legal control or jurisdiction over the water resources to be regulated, *see id.* § 1377(e)(2) ("water resources which are held by an Indian tribe . . . or otherwise within the borders of an Indian reservation"). Of course, either one of these additional criteria may present significant hurdles for some tribes, and each case must be considered individually. *See, e.g.*, Rebecca M. Mitchell, *"People of the Outside": The Environmental Impact of Federal Recognition of American Indian Nations*, 42 B.C. Envtl. Aff. L. Rev. 507 (2015) (Duwamish Tribe, native people of the area including present-day Seattle, denied federal recognition despite more than 45 years of petitions); *Idaho v. U.S.*, 533 U.S. 262 (2001) (epic litigation to establish jurisdiction of Coeur d'Alene Tribe over lower part of Idaho's Lake Coeur d'Alene).

Despite these sometimes extraordinary hurdles, however, many tribes today do indeed administer NPDES permit programs successfully, and this number may be expected to expand in the future as tribes develop the resources and institutional capacity to carry out these programs.

A common concern is how closely a state or tribal CWA program must reflect the federal program in order to receive authorization. Should a state program mirror the federal program in order to discourage polluting industries from "forum shopping"? Or should states retain some flexibility in designing their programs, as long as they meet the minimum criteria specified in the statute? EPA's rules governing state authorization, promulgated at 40 C.F.R. Part 123, do indeed allow for state flexibility. These rules, however, were challenged by environmental organizations, which resulted in the following decision.

Natural Resources Defense Council, Inc. v. U.S. EPA
859 F.2d 156 (D.C. Cir. 1988)

PER CURIAM:

* * *

1. *Regulatory Uniformity and State Autonomy.* Petitioners challenge two regulations implementing the Act's provisions on state assumption of the permit program. Citizens for a Better Environment (CBE) attacks the standards for minimum public participation at the state level. NRDC complains of the absence of state authority to impose a given maximum penalty. Both protests rest on the assumption that congressional emphasis on uniformity was directed to procedural as well as substantive standards, and that as a result federal requirements respecting public participation and penalties must be mirrored on the state level.

Uniformity is indeed a recurrent theme in the Act, a direct manifestation of concern that the permit program be standardized to avoid the "industrial equivalent of forum shopping" and the creation of "pollution havens" by migration of dischargers to areas having lower pollution standards. The desired uniformity, however, is spoken of almost exclusively in relation to effluent limitations. Moreover, Congress' quest for homogeneity is in tension with its independent emphasis on state autonomy, which is repeated throughout the legislative history of the Act, is enshrined in the Act as the basic policy to "recognize, preserve, and protect the primary responsibilities and rights of States," and is the very foundation of the permit program . . . .

In fashioning its guidelines on both participation and penalties, EPA endeavored to reconcile the competing objectives of regulatory uniformity and state autonomy by establishing a floor for citizen participation and state enforcement authority, while ensuring that states have the maximum possible independence. We are fully mindful of the rule that an agency is entitled to special deference when it harmonizes competing policies; "'[i]f this choice represents a reasonable accommodation of conflicting policies that were committed to the agency's care by the statute, we should not disturb it unless it appears from the statute or its legislative history that the accommodation is not one that Congress would have sanctioned.'" The regulations at issue are classic examples of such administrative balancing, and we find that they fall well within the permissible bounds of the agency's discretion.

2. *Public Participation.* CBE assails on two grounds EPA's regulations specifying the minimum level of public participation that states must afford. CBE first claims that the regulations are inadequate because they do not include all of the protections built into the federal permit program. Alternatively, it contends that they fail to provide any meaningful right.

The requirement of public participation in efforts to control water pollution is established in the congressional declaration of policy and goals of the Act . . .

The statutory text does not, however, elaborate on the extent of public participation contemplated by Congress . . . .

As CBE insists, Congress considered the citizen suit provision to be of dual importance, serving both as a method of prodding the agency, and as a backup means of enforcing the Act. On the other hand, Congress also expressed reservations about potential abuses of citizen suits, and expressly noted its concern "with protecting local government, industry, and individuals from harassing law suits while still keeping the courts open to responsible parties concerned with environmental protection." Nowhere in either the Act or its legislative history is there any express statement that the provisions of Section [505] extend to states, nor do we find persuasive any equivocal intimation in that direction. It would have been very easy for Congress to say so if that was what it had in mind; instead, even intervention as of right was restricted to litigation in federal courts . . . .

CBE would also bootstrap a prescription for state-level citizen suits from the statutory mandate that "[t]he permit program of the Administrator . . . shall be subject to the same terms, conditions, and requirements as apply to a State program . . . under subsection [402(b)]." 33 U.S.C. § 1342(b). As the Seventh Circuit has noted, however, this provision on its face applies in only one direction: the federal program must meet specific requirements set out in subsection (b), such as a five-year fixed permit term and incorporation of effluent limitations. Furthermore, the section cross-references only "terms, conditions, and requirements . . . under subsection (b)." Subsection (b) already applies to states, rendering CBE's argument empty, and refers only generally to public participation without any requirement of citizen suits.

Finally, we note that EPA maintains that "[n]othing in the Act or its legislative history indicates that Congress intended that states be required to provide identical rights to those Congress specified for citizens in Federal court." Because we have found that "Congress has not directly addressed the precise question at issue," and determined that "the agency's answer is based on a permissible construction of the statute," we defer to EPA's reading. We therefore hold that state-level citizen suits are not commanded by the Act, and find no impropriety in the Administrator's failure to require state programs to afford them.

CBE asks that, should we decide that state public participation specifications need not match the federal requirements, we hold that the present regulations are incapable of producing meaningful public involvement. We decline this invitation . . . .

[W]e conclude that the regulations, as interpreted, provide meaningful and adequate opportunity for public participation consistent with the statutory mandate. The regulations reasonably accommodate conflicting statutory prescriptions by "establish[ing] requirements which ensure the benefits of public participation, while intruding less into the States' management of their judicial and administrative systems." We accordingly reject CBE's challenge.

3. *Maximum Penalties.* Section [309], as amended by the Water Quality Act of 1987, specifies the penalties assessable on the federal level . . . .

States are required to have "adequate authority" "[t]o abate violations of the permit or the permit program, including civil and criminal penalties and other ways and means of enforcement." The Administrator was charged with the responsibility of fashioning guidelines defining the minimum enforcement provisions deemed adequate. Pursuant to this mandate, the Administrator promulgated the regulations here in question, which require state authority

[t]o assess or sue to recover in court civil penalties and to seek criminal remedies, including fines, as follows:

(i) Civil penalties . . . shall be assessable in at least the amount of $5,000 a day for each violation.

(ii) Criminal fines [for permit or filing violations] . . . shall be assessable in at least the amount of $10,000 a day for each violation.

(iii) Criminal fines [for falsification of reports or monitoring] . . . shall be recoverable in at least the amount of $5,000 for each instance of violation. 40 C.F.R. § 123.27(a)(3).

Petitioner NRDC contends that these regulations are invalid because they do not compel the states to provide authority to levy the maximum penalties assessable in federal enforcement programs.

Throughout its consideration of the Act, Congress reiterated the important role penalties play in enforcement of water pollution standards, and emphasized the need for substantial penalties . . . .

In this articulation of congressional purpose, coupled with the congressional expectation that states would bear the primary enforcement burdens of the Act, NRDC would find a mandate for state ability and willingness to assess the federally required maximum penalties.

NRDC also relies on Section [510], which provides that states "may not adopt or enforce any effluent limitation, or other limitation, effluent standard, prohibition, pretreatment standard, or standard of performance which is less stringent than the effluent limitation, or other limitation, effluent standard, prohibition, pretreatment standard, or standard of performance under this chapter." NRDC asserts that this means that states also may not adopt penalty provisions less stringent than those that the Act prescribes for federal enforcement. We note, however, that this section refers, not to enforcement powers, but only to effluent limitations and similar standards.

The Water Quality Act of 1987 contained a provision amending Section 309 that weighs heavily against NRDC's contentions. The section laying out increased maximum civil penalties states:

> INCREASED PENALTIES NOT REQUIRED UNDER STATE PROGRAMS.— The Federal Water Pollution Control Act shall not be construed as requiring a State to have a civil penalty for violations described in section 309(d) of such Act which has the same monetary amount as the civil penalty established by such section, as amended by paragraph (1). Nothing in this paragraph shall affect the Administrator's authority to establish or adjudge by regulation a minimum acceptable State civil penalty.

NRDC concedes that this section relieves state programs from any obligation to match the maximum federal civil penalties set forth in the Water Quality Act. But, NRDC says, the quoted language should be read as a narrow exception applicable only to the federal penalties to which it expressly refers, with the result that state programs must adopt the federal civil penalties in force prior to the passage of the Water Quality Act and, more clearly than ever, must incorporate the maximum federal criminal penalties into their programs. EPA's reply is that the new provision should be understood as simply a confirmation of the broad authority the Administrator already enjoyed in crafting state program requirements. We accept EPA's position.

This challenge by NRDC exposes the same logical infirmity flawing the attack leveled by CBE. It presumes an unexpressed congressional intent that state requirements must mirror the federal ones, a presumption inconsistent with the elements of the statutory scheme limiting operation of the provisions to enforcement efforts at the national level and explicitly empowering the Administrator to set the prerequisites for state plans. Nothing in the Act or its legislative history supports a reduction of the Administrator's discretion to activity purely ministerial, as approval of NRDC's thesis would do, and the Administrator's conclusion to the contrary is eminently reasonable . . . .

The rationale EPA offers for its disinclination to adopt the statutory maxima also buttresses this conclusion. The proposed regulations would have required the states to exert enforcement authority virtually identical with the federal, including the same levels of minimum and maximum fines. In final structure, however, the regulations, changed largely in response to state comments, reflect the balancing of uniformity and state autonomy contemplated by the Act:

> The Agency has determined that it is necessary to set specific minimum levels of fines and penalties which States must have the authority to recover in

order to ensure effective State enforcement programs. Without such minimum levels, EPA would often be forced to take its own enforcement action in approved States because the State action imposed inadequate penalties. Such EPA action, while available as a backup, is not intended to be relied upon as the prime enforcement mechanism in approved States. Accordingly, the Agency has set minimum levels of fines and penalties. However, it has reduced the levels below those' available to EPA based on the large volumes of comments from states requesting such relief.

We will not disturb this "reasonable accommodation of manifestly competing interests," and consequently we uphold the agency's penalty regulations.

Judgment accordingly.

2. How State and Tribal Implementation Is Overseen

After a CWA program is delegated to a state or tribal government for implementation, there remain many mechanisms for EPA to ensure that the delegated authority is administered properly in order to meet the objectives of the program. According to § 402(c), in the event that EPA determines a state is not administering a CWA program properly, it "shall withdraw approval such program." 33 U.S.C. § 1342(c). This extraordinary authority is rarely, if ever, used, however. More commonly, if EPA believes the state or tribe is proposing to issue an NPDES that does not meet CWA requirements, the EPA will provide written comments identifying the problems. *See* 33 U.S.C. § 1342(d)(1) ("Each State shall transmit to the Administrator a copy of each permit application received"). If EPA's comments are not resolved by the state, EPA then has the statutory authority to veto the proposed permit. *Id.* § 1342(d)(2) ("No permit shall issue (A) if the Administrator within ninety days . . . objects in writing"). Again, this is also a drastic authority and unlikely to be used by EPA in any typical case. But the EPA's permit veto authority does give EPA comments substantial weight in the permitting process.

The most common way EPA ensures compliance with CWA requirements in authorized jurisdictions comes in the form of EPA periodic reviews of state enforcement data and in regular coordination between EPA regional offices and state environmental agencies. EPA may also ensure compliance directly by reviewing facility monitoring data and by taking enforcement actions in response to facility violations. Under § 308(a), and consistent with § 402(i) ("Nothing in this section shall be construed to limit the authority of the Administrator to take action pursuant to section [309] of this title"), EPA reserves the authority to "inspect, monitor, enter, and require reports" from facilities with permits issued by an authorized state to the same extent as EPA may do in non-authorized states. Moreover, EPA retains full authority to bring enforcement actions in authorized states, including the assessment of administrative, civil, and criminal sanctions. CWA § 309(a)(1). Knowing this, many environmental defense counsel prefer to resolve violations with state regulators before EPA becomes involved. In turn, many state regulators may invoke the threat of enforcement by EPA (the "800-pound gorilla") in order to encourage violators to settle quickly.

VII. Protection of Wetlands

A. Introduction

One of the most controversial but important elements of the Clean Water Act is the program for protecting wetlands, principally under CWA §404. As we have seen, "adjacent wetlands" are included in the regulatory definition of "waters of the United States." Wetlands have been included in the regulatory definition promulgated by EPA and the Corps of Engineers since 1975, and this inclusion was generally approved by the U.S. Supreme Court in 1985. See *United States v. Riverside Bayview Homes, Inc.*, 474 U.S. 121 (1985) ("We cannot say that the Corps' conclusion that adjacent wetlands are inseparably bound up with the 'waters' of the United States . . . is unreasonable"). Notwithstanding the controversy engendered by *SWANCC* in 2001 and *Rapanos* in 2006, today the regulation of at least *some* wetlands under the Clean Water Act is no longer in doubt. This conclusion, of course, begs the question of what are "wetlands" for purposes of Clean Water Act regulation, as well as the question of what are the substantive requirements for wetlands subject to Clean Water Act regulation. We will address each of those questions in turn below. First, however, we consider the question of why we should protect wetlands at all.

The idea that wetlands should be protected from destruction is a relatively recent notion in American history. For much of our history, swamps, marshes, and other features that today we would call wetlands were considered wastelands and vile places, the haunts of serpents and the breeding grounds of malaria. They were also considered a major impediment to agriculture, and as such were methodically drained and filled across the United States, often with government assistance. *See, e.g.,* Swamp Lands Act of 1850, 43 U.S.C. §982 (authorizing federal grants "to enable the several States . . . to construct the necessary levees and drains, to reclaim the swamp").

According to the U.S. Fish and Wildlife Service, at the time of our country's founding, the lower 48 states had approximately 221 million acres of wetlands. Since that time, within the same area, more than half of our wetlands have been lost. Thomas E. Dahl, U.S. Fish and Wildlife Service, Status and Trends of Wetlands in the Coterminous United States: 2004 to 2009, at 16 (2011). Of the staggering amount of wetlands lost in the United States, agriculture has been by far the largest cause, representing approximately 87 percent of the acres lost between the 1950s and 1970s. Ralph W. Tiner Jr., U.S. Fish & Wildlife Service, Wetlands of the United States: Current Status and Recent Trends 31 (1984).

Since the dawn of wetlands protections under the Clean Water Act, the rate of wetlands losses has fallen dramatically. Before the Clean Water Act, between the 1950s and 1970s, the U.S. Fish and Wildlife Service estimates that the United States lost approximately 458,000 acres of wetlands per year. Between the 1970s and 1980s, the U.S. lost approximately 290,000 acres of wetlands per year. Most recently, between 2004 and 2009, the annual loss of wetlands was estimated at 13,800 acres per year. Dahl, *supra*, at 40.

The dramatic reduction in wetlands losses over the last several decades reflects the establishment of legal protections under the Clean Water Act, of course. But it also reflects the growing public recognition of the benefits provided by wetlands. As the U.S. Fish and Wildlife Service succinctly states:

> Wetlands provide a multitude of ecological, economic and social benefits. They provide habitat for fish, wildlife and a variety of plants. Wetlands are nurseries for many saltwater and freshwater fishes and shellfish of commercial and recreational importance. Wetlands are also important landscape features because they hold and slowly release flood water and snow melt, recharge groundwater, acts as filters to cleanse water of impurities, recycle nutrients, and provide recreation and wildlife viewing opportunities for millions of people. http://www.fws.gov/wetlands/Other/What-are-wetlands.html (last visited 4/24/2016).

Emphasizing the importance of wetlands as habitat for fish and wildlife, the U.S. EPA has reported that more than one-third of all threatened and endangered species in the United States live only in wetlands, and almost one-half use wetlands at some point in their lives. http://www.epa.gov/owow/wetlands/fish.html (visited 4/24/2016). Recognizing the economic importance of wetlands, the U.S. EPA reported that wetlands-related tourism activities such as hunting, fishing, bird-watching, and photography contributed approximately $50 billion to the national economy in 1991 and contributes almost $79 billion per year in the commercial and recreational fishing industry. U.S. EPA, Functions and Values of Wetlands (2002), available at http://nepis.epa.gov/Exe/ZyPDF.cgi/200053Q1.PDF?Dockey=200053Q1.PDF (last visited on 4/24/2016). In the era of climate change, the protections of wetlands may become more vital, both for purposes of climate change mitigation and climate change adaptation. On the mitigation side, according to the U.S. EPA, "Wetlands store carbon within their plants, communities, and soil instead of releasing it to the atmosphere as carbon dioxide." http://www.epa.gov/owow/wetlands.html (last visited on 4/24/2016). On the climate change adaptation side, wetlands such as mangrove swamps may play key roles now and increasingly in the future in helping to protect coastal communities from the ravaging effects of storm surge as a result of rising sea levels and more frequent and violent weather events. Robert R.M. Verchick, Facing Catastrophe (2012).

B. Wetlands Determinations

The Clean Water Act does not define "wetlands," but since 1977 the EPA and Corps of Engineers in their regulations have defined "wetlands" to mean:

> those areas that are inundated or saturated by surface or ground water at a frequency and duration sufficient to support, and that under normal circumstances do support, a prevalence of vegetation typically adapted for life in saturated soil conditions. Wetlands generally include swamps, marshes, bogs, and similar areas. 33 CFR § 328.3(b); 40 CFR § 230.3(t).

Wetlands are thus defined, in part, by the plant communities associated with wetlands—a definition that may seem a bit circular. Another common challenge, even where wetlands are unquestionably present, is the determination of *how far* those wetlands extend in any direction. To help provide useful instruction to its field offices on this question of *wetlands delineation*, the Corps of Engineers in 1987 adopted a Wetlands Delineation Manual that is still in use by the Corps today. WATERWAYS EXPERIMENT STATION, U.S. DEPARTMENT OF THE ARMY, ARMY CORPS OF ENGINEERS WETLANDS DELINEATION MANUAL (Jan. 1987), available at http://www.wetlands.com/regs/tlpage02e.htm. Other federal agencies may use different guidances and criteria for delineating wetlands for different purposes. For example, the Natural Resources Conservation Service within the U.S. Department of Agriculture delineates wetlands in "agricultural areas" for purposes of enforcing the Swampbuster program under the Food Security Act of 1985, Pub. L. No. 99-198, 99 Stat. 1504 (1985), which generally denies subsidies to farmers if they produce agricultural products on converted wetlands. 16 U.S.C. §§ 3801, 3821–3824. The U.S. Fish and Wildlife Service also conducts wetlands delineations for purposes of carrying out its charge with mapping the nation's wetlands. *See generally* http://www.fws.gov/wetlands/ (last visited 4/26/16). In general, the Corps of Engineers remains the lead agency for *jurisdictional determinations* (i.e., determining the presence or absence of wetlands and other "waters of the United States") for purposes of the enforcing provisions of the Clean Water Act and the Corps continues to apply the 1987 WETLANDS DELINEATION MANUAL for this purpose.

What is the legal effect of a jurisdictional determination (JD) by the Corps of Engineers? At least until recently, it might have depended on whom you asked. With no statutory requirement in the Clean Water Act compelling the Corps to perform jurisdictional determinations, the Corps considered its JDs to be primarily for the benefit of landowners who wanted to know whether permitting requirements might apply to the development of their property. Property owners, however, began to see JDs differently, as an agency determination that their property could not be developed as they desired. If a JD indeed has this effect, with consequent impacts on property value, should property owners have some right, grounded perhaps in either due process or the Administrative Procedure Act, to challenge the JDs? Or must they wait until after the Corps or EPA brings an enforcement action in response to an asserted Clean Water Act violation? That was the question that went before the U.S. Supreme Court in 2016 for decision.

U.S. Army Corps of Engineers v. Hawkes Co. Inc.

136 S. Ct. 1807 (2016)

Chief Justice ROBERTS:

The Clean Water Act regulates the discharge of pollutants into "the waters of the United States." 33 U.S.C. §§ 1311(a), 1362(7), (12). Because it can be difficult to determine whether a particular parcel of property contains such waters, the U.S. Army Corps of Engineers will issue to property owners an "approved jurisdictional

Issue

determination" stating the agency's definitive view on that matter. See 33 CFR § 331.2 and pt. 331, App. C (2015). The question presented is whether that determination is final agency action judicially reviewable under the Administrative Procedure Act . . . .

The Corps specifies whether particular property contains "waters of the United States" by issuing "jurisdictional determinations" (JDs) on a case-by-case basis. § 331.2. JDs come in two varieties: "preliminary" and "approved." While preliminary JDs merely advise a property owner "that there *may* be waters of the United States on a parcel," approved JDs definitively "stat[e] the presence or absence" of such waters. *Ibid.* (emphasis added). Unlike preliminary JDs, approved JDs can be administratively appealed and are defined by regulation to "constitute a Corps final agency action." §§ 320.1(a)(6), 331.2. They are binding for five years on both the Corps and the Environmental Protection Agency, which share authority to enforce the Clean Water Act. See 33 U.S.C. §§ 1319, 1344(s); 33 CFR pt. 331, App. C; EPA, Memorandum of Agreement: Exemptions Under Section 404(F) of the Clean Water Act § VI-A (1989) (Memorandum of Agreement).

Respondents are three companies engaged in mining peat in Marshall County, Minnesota. Peat is an organic material that forms in waterlogged grounds, such as wetlands and bogs. See Xuehui & Jinming, Peat and Peatlands, in 2 Coal, Oil Shale, Natural Bitumen, Heavy Oil and Peat 267–272 (G. Jinsheng ed. 2009) (Peat and Peatlands). It is widely used for soil improvement and burned as fuel. *Id.,* at 277. It can also be used to provide structural support and moisture for smooth, stable greens that leave golfers with no one to blame but themselves for errant putts. See Monteith & Welton, Use of Peat and Other Organic Materials on Golf Courses, 13 Bulletin of the United States Golf Association Green Section 90, 95-100 (1933). At the same time, peat mining can have significant environmental and ecological impacts, see Peat and Peatlands 280–281, and therefore is regulated by both federal and state environmental protection agencies, see, *e.g.,* Minn.Stat. § 103G.231 (2014).

Respondents own a 530-acre tract near their existing mining operations. The tract includes wetlands, which respondents believe contain sufficient high quality peat, suitable for use in golf greens, to extend their mining operations for 10 to 15 years.

In December 2010, respondents applied to the Corps for a Section 404 permit for the property. A Section 404 permit authorizes "the discharge of dredged or fill material into the navigable waters at specified disposal sites." 33 U.S.C. § 1344(a). Over the course of several communications with respondents, Corps officials signaled that the permitting process would be very expensive and take years to complete. The Corps also advised respondents that, if they wished to pursue their application, they would have to submit numerous assessments of various features of the property, which respondents estimate would cost more than $100,000.

In February 2012, in connection with the permitting process, the Corps issued an approved JD stating that the property contained "water of the United States" because its wetlands had a "significant nexus" to the Red River of the North, located some 120 miles away. Respondents appealed the JD to the Corps' Mississippi Valley Division Commander, who remanded for further factfinding. On remand, the Corps reaffirmed its original conclusion and issued a revised JD to that effect.

Respondents then sought judicial review of the revised JD under the Administrative Procedure Act (APA), 5 U.S.C. § 500 *et seq.* The District Court dismissed for want of subject matter jurisdiction, holding that the revised JD was not "final agency action for which there is no other adequate remedy in a court," as required by the APA prior to judicial review. The Court of Appeals for the Eighth Circuit reversed and we granted certiorari.

The Corps contends that the revised JD is not "final agency action" and that, even if it were, there are adequate alternatives for challenging it in court. We disagree at both turns.

In *Bennett v. Spear*, 520 U.S. 154 (1997), we distilled from our precedents two conditions that generally must be satisfied for agency action to be "final" under the APA. "First, the action must mark the consummation of the agency's decisionmaking process—it must not be of a merely tentative or interlocutory nature. And second, the action must be one by which rights or obligations have been determined, or from which legal consequences will flow." *Id.,* at 177–178 (internal quotation marks and citation omitted).

The Corps does not dispute that an approved JD satisfies the first *Bennett* condition. Unlike preliminary JDs—which are "advisory in nature" and simply indicate that "there may be waters of the United States" on a parcel of property, 33 CFR § 331.2— an approved JD clearly "mark[s] the consummation" of the Corps' decisionmaking process on that question. . . .

The definitive nature of approved JDs also gives rise to "direct and appreciable legal consequences," thereby satisfying the second prong of *Bennett*, 520 U.S., at 178, 117 S.Ct. 1154. Consider the effect of an approved JD stating that a party's property does *not* contain jurisdictional waters—a "negative" JD, in Corps parlance. As noted, such a JD will generally bind the Corps for five years. See 33 CFR pt. 331, App. C; 2005 Guidance Letter § 1. Under a longstanding memorandum of agreement between the Corps and EPA, it will also be "binding on the Government and represent the Government's position in any subsequent Federal action or litigation concerning that final determination." . . .

It follows that affirmative JDs have legal consequences as well: They represent the denial of the safe harbor that negative JDs afford. See 5 U.S.C. § 551(13) (defining "agency action" to include an agency "rule, order, license, sanction, relief, or the equivalent," or the "denial thereof"). Because "legal consequences . . . flow" from approved JDs, they constitute final agency action.

Even if final, an agency action is reviewable under the APA only if there are no adequate alternatives to APA review in court. 5 U.S.C. § 704. The Corps contends that respondents have two such alternatives: either discharge fill material without a permit, risking an EPA enforcement action during which they can argue that no permit was required, or apply for a permit and seek judicial review if dissatisfied with the results.

Neither alternative is adequate. As we have long held, parties need not await enforcement proceedings before challenging final agency action where such proceedings carry the risk of "serious criminal and civil penalties." *Abbott*, 387 U.S., at 153. If respondents discharged fill material without a permit, in the mistaken belief that their property did not contain jurisdictional waters, they would expose themselves to civil penalties of up to $37,500 for each day they violated the Act, to say nothing of potential criminal liability. See 33 U.S.C. §§ 1319(c), (d); *Sackett*, 132 S.Ct., at 1370, n. 1 (citing 74 Fed.Reg. 626, 627 (2009)). Respondents need not assume such risks while waiting for EPA to "drop the hammer" in order to have their day in court. *Sackett*, 132 S.Ct., at 1372.

Nor is it an adequate alternative to APA review for a landowner to apply for a permit and then seek judicial review in the event of an unfavorable decision. As Corps officials indicated in their discussions with respondents, the permitting process can be arduous, expensive, and long. See *Rapanos*, 547 U.S., at 721(plurality opinion). On top of the standard permit application that respondents were required to submit, see 33 CFR § 325.1(d) (detailing contents of permit application), the Corps demanded that they undertake, among other things, a "hydrogeologic assessment of the rich fen system including the mineral/nutrient composition and pH of the groundwater; groundwater flow spatially and vertically; discharge and recharge areas"; a "functional/ resource assessment of the site including a vegetation survey and identification of native fen plan communities across the site"; an "inventory of similar wetlands in the general area (watershed), including some analysis of their quality"; and an "inventory of rich fen plant communities that are within sites of High and Outstanding Biodiversity Significance in the area." Respondents estimate that undertaking these analyses alone would cost more than $100,000. *Id.*, at 17. And whatever pertinence all this might have to the issuance of a permit, none of it will alter the finality of the approved JD, or affect its suitability for judicial review. The permitting process adds nothing to the JD.

The Corps nevertheless argues that Congress made the "evident [ ]" decision in the Clean Water Act that a coverage determination would be made "as part of the permitting process, and that the property owner would obtain any necessary judicial review of that determination at the conclusion of that process." But as the Corps acknowledges, the Clean Water Act makes no reference to standalone jurisdictional determinations, so there is little basis for inferring anything from it concerning the reviewability of such distinct final agency action. And given "the APA's presumption of reviewability for all final agency action," *Sackett*, 132 S.Ct., at 1373, "[t]he mere fact" that permitting decisions are "reviewable should not suffice to support an implication of exclusion as to other[ ]" agency actions, such as approved JDs.

Finally, the Corps emphasizes that seeking review in an enforcement action or at the end of the permitting process would be the only available avenues for obtaining review "[i]f the Corps had never adopted its practice of issuing standalone jurisdictional determinations upon request." True enough. But such a "count your blessings" argument is not an adequate rejoinder to the assertion of a right to judicial review under the APA.

Justice KENNEDY, with whom Justice THOMAS and Justice ALITO join, concurring.

My join extends to the Court's opinion in full. The following observation seems appropriate not to qualify what the Court says but to point out that, based on the Government's representations in this case, the reach and systemic consequences of the Clean Water Act remain a cause for concern. As Justice ALITO has noted in an earlier case, the Act's reach is "notoriously unclear" and the consequences to landowners even for inadvertent violations can be crushing. See *Sackett v. EPA*, 132 S.Ct. 1367 (2012) (concurring opinion).

An approved Jurisdictional Determination (JD) gives a landowner at least some measure of predictability, so long as the agency's declaration can be relied upon. Yet, the Government has represented in this litigation that a JD has no legally binding effect on the Environmental Protection Agency's (EPA) enforcement decisions. It has stated that the memorandum of agreement between the EPA and the Army Corps of Engineers, which today's opinion relies on, does not have binding effect and can be revoked or amended at the Agency's unfettered discretion. If that were correct, the Act's ominous reach would again be unchecked by the limited relief the Court allows today. Even if, in an ordinary case, an agency's internal agreement with another agency cannot establish that its action is final, the Court is right to construe a JD as binding in light of the fact that in many instances it will have a significant bearing on whether the Clean Water Act comports with due process.

The Act, especially without the JD procedure were the Government permitted to foreclose it, continues to raise troubling questions regarding the Government's power to cast doubt on the full use and enjoyment of private property throughout the Nation.

[The concurring opinion of Justice KAGAN has been omitted.]

Justice GINSBURG, concurring in part and concurring in the judgment.

I join the Court's opinion, save for its reliance upon the Memorandum of Agreement between the Army Corps of Engineers and the Environmental Protection Agency (construing the memorandum to establish that Corps jurisdictional determinations (JDs) are binding on the Federal Government in litigation for five years). The Court received scant briefing about this memorandum, and the United States does not share the Court's reading of it. But the JD at issue is "definitive," not "informal" or "tentative," *Abbott Laboratories v. Gardner*, 387 U.S. 136, 151 (1967), and has "an immediate and practical impact," *Frozen Food Express v. United States*, 351 U.S. 40, 44 (1956). Accordingly, I agree with the Court that the JD is final.

Notes and Questions

1. After the Supreme Court's decision in *Hawkes,* which concluded that jurisdictional determinations are subject to judicial review, how do you think the EPA and Corps of Engineers should respond? Should the agencies prepare a comprehensive record in order to defend every single approved JD in anticipation of litigation? What might that do, then, to the number of approved JDs that the agencies can complete each year, given limited agency resources? Should the agencies simply discontinue the practice and allow property owners to take their chances with enforcement in the event their property contains waters of the United States? What advantages or disadvantages would you see to both the agencies and property owners if approved JDs were discontinued? Why do you think the agencies would agree that the findings of an approved JD would be binding on the agencies for five years — or for any time at all? Doesn't that constrain their agency discretion? For purposes of protecting wetlands and other waters of the U.S., should the practice of issuing JDs be continued?

2. Given that there is no requirement in the Clean Water Act to provide JDs to property owners, can the agencies now legally refuse to provide any JDs, preliminary or approved? What arguments might property owners make to seek to compel JDs even if the Corps refused? How would you expect Justice Kennedy to respond, given the concluding comments in his concurrence?

3. The Court's unanimous decision in *Hawkes* cites and reflects the Court's unanimous decision four years earlier in *Sackett v. U.S. Environmental Protection Agency,* 132 S. Ct. 1367 (2012), which similarly found that administrative orders to enforce the Clean Water Act are subject to judicial review. The Court's analysis in *Sackett* will be examined more thoroughly in Chapter 11. For now, consider the procedural posture leading up to the Court's grant of certiorari in this case. In the underlying district court case, the trial judge found that approved JDs do not constitute a "final agency action" subject to judicial review. *Hawkes Co., Inc. v. U.S. Army Corps of Engineers,* 963 F. Supp. 2d 868 (D. Minn. 2013). A panel of the Fifth Circuit Court of Appeals also found the same. *Belle Co., LLC v. U.S. Army Corps of Engineers,* 761 F.3d 383 (5th Cir. 2014). After considering both of these decisions, the Eighth Circuit Court of Appeals went the opposite way, declining to follow the Fifth Circuit and reversing the underlying district court decision. In reversing the district court, the Eighth Circuit found that approved JDs do indeed constitute "final agency action," as the approved JD represented "a final decision from which legal consequences flowed." *Hawkes Co., Inc. v. U.S. Army Corps of Engineers,* 782 F.3d 994 (8th Cir. 2015). Given the circuit split on this question, then, what do you think of the decision by the United States to seek certiorari in this case? Should the United States have been content with applying different rules in different circuits?

4. What do you think of Justice Ginsburg's concern about the Memorandum of Agreement between EPA and the Corps of Engineers? Can "legal consequences" really flow to third parties (such as Hawkes Co.) from an agreement between two federal agencies? If EPA and the Corps renegotiated the Memorandum of Agreement to provide heightened standards for a JD, or if the agencies rescinded the Memorandum of

Agreement entirely, would either action be subject to judicial review? Could "legal consequences" still flow to third parties if the Corps had a consistent practice—but no written agreement—providing for the issuance of JDs?

§404 Dredge + Fill

C. Dredge-and-Fill Requirements

For wetlands that are subject to Clean Water Act regulation as "waters of the United States," what exactly is required of a landowner? First, it may be important to recognize that the presence of wetlands on a property may create no legal requirements for a landowner, unless the landowner desires to engage in certain activities that would trigger CWA jurisdiction. Recall that CWA § 301 makes it unlawful for any person to "discharge [] any pollutant," 33 U.S.C. § 1311(a), into the waters of the United States, except as in compliance with other parts of the statute, including § 404. Section 404, in turn, creates a special permitting program for the subcategory of pollutants known as "dredged or fill material." 33 U.S.C. § 1344(a).

The Clean Water Act does not define "dredged or fill material," but the terms are defined in regulations promulgated by the Corps of Engineers, 33 C.F.R. § 323.2, with matching regulations promulgated by EPA, 40 C.F.R. § 232.2. Specifically, the agency regulations define "dredged material" to mean "material that is excavated or dredged from waters of the United States." 33 C.F.R. § 323.2(c). The regulations define "fill material" as "material placed in waters of the United States where the material has the effect of: (i) Replacing any portion of a water of the United States with dry land; or (ii) Changing the bottom elevation of any portion of a water of the United States." 33 C.F.R. § 323.2(e). The regulations provide examples of "fill material" to include "rock, sand, soil, clay, plastics, construction debris, wood chips, overburden from mining or other excavation, and materials used to create any structure or infrastructure in the waters of the United States." *Id.* § 323.2(e)(2). The regulations also make a specific exception from the term "fill material" for "trash or garbage." *Id.* § 323.2(e)(3). Thus, the disposal of "trash or garbage" within the "waters of the United States" is excluded from the 404 program administered by the Corps of Engineers and so is generally regulated by the EPA under CWA § 402.

The breadth of the regulatory definitions of "dredged or fill material" clearly reaches a significant share of productive activity in the United States, to include almost any dredging operation with wetlands, the placement or removal of almost any bridge or pier, and almost any highway construction near open water. Significantly, with "overburden from mining" included within the definition of "fill material," the activity known as "mountain-top mining," which involves the massive removal of soil pushed down into "valley fills," remains subject to Corps regulation under 404, to the wide consternation of environmentalists. *See, e.g., Kentuckians for Commonwealth, Inc., v. Riverburgh*, 317 F.3d 425 (4th Cir. 2003) (dismissing challenge by environmentalists to rule including "overburden" within definition of "fill material").

Discharges of dredged or fill material into open waters present relatively easy cases for 404 regulation. The more challenging cases, as we have already seen with *SWANCC*

(2001) and *Rapanos* (2006), are cases involving the discharge of dredged or fill material into wetlands. This is in part due to the unresolved scope of "waters of the United States," but also due to the frequent contact between human industry and regulated wetlands in the United States. Thus, the construction of an ordinary home on property containing wetlands may raise questions of 404 permitting, *see, e.g., Sackett v. EPA*, 132 S. Ct. 1367 (2012) (filling wetlands for home construction without 404 permit may trigger enforcement order subject to judicial review), as may certain agricultural practices, *see, e.g., Borden Ranch Partnership v. U.S Army Corps of Engineers*, 261 F.3d 810 (9th Cir. 2001) ("deep-ripping" of wetlands, through use of large metal prongs pulled by tractors, may require 404 permit); *Avoyelles Sportsmen's League v. Marsh*, 715 F.2d 897 (5th Cir. 1983) (clearing of bayou forest for soybean production may require 404 permit).

While the scope of "dredged or fill material" may appear exceedingly broad, both the statute and the implementing regulations provide some substantial limitations. In 1977, Congress amended § 404 itself to provide exceptions from Clean Water Act regulation for industrial activities, including "normal farming, silviculture, and ranching activities . . . ." 33 U.S.C. § 1344(f)(1). Likewise, over time, implementing regulations have established a number of limitations on 404 permitting requirements. For example, the regulations elaborate on the "normal farming" exemption to provide examples such as "plowing, seeding, cultivating, minor drainage, and harvesting for the production of food, fiber, and forest products . . . ." 33 C.F.R. § 323.4(a)(1). The regulations also exempt from 404 permit requirements "normal dredging operations" within traditionally navigable waterways. 33 C.F.R. § 323.2(d)(3)(ii). The regulations also create a *de minimis* 404 permit exemption for "incidental fallback" from dredging operations, 33 C.F.R. § 323.2(d)(2)(iii), if the project proponent is able to demonstrate to EPA or the Corps that such "incidental addition . . . would not have the effect of destroying or degrading any area of waters of the United States." 33 C.F.R. § 323.2(d)(3)(i). Before seeking any permit under § 404, good practitioners will thoroughly exhaust the possibilities that a permit may not be needed.

If a permit is required under Clean Water Act § 404, what exactly is needed? § 404(b)(1) provides that each permit shall be subject to "application of guidelines developed by" EPA. 33 U.S.C. § 1344(b)(1). EPA's "404(b)(1) Guidelines" have been promulgated at 40 C.F.R. Part 230. If a proposed dredge-and-fill activity does not appear to comply with the 404(b)(1) Guidelines, the Corps of Engineers will deny the permit. 33 C.F.R. § 323.6(a); *Fox Bay Partners v. U.S. Corps of Engineers*, 831 F. Supp. 605 (N.D. Ill. 1993) (upholding Corps denial of 404 permit for proposed construction of commercial marina). On the other hand, if a proposed activity appears to comply with the 404(b)(1) Guidelines, the Corps will approve the permit "unless issuance would be contrary to the public interest." 33 C.F.R. § 323.6(a).

In general, consistent with the overall purpose of the Clean Water Act and § 404 in particular, the 404(b)(1) Guidelines reflect a "fundamental precept" that "dredged or fill material should not be discharged into the aquatic ecosystem," unless the project proponent can demonstrate that the discharge "will not have an unacceptable adverse impact either individually or in combination" with other activities affecting that ecosystem. 40 C.F.R. § 230.1(c). Another fundamental precept of the Guidelines is that "no discharge of dredged or fill material shall be permitted if there is a <u>practicable</u> <u>alternative</u> to the proposed discharge . . . ." *Id.* § 230.10(a). An alternative is "practicable" if it is "available and capable of being done after taking into consideration cost, existing technology, and logistics in light of the overall project purpose." *Id.* § 230.10(a)(2). For proposed discharges into wetlands and other "special aquatic sites," the existence of practicable alternatives will be presumed, unless demonstrated otherwise. *Id.* § 230.10(a)(3).

If no practicable alternatives are available, the 404 permit still will not be issued if it would <u>violate state water quality standards</u>, violate any applicable toxic effluent standard, violate protections for marine sanctuaries, or jeopardize the continued existence of species protected under the Endangered Species Act. *Id.* § 230.10(b). Perhaps most significantly under the Guidelines, no 404 permit shall be issued "unless appropriate and practicable steps have been taken which will minimize potential adverse impacts of the discharge on the aquatic ecosystem." *Id.* § 230.10(d). The Guidelines provide a number of potential measures to minimize impacts on aquatic ecosystem, *see id.* §§ 230.70–230.77, and failure to adopt sufficient minimization measures may be grounds for denial of a permit by the Corps. *See Town of Norfolk v. U.S. Army Corps of Engineers*, 968 F.2d 1438 (1st Cir. 1992) (upholding Corps denial of 404 permit).

In practice, one of the most challenging mitigation measures has been the restoration or development of new habitat to compensate for potential adverse ecological impacts from the proposed project. *See* 40 C.F.R. § 230.75(d) ("habitat development and restoration"). In 2008, EPA and the Corps issued the "Mitigation Rule" to establish requirements for compensatory mitigation. 73 Fed. Reg. 19,670 (April 10, 2008), codified at 33 C.F.R. Part 332. Consistent with the national policy for no net loss of wetlands, the regulations generally require at least a one-to-one replacement for impacted wetlands, as measured by acreage or linear feet. 33 C.F.R. § 332.3(f). In order to achieve the required mitigation most efficiently and reliably, the regulations promote the use of "mitigation bank credits," which allow developers to purchase shares of approved mitigation projects conducted by third parties. Developers may also agree to conduct their own mitigation projects with agency oversight, financial assurance, and other required elements. Preferred mitigation projects will be within the same watershed as the site disturbed by the permitted activity and will be "in-kind"—for example, restoring a perennial stream in compensation for permitted impacts to a perennial stream. *See generally* 33 C.F.R. § 332.1.

[handwritten margin note: 1-to-1 restoration]

While the requirements to obtain a 404 permit may appear daunting, if not impossible, in many cases, thousands of dredge-and-fill operations proceed every year. Many of these actions are covered by "general permits" under CWA § 404(e), which allows the Corps to identify "categories of activities" where the discharge of dredged or fill material "will cause only minimal adverse environmental effects" either individually or in combination with other activities. 33 U.S.C. § 1344(f) and implementing regulations at 33 C.F.R. Part 330. As of 2016, the Corps has issued 50 Nationwide Permits (NWPs) for categories of activities including aids to navigation (NWP 1), maintenance of previously permitted structures (NWP 3), bank stabilization projects (NWP 13), response to oil and hazardous substance spills (NWP 20), construction of single-family homes (NWP 29), and commercial shellfish operations (NWP 48). *See* 77 Fed. Reg. 10,184 (Feb. 21, 2012).

For activities subject to a NWP, project proponents often may simply proceed with the project, in compliance with all terms and conditions of the NWP. For some activities, such as those that discharge dredged or fill material directly into wetlands, proponents must first conduct a wetlands delineation and provide a "Predischarge Notification" (PDN) to the Corps of Engineers. If the Corps does not object within 30 days from receipt of the PDN, the activity may proceed. 33 C.F.R. § 330.1(e).

In addition to Nationwide Permits, District Engineers for the Corps of Engineers may develop Regional Permits to address activities and water bodies in designated geographic areas. 33 C.F.R. § 325.2(e)(2). Moreover, in the event the Corps discovers an unpermitted discharge of dredged or fill material in violation of § 404, the Corps has authority to issue "After-the-Fact" permits to authorize the discharge *post hoc* and bring the violator into compliance with other applicable requirements. 33 C.F.R. § 326.3(e).

If an exemption or general permit does not apply, and the project proponent still wants to proceed with the dredge or fill activity, individual 404 permits may be pursued from the Corps of Engineers. This application process may involve many different agencies and trigger a number of other statutes beyond the Clean Water Act, to include NEPA, the Endangered Species Act, and the National Historic Preservation Act. As a result, this process often requires considerable time and expense. For more on permitting generally, see Chapter 12. For a thorough, practical guide to wetlands regulation and permitting, see the Envtl L. Institute, Wetlands Deskbook (4th ed. 2015).

Notes and Questions

1. Consider the permit exemption for "incidental fallback." 33 C.F.R. § 323.2(d)(2)(iii). If some "fallback" of material is always incidental to dredging operations, could this exemption potentially consume the rule so that no dredging operations would be subject to § 404 unless the fallback was intentional? The rule as it appears today evolved over decades of agency rulemaking and litigation brought by both environmentalists and industry advocates. In *North Carolina Wildlife Federation v. Tulloch*, C90-713-CIV-5-BO (E.D.N.C. 1992), environmentalists challenged a finding by the Corps that a developer's draining of 700 acres of wetlands in North Carolina was not subject to § 404 because the challenged action only involved incidental releases of material. As a result of the litigation, EPA and the Corps agreed to promulgate more protective regulations that came to be known as the *Tulloch* Rule. The *Tulloch* Rule essentially did away with the exemption for incidental fallback, triggering a successful challenge by industry. *See National Mining Association v. U.S. Army Corps of Engineers*, 145 F.3d 1399 (D.C. Cir. 1998). In response, EPA and the Corps reinstated the incidental fallback exemption, but included a new paragraph that places the burden squarely upon project proponents to show that the proposed activity "would not destroy or degrade any area of waters of the United States." 33 C.F.R. § 323.2(d)(3).

2. In the *Sackett* case referenced above and excerpted in Chapter 11, the plaintiffs were a husband and wife who wanted to build a home near Priest Lake in northern Idaho. The Sacketts begin filling an area on their property that the Corps and EPA immediately identified as wetlands subject to § 404 of Clean Water Act, an opinion confirmed by a private consultant hired by Mrs. Sackett. If the Sacketts' activity was subject to § 404, wouldn't it be covered by Nationwide Permit 29? What would you need to know in order to be sure? *See* 77 Fed. Reg. 10,217 (requirements including disturbance of no more than half-acre or 300 linear feet). If the application and compliance with the Nationwide Permit cost as little as $2,000, as suggested by amicus curiae Natural Resources Defense Council, why would the Sacketts choose to oppose the Clean Water Act enforcement order all the way to the U.S. Supreme Court?

[handwritten margin note: Only covered → more than ½ acre]

3. In addition to the 50 existing Nationwide Permits in 2016, the Corps of Engineers recently proposed two more: Land-Based Renewable Energy Generation Facilities (NWP 51) and Water-Based Renewable Energy Generation Pilot Projects (NWP 52). 81 Fed. Reg. 35,186 (June 1, 2016). Both permits appear directed at promoting clean energy development, consistent with national goals and international agreements to address climate change. As proposed, NWP 52 would be limited to projects covering no more than half an acre of open water, although the Corps solicited comments on whether that areal limit should be expanded. 81 Fed. Reg. 35,203. What do you think? In the interest of combating climate change, should greater use of lakes, bays, and coastal waters be considered for deployment of solar generating facilities? What other laws might apply to check the potential proliferation of solar facilities upon open waters if NWP 52 were allowed to expand beyond a half-acre?

4. As with the NPDES permit program under § 402, states and tribes may be authorized to carry out the permit program under § 404. 33 U.S.C. § 1344(g). As noted previously, all but a few states do indeed administer the NPDES permit programs in their states. However, only two states, Michigan and New Jersey, have elected to administer the 404 permit program. Why this striking difference? Can it be explained by the broad use of Nationwide Permits or perhaps an approach the Corps of Engineers takes toward 404 permit applications that is different from EPA's approach to permit applications under 402?

Practice Problem

The New England town of Jules Junction is planning to construct a large municipal golf course on property it owns near Jordan River. The town property covers approximately 140 acres and features a natural depression that is ringed by willows and filled with mud or standing water for many months of the year. The eastern edge of the depression is located approximately 42 feet from the Jordan River. The town notes that this proximity would facilitate construction of the golf course, as tons of fill materials

586 7 · THE CLEAN WATER ACT

could be delivered by barge instead of by truck, thus reducing the carbon footprint that would otherwise be associated with delivering all this material by truck.

1. Does construction of the golf course on the Jules Junction property near the Jordan River appear to impact "waters of the United States" for the purposes of the Clean Water Act? Explain your reasoning.

2. If you conclude that construction of the golf course does trigger Clean Water Act jurisdiction, as town attorney, what steps might you advise the town take in order to comply with the Clean Water Act with the minimum expenditure of time and effort?

VIII. Substantive Standards

While the Clean Water Act begins with the stated goal of eliminating the discharge of pollutants into waters of the United States by 1985, the heart of the CWA is really the program established by § 402 that allows the continued discharge of pollutants through permits under the National Pollutant Discharge Elimination System (NPDES). Of course, at the same time that the NPDES permits allow the continued discharge of pollutants, they also regulate and restrict these discharges principally through the establishment of effluent limitations. Permit writers for either EPA or authorized states or tribes develop effluent limitations for each NPDES permit through the consideration of two major elements: technology-based standards and water quality-based standards. Once the applicable standards have been identified, the most stringent standard will usually be incorporated into the permit. Technology-based standards and water quality-based standards will both be discussed in this section.

A. Technology-Based Standards

The 1972 Clean Water Act established a "technology-first" approach to effluent limitations, specifying the use of available water treatment technologies and leaving water quality standards as a back-up if necessary to meet the objectives of the Act. In general, the CWA imposes different technology standards for different industries and categories of dischargers. Three broad categories of dischargers are known as "direct dischargers," "Publicly Owned Treatment Works," and "pretreaters" (or "tie-in dischargers"). Publicly Owned Treatment Works, or "POTWs," are largely sewage treatment plants that collect and treat liquid wastes from other dischargers before releasing the effluent into waters of the United States. POTWs are subject to standards established under CWA § 301(b)(1)(B). Pretreaters are industrial dischargers who discharge their liquid wastes into sewage treatment systems. Pretreaters must meet a set of "pretreatment standards" established under CWA § 307(b) and (c). This section will focus on technology standards for "direct dischargers"—parties that discharge directly into waters of the United States.

Like the Clean Air Act, the Clean Water Act distinguishes between new and existing sources of water pollution, with new sources generally held to the most stringent standards. For all dischargers, Congress sought to phase-in advances in treatment technologies over time. According to this phased approach, the first technology standard for existing sources was known as "best practicable control technology" (BPT), which Congress required existing sources to meet by July 1, 1977. CWA § 301(b)(1). BPT would be defined by EPA as the technology reflecting the "average" of the best existing facilities. After BPT, Congress required that many existing facilities meet the standard for the "best available control technology economically achievable" ("BAT"). CWA § 301(b)(2). Congress originally required that existing sources meet BAT by 1983, but extended that deadline twice, establishing the final deadline for BAT as 1989. For new sources, Congress required the use of "best available demonstrated control technology" (BADT), a standard theoretically more stringent than BPT or BAT, akin to New Source Performance Standards under the Clean Air Act. CWA § 306(a)(1). *See also* CWA § 306(a)(2) (definition of "new source").

In the years that followed the Clean Water Act of 1972, much uncertainty remained concerning how technology-based standards for individual industries would be set and who exactly (between EPA and authorized states) would set them. The following case helped resolve some of this early uncertainty and remains one of the most cogent analyses of the CWA's technology-based scheme.

Weyerhaeuser Co. v. Costle
590 F.2d 1011 (D.C. Cir.1978)

Judge McGOWAN:

Under the aegis of the Federal Water Pollution Control Act Amendments of 1972 (the Act), the Environmental Protection Agency has embarked upon a step-by-step process of issuing effluent limitations for each industry that discharges pollutants into the waters of the United States. By these consolidated petitions, members of one such industry, American pulp and paper makers, challenge the validity of EPA regulations limiting the 1977–83 effluent discharges of many pulp, paper, and paperboard mills. We are satisfied that EPA properly construed and rationally exercised the authority delegated to it by Congress. . . . Accordingly, we uphold the resulting effluent limitations. . . .

To make paper from trees is an old art; to do it without water pollution is a new science. In papermaking, logs or wooden chips must be ground up or "cooked" in one of several processes until only cellulose pulp is left. The pulp is bleached and made into various types and grades of paper. The cooking solutions and wash water that are left contain a variety of chemicals produced during "cooking" and other processes, including acids and large quantities of dissolved cellulose-breakdown products. Indeed, in some pulping processes, more of the wood is discarded in the waste water than is used to make paper. EPA has selected three parameters for measuring the pollutant content of the industry's effluent, all of which have been used extensively in this and

A lot of waste

other industries' measurements: total suspended solids (TSS), biochemical oxygen demand (BOD), and pH. TSS reflects the total amount of solids in solution, while BOD reflects the amount of biodegradable material in solution, and pH measures the acidity of the solution.

EPA has divided this segment of the industry into 16 subcategories, and further subdivided it into 66 subdivisions, for the purposes of its rulemaking effort. . . . Actually, of the 16 subcategories in the whole industry, only three — the three that use some form of the "sulfite process" — have evoked particularized challenges. The reaction of sulfite mill operators stems from the limitations' greater economic impact on them. That impact in turn results from the fact that the sulfite process creates one of the highest pollution loads of any industrial process, and certainly the highest within the pulping industry. . . .

Petitioner argument

Some of the paper mills that must meet the effluent limitations under review discharge their effluents into the Pacific Ocean. Petitioners contend that the ocean can dilute or naturally treat effluent, and that EPA must take this capacity of the ocean ("receiving water capacity") into account in a variety of ways. They urge what they term "common sense," i.e., that because the amounts of pollutant involved are small in comparison to bodies of water as vast as Puget Sound or the Pacific Ocean, they should not have to spend heavily on treatment equipment, or to increase their energy requirements and sludge levels, in order to treat wastes that the ocean could dilute or absorb.

EPA argument

EPA's secondary response to this claim was that pollution is far from harmless, even when disposed of in the largest bodies of water. As congressional testimony indicated, the Great Lakes, Puget Sound, and even areas of the Atlantic Ocean have been seriously injured by water pollution. Even if the ocean can handle ordinary wastes, ocean life may be vulnerable to toxic compounds that typically accompany those wastes. In the main, however, EPA simply asserted that the issue of receiving water capacity could not be raised in setting effluent limitations because Congress had ruled it out. We have examined the previous legislation in this area, and the 1972 Act's wording, legislative history, and policies, as underscored by its 1977 amendments. These sources, which were thoroughly analyzed in a recent opinion of the administrator of the Agency, fully support EPA's construction of the Act. They make clear that based on long experience, and aware of the limits of technological knowledge and administrative flexibility, Congress made the deliberate decision to rule out arguments based on receiving water capacity.

The earliest version of the Federal Water Pollution Control was passed in 1948 and amended five times before 1972. Throughout that 24 year period, Congress attempted to use receiving water quality as a basis for setting pollution standards. W. Rodgers, Environmental Law 355–57 (1977). At the end of that period, Congress realized not only that its water pollution efforts until then had failed, but also that reliance on receiving water capacity as a crucial test for permissible pollution levels had contributed greatly to that failure.

Based on this experience, Congress adopted a new approach in 1972. Under the Act, "a discharger's performance is . . . measured against strict technology-based effluent limitations specified levels of treatment to which it must conform, rather than against limitations derived from water quality standards to which it and other polluters must collectively conform." *EPA v. State Water Resources Control Board*, 426 U.S. 200, 204–05 (1976).

This new approach reflected developing views on practicality and rights. Congress concluded that water pollution seriously harmed the environment, and that although the cost of control would be heavy, the nation would benefit from controlling that pollution. Yet scientific uncertainties made it difficult to assess the benefits to particular bodies of receiving water. Even if the federal government eventually could succeed at the task at which had failed for 24 years and thus could determine benefits and devise water quality standards, Congress concluded that the requisite further delay was too long for the nation to wait.

Moreover, by eliminating the issue of the capacity of particular bodies of receiving water, Congress made nationwide uniformity in effluent regulation possible. Congress considered uniformity vital to free the states from the temptation of relaxing local limitations in order to woo or keep industrial facilities. In addition, national uniformity made pollution clean-up possible without engaging in the divisive task of favoring some regions of the country over others.

More fundamentally, the new approach implemented changing views as to the relative rights of the public and of industrial polluters. Hitherto, the right of the polluter was pre-eminent, unless the damage caused by pollution could be proven. Henceforth, the right of the public to a clean environment would be pre-eminent, unless pollution treatment was impractical or unachievable. The Senate Committee declared that "(t)he use of any river, lake, stream or ocean as a waste treatment system is unacceptable" regardless of the measurable impact of the waste on the body of water in question. Legislative History at 1425 (Senate Report). The Conference Report stated that the Act "specifically bans pollution dilution as an alternative to waste treatment." Id. at 284. This new view of relative rights was based in part on the hard-nosed assessment of our scientific ignorance: "we know so little about the ultimate consequences of injection of new matter into water that (the Act requires) a presumption of pollution. . . ." Id. at 1332 (remarks of Sen. Buckley). It also was based on the widely shared conviction that the nation's quality of life depended on its natural bounty, and that it was worth incurring heavy cost to preserve that bounty for future generations.

The Act reflects the new approach in a number of provisions. As noted, its goal was Zero discharge of pollutants by 1985, section 101(a)(1), 33 U.S.C. s 1251(a)(1), *not* discharges at acceptable or tolerable levels for receiving water . . . In only one limited instance, thermal pollution, is receiving water capacity to be considered in relaxing standards, and the section allowing such consideration was drafted as a clear exception. Section 316(a). Otherwise, receiving water quality was to be considered only in setting "more stringent" standards than effluent limitations otherwise would prescribe. Section 301(b)(1)(C).

The Act was passed with an expectation of "mid-course corrections," Legislative History, at 175 (statement of Sen. Muskie), and in 1977 Congress amended the Act, although generally holding to the same tack set five years earlier. Notably, during those five years, representatives of the paper industry had appeared before Congress and urged it to change the Act and to incorporate receiving water capacity as a consideration. Nonetheless, Congress was satisfied with this element of the statutory scheme. Except for a provision specifically aimed at discharges from "publicly owned treatment plants," section 301(h) of the Act, it resolved in the recent amendments to continue regulating discharges into all receiving waters alike.

Our experience with litigation under the Act, and particularly with this case, emphasizes the weight of Congress' policies. Even without receiving water capacity as an issue to delay it, EPA was late in promulgating these regulations. We have wrestled with the problems of weighing technological imponderables and can understand the greater difficulties that would have arisen if the receiving water issues involving even greater imponderables had also been involved. Historically, the paper industry itself, and particularly the sulfite process sector, avoided the impact of regulation because of the difficulty of proving that its discharges adversely affected receiving water.

Under the new statutory scheme, Congress clearly intended us to avoid such problems of proof so that a set of regulations with enforceable impact is possible . . . .

P Argument

Petitioners also challenge EPA's manner of assessing two factors that all parties agree must be considered: cost and non-water quality environmental impacts. They contend that the Agency should have more carefully balanced costs versus the effluent reduction benefits of the regulations, and that it should have also balanced those benefits against the non-water quality environmental impacts to arrive at a "net" environmental benefit conclusion. Petitioners base their arguments on certain comments made by the Conferees for the Act, and on the fact that the Act lists non-water quality environmental impacts as a factor the Agency must "take into account."

In order to discuss petitioners' challenges, we must first identify the relevant statutory standard. Section 304(b)(1)(B) of the Act identifies the factors bearing on [BPT] in two groups. First, the factors shall

> include consideration of the total cost of application of technology in relation to the effluent reduction benefits to be achieved from such application,

and second, they

> shall also take into account the age of equipment and facilities involved, the process employed, the engineering aspects of the application of various types of control techniques, process changes, non-water quality environmental impact (including energy requirements), and such other factors as the Administrator deems appropriate(.)

The first group consists of two factors that EPA must compare: total cost versus effluent reduction benefits. We shall call these the "comparison factors." The other group is a list of many factors that EPA must "take into account:" age, process, engineering aspects, process changes, environmental impacts (including energy), and any others EPA deems appropriate. We shall call these the "consideration factors."

Notably, section 304(b)(2)(B) of the Act, which delineates the factors relevant to setting [BAT], tracks the [BPT] provision before us except in one regard: in the [BAT] section, All factors, including costs and benefits, are consideration factors, and no factors are separated out for comparison.

Based on our examination of the statutory language and the legislative history, we conclude that Congress mandated a particular structure and weight for the [BPT] comparison factors, that is to say, a "limited" balancing test. In contrast, Congress did not mandate any particular structure or weight for the many consideration factors. Rather, it left EPA with discretion to decide how to account for the consideration factors, and how much weight to give each factor. In response to these divergent congressional approaches, we conclude that, on the one hand, we should examine EPA's treatment of cost and benefit under the [BPT] standard to assure that the Agency complied with Congress' "limited" balancing directive. On the other hand, our scrutiny of the Agency's treatment of the several consideration factors seeks to assure that the Agency informed itself as to their magnitude, and reached its own express and considered conclusion about their bearing. More particularly, we do not believe that EPA is required to use any specific structure such as a balancing test in assessing the consideration factors, nor do we believe that EPA is required to give each consideration factor any specific weight.

Our conclusions are based initially on the section's wording and apparent logic. By singling out two factors (the comparison factors) for separate treatment, and by requiring that they be considered "in relation to" each other, Congress elevated them to a level of greater attention and rigor. Moreover, the comparison factors are a closed set of two, making it possible to have a definite structure and weight in considering them and preventing extraneous factors from intruding on the balance.

By contrast, the statute directs the Agency only to "take into account" the consideration factors, without prescribing any structure for EPA's deliberations. As to this latter group of factors, the section cannot logically be interpreted to impose on EPA a specific structure of consideration or set of weights because it gave EPA authority to "upset" any such structure by exercising its discretion to add new factors to the mix. Instead, the listing of factors seems aimed at noting all of the matters that Congress considered worthy of study before making limitation decisions, without preventing EPA from identifying other factors that it considers worthy of study. So long as EPA pays some attention to the congressionally specified factors, the section on its face lets EPA relate the various factors as it deems necessary . . . .

Notes and Questions

1. While industrial dischargers were required to implement BPT by 1977, obviously that did not happen. Much of the delay could be explained by the time it took EPA to get BPT standards in place due to the technological complexities and magnitude of the job. Note that in *Weyerhaeuser*, EPA had to define technology standards not just for one homogenous pulp and paper industry, but for 16 subcategories of this industry, with 66 subdivisions, including three that employed the highly polluting "sulfite

process." Is it realistic for one federal agency to comprehend every polluting industry so thoroughly as to assign technology standards for every industry and every variation within every industry? If this does not seem realistic, what is the alternative?

2. Pollutant Categories. While the Clean Water Act of 1972 required technology-based standards based upon industrial standards, CWA amendments in 1977 created a scheme requiring different standards based upon categories of pollutants. These are generally described below.

- **"Toxic pollutants"** are pollutants subject to a list maintained by EPA and revised periodically. *Id.* § 1317(a)(1). The list is maintained at 40 C.F.R. § 401.15 and currently contains 65 pollutants or classes of pollutants, including industrial materials such as asbestos, DDT, and polychlorinated biphenyls (PCBs); and metals such as arsenic, cadmium, lead, mercury, and zinc. (Note that each of these particular examples is also listed as a "hazardous substance" subject to the Comprehensive Environmental Response, Compensation and Liability Act, as discussed in Chapter 9.)

- **"Nonconventional pollutants"** include pollutants that fall in between the categories of "toxic pollutants" and "conventional pollutants." Nonconventional pollutants include such common pollutants as ammonia, chlorine, color, iron, and phosphorus. Nonconventional pollutants may also include heat (also known as "thermal discharges"); however, this particular category of pollutant is often subject to standards set through ad hoc variances. *See* CWA § 316(a), 33 U.S.C. § 1326(a).

- **"Conventional pollutants"** were defined by CWA § 304 to include biological oxygen demand, suspended solids, fecal coliform, and pH. *Id.* § 1314(a)(4). To this short list of conventional pollutants, EPA by regulation added oil and grease in 1979. *See* 44 Fed. Reg. 44,501 (July 30, 1979).

The significance of these pollutant categories is this: while all facilities were originally required to meet BPT standards by 1977, Congress eventually required all facilities discharging toxic pollutants and nonconventional pollutants to meet BAT standards by 1989. 33 U.S.C. § 1311(b)(2)(A), (D), and (F). At the same time, conventional pollutants had to meet a different standard known as "best conventional pollutant control technology" (BCT). *Id.* § 1311(b)(2)(E). In practice, BCT is often set at the less stringent standard of BPT, giving dischargers of conventional pollutants only some relief from having to meet standards for BAT or BADT.

3. As we have seen already, challenges to standards promulgated under the Clean Water Act must be brought in the federal circuit court of appeals. CWA § 509(b)(1). When setting deadlines for compliance with standards, should Congress allow time for the inevitable judicial challenges to every final standard? If so, how much time should Congress allow?

4. Over time, EPA eventually promulgated (and defended) technology-based standards for more than 500 industries and subcategories in the United States. Looking back at the dramatic improvements in U.S. water quality since the "technology-first" approach was established in 1972, most observers agree that this approach worked. Contrasting the technology-first approach with the water quality-based approach that failed before it, the Supreme Court noted in one of the early CWA cases, "[D]irect restrictions on discharges facilitate enforcement by making it unnecessary to work backward from an overpolluted body of water to determine which point sources are responsible and which must be abated." *EPA v. State Water Resources Control Board*, 426 U.S. 200, 204, 96 S. Ct. 2022, 2024 (1976).

5. In *Weyerhaeuser*, the D.C. Circuit upheld EPA's BPT standard even though EPA determined that the standard would likely result in the closure of three sulfite mills, with 550 workers being laid off. The Supreme Court two years later tacitly approved of this difficult choice, recognizing that "Congress anticipated that the [BPT] regulations would cause economic hardship and plant closings." *EPA v. National Crushed Stone Ass'n*, 449 U.S. 64, 83, 101 S. Ct. 295, 307 (1980). Other courts have also upheld BPT standards despite potentially grave economic impacts. *See, e.g., National Ass'n of Metal Finishers v. EPA*, 719 F.2d 624 (3ᵈ Cir. 1983) (upholding BPT despite possible closing of 20 percent of electroplating shops, with potential loss of 10,000 jobs). What factors do you think EPA, the courts, or Congress should consider before mandating an environmental standard that could put people out of work? Given the tremendous political shifts in the United States since the early 1970s, do you think these types of difficult choices will need to be made again soon?

6. BPT versus BAT. What is the real difference between the "best practicable control technology" (BPT) and the "best available control technology economically achievable" (BAT)? As indicated in *Weyerhaeuser*, the statutory factors for defining BAT track very closely the factors for defining BPT, with both standards requiring consideration of "age of equipment and facilities," "the process employed," and "non-water quality environmental impact," among other things. *Cf.* § 304(b)(1)(B) with 304(b)(2)(B). Nevertheless, as courts have recognized, Congress clearly intended BAT to be more stringent. In 1974, EPA defined BPT as "the average of the best existing performance by plants of various sizes, ages and unit processes within each industrial category or subcategory." *See EPA v. National Crushed Stone Ass'n*, 449 U.S. 64, 76, n.15, 101 S. Ct. 295 (1980), quoting 39 Fed. Reg. 6580 (1974). BAT, on the other hand, would be defined not by the "average" of the best existing technology, but by technology that reflected the latest scientific research and development, even (theoretically) if this latest technology had not yet been deployed in any fully operational facilities. As one court described it, "In setting BAT, EPA uses not the average plant, but the optimally operating plant, the pilot plant which acts as a beacon to show what is possible." *Kennecott v. EPA*, 780 F.2d 445, 448 (4ᵗʰ Cir. 1985).

7. "Economically Achievable." For purposes of defining BAT, what does it mean to be "economically achievable"? Achievable by whom? Obviously, BAT does not have to be a standard achievable by every individual facility within an industrial sector; if BPT can compel facility closures, the more stringent BAT certainly can, too. But the statute does provide some useful guidance here: BAT must be economically achievable "for such category or class." § 301(b)(2)(A). In other words, the particular industry subject to the standard must be able to achieve it, even if individual facilities cannot. This gives EPA the opportunity both to challenge an industry to improve its performance and also to reject a technology standard where it might have serious economic impacts on the sector. *See, e.g., National Wildlife Federation v. EPA*, 286 F.3d 554 (D.C. Cir. 2002) (upholding EPA determination that "Option B" technology was not economically achievable by a subcategory of the pulp and paper industry where evidence existed that the technology would result in multiple mill closures).

8. Variances. For existing sources, the statute allowed individual facilities to seek variances from technology-based standards on various bases. Section 301(c), for example, allowed facilities to seek a temporary variance if the upgrade from BPT to BAT entailed costs beyond the "economic capability of the owner or operator" and the technology employed by the facility would still allow "reasonable further progress" toward the goal of eliminating the discharge of pollutants. 33 U.S.C. § 1311(c). This cost variance should see little application now because most facilities should have been implementing BAT since 1989. More significant today is the variance for "fundamentally different factors" (FDF). The FDF variance was created by EPA regulations that were challenged by environmental organizations and upheld upon judicial review. *See, e.g., EPA v. National Crushed Stone Ass'n*, 449 U.S. 64 (1980); *Chem. Mfrs. Ass'n v. NRDC*, 470 U.S. 116 (1985). The FDF variance was subsequently codified by Congress in the Water Quality Amendments of 1987. The FDF variance now appears in Clean Water § 301(n). Read the requirements of § 301(n)(1)–(2) carefully. If you represented a new business seeking an NPDES permit today, would you have any ability to obtain an FDF variance if the applicable technology standards were established 10 years ago?

9. New Sources. The variances established under §§ 301(c) and 301(n) only apply to existing sources, not new sources. "New sources" are required by § 306 to meet standards for "best available demonstrated control technology" (BADT). 33 U.S.C. § 1316(a)(1). These standards are also sometimes referred to as "new source performance standards" (NSPS). *See* 40 C.F.R. § 440.104. Section 306 defines "new source" to mean "any source, the construction of which is commenced after the publication of proposed regulations prescribing [an applicable] standard of performance. . . ." 33 U.S.C. § 1316(a)(2). In turn, the statute defines "source" to mean "any building, structure, facility, or installation from which there is or may be the discharge of pollutants." *Id.* § 1316(a)(3). Given this definition, could a single industrial facility with multiple operating units be subject to differing treatment standards? What would be the applicable standard if a facility constructs a new plant that would contribute a new discharge for which no BADT has been established? In such a case, the permit writer will often apply the underlying standard for BAT.

10. What if no standard at all has been established for a certain industrial category? In that case, the permitting authority must develop a technology-based limitation for the facility based upon exercise of "best professional judgment" (BPJ). *Id.* § 1342(a)(1)(B); 40 C.F.R. § 125.3(b). Can BPJ be less than BAT or BPT? Can it ever be subject to judicial review?

11. Can technology-based standards change over time with advances in technology? Read CWA § 304(b). How compelling do you find this language for making regular updates to effluent standards? Perhaps to address the loose standard of "if appropriate," Congress in 1987 amended the Clean Water Act to add § 304(m), which requires EPA to publish a plan biennially that sets forth a schedule for revising existing standards or developing new standards for categories of sources discharging toxic or nonconventional pollutants for which standards have not previously existed. 33 U.S.C. § 1314(m)(1). EPA immediately fell out of compliance with § 304(m), prompting a citizen suit and judgment against EPA to compel the timely issuance of effluent guidelines. *Natural Resources Defense Council v. Reilly*, No. 89-2980 (D.D.C. 1991). Consistent with § 304(m) today, EPA publishes an *Effluent Guidelines Program Plan* at least every two years, providing schedules for proposed or final revisions to existing standards or development of new standards. In the 2016 plan, for example, EPA announced the development of new effluent standards for the "Canned and Preserved Seafood Category" of the Alaska Seafood Processing industrial sector. For the latest plan and proposed updates, see www.epa.gov/eg/effluent-guidelines-plan (last visited 7/11/2016). However, because EPA can only update a handful of technology-based standards every two years, the vast majority of the 500-plus established standards grow older and potentially more stale each year.

12. So what do these technology-based standards really look like? Perhaps surprisingly, standards such as BPT, BAT, BADT generally do not specify the use of any particular technologies. Rather, they establish "performance standards"—standards for pollution reduction that could be achieved by dischargers using available technologies. For example, recall that in the *Coeur Alaska* (2009) case involving discharges into Lower Slate Lake, EPA had promulgated BADT for new gold mines employing the "froth-flotation" process. For this industrial subcategory, BADT consisted largely of a narrative performance standard of "no discharge of process wastewater" from the mill. 40 CFR § 440.104(b)(1). However an individual meets this narrative standard, then, is often up to the discretion of the facility, consistent with any specific permit conditions developed by the permit writer with EPA or the authorized permitting agency.

B. Water Quality-Based Standards

While the modern Clean Water Act emphasized technology-based effluent limitations over the focus on the quality of receiving waters that came before 1972, the Clean Water Act has always maintained an important role for water quality standards. The gist of the "new" role for water quality consideration is set forth in CWA § 302:

> Whenever, in the judgment of [EPA], discharges of pollutants from a point source . . . with the application of effluent limitations . . . would interfere with the attainment or maintenance of [water quality], effluent limitations . . . for such point source . . . shall be established which can reasonably be expected to contribute to the attainment or maintenance of such water quality. 33 U.S.C. § 1312(a).

In other words, if technology-based standards are not enough to protect water quality, then the effluent standards included in any individual NPDES permit may be enhanced by standards specifically to ensure the protection of water quality.

The process for establishing water quality standards can be complicated, particularly because such standards are often subject to legal challenges from both environmental and industry advocates that may linger for years. Once a water quality standard does become final, another major challenge may be how to implement that standard. With an eye toward simplifying these complicated questions, this subsection will first examine how water quality standards are set, and then how they may be implemented.

1. How Water-Quality Standards Are Established

Carrying forward the pre-1972 primacy of state regulation, the Clean Water Act intended water quality standards to be established largely by states and tribes. CWA § 303(c) requires states to develop water quality standards for their states and to submit these standards to EPA for review and approval. 33 U.S.C. § 1313(c). If EPA disapproves the state's submission, EPA must provide notice to the state and allow the state an opportunity to fix identified problems. If these problems are not fixed within 90 days, "[EPA] shall promulgate such standard" on behalf of the state. *Id.* § 1313(c)(3). Once water quality standards are established for a state, the states must review them at least every three years and, "as appropriate," modify the existing standards or adopt new ones. *Id.* § 1313(c)(1). This process is known as the "triennial review."

Water quality standards developed by the states (or tribes, or EPA) consist of two major elements: (1) "designated uses" and (2) "water quality criteria" determined to protect such uses. *Id.* § 1313(c)(2)(A). These two major elements are then subject to an "antidegradation" policy that may provide an additional layer of water quality protection.

Designated uses are to be developed by states for all water bodies in their states. Under § 303(c), these designated uses shall be consistent with the national goal of "fishable/swimmable" waters, while also protecting public water supplies and other uses. 33 U.S.C. § 1313(c)(2)(A). By EPA regulation, 40 C.F.R. § 131.12(a)(1), one fundamental rule is that all existing uses of a water body shall be maintained, consistent with the express CWA goal "to restore and *maintain* the chemical, physical, and biological integrity of the Nation's waters." 33 U.S.C. § 1251(a) (emphasis added). In addition to existing uses, states may also designate other uses, whether or not they are currently being attained. For one current example of designated uses from one subbasin in the State of Idaho, see Figure 7-1.

Figure 7-1, in scientific terms, reflects the "fishable/swimmable" use designation. The designation indicates that the six water bodies listed here may be used to support "cold water" aquatic communities native to the mountains of northern Idaho. These same water bodies may also be used to support successful spawning

Figure 7-1. Designated Uses for Six Water Bodies within "Upper Kootenai Subbasin"

IDAHO ADMINISTRATIVE CODE
Department of Environmental Quality

IDAPA 58.01.02
Water Quality Standards

Unit	Waters	Aquatic Life	Recreation	Other
P-1	Star Creek - source to Idaho/Montana border	COLD SS	PCR	
P-2	North Callahan Creek - source to Idaho/Montana border	COLD SS	PCR	
P-3	South Callahan Creek - Glad Creek to Idaho/Montana border	COLD SS	PCR	
P-4	South Callahan Creek - source to Glad Creek	COLD SS	PCR	
P-5	Glad Creek - source to mouth	COLD SS	PCR	
P-6	Keeler Creek - source to Idaho/Montana border	COLD SS	PCR	

(3-30-01)

Key: COLD = Cold Water Communities
SS = Salmonid Spawning
PCR = Primary Contact Recreation

of "salmonid" fishes, which include native species of salmon and trout. The designation is further set to allow direct human contact with the water during recreational activities such as swimming.

Once a state sets one or more designated uses for a water body, they can only be removed if the state can demonstrate that attaining it is not feasible. In order to demonstrate that a particular designated use is not attainable, the state must prepare an assessment called a Use Attainability Analysis. 40 C.F.R. § 131.10(g). In order to justify not attaining the designated use, the Use Attainability Analysis must demonstrate to EPA at least one of six conditions, such as that low stream flow prevents aquatic life or that more stringent controls would result in "substantial and widespread economic and social impact."

Water quality criteria are narrative statements or numeric standards intended to protect designated uses for a water body. CWA § 304(a) requires EPA to develop and publish water quality criteria "accurately reflecting the latest scientific knowledge . . . ." 33 U.S.C. § 1314(a)(1). EPA periodically publishes water quality criteria in comprehensive collections such as the "Gold Book" of 1986. States have some discretion whether to adopt these criteria for their own water quality standards. However, states may be compelled by EPA to justify adopting any criteria that are less stringent. *See, e.g., Mississippi Commission on Natural Resources v. Costle*, 625 F.2d 1269 (5th Cir. 1980). As such, many states set their water quality criteria neither above nor below the EPA criteria, but precisely the same.

For some time after 1972, many states avoided the strictures of numeric criteria by favoring broad narrative criteria such as "no toxics in toxic amounts" or statements concerning aesthetics. *See, e.g.,* WAC 173-201A-260(2) (2016) (Washington State water quality criteria) ("Aesthetic values shall not be impaired by the presence of materials . . . which offend the senses of sight, smell, touch, or taste"). While such narrative standards may prove useful in certain circumstances, EPA has traditionally encouraged states to adopt more readily identifiable and enforceable numeric criteria. 40 C.F.R. § 131.11(b)(1). This preference was embraced by Congress in the Water Quality Act of 1987, which added § 303(c)(2)(B) to the Clean Water Act. This new provision specifically required states to adopt numeric criteria at least for toxic pollutants. 33 U.S.C. § 1313(c)(2)(B). Where such numeric criteria remain unavailable, states must adopt reliable methodologies for determining water quality criteria in order to ensure the protection of designated uses. *Id.*

Where states have not adopted water quality criteria as required, EPA can and does adopt water quality criteria that will apply in these states. In 1992, for example, EPA promulgated the National Toxics Rule to establish numeric criteria for toxic pollutants that would apply to all states that had not by then adopted their own water quality criteria for these pollutants as required by CWA § 303(c)(2)(B). 57 Fed. Reg. 60,848 (Dec. 22, 1992). Failures by states to adopt water quality criteria and by EPA to promulgate water quality criteria in the absence of state criteria have inspired many citizen suits by environmental advocates to compel compliance with the substantive requirements and deadlines included in § 303. *See, e.g., Northwest Envt'l Advocates v. U.S. EPA*, 855 F. Supp. 2d 1199 (D. Or. 2012) (recounting 16-year saga of citizen suit seeking revised criteria for temperature to protect endangered salmon in Oregon).

Antidegradation flows from the basic CWA premise that water quality in the United States should be restored or maintained, and never allowed to deteriorate. Like the Prevention of Significant Deterioration program of the Clean Air Act, the CWA antidegradation program specifically seeks to keep pristine waters pristine and to restore other waters to attain all designated uses. The antidegradation program began as an EPA policy promulgated at 40 C.F.R. § 131.12. Subsequently, the antidegradation program was endorsed in part by Congress in the 1987 CWA amendments, which added § 303(d)(4)(B) (requiring compliance with "antidegradation policy" for certain categories of discharges).

Substantively, the antidegradation program requires states to develop their own antidegradation policies that establish water quality standards according to three tiers of protection as described in brief below:

- For every water body, all existing water uses shall be maintained and protected.
- For every water body where the "fishable/swimmable" standard has been fully met, lower water quality may be allowed if the State finds it is "necessary to accommodate important economic or social development in the area. . . ."
- For "high quality waters" (sometimes known as "Tier 3 waters") that constitute "an outstanding National resource," such as waters of national parks and

wildlife refuges, water quality shall be maintained and protected without exception.

40 C.F.R. § 131.12(a)(1)–(3).

Both the statutory provisions and the implementing regulations concerning water quality standards left many questions to be resolved by implementing agencies, inviting legal challenges from all sides and judicial review. The following case focuses on the determination of designated uses while providing an excellent review of the applicable legal framework for developing water quality standards under the Clean Water Act.

Idaho Mining Ass'n v. Browner

90 F. Supp. 2d 1078 (D. Idaho 2000)

Chief United States Magistrate Judge WILLIAMS:

Background

In the instant action, the Court is asked to determine whether the Environmental Protection Agency ("EPA") exceeded its authority under the Administrative Procedures Act ("APA"), 5 U.S.C. § 551, *et seq.,* and the Clean Water Act ("CWA" or "Act"), 33 U.S.C. § 1251, *et seq.,* when it promulgated a rule establishing revised water quality standards for three (3) water body segments in Northern Idaho. Plaintiff, Idaho Mining Association, challenges the revised standards and seeks a declaration from this Court that the EPA's rulemaking was arbitrary and capricious, an abuse of discretion and otherwise not in accordance with the law. Plaintiff also seeks an order vacating the challenged rule and remanding the matter back to the EPA for further proceedings in accordance with the requirements of the APA and CWA.

The Clean Water Act

The primary objective of the Clean Water Act ("CWA") is to "restore and maintain the chemical, physical, and biological integrity of the Nation's waters" through the implementation of goals and policies designed to eliminate the discharge of pollutants into these waters. Section 101(a), 33 U.S.C. § 1251(a). To this end, Congress has declared that "wherever attainable, an interim goal of water quality which provides for the protection and propagation of fish, shellfish, and wildlife and provides for recreation in and on the water be achieved." Section 101(a)(2), 33 U.S.C. § 1251(a)(2). These so-called "fishable/swimmable" uses are primarily achieved through the implementation of two mechanisms: (1) technology-based requirements, i.e. "effluent limitations guidelines;" and (2) water-quality based requirements, i.e. water quality standards. *See* Sections 301 and 303, 33 U.S.C. §§ 1311 and 1313.

Technology-based requirements impose stringent limitations upon the types and amounts of pollutants which may be discharged into the nation's waters by point sources. Section 301, 33 U.S.C. § 1311. Water quality-based requirements, on the other hand, specify the desired condition of a waterway in terms of the standard (i.e.

fishable/swimmable, agricultural, industrial, etc.) to be achieved. Section 303, 33 U.S.C. § 1313. Thus, water quality standards generally consist of three elements: (1) one or more designated uses for the water body at issue; (2) water quality criteria which express the concentrations or levels of pollutants which may be present in the water and still support the designated use(s); and (3) an anti-degradation policy. Section 303(c)(2), 33 U.S.C. § 1313(c)(2); Section 303(d)(4)(B), 33 U.S.C. § 1313(d)(4) (B); 40 C.F.R. § 131.3(i). As the United States Supreme Court has explained, water quality standards "supplement effluent limitations 'so that numerous point sources, despite individual compliance with effluent limitations, may be further regulated to prevent water quality from falling below acceptable levels.'" *Arkansas v. Oklahoma*, 503 U.S. 91 (1992) (quoting *EPA v. California ex rel. State Water Resources Control Bd.*, 426 U.S. 200, 205 n. 12 (1976)).

Under the CWA, individual states are primarily responsible for the prevention, reduction and elimination of pollution of waterways within their boundaries. Section 101(b), 33 U.S.C. § 1251(b). . . .

The CWA does not impose upon states the obligation to designate any particular use(s) for water bodies. At a minimum, however, states must revise their water quality standards to reflect existing uses, i.e. those uses which are actually being attained. 40 C.F.R. § 131.10(i); 40 C.F.R. § 131.10(e). Furthermore, fishable/swimmable uses are favored. Section 101(a)(2), 339 U.S.C. § 1251(a)(2). Thus, where a state fails to designate a water body for fishable/swimmable uses, the state must conduct a use attainability analysis ("UAA") in accordance with the provisions of the CWA. 40 C.F.R. § 131.10(j)(1). Conversely, a UAA is not required whenever fishable/swimmable uses are designated. 40 C.F.R. § 131.10(k). . . .

B. Procedural History

Plaintiff, Idaho Mining Association, is a non-profit corporation whose members include industrial facilities that conduct mining activities in the State of Idaho. Plaintiff's members hold National Pollutant Discharge Elimination System ("NPDES") permits and are authorized to discharge certain amounts of industrial wastewater to particular waters in Northern Idaho. On October 2, 1998, Plaintiff filed a Complaint in the instant action naming the United States Environmental Protection Agency and the following individuals as defendants: Carol M. Browner, Administrator, U.S. Environmental Protection Agency; and Charles C. Clarke, Regional Administrator, Environmental Protection Agency, Region 10 (hereinafter collectively referred to as "EPA"). In its Complaint, Plaintiff alleges that the EPA failed to comply with the requirements of the APA when it promulgated revised water quality standards for certain Idaho waters in 1997. The revised standards establish new designated uses for certain stream segments in Northern Idaho and impose more stringent water quality criteria to protect the new uses. Plaintiff alleges that the new standards will significantly affect the ability of Plaintiff's members to discharge mining pollutants into the affected waters pursuant to their NPDES permits and will negatively impact the economic viability of the mining industry in Idaho. Plaintiff seeks an order vacating that portion of the EPA rule which establishes the new designated uses on the grounds that the EPA rulemaking as to the revised standards was arbitrary and capricious, an abuse of discretion and otherwise not in accordance with the law. . . .

C. Factual History

The material facts underlying this matter are not in dispute. On July 11, 1994, the State of Idaho fulfilled its obligations under section 303(c) of the CWA by submitting a complete set of water quality standards to the EPA for review. Almost two years later, on June 25, 1996, the EPA issued an official notification approving Idaho's 1994 water quality standards with certain exceptions. However, this notification came only after the Conservation Groups filed a citizen suit against the EPA to compel it to comply with its mandatory duties under sections 303(c)(3) and 303(c)(4)(A) of the CWA to formally approve or disapprove Idaho's proposed water quality standards and, if necessary, to adopt replacement standards for those state standards which it disapproved. *See Idaho Conservation League v. Browner*, 968 F.Supp. 546 (W.D.Wash.1997) (hereinafter "*ICL v. Browner*").

One group of standards which the EPA disapproved in its June 1996 letter concerned the designation of 53 Idaho stream segments for uses less protective than fishable/swimmable. . . . . .

Having disapproved Idaho's use designations for the specified stream segments, and consistent with its obligations under section 303(c)(3) of the CWA, the EPA informed the IDEQ that it must undertake certain revisions in order to bring Idaho's 1994 water quality standards in conformity with the purposes and requirements of the CWA. In this respect, the EPA provided the IDEQ with two options, either of which it determined to be an appropriate resolution to remedy the deficient water quality standards:

> The State can either a) conduct and submit to EPA acceptable use attainability analyses to justify the existing classification for the above listed water bodies, or b) adopt designated uses for each water body which provides for the protection and propagation of aquatic life and recreation in and on the water where applicable.

However, Idaho failed to undertake either of these revisions within the ninety (90) day time period prescribed by section 303(c)(4)(A) of the CWA. Thus, it became the EPA's responsibility to "promptly prepare and publish" replacement standards in accordance with the CWA. Section 303(c)(4)(A), 33 U.S.C. § 1313(c)(4)(A); 40 C.F.R. § 131.22(a).

By February, 1997, neither the IDEQ nor the EPA had promulgated new or revised water quality standards for Idaho. Consequently, the Conservation Groups took it upon themselves to seek a court order requiring the EPA to adopt replacement standards in accordance with its duties under section 303(c)(4)(A) of the CWA. On February 20, 1997, the presiding judge in *ICL v. Browner*, granted the Conservation Groups' motion for summary judgment and entered an order directing the EPA to act within sixty (60) days to "promulgate water quality standards for Idaho in accordance with its June 1996 letter of disapproval." *ICL v. Browner,* 968 F.Supp. at 549. The court order was subsequently modified to allow the EPA sixty (60) days in which to propose revised standards and ninety (90) days thereafter in which to promulgate a final rule.

On April 28, 1997, the EPA published a proposed rule introducing several tentative revisions to those Idaho water quality standards which the EPA had disapproved in 1996. 62 Fed.Reg. 23,003 (April 28, 1997). Included within the proposed revisions was a new federal use designation establishing aquatic life and recreation uses for the specific water body segments whose use designations EPA had disapproved in 1996. The EPA explained that it had previously disapproved Idaho's regulations with respect to those waters because, in many cases, the regulations only protected the stream segments for recreation and did not provide any protection for aquatic life. The EPA determined that Idaho's failure to adopt water quality standards which provided protection for the fishable component of fishable/swimmable uses was inconsistent with the goals and requirements of the CWA because Idaho had not undertaken a UAA to demonstrate that such uses were unattainable. Thus, the EPA proposed to promulgate a rule establishing aquatic life and recreation designated uses for the water body segments of concern, unless it was demonstrated to the EPA for a particular water body that such uses were unattainable. In proposing this rule, the EPA expressly stated that it was relying on a rebuttable presumption implicit in its regulations at 40 C.F.R. Part 131 that fishable/swimmable uses are attainable unless the uses have been shown by a UAA to be unattainable. In addition, the EPA specifically proposed that 35 of the 53 stream segments be designated for cold water biota use because "[t]he majority of native Idaho fish are classified as cold water species and the presence of the species occurs throughout the entire State."

The EPA held a public hearing and took comments on all aspects of the proposed rule for a period of thirty (30) days.... [A]fter reviewing the information submitted, the EPA concluded that the data did not demonstrate that the aquatic life uses—and specifically, the cold water biota uses—could not be attained.

On July 31, 1997, the EPA published the final rule establishing cold water biota designated uses for several Idaho waterways, including the South Fork of the Coeur d'Alene River and two of its tributaries, Canyon Creek and Shields Gulch (hereinafter collectively referred to as the "affected waters"). *See* 40 C.F.R. § 131.33(b). In doing so, the EPA again stated that it was "relying on the rebuttable presumption implicit in the CWA and EPA's regulations at 40 C.F.R. part 131, that in the absence of data to the contrary, 'fishable' uses are attainable."

* * *

Whether the EPA Reasonably Interpreted Its Own Regulations as Requiring a Rebuttable Presumption in Favor of Aquatic Life Use Designations

It is undisputed that one of the primary goals of the CWA is to achieve water quality that provides for fishable/swimmable uses wherever such uses are attainable. Section 101(a)(2), 33 U.S.C. § 1251(a)(2). It is further undisputed that when establishing new or revised water quality standards, states are required to adopt standards that "protect the public health or welfare, enhance the quality of water and serve the purposes" of the CWA. Section 303(c)(2)(A), 33 U.S.C. § 1313(c)(2)(A). While these provisions plainly express a preference for fishable/swimmable use designations, all parties agree that the CWA does not itself create a rebuttable presumption that such uses are always attainable. Rather, the CWA directs states to consider numerous factors when adopting water quality standards, including the water body's "use and value for public water supplies, propagation of fish and wildlife, recreational purposes," and other purposes enumerated by the Act. *Id. See also,* 40 C.F.R. § 131.10(a). Nevertheless, the EPA contends that a rebuttable presumption of aquatic life attainability is clearly supported by EPA regulations implementing the CWA . . . .

It is well-settled that an agency's reasonable interpretation of its own regulations is entitled to substantial deference . . . Accordingly, the threshold inquiry to be resolved on summary judgment is whether the EPA reasonably interpreted its water quality standards regulations as requiring a rebuttable presumption in favor of aquatic life use designations. Plaintiff contends that it did not. . . .

While Plaintiff expressly acknowledges that subsection (k) of 40 C.F.R. § 131.10 authorizes states to establish fishable/swimmable use designations without performing a UAA, it nevertheless argues that the EPA does not have that same authority. However, as both Defendants and the Intervenors point out, this argument carries little force. Because Idaho failed to correct the deficiencies in its 1994 water quality standards, the EPA was under a mandatory duty pursuant to section 303(c) of the CWA to promptly adopt replacement standards for those standards which it had disapproved. In doing so, the EPA was "subject to the same policies, procedures, analyses, and public participation requirements established for States in [the EPA] regulations." 40 C.F.R. § 131.22(c). Thus, despite Plaintiff's assertions to the contrary, section 131.10(k) authorized the EPA to establish aquatic life uses for the affected waters without performing a UAA. . . .

Based on the foregoing, the Court concludes that the EPA reasonably interpreted its regulations at 40 C.F.R. § 131.10(j) and (k) as requiring an aquatic life use designation unless a UAA demonstrates that aquatic life uses are unattainable. Although the regulations do not explicitly contain the phrase "rebuttable presumption," the Court finds that it was neither arbitrary and capricious, an abuse of discretion, nor contrary to law for the EPA to construe them as such. . . .

Whether the CWA Authorizes a Rebuttable Presumption in Favor of Fishable/ Swimmable Uses

The threshold issue before the Court is whether the EPA was authorized under the CWA to promulgate regulations which effectively created a rebuttable presumption in favor of fishable/swimmable uses. Resolution of this issue will require the Court to determine whether the applicable language of the statute is plain and unambiguous or whether the language is subject to multiple interpretations. The parties take entirely different positions as to this issue. . . .

In this case, Plaintiff argues that the plain language of section 303(c)(2)(A) of the CWA prohibits "default" use designations such as the presumptive aquatic life use designation relied upon by the EPA in this case. Section 303(c)(2)(A) provides:

> Whenever the State revises or adopts a new standard, such revised or new standard shall be submitted to the Administrator. Such revised or new water quality standard shall consist of the designated uses of the navigable waters involved and the water quality criteria for such waters based upon such uses. Such standards shall be such as to protect the public health or welfare, enhance the quality of water and serve the purposes of this chapter. Such standards shall be established taking into consideration their use and value for public water supplies, propagation of fish and wildlife, recreational purposes, and agricultural, industrial, and other purposes, and also taking into consideration their use and value for navigation.

33 U.S.C. § 1313(c)(2)(A). As Plaintiff points out, this provision does not establish a "presumptive use" for waters of the United States. Instead, it directs the states to consider a variety of factors when establishing water quality standards, including the waters' use and value for recreational, agricultural, industrial and aquatic life uses. Plaintiff contends that in drafting this provision, Congress expressly left it to the discretion of the each individual state to determine the appropriate use designation for each of its water bodies. Plaintiff also argues that the EPA's presumptive use interpretation "essentially reads out of the statute the *selection* authority that Congress vested exclusively in the states under this section." Plaintiff contends that had Congress intended that all waters of the United States be designated as fishable/swimmable, it would have expressly provided for it in Section 303(c)(2)(A). . . .

[The Court then summarized the two-step analysis required in the *Chevron* case for judicial review of an agency's construction of a statute that it administers.]

In this case, the Court agrees with Defendants that Congress has not directly spoken to the precise question at issue, i.e. "what showing should be required for a water body to avoid (or receive) a particular designated use." Instead, Section 303(c)(2)(A) of the CWA merely provides a list of competing factors/uses to be considered when establishing water quality standards without providing any specific guidance as to how those factors should be weighed or balanced against one another. In light of this ambiguity, the Court must proceed to the second step of the *Chevron* inquiry and determine whether the EPA's presumptive fishable/swimmable use interpretation is a permissible construction of the statute. For the following reasons, the Court finds that it is.

In promulgating its 1983 regulations and the challenged rule, the EPA did not unreasonably exclude any of the factors contained in section 303(c)(2)(A) from consideration. Instead, it merely exercised its discretion to balance those factors in favor of a fishable/swimmable use designation unless a UAA demonstrates that such uses are not attainable. In the Court's view, the EPA's presumptive use interpretation is consistent with Congress' express directive that water quality standards be such as to "protect the public health or welfare, enhance the quality of water and serve the purposes of [the CWA]." Section 303(c)(2)(A), 33 U.S.C. § 1313(c)(2)(A). Undeniably, one of the over-arching purposes of the CWA is to achieve fishable/swimmable uses wherever attainable. Section 101(a)(2), 33 U.S.C. § 1251(a)(2). Thus, although Congress recognized that the achievement of fishable/swimmable uses will not always be possible, it clearly indicated an intent that states move toward more protective water quality standards to preserve the nation's waters for human uses as well as for aquatic life. The EPA's regulations at 40 C.F.R. § 131.10(j) and (k), and the rebuttable presumption stemming therefrom, are plainly consonant with this intent and represent a "reasonable accommodation of conflicting policies that were committed to the agency's care by" section 303(c)(2)(A) of the CWA. *Chevron*, 467 U.S. at 845 (quoting *Shimer*, 367 U.S. at 383). Accordingly, the Court finds that the EPA's presumptive use interpretation is a permissible construction of the statute and is therefore entitled to deference from this Court. . . .

[The court rejected the plaintiff's contention that EPA did not have a sufficient factual basis to conclude that aquatic life users could be attained in the affected waters. It found that EPA's determination was clearly supported by the available biological data and was neither arbitrary nor capricious.]

Notes and Questions

1. The extensive mining contamination in the Coeur d'Alene Basin, at issue in *Idaho Mining Ass'n*, affects many communities and jurisdictions, including the Coeur d'Alene Tribe. Like states, tribes may have the ability—though not necessarily the *responsibility*—to establish their own water quality standards, after receiving Treatment as State (TAS) status. *See* CWA § 518(e), 33 U.S.C. § 1377 (authorizing EPA to treat tribes as states for purposes including § 303, relating to development of water quality standards). Under § 518, the Coeur d'Alene Tribe applied for and received TAS status in 2005, allowing the Tribe to establish water quality standards for waters impacted by the mining contamination in the Coeur d'Alene Basin. *See* Letter from Ronald A. Kreizenbeck, EPA Region 10, to Chief J. Allan, Chairman, Coeur d'Alene Tribe, Aug. 5, 2005. Through TAS status, tribes may seek to protect designated uses of water that may not be protected otherwise by states, including for cultural and religious practices. *See, e.g.*, City of Albuquerque v. Browner, 97 F.3d 415 (10th Cir. 1996), *cert. denied*, 522 U.S. 965 (1997) (water quality standards of Isleta Pueblo to protect ceremonial uses of water in Rio Grande are enforceable against upstream City of Albuquerque).

2. What does it mean for a designated use to be "attainable" per CWA § 101(a)(2)? Is there both a technological and a time dimension? In other words, attainable *when*? If it appears that a use in a heavily polluted area cannot be achieved within a reasonable amount of time, is it still "attainable"? In fact, within the Coeur d'Alene Basin, computer modeling indicated that some polluted stream segments could not meet standards for dissolved zinc (highly toxic to native trout) in less than 200 years, no matter how aggressive the cleanup actions that might be taken. *See* Clifford J. Villa, *Superfund vs. Mega-Sites: The Coeur d'Alene River Basin Story*, 28 COLUM. J. ENVTL. LAW 255, 303

and n.294 (2003). Does this mean that these water quality standards should be ignored or removed from the NPDES permits held by the mining companies?

3. In *Idaho Mining Ass'n*, the mining industry itself argued that water quality was so degraded ("orders of magnitude" above applicable criteria for the South Fork of the Coeur d'Alene River), that designated use for cold water biota was inappropriate. If this argument had been accepted by the court, consider the implications. Would this allow courts to dismiss water quality standards for polluted water bodies if they are too polluted? How does this comport with the national goals of the Clean Water Act? Consider also the argument of the mining industry emphasizing the extreme levels of mining contamination in the Coeur d'Alene Basin. If you represented the mining industry in this case, do you think you would have pursued this strategy? Why or why not? In this context, are there laws beyond the Clean Water Act that should concern the mining companies? *See, e.g., U.S. v. ASARCO Inc.,* 280 F. Supp. 2d 1094 (D. Id. 2003) (finding mining companies liable for mining contamination in the Coeur d'Alene Basin under the Comprehensive Environmental Response, Compensation, and Liability Act).   SUPERFUND LAW

4. In addition to the Comprehensive Environmental Response, Compensation, and Liability Act (CERCLA), a number of other environmental statutes may also be implicated in the development and implementation of water quality standards. Chief among these may be the National Environmental Policy Act (NEPA) and the Endangered Species Act. In developing water quality standards, failure to complete a required NEPA environmental impact statement (EIS) or environmental assessment (EA) and failure to complete the ESA § 7 consultation process may lead to legal challenges and years of delay. *See, e.g., Northwest Envt'l Advocates v. U.S. EPA,* 855 F. Supp. 2d 1199 (D. Or. 2012) (invalidating Oregon water quality standards for failure of federal wildlife agencies to conduct adequate ESA Biological Opinion).

2. How Water Quality Standards Are Implemented

While the Clean Water Act has much to say about how water quality standards are to be developed, it has little to say directly about how they are to be implemented. In the context of point sources, § 301(b) suggests that NPDES permits must ensure compliance with any applicable state water quality standards. 33 U.S.C. § 1311(b)(1)(C). Beyond that, EPA has promulgated regulations that seek to compel compliance with water quality standards in certain circumstances. Among these circumstances, EPA regulations preclude the issuance of any NPDES permits "when the imposition of conditions cannot ensure compliance with the applicable water quality requirements of all affected States." 40 C.F.R. § 122.4(d). EPA regulations also preclude permits for new discharges if such discharges will "cause or contribute to the violation of water quality standards." *Id.* § 122.4(i).

Note that each of the circumstances identified above requires the issuance (or denial) of an NPDES permit. Water quality standards are not self-implementing. While environmental groups may spend years in litigation to compel more stringent water quality standards, such standards by themselves do nothing to improve the quality of the environment. By the same token, industrial concerns may spend years opposing water quality standards, but the standards by themselves may pose no additional obligations upon them. Water quality standards require some vehicle for implementation: most commonly, an NPDES permit. As the Supreme Court has observed, the NPDES permit "serves to transform generally applicable effluent limitations and other standards including those based on water quality into the obligations . . . of the individual discharger. . . ." *EPA v. California ex rel. State Water Resources Control Board*, 426 U.S. 200, 205 (1976).

The district court in the *Idaho Mining Ass'n* case above explicitly recognized this dynamic as well, observing:

> In promulgating the final rule, the EPA made clear that a discharger with an existing NPDES permit is not subject to permit conditions reflecting the heightened water quality standards for the affected waters until such time as the discharger's permit is renewed. However, the EPA recognized that additional data material to the attainability of the cold water biota uses might become available in the future. Thus, the EPA rule also established a procedure by which an individual discharger can obtain a variance from the water quality standards by demonstrating that the cold water biota use is unattainable due to the presence of certain chemical or physical conditions, or because compliance with the fishable use criteria would cause "substantial and widespread economic and social impact." 40 C.F.R. § 131.33(d)(3). Pursuant to the variance procedure, application for the water quality standards variance is timed to coincide with the NPDES permit renewal process. 40 C.F.R. § 131.33(d)(4). Thus, an individual NPDES regulated discharger who establishes that the cold water biota use is unattainable for a particular water body will escape the more stringent permit limits imposed by cold water biota use designation. However, the variance applies only to the permit holder requesting the variance; the underlying cold water biota use designation otherwise remains in effect. 40 C.F.R. § 131.33(d)(1).

Idaho Mining Ass'n v. Browner, 90 F. Supp. 2d 1078, 1085 (D. Id. 2000). Thus, even though the court in that case upheld EPA's water quality standards including the fishable/swimmable use designation, the individual mining companies concerned have no obligation to comply with these new standards, at least until their individual NPDES permits have been issued or renewed.

The *Idaho Mining Ass'n* case dealt in part with mining pollution in northern Idaho affecting the watershed of the Coeur d'Alene River. This pollution impacts resources of the Coeur d'Alene Tribe and also the downstream State of Washington. As navigable waters in the United States often cross political boundaries, permitting agencies often must determine *whose* water quality standards should be incorporated into any individual NPDES permit. In 1992, the Supreme Court was called to review one such determination, resulting in the landmark decision excerpted below.

Arkansas v. Oklahoma

503 U.S. 91 (1992)

Justice STEVENS:

Pursuant to the Clean Water Act, 86 Stat. 816, as amended, 33 U.S.C. § 1251 *et seq.,* the Environmental Protection Agency (EPA or agency) issued a discharge permit to a new point source in Arkansas, about 39 miles upstream from the Oklahoma state line. The question presented in this litigation is whether the EPA's finding that discharges from the new source would not cause a detectable violation of Oklahoma's water quality standards satisfied the EPA's duty to protect the interests of the downstream State. Disagreeing with the Court of Appeals, we hold that the Agency's action was authorized by the statute.

In 1985, the city of Fayetteville, Arkansas, applied to the EPA, seeking a permit for the city's new sewage treatment plant under the National Pollution [sic] Discharge Elimination System (NPDES). After the appropriate procedures, the EPA, pursuant to § 402(a)(1) of the Act, 33 U.S.C. § 1342(a)(1), issued a permit authorizing the plant to discharge up to half of its effluent (to a limit of 6.1 million gallons per day) into an unnamed stream in northwestern Arkansas. That flow passes through a series of three creeks for about 17 miles, and then enters the Illinois River at a point 22 miles upstream from the Arkansas-Oklahoma border.

The permit imposed specific limitations on the quantity, content, and character of the discharge and also included a number of special conditions, including a provision that if a study then underway indicated that more stringent limitations were necessary to ensure compliance with Oklahoma's water quality standards, the permit would be modified to incorporate those limits.

Respondents challenged this permit before the EPA, alleging, *inter alia,* that the discharge violated the Oklahoma water quality standards. Those standards provide that "no degradation [of water quality] shall be allowed" in the upper Illinois River, including the portion of the river immediately downstream from the state line.

Following a hearing, the Administrative Law Judge (ALJ) concluded that the Oklahoma standards would not be implicated unless the contested discharge had "something more than a mere *de minimis* impact" on the State's waters. He found that the discharge would not have an "undue impact" on Oklahoma's waters and, accordingly, affirmed the issuance of the permit.

On a petition for review, the EPA's Chief Judicial Officer first ruled that § 301(b)(1)(C) of the Clean Water Act "requires an NPDES permit to impose any effluent limitations necessary to comply with applicable state water quality standards." He then held that the Act and EPA regulations offered greater protection for the downstream State than the ALJ's "undue impact" standard suggested. He explained the proper standard as follows:

"[A] mere theoretical impairment of Oklahoma's water quality standards — *i.e.,* an infinitesimal impairment predicted through modeling but not expected to be actually detectable or measurable—should not by itself block the issuance of the permit. In this case, the permit should be upheld if the record shows by a preponderance of the evidence that the authorized discharges would not cause an actual *detectable* violation of Oklahoma's water quality standards." *Id.,* at 117a (emphasis in original).

On remand, the ALJ made detailed findings of fact and concluded that the city had satisfied the standard set forth by the Chief Judicial Officer. Specifically, the ALJ found that there would be no detectable violation of any of the components of Oklahoma's water quality standards. The Chief Judicial Officer sustained the issuance of the permit.

Both the petitioners ... and the respondents in this litigation sought judicial review. Arkansas argued that the Clean Water Act did not require an Arkansas point source to comply with Oklahoma's water quality standards. Oklahoma challenged the EPA's determination that the Fayetteville discharge would not produce a detectable violation of the Oklahoma standards.

The Court of Appeals did not accept either of these arguments. The court agreed with the EPA that the statute required compliance with Oklahoma's water quality standards ..., and did not disagree with the Agency's determination that the discharges from the Fayetteville plant would not produce a detectable violation of those standards. Nevertheless, relying on a theory that neither party had advanced, the Court of Appeals reversed the Agency's issuance of the Fayetteville permit. The court first ruled that the statute requires that "where a proposed source would discharge effluents that would contribute to conditions currently constituting a violation of applicable water quality standards, such [a] proposed source may not be permitted." Then the court found that the Illinois River in Oklahoma was "already degraded," that the Fayetteville effluent would reach the Illinois River in Oklahoma, and that that effluent could "be expected to contribute to the ongoing deterioration of the scenic [Illinois R]iver" in Oklahoma even though it would not detectably affect the river's water quality.

The importance and the novelty of the Court of Appeals' decision persuaded us to grant certiorari. We now reverse. ...

The parties have argued three analytically distinct questions concerning the interpretation of the Clean Water Act. First, does the Act require the EPA, in crafting and issuing a permit to a point source in one State, to apply the water quality standards of downstream States? Second, even if the Act does not *require* as much, does the Agency have the statutory authority to mandate such compliance? Third, does the Act provide, as the Court of Appeals held, that once a body of water fails to meet water quality standards no discharge that yields effluent that reach the degraded waters will be permitted?

In these cases, it is neither necessary nor prudent for us to resolve the first of these questions. In issuing the Fayetteville permit, the EPA assumed it was obligated by both the Act and its own regulations to ensure that the Fayetteville discharge would not violate Oklahoma's standards. As we discuss below, this assumption was permissible and reasonable and therefore there is no need for us to address whether the Act requires as much. . . .

Our decision not to determine at this time the scope of the Agency's statutory *obligations* does not affect our resolution of the second question, which concerns the Agency's statutory *authority*. Even if the Clean Water Act itself does not require the Fayetteville discharge to comply with Oklahoma's water quality standards, the statute clearly does not limit the EPA's authority to mandate such compliance.

Since 1973, EPA regulations have provided that an NPDES permit shall not be issued "[w]hen the imposition of conditions cannot ensure compliance with the applicable water quality requirements of all affected States." 40 CFR § 122.4(d) (1991); see also 38 Fed.Reg. 13533 (1973); 40 CFR § 122.44(d) (1991). Those regulations—relied upon by the EPA in the issuance of the Fayetteville permit—constitute a reasonable exercise of the Agency's statutory authority. . . .

The application of state water quality standards in the interstate context is wholly consistent with the Act's broad purpose "to restore and maintain the chemical, physical, and biological integrity of the Nation's waters." 33 U.S.C. § 1251(a). Moreover, as noted above, § 301(b)(1)(C) expressly identifies the achievement of state water quality standards as one of the Act's central objectives. The Agency's regulations conditioning NPDES permits are a well-tailored means of achieving this goal. . . .

For these reasons, we find the EPA's requirement that the Fayetteville discharge comply with Oklahoma's water quality standards to be a reasonable exercise of the Agency's substantial statutory discretion. Cf. *Chevron U.S.A. Inc. v. Natural Resources Defense Council, Inc.,* 467 U.S. 837, 842–845 (1984).

The Court of Appeals construed the Clean Water Act to prohibit any discharge of effluent that would reach waters already in violation of existing water quality standards. We find nothing in the Act to support this reading. . . .

Although the Act contains several provisions directing compliance with state water quality standards, *see, e.g.,* § 1311(b)(1)(C), the parties have pointed to nothing that mandates a complete ban on discharges into a waterway that is in violation of those standards. The statute does, however, contain provisions designed to remedy existing water quality violations and to allocate the burden of reducing undesirable discharges between existing sources and new sources. *See, e.g.,* § 1313(d). Thus, rather than establishing the categorical ban announced by the Court of Appeals—which might frustrate the construction of new plants that would improve existing conditions—the Clean Water Act vests in the EPA and the States broad authority to develop long-range, area-wide programs to alleviate and eliminate existing pollution.

To the extent that the Court of Appeals relied on its interpretation of the Act to reverse the EPA's permitting decision, that reliance was misplaced. . . .

Notes and Questions

1. In *Arkansas v. Oklahoma*, the State of Arkansas objected to a condition in their NPDES permit that would have required their compliance with a water quality standard established by the downstream State of Oklahoma. Note that the particular condition at issue was a narrative criterion providing that "no degradation [of water quality] shall be allowed" in the upper Illinois River. Could such a loose standard be challenged by permit holders as void for vagueness? On the other hand, can such a loose narrative be enforced? *See, e.g., Northwest Envt'l Advocates v. City of Portland*, 56 F.3d 979, 985 (9th Cir. 1995), *cert. denied,* 518 U.S. 1018 (1996) (dismissing the city's vagueness argument and finding that citizens may enforce permit condition that "no wastes shall be discharged . . . which will violate [water quality standards]").

2. In *Arkansas v. Oklahoma*, who has the burden of proving that an individual discharge in Arkansas (39 miles upstream from the state border) will *not* allow degradation of water quality in Oklahoma? On this note, compare 40 C.F.R. § 122.4(d) (precluding issuance of any permit "when the imposition of conditions cannot ensure compliance with the applicable water quality requirements of all affected States") with Justice Stevens' pragmatic approach to determining degradation of water quality as a factual matter.

3. Does compliance with all applicable water quality standards in a water body mean that all designated uses are safe? For example, does full compliance with the "fishable/ swimmable" standard in a particular river mean that river is safe for swimming? For fishing? For eating the fish? Obviously, water quality standards are only designed to protect against exposure to pollution, not physical hazards such as currents or sharp rocks on the bottom of a river. Moreover, even when it comes to questions of pollution, recall that water quality standards currently in place may be many years or even decades old, falling behind advances in science and technology. The impacts of lead on human health, for example, were gravely underestimated in the past, and those misapprehensions may still be reflected in standards today. *See* David C. Bellinger and Andrew M. Bellinger, *Childhood Lead Poisoning: The Tortuous Path from Science to Policy*, 116 J. Clinical Investigation 853 (April 2006). In addition, what is deemed "safe" for one individual or group may not be safe for others. For example, while an occasional dinner of fileted trout may be safe for recreational fishermen, the more regular consumption of fish (including whole fish) by some indigenous or immigrant communities may pose a much greater threat to their health. *See* Catherine O'Neill, *Fishable Waters*, 1 Am. Indian L. J. 181 (2013) (noting that water quality standards in Washington, Idaho, and Alaska assume that individuals eat no more than 12 fish meals a year, despite evidence that Northwest tribes may consume hundreds of times that much fish). Thus, water quality standards may raise serious concerns for environmental justice, failing to protect the health of all people and communities.

Finally, note that water quality standards may only address pollution in the "water column" (the open water between the surface and bottom of a river, lake, or bay). Measurement of pollutants limited to this space may miss the significant contamination in other media, including the sediments at the bottom of a lake or river. Particularly in urban waterways, sediments may often be contaminated with toxic pollutants, including heavy metals, such as lead and mercury, and industrial compounds such as polychlorinated biphenyls (PCBs). Contaminants in sediments may pose serious threats to human health and the environment through the food chain or other release mechanisms, even if monitoring in the water column indicates compliance with water quality standards. *See, e.g., Friends of the Earth v. Laidlaw Envt'l Services*, 528 U.S. 167 (2000) (no violations of water quality standard for mercury detected in North Tyger River, despite evidence of 489 violations of NPDES permit standard for mercury).

4. Mixing Zones. The question of monitoring in order to ensure compliance with water quality standards raises many other questions, including the use of "mixing zones." Mixing zones are authorized by EPA regulation, 40 C.F.R. § 131.13, and defined by EPA to represent "a limited area or volume of water where initial dilution of a discharge takes place and where certain numeric criteria may be exceeded." EPA, *Water Quality Standards Handbook* § 5.1 (2016), available online at https://www.epa.gov/ wqs-tech/water-quality-standards-handbook. Through the use of mixing zones, water samples for purposes of compliance monitoring may be taken not at the end of a pipe or other discharge point, but at some distance from the outfall in the water body itself. This allows the discharger some benefit of dilution in order to meet the standard. Obviously, most dischargers would prefer larger mixing zones and environmental interests would prefer smaller. A typical mixing zone would have a radius of 100 feet, but the specific dimensions and conditions for each mixing zone should be defined in an individual NPDES permit. For further guidance on the proper development and use of mixing zones, see the EPA *Water Quality Standards Handbook* at § 5.1.

Practice Problem

Jules Junction in the State of Portlandia, is planning to construct a large municipal golf course on town property near the Jordan River. Liquid wastes from the golf course, including sanitation from the golf course club house, runoff of oil and grease from the parking lot, and herbicides and pesticides from maintenance of the greens, will be captured and pumped into the Jordan River, which lies less than 50 feet from the edge of the golf course. Given the relatively light concentration of these pollutants, no violations of water quality standards in the Jordan River are anticipated more than a mile and a half downstream from the golf course.

1. If Jules Junction agrees to meet all applicable technology standards for its discharge from the golf course, should it expect to receive a permit allowing this discharge? If you were EPA legal counsel providing advice to the permit writer, what factors might you suggest evaluating before the permit was issued?

2. If the State of Armisen, 34 miles downstream from the Portlandia state line, objects to issuance of the permit, asserting that the discharge from the golf course would cause violations of its own water quality standards for the Jordan River, should the permit still be issued? Why or why not?

IX. Other Water-Quality Based Programs

NPDES permits are one important means of implementing water quality standards. However, as noted earlier in this chapter, NPDES permits are only required for point sources. As noted above, the largest source of water pollution in the United States is nonpoint sources, including runoff of nutrients (especially nitrogen and phosphorus) from agriculture, pathogens (e.g., bacteria) from livestock operations, sediment from forestry and construction, and oil and grease from urban runoff. EPA, *National Water Quality Inventory: Report to Congress* (Jan. 2009). To reach these nonpoint sources, and to continue making progress toward the Clean Water Act goal of eliminating the discharge of pollutants into the waters of the United States, the CWA establishes three major programs that will be discussed here: the 319 grant program; the 401 certification program; and the TMDL program.

A. 319 Grants

The 1972 Clean Water Act included § 208, which encouraged states to engage in "areawide" planning processes to address water pollution concerns, including nonpoint runoff. 33 U.S.C. § 1288(a). The provision also authorized EPA to make grants to states that engaged in "areawide" planning. *Id.* § 1288(f)(1). When this areawide planning approach failed to achieve notable reductions in nonpoint source pollution, Congress tried again through enactment of § 319 in the Water Quality Act of 1987. Specifically targeted at nonpoint source pollution, § 319 required states to produce a report assessing the nonpoint sources of pollution in their state and prepare a management plan identifying best management practices and strategies for addressing those sources. 33 U.S.C. § 1329(a), (b). After completing those two reports, states could apply to EPA for annual grant funding to work on specific nonpoint source issues in their state. CWA § 319(h), 33 U.S.C. § 1319(h).

Since 1987, the 319 grant program has proven very popular for states, tribes, and territories, funding a variety of activities, including education, training, technical assistance, and demonstration projects in impaired watersheds. Beginning in 1999, annual funding for the 319 grant program nearly doubled to $200 million. Under EPA guidance, approximately half of a state's grant allocation may go toward program funding supporting broad solutions, such as public education and worker training to prevent nonpoint source pollution. The other half of the state's allocation must go toward specific projects identified by the state to protect or restore local watersheds. EPA, *Nonpoint Source Program and Grants Guidelines for States and Territories* (April 2013).

Together with state matching funds—typically 40 percent per § 319(h)(3)—and other public and private resources, the 319 grant program has led to achievements toward addressing nonpoint source pollution in every state and on many tribal lands. *See* EPA, *Nonpoint Source Success Stories* (available online at https://www.epa.gov/nps/success). Nonetheless, given the magnitude of the program, the 319 program cannot be seen as the final solution for nonpoint source pollution in the United States.

Indeed, one study revealed that while the 319 program had succeeded in restoring 355 impaired water bodies by 2011, that represented just one percent of all impaired water bodies in the U.S. EPA, *A National Evaluation of the Clean Water Act Section 319 Program* 1 (Nov. 2011).

B. 401 Certification

Section 401(a) of the Clean Water Act provides that "Any applicant for a Federal license or permit ... which may result in any discharge into the navigable waters, shall provide the licensing or permitting agency a certification from the State in which the discharge originates ... that any such discharge will comply with" requirements including water quality standards under CWA § 303. Note that this rather straightforward proposition carries potentially substantial implications. By requiring "any" applicant for a federal license or permit to obtain this certification, § 401 expands compliance with water quality standards beyond the realm of NPDES permits. Thus, 401 certification must also be obtained by applicants for a 404 permit from the Corps of Engineers under the wetlands program and by applicants for a license from the Federal Energy Regulatory Commission (FERC) under the Federal Power Act, 16 U.S.C. § 791 *et seq.*

One 401 certification case concerning an application for a FERC license reached the U.S. Supreme Court and resulted in the following decision:

PUD No. 1 Of Jefferson County v. Washington Dept. of Ecology
511 U.S. 700 (1994)

Justice O'CONNOR:

Petitioners, [the City of Tacoma] and a local utility district, want to build a hydroelectric project on the Dosewallips River in Washington State. We must decide whether respondent state environmental agency (hereinafter respondent) properly conditioned a permit for the project on the maintenance of specific minimum stream flows to protect salmon and steelhead runs. . . .

Petitioners propose to build the Elkhorn Hydroelectric Project on the Dosewallips River. If constructed as presently planned, the facility would be located just outside the Olympic National Park on federally owned land within the Olympic National Forest. The project would divert water from a 1.2-mile reach of the river (the bypass reach), run the water through turbines to generate electricity and then return the water to the river below the bypass reach. Under the Federal Power Act (FPA), 41 Stat. 1063, as amended, 16 U.S.C. § 791a *et seq.*, the Federal Energy Regulatory Commission (FERC) has authority to license new hydroelectric facilities. As a result, petitioners must get a FERC license to build or operate the Elkhorn Project. Because a federal license is required, and because the project may result in discharges into the Dosewallips River, petitioners are also required to obtain state certification of the project pursuant to § 401 of the Clean Water Act, 33 U.S.C. § 1341.

The water flow in the bypass reach, which is currently undiminished by appropriation, ranges seasonally between 149 and 738 cubic feet per second (cfs). The Dosewallips supports two species of salmon, coho and chinook, as well as steelhead trout. As originally proposed, the project was to include a diversion dam which would completely block the river and channel approximately 75% of the river's water into a tunnel alongside the streambed. About 25% of the water would remain in the bypass reach, but would be returned to the original riverbed through sluice gates or a fish ladder. Depending on the season, this would leave a residual minimum flow of between 65 and 155 cfs in the river. Respondent undertook a study to determine the minimum stream flows necessary to protect the salmon and steelhead fishery in the bypass reach. On June 11, 1986, respondent issued a § 401 water quality certification imposing a variety of conditions on the project, including a minimum stream flow requirement of between 100 and 200 cfs depending on the season.

A state administrative appeals board determined that the minimum flow requirement was intended to enhance, not merely maintain, the fishery, and that the certification condition therefore exceeded respondent's authority under state law. On appeal, the State Superior Court concluded that respondent could require compliance with the minimum flow conditions. The Superior Court also found that respondent had imposed the minimum flow requirement to protect and preserve the fishery, not to improve it, and that this requirement was authorized by state law.

The Washington Supreme Court held that the antidegradation provisions of the State's water quality standards require the imposition of minimum stream flows. The court also found that § 401(d), which allows States to impose conditions based upon several enumerated sections of the Clean Water Act and "any other appropriate requirement of State law," 33 U.S.C. § 1341(d), authorized the stream flow condition. Relying on this language and the broad purposes of the Clean Water Act, the court concluded that § 401(d) confers on States power to "consider all state action related to water quality in imposing conditions on section 401 certificates." We granted certiorari [and] now affirm.

The principal dispute in this case concerns whether the minimum stream flow requirement that the State imposed on the Elkhorn Project is a permissible condition of a § 401 certification under the Clean Water Act. . . .

There is no dispute that petitioners were required to obtain a certification from the State pursuant to § 401. Petitioners concede that, at a minimum, the project will result in two possible discharges—the release of dredged and fill material during the construction of the project, and the discharge of water at the end of the tailrace after the water has been used to generate electricity. Petitioners contend, however, that the minimum stream flow requirement imposed by the State was unrelated to these specific discharges, and that as a consequence, the State lacked the authority under § 401 to condition its certification on maintenance of stream flows sufficient to protect the Dosewallips fishery.

If § 401 consisted solely of subsection (a), which refers to a state certification that a "discharge" will comply with certain provisions of the Act, petitioners' assessment of the scope of the State's certification authority would have considerable force. Section 401, however, also contains subsection (d), which expands the State's authority to impose conditions on the certification of a project. Section 401(d) provides that any certification shall set forth "any effluent limitations and other limitations . . . necessary to assure that *any applicant* " will comply with various provisions of the Act and appropriate state law requirements. 33 U.S.C. § 1341(d) (emphasis added). The language of this subsection contradicts petitioners' claim that the State may only impose water quality limitations specifically tied to a "discharge." . . . § 401(d) is most reasonably read as authorizing additional conditions and limitations on the activity as a whole once the threshold condition, the existence of a discharge, is satisfied.

Our view of the statute is consistent with EPA's regulations implementing § 401. The regulations expressly interpret § 401 as requiring the State to find that "there is a reasonable assurance that the *activity* will be conducted in a manner which will not violate applicable water quality standards." 40 CFR § 121.2(a)(3) (1993) (emphasis added). EPA's conclusion that *activities* — not merely discharges — must comply with state water quality standards is a reasonable interpretation of § 401, and is entitled to deference. See, *e.g., Arkansas v. Oklahoma,* 503 U.S. 991, 110 (1992); *Chevron U.S.A. Inc. v. Natural Resources Defense Council, Inc.,* 467 U.S. 837 (1984).

Although § 401(d) authorizes the State to place restrictions on the activity as a whole, that authority is not unbounded. The State can only ensure that the project complies with "any applicable effluent limitations and other limitations, under [33 U.S.C. §§ 1311, 1312]" or certain other provisions of the Act, "and with any other appropriate requirement of State law." 33 U.S.C. § 1341(d). The State asserts that the minimum stream flow requirement was imposed to ensure compliance with the state water quality standards adopted pursuant to § 303 of the Clean Water Act, 33 U.S.C. § 1313.

We agree with the State that ensuring compliance with § 303 is a proper function of the § 401 certification. Although § 303 is not one of the statutory provisions listed in § 401(d), the statute allows States to impose limitations to ensure compliance with § 301 of the Act, 33 U.S.C. § 1311. Section 301 in turn incorporates § 303 by reference. . . . [A]t a minimum, limitations imposed pursuant to state water quality standards adopted pursuant to § 303 are "appropriate" requirements of state law. Indeed, petitioners appear to agree that the State's authority under § 401 includes limitations designed to ensure compliance with state water quality standards. . . .

[The Court went on to conclude that the minimum flow conditions imposed by the State were an "appropriate requirement" of State law, that narrative descriptions for designated uses may be directly enforceable, that water quality standards may be based on an antidegradation approach, and that they may also regulate water quantity.]

In summary, we hold that the State may include minimum stream flow requirements in a certification issued pursuant to § 401 of the Clean Water Act insofar as necessary to enforce a designated use contained in a state water quality standard. The judgment of the Supreme Court of Washington, accordingly, is affirmed.

[The concurring opinion of Justice STEVENS and the dissenting opinion of Justice THOMAS have been omitted.]

Notes and Questions

1. Section 401 begins with an application to conduct any activity "which may result in a *discharge* into the navigable waters" (emphasis added). What kind of "discharge" should trigger the need for 401 certification? What was the discharge that triggered the need for 401 certification in *PUD No. 1*? If the discharge was only clean water around a dam, would that constitute a "discharge" for purposes of § 401? The Supreme Court in *PUD No. 1* seemed to assume so. 14 years later, the Court confirmed that assumption in *S.D. Warren Co. v. Maine Bd. of Envtl. Protection*, 547 U.S. 370 (2006), another 401 certification case involving application for a FERC license. Beyond discharges of clean water, what other kinds of discharges would trigger 401 certification? Could the discharge of contaminated runoff from nonpoint sources such as a forest road or construction site trigger 401 certification? In 1998, the Ninth Circuit Court of Appeals suggested it should not. In a case involving an environmental challenge to grazing permits on federal lands, the Ninth Circuit rejected the argument that nonpoint source pollution from grazing activities constituted a "discharge" for purposes of § 401. *Oregon Natural Desert Ass'n v. Dombeck*, 172 F.3d 1092 (9th Cir. 1998). The Ninth Circuit based its conclusion in part on its observation that "the word 'discharge' is used consistently [in the CWA] to refer to the release of effluent from a point source." *Id.* at 1098. Even so, notice that CWA § 502 provides separate definitions for "discharge of a pollutant" and "discharge." § 502(12), (16). Read each definition carefully. How are they different? Which one do you think should be applied for purposes of § 401? Would the different definitions result in different conclusions?

2. Which states hold the power and responsibility for 401 certifications? Is it only those states authorized to administer the NPDES program? Is it some smaller subset of states? Or all of them? Read § 401(a) closely. Do you find any limitations here?

3. In her opinion for the Court, Justice O'Connor appears to decide as a matter of law that use designations can be enforced independently of water quality criteria. In *PUD No. 1*, this allows the State of Washington to impose stream flow conditions in order to support the use designation for fish habitat. What other conditions might the State of Washington reasonably impose to support this use? Wetlands restoration projects? Fish-rearing operations? Fish wardens to patrol and protect the habitat?

4. Justice O'Connor appears to assume that water quality criteria may be directly enforced. However, as she points out, the particular demands of water quality criteria are not always readily discernible. Justice O'Connor writes, "We think petitioners' attempt to distinguish between uses and criteria loses much of its force in light of the fact that the [CWA] permits enforcement of broad, narrative criteria based on, for example, 'aesthetics.'" While criteria for "aesthetics" may thus be enforceable as a matter of law, how would any regulator pursue a case based on aesthetics? Consider the particular Washington State criteria for aesthetics at issue in *PUD No. 1*: "Aesthetic values shall not be impaired by the presence of materials . . . which offend the senses of sight, smell, touch, or taste." WAC 173-201A-260(2) (2016). If you were a regulator, what kind of offensive conditions might prompt you to consider enforcing this standard? How would you prepare and present that case?

5. Justice O'Connor's opinion for the majority raises the relation between water *quality* (the focus of the federal CWA) and water *quantity* (the usual province of state and local jurisdictions). What is this relationship? Besides the link between stream flows and fish habitat in *PUD No. 1*, are there other cases you might imagine where the need to protect water quality may implicate needs for water quantity? *See, e.g., National Wildlife Fed. v. U.S. Army Corps of Engineers*, 384 F.3d 1163 (9th Cir. 2004) (link between dam operations and violation of water temperature standards for protection of salmon spawning habitat).

6. In dissent, Justice Thomas expresses concern that the Court's decision in *PUD No. 1* would allow a state to impose any condition whatsoever as long as it could support a designated use for a water body. Could a state then require a permit applicant to provide state residents with swim areas for swimming, hatchery fish for fishing, or boats for boating? What about providing transportation, lodging, or guide services to ensure that existing recreational uses of a water body are maintained? If at some point such hypothetical conditions begin to seem absurd, what effective checks remain? Imagine that you are an Assistant Attorney General for the State of Washington, and your client in the Department of Ecology proposes a 401 certification condition that would require the utility to provide fishing boats to all fishermen on the Dosewallips River. How would you respond? Would you support the condition or advise against it? Would reading the Supreme Court's decision in *PUD No. 1* change your advice in any way? Now consider the same question from the perspective of petitioners in this case: if you represented the utility or City of Tacoma, would you advise your client to accept this condition of providing fishing boats to all fishermen? Why or why not? In general, more than 20 years after *PUD No. 1*, why do you imagine that 401 certifications have not become overrun with outrageous conditions as Justice Thomas seemed to fear?

C. Total Maximum Daily Loads

In 1972, § 303(d) of the Clean Water Act created a program of Total Maximum Daily Loads (TMDLs). Under the TMDL program, states were charged with identifying water bodies for which technology-based standards were "not stringent enough to implement any water quality standard applicable to such waters." 33 U.S.C. § 1313(d)(1). The tabulation of these "water-quality limited" waters (or "segments") would come to be known as the "303(d) list." For each water or segment included on the 303(d) list, states were to develop a "total maximum daily load" that would be set at "a level necessary to implement the applicable water quality standards." § 303(d)(1)(C), 33 U.S.C. § 1313(d)(1)(C). In essence, the TMDL would represent a pollutant budget, defining how much of certain pollutants could go into a water body and still allow that water body to meet water quality standards.

Because the TMDL calculation would depend on a number of variables, § 303(d) required that the TMDL adjust for "seasonal variances" and include a "margin of safety" that takes into account technical uncertainties. Like the process for water quality standards, states were to develop and submit their TMDLs to EPA for approval. If EPA disapproves the TMDL, EPA "shall" then have 30 days develop such TMDL for the state. *Id.* § 1313(d)(D)(2).

States were originally required to develop their TMDLs by 1973. However, for various reasons, including some delay by EPA in promulgating necessary instructions, states did not come close to meeting this deadline. By the early 1980s, some environmental organizations became frustrated with the delay and filed lawsuits to compel the development of TMDLs. Responding to one of these suits, the Seventh Circuit concluded in 1984 that a state's "prolonged failure" to develop and submit a TMDL to EPA represented constructive submission of no TMDL. The EPA was thus in violation of its nondiscretionary duty under § 303(d)(2) for failure to develop a TMDL within 30 days of this constructive submission. *Scott v. City of Hammond*, 741 F.2d 992, 998 (7th Cir. 1984). Soon after *Hammond*, courts across the country found EPA in violation of this same duty, leading to court orders and consent decrees with schedules for developing TMDLs for hundreds or thousands of water bodies.

At about the same time, EPA promulgated rules imposing some structure upon the TMDL program. In particular, EPA required that TMDLs establish a "wasteload allocation" for point sources and "load allocation" for nonpoint sources. 40 C.F.R. § 130.2. Thus, as one might surmise from the "total" in "total maximum daily load," TMDLs must generally be developed for any water quality limited water body, regardless of whether it was impacted solely by point sources or nonpoint sources, or some combination. In 2002, the Ninth Circuit confirmed this interpretation. *Pronsolino v. Nastri*, 291 F.3d 1123 (9th Cir. 2002).

TMDLs, like water quality standards, are not self-executing. They require some vehicle, whether under the Clean Water Act or some other statute or program, in order to achieve any improvements in water quality. In cases involving point sources, wasteload allocations may be addressed at least in part through revised discharge limits in NPDES permits. For nonpoint sources, many states have found creative means to implement the load allocations in their TMDLs. In *Pronsolino*, for example, the Ninth Circuit upheld a decision by the California Department of Forestry that conditioned a timber harvest permit on mitigation to reduce the nonpoint sediment loading from timber roads and timber-cutting operations, consistent with the Garcia River TMDL.

As the TMDL program matured, the question naturally arose of what exactly a TMDL could or should encompass. Should a TMDL consist of nothing more than a matrix of numbers establishing a pollution budget for an impaired water body under various conditions? Or could the TMDL include more, such as allocations to different industries and discrete facilities, and implementation plans to achieve these allocations? That question was most recently decided in the following opinion, in which the circuit judge also took the opportunity to provide an extraordinary accounting of the TMDL program as a whole and its particular application to the nation's largest estuary, the Chesapeake Bay.

American Farm Bureau Fed. v. U.S. EPA
792 F.3d 281 (3d Cir. 2015)

Judge AMBRO:

The Environmental Protection Agency ("EPA") published in 2010 the "total maximum daily load" ("TMDL") of nitrogen, phosphorous, and sediment that can be released into the Chesapeake Bay (the "Bay") to comply with the Clean Water Act, 33 U.S.C. § 1251 *et seq.* The TMDL is a comprehensive framework for pollution reduction designed to "restore and maintain the chemical, physical, and biological integrity" of the Bay, 33 U.S.C. § 1251, the subject of much ecological concern over several decades.

Trade associations with members who will be affected by the TMDL's implementation — the American Farm Bureau Federation, the National Association of Home Builders, and other organizations for agricultural industries that include fertilizer, corn, pork, and poultry operations (collectively, "Farm Bureau") — sued. They allege that all aspects of the TMDL that go beyond an allowable sum of pollutants (*i.e.,* the most nitrogen, phosphorous, and sediment the Bay can safely absorb per day) exceeded the scope of the EPA's authority to regulate, largely because the agency may intrude on states' traditional role in regulating land use.

The District Court ruled against Farm Bureau, and it appeals. For the reasons that follow, we side with the EPA and affirm the District Court's ruling.

The EPA and seven states — Virginia, West Virginia, Maryland, Delaware, Pennsylvania, New York, and the District of Columbia, which is a "state" for Clean Water Act purposes, 33 U.S.C. § 1362(3) — have engaged in a decades-long process to develop a plan to improve the quality of the water in the Chesapeake Bay, the largest estuary in North America. The Bay's watershed area of 64,000 square miles contains tens of thousands of lakes, rivers, streams and creeks. The Bay itself has a surface area of 4,500 square miles, and it has 11,684 miles of shoreline, longer than the coastline from San Diego, California to Seattle, Washington.

Before Europeans settled the Bay, it supported much sea life. As two associates of John Smith wrote, "Neither better fish more plenty or variety had any of us ever seene, in any place swimming in the water, then in the bay of Chesapeack." Walter Russell & Anas Todkill *et al.,* The Accidents that Happened in the Discoverie of the Bay, *in* 1 *The Complete Works of Captain John Smith (1580 — 1631)* Philip L. Barbour, ed., 224, 228 (1986). The fertile land of the watershed and the beauty and commercial value of the Bay proved attractive. By 1950 about 7,000,000 people lived in the watershed; today it is home to 17,000,000, and by 2030 the population may reach 20,000,000.

The watershed area not only sustains its growing human population; it also supports a great deal of commerce, including fishing, shipping, farming, and tourism. All these activities, as well as other incidents of daily life, contribute pollutants to the Bay.

As a result, it is plagued by dead zones with opaque water and algae blooms that render significant parts of it unable to support aquatic life. Surrounding jurisdictions recognize that the Bay absorbs far too much nitrogen, phosphorous, and sediment to be the healthy ecosystem it once was. These threats to the Bay (and to the livelihood of many who depend on its bounty) have been known for a long time both to scientists and to observant lay people. . . .

[Clean Water Act Section 303, 33 U.S.C. §] 1313 anticipates that effluent limitations on point sources will be the front line of the defense against water pollution. But, acknowledging that effluent limitations may not be enough, § 1313(d) requires the states to submit to the EPA a list of all bodies of water (or, by regulation, any segment of a body of water) for which effluent limitations and technology-based point source controls are insufficient to meet the applicable water quality standard. These areas are known as "water quality limited segment[s]," 40 C.F.R. § 131.3(h), and the list on which they appear often goes by the "Section 303(d) list" after the part of the uncodified Clean Water Act to which 33 U.S.C. § 1313(d) corresponds.

Together with the Section 303(d) list, states must submit "total maximum daily loads" for those pollutants that cannot be brought to an acceptable level by point source controls. 33 U.S.C. § 1313(d)(1)(A) & (C). After a state submits its Section 303(d) list and TMDL, the EPA must approve or disapprove them; if it disapproves, it must create its own list and TMDL. 33 U.S.C. § 1313(d)(2).

* * *

This case primarily concerns the meaning of "total maximum daily load," words that occur in the part of the Clean Water Act that requires states (or, in this case, the EPA) to:

> establish . . . the total maximum daily load[ ] for those pollutants which the Administrator identifies under section 1314(a)(2) of this title as suitable for such calculation. Such load shall be established at a level necessary to implement the applicable water quality standards with seasonal variations and a margin of safety which takes into account any lack of knowledge concerning the relationship between effluent limitations and water quality.

33 U.S.C. § 1313(d)(1)(C). The Act directed states to include "total maximum daily load[s]" in their required "continuing planning process[es]" no later than February 15, 1973. 33 U.S.C. § 1313(e)(2).

This deadline, it turns out, was overly optimistic, as both states and the EPA have been slow in establishing TMDLs. *See* Oliver A. Houck, *TMDLs, Are We There Yet?: The Long Road Toward Water Quality—Based Regulation under the Clean Water Act*, 27 Envtl. L. Rep. (Envtl. L. Inst.) 10,391, 10,392–93 (1997). . . .

The EPA's regulations define "total maximum daily load" as the sum of "waste load allocations" and "load allocations." 40 C.F.R. § 130.2(i). Also by regulatory definition, waste load allocations are pollutant loads that come from point sources; load allocations come from nonpoint sources. 40 C.F.R. § 130.2(g) & (h). The EPA applies these

Farm/Agriculture = nonpoint sources

allocations to any pollutant that brings a body of water below an acceptable standard of cleanliness. *See* 43 Fed.Reg. 60,662 (Dec. 28, 1978) (identifying "all pollutants" as suitable for TMDL development).

Once the EPA had laid out the required contents of TMDLs, it and the states remained tardy in establishing them. As a result, a wave of citizen-suits in the 1980s led to a consensus that a state's failure to submit a TMDL should be deemed a "constructive submission" that no TMDL is needed, triggering the EPA's duty to accept that conclusion or promulgate its own TMDL. *Kingman Park Civic Ass'n v. EPA,* 84 F.Supp.2d 1, 5 (D.D.C.1999) (collecting cases). Even these successes did not spur immediate action, as courts initially would not follow the "constructive submission" theory "in cases brought against states which engaged in some level of TMDL activity, no matter how minute." Conway, *TMDL Litigation,* 17 Va. Envtl. L.J. at 95.

In the mid-1990s, nearly a quarter century past the Clean Water Act's "deadline," courts became frustrated with the prevailing "wait-and-see" approach and directed states and the EPA to develop TMDLs with more dispatch. *See Sierra Club v. Hankinson,* 939 F.Supp. 865 (N.D.Ga.1996), 939 F.Supp. 872 (N.D.Ga.1996); *Idaho Sportsmen's Coalition v. Browner,* 951 F.Supp. 962 (W.D.Wash.1996). Following the success of these cases, "citizen-plaintiffs, imbued with the ecosystem consciousness, launched a tidal wave of lawsuits to force the EPA and the states to implement the TMDLs process." Michael M. Wenig, *How "Total" Are "Total Maximum Daily Loads"?—Legal Issues Regarding the Scope of Watershed-Based Pollution Control Under the Clean Water Act,* 12 Tul. Envtl. L.J. 87, 94 (1998).

The lawsuits of the 1990s were followed by the actual drafting of thousands of TMDLs, which the EPA has described as "the technical backbone" of its approach to cleaning the Nation's waters. EPA Office of Water, *Total Maximum Daily Load (TMDL) Program Draft TMDL Program Implementation Strategy* § 1.2 (1996). TMDLs are now thorough "informational tools that allow the states to proceed from the identification of waters requiring additional planning to the required plans." *Pronsolino v. Nastri,* 291 F.3d 1123, 1129 (9th Cir.2002). TMDLs are not self-executing, but they serve as the cornerstones for pollution-reduction plans that do create enforceable rights and obligations.[+]

D. The Chesapeake Bay TMDL, 2000–2010

[The court then described the history of the development of the Chesapeake Bay TMDL.]

The final Chesapeake Bay TMDL . . . is detailed, as it includes point- and nonpoint-source limitations on nitrogen, phosphorous, and sediment for 92 segments of the Bay identified as overpolluted and further allocates those limits to specific point sources and to nonpoint source sectors. The TMDL sets target dates, anticipating that 60% of its proposed actions will be complete by 2017, with all pollution control measures in place by 2025. The next step, yet to happen, is for the states to develop their Phase II Watershed Improvement Plans to implement the TMDL.

On December 29, 2010, the EPA promulgated the TMDL through the notice-and-comment rulemaking process of the Administrative Procedure Act ("APA"). Over 45 days, the EPA held 18 public meetings (at which 2,500 members of the public attended), and it received more than 14,000 comments. It took these comments and meetings into account when publishing the final TMDL....

In January 2011, Farm Bureau sued the EPA under the APA and the citizen-suit provision of the Clean Water Act. It asserted that the EPA exceeded its statutory authority by including deadlines and allocations in the TMDL and by requiring "reasonable assurance" from the states in drafting that document. The District Court granted summary judgment in favor of the EPA, and this appeal followed....

Farm Bureau interprets the words "total maximum daily load" in the Clean Water Act, codified at 33 U.S.C. § 1313(d)(1)(C), as unambiguous: a TMDL can consist only of a number representing the amount of a pollutant that can be discharged into a particular segment of water and nothing more. Thus it argues that the EPA overstepped its statutory authority in drafting the Chesapeake Bay TMDL when the agency (1) included in the TMDL allocations of permissible levels of nitrogen, phosphorous, and sediment among different kinds of sources of these pollutants, (2) promulgated target dates for reducing discharges to the level the TMDL envisions, and (3) obtained assurance from the seven affected states that they would fulfill the TMDL's objectives. In Farm Bureau's view, even if allocations, target dates, and reasonable assurance are useful in calculating the number that is the TMDL, the final document may not specify a distribution of pollutants from point and nonpoint sources or deadlines for meeting the target reductions in pollutant discharge, nor may the EPA in drafting the document obtain any assurance from states that they will meet the targets....

The parties agree that this case is governed by *Chevron v. NRDC,* 467 U.S. 837 (1984)....

The District Court noted that it was a question of first impression whether a TMDL could include more than a quantity of a pollutant. *Am. Farm Bureau Fed'n v. EPA,* 984 F.Supp.2d 289, 316–18 (M.D.Pa.2013). Since its decision, there has been no development in the case law on that point. However, we do not write on a completely blank slate. As the District Court also observed, many circuit and district courts have defined TMDLs to accord with the EPA's regulations (implying they did not present a problem). If Farm Bureau were correct that the statute unambiguously supports its reading, we would expect one of the judges who has presided over TMDL litigation to have noticed the disconnect between the statute and the regulation, but there has been none.

Additionally, in response to challenges from both environmental and industry groups, courts have recognized the EPA's authority to fill the Clean Water Act's considerable gaps on how to promulgate a "total maximum daily load." *Pronsolino,* 291 F.3d at 1131 ("[T]he EPA has the delegated authority to enact regulations carrying the force of law regarding the identification of § 303(d)(1) waters and TMDLs.")....

Farm Bureau's strongest argument is that Congress specifically authorized the EPA to publish "*total* maximum daily *load* [s] ... at a *level* necessary to implement the applicable water quality standards. . . ." 33 U.S.C. § 1313(d)(1)(C) (emphases added). Under Farm Bureau's reading, a "total load" is just a number, like the "total" at the bottom of a restaurant receipt. This ordinary understanding of the word "total" is supported, the argument continues, because the load is to be established at a "level," which can be high or low (so long as it is necessary to implement the water quality standards); in any event it should not be expressed as a comprehensive framework, and in no event can a TMDL include allocations among point and nonpoint sources, deadlines, and the reasonable assurance requirement.

This argument has some intuitive appeal, but other readings are possible. Our most significant textual concern is that Farm Bureau's analysis makes the word "total" redundant. "Maximum daily load[s]. . . . established at a level necessary to implement the applicable water standard" would mean the same thing that Farm Bureau argues "total maximum daily load" means: a number set at a level needed to alleviate water pollution. Applying the canon against surplusage, a plausible understanding of "total" is that it means the sum of the constituent parts of the load. The load is still set at the level necessary to fight pollutants, but it is expressed in terms of a total of the different relevant allocations.

Other uses of "total" in the Clean Water Act support this reading. For example, in a section relating to the EPA's power to grant funds to publicly owned treatment works, the agency must consider "the *total* cost of operation and maintenance of such works by each user class (taking into account total waste water loading of such works, the constituent elements of the wastes, and other appropriate factors)." 33 U.S.C. § 1284(b)(1) (emphasis added). Admittedly, the explicit listings of factors in calculating the "total cost" under § 1284 distinguishes that use of "total" from the language in § 1313, yet it indicates that Congress does use the word to mean something more than a single number. . . .

As far as allocations are concerned, the EPA's construction of the TMDL requirement comports well with the Clean Water Act's structure and purpose. Specifically allocating the pollution load between point sources (primarily the EPA's responsibility) and nonpoint sources (the states' dominion) is a commonsense first step to achieve the target water quality.

Because TMDLs only relate to bodies of water for which point source limitations are insufficient, they must take into account pollution from both point and nonpoint sources. We believe the congressional silence on how to promulgate a TMDL and the congressional command that a TMDL be established only for waters that cannot be cleaned by point-source limitations alone (necessarily implying that, whatever form the TMDL takes, it must incorporate nonpoint source limitations) combine to authorize the EPA to express load and waste load allocations. To be sure, the statute does not command the EPA's final regulation to allocate explicitly parts of a load among different kinds of sources, but we agree with the EPA that it may do so.

Similarly, it is common sense that a timeline complements the Clean Water Act's requirement that all impaired waters achieve applicable water quality standards. The amount of acceptable pollution in a body of water is necessarily tied to the date at which the EPA and the states believe the water should meet its quality standard; if the target date is 100 years from now, more pollution per day will be allowable than if the target date is five years from now. . . . .

Farm Bureau's argument that the Act forbids the EPA from seeking reasonable assurance from the states that their Watershed Improvement Plans will meet their stated goals is also inconsistent with the purpose and structure of the Clean Water Act. The TMDL must be set "at a level necessary to implement the applicable water quality standards." 33 U.S.C. § 1313(d)(1)(C). The EPA chose to set the TMDL with substantial input from the states but, in order to comply with the Clean Water Act and the APA, the EPA would not blindly accept states' submissions. Instead it decided to satisfy itself that the states' proposals would actually "implement the applicable water quality standards." *Id.* This requirement made sure that the EPA could exercise "reasoned judgment" in evaluating the states' proposed standards and was thus consistent with the Clean Water Act. *Ctr. for Biological Diversity v. EPA,* 749 F.3d 1079, 1087 (D.C.Cir.2014).

The point of the TMDL is to take into consideration nonpoint-source pollution; no meaningful decision about limiting pollution can be made without specifying a time frame within which pollution is to be eliminated; and the Clean Water Act envisions assurance of effective pollution controls. Preventing the EPA from expressing allocations and timelines and from obtaining reasonable assurance from affected states appears to frustrate those goals, and thus the phrase "total maximum daily load" has enough play in the joints to allow the EPA to consider and express these factors in its final action. . . .

Perhaps we would reach a different result if the TMDL in fact made land-use decisions diminishing state authority in a significant way; we might then say that Congress delegated some authority over the definitions of technical terms in the Clean Water Act but not so much discretion as to usurp states' zoning powers. Indeed, the heart of Farm Bureau's federalism argument is that the TMDL impermissibly grants the EPA the authority to make land-use and zoning regulations. The challenge is long on swagger but short on specificity. That is likely because the TMDL's provisions that could be read to affect land use are either explicitly allowed by federal law or too generalized to supplant state zoning powers in any extraordinary way. . . .

Water pollution in the Chesapeake Bay is a complex problem currently affecting at least 17,000,000 people (with more to come). Any solution to it will result in winners and losers. To judge from the arguments and the *amici* briefs filed in this case, the winners are environmental groups, the states that border the Bay, tourists, fishermen, municipal waste water treatment works, and urban centers. The losers are rural counties with farming operations, nonpoint source polluters, the agricultural industry, and those states that would prefer a lighter touch from the EPA. Congress made a judgment in the Clean Water Act that the states and the EPA could, working together, best allocate the benefits and burdens of lowering pollution. The Chesapeake Bay TMDL will require sacrifice by many, but that is a consequence of the tremendous effort it will take to restore health to the Bay—to make it once again a part of our "land of living," Robert Frost, *The Gift Outright* line 10—a goal our elected representatives have repeatedly endorsed. Farm Bureau's arguments to the contrary are unpersuasive, and thus we affirm the careful and thorough opinion of the District Court.

Notes and Questions

1. After the Third Circuit's decision in *American Farm Bureau*, issued in July 2015, Farm Bureau petitioned the U.S. Supreme Court for review and many Court-watchers assumed the Court would grant certiorari or otherwise insert itself, as it had for a number of other recent high-profile environmental cases. *See, e.g., U.S. Army Corps of Engineers v. Hawkes Co., Inc.,* 136 S. Ct. 1807 (2016); *Chamber of Commerce, et al., v. U.S. EPA,* 577 U.S. ___ (Feb. 9, 2016) (Order in Pending Case) (granting stay of agency action on Clean Power Plan). However, it may be that fate intervened with the unexpected passing of Justice Scalia on Feb. 13, 2016. Two weeks later, the Supreme Court denied certiorari in this case, 136 S. Ct. 1246 (Feb. 29, 2016), marking perhaps the first major environmental decision of the post-Scalia era.

2. The Chesapeake Bay TMDL, available online at https://www.epa.gov/chesapeake-bay-tmdl (last visited July 20, 2016), addresses the three pollutants of nitrogen, phosphorus, and sediment within the 64,000-mile Chesapeake Bay watershed. The TMDL is actually comprised of 276 smaller TMDLs for each of these three pollutants across 92 listed segments within the watershed. In order to meet water quality standards for the Chesapeake Bay, it sets limits of "185.9 million pounds of nitrogen per year, 12.5 million pounds of phosphorus and 6.45 billion pounds of sediment per year—a 25 percent reduction in nitrogen, 24 percent reduction in phosphorus and 20 percent reduction in sediment." EPA, *Total Maximum Daily Load for Nitrogen, Phosphorus, and Sediment* at ES-1 (Dec. 29, 2010). Beyond these numerical limits, it also includes a series of technical analyses and Watershed Implementation Plans (WIPs), developed by the individual states and approved and incorporated into the TMDL. According to these plans and schedules, at least 60 percent of the pollution control measures described in the WIPs should be in place by 2017, with all control measures needed to fully restore the Bay in place by 2025. *Id.*

3. What do you think of Farm Bureau's argument that TMDLs are "just a number"? Do you agree that this understanding appears to flow from the plain language of "*total* maximum daily loads" (emphasis added)? In fact, Farm Bureau's view of the limited scope of TMDLs was widely shared by regulators, the regulated community, and the courts in the early days of the TMDL program. In 2000, EPA attempted to expand the scope of TMDLs by promulgating a rule that would have required, in addition to numerical calculations, the development of "comprehensive implementation plans providing 'reasonable assurance' that the TMDL would actually be implemented." 65 Fed. Reg. 43,591 (July 13, 2000). This rule, however, generated significant controversy and was later withdrawn by EPA in 2003. 68 Fed. Reg. 13,608 (Mar. 19, 2003). Left without regulatory interpretation, the Third Circuit in *American Farm Bureau* recognized the "intuitive appeal" of Farm Bureau's plain language argument that "total" means a total, like at "the bottom of a restaurant receipt." How did the Third Circuit come to embrace EPA's expansive TMDL for the Chesapeake Bay? What, if any, statutory bases supported this broader view?

4. Consider the role of the states in *American Farm Bureau*. The Chesapeake Bay TMDL reflected the cooperative development and support of the District of Columbia and the six bay states of Virginia, West Virginia, Maryland, Delaware, Pennsylvania, and New York. And yet the Chesapeake Bay TMDL was opposed by 21 states (including West Virginia) in an amicus brief in support of Farm Bureau before the Third Circuit. How does Judge Ambro in *American Farm Bureau* address the issues of federalism and state powers in matters of land use and zoning? Would the court support the TMDL if it required a 20 percent reduction in nitrogen discharges from agriculture? What about a 20 percent reduction in watershed acreage committed to agriculture? In fact, one Watershed Implementation Plan prepared by Virginia anticipates a reduction of nearly 500,000 acres of agriculture in the state. Commonwealth of Virginia, Chesapeake Bay TMDL Phase II Watershed Implementation Plan 43, 45–46 (Mar. 30, 2012). Does this anticipated reduction intrude on state powers of land use and zoning? Why or why not?

5. Following up on the example immediately above, what would happen if the anticipated reduction in agricultural acreage does not occur? More broadly, what happens if any of the pollution reduction measures identified in the Chesapeake Bay TMDL fails to meet expectations? Can EPA sue Virginia for failing to reduce agricultural acreage? Can citizens sue EPA or Virginia for the same failure? Short of lawsuits, are there other means that would allow EPA or citizens to encourage compliance with the TMDL pollution control measures? In that regard, see Chesapeake Bay TMDL at § 7-11 (listing "potential actions EPA may take to ensure that [states] develop and implement appropriate WIPs").

6. Recall that CWA § 303(d) requires that a TMDL be set with a "margin of safety." 33 U.S.C. § 1313(d)(1)(C). How much is a reasonable margin of safety? Ten percent? Twenty? In actuality, there is no set percentage or amount that must be applied and this figure is left to EPA's discretion. *See NRDC v. Muszynski*, 268 F.3d 91 (2[d] Cir. 2001) (10 percent margin of safety supported by EPA's use of professional judgment for particular water body). Depending on the level of technical uncertainty concerning a particular water body, courts have recognized, "In many cases, a separate margin of safety is not used, but is inherent in the conservative assumptions used in the model." *Id.* In fact, for the Chesapeake Bay TMDL, such "implicit" margins of safety were used where EPA concluded that "the extensive development and refinement of the Bay models provides for excellent confidence in the modeling accuracy . . . ." Chesapeake Bay TMDL at 6–15.

7. Water Quality Trading. The overall objective of meeting water quality standards in a large, complex watershed may allow for some creative solutions, including what is known as "water quality trading." In essence, if one particular pollution source finds it more efficient, it might encourage another source to reduce its pollution contribution rather than reducing its own contribution. *See* EPA, *Water Quality Trading*

Policy, 68 Fed. Reg. 1608 (Jan. 13, 2003). Water quality trading is explicitly authorized by the Chesapeake Bay TMDL and the TMDL recognizes that a number of Bay states are already implementing water quality trading programs in their jurisdictions. See Chesapeake Bay TMDL at 10–3. Note that water quality trading may also create opportunities for new businesses to open in the watershed through the purchase or acquisition of pollution reduction credits.

8. Cost? What will it cost to implement the Chesapeake Bay TMDL? EPA has not calculated a total cost for implementing the Chesapeake Bay TMDL. However, the State of Maryland estimated its costs for TMDL implementation through 2025 at approximately $14.4 billion, including costs to upgrade wastewater treatment facilities and implement Best Management Practices to control runoff from agricultural fields. Maryland's Phase II Watershed Implementation Plan for the Chesapeake Bay TMDL 55 (Oct. 26, 2012), available at http://perma.cc/P3WK-H5XA. Virginia estimated its implementation costs at between $13.6 and $15.7 billion. Virginia Senate Finance Comm., *Chesapeake Bay TMDL Watershed Implementation Plan: What Will It Cost to Meet Virginia's Goals?* 17 (Nov. 18, 2011), available at http://perma.cc/88EG-EBX4. Against these costs, however, substantial economic benefits may flow from the improvement in water quality following full implementation of the Chesapeake Bay TMDL. As Judge Ambro recognized in his opinion in *American Farm Bureau*, the pollution of the Chesapeake Bay affected not only the lives of the millions of residents of the watershed, but also the "livelihood of many who depend on its bounty." By one estimate, full implementation of the Chesapeake Bay TMDL will result in economic gains of between $22.5 billion and $129.7 billion *every year*, making the TMDL implementation a very smart economic, as well as ecological, investment. Chesapeake Bay Foundation, *The Economic Benefits of Cleaning Up the Chesapeake* 1 (Oct. 2014), available online at www.cbf.org/document.doc?id=2258 (last visited July 20, 2016).

9. In addition to the Clean Water Act, what other federal environmental statutes might help achieve the goals of the more 40,000 TMDLs that have now been completed across the country? The Chesapeake Bay TMDL itself provides one answer: "EPA has committed to reducing air deposition of nitrogen to the tidal waters of the Chesapeake Bay from 17.9 to 15.7 million pounds per year. The reductions will be achieved through implementation of federal air regulations during the coming years." Chesapeake Bay TMDL at ES-6. In the Coeur d'Alene Basin of northern Idaho, severely impacted by a century of mining contamination, TMDL goals might be met in part through the completion of cleanup actions under the Comprehensive Environmental Response, Compensation and Liability Act (CERCLA), better known as Superfund. *See* Villa, *supra*, at 271–273 (arguing that "Direct means to address nonpoint sources, such as the contaminated sediments in the Coeur d'Alene Basin, may be found in the Superfund [cleanup] authorities").

In addition to CERCLA, the Clean Water Act, and the Clean Air Act, are there other federal statutes that might help restore the quality of impaired waters across the United States? Keep this question in mind as you work through the further chapters of this book.

Chapter 8

Dealing with the Detritus of Production and Consumption: The Resource Conservation and Recovery Act

[handwritten annotations:]
Subtitle D: solid waste mgmt.
Subtitle C: "cradle to grave"
Federal Regulation of HAZARDOUS WASTE (direct federal regulation)

I. Introduction

Waste happens. For every organism, waste is a biological fact of life. Humans, for example, must exhale carbon dioxide created during respiration, must urinate to excrete the chemical remnants of broken-down proteins and other metabolic products, and must defecate to eliminate undigested food. Every animal species has the same or analogous physiological needs and responses. Nor is waste only a function of biochemistry, even for nonhuman species: the lion does not eat all of its kill.

Natural processes, up to a point, can cope with waste without undue ecological disruption or, from a human perspective, threats to public health. Plants use carbon dioxide in photosynthesis (and in turn release their own waste product, oxygen). Protein wastes are recycled by bacterial and abiotic processes into the nitrogen cycle. Flies and other organisms, including bacteria, consume fecal matter. And the savanna is not littered with the uneaten remains of lion kills thanks to scavengers and decomposers.

Too much waste or badly managed waste can pose problems, however. To take a simple example, a small human settlement might manage its fecal matter with a septic system, which could be harmless to the members of the community—but not if it is placed where bacteria from the septic field can leach into the community's drinking water well.

Human population growth, intensification of agriculture, industrialization, urbanization, and increased resource consumption contributed to increased production of waste. "For every 1 percent increase in GDP, resource use has risen 0.4 percent. Data indicate that global material resource use during the 20th century rose at about twice the rate of population . . . . According to the World Resources Institute, 'one half to three quarters of annual resource inputs to industrial economies is returned to the environment as wastes within just one year.'" U.S. EPA, Advancing Sustainable Materials Management: Facts and Figures 2013 1–2 (June 2015), https://www.epa .gov/sites/production/files/2015-09/documents/2013_advncng_smm_rpt.pdf. The amount and types of waste, the methods of disposal, and the resultant environmental and public health problems, of course, have changed with social and technological change. In the United States,

> In the 1880's, the most prevalent wastes posing difficult challenges to garbage collectors were coal and wood ash, seasonal food waste, and horse manure. While these wastes were not always pleasant to remove, they were not nearly as diverse, complex or dangerous as our waste streams today. Today such wastes can include electronics, paper, glass, plastics, rubbers, metals, leather goods, yard wastes, household chemicals and cleaners, as well as a host of other commercial chemicals and industrial byproducts that are dangerous to human health and the environment.

OLGA L. MOYA & ANDREW L. FONO, FEDERAL ENVIRONMENTAL LAW: THE USER'S GUIDE 93 (3d ed. 2011). For most of the country's history, waste management was a mélange of private and local government activity, sometimes unregulated and sometimes subject to state or local sanitation or anti-dumping legislation that was inconsistently enforced. By the mid-1960s, however, the problem of waste disposal garnered congressional attention.

II. Legislating by Accretion to Address the Problem of Solid and Hazardous Waste: Origins and History of the Resource Conservation and Recovery Act

The federal government's first significant—albeit limited—involvement with solid waste came with enactment of the Solid Waste Disposal Act of 1965 (SWDA). The Congress found:

> (1) that the continuing technological progress and improvement in methods of manufacture, packaging, and marketing of consumer products has resulted in an ever-mounting increase, and in a change in the characteristics, of the mass of material discarded by the purchase of such products;

> (2) that the economic and population growth of our Nation, and the improvements in the standard of living enjoyed by our population, have required increased industrial production to meet our needs, and have made necessary the demolition of old buildings, the construction of new buildings, and the provision of highways and other avenues of transportation, which, together with related industrial, commercial, and agricultural operations, have resulted in a rising tide of scrap, discarded, and waste materials;

> (3) that the continuing concentration of our population in expanding metropolitan and other urban areas has presented these communities with serious financial, management, intergovernmental, and technical problems in the disposal of solid wastes resulting from the industrial, commercial, domestic, and other activities carried on in such areas;

. . . .

(6) that while the collection and disposal of solid wastes should continue to be primarily the function of State, regional, and local agencies, the problems of waste disposal . . . have become a matter national in scope and in concern and necessitate Federal action through financial and technical assistance and leadership . . . .

P.L. 89-272 §202(a)(1–3, 6), *now codified at* 42 U.S.C. §6901(a)(1–4). The focus of congressional concern in 1965 was clear from the SWDA's original definition of "solid waste" to include "garbage, refuse, and other discarded solid materials . . . ." but to exclude water pollutants, even if those pollutants were in solid form. *Id.* §203(4). SWDA also made clear the limited federal role the Congress envisioned in 1965; the purposes of the act were "to initiate and accelerate a national research and development program for new and improved methods of . . . solid-waste disposal, . . ." *id.* §202(b)(1), and "to provide technical and financial assistance to State and local governments . . . ." *id.* §202(b)(2).

Within a decade, Congress concluded that the 1965 SWDA was insufficient. The continued reliance on landfills and open dumps for solid waste disposal was consuming land and causing pollution of land, air, and water resources. *See* 42 U.S.C. §6901(a)(1)-(4) (congressional findings). Disposal capacity was becoming scarce. H.R. Rep. 94-1491 9 (94th Cong., 2d Sess., Sept. 9, 1976) ("Projections of land fill capacity show that 50 of the nation's largest cities will run out of capacity by the end of the decade . . . . As present capacity is expended, the cost of waste disposal increases."). Careless handling or disposal of industrial waste was causing a continuing litany of incidents of environmental and public health harms, such as fish and cattle kills, contamination of water supplies, and human poisonings. *Id.* at 17–23 (giving examples of harmful episodes involving hazardous waste). In response, Congress amended the SWDA. The amendment was such a dramatic rewrite that the statute is now generally known by the amending bill's name: the Resource Conservation and Recovery Act of 1976 (RCRA).

In 1991, an EPA attorney (writing in his personal capacity) provided an overview of RCRA and the most important subsequent amendment to RCRA, the Hazardous and Solid Waste Amendments of 1984. Do not be dismayed by the article's subtitle: although RCRA is complex, we will break it down into digestible pieces.

Randolph L. Hill, *An Overview of RCRA: The "Mind-Numbing" Provisions of the Most Complicated Environmental Statute*

21 Envtl. L. Rep. 10,254 (May 1991)

C = hazardous waste

D = non-haz waste

Congress adopted the basic outlines of RCRA in 1976. Included in the Act were the key provisions of subtitle C (i.e., a program for federal regulation of hazardous wastes) and subtitle D (i.e., a separate program for state regulation of other (non-hazardous) wastes pursuant to federal guidelines). Congress instructed EPA to develop regulations within 18 months to put the subtitle C program in place and to set similar deadlines for new criteria under subtitle D.

Despite the congressional mandate, funding for the RCRA program under the Carter Administration was a low priority. As a result, EPA failed to meet the initial statutory deadlines for promulgating regulations under both subtitles C and D. EPA's failure to promulgate timely subtitle C regulations led to a citizens suit to compel their issuance. The Agency eventually issued the subtitle C regulations in three phases pursuant to court order: February 1980, May 1980, and July 1982. The subtitle D regulations were issued in 1979.

Soon after the first subtitle C regulations were promulgated, the Reagan Administration took office, with its plan for the significant deregulation of U.S. industry. Environmental standards were at the top of the list of the regulations to be relaxed or eliminated. Under the Reagan appointees, EPA continued to delay developing additional subtitle C regulations and failed to develop an adequate enforcement scheme for the program. In addition, top EPA officials became embroiled in a huge scandal over alleged mismanagement and political favoritism in their handling of the hazardous waste and Superfund programs. It was no surprise that Congress became dubious of EPA's ability to develop and implement an effective program for regulating hazardous wastes.

. . . .

The climate created by the Reagan Administration's handling of the hazardous waste program led to Congress' response: the Hazardous and Solid Waste Amendments of 1984 (HSWA, or the 1984 Amendments). HSWA significantly expanded the size, complexity, and detail of subtitle C, and severely curtailed EPA's discretion to implement congressional mandates. HSWA addressed four key congressional concerns with the subtitle C program: delays in regulatory development, loopholes in the regulations, inadequate enforcement, and an unclear direction for overarching hazardous waste policy. HSWA addressed these problems by establishing many overlapping and tight regulatory deadlines and by setting detailed minimum standards to be implemented by EPA through regulations or very stringent standards that would take effect if EPA failed to adopt the required regulations (through use of statutory "hammers," which are tight deadlines for regulatory development). Today, the solid and hazardous waste program focuses almost exclusively on implementing the HSWA requirements . . . .

Notes and Questions

1. RCRA included other subtitles (codified as "subchapters" in the United States Code), but as the excerpt describes, the core programs established by RCRA are the Subtitle C hazardous waste regulation program and the Subtitle D program of guidelines for state regulation of non-hazardous solid waste. Of the two, the hazardous waste program—which involves direct federal regulation of specified conduct—is much more intricate and controversial. Before we turn to Subtitle C, however, in the next section we will take a brief look at "ordinary" waste and RCRA Subtitle D.

2. As you can tell from the excerpt, neither Subtitle C nor Subtitle D of RCRA supplied a fully elaborated, self-executing regulatory program. Rather, Congress tasked

EPA with promulgating rules and guidelines to implement the statute's policies. As of 2015, the guidelines developed under Subtitle D spanned nearly 150 pages of the Code of Federal Regulations; the Subtitle C hazardous waste rules filled two volumes totaling about 1,500 pages. 40 C.F.R. Parts 239–259 (2015) (Subtitle D guidelines); *Id.* Parts 260–299 (Subtitle C regulations). The regulations change fairly frequently as EPA learns from experience and responds to changing conditions. *E.g.,* 80 Fed. Reg. 1694 (Jan. 13, 2015) (revising certain provisions that determine whether materials are subject to regulation as hazardous waste). These voluminous regulations are the daily bread for attorneys who counsel their clients about how to comply with RCRA, represent clients claiming that other parties have violated RCRA, or defend clients alleged to have violated RCRA. Many RCRA cases turn on whether EPA's regulations are valid or whether EPA's regulations have been properly applied to a particular set of facts.

3. Provisions of RCRA, both as enacted in 1976 and especially as amended by HSWA in 1984, evince congressional concern that EPA might not promulgate regulations with suitable alacrity. The Hill excerpt noted that a citizen suit dictated the timing of EPA's promulgation of its first batches of hazardous waste regulations. RCRA's citizen suit provision states, in pertinent part, that "any person may commence a civil action on his own behalf . . . . against the Administrator [of EPA] when there is alleged a failure of the Administrator to perform any act or duty under this chapter which is not discretionary with the Administrator." 42 U.S.C. § 6972(a) (RCRA § 7002(a)). The excerpt attributes early delays in promulgating hazardous waste regulations to a "low priority" for funding "under the Carter Administration." Is the executive or legislative branch responsible for determining such funding priorities?

Assuming that the excerpt's explanation of the Carter Administration is correct, is it a good idea to allow citizens to bring lawsuits seeking to reorder EPA's (or the President's) priorities? Many other environmental statutes include a similar provision. (The citizen suit provision also provides for citizen enforcement against alleged violators of RCRA; we take up that provision in Section VII, below).

4. In HSWA Congress used the "hammer" approach described in the excerpt to secure EPA's prompt rulemaking: a tight deadline with an *in terrorem* regulatory consequence to be triggered by failure to meet the deadline. Congress assumed that no EPA Administrator (and by extension, no President) would be willing to be blamed for causing the backstop "very stringent standard" to take effect. Recent years have seen similar games of chicken played out at times when the legislative and executive branches have had very different policy perspectives. Are legislative "hammers" a good idea?

The HSWA hammers succeeded in prompting EPA to meet the statute's deadlines for promulgating regulations. But note the effect, according to the Hill excerpt: "Today, the solid and hazardous waste program focuses almost exclusively on implementing the HSWA requirements." Inevitably, focusing the agency's resources in this way means that something else will not be getting done. Is it appropriate for Congress to make policy choices in this manner? Would it be feasible for Congress to use similar hammers in multiple statutes? What if meeting the deadline results in a poorly crafted regulation? What, if any, responsibility should Congress bear for its choices about how much funding to appropriate to EPA for carrying out the Agency's statutory obligations?

5. Congressional impatience with the pace of EPA's work may be understandable, particularly in light of the political circumstances of the early 1980s: Congress, which had fairly recently enacted much environmental legislation, was controlled by the Democratic Party, and President Reagan was a Republican President pursuing a deregulatory agenda. As we will see, however, the statutory mandate "to develop regulations within 18 months," so easily described, actually embodied a staggering amount of difficult work requiring massive amounts of information and innumerable decisions that Congress delegated to EPA.

The agency's engineers, scientists, and attorneys undertook this effort in an atmosphere of limited resources, uncertain political support for (or even political hostility to) the effort, and the near-certainty of judicial challenges by both regulated industry contending the Agency had gone too far and environmental groups contending the Agency had not gone far enough. One wonders whether any agency could have completed this task and completed it well in the 18 months that RCRA allotted.

Consider just one problem EPA faced: knowing enough about the activities it was charged with regulating. The Agency's staff could hardly be expected to have expertise covering all of the myriad enterprises and processes that might generate hazardous waste. Indeed, in a remarkably candid self-assessment prepared by a team of career employees, EPA itself noted that "[s]taff writing EPA regulations often are not familiar enough with or do not have enough exposure to the types of facilities and industrial groups they are trying to regulate." U.S. EPA, The Nation's Hazardous Waste Management Program at a Crossroads: The RCRA Implementation Study 37 (1990); *see generally* Cary Coglianese et al., *Seeking Truth for Power: Informational Strategy and Regulatory Policymaking*, 89 Minn. L. Rev. 277 (2004) (discussing and comparing approaches available to government agencies to obtain information about regulated industry). On the other hand, a regulatory agency staffed with former or future employees of the industry it regulates is often accused of being "captured" via the "revolving door." *E.g.,* Sidney A. Shapiro, *The Complexity of Regulatory Capture: Diagnosis, Causality, and Remediation*, 17 Roger Williams U.L. Rev. 221, 230, 251 (2012) (discussing the revolving door with respect to agency officials and staff).

III. Improving Disposal of Non-Hazardous Solid Waste: RCRA Subtitle D

RCRA prohibits placing solid waste[1] in "open dumps." 42 U.S.C. § 6945(a) (RCRA § 4005(a)). An "open dump" is

---

1. As we will see, Section V.A, below, RCRA also gave "solid waste" a much broader meaning than originally prescribed in the 1965 Solid Waste Disposal Act.

"open dump":

> Any facility or site where solid waste is disposed of which is not a sanitary landfill which meets the criteria promulgated under section 6944 of this title and which is not a facility for disposal of hazardous waste.

42 U.S.C. §6903(14) (RCRA §1004(14)). Section 6944, in turn, requires EPA to promulgate criteria for sanitary landfills that "[a]t a minimum, . . . shall provide that a facility may be classified as a sanitary landfill and not an open dump only if there is no reasonable probability of adverse effects on health or the environment from disposal of solid waste at such facility." 42 U.S.C. §6944(a) (RCRA §4004(a)). The detailed and technical criteria EPA promulgated for municipal solid waste (MSW) landfills are codified at 40 C.F.R. Part 258; criteria for certain other types of non-hazardous-waste landfills are at 40 C.F.R. Part 257.

As noted above, however, RCRA recognizes that solid waste collection and disposal are "primarily the function" of non-federal governmental entities. Accordingly, RCRA Subtitle D aims to improve solid waste management by providing federal technical and financial assistance and by requiring EPA to develop guidelines for better state and local solid waste management rather than by direct federal regulation of landfills. 42 U.S.C. §6941 (RCRA §4001). Under Subtitle D each state is to develop, and submit to EPA for approval, a plan for solid waste management. *Id.* §§6942, 6943, 6944(b), 6946 (RCRA §§4002, 4003, 4004(b), 4006). EPA is required to approve plans that meet specified requirements, including the ban on open dumps, *id.* §6947(a) (RCRA §4007(a)). The carrot offered to states for submitting a plan that EPA approves is eligibility for federal financial assistance, *id.* §6947(b) (RCRA §4007(b)). Congressional appropriations for such financial assistance dried up after 1980, however.

Nevertheless, most states have established solid waste programs. By 1988, EPA reported that 46 states and one territory had obtained full or partial approval of their MSW landfill programs. 63 Fed. Reg. 57,026, 57,027 (Oct. 23, 1988). At that time, EPA began requiring states to satisfy new permitting requirements added by the 1984 HSWA amendments. These requirements were designed to prevent MSW landfills and other non-hazardous-waste landfills from releasing the small quantities of hazardous waste inevitably disposed of in such locations. At least 38 states, two territories, and one Indian tribe have since received partial or full approval of their MSW landfill permitting program.

A moment's reflection about one's own personal production of garbage demonstrates what a monumental task it is to manage the waste of some 300 million Americans. The following excerpt provides data to confirm that intuition.

U.S. ENVIRONMENTAL PROTECTION AGENCY
ADVANCING SUSTAINABLE MATERIALS MANAGEMENT:
FACTS AND FIGURES 2013

(June 2015)

Our trash, or MSW, is comprised of various items Americans commonly throw away after being used. These items include packaging, food, grass clippings, sofas, computers, tires, and refrigerators. Not included are materials that also may be disposed in landfills but are not generally considered MSW, such as C&D [construction and demolition] debris, municipal wastewater treatment sludges, and non-hazardous industrial wastes.

. . . .

In the United States, we generated 254 million tons . . . of MSW in 2013—3 million tons more than generated in 2012. MSW generation in 2013 increased to 4.40 pounds per person per day. This is an increase of less than 1 percent from 2012 to 2013.

About 87 million tons of MSW were recycled and composted. Excluding composting, 65 million tons of MSW were recycled, similar to the tons recycled in 2012. The tons of food and yard trimmings recovered for composting were 22 million tons in 2013, an increase of 1 million tons compared to 2012. The recovery rate for recycling (including composting) was 34.3 percent in 2013, slightly lower than the 34.5 percent in 2012 . . . . The recycling rate in 2013 (including composting) was 1.51 pounds per person per day. This is 1.12 pounds per person per day for recycling and 0.39 pounds per person per day for composting.

Three materials whose recycling rates rose from 2012 to 2013 are yard trimmings, selected consumer electronics, and food. In 2013, the rate of yard trimmings composting was 60.2 percent (20.60 million tons), up from 57.7 percent (19.59 million tons). This translates to 130 pounds per person per year of yard trimmings composted in 2013. In 2013, the rate of selected consumer electronics recovery was 40.4 percent (1.27 million tons) up from 30.6 percent in 2012 (1.00 million tons). This translates to 8 pounds per person per year recovered in 2013. In 2013, the rate of food recovery was 5.0 percent (1.84 million tons), up from 4.8 percent in 2012 (1.74 million tons). This translates to 12 pounds per person per year composted in 2013 . . . .

[There was] a decrease in MSW generation and an increase in recycling from 2000 to 2013. The state of the economy has a strong impact on consumption and waste generation. Waste generation increases during times of strong economic growth and decreases during times of economic decline . . . .

U.S. Environmental Protection Agency (EPA) uses two methods to characterize the 254 million tons of MSW generated in 2013. The first is by material (paper and paperboard, yard trimmings, food, plastics, metals, glass, wood, rubber, leather and textiles, and other); the second is by several major product categories. The product-based categories are containers and packaging; nondurable goods (e.g., newspapers); durable goods (e.g., appliances); food; yard trimmings; and other materials.

Notes and Questions

1. EPA's 2014 report, released shortly before this book went to press, described only modest changes from 2013. Total MSW generation ticked up from 254 million tons to 258 million tons; daily per capita MSW generated increased to 4.44 pounds per person per day (less than a one percent year-to-year increase). But recycling and composting increased too, both in absolute and percentage terms: 89.4 million tons of MSW, or 36.4 percent of the total amount generated, was recycled or composted. The same three materials—yard trimmings, consumer electronics, and food—led the increase in recycling or composting in 2014 as in 2013. U.S. EPA, Advancing Sustainable Materials Management: Facts and Figures 2014 2–3 (November, 2016) (hereafter, "EPA, Materials Management 2014").

2. The quantitative trends described in EPA's annual reports on waste generation and recycling are easier to understand if presented graphically. The total amount of MSW generated has increased steadily since 1960, although the amount generated per capita leveled off after 1990. See Figures 8-1 and 8-2 (following Note 3).

Even as the United States increased its generation of MSW, however, an increasing percentage of the waste has been recycled or composted. The rate of growth in the recycling rate, however, may be slowing. See Figure 8-3 (following Note 3).

Combining data on the growth of MSW generation and MSW recycling and composting provides a picture of the amount of trash that is generated but not recycled or composted. Some of this material is burned with some recovery of energy from the waste (typically by using the heat of incineration to generate electricity). Despite the increase in MSW generation, the total amount of municipal solid waste that is burned or buried has leveled off or declined. See Figure 8-4 (following Note 3).

3. As you read in the excerpt, in addition to collecting data about the aggregate amount of MSW, EPA also studies the materials that comprise our waste. Because the percentage of each waste material recycled, composted, and burned varies, the composition of the waste that goes into our landfills is markedly different from the composition of the waste we generate. See Figure 8-5 (following Note 3).

The categories of paper (including paperboard) and yard trimmings accounted for almost three-fourths of all the MSW recycled and composted in 2014. As a result, only about 22 percent of the mass of landfilled MSW consisted of these materials, even though they were about 40 percent of the mass of MSW generated. By contrast, plastics and food together represented only about 28 percent of the MSW generated, but about 40 percent of the mass of MSW placed in landfills.

Figure 8-1. MSW Generated in the United States, 1960–2014.

Amount (Million tons)

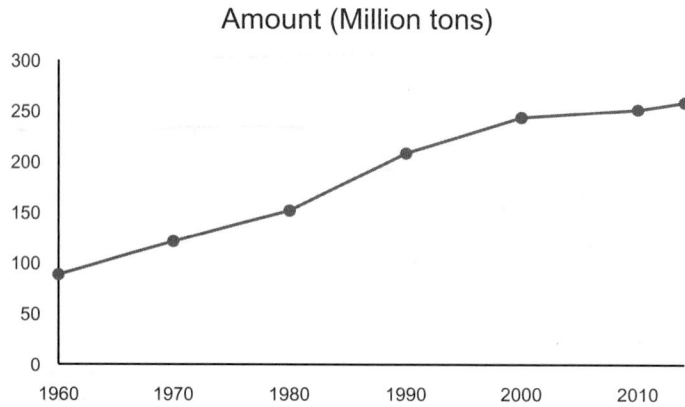

Source: EPA, Materials Management 2014 2 (Figure 1).

Figure 8-2. MSW Generated Per Capita in the United States, 1960-2014.

Amount (lb/person/day)

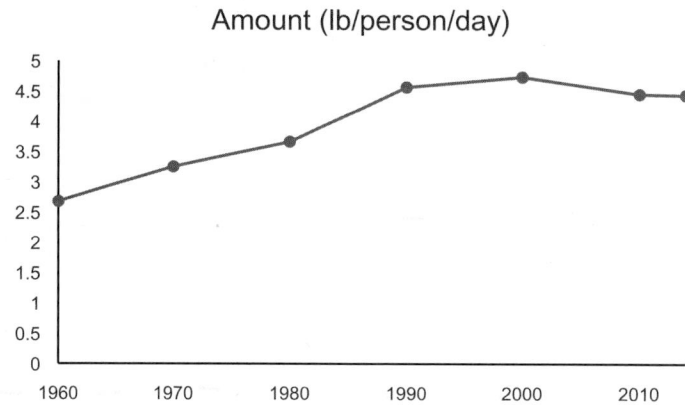

Source: EPA, Materials Management 2014 2 (Figure 1).

Figure 8-3. Fraction of MSW Recycled or Composted, 1960-2014.

Percent recycled or composted

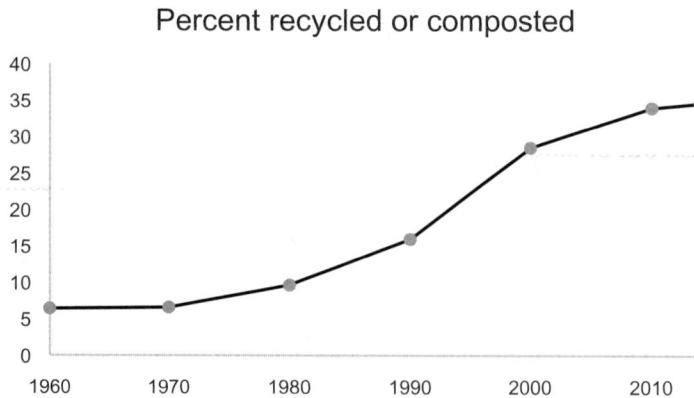

Source: EPA, *Materials Management 2014* 3 (Figure 2).

Figure 8-4. MSW Not Recycled, Composted, or Burned with Energy Recovery in the United States, 1960-2014.

Amount (million tons)

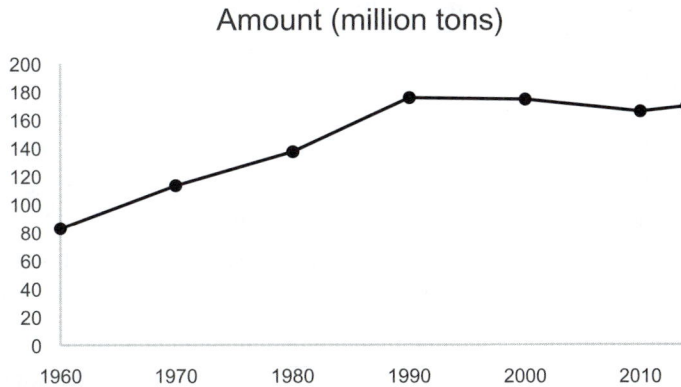

Source: EPA, MATERIALS MANAGEMENT 2014 2-3 (Figures 1, 2).

Figure 8-5. Fraction of Mass, by Material, of MSW Generated and Landfilled in the United States, 2014.

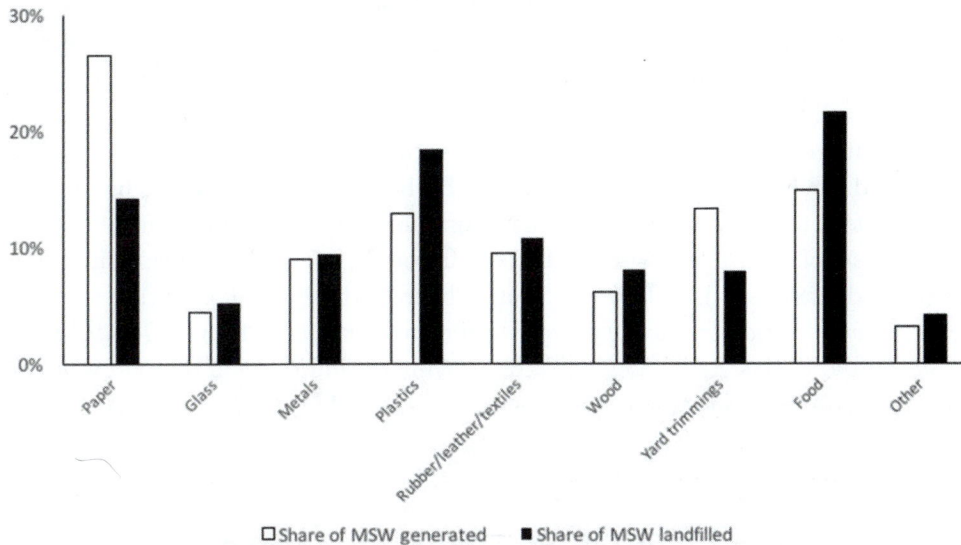

☐ Share of MSW generated   ■ Share of MSW landfilled

Source: EPA, MATERIALS MANAGEMENT 2014 7 (Figures 5, 8).

4. Often, solving one waste disposal problem can create another. For example, one way to get trash out of landfills is to burn the trash for energy recovery. But burning trash emits carbon dioxide and other air pollutants. Some air pollution control devices, in turn, may produce wastes that present disposal problems of their own. On the other hand, burying trash in landfills also can cause greenhouse gas emissions (notably of methane, a very potent contributor to atmospheric warming), and can also leach pollutants into underground and surface water bodies. Thus, although the pollution laws evolved to address pollution of one environmental medium at a time—air, water, land—a comprehensive environmental policy should take into account the phenomenon of "cross-media" pollution.

Life Cycle
Analysis

5. The cross-media challenges inherent to solid waste disposal partly explain why EPA shifted its rhetorical and policy emphasis away from waste management and toward "sustainable materials management." As described by EPA, sustainable materials management "starts with extraction of natural resources and material processing through product design and manufacturing, then the product use stage, followed by collection/processing and final end of life." EPA, Materials Management 2014 at 19. It "seeks to use materials in the most productive way . . . [,] using fewer materials and products, reducing toxic chemicals and environmental impacts throughout the material's life cycle and assuring we have sufficient resources" to meet present and future needs. *Id.* As you study RCRA, consider whether the statute is a well-designed tool for implementing a sustainable materials management strategy.

6. Solving some solid waste problems could also help solve other social problems that are not often included in the "environmental" rubric. Food waste is an important example that is garnering increased attention from environmental and social activists, as well as from various participants in the food industry. In 2012, the Natural Resources Defense Council reported that "40 percent of food in the United States today goes uneaten." Dana Gunders, Wasted: How America is Losing Up to 40 Percent of Its Food from Farm to Fork to Landfill 4 (Aug. 2012). Much of that wasted food rots in landfills, needlessly consuming disposal facility resources and emitting methane gas. *Id.* It also represents a huge waste of money and a missed opportunity to provide adequate nutrition for the American people. *Id.* This joint social and environmental problem would be better addressed by reducing the amount of food that is wasted, rather than improving the management of solid waste that consists of food. For an internationally flavored taste of the growing literature about food waste, see Jack Bobo & Sweta Chakraborty, *Pink Slime versus Garbage Chic: A Consideration of the Impact of Framing on Consumer Behavior Toward Food Waste*, 6 Eur. J. Risk Reg. 445 (2015). EPA maintains information on food waste at https://www.epa.gov/sustainable-management-food (last visited Dec. 14, 2016).

IV. "Cradle to Grave" Regulation of Hazardous Wastes: An Overview of RCRA Subtitle C

As described above, the enactment of RCRA initiated direct federal regulation of hazardous waste. As further articulated in the 1984 HSWA amendments, RCRA aims:

to promote the protection of health and the environment . . . by— . . .

(4) assuring that hazardous waste management practices are conducted in a manner which protects human health and the environment;

(5) requiring that hazardous waste be properly managed in the first instance thereby reducing the need for corrective action at a future date;

(6) minimizing the generation of hazardous waste and the land disposal of hazardous waste by encouraging process substitution, materials recovery, properly conducted recycling and reuse, and treatment . . .

42 U.S.C. § 6902 (RCRA § 1003 as amended by HSWA § 101); *see* 42 U.S.C. §§ 6921–6939g (codifying Subtitle C of RCRA as amended). To achieve these goals, the statute, both as originally enacted and as amended by HSWA, requires EPA to take specific regulatory actions.

RCRA's hazardous waste provisions are a quintessential example of Congress articulating a list of things it wants regulated and entrusting the details ("hammers" notwithstanding) to an executive agency. Many (not all) of the statutory provisions do not impose legal requirements on industry directly but function almost like a table of contents for the EPA regulations that spell out the specific requirements. Thus, to understand how RCRA actually works, reference to the regulations, as well as the statute, is essential.

Subtitle C's fundamental provisions mandate the creation of a regulatory scheme to track comprehensively the creation, movement, and disposition of hazardous waste. 42 U.S.C. §§ 6922–6925 (RCRA §§ 3002–3005). Subtitle C's regulatory scheme applies from the moment hazardous waste comes into existence until it reaches its final resting place (or is transformed into something other than hazardous waste): from "cradle to grave."

A. Generators

Hazardous waste regulation begins with the generation of hazardous waste: "the act or process of producing hazardous waste." 42 U.S.C. § 6903(6) (RCRA § 1004(6)). The statute requires EPA to create standards for hazardous waste generators with respect to hazardous waste containers and their labels, as well as a variety of record-keeping and reporting requirements to track the quantity and nature of hazardous waste generated. *Id.* § 6922 (RCRA § 3002); *see generally* 40 C.F.R. Part 262 (EPA regulations specifying standards for hazardous waste generators). Most important, RCRA requires EPA to promulgate regulations for:

> use of a manifest system and any other reasonable means necessary to assure that all such hazardous waste generated is designated for treatment, storage, or disposal in, and arrives at, treatment, storage, or disposal facilities (other than facilities on the premises where the waste is generated) for which a permit has been issued . . .

Id. § 6922(a)(5). A "manifest" is a "form used for identifying the quantity, composition, and the origin, routing, and destination of hazardous waste during its transportation from the point of generation to the point of disposal, treatment, or storage." *Id.* § 6903(12) (RCRA § 1004(12)); *see* 40 C.F.R. §§ 262.20–262.27 (EPA regulations setting standards for hazardous waste manifests). Like a tracking number for a product ordered online, then, the manifest is designed to ensure that hazardous waste reaches its intended destination—a permitted treatment, storage, or disposal facility—or to inform government authorities if hazardous waste ends up somewhere else. (And like such tracking numbers, manifests can now be in electronic rather than paper form. *See* 42 U.S.C. § 6939(g); 40 C.F.R. § 262.24). In HSWA, Congress also enlisted the manifest to do policy work, by requiring generators to certify in their manifests that they have a system in place to reduce the amount and toxicity of hazardous waste they generate and that "the proposed method of treatment, storage, or disposal is that practicable method currently available to the generator which minimizes the present and future threat to human health and the environment." 42 U.S.C. § 6922(b)(2).

B. Transporters

Hazardous waste's route from cradle to grave is sometimes short—some generators of hazardous waste treat, store, or dispose of that waste at the same site where it is generated. Often, however, hazardous waste must be shipped, and to keep it safe in transit RCRA requires EPA, "after consultation with the Secretary of Transportation and the States," to promulgate regulations applicable to transporters of hazardous waste. 42 U.S.C. § 6923; *see* 40 C.F.R. Part 263 (EPA regulations setting standards for hazardous waste transporters).

Overall, the RCRA regulations for transporters are not as onerous as those for generators. Like generators, transporters are subject to various recordkeeping requirements. They must use the manifest started by the generator to track each shipment of hazardous waste and must comply with the manifest by bringing the shipment to the destination designated by the generator (either the next transporter in a sequence or a facility for treatment, storage, or disposal of the waste). 40 C.F.R. §§ 263.20, 263.21. EPA's regulations incorporate by reference the very detailed rules promulgated by the Department of Transportation that regulate how hazardous materials are hauled (for example, setting standards for shipping containers depending on the material being transported and its hazards, and requiring labeling with the familiar diamond-shaped placards). In the event of a spill, EPA's rules require transporters to take immediate action to protect human health and the environment, to notify appropriate government authorities, and to clean up the discharge. 40 C.F.R. §§ 263.30, 263.31.

C. Treatment, Storage and Disposal Facilities (TSDFs)

Eventually, the journey of hazardous waste stops—the waste arrives at a facility for, in RCRA's words, "the treatment, storage, or disposal of hazardous waste." 42 U.S.C. § 6924(a) (RCRA § 3004(a)). We will consider what these terms mean, and how they differ from one another, in Section VI.B, below. For such facilities, which RCRA practitioners know by the acronym TSDFs ("treatment, storage, or disposal facilities"), the statute requires EPA to promulgate "performance standards." *Id.* The statute also requires EPA "to promulgate regulations requiring each person owning or operating an existing [TSDF] or planning to construct a new [TSDF] . . . to have a permit issued pursuant to this section." *Id.* § 6925(a) (RCRA § 3005(a)). Thus, once

permit
required

the permitting regulations went into effect, it became illegal to own, operate or construct a TSDF without having a valid permit and complying with the permit's conditions. *See generally* 40 C.F.R. § 270.1.

Congress recognized, however, that many hazardous waste treatment, storage, and disposal facilities already existed at the time of RCRA's enactment, and that it would be impractical and unwise to put them all instantly out of business for lack of a permit. Therefore RCRA includes provisions allowing previously existing TSDFs to operate in a lawful "interim status" while in the process of obtaining a permit. 42 U.S.C. § 6925(c).

Section 3004 of RCRA, as originally enacted, was a relatively short provision requiring EPA to issue regulations prescribing performance standards for TSDFs within 18 months. The slow pace of EPA regulation that ensued made this section a major focus of the 1974 amendments to the statute. As amended, § 3004 includes lengthy and numerous provisions with respect to various particular types of hazardous wastes, disposal methods, types of disposal facilities, types of treatment, and related matters. 42 U.S.C. § 6924(b)–(y).

Because the risks posed by hazardous waste are greatest if the waste is improperly disposed of, the RCRA Subtitle C rules for TSDFs are more onerous than those for generators or transporters "by several orders of magnitude." Richard G. Stoll, *Coping with the RCRA Hazardous Waste System: A Few Practical Points for Fun and Profit*, C414 ALI-ABA 167, 172 (1989). The TSDF regulations are varied, detailed, and expensive to comply with. *See generally* 40 C.F.R. Parts 264–270. No survey course in environmental law can address them comprehensively; we discuss a few issues related to TSDF regulation in Section VI.B, below.

D. Corrective Action

What if, despite all the regulations that apply to treatment, storage, or disposal facilities, hazardous waste escapes from a facility and threatens to harm human health or the environment? As amended, RCRA provides that all TSDF permits must require "corrective action for all releases of hazardous waste . . . from any solid waste management unit at a [TSDF] . . . regardless of the time at which waste was placed in such unit." 42 U.S.C. § 6924(u) (HSWA § 206, adding RCRA § 3004(u)). Corrective action is required "where necessary to protect human health and the environment," even beyond the facility boundary. *Id.* § 6924(v) (HSWA § 207, adding RCRA § 3004(v)). Such a situation might arise, for example, if toxic constituents such as metals or solvents leached from a hazardous waste landfill into groundwater and then migrated away from the facility with groundwater movement.

E. The Role of States

Like many environmental statutes, RCRA embraces a model of cooperative federalism. A state may apply for and receive EPA's authorization to administer the Subtitle C hazardous waste regulation program. 42 U.S.C. § 6926(b) (RCRA § 3006(b)). To receive EPA's authorization, a state's program must be "equivalent to the Federal program" as well as "consistent with the Federal or State programs applicable in other States," and must "provide adequate enforcement." *Id.*; *see* 40 C.F.R. §§ 271.1–271.27 (EPA regulations setting out requirements for final authorization of state programs). RCRA expressly preempts any state or local regulations less stringent than EPA's promulgated federal requirements, but expressly reserves state authority to impose requirements that are more stringent. 42 U.S.C. § 6929 (RCRA § 3009, as amended by P.L. 96-482 (1980)); *see* 40 C.F.R. § 271.1(i).

In states without authorized programs, EPA's federal regulations apply directly and EPA operates the hazardous waste regulation program—for example, deciding whether to grant TSDF permits. After RCRA's enactment and EPA's initial promulgation of federal regulations, many states sought and obtained authorization to operate their own equivalent hazardous waste programs in lieu of the federal program. With subsequent amendments to RCRA and additional EPA rule promulgations, states have not always kept up. Therefore, in some states the authority over hazardous waste regulation is divided, with the state responsible for its authorized program and EPA responsible for the remaining regulatory provisions. Today, 48 states and the territory of Guam have authorization for all or part of the RCRA Subtitle C regulatory program. *See* https://www3.epa.gov/epawaste/laws-regs/state/stats/authall.pdf (last visited August 4, 2016).

The partnerships between EPA's regional offices and their state agency counterparts function more or less well depending on the relations among agency staff and agency leadership, as well as the political relationship between the state and federal executive branches. *See* 40 C.F.R. § 271.8 (requiring execution of a Memorandum of Understanding between a state and the appropriate EPA regional office as a prerequisite for approval of an authorization request). Even in an authorized state, EPA retains the authority to conduct inspections of generators, transporters, or TSDFs, and after notice to the state, to take enforcement action on its own against alleged violators. *See id.*; 42 U.S.C. § 6927 (RCRA § 3007) (authorizing EPA inspections); *id.* § 6928(a)(2) (RCRA § 3008(a)(2)) (authorizing EPA enforcement actions).

In this chapter, for syntactic simplicity we will generally refer to EPA and to EPA regulations. This allows us, for example, to refer to a permit issued by "EPA" instead of by "the permitting authority" (which could be EPA or a state). You should always bear in mind, however, that an authorized state environmental agency may be wholly or partly responsible for implementing the provisions you read about. So, for example, when seeking a permit for a new hazardous waste disposal facility, the owner or operator may have to apply only to EPA, or only to a state agency, or to EPA for some parts of the permit and to a state agency for other parts.

F. Enforcement

RCRA § 3008 provides the framework for enforcement action against violators of Subtitle C and its implementing regulations. RCRA authorizes the United States government to take administrative, civil judicial, and criminal enforcement actions. All these enforcement authorities must be available under state law in any authorized state hazardous waste program. 40 C.F.R. § 271.16.

Administrative enforcement is the predominant method. Section 3008(a)(1) of RCRA grants EPA the authority to issue an order to an alleged violator requiring the violator to come into compliance and to pay a civil penalty for the violations. 42 U.S.C. § 6928(a)(1). Violating the order itself carries additional penalties, *id.* § 6928(c). A respondent to a compliance order is entitled to a hearing, *id.* § 6928(b), and to judicial review under the Administrative Procedure Act.

Section 3008(a)(1) also authorizes civil judicial enforcement as an alternative to administrative action. EPA, represented by the Department of Justice, may bring a civil action against an alleged violator "for appropriate relief," including injunctive relief. *Id.* § 6928(a)(1). These same administrative and judicial options are available to secure corrective action in the event of a release of hazardous waste from an interim status TSDF. *Id.* § 6928(h) (RCRA § 3008(h) as amended by HSWA § 233). Finally, certain knowing violations of RCRA are federal crimes. 42 U.S.C. § 6928(d), (e) (RCRA § 3008(d), (e), as amended).

RCRA, like many other environmental statutes, also enlists the aid of "private attorneys general" to enforce its provisions. Under RCRA's citizen suit provision, if the federal or state government is notified of a violation and does not commence and diligently prosecute an enforcement action, any person may bring a citizen suit seeking the same relief the government could obtain. 42 U.S.C. § 6972 (RCRA § 7002).

In addition to § 3008, which applies specifically to the Subtitle C hazardous waste program, violators of RCRA's hazardous waste provisions may also face enforcement through a broader provision of the statute. Section 7003(a) of RCRA provides:

> Notwithstanding any other provision of this chapter, upon receipt of evidence that the past or present handling, storage, treatment, transportation or disposal of any solid waste or hazardous waste may present an imminent and substantial endangerment to health or the environment, the Administrator may bring suit on behalf of the United States in the appropriate district court against any person (including any past or present generator, past or present transporter, or past or present owner or operator of a treatment, storage, or disposal facility) who has contributed or who is contributing to such handling, storage, treatment, transportation or disposal to restrain such person from such handling, storage, treatment, transportation, or disposal, to order such person to take such other action as may be necessary, or both . . . . The Administrator shall provide notice to the affected State of any such suit. The Administrator may also, after notice to the affected State, take other action under this section including, but not limited to, issuing such orders as may be necessary to protect public health and the environment.

42 U.S.C. § 6973(a). Violating a § 7003 order subjects the violator to civil penalties. *Id.* § 6973(b).

Note two important distinctions between § 7003 and § 3008. First, relief under § 7003 requires proof that solid or hazardous waste "may present an imminent and substantial endangerment to health or the environment" but does not require proof of a violation of a specific RCRA statutory provision or regulation. Second, § 3008 applies only to RCRA's hazardous waste provisions, but § 7003 applies to "solid waste *or* hazardous waste" (emphasis added). We defer further discussion of the meaning of "imminent and substantial endangerment" to Section VII, p. 714, below, but the difference in applicability of the two enforcement provisions figures prominently in some of the cases in the next Section of this chapter, below.

G. Summary

To sum up: Subtitle C of RCRA aims to protect human health and the environment from the risks posed by hazardous waste. The statute divides the participants in the life cycle of hazardous waste into three categories: (1) generators, (2) transporters, and (3) owners and operators of treatment, storage, or disposal facilities (TSDFs). For the most part, the statute describes the subjects to be regulated for each category of participants and directs EPA to promulgate the actual requirements, although the HSWA amendments included numerous prescriptions for TSDFs. The regulatory system relies heavily on recordkeeping and in particular on the manifest system that tracks the creation, movement, and disposition of hazardous waste. The regulations also specify in detail how generators, transporters, and TSDFs must handle hazardous waste to protect human health and the environment. A TSDF must have a permit that specifies in detail the hazardous waste it will manage and prescribes methods for doing so. If hazardous waste is released to the environment despite these requirements, corrective action is required. States may obtain authorization to run hazardous waste programs that are at least as stringent as the federal program. The federal government and authorized state governments may bring criminal, administrative, or civil actions in response to alleged violations of the hazardous waste requirements or to imminent and substantial endangerments presented by solid or hazardous wastes; absent government action, citizens may bring civil suits under either enforcement provision.

In providing this capsule description of RCRA's hazardous waste program, we have deliberately omitted the issue that has proven to be most contentious in RCRA enforcement: to what and whom does that program apply? That is, what is "hazardous waste"?

V. Triggering RCRA Subtitle C: Defining and Identifying Hazardous Waste

In RCRA, Congress directed EPA — within 18 months after enactment — to:

develop and promulgate criteria for identifying the characteristics of hazardous waste, and for listing hazardous waste, which should be subject to the provisions of this subchapter, taking into account toxicity, persistence, and degradability in nature, potential for accumulation in tissue, and other related factors such as flammability, corrosiveness, and other hazardous characteristics.

42 U.S.C. § 6921(a) (RCRA § 3001(a)). You should pause for a moment to consider the enormity of the task Congress assigned EPA. Think about the vast range of activities in the huge American economy that produce waste that could be considered "hazardous." Manufacturing operations, large and small: steel mills, chemical and pharmaceutical factories, oil refineries, textile factories, auto and aircraft factories, power plants, metal plating shops, machine shops, to name a few. Service industries like dry cleaners, auto repair shops, even universities, hospitals, and medical offices. Extractive industries like oil and gas, coal, and minerals. Farms. Construction and demolition activities. Not to mention business and individual consumers of useful products—solvents, metals, solders, pesticides, herbicides, sealants, glues, paints, building materials, and many others—that might present health or environmental hazards when thrown away. EPA, which had not previously been involved in hazardous waste regulation, was required to survey these activities and decide which wastes "should be subject to the provisions of this subchapter," taking into account a handful of specific possible attributes—which might or might not have been studied or documented for any individual waste or waste stream—as well as a catchall "other hazardous characteristics" not further defined.

RCRA industries

Congress did provide EPA with some additional guidance, however. RCRA defines "hazardous waste" as follows:

> The term "hazardous waste" means a solid waste, or combination of solid wastes, which because of its quantity, concentration, or physical, chemical, or infectious characteristics may—
>
> > (A) cause, or significantly contribute to an increase in mortality or an increase in serious irreversible, or incapacitating reversible, illness; or
> >
> > (B) pose a substantial present or potential hazard to human health or the environment when improperly treated, stored, transported, or disposed of, or otherwise managed.

"hazardous waste" definition

42 U.S.C. § 6903(5) (RCRA § 1004(5)). Compare this definition of hazardous waste to the provision that tells EPA what to consider when identifying the characteristics of hazardous waste and listing hazardous waste. How are the two statutory provisions different? How do they overlap? Does one expand or limit the other?

A. Is It "Solid Waste"?

The definition of hazardous waste makes one thing clear: to be a "hazardous waste," a substance must first be "a solid waste" (or a combination of solid wastes). What is a solid waste? RCRA tells us that too:

"solid waste" definition

The term "solid waste" means any garbage, refuse, sludge from a waste treatment plant, water supply treatment plant, or air pollution control facility and other discarded material, including solid, liquid, semisolid, or contained gaseous material resulting from industrial, commercial, mining, and agricultural operations, and from community activities, but does not include solid or dissolved material in domestic sewage, or solid or dissolved materials in irrigation return flows or industrial discharges which are point sources subject to permits under section 1342 of Title 33, or source, special nuclear, or byproduct material as defined by the Atomic Energy Act of 1954, as amended (68 Stat. 923) [42 U.S.C.A. § 2011 et seq.].

NOT Solid waste

42 U.S.C. § 6903(27) (RCRA § 1004(27)). It is worth taking a moment to parse the way this definition works. It begins by defining solid waste as any member of a set, then elaborates on that set with a broad description of what is included, and finally excludes particular items that otherwise might seem to fit the definition. We examine each part of the definition, working backward.

The exclusions are easy to understand: Congress intended certain types of waste streams to be regulated under statutes *other* than RCRA. Thus, domestic sewage and point sources of water pollution are regulated under the Clean Water Act; nuclear wastes are regulated under the Atomic Energy Act.

The inclusions achieve two major purposes. They make clear that RCRA's reach was not limited to waste generated by any particular type of activity: what matters is whether something fits the description of solid waste, not whether it resulted from "industrial, commercial, mining, . . . agricultural . . . [or] community" sources. The inclusions also make clear that "solid waste" is a term of convenience rather than a reference to a specific state of matter: a "solid waste" need not be solid; "solid, liquid, semisolid, or contained gaseous material" can be solid waste. If you toss a half-consumed bottle of water into a trash bin, is the bottle "solid waste"? Is the water inside the bottle "solid waste"? What about helium that you let out of a balloon at the end of a party?

Now that we know solid waste includes a range of states of matter generated by a range of types of activities, we still need to know what makes something solid waste. To tell us that, Congress provided the list of items at the beginning of the "solid waste" definition. Note that the list includes only a few items that are specifically identified: "sludge from a waste treatment plant, water supply treatment plant, or air pollution control facility." Otherwise, a solid waste is "garbage, refuse, . . . and other discarded material . . . ." How much do these terms clarify, as compared to just the term "solid waste?"

The distinction between waste and non-waste—or between that which is "garbage, refuse, . . . and other discarded material" and that which is not—might seem obvious. That half-consumed bottle of water you toss in a trash bin is garbage; the full, new bottle you put in the refrigerator is not. What about the half-consumed bottle that you put in the refrigerator, intending to drink the rest later? The half-consumed bottle you leave untouched in your fridge for a month while you open and drink many new bottles? The full, new bottle you leave behind in a cupboard when you move out of your apartment? The empty bottle you put in a recycling bin?

As we will see, deciding when something has been "discarded" is not always so easy. And it is important: if something has not been discarded, it is not solid waste; if it is not solid waste, it cannot be hazardous waste; if it is not hazardous waste, it cannot be subject to the protective but onerous requirements of the RCRA Subtitle C treatment, storage, and disposal regulations. Because classifying a material as "solid waste" has such great consequences, the meaning of "discarded" has elicited a great deal of ingenuity from parties who want certain hazardous materials to be subject to the Subtitle C rules, as well as from parties seeking to avoid such regulation.

"discarded"

No Spray Coalition, Inc. v. City of New York
252 F.3d 148 (2d Cir. 2001)

PER CURIAM.

In an effort to control West Nile Virus—a fatal, mosquito-borne disease—the City of New York last summer undertook an insecticide spraying program, and may renew that program in the summer of 2001. Plaintiffs appeal an order of the United States District Court ... denying ... a preliminary injunction against the renewed spraying and dismissing the claim under the citizens suit provision of the Resource Conservation and Recovery Act ("RCRA") ....

[Under RCRA] the term "solid waste"

means any garbage, refuse, [...] and *other discarded material* ...

[42 U.S.C.] § 6903(27) (emphasis added).

Plaintiffs claim, in essence, that ... the spraying of the pesticides constitutes the "disposal" of a "solid waste" in a manner that renders it "discarded material" ....

....

Plaintiffs argue that "[o]nce pesticides are sprayed onto or into the air, land, and waters of New York City, they become discarded solid wastes within the meaning of RCRA § 1004(27)." But we have indicated that material is not discarded until after it has served its intended purpose. We therefore agree with the district court that the pesticides are not being "discarded" when sprayed into the air with the design of effecting their intended purpose: reaching and killing mosquitoes and their larvae.

....

The denial of the preliminary injunction and the dismissal of the claims under RCRA are affirmed.

Notes and Questions

1. Do you think the *No Spray* plaintiffs would have been satisfied if the City government had gotten a permit allowing it to "dispose" of the pesticides by spraying them around New York? If not, then what was the plaintiffs' real goal or real concern? Instead of trying to use the hazardous waste laws, might the plaintiff have invoked a regulatory regime aimed directly at pesticide use? See Chapter 10 for an introduction to the Federal Insecticide, Fungicide, and Rodenticide Act, which takes a quite different regulatory approach.

2. What becomes of the insecticides after they are sprayed? Is the result any different than if the City had just taken drums of insecticide and dumped their contents?

3. Should it matter that the City's spraying program was aimed at combating a "fatal" virus? In fact, West Nile disease is not so fatal after all. According to the United States Centers for Disease Control and Prevention, 70 to 80 percent of all people infected with West Nile virus have no symptoms; about 20 percent develop flu-like symptoms from which recovery can be lengthy; about one percent develop severe neurological symptoms, and of that one percent, about 10 percent (0.1% of all infected people) die. Centers for Disease Control and Prevention, General Questions About West Nile Virus, https://www.cdc.gov/westnile/faq/genquestions.html (last visited Nov. 23, 2016). "Influenza kills more than 30,000 people each year in the United States, compared with fewer than 300 who died from West Nile last year. Yet rarely does a flu outbreak inspire the kind of dread West Nile does." Richard Perez-Pena, *Who's Afraid of This Little Fellow? West Nile Is Still Here, but the Furor and Anxiety Have Ebbed*, N.Y. TIMES Sept. 21, 2003, p. 41.

4. Did the *No Spray* case have environmental justice implications?

5. Is "intended purpose" a useful distinction? What if a business sprays dioxin-contaminated chemical wastes on rural dirt roads with the "intended purpose" of suppressing dust? What if farmers spray nitrate fertilizer with the "intended purpose" of improving crop yields but excess fertilizer leaches into drinking water wells and causes "blue baby" syndrome?

6. In *No Spray* it was at least clear that the intended use of the insecticide involved broadcasting it into the environment. What if the environmental dispersal of a product is only a consequence of the product's use for its intended purpose? Consider the following case.

Connecticut Coastal Fishermen's Ass'n v. Remington Arms Co., Inc.
989 F.2d 1305 (2d Cir.)

Judge CARDAMONE.

Critical on this appeal is the meaning of the terms "solid waste" and "hazardous waste," as these terms are defined in [RCRA]. Defining what Congress intended by these words is not child's play, even though RCRA has an "Alice in Wonderland" air about it. We say that because a careful perusal of RCRA and its regulations reveals that "solid waste" plainly means one thing in one part of RCRA and something entirely different in another part of the same statute.

. . . .

Remington Arms Co., Inc. (Remington or appellant) has owned and operated a trap and skeet shooting club—originally organized in the 1920s—on Lordship Point in Stratford, Connecticut since 1945. Trap and skeet targets are made of clay, and the shotguns used to knock these targets down are loaded with lead shot. The Lordship Point Gun Club (the Gun Club) was open to the public and it annually served 40,000 patrons. After nearly 70 years of use, close to 2,400 tons of lead shot (5 million pounds) and 11 million pounds of clay target fragments were deposited on land around the club and in the adjacent waters of Long Island Sound. Directly to the north of Lordship Point lies a Connecticut state wildlife refuge at Nells Island Marsh, a critical habitat for one of the state's largest populations of Black Duck. The waters and shore near the Gun Club feed numerous species of waterfowl and shorebirds.

Plaintiff, Connecticut Coastal Fishermen's Association (Coastal Fishermen or plaintiff) brought suit against defendant Remington alleging that the lead shot and clay targets are hazardous wastes under RCRA . . . . Remington has never obtained a permit under § 3005 of RCRA for the storage and disposal of hazardous wastes, 42 U.S.C. § 6925 . . . . Plaintiff insists that Remington must now clean up the lead shot and clay fragments it permitted to be scattered on the land and in the sea at Lordship Point. Because the debris constitutes an imminent and substantial endangerment to health and the environment under RCRA, we agree.   *decision*

[In 1985, the Connecticut Department of Environmental Protection (DEP), which did not at the time have the authority to issue RCRA permits, ordered Remington to investigate, and if necessary to remedy, lead contamination and the potential for lead poisoning of waterfowl resulting from the gun club's activities. After several years of study, Remington submitted a cleanup plan. DEP was still considering whether to approve the plan at the time of the opinion.] . . . . To date, none of the lead shot or the clay target fragments has been removed from Lordship Point or the surrounding waters of Long Island Sound.

[The Coastal Fishermen's Association's complaint alleged that (1) the lead shot and   *Petitioner's* clay targets are hazardous waste under RCRA; (2) therefore the Gun Club is a haz-   *arguments* ardous waste storage and disposal facility unlawfully operating without a RCRA permit; and (3) that the Gun Club's handling of hazardous waste had contributed to conditions which may present an imminent and substantial endangerment to human health and the environment. On cross-motions for summary judgment,] the district court held that the lead shot and clay targets were "discarded material" under 42 U.S.C. § 6903(27) (RCRA § 1004(27)), were "solid waste" under that statute, and therefore were subject to regulation under RCRA. It further stated that the lead shot was a "hazardous waste," but believed there were genuine issues of material fact as to whether the clay targets were "hazardous waste" under RCRA.

. . . .

. . . . With respect to the RCRA holding, we reverse in part and affirm in part.

. . . .

II *RESOURCE CONSERVATION AND RECOVERY ACT*

A. Overview

Defendant argument

. . . . Remington . . . contends that . . . lead shot and clay target debris are not "solid wastes"—and hence cannot be "hazardous wastes" regulated by RCRA . . . . In essence, Remington contends that RCRA does not apply to the Gun Club because any disposal of waste that occurred there was merely incidental to the normal use of a product.

Issue #1

. . . . Under RCRA "hazardous wastes" are a subset of "solid wastes." *See* 42 U.S.C. § 6903(5). Accordingly, for a waste to be classified as hazardous, it must first qualify as a solid waste under RCRA. We direct our attention initially therefore to whether the lead shot and clay targets are solid waste.

B. *Chevron* Analysis

Our analysis of the definition of solid waste entails statutory interpretation as outlined in [*Chevron*, p. 52 above] . . . .

. . . .

We consider first the statutory definition of solid waste. RCRA defines solid waste as:

> any garbage, refuse, sludge from a waste treatment plant, water supply treatment plant, or air pollution control facility *and other discarded material . . .* resulting from industrial, commercial, mining and agricultural operations, and from community activities . . .

42 U.S.C. § 6903(27) (emphasis added). Remington admits that its Gun Club is a "commercial operation" or a "community activity;" it challenges the district court's finding that the lead shot and clay target debris are "discarded material." The statute itself does not further define "discarded material," and this creates an ambiguity with respect to the specific issue raised by Remington: At what point after a lead shot is fired at a clay target do the materials become discarded? Does the transformation from useful to discarded material take place the instant the shot is fired or at some later time?

The legislative history does not satisfactorily resolve this ambiguity. It tells us that . . . the reach of RCRA was intended to be broad.

> It is not only the waste by-products of the nation's manufacturing processes with which the committee is concerned: *but also the products themselves once they have served their intended purposes and are no longer wanted by the consumer.* For these reasons the term discarded materials is used to identify collectively those substances often referred to as industrial, municipal or post-consumer waste; refuse, trash, garbage and sludge.

[H.R.Rep. No. 1491, 94th Cong., 2d Sess. 4 (1976)] . . . (emphasis added). Yet, the legislative history does not tell us at what point products have served their intended purposes. The statutory definition of "disposal" as "the discharge, deposit, injection, dumping, spilling, leaking, or placing of any solid waste or hazardous waste into or on any land or water," 42 U.S.C. § 6903(3), while broad, sheds little light on this question. Remington's focus on RCRA as being intended to address only solid waste "disposal"—in the sense of the affirmative acts of collecting, transporting, and treating manufacturing or industrial by-products—clearly is too narrow because it ignores legislative aim and fails to take into account the often non-voluntary acts of depositing, spilling and leaking. The statute and legislative history do not instruct as to how far the reach of RCRA extends. Thus, we proceed to the second step of the *Chevron* analysis and consider the EPA's interpretation.

The RCRA regulations create a dichotomy in the definition of solid waste. The EPA distinguishes between RCRA's regulatory and remedial purposes and offers a different definition of solid waste depending upon the statutory context in which the term appears. In its *amicus* brief, the EPA tells us that the regulatory definition of solid waste—found at 40 C.F.R. § 261.2(a)—is narrower than its statutory counterpart. The regulations define solid waste as "any discarded material" and further define discarded material as that which is "abandoned." 40 C.F.R. § 261.2(a). Materials that are abandoned have been "disposed of." 40 C.F.R. § 261.2(b). According to RCRA regulations, this definition of solid waste "applies only to wastes that also are hazardous for purposes of the regulations implementing Subtitle C of RCRA." 40 C.F.R. § 261.1(b)(1). As previously noted, Subtitle C [Subchapter III] contains more stringent handling standards for hazardous waste, and hazardous waste is a subset of solid waste.

The regulations further state that the statutory definition of solid waste, found at 42 U.S.C. § 6903(27), applies to "imminent hazard" lawsuits brought by the United States under § 7003, 42 U.S.C. § 6973. *See* 40 C.F.R. § 261.1(b)(2)(ii). This statement recognizes the special nature of the imminent hazard lawsuit under RCRA. Currently, RCRA authorizes two kinds of citizen suits. The first, under § 7002(a)(1)(A), 42 U.S.C. § 6972(a)(1)(A), enables private citizens to enforce the EPA's hazardous waste regulations and—according to 40 C.F.R. § 261.1(b)(1)—invokes the narrow regulatory definition of solid waste. The second type of citizen suit, under § 7002(a)(1)(B), 42 U.S.C. § 6972(a)(1)(B), authorizes citizens to sue to abate an "imminent and substantial endangerment to health or the environment." While the regulations do not specifically mention this second category of citizen suit, regulatory language referring to § 7003 must also apply to § 7002(a)(1)(B) because the two provisions are nearly identical. Consequently, the broader statutory definition of solid waste applies to citizen suits brought to abate imminent hazard to health or the environment.

We recognize the anomaly of using different definitions for the term "solid waste" and that such view further complicates an already complex statute. Yet, we believe on balance that the EPA regulations reasonably interpret the statutory language. Hence, we defer to them. Dual definitions of solid waste are suggested by the structure and language of RCRA. Congress in Subchapter III [Subtitle C] isolated hazardous wastes for more stringent regulatory treatment. Recognizing the serious responsibility that such regulations impose, Congress required that hazardous waste—a subset of solid waste as defined in the RCRA regulations—be clearly identified. The statute directs the EPA to develop specific "criteria" for the identification of hazardous wastes as well as to publish a list of particular hazardous wastes. By way of contrast, Subchapter IV [Subtitle D] that empowers the EPA to publish "guidelines" for the identification of problem solid waste pollution areas, does not require explanation beyond RCRA's statutory definition of what constitutes solid waste. Hence, the words of the statute contemplate that the EPA would refine and narrow the definition of solid waste for the sole purpose of Subchapter III [Subtitle C hazardous waste] regulation and enforcement.

C. Regulatory Definition of Solid Waste

[EPA, as *amicus*, argued that the Gun Club's lead shot and clay targets do not fall within the narrow regulatory definition of solid waste and therefore do not trigger EPA's TSDF regulations. However, the Court declined to decide the issue. Instead, the court held on other grounds that plaintiff had not alleged a valid claim that the Gun Club was operating a hazardous waste storage or disposal facility under RCRA § 3005.]

. . . .

D. Statutory Definition of Solid Waste

. . . .

As already noted, RCRA regulations apply the broader statutory definition of solid waste to imminent hazard suits. The statutory definition contains the concept of "discarded material," but it does not contain the terms "abandoned" or "disposed of" as required by the regulatory definition. 40 C.F.R. §§ 261.2(a)(2), (b)(1). Amicus [EPA] interprets the statutory definition of solid waste as encompassing the lead shot and clay targets at Lordship Point because they are "discarded." Specifically, the EPA states that the materials are discarded because they have been "left to accumulate long after they have served their intended purpose." Without deciding how long materials must accumulate before they become discarded — that is, when the shot is fired or at some later time — we agree that the lead shot and clay targets in Long Island Sound have accumulated long enough to be considered solid waste.

[Having decided that the lead shot and clay targets were "solid waste" under the statutory definition, the court of appeals affirmed the district court's rulings that the lead shot was also hazardous waste as a matter of law and that whether the clay targets were hazardous waste could not be decided on summary judgment because disputed issues of material fact existed.] . . . .

Notes and Questions

1. The Connecticut Coastal Fishermen's Association is a private entity. Why was it able to bring this case? [*citizen suit*] What was the consequence of the Second Circuit's resolution of the RCRA issues in the appeal?

2. Section 1004(27) of RCRA provides a detailed definition of "solid waste." Why did EPA think it necessary to add a regulatory definition that is different from the statutory definition? [*Clarity*]

3. Which definition of *solid waste* includes a broader range of materials? Which definition applies to a broader range of regulatory requirements and enforcement options?

As the *Connecticut Coastal Fishermen's* opinion described, only material within the regulatory definition of solid waste is subject to the extensive cradle-to-grave regulations that govern the generation, treatment, storage, and disposal of hazardous waste. Thus the regulatory definition deserves a closer look.

Regulations of the Environmental Protection Agency

Code of Federal Regulations, Title 40 (2015)

§ 261.2 Definition of solid waste.

(a)

(1) A solid waste is any discarded material that is not excluded under [several other regulations].

(2)

(i) A discarded material is any material which is:

(A) Abandoned, as explained in paragraph (b) of this section; or

(B) Recycled, as explained in paragraph (c) of this section; or

(C) Considered inherently waste-like, as explained in paragraph (d) of this section; or

(D) A military munition identified as a solid waste [because of the way it was handled, which does not include being used or detonated for training or other intended purposes] . . . .

. . . .

(b) Materials are solid waste if they are abandoned by being:

(1) Disposed of; or

(2) Burned or incinerated; or

(3) Accumulated, stored, or treated (but not recycled) before or in lieu of being abandoned by being disposed of, burned or incinerated; or

(4) Sham recycled, as explained in paragraph (g) of this section.

(c) Materials are solid wastes if they are recycled — or accumulated, stored, or treated before recycling — [in certain specified ways] . . . .

. . . .

(d) Inherently waste-like materials. The following materials are solid wastes when they are recycled in any manner: [The regulation lists several specific types of waste] . . . .

. . . .

(g) Sham recycling. A hazardous secondary material found to be sham recycled is considered discarded and a solid waste. Sham recycling is recycling that is not legitimate recycling as defined in § 260.43.

Notes and Questions

1. Because EPA's definition of solid waste for RCRA Subtitle C purposes is so consequential, it has frequently been challenged. EPA has tweaked the definition repeatedly, sometimes in response to the outcomes of lawsuits. The version excerpted above is as of March 2016 and includes changes that became effective on July 13, 2015. *See* 80 Fed. Reg. 1774 (Jan. 13, 2015). As you read the cases that follow, be aware that the rules at issue in those cases may be different from the rule excerpted above.

2. Note the structure of EPA's regulatory definition, which begins with the general and becomes progressively more specific. First, the rule says that a solid waste is "discarded" material (why?), then gives four ways in which a material can be discarded, then elaborates (with cross-references) on each of those four. The definition also has a recursive quality, because a material cannot be hazardous waste unless it is solid waste, but the definition of solid waste only applies to materials that are both discarded and regulated as "hazardous" under RCRA Subtitle C. Thus, recycled paper — even if it might otherwise fit the regulatory definition of solid waste — is outside that definition because recycled paper is not hazardous. 40 C.F.R. § 261.1(b)(1).

3. A discarded material is also not solid waste under EPA's regulatory definition if another section of the RCRA regulations excludes that material from the definition. *See* 40 C.F.R. § 261.2(a)(1) (excerpted above). The regulations provide two types of exclusion. First, certain classes of materials that would otherwise fit the definition are excluded on a categorical basis. *Id.* § 261.4. Most, but not all, of these exclusions are required by the statute itself, such as the exclusions of sewage sludge and irrigation return flows, p. 648, above. Second, on a case-by-case basis EPA may grant variances from the definition of solid waste for materials being recycled that would otherwise be considered solid wastes, provided the applicant for a variance can satisfy the applicable criteria. *See id.* §§ 260.30–260.34.

4. It makes sense that material that has been "abandoned," 40 C.F.R. § 261.2(a)(2)(A), should be considered discarded. (Can you see why EPA included subsection 261.2(b)(3) in its description of when a material is abandoned?) So too for material that is "inherently waste-like," *id.* § 261.2(a)(2)(C). These issues can be disputed — recall that in *Connecticut Coastal Fishermen's* Remington argued (and EPA agreed) that the lead shot and clay target fragments deposited at the firing range were not "abandoned" materials and therefore were not "solid waste." The most interesting and contested aspects of EPA's regulatory definition of solid waste, however, have arisen from EPA's efforts to apply RCRA Subtitle C regulations to materials being recycled.

Consider, for example, the metal, plastic, and glass containers you toss in your recycling bin. From your perspective, you are disposing of them. But they are not destined for a landfill or incinerator. From the perspective of the facility that acquires them, your discarded containers are raw materials to be made into some other product. If that facility used virgin raw materials to manufacture its products, the raw materials would never be considered "waste." So why should EPA ever regulate recycled hazardous materials as "waste"?

The answer comes from contemplating *hazardous* materials generated and used on an industrial scale in complex, multi-pronged processes. Some methods of handling materials that might be characterized as "recycling" (say, extracting lead from large used batteries) may entail the same environmental harms and public health risks that result from materials handling methods that look more like "storage" or "disposal" of waste (say, allowing lead to spill on the ground and leach into water supplies). You will see several examples of the consequences of unregulated recycling processes in Chapter 9, which describes the Superfund program. On the other hand, EPA has not found it desirable to regulate under RCRA Subtitle C *all* hazardous materials that are recycled. After all, properly recycling hazardous materials can reduce the amount of hazardous waste, and its attendant risks, that must be managed. Therefore some recycled material is *not* within the regulatory definition of solid waste.

EPA defines a material as "recycled" if it is "used, reused or reclaimed." 40 C.F.R. § 261.1(c)(7). For recycled material to avoid being considered solid waste, the recycling must be "legitimate"—it must provide a useful contribution to a recycling process that produces a valuable output. *Id.* § 260.43. Sham recycling—such as using more material than is needed to produce the output, or using material to produce a useless or ineffective output—is considered a form of abandonment, and the material being sham recycled is solid waste. *Id.* §§ 261.2(b)(4), (g).

Even if recycling is legitimate, however, some recycled material *is* within the regulatory definition of solid waste. Solid waste includes certain materials that are recycled by being: (1) used in a manner constituting disposal, e.g., applied directly to the land; (2) burned for energy recovery; (3) reclaimed, i.e., regenerated or processed to recover a usable product; or (4) speculatively accumulated (described in the next paragraph). 40 C.F.R. § 261.2(c)(1)–(4); *see also id.* 261.1(c)(4) (defining "reclaimed"). The definition includes a chart showing which classes of materials are solid waste if recycled in each of these four ways. *Id.* § 261.2(c) Table 1.

What does it mean to "speculatively accumulate" a waste material? Recall that RCRA regulates not only treatment and disposal of hazardous waste but also *storage.* Imagine that the operator of a facility accumulates—keeps—material that would be hazardous waste unless it is recycled. The operator claims that the material will be recycled someday, and therefore the facility need not comply with the hazardous waste storage regulations. But the material just keeps on piling up indefinitely. To close this potential loophole, EPA categorizes such accumulated material as solid waste unless the person accumulating the material shows that the material can be recycled and that during each year an amount equal to at least three-quarters of the material on hand at the beginning of each year is actually recycled (or sent to a recycler). 40 C.F.R. § 262.1(c)(8).

We have thus summarized EPA's current regulations defining whether recycled material is or is not solid waste. The road to today's regulations, however, was anything but smooth, as the following opinion demonstrates.

American Mining Congress v. United States Environmental Protection Agency
824 F.2d 1177 (D.C. Cir. 1987)

Recycled industrial materials

Judge STARR:

. . . . Petitioners . . . challenge regulations promulgated by EPA that amend the definition of "solid waste" to establish and define the agency's authority to regulate secondary materials reused within an industry's ongoing production process. In plain English, petitioners maintain that EPA has exceeded its regulatory authority in seeking to bring materials that are not discarded or otherwise disposed of within the compass of "waste."

. . . .

Congress' "overriding concern" in enacting RCRA was to establish the framework for a national system to insure the safe management of hazardous waste. In passing RCRA, Congress expressed concern over the "rising tide" in scrap, discarded, and waste materials. 42 U.S.C. § 6901(a)(2). As the statute itself puts it, Congress was concerned with the need "to reduce the amount of waste and unsalvageable materials and to provide for proper and economical solid waste disposal practices." Id. § 6901(a)(4) . . . .

. . . EPA's authority [under RCRA subtitle C], however, extends only to the regulation of "hazardous waste." Because "hazardous waste" is defined as a subset of "solid waste," the scope of EPA's jurisdiction is limited to those materials that constitute "solid waste." That pivotal term is defined by RCRA as

> any garbage, refuse, sludge from a waste treatment plant, water supply treatment plant, or air pollution control facility *and other discarded material,* including solid, liquid, semisolid or contained gaseous material, resulting from industrial, commercial, mining, and agricultural operations, and from community activities. . . .

42 U.S.C. § 6903(27) (emphasis added). As will become evident, this case turns on the meaning of the phrase, "and other discarded material," contained in the statute's definitional provisions.

EPA's interpretation of "solid waste" has evolved over time . . . .

. . . .

[The court described EPA's 1980 interim rule defining solid waste, an amended rule that EPA proposed in 1983, and the final rule that EPA adopted in 1985 after considering comments on its 1983 proposal.] Under the final rule, materials are considered "solid waste" if they are abandoned by being disposed of, burned, or incinerated; or stored, treated, or accumulated before or in lieu of those activities. In addition, certain recycling activities fall within EPA's definition. EPA determines whether a material is a RCRA solid waste when it is recycled by examining both the material or substance itself and the recycling activity involved. The final rule identifies five categories of "secondary materials" (spent materials, sludges, by-products, commercial chemical products, and scrap metal). These "secondary materials" constitute "solid waste" when they are disposed of; burned for energy recovery or used to produce a fuel; reclaimed; or accumulated speculatively. Under the final rule, if a material constitutes "solid waste," it is subject to RCRA regulation unless it is directly reused as an ingredient or as an effective substitute for a commercial product, or is returned as a raw material substitute to its original manufacturing process . . . . In either case, the material must not first be "reclaimed" (processed to recover a usable product or regenerated). EPA exempts these activities "because they are like ordinary usage of commercial products."

Petitioners, American Mining Congress ("AMC") and American Petroleum Institute ("API"), challenge the scope of EPA's final rule. Relying upon the statutory definition of "solid waste," petitioners contend that EPA's authority under RCRA is limited to controlling materials that are discarded or intended for discard. They argue that EPA's reuse and recycle rules, as applied to in-process secondary materials, regulate materials that have not been discarded, and therefore exceed EPA's jurisdiction.

To understand petitioners' claims, a passing familiarity with the nature of their industrial processes is required.

Petroleum. Petroleum refineries vary greatly both in respect of their products and their processes. Most of their products, however, are complex mixtures of hydrocarbons produced through a number of interdependent and sometimes repetitious processing steps. In general, the refining process starts by "distilling" crude oil into various hydrocarbon streams or "fractions." The "fractions" are then subjected to a number of processing steps. Various hydrocarbon materials derived from virtually all stages of processing are combined or blended in order to produce products such as gasoline, fuel oil, and lubricating oils. Any hydrocarbons that are not usable in a particular form or state are returned to an appropriate stage in the refining process so they can eventually be used. Likewise, the hydrocarbons and materials which escape from a refinery's production vessels are gathered and, by a complex retrieval system, returned to appropriate parts of the refining process. Under EPA's final rule, this reuse and recycling of materials is subject to regulation under RCRA.

Mining. In the mining industry, primary metals production involves the extraction of fractions of a percent of a metal from a complex mineralogical matrix (i.e., the natural material in which minerals are embedded). Extractive metallurgy proceeds incrementally . . . . [M]aterials are reprocessed in order to remove as much of the pure metal as possible from the natural ore. Under EPA's final rule, this reprocessed ore and the metal derived from it constitute "solid waste." What is more, valuable metal-bearing and mineral-bearing dusts are often released in processing a particular metal. The mining facility typically recaptures, recycles, and reuses these dusts, frequently in production processes different from the one from which the dusts were originally emitted. The challenged regulations encompass this reprocessing, to the mining industry's dismay.

Against this factual backdrop, we now examine the legal issues presented by petitioners' challenge.

We observe at the outset of our inquiry that EPA's interpretation of the scope of its authority under RCRA has been unclear and unsteady . . . . Under settled doctrine, "an agency interpretation of a relevant provision which conflicts with the agency's earlier interpretation is 'entitled to considerably less deference' than a consistently held agency view."

Because the issue is one of statutory interpretation, ...

. . . .

[w]e . . . begin our inquiry with the first step of _Chevron's_ analysis: did Congress clearly intend to limit EPA's regulatory jurisdiction to materials disposed of or abandoned, as opposed to materials reused within an ongoing production process? . . . .

. . . .

. . . Congress . . . granted EPA power to regulate "solid waste." Congress specifically defined "solid waste" as "discarded material." EPA then defined "discarded material" to include materials destined for reuse in an industry's ongoing production processes. The challenge to EPA's jurisdictional reach is founded, again, on the proposition that in-process secondary materials are outside the bounds of EPA's lawful authority. Nothing has been discarded, the argument goes, and thus RCRA jurisdiction remains untriggered.

The first step in statutory interpretation is, of course, an analysis of the language itself. In pursuit of Congress' intent, we "start with the assumption that the legislative purpose is expressed by the ordinary meaning of the words used." . . . . Here, Congress defined "solid waste" as "discarded material." The ordinary, plain-English meaning of the word "discarded" is "disposed of," "thrown away" or "abandoned." Encompassing materials retained for immediate reuse within the scope of "discarded material" strains, to say the least, the everyday usage of that term.

. . . .

. . . [A] complete analysis of the statutory term "discarded" calls for more than resort to the ordinary, everyday meaning of the specific language at hand. For, "the sense in which [a term] is used in a statute must be determined by reference to the purpose of the particular legislation." The statutory provision cannot properly be torn from the law of which it is a part; context and structure are, as in examining any legal instrument, of substantial import in the interpretive exercise.

. . . [T]he broad objectives of RCRA are "to promote the protection of health and the environment and to conserve valuable material and energy resources. . . ." But that goal is of majestic breadth, and it is difficult . . . to pour meaning into a highly specific term by resort to grand purposes. Somewhat more specifically, we have seen that RCRA was enacted in response to Congressional findings that the "rising tide of scrap, discarded, and waste materials" generated by consumers and increased industrial production has presented heavily populated urban communities with "serious financial, management, intergovernmental, and technical problems in the disposal of solid wastes." In light of this problem, Congress determined that "federal action through financial and technical assistance and leadership in the development, demonstration, and application of new and improved methods and processes to reduce the amount of waste and unsalvageable materials and to provide for proper and economical solid waste disposal practices was necessary." Also animating Congress were its findings that "disposal of solid and hazardous waste" without careful planning and management presents a danger to human health and the environment; that methods to "separate usable materials from solid waste" should be employed; and that usable energy can be produced from solid waste.

The question we face, then, is whether, in light of the National Legislature's expressly stated objectives and the underlying problems that motivated it to enact RCRA in the first instance, Congress was using the term "discarded" in its ordinary sense—"disposed of" or "abandoned"—or whether Congress was using it in a much more open-ended way, so as to encompass materials no longer useful in their original capacity though destined for immediate reuse in another phase of the industry's ongoing production process.

For the following reasons, we believe the former to be the case. RCRA was enacted, as the Congressional objectives and findings make clear, in an effort to help States deal with the ever-increasing problem of solid waste disposal by encouraging the search for and use of alternatives to existing methods of disposal (including recycling) and protecting health and the environment by regulating hazardous wastes. To fulfill these purposes, it seems clear that EPA need not regulate "spent" materials that are recycled and reused in an ongoing manufacturing or industrial process.[11] These materials have not yet become part of the waste disposal problem; rather, *they are destined for beneficial reuse or recycling in a continuous process by the generating industry itself.*

. . . .

Our task in analyzing the statute also requires us to determine whether other provisions of RCRA shed light on the breadth with which Congress intended to define "discarded." As the Supreme Court reiterated a few years ago, in interpreting a statute, we do not . . . "construe statutory phrases in isolation; we read statutes as a whole." The structure of a statute, in short, is important in the sensitive task of divining Congress' meaning.

. . . .

EPA . . . argues that § 6924(r)(2) of RCRA implicitly authorizes the agency to regulate recycled secondary materials. That subsection . . . exempts from a general labelling requirement fuels produced from petroleum refining waste containing oil if

---

11. . . . . We . . . . fail to see how not regulating in-process secondary materials in an on-going production process will subvert RCRA's waste disposal management goals . . . .

such materials . . . are "generated and reinserted on-site into the refining process" . . . It cannot go unnoticed that this subsection can be interpreted to come into play only where the material has become "hazardous waste" by being disposed of, and then is generated and reinserted on-site into the refining process. This interpretation, needless to say, would be singularly unhelpful to the agency's case . . . . EPA asserts, however, that the more natural reading of this provision is that materials generated and reinserted on-site into the refining process can be "hazardous waste," and are exempted from the otherwise applicable labelling requirement . . . .

    . . . .

Although we frankly agree that EPA's reading of this specific provision provides some support for its construction of RCRA's reach, it is, dispassionately viewed, of marginal force. For one thing, the provision has "no application to conventional fuels made by normal refining processes from recaptured hydrocarbon materials never intended to be discarded and never discarded." And, even more significantly, § 6924 itself is a provision defining "standards applicable to owners and operators of hazardous waste treatment, storage, and disposal facilities." This strongly suggests that the labelling subsection is directed at material which has indeed become hazardous waste, has reached a hazardous waste treatment facility, and is being recycled at that point.[16] . . . .

    . . . .

After this mind-numbing journey through RCRA, we return to the provision that is, after all, the one before us for examination. And that definitional section, we believe, indicates clear Congressional intent to limit EPA's authority. First, the definition of "solid waste" is situated in a section containing thirty-nine separate, defined terms. This is definitional specificity of the first order. The very care evidenced by Congress in defining RCRA's scope certainly suggests that Congress was concerned about delineating and thus cabining EPA's jurisdictional reach.

Second, the statutory definition of "solid waste" is quite specific. Although Congress well knows how to use broad terms and broad definitions, . . . the definition here is carefully crafted with specificity. It contains three specific terms and then sets forth the broader term, "other discarded material." That definitional structure brings to mind a long-standing canon of statutory construction, *ejusdem generis*. Under that familiar canon, where general words follow the enumeration of particular classes of

---

16. The dissent's argument that § 6924(q)(2)(A), which excepts from the labelling requirement of subsection (r) "petroleum refinery wastes containing oil which are converted into petroleum coke at the same facility at which such wastes were generated," is rendered a nullity by our interpretation of § 6924(r) demonstrates, with all respect, confusion with regard to this complex statute. Under our interpretation, the labelling requirement can indeed be applied to materials generated (presumably in a recycling procedure) on-site at a hazardous waste treatment facility. The exemption contained in § 6924(q)(2)(A) is fully consistent with this interpretation. It allows one particular type of recycled waste—petroleum refinery wastes containing oil which are converted into petroleum coke—to be excepted from the labelling requirement. Section 6924(q)(2)(A) thus does not "go without saying" under our interpretation of § 6924(r).

things, the general words are most naturally construed as applying only to things of the same general class as those enumerated . . . . Here, the three particular classes— garbage, refuse, and sludge from a waste treatment plant, water supply treatment plant, or air pollution control facility—contain materials that clearly fit within the ordinary, everyday sense of "discarded." It is most sensible to conclude that Congress, in adding the concluding phrase "other discarded material," meant to grant EPA authority over similar types of waste, but not to open up the federal regulatory reach of an entirely new category of materials, i.e., materials neither disposed of nor abandoned, but passing in a continuous stream or flow from one production process to another.

In sum, our analysis of the statute reveals clear Congressional intent to extend EPA's authority only to materials that are truly discarded, disposed of, thrown away, or abandoned. EPA nevertheless submits that the legislative history evinces a contrary intent . . . .

. . . .

. . . EPA argues that the 1984 legislative history of RCRA amendments ratifies the agency's interpretation. The agency relies heavily on the following passage from the Report of the House Committee on Energy and Commerce, which states:

> This proposed section of the bill amends [Section 6921] of RCRA to require the Administrator to issue regulations regarding use, reuse, recycling, and reclamation of hazardous wastes. This provision is intended to reaffirm the Agency's existing authority to regulate as [sic] hazardous waste to the extent it may be necessary to protect human health and the environment. The Committee affirms that RCRA already provides regulatory authority over *these activities* (which authority the Agency has exercised to a limited degree) and in this provision is amending to clarify that materials being used, reused, recycled, or reclaimed can indeed be solid and hazardous wastes and that these various recycling activities may constitute hazardous waste treatment, storage, or disposal.

H.R. Rep. No. 198, 98th Cong., 2d Sess. at 46 (1984) (emphasis added). This language is ambiguous at best. The Report refers to the agency's existing authority to regulate hazardous waste, which . . . renders EPA's argument circular. It is only in the context of "these activities"—regulation of "hazardous waste"—that the Report states that materials being used, reused, recycled, or reclaimed can be solid and hazardous wastes. Moreover, the Conference Report accompanying the bill enacted into law states: "The Conference substitute does not include the House provision on the use, reuse, recycling, and reclamation of hazardous waste. EPA has the authority to regulate such activities and an explicit mandate is not necessary." Thus, with the exception of one passing phrase, which seems to us of limited probative value, EPA is unable to point to any portion of the legislative history which supports its expansive and counterintuitive interpretation of the pivotal term, "discarded."

To the contrary, a fair reading of the legislative history reveals intimations of an intent to regulate under RCRA only materials that have truly been discarded . . . . Most significantly, in discussing its choice of the words "discarded materials" to define "solid waste," the House Committee stated:

> Not only solid wastes, but also liquid and contained gaseous wastes, semi-solid wastes and sludges are the subjects of this legislation. Waste itself is a misleading word in the context of the committee's activity. *Much industrial and agricultural waste is reclaimed or put to new use and is therefore not a part of the discarded materials disposal problem the committee addresses.*

H.R. Rep. No. 1491, 94th Cong., 2d Sess. at 2 (emphasis added) . . . . Throughout the Report, the Committee refers time and again to the problem motivating the enactment of RCRA as the disposal of waste.

. . . .

. . . [W]e are satisfied that the legislative history, rather than evincing Congress' intent to define "discarded" to include in-process secondary materials employed in an ongoing manufacturing process, confirms that the term was employed by the Article I branch in its ordinary, everyday sense.

We are constrained to conclude that, in light of the language and structure of RCRA, the problems animating Congress to enact it, and the relevant portions of the legislative history, Congress clearly and unambiguously expressed its intent that "solid waste" (and therefore EPA's regulatory authority) be limited to materials that are "discarded" by virtue of being disposed of, abandoned, or thrown away. While we do not lightly overturn an agency's reading of its own statute, we are persuaded that by regulating in-process secondary materials, EPA has acted in contravention of Congress' intent. Accordingly, the petition for review is

Granted.

Judge MIKVA, dissenting:

The court today strains to overturn the Environmental Protection Agency's interpretation of the Resource Conservation and Recovery Act to authorize the regulation of certain recycled industrial materials. Under today's decision, the EPA is prohibited from regulating in-process secondary materials that contribute to the ominous problem that Congress sought to eradicate by passing the RCRA. In my opinion, the EPA has adequately demonstrated that its interpretation is a reasonable construction of an ambiguous term in a statute committed to the agency's administration. We therefore are obliged to defer to the agency's interpretation under the principles of *[Chevron]* . . . .

I agree with the majority that the case turns on the definition of solid waste as "discarded material" in RCRA. On its face, this definition would not necessarily encompass the in-process secondary materials at issue in this case. However, the EPA has pointed us to an important statutory provision and a key passage from the legislative history that strongly support the agency's interpretation. At a minimum, they establish that the issue is ambiguous, so that we must defer to the agency's solution if it is reasonable.

Section 6924 of RCRA, when carefully parsed, provides direct support for the EPA's interpretation. Two provisions in section 6924 are especially relevant to EPA's claim.

Section 6924(r)(2) provides an exemption from RCRA's general labelling requirement for materials "generated and reinserted onsite into the refining process." The accompanying legislative history specifies that the provision is a special and narrow exemption that "applies only to wastes generated on-site in the refining process itself." The clear implication of this statutory provision is that RCRA establishes the EPA's general jurisdiction to regulate wastes generated on-site but cabins that power in one particular area. If, as the majority contends, these materials were clearly meant to be beyond EPA's regulatory scope anyway, this exemption would be unnecessary.

The majority acknowledges the "marginal force" of the EPA's reading of section 6924(r)(2). That would appear to be an implicit concession that the provision at least provokes ambiguity about the meaning of solid waste under RCRA. The majority then tries to finesse its way around the provision by claiming that it applies only to materials that already have been abandoned by the manufacturer and transported to a hazardous waste treatment facility. A neighboring provision, however, plainly demonstrates the inadequacy of the majority's explanation. Section 6924(q)(2)(A) specifies that subsection (r), the labeling provision, normally "shall not apply to petroleum refinery wastes containing oil which are converted into petroleum coke *at the same facility at which such wastes were generated.*" (emphasis added.) This provision excepts from the labelling requirements one particular kind of material that is generated on-site and then reintroduced into the refining process. The majority's interpretation of subsection (r) makes nonsense of Congress' carefully drawn exception. If subsection (r) were intended to apply only to abandoned materials, 6924(q)(2)(A) would go without saying. The provision therefore indicates that subsection (r) in particular, and RCRA in general, are intended to reach certain materials recycled on-site.

More generally, 6924(q)(2)(A) refers directly to wastes that are generated in the refining process and then put to further beneficial use by being converted to petroleum coke. It provides specific textual evidence that RCRA's definition of the pivotal term "waste" comprises at least some materials that are generated in a primary process and then recycled into another on-site process.

The majority attempts to square its position with the apparently irreconcilable directive in § 6924(q)(2)(A) by arguing that "under our interpretation, the labelling requirement can indeed be applied to materials generated (presumably in a recycling procedure) on-site at a hazardous waste treatment facility." The majority apparently is asserting that Congress' use of the term "wastes" in 6024(q)(2)(A) [sic] was meant to refer only to wastes generated from other wastes. This highly conclusory and unnatural reading demonstrates that the majority has lost its way through this complex statute. The complexity of a statute does not give courts additional leeway to ignore the deference due an agency interpretation; on the contrary, when the complexity stems from technical definitions and procedures, that deference is enhanced.

The legislative history of the 1984 RCRA amendments also cuts firmly in EPA's favor. The version of the bill passed by the House contained a section directing the agency to regulate hazardous wastes that are used, reused, recycled, or reclaimed. (This provision eventually was deleted on the ground that RCRA already provided the EPA with authority to regulate these materials.) The report accompanying this provision explained:

> This provision is intended to reaffirm the Agency's existing authority to regulate as [sic] hazardous waste to the extent it may be necessary to protect human health and the environment. The Committee affirms that RCRA already provides regulatory authority over these activities (which authority the Agency has exercised to a limited degree) and in this provision is amending to clarify that materials being used, reused, recycled, or reclaimed can indeed be solid and hazardous wastes and that these various recycling activities may constitute hazardous waste treatment, storage, or disposal.

H.R. Rep. No. 198, 98th Cong., 2d Sess. (1984) (emphasis added).

It is hard to see how the majority can hold to its position that on-site recycled materials can never be waste in the face of this clear legislative history to the contrary. The majority grudgingly allows that this language is "ambiguous at best," apparently forgetting that EPA has only to demonstrate ambiguity to earn its reasonableness review. The majority then posits the theory that the legislative history pertains only to materials that already have been abandoned and thereby become hazardous waste. This interpretation is not credible. The legislative history states that materials being recycled can be solid and hazardous wastes. If the materials referred to already were hazardous wastes, this statement would be absurd. The statement rather indicates that recycled materials can constitute solid waste where they present the dangers to human health and the environment that RCRA is designed to control.

. . . .

I acknowledge that the majority cites other evidence that casts some doubt on the agency's interpretation. But this is a concession that the agency can afford, while the majority cannot. EPA need demonstrate only that its definition of solid waste does not clearly contradict congressional intent. Section 6924 as well as the key piece of legislative history cited above provide ample evidence for that modest proposition. *Chevron* therefore requires us to give effect to the agency interpretation if it is reasonable.

In my opinion, the EPA's interpretation of solid waste is completely reasonable in light of the language, policies, and legislative history of RCRA. Congress had broad remedial objectives in mind when it enacted RCRA, most notably to "regulat[e] the treatment, storage, transportation, and disposal of hazardous wastes which have adverse effects on the environment." 42 U.S.C. § 6902(4). The disposal problem Congress was combatting encompassed more than just abandoned materials. RCRA makes this clear with its definition of the central statutory term "disposal":

> the discharge, deposit, injection, dumping, spilling, leaking, or placing of any solid waste or hazardous waste into or on any land or water so that such solid waste or hazardous waste or any constituent thereof may enter the environment or be emitted into the air or discharged into any waters, including ground waters.

42 U.S.C. § 6903(3). This definition clearly encompasses more than the everyday meaning of disposal, which is a "discarding or throwing away." Webster's Third International Dictionary 654 (2d ed. 1981). The definition is functional: waste is disposed under this provision if it is put into contact with land or water in such a way as to pose the risks to health and environment that animated Congress to pass RCRA . . . .

Faithful to RCRA's functional approach, EPA reasonably concluded that regulation of certain in-process secondary materials was necessary to carry out its mandate. The materials at issue in this case can pose the same risks as abandoned wastes, whether or not the manufacturer intends eventually to put them to further beneficial use. As the agency explained, "simply because a waste is likely to be recycled will not ensure that it will not be spilled or leaked before recycling occurs." The storage, transportation, and even recycling of in-process secondary materials can cause severe environmental harm. Indeed, the EPA documented environmental disasters caused by the handling or storage of such materials. It also pointed out the risk of damage from spills or leaks when certain in-process secondary materials are placed on land or in underground product storage.

Moreover, the agency's action is carefully aligned with Congress' functional approach to problems of waste disposal . . . . EPA stressed that "to determine if a secondary material is a RCRA solid waste when recycled, one must examine both the material and the recycling activity involved. A consequence is that the same material can be a waste if it is recycled in certain ways, but would not be a waste if it is recycled in other ways." Thus, the agency has sought to regulate these materials only when they present the risks Congress was combatting in RCRA.

. . . .

. . . [T]he EPA has interpreted solid waste in a manner that seems to expand the everyday usage of the word "discarded." Its conclusion, however, is fully supportable in light of the statutory scheme and legislative history of RCRA. The agency concluded that certain on-site recycled materials constitute an integral part of the waste disposal problem. This judgment is grounded in the EPA's technical expertise and is adequately supported by evidence in the record. The majority nevertheless reverses the agency because it believes that the materials at issue "have not yet become part of the wast[e] disposal problem." This declaration is nothing more than a substitution of the majority's own conclusions for the sound technical judgment of the EPA. The EPA's interpretation is a reasonable construction of an ambiguous statutory provision and should be upheld . . . .

I dissent.

Notes and Questions

1. According to the majority, at which step of the two-step *Chevron* analysis did EPA's interpretation of "solid waste" fail? Did EPA interpret RCRA in a manner inconsistent with unambiguous congressional meaning, or did EPA unreasonably interpret an ambiguous statutory provision?

2. How did the majority and the dissenting judge disagree about the underlying statutory purposes of RCRA? How did that disagreement affect their respective analyses of the challenged EPA rule?

3. EPA and the dissenting judge argued that two subsections of RCRA § 3004, 42 U.S.C. §§ 6924(r)(2) and (q)(2)(B), demonstrated that Congress intended that recycled secondary materials could be regulated as solid waste and thus hazardous waste. The majority interpreted these subsections differently and concluded that, in any event, they did not change the statute's general definition of solid waste. Which interpretation of these subsections is more persuasive? If EPA and the dissent interpreted these subsections correctly, would it follow that EPA had the regulatory authority that EPA claimed? Or do these subsections simply show that for a complicated statute like RCRA, it is hard to draft every last subsection in an entirely coherent way? But in that case, why shouldn't the court defer to EPA's interpretation? Does it matter that these subsections were added in the 1984 Hazardous and Solid Waste Amendments rather than included in the original 1976 enactment?   *Dissent ≠ Law*

4. How much did *American Mining Congress* limit EPA's regulatory authority under RCRA? The D.C. Circuit considered that issue in a later challenge to another EPA regulation.

American Petroleum Inst. v. United States Environmental Protection Agency

216 F.3d 50 (D.C. Cir. 2000)

PER CURIAM:

. . . .

Industry petitioners, American Petroleum Institute ("API"), the Chemical Manufacturers Association ("CMA"), and Texaco, Inc. (collectively, "industry petitioners") . . . . challenge[ ] EPA's regulation under RCRA of two materials as solid waste . . . .

. . . .

In 1994 and 1998 rulemakings in pursuit of its RCRA obligations, the EPA examined the production processes of the petroleum refining industry. As pertinent to the issue before us, EPA considered whether to exclude from the definition of solid waste two secondary materials: oil-bearing wastewaters generated by the petroleum refining industry and recovered oil produced by the petrochemical manufacturing industry. EPA determined that oil-bearing wastewaters are solid waste for purposes of RCRA regulation, and that recovered oil from petrochemical facilities is excluded from the definition of solid waste only when specified conditions are met. Industry petitioners challenge these conclusions.

B. Oil-Bearing Wastewaters

In petroleum refining, impurities are removed and usable hydrocarbon fractions are isolated from crude oil feedstock. Large quantities of water are used, and the resulting wastewaters contain a small percentage of residual oil. These "oilbearing wastewaters" are destined for ultimate discharge, but only after a three-step treatment process is first applied. The first phase of treatment, known as "primary treatment," removes certain materials including the oil. This phase has at least two beneficial consequences: (1) it meets a Clean Water Act requirement that refineries remove oil from their wastewater, and (2) it allows refineries to recover a not insignificant quantity of oil (which industry claims can range up to 1,000 barrels a day at certain refineries) which is cycled back into the refinery production process.

Industry petitioners and EPA disagree over when these wastewaters become discarded for purposes of the solid waste definition. While no one disputes that discard has certainly occurred by the time the wastewaters move into the later phases of treatment, the question is whether discard happens before primary treatment, allowing regulation of wastewater as solid waste at that point, or not until primary treatment is complete and oil has been recovered for further processing.

EPA's initial proposal excluded oil-bearing wastewaters. However, it changed its mind in 1994 and concluded that even before the oil is recovered in primary treatment, "the wastewaters are discarded materials and hence solid wastes subject to regulation under RCRA." EPA stated: "Primary wastewater treatment operations exist to treat plant wastewaters." It noted that the percentage of oil in the wastewater is very small and "not significant in the context of a refinery's overall production activities," and that the Clean Water Act mandates such treatment. For these stated reasons, EPA concluded that "clearly, wastewater treatment is the main purpose of the systems in question, and any oil recovery is of secondary import."

EPA restated its conclusion in its subsequent 1995 Proposed Rule and retained it in the Final Rule. The actual regulation does not mention wastewaters. But by not being excluded, all wastewaters including oil-bearing wastewaters are considered to fall under EPA's general regulatory definition of solid waste.

Whether a material has been "discarded," subjecting it to RCRA regulation, is a question we have considered in four prior cases. First, in *American Mining Congress v. EPA*, 824 F.2d 1177 (D.C.Cir.1987) ("*AMC I*"), we held that the term "discarded" conforms to its plain meaning. Thus, items that are "disposed of, abandoned, or thrown away" are discarded. *AMC I* concluded that "in-process secondary materials," that is, materials "destined for immediate reuse in another phase of [an] industry's ongoing production process," are not discarded under RCRA. We recently reaffirmed that holding . . . [and] reiterated that EPA cannot regulate as solid waste secondary materials "destined for reuse as part of a continuous industrial process" that is therefore "not abandoned or thrown away."

At the other end of the spectrum we have held that a material that has been "indisputably 'discarded'" can, of course, be subjected to regulation as solid waste. Where a material was "delivered to [a metals reclamation] facility not as part of an 'ongoing manufacturing or industrial process' within 'the generating industry,' but as part of a mandatory waste treatment plan prescribed by EPA," we concluded that a material was not precluded from being classified by EPA as a solid waste.

A material somewhere between the extremes of ongoing production and indisputable discard was addressed in *American Mining Congress v. EPA*, 907 F.2d 1179 (D.C.Cir.1990) ("*AMC II*"). Industry petitioners claimed that sludges from wastewater stored in surface impoundments, which "may" later be reclaimed for treatment, could not be regulated. We disagreed and deferred to EPA's determination that such sludges have been discarded. Nothing, we reasoned, prevents EPA from regulating as "solid wastes" materials managed in land disposal units which are no longer part of an industrial process.

Industry petitioners rely primarily on *AMC I*. They first contend that the oil-bearing wastewaters at issue in this case cannot be classified as discarded because *AMC I* already said they are not. We disagree. True, API's brief in *AMC I* characterized oil-bearing wastewaters as part of an ongoing industrial process. Our opinion in *AMC I*, however, did not decide this question. We only held that in-process secondary materials are not "discarded" so that EPA could not regulate them; we did not address the discard status of any of the particular materials discussed in the briefs.

Industry petitioners also contend that . . . oil-bearing wastewaters cannot be regulated because they are . . . unquestionably in-process materials not yet discarded. Alternately, even if the status of oil-bearing wastewaters is not so plain, petitioners assert that EPA's conclusion is arbitrary and capricious because it is not based on reasoned decisionmaking. Petitioners emphasize that primary treatment yields valuable oil that is reinserted into the refining processes in a continuous operation. They also claim that oil recovery operations began long before Clean Water Act regulations required it. In sum, they contend that oil recovery in primary treatment is a part of in-process oil production.

At bottom, the parties disagree over the proper characterization of primary treatment. Is it simply a step in the act of discarding? Or is it the last step in a production process before discard? . . . .

It may be permissible for EPA to determine that the predominant purpose of primary treatment is discard. Legal abandonment of property is premised on determining the intent to abandon, which requires an inquiry into facts and circumstances. Where an industrial by-product may be characterized as discarded or "in process" material, EPA's choice of characterization is entitled to deference. However, the record must reflect that EPA engaged in reasoned decisionmaking to decide which characterization is appropriate. The record in this case is deficient in that regard. EPA has noted two purposes of primary treatment and concludes, "[c]learly, wastewater treatment is the main purpose." As English teachers have long taught, a conclusion is not "clear" or "obvious" merely because one says so.

EPA points out that primary treatment only recovers a small amount of oil relative to the entire output of a typical refining facility. However, the oil is still valuable and usable, so that reason alone cannot show discard. The rock of a diamond mine may only contain a tiny portion of precious carbon, but that is enough to keep miners busy . . . .

EPA also notes that the Clean Water Act requires primary treatment before discharge. If refiners got nothing from primary treatment, this might be a compelling rationale because it would be hard to explain why, other than to discard, refiners would engage in a costly treatment activity with no economic benefits. However, petitioners claim they would engage in primary treatment regardless of the treatment standards in order to recover the desired oil. EPA does not explain why this possibly valid motivation is not compelling . . . . Indeed, without further explanation, it is not inherently certain why a substance is definitively "discarded" if its possessor is continuing to process it, even though the possessor's decision to continue processing may have been influenced, or even predominantly motivated, by some external factor . . . .

In short, EPA has not set forth why it has concluded that the compliance motivation predominates over the reclamation motivation. Perhaps equally importantly it has not explained why that conclusion, even if validly reached, compels the further conclusion that the wastewater has been discarded. Therefore, because the agency has failed to provide a rational explanation for its decision, we hold the decision to be arbitrary and capricious. We therefore vacate the portion of EPA's decision declining to exclude oil-bearing wastewaters from the statutory definition of solid waste, and remand for further proceedings. We do not suggest any particular result on remand, only a reasoned one demonstrating when discard occurs if EPA wishes to assert jurisdiction.

C. Petrochemical Recovered Oil

Unlike petroleum refiners, petrochemical manufacturers do not refine crude oil but instead use refined petroleum products and other feedstocks to produce petrochemical products such as organic chemicals. These production processes can produce residual oil, known as "petrochemical recovered oil." This oil can be inserted into the petroleum refining process.

EPA crafted a regulation excluding petrochemical recovered oil from the definition of solid waste, provided that certain conditions are met. These conditions are designed to disqualify from the exclusion oil that contains non-refinable hazardous materials. EPA was concerned that if additional unneeded materials present in petrochemical recovered oil were covered by the exclusion, it would allow for the improper disposal of waste materials through adulteration. Such activity is called "sham recycling." Simply put, if extra materials are added to petrochemical recovered oil that provide no benefit to the industrial process, EPA finds this to be an act of discard under the guise of recycling. Although EPA apparently does not know if sham recycling actually occurs in this industry, it was concerned because some of the petrochemical recovered oil samples it tested were contaminated with chlorinated or other halogenated materials that were unexpected.

The EPA rule promulgated excludes from its solid waste definition "petrochemical recovered oil . . . to be inserted into the petroleum refining process . . . along with normal petroleum refinery process streams, provided [that] [t]he oil is hazardous only because it exhibits the characteristic of ignitability . . . and/or toxicity for benzene. . . ." EPA explained that the ignitability and benzene toxicity properties are typical of or very similar to basic petroleum refining feedstocks. Thus, the exclusion does not cover petrochemical recovered oil that is hazardous due to the presence of other hazardous materials. The exclusion also contains other conditions meant to help curb sham recycling, such as when petrochemical recovered oil is "speculatively accumulated before being recycled into the petroleum refining process."

Industry petitioner CMA makes one argument, premised solely on *Chevron* step one. CMA argues that EPA has no authority to regulate any petrochemical recovered oil under any circumstances because such materials are not "discarded." . . .

This *Chevron* plain meaning argument fails because EPA is correct that abandoning a material is discarding even if labeled recycling. EPA is not violating *AMC I*'s definition of discard. To the contrary, the premise of EPA's rule is sound precisely because it is meant to regulate only discarded materials. EPA can regulate material "discarded" through sham recycling even though it cannot regulate under RCRA materials that are not discarded. Speculatively accumulated recovered oil is a clear example of a condition imposed under the exclusion which shows that some petrochemical recovered oil can indeed be considered as discarded . . . . We therefore deny CMA's petition as to petrochemical recovered oil.

Notes and Questions

1. Why did EPA decide to regulate oil-bearing wastewaters and petrochemical recovered oil as hazardous waste?

2. Why did the court reject the oil industry's assertion that *AMC I* precluded regulation of its oil-bearing wastewaters as hazardous waste?

3. The court remanded to EPA the agency's "decision declining to exclude oil-bearing wastewaters" from the definition of hazardous waste. The court explicitly left EPA's options open on remand; EPA remained free to reconfirm its decision or to change its mind again. Why did the court structure the petitioners' relief in that way?

If you were an attorney in EPA's Office of General Counsel and the agency's RCRA program staff informed you that it was important to regulate oil-bearing wastewaters as hazardous waste, what advice would you give the staff? What findings, supported by what type of evidence, would EPA need to be able to make in order to adhere to its prior decision and have the rule survive the next challenge? As it happens, in the 16 years since the *American Petroleum Institute* opinion, EPA has not accepted the D.C. Circuit's invitation to make a new decision about the exclusion of the oil-bearing wastewaters.

4. "Spent" materials are another controversial category of materials that EPA considers discarded. If you have ever cleaned a floor, you know what a "spent" solution of floor cleaner and water looks like — it is too dirty to keep using as a cleaning solution. Suppose company A purchases a substance for a certain purpose and then, after the substance becomes unfit for that purpose, sends it to company B, which uses the dirty substance for some other purpose. Did company A discard a spent material? See *Howmet Corp. v. EPA*, 614 F.3d 544 (D.C. Cir. 2010), discussed at p. 716, below.

B. Is It Hazardous Waste?

Not all solid wastes, of course, are hazardous wastes for which stringent regulation is needed to protect human health and the environment. As we saw, p. 647 above, RCRA includes a definition of hazardous waste, but it is hardly self-evident whether a particular waste satisfies the requirements of the statutory definition. 42 U.S.C. § 6903(5) (RCRA § 1004(5)). Instead, RCRA directs EPA to "develop and promulgate criteria for identifying the characteristics of hazardous waste, and for listing hazardous waste, which should be subject to the provisions of this subchapter [RCRA Subtitle C]," *id.* § 6921(a) (RCRA § 3001(a)), and then, based on these criteria, to "promulgate regulations identifying the characteristics of hazardous waste, and listing particular hazardous wastes (within the meaning of section 6903(5) of this title), which shall be subject to the provisions of this subchapter." *Id.* § 6921(b)(1) (RCRA § 3001(b)(1)).

1. Listed and Characteristic Hazardous Wastes

As § 3001 of RCRA implies, EPA's regulations include two ways of identifying a solid waste as "hazardous waste": by being specifically listed as a hazardous waste or by having one or more hazardous characteristics. The following excerpt describes generally the "listed hazardous wastes" and "characteristic hazardous wastes" regulated under Subtitle C of RCRA.

UNITED STATES ENVIRONMENTAL PROTECTION AGENCY
RCRA ORIENTATION MANUAL
(2014)

IS THE WASTE A LISTED HAZARDOUS WASTE?

. . . .

Before developing each hazardous waste listing, EPA thoroughly studies a particular wastestream and the threats that it can pose to human health and the environment. If the waste poses sufficient threat, EPA includes a precise description of that waste on one of four hazardous waste lists within the regulations.

In order to determine whether a waste should be listed in the first place, the Agency developed a set of criteria to use as a guide and a consistent frame of reference when considering listing a wastestream . . . .

. . . . The three criteria are:

- The waste typically contains toxic chemicals at levels that could pose a threat to human health and the environment if improperly managed. Such wastes are known as toxic listed wastes.

- The waste contains such dangerous chemicals that it could pose a threat to human health and the environment even when properly managed. These wastes are fatal to humans and animals even in low doses. Such wastes are known as acute hazardous wastes.

Criteria:
① contains toxic materials
② dangerous chemicals
③ exhibits characteristics of hazardous waste:
- ignitibility
- corrosive
- reactive (explosive)
- toxic

- The waste typically exhibits one of the four of specific characteristics of hazardous waste: <u>ignitability, corrosivity, reactivity, and toxicity</u>.

In addition, EPA may list a waste as hazardous, if it has cause to believe that, for some other reason, the waste typically fits within the statutory definition of hazardous waste developed by Congress.

EPA has applied the listing criteria to hundreds of specific industrial wastestreams. These wastes are grouped into . . . four lists . . . organized as follows:

- The F list — The F list includes wastes from certain common industrial and manufacturing processes. Because the processes generating these wastes can occur in different sectors of industry, the F list wastes are known as wastes from nonspecific sources. The F list is codified in the regulations in 40 CFR § 261.31.

- The K list — The K list includes wastes from specific industries. As a result, K list wastes are known as wastes from specific sources. The K list is found in 40 CFR § 261.32.

- The P list and the U list — These two lists include pure or commercial grade formulations of specific unused chemicals. Chemicals are included on the P list if they are acutely toxic. A chemical is acutely toxic if it is fatal to humans in low doses, if scientific studies have shown that it has lethal effects on experimental organisms, or if it causes serious irreversible or incapacitating illness. The U list is generally comprised of chemicals that are toxic, but also includes chemicals that display other characteristics, such as ignitability or reactivity. Both the P list and U list are codified in 40 CFR § 261.33.

Each list includes anywhere from 30 to a few hundred listed hazardous wastestreams. All of the wastes on these lists are assigned an identification number (i.e., a waste code) consisting of the letter associated with the list (i.e., F, K, P, or U) followed by three numbers. For example, wastes on the F list may be assigned a waste code ranging from F001 to F039, while wastes on the K list may be assigned a waste code ranging from K001 to K181 . . . .

. . . .

IS THE WASTE A CHARACTERISTIC HAZARDOUS WASTE?

. . . .

Characteristic wastes are wastes that exhibit measurable properties which indicate that a waste poses enough of a threat to warrant regulation as hazardous waste. EPA tried to identify characteristics that, when present in a waste, can cause death or injury to humans or lead to ecological damage. The characteristics identify both acute (near-term) and chronic (long-term) hazards, and are an essential supplement to the hazardous waste listings. For example, some wastes may not meet any listing description because they do not originate from specific industrial or process sources, but the waste may still pose threats to human health and the environment . . . .

. . . .

EPA decided that the characteristics of hazardous waste should be detectable by using a standardized test method or by applying general knowledge of the waste's properties. Given these criteria, EPA established four hazardous waste characteristics:

- Ignitability
- Corrosivity
- Reactivity
- Toxicity.

Ignitability

The ignitability characteristic identifies wastes that can readily catch fire and sustain combustion. Many paints, cleaners, and other industrial wastes pose such a hazard . . . .

Most ignitable wastes are liquid in physical form. EPA selected a flash point test as the method for determining whether a liquid waste is combustible enough to deserve regulation as hazardous. The flash point test determines the lowest temperature at which the fumes above a waste will ignite when exposed to flame. Liquid wastes with a flash point of less than 60°C (140°F) in closed-cup test are ignitable.

Many wastes in solid or nonliquid physical form (e.g., wood or paper) can also readily catch fire and sustain combustion, but EPA did not intend to regulate most of these nonliquid materials as ignitable wastes. A nonliquid waste is considered ignitable only if it can spontaneously catch fire or catch fire through friction or absorption of moisture under normal handling conditions and can burn so vigorously that it creates a hazard. Certain compressed gases are also classified as ignitable. Finally, substances meeting the DOT's definition of oxidizer are classified as ignitable wastes. Ignitable wastes carry the waste code D001 and are among some of the most common hazardous wastes. The regulations describing the characteristic of ignitability are codified in 40 CFR § 261.21.

Corrosivity

The corrosivity characteristic identifies wastes that are acidic or alkaline (basic). Such wastes can readily corrode or dissolve flesh, metal, or other materials. They are also among some of the most common hazardous wastes.

An example is waste sulfuric acid from automotive batteries. EPA uses two criteria to identify liquid and aqueous corrosive hazardous wastes. The first is a pH test. Aqueous wastes with a pH greater than or equal to 12.5 [strong bases] or less than or equal to 2 [strong acids] are corrosive. A liquid waste may also be corrosive if it has the ability to corrode steel under specific conditions . . . . Corrosive wastes carry the waste code D002. The regulations describing the corrosivity characteristic are found in 40 CFR § 261.22.

Reactivity

The reactivity characteristic identifies wastes that readily explode or undergo violent reactions or react to release toxic gases or fumes. Common examples are discarded munitions or explosives . . . .

. . . .

Wastes exhibiting the characteristic of reactivity are assigned the waste code D003. The reactivity characteristic is described in the regulations in 40 CFR § 261.23.

Toxicity

When hazardous waste is disposed of in a land disposal unit, toxic compounds or elements can leach into underground drinking water supplies and expose users of the water to hazardous chemicals and constituents. EPA developed the toxicity characteristic (TC) to identify wastes likely to leach dangerous concentrations of toxic chemicals into ground water.

In order to predict whether any particular waste is likely to leach chemicals into ground water at dangerous levels, EPA designed a lab procedure to estimate the leaching potential of waste when disposed in a municipal solid waste landfill. This lab procedure is known as the Toxicity Characteristic Leaching Procedure (TCLP).

The TCLP requires a generator to create a liquid leachate from its hazardous waste samples. This leachate would be similar to the leachate generated by a landfill containing a mixture of household and industrial wastes. Once this leachate is created via the TCLP, the waste generator must determine whether it contains any of 40 different toxic chemicals in amounts above the specified regulatory levels . . . . If the leachate sample contains a concentration above the regulatory limit for one of the specified chemicals, the waste exhibits the toxicity characteristic and carries the waste code associated with that compound or element . . . . The regulations describing the toxicity characteristic are codified in 40 CFR § 261.24, and the TC regulatory levels appear in Table 1 of that same section.

Notes and Questions

1. As the excerpt from EPA's manual suggests, the four sets of listed hazardous wastes are extensive and detailed. Here are some examples:

A variety of solvents are used in many industrial processes; for example, to serve as a medium in which chemical reactions occur or to remove grease or other residues from manufactured parts. As a solvent in use accumulates dirt or contamination, the solvent eventually becomes "spent," or unusable. Many solvents are toxic or ignitable, and therefore hazardous. Such spent solvents are classified as F wastes because they may be generated by many different industries. F005 waste, for example, includes spent "[t]oluene, methyl ethyl ketone, carbon disulfide, isobutenol, pyridine, benzene, 2-ethoxyethanol, and 2-nitropropane," among other spent solvents.

Aniline is a toxic and carcinogenic organic chemical that is used as a reactant in the production of many other chemicals. Aniline is manufactured by a chemical reaction and then separated and purified by a distillation process. After the aniline has been recovered, the material left in the still—"[d]istillation bottoms from aniline production"—is a listed hazardous waste from a specific source, K083.

Aniline itself, if discarded (e.g., by being spilled, or because a batch of aniline failed to meet manufacturing specifications) is a listed U waste, U012. By contrast, discarded strychnine is a listed P waste, P108. Strychnine is a poison registered for use (see Chapter 10, below) as a below-ground bait to control pocket gophers. It is listed as a P waste rather than as a U waste because of its acute toxicity to humans.

2. The listed and characteristic categories of hazardous waste are not mutually exclusive. A listed hazardous waste is also a characteristic hazardous waste if it displays one or more of the four hazardous characteristics (ignitability, corrosivity, reactivity, and toxicity). This may affect the regulatory requirements for treating, storing, or disposing of the hazardous waste in question.

3. The criteria for deciding whether a solid waste should be listed as hazardous waste are codified at 40 C.F.R. § 261.11. The regulation is considerably more detailed than the summary description given in the excerpt from EPA's manual. For example, the regulation lists 10 specific factors, plus a catchall factor, that EPA considers when deciding whether a waste that contains toxic constituents should be listed as a "toxic listed waste." *See* 40 C.F.R. § 261.11(a)(3)(i)–(xi) (listing factors including, among others, the concentration of the toxic constituent, its persistence and bioaccumulation, the human health and environmental effects that have resulted from mismanagement of the waste, and action taken by other agencies or regulatory programs based on the hazard posed by the waste or the constituent).

4. EPA's regulations listing hazardous wastes are, of course, subject to judicial review. As often happens when EPA exercises congressionally granted regulatory authority, some challenges have asserted that EPA's listings are underinclusive, while others have asserted that EPA's listings are overinclusive.

In the former category, environmental groups challenged EPA's decision not to list used motor oil as a hazardous waste. Congress required EPA to make a decision on "whether to list or identify used automobile and truck crankcase oil and other used oil as hazardous wastes" no later than 24 months after enactment of the 1984 HSWA amendments. 42 U.S.C. § 6935(b) (HSWA § 241(b)). In 1986, EPA decided not to list *recycled* used oil as a hazardous waste because EPA feared that the stigma of such listing would discourage recycling. An environmental organization (along with trade associations whose members were involved in hazardous waste treatment and oil refining) challenged the decision. The D.C. Circuit held that EPA's desire to avoid stigmatization and to encourage recycling were not acceptable considerations under § 3001 of RCRA. The court ordered EPA to decide whether recycled used oil meets the hazardousness criteria established pursuant to § 3001. *Hazardous Waste Treatment Council v. U.S. EPA*, 861 F.2d 270 (D.C. Cir. 1988). Four years after the court's opinion, EPA finally decided not to list *any* used motor oil (recycled or not) as hazardous waste. The environmental organization challenged that decision as well. The D.C. Circuit denied the petition for review, holding that EPA properly applied the hazardousness criteria (particularly the "toxic listed waste" factors at 40 C.F.R. § 261.11(a)(3)) and adequately explained its decision. *Natural Resources Defense Council, Inc. v. U.S. EPA*, 25 F.3d 1063 (D.C. Cir. 1994). Judge Wald dissented. Her description of the regulatory history gave some insight into the concerns that motivated Congress to enact HSWA and testified to the complexity of hazardous waste regulation:

> Over the course of the last fifteen years the EPA has repeatedly announced that it would seek listing used oil as hazardous under the RCRA. Each time it began its venture with a host of reasons arguing in favor of a decision to list, and each time it ended its rulemaking in withdrawal.

Id. at 1080. For another example of an environmental group challenge to an EPA decision against listing, see *Environmental Defense Fund v. EPA*, 210 F.3d 396 (D.C. Cir. 2000) (denying petition for review of EPA's decision not to add 14 solvent wastes to the F waste list).

By contrast, EPA's effort to list carbamate wastes and discarded carbamate products as hazardous wastes elicited a challenge from industry. Carbamates and their derivatives are used as pesticides, herbicides, and fungicides. In 1995, EPA added certain waste from carbamate manufacturing or processing to the K waste list, added 40 discarded carbamate products to the U list (for toxicity), and added 18 discarded carbamate products to the P list (for acute toxicity). Three companies and a trade association challenged most of the U and K listings. In considering the petition for review, the D.C. Circuit closely compared EPA's explanation for each listing against the 10 "listed toxic waste" factors, 40 C.F.R. § 261.11(a)(3)(i)–(x). The court vacated the challenged U listings because EPA had failed to consider all 10 of the factors. The court also vacated some of the K listings, holding that for the wastes in question EPA had not adequately identified plausible mismanagement scenarios, which is one of the factors EPA must consider, *id.* § 261.11(a)(3)(vii). *Dithiocarbamate Task Force v. EPA*, 98 F.3d 1394 (D.C. Cir. 1996).

5. Disputes may arise even after EPA has validly listed a hazardous waste. To make compliance decisions, a regulated entity must decide whether each of its waste streams fits within EPA's narrative description of a listed hazardous waste and manage the waste accordingly. If EPA's view differs, enforcement action may ensue. The following two court opinions illustrate the practicalities of compliance decisions and enforcement actions—the first with respect to an alleged characteristic waste and the second with respect to an alleged listed waste.

United States v. Mobil Oil Corp.

1997 WL 1048911 (E.D.N.Y. 1989)

Judge GLEESON:

In this action against the Mobil Oil Corporation ("Mobil"), the United States alleges that Mobil illegally treated, stored, or disposed of hazardous waste at its Port Mobil Marine Terminal ("Port Mobil") in violation of the Resource Conservation and Recovery Act ("RCRA") . . . .

BACKGROUND

A. *The Alleged Permit Violations*

Port Mobil is a petroleum receiving, storage, and distribution facility. Barges, ocean-going tankers, and other ships dock there and the petroleum products they carry are pumped into holding tanks for later distribution. The facility covers approximately 200 acres on Staten Island.

. . . Mobil operated a barge cleaning operation at Port Mobil. After the barges were unloaded, hot water was injected into their nearly empty holds. The resulting water/petroleum product mixture was siphoned from the barge and routed to one of two holding tanks at Port Mobil. In the holding tank, the water separated from the bulk of the petroleum product as the water settled to the bottom of the tank. Mobil removed the petroleum product from the top of the tank for recovery and resale. The water/petroleum mixture remaining at the bottom was drained from the tank and carried, via open concrete ditches, to an oil/water separator known as an "API separator." The API separator removed more of the petroleum product from the water, after which the water (along with any unremoved petroleum product) flowed to a concrete "separator box" adjacent to a fully lined "surface impoundment" (an artificial pond). According to Mobil, the separator box removed still more petroleum from the mixture before it was dumped into the pond.

The barge waste was not the only waste Mobil dumped into the pond: the company also dumped storm water and wastewater from a well into the pond.[3] Mobil claims that sometimes the barge waste was mixed with the other wastes before it reached the pond, and sometimes it was not.

In September 1990, the EPA promulgated the Toxicity Characteristic Rule ("TC Rule"), which added to the list of hazardous substances regulated by RCRA. Among other additions, the TC Rule defined waste containing benzene at levels in excess of .5 milligrams/liter ("mg/l") as hazardous. 40 C.F.R. § 261.24. RCRA requires any owner or operator of a facility which treats, stores, or disposes of hazardous waste to obtain a permit. Accordingly, any owner of a facility which treats, stores, or disposes of water with a concentration of benzene in excess of .5 mg/l is required to obtain a permit.

In contemplation of the promulgation of the TC Rule, Mobil took samples at Port Mobil in June 1990 and determined that the waste being dumped into the pond was hazardous as defined by the TC Rule. The company accordingly applied for and received an interim permit, which was valid until September 1991. In September 1991, Mobil applied for a permanent permit, but failed to meet the requirements set forth by RCRA, and no permit was granted.

Despite its failure to obtain a permit, Mobil continued to dump barge waste into the pond. In 1992, Mobil took additional tests and told the EPA that in fact the barge waste was not hazardous. In March and April of 1993, the EPA took five samples. According to the EPA's analysis, each of the five samples proved hazardous for benzene; one of the samples contained twenty times the regulatory limit. Mobil was provided a portion of each sample and concluded that four of the five samples tested for benzene in excess of the .5 mg/l limit.

---

3. The well water came from an area at Port Mobil where Mobil found oil floating on the water table. The oil was recovered for resale, and the wastewater was routed to the artificial pond.

On August 23, 1993, the EPA issued a Notice of Violation. In September 1993, Mobil stopped dumping barge waste into the pond. In this action, filed in March 1996, the EPA alleges that Mobil illegally treated, stored, and/or disposed of hazardous waste from September 1991 until September 1993. The EPA seeks to impose civil penalties of up to $25,000 per day of the violation, and also seeks injunctive relief.

. . . .

C. *Mobil's Defenses . . .*

Currently at issue are affirmative defenses raised by Mobil to fend off the EPA's allegations . . . . Mobil claims that the barge waste is not hazardous as defined by RCRA, the TC Rule, and other governing law. According to Mobil, since the barge waste is not hazardous, the company needed no permit to dump it into the pond at Port Mobil. Therefore, Mobil contends, it has never been in violation of RCRA and cannot be liable for civil penalties and injunctive relief . . . .

Mobil's claim that the barge wastewater is not hazardous is based on its assertion that the EPA used an improper testing method when evaluating the waste being dumped in the pond.[5] Mobil's argument boils down to this: the EPA's tests are flawed because they only measure one of the sources of discharge into the pond, namely, the barge waste. Mobil dumps several different types of waste into the pond, including storm water runoff and water taken from recovery wells elsewhere at the facility. Mobil argues that the proper way to test for hazardousness is to take a long-term average of all of the waste it dumps, measured at the point where the waste is dumped into the pond.

D. *The Government's Motion to Strike . . .*

The EPA argues that the "long-term averaging" advocated by Mobil is wrong as a matter of law. Accordingly, the EPA has moved . . . strike each defense that relies on the averaging theory . . . .

DISCUSSION

. . . .

B. *Long-Term Averaging*

1. *The Standard of Review*

. . . . Courts are generally "very reluctant to determine disputed or substantial issues of law on a motion to strike." Motions to strike will be granted only where it appears to a certainty that a defense would fail despite any state of facts which could be proved.

While the government has a heavy burden, it is important to bear in mind the standard by which Mobil's claims would be measured at trial. Mobil is challenging an agency's interpretation of its own regulations. The Supreme Court recently explained the appropriate standard of review in this circumstance:

---

5. Mobil asserts that its initial tests, which indicated the waste was hazardous, were likewise mistaken because they were based on an improper testing method.

> We must give substantial deference to an agency's interpretation of its own regulations. Our task is not to decide which among several competing interpretations best serves the regulatory purpose. Rather, the agency's interpretation must be given controlling weight unless it is plainly erroneous or inconsistent with the regulation.[. . .]

Highly technical regulations like those at issue in this case underscore the importance of deference to agency expertise. "This broad deference is all the more warranted when, as here, the regulation concerns a 'complex and highly technical regulatory program'" that depends on "'significant expertise and entail[s] the exercise of judgment grounded in policy concerns.'"

Applying the Supreme Court's deferential approach to an agency's interpretation of its own regulations, the standard of review for the government's motion is as follows: Mobil's claims fail unless its allegations could lead to the conclusion that the EPA's method of testing is plainly erroneous and that an alternative testing method is compelled by the regulation's plain language or by other indications of the Administrator's intent.

2. The Statutory and Regulatory Framework

. . . .

. . . The testing procedure referred to in the TC Rule, the Toxicity Characteristic Leaching Procedure ("TCLP") is described in an EPA guidance document known as SW-846. This document discusses, among other things, appropriate sampling techniques.

Mobil dumps a number of different wastes into the pond: the barge waste, the storm water runoff, and the residual water from recovery wells. Sometimes the wastes are mixed before they are dumped, sometimes they are not. The government says that in order to determine if the waste is hazardous, one must take a representative sample of each waste stream to see if it is hazardous. Mobil disagrees. There is one culvert from which the relevant waste is dumped into the pond. To determine if the waste is hazardous, the company contends, one must take a representative sample of everything that is dumped from that culvert.

3. The Appropriate Deference to Agency's Interpretation of Its Own Regulations

Given the "broad deference" due an agency's interpretation of its own regulations, Mobil's claims must be rejected. Mobil simply has provided no basis for the conclusion that EPA's interpretation of the TC Rule is "plainly erroneous or inconsistent with the regulation." EPA says "representative sample" refers to each waste stream. Mobil says "representative sample" refers to all the waste streams. While Mobil has offered an alternative reading of the law, it has failed to establish that its reading is "compelled by the regulation's plain language" or the Administrator's intent at the time the regulation was promulgated.

Indeed, Mobil does not even allege that the agency's interpretation is plainly erroneous. In its affirmative defenses, the company simply claims that the government's samples were not "representative" according to Mobil's reading of the law, and that its own "method accords with EPA's definition of 'representative' sample." . . . The company frames the issue this way: "The question, therefore, is which calculation is correct: Mobil's or the government's." But that is not the question. The Supreme Court has expressly forbidden the type of choice Mobil suggests. The question in a challenge to an agency's interpretation of its own regulations is whether the agency's interpretation is "plainly erroneous." Mobil has failed even to allege that EPA's reading is "plainly erroneous," and its averaging-based defenses . . . must therefore be struck.

4. *The Merits of the Averaging Theory*

Even if I were not bound to apply such a deferential standard, Mobil's defenses would fail, for the company's averaging theory is wrong as a matter of law. The plain language of the TC Rule is contrary to Mobil's reading. The TC Rule requires testing a representative sample of "the waste." If the EPA had intended to refer to multiple waste streams, it easily could have done so. Mobil's proposed reading of the law would have me conclude that the singular "waste" in fact requires a representative sample of several different waste streams which (by Mobil's admission) (1) have different contents; (2) come from three unrelated sources; (3) are dumped on different days; and (4) are sometimes commingled and sometimes not. I do not read the EPA's requirement to test "a representative sample of the waste" to include multiple waste streams which are so obviously unrelated. The EPA would certainly have given some indication if it intended such an open-ended testing methodology. Mobil points to no such indication and I have identified none.

The impact Mobil's averaging theory would have on the effectiveness of RCRA permitting requirements likewise leads me to the conclusion that Mobil's reading of the regulations is wrong as a matter of law. Under Mobil's theory, it could dump any amount of highly hazardous waste in the pond on Staten Island, so long as it also dumped enough non-hazardous waste such that, "on average," the material dumped was not hazardous. This is entirely inconsistent with the "cradle-to-grave" regulatory structure that RCRA establishes . . . . Under Mobil's reading of the TC Rule, a hazardous waste (such as the allegedly hazardous barge waste) could be cloaked in a mix of non-hazardous waste and thus avoid regulation. Under Mobil's theory, hazardous waste would skip the cradle altogether and could be disposed of as non-hazardous waste.

In practical terms, it is impossible to distinguish Mobil's averaging theory from a rule providing that hazardous waste may be diluted before testing. If, as Mobil insists, the barge waste is not hazardous because it is only a fraction of the waste that is dumped, it is the ultimate mixing with non-hazardous waste which leads to the conclusion that the barge waste is not hazardous. Dilution, however, is forbidden by RCRA absent a permit. *See* 42 U.S.C. § 6903(34) (treatment includes "any method . . . designed to change the . . . character or composition of any hazardous waste so as to neutralize such waste or so as to render such waste nonhazardous").

EPA regulations requiring that waste dumped in ponds be tested at the "point of generation" further support my conclusion that averaging is wrong as a matter of law.

The point of generation rule ensures detection of hazardous wastes which would be overlooked if testing happened after the waste is mixed with other wastes in the pond. Mobil concedes that testing after the waste has mixed in the pond is not appropriate. Yet Mobil's averaging theory appears to lead to the same result as testing post-mixture: a hazardous waste stream may be rendered legally non-hazardous simply by averaging its hazardous properties with the properties of non-hazardous wastes.

. . . .

Mobil's affirmative defenses based on averaging are not sufficient to withstand a motion to strike . . . . Indeed, Mobil's averaging theory is contrary to the plain language and objectives of RCRA, and is wrong as a matter of law. Accordingly, the motion to strike Mobil's third and eleventh affirmative defenses, which rely on the averaging theory, is granted.

. . . .

United States v. Bethlehem Steel Corp.

38 F.3d 862 (7th Cir. 1994)

Judge KANNE:

The United States brought this penal enforcement action on behalf of the United States Environmental Protection Agency ("EPA") against Bethlehem Steel Corporation to enforce hazardous waste requirements under [RCRA] . . . .

Bethlehem Steel Corporation owns and operates an integrated steelmaking facility at Burns Harbor, Indiana. The United States alleges that a series of environmental violations have occurred (and continue to occur) at Burns Harbor . . . . The government's second through sixth claims pertain to sludges the plant previously generated from the treatment of electroplating and other wastewaters. These sludges are currently stored or disposed of in two finishing lagoons and a landfill, also at the plant site.

[handwritten margin note: mixed sludges w/ other wastewaters]

. . . The district court granted partial summary judgment in favor of the United States . . . . [and] issued a permanent injunction, ordering Bethlehem to comply with its hazardous waste obligations . . . . Bethlehem appeals . . . .

I. BACKGROUND

. . . Section 3005(a) of RCRA, 42 U.S.C. § 6925(a), generally prohibits the operation of hazardous waste management facilities or units, except in accordance with a RCRA permit or with established interim status requirements . . . .

. . . .

B. United States' Second through Sixth Claims for Relief

In its second through sixth claims for relief, the United States alleges that Bethlehem violated RCRA by failing to comply with RCRA "interim status performance standards" for its landfill and two terminal polishing lagoons.

From the mid-1960's until June 16, 1983, Bethlehem conducted tin and chromium electroplating at its Burns Harbor facility, generating electroplating wastewater as a by-product. Bethlehem treated this electroplating wastewater by, among other things, mixing it with other kinds of wastewaters, then adding a flocculent or thickener and allowing the resulting solids to settle to the bottom as sludge. After the clarified water was drawn off, the sludge was filtered. The clarified water was sent to two terminal polishing lagoons to allow further settling and to allow the temperature and chemical composition of the water to equilibrate. The filtered sludge was disposed of in the landfill. The United States contends that because 40 C.F.R. § 261.31 lists "wastewater treatment sludges from electroplating operations" as F006 hazardous waste, Bethlehem's landfill and lagoons are "hazardous waste management units" subject to 42 U.S.C. § 6925(a)'s permit requirements.

In enacting RCRA, Congress recognized that the EPA could not issue permits to all applicants before RCRA's effective date. Thus, RCRA provides that facilities already in existence on November 19, 1980, could continue to manage hazardous waste without a permit on an "interim status" basis, until the EPA made a final administrative disposition of their submitted permit applications. 42 U.S.C. § 6925(e). To obtain interim status, existing facilities were required to submit a "Part A application" by a certain date and then were to be "treated as having been issued [a] permit." 42 U.S.C. § 6925(e).

Such facilities nonetheless were required to conduct their hazardous waste management in compliance with the "interim status standards" set forth at 40 C.F.R. Pt. 265. In the last five counts of its complaint, the government alleges that Bethlehem did not meet its interim status obligations . . . .

. . . .

II. DISCUSSION

. . . .

B. Landfill and Polishing Lagoons

. . . .

The United States maintains that the settled sludge at the bottom of Bethlehem's finishing lagoons and the filtered sludge disposed of in its landfill are F006 listed waste, because the sludges are properly classified as "wastewater treatment sludges from electroplating operations." *See* 40 C.F.R. § 261.31 . . . .

. . . .

If Bethlehem's sludges are listed waste, they would be considered hazardous until delisted. Bethlehem's sludges were not delisted; therefore, Bethlehem's lagoons and landfill would be subject to RCRA's section 3005 interim status requirements, if indeed they contain F006. (Recall that Bethlehem was a pre-November 19, 1980 facility with a permit application pending with the EPA and was thus qualified to be an interim status facility). Bethlehem has failed to meet a slew of the EPA's interim status standards; thus, if the government's arguments are correct, Bethlehem would potentially be liable for injunctive relief and penalties.

. . . .

. . . We must first acknowledge that the plain language of the F006 listing is not particularly instructive in this case. Although the district court notes that "the term 'wastewater treatment sludges from electroplating operations' does not have the words 'solely', 'only', or 'exclusively' in it, to imply that only wastewater treatment sludges from electroplating operations and not a mixture thereof is hazardous waste," we are equally persuaded by Bethlehem's observation that the listing also "does not contain the words, 'partly,' 'mixed with,' or 'in trace amount' either."

Similarly, we find it significant that the F006 listing lacks the phrase "mixtures/blends," or any mention of a threshold concentration percentage (for instance, ten percent or more electroplating wastewater). The F001-F005 listings immediately preceding F006 contain both.[12] A facility may reasonably infer that when the EPA intends to include waste mixtures in its listings, it knows how to do so, and that in the F006 listing, such mixture language is conspicuously absent. Subsequently, the EPA explicitly "amend[ed] . . . [the F001-F005] spent solvent listings to include solvent mixtures," 40 C.F.R. §271.1 (table 1); 50 Fed.Reg. 53318 (December 31, 1985) ("Today's amendment will close a major regulatory loophole which allows toxic solvent mixtures to remain unregulated."), but did not amend the F006 listing to include electroplating wastewater mixtures.

. . . .

. . . We conclude that the F006 listing does not . . . include Bethlehem's mixed wastewater treatment sludges.

. . . .

CONCLUSION

. . . .

. . . Bethlehem's wastewater treatment sludges do not fall within the listing for F006 hazardous waste. The parties agree that the sludges are a mixture of F006 and non-hazardous waste, and the government does not allege that Bethlehem's sludges are hazardous waste by virtue of any theory other than its listing as F006 waste. As such, the sludges in Bethlehem's two lagoons and landfill are not subject to RCRA subtitle C requirements as a listed hazardous waste. We therefore VACATE the portion of the district court's opinion that grants partial summary judgment and injunctive relief against Bethlehem on the United States' second through sixth claims, and REMAND the case with instructions to enter partial summary judgment in favor of Bethlehem with regard to those five claims.

---

12. For example, the F004 listing specifies "the following spent non-halogenated solvents: Cresols and cresylic acid, and nitrobenzene; all spent solvent mixtures/blends containing, before use, a total of ten percent or more (by volume) of one or more of the above non-halogenated solvents or those solvents listed in F001, F002, and F005; and still bottoms from the recovery of these spent solvents and spent solvent mixtures."

Judge RIPPLE, concurring in part and dissenting in part:

. . . .

I believe that the sludge at the bottom of Bethlehem's finishing lagoons and the filtered sludge in its landfill are properly classified as F006 listed waste because these sludges are "wastewater treatment sludges from electroplating operations." 40 C.F.R. § 261.31. In my view, the agency's description is very clear and further specificity is not required. I note that the F006 listing specifically eliminates from its scope sludges produced by certain processes. If the agency believed that other exclusions, based for instance on the percentage of the sludge attributable to hazardous waste, were appropriate, it would have included such a specification.

Notes and Questions

1. The defendants in the case excerpts, Mobil Oil and Bethlehem Steel, were large, sophisticated corporations. Each, by behaving as if its waste was not hazardous, took a major risk that it would face a government enforcement action and that it might lose. Why do you suppose the companies were willing to take that risk?

2. Does the difference between characteristic hazardous waste and listed hazardous waste help to explain why the United States prevailed in the *Mobil* opinion but not in the *Bethlehem* opinion?

3. Mobil initially concluded that its waste stream was hazardous waste and even obtained an interim permit for its treatment, storage, or disposal of that waste, but never obtained a final permit. Instead, Mobil argued that its initial characterization of its waste was incorrect. What might explain this? We discuss TSDF permitting procedures and requirements in Section VI.B.2, below.

4. In *Mobil*, the United States moved to strike Mobil's affirmative defenses that were based on the defendant's long-term averaging theory. Rule 12(f) of the Federal Rules of Civil Procedure provides that a trial court, on its own or on motion by a party, "may strike from a pleading an insufficient defense." Thus, as the court's description of the standard of review shows, a Rule 12(f) motion to strike an affirmative defense is analogous to a motion under Rule 12(b)(6) to dismiss all or part of a complaint "for failure to state a claim upon which relief can be granted." Motions to strike defenses are not terribly common in civil litigation, but they have become part of the toolkit of government attorneys bringing enforcement actions under some environmental statutes that allow only limited defenses.

5. In *Mobil*, the court deferred to EPA's interpretation of its own regulation. The TC Rule, 40 C.F.R. § 261.24, requires testing of a "representative sample of the waste." Where can EPA's interpretation of this rule, to which the court deferred, be found?

6. In *Bethlehem*, how did the majority's reading of EPA's F006 listing differ from the dissenting judge's reading? Why, according to the majority, were Bethlehem's mixed wastewater treatment sludges not F006 waste? Could EPA have written the F006 listing in a way that would have included Bethlehem's waste to the majority's satisfaction?

7. In *Bethlehem*, the court stated that EPA and the defendant agreed "that the sludges are a mixture of F006 and non-hazardous waste." As a matter of policy, does it make more sense to treat such a mixture as hazardous waste or as nonhazardous waste? In a portion of the opinion not excerpted above, the majority rejected EPA's argument that Bethlehem's mixed sludges should be treated as hazardous waste because of a "general principle . . . that a hazardous waste does not lose its hazardous character simply because it changes form or is combined with other substances." The government warned the court that "[t]o fail to do so . . . would effectively gut RCRA." Do you understand the basis of EPA's concern? If you had been responsible for drafting EPA's hazardous waste regulations, how would you have tried to address the concern? We turn to EPA's actual approach.

2. The Mixture and Derived-From Rules

After publishing the first proposed regulations for the identification of hazardous waste pursuant to § 3001 of RCRA, EPA received public comments that revealed a problem. In the final rule, "in response to inquiries about whether mixtures of hazardous and nonhazardous wastes would be subject to Subtitle C requirements," EPA added "a clarification" that had not been included in the proposed rule. 45 Fed. Reg. 33084, 33095 (May 19, 1980). EPA explained:

> This is a very real issue in real-world waste management, since many hazardous wastes are mixed with non-hazardous wastes or other hazardous wastes during storage, treatment, or disposal.
>
> Although it was not expressly stated in the proposed regulation, EPA intended waste mixtures containing listed hazardous wastes to be considered a hazardous waste and managed accordingly. Without such a rule, generators could evade Subtitle C requirements simply by commingling listed wastes with non-hazardous solid waste. Most of these waste mixtures would not be caught by the Subpart C characteristics because they would contain wastes which were listed for reasons other than that they exhibit the characteristics (e.g., they contain carcinogens, mutagens or toxic organic materials). Obviously, this would leave a major loophole in the Subtitle C management system and create inconsistencies in how wastes must be managed under that system.

Id. To address this concern, EPA's final rule provided that any "waste mixtures containing *listed* hazardous wastes," *id.* (emphasis added) would be regulated as hazardous waste—regardless of the proportion of hazardous to non-hazardous waste and regardless of the actual hazardous properties of the mixture. EPA acknowledged that this rule might include some waste mixtures unnecessarily, but concluded that overinclusion was a necessary price to pay in order to avoid risking the possibility of leaving dangerous waste mixtures unregulated. The final rule also deemed hazardous waste any waste "derived from" a listed hazardous waste. This provision referred to "solid wastes generated by storage, disposal and treatment" of listed hazardous waste. *Id.* at 33096. EPA reasoned that "it is reasonable to assume that these wastes, which are derived from hazardous wastes, are themselves hazardous."

By contrast, the so-called mixture rule and derived-from rule did not apply to *characteristic* hazardous waste. Waste mixtures containing (or wastes derived from) only *characteristic* hazardous waste would "be considered hazardous only if they exhibit the characteristics"—because, after all, it was only the presence of the characteristics that made the waste hazardous in the first place. *Id.* at 33095.

A number of corporations and trade associations sought judicial review of the mixture and derived-from rules. The D.C. Circuit vacated the rules on procedural grounds. The court held that because these provisions were not included in EPA's proposed rule, and were not a "logical outgrowth" of the proposed rule, EPA had not provided the affected industries with adequate notice and opportunity to comment on the rule as required by the Administrative Procedure Act. *Shell Oil Co. v. EPA*, 950 F.2d 741 (D.C. Cir. 1992). But even as it remanded the rules to EPA, the D.C. Circuit acknowledged "the dangers that may be posed by a discontinuity in the regulation of hazardous wastes" and therefore suggested to EPA that "the agency may wish to consider reenacting the rules . . . on an interim basis under the [APA's] 'good cause' exemption" to the notice-and-comment requirement. *Id.* at 752. That is exactly what EPA did, so the mixture rule and the derived-from rule remained in effect, albeit on an "interim" basis. And there matters stood for nearly a decade.

— END ——————

American Chemistry Council v. EPA

337 F.3d 1060 (D.C. Circuit 2003)

Judge GINSBURG:

The American Chemistry Council (ACC) petitions for review of a rule promulgated by the Environmental Protection Agency pursuant to [RCRA], treating as a "hazardous waste" any substance that is either mixed with or derived from a listed hazardous waste. The effect is to render such mixtures and derivatives subject to the stringent standards for the management of hazardous waste. We reject the ACC's argument that the EPA lacked authority for the rule under the RCRA and hence we deny the petition for review.

I. Background

The RCRA . . . requires the EPA to regulate the identification, disposal, and treatment of "hazardous waste[.]" . . . .

[The court quoted RCRA's definitions of "hazardous waste" and "solid waste", 42 U.S.C. §§ 6903(5), (27), see pp. 647–648 above, and described EPA's obligation to promulgate criteria for identifying the characteristics of hazardous waste, regulations identifying those characteristics, and regulations listing particular hazardous wastes, id. § 6921(a), (b)(1), see pp. 646–647, above.]

. . . .

Both characteristic hazardous wastes and listed hazardous wastes are subject to regulation under Subtitle C of the RCRA, which applies stringent management standards to the generation, transportation, treatment, storage, and disposal of hazardous waste. Under the "delisting process" provided in the Act, a listed hazardous waste will be deemed non-hazardous at a particular facility if a petitioner demonstrates that the waste no longer meets any of the criteria for which it was listed, and that it is not hazardous because of any other factor reasonably identified by the EPA. 42 U.S.C. § 6921(f), 40 C.F.R. § 260.22.

In the proceeding here under review, the EPA modified the regulatory definition of "hazardous waste" to include, subject to certain exceptions, "a mixture of solid waste and one or more hazardous wastes," 40 C.F.R. § 261.3(a)(2)(iv), and "any solid waste generated from the treatment, storage, or disposal of a hazardous waste, including any sludge, spill residue, ash emission control dust, or leachate." 40 C.F.R. § 261.3(c)(2)(i). The EPA's new definition went into effect on an interim basis in 1992. In 1999 the EPA proposed in substance to make permanent the 1992 rule, with some minor alterations not relevant to this case. The EPA issued the Final Rule so doing on May 16, 2001.

II. Analysis

. . . .

A. *Chevron* step one

The ACC argues first that the EPA's interpretation is inconsistent with the statutory definition of hazardous waste, because the rule brings within that definition substances that do not exhibit a harmful "characteristic." The ACC points to the "EPA['s] acknowledgement that not all mixtures and derivatives pose hazards to human health and the environment." According to the ACC, the Congress could not possibly have meant to include in the definition of hazardous waste solid wastes that do not pose a threat to human health or the environment . . . .

In our view, however, the Congress did not speak directly, let alone clearly, to this issue. As the EPA points out, the definition of "hazardous waste" in the statute has a broad sweep. It includes not only those solid wastes that do pose hazards to human health or the environment, but also those that "may" do so. In addition, the definition includes those wastes in which the "potential hazard" becomes an actual hazard only if the waste is "improperly treated, stored, transported, or disposed of, or otherwise managed." 42 U.S.C. § 6903(5)(B). This provision does not make mixtures and derivatives clearly hazardous wastes or clearly non-hazardous wastes. The element of judgment imported into the definition of hazardous waste by the use of "may" and the inclusion of waste that may be hazardous only if mismanaged necessarily makes the statute ambiguous on this score.

The ACC argues nonetheless that the Final Rule simply cannot be squared with the Act because it allows the EPA to classify a substance as hazardous without "taking into account toxicity, persistence, and degradability in nature, potential for accumulation in tissue, and other related factors," as required by § 6921(a). Amicus American Petroleum Institute adds that the legislative history of § 6921 indicates the EPA must follow a two-step process in order to regulate a solid waste as hazardous: it must first determine the characteristics of a hazardous waste and then show that a particular solid waste has at least one such characteristic. *See* H.R.Rep. No. 1491, 94th Cong., 2d Sess. 25 ("Only after the criteria for determining what is hazardous has [sic] been developed can the Administrator determine which specific wastes are hazardous").

According to the EPA, however, when it lists a waste as hazardous it could, in principle, automatically list its mixtures and derivatives as well. That is, the mixture rule and the derived-from rule are consistent with § 6921 because mixtures and derivatives are "a second generation of the listed hazardous wastes from which they originate, [and] it is reasonable to presume, until demonstrated otherwise, that these wastes are also hazardous."

We think the EPA's response is sufficient, at the least, to demonstrate that the statute does not directly answer the issue before us. For the reason just quoted, § 6921 cannot be understood to preclude the EPA from regulating mixtures and derivatives until such time as they may be shown to be non-hazardous. Some—perhaps most—mixtures and derivatives maintain the characteristics of their parent hazardous waste .... Any mixture or derivative that does not remain hazardous may be exonerated either by an explicit exclusion in the initial listing or through the delisting process of § 6921(f).

In sum, neither the definition of "hazardous waste" nor § 6921 answers the question whether that definition or any other provision of the RCRA authorizes the EPA to regulate a mixture or derivative that may be, but has not yet been shown to be, a hazardous waste. We must go on to determine, therefore, whether the EPA's interpretation of 42 U.S.C. § 6903(5) is reasonable.

B. *Chevron* step two

The EPA persuasively argues that it reasonably interpreted the term "hazardous waste" presumptively to include mixtures and derivatives: "[The Final Rule] assures that hazardous mixtures and derivatives do not imprudently escape Subtitle C requirements." We agree. The Final Rule fulfills the purpose for which the Congress passed the RCRA, namely to subject hazardous waste to "cradle-to-grave" regulation in order to protect public health and the environment. To that end, too, the Congress "required that hazardous waste be properly managed in the first instance thereby reducing the need for corrective action at a future date." 42 U.S.C. § 6902(a)(5). We also agree that, because many mixtures of and derivatives from hazardous wastes are themselves hazardous, it is reasonable for the EPA to assume that all such mixtures and derivatives are hazardous until shown otherwise. For that reason we have already endorsed a similar action by the EPA with respect to hazardous wastes that mix with soil and groundwater. Placing the burden upon the regulated entity to show the lack of a hazardous characteristic in a mixture or derivative it manages avoids placing upon the EPA what the agency persuasively describes as "the nearly impossible affirmative burden of anticipating and analyzing, in a listing decision, the hazardousness or non-hazardousness [of] every conceivable mixture or derivative that a generator might create." In addition, the dozen or more exceptions already contained in the rule—such as those for used oil, certain laboratory wastewaters, and certain carbamate wastewaters,—prevent it from casting too wide a net over nonhazardous mixtures and derivatives.

The ACC objects that the delisting mechanism does not provide any realistic relief to the potential over-inclusiveness of the rule because it is "slow, onerous, ineffective, and at times controversial." [quoting EPA's 1990 study of the RCRA program]. The cumbersome nature of the delisting process, however, says nothing about the reasonableness of the EPA's interpretation of the statute. And in any event, even if the delisting process were impossibly cumbersome, a party could still head off the initial listing of the mixture or derivative by proposing that the initial listing of a particular waste as hazardous include the qualification that certain specified mixtures and derivatives are not included in the listing.

The ACC claims the EPA has available to it other "lawful and adequate alternatives to the mixture rule and the derived-from rule," such as adopting broader listings or modifying the current prohibition on dilution of hazardous waste. *See* 40 C.F.R. § 268.3. We disagree because the EPA has shown not only that the Final Rule prevents hazardous mixtures and derivatives from evading proper treatment under the RCRA but also that the alternatives proposed by the ACC would not be as effective. For example, using broader listings would place upon the EPA the very administrative burden we deemed above to be impractical; the Agency would have to identify not only the hazardous waste but also to determine whether all second-generation wastes are hazardous. The anti-dilution rule makes unlawful the expedient of simply diluting hazardous waste in order to lower the concentration of hazardous constituents and thereby circumvent regulation under the RCRA. The ACC does not explain how modifying the anti-dilution rule would make it an effective substitute for the Final Rule.

Finally, the ACC argues that the Final Rule imposes a significant cost upon industry without any showing of a concomitant public benefit. The ACC, however, does not identify any provision of the RCRA requiring the benefits of a regulation to equal or exceed its costs. And the EPA has submitted evidence that some mixtures and derivatives display the hazardous characteristics of their parent waste, which suggests the rule will provide at least some added protection of the environment and public health.

We think the Congress wanted the EPA, in deciding which substances to regulate as "hazardous" under the RCRA, to err on the side of caution; the Final Rule is a reasonable exercise of such caution. Therefore, we cannot say the rule is an unreasonable interpretation of the agency's statutory mandate comprehensively to regulate hazardous waste.

III. Conclusion

For the foregoing reasons, the petition for review is

Denied.

Notes and Questions

1. EPA appeared to admit that the mixture rule and derived-from rule may subject to RCRA Subtitle C regulation wastes that do not in fact present the types of hazards against which the statute and regulations are designed to protect. Do you agree with the court of appeals that the rules are nevertheless reasonable interpretations of the statute?

2. Think about the wastes that were at issue in the *Mobil* and *Bethlehem* cases. How would these wastes fare in light of the mixture rule and the *American Chemistry Council* decision? More generally, suppose that a company legitimately generated wastes composed of a mixture of hazardous waste and non-hazardous waste. Could that company avoid complying with RCRA's hazardous waste regulations if the hazardous waste part of the mixture were composed of: (a) listed hazardous waste; (b) characteristic hazardous waste; or (c) a waste that is both listed hazardous waste and characteristic hazardous waste? If so, how?

3. Recall that the waste at issue in *Bethlehem* was, by Bethlehem's own admission, a mixture of a listed hazardous waste and non-hazardous waste. Why wasn't the entire mixture deemed hazardous waste by application of the mixture rule? The Seventh Circuit concluded that EPA's acknowledged *need* for a mixture rule meant that the specific listing of "wastewater treatment sludges from electroplating operations" (F006) did not include mixed sludges; at the same time, because the mixture rule had been invalidated, EPA could not apply the principle behind the mixture rule as an independent basis for regulating Bethlehem's mixed waste as hazardous waste.

3. Exclusions from RCRA Hazardous Waste Regulation

We have seen that, pursuant to RCRA's requirements, EPA identified criteria for listing hazardous waste as well as characteristics that make waste hazardous. Certain waste streams that might literally satisfy the criteria or display the characteristics are nevertheless excluded from EPA's regulatory definition of "hazardous waste." Wastes covered by an exclusion are not subject to the Subtitle C "cradle-to-grave" regulatory scheme.

The various exclusions are based on EPA's interpretation of particular statutory provisions, EPA's view of overall congressional intent, or EPA's identification of policy considerations in light of the statutory objectives. Currently, EPA regulations list 17 exclusions, which vary greatly in scope and complexity. *See* 40 C.F.R. 261.4(b). We focus on two of the most important exclusions: household waste and certain wastes from mining and mineral processing.

Household waste exclusion: You may not think of yourself as a generator of hazardous waste, but almost certainly you discard materials that (as RCRA defines hazardous waste) "may . . . pose a substantial present or potential hazard to human health and the environment when improperly treated, stored, transported, or disposed of . . . ." 42 U.S.C. § 6903(5). Waste or residual oil-based paints, paint thinners and other solvents, mercury-containing thermometers or fluorescent lights, cleaning fluids and polishes, drain openers, batteries, motor oils, insecticides, herbicides, fungicides, and moth balls are some examples. According to EPA, each person in the United States produces an average of four pounds of household hazardous waste per year. EPA Region 9, Household Hazardous Waste, https://www3.epa.gov/region9/waste/solid /house.html (last visited Nov. 15, 2016). Sum that up among the American population and pretty soon you're talking about a real mass of hazardous material in household garbage.

EPA, however, recognized from the inception of its RCRA program that "subjecting households to the strict RCRA waste management regulations would create a number of practical problems." EPA, RCRA ORIENTATION MANUAL 2014 III-8–III-9. EPA concluded that Congress did not intend for EPA to regulate household waste as hazardous waste:

> The exclusion is based on language in the Senate Report, which states:
>
> > (The hazardous waste program) is not to be used to control the disposal of substances used in households or to extend control over general municipal wastes based on the presence of such substances.
>
> (S. Rep. No. 94-988, 94th Cong.. 2nd Sess., at 16.)
>
> This indicates Congressional intent to exclude waste streams generated by consumers at the household level . . . .
>
> The Senate language makes it clear that household waste does not lose the exclusion simply because it has been collected. Since household waste is excluded in all phases of its management, residues remaining after treatment (e.g. incineration, thermal treatment) are not subject to regulation as hazardous waste.

45 Fed. Reg. 33084, 33099 (May 19, 1980). Accordingly, since 1980, EPA's regulations have provided:

> The following solid wastes are not hazardous wastes:
>
> (1) Household waste, including household waste that has been collected, transported, stored, treated, disposed, recovered (e.g., refuse-derived fuel) or reused . . . .

40 C.F.R. § 261.4(b) (2015); *see* 45 Fed. Reg. 33084, 33120 (May 19, 1980) (containing the same provision).

But what *is* household waste? If household waste is excluded because Congress did not intend "to extend control over general municipal wastes," should the ordinary trash from an office building be considered "household waste"? If an individual homeowner's trash can placed at the curb contains "household waste," should the contents of a 30-cubic-yard container at a large apartment building, which includes material disposed of by both the residents and the building's management company, also be considered "household waste"? What if part of the building is a hotel? What if the building is *only* a hotel? Here is EPA's answer, which has evolved somewhat from the original regulation:

> "Household waste" means any material (including garbage, trash and sanitary wastes in septic tanks) derived from households (including single and multiple residences, hotels and motels, bunkhouses, ranger stations, crew quarters, campgrounds, picnic grounds and day-use recreation areas).

40 C.F.R. § 264.1(b)(1) (2015).

Notice that, as EPA explained in 1980 and stated in the promulgated regulation, household waste is excluded from the definition of hazardous waste, as it were, from cradle to grave: you do not generate hazardous waste when you put out your household waste; your trash hauler does not transport hazardous waste when it collects your household waste; your local government does not store, treat or dispose of hazardous waste when it puts your household waste in a transfer station, landfill, or incinerator. Household waste is thus granted "what is known as a 'waste stream' exemption . . . , *i.e.*, an exemption covering that category of waste from generation through treatment to final disposal of residues." *City of Chicago v. Environmental Defense Fund*, 511 U.S. 328, 333 (1994).

The *City of Chicago* case concerned Chicago's trash-to-energy facility. The combustion of municipal waste in that facility produced energy but also created ash — more than 100,000 tons of it per year. Do you think the ash should have been covered by the municipal waste exclusion? What if the ash, when subjected to EPA's TCLP test, displayed the toxicity characteristic? Should Chicago have been required to manage the ash as a hazardous waste, that is, to dispose of it only at a licensed hazardous waste disposal facility?

Chicago disposed of the ash in ordinary municipal landfills. But there was a wrinkle: Chicago's trash-to-energy plant burned not only household waste, but also some industrial waste. The industrial waste was *not* hazardous waste, and of course the household waste (by definition) also was not hazardous waste. But the Environmental Defense Fund (EDF) alleged that the *ash* from the incinerator *was* hazardous waste — and therefore subject to RCRA's cradle-to-grave regulatory scheme — by virtue of the toxicity characteristic.

The Supreme Court observed that the broad "waste stream exemption" of 40 C.F.R. § 261.4(b)(1) did not apply to the waste burned in Chicago's incinerator. Can you see why not?

But Chicago argued that the incinerator ash was exempted from the hazardous waste regulations by virtue of a "Clarification of Household Waste Exclusion" that Congress enacted in 1984, 42 U.S.C. § 6921(i) (RCRA § 3001(i), added by HSWA § 233). The amendment, as reproduced virtually verbatim in the EPA regulation, provided that:

> A resource recovery facility managing municipal solid waste shall not be deemed to be treating, storing, disposing of, or otherwise managing hazardous wastes for the purposes of regulation under this subtitle, if such facility:

(i) Receives and burns only

(A) Household waste (from single and multiple dwellings, hotels, motels, and other residential sources) and

(B) Solid waste from commercial or industrial sources that does not contain hazardous waste; and

(ii) Such facility does not accept hazardous wastes and the owner or operator of such facility has established contractual requirements or other appropriate notification or inspection procedures to assure that hazardous wastes are not received at or burned in such facility.

40 C.F.R. § 261.4(b)(1) (2015). How is the scope of this provision different from the general household waste exclusion? Chicago argued that its incinerator satisfied all of the requirements of this provision and therefore gained the protection of the household waste "waste stream" exclusion.

The Supreme Court, relying on a literal reading of the statute and regulation, ruled in EDF's favor. The Court held that the statutory "clarification" protected Chicago's *incinerator* from being regulated as a hazardous waste TSDF, but did *not* exclude the *ash generated by* the incinerator from the definition of hazardous waste. The court reasoned that, by creating ash, Chicago generated a new waste. The ash was not a residue from treating household waste because some of what the incinerator waste burned was industrial waste rather than household waste. And the clarifying amendment only said that facilities like Chicago's would not be deemed to treat, store, or dispose of hazardous waste; it did not say they could not be deemed to be hazardous waste *generators*. Two justices dissented, arguing that the statute was ambiguous and the majority's interpretation disserved RCRA's purpose of encouraging energy recovery from solid waste.

Local governments increasingly require or encourage special treatment of household hazardous wastes by various means, such as providing special collection days when residents may bring such materials to designated collection points. Even though household waste is not regulated as hazardous waste under Subtitle C of RCRA, EPA's criteria for municipal solid waste (MSW) landfills require groundwater monitoring for hazardous constituents and corrective action in case of releases. *See* 40 C.F.R. Part 258, Subpart E.

"Bevill" mining waste exclusion: The process of obtaining usable metals and other materials from the rocks in the Earth's crust generates a prodigious amount of waste. Often the sought-after materials constitute only a fraction of a percent of the ore that contains them. Much of the remaining material that is mined and processed, together with some of the materials needed for processing it, becomes waste. EPA, REPORT TO CONGRESS: WASTES FROM THE EXTRACTION AND BENEFICIATION OF METALLIC ORES, PHOSPHATE ROCK, ASBESTOS, OVERBURDEN FROM URANIUM MINING, AND OIL SHALE ES-4–ES-6 (Dec. 1985) (describing and quantifying waste generation during mining activities); *id.* at 2–11 Table 2-5 (showing that for most metals mined, concentration of marketable metal in ore is less than one percent). Some of this waste meets EPA's

hazardousness criteria, especially the toxicity and sometimes the corrosivity characteristics. But the sheer volume of mining waste presents daunting problems of practicality and cost for any attempt to manage mining waste in the same manner as other
hazardous wastes.

Early in its effort to implement Subtitle C of RCRA, EPA recognized the special
difficulty of regulating hazardous wastes resulting from mining and mineral processing. Congress then made known its views of the problem as well. The result was
a lengthy dance of legislation, regulation, and litigation that well illustrates the interplay
among the three branches of government in fashioning environmental policy as well as
the process of legislating by accretion that has characterized the history of RCRA.

First, EPA in 1980 proposed to establish a category of "special waste," including
certain mining wastes, that might technically be hazardous waste but that, because of
its high volume and relatively low hazard, might not be amenable to the same type of
regulation appropriate to industrial hazardous waste. EPA's final regulations, however, modified the originally proposed hazardousness criteria and therefore "abandoned the concept of special waste." *Solite Corp. v. U.S. EPA*, 952 F.2d 473, 478 (D.C.
Cir. 1991). Just before the effective date of EPA's 1980 rules, however, Congress
enacted the "Bevill Amendment," named after its sponsor, Representative Thomas
Bevill of Alabama. *Environmental Defense Fund v. EPA*, 852 F.2d 1316 (D.C. Cir.
1988) ("*EDF II*"). For wastes within its purview—as pertinent here, "solid waste
from the extraction, beneficiation, and processing of ores and minerals"—the Bevill
Amendment did three things: (1) it required EPA to study and report to Congress on
the environmental and health effects of those wastes, the current and possible alternative disposal methods, and the costs and other market effects of switching to alternative disposal methods; (2) it prohibited EPA from regulating those wastes under
Subtitle C until at least six months after the study's completion; and (3) it required
EPA to determine, within six months after the study's completion, whether such wastes
should or should not be regulated under Subtitle C. *See* 42 U.S.C. §§ 6982(n)–(p),
6921(b)(3).

EPA missed the original deadline for producing the study and making its regulatory determinations, but eventually, after being sued and given revised court-ordered
deadlines, EPA did what Congress demanded. Pending its study, however, EPA excluded
the types of waste specified in the Bevill Amendment from RCRA's hazardous waste
regulatory scheme, as the statute required.

While EPA was studying, Congress kept legislating. As the D.C. Circuit explained
in *EDF II*, 852 F.2d at 1321:

> [T]he Hazardous and Solid Waste Amendments of 1984 ... added subsection
> 3004(x), 42 U.S.C. § 6924(x), which explicitly gives EPA flexibility in fashion-
> ing Subtitle C standards for wastes from the extraction, beneficiation and
> processing of ores and minerals. EPA was given the authority to modify vari-
> ous of the standards for hazardous waste disposal under Subtitle C
>
> > to take into account the special characteristics of such wastes, the prac-
> > tical difficulties associated with implementation of such requirements,

and site-specific characteristics, including but not limited to the climate, geology, hydrology and soil chemistry at the site, so long as such modified requirements assure protection of human health and the environment.

42 U.S.C. § 6924(x) [RCRA § 3004(x)].

EPA completed its work with respect to wastes from mining and beneficiation [2] first. On December 31, 1985, EPA submitted its report to Congress on these wastes. EPA then decided to exclude wastes from mining (extraction) and beneficiation of various minerals from the definition of hazardous waste. EPA "rejected the option [granted by § 3004(x)] to tailor Subtitle C requirements" to mining and beneficiation wastes. *Environmental Defense Fund v. U.S. EPA*, 852 F.2d 1309, 1313 (D.C. Cir. 1988) ("*EDF I*"). The D.C. Circuit upheld EPA's choices. *Id.* at 1316. Today, EPA's regulations provide that, subject to a limited exception, solid waste from the extraction and beneficiation of ores and minerals is not hazardous waste. 40 C.F.R. § 261.4(b)(7).

EPA had more trouble figuring out how to apply the Bevill Amendment to wastes from the "processing" of ores and minerals. How much of the pathway from beneficiation to final product did Congress intend "processing" to cover?

Initially, EPA temporarily decided to treat all waste from ore and mineral processing, including waste from smelting and refining, as within the scope of the Bevill Amendment. This was a pragmatic decision that gave the mining industry certainty that EPA would not regulate these wastes under Subtitle C at least until EPA completed a study of the wastes. *See EDF II*, 852 F.2d at 1320. It also meant that several smelting wastes that EPA had *previously* listed as hazardous waste became exempt—at least temporarily—from the Subtitle C regulations. *Id.*

As EPA vacillated about how to address smelting wastes, its temporary interpretation of the term "processing," as used in the Bevill Amendment, lasted from 1980 until 1986—when EPA effectively made that interpretation permanent. *Id.* at 1325. The Environmental Defense Fund challenged EPA's decision. The D.C. Circuit, relying primarily on the legislative history of the Bevill Amendment, held that EPA's decision to exclude all ore and mineral processing wastes from Subtitle C regulation was arbitrary and capricious and based on an impermissible interpretation of the Bevill Amendment. *Id.* at 1326, 1330. The court held that the Bevill Amendment covered only "high volume, low hazard" processing wastes. The court ordered EPA to decide which processing wastes fit that description, to study those wastes as required by the

---

2. In the mining industry, "beneficiation" refers to a variety of processes "to improve physical or chemical properties [of ore] especially in preparation for smelting." Merriam-Webster Dictionary, https://www.merriam-webster.com/dictionary/beneficiation (last visited Dec. 13, 2016). Under EPA's RCRA regulations, beneficiation includes any of about twenty-five specific activities. 40 C.F.R. § 261.4(b)(7)(i). "Smelting" is a later stage of processing that uses physical and chemical methods to release desired metals from the minerals containing them. *See* Merriam-Webster Dictionary, https://www.merriam-webster.com/dictionary/smelt (last visited Dec. 13, 2016); *see also* "Smelting," ENCYCLOPAEDIA BRITANNICA, https://www.britannica.com/technology/smelting (July 18, 2007) (last visited Dec. 13, 2016).

Bevill Amendment, and then to decide whether to regulate the studied wastes under Subtitle C. *Id.* at 1331.

EPA obeyed the court's order. EPA promulgated regulations defining "high volume" and "low hazard" so EPA could decide which processing wastes might *potentially* be excluded pursuant to the Bevill Amendment. Applying these criteria to a number of ore and mineral processing wastes, EPA eventually concluded that 20 specific wastes qualified for consideration under the Bevill Amendment. The D.C. Circuit upheld EPA's criteria and (with two exceptions) upheld EPA's decisions about which wastes fit the criteria. *Solite Corp. v. U.S. EPA*, 952 F.2d 473 (D.C. Cir. 1991). Today, EPA's regulations exclude from the definition of "hazardous waste" 20 specific wastes from various types of ore and mineral processing. 40 C.F.R. § 261.4(b)(7)(ii)(A)–(T). Other mineral processing wastes, of course, are hazardous waste only *if* they are listed as such or display one of the hazardous waste characteristics.

Practice Problem: Identifying Hazardous Waste

Responding to needs in the Tri-State area, Geleroton Township constructed a regional landfill to accept solid and hazardous wastes. The Township does not place incoming hazardous wastes directly into the landfill, however. Instead, before placing hazardous wastes in the landfill, the Township treats the wastes in an on-site incinerator. After thus reducing the volume of the incoming hazardous waste material, the Township then places the incinerator ash and residue in the landfill.

Five years into the operation, the incineration-and-landfill process appears to be working, with no known threats to human health or the environment. However, a records request to the Township recently revealed that the Township failed to obtain any permit under RCRA or a state-authorized RCRA program that would allow it to dispose of hazardous wastes.

In response to a civil complaint from a national environmental group, alleging illegal disposal of hazardous waste without a permit, the Township acknowledges that wastes it has accepted for disposal may be considered hazardous wastes. However, the Township argues that the incineration of these materials renders them no longer "hazardous," so that rules regarding disposal of hazardous wastes do not apply to the disposal of the incinerator ash and residue.

1. On competing motions for summary judgment on this point, how do you believe a federal judge should rule, and why?

2. To settle litigation on this question, instead of disposing of the incinerator ash in the landfill, the Township offers to store the ash while it looks for productive uses for this material. A Township official recently returned from the Pacific Northwest, where she learned that volcanic ash from Mount St. Helens has been used to form figurines and other knick-knacks for sale in the gift shop of the Mount St. Helens observatory. As an attorney representing the environmental plaintiffs in this case, would you be prepared to accept an offer from the Township to turn

their incinerator ash into figurines for sale? If not, why not? If you would be willing to entertain this offer, what conditions might you require as a matter of settlement?

VI. Implementing RCRA Subtitle C

In the preceding sections, we considered in great detail whether particular wastes are or are not within the hazardous waste subset of solid waste. That determination is vitally important to regulated industries and to people and ecosystems potentially affected, because it determines whether Subtitle C's cradle-to-grave regulatory apparatus — especially the costly and protective requirements for hazardous waste treatment, storage, and disposal facilities (TSDFs) — must be followed.

In this section we discuss some of Subtitle C's regulatory requirements. You may want to review the general description of Subtitle C (Section IV, pp. 640–646 above), as we do not repeat it here; instead, we fill in certain important details.

A. Generators

As you know, hazardous waste generation is the starting point of Subtitle C regulation. A "generator" is "any person, by site, whose act or process produces hazardous waste identified or listed in part 261 of this chapter [*i.e.,* 40 C.F.R. Part 261] or whose act first causes a hazardous waste to become subject to regulation." 40 C.F.R. § 260.10.

As we noted in the overview, a key requirement for generators is creation of the manifest that will accompany hazardous waste from generation through transport to storage and ultimate treatment or disposal. Generators also have obligations to package and label their hazardous waste properly, to keep records of their hazardous waste activities, and periodically to report those activities to EPA. Special requirements apply if generators export their hazardous waste to a foreign country. Personnel training and emergency planning and preparedness (for spills and other incidents) are mandated as well. *See generally* 40 C.F.R. Part 262.

The precise obligations of hazardous waste generators vary with the amount of waste they generate. EPA regulates generators in three size categories, based on the amount of various kinds of hazardous waste generated in a calendar month. A "large quantity generator" generates more than 1,000 kilograms of non-acute hazardous waste, or more than 100 kilograms of residues from a cleanup of acute hazardous waste, or one kilogram or more of acute hazardous waste, in a single month. A generator that generates amounts smaller than these thresholds is a "small quantity generator" unless the amount of non-acute hazardous waste generated is less than or equal to 100 kilograms, in which case the generator qualifies as a "very small quantity generator." A generator's classification can change from month to month if the amount of hazardous waste generated varies. Figure 8-6 summarizes the size classifications for hazardous waste generators:

Figure 8-6. Hazardous Waste Generator Categories.

A generator is classified as a:	If, in one calendar month, the generator generates this quantity of:		
	Non-acute hazardous waste	Acute hazardous waste	Residues from a cleanup of acute hazardous waste
Large Quantity Generator (LQG)	Any amount	More than 1 kilogram	Any amount
	Any amount	Any amount	More than 100 kilograms
	1,000 kilograms or more	Any amount	Any amount
Small Quantity Generator (SQG)	More than 100 kilograms but less than 1,000 kilograms	No more than 1 kilogram	No more than 100 kilograms
Very Small Quantity Generator (VSQG)	No more than 100 kilograms	No more than 1 kilogram	No more than 100 kilograms

Source: Adapted from 40 C.F.R. § 262.13 Table 1.[3]

As you might expect, the requirements for Large Quantity Generators are more stringent than the requirements for Small Quantity Generators. Very Small Quantity Generators (VSQGs), if they satisfy certain conditions, are exempt from most of the Subtitle C requirements for hazardous waste generators. Because of this conditional exemption, this class of generators was known as "Conditionally Exempt Small Quantity Generators" until EPA replaced that unwieldy nomenclature with the pithier and more descriptive "Very Small" appellation.

To qualify for the exemption, a VSQG must properly characterize and label its waste as hazardous or non-hazardous, must generate no more than the prescribed quantity of hazardous waste, and must have its hazardous waste treated or disposed of at an approved facility. Significantly, VSQGs are allowed to treat or dispose of their hazardous waste on-site or at certain non-hazardous-waste landfills. This contrasts with other generators, who must have their hazardous waste treated or disposed of at a TSDF. *See* 40 C.F.R. § 262.14 (provisions formerly codified in § 261.5)

Inevitably, a hazardous waste generator must hold on to some of the generated waste before shipping it off to be treated or disposed of. Rarely, if ever, is it technically and economically feasible for a generator to whisk its hazardous waste off to

---

3. The cited table is part of a final rule that revised and reorganized the regulations applicable to hazardous waste generators, effective May 30, 2017. 81 Fed. Reg. 85732 (Nov. 28, 2016). Previously, the size classifications for generators were found in 40 C.F.R. §§ 260.10 (defining "Small Quantity Generator"); 261.5(a), (e) (describing requirements for Conditionally Exempt Small Quantity Generators, now called Very Small Quantity Generators); 262.34 (b), (d) (describing requirements for Large Quantity Generators and Small Quantity Generators).

another facility instantaneously as the waste is produced. But if a generator "stores" hazardous waste it becomes a storage facility, subject to a whole new set of regulations applicable to TSDFs. To accommodate generators' need to temporarily keep their hazardous waste on-site, EPA devised the concept of "accumulation" as distinct from "storage." A generator is allowed to accumulate a certain amount of hazardous waste for a limited period without thereby engaging in the storage of hazardous waste. For Large Quantity Generators, the amount is unlimited but the maximum period is 90 days; for Small Quantity Generators, the maximum amount is 6,000 kilograms but the maximum period is 180 or 270 days depending on the shipping distance; for Very Small Quantity Generators, the maximum amounts are much smaller (1,000 kilograms of non-acute hazardous waste, one kilogram of acute hazardous waste, or 100 kilograms of acute spill residue) but the accumulation time is unlimited. *See* 40 C.F.R. §§ 261.5, 262.34. The accumulation allowance is quite important to generators for reasons that will become apparent as we consider the regulatory requirements faced by hazardous waste treatment, storage, and disposal facilities.

B. Treatment, Storage, and Disposal Facilities (TSDFs)

Some generators handle the ultimate disposition of their hazardous waste on-site; others hire transporters to bring their waste to its final destination.[4] Either way, the waste eventually makes its way to a "facility for the treatment, storage, or disposal of hazardous waste," i.e., a TSDF. The "owners and operators" of such facilities must have and comply with a permit, 42 U.S.C. § 6925 (RCRA § 3005), and must comply with EPA's "performance standards" for TSDFs, *id.* § 6924 — the most comprehensive and complex set of RCRA Subtitle C regulations.

As we explained in the overview of Subtitle C, p. 643 above, no casebook (and few practicing attorney specialists) can possibly explain the TSDF regulations in comprehensive detail. Instead, we lay out the pieces of the basic regulatory structure that applies to TSDFs.

---

4. With respect to transporter regulations, we have nothing to add here to the brief synopsis provided above (Section IV.B, p. 642). EPA's RCRA regulations for hazardous waste transporters are brief and address only requirements for keeping records and cleaning up spills. 40 C.F.R. Part 263. EPA's rules incorporate by reference the Department of Transportation's (DOT) extensive and detailed requirements "for the safe and secure transportation of hazardous materials in commerce," 49 C.F.R. § 171.1. The DOT rules in turn define hazardous waste as "any material subject to" EPA's hazardous waste manifesting requirement, *id.* § 171.8, and prohibit transporting or offering for transportation a hazardous waste "except in accordance with" the DOT requirements, *id.* § 171.3. Those technical requirements, unsurprisingly, vary depending on the nature of the material transported and the manner of transportation. They are codified at 49 C.F.R. Parts 171–180.

1. Definitions and Scope of the Regulations

The statute provides definitions to help regulators and the regulated community determine whether a particular facility is engaged in treatment, storage, or disposal of hazardous waste:

(3) The term "disposal" means the discharge, deposit, injection, dumping, spilling, leaking, or placing of any solid waste or hazardous waste into or on any land or water so that such solid waste or hazardous waste or any constituent thereof may enter the environment or be emitted into the air or discharged into any waters, including ground waters.

. . . .

(33) The term "storage", when used in connection with hazardous waste, means the containment of hazardous waste, either on a temporary basis or for a period of years, in such a manner as not to constitute disposal of such hazardous waste.

(34) The term "treatment", when used in connection with hazardous waste, means any method, technique, or process, including neutralization, designed to change the physical, chemical, or biological character or composition of any hazardous waste so as to neutralize such waste or so as to render such waste nonhazardous, safer for transport, amenable for recovery, amenable for storage, or reduced in volume. Such term includes any activity or processing designed to change the physical form or chemical composition of hazardous waste so as to render it nonhazardous.

42 U.S.C. § 6903 (RCRA § 1004). As you can see, the statutory definitions are commodious. As with the definitions of "solid waste" and "hazardous waste," EPA found it necessary to promulgate regulatory refinements of these terms to tailor the scope of the Subtitle C requirements.

With respect to "treatment," the regulatory definition is broader than the statutory definitions, or at least clarifies that the regulation includes some activities not explicitly identified as treatment in the statute:

Treatment means any method, technique, or process, including neutralization, designed to change the physical, chemical, or biological character or composition of any hazardous waste so as to neutralize such waste, or so as to recover energy or material resources from the waste, or so as to render such waste non-hazardous, or less hazardous; safer to transport, store, or dispose of; or amenable for recovery, amenable for storage, or reduced in volume.

40 C.F.R. § 260.10; *see also id.* § 270.2 (specifying the same definition of "treatment" for the TSDF permitting program). In what ways did EPA make the statutory definition of "treatment" easier to apply and understand?

The regulatory definition of "storage" also indicates an attempt by EPA to make the statutory definition easier to apply in practice. According to the regulations, "[s]torage means the holding of hazardous waste for a temporary period, at the end of which the hazardous waste is treated, disposed of, or stored elsewhere." 40 C.F.R. § 260.10; *see also id.* § 270.2 (specifying the same definition of "storage" for the TSDF permitting program). Is the regulatory definition clearer than the statute? Recall that in addition to formally defining "storage," EPA functionally limited the scope of "storage" by allowing generators to "accumulate" wastes for limited periods without thereby subjecting themselves to regulation as storage facilities. See p. 701, above.

For the general regulatory definition of "disposal," EPA simply repeated the statutory definition. 40 C.F.R. § 260.10. But the statutory definition (quoted at p. 702, above) presented problems for the regulation of TSDFs. First, the statutory definition referred to both solid waste and hazardous waste, but only treatment, storage, or disposal of hazardous waste triggers the Subtitle C permitting requirement. *See* 42 U.S.C. § 6925. For the permitting program, therefore, EPA defined "disposal" only to apply to hazardous waste. 40 C.F.R. § 270.2. Second, the statutory definition of "disposal" includes things that might occur without deliberate human agency, such as "leaking" and "spilling." For enforcement purposes, this broad definition makes a great deal of sense, as we will see in the *Waste Industries* case, p. 718 below. *See, e.g., United States v. Power Eng'g Co.,* 10 F. Supp. 2d 1145 (D. Colo. 1988) (holding that continued leaching of hazardous waste from contaminated soil into groundwater, as well as original leaking of hazardous waste from equipment into soil, constituted disposal). But would it make sense to say that someone who accidentally spills hazardous waste thereby operates a hazardous waste disposal facility and was legally required to have a permit beforehand? EPA's answer is that "[d]isposal *facility* means a facility or part of a facility at which hazardous waste is *intentionally* placed into or on the land or water, and at which hazardous waste will remain after closure . . . ." 40 C.F.R. § 270.2 (emphasis added); *see also id.* § 260.10 (stating very similar definition for Subtitle C regulations generally).

And what is a facility? The statute itself does not say. For RCRA Subtitle C regulations, EPA defines "facility" in general to mean:

> . . . All contiguous land, and structures, other appurtenances, and improvements on the land, used for treating, storing, or disposing of hazardous waste, or for managing hazardous secondary materials prior to reclamation. A facility may consist of several treatment, storage, or disposal operational units (e.g., one or more landfills, surface impoundments, or combinations of them).
>
> . . . .

40 C.F.R. § 260.10; *see also id.* § 270.2 (stating that for permitting purposes, "[f]acility . . . means any [hazardous waste management] facility . . . (including land or appurtenances thereto) that is subject to regulation under the RCRA program").

Of course, RCRA does not impose obligations on facilities (the physical objects) but rather on their human or human-run owners and operators. *See* 42 U.S.C. § 6924(a) (RCRA § 3004(a)) (requiring EPA to promulgate standards "applicable to owners and operators" of TSDFs); *id.* § 6925(a) (RCRA § 3005(a)) (requiring EPA to promulgate standards obligating "each person owning or operating an existing facility or planning to construct a new facility" to obtain a permit). RCRA broadly defines "person" to mean "an individual, trust, firm, joint stock company, corporation (including a government corporation), partnership, association, State, municipality, commission, political subdivision of a State, or any interstate body and . . . each department, agency, and instrumentality of the United States," *id.* § 6903 (RCRA § 3004), but does not define the terms "owner" and "operator."

EPA, however, has supplied definitions of these critical terms. In the RCRA Subtitle C regulatory program, "Operator means the person responsible for the overall operation of a facility. Owner means the person who owns a facility or part of a facility." 40 C.F.R. § 260.10. Are these definitions helpful?

What if a corporate "person" owns and operates a TSDF? Can the human people who are responsible for the corporation's acts be held accountable for RCRA compliance? Courts have held that individuals as well as corporations can simultaneously operate a facility, notwithstanding regulations referring to "the" operator. *See, e.g., United States v. Production Plated Plastics, Inc.*, 742 F. Supp. 956, 963 (W.D. Mich. 1990) (holding corporate officer and corporation jointly liable as operators where officer was the "ultimate decision-making authority" and "personally involved in or directly responsible for acts in violation of RCRA"); *United States v. Conservation Chem. Co. of Illinois*, 733 F. Supp. 1215, 1222 (N.D. Ind. 1989) (holding that individual who was corporation's president, chairman of the board, treasurer, and principal shareholder, who designed facility's treatment processes, and who was responsible for facility's environmental compliance, would be liable as operator for any proven violations of RCRA at the facility).

The foregoing definitions govern whether a particular enterprise qualifies as a TSDF and whether a particular individual or entity is the facility's owner or operator. Armed with these definitions, we next examine what RCRA requires of the owners and operators of TSDFs.

2. TSDF Permits

RCRA demands that each person owning or operating or planning to construct a new TSDF must obtain a permit to do so. 42 U.S.C. § 6925(a) (RCRA § 3005(a)). Facilities in existence at the time of RCRA's enactment could continue to operate lawfully in an "interim status" provided they applied for a permit and complied with EPA's regulatory requirements for interim status facilities. *See id.* § 6925(e) (RCRA § 3005(e)) (describing interim status). In recognition of the difficulty of retrofitting existing RCRA facilities to comply with new regulatory standards, the requirements for interim status facilities are less extensive than those for fully permitted facilities. *See* 40 C.F.R. Part 265 (specifying requirements for TSDFs in interim status).

The statute makes interim status available to a TSDF owner or operator only if that person "has made an application for a permit." 42 U.S.C. § 6925(e)(1)(c). EPA's regulations divide the permit application into two parts—a relatively simple Part A application and a much more detailed, much more cumbersome Part B application. *See* 40 C.F.R. §§ 270.1(b) (describing permit process), 270.13 (identifying required contents of Part A), 270.14–270.28 (identifying requirements for Part B). Under the rules, an existing facility initially can obtain interim status by submitting Part A, but to maintain interim status must then submit Part B by a specified date, usually within 12 months. *Id.* §§ 270.10(e)(5), 270.70(a)(2), 270.73(c)–(g). Interim status then continues while the permit application is pending. Interim status ends when a permit is granted — in which case the facility must then operate in compliance with its permit — or when a permit is finally denied — in which case the facility may no longer lawfully operate.

Interim status is thus a type of limited "grandfather clause," which allowed pre-existing TSDFs to stay in operation as they came into compliance with new requirements. During the early 1990s, enforcement staff at EPA and the Justice Department did a fairly brisk business taking action against facilities that had failed to submit timely and complete Part B applications or had otherwise lost their interim status. You might think that, with so many years elapsed since RCRA was enacted, interim status has become a dead letter. Interim status applies, however, not only to facilities that were in existence when RCRA (and then HSWA) was enacted, but to any existing facility that newly becomes subject to Subtitle C's TSDF regulations. 42 U.S.C. § 6925(e)(1)(A)(ii); 40 C.F.R. § 270.70(a). Thus, for example, if EPA adds a new waste stream to its list of hazardous waste, facilities that already treat, store, or dispose of that waste stream would need to qualify for interim status and then obtain a final TSDF permit.

You might wonder why any business, after going to the trouble to submit Part A of a permit application, might not complete an acceptable Part B application and obtain a permit. To understand this you must appreciate that a TSDF permit under RCRA is far more than a document that tells an applicant, "OK, now you may operate a facility that treats, stores or disposes of hazardous waste." As EPA describes them, permits embody a "tangible guarantee that TSDFs . . . comply with their extensive management standards" in order to protect human health and the environment. EPA, RCRA ORIENTATION MANUAL 2014 III-107. "Permits provide TSDF owners and operators with the legal authority to treat, store and dispose of hazardous waste *and detail how the facility must comply with the regulations*." *Id.* (emphasis added). In Part B applications, would-be TSDF owners and operators specify detailed plans for compliance. To get a feeling for the information required (and a preview of the TSDF regulations described in the next subsection of this chapter), consider this partial list of the general requirements for a Part B application.

Regulations of the Environmental Protection Agency

40 C.F.R. § 270.14 (2015)

(a) Part B of the permit application consists of the general information requirements of this section, and the specific information requirements in [40 C.F.R.] §§ [270.14] through 270.29 applicable to the facility. The part B information requirements presented in §§ 270.14 through 270.29 reflect the standards [for TSDF design, construction, operation and maintenance] promulgated in 40 CFR part 264 . . . .

(b) General information requirements. The following information is required for all HWM [hazardous waste management] facilities, except as § 264.1 provides otherwise:

(1) A general description of the facility.

(2) Chemical and physical analyses of the hazardous waste and hazardous debris to be handled at the facility . . . .

(3) A copy of the waste analysis plan . . . .

(4) A description of the security procedures and equipment . . . .

(5) A copy of the general inspection schedule . . . .

. . . .

(7) A copy of the contingency plan . . . .

(8) A description of procedures, structures, or equipment used at the facility to:

   (i) Prevent hazards in unloading operations . . . ;

   (ii) Prevent runoff from hazardous waste handling areas to other areas of the facility or environment, or to prevent flooding . . . ;

   (iii) Prevent contamination of water supplies;

   (iv) Mitigate effects of equipment failure and power outages;

   (v) Prevent undue exposure of personnel to hazardous waste . . . ; and

   (vi) Prevent releases to atmosphere.

(9) A description of precautions to prevent accidental ignition or reaction of ignitable, reactive, or incompatible wastes . . . .

(10) Traffic pattern, estimated volume . . . and control . . . .

(11) Facility location information [sufficient among other things to determine whether the facility must satisfy standards with respect to earthquakes and floods];

(12) An outline of both the introductory and continuing training programs . . . to prepare persons to operate or maintain the HWM facility in a safe manner . . . .

. . . .

(19) A topographic map showing a distance of 1,000 feet around the facility at a scale of 2.5 centimeters (1 inch) equal to not more than 61.0 meters (200 feet). Contours must be shown on the map. The contour interval must be sufficient to clearly show the pattern of surface water flow in the vicinity of and from each operational unit of the facility . . . . The map shall clearly show the following:

   (i) Map scale and date.

   (ii) 100-year floodplain area.

   (iii) Surface waters including intermittent streams.

(iv) Surrounding land uses (residential, commercial, agricultural, recreational).

(v) A wind rose (i.e., prevailing wind-speed and direction).

. . . .

(viii) Access control (fences, gates).

(ix) Injection and withdrawal wells both on-site and off-site.

(x) Buildings; treatment, storage, or disposal operations . . . .

(xi) Barriers for drainage or flood control.

(xii) Location of operational units within the HWM facility site . . . .

. . . .

(c) Additional information . . . regarding protection of groundwater is required from owners or operators of hazardous waste facilities containing a regulated unit . . . .

Notes and Questions

1. As stated, the above excerpt includes only some of the requirements for Part B permit applications. In particular, we omitted from subsection (c) a great many detailed requirements for information about groundwater protection. We also omitted a number of requirements that relate to making certain that human health and the environment remain protected even after a TSDF closes, *see* p. 711, below. Moreover, as the regulation stated, the Part B application must include not only the general facility information listed in 40 C.F.R. § 270.14, but also specific information showing how each of the facility's hazardous waste management units will comply with the specific requirements applicable to that particular type of unit, *see* p. 709, below. Based on the excerpt, can you understand why simply applying for a TSDF permit entails a substantial investment of time and money? Nevertheless, some businesses find that investment worthwhile because of the demand for the services of facilities that provide safe and lawful management of hazardous waste.

2. TSDF permitting is not like applying to law school, where candidates for admission submit their materials and then simply wait for a yes-or-no decision. EPA views the permitting process as an iterative dialectic between the applicant and the permitting authority, in which more information may be repeatedly requested from the applicant until the agency is ready to make a final decision. Moreover, the applicant is not the only participant in the conversation: pursuant to RCRA and EPA regulations, the public is also part of the permitting process. *See generally* 40 C.F.R. Part 124, Subparts A, B (providing procedures for public participation in EPA permitting generally and under RCRA); *see also* Chapter 12, below. One attorney described the industry's perspective on the TSDF permitting process this way: "Because of public hysteria over the words 'hazardous waste,' a permit process often brings demons out of the vapors and projects can be delayed for months if not years. Administrative and judicial challenges are common." Richard G. Stoll, *Coping with the RCRA Hazardous Waste System: A Few Practical Points for Fun and Profit*, C414 ALI-ABA 167, 172 n.7 (1989).

3. Does the TSDF permitting process invoke environmental justice concerns? As the quote from Mr. Stoll suggested, many people do not consider a hazardous waste management facility to be a welcome neighbor. Nevertheless, a study published in 2007 estimated that more than nine million Americans lived within three kilometers of a TSDF. ROBERT B. BULLARD ET AL., TOXIC WASTES AND RACE AT TWENTY 1987–2007 52 (2007). Analyzing the characteristics of the populations living in census tracts that are close to TSDFs, the authors concluded that "[a]ll race variables (percentages of Hispanics, African Americans and Asians/Pacific Islanders)" as well as "mean income and percent employed in blue collar occupations" were statistically significantly associated with proximity to a TSDF. *Id.* at 63. EPA has acknowledged the need to consider environmental justice in permitting decisions generally and in RCRA permitting specifically. *See* National Environmental Justice Advisory Council, ENHANCING ENVIRONMENTAL JUSTICE IN EPA PERMITTING PROGRAMS (April 2011) (available at https://www.epa.gov/sites/production/files/2015-02/documents/ej-in-permitting-report-2011.pdf) (describing charge from EPA and making recommendations).

3. Regulating the Operation of TSDFs

Since RCRA's original enactment, section 3004 of the statute has required EPA to promulgate regulations establishing "performance standards, applicable to owners and operators" of TSDFs, that include "requirements respecting"

(1) maintaining records of all hazardous wastes ... which is [sic] treated, stored, or disposed of, ... and the manner in which such wastes were treated, stored, or disposed of;

(2) satisfactory reporting, monitoring, and inspection and compliance with the manifest system referred to in section 6922(5) of this title;

(3) treatment, storage, or disposal of all such waste received by the facility pursuant to such operating methods, techniques, and practices as may be satisfactory to the Administrator;

(4) the location, design, and construction of such hazardous waste treatment, disposal, or storage facilities;

(5) contingency plans for effective action to minimize unanticipated damage from any treatment, storage, or disposal of any such hazardous waste;

(6) the maintenance of operation of such facilities ...;

(7) compliance with the requirements of section 6925 of this title [RCRA § 3005] respecting permits for treatment, storage, or disposal.

42 U.S.C. § 6924(a). The purpose of these required regulations is "to protect human health and the environment." *Id.* Pursuant to § 3004(a), EPA has promulgated TSDF regulations that include both generally applicable requirements addressing various subjects listed in the statute, as well as technical requirements for particular types of treatment, storage, or disposal "units" that may be found at a given TSDF.

The general requirements for TSDFs begin with tracking and recordkeeping. Facilities must ensure that incoming waste is manifested, must return a copy of the manifest to the generator in order to document safe receipt of the waste, must keep its own copy of the manifest and must submit periodic reports to EPA (and sometimes an authorized state agency). Facilities also must ensure that their personnel meet training requirements and must plan to prevent and respond to leaks, spills, and other emergencies. *See generally* 40 C.F.R. Part 264, Subparts B–E.

EPA's rules also regulate how TSDFs handle hazardous waste. To ensure proper management of waste received, facilities must test incoming waste to confirm it is as described in the manifest. *See* 40 C.F.R. § 264.13(a)(1) ("Before an owner or operator treats, stores, or disposes of any hazardous wastes . . . he must obtain a detailed chemical and physical analysis of a representative sample of the wastes."). Facilities must make certain to keep separate wastes that if mixed would present explosion, fire, or other risks, or to otherwise protect against those risks. *See id.* § 264.17.

EPA's technical requirements for hazardous waste treatment, storage, or disposal units aim to reduce the ecological and human health risks of hazardous waste by preventing the escape of hazardous waste into the environment. These requirements are detailed and as varied as the types of units (e.g., containers, containment buildings, tanks, landfills, impoundments, surface treatment units or "land farms," incinerators, drip pads, and waste piles). *See generally* 40 C.F.R. Part 264, Subparts I–EE (specifying requirements for various types of units); *see also id.* Part 266 (specifying standards for specific types of hazardous wastes and hazardous waste management facilities).

Some general principles emerge from the mass of rules that apply specifically to particular types of hazardous waste management units. First, the regulations require units that hold hazardous waste to be designed, constructed, operated, and maintained so as to prevent the release of waste to soil, surface water or ground water, or the air. Thus, for example, drums must be kept closed when not actually being filled or emptied; landfills must be designed and built to keep water from flowing onto the landfill from adjacent areas; landfills and impoundments must be lined with impermeable material to prevent leachate from escaping; land farms must be covered to prevent wind from blowing particles of hazardous waste away; concrete pads must be maintained without cracks; emissions of volatile materials from storage tanks must be controlled; etc. Second, the regulations require TSDFs to install and maintain secondary containment to intercept any spills or leaks of hazardous waste. Thus, for example, drums must be stored in such a way that any leaks will be collected; tanks must have double walls or be surrounded by a liner; liners under landfills and impoundments must be doubled so as to catch any liquid that leaks through the first layer; systems must be installed to collect leachate; etc.

4. Land Disposal Restrictions

Some facilities recycle certain hazardous wastes or subject certain hazardous wastes to chemical or physical treatment (such as neutralization or incineration) that eliminate the hazard. But most of the hazardous waste management units you read about in the preceding subsection have something in common: they all involve disposal of hazardous waste on land.

Land disposal of hazardous wastes, of course, was precisely the cause of the problems that motivated Congress to enact RCRA in 1976. Dissatisfied with the performance of the original statute's implementation by EPA, Congress in 1984 added to the statute a series of provisions colloquially known as the "land ban." 42 U.S.C. § 6924(b)–(m) (RCRA § 3004(b)–(m), added by HSWA § 201).

The new statute sections "shifted the focus of hazardous waste management away from land disposal to treatment alternatives," making "land disposal . . . the least favored method for managing hazardous wastes." *American Petroleum Inst. v. EPA*, 906 F.2d 729, 733 (D.C. Cir. 1990) (quoting 42 U.S.C. § 6901(b)(7)). Some of these provisions literally ban certain types of land disposal of specified types of hazardous waste (e.g., *id.* § 6924(b), prohibiting placement of bulk or noncontainerized liquid hazardous waste in landfills). For the most part, however, the land ban was a hammer designed to get EPA to promulgate "land disposal restrictions" in a timely manner. *See id.* § 6924(d), (e), (g), (m).

Specifically, HSWA required EPA to "promulgate regulations specifying those levels or methods of treatment, if any, which substantially diminish the toxicity of the waste or substantially reduce the likelihood of migration of hazardous constituents from the waste so that short-term and long-term threats to human health and the environment are minimized." 42 U.S.C. § 6924(m). These regulations prohibit land disposal of hazardous waste unless the wastes are first treated (not diluted) to attain concentrations of hazardous constituents lower than standards specified in the regulations. 40 C.F.R. §§ 268.1, 268.3.

For example, K170 waste—clarified slurry oil sediment from petroleum refining operations—is prohibited from land disposal unless the concentration of 13 particular hydrocarbons in the waste is reduced below specified levels. *Id.* §§ 268.35, 268.40 Table. For some hazardous wastes, EPA promulgated treatment standards that require application of a particular "best demonstrated available technology" rather than achievement of a quantitative concentration of hazardous constituents. For example, waste elemental mercury contaminated with radioactive materials is prohibited from land disposal unless first treated by amalgamation with other metals to produce a semi-solid material that is less likely to release mercury vapor into the air. *Id.* §§ 268.40 Table, 268.41 Table 1. Thus the "land ban" did not end land disposal of hazardous waste, but it made land disposal of hazardous waste safer.

In *American Petroleum Inst. v. EPA, supra*, the court rejected an industry challenge to some of EPA's land disposal restrictions. EPA had concluded that so-called "land treatment" was a prohibited form of land disposal and therefore would not be considered as a treatment technology that might avoid the land ban. Several trade associations argued that for certain hazardous wastes EPA should have permitted land treatment as a best demonstrated available technology. The D.C. Circuit observed, 906 F.2d at 735–36, that HSWA defined "land disposal" to include "placement of . . . hazardous waste in a . . . land treatment facility," 42 U.S.C. § 6924(k), and required hazardous waste to be treated *before* land disposal, *id.* § 6924(m)(2). "Thus, it was eminently reasonable for EPA to conclude that Industry Petitioners were requesting the agency to consider a BDAT [best demonstrated available technology] that clearly contravened the strictures of the RCRA," the court concluded. 906 F.2d at 737.

5. Corrective Action

Sometimes, even with a facility's best efforts at compliance, hazardous waste or hazardous constituents of waste are released into the environment. Or releases may have occurred at a facility that existed before the regulations to prevent such releases came into effect. As we have seen, the TSDF standards require facilities to monitor for one of the most commonly observed types of releases, contamination of groundwater.

As mentioned in our overview of Subtitle C, p. 643 above, to address such situations HSWA added §§ 3004(u) and 3004(v) to RCRA. These sections provide that:

> (u) . . . Standards promulgated under this section shall require, and a permit issued after November 8, 1984, by the Administrator or a State shall require, corrective action for all releases of hazardous waste or constituents from any solid waste management unit at a treatment, storage, or disposal facility seeking a permit under this subchapter, regardless of the time at which waste was placed in such unit . . . .

> (v) . . . [T]he Administrator shall amend the standards under this section . . . to require that corrective action be taken beyond the [treatment, storage or disposal] facility boundary where necessary to protect human health and the environment . . . .

42 U.S.C. §§ 6924(u), (v). "Corrective action permits" issued pursuant to this authority are not grants of authority to operate but rather affirmative requirements to undertake the actions needed to clean up releases of hazardous waste as necessary to achieve the protectiveness standard mandated by the statute.

Unlike the detailed, prescriptive requirements that characterize most of the regulatory scheme for TSDFs, EPA's corrective action rules are general and procedural. *See* 40 C.F.R. §§ 264.100, 264.101. This reflects a recognition that corrective action choices will depend on highly variable conditions at individual facilities. Much of EPA's approach to corrective action is articulated in guidance documents rather than in promulgated regulations. *See, e.g.,* 68 Fed. Reg. 8757 (Feb. 25, 2003) (announcing EPA's final guidance on how to tell when corrective action is complete).

6. Closure and Post-Closure Requirements

Nothing lasts forever, not even a hazardous waste treatment, storage, or disposal facility. Eventually a landfill or impoundment fills to capacity. Or a once-profitable business stops being so. What happens when and after a TSDF closes?

If the facility is still laden with hazardous waste, it is obviously untenable to allow the owner or operator simply to turn out the lights, lock the gates, and walk away. Many of the nation's worst Superfund sites (see Chapter 9) were created in just such a fashion. EPA accordingly imposes strict technical and financial requirements for the closure of TSDFs and for their continued safety after being closed ("post-closure"). These regulations begin with a general performance standard requiring the owner or operator of a TSDF to "close the facility in a manner that (a) Minimizes the need for further maintenance; and (b) Controls, minimizes or eliminates, to the extent necessary to protect human health and the environment, post-closure escape of hazardous waste . . . ." 40 C.F.R. § 264.111. The owner and operator must prepare plans for closure and post-closure care of the facility. *Id.* §§ 264.112, 264.118. And through one of a variety of financial mechanisms, the owner and operator must assure that funds are available to follow through on the closure and post-closure plans. *See generally id.* §§ 264.140–264.151. These regulations specify detailed requirements for the use of such devices as trust funds, surety bonds, letters of credit, and insurance policies to provide financial assurance. Do these requirements strike you as "environmental" regulations? Can you see why financial assurance is important?

The owners and operators of TSDFs do not have the luxury of thinking about closure only when it is time to close. EPA requires that a facility's closure and post-closure plans, as well as documentation of financial assurance, be included in the facility's Part B permit application. 40 C.F.R. § 270.14(13), (15–18).

United States v. Conservation Chemical Co. of Illinois, 733 F. Supp. 1215 (N.D. Ind. 1989) illustrates how a TSDF can run afoul of the closure and post-closure planning requirements as well as the procedural intricacies of TSDF permitting. In that case, the United States sought "a court order requiring defendants to close" their TSDF "in accordance with the closure and post-closure requirements of RCRA" and awarding "civil penalties for defendants' alleged failure to submit and implement adequate closure and post-closure plans . . . ." 733 F. Supp. at 1217.

As described in the court's findings of fact, Conservation Chemical Company of Illinois ("CCCI") began operating an industrial waste facility in Gary, Indiana, in 1968. After RCRA's enactment, CCCI submitted a Part A TSDF permit application on November 18, 1980 and attained interim status. CCCI submitted its Part B application to EPA on July 13, 1984. *Id.* at 1218–19. On January 30, 1985, EPA informed CCCI that the Part B application was deficient for various reasons, including a deficient closure plan. On May 14, 1985, CCCI submitted a revised Part B application, but EPA again rejected the closure plan as deficient. *Id.* at 1219. On January 31, 1986, EPA granted the State of Indiana final authorization to carry out the RCRA Subtitle C program in Indiana. *Id.* at 1217–18. Thereafter CCCI apparently submitted its RCRA documents to the Indiana Department of Environmental Management (IDEM), including a closure plan submitted on May 23, 1986. IDEM's review of that plan identified dozens of deficiencies, some "clearly *de minimis*" but others "just as clearly basic and major." *Id.* at 1227.

The court noted that Indiana's RCRA regulations (which were identical to the corresponding EPA regulations) required only submission of a closure plan with the Part B application; "[t]he words "proper" and "acceptable" do not appear in the regulation." *Id.* at 1226. Moreover, the regulations plainly contemplated the possibility that an initial submission would require revision before approval. *Id.* Nevertheless, the court refused to elevate form wholly above function:

> In sum, because the court finds there is an implied requirement that a closure plan be substantially acceptable once it has been reviewed, rejected, and resubmitted, and because defendants have not controverted the United States' submissions establishing that CCCI has failed, after at least two tries, to submit a closure plan that is even close to being acceptable, the court finds defendants liable for failing to submit a substantially acceptable closure plan in a timely fashion.

Id. at 1228. Although failing to submit an acceptable closure "plan" may seem to be a "paperwork" violation, imagine the potential consequences of a facility's actually *closing* without a plan to protect human health and the environment. The CCCI facility had lost interim status, *id.*, was therefore operating illegally, and (as revealed by two state agency inspections) had violated numerous substantive requirements applicable to interim status TSDFs. *Id.* at 1219–20, 1229–31.

7. Avoiding TSDF Requirements

As the preceding sections suggest, owning or operating a law-abiding hazardous waste treatment, storage, or disposal facility is hard, expensive work. The stringency of the TSDF regulations creates a strong incentive for businesses to try to avoid being subject to those regulations. Finding cost-effective ways to do so (short of flouting the law outright) is a major focus for executives in certain industries—and for their attorneys. Often, the most expedient method is to arrange a company's activities so as to exclude the materials being managed from EPA's regulatory definition of "hazardous waste."

We have seen these incentives at work in several court opinions excerpted earlier in this chapter. If the lead shot in *Connecticut Coastal Fishermen's Ass'n* had been hazardous waste, the gun club would have been a TSDF. If the in-process secondary materials in *American Mining Congress* had been hazardous waste, the companies creating and recycling that waste would have been generators, but might also have been operating TSDFs if the recycling activities qualified as "treatment." In *Mobil Oil*, the court's conclusion that Mobil's barge waste was a hazardous waste subjected Mobil to liability for operating an unpermitted TSDF. In *Bethlehem Steel*, the court's conclusion that Bethlehem's polishing lagoons and landfill did not contain hazardous waste meant that Bethlehem was not liable for alleged violations of the interim status requirements applicable to TSDFs.

In a 1989 article, a lawyer who had worked for EPA and a trade association before joining a law firm representing industry clients gave several examples of how to avoid triggering TSDF regulations—by avoiding handling "hazardous waste," by avoiding engaging in "treatment, storage or disposal," or by taking advantage of other exemptions in the complex RCRA regulations. Richard G. Stoll, *Coping with the RCRA Hazardous Waste System: A Few Practical Points for Fun and Profit*, C414 ALI-ABA 167 (1989). The article emphasized that finding these opportunities required extensive knowledge of the codified RCRA regulations as well as less formal statements of agency policy.

For example, Mr. Stoll's article hypothesized a plant manager seeking to save money by replacing the purchase of an expensive raw material with the purchase of a material containing the same chemical that is a hazardous waste but could be recycled into a usable feedstock for the plant's manufacturing process. Although doing this might appear to be treatment of hazardous waste, the article noted that EPA regulations state that the "recycling process itself is exempt from" RCRA regulation—but that "EPA buried this fundamental in a parenthetical near the end of a paragraph dealing with storage." Stoll, *supra*, at 174 (quoting 40 C.F.R. § 261.6(c)(1)). The author argued that "[f]or the most part, . . . these pathways are not really suggestive of 'loopholes' in the RCRA system. Rather, they show that recycling is something that is generally encouraged by RCRA." *Id.* at 185.

VII. Enforcing RCRA

As we described in the overview of Subtitle C, p. 645 above, § 3008 of RCRA, 42 U.S.C. § 6928, provides the federal government with criminal, civil judicial, and administrative tools with which to enforce the requirements of RCRA's statutory and regulatory requirements for hazardous waste. Administrative enforcement actions occur much more frequently than civil judicial enforcement actions, which occur much more frequently than criminal enforcement actions.

Criminal enforcement is reserved for a set of specified knowing violations of RCRA, 42 U.S.C. § 6928(d). One of these provisions gives teeth to the many provisions of RCRA that depend on certifications and reporting by regulated entities: it is a crime to "knowingly omit[ ] material information or make[ ] any false material statement or representation" on any document prepared for compliance with Subtitle C. *Id.* § 6928(d)(3); *see also* 18 U.S.C. § 1001 (making it a crime to make a "materially false, fictitious or fraudulent statement or representation" in any matter within the jurisdiction of the United States government). For knowing violations with more serious actual or threatened real-world consequences, RCRA provides an additional criminal penalty if the violator "knows at that time that he thereby places another person in imminent danger of death or serious bodily injury," *Id.* § 6928(e).

RCRA violations become criminal prosecutions only if the government believes the elements of the crime can be proven beyond a reasonable doubt, and typically only if a case involves egregious violations or severe harm, or risk of harm, to people or to the environment. For examples, see *United States v. Hansen*, 262 F.3d 1217, 1243–45 (11th Cir. 2001) (affirming conviction for knowing endangerment where corporate officers' improper storage of hazardous waste exposed employees to mercury-laden and caustic waste); *United States v. Laughlin*, 10 F.3d 961, 964–66 (2d Cir. 1993) (affirming conviction for operating a TSDF without a permit, where a corporate officer directed disposal of waste that included spilled creosote on remote portions of the property and personally emptied creosote sludge from a tanker car onto the ground and then ordered the sludge covered with dirt).

For the many situations in which criminal prosecution is not appropriate, § 3008 of RCRA includes two provisions authorizing other enforcement mechanisms. First, under § 3008(a),

> ... whenever ... the Administrator determines that any person has violated or is in violation of any requirement of this subchapter, the Administrator may issue an order assessing a civil penalty for any past or current violation, requiring compliance immediately or within a specified time period, or both, or ... may commence a civil action ... for appropriate relief, including a temporary or permanent injunction.

42 U.S.C. §§ 6928(a). Second, under § 3008(h)(1):

> Whenever ... the Administrator determines that there is or has been a release of hazardous waste into the environment from a facility authorized to operate under [interim status] ..., the Administrator may issue an order requiring corrective action or such other response measure as he deems necessary to protect human health or the environment or ... may commence a civil action ... for appropriate relief, including a temporary or permanent injunction.

Id. § 6928(h)(1).

Both provisions offer a choice of administrative or judicial enforcement mechanisms. Generally, civil judicial enforcement involves relatively severe violations or cases in which administrative action has not sufficed to bring a violator into compliance (and EPA hopes a judicial injunction backed by the threat of being held in contempt of court will suffice).

We saw examples of civil judicial enforcement in the *Mobil* and *Bethlehem* cases in which defendants were alleged to have operated TSDFs without a permit, pp. 678, 683, above. The *CCCI* case, which we described in the section on closure and post-closure plans, p. 712 above, also was a civil enforcement case. In *CCCI*, the defendant was alleged to have violated RCRA not only by failing to submit an adequate closure plan, but also by violating numerous interim status requirements. For example, the United States alleged that CCCI had leaking tanks of hazardous waste, allowed a surface impoundment of hazardous waste to overflow, had no protective cover on earthen dikes, did not install a groundwater monitoring system, and failed to provide adequate security. *See* 733 F. Supp. at 1219–20, 1229–30.

In civil judicial enforcement cases, the government typically seeks civil penalties and injunctive relief (for example, requiring the defendant to correct the violations, to comply in the future, to take corrective action for releases of hazardous substances to the environment, or to close the facility in accordance with RCRA requirements). Civil penalties available under RCRA can be quite large. They were originally set at a maximum of $25,000 per violation of "any requirement" of Subtitle C, with "[e]ach day of such violation" to "constitute a separate violation." 42 U.S.C. § 6928(g) (RCRA

§ 3008(g)). Pursuant to the Federal Civil Penalties Inflation Adjustment Act of 1990, P.L. 101-410, however, the maximum penalty has increased to $70,117 per day for penalties assessed after August 1, 2016, for violations that occurred after November 2, 2015. 40 C.F.R. § 19.4 Table 2. This can quickly add up to tens or even hundreds of millions of dollars in a case of numerous violations that persist for months or years, although judgments and settlement usually assess penalty amounts much smaller than the theoretical maximum. The cost of injunctive relief imposed on a violator, of course, depends on the nature of the injunction. Often, however, complying with the injunction embodied in a court judgment or consent decree requires a greater outlay than paying the civil penalty actually assessed.

Administrative enforcement begins with EPA issuing an order rather than filing a lawsuit. In addition to compliance orders under § 3008(a) and corrective action orders under § 3008(h), § 3013 of RCRA authorizes EPA to issue another type of administrative order:

> If the Administrator determines . . . that—
>
> (1) the presence of any hazardous waste at a facility or site at which hazardous waste is, or has been, stored, treated, or disposed of, or
>
> (2) the release of any such waste from such facility or site
>
> may present a substantial hazard to human health or the environment, he may issue an order requiring the owner or operator of such facility or site to conduct such monitoring, testing, analysis, and reporting with respect to such facility or site as the Administrator deems reasonable to ascertain the nature and extent of such hazard.

42 U.S.C. § 6934(a). A "3013 order" is not per se an enforcement action, but the order has the force of law and may be enforced by a civil judicial action for penalties and injunctive relief. *Id.* § 3013(e).

Howmet Corp. v. EPA, 614 F.3d 544 (D.C. Cir. 2010), illustrates the process of administrative enforcement. Howmet made precision investment castings for industry, using a solution of potassium hydroxide—KOH, a corrosive strong base—to clean the ceramic core from the metal castings. *Id.* at 548. When the KOH became too contaminated to clean the castings effectively, Howmet typically accumulated "the used KOH in storage tanks at an authorized hazardous waste disposal facility." *Id.* In one 13-month period, however, Howmet sent some of the used KOH to a fertilizer manufacturer, which added the used KOH to its product to reduce the fertilizer's acidity and to provide a source of potassium. *Id.*

EPA issued a compliance order, alleging that the used KOH was a hazardous waste that Howmet transported without preparing a manifest and without complying with several other record-keeping requirements. *Id.* The order alleged that the used KOH was a solid waste because it was "spent" material—defined in the regulations as material that can no longer serve "the purpose for which it was produced" without processing—and was a characteristic hazardous waste because of its corrosivity. *Id.*

Howmet contested the compliance order and requested a hearing before an Administrative Law Judge—an EPA employee whose job is to independently and neutrally adjudicate such disputes. *Id.* at 549. Howmet argued that the used KOH was not "spent" because it could still be used as a component of fertilizer, which is one purpose for which KOH is produced. *Id.* at 548. EPA argued that in the context of Howmet's activities, cleaning was the "purpose for which [the KOH] was produced," and once the KOH could no longer be used that way, it became "spent material." *Id.* The ALJ agreed with EPA and assessed a civil penalty of more than $300,000. *Id.* at 549. Howmet then filed an administrative appeal to EPA's Environmental Appeals Board (EAB). The EAB affirmed the ALJ's decision. At that point the decision became EPA's final agency action subject to judicial review. *Id.* Howmet sought judicial review by filing a complaint in district court. In court, Howmet alleged that EPA's decision—in particular EPA's interpretation of its regulation defining "spent material"—was arbitrary and capricious. The district court granted EPA's motion for summary judgment and upheld EPA's decision. *Id.* On appeal, the D.C. Circuit affirmed by a 2–1 vote, holding that EPA had reasonably interpreted its own ambiguous regulation. *Id.* at 550–53.

We have thus far discussed RCRA's enforcement provisions in connection with enforcement by the federal government. In states that are authorized to administer the RCRA Subtitle C regulatory program, state law must provide equivalent criminal, civil judicial, and administrative enforcement tools as a condition to receive authorization. *See* 40 C.F.R. § 271.16. But RCRA also allows EPA to take administrative or civil judicial enforcement actions even for violations in an authorized state, provided EPA gives the state prior notice. 42 U.S.C. § 6928(a)(2). The apparent duality of enforcement authority in authorized states has sometimes led to conflicts when EPA and a state have viewed the same violations from different perspectives.

In *Harmon Industries Inc. v. Browner*, 191 F.3d 894 (8th Cir. 1999), Harmon reported to the authorized state agency, the Missouri Department of Natural Resources (MDNR) that for a period of about 14 years its employees had "routinely discarded volatile solvent residue" on the ground behind the plant, *id.* at 896. While Harmon was negotiating with MDNR, EPA gave the state notice of, and initiated, an administrative enforcement action against Harmon; before EPA's final decision, however, Harmon and MDNR finalized a settlement under which Harmon would agree to a compliance plan, but not pay any penalty for the illegal disposal. After EPA imposed a civil penalty of nearly $600,000, Harmon sought judicial review. Harmon obtained summary judgment in the district court, and EPA appealed. *Id.*

On appeal, the Eighth Circuit held that RCRA did not authorize EPA's "overfiling" of a federal enforcement action if an authorized state had taken enforcement action with respect to the same violations. *Id.* at 901–02. The Eighth Circuit reasoned that the structure of RCRA, including the requirement that EPA give notice before taking an enforcement action against a violation in an authorized state, manifested a congressional intent to give authorized states primary enforcement responsibility. Other courts, however, have not followed *Harmon*. *See, e.g., United States v. Power Engineering Co.*, 303 F.3d 1232 (10th Cir. 2002) (disagreeing expressly with *Harmon*); *see also, e.g., United States v. Elias,* 269 F.3d 1003 (9th Cir. 2001) (stating that the United States retains all its RCRA enforcement authorities even in authorized states, and that even under *Harmon,* federal enforcement would not be limited in the *absence* of state enforcement action).

We have considered, then, the three types of enforcement action authorized by §3008 of RCRA. As we noted above, however (pp. 645–646), elsewhere in the statute Congress authorized a different, more sweeping authority for injunctive relief in cases of "imminent and substantial endangerment." 42 U.S.C. §6973 (RCRA §7003). We conclude our study of RCRA by considering two cases that illustrate how §7003 works.

United States v. Waste Industries, Inc.
734 F.2d 159 (4th Cir. 1984)

Judge SPROUSE:

After the Environmental Protection Agency (EPA) investigated the Flemington landfill waste disposal site in New Hanover County, North Carolina (the Flemington landfill) for possible water pollution in the surrounding area, the United States of America for the Administrator of the EPA initiated this action against [several defendants] . . . referred to collectively as the landfill group . . . . The EPA demanded affirmative action by the landfill group under section 7003 of [RCRA], 42 U.S.C. §6973, to abate alleged threats to public health and the environment posed by hazardous chemicals leaking from the Flemington landfill, to monitor the area for further contamination, to reimburse the EPA for money spent on the area, and to provide residents with a permanent potable water supply. The district court granted the landfill group's motion to dismiss under Federal Rule of Civil Procedure 12(b)(6) for failure to state a cause of action and the EPA brought this appeal. We reverse.

I

[The district court accepted the following facts as true for purposes of the motion to dismiss] . . . . [B]efore 1968, New Hanover County, North Carolina (County) had no trash or solid waste disposal programs or facilities. Private trash and garbage dumps existed throughout the County, but most were simply the result of the public's disposal of garbage and waste on private property without the permission of the property owners. [After trying several landfills between 1968 and 1972,] . . . the County Board granted Waste Industries, Inc. and Waste Industries of New Hanover County, Inc. (referred to collectively as Waste Industries) an exclusive license to dispose of solid waste generated in the County.

Under the terms of the license, Waste Industries was to establish and operate landfills for the sanitary disposal of solid waste generated within the County on sites Waste Industries owned. Waste Industries was to obtain all licenses and permits for operation of the landfills . . . . In return, Waste Industries gained an exclusive franchise to operate sanitary landfills within the County to provide sanitary disposal of solid waste, such as inflammable or toxic materials and industrial, commercial, and agricultural by-products . . . .

. . . Waste Industries obtained several landfill sites, including the seventy-acre Flemington site leased from private owners . . . . The [Flemington] landfill . . . is situated in a hole from which sand has been removed, known as a "sand barrow pit"; the surrounding soil is composed of highly permeable sand. The Flemington landfill is within a mile of both the Cape New Fear and Northeast Cape New Fear Rivers. During the operation of the landfill, unknown quantities of solid and hazardous waste were buried at the site. These wastes began leaching through the sandy soil beneath them and into the groundwater aquifer below.

Before Waste Industries began operating the landfill, the residents of the Flemington community had high quality groundwater. Flemington area residents first noticed a decline in water quality in autumn 1977, when their water became foul in color, taste, and smell. Some residents suffered illnesses or side effects such as blisters, boils, and stomach distress they attribute to their use of well water. Residents complained to the County Board and demanded help.

In response to residents' demands, the County in 1978 placed surplus water tanks that it still operates in the Flemington area. Many residents, however, had found it difficult to use these tanks because of infirmity or disability. Many families wash their clothes at laundromats and drive to the homes of friends or relatives elsewhere to bathe. Others have abandoned their homes because of the contaminated water.

. . . [T]he North Carolina Department of Natural Resources and Community Development . . . . directed Waste Industries to cease disposing of waste at the Flemington landfill, which it did on June 30, 1979.

Meanwhile, . . . the EPA's regional office . . . conducted hydrologic investigations of Flemington groundwater and well water in April, July, and September 1979 . . . . Analysis of Flemington area groundwater samples taken by the EPA revealed a large number of toxic, organic, and inorganic contaminants, including known carcinogens, resulting from improper disposal of waste at the Flemington landfill. The contaminants found beneath the landfill and in residential wells include tetrachloroethylene, benzene, trichloroethylene; 1, 2-dichloroethane; vinyl chloride, methylene chloride, and lead. These chemicals, migrating from the Flemington landfill, have been detected in residential wells at levels sufficient to affect adversely human health and the environment. The presence of chlorides, dichlorophenol, chlorobenzene, iron, manganese, phenol, and zinc has rendered the water in the wells unfit for human consumption because some of these chemicals are suspected carcinogens and all of them are a source of extremely bad taste or odor in water. Concentrations of lead, benzene, tetrachloroethylene, trichlorethylene, 1, 2-dichloroethane, and vinyl chloride found in three residential wells pose an unacceptably high risk of neurological damage in children and cancer in humans of any age.

. . . [T]he EPA warned many local residents that continued use of their wells for any purpose would endanger their health . . . . [T]he EPA demanded that the County provide an adequate water supply to Flemington residents. A water system funded with federal, state, and local money is now in operation.

The new water system, however, has not solved the problem of escaping waste. As precipitation infiltrates the landfill waste and transports contaminants through permeable soil, the contaminants reach the local aquifer and move laterally through the aquifer in the direction of groundwater flow to the south and east. Tests indicate that the process of leaching and migration of contaminants will continue indefinitely unless remedial action is taken.

II

The EPA . . . requested . . . injunctive relief requiring the appropriate parties: (1) to supply affected residents with a permanent and potable source of water; (2) to develop and implement a plan to prevent further contamination; (3) to restore the groundwater; (4) to monitor the area for further contamination; and (5) to reimburse the EPA for money spent in connection with the Flemington landfill . . . .

The district court . . . found that the EPA's claim for permanent injunctive relief failed to state a cause of action. It concluded that Waste Industries' failure to abate the leaching of contaminants was not actionable under section 7003 of the Act, because the provision was not intended to apply to past conduct that terminated before enforcement was sought . . . .

. . . .

III

Section 7003 of the Act provides that

> [n]otwithstanding any other provision of this chapter, upon receipt of evidence that the handling, storage, treatment, transportation or disposal of any solid waste or hazardous waste may present an imminent and substantial endangerment to health or the environment, the Administrator may bring suit on behalf of the United States in the appropriate District Court to immediately restrain any person contributing to such handling, storage, treatment, transportation or disposal to stop such handling, storage, treatment, transportation, or disposal or to take such other action as may be necessary.

The landfill group contends, and the district court held, that this section does not authorize an action to correct hazardous conditions because it only regulates the wastes themselves before or as they are produced, not the conditions they later create. The fallacy of that contention is demonstrated by the indication of Congress that section 7003 remedies exist apart from the other provisions in the Act's structure. In addition, section 7003 stands apart from the other sections of the Act defining the EPA's regulatory authority. The regulatory scheme for hazardous wastes appears in subtitle C of the Act; the scheme for solid wastes, in subtitle D. In contrast, section 7003 appears in subtitle G, and it is designed to deal with situations in which the regulatory schemes break down or have been circumvented.

. . . . This section is logically placed in the statutory structure to provide a remedy for environmental endangerment by hazardous or solid waste, whether or not those engaging in the endangering acts are subject to any other provision of the Act. Its application "notwithstanding any other provision of this chapter" indicates a congressional intent to include a broadly applicable section dealing with the concerns addressed by the statute as a whole.

The operative language of section 7003 authorizes the administrator to bring an action against any person contributing to the alleged disposal to stop such disposal "*or* to take such other action as may be necessary." 42 U.S.C. § 6973(a) (emphasis added). "Disposal" is defined in 42 U.S.C. § 6903(3) as follows:

> The term "disposal" means the discharge, deposit, injection, dumping, spilling, leaking, or placing of any solid waste or hazardous waste into or on any land or water so that such solid waste or hazardous waste or any constituent thereof may enter the environment or be emitted into the air or discharged into any waters, including ground waters.

The district court held . . . that this language means only disposal by "active human conduct." We cannot agree. The term "disposal," it is true, is used throughout subtitle C in the sense that the Administrator can regulate current disposal of hazardous waste. In this way, the Act regulates current conduct of would-be polluters. But a strained reading of that term limiting its section 7003 meaning to active conduct would so frustrate the remedial purpose of the Act as to make it meaningless. Section 7003, unlike the provisions of the Act's subtitle C, does not regulate conduct but regulates and mitigates endangerments. The Administrator's intervention authorized by section 7003 is triggered by evidence that the "disposal of . . . hazardous waste *may present* an imminent and substantial endangerment." (emphasis added).

The inclusion of "leaking" as one of the diverse definitional components of "disposal" demonstrates that Congress intended "disposal" to have a range of meanings, including conduct, a physical state, and an occurrence. Discharging, dumping, and injection (conduct), hazardous waste reposing (a physical state) and movement of the waste after it has been placed in a state of repose (an occurrence) are all encompassed in the broad definition of disposal. "Leaking" ordinarily occurs when landfills are not constructed soundly or when drums and tank trucks filled with waste materials corrode, rust, or rot. Thus "leaking" is an occurrence included in the meaning of "disposal."

The district court's statutory analysis relied heavily upon the present-tense definition of "disposal" as indicative of an intent to restrain only ongoing human conduct. The Act, however, permits a court to order a responsible party to "stop" activities "*or* to take such other action as may be necessary" (emphasis added) to abate the endangerment. Such grammatical niceties as tense may be useful in arriving at a narrowly-sculpted meaning, but they are of little help in interpreting remedial statutes in which actions such as "may be necessary" are contemplated in order to abate gross dangers to a community. Since the term "disposal" is used throughout the Act, its definition in section 6903(3) must necessarily be broad and general to encompass both routine regulatory and the less common emergency situations . . . . We conclude that Congress made "leaking" a part of the definition of "disposal" to meet the need to respond to the possibility of endangerment, among other reasons.

. . . .

IV

The landfill group argues that section 7003 was designed to control pollution only in emergency situations. The district court agreed, concluding that it was similar to other statutes designed by Congress solely to eliminate emergency problems. We find this position unsupportable, for the section's language stands in contrast to "emergency" type statutes. The language of section 7003 demonstrates that Congress contemplated circumstances in which the disposal of hazardous waste "*may present* an imminent and substantial endangerment" (emphasis added); therefore, the section's application is not specifically limited to an "emergency."

The Third Circuit . . . reached the same conclusion. It described section 7003 as having "enhanced the courts' traditional equitable powers by authorizing the issuance of injunctions when there is but a risk of harm, a more lenient standard than the traditional requirement of threatened irreparable harm." . . . .

V

. . . . The legislative history of the Act as originally enacted contains no specific discussion of the reach of section 7003 and no mention of the reasons for its insertion. The hastiness of the Act's passage in the final days of a congressional session has been well-documented . . . .

The focus of our attention, then, is not on the Act's legislative history, but on the legislative history of its 1980 amendments, in which various congressional committees addressed the issues of EPA authority under section 7003 and the purposes of this section. Later congressional ratification of the availability of section 7003 as a tool for abating hazards created by inactive solid and hazardous waste disposal sites such as the Flemington landfill has been consistent and authoritative. Although this is not legislative history as such, the views of subsequent Congresses on the same or similar statutes are entitled to some weight in the construction of previous legislation . . . . To the extent that the precise intent of the enacting Congress may be obscure, the views of subsequent Congresses should be given greater deference than they would be otherwise entitled to receive.

. . . . [A] congressional report on hazardous waste disposal issued when the 1980 amendments were being drafted observed:

> Imminence in this section [7003] applies to the nature of the threat rather than identification of the time when the endangerment initially arose. The section, therefore, may be used for events which took place at some time in the past but which continue to present a threat to the public health or the environment.

After noting that "RCRA is basically a prospective act designed to prevent improper disposal of hazardous wastes in the future," the . . . Report points out: "The only tool that [the Act] has to remedy the effects of past disposal practices which are not sound is its imminent hazard authority [section 7003]." Accordingly, the authority to abate waste hazards is expansive:

Section 7003 is designed to provide the Administrator with overriding authority to respond to situations involving a substantial endangerment to health or the environment, regardless of other remedies available through the provisions of the Act.

It is true that some confusion has been created in the interpretation of section 7003 by the EPA's own earlier interpretation — since abandoned — ... that because of its present tense language the statute was not intended to apply to inactive disposal facilities . . . . Not only did Congress [in a Committee report] reject the EPA's narrow view of its own authority, but the EPA later reversed its own early interpretation of section 7003. The agency's current view is, of course, entitled to substantial deference.

. . . .

VIII

Contrary to the district court holding, we conclude on the peculiar facts of this case that permanent mandatory injunctive relief is an appropriate remedy . . . . The EPA need not prove that an emergency exists to prevail under section 7003, only that the circumstances may present an imminent and substantial endangerment. It has been alleged that an imminent and substantial endangerment exists. We make no finding on whether the EPA will be able to meet its burden at trial. Since this case came to us in the posture of an appeal from the grant of a Rule 12(b)(6) motion to dismiss, we have viewed all the evidence in the light most favorable to the party opposing the motion, the EPA.

. . . .

For the reasons stated we reverse the district court's grant of the landfill group's motion to dismiss and remand for further proceeding consistent with this opinion.

Notes and Questions

1. How does EPA's enforcement authority under § 7003 differ from its enforcement authority under § 3008? For a discussion of the breadth and power of § 7003, see Joel A. Mintz, *Abandoned Hazardous Waste Sites and the RCRA Imminent Hazard Provision: Some Suggestions for a Sound Judicial Construction*, 11 Harv. Envtl. L. Rev. 247 (1987).

2. What, according to the court of appeals, was the significance of the location of § 7003 within the structure of RCRA? Should such structural considerations affect a court's construction of a statutory provision?

In a portion of the opinion not included in the excerpt, the court stated that the promulgation of EPA's hazardous waste regulations had no effect on the case, because "the regulations issued under the Act pertain to subtitle C and establish rules for safe management practices for persons handling hazardous wastes, not for situations covered by § 7003."

3. As the court observed, the term "disposal" is used throughout RCRA. Did the court's decision suggest a consistent meaning of "disposal" as used in the statute? If not, how does the court suggest the term's meaning varies in different parts of the statute?

4. Just as a corporate officer's personal involvement in a TSDF's activities can make the officer an "operator" of the facility alongside the corporation, see p. 704, above, under § 7003 a corporate officer can be individually liable as a "person" who "has contributed or is contributing to" an imminent and substantial endangerment. *United States v. Northeastern Pharm. & Chem. Co., Inc.*, 810 F.2d 726, 745 (8th Cir. 1986) (holding liable two corporate officers who were personally involved in the decisions and conduct that created the imminent and substantial endangerment).

5. The court noted that EPA originally interpreted the scope of § 7003 in a manner similar to the interpretation for which the landfill group advocated in *Waste Industries*, but that EPA later changed its view. EPA set forth, in the Federal Register, its original interpretation in 1978 and its revised interpretation in 1980. The court stated that EPA's revised interpretation "is, of course, entitled to substantial deference." Should that be true when the agency itself seemed to be of two minds? Agency reversals of position are a recurring topic in administrative law, particularly as Presidential Administrations (and their policy preferences) change. For landmark cases on this subject in regulatory contexts other than environmental law, see *Motor Vehicle Manufacturers Assn. v. State Farm Mutual Automobile Ins. Co.*, 463 U.S. 29 (1983) and *FCC v. Fox Television Stations, Inc.*, 556 U.S. 502 (2009).

6. In addition to authorizing the government to bring civil suits for injunctive relief as in *Waste Industries*, § 7003 authorizes EPA to "take other action . . . including, but not limited to, issuing such orders as may be necessary to protect public health and the environment." 42 U.S.C. § 6973(a). Willful violation or failure or refusal to comply with an order issued under § 7003(a) subjects the violator to a civil penalty, originally set at up to $5,000 per day, now increased with inflation adjustments to $14,023 per day. *Id.* § 6973(b); 40 C.F.R. § 19.4 Table 2.

7. In certain respects, the authorities granted under § 7003 of RCRA parallel some of the powers to compel environmental cleanups that Congress bestowed on EPA in the Comprehensive Environmental Response, Compensation and Liability Act (CERCLA), described in Chapter 9. As you will see, CERCLA is in many ways a more powerful tool than § 7003. But § 7003 reaches at least one place where CERCLA does not: unlike CERCLA, see p. 740, RCRA does not exclude petroleum from its regulatory reach, so § 7003 can be used to compel the cleanup of petroleum wastes.

8. Section 7003 authorizes relief only if the management of solid waste or hazardous waste "may present an imminent and substantial endangerment to health or the environment." 42 U.S.C. § 6973(a). How stringent a condition is this? What "imminent and substantial endangerment" did the United States allege in *Waste Industries*? Why were the allegations sufficient to state a claim for relief and therefore to withstand a motion to dismiss? How did the court interpret the terms used by the statute: "may present," "imminent," "substantial," and "endangerment"? Is there room between the court's interpretation and the defendants' assertion that an imminent and substantial endangerment must be an "emergency"?

9. Was the Third Circuit, favorably quoted in *Waste Industries*, correct to hold that § 7003 authorizes injunctions based on "a risk of harm, a more lenient standard than the traditional" standard for injunctive relief? These issues are further explored in the next case, brought not by a government environmental agency, but by a citizens' organization under a different provision of RCRA.

Interfaith Community Organization v. Honeywell Int'l, Inc.
399 F.3d 248 (3d Cir. 2005)

Judge VAN ANTWERPEN:

Appellant Honeywell International, Inc. challenges an injunction entered against it after the District Court found it had violated the citizen suit provision of the Resource Conservation and Recovery Act, ("RCRA"), 42 U.S.C. § 6972(a)(1)(B) . . . .

I. Background Facts

Starting in 1895, Mutual Chemical Company of America ("Mutual"), later the largest chrome manufacturer in the world, operated a chromate chemical plant in Jersey City, New Jersey. Its process resulted in a waste residue that had a high pH and high concentrations of hexavalent chromium. Mutual piled this waste at a tidal wetlands site along the Hackensack River. The piling of the waste created a land-mass (the "Site") which is the subject of this appeal. The Site consists of some 1,500,000 tons of the waste, 15 to 20 feet deep, on some 34 acres. The Site's high pH prevents the hexavalent chromium from reducing naturally to its less-toxic trivalent form, and enhances its ability to leach freely into surface water and groundwater. The hexavalent chromium is highly soluble, a known carcinogen to humans, and toxic to the environment.

Mutual continued dumping until 1954, when it was succeeded by the Allied Corporation, in turn succeeded by AlliedSignal, Inc., and then Honeywell. The site was never cleaned up.

The State of New Jersey first sought a permanent remedy for the Site in 1982, about the time a "green stream" and "yellowish-green plumes" were observed in surface water on the Site . . . . Honeywell did not act, however, until seven years later, about two years after NJDEP [New Jersey Department of Environmental Protection] had ordered it to do so. The result was not a permanent remedy but rather an "interim" measure consisting of poured concrete and asphalt over 17 acres of the Site and a plastic liner "cap" over the remaining 17 acres. This was intended to last only five years while a permanent remedy was to be studied and implemented . . . .

In a 1993 consent order arising from litigation over the Site, AlliedSignal promised $60 million towards a permanent containment solution and NJDEP reserved the right to compel a full cleanup at higher cost. The order also stated that the permanent remedy would be put in place through the NJDEP's usual process, which was to: (i) delineate, or identify, all of the conditions needing remedy; (ii) analyze remedial alternatives and select a remedy; and (iii) take "remedial action." The District Court found, and the record shows, that these steps were not taken or completed.

In 1995, a local community organization, Interfaith Community Organization ("ICO"), and five individual plaintiffs sued Honeywell's predecessor AlliedSignal and the then-owners of the Site under the citizen suit provision of RCRA, § 6972(a)(1)(B), alleging the Site "may present an imminent and substantial endangerment to health or the environment." At the conclusion of a two-week bench trial, the District Court found for plaintiffs and enjoined Honeywell to clean up the Site through excavation of the contamination.

. . . .

III. Analysis

. . . .

B. Imminent and Substantial Endangerment

1. Legal Standard

Honeywell contends it did not violate § 6972(a)(1)(B) . . . . [A] person may bring suit under this provision

> against any person . . . who has contributed or who is contributing to the past or present handling, storage, treatment, transportation, or disposal of any solid or hazardous waste which may present an imminent and substantial endangerment to health or the environment.

42 U.S.C. § 6972(a)(1)(B). This provision explicitly allows the consideration of environmental or health effects arising from waste and authorizes suit any time there may be a present threat — an imminent and substantial endangerment — to health or the environment. To prevail under § 6972(a)(1)(B), a plaintiff must prove:

> (1) that the defendant is a person, including, but not limited to, one who was or is a generator or transporter of solid or hazardous waste or one who was or is an owner or operator of a solid or hazardous waste treatment, storage, or disposal facility; (2) that the defendant has contributed to or is contributing to the handling, storage, treatment, transportation, or disposal of solid or hazardous waste; and (3) that the solid or hazardous waste may present an imminent and substantial endangerment to health or the environment.

Because Honeywell concedes that it is legally responsible for the Site and that chromium is both a solid and a hazardous waste under RCRA, the only remaining issue is whether it "may present an imminent and substantial endangerment to health or the environment." The meaning of this statutory language has been summarized as follows:

> The operative word . . . [is] "may". . . .
>
> [P]laintiffs need only demonstrate that the waste . . . "may present" an imminent and substantial threat. . . . Similarly, the term "endangerment" means a threatened or potential harm, and does not require proof of actual harm. . . . The endangerment must also be "imminent" [meaning] threatens to occur immediately. . . . Because the operative word is "may," however, the plaintiffs must [only] show that there is a potential for an imminent threat of serious

harm . . . [as] an endangerment is substantial if it is "serious" . . . to the environment or health.

This approach, we believe, is most faithful to the statutory language, especially as to the word "substantial." *See, e.g., United States v. Union Corp.*, 259 F.Supp.2d 356, 399–400 (E.D.Pa.2003) (observing that RCRA's "substantial" requirement "'does not require quantification of the endangerment (*e.g.*, proof that a certain number of persons will be exposed . . . or that a water supply will be contaminated to a specific degree)'") . . . .

Here, the District Court added four additional requirements to the endangerment showing . . . . as follows:

> [A] site "may present an imminent and substantial endangerment" within the meaning of RCRA where: (1) there is a potential population at risk; (2) the contaminant at issue is a RCRA "solid" or "hazardous waste"; (3) the contaminant is present at levels above that considered acceptable by the state; and (4) there is a pathway for current and/or future exposure.

At least two of these requirements are irreconcilable with § 6972(a)(1)(B).[5] The first requirement requires a "population," but § 6972(a)(1)(B)'s disjunctive phrasing, "*or* environment," means a living population is not required for success on the merits . . . . The third requirement, apparently intended by the District Court to give quantitative meaning to the word "substantial" in § 6972(a)(1)(B), is similarly without support. The word "substantial" is not defined by the statute or its legislative history. Turning to a dictionary, we find that "substantial" means "having substance" and "not imaginary"; only as the last of several definitions does the dictionary offer "of considerable size or amount." These definitions do not support one particular type of quantification measurement, such as the District Court's requirement that there be an exceedance of state standards . . . .

. . . .

. . . . [A] discussion of RCRA's amendments observes that § 6972(a)(1)(B) is "'intended to confer upon the courts the authority to eliminate any risks posed by toxic wastes,'" S.Rep. No. 98-284, 98th Cong., 1st Sess. at 59 (1983), and further that courts should "recogniz[e] that risk may be assessed from suspected, but not completely substantiated, relationships between imperfect data, or from probative preliminary data not yet certifiable as fact." This supports neither the District Court's particular quantitative requirement nor the even higher and more narrow quantitative standards that Honeywell would have us impose.

. . . .

Plaintiffs in this case were required to make a merits showing higher than that actually contemplated by the statute. Even under the higher requirements, the District

---

5. The second requirement is superfluous as it merely repeats the second element of § 6972(a)(1)(B), which requires a "solid or hazardous waste." Although not expressly stated, the fourth requirement is implicit in a finding of liability under § 6972(a)(1)(B).

Court found endangerments as to both human health and the environment as well as *actual* harm to the environment. As we will discuss below, these findings are not clearly erroneous. The District Court's inadvertent legal error with respect to the higher requirements it applied is therefore harmless . . . .

2. Evidence of Endangerment

. . . The District Court first found that the amounts of hexavalent chromium for which Honeywell was responsible far exceeded all applicable NJDEP contamination standards . . . . The evidence shows this finding was not clearly erroneous. . . . [I]n the soil at the Site . . . ., the average level of contamination was over 30 times higher than the state standard, and, at its highest, was about 75 to 90 times higher. Similarly, hexavalent concentrations in surface water at the Site . . . . [were] over 350 times higher than New Jersey's acceptable limit. Next, concentrations in the groundwater . . . . ranged from about 200 to 8,000 times higher than acceptable. Finally, concentrations in the river sediments adjacent to the Site were . . . . roughly 90 to 400 times higher than allowed.[6]

The District Court then found that there existed present and continuing pathways for exposure such that both human health and the environment were endangered. The evidence showed, among other things, breaches in the 17-acre plastic liner, estimated at the rate of over one million holes per acre; "ponding" of contaminated, high pH water on the Site's surface; percolation of contaminated water to the surface and through the breaches in the liner, as well as through cracks in the asphalt cap; Honeywell's admission that its hexavalent chromium is discharging from the Site's shallow groundwater into the Hackensack River; Honeywell's admission that hexavalent chromium is also seeping to the surface of the Site, mingling with surface water runoff, and entering the river; Honeywell's admission that chromium from its Site has already contaminated river sediments, which would not be possible absent a pathway; and Honeywell's admission that the interim measures it had installed to date were not preventing all discharges of chromium residue from the Site . . . .

There was also evidence . . . that Honeywell had expressly informed NJDEP at the time of Honeywell's installation of its "interim" measures that they could not prevent all discharges of chromium contamination from the Site, but would rather only "substantially reduce" discharges through their "various routes." The evidence showed that these measures, as built and maintained, were now severely compromised because the 17-acre plastic liner, or "cap," had been used years beyond its intended useful life and was ripped and leaking due to, among other things, wind damage. Similarly, the asphalt portion of the cap used to cover the remaining 17 acres of the site was buckled and cracked in numerous places due to "heaving" caused by the chromium at the Site. [The court explained "that chromium waste at the Site is literally 'heaving the ground vertically and horizontally, without warning, causing peaks and valleys of two feet or more in the interim measure "cap," compromising it.'"]

---

6. As we have previously indicated, state standards do not define a party's federal liability under RCRA. However, we find New Jersey's standards relevant and useful in determining the existence of an imminent and substantial endangerment.

Additionally as to pathways for human endangerment, the evidence showed ample evidence of human trespass at the Site and in and around the river, including holes and damage to the Site's fence and fencing around the river, discarded food and wrappers, toys, fishing poles and equipment, and graffiti. Our review of the record reveals additional evidence of humans at the Site, including soccer balls and soda bottles. Additionally as to pathways for endangerment to the environment, the District Court found, and the evidence shows, discharges into the groundwater, the river, and river's sediments through multiple routes . . . .

. . . .

In addition to the evidence of contamination of water, river sediments, and the river itself, the record also shows evidence of dogs and birds at and around the Site, as well as fish, invertebrates, benthic organisms, barnacles, mussels, crabs, clams, and crustaceans in the river; and seagulls, owls, pigeons, mice, and Canadian [sic] geese around both the Site and the river. As to other organisms living in the river's sediments, an expert in the fields of ecological risk and sediment contamination conducted standard bioassay tests on sediment dwelling organisms, taking sediment samples directly adjacent to the Site. These tests exhibited mortality rates of 50 to 100 percent for those organisms, which the expert attributed to the Site's contamination . . . .

. . . .

Even assuming *arguendo* the District Court clearly erred with respect to its findings relating to human endangerment, the findings with respect to environmental endangerment are manifestly correct on this record. That is all that is required under § 6972(a)(1)(B), which imposes liability for endangerments to the environment, including water in and of itself . . . .

. . . The extensive trial record includes the testimony of ten exceptionally qualified experts in the fields of health and environmental risk, ecological and aquatic toxicology, hydrogeology, environmental engineering and geochemistry, environmental remediation, dermatology, and "heaving." Their testimony rested upon legally relevant and permissible facts and assumptions, and had sound factual and scientific basis. We will not disturb findings supported by their testimony.

In sum, on the basis of all of the above evidence, the imminent and substantial endangerment determination was not clearly erroneous.

IV. Propriety of the Injunction

Honeywell argues the District Court erred in enjoining Honeywell to clean up its Site through excavation and removal of the contaminated waste . . . . [T]he District Court . . . found . . . that a permanent solution (as opposed to an interim solution) was necessary within the meaning of the statute to eliminate the established endangerments; . . . that Honeywell presented no credible evidence at trial that either a containment "cap" or shallow groundwater treatment, or both, would be an effective permanent remedy; and that excavation and removal of the contamination from the Site was necessary within the meaning of the statute to ensure a permanent remedy. The evidence shows that experts presented all other conceivable remedial options known to be potentially available, and . . . demonstrated why none were appropriate for the site except excavation. These included capping, encapsulation, reactive barriers, vitrification, solidification and stabilization, bioremediation, chemical reduction, chemical stabilization, chemical extraction, electrokinetics, soil washing, and, finally, "pump and treat" remedies.

The evidence also shows . . . a Site with unusually high levels of contamination and other unique characteristics, such as the high pH level . . . . Honeywell's own consultants called the heaving at the Site "erratic" and "unpredictable," and estimated it will occur for at least another 50 years. Honeywell's experts also conceded there is no viable treatment method capable of stopping heaving, except to remove the chromium waste that causes it . . . .

. . . .

Honeywell next argues that the injunction does not serve a public interest. In its brief, Honeywell poses the question as follows: even if cleaning up hexavalent chromium would be "better" for humans living near the site "and for some barnacles and clams in the Hackensack River . . . is it worthwhile to move over 1,500,000 tons of fill" and replace it with "over 1,500,000 tons of clean fill?" Honeywell asserts that environmental agencies would answer this question in the negative, and that therefore the District Court erred in reaching a different conclusion.

Without a doubt, the injunction will require the movement of a substantial amount of fill. Nevertheless, Honeywell's framing of the issue misses the point in several respects: the 1,500,000 tons of fill are all contaminated with a hazardous waste; plaintiffs have satisfied the standard for liability; and the evidence they adduced persuaded the District Court that a cleaning up through excavation was necessary, even in light of the monetary and other costs associated with that remedy, including the use of hazardous waste landfill capacities. The record shows the District Court considered the cost-benefit analysis evidence appropriately and made findings consistent with the public interest as reflected in the applicable statutory scheme.

. . . .

Honeywell next suggests the public interest requires a sophisticated, step-by-step, "sound" analysis appropriate for the permanent cleanup of a site as large and as contaminated as Honeywell's Site is, and that the District Court lacked the ability to "appreciate the inherent complexity and difficulty" of making "sound" remedial decisions. The District Court was very thorough and its decision is not lacking in any of these respects . . . .

Honeywell's final argument is that the District Court improperly overrode an ongoing administrative process . . . . [T]he District Court's findings as to Honeywell's dilatory tactics and NJDEP's inability to deal effectively with those tactics are not clear error. Indeed, a fair reading of the record casts strong doubt as to whether there *is* a process to override in this case. Honeywell next suggests that NJDEP's presence alone precludes a judicial remedy, given Congress' preference for agency-directed cleanups. Not only does the statute not bar the remedy here, but Congress has rejected

Honeywell's argument outright. *See* S.Rep. No. 98-284, 98th Cong., 1st Sess. at 57 (1983) "[C]itizens need not exhaust or rely upon other resources or remedies before seeking relief under these amendments. As with Section 7003, these amendments are to be an alternative and supplement to other remedies." . . . .

More fundamentally, Honeywell argues the remedial injunction usurps agency power. The reconciliation of such power in the injunctive context, however, is not difficult. Honeywell has violated the statute; and, despite Honeywell's argument to the contrary, nothing in the statute precludes the nature of the injunctive relief ordered here. Depending on the particular characteristics of a given RCRA site, as found by a district court on a case-by-case basis, particular types of injunctive relief may not be circumscribed by arguments as to what an agency might have done . . . .

. . . . On appeal, Honeywell contends the allowed injunctive relief on such facts may only be, at most, an order "directing Honeywell not to miss NJDEP deadlines." We do not agree. Given the severity of the contamination at the Site and its other unique characteristics, precisely established in the evidence, the injunction was reasonably calculated, narrowly tailored, and thus necessary to remedy an established wrong. As the District Court did not abuse its discretion, the injunction is affirmed.

. . . .

[The concurring opinion of Judge Ambro is omitted.]

Notes and Questions

1. Compare the citizen suit "imminent and substantial endangerment" provision quoted in *Interfaith Community*, 42 U.S.C. § 6972(a)(1)(B) (RCRA § 7002(a)(1)(B)), with the "imminent and substantial endangerment" provision quoted in *Waste Industries, id.* § 6973 (RCRA § 7003(a)). How are these provisions similar or different? To what extent would judicial interpretations of either provision apply to construction of the other?

2. Why did the court of appeals reject the district court's enumeration of the elements the plaintiffs needed to prove to establish an imminent and substantial endangerment? What does the Third Circuit's reasoning teach us about the stringency of the statutory standard? Why did the Third Circuit construe the statutory provision as it did? On this issue, is *Interfaith Community* consistent with *Waste Industries*?

3. After stating the legal standard for an imminent and substantial endangerment, the Third Circuit, applying the "clearly erroneous" standard of review, considered whether the evidence supported the district court's finding that an endangerment existed. Why did the court of appeals affirm the district court's findings?

4. The district court found an imminent and substantial endangerment to both health and the environment. The court of appeals affirmed both findings. Nevertheless, the court of appeals entertained the possibility that, even if, "*arguendo*," the district court clearly erred in finding an endangerment to health, the finding of an environmental endangerment was "manifestly correct." Why do you think the court made this point? Was there a distinction between the evidence presented in support of the human health endangerment and the evidence presented in support of the environmental endangerment?

5. Speaking of evidence, why did the plaintiffs introduce testimony from so many experts in so many diverse fields? Environmental lawyers need not be scientists, but they often find it very helpful to be able to communicate with scientists and to learn scientific principles. It also helps if lawyers are able to teach scientists to communicate with judges and juries. In many instances that were omitted from the excerpt you read, the Third Circuit in *Interfaith Community* noted that the district court explicitly found particular expert witnesses credible.

6. In the *Waste Industries* case, EPA—a presumably expert government agency—determined what needed to be done to address the groundwater contamination emanating from the Flemington landfill and asked the court to issue an injunction requiring the defendants to perform that work. By contrast, in *Interfaith Community*, the plaintiff demanding a specific type of cleanup was a citizens' organization. Honeywell contended—rightly or wrongly—that no environmental agency would impose on Honeywell the remedy that the plaintiffs sought from the court.

Fundamentally, Honeywell argued in several different ways that the district court's injunction improperly intruded on the authority of New Jersey's environmental agencies to select the best "permanent cleanup" for Honeywell's contaminated site. The court of appeals, however, condemned the administrative process as applied to this site in no uncertain terms: "a fair reading of the record casts strong doubt as to whether there *is* a process to override in this case." Why?

Agency and defendant dilatoriness aside, does it make sense to have judges decide the best way to clean up dangerous hazardous waste sites? Do you agree with the court of appeals' defense of the district court's ability to make this decision and its thoroughness in doing so? Or do you think that issues of institutional competence suggest that courts should defer to agency expertise on such issues?

If you prefer deference to agencies, how do you think the court in *Interfaith Community* could have deferred to agency decision-making in light of the history of the site? If you believe in courts' ability to fashion remedies, do you think the trial judge in *Waste Industries* should have been free to disregard EPA's request for relief and craft a different injunction (assuming that the United States proved its claim of an imminent and substantial endangerment)? We discuss an analogous issue, relating to cleanup orders and injunctions under the "Superfund" statute, in Chapter 9. See p. 760, below.

7. Courts have generally agreed that "may present an imminent and substantial endangerment" is a relatively low threshold for obtaining relief. As the First Circuit summarized the case law:

> . . . To date, at least four of our sister circuits have construed [section 7003 and its "counterpart language" in section 7002(a)(1)(B)] . . . expansively. In taking this position, all four courts have emphasized the preeminence of the word "may" in defining the degree of risk needed to support [the] . . . liability standard.

> This expansiveness in construing the requisite degree of risk has largely been matched in the courts' assessment of the gravity and immediacy of the threatened harm. With one possible exception, the courts have agreed that the word "substantial" implies serious harm. There has, however, been some reluctance to quantify the needed level of harm more precisely. Imminence generally has been read to require only that the harm is of a kind that poses a near-term threat; there is no corollary requirement that the harm necessarily will occur or that the actual damage will manifest itself immediately.

Maine People's Alliance v. Mallinckrodt, Inc., 471 F.3d 277, 288 (1st Cir. 2006). The First Circuit joined its sister circuits, concluding "that a reasonable prospect of future harm is adequate to engage the gears of RCRA § 7002(a)(1)(B) so long as the threat is near-term and involves potentially serious harm." *Id.* at 296.

  8. RCRA authorizes citizens to bring suit in other circumstances as well. § 7002(a)(1)(A) authorizes citizen suits

> against any person (including (a) the United States, and (b) any other governmental instrumentality or agency, to the extent permitted by the eleventh amendment to the Constitution) who is alleged to be in violation of any permit, standard, regulation, condition, requirement, prohibition, or order which has become effective pursuant to this chapter . . .

42 U.S.C. § 6972(a)(1)(A). § 7002(a)(2) authorizes citizen suits "against the Administrator [of EPA] where there is alleged a failure of the Administrator to perform any act or duty under this chapter which is not discretionary with the Administrator." *Id.* § 6972(a)(2). RCRA requires notice before commencement of a citizen suit. *Id.* § 6972(b)(1)(A), (b)(2)(A), (c). Citizen suits against violators are barred "if the Administrator or State has commenced and is diligently prosecuting a civil or criminal action in a court of the United States or a State to require compliance . . . ," *id.* § 6972(b)(1)(B). Citizen suits against imminent and substantial endangerments are barred if EPA or a state agency is already taking one of several types of authorized actions to address the conditions creating the endangerment. *Id.* § 6972(b)(2)(B), (C). In many situations, citizen suits are a vital adjunct to government enforcement authorities that the government cannot or will not exercise, perhaps because of limited government resources, varying government priorities, or government reluctance to pursue a particular case.

"Superfund" statute
— made liable "persons" who have certain types of involvement w/ facilities from which hazardous substances are released
— "person" = individuals, business entities, gov't agencies

Chapter 9

SUPERFUND

Addressing a Legacy of Contamination: The Comprehensive Environmental Response, Compensation and Liability Act

You own your manifested waste from cradle to grave.

I. Introduction

The residents of a low-lying neighborhood in Niagara Falls, New York, grappled with a problem familiar to many people: water was seeping into their basements. In the spring and summer of 1978, however, they—and the nation and the world—learned that the water and soil beneath their neighborhood were laden with chemical waste, including solvents, heavy metals, and dioxins. State health officials quickly concluded that long-term exposure to this toxic soup posed a health risk. The neighborhood's name, Love Canal, became a symbol of the lurking legacy of industrial waste that was dumped long before its disposal was regulated.

The people of Love Canal, fearing for their health, concerned about the value and habitability of their property, and unable to fix the problem on their own, organized. They demanded government action. Their predicament became a media sensation and a potent political issue.

Domestic policy advisers at the highest level of the federal government tried to respond to the urgent demand to "do something," only to confront an awful realization: in the entire body of federal statutes, there did not seem to be any that clearly conferred the authority to address a situation like Love Canal. Eventually President Carter turned to the Federal Disaster Relief Act and declared an emergency in Love Canal. The government's disaster assistance machinery sprang to life: officials of the Federal Disaster Assistance Agency (later the Federal Emergency Management Agency), with environmental engineers from the Environmental Protection Agency (EPA) riding shotgun, toured the neighborhood, conducting a "windshield survey" of the "damage," which they dutifully recorded on forms plainly designed for hurricanes, tornadoes, and floods rather than for public health threats resulting from toxic chemicals. With this somewhat odd beginning, EPA commenced a series of both immediate and long-term efforts, which culminated only in 2004, to protect the citizens of Love Canal and the environment from the risks posed by the chemical wastes within.

In the immediate aftermath of the discovery of contamination at Love Canal, the most urgent question was "what do we do?" But another urgent question soon arose:

735

Landfill ≠ grave

"how could this happen?" How did an entire neighborhood, including a school, come to exist directly atop what turned out to be some 43 million pounds of chemical waste?

Investigators learned that Love Canal had indeed begun its life as a canal, the brain-child of a late-nineteenth-century entrepreneur named William Love. Mr. Love abandoned the project in the wake of an economic downturn, leaving the canal partly dug. Decades later, in the industrial heyday of the Buffalo-Niagara Falls region, the Hooker Chemical Company found the ready-made pit a convenient place to dump its process waste, first by arrangement with the landowner and then, after buying the property, as the landowner. In 1953, Hooker sold the land to the City of Niagara Falls Board of Education. Thereafter a residential neighborhood and a school to serve it were built on and adjacent to the former Hooker chemical waste landfill.

By 1978, of course, as you read in Chapter 8, RCRA was supposed to have prohibited the type of haphazard disposal of hazardous wastes that led to the seepage of toxins into the Love Canal neighborhood. But by 1978, Hooker and its corporate successors had long since stopped owning or operating the landfill.

Thus Love Canal illustrated twin gaps in federal law: a lack of clear authority to respond to the environmental and public health threats posed by releases of hazardous substances, and a lack of clear authority to hold accountable the persons or entities responsible for the conditions that led to such releases. To try to fill those gaps, Congress passed and President Carter signed the Comprehensive Environmental Response, Compensation and Liability Act (CERCLA), often called the "Superfund" law.

Although the antecedents of CERCLA began kicking around Congress no more than a year after the first federal involvement at Love Canal, *see* President Jimmy Carter, Message to Congress: Environmental Priorities and Programs (Aug. 2, 1979) *in* 15 WEEKLY COMP. PRES. DOCS i 1979 1353, 1357 (noting proposed legislation submitted to Congress the previous month), the statute did not pass Congress until December 11, 1980. By then Ronald Reagan had won the 1980 presidential election, and the lame-duck, Democratic-controlled Congress hastened to finish the complex legislation in time for President Carter to sign it. This haste contributed to drafting problems that courts have often lamented as they struggled to apply and interpret the statute's provisions. Congress has amended CERCLA several times, including a major overhaul in 1986, the Superfund Amendments and Reauthorization Act (SARA). SARA was designed to clarify some ambiguities in CERCLA and to correct several perceived problems with the way EPA implemented the original statute, although the corrections added considerable procedural complexity to an already complex law.

CERCLA's ambiguities and amendments, however, have neither obscured nor altered its core dual purposes. In one of the first court opinions to interpret CERCLA, a federal district judge described those purposes (in a passage later quoted by five federal courts of appeals) as follows:

> First, Congress intended that the federal government be immediately given the tools necessary for a prompt and effective response to problems of national magnitude resulting from hazardous waste disposal. Second, Congress

intended that those responsible for problems caused by the disposal of chemical poisons bear the costs and responsibility for remedying the harmful conditions they created.

United States v. Reilly Tar & Chem. Corp., 546 F. Supp. 1100, 1112 (D. Minn. 1982). We begin our study of CERCLA by considering its provisions aimed at achieving the first of these goals.

II. Response Authority

Congress ensured that no future President would face the problem President Carter faced as he and his staff cast about for legal authority to take action at Love Canal.

> Whenever (A) any hazardous substance is released or there is a substantial threat of such a release into the environment, or (B) there is a release or substantial threat of release into the environment of any pollutant or contaminant which may present an imminent and substantial danger to the public health or welfare, the President is authorized to act, consistent with the national contingency plan, to remove or arrange for the removal of, and provide for remedial action relating to such hazardous substance, pollutant, or contaminant at any time (including its removal from any contaminated natural resource), or take any other response measure consistent with the national contingency plan which the President deems necessary to protect the public health or welfare or the environment . . . .

42 U.S.C. § 9604(a)(1) (CERCLA § 104(a)(1)). Section 104(a) authorizes two different types of "response" actions—"removal" and "remedial action." The statute distinguishes those responses in its definitions section:

> (23) The terms "remove" or "removal" means [sic] the cleanup or removal of released hazardous substances from the environment, such actions as may be necessary [sic] taken in the event of the threat of release of hazardous substances into the environment, such actions as may be necessary to monitor, assess, and evaluate the release or threat of release of hazardous substances, the disposal of removed material, or the taking of such other actions as may be necessary to prevent, minimize, or mitigate damage to the public health or welfare or to the environment, which may otherwise result from a release or threat of release. The term includes . . . security fencing or other measures to limit access, provision of alternative water supplies, temporary evacuation and housing of threatened individuals . . . , action taken under [CERCLA § 104(b), which authorizes the President to "undertake . . . investigations, monitoring, surveys, testing and other information gathering" with respect to releases], and any emergency assistance which may be provided under the Disaster Relief and Emergency Assistance Act.

> (24) The terms "remedy" or "remedial action" means [sic] those actions consistent with permanent remedy taken instead of or in addition to removal actions in the event of a release or threatened release of a hazardous substance

into the environment, to prevent or minimize the release of hazardous substances so that they do not migrate to cause substantial danger to present or future public health or welfare or the environment. The term includes . . . such actions at the location of the release as storage, confinement, perimeter protection using dikes, trenches, or ditches, clay cover, neutralization, cleanup of released hazardous substances and associated contaminated materials, recycling or reuse, diversion, destruction, segregation of reactive wastes, dredging or excavations, repair or replacement of leaking containers, collection of leachate and runoff, onsite treatment or incineration, provision of alternative water supplies, and any monitoring reasonably required to assure that such actions protect the public health and welfare and the environment. The term includes . . . permanent relocation of residents and businesses and community facilities . . . ; the term includes offsite transport and offsite storage, treatment, destruction, or secure disposition of hazardous substances and associated contaminated materials.

42 U.S.C. § 9601(23), (24) (CERCLA § 101(23), (24)). For good measure, the statute further defines "respond" or "response" to include "remove, removal, remedy, and remedial action." *Id.* § 9601(25) (CERCLA § 101(25)). These definitions provide a glimpse into the syntactic complexity of CERCLA. Having read them, can you say what the difference is between a removal and a remedial action?

The necessary predicate for either removal or remedial action is a release or substantial threat of release of either: (1) "any hazardous substance" or (2) "any pollutant or contaminant which may present an imminent and substantial danger to the public health or welfare." It is often true that a "pollutant or contaminant" is also a "hazardous substance," but the statutory definitions of these terms are not identical. CERCLA defines "pollutant or contaminant" functionally, as something "which after release into the environment and upon exposure, ingestion, inhalation, or assimilation into any organism . . . will or may reasonably be anticipated to cause death, disease, behavioral abnormalities, cancer, genetic mutation, physiological malfunctions . . . or physical deformations . . . ." 42 U.S.C. § 9601(33) (CERCLA § 101(33)). "Hazardous substance," by contrast, is defined mainly by reference to several lists of materials deemed hazardous pursuant to other environmental statutes. Any of the following is a CERCLA hazardous substance:

- a listed or characteristic "hazardous waste" regulated under the Resource Conservation and Recovery Act (RCRA) (see Chapter 8, pp. 673–678);

- a "toxic pollutant" or "hazardous substance" designated or listed by EPA under sections 307(a) or 311(b)(2)(A) of the Clean Water Act, respectively (see Chapter 7, p. 592);

- a "hazardous air pollutant" listed under § 112 of the Clean Air Act (see Chapter 5, pp. 329–336);

- an "imminently hazardous chemical substance or mixture" as to which EPA has taken action under § 7 of the Toxic Substances Control Act (TSCA) (see Chapter 10 Section IV.A).

42 U.S.C. § 9601(14) (CERCLA § 101(14)). Lest these lists from other statutes be incomplete, CERCLA empowers EPA to identify additional hazardous substances that "when released into the environment may present substantial danger to the public health or welfare or the environment." *Id.* §§ 9602(a) (CERCLA § 102(a)) (authorizing designation of additional hazardous substances), 9601(14) (CERCLA § 101(14)) (including a substance designated under § 102(a) in the definition of "hazardous substance"). Because CERCLA's definition of hazardous substances incorporates materials designated under disparate criteria pursuant to statutes serving diverse purposes, the list of CERCLA hazardous substances includes many redundant or overlapping entries. Thus, for example, "lead," "lead and compounds," "lead compounds," and 14 specified chemical compounds of lead all are hazardous substances. *See generally* 40 C.F.R. § 302.4 (listing hazardous substances under CERCLA).

Despite the overlap between "hazardous substances" and "pollutants and contaminants," as a practical matter CERCLA in operation is much more concerned with hazardous substances than with pollutants or contaminants, for at least three reasons. First, CERCLA defines pollutants or contaminants based on their capacity to cause death or illness, which might become a contested issue. By contrast, it is difficult to contest that a hazardous substance is on the CERCLA list. Second, CERCLA authorizes response to a release of pollutants or contaminants only if the release "may present an imminent and substantial danger." This standard is not terribly difficult to satisfy (see pp. 732–733, above), and is often invoked for other purposes under CERCLA, but it is not a prerequisite for taking action in response to hazardous substance releases. Therefore it can be somewhat easier to demonstrate statutory authorization for a response to a hazardous substance release. Third, CERCLA's liability provision, which we describe in Section III below, applies only to releases of hazardous substances. Therefore the usual trigger for CERCLA response action, and the only trigger for CERCLA liability, is a release or threatened release of at least one hazardous substance.

The Congress that enacted CERCLA understood that responding to the nation's legacy of abandoned chemical waste would not be cheap, because Love Canal was not unique. A congressional subcommittee had persuaded the 53 largest chemical companies in America to disclose voluntarily information they had on their past waste disposal practices. The responses showed that just these companies had dumped 762 million tons of chemical process waste at more than 3,000 sites, any one of which might become a threat to human health or the environment. Subcomm. on Oversight & Investigations, House Comm. on Interstate & Foreign Commerce, WASTE DISPOSAL SITE SURVEY iii (96th Cong. 1st Sess., Oct. 1979). Anticipating a need to pay for removal and remedial action at many of these sites and others, Congress created the Hazardous Substance Response Trust Fund, a repository within the Treasury initially financed mainly by a new tax on certain petroleum products and chemicals. 26 U.S.C. §§ 4661, 4662 (CERCLA § 211) (imposing tax); (CERCLA § 221) (creating trust fund, formerly codified at 42 U.S.C. § 9631). This trust fund, at first colloquially and now officially known as the "Superfund," 26 U.S.C. § 9507 (added by SARA § 204), gave a widely used nickname to the statute, the government program administering the statute, and the sites that the program cleans up.

Notes and Questions

1. Section 104 of CERCLA authorizes "the President" to take response actions. By Executive Order, President Reagan delegated almost all of this authority to the Environmental Protection Agency. Exec. Order 12580 (Jan. 23, 1987); *see* 42 U.S.C. § 9615 (CERCLA § 115) (authorizing Presidential delegation of authority). Within EPA, the Office of Land and Emergency Management (OLEM), headed by an Assistant Administrator, is responsible for the overall Superfund program; an analogous office in each EPA regional office manages response actions within its geographic domain.

2. Although CERCLA defines "hazardous substances" very broadly, the definition specifically excludes both "petroleum, including crude oil or any Fraction [sic] thereof which is not otherwise specifically listed . . . as a hazardous substance" and "natural gas, natural gas liquids, liquefied natural gas, or synthetic gas . . . ." 42 U.S.C. § 9601(14). The same materials are excluded from CERCLA's definition of "pollutant or contaminant." *Id.* § 9601(33). Thus, the presence of, for example, crude oil at an abandoned dump site would not authorize a CERCLA response action (and would not give rise to CERCLA liability). Oil spills into waters and coastal areas are addressed under § 311 of the Clean Water Act, 33 U.S.C. § 1321; liability for oil spills is governed by the Oil Pollution Act, *id.* §§ 2701–2762, enacted after the massive release of oil into Prince William Sound from the grounded *Exxon Valdez* in 1989. Courts have held, however, that EPA can use CERCLA to respond to releases of petroleum products to which hazardous substances have been *added*, such as the metals found in used motor oil. *E.g. Wilshire Westwood Assoc. v. Atl. Richfield Corp.*, 881 F.2d 801 (9th Cir. 1989); *Esso Standard Oil Co. v. Perez*, 2004 U.S. Dist. LEXIS 19954 (D.P.R. Oct. 1, 2004). Why do you think Congress excluded petroleum and natural gas from the scope of CERCLA?

3. CERCLA provides a uniquely *federal* grant of authority to take response action. Unlike many of the environmental statutes you have studied, CERCLA does not authorize the wholesale delegation of its program to state governments. But states still have a role in the Superfund process. EPA may not use federal Superfund monies for remedial action unless the state in which the release is located has assured that it will contribute 10 percent of the cost of the remedial action (at least 50 percent for releases from state-operated facilities), including all future maintenance of the remedial action once construction is complete. 42 U.S.C. § 9604(c) (CERCLA § 104(c)). Moreover, although EPA retains ultimate authority to select removal and remedial action, CERCLA requires the President to provide "substantial and meaningful involvement by each State in initiation, development, and selection of remedial actions to be undertaken in the State." *Id.* § 9621(f)(1) (CERCLA § 121(f)(1), added by SARA).

Most state environmental agencies today have at least some sort of legal authority analogous to the federal authority granted by CERCLA. EPA's ten regional offices and these state agencies coexist and cooperate with varying degrees of congeniality. Typically, the federal and state agencies enter into a memorandum of agreement that governs the general conduct of their relationship. For reasons of intergovernmental comity, efficient resource allocation, or politics, EPA sometimes defers federal action in favor of state response at a site. Sometimes states invite EPA to take over a state-run cleanup when state resources prove inadequate. Often EPA and a state agency enter into a cooperative agreement under which the state agency takes the lead on a response action project using federal Superfund monies—essentially a grant to the state from EPA, with EPA retaining ultimate responsibility and authority to ensure that the response action meets federal standards.

CERCLA response actions, especially remedial actions, can be controversial and can raise environmental justice concerns. The discovery of a contaminated site releasing hazardous substances may be traumatic to the community surrounding the site. The decisions that must be made about how to respond to the release, no less than the release itself, can have dramatic effects on that community. Many removal and remedial actions amount to major excavation and construction projects. They are rarely quiet, pretty, or short-lived. Furthermore, they may have long-term environmental consequences. Some communities, for example, opposed EPA efforts to incinerate wastes at the site of the contamination, not believing that incineration would truly neutralize the wastes and fearing danger from the incinerator's emissions. Other communities objected to EPA plans to cap and contain buried chemical wastes in place, preferring that the wastes be excavated and hauled away for treatment somewhere else.

Community relations work is an important and sometimes underappreciated part of any response action. Hazardous substance removal and remedial actions require risk-benefit trade-offs, which different constituencies are apt to value differently. Mutual trust between the affected citizens and government officials (in federal and state agencies) makes the process smoother and more satisfying for all concerned.

4. EPA, obviously, usually cannot walk onto the site of a newly discovered release of hazardous substances and just begin cleaning up (although some emergencies require EPA to do just that). Most often, taking a proper response action requires knowing a great deal about the release or threatened release (for example, knowing the chemical composition of liquids in old drums). It also requires access to and control of the site of the release, which is often on private property and may cross property lines. CERCLA facilitates the exertion of § 104(a)'s response authority by granting substantial investigatory and access powers. § 104(b) provides:

> Whenever the President is authorized to act pursuant to subsection (a) of this section . . . he may undertake such investigations, monitoring, surveys, testing, and other information gathering as he may deem necessary or appropriate to identify the existence and extent of the release or threat thereof, the source and nature of the hazardous substances, pollutants or contaminants involved, and the extent of danger to the public health or welfare or to the environment. In addition, the President may undertake such planning, legal, fiscal, economic, engineering, architectural, and other studies or investigations as he may deem necessary or appropriate to plan and direct response actions . . . .

42 U.S.C. § 9604(b). Section 104(e) of CERCLA authorizes any "duly designated" "officer, employee, or representative of the President"

- to require any person to provide information and documents relating to the materials brought to the site of a release as well as the nature and extent of the release, 42 U.S.C. § 9604(e)(2);

- to enter any property "where any hazardous substance or pollutant or contaminant may be or has been generated, stored, treated, disposed of, or transported from," or where there has been or may be a release or threatened release, or where entry is needed for purposes of a response action (even if not the actual site of a release), *id.* § 9604(e)(3); and

- to inspect and obtain samples from any such location, *id.* § 9604(e)(4)(A),

for the purpose of determining the need for a response action, planning or taking a response action, or "otherwise enforcing" the provisions of CERCLA. If necessary, EPA's request for information, access, or sampling can be backed by legal compulsion, either by directly seeking a judicial injunction or by issuing an administrative order and then enforcing that order in court. Unreasonable noncompliance with a request or order issued under § 104(e) subjects the violator to civil penalties. *Id.* § 9604(e)(5).

5. As you just read, the information-gathering, access, and sampling authorities granted by § 104(e) may be used not only for response actions, but also for enforcement actions. Similarly, the investigative authority granted by § 104(b) may be used not only to plan and direct response actions, but also "to recover the costs thereof, and to enforce the provisions" of CERCLA. These authorities provide powerful tools to help EPA identify and pursue parties who may be ordered to take response actions, *see* Section II.B, p. 759, below, or who may be subject to CERCLA liability, *see* Section III, p. 765 below. Although § 104(e) seems to distinguish "response" from "enforcement," CERCLA also paradoxically defines removal, remedial action, and response to "include enforcement activities related thereto." 42 U.S.C. § 9601(25) (CERCLA § 101(25). This definition has consequences for CERCLA liability. *See* p. 821, below.

6. Why did Congress find it necessary to create the Superfund? After all, there is no special trust fund for national defense or the federal prisons or nearly any other important government function. One reason is that a dedicated source of funding provided at least some freedom from the waiting game that is the annual appropriations process, enabling EPA to plan multi-year response actions. Another reason is that the Superfund was expected to act as a revolving fund—diminishing as EPA drew upon it to pay for response actions, but being replenished as the government recovered money pursuant to CERCLA's liability provisions, making the recovered money available for the next round of response actions. Thus EPA's Superfund program stands as an exception to the general rule that when a federal agency program collects revenue, it cannot reserve those receipts for the agency's own use but must remit them to the general Treasury. Nevertheless, Congress and EPA always understood that the Fund could never be fully self-sustaining on a revolving basis—inevitably, despite CERCLA's liability provisions, some of EPA's response costs would be uncollectable (because all liable parties in a particular case might be insolvent, because some claims brought by EPA might not succeed, and because EPA might compromise some claims).

CERCLA put a time limit on the taxes that filled the Fund's coffers, which Congress extended in the 1986 Superfund Amendments and Reauthorization Act (SARA). The taxing authority expired on December 31, 1995, however, and has not been reauthorized since. After the tax ended, withdrawals from the Fund generally exceeded deposits, so the amount of money in the Superfund has trended downward. The balance actually reached zero at least twice. But EPA's Superfund program did not grind to a halt, because Congress made up most of the shortfall by appropriating general revenues to EPA. Since 1986, EPA's Superfund appropriations have averaged about $1.3 billion per year.

7. CERCLA assigned to the executive branch an unprecedented, technically challenging task: responding to *in situ* chemical contamination to protect human health and welfare and the environment from hazardous substance releases. Among the myriad problems implicit in that assignment, one of the most vexing was easily stated: How? Until the beginning of the Superfund program, environmental engineering had focused mainly on pollution control, aiming to design facilities and to dispose of waste in a way that reduced emissions and releases. Early efforts to devise response actions, beginning with Love Canal itself, required ingenuity and innovation. The scale of the task was enormous; there were thousands of sites where releases or threatened releases of hazardous substances existed. And, as a small sample shows, the releases and threatened releases presented a breathtaking variety of environmental and public health hazards:

- at sites like Love Canal, a diverse group of organic and inorganic hazardous substances contaminated a range of media, including not only basements but also flowing groundwater, soil, and sediments in surface water;

- at defunct industrial facilities across the nation, all manner of deteriorating containers of diverse hazardous substances, abandoned by insolvent enterprises large and small, were found stored in ways that presented risks of explosions, reactions that would produce poisonous vapors, or contamination of water supplies;

- at a factory in Connecticut, where a company failing under the weight of asbestos tort suits had manufactured brake linings, old settling ponds—now filled with 17 feet of lead and asbestos debris—were left exposed and accessible to trespassers, including kids who kicked up clouds of dust with their mountain bikes;

- in water bodies such as the Acushnet River and New Bedford Harbor in Massachusetts, the Housatonic River in Massachusetts and Connecticut, the Hudson River and New York Harbor in New York and New Jersey, the Passaic River and Newark Bay in New Jersey, and the Fox River in Wisconsin, sediments contaminated by industrial discharges of carcinogenic PCBs and dioxins were spread over large areas by currents and tides;

- in several Eastern cities, homes were contaminated by neurotoxic or carcinogenic metals, released from industrial operations, that were carried by groundwater or were deposited from the air—or were simply left in factory buildings that were reused for residential purposes without being decontaminated first;

- in several central states, aquifers providing municipal water supplies were contaminated by solvents released from multiple industrial facilities spread across entire cities or neighborhoods;

- in several western regions, large areas were contaminated by mining and ore processing operations—such as the previously pristine Clark Fork River, which was polluted by leaching copper, arsenic, cadmium, lead, and other metals, or the town of Libby, Montana, which was contaminated by dust blown off piles of asbestos-bearing material;

- in many places, mixtures of many companies' chemical wastes were found where they had been dumped: in trenches, in pits dug in remote corners of no-longer-profitable farms, in ready-made holes formed by old gravel pits, in the water-filled remains of old gravel pits, or elsewhere.

The early years of the Superfund program were, no doubt, made even more difficult by the fact that they coincided with the beginning of the Reagan Administration, which had little appetite for a massive, costly, federal environmental protection initiative. *See* JOEL A. MINTZ, ENFORCEMENT AT THE EPA 41–61 (Revised ed. 2012). Political opponents of the Administration, notably in Congress, seized on the real and perceived problems in the management of the CERCLA program. In 1983, first the Assistant Administrator in charge of the program and then the EPA Administrator herself were forced to resign. Rita Lavelle, the Assistant Administrator, was convicted of perjury and obstructing a congressional investigation. In 1986 Congress enacted SARA, in no small part to rein in EPA practices and policies that had led to inadequate cleanups and lax enforcement.

Through all this turmoil, the environmental engineers, risk assessors, scientists, and attorneys at EPA were gaining experience in investigating and assessing releases, selecting the removal or remedial action to take in response, and implementing response actions. Even today, no response action is truly routine. Nonetheless, after more than 35 years of CERCLA implementation, some patterns have emerged. Best practices have spread. For example, when an abandoned bunch of drums is discovered, typically each drum is sampled, "overpacked" into a larger drum to prevent leakage, and shipped to a permitted hazardous waste disposal facility appropriate to the chemical nature of its contents. An unlined chemical waste landfill leaking its contents into groundwater, most often, is capped with impermeable material to prevent additional leaching and then fitted with some method to manage the migration of contamination already in the aquifer, which might include a well that pumps contaminated water to a treatment plant.

Reams of detailed guidance documents help EPA's Superfund staff—especially the on-scene coordinators (OSCs) in charge of removal actions and the remedial project managers (RPMs) in charge of remedial actions—make the daily decisions they must make (or that they recommend to executives who have the decision-making authority). All of these decisions, according to CERCLA, must be guided by one overarching principle. Section 104(a) of CERCLA authorizes the President to take removal or remedial action that is "consistent with the National Contingency Plan."

A. The Response Action Process: The National Contingency Plan and the National Priorities List

Before CERCLA's enactment, the Council on Environmental Quality, pursuant to a requirement of the Clean Water Act, had prepared a plan for responding to oil spills and other incidents involving discharge of hazardous substances into the nation's waters. Section 105(a) of CERCLA directed the President (and thus EPA by delegation), within 180 days of enactment, to revise the plan "to reflect and effectuate the responsibilities and powers created" by CERCLA. Specifically, CERCLA requires the plan to include:

> (1) methods for discovering and investigating facilities at which hazardous substances have . . . come to be located;

> (2) methods for evaluating . . . and remedying any releases or threats of releases from facilities which pose substantial danger to the public health or the environment;

> (3) methods and criteria for determining the appropriate extent of removal, remedy, and other measures authorized by [CERCLA] . . . .

42 U.S.C. § 9605(a). This was a tall order. EPA missed the deadline by about a year, promulgating the revised "National Oil and Hazardous Substances Contingency Plan"—usually known simply as the National Contingency Plan or NCP—in July 1982. EPA promulgated major revisions to the NCP in 1985, in 1990 after enactment of SARA, and in 1994 after enactment of the Oil Pollution Act. The current version of the NCP, including several important appendices, consumes approximately 280 pages of the Code of Federal Regulations. *See* 40 C.F.R. Part 300.

The first two appendices to the NCP are especially noteworthy. Appendix A is the Hazard Ranking System, a technical algorithm for assessing "the potential for releases of uncontrolled hazardous substances to cause human health or environmental damage." 40 C.F.R. Part 300 App. A § 1.0. The Hazard Ranking System responds to the statutory requirement that the NCP include

> criteria for determining priorities among releases or threatened releases throughout the United States for the purpose of taking remedial action and . . . removal action. Criteria and priorities under this paragraph shall be based upon relative risk or danger to public health or welfare or the environment, in the judgment of the President, taking into account to the extent possible [eight itemized factors] and other appropriate factors . . . .

42 U.S.C. § 9605(a)(8)(A) (CERCLA § 105(a)(8)(A)). In evaluating a release of hazardous substances, EPA collects data about the relevant factors. Then, in a process somewhat analogous to the way various entities develop rankings of law schools and other institutions, the Hazard Ranking System uses the data to compare highly disparate releases of hazardous substances along a single quantitative scale.

CERCLA directs that, based upon the above criteria, "the President shall list . . . national priorities among the known releases or threatened releases throughout the United States . . . ." 42 U.S.C. § 9605(a)(8)(B) (CERCLA § 105(a)(8)(B)). EPA employs the Hazard Ranking System as a screening device to help determine those priorities. Releases that exceed a threshold score, specified in the NCP, are eligible for placement on the National Priorities List (NPL). Listing on the NPL makes a release eligible for remedial action funded by the Superfund and usually is a precursor to years of study and cleanup efforts. EPA uses notice-and-comment rulemaking to add sites to the NPL. The NPL is Appendix B to the NCP, 40 C.F.R. Part 300 App. B.

The National Contingency Plan, of course, does not specify the action to be taken in response to any particular release of hazardous substances. It functions more like a decision tree to guide the choice of response actions and a checklist of the steps to be taken in implementing the selected response action. Figure 9-1 schematically illustrates the response action process for a generic Superfund site. You should bear in mind that a Superfund "site," a term widely used by lawyers, environmental professionals, and the public (as well as by this book), is a conceptual convenience; the operative statutory provisions refer to releases or threatened releases of hazardous substances—which of course take place at an actual geographic "site."

Figure 9-1. Schematic of CERCLA Response Action Procedures

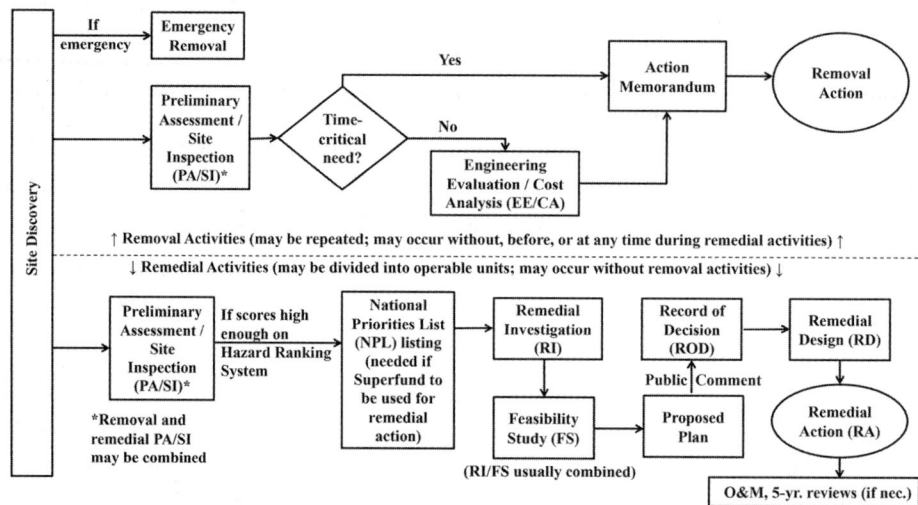

The CERCLA response process begins with the discovery of a release or threatened release of hazardous substances. A site may be discovered in numerous ways. The congressional investigation that preceded CERCLA's enactment might have identified it. EPA or a state or local agency might become aware of a site through regulatory involvement, under RCRA for example. An agency might receive a tip from someone who knows or suspects that hazardous substances are being released. A property owner might discover contamination, for example by testing well water or by finding suspicious material oozing into the basement. Or a site might reveal itself, quite literally, with a bang—an explosion, fire, or some other dramatic event that requires an immediate emergency response. Finally, since CERCLA's enactment, a "person in charge" of a facility has had a legal obligation to report any release of a hazardous substance that equals or exceeds a "reportable quantity" established by EPA regulation.

See 42 U.S.C. §§ 9602, 9603 (CERCLA §§ 102, 103) (providing for designation of reportable quantities and obligation to report); 40 C.F.R. § 302.4 (listing hazardous substances and reportable quantities).

Emergency situations aside, if EPA believes a response action may be warranted, the next step is to evaluate the release to determine if a removal action is needed. A removal site evaluation generally consists of a Preliminary Assessment, which collects readily available information about the release, and a Site Inspection (PA/SI). If the PA/SI reveals a threat that requires immediate or relatively prompt response, EPA may select and perform a removal action. If the PA/SI reveals a need for removal action but EPA concludes that it is safe to delay on-site activities for a planning period of at least six months, EPA performs an Engineering Evaluation and Cost Analysis (EE/CA) to help it choose among possible alternatives for the removal action. Under either scenario, EPA prepares a document called an Action Memorandum, setting forth its decision to conduct a particular removal action. *See* 40 C.F.R. §§ 300.410, 300.415.

Most often, removal action suffices to address the threat to public health and the environment that a release presents. If EPA believes that a further, long-term response may be required, EPA begins the remedial action process for the site. Like the removal action process, the remedial action process begins with a PA/SI. A remedial PA/SI, mainly, gathers the data needed to assign the site a Hazard Ranking System score. Based on that score, EPA may propose the site for listing on the National Priorities List and, after public comment, may add the site to the NPL. *See* 40 C.F.R. § 300.420.

EPA may use Superfund money for a remedial action at a site only if the site is listed on the NPL. The process of selecting a remedial action is substantially more complex than the process of selecting a removal action. First, EPA performs a Remedial Investigation (RI)—an effort "to assess the risks to human health and the environment and to support the development, evaluation, and selection of appropriate response alternatives." 40 C.F.R. § 300.430. After (or, often, concurrently with) the RI, EPA performs a Feasibility Study (FS), which develops and evaluates remedial alternatives so EPA can select an appropriate remedial action (or "remedy"). The results of both these steps are usually reported in a combined document referred to as an RI/FS.

With RI/FS results in hand, EPA proceeds to select the remedial action from among the alternatives presented. In evaluating alternatives, EPA applies a set of criteria, some mandated by the statute and some adopted by EPA rulemaking, listed in the NCP. The minimum requirement is that the selected remedy must protect human health and the environment. EPA also considers the feasibility and cost of each alternative; how well each alternative complies with cleanup standards specified in CERCLA; the short-term and long-term effectiveness of each alternative; whether each alternative includes treatment of the hazardous substances; and the degree of acceptability of each alternative to the state and the affected community. *See* 40 C.F.R. § 300.430(e)(9)(3) (identifying nine criteria against which remedial alternatives must be evaluated); *see also* 42 U.S.C. § 9621 (CERCLA § 121) (specifying factors to be considered, requiring selection of "cost-effective response," and mandating preference for treatment to permanently reduce volume, toxicity, or mobility of hazardous substances).

EPA announces its tentative remedial choice in a "proposed plan" and invites public comment. After public comment, EPA prepares a Record of Decision (ROD) formally selecting a particular remedial action. *See* 42 U.S.C. § 9617 (CERCLA § 117, added by SARA) (providing for public participation in remedy selection). Once the ROD is issued, the next steps are to design and construct the selected remedy ("Remedial Design and Remedial Action," or RD/RA). For particularly complex sites, EPA may divide the remedial action into "Operable Units" and produce a ROD for each one. *See generally* 40 C.F.R. §§ 300.430, 300.435 (describing selection of remedy and implementation of RD/RA). EPA guidance also includes procedures to alter aspects of a selected remedy if warranted by new information or changed circumstances.

Some remedial actions—a groundwater treatment plant, or an impermeable cap placed on a former landfill—require long periods of operation and maintenance after initial construction is complete. If the remedy entails leaving hazardous substances *in situ*, CERCLA requires EPA to review the remedial action every five years to make sure the remedy remains protective of human health and the environment. 42 U.S.C. § 9621(c). When EPA concludes that all response action has been implemented and no further response action is appropriate, it may, by notice-and-comment rulemaking, delete a release from the NPL. 40 C.F.R. § 300.425(e).

Although we have described the removal and remedial action processes as distinct and sequential, in practice neither the sequence nor the distinction is always so clear-cut. At a complex site, EPA might conduct removal actions to respond to acute threats even while planning or performing longer-term remedial action. Some tasks carried out as a removal action could also be part of a remedial action, and vice versa. But as you have seen, EPA's characterization of a response action as removal or remedial action has important procedural consequences. In litigation about CERCLA liability (see Section III), that characterization can be controversial, as in the case that follows.

United States v. W.R. Grace & Co.
429 F.3d 1224 (9th Cir. 2005)

Judge MCKEOWN:

Libby, Montana, sits sixty-five miles south of the Canadian border. The seemingly rustic and picturesque environment of this area masks a troubling history—the community has been plagued with asbestos-related contamination. In 1999, the Environmental Protection Agency ("EPA") was called in to address disturbing health reports due to asbestos-related contamination. We must decide whether, in responding to this threat, the EPA exceeded the bounds of its authority to conduct cleanup activities under the Comprehensive Environmental Response, Compensation, and Liability Act ("CERCLA") . . . .

Defendants . . . (collectively, "Grace") do not dispute that they are financially obligated under CERCLA to assist with the cleanup of asbestos originating from their former mining and processing operations near Libby. Instead, Grace contests the EPA's characterization of the cleanup as a removal action rather than a remedial action under CERCLA. If the cleanup is a remedial action, . . . then Grace argues that the EPA did not fulfill the regulatory requirements for remedial actions . . . .

Grace argues that the EPA circumvented the regulatory safeguards by conducting a remedial action under the guise of a removal, thereby giving the EPA free rein to conduct what Grace styles as "the *quintessential* remedial action" under the less-restrictive requirements applied to removals . . . .

Grace further contends that even if the action is appropriately classified as a removal action, the district court erred in exempting the action from CERCLA's general 12-month, $2 million cap for removal actions . . . .

The situation confronting the EPA in Libby is truly extraordinary . . . . [T]he population of Libby and nearby communities, which the EPA estimates at about 12,000, faces ongoing, pervasive exposure to asbestos particles being released through documented exposure pathways. We cannot escape the fact that people are sick and dying as a result of this continuing exposure. Confronted with this information, the EPA determined on the basis of its professional judgment, and in accord with its administrative interpretation of the scope of removal actions, that the situation warranted an immediate, aggressive response to abate the public health threat.

. . . [W]e reach the same ultimate conclusion [as the district court]: The EPA's cleanup in Libby was a removal action that was exempt from the temporal and monetary cap . . . . We therefore affirm the judgment of the district court.

BACKGROUND

I. CERCLA

. . . .

CERCLA and the National Contingency Plan divide response actions into two broad categories: removal actions and remedial actions. Removal actions are typically described as time-sensitive responses to public health threats for which the EPA is granted considerable leeway in structuring the cleanup. Superfund-financed removal actions generally are required to "be terminated after $2 million has been obligated for the action or 12 months have elapsed from the date removal activities begin on-site." 40 C.F.R. § 300.415(b)(5). These limitations are not, however, inviolate. The EPA may exceed this cap if it determines one of two exemptions applies:

> (i) There is an immediate risk to public health or welfare of the United States or the environment; continued response actions are immediately required to prevent, limit, or mitigate an emergency; and such assistance will not otherwise be provided on a timely basis; or

> (ii) Continued response action is otherwise appropriate and consistent with the remedial action to be taken.

[*Id.*; 42 U.S.C. § 9605(c)(3) (CERCLA § 105(c)(3)) (imposing monetary cap and stating grounds for waiver]. Remedial actions, on the other hand, are often described as permanent remedies to threats for which an urgent response is not warranted.

The distinction between removal and remedial actions is critical under CERCLA because "[b]oth types of actions have substantial requirements, but the requirements for remedial actions are much more detailed and onerous." . . . .

II. HISTORY OF THE EPA'S CLEANUP ACTIVITIES IN LIBBY

. . . .

A. ASBESTOS CONTAMINATION IN LIBBY

From the 1920s until 1990, Grace and its predecessors mined and processed vermiculite—a mineral containing a type of asbestos called tremolite—at a mine approximately seven miles northeast of Libby. Processed ore was trucked to screening plants and expansion/export plants from which the materials were distributed nationwide. Vermiculite was also available for employees to take home for their personal use, and Grace donated vermiculite to the local schools . . . .

. . . .

B. THE EPA'S INVOLVEMENT IN LIBBY

. . . .

. . . EPA's . . . initial investigation confirmed two things: (1) "a large number of current and historic cases of asbestos related diseases centered around Libby," including "33 incidents of apparently non-occupational exposures"; and (2) a "high likelihood that significant amounts of asbestos contaminated vermiculite still remain in and around Libby." . . . [S]ubsequent testing showed asbestos contamination to be pervasive.

. . . [T]he EPA documented "complete human exposure pathways" through which asbestos particles were becoming airborne as a result of normal human activities, such as foot traffic and vacuuming, and natural forces, such as wind—especially during the dry summer months. This migration transformed the latent threat of undisturbed asbestos into a current hazard to anyone breathing the airborne particles . . . . A study of Libby residents conducted in 2000 by the Agency for Toxic Substances and Disease Registry . . . found . . . that 18% of those x-rayed had abnormalities in the lining of their lungs—as compared with the expected rate of 0.2% to 2.3% for groups living in the United States who have no known asbestos exposures.

These findings led the EPA to set out the intended removal action in a series of three memoranda . . . which progressively broadened the scope of the cleanup. The original action memorandum, dated May 23, 2000 ("First Action Memo"), covered a former vermiculite export plant and screening plant, the former of which was being used as a retail lumber mill and the latter as a combined commercial/residential property. The First Action Memo authorized a time-critical removal action to be completed by spring/summer 2001 with a total project ceiling of approximately $5.8 million for the two sites. The EPA determined that the action met the requirements to exceed the $2 million, 12-month cap . . . .

The EPA then broadened the scope of the cleanup in an action memorandum amendment, dated July 20, 2001 ("Second Action Memo"), which covered "newly identified risks" at six additional locations . . . . The six sites included two private residences, three local schools, and a public road running past the mine site . . . . As with the First Action Memo, the EPA determined that the situation warranted an exemption from the cap and, consequently, authorized a total site removal ceiling of approximately $20.1 million with an estimated completion date for most of the work by winter 2001/02.

The EPA expanded the removal action again in an action memorandum amendment, dated May 2, 2002 ("Third Action Memo"), which brought a number of homes and businesses in Libby within the ambit of the removal action. The EPA again determined that an exemption from the statutory cap was warranted. In addition, although Libby was not added to the National Priorities List until October 2002, the EPA proposed that the site be added in February 2002. The Third Action Memo also explained that the removal action was consistent with a planned future remedial action. The EPA estimated that the proposed work would take two to three construction seasons, and it raised the total project ceiling to approximately $55.6 million . . . .

C. COST-RECOVERY ACTION AGAINST GRACE

[The United States filed a cost recovery action (see Section III, p. 765, below) against Grace. The district court held Grace liable for $54.53 million in response costs and entered a declaratory judgment that Grace would be liable for future response costs.]

ANALYSIS

The EPA's ability to recover the costs of its cleanup in Libby hinges on whether its response is properly characterized as a removal action, as argued by the EPA and found by the district court, or a remedial action, as argued by Grace . . . .

We emphasize at the outset that the EPA's response action in Libby is no mere run-of-the-mill CERCLA cleanup. As the EPA itself recognizes, the Libby cleanup is a unique removal action of a size and cost not previously seen. But the situation in Libby was, and remains today, truly extraordinary.

I. REMOVAL OR REMEDIAL ACTION: STRUCTURE OF THE TWO-STEP INQUIRY AND APPLICATION TO THE CLEANUP IN LIBBY

. . . CERCLA provides that the selection of response actions shall be upheld "unless arbitrary and capricious or otherwise not in accordance with the law." 42 U.S.C. § 9613(j)(2). We agree that it was not arbitrary and capricious for the EPA "to approve a time-critical removal action." However, the statutory scheme compels us to take the inquiry one step further.

. . . [E]ven if the EPA's *selection* of a removal action was proper, the question remains whether the actions *actually taken* by the EPA to combat the threat are properly categorized as such.

We agree with Grace that this second step of our inquiry is a question of law: Does the EPA's response action in Libby fall within the statutory limits of a removal action? Grace's challenge is built on the premise that the EPA termed its cleanup in Libby a removal action as a subterfuge when the response was, in substance, a remedial action . . . .

A. DECISION TO CONDUCT A REMOVAL ACTION IN LIBBY

The EPA's initial decision to conduct a removal action must be upheld unless Grace can demonstrate on the administrative record that the decision was arbitrary and capricious or otherwise not in accordance with law. Grace has not met this burden.

The National Contingency Plan requires the EPA to consider a series of factors[15] to determine that it was appropriate to initiate a removal action. The EPA did so and its findings are extensively documented.

[The court described EPA's explanation of the factors considered in each Action Memo.] . . . .

. . . In light of the EPA's carefully documented reasoning in the three Action Memos, we agree with the district court that the EPA's decision to approve a removal action was not arbitrary and capricious. . . .

B. CHARACTERIZATION OF THE EPA'S RESPONSE ACTION

The question remains whether the steps actually taken by the EPA to combat the threat are properly characterized as a removal action. Whether the EPA's cleanup activity was a removal action—or, on the other hand, a remedial action in removal action's clothing—is a question of statutory interpretation . . . . that we review as a matter of law . . . .

. . . .

Grace contests the denomination of the action as a removal by cherry-picking discrete cleanup activities which, standing alone, might fall within the ambit of a remedial action. We refrain from slicing and dicing the EPA's single, cohesive removal action into a myriad of fractured parts . . . . Instead, we take a more comprehensive view of the administrative record in concluding that the EPA's response was a removal action.

---

15. 40 C.F.R. § 300.415(b)(2) [lists]

(i) Actual or potential exposure to nearby human populations, animals, or the food chain[. . .];

(ii) Actual or potential contamination of drinking water supplies or sensitive ecosystems;

(iii) Hazardous substances [. . .] in drums, barrels, tanks, or other bulk storage containers, that may pose a threat of release;

(iv) High levels of hazardous substances [. . .] in soils largely at or near the surface, that may migrate;

(v) Weather conditions that may cause hazardous substances [. . .] to migrate or be released;

(vi) Threat of fire or explosion;

(vii) The availability of other appropriate federal or state response mechanisms[. . .]; and

(viii) Other situations or factors that may pose threats to public health or welfare of the United States or the environment.

1. STATUTORY INTERPRETATION: REMOVAL AND REMEDIAL ACTIONS

The first step under *Chevron* requires a straightforward exercise in statutory interpretation: "If a court, employing traditional tools of statutory interpretation, ascertains that Congress had an intention on the precise question at issue, that intention is the law and must be given effect."

We begin with the statutory definitions because "[w]hen a statute includes an explicit definition, we must follow that definition, even if it varies from that term's ordinary meaning." It has become de rigueur to criticize CERCLA as a hastily passed statute that is far from a paragon of legislative clarity. The definitions of removal and remedial action exemplify this muddled language.

The definition of "removal" . . . begins with the general statement that "removal" means "the cleanup or removal of released hazardous substances from the environment." The definition goes on to describe three categories of events that trigger removal . . . . Finally, the definition lists a number of specific activities that fall within the definition of "removal"—"alternative water supplies," "temporary evacuation and housing," and "emergency assistance." Although at first glance this half of the definition appears to provide concrete guidance by listing identifiable activities such as "security fencing," this part too is left vague by the opening caveat that the term "removal" "includes, in addition, without being limited to, security fencing. . . ." Consequently, "these examples serve only as a guide to what activities may appropriately be classified as 'removal action.'"

The definition of "remedial action" is similarly broad, but can be distinguished from "removal" because it refers to "permanent" remedies and its list of specific actions is, in large part, distinct from the list included under "removal." (For example, "removal" is focused on temporary and emergency activities.) . . . . The definition concludes with three lists of specific examples classified as a remedy, such as "segregation of reactive wastes." . . . .

Adding to the confusion is the overlap between the two definitions. Attempting to untie the Gordian knot of these definitions solely based on their plain meanings is thus unavailing.

. . . .

CERCLA makes clear that the EPA has the tools of both removal and remedial actions at its fingertips when there is a release or threatened release of a hazardous substance . . . . The statute as a whole, however, does little to clarify how to categorize a given response action except to suggest that remedial actions may be "long term."

Nor does the purpose of the statute provide definitive guidance, though it points towards a liberal reading of "removal" in order to effectuate CERCLA's underlying purpose of "protect[ing] and preserv[ing] public health and the environment by facilitating the expeditious and efficient cleanup of hazardous waste sites." Specifically, because a removal action can be initiated promptly after notification of a threat, a liberal reading provides the EPA with greater flexibility to use this tool for the protection of the public health.

Last, we turn to CERCLA's legislative history for guidance.

Unfortunately, legislative history is particularly unhelpful because of the haphazard passage of CERCLA with many of the more lucid descriptions of the statute falling under the oxymoronic category of post-enactment "history." Considering that no committee or conference reports address the version of CERCLA that ultimately became law, it is apt to describe the search for legislative history as "somewhat of a snark hunt."

. . . .

In sum, we are unable to discern Congress's clear intent through the normal tools of statutory interpretation. The meanings of "removal" and "remedial action" under CERCLA are inescapably vague.

2. DEFERENCE TO THE EPA'S CHARACTERIZATION

Having concluded that Congress did not draw a clear line between removal and remedial actions, we turn to the second step under *Chevron* and ask whether, in view of the deference owed to the EPA, the Libby cleanup was a removal action as a matter of law . . . .

. . . We hold that the EPA has rationally construed CERCLA and that construction deserves our respect. As interpreted by the EPA, the removal/remedial distinction boils down to whether the exigencies of the situation were such that the EPA did not have time to undertake the procedural steps required for a remedial action, and, in responding to such a time-sensitive threat, the EPA sought to minimize and stabilize imminent harms to human health and the environment. The EPA did so here.

The definitions of "removal" and "remedial action" in the EPA-promulgated National Contingency Plan merely parrot CERCLA's definitions . . . . Because these definitions do nothing to interpret the definitions in CERCLA, they are unhelpful to our inquiry.

That being said, other parts of the National Contingency Plan offer some guidance. For instance, 40 C.F.R. § 300.415(e) sets forth examples of activities that are "as a general rule," appropriate as part of a removal action, but notes that the list "is not exhaustive and is not intended to prevent the lead agency from taking any other actions deemed necessary under CERCLA." . . . The bulk of activities carried out in Libby easily fall within the scope of the listed examples . . . .

The need for immediate action permeates the EPA's activities in Libby . . . . [T]he carcinogenic fibers were widespread and . . . were not contained such that they would not be inhaled. As ominously observed by the EPA, "Of course once airborne, the fibers will migrate whichever way the wind blows."

The sequence of activities in Libby further comports with the EPA's description in the National Contingency Plan of the preferred development of response actions. The National Contingency Plan provides that the agency should orderly transition from a removal to a remedial action if it "determines that the removal action will not fully address the threat posed by the release." This progression is evidenced by the three

Action Memos for Libby, which began by calling for a removal action but later paved the way for a remedial action . . . . Thus, the EPA conducted its removal action in Libby not in lieu of a remedial action, but rather as a prelude to a comprehensive remedial action.

Looking beyond the National Contingency Plan, the EPA's characterization of response actions in documents that do not have the heft of regulations still carry weight because "[c]ogent 'administrative interpretations . . . not [the] products of formal rulemaking . . . nevertheless warrant respect.'" . . .

Most notably, the EPA issued a memo in 2000 to guide project managers during the decisionmaking process of selecting between remedial and removal actions (hereinafter "Removal Memo") . . . . [T]he Removal Memo emphasizes "time sensitivity," i.e., "the need to take relatively prompt action," as a key characteristic of removal actions: "[E]ven expensive and complex response actions may be removal action candidates if they are relatively time-sensitive."[23] . . .

Courts have also stressed the immediacy of a threat in deciding whether a cleanup is a removal action.

While stressing time sensitivity, the Removal Memo downplays the importance that some courts have placed on duration, i.e., "how long the response action will take to build or implement," because "removal actions are most often of short duration, but they certainly can be long-running responses, too, thereby undercutting the probative value of duration . . . in deciding whether an action is removal rather than remedial in nature." Accordingly, the action in Libby is not disqualified from being a removal action just because it took several years. The length of the cleanup in Libby is especially understandable given that harsh winters truncated the construction season and that the sheer magnitude of the initial cleanup far exceeded the normal situation faced by the EPA.

Likewise, the Removal Memo describes courts' reliance on the "permanence" of the response as "sometimes misleading": "As a practical matter, removal actions are often permanent solutions such as can be the case in a typical soil or drum removal." This observation seems logical, as we do not want to tie the EPA's hands or compel it to adopt short-term remedies for fear that any more permanent solutions automatically will be dubbed "remedial actions." Nor would it make economic or practical sense to impose a requirement that removal actions must be only temporary in nature. The Removal Memo instead uses the term "comprehensiveness" to distinguish between the use of removal authority to conduct interim or partial response actions that are focused on immediate risk reduction as compared with a final or "comprehensive" response at the site. The Libby cleanup exhibits this two-tier approach . . . .

---

23. The three Action Memos all categorize the action in Libby as "Time Critical." The EPA may also choose to conduct "non-time-critical" removal actions "when the lead Agency determines, based on the site evaluation, that a removal action is appropriate, and a planning period of at least six months is available before on-site activities must begin." . . . .

Rationale

These informal interpretations combined with the descriptions in the National Contingency Plan provide a persuasive interpretation that removal actions encompass interim, partial time-sensitive responses taken to counter serious threats to public health . . . .

. . . .

The EPA's scientific basis for finding an immediate threat to the public health is thoroughly documented over thousands of pages. In addition to the detailed evaluation of the threat in the three Action Memos, the administrative record includes, for example, comprehensive reports by both the EPA's regional toxicologist and senior toxicologist explaining the imminent and substantial endangerment to public health in Libby, extensive responses by the EPA to Grace's comments on the cleanup, and lengthy findings by the Agency for Toxic Substances and Disease Registry on medical testing conducted on Libby residents . . . .

. . . .

In sum, given the sweeping language in the definition of "removal," the significant deference due to the EPA's interpretation of this language, and the scope of the interim cleanup, we hold that the EPA's cleanup in Libby falls within the bounds of a removal action . . . . This holding comports with CERCLA's fundamental goal of protecting the public health . . . .

In so holding, we recognize that Congress created a bifurcated scheme of removal and remedial actions and, accordingly, there must be outer limits to removal actions. But the EPA did not exceed these limits in this case. Nor need we delineate the outer parameters. We simply conclude that the EPA's characterization of the cleanup in Libby as a removal action is amply supported by the administrative record and easily withstands scrutiny . . . .

. . . .

II. EXEMPTIONS FROM THE $2 MILLION, 12-MONTH STATUTORY CAP APPLICABLE TO REMOVAL ACTIONS

Having determined that the action is properly characterized as a removal action, the inquiry turns to whether the EPA can recover costs in excess of the $2 million, 12-month statutory cap on removal actions . . . .

. . . .

[The court described EPA's findings, in each of the three Action Memos,] that the removal action met the three statutory elements required to exceed the cap. Namely, (1) the asbestos in the environment posed an immediate threat to the local population; (2) a cleanup beyond the cap was required to prevent, limit, or mitigate an emergency because of the size of the cleanup and the short construction season; and (3) assistance from other government agencies was not anticipated on a timely basis. [The court also described EPA's reliance, in the Third Action Memo,] on the "consistency exemption," which allows for a continued removal action over the cap when it is "otherwise appropriate and consistent with the remedial action to be taken."

On a practical level, the need to exceed the cap is not surprising given the urgency, magnitude, and long-standing nature of the problem. First, the tremendous scope of the removal in Libby made the $2 million ceiling unworkable. An entire town needed to be cleaned up . . . .

The 12-month limit was also impractical given both the scale of the effort and the meteorological reality of the harsh conditions, which result in a short construction season and thus necessitate several years to complete cleanup activities that might be completed considerably faster in a more temperate climate . . . .

Given these daunting realities and the EPA's careful documentation of its reasons for invoking the emergency and consistency exemptions, we hold that the EPA's decision to exceed the statutory cap was based on the relevant factors, there has been no clear error of judgment, and the decision was not arbitrary and capricious.

. . . .

AFFIRMED.

[The concurring opinion of Judge Bea is omitted.]

Notes and Questions

1. Do you agree with the court's conclusion that all of EPA's response actions in Libby were appropriately characterized as "removal"? In reviewing EPA's actions, what standard of review did the Ninth Circuit apply? Why did the court use that standard?

2. Why did W.R. Grace argue that EPA's response actions in Libby should have been considered "remedial action"? If the Ninth Circuit had agreed with Grace, what would the consequences have been? The answer will become clearer when we consider CERCLA's liability provisions, see pp. 765, 815–21, below.

3. If Grace believed so strongly that EPA's actions in Libby were procedurally improper, why didn't Grace challenge those actions before EPA spent millions of dollars implementing them? Section 113(h) of CERCLA, 42 U.S.C. § 9613(h), bars pre-enforcement review of "any challenges to removal or remedial action selected under" § 104. Thus, although Grace could challenge the legality of EPA's removal actions, Grace had to wait until EPA sued Grace for cost recovery. Courts have held that the provision bars pre-enforcement challenges alleging violations of other federal statutes (such as NEPA), as well as challenges based on CERCLA's requirements.

4. Whether a response action is classified as removal or remedial action also affects the trigger of CERCLA's complicated statute of limitations for liability suits, § 113(g), 42 U.S.C. § 9613(g). In that context, courts have held that all steps short of actual construction of a selected remedy qualify as "removal," even if those steps (such as an RI/FS or remedial design) are part of the process leading up to selection and implementation of remedial action.

5. In our description of the removal and remedial action process provided above, we focus on EPA as the actor. The NCP itself, however, speaks more generally in terms of a "lead agency." *See* 40 C.F.R. § 300.5 (defining "lead agency"). The lead agency is usually, but not always, EPA. A state agency, conducting a CERCLA response action by agreement with EPA, may be the lead agency. For spills into coastal waters of the United States, the Coast Guard is the lead agency. For releases at or from federal facilities, the federal agency in charge of the facility is the lead agency. Many Superfund sites are found on military bases, a legacy of past war preparation or military production during which environmental considerations were far from the topmost priority. The Department of Energy operates the site of by far the most expensive Superfund cleanup: the Hanford Nuclear Reservation, where (among other activities) plutonium was produced for use in nuclear weapons; response actions may eventually cost tens of billions of dollars. But other federal properties—from office buildings to national forests—may also host releases of hazardous substances as a result of government or private activity. Each federal agency is responsible for CERCLA cleanups on the property it manages. The NCP applies to all response actions taken under the authority of CERCLA regardless of the identity of the lead agency. 40 C.F.R. § 300.2; *see also* 42 U.S.C. §§ 9620 (CERCLA § 120, added by SARA) (applying NCP to federal facilities and requiring agencies that own or operate federal facilities on the NPL to perform RI/FSs and remedial actions).

6. How clean is clean? The goal of a CERCLA response action is to protect human health and the environment from the risks posed by releases and threatened releases of hazardous substances. This is hardly an objective or self-explanatory standard. In attempting to satisfy it, EPA has placed central importance on risk assessment: assessing the health and environmental hazards presented by a release, identifying the pathways by which human and non-human receptors might be exposed, and quantifying the resulting risk to health or ecological conditions.

Congressional dissatisfaction with some of EPA's remedial choices in the first years of the Superfund program led to the enactment, in SARA, of a statutory standard for the degree of cleanup that remedial actions (not removals) must achieve. Beneath an overarching requirement of protectiveness, the provision in essence borrows cleanup standards from other federal and state environmental statutes. For example, a remedial action responding to contamination of an actual or potential source of drinking water must generally meet the maximum contaminant level goals provided by the federal Safe Drinking Water Act. The borrowed cleanup standards are referred to by the tongue-twisting acronym ARARs, for "applicable or relevant and appropriate requirements." *See* 42 U.S.C. § 9621(d) (CERCLA § 121(d)).

A specific ARAR might not exist for a particular hazardous substance released into a particular environmental medium at a Superfund site. For such circumstances, EPA has established general rules of thumb for the degree of risk reduction to be obtained. For carcinogens, the general policy is to reduce the additional cancer risk resulting from the release below one in 10,000 and preferably below one in one million. For non-carcinogens, the general policy is to eliminate exposures that would produce adverse health effects. Obviously, the circumstances of individual remedial actions sometimes cause EPA to deviate from these rules of thumb. Section 121(d) allows EPA to waive even ARARs in specified conditions.

7. Love Canal illustrates the complexity that a CERCLA response action can entail. State and federal efforts at Love Canal included fencing contaminated areas (quintessentially a removal action); construction of drain systems to collect contaminated leachate; construction and then operation and maintenance of a plant to treat contaminated leachate; demolishing contaminated homes and relocating residents; installing and maintaining an impermeable cap over the old landfill; cleaning out sewers and incinerating or disposing of contaminated sediment removed from the sewers; disposing of residue from the incinerator; excavating and treating or disposing of contaminated soil next to the school at the site. In September 2004, EPA removed Love Canal from the National Priorities List. In the course of the overall response to the release of hazardous substances at Love Canal, EPA issued several RODs. *See* Love Canal, Niagara Falls, NY, EPA.gov (Dec. 19, 2016), https://cumulis.epa.gov/super cpad/cursites/csitinfo.cfm?id=0201290; Site Information for Love Canal, EPA.gov (Dec. 19, 2016), https://cumulis.epa.gov/supercpad/cursites/dsp_ssppSiteData1.cfm ?id=0201290#Why.

B. Response Action Orders

In Libby, EPA used the authority granted by § 104 of CERCLA, and the money made available to EPA through the Superfund, to perform a removal action. When enacting CERCLA, however, Congress understood that, despite the availability of the Superfund, more cleanups would happen more quickly if EPA could also bring private resources to bear on the task. Mindful of the statute's second major goal—"that those responsible for problems caused by the disposal of chemical poisons bear the costs and responsibility for remedying the harmful conditions they created"—Congress gave EPA powerful tools to compel such parties to undertake response actions themselves, rather than waiting for EPA to clean up their mess.

Section 106(a) of CERCLA provides that:

> when the President determines that there may be an imminent and substantial endangerment to the public health or welfare or the environment because of an actual or threatened release of a hazardous substance from a facility, he may require the Attorney General of the United States to secure such relief as may be necessary to abate such danger or threat, and the district court of the United States in the district in which the threat occurs shall have jurisdiction to grant such relief as the public interest and the equities of the case may require. The President may also, after notice to the affected State, take other action under this section including, but not limited to, issuing such orders as may be necessary to protect public health and welfare and the environment.

42 U.S.C. § 9606(a). In addition to the coercive authorities granted by § 106, CERCLA expressly authorizes consensual agreements under which responsible parties perform removal or remedial action. *See id.* § 9622 (CERCLA § 122, added by SARA) (imposing requirements on settlement agreements for performance of response actions); § 9604(a) (CERCLA § 9604(a)) (authorizing agreements for performance of RI/FSs).

Notes and Questions

1. Why would a Superfund, or any authority for a government-conducted response action, be needed in light of § 106(a) of CERCLA? *Why spend Treasury $ $ when dealing w/ corporation?*

2. What is the difference between the authority granted in the first sentence of § 106(a) of CERCLA and the authority granted in the second sentence? Which of these two authorities is the President more likely to invoke? Why? *See United States v. Ottati & Goss, Inc.*, 900 F.2d 429, 434 (1st Cir. 1990) (stating that EPA's remedy selection process did not constrain court's choice of injunctive relief).

3. Pursuant to the second sentence of § 106(a), EPA may select a removal or remedial action and then issue an order (known as an "administrative order" because it is issued by an agency instead of a court) requiring one or more parties ("respondents") to carry out the response action. Sometimes a respondent or a group of them agrees in advance to perform the response action and negotiates with EPA the other terms of an "administrative order on consent (AOC)," a form of settlement agreement (see pp. 854–59, below) that remains enforceable as an EPA order in the event of non-performance.[1] An administrative order issued under § 106(a) without such an agreement is denominated a "unilateral administrative order (UAO)."

4. Before issuing a § 106 order, EPA must find "that there may be an imminent and substantial endangerment to the public health or welfare or the environment." As with RCRA § 7003 orders, pp. 724–25, above, this is not a high hurdle when hazardous substances are released (or a release is threatened). Courts have held that the word "may" means that EPA need only show a threat of an imminent and substantial endangerment, not an existing endangerment; that "endangerment" means only a risk of harm and not actual harm; that "imminent" refers to the conditions that give rise to the endangerment, not to the endangerment itself; and that "substantial" does not require quantification of the risk. Moreover, CERCLA orders may be predicated on endangerment of not only health or the environment (as in RCRA), but also on endangerment of "public . . . welfare," a very broad concept. *See, e.g., United States v. Conservation Chem. Co.*, 619 F. Supp. 162, 192 (W.D. Mo. 1985).

5. In the early days of the Administration of President George H.W. Bush, newly installed EPA Administrator William Reilly ordered a study of EPA's implementation of the CERCLA program. Responding to criticism about the slow pace of "Fund-lead" CERCLA cleanups (i.e., response actions performed by EPA with Superfund money), the EPA under Administrator Reilly adopted a policy that called for greater reliance on "Enforcement-lead" response actions (i.e., those performed by responsible parties under an injunction, administrative order, or settlement agreement). The "enforcement first" policy expressed a general preference for trying to secure response actions by responsible parties as early as possible, rather than stressing prompt initiation of response action by the government, followed by enforcement action later (see

---

1. A settlement agreement for performance of remedial action, however, must be memorialized in a consent decree approved by a court rather than in an AOC. 42 U.S.C. § 9622(d)(1) (CERCLA § 122(d)(1), added by SARA).

Section III, below). EPA emphasized that although it would rather reach negotiated agreements for performance of response actions, it would rely on unilateral administrative orders if negotiations failed. Since its formal nationwide adoption in 1989, EPA has reiterated the enforcement-first policy repeatedly.

6. Failing to comply with a § 106(a) order can have serious consequences. A "person who, without sufficient cause, willfully violates, or fails or refuses to comply with" an order may be liable for a civil penalty "for each day in which such violation occurs or such failure to comply continues." 42 U.S.C. § 9606(b)(1) (CERCLA § 106(b)(1)). CERCLA set the maximum penalty at $25,000 per day; the maximum penalty has increased to $53,907 per day by operation of the Federal Civil Penalties Adjustment Act of 1990, P.L. 101-410, 28 U.S.C. § 2461 Note. *See* 40 C.F.R. § 19.4 (showing inflation adjustments). Moreover, a liable person (see Section III.C, below) who "fails without sufficient cause to properly provide removal or remedial action upon order of the President pursuant to" § 104 or § 106 "may be liable to the United States for punitive damages in an amount at least equal to, and not more than three times, the amount of any costs incurred by the Fund as a result . . . ." 42 U.S.C. § 9607(c)(3) (CERCLA § 107(c)(3)). A corporation that frequently has been on the receiving end of EPA orders challenged the constitutionality of this statutory scheme.

General Electric Co. v. Jackson
610 F.3d 110 (D.C. Cir. 2010)

In this case, appellant challenges the constitutionality of a statutory scheme that authorizes the Environmental Protection Agency to issue orders, known as unilateral administrative orders (UAOs), directing companies and others to clean up hazardous waste for which they are responsible. Appellant argues that the statute, as well as the way in which EPA administers it, violates the Due Process Clause because EPA issues UAOs without a hearing before a neutral decisionmaker. We disagree . . . .

. . . .

When EPA determines that an environmental cleanup is necessary at a contaminated site, CERCLA gives the agency four options: (1) it may negotiate a settlement with potentially responsible parties (PRPs); (2) it may conduct the cleanup with "Superfund" money and then seek reimbursement from PRPs by filing suit; (3) it may file an abatement action in federal district court to compel PRPs to conduct the cleanup; or (4) it may issue a UAO instructing PRPs to clean the site. This last option, authorized by CERCLA section 106, is the focus of this case.

. . . .

Once EPA issues a UAO, the recipient PRP has two choices. It may comply and, after completing the cleanup, seek reimbursement from EPA. If EPA refuses reimbursement, the PRP may sue the agency in federal district court to recover its costs on the grounds that (1) it was not liable for the cleanup; or (2) it was liable but EPA's selected response action (or some portion thereof) was "arbitrary and capricious or . . . otherwise not in accordance with law[.]" Alternatively, the PRP may refuse to comply with the UAO, in which case EPA may either bring an action in federal district court to enforce the UAO against the noncomplying PRP, or clean the site itself and then sue the PRP to recover its costs. In either proceeding, if the court concludes that the PRP "willfully" failed to comply with an order "without sufficient cause," it "may" (but need not) impose fines, which are currently set at $37,500 per day, and accumulate until EPA brings a recovery or enforcement action—a period of up to six years [based on possibly applicable statutes of limitations]. If EPA itself undertakes the cleanup and the district court finds that the PRP "fail[ed] without sufficient cause" to comply with the UAO, the court "may" impose punitive damages of up to "three times[] the amount of any costs" the agency incurs.

Central to this case, these two options—comply and seek reimbursement, or refuse to comply and wait for EPA to bring an enforcement or cost recovery action—are exclusive. CERCLA section 113(h) bars PRPs from obtaining immediate judicial review of a UAO ....

Over the years, appellant General Electric (GE) has received at least 68 UAOs. In addition, GE "is currently participating in response actions at 79 active CERCLA sites" where UAOs may issue, including the cleanup of some 200 miles of the Hudson River stretching from Hudson Falls to the southern tip of Manhattan .... Although EPA has yet to issue GE a UAO for the Hudson River, the agency has reserved the right to do so, and the company suspects it will receive UAOs at other sites as well.

... According to GE, "[t]he unilateral orders regime ... imposes a classic and unconstitutional Hobson's choice": because refusing to comply "risk[s] severe punishment [i.e., fines and treble damages]," UAO recipients' only real option is to "comply ... before having any opportunity to be heard on the legality and rationality of the underlying order." ...

... [The district court granted summary judgment to EPA on both "facial" and "pattern and practice" constitutional claims.]

We begin with GE's facial challenge ....

The Fifth Amendment to the United States Constitution provides that "No person shall ... be deprived of life, liberty, or property, without due process of law." "The first inquiry in every due process challenge is whether the plaintiff has been deprived of a protected interest in 'liberty' or 'property.' Only after finding the deprivation of a protected interest do we look to see if the [government's] procedures comport with due process." ...

 ....

The parties agree that the costs of compliance and the monetary fines and damages associated with noncompliance qualify as protected property interests. They disagree, however, as to whether judicial review is available before any deprivation occurs. EPA contends that CERCLA gives PRPs the right to pre-deprivation judicial review: by refusing to comply with a UAO, a PRP can force EPA to file suit in federal court, where the PRP can challenge the order's validity before spending a single dollar on compliance costs, damages, or fines. GE responds that noncompliance—and thus pre-deprivation judicial review—is but a theoretical option. According to GE, daily fines and treble damages "are so severe that they . . . intimidate[] PRPs from exercising the purported option of electing not to comply with a UAO so as to test an order's validity" via judicial review. PRPs are thus forced to comply and spend substantial sums prior to any hearing before a neutral decisionmaker . . . .

GE's argument hinges on the Supreme Court's decision in *Ex Parte Young*, 209 U.S. 123 (1908), and its progeny. Under those cases, a statutory scheme violates due process if "the penalties for disobedience are by fines so enormous . . . as to intimidate the [affected party] from resorting to the courts to test the validity of the legislation [because] the result is the same as if the law in terms prohibited the [party] from seeking judicial [review]" at all. The Supreme Court has made clear, however, that statutes imposing fines—even "enormous" fines—on noncomplying parties may satisfy due process if such fines are subject to a "good faith" or "reasonable ground[s]" defense. Courts have also held that "there is no constitutional violation if the imposition of penalties is subject to judicial discretion."

CERCLA guarantees these safeguards. Indeed, the statute offers noncomplying PRPs several levels of protection: a PRP faces daily fines and treble damages only if a federal court finds (1) that the UAO was proper; (2) that the PRP "willfully" failed to comply "without sufficient cause"; and (3) that, in the court's discretion, fines and treble damages are appropriate . . . . CERCLA's "willfulness" and "sufficient cause" requirements are quite similar to the good faith and reasonable grounds defenses the Supreme Court has found sufficient to satisfy due process, and GE does not argue otherwise. Moreover, PRPs receive added protection from the fact that the district court has authority to decide not to impose fines even if it concludes that a recipient "without sufficient cause, willfully violate[d], or fail[ed] or refuse[d] to comply with" a UAO . . . . Contrary to GE's claim, then, PRPs face no Hobson's choice. We therefore join three of our sister circuits that have rejected similar *Ex Parte Young* challenges to CERCLA's UAO regime.

. . . .

GE contends that even if CERCLA's UAO provisions are facially constitutional, EPA administers the statute in a way that denies PRPs due process . . . .

. . . .

. . . GE . . . contends that . . . EPA administers the statute in a way that "intimidate[s] PRPs from exercising the purported option of electing not to comply with a UAO so as to test an order's validity, giving rise to an independent due process violation under *Ex Parte Young*." . . . GE . . . urges us to infer coercion from the fact that the vast majority of PRPs elect to comply with UAOs . . . .

Rejecting this argument, the district court began by explaining, properly in our view, that the pattern and practice claim added little to GE's facial *Ex Parte Young* challenge: regardless of EPA's policies—for example, GE alleges that the agency coerces PRPs into compliance by threatening to seek multiple penalties for violations at a

Due process is satisfied if non-complying parties have a reasonable or good faith defense.

single UAO site—"a *judge* ultimately decides what, if any, penalty to impose." . . . As to GE's argument that the high incidence of UAO compliance evidences coercion, the district court found that "GE's own expert . . . demonstrate[d] that instances of noncompliance are sufficiently numerous to suggest that PRPs are not, in fact, forced to comply." And for our part, we observe that . . . recipients may be complying in large numbers not because they feel coerced, but because they believe that UAOs are generally accurate and would withstand judicial review . . . .

We fully understand, as GE argues, that the financial consequences of UAOs can be substantial. We also understand that other administrative enforcement schemes that address matters of public health and safety may provide greater process than does CERCLA. Such concerns, however, do not implicate the constitutionality of CERCLA or of the policies and practices by which EPA implements it . . . . [W]e affirm the decisions of the district court.

Notes and Questions

1. As the D.C. Circuit noted, § 113(h) of CERCLA, 42 U.S.C. § 9613(h), precludes a UAO respondent from immediately challenging the order. Why would Congress have included that provision? Should other environmental protection statutes include similar prohibitions on pre-enforcement review of administrative orders? *See Sackett v. Envtl. Protection Agency*, 132 S. Ct. 1367 (2012), p. 960, below.

2. Under § 113(h), a respondent who believes a § 106 UAO is unlawful and chooses *not* to comply may challenge the order only when and if EPA sues to enforce the order or to obtain penalties for the violation, while in the meantime potential daily penalties accumulate (as well as punitive damages if EPA performs the response action with Superfund money). What if a respondent *does* comply with an order, but nevertheless believes the order is unlawful? After completing the response action, the respondent may seek to be reimbursed for its costs from the Superfund. 42 U.S.C. § 9606(b)(2) (CERCLA § 106(b)(2)). These petitions are directed to EPA and initially decided by EPA's Environmental Appeals Board. A petitioner dissatisfied with EPA's decision may obtain judicial review in federal district court. *Id.*

3. The courts have not comprehensively defined the outer limits of the "sufficient cause" defense available to a non-complying respondent. In general, however, the sufficient causes for violating an order seem to be the same as the reasons for granting reimbursement to a complying respondent. According to § 106(b) of CERCLA, there are two of these. First, a party ordered to perform a response action must be reimbursed (or can avoid penalties and punitive damages) if it proves that EPA's "decision in selecting the response action ordered was arbitrary and capricious or was otherwise not in accordance with law." 42 U.S.C. § 9606(b)(2)(D). We saw this standard of review at work, in a different context, in *W.R. Grace*, p. 754, above. Second, a party ordered to perform a response action must be reimbursed (or can avoid penalties and punitive damages) if it proves that "it is not liable for response costs under" § 107 of CERCLA. We address § 107, CERCLA's basic liability provision, in the next section.

III. Liability

As we have seen, § 106 of CERCLA provides one tool for imposing the costs of response actions on the parties Congress deemed responsible for hazardous substance releases: judicial or administrative orders requiring responsible parties to perform response actions at their own expense. Section 107 provides a way for EPA to take response actions initially at its own expense but then to recover from responsible parties the costs that EPA incurred. Section 107(a), 42 U.S.C. § 9607(a), makes four categories of persons liable to reimburse a sovereign's response costs:

Notwithstanding any other provision or rule of law . . . —

(1) the owner and operator of a vessel or a facility,

(2) any person who at the time of disposal of any hazardous substance owned or operated any facility at which such hazardous substances were disposed of,

(3) any person who by contract, agreement, or otherwise arranged for disposal or treatment, or arranged with a transporter for transport for disposal or treatment, of hazardous substances owned or possessed by such person, by any other party or entity, at any facility or incineration vessel owned or operated by another party or entity and containing such hazardous substances, and

(4) any person who accepts or accepted any hazardous substances for transport to disposal or treatment facilities, incineration vessels or sites selected by such person, from which there is a release, or a threatened release which causes the incurrence of response costs, of a hazardous substance, shall be liable for [among other things, the government's response costs, see Section III.D, below] . . . .

A "person" is "an individual, firm, corporation, association, partnership, consortium, joint venture, commercial entity, United States Government, State, municipality, commission, political subdivision of a State, or any interstate body." *Id.* § 9601(21) (CERCLA § 101(21)). This definition notably includes both private and government entities. Thus the federal government may be liable under CERCLA if a federal agency fits into one of the classes of liable persons. The federal government does not sue itself, but may nevertheless be liable to a State or even to a private CERCLA plaintiff (in circumstances we explore below, p. 859). *See* 42 U.S.C. § 9620(a)(1) (CERCLA § 120(a)(1)) (waiving sovereign immunity for suits under § 107(a)); *see generally FMC Corp. v. U.S. Dept. of Commerce*, 29 F.3d 833 (3d Cir. 1994) (describing scope and limits of CERCLA's waiver of sovereign immunity). As to states, however, the Supreme Court, after initially upholding Congress's apparent abrogation of the states' Eleventh Amendment immunity from suit, reversed itself and held that the Commerce Clause did not give Congress the authority to make a state liable under CERCLA absent a state's consent to be sued. *Pennsylvania v. Union Gas Co.*, 491 U.S. 1 (1989), *overruled, Seminole Tribe of Fla. v. Florida*, 517 U.S. 44 (1996).

We will examine in detail the elements of CERCLA liability, including each class of responsible party described in § 107(a). Before doing so, however, we consider some general issues about how CERCLA's liability scheme works.

A. The Structure of CERCLA Liability

After CERCLA's enactment, EPA began exercising its new authorities to respond to releases and threatened releases of hazardous substances. In due course the government brought suit to recover the response costs it had incurred. Defendants in these cost recovery cases raised a host of fundamental issues about how Congress intended CERCLA's liability scheme to function.

United States v. Monsanto Co.

858 F.2d 160 (4th Cir. 1986)

Judge SPROUSE:

Oscar Seidenberg and Harvey Hutchinson (the site-owners) and Allied Corporation, Monsanto Company, and EM Industries, Inc. (the generator defendants), appeal from the district court's entry of summary judgment holding them liable to the United States and the State of South Carolina (the governments) under section 107(a) of the Comprehensive Environmental Response, Compensation, and Liability Act of 1980 (CERCLA) . . . .

I.

In 1972, Seidenberg and Hutchinson leased a four-acre tract of land they owned to the Columbia Organic Chemical Company (COCC), a South Carolina chemical manufacturing corporation. The property, located along Bluff Road near Columbia, South Carolina, consisted of a small warehouse and surrounding areas. The lease was verbal, on a month-to-month basis, and according to the site-owners' deposition testimony, was executed for the sole purpose of allowing COCC to store raw materials and finished products in the warehouse. Seidenberg and Hutchinson received monthly lease payments of $200, which increased to $350 by 1980.

In the mid-1970s, COCC expanded its business to include the brokering and recycling of chemical waste generated by third parties. It used the Bluff Road site as a waste storage and disposal facility for its new operations. In 1976, COCC's principals incorporated South Carolina Recycling and Disposal Inc. (SCRDI), for the purpose of assuming COCC's waste-handling business, and the site-owners began accepting lease payments from SCRDI.

SCRDI contracted with numerous off-site waste producers for the transport, recycling, and disposal of chemical and other waste . . . . SCRDI . . . deposited much of the waste it received at the Bluff Road facility. The waste stored at Bluff Road contained many chemical substances that federal law defines as "hazardous."

Between 1976 and 1980, SCRDI haphazardly deposited more than 7,000 fifty-five gallon drums of chemical waste on the four-acre Bluff Road site. It placed waste laden drums and containers wherever there was space, often without pallets to protect them from the damp ground. It stacked drums on top of one another without regard to the chemical compatibility of their contents. It maintained no documented safety procedures and kept no inventory of the stored chemicals.

Over time many of the drums rusted, rotted, and otherwise deteriorated. Hazardous substances leaked from the decaying drums and oozed into the ground. The substances commingled with incompatible chemicals that had escaped from other containers, generating noxious fumes, fires, and explosions.

On October 26, 1977, a toxic cloud formed when chemicals leaking from rusted drums reacted with rainwater. Twelve responding firemen were hospitalized. Again, on July 24, 1979, an explosion and fire resulted when chemicals stored in glass jars leaked onto drums containing incompatible substances . . . .

In 1980, the Environmental Protection Agency (EPA) inspected the Bluff Road site. Its investigation revealed that the facility was filled well beyond its capacity with chemical waste. The number of drums and the reckless manner in which they were stacked precluded access to various areas in the site. Many of the drums observed were unlabeled, or their labels had become unreadable from exposure, rendering it impossible to identify their contents. The EPA concluded that the site posed "a major fire hazard."

Later that year, the United States filed suit under section 7003 of the Resource [RCRA] Conservation and Recovery Act against SCRDI, COCC, and Oscar Seidenberg. The complaint was filed before the December 11, 1980, effective date of CERCLA, and it sought only injunctive relief. Thereafter, the State of South Carolina intervened as a plaintiff . . . .

In the course of discovery, the governments identified a number of waste generators, including the generator defendants in this appeal, that had contracted with SCRDI for waste disposal. The governments notified the generators that they were potentially responsible for the costs of cleanup at Bluff Road under section 107(a) of the newly-enacted CERCLA. As a result of these contacts, the governments executed individual settlement agreements with twelve of the identified off-site producers. The generator defendants, however, declined to settle.

. . . [T]he governments contracted [for] . . . a partial surface cleanup at the site . . . . The [contractor] documented that it had removed containers and drums bearing the labels or markings of each of the three generator defendants.

The EPA reinspected the site after the first phase of the cleanup had been completed. The inspection revealed that closed drums and containers labeled with the insignia of each of the three generator defendants remained at the site. The EPA also collected samples of surface water, soil, and sediment from the site. Laboratory tests of the samples disclosed that several hazardous substances contained in the waste the generator defendants had shipped to the site remained present at the site.[5]

. . . .

---

5. It is undisputed that hazardous substances of the sort contained in each of the generator defendants' waste materials were found at the site. These substances included 1,1,1-Trichloroethane, acetone, phenol, cresol (methyl phenol), chlorophenol, and 2,4-dichlorophenol.

In 1982, the governments filed an amended complaint, adding the three generator defendants and site-owner Harvey Hutchinson, and including claims under section 107(a) of CERCLA against all of the nonsettling defendants . . . .

. . . .

. . . All parties thereafter moved for summary judgment.

After an evidentiary hearing, the district court granted the governments' summary judgment motion on CERCLA liability . . . .

As to the site-owners' liability, the court found it sufficient that they owned the Bluff Road site at the time hazardous substances were deposited there. It rejected their contentions that Congress did not intend to subject "innocent" landowners to CERCLA liability. The court similarly found summary judgment appropriate against the generator defendants because it was undisputed that (1) they shipped hazardous substances to the Bluff Road facility; (2) hazardous substances "like" those present in the generator defendants' waste were found at the facility; and (3) there had been a release of hazardous substances at the site. In this context, the court rejected the generator defendants' arguments that the governments had to prove that their specific waste contributed to the harm at the site, and it found their constitutional contentions to be "without force." . . . This appeal followed.

II.

. . . .

In our view, the plain language of section 107(a) clearly defines the scope of intended liability under the statute and the elements of proof necessary to establish it. We agree with the overwhelming body of precedent that has interpreted section 107(a) as establishing a strict liability scheme.[11] Further, in light of the evidence presented here, we are persuaded that the district court correctly held that the governments satisfied all the elements of section 107(a) liability as to both the site-owners and the generator defendants.

A. *Site-Owners' Liability*

In light of the strict liability imposed by section 107(a), we cannot agree with the site-owners [sic] contention that they are not within the class of owners Congress intended to hold liable. The traditional elements of tort culpability on which the site-owners rely simply are absent from the statute. The plain language of section 107(a)(2) extends liability to owners of waste facilities regardless of their degree of participation in the subsequent disposal of hazardous waste.

---

11. In addition to the unanimous judicial viewpoint that Congress intended CERCLA liability to be strict, we observe that CERCLA section 101(32) provides that the standard of liability applicable to CERCLA actions shall be that which governs actions under section 311 of the Clean Water Act, 33 U.S.C. § 1321. In [an earlier case] we held that the standard of liability under section 311 is strict liability.

Under section 107(a)(2), *any* person who owned a facility at a time when hazardous substances were deposited there may be held liable for all costs of removal or remedial action if a release or threatened release of a hazardous substance occurs. The site-owners do not dispute their ownership of the Bluff Road facility, or the fact that releases occurred there during their period of ownership. Under these circumstances, all the prerequisites to section 107(a) liability have been satisfied.

. . . .

. . . The district court committed no error in entering summary judgment against the site-owners.

B. *Generator Defendants' Liability*

The generator defendants first contend that the district court misinterpreted section 107(a)(3) because it failed to read into the statute a requirement that the governments prove a nexus between the waste they sent to the site and the resulting environmental harm. They maintain that the statutory phrase "containing such hazardous substances" requires proof that the specific substances they generated and sent to the site were present at the facility at the time of release. The district court held, however, that the statute was satisfied by proof that hazardous substances "like" those contained in the generator defendants' waste were found at the site. We agree with the district court's interpretation.

Reduced of surplus language, sections 107(a)(3) and (4) impose liability on off-site waste generators who:

> "arranged for disposal . . . of hazardous substances . . . at any facility . . . *containing such hazardous substances* . . . from which there is a release . . . of a hazardous substance."

In our view, the plain meaning of the adjective "such" in the phrase "containing such hazardous substances" is "alike, similar, of the like kind." *Black's Law Dictionary* 1284 (5th ed. 1979). As used in the statute, the phrase "such hazardous substances" denotes hazardous substances alike, similar, or of a like kind to those that were present in a generator defendant's waste or that could have been produced by the mixture of the defendant's waste with other waste present at the site. It does not mean that the plaintiff must trace the ownership of each generic chemical compound found at a site. Absent proof that a generator defendant's specific waste remained at a facility at the time of release, a showing of chemical similarity between hazardous substances is sufficient.

The overall structure of CERCLA's liability provisions also militates against the generator defendants' "proof of ownership" argument. . . . As the statute provides— "notwithstanding any other provision or rule of law"—liability under section 107(a) is "subject *only* to the defenses set forth" in section 107(b). Each of the three defenses established in section 107(b) "carves out from liability an exception based on causation." Congress has, therefore, allocated the burden of disproving causation to the defendant who profited from the generation and inexpensive disposal of hazardous waste. We decline to interpret the statute in a way that would neutralize the force of Congress' intent.[17]

Finally, the purpose underlying CERCLA's liability provisions counsels against the generator defendants' argument. Throughout the statute's legislative history, there appears the recurring theme of facilitating prompt action to remedy the environmental blight of unscrupulous waste disposal. In deleting causation language from section 107(a), we assume as have many other courts, that Congress knew of the synergistic and migratory capacities of leaking chemical waste, and the technological infeasibility of tracing improperly disposed waste to its source. In view of this, we will not frustrate the statute's salutary goals by engrafting a "proof of ownership" requirement, which in practice, would be as onerous as the language Congress saw fit to delete.

. . . .

IV.

The generator defendants . . . contend that the imposition of "disproportionate" liability without proof of causation violated constitutional limitations on retroactive statutory application . . . .

. . . .

Many courts have concluded that Congress intended CERCLA's liability provisions to apply retroactively to pre-enactment disposal activities of off-site waste generators. They have held uniformly that retroactive operation survives the Supreme Court's tests for due process validity.[31] We agree with their analyses.

In *Usery v. Turner Elkhorn Mining Co.,* 428 U.S. 1 . . . (1976), the Supreme Court, in a different context, rejected a due process challenge to the retroactive operation of the liability provisions in the Black Lung Benefits Act of 1972. The Court stated that "a presumption of constitutionality" attaches to "legislative Acts adjusting the burdens and benefits of economic life," and that "the burden is on one complaining of a due process violation to establish that the legislature has acted in an arbitrary and irrational way." It reasoned that although the Act imposed new liability for disabilities developed prior to its enactment, its operation was "justified as a rational measure to spread the costs of the employees' disabilities to those who have profited from the fruits of their labor."

The reasoning of *Turner Elkhorn* applies with great force to the retroactivity contentions advanced here. While the generator defendants profited from inexpensive waste disposal methods that may have been technically "legal" prior to CERCLA's

---

17. . . . . [A]n early House version of what ultimately became section 107(a) limited liability to "any person who caused or contributed to the release or threatened release." As ultimately enacted after House and Senate compromise, however, CERCLA "imposed liability on classes of persons without reference to whether they caused or contributed to the release or threat of release." The legislature thus eliminated the element of causation from the plaintiff's liability case.

31. These decisions hold that CERCLA's legislative history and the past-tense language of section 107(a) evince congressional intent to apply CERCLA retroactively.

enactment, it was certainly foreseeable at the time that improper disposal could cause enormous damage to the environment. CERCLA operates remedially to spread the costs of responding to improper waste disposal among all parties that played a role in creating the hazardous conditions . . . . We do not think these consequences are "particularly harsh and oppressive," and we agree . . . that retroactive application of CERCLA does not violate due process.

. . . .

In view of the above, the judgment of the district court as to the CERCLA liability of the site-owners and generator defendants is affirmed . . . .

[The concurring and dissenting opinion of Judge Widener is omitted.]

Notes and Questions

1. Before CERCLA's enactment, the United States sued the owners and operators of the Bluff Road site under § 7003 of RCRA, the "imminent and substantial endangerment" provision (see pp. 645–646, above). Why did the United States need to add a CERCLA claim after CERCLA was enacted? What advantages did the new statute provide?

After Love Canal and other widely publicized hazardous waste episodes, but before the enactment of CERCLA, the federal government had attempted to use the then-available legal tools to secure cleanup of hazardous waste sites. Those tools were limited because, as described in the article by Randolph Hill (p. 631 above), EPA had not yet promulgated hazardous waste regulations under Subtitle C of RCRA. Nevertheless, EPA and the Department of Justice mounted an aggressive enforcement effort, relying primarily on § 7003 of RCRA, that included filing 54 civil actions in about a year. The effort is described in JOEL A. MINTZ, ENFORCEMENT AT THE EPA 36–40 (revised ed. 2012). After CERCLA's enactment, CERCLA claims were added to the pending suits, as in *Monsanto*.

2. What is the significance of the court's holding that CERCLA provides for strict liability? How does this holding relate to the court's conclusion that the "traditional elements of tort culpability" are absent from CERCLA's liability scheme?

3. What must a plaintiff prove in order to hold site owners such as Seidenberg and Hutchinson liable? The court rejected the owners' claim that they were "innocent" parties whom Congress did not intend to make liable. In the 1986 SARA amendments to CERCLA, Congress did extend a limited affirmative defense to CERCLA liability for innocent purchasers of contaminated property. We discuss CERCLA's innocent purchaser provision, which would not have applied to Seidenberg and Hutchinson, on p. 783, below.

4. The "generator" defendants in *Monsanto* argued that they could not be held liable unless the United States established the presence of each defendant's particular hazardous substances at the Bluff Road facility at the time of the response action. Suppose the court had accepted this argument and imposed a "waste fingerprinting" requirement. What would have been the practical result?

5. The Fourth Circuit reasoned that to accept the "fingerprinting" argument would have been inconsistent with the structure of CERCLA's causation-based affirmative defenses. As the court noted, § 107(a) provides that the liability it creates is "subject only to the defenses set forth in subsection (b) of this section." Section 107(b), in turn, provides that "[t]here shall be no liability . . . for a person otherwise liable who can establish by a preponderance of the evidence that the release or threat of release of a hazardous substance and the damages resulting therefrom were caused solely by" an act of God, an act of war, an act or omission of a third party, or any combination thereof. 42 U.S.C. § 9607(b). Only rarely could a defendant invoke an act of God or act of war as a defense, but a number of defendants have attempted to establish the so-called "third-party defense." The statute, however, requires satisfaction of quite stringent conditions for the defense to succeed.

First, the third party who allegedly was the sole cause of the release must not be an "employee or agent of the defendant" or "one whose act or omission occurs in connection with a contractual relationship, existing directly, or indirectly, with the defendant." *Id.* § 9607(b)(3). This means, for example, that a person who arranged for disposal of a hazardous substance cannot avoid liability by blaming the release on the owner or operator of the disposal site or on the transporter who brought the hazardous substance there, and vice versa. Can you think of circumstances in which a third party who caused the release would not have a direct or indirect contractual relationship with an otherwise liable party?

To maintain defense *

Second, even if the third party is unrelated to the defendant as just described, the defendant must establish

> by a preponderance of the evidence that (a) he exercised due care with respect to the hazardous substance concerned, taking into consideration the characteristics of such hazardous substance, in light of all relevant facts and circumstances, and (b) he took precautions against foreseeable acts or omissions of any such third party and the consequences that could foreseeably result from such acts or omissions.

Id. There has not been very much litigation to clarify the meaning of the due care and precautions requirements. For one example, see *Franklin County Convention Facilities Auth. v. American Premier Underwriters, Inc.,* 240 F.3d 53 (6th Cir. 2001) (holding that a landowner failed to exercise due care when, after its contractor accidentally split open a long-buried box containing hazardous substances, the substances migrated into an open sewer and the landowner waited more than a year before erecting a barrier against migration).

To successfully assert a § 107(b) defense, a defendant must prove that the act of God, war, or a third party was the sole cause of the release or threatened release of hazardous substance. Putting aside the philosophical impossibility of any one act being the "sole" cause of any outcome, a plausible interpretation of this requirement would be that it means the defendant must not in any way have caused the release. That, too, would be a difficult if not impossible burden to satisfy for a party that transported hazardous substances to the site, arranged for disposal of hazardous substances, or operated a facility from which hazardous substances were released, and possibly even for the owner of a facility.

In *Monsanto*, the owner defendants attempted to assert the third-party defense, arguing that only SCRDI and COCC had caused the release of hazardous substances. Why did the attempt fail?

May a CERCLA defendant rely on any other affirmative defenses? Courts have uniformly held that the statutory affirmative defenses are exclusive. *See* 42 U.S.C. § 9607(a) (creating liability "[n]otwithstanding any other provision or rule of law" subject "only" to the defenses set forth in § 107(b)). Thus, defenses that might be available, for example, in a tort suit, such as contributory negligence, and equitable defenses such as laches, unclean hands, waiver, estoppel, etc., are not available to a CERCLA defendant. *See, e.g., California* ex rel. *California Dept. of Toxic Substances Control v. Neville Chem. Co.*, 358 F.3d 661 (9th Cir. 2004) (holding that only statutory defenses are permitted and defendant may not raise equitable defenses).

6. Releases and threatened releases of hazardous substances existed at Bluff Road before CERCLA's enactment. The "generator" defendants' wastes were disposed of at Bluff Road before CERCLA's enactment. The Eighth Circuit held that the defendants could be liable nevertheless. The courts of appeals have uniformly agreed that CERCLA applies retroactively to create liability for pre-enactment conduct (much of which was legal at the time it was undertaken) and that such application is constitutional. *E.g., ASARCO LLC v. Goodwin*, 756 F.3d 191 (2d Cir. 2014); *United States v. Dico, Inc.*, 266 F.3d 864 (8th Cir. 2001); *Franklin County Convention Facilities Auth. v. American Premier Underwriters, Inc.*, 240 F.3d 534 (6th Cir. 2001); *United States v. Olin Corp.*, 107 F.3d 1225 (11th Cir. 1997); *O'Neil v. Picillo*, 883 F.2d 176 (1st Cir. 1989).

In *Monsanto*, the disposal of hazardous substances occurred only a few years before CERCLA became law. But CERCLA's retroactivity has been described as "unlimited." *Commonwealth Edison Co. v. United States*, 271 F.3d 1327, 1351 (Fed. Cir. 2001). At Love Canal, for example, EPA responded to releases of hazardous substances dumped before 1953. CERCLA claims have been predicated on the rupture of a wooden box of hazardous substances buried before 1901, *Franklin County, supra,* and on nineteenth-century contamination of the grounds of manufactured gas plants, *e.g. Atlanta Gas Light Co. v. UGI Utilities, Inc.*, 463 F.3d 1201 (11th Cir. 2006) (describing recent landowner's settlement with EPA for response to releases of hazardous substances deposited at the facility beginning in 1886); *Consolidated Edison Co. of N.Y., Inc. v. UGI Utilities, Inc.*, 153 Fed. Appx. 749 (2d Cir. 2005) (describing effort by utility to recover costs of responding to releases of hazardous substances deposited at 10 plants between 1887 and 1904). → *Can't be too early for you to be responsible*

Because CERCLA liability reaches so far back in time, inevitably parties that would otherwise be liable have undergone bankruptcy, dissolution, sale, or changes in corporate form. Principles of bankruptcy and corporate law, therefore, are often important in CERCLA cases. In particular, plaintiffs often allege that a defendant is liable as the successor to an entity that was within one of CERCLA's classes of liable persons. The buried box in *Franklin County*, for example, was placed on land owned by two

↳ Successor corps are liable as well.

small railroads that were later purchased by the Pennsylvania Railroad, which later merged with the New York Central Railroad to form the Penn Central Company, which after a bankruptcy reorganization became the defendant, American Premier Underwriters.

Courts have unanimously agreed that by including a "corporation" within CERCLA's definition of "person," Congress intended to extend liability to corporate successors. They have differed, however, on the test to be applied to determine whether a business organization is subject to liability as the successor to a prior entity. *Compare, e.g., United States v. Carolina Transformer Co.*, 978 F.2d 832 (4th Cir. 1992) (adopting broad, federal-law test for successor liability under CERCLA) and *Smith Land & Improvement Corp. v. Celotex Corp.*, 851 F.2d 86 (3d Cir. 1988) (emphasizing need for nationwide, uniform liability rules) with *Anspec Co. v. Johnson Controls, Inc.*, 922 F.2d 1240 (6th Cir. 1991) (finding that it is not necessary to fashion a federal common law rule of successor liability).

7. The generator defendants in *Monsanto* complained that their liability was disproportionate to their respective roles in creating the release of hazardous substances and thus the need for response action. The same issue looms much larger in the next case.

United States v. Alcan Aluminum Corp.
964 F.2d 252 (3d Cir. 1992)

Judge GREENBERG:

This matter is before the court on appeal by Alcan Aluminum Corporation ("Alcan") from a summary judgment entered in favor of the United States (the "Government") for response costs incurred by the Government in cleaning the Susquehanna River.

... [T]he Government filed a complaint ... under section 107(a) of ... [CERCLA] against 20 defendants, including Alcan, for the recovery of clean-up costs it incurred in response to a release of hazardous substances into the Susquehanna River. [The Government and Alcan both moved for summary judgment.]

The district court ... issued a memorandum and order granting the Government's motion .... Accordingly ..., the court entered judgment against Alcan in the amount of $ 473,790.18, which was the difference between the full response costs the Government had incurred in cleaning the Susquehanna River and the amount the Government had recovered from the settling defendants.

I.

FACTS AND PROCEDURAL HISTORY

Virtually all of the facts in this case to the extent developed at this point are undisputed. The Butler Tunnel Site (the "Site") is listed on the National Priorities List .... The Site includes a network of approximately five square miles of deep underground mines and related tunnels, caverns, pools and waterways bordering the east bank of the Susquehanna River in Pittston, Pennsylvania. The mine workings at the Site are drained by the Butler Tunnel (the "Tunnel"), a 7500 foot tunnel which feeds directly into the Susquehanna River.

The mines are accessible from the surface by numerous air shafts or boreholes. One borehole (the "Borehole") is located on the premises of Hi-Way Auto Service, an automobile fuel and repair station situated above the Tunnel. The Borehole leads directly into the mine workings at the Site.

In the late 1970's, the owner of Hi-Way Auto Service permitted various liquid waste transport companies, including those owned and controlled by Russell Mahler (the "Mahler Companies"), to deposit oily liquid wastes containing hazardous substances into the Borehole. The Mahler Companies collected the liquid wastes from numerous industrial facilities located in the northeastern United States and, in total, disposed of approximately 2,000,000 gallons of oily wastes containing hazardous substances through the Borehole. Apparently, it was contemplated that the waste would remain at the Site indefinitely.

Alcan is an Ohio corporation which manufactures aluminum sheet and plate products in Oswego, New York. From 1965 through at least 1989, Alcan's manufacturing process involved the hot-rolling of aluminum ingots. To keep the rolls cool and lubricated during the hot-rolling process, Alcan circulated an emulsion through the rolls, consisting of 95% deionized water and 5% mineral oil. At the end of the hot-rolling process, Alcan removed the used emulsion and replaced it with unused emulsion.

During the rolling process, fragments of the aluminum ingots, which also contained copper, chromium, cadmium, lead and zinc, hazardous substances under CERCLA, broke off into the emulsion. In an effort to remove those fragments, Alcan then filtered the used emulsion prior to disposing of it, but the filtering process was imperfect and hence some fragments remained. According to Alcan, however, the level of these compounds in the post-filtered, used emulsion was "far below the EP toxic or TCLP toxic levels [for characteristic hazardous waste under RCRA] and, indeed, orders of magnitude below ambient or naturally occurring background levels. Moreover, the trace quantities of metal compounds in the emulsion [were] immobile. . . ." The Government does not specifically challenge Alcan's assertion that the used emulsion contained only low levels of these metallic compounds . . . .

From mid-1978 to late 1979, Alcan contracted with the Mahler Companies to dispose of at least 2,300,950 gallons of used emulsion from its Oswego, New York, facility. During that period, the Mahler Companies disposed of approximately 32,500–37,500 gallons (or five 6500–7500 gallon loads) of Alcan's liquid waste through the Borehole into the Site.[3]

In September 1985, approximately 100,000 gallons of water contaminated with hazardous substances were released from the Site into the Susquehanna River. It appears that this discharge was composed of the wastes deposited into the Borehole in the late

---

3. . . . . Alcan asserts that it was not aware that Mahler was disposing of the oily waste in this fashion, but the Government does not contend otherwise, and in any event Alcan does not contend that this should affect our result.

1970's. Between September 28, 1985, and January 7, 1987, EPA incurred significant response costs due to the release and the threatened release of hazardous substances from the Site. According to the Government, EPA's response actions included "containing an oily material on the river through the use of absorbent booms; immediately removing and disposing of 161,000 pounds (over 80 tons) of oil and chemical-soaked debris and soil, monitoring, sampling and analysis of air and water, and conducting hydrogeologic studies."

. . . .

In November 1989, the Government filed a complaint against 20 defendants, including Alcan, for the recovery of costs incurred as a result of the release of hazardous wastes from the Site into the Susquehanna River. [In two consent decrees entered by the district court, every defendant except Alcan settled with the Government by agreeing to reimburse certain removal costs.]

The Government then moved for summary judgment against Alcan, the only nonsettling defendant, to collect the balance of its response costs. Alcan cross-moved for summary judgment, arguing that its emulsion did not constitute a "hazardous substance" as defined by CERCLA due to its below-ambient levels of copper, cadmium, chromium, lead and zinc, and further contending that its emulsion could not have caused the release or any response costs incurred by the Government.

[After the district court granted the Government's motion and denied Alcan's, Alcan appealed.]

II.

DISCUSSION

A. CERCLA FRAMEWORK:

. . . .

CERCLA's bite lies in its requirement that responsible parties pay for actions undertaken pursuant to section 104. Under section 107, CERCLA liability is imposed where the plaintiff establishes the following four elements:

(1) the defendant falls within one of the four categories of "responsible parties";

(2) the hazardous substances are disposed at a "facility";[8]

(3) there is a "release" or threatened release of hazardous substances from the facility into the environment;[9]

(4) the release causes the incurrence of "response costs".

. . . .

. . . CERCLA imposes strict liability on responsible parties.

---

8. . . . . The parties have agreed that the Site is a "facility" within the meaning of CERCLA.
9. . . . . The parties in this suit have also agreed that a "release" has occurred.

B. CERCLA CONTAINS NO QUANTITATIVE REQUIREMENT IN ITS DEFINITION OF "HAZARDOUS SUBSTANCE":

Alcan argues that it should not be held liable for response costs incurred by the Government in cleaning the Susquehanna River because the level of hazardous substances in its emulsion was below that which naturally occurs and thus could not have contributed to the environmental injury. It asserts that we must read a threshold concentration requirement into the definition of "hazardous substances" for the term "hazardous" to have any meaning. The United States Chamber of Commerce (the "Chamber") as *amicus curiae* .... states that "the uncontested facts show that Alcan's waste contained less of these [hazardous] elements than can be found in clean dirt." ...

The Government responds that under a plain reading of the statute, there is no quantitative requirement in the definition of "hazardous substance." Therefore, the Government asserts that Alcan's argument that substances containing below-ambient levels of hazardous substances are not really "hazardous" is properly directed at Congress, not the judiciary.

... [T]he district court ... agreed with the Government. ...

. . . .

For the reasons that follow, we are satisfied that the court was correct ....

1. Plain Meaning:

[The court quoted the definition of "hazardous substance" in CERCLA § 9601(14), 42 U.S.C. § 9601(14).]

Hence, the statute does not, on its face, impose any quantitative requirement or concentration level on the definition of "hazardous substances." Rather, the substance under consideration must simply fall within one of the designated categories.

2. Legislative History:

Since the statute is plain on its face, we need not resort to legislative history to uncover its meaning. In any event, the legislative history is barren of any remarks directly revealing Congress' intent vis-a-vis a threshold requirement on the definition of hazardous substances. Significantly, however, the available legislative history of CERCLA *does* indicate that Congress created the statute to force all polluters to pay for their pollution. It is difficult to imagine that Congress intended to impose a quantitative requirement on the definition of hazardous substances and thereby permit a polluter to add to the total pollution but avoid liability because the amount of its own pollution was minimal.

3. Jurisprudence:

In addition, courts that have addressed this issue have almost uniformly held that CERCLA liability does not depend on the existence of a threshold quantity of a hazardous substance.

4. Congressional Matter:

It may be that Congress did not intend such an all-encompassing definition of "hazardous substances," but this argument is best directed at Congress itself. If Congress had intended to impose a threshold requirement, it could easily have so indicated. We should not rewrite the statute simply because the definition of one of its terms is broad in scope.

. . . .

D. CAUSATION:

Alcan maintains that . . . we must at least require the Government to prove that *Alcan's emulsion* caused or contributed to the release or the Government's incurrence of response costs. The Government contends, and the district court . . . agreed, that the statute imposes no such causation requirement, but rather requires that the plaintiff in a CERCLA proceeding establish that the *release* or *threatened release* caused the incurrence of response costs; it underscores the difficulty CERCLA plaintiffs would face in the multi-generator context if required to trace the cause of the response costs to each responsible party.

1. Plain Meaning:

The plain meaning of the statute supports the Government's position . . . . The statute does not, on its face, require the plaintiff to prove that the generator's *hazardous substances* themselves caused the release or caused the incurrence of response costs; rather, it requires the plaintiff to prove that the *release or threatened release* caused the incurrence of response costs, and that the defendant is a generator of hazardous substances at the facility.

2. Legislative History:

The legislative history also . . . . indicates that Congress considered and rejected a requirement that the plaintiff establish that the defendant's waste caused or contributed to the release or the incurrence of response costs.

3. Jurisprudence:

Further, virtually every court that has considered this question has held that a CERCLA plaintiff need not establish a direct causal connection between the defendant's hazardous substances and the release or the plaintiff's incurrence of response costs . . . .

. . . .

. . . Accordingly, we reject Alcan's argument that the Government must prove that Alcan's emulsion deposited in the Borehole caused the release or caused the Government to incur response costs. Rather, the Government must simply prove that the defendant's hazardous substances were deposited at the site from which there was a release and that the *release* caused the incurrence of response costs.

Notes and Questions

1. In *Alcan*, the Third Circuit concluded that Congress intended for a party like Alcan to be liable under CERCLA regardless of the amount or concentration of hazardous substances that Alcan contributed to the facility from which hazardous substances were released. Assuming Congress so intended, is the result a sensible policy? The *Alcan* court was persuaded by the government's argument that if many parties deposited small amounts of hazardous substances to a facility, imposing a quantitative threshold could lead to the perverse result that *none* of the contributors would be liable, even though all contributed to a release of hazardous substances that posed a serious environmental problem and required a substantial expenditure of response costs. Nevertheless, the court of appeals was troubled by Alcan's argument that without a quantitative threshold and a causation requirement, parties could be held liable for disposing of everyday, harmless materials that contained minute quantities of hazardous substances. We discuss the court's solution, which gives parties like Alcan a second bite at the causation apple in a "divisibility of harm" inquiry, below (p. 840).

2. Alcan, like the defendants in *Monsanto*, argued that, in order to establish liability, the plaintiff must establish causation with respect to Alcan's emulsion. The court rejected Alcan's argument, citing *Monsanto* among other cases. Are the causation arguments in the two cases identical?

3. Do you think the CERCLA liability scheme as explained in *Monsanto* and *Alcan* is fair? Do you think it is effective at achieving the goals of CERCLA?

B. The Common Elements of CERCLA Liability

The *Alcan* opinion recited the elements of CERCLA liability, which require a bit of teasing out of the statute because of the way § 107(a) is structured. (See p. 776 for the list of elements and p. 765 for the statutory text, above). Reframing slightly the Third Circuit's statement of the elements, for a defendant to be liable there must be: (1) a release or threatened release of (2) a hazardous substance from (3) a facility;[2] (4) the release or threatened release must have caused incurrence of response costs; and (5) the defendant must be in one of the four categories of liable parties listed in § 107(a). The first four elements are sometimes called the "common elements" because they apply to a claim against any category of CERCLA defendant.

In CERCLA litigation, the common elements rarely are seriously disputed. CERCLA defines the terms of the common elements very broadly. It is unlikely that EPA or anyone else would take response action and sue for cost recovery in their absence.

We have already seen, p. 738 above, that the definition of "hazardous substance" relies primarily on designations under other statutes and that in almost all cases it is possible to decide whether a particular substance is a hazardous substance simply by

---

2. CERCLA also imposes liability for a release from a "vessel" but few CERCLA cases have involved vessels.

referring to a published list. Congress conceivably might have given limiting content to the concept of a "release" but CERCLA defines release very broadly to include "any spilling, leaking, pumping, pouring, emitting, emptying, discharging, injecting, escaping, leaching, dumping, or disposing into the environment (including the abandonment or discarding of barrels, containers, and other closed receptacles containing any hazardous substance or pollutant or contaminant)." 42 U.S.C. § 9601(22) (CERCLA § 101(22)). A release must be "into the environment" but "environment" is defined to include air, land, and water and thus is not much of a constraint on the breadth of the term "release." *Id.* § 9601(8). The definition of release notably includes movement of hazardous substances both with and without human agency (dumping and disposing but also leaking and leaching) as well as the abandonment or discarding of *closed* hazardous substance containers.

CERCLA Exclusions

A few things that would otherwise fall within the definition of release are excluded. Workplace exposures, engine emissions, and nuclear incidents are excluded, presumably because other statutes address these things. The normal application of fertilizer is excluded — a policy choice that seems to indicate Congress understood how broad the scope of "releases of hazardous substances" could be. *Id.*

Whether the release was from a "facility" rarely, if ever, becomes an issue. Under CERCLA

Oil exclusion

> the term "facility" means any building, structure, installation, equipment, pipe or pipeline (including any pipe into a sewer or publicly owned treatment works), well, pit, pond, lagoon, impoundment, ditch, landfill, storage container, motor vehicle, rolling stock, or aircraft, or (B) any site or area where a hazardous substance has been deposited, stored, disposed of, or placed, or otherwise come to be located; but does not include any consumer product in consumer use or any vessel.

42 U.S.C. § 9601(9) (CERCLA § 101(9)). The breadth of this definition, particularly part (B), is such that, as in *Monsanto* and *Alcan*, defendants usually concede the "facility" element.

Finally, as described in *Alcan*, CERCLA liability requires that the release or threatened release caused the incurrence of response costs. CERCLA does not define "incurrence of response costs" but, as we have seen, it does define "response." To satisfy this last common element, then, a CERCLA plaintiff must simply prove that it carried out some type of CERCLA removal or remedial action with respect to the release or threatened release at issue and that it spent at least some money doing so — even if the exact amount of recoverable costs might be disputed.

C. Responsible Parties

The common elements of liability under § 107(a) rarely present difficulties for plaintiffs. The action in CERCLA cost recovery cases is almost always about the fifth element: whether the defendant is within one of the categories of responsible parties.

1. Owners and Operators

The "owner and operator of a ... facility" is liable under § 107(a)(1), 42 U.S.C. § 9601. Identifying the "owner" would seem to be an easy task. But is an owner liable even if it had nothing to do with the placement of hazardous substances at the facility?

New York v. Shore Realty Corp.
759 F.2d 1032 (2d Cir. 1985)

Judge OAKES:

[Donald LeoGrande incorporated the Shore Realty Corp. for the sole purpose of purchasing a piece of property on which he hoped to build condominiums. LeoGrande knew that the seller's tenants were operating a hazardous waste storage facility and that tanks and a warehouse containing chemical waste were on the property. The purchase agreement provided that Shore could void the contract after conducting an environmental review. The review, performed by a consultant Shore hired, disclosed releases and threatened releases of hazardous substances. Nevertheless, Shore completed the sale and took title to the property, even after requesting but failing to obtain a waiver of liability from the New York State Department of Environmental Conservation (DEC). The tenants continued adding hazardous waste to the tanks until Shore evicted the tenants a few months after the sale. The DEC investigated the conditions at the property, ordered Shore to remove the drums, and supervised Shore's actions. The State then sued Shore and LeoGrande under CERCLA, alleging that the costs of DEC's investigation were within CERCLA's definition of "response costs." The district court granted the State's motion for partial summary judgment, holding Shore and LeoGrande liable under section 107(a) of CERCLA.]

We hold that the district court properly awarded the State response costs under section 9607(a)(4)(A). The State's costs in assessing the conditions of the site and supervising the removal of the drums of hazardous waste squarely fall within CERCLA's definition of response costs, even though the State is not undertaking to do the removal . . . .

Shore argues that it is not covered by section 9607(a)(1) because it neither owned the site at the time of disposal nor caused the presence or the release of the hazardous waste at the facility . . . . Shore claims that Congress intended that the scope of section 9607(a)(1) be no greater than that of section 9607(a)(2) and that both should be limited by the "at the time of disposal" language . . . . We agree with the State, however, that section 9607(a)(1) unequivocally imposes strict liability on the current owner of a facility from which there is a release or threat of release, without regard to causation.

. . . . Congress intended to cover different classes of persons differently. Section 9607(a)(1) applies to all current owners and operators, while section 9607(a)(2) primarily covers prior owners and operators. Moreover, section 9607(a)(2)'s scope is more limited than that of section 9607(a)(1). Prior owners and operators are liable only if they owned or operated the facility "at the time of disposal of any hazardous substance"; this limitation does not apply to current owners, like Shore . . . .

. . . .

. . . [A]s the State points out, accepting Shore's arguments would open a huge loophole in CERCLA's coverage. It is quite clear that if the current owner of a site could avoid liability merely by having purchased the site after chemical dumping had ceased, waste sites certainly would be sold, following the cessation of dumping, to new owners who could avoid the liability otherwise required by CERCLA. Congress had well in mind that persons who dump or store hazardous waste sometimes cannot be located or may be deceased or judgment-proof. We will not interpret section 9607(a) in any way that apparently frustrates the statute's goals, in the absence of a specific congressional intention otherwise . . . .

Notes and Questions

1. In reciting the facts (paraphrased in the excerpt), the Second Circuit pointed out that LeoGrande (and thus his corporation, Shore) was "fully aware" of the hazardous waste storage facility before buying the property. If Shore had not known about the tenants' activities, would Shore have been liable?

2. CERCLA defines the term "owner or operator," but the basic definition — "'owner or operator' means . . . any person owning or operating" a facility, 42 U.S.C. § 9601(20)(A), CERCLA § 101(20)(A) — is uninformative. The title holder of record presumably is an owner, but might anyone else qualify?

As you know from your course in property law, ownership involves a bundle of rights. Can CERCLA "owner" liability attach to a person who does not have all rights of ownership? In commercial settings, for example, leases often grant the nominal tenant significant rights and responsibilities with respect to the leased property (although not the power to sell or transfer it). Some courts have held that a tenant with sufficient authority over the property might be an "owner" for purposes of CERCLA liability. *See Commander Oil Corp. v. Barlo Equipment Corp.*, 215 F.3d 321 (2d Cir. 2000) (explaining this principle and describing cases).

What about a lender who takes a mortgage on a property? CERCLA's definition of "owner or operator" excludes "a person who, without participating in the management of a . . . facility, holds indicia of ownership primarily to protect his security interest in the . . . facility." 42 U.S.C. § 9601(20)(A). But what if a lender imposed requirements on the borrower to ensure that the borrower did not diminish the value of the property — would that be "participating in management"? And what if a lender foreclosed on a property and thereby became the title holder? Some early court opinions limited the scope of the "security interest" exclusion. In response to concerns of the banking industry, Congress in 1997 added provisions to CERCLA that: (1) exclude from the definition of "owner or operator" a lender who took title by foreclosure and (2) define "participation in management" narrowly, thereby making certain that many common lender activities would not subject a lender to CERCLA owner liability. *See* 42 U.S.C. § 9601(20)(E), (F) (CERCLA § 101(20)(E), (F)).

CERCLA also excludes from "owner or operator" a government agency that "involuntarily acquires title by virtue of its function as sovereign," as in a foreclosure for tax delinquency. 42 U.S.C. §9601(20)(D)) (CERCLA §101(20)(D)). In such circumstances, a person who owned or operated the facility immediately before the government took title or control is still considered an "owner or operator." *Id.* §9601(20)(A)(iii). This provision applies in many situations in which the owner simply abandoned a property because the likely cost of response actions exceeded the property's value.

3. As *Shore Realty* and many other court opinions held, §107(a)(1) pays no heed to an owner's "innocence" of causing the contamination; an owner is liable purely by virtue of ownership. Should owners who did not themselves contaminate a property be liable under CERCLA? Consider the possibilities: under the terms of §107(a)(1), would a homeowner at Love Canal be liable for the flow of hazardous substances off her or his property?

One possible answer for an innocent owner—who unwittingly bought property contaminated by a previous owner's behavior—might have been the third-party defense of CERCLA §107(b)(3). The owner could have argued that acts or omissions of the prior owner(s) had been the sole cause of the release of hazardous substances. There was a problem, however. Recall that the "third party," under §107(b)(3), may not be a party "whose act or omission occurs in connection with a contractual relationship, existing directly or indirectly, with the defendant." Wouldn't the seller and the buyer have a contractual relationship that defeated the defense? For that matter, wouldn't any prior owner have an indirect contractual relationship with the current owner by virtue of the chain of title?

The 1986 SARA amendments to CERCLA clarify the liability of so-called "innocent landowners." Rather than amend the liability provisions of §107, however, Congress added a new and complex definition of "contractual relationship" to the statute.

The definition first makes clear that a "contractual relationship" generally includes a land contract, deed, or other instrument transferring an interest in real property. But such an instrument is *not* considered a contractual relationship for purposes of the third-party defense if the defendant acquired the facility after the disposal or placement of hazardous substances and the defendant can prove by a preponderance of the evidence that:

> (i) At the time the defendant acquired the facility the defendant did not know and had no reason to know that any hazardous substance which is the subject of the release or threatened release was disposed of on, in, or at the facility. [or]
>
> (ii) The defendant is a government entity which acquired the facility by escheat, or through any other involuntary transfer or acquisition, or through the exercise of eminent domain authority by purchase or condemnation. [or]
>
> (iii) The defendant acquired the facility by inheritance or bequest.

42 U.S.C. §9601(35)(A) (CERCLA §101(35)(A), added by SARA §101(f)). Of these bases for "innocence," the most commonly invoked is the first: that the landowner "did

not know and had no reason to know" of the presence of hazardous substances. SARA further specified that to "establish that the defendant had no reason to know, . . . the defendant must have undertaken, at the time of acquisition, all appropriate inquiry into the previous ownership and uses of the property consistent with good commercial or customary practice in an effort to minimize liability." SARA, P.L. 99-499 § 101(f). After further amendment, the statute now requires proof that a purchaser "carried out all appropriate inquiries" before buying the property, 42 U.S.C. § 9601(35)(B)(i), and identifies facts to be considered in determining whether a purchaser met its burden of proof, *id.* § 9601(35)(B)(ii)–(iv). Among other things, Congress directed EPA to promulgate regulations specifying standards and practices that would constitute "all appropriate inquiries." *Id.* § 9601(35)(B)(ii).

Because of the way the statute's "innocent landowner" provision is structured, even proof that a landowner did not know or have reason to know of the presence of hazardous substances at the time of acquisition does not, by itself, protect the owner from liability. The landowner must still establish the other elements of the § 107(b)(3) third-party defense, see p. 772 above, including the requirements that the owner exercised due care and took precautions against foreseeable third-party acts. *Id.* § 9601(35)(A), (B)(i)(II) (specifying additional requirements).

In 2002, Congress created two additional, limited exemptions from "owner" liability. P.L. 107-118 §§ 221, 222. The first protected from liability the owners (and operators) of property contaminated by a hazardous substance release that spread from adjacent property. 42 U.S.C. § 9607(q) (CERCLA § 107(q)). The second, intended to encourage sale and re-use of contaminated properties, defined and insulated from liability "bona fide prospective purchasers" of previously contaminated land. *Id.* § 9607(r) (CERCLA § 107(r)). Each exemption includes detailed requirements that a person must satisfy in order to qualify.

brownfields

Review the summarized facts of *Shore Realty*. If CERCLA's innocent landowner provision had been in effect at the time New York sued Shore Realty Corp., would the provision have shielded the defendant from liability? Why or why not? What about the owner-defendants in *United States v. Monsanto*, p. 766 above?

4. The Second Circuit held that LeoGrande's corporation, Shore Realty, was liable as an owner. What about LeoGrande himself? The Second Circuit decided whether he was liable, too.

New York v. Shore Realty Corp.
759 F.2d 1032 (2d Cir. 1985)

Judge OAKES:

. . . .

LeoGrande incorporated Shore solely for the purpose of purchasing the Shore Road property. All corporate decisions and actions were made, directed, and controlled by him . . . .

. . . .

Needless to say, the tenants did not clean up the site before they left. Thus, . . . when Shore employees first entered the site[,] . . . [a]s LeoGrande admitted by affidavit, "the various storage tanks, pipe lines and connections between these storage facilities were in a bad state of repair." While Shore claims to have made some improvements, such as sealing all the pipes and valves and continuing the cleanup of the damage from earlier spills, Shore did nothing about the hundreds of thousands of gallons of hazardous waste standing in deteriorating tanks. In addition, although a growing number of drums were leaking hazardous substances, Shore essentially ignored the problem until June, 1984.

. . . .

We hold LeoGrande liable as an "operator" under CERCLA . . . . Under CERCLA "owner or operator" is defined to mean "any person owning or operating" an onshore facility, and "person" includes individuals as well as corporations. More important, the definition of "owner or operator" excludes "a person, who, without participating in the management of a . . . facility, holds indicia of ownership primarily to protect his security interest in the facility." The use of this exception implies that an owning stockholder who manages the corporation, such as LeoGrande, is liable under CERCLA as an "owner or operator." That conclusion is consistent with that of other courts that have addressed the issue. In any event, LeoGrande is in charge of the operation of the facility in question, and as such is an "operator" within the meaning of CERCLA . . . .

Notes and Questions

1. What principles of statutory interpretation did the Second Circuit use to conclude that LeoGrande was liable as an operator? Does the court's reasoning persuade you?

2. Notice the Second Circuit's implicit interpretation of the phrase "owner and operator." To be liable, a party need not be "the owner and operator" of a facility. Rather, one person may be an "owner" and another person an "operator," and both are liable.

3. What was the "operation" that LeoGrande was "in charge of"? Suppose that, instead of being "in charge of" anything, LeoGrande had simply owned some of the stock of Shore Realty Corporation. Would he have been liable under CERCLA? The Supreme Court had its say on that question in the context of a claim under § 107(a)(2) of CERCLA, which we turn to next.

2. Owners and Operators at the Time of Disposal

Section 107(a)(2) of CERCLA makes liable "any person who at the time of disposal of any hazardous substance owned or operated any facility at which such hazardous substances were disposed of." How does liability under § 107(a)(2) differ from liability under § 107(a)(1)? As the Second Circuit explained in *Shore Realty*, § 107(a)(1) applies only to those who currently own or operate a facility. Section 107(a)(2), however, applies also to those who no longer own or operate a facility but did so in the past—provided that *while* they owned or operated the facility, hazardous substances were disposed of at the facility. CERCLA includes no special definition of "owner" or "operator" with respect to § 107(a)(2), so issues regarding whether a particular defendant fits that category are similar to those under § 107(a)(1).

United States v. Bestfoods

524 U.S. 51 (1998)

Justice SOUTER:

The United States brought this action for the costs of cleaning up industrial waste generated by a chemical plant. The issue . . . is whether a parent corporation that actively participated in, and exercised control over, the operations of a subsidiary may, without more, be held liable as an operator of a polluting facility owned or operated by the subsidiary. We answer no, unless the corporate veil may be pierced. But a corporate parent that actively participated in, and exercised control over, the operations of the facility itself may be held directly liable in its own right as an operator of the facility.

. . . The term "person" is defined in CERCLA to include corporations and other business organizations, and the term "facility" enjoys a broad and detailed definition as well. The phrase "owner or operator" is defined only by tautology, however, as "any person owning or operating" a facility, and it is this bit of circularity that prompts our review.

In 1957, Ott Chemical Co. (Ott I) began manufacturing chemicals at a plant near Muskegon, Michigan, and its intentional and unintentional dumping of hazardous substances significantly polluted the soil and ground water at the site. In 1965, respondent CPC International Inc. [now known as Bestfoods but herein referred to as CPC] incorporated a wholly owned subsidiary to buy Ott I's assets in exchange for CPC stock. The new company, also dubbed Ott Chemical Co. (Ott II), continued chemical manufacturing at the site, and continued to pollute its surroundings. CPC kept the managers of Ott I, including its founder, president, and principal shareholder, Arnold Ott, on board as officers of Ott II. Arnold Ott and several other Ott II officers and directors were also given positions at CPC, and they performed duties for both corporations.

In 1972, CPC sold Ott II to Story Chemical Company, which operated the Muskegon plant until its bankruptcy in 1977. Shortly thereafter, when respondent Michigan Department of Natural Resources (MDNR) examined the site for environmental damage, it found the land littered with thousands of leaking and even exploding drums of waste, and the soil and water saturated with noxious chemicals. MDNR sought a buyer for the property who would be willing to contribute toward its cleanup . . . [R]espondent Aerojet-General Corp. . . . created a wholly owned California subsidiary, Cordova Chemical Company (Cordova/California), to purchase the property, and Cordova/California in turn created a wholly owned Michigan subsidiary, Cordova

(margin note: Corporate Liability)

Chemical Company of Michigan (Cordova/Michigan), which manufactured chemicals at the site until 1986.

By 1981, the federal Environmental Protection Agency had undertaken to see the site cleaned up, and its long-term remedial plan called for expenditures well into the tens of millions of dollars. To recover some of that money, the United States filed this action under § 107 in 1989, naming five defendants as responsible parties: CPC, Aerojet, Cordova/California, Cordova/Michigan, and Arnold Ott.[6] (By that time, Ott I and Ott II were defunct.) . . . . [T]he District Court held a 15-day bench trial on the issue of liability. Because the parties stipulated that the Muskegon plant was a "facility" within the meaning of [CERCLA], that hazardous substances had been released at the facility, and that the United States had incurred reimbursable response costs to clean up the site, the trial focused on the issues of whether CPC and Aerojet, as the parent corporations of Ott II and the Cordova companies, had "owned or operated" the facility within the meaning of § 107(a)(2).

The District Court said that operator liability may attach to a parent corporation both directly, when the parent itself operates the facility, and indirectly, when the corporate veil can be pierced under state law . . . . As the District Court put it,

> "a parent corporation is directly liable under section 107(a)(2) as an operator only when it has exerted power or influence over its subsidiary by actively participating in and exercising control over the subsidiary's business during a period of disposal of hazardous waste. A parent's actual participation in and control over a subsidiary's functions and decision-making creates 'operator' liability under CERCLA; a parent's mere oversight of a subsidiary's business in a manner appropriate and consistent with the investment relationship between a parent and its wholly owned subsidiary does not."

Applying that test to the facts of this case, the District Court held both CPC and Aerojet liable under § 107(a)(2) as operators. As to CPC, the court found it particularly telling that CPC selected Ott II's board of directors and populated its executive ranks with CPC officials, and that a CPC official, G.R.D. Williams, played a significant role in shaping Ott II's environmental compliance policy.

[A 7–6 majority of the *en banc* Sixth Circuit stated]: "At least conceivably, a parent might independently operate the facility in the stead of its subsidiary; or, as a sort of joint venturer, actually operate the facility alongside its subsidiary." But the court refused to go any further and rejected the District Court's analysis with the explanation:

> "[W]here a parent corporation is sought to be held liable as an operator [. . .] based upon the extent of its control of its subsidiary which owns the facility, the parent will be liable only when the requirements necessary to pierce the corporate veil [under state law] are met. In other words, . . . whether the parent will be liable as an operator depends upon whether the degree to which it

---

6. Arnold Ott settled out of court with the Government on the eve of trial.

controls its subsidiary and the extent and manner of its involvement with the facility, amount to the abuse of the corporate form that will warrant piercing the corporate veil and disregarding the separate corporate entities of the parent and subsidiary."

Applying Michigan veil-piercing law, the Court of Appeals decided that neither CPC nor Aerojet was liable for controlling the actions of its subsidiaries . . . .

We granted certiorari to resolve a conflict among the Circuits over the extent to which parent corporations may be held liable under CERCLA for operating facilities ostensibly under the control of their subsidiaries . . . .

It is a general principle of corporate law deeply "ingrained in our economic and legal systems" that a parent corporation (so-called because of control through ownership of another corporation's stock) is not liable for the acts of its subsidiaries. Thus it is hornbook law that "the exercise of the 'control' which stock ownership gives to the stockholders . . . will not create liability beyond the assets of the subsidiary. That 'control' includes the election of directors, the making of by-laws . . . and the doing of all other acts incident to the legal status of stockholders. Nor will a duplication of some or all of the directors or executive officers be fatal." Although this respect for corporate distinctions when the subsidiary is a polluter has been severely criticized in the literature, nothing in CERCLA purports to reject this bedrock principle, and against this venerable common-law backdrop, the congressional silence is audible. The Government has indeed made no claim that a corporate parent is liable as an owner or an operator under § 107 simply because its subsidiary is subject to liability for owning or operating a polluting facility.

But there is an equally fundamental principle of corporate law, . . . that the corporate veil may be pierced and the shareholder held liable for the corporation's conduct when, inter alia, the corporate form would otherwise be misused to accomplish certain wrongful purposes, most notably fraud, on the shareholder's behalf. Nothing in CERCLA purports to rewrite this well-settled rule, either. CERCLA is thus like many another congressional enactment in giving no indication "that the entire corpus of state corporation law is to be replaced simply because a plaintiff's cause of action is based upon a federal statute," and the failure of the statute to speak to a matter as fundamental as the liability implications of corporate ownership demands application of the rule that "in order to abrogate a common-law principle, the statute must speak directly to the question addressed by the common law[.]" The Court of Appeals was accordingly correct in holding that when (but only when) the corporate veil may be pierced,[9] may a parent corporation be charged with derivative CERCLA liability for its subsidiary's actions.

---

9. There is significant disagreement among courts and commentators over whether, in enforcing CERCLA's indirect liability, courts should borrow state law, or instead apply a federal common law of veil piercing . . . . Since none of the parties challenges the Sixth Circuit's holding that CPC and Aerojet incurred no derivative liability, the question is not presented in this case, and we do not address it further.

If the act rested liability entirely on ownership of a polluting facility, this opinion might end here; but CERCLA liability may turn on operation as well as ownership, and nothing in the statute's terms bars a parent corporation from direct liability for its own actions in operating a facility owned by its subsidiary. As Justice (then-Professor) Douglas noted almost 70 years ago, derivative liability cases are to be distinguished from those in which "the alleged wrong can seemingly be traced to the parent through the conduit of its own personnel and management" and "the parent is directly a participant in the wrong complained of." In such instances, the parent is directly liable for its own actions. The fact that a corporate subsidiary happens to own a polluting facility operated by its parent does nothing, then, to displace the rule that the parent "corporation is [itself] responsible for the wrongs committed by its agents in the course of its business," and whereas the rules of veil-piercing limit derivative liability for the actions of another corporation, CERCLA's "operator" provision is concerned primarily with direct liability for one's own actions. It is this direct liability that is properly seen as being at issue here.

Under the plain language of the statute, any person who operates a polluting facility is directly liable for the costs of cleaning up the pollution. This is so regardless of whether that person is the facility's owner, the owner's parent corporation or business partner, or even a saboteur who sneaks into the facility at night to discharge its poisons out of malice. If any such act of operating a corporate subsidiary's facility is done on behalf of a parent corporation, the existence of the parent-subsidiary relationship under state corporate law is simply irrelevant to the issue of direct liability.

This much is easy to say; the difficulty comes in defining actions sufficient to constitute direct parental "operation." Here of course we may again rue the uselessness of CERCLA's definition of a facility's "operator" as "any person . . . operating" the facility, which leaves us to do the best we can to give the term its "ordinary or natural meaning." In a mechanical sense, to "operate" ordinarily means "to control the functioning of; run: operate a sewing machine." American Heritage Dictionary 1268 (3d ed. 1992); see also Webster's New International Dictionary 1707 (2d ed. 1958) ("to work; as, to operate a machine"). And in the organizational sense more obviously intended by CERCLA, the word ordinarily means "to conduct the affairs of; manage: operate a business." American Heritage Dictionary, *supra*, at 1268; see also Webster's New International Dictionary, *supra*, at 1707 ("to manage"). So, under CERCLA, an operator is simply someone who directs the workings of, manages, or conducts the affairs of a facility. To sharpen the definition for purposes of CERCLA's concern with environmental contamination, an operator must manage, direct, or conduct operations specifically related to pollution, that is, operations having to do with the leakage or disposal of hazardous waste, or decisions about compliance with environmental regulations.

With this understanding, we are satisfied that the Court of Appeals correctly rejected the District Court's analysis of direct liability. But we also think that the appeals court erred in limiting direct liability under the statute to a parent's sole or joint venture operation, so as to eliminate any possible finding that CPC is liable as an operator on the facts of this case.

By emphasizing that "CPC is directly liable under section 107(a)(2) as an operator because CPC actively participated in and exerted significant control over Ott II's business and decision-making," the District Court applied the "actual control" test of whether the parent "actually operated the business of its subsidiary," as several Circuits have employed it.

The well-taken objection to the actual control test, however, is its fusion of direct and indirect liability; the test is administered by asking a question about the relationship between the two corporations (an issue going to indirect liability) instead of a question about the parent's interaction with the subsidiary's facility (the source of any direct liability). If, however, direct liability for the parent's operation of the facility is to be kept distinct from derivative liability for the subsidiary's own operation, the focus of the enquiry must necessarily be different under the two tests. "The question is not whether the parent operates the subsidiary, but rather whether it operates the facility, and that operation is evidenced by participation in the activities of the facility, not the subsidiary. Control of the subsidiary, if extensive enough, gives rise to indirect liability under piercing doctrine, not direct liability under the statutory language." The District Court was therefore mistaken to rest its analysis on CPC's relationship with Ott II, premising liability on little more than "CPC's 100-percent ownership of Ott II" and "CPC's active participation in, and at times majority control over, Ott II's board of directors." The analysis should instead have rested on the relationship between CPC and the Muskegon facility itself.

. . . [E]ven those findings of the District Court that might be taken to speak to the extent of CPC's activity at the facility itself are flawed, for the District Court wrongly assumed that the actions of the joint officers and directors are necessarily attributable to CPC. The District Court emphasized the facts that CPC placed its own high-level officials on Ott II's board of directors and in key management positions at Ott II, and that those individuals made major policy decisions and conducted day-to-day operations at the facility . . . .

In imposing direct liability on these grounds, the District Court failed to recognize that "it is entirely appropriate for directors of a parent corporation to serve as directors of its subsidiary, and that fact alone may not serve to expose the parent corporation to liability for its subsidiary's acts."

This recognition that the corporate personalities remain distinct has its corollary in the "well established principle [of corporate law] that directors and officers holding positions with a parent and its subsidiary can and do 'change hats' to represent the two corporations separately, despite their common ownership." Since courts generally presume "that the directors are wearing their 'subsidiary hats' and not their 'parent hats' when acting for the subsidiary," it cannot be enough to establish liability here that dual officers and directors made policy decisions and supervised activities at the facility. The Government would have to show that, despite the general presumption to the contrary, the officers and directors were acting in their capacities as CPC officers and directors, and not as Ott II officers and directors, when they committed those acts.[13] The District Court made no such enquiry here . . . .

In sum, the District Court's focus on the relationship between parent and subsidiary (rather than parent and facility), combined with its automatic attribution of the actions of dual officers and directors to the corporate parent, erroneously, even if unintentionally, treated CERCLA as though it displaced or fundamentally altered common law standards of limited liability. Indeed, if the evidence of common corporate personnel acting at management and directorial levels were enough to support a finding of a parent corporation's direct operator liability under CERCLA, then the possibility of resort to veil piercing to establish indirect, derivative liability for the subsidiary's violations would be academic. There would in essence be a relaxed, CERCLA-specific rule of derivative liability that would banish traditional standards and expectations from the law of CERCLA liability. But, as we have said, such a rule does not arise from congressional silence, and CERCLA's silence is dispositive.

We accordingly agree with the Court of Appeals that a participation-and-control test looking to the parent's supervision over the subsidiary, especially one that assumes that dual officers always act on behalf of the parent, cannot be used to identify operation of a facility resulting in direct parental liability. Nonetheless, a return to the ordinary meaning of the word "operate" in the organizational sense will indicate why we think that the Sixth Circuit stopped short when it confined its examples of direct parental operation to exclusive or joint ventures, and declined to find at least the possibility of direct operation by CPC in this case.

In our enquiry into the meaning Congress presumably had in mind when it used the verb "to operate," we recognized that the statute obviously meant something more than mere mechanical activation of pumps and valves, and must be read to contemplate "operation" as including the exercise of direction over the facility's activities. The Court of Appeals recognized this by indicating that a parent can be held directly liable when the parent operates the facility in the stead of its subsidiary or alongside the subsidiary in some sort of a joint venture. We anticipated a further possibility above, however, when we observed that a dual officer or director might depart so far from the norms of parental influence exercised through dual officeholding as to serve the parent, even when ostensibly acting on behalf of the subsidiary in operating the facility. Yet another possibility, suggested by the facts of this case, is that an agent of the parent with no hat to wear but the parent's hat might manage or direct activities at the facility.

Identifying such an occurrence calls for line drawing yet again, since the acts of direct operation that give rise to parental liability must necessarily be distinguished

---

13. We do not attempt to recite the ways in which the Government could show that dual officers or directors were in fact acting on behalf of the parent. Here, it is prudent to say only that the presumption that an act is taken on behalf of the corporation for whom the officer claims to act is strongest when the act is perfectly consistent with the norms of corporate behavior, but wanes as the distance from those accepted norms approaches the point of action by a dual officer plainly contrary to the interests of the subsidiary yet nonetheless advantageous to the parent.

from the interference that stems from the normal relationship between parent and subsidiary. Again norms of corporate behavior (undisturbed by any CERCLA provision) are crucial reference points. Just as we may look to such norms in identifying the limits of the presumption that a dual officeholder acts in his ostensible capacity, so here we may refer to them in distinguishing a parental officer's oversight of a subsidiary from such an officer's control over the operation of the subsidiary's facility. "Activities that involve the facility but which are consistent with the parent's investor status, such as monitoring of the subsidiary's performance, supervision of the subsidiary's finance and capital budget decisions, and articulation of general policies and procedures, should not give rise to direct liability." The critical question is whether, in degree and detail, actions directed to the facility by an agent of the parent alone are eccentric under accepted norms of parental oversight of a subsidiary's facility.

There is, in fact, some evidence that CPC engaged in just this type and degree of activity at the Muskegon plant. The District Court's opinion speaks of an agent of CPC alone who played a conspicuous part in dealing with the toxic risks emanating from the operation of the plant. G.R.D. Williams worked only for CPC; he was not an employee, officer, or director of Ott II, and thus, his actions were of necessity taken only on behalf of CPC. The District Court found that "CPC became directly involved in environmental and regulatory matters through the work of . . . Williams, CPC's governmental and environmental affairs director. Williams . . . became heavily involved in environmental issues at Ott II." He "actively participated in and exerted control over a variety of Ott II environmental matters," and he "issued directives regarding Ott II's responses to regulatory inquiries[.]"

We think that these findings are enough to raise an issue of CPC's operation of the facility through Williams's actions, though we would draw no ultimate conclusion from these findings at this point. Not only would we be deciding in the first instance an issue on which the trial and appellate courts did not focus, but the very fact that the District Court did not see the case as we do suggests that there may be still more to be known about Williams's activities. Indeed, even as the factual findings stand, the trial court offered little in the way of concrete detail for its conclusions about Williams's role in Ott II's environmental affairs, and the parties vigorously dispute the extent of Williams's involvement. Prudence thus counsels us to remand, on the theory of direct operation set out here, for reevaluation of Williams's role, and of the role of any other CPC agent who might be said to have had a part in operating the Muskegon facility.[14]

---

14. There are some passages in the District Court's opinion that might suggest that, without reference to Williams, some of Ott II's actions in operating the facility were in fact dictated by, and thus taken on behalf of, CPC . . . . But nothing in the District Court's findings of fact, as written, even comes close to overcoming the presumption that Ott II officials made their decisions and performed their acts as agents of Ott II . . . . Still, the Government is, of course, free on remand to point to any additional evidence, not cited by the District Court, that would tend to establish that Ott II's decisionmakers acted on specific orders from CPC.

The judgment of the Court of Appeals for the Sixth Circuit is vacated, and the case is remanded with instructions to return it to the District Court for further proceedings consistent with this opinion.

Notes and Questions

1. *Bestfoods* highlights the intersection of environmental law with other substantive law. Most obviously, *Bestfoods* is also about corporate law. Consider the way Aerojet organized its acquisition of the Ott Chemical plant. What might explain the structure Aerojet chose?

It is also worth noting that Aerojet acquired the plant "from the Story bankruptcy trustee." Bankruptcy is available to any business and may affect any type of claim against a business, of course, but bankruptcy law has played a particularly prominent role in CERCLA cases. Why?

2. In *Bestfoods* the Court identified two distinct ways a parent corporation (or, in principle, any shareholder) can be liable as a CERCLA operator: indirectly by piercing the corporate veil, and directly by operating the facility itself in lieu of or in addition to its subsidiary. Which type of claim would be easier to prove?

3. In deciding that the corporate parents were not subject to indirect, veil-piercing liability, the Sixth Circuit applied Michigan law. The Supreme Court declined to decide whether state law or a federal common law of veil piercing should apply. What are the arguments in favor of applying state law? What are the arguments in favor of developing federal common law in this area?

4. According to *Bestfoods*, how does a parent corporation become a direct operator of a subsidiary's facility instead of just an owner of the subsidiary's stock? Direct liability will attach "[i]f any ... act of operating a corporate subsidiary's facility is done on behalf of a parent corporation." In a parent-subsidiary situation, how is it possible to distinguish which corporation an act is "on behalf of"? The Supreme Court emphasized that courts should scrutinize whether the parent corporation (or officers and directors with roles in both corporations) behaved in ways that are "eccentric" to "norms of corporate behavior." Where do those norms come from? In view of the emphasis on corporate norms, how different is the Court's test for direct operator liability from the test for indirect liability? Can you think of any other way to determine whether a parent company acts on its own behalf rather than on its subsidiary's behalf? Can you think of a test for direct operator liability of a parent corporation that does not depend on deciding which corporation the parent acts "on behalf of"?

5. Relying on the language of § 107(a)(2) of CERCLA, the Court emphasized that to be directly liable, a parent corporation must operate the subsidiary's facility, not simply the subsidiary. "To sharpen the definition," the Court held that "an operator must manage, direct, or conduct operations specifically related to pollution ...." What statutory text is the basis for this requirement? Does this requirement apply to the operator of a facility in the absence of a corporate parent-subsidiary relation?

What does "specifically related to pollution" mean? To be liable, must a parent take an action that leads to disposal of hazardous substances at the facility? Or, even more strongly, must a parent take an action that leads to a release of hazardous substances at the facility? Or does any management or conduct of pollution-related activities satisfy the standard?

Suppose a corporation owns several subsidiaries, but the parent corporation uses a centralized environmental management system to manage permitted water pollution discharges and air pollution emissions for all of its subsidiaries' facilities. In all other respects, each facility is managed by one of the subsidiary corporations. At one facility that has (and complies with) permits for water discharges and air emissions, a manager who is employed only by the subsidiary directs employees to dump used solvent in a wooded part of the property near a stream. The solvents migrate to the stream and a costly removal action ensues. The parent thus directly managed operations of the facility that were "specifically related to pollution"—but not the pollution that was the subject of a CERCLA response action. Would the parent company be liable as an operator under *Bestfoods*? Should the parent corporation be liable as an operator under CERCLA?

Did the Supreme Court give parent corporations an incentive to try to avoid managing activities related to pollution, even if the parent directly manages everything else about the way a subsidiary's facility operates? Suppose a subsidiary corporation operates a plant that generates hazardous waste. The parent company's CEO, who is not an officer or director of the subsidiary, directs the plant manager to increase the plant's profits to a specified target. The manager replies that the only way to meet the target is to reduce costs by illegally burying the hazardous waste on-site instead of sending it to a licensed disposal facility. The CEO says, "I am not telling you how to run the plant, I am just telling you the profit target you need to hit." If the manager buries the hazardous waste on site and EPA later responds to a release of hazardous substances from the pit, would the parent corporation be liable as an operator under *Bestfoods*? Should the parent corporation be liable as an operator under CERCLA? Would your answers be different if the plant manager had not told the CEO what the plant would do to hit the profit target?

6. The Supreme Court stated that, absent an express provision in CERCLA, it would assume that Congress intended ordinary principles of corporate law to constrain CERCLA liability. Many courts, including most of the federal courts of appeals, have stated that CERCLA is a remedial statute that should be construed broadly to serve its statutory purposes. Is this view in tension with the approach the Supreme Court took in *Bestfoods*?

7. The Supreme Court stated that to operate a facility means "something more than mere mechanical activation of pumps and valves." At a Superfund site in New Jersey, a corporation recycled used motor oil by mixing the oil with acid in a tank. The process produced hazardous substances, which the corporation disposed by opening a valve on the tank and allowing the hazardous substances to run over the ground into a waste lagoon. Would the person who opened the valve be liable as an operator? Would the corporate executive who told that person to open the valve be liable as an operator?

8. In *Bestfoods*, which side won in the Supreme Court? The United States was the petitioner and the decision below was vacated, so in that sense the plaintiff won. But the Supreme Court's decision did not reinstate the district court judgment in favor of the government. On remand, the government failed to persuade the district judge that the evidence established operator liability under the standard set by the Supreme Court. *Bestfoods v. Aerojet-General Corp.*, 173 F. Supp. 2d 729 (W.D. Mich. 2001).

9. Not every past owner or operator of a facility that becomes the subject of a CERCLA response action is liable under § 107(a)(2); to be liable, a person must have owned or operated the facility "at the time of disposal" of hazardous substances. Thus, a person who owned or operated a facility *before* hazardous substances were disposed of there — say, a gravel company that sold an old quarry to a company that then used the quarry pit as a hazardous waste dump — would not be liable. What about a developer who bought the dump after it was closed, dumped nothing at the site, built a retail building on top of the landfill cover, and sold the building to a retailer who is the current landowner?

Suppose EPA discovered that, beneath the retail building, hazardous substances had leached out of the buried hazardous waste and contaminated the underlying aquifer. To hold the developer liable, a court would have to find that a "disposal" of hazardous substances occurred during the time the developer owned or operated the facility. Our hypothetical developer did not place any hazardous substances in the dump. Is that dispositive?

Section 101(29) of CERCLA, 42 U.S.C. § 9601(29), borrows the definition of "disposal" from RCRA. Thus "disposal," under both statutes, means:

> the discharge, deposit, injection, dumping, spilling, leaking, or placing of any solid waste or hazardous waste into or on any land or water so that such solid waste or hazardous waste or any constituent thereof may enter the environment or be emitted into the air or discharged into any waters, including ground waters.

42 U.S.C. § 6903(3) (RCRA § 1004(3)). What if our hypothetical developer, in regrading the site for a building, spread contaminated soil around and thereby "placed" hazardous substances on a previously uncontaminated part of the site? What if, while our hypothetical developer owned the facility, hazardous substances "leaked" out of drums buried in the dump? Would these things constitute "disposal"? Courts have divided on such issues; the factual circumstances of each case seem to matter greatly.

Courts generally agree that a "disposal" can occur even after hazardous substances are first brought to or dumped at a site — but only if something happens to the hazardous substances that fits within the statutory definition. *See Tanglewood East Homeowners v. Charles Thomas, Inc.*, 849 F.2d 1568 (5th Cir. 1988) (holding, in affirming district court's denial of motion to dismiss, that alleged moving of previously dumped hazardous substances during excavation could constitute disposal); *accord Kaiser*

Aluminum & Chem. Corp. v. Catellus Dev't Corp., 976 F.2d 1338 (9th Cir. 1992). The Third Circuit, citing its *Alcan* opinion, held that the movement of any amount of hazardous substances, no matter how small, could constitute a "discharge" or "placing" and therefore a "disposal" of the hazardous substances involved. *United States v. CDMG Realty Co.*, 96 F.3d 706 (3d Cir. 1996).

The situation becomes more complicated if the hazardous substances move on their own. In *Nurad, Inc. v. William E. Hooper & Sons Co.*, 966 F.2d 837 (4th Cir. 1992), the court rejected the view that "affirmative human conduct" is required to effect a disposal. In *Nurad*, a developer bought a former textile plant where underground storage tanks contained hazardous substances. For a time the developer leased the property to a tenant, but neither the developer nor the tenant used the tanks before the property was subdivided and sold. The Fourth Circuit held that because the record supported a finding that the tanks leaked during the developer's ownership, the developer was an owner at the time of disposal of hazardous substances.

The Third Circuit distinguished *Nurad* in a case in which the court described the alleged disposal as "passive spreading [of hazardous substances] in a landfill" rather than leakage from a tank or a drum. *United States v. CDMG Realty Co.*, 96 F.3d 706 (3d Cir. 1996). The Third Circuit held that none of the words in the statutory definition of disposal encompassed the migration of previously deposited hazardous substances through environmental media. The court also noted that "there is a strong argument . . . that in the context of this definition, 'leaking' and 'spilling' should be read to require affirmative human action," but the court expressly left the question open. *Id.*; *see also ABB Industrial Systs., Inc. v. Prime Technology, Inc.*, 120 F.3d 351 (2d Cir. 1997) (agreeing with and following *CDMG Realty*); *Bob's Beverage, Inc. v. Acme, Inc.*, 264 F.3d 692 (6th Cir. 2001) (holding that no disposal occurred where an owner, after learning that hazardous substances deposited by an earlier owner were on the soil, took no affirmative act that spread the contamination but did not prevent migration of the hazardous substances).

In *Carson Harbor Village v. Unocal, Inc.*, 270 F.3d 863 (9th Cir. 2001), the court criticized the active/passive distinction as too simplistic, holding that a court must examine the factual record of a particular case in light of CERCLA's definition of disposal. In *Carson Harbor*, a "tar-like" waste containing hazardous substances slowly moved through the soil. The court held that words like *spreading, seeping, oozing,* or *leaching* might describe this movement — but that because the definition of disposal does not include any of those words, no disposal occurred during the property developer's ownership.

Is the treatment of "passive" "disposal" in these CERCLA cases the same as or different from the way the issue has been addressed in cases under RCRA? Review the *Connecticut Coastal Fisherman's* and *Waste Industries* cases, pp. 650 and 718, above.

The statutory term "disposal" also figures prominently in deciding whether parties fit into the next, and perhaps most important, class of liable persons listed in § 107(a). We now turn to the "arranger" category.

3. Arrangers

The third category of responsible person under § 107(a) of CERCLA is

> (3) any person who by contract, agreement, or otherwise arranged for disposal or treatment, or arranged with a transporter for transport for disposal or treatment, of hazardous substances owned or possessed by such person, by any other party or entity, at any facility or incineration vessel owned or operated by another party or entity and containing such hazardous substances

42 U.S.C. § 9607(a)(3). Notice that this subsection distinguishes arrangers from transporters (because an arranger can "arrange" with a transporter rather than directly with the owner or operator of a disposal or treatment facility) and from owners and operators (because arranger liability only attaches for arrangements for disposal or treatment at facilities "owned or operated by *another* party").

We have already seen arranger liability in action. In the *Monsanto* case (p. 766 above), several parties that contracted with SCRDI to take away, recycle, or dispose of hazardous substances that SCRDI deposited at the Bluff Road site were held liable. They disputed their liability but did not contest that they had arranged for the disposal of their materials. In *Alcan* (p. 774 above), Alcan disputed that its waste emulsion constituted a hazardous substance, but did not dispute that it had arranged for disposal of the emulsion by contract with the Mahler companies. Sometimes, however, the existence of an arrangement for disposal or treatment is at the heart of the dispute.

Burlington Northern and Santa Fe Railway Co. v. United States
556 U.S. 599 (2009)

Justice STEVENS:

. . . .

In 1960, Brown & Bryant, Inc. (B&B), began operating an agricultural chemical distribution business, purchasing pesticides and other chemical products from suppliers such as Shell Oil Company (Shell). Using its own equipment, B&B applied its products to customers' farms. [The land on which B&B operated its business] graded toward a sump and drainage pond . . . . Neither the sump nor the drainage pond was lined until 1979, allowing waste water and chemical runoff from the facility to seep into the ground water below.

During its years of operation, B&B stored and distributed various hazardous chemicals on its property. Among these were . . . the pesticides D-D and Nemagon, both sold by Shell . . . . Nemagon was stored in 30-gallon drums and 5-gallon containers inside the [B&B] warehouse. Originally, B&B purchased D-D in 55-gallon drums; beginning in the mid-1960's, however, Shell began requiring its distributors to maintain bulk storage facilities for D-D. From that time onward, B&B purchased D-D in bulk.[1]

---

1. Because D-D is corrosive, bulk storage of the chemical led to numerous tank failures and spills as the chemical rusted tanks and eroded valves.

... When the product arrived, it was transferred from tanker trucks to a bulk storage tank . . . . From there, the chemical was transferred to bobtail trucks, nurse tanks, and pull rigs. During each of these transfers leaks and spills could — and often did — occur. Although the common carrier and B&B used buckets to catch spills from hoses and gaskets connecting the tanker trucks to its bulk storage tank, the buckets sometimes overflowed or were knocked over, causing D-D to spill onto the ground during the transfer process.

Aware that spills of D-D were commonplace among its distributors, in the late 1970's Shell took several steps to encourage the safe handling of its products. . . . Later, Shell . . . require[d] distributors to obtain an inspection by a qualified engineer and provide self-certification of compliance with applicable laws and regulations. B&B's Arvin facility was inspected twice, and in 1981, B&B certified to Shell that it had made a number of recommended improvements to its facilities.

Despite these improvements, B&B remained a "'[s]loppy' [o]perator." Over the course of B&B's 28 years of operation, delivery spills, equipment failures, and the rinsing of tanks and trucks allowed Nemagon [and] D-D . . . to seep into the soil and upper levels of ground water of the Arvin facility. In 1983, the California Department of Toxic Substances Control (DTSC) began investigating B&B's violation of hazardous waste laws, and the United States Environmental Protection Agency (EPA) soon followed suit, discovering significant contamination of soil and ground water. Of particular concern was a plume of contaminated ground water located under the facility that threatened to leach into an adjacent supply of potential drinking water.

Although B&B undertook some efforts at remediation, by 1989 it had become insolvent and ceased all operations. That same year, the Arvin facility was added to the National Priority List, and subsequently, DTSC and EPA (Governments) exercised their authority . . . to undertake cleanup efforts at the site. By 1998, the Governments had spent more than $8 million responding to the site contamination; their costs have continued to accrue.

. . . .

[The Governments sued Shell. After a bench trial, the district court held Shell liable] because it had "arranged for" the disposal of hazardous substances through its sale and delivery of D-D. [Shell appealed.]

. . . The Court of Appeals acknowledged that Shell did not qualify as a "traditional" arranger under § 9607(a)(3), insofar as it had not contracted with B&B to directly dispose of a hazardous waste product. Nevertheless, the court stated that Shell could still be held liable under a "'broader' category of arranger liability" if the "disposal of hazardous wastes [wa]s a foreseeable byproduct of, but not the purpose of, the transaction giving rise to" arranger liability. Relying on CERCLA's definition of "disposal," which covers acts such as "leaking" and "spilling," the Ninth Circuit concluded that an entity could arrange for "disposal" "even if it did not intend to dispose" of a hazardous substance.

. . . .

. . . We granted certiorari . . . . [W]e now reverse.

... To determine whether Shell may be held liable as an arranger, we begin with the language of the statute. As relevant here, § 9607(a)(3) applies to an entity that "arrange[s] for disposal ... of hazardous substances." It is plain from the language of the statute that CERCLA liability would attach under § 9607(a)(3) if an entity were to enter into a transaction for the sole purpose of discarding a used and no longer useful hazardous substance. It is similarly clear that an entity could not be held liable as an arranger merely for selling a new and useful product if the purchaser of that product later, and unbeknownst to the seller, disposed of the product in a way that led to contamination. Less clear is the liability attaching to the many permutations of "arrangements" that fall between these two extremes — cases in which the seller has some knowledge of the buyers' planned disposal or whose motives for the "sale" of a hazardous substance are less than clear. In such cases, courts have concluded that the determination whether an entity is an arranger requires a fact-intensive inquiry that looks beyond the parties' characterization of the transaction as a "disposal" or a "sale" and seeks to discern whether the arrangement was one Congress intended to fall within the scope of CERCLA's strict-liability provisions.

Although we agree that the question whether § 9607(a)(3) liability attaches is fact intensive and case specific, such liability may not extend beyond the limits of the statute itself. Because CERCLA does not specifically define what it means to "arrang[e] for" disposal of a hazardous substance, we give the phrase its ordinary meaning. In common parlance, the word "arrange" implies action directed to a specific purpose. *See* Merriam-Webster's Collegiate Dictionary 64 (10th ed. 1993) (defining "arrange" as "to make preparations for: plan[;] ... to bring about an agreement or understanding concerning"). Consequently, under the plain language of the statute, an entity may qualify as an arranger under § 9607(a)(3) when it takes intentional steps to dispose of a hazardous substance. The Governments do not deny that the statute requires an entity to "arrang[e] for" disposal; however, they interpret that phrase by reference to the statutory term "disposal," which the Act broadly defines as "the discharge, deposit, injection, dumping, spilling, leaking, or placing of any solid waste or hazardous waste into or on any land or water." The Governments assert that by including unintentional acts such as "spilling" and "leaking" in the definition of disposal, Congress intended to impose liability on entities not only when they directly dispose of waste products but also when they engage in legitimate sales of hazardous substances knowing that some disposal may occur as a collateral consequence of the sale itself. Applying that reading of the statute, the Governments contend that Shell arranged for the disposal of D-D within the meaning of § 9607(a)(3) by shipping D-D to B&B under conditions it knew would result in the spilling of a portion of the hazardous substance by the purchaser or common carrier. Because these spills resulted in wasted D-D, a result Shell anticipated, the Governments insist that Shell was properly found to have arranged for the disposal of D-D.

While it is true that in some instances an entity's knowledge that its product will be leaked, spilled, dumped, or otherwise discarded may provide evidence of the entity's intent to dispose of its hazardous wastes, knowledge alone is insufficient to prove that an entity "planned for" the disposal, particularly when the disposal occurs as a peripheral result of the legitimate sale of an unused, useful product. In order to qualify as an arranger, Shell must have entered into the sale of D-D with the intention that at least a portion of the product be disposed of during the transfer process by one or more of the methods described in § 6903(3). Here, the facts found by the District Court do not support such a conclusion.

Although the evidence adduced at trial showed that Shell was aware that minor, accidental spills occurred during the transfer of D-D from the common carrier to B&B's bulk storage tanks after the product had arrived at the Arvin facility and had come under B&B's stewardship, the evidence does not support an inference that Shell intended such spills to occur. To the contrary, the evidence revealed that Shell took numerous steps to encourage its distributors to reduce the likelihood of such spills . . . . Although Shell's efforts were less than wholly successful, given these facts, Shell's mere knowledge that spills and leaks continued to occur is insufficient grounds for concluding that Shell "arranged for" the disposal of D-D within the meaning of § 9607(a)(3). Accordingly, we conclude that Shell was not liable as an arranger for the contamination that occurred at B&B's Arvin facility.

. . . .

Justice GINSBURG, dissenting:

Although the question is close, I would uphold the determinations of the courts below that Shell qualifies as an arranger . . . . As the facts found by the District Court bear out, Shell "arranged for disposal . . . of hazardous substances" owned by Shell when the arrangements were made.

In the 1950's and early 1960's, Shell shipped most of its products to . . . B&B in 55-gallon drums, thereby ensuring against spillage or leakage during delivery and transfer. Later, Shell found it economically advantageous . . . to require B&B to maintain bulk storage facilities for receipt of the chemicals B&B purchased from Shell. By the mid-1960's, Shell was delivering its chemical to B&B in bulk tank truckloads. As the Court recognizes, "bulk storage of the chemical led to numerous tank failures and spills as the chemical rusted tanks and eroded valves."

Shell furthermore specified the equipment to be used in transferring the chemicals from the delivery truck to B&B's storage tanks. In the process, spills and leaks were inevitable; indeed spills occurred every time deliveries were made.

That Shell sold B&B useful products . . . did not exonerate Shell from CERCLA liability, for the sales "necessarily and immediately result[ed] in the leakage of hazardous substances." The deliveries, Shell was well aware, directly and routinely resulted in disposals of hazardous substances (through spills and leaks) for more than 20 years . . . . Given the control rein held by Shell over the mode of delivery and transfer, . . . Shell was properly ranked as an arranger. Relieving Shell of any obligation to pay for the cleanup . . . is surely at odds with CERCLA's objective to place the cost of remediation on persons whose activities contributed to the contamination rather than on the taxpaying public.

. . . .

Notes and Questions

1. Compare and contrast the majority and dissenting opinions. Do Justice Ginsburg and the majority disagree about the interpretation of the statutory phrase "arranged for disposal"? On what tools of statutory interpretation does each opinion rely?

2. Did the Court focus its interpretive effort on the correct word? Even if "arrange" implies a volitional act, might it be possible for a person (as the Government argued) to "arrange" for an act constituting "disposal" under CERCLA even without an "intent" to dispose of a hazardous substance? Or did the Court correctly interpret the phrase "arranged for disposal" as a whole? After *Burlington Northern*, is it possible that any "legitimate sale of an unused, useful product" could include an arrangement for disposal?

3. The majority emphasized that Shell, in selling D-D and Nemagon, tried to reduce the amount of product that its distributors spilled. The dissent emphasized that Shell, at least in selling D-D, for its own economic advantage forced distributors to accept and store product in a manner guaranteed to result in spills. Does the issue of Shell's arranger liability turn on which of these competing characterizations is accepted? If so, how would the majority address a situation in which a seller knew that its method of sale would result in significant spillage of hazardous substances despite its efforts to encourage buyers to try to avoid spills? Under the majority's approach, what would stop sellers from making nominal efforts to educate purchasers about safe handling of their hazardous substance products while tolerating leaks and spills with a wink and a nod? Would the dissent's approach create perverse incentives for sellers to avoid giving purchasers of hazardous substances instructions about how to store and handle the products? Or would the dissent's approach leave sellers whose buyers are likely to spill a hazardous substance product in an insoluble dilemma: liable if they made no effort to make purchasers limit spills (because the sale would then necessarily entail the disposal) but also liable if they tell the purchasers what to do (because the seller would then have control of the handling method causing the disposal)?

4. The CERCLA categories of responsible parties—present and past owners and operators, transporters, and arrangers—seem somewhat parallel to the categories of entities regulated under Subtitle C of RCRA (see pp. 641–43, above)—owners and operators of TSDFs, hazardous waste transporters, and hazardous waste generators. Moreover, as we noted above, p. 771, early CERCLA cases often began as RCRA cases. Thus, early CERCLA decisions, such as *Monsanto*, p. 766 above, often used the RCRA term "generators" to refer to persons liable under § 107(a)(3). The structure and function of CERCLA's liability scheme and of RCRA's regulatory scheme differ from one another, however, and there are significant differences between the seemingly parallel categories as well. For example, to be liable as a CERCLA arranger, a person must arrange for "disposal or treatment" of "hazardous substances," but not necessarily of "hazardous waste." *B.F. Goodrich v. Murtha*, 958 F.2d 1192, 1202 (2d Cir. 1992) (holding that CERCLA arranger liability does not require disposal of material defined as or regulated as "hazardous waste"); *but cf. Pneumo Abex Corp. v. High Point,*

Thomasville & Denton R.R. Co., 142 F.3d 769 (4th Cir. 1998) (holding that to prove that defendant "arrange[d] for treatment," plaintiff must show treatment of "hazardous waste" as defined in RCRA). Furthermore, a CERCLA arranger need not "generate" the hazardous substances being disposed of. A party that receives hazardous waste from a generator for temporary storage, for example, might then arrange by contract or otherwise to dispose of the hazardous substances in that waste. *E.g.,* *United States v. Bliss*, 667 F. Supp. 1298, 1306 (E.D. Mo. 1987) (holding liable under § 107(a)(3) a party that acted as a broker between the waste generator and the disposal facility). More recent CERCLA case law, such as *Burlington Northern*, has tended to more precisely discuss "arranger" rather than "generator" liability.

5. Although liability under § 107(a)(3) attaches only to a person who "arranges for disposal or treatment" of a hazardous substance, the arranger need not have arranged specifically for the waste to be disposed at the *facility* from which the hazardous substance is released. To the contrary, numerous courts have held arrangers liable for releases at facilities where the arrangers' waste was disposed of, even if the arrangers expressly directed that the disposal occur at a *different* facility. *See, e.g., Ekotek Site PRP Comm. v. Self*, 932 F. Supp. 1328 (D. Utah 1996) (granting summary judgment of liability against a corporation that admitted arranging for disposal with a transporter despite corporation's assertion that it had "no idea" where transporter would dispose of hazardous substances); *United States v. Bliss*, 667 F. Supp. 1298 (E.D. Mo. 1987) (holding arranger liable for response costs at facilities where its hazardous substances were sprayed for dust suppression after being held at a storage facility by the entity that did the spraying); *Violet v. Picillo,* 648 F. Supp. 1283 (D.R.I. 1986) (holding that arranger could be liable for response costs at farm where its waste was buried although it contracted to have the waste hauled to a landfill); *Missouri v. Independent Petrochemical Corp.*, 610 F. Supp. 4 (E.D. Mo. 1985) (denying motion to dismiss complaint that alleged that defendant arranged disposal of hazardous substances at one facility, from which the substances were brought by a third party to another facility from which there was a release that caused incurrence of response costs). Are these holdings fair? Do they serve CERCLA's statutory purposes? Do they preserve a meaningful limit on potential arranger liability?

6. As with operator liability, arranger liability can attach to the individual officials of a corporation who make the arrangements for disposal of hazardous substances. The leading opinion is *United States v. Northeastern Pharm. & Chem. Co. ("NEPACCO")*, 810 F.2d 726 (8th Cir. 1986). NEPACCO hired a transporter to haul chemical waste containing hazardous substances to a farm where the waste was dumped in a trench. Edwin Lee, a NEPACCO shareholder, vice-president, and plant supervisor, approved both the transporter and the disposal site. By the time EPA sought to recover the costs of responding to the release of hazardous substances at the farm, NEPACCO had dissolved and distributed its assets to shareholders. The district court held Lee liable as an arranger. The court of appeals affirmed, holding that Lee's personal involvement sufficed to make him a "person who . . . arranged for disposal" without any need to pierce the corporate veil. *Id.* at 744. The court also held that Lee "owned or possessed"

the hazardous substances, within the meaning of § 107(a)(3), because he personally had "the authority to control the handling and disposal of hazardous substances." *Id.* at 743.

7. For parties that are "repeat players" in CERCLA disputes, the statute can make it difficult to maintain a consistent position. This is true for the United States (which, as we have seen, often plays the role of a plaintiff seeking to recover response costs but can also be a liable party pursuant to CERCLA's waiver of sovereign immunity), but it is also true for private parties. In *Burlington Northern*, the United States alleged that Shell was liable as an arranger, and Shell argued that to arrange for disposal required an intentional act aimed at achieving a disposal. But the year before the Supreme Court decided *Burlington Northern*, Shell lost a case in which it alleged that the United States had arranged for disposal on a "broader" rather than "traditional" theory.

During World War II, Shell and other petroleum refiners produced large quantities of high-octane aviation gasoline under contract with the United States government. The "avgas" was "critical to the war effort," so the government "exercised significant control over the means of its production." *United States v. Shell Oil Co.*, 294 F.3d 1045, 1049 (9th Cir. 2008). The avgas refining process produced contaminated, acidic waste. The oil companies contracted with the owner of a tract of land who agreed to dump the waste in earthen sumps on his land — a classic, "traditional" arrangement for disposal. Decades later, EPA conducted a remedial action costing nearly $100 million at the disposal facility. Shell and the other oil companies (using a mechanism we discuss below, p. 847) sought to require the United States to contribute to the response costs. They alleged that the government, by virtue of its control over the process that generated the waste, had also arranged for the disposal of the waste at the dump site. The Ninth Circuit agreed that such a "broader" theory could support arranger liability, but held that the evidence at trial did not establish that the government had the requisite amount of control over the manufacturing process. *See also United States v. Vertac Chem. Corp.*, 46 F.3d 803 (8th Cir. 1995) (holding that the government did not arrange for disposal of wastes resulting from a chemical company's production of Agent Orange during the Vietnam War because the production contracts did not give the government control over the manufacturing or waste disposal process).

8. The Supreme Court and the Ninth Circuit apparently agreed that § 107(a)(3) creates liability for so-called "traditional" arrangers — parties that "enter into a transaction for the sole purpose of discarding a used and no longer useful hazardous substance," paying a hauler or a facility to make their junk disappear. Why should any court recognize arranger liability in any other circumstance?

Even before *Burlington Northern*, courts had recognized that whether a particular course of conduct entailed an arrangement for disposal is a "fact intensive and case specific" inquiry, as the Supreme Court put it. The granddaddy of these cases is *United States v. Aceto Agricultural Chem. Corp.*, 872 F.3d 1373 (8th Cir. 1989).

In *Aceto*, the United States and the State of Iowa incurred more than $10 million in costs responding to the release of hazardous substances from a pesticide formulation facility owned and formerly operated by Aidex, a defunct corporation. As a formulator, Aidex did not synthesize chemical pesticides, but provided a service to pesticide manufacturers by mixing various industrial-grade pesticides and other components to create commercial-grade products. By the time of suit, Aidex had no assets, so the governments sued the pesticide manufacturers, alleging that the manufacturers had arranged for disposal of pesticides found at and emanating from the Aidex facility. The complaints alleged that the manufacturers, under the terms of their contracts with Aidex, maintained ownership of the chemicals throughout Aidex's process, and that "disposal"—leaking and spilling of pesticides, and production of some unusable off-spec pesticide products—were inherent parts of Aidex's work. The Eighth Circuit held that these allegations stated a claim for arranger liability. For examples of courts' varying treatment of similar theories, see *United States v. Hercules, Inc.*, 247 F.3d 706 (8th Cir. 2001) (affirming district court judgment holding arranger liable after trial established facts similar to those in *Aceto*); *General Electric Co. v. AAMCO Transmissions, Inc.*, 962 F.2d 281 (1st Cir. 1992) (holding that defendant oil companies, by selling motor oil to service stations and leasing underground tanks for storage of contaminated used oil, did not arrange for disposal of hazardous substances, even though used oil collected at the service stations was later dumped at a facility from which hazardous substances were released).

In other cases courts have scrutinized "sales" of goods to see if the sellers were really arranging for disposal of hazardous substances in the materials. Thus sales of used batteries and battery parts to reclaimers have been held to be arrangements for disposal, because the reclaimers inevitably spilled lead and other hazardous substances in the batteries onto the ground (which later resulted in a release of hazardous substances that caused the incurrence of response costs). *E.g., United States v. Atlas-Lederer Co.*, 282 F. Supp. 2d 687 (S.D. Ohio 2001); *cf.* 42 U.S.C. § 9627 (exempting from liability persons who arranged for certain types of recycling of materials containing hazardous substances, including lead batteries, provided specified conditions were satisfied) (CERCLA § 127, added in 1999 by the Superfund Recycling Equity Act, P.L. 106-113 § 6001); *see also United States v. Summit Equip. Supplies, Inc.*, 805 F. Supp. 1422 (N.D. Ohio 1992) (holding that sellers of used, surplus equipment could not avoid arranger liability by keeping blinders on during sale).

On the other hand, even before *Burlington Northern*, courts had held that a bona fide sale of a useful product was not an arrangement for disposal even if the seller knew that the transaction inevitably entailed the disposal of hazardous substances. *E.g. Ekotek Site PRP Comm. v. Self*, 932 F. Supp. 1328 (D. Utah 1996) (holding that although defendant admitted selling used mineral oil to the owner of a Superfund site, evidence that before the sale the defendant treated its waste to extract usable oil was sufficient to create a material issue of fact as to whether defendant arranged for disposal or sold a useful product); *Edward Hines Lumber Co. v. Vulcan Materials Co.*, 685 F. Supp. 651 (N.D. Ill. 1988) (holding that chemical companies did not arrange for disposal by selling wood treatment chemicals to a company that used the chemicals and then deposited run-off from the process in a holding pond).

9. In *Burlington Northern* the Supreme Court described the easy extremes of alleged arranger liability, distinguishing the sale of a useful product that contains hazardous substances and is separately disposed of later by the buyer (in which case the seller is not an arranger) from an agreement to pay for a service with no other purpose than disposing of a waste that contains hazardous substances (in which case the payor is an arranger). For cases in between these extremes, how much guidance did *Burlington Northern* give lower courts?

United States v. General Electric Co.

670 F.3d 377 (1st Cir. 2012)

Judge TORRUELLA:

Defendant-Appellant General Electric Company ("GE") appeals from a district court judgment holding it liable . . . for response costs incurred by the United States Environmental Protection Agency ("EPA") in the unfinished cleanup of the Fletcher's Paint Works and Storage Facility Superfund Site in Milford, New Hampshire (the "Fletcher Site" or the "Site") . . . .

[For thirty years, GE manufactured "Pyranol" at two plants in upstate New York. GE purchased polychlorinated biphenyls (PCBs) from a chemical company and refined the PCBs to make Pyranol, a dielectric fluid used in capacitors and other electrical equipment made by GE and others.]

PCBs

[Between 1953 and 1967, Fred Fletcher's paint manufacturing business added PCBs as a "plasticizer" to the paints being produced. Fletcher purchased PCBs from the same company that supplied PCBs to GE.]

To be of use to GE, the processed Pyranol had to meet and retain demanding purity specifications. Pyranol that fell short of these standards was deemed "scrap Pyranol" and was stored away in 55-gallon drums in designated scrap areas.

Over time, GE accumulated a glut of scrap Pyranol . . . . Seemingly recognizing a mutually-advantageous situation, Fletcher and GE . . . entered into an informal agreement whereby Fletcher purchased scrap Pyranol from GE at bargain prices for his industrial needs.

For approximately ten years ending in 1967, Fletcher regularly purchased 55-gallon drums of scrap Pyranol from GE. GE records indicate that in this period, Fletcher availed himself of over 200,000 gallons of GE's scrap Pyranol. Accordingly, for the better part of a decade, 55-gallon drums full of scrap Pyranol—about 3,600 worth of them—routinely traveled by truck from [GE's plants] to the Fletcher Site. . . . .

. . .

In 1987, EPA found hundreds of drums containing scrap Pyranol and other chemicals at the Fletcher Site. The drums were unmarked and several had leaked. Subsequent testing detected hazardous substances at the Site, including tricholoroethylene

("TCE"), trichlorobenzene ("TCB"), and PCBs. As a result, EPA placed a temporary cap on the Site and, in 1989, added it to its National Priorities, or "Superfund," List.

. . . .

[After a bench trial, the district court held] that GE had arranged to dispose of hazardous substances at the Fletcher Site and was liable for response costs incurred by EPA. [GE appealed.]

. . . .

GE's appeal largely hinges on its reading of the Supreme Court's *Burlington Northern* decision . . . . GE's contention is that only an entity that enters into an arrangement with a transparently evident desire to have its hazardous substances enter the environment properly comes into § 9607(a)(3)'s purview.

We do not agree . . . .

. . . .

In contrast to *Burlington Northern*, where Shell's exposure to liability stemmed from its sale of a legitimate new and useful product, the record here contains ample evidence that GE viewed scrap Pyranol as waste material and that any profit it derived from selling scrap Pyranol to Fletcher was subordinate and incidental to the immediate benefit of being rid of an overstock of unusable chemicals. GE stored scrap Pyranol, a byproduct of its capacitor manufacturing operations, in second-hand 55-gallon drums — often labeled "scrap Pyranol," "waste Pyranol," "scrap oil," or otherwise, depending on the manner in which it was collected — which were then placed in its facilities' salvage areas . . . . GE pursued varied arrangements by which to deplete its scrap Pyranol stockpile, for example, by transferring scrap Pyranol to local landfills, selling it to local government entities which could use it as dust suppressant, giving it away to its employees for use as a weed killer, or discharging it into the Hudson River . . . . This evidence is inconsistent with the notion that GE ever viewed scrap Pyranol as the archetypal "useful substance [conveyed] for a useful purpose" that has commonly been found to lie outside of § 9607(a)(3)'s reach.

Also telling in this regard is what the record does not reveal: any attempt by GE to market scrap Pyranol as a viable product to any entity or person other than Fletcher . . . . Although it is clear that Fletcher used an unknown amount of scrap Pyranol as a plasticizer agent in his paint making operations, evidence proffered by the government's expert suggested that the uncertain and inconsistent quality of scrap Pyranol rendered it a poor choice even for that purpose . . . . Relying on this evidence, the district court reasoned that if use as a plasticizer ingredient was indeed a practical or sustainable application for scrap Pyranol, then GE, a sophisticated profit-seeking entity, would have either used it as an additive in its own paint making operations or sought to expand the market for its scrap Pyranol to purchasers other than Fletcher . . . .

. . . .

The fact that GE viewed the scrap Pyranol in its scrap and salvage yards as a waste product does not, by itself, bring GE within the purview of § 9607(a)(3) arranger liability.

Our focus now turns to GE's dealings with Fletcher to determine whether GE possessed the element of intent necessary to qualify as an arranger under § 9607(a)(3) . . . .

. . . [T]he record sustains an inference that GE knew or otherwise understood that Fletcher used an unknown amount of the scrap Pyranol he purchased as a plasticizer in his paint manufacturing operations. At a minimum, GE also likely understood that Fletcher saw some value in the scrap Pyranol because Fletcher paid (or said he would pay) for these materials . . . . Because Fletcher alleged certain drums were unusable to him one can also infer that, from early on, GE understood some drums of scrap Pyranol contained materials of such poor quality so as to not be of any value whatsoever to Fletcher.

. . . Though GE was content at first giving Fletcher between 100 and 500 drums of scrap Pyranol at no charge, starting in 1956 GE required payment of $3.50 to $4.00 per 55-gallon drum . . . . Before 1964, Fletcher was able to replace drums containing scrap Pyranol he claimed to be unusable free of charge; not so between 1964–66, a period during which GE required Fletcher to pay for each drum that Fletcher transported from GE facilities to the Site. Not surprisingly, during this period, Fletcher's employees tested drums of scrap Pyranol for quality assurance at GE facilities before loading them onto Fletcher's truck, rejecting those Fletcher could not use.

The arrangement between Fletcher and GE again shifted at some point during 1966, and GE's conduct over the following two years leaves little doubt that GE availed itself of its relationship with Fletcher to rid itself of the scrap Pyranol in its inventory. During this period, GE, not Fletcher, loaded the trucks that traveled from GE facilities to the Fletcher Site, and the frequency with which GE sent Fletcher shipments of scrap Pyranol drastically increased. There is no indication in the record that Fletcher solicited or wanted the increase. Importantly, from February 1966 onwards, Fletcher routinely missed payments and did not compensate GE for any shipments of scrap Pyranol. However, Fletcher's failure to pay for its shipments notwithstanding, GE's scrap Pyranol deliveries continued apace, with Fletcher receiving three more shipments between August and November 10, 1967.

Evidence in the record suggests that during this final stage of the GE-Fletcher relationship, GE largely controlled the flow of scrap Pyranol between GE facilities and the Fletcher Site . . . .

. . . .

[In 1968, Fletcher] put GE on notice that (1) large quantities of the hazardous substances that it had provided were of absolutely no use to Fletcher and were, at that moment, "piled" at the Fletcher Site, (2) Fletcher had not consciously accepted large quantities of the chemicals GE had delivered . . . and (3) importantly, that Fletcher expected GE's cooperation in resolving the matter of the more than 1,800 55-gallon drums of unusable chemicals sitting at the Site.

. . . [I]n *Burlington Northern*, the Supreme Court underscored the fact that Shell took varied active steps to reduce chemical spillage as evidence supportive of an inference that Shell did not intend the spills to occur in the first place. In contrast—once apprised that Fletcher had no use for large quantities of the scrap chemicals GE had sent to his facilities, aware that Fletcher blamed GE for (either deliberately or negligently) sending contaminated shipments of scrap Pyranol to his attention, and conscious of the fact that Fletcher desired to transfer these chemicals back to GE—GE took at least three well-documented steps the collective effect of which, rather than prevent or reduce the likelihood of disposal, was to ensure it.

First, GE undertook to corroborate Fletcher's claims regarding the poor quality of the scrap Pyranol . . . . [I]n an internal GE letter dated August 6, 1968 . . . Senior Buyer Albert C. Clark informed GE Manager of General Accounting . . . "[. . .] that [Fletcher] has a valid claim[ ]" [and] . . . that the scrap Pyranol Fletcher had received was inconsistent and/or contaminated in nature, noting "[t]he material in question contained anything from water to [TCE] (as much as 22% [TCE] was found)." . . . "This certainly is not the material that [Fletcher] agreed to buy at $3.75 per drum."

Second, once its own testing had confirmed Fletcher's claim that much of the scrap Pyranol it sent Fletcher in recent years was contaminated and/or unusable, GE decided to forgive Fletcher's debt . . . . [T]his recommendation reflected a deliberate financial calculus that accounted for the fact that GE viewed scrap Pyranol as a waste product that should have been discarded and the company stood to benefit financially by leaving Fletcher to deal with the issue of disposal.

Third, consistent with this recommendation and cost analysis, GE made no effort, either then or at a later date, to retrieve, cleanup [sic], or otherwise properly dispose of the thousands of drums of scrap Pyranol Fletcher had claimed were unusable to him. Evidence in the record supports the district court's conclusion that GE's non-action in this regard flowed from a deliberate decision to wash its hands of the issue of the scrap Pyranol's disposal in the belief that GE could benefit by shifting that responsibility to Fletcher . . . .

. . . .

Properly connected, these points establish that GE purposefully entered into its arrangement with Fletcher with the desire to be rid of the scrap Pyranol. Though the initial arrangement (informal as it was) may not have, in express terms, directed Fletcher to dispose of GE's scrap Pyranol, GE certainly understood this would be the result of its actions and took the conscious and intentional step of leaving Fletcher to dispose of the materials . . . . We therefore hold that GE's actions in relation to the Fletcher Site render it liable for arranging for disposal of a hazardous substance pursuant to § 9607(a)(3).

They were disposing of waste, not arranging transport of useful product.

Notes and Questions

1. In a passage not included in the excerpt, the First Circuit stated that this case "comfortably" fits into the middle ground between an obvious arrangement for disposal and an obvious sale of a useful product. Do you agree? Did the court correctly apply *Burlington Northern*?

2. Although the court held General Electric liable for arranging disposal of Pyranol at the Fletcher Paint site, alleged arrangers who did not make "traditional" arrangements for disposal have prevailed in a number of other cases decided after *Burlington Northern*. In every case, the court delved deeply into, as the Supreme Court put it, "a fact-intensive inquiry." *See, e.g., Consolidation Coal Co. v. Georgia Power Co.*, 781 F.3d 129 (4th Cir. 2015) (holding that seller of used transformers did not arrange to dispose of residual PCB oil in the transformers because evidence showed that the seller intended to maximize revenue from the sales, the buyer intended to reuse whole transformers where possible, PCB residues could not practically be separated from the used transformers, and the seller obtained more than scrap value for them); *NCR Corp. v. George A. Whiting Paper Co.*, 768 F.3d 682 (7th Cir. 2014) (holding that a paper manufacturer, which sold unusable carbonless paper coated with PCBs to a company that used such scrap to make recycled paper, did not arrange for disposal of the PCBs); *Team Enterprises, LLC v. Western Investment Real Estate Trust*, 647 F.3d 901 (9th Cir. 2011) (holding that the manufacturer of a dry cleaning machine did not arrange for disposal by selling the machine to dry cleaners despite knowing that the machine produced waste water containing a hazardous substance).

3. In several contexts, plaintiffs have argued that emitting hazardous substances into the air can be an arrangement for disposal if the emitted substances end up being deposited at a CERCLA "facility." It remains to be seen whether such arguments will succeed. In *Pakootas v. Teck Cominco Metals, Inc.*, 830 F.3d 975, 978 (9th Cir. 2016), a smelter had "emit[ted] lead, arsenic, cadmium, and mercury compounds through a smokestack and those compounds contaminate[d] land or water downwind." The court held that the smelter's owner did not arrange for disposal of the hazardous substances, but only because it was constrained by the Ninth Circuit's *Carson Harbor* precedent, see p. 796 above. "Plaintiffs' interpretation appears a reasonable enough construction of § 9607(a)(3), and if we were writing on a blank slate, we might be persuaded to adopt it." *Pakootas*, 833 F.3d at 983.

4. Factual investigation is as critical to environmental law cases as to any category of cases. Often the most important facts developed do not seem to have much to do with the environment. In *United States v. General Electric*, the plaintiff had to establish that PCBs are a hazardous substance, that there was a release or threat of release of PCBs at the Fletcher Paint site, that GE's PCBs had come to be present at the site, and that the United States incurred response costs because of the release or threatened release. Yet all these "environmental" facts were not seriously disputed. The big issue was whether GE intended to arrange for disposal of the scrap Pyranol sent to Fletcher. On this issue the plaintiff assembled copious direct and circumstantial evidence of GE's intent based on the *business* dealings between GE and Fletcher: the price Fletcher paid for the scrap Pyranol, the absence of other buyers, the changing arrangements regarding drums of Pyranol that Fletcher deemed unusable, the correspondence between GE and Fletcher, GE's internal memoranda, the sudden increase in the volume of Pyranol shipped once GE took control of the pace of shipments, GE's forgiveness of Fletcher's debt, etc. The nature of environmental law work — especially, perhaps, CERCLA work — requires practitioners to have a broad perspective, to be

comfortable with diverse sources and types of evidence, and to be cognizant of many areas of law beyond their specialty field.

5. Business arrangements and internal motivations also play a role in assessing allegations of liability under CERCLA's fourth category of responsible person— transporters.

4. *Transporters*

The final category of responsible party under CERCLA § 107 is "any person who accepts or accepted any hazardous substances for transport to disposal or treatment facilities, incineration vessels or sites selected by such person." 42 U.S.C. § 9607(a)(4). "Transport" means "the movement of a hazardous substance by any mode. . . ." *Id.* § 9601(26) (CERCLA § 101(26)).

Transporters tied together many CERCLA cases that involved cleanups of unregulated or illicit dumps in the nation's old industrial heartland. In a common scenario, evidence showed that someone who owned a truck, or a few trucks, or a fleet of trucks, had agreed for a relatively small fee to haul chemical waste from a factory or other industrial location—or a slew of locations. To maximize profits, the transporter then dumped each load of waste at the closest, cheapest, or most convenient place—a chemical waste land-fill, a municipal waste landfill, a junkyard, a farm whose owner would accept the waste to make a little more money, or even a roadside drainage ditch. Or, as we saw in *Alcan* (p. 774 above), down a borehole that seemed to just disappear into the bowels of the earth.

In this way transporters might make many arrangers liable for releases from a single facility, might make a single arranger liable for releases from many facilities, or might make many arrangers liable for releases from many facilities. Untangling the web of links connecting arrangers, transporters, and facilities has often been a major challenge for CERCLA litigators.

Of course, arrangers sometimes chose the disposal location and thus brought on themselves the eventual liability for response actions at that facility. Sometimes, how-ever, transporters brought hazardous substances to illicit disposal facilities despite contractual agreements with arrangers that specified a different location (see p. 802 above). Sometimes the arranger gave no directions about where to take the material being disposed of. An arranger may be liable even if it did not select or know the location where its hazardous substances went, but CERCLA makes a transporter lia-ble only for a release from a facility "selected by such person." The meaning of this limitation is the subject of the following court opinion.

Tippins Inc. v. USX Corp.

37 F.3d 87 (3d Cir. 1994)

Judge BECKER:

   . . . .

In September 1987, [plaintiff] Tippins signed an agreement with Sydney Steel Cor-poration of Nova Scotia to provide equipment for electric arc furnace ("EAF") steelmaking. Included in this agreement was a provision that required Tippins to furnish and install an EAF baghouse.[2] Tippins [agreed to purchase a used EAF baghouse from USX Corporation] . . . . Under the purchase agreement, Tippins was responsible for the dismantling and load-out of the baghouse.

As a result of USX's manufacturing and processing of steel . . . , EAF dust was present in and around the baghouse. To effect cleanup of the EAF dust, Tippins solicited bids from contractors to pick up and transport the dust for disposal. Tippins eventually contracted with Petroclean, which is licensed to haul hazardous waste and specializes in the transport and disposal of hazardous substances, to transport the dust for disposal. The transportation agreement provided that Petroclean would supply the labor, equipment, and material for removal and transport of the EAF dust as well as obtain a provisional EPA identification number for the generation of the hazardous waste.

Petroclean = transporter ⤷ they selected the site

The CECOS International facility in Williamsburg, Ohio was chosen after Petroclean gathered information on the site and submitted a proposal to Tippins based on certain cost parameters. Those cost parameters involved the use of a certain type of container for the dust known as a bulk lift disposal bag. The parties subsequently learned that the CECOS site would accept EAF dust only if packaged in its own containers. Since those containers were "prohibitively" expensive, Tippins and Petroclean agreed to transport the dust to another disposal site. Petroclean, having surveyed substitute disposal sites, identified two landfills that would accept the dust, the Four County Landfill in Rochester, Indiana and Wayne Disposal, Inc. in Detroit, Michigan. Petroclean contacted each site, gathered financial information as to disposal costs, and offered Tippins both sites as possible disposal locations from which Tippins could choose. Tippins subsequently picked Four County, where Petroclean disposed of the EAF dust.

Later, . . . [t]he EPA . . . notified Tippins that it was a potentially responsible party for environmental contamination at Four County . . . .

In August 1992, Tippins filed an action in the District Court for the Western District of Pennsylvania against Petroclean . . . . Tippins alleged that . . . Petroclean was liable as a transporter under § 107(a)(4). [On cross-motions for summary judgment, the district court held Petroclean liable. Petroclean appealed.]

. . . .

Petroclean contends . . . that it cannot be liable unless the court finds that Petroclean made the ultimate selection of Four County as the disposal location. Petroclean further submits that the record is "vague at best" regarding its role in site selection and, thus, that a genuine issue of material fact exists as to this issue.

Transporter selected the disposal location

---

2. EAF dust is a byproduct of the manufacture of steel using electric furnaces. A baghouse, a large, fabricated structure, vacuums contaminated air inside to filter out the EAF dust. The dust is collected inside a hopper or dumpster, and clean air is exhausted from the structure. The EPA listed EAF dust as a hazardous substance in 1980, designating it as K061. *See* 40 C.F.R. § 261.32.

In response, Tippins argues that . . . the record demonstrates that, as a matter of fact, Petroclean did select the Four County facility.

. . . .

Since a transporter must select the disposal location to be liable under § 107(a)(4), we must determine whether Petroclean selected Four County as the disposal facility. Tippins argues that Petroclean selected the site because it was actively involved in the selection process. Not surprisingly, Petroclean counters this contention and would construe § 107(a)(4) narrowly to hold a transporter liable only when it made the final decision to select the disposal facility. CERCLA does not unequivocally resolve the question of what particular acts by a transporter constitute selection, as it does not define the term "select." Nor did the drafters of CERCLA or SARA provide any explanation for the site selection language.

. . . [W]e believe that a person is liable as a transporter not only if it ultimately selects the disposal facility, but also when it actively participates in the disposal decision to the extent of having had substantial input into which facility was ultimately chosen. The substantiality of the input will be a function, in part, of whether the decisionmaker relied upon the transporter's special expertise in reaching its final decision. In other words, the selection process is a continuum and, in the circumstances we have described, the selection is done jointly.

Construing the term "selected" to encompass those persons whose participation in the selection process is as described takes no liberties with the statute. In Justice Holmes' oft quoted words, "[a] word is not a crystal, transparent and unchanged, it is the skin of a living thought and may vary greatly in color and content according to the circumstances and the time in which it is used." In a case such as this, where the statute does not define the term at issue and the legislative history is unavailing, we must define the term "selected" in light of its ordinary use and the overall policies and objectives of CERCLA.

First, we note that our construction of "selected" is within the term's ordinary meaning. To "select" is "to choose from a number or group usu[ally] by fitness, excellence, or other distinguishing feature." WEBSTER'S THIRD NEW INTERNATIONAL DICTIONARY 2058 (Philip B. Gove ed. 1966). When a transporter with a knowledge and understanding of the industry superior to its customer's investigates a number of potential disposal sites and suggests several to the customer from which it may pick, and the customer relies upon the transporter's knowledge and experience by choosing one of the winnowed sites, the transporter has performed a selection. Although the transporter has not made the ultimate decision, it has made the penultimate one; for all intents and purposes, the transporter has selected the facility by presenting it as one of a few disposal alternatives. In such cases of cooperation, the customer and transporter have jointly selected an appropriate disposal facility.

The "active participation" standard advances the objectives of CERCLA by recognizing the reality that transporters often play an influential role in the decision to dispose waste at a given facility. Generators undoubtedly regularly rely upon a transporter's expertise in hazardous waste management when considering disposal alternatives. A sophisticated transporter specializing in the transportation of hazardous material is accordingly frequently in the best position to ensure safe and proper disposal of the waste. There is no sound reason for such parties to escape CERCLA liability while the generators, owners, and operators are held liable, when they essentially determined the disposal location subjected to the remedial actions and incurring the response costs. This approach also comports with the need to interpret a remedial statute such as CERCLA liberally.

We emphasize that for liability to attach, a transporter must be so involved in the selection process that it has substantial input into the disposal decision. A transporter clearly does not select the disposal site merely by following the directions of the party with which it contracts. In such cases, the transporter is no more than a conduit of the waste and its "connection with the material is the most attenuated among potentially responsible parties." Congress intended such transporters to avoid liability. To be held liable under § 107(a)(4), the transporter must be so engaged in the selection process that holding it liable furthers one of CERCLA's central objectives: to hold all persons actively involved in the storage or disposal of hazardous waste financially accountable for the cost of remedying resulting harm to the human health or environment.

Applying this standard to the instant case, we conclude that the district court appropriately granted summary judgment against Petroclean . . . . As a company specializing in site remediation and hazardous waste and transportation services, Petroclean had substantial input into the selection process, and Tippins clearly relied on its special expertise in ultimately choosing Four County.

Petroclean first identified the CECOS facility as the disposal site for the EAF dust and subsequently contracted with Tippins to dispose of the waste there. Later, after discussions with CECOS about disposal costs, ... Petroclean . . . completed applications for two possible disposal locations . . . . After receiving estimated disposal costs for the EAF dust from those sites, Petroclean forwarded the financial information to Tippins, which relied upon it to make its final selection of Four County as the disposal facility.

Although Petroclean did not make the *final* decision to dispose of the dust at *Rationale* Four County, it substantially contributed to and shared in that decision by locating and submitting a limited number of potential disposal sites from which Tippins could select. Moreover, it is evident from the record that Tippins at all times relied upon Petroclean's expertise in the field of hazardous waste management when deciding the appropriate means and location to dispose of the EAF dust. On these facts, Petroclean was far more than a mere conduit of the hazardous waste; rather, it actively participated in the site selection decision, such that Petroclean and Tippins, working together, selected Four County as the disposal site. Consequently, Petro- *Decision* clean is liable under CERCLA § 107(a)(4) as a transporter which selected the disposal facility.

. . . .

Notes and Questions

1. You may have noticed that although EPA identified Tippins as potentially *liable* for response costs incurred (by EPA and the State of Indiana) at the Four County Landfill, Tippins was the *plaintiff* in the excerpted opinion. Tippins sued Petroclean and USX for contribution under CERCLA §§ 107(a) and 113(f). We discuss § 113(f), and the relation between it and § 107(a) below, p. 846.

2. The *Tippins* court discussed only Petroclean's liability. Can you explain why Tippins might have been liable for actions taken in response to the release of hazardous substances at Four County?

3. If you had been counsel for Tippins, would you have recommended suing USX as well as Petroclean? If so, on what theory? If not, why not?

4. Why was it important for Tippins to install a baghouse to capture the dust from its EAF steelmaking operation?

5. Why was it so hard for Petroclean and Tippins to find facilities at which they could dispose of the baghouse dust? Why was the EAF baghouse dust a hazardous substance under CERCLA?

6. In its introduction to the opinion (not included in the excerpt), the Third Circuit stated: "We basically agree with Tippins that § 107(a)(4) applies if the transporter's advice was a substantial contributing factor in the decision to dispose of the hazardous waste at a particular facility." Is this standard the same as the one set forth at the end of the opinion (quoted in the excerpt above)? Where does the idea of a "substantial contributing factor" come from? Is it appropriate to borrow that concept from its source?

7. In addition to arguing that Petroclean had, in fact, "selected" Four County, Tippins also argued that § 107(a)(4), properly construed, does not even require that a transporter select the disposal facility. Tippins based this argument on the structure of the transporter liability provision, which makes liable "any person who accepts or accepted any hazardous substances for transport to disposal or treatment facilities, incineration vessels or sites selected by such person." Tippins argued that the phrase "selected by such person" modifies only the immediately preceding word "sites." Because the parties agreed that Four County Landfill was a CERCLA "facility"—a place where hazardous substances had come to be located—Tippins reasoned that Petroclean was liable for transporting hazardous substances to Four County regardless of whether Petroclean selected that facility.

The court agreed with Tippins that "in view of the absence of a comma after 'sites'" the provision was ambiguous. The court further acknowledged that under a general canon of statutory construction, a modifier is deemed to modify only the closest noun. But the court also concluded that the construction Tippins advocated was absurd: why would Congress want to hold a transporter liable for bringing hazardous substances to a "facility" no matter who selected the facility, but for bringing hazardous substances to a "site" (whatever that means) only if the transporter selected the site? Therefore, with a nod to CERCLA's "inartful crafting," the court rejected Tippins' argument. The court's discussion illustrates that clever lawyerly arguments work best if they are supported by a reasonable explanation of why they make sense, and that statutes (and other legal documents) work best if they are carefully drafted.

8. Speaking of congressional intent, why did Congress decide to hold an arranger liable regardless of its role in selecting the facility, but to hold a transporter liable only if the transporter selected the facility? Do you agree with this policy choice?

And speaking of inartful crafting, after listing the classes of responsible parties in §§ 107(a)(1) through 107(a)(4), CERCLA then uses the letters A through D to list four categories of costs or damages that a plaintiff may recover from liable parties. This makes it appear as if the list of recoverable items is a sub-sub-section of § 107(a)(4), but in practice any liable party can be liable for any item on the list. What are those items?

D. Liability for What?

It should already be clear to you that CERCLA "cost recovery" cases involve claims for the money the government spends implementing response actions pursuant to the government's authority under § 104. CERCLA, however, provides liability for more than just that.

1. Government Response Costs

Section 107(a)(4)(A) of CERCLA makes responsible parties liable for "all costs of removal or remedial action incurred by the United States Government or a State or an Indian tribe not inconsistent with the national contingency plan." The phrase "all costs" might seem self-explanatory. But after early CERCLA cases made it clear that potentially responsible parties would find it difficult to avoid liability, and defendants realized that CERCLA response actions would be very expensive, the amount of the government's recoverable costs for a time became a major battleground in CERCLA litigation.

United States v. American Cyanamid Co.
786 F. Supp. 152 (D.R.I. 1992)

Judge PETTINE:

Once again, the Court visits the Picillo Pig Farm, a hazardous waste site in Coventry, Rhode Island. The United States government, through the Environmental Protection Agency, sued American Cyanamid Company and Rohm & Haas Company for recovery of clean-up ("response") costs under [CERCLA]. The Court found the defendants liable . . . ; the only remaining issue is the amount of recovery the United States may demand from defendants . . . .

I. CASE HISTORY

. . . Litigation surrounding this hazardous waste site began in 1977, when the problem was first recognized.

> State environmental authorities discovered this chemical wasteland in 1977 after combustible chemicals caused a dramatic explosion and towering flames to rip through the waste disposal site. After the fire, state investigators discovered large trenches and pits filled with free-flowing, multicolored, pungent liquid wastes; they also excavated approximately 10,000 barrels and containers in varying states of decay containing hazardous chemical wastes.

Violet v. Picillo, 648 F. Supp. 1283, 1286 (D.R.I. 1986) . . . .

[The court "found American Cyanamid and Rohm & Haas jointly and severally liable to the State of Rhode Island." In a later cost recovery suit brought by the United States, the court "granted partial summary judgment to the government regarding defendants' liability."]

Liability established, only the issue of the amount of recovery remained. On June 26, 1991, the Court referred this action to Special Master Stephen D. Anderson, Esq., for determination of the factual issues regarding the costs incurred by the United States in connection with the site. Special Master Anderson submitted his thorough and well-organized Report to the Court on November 13, 1991. Both parties, the United States and the generator defendants, have objected to certain findings of fact made by the Master. According to the Order of this Court dated June 26, 1991, the Court will decide de novo any of the Master's factual findings objected to by a party, as well as all questions of law . . . .

. . . .

II. CERCLA "SUPERFUND" LAW

A. CERCLA AUTHORIZES AWARDING RESPONSE COSTS TO THE UNITED STATES GOVERNMENT

. . . .

It is worth reiterating that all costs incurred by the government are recoverable under . . . section [107(a)(4)(A)]. This includes indirect costs and administrative expenses.

. . . [T]he government's response costs . . . include:

(a) Investigations, monitoring and testing to identify the extent of danger to the public health or welfare or the environment.

(b) Investigations, monitoring and testing to identify the extent of the release or threatened release of hazardous substances.

(c) Planning and implementation of a response action.

(d) Recovery of the costs associated with the above actions, and to enforce the provisions of CERCLA, including the costs incurred for the staffs of the EPA and the Department of Justice.

. . . .

Under Section 104(b), courts have held that the United States is entitled to recover its litigation costs from liable parties.

B. THE GOVERNMENT'S PRIMA FACIE CASE

The National Contingency Plan ("NCP") . . . outlines procedures for selecting response actions to hazardous substance releases . . . .

Once the government meets the threshold criteria [of accounting for and documenting the amount of its costs], the burden of proof shifts to the defendants.

C. BURDEN OF PROOF IN AREA OF RESPONSE COSTS

Liable defendants must pay "*all* costs . . . not inconsistent with the national contingency plan." 42 U.S.C. § 9607(a)(4)(A) (emphasis added). The NCP establishes detailed procedures for choosing appropriate response actions. "As long as the actions taken by the government were in harmony with the NCP, the costs incurred pursuant to those actions are presumed to be reasonable and therefore are recoverable."

Defendants bear the burden of proving that the response costs claimed by the United States are inconsistent with the NCP. To establish such inconsistency, defendants must prove that the agency's actions were arbitrary and capricious . . . .

III. SPECIAL MASTER'S REPORT AND RECOMMENDATION

Special Master Anderson conducted ten days of evidentiary hearings, received testimony from thirteen witnesses, and took into evidence thousands of pages of documents. In his Report, the Master addressed the two crucial issues which form the basis of the parties' objections. First, does the government's documentation of expenses . . . form an adequate basis for cost recovery from the defendants? Second, should certain costs be disallowed because of a substantive inconsistency with the NCP?

Before deducting settlement costs recovered from other parties with respect to the site, and before assessing prejudgment interest, the government initially claimed $5,817,063.43 for EPA and Department of Justice ("DOJ") expenditures. During the course of the proceedings, the government reduced its claim by $543,882.57. The Master recommended the additional disallowance of $276,846.32 based on inadequate documentation.

Defendants urge this Court to reject the Master's Report in its entirety save for the above mentioned disallowances. Concomitantly, the government requests that the Court affirm the Master's Report except for four disallowances . . . .

All other disallowances recommended by the Special Master have not been objected to by the United States; the Court need not discuss those areas . . . .

IV. OBJECTIONS TO THE MASTER'S REPORT

A. DEFENDANTS' OBJECTIONS BASED ON ADEQUACY OF DOCUMENTATION

Defendants continue to claim that the documentation maintained by the government in this case is inadequate. The Master, through hours of testimony and thousands of pages of documents, evaluated each area of documentation for adequacy.

After reviewing the Master's Report, the transcripts, and the documentary evidence, this Court accepts all but one of the Master's recommendations as to the adequacy of the documentation for allowed and disallowed expenses . . . .

1. Direct Payroll Expenses

The Court finds the documentation of the payroll expenses adequate. Additionally, the Court will not second-guess the EPA as to the appropriate number of employees necessary for the cleanup of the site.

2. Indirect Cost Allocation

The government claims $447,442.00 in EPA indirect costs. "[O]rdinarily courts should allow recovery of these indirect costs." . . . The Master's Report explains in detail the methodology used by the EPA. The Court accepts these costs as adequately documented.

[The court then addressed the adequacy of documentation submitted in support of several specific direct cost items that the government had claimed and the defendants had challenged. Based on an item-by-item review of the documents, the court accepted all of the Special Master's recommendations to allow particular costs, accepted some of the Special Master's recommendations to disallow particular costs, and rejected some of the Special Master's recommendations to disallow particular costs.]

B. INCONSISTENCY WITH NCP

Once the United States presents its prima facie case for response costs, the burden shifts to the defendants to show that these response costs are inconsistent with the NCP.

Defendants, like other parties liable under CERCLA, "shall be liable for . . . all costs of removal or remedial action incurred by the United States . . . not inconsistent with the national contingency plan." Consistency with the NCP is "the only criterion for the recoverability of response costs under CERCLA."

The burden of proving inconsistency with the NCP is on the defendants. To meet that burden, defendants must identify a particular provision in the NCP with which a specific response action is inconsistent.

Even if a response action is shown to be inconsistent with the NCP, defendants still have not triumphed. In order to establish the amount of costs to be disallowed, "the defendants have the burden of demonstrating that the clean-up, because of some variance from the Plan, resulted in demonstrable excess costs. . . ."

CERCLA imposes no obligation on the United States to minimize its response costs for the benefit of responsible parties who are liable for the costs. As one court recently noted, "'all costs' incurred by the United States not inconsistent with the NCP are conclusively presumed to be reasonable, and whether costs are 'necessary' or 'cost-effective' are relevant only to the extent that the NCP imposes those requirements."

Reasonableness of costs for clean-up is not a defense to recovery.[5] The requirement of NCP consistency "addresses the nature of the response action for which costs can be recovered," not how much the response action costs. As long as the actions taken by the government fit within the NCP, the costs are presumed reasonable.

Defendants charge that the response costs are not "cost-effective" and are therefore inconsistent with the NCP. This challenge is inapposite.

. . . .

Cost effectiveness is a criteria [sic] for the EPA only when choosing a permanent remedy for a site among competing alternatives. This is the only reference to cost-effectiveness of hazardous substance response actions in the NCP . . . . The NCP directs EPA to prospectively choose a remedial action that EPA believes will clean-up the site for the least cost. Once EPA validly chooses a permanent remedy for a site, cost-effectiveness is no longer a viable challenge to the implementation of that remedy.

When the United States is required to take response action on its own, responsible parties must accept the government's judgments as to the proper allocation of resources consistent with the government's own procedures and cost controls.[6] "Defendants chose to pay the piper after the dance and, the dance now concluded, they seek to extricate every sour note along the way from the fee."

1. Defendants' Challenges

Aside from documentary adequacy, defendants' challenges to the Master's Report primarily center on the cost of the action, not the action itself. The generator defendants appear to challenge all of the allowed costs as inconsistent with the NCP . . . .

Defendants maintain that certain studies failed to address contaminated soils remaining at the site, ignored or mislocated a groundwater divide, failed to implement specific recommendations, failed to develop monitoring data, lacked essential information to evaluate remedial alternatives, and duplicated field work and report preparation. However, defendants fail to meet their burden of proof regarding inconsistency with the NCP. Defendants' claims and challenges are not supported by reference to the administrative record or through testimony.

Defendants do not adequately prove inconsistency with specific provisions of the NCP. All charges allowed by the Special Master in this section of his Report are adopted by the Court.

---

5. In contrast, Congress did impose "reasonable cost" limits on private parties seeking to recover response costs. 42 U.S.C. §9606(b)(2)(D). Congress created a statutory difference between government action and private action. To read "reasonable" into the statute (as defendants advocate) would nullify this congressional differentiation.

6. Defendants complain about the "government's callous attitude towards conservation of scarce financial resources." However, this Court notes that defendants could have taken [it] upon themselves to clean-up the Picillo Pig Farm . . . . Indeed, if defendants had taken this path, they would have controlled costs at the site themselves. Additionally, defendants should be embarrassed, after all the proceeding [sic] litigation, to claim that they understand the conservation of financial resources.

2. Governmental Challenges

The United States challenges [one disallowance] . . . recommended by the Special Master . . . . because of supposed inconsistency with the NCP.

The Court rejects the Special Master's recommendation of the disallowance under the Arthur D. Little contract. ADL has been and continues to conduct studies aimed at selecting and implementing a permanent remedy for the groundwater contamination at the site. The recommended disallowance is based on EPA's rather sudden change of contractors for this investigation. Due to the change in contractors, a certain amount of ADL's work overlapped with previous contractor costs. The Court cannot second-guess the underlying reason for the change in contractors. However, the overlap does not rise to the level of inconsistency with NCP; the entire cost of ADL's work must be allowed.

. . . .

V. CONCLUSION

. . . .

. . . Defendants American Cyanamid and Rohm & Haas are liable for . . . [$5,020,829.89, with the judgment amount to be reduced by the amount recovered in settlements from other defendants and increased by computed pre-judgment interest as allowed by section 107(a)].

Notes and Questions

1. Obviously, to recover the costs of responding to a release of hazardous substances, EPA must keep track of how much it spends on each release. Until EPA developed a system for documenting costs in a routine way, doing so was something of an ad hoc endeavor. In *American Cyanamid*, the defendants disputed the adequacy of EPA's documentation of a few particular cost items, but more broadly challenged EPA's cost accounting method as a whole. A few of the specific challenges succeeded, but the broad attack failed.

2. What are the "indirect costs" that the court allowed EPA to recover? They are costs that are not incurred specifically for a particular response action, but that support the Superfund program, which allows EPA to undertake *any* response actions. For example, EPA has an office that prepares guidance documents to help remedial project managers perform their tasks. The money spent on that office does not clean up any particular Superfund site, but the cleanup of every Superfund site benefits from the work of that office. EPA's cost accountants devised a methodology to distribute a portion of such "indirect costs" to the various response actions. In *American Cyanamid* and other cases, courts have approved EPA's approach.

Accounting for indirect costs, also called "overhead" costs, is not unique to EPA. The price you pay when you buy a new car, for example, includes not only the direct cost of manufacturing that particular car, but also a fraction of the cost of all the manufacturer's corporate infrastructure—the CEO's salary, the cost of producing the annual report, the mortgage payments on the corporate headquarters, etc.

3. Why did the *American Cyanamid* court hold that the government may recover its litigation costs? Recall that the definition of "response," "removal," and "remedial action" includes "enforcement activities related thereto." 42 U.S.C. § 9601(25). If "enforcement activities" are response actions, then the costs of enforcement activities are recoverable response costs.

4. The *American Cyanamid* defendants broadly attacked the government's response costs as excessive and unreasonable, to the point of questioning the number of EPA employees assigned to certain tasks. The court, consistent with the holdings of other courts, held that such arguments fail because inconsistency with the NCP is the only basis for denying recovery of a proven response cost. Why is that so?

Why did the court assign the defendants the burden of proving that the government incurred costs that were inconsistent with the NCP, instead of requiring the government to prove that its costs were consistent with the NCP? How could a defendant satisfy that burden of proof?

The *American Cyanamid* court held that inconsistency with the NCP can only be established by showing, on the administrative record, that EPA made a response action decision that was arbitrary and capricious. Why is that the appropriate standard? Section 113(j)(1) of CERCLA provides that "judicial review of any issues concerning the adequacy of any response action taken or ordered by the President shall be limited to the administrative record." 42 U.S.C. § 9613(j)(1). Section 113(j)(2) provides the standard of review: "the court shall uphold the President's decision in selecting the response action unless the objecting party can demonstrate, on the administrative record, that the decision was arbitrary and capricious or otherwise not in accordance with law." *Id.* § 9613(j)(2). If the objecting party satisfies that standard, "the court shall award . . . only the response costs . . . that are not inconsistent with the national contingency plan." *Id.* § 9613(j)(3).

2. Response Costs of Others

In contrast with § 107(a)(4)(A), which creates liability for response costs incurred by a federal, state or tribal government, § 107(a)(4)(B) makes responsible parties liable for "any other necessary costs of response incurred by any other person consistent with the national contingency plan." 42 U.S.C. § 9607(a)(4)(A). What type of "other person" might incur response costs? Two possibilities come readily to mind: an innocent landowner who cleans up a release caused by some other party, or a volunteer who cleans up a release despite not being liable to do so, might seek to recover the costs of their response actions from responsible parties. We will consider other types of "other person" in Section III.F, below.

Compare the language of § 107(a)(4)(B) with that of § 107(a)(4)(A). How do the subsections differ? Are the differences significant?

Courts have found two significant differences between these two provisions. First, a government is entitled to recover "all costs of removal or remedial action," but other plaintiffs may only recover "necessary costs of response." As you read in the *American Cyanamid* opinion, courts have interpreted "all costs" to create a conclusive presumption of reasonableness for response costs incurred by the government, so long as those costs are not inconsistent with the NCP. By contrast, a defendant could contend that certain costs incurred by any other person should not be recovered because they were not necessary, even if the plaintiff proved the amount of the costs and that the costs were incurred for response action. *See, e.g., Young v. United States*, 394 F.3d 858 (10th Cir. 2005) (holding that plaintiff's costs, even if within the definition of "response costs," were not "necessary" because "the costs were not tied in *any* manner to the actual cleanup").

Second, courts have found meaning in the difference between liability to the government for response costs "not inconsistent with" the NCP and liability to other parties for costs "consistent with" the NCP. As explained in *American Cyanamid*, courts have uniformly held that a government's right to recover costs not inconsistent with the NCP makes NCP inconsistency an affirmative defense to recovery—meaning a defendant must prove that particular costs were inconsistent with the NCP. By contrast, any other plaintiff must affirmatively prove that the costs it incurred were consistent with the NCP. *See, e.g., Carson Harbor Village v. County of Los Angeles*, 433 F.3d 1260 (9th Cir. 2006) (holding that plaintiff must prove response costs were necessary and consistent with the NCP and affirming summary judgment that costs were not consistent with NCP); *Union Pacific R. Co. v. Reilly Inds., Inc.*, 215 F.3d 830 (8th Cir. 2000) (same).

But the NCP is a regulation that applies to response actions selected (and undertaken or overseen) by the federal government. How can a response action undertaken by someone else be "consistent" with the NCP? The NCP itself supplies an answer, which courts have willingly applied. A non-government response action that is neither selected nor supervised by EPA "will be considered 'consistent with the NCP'" if "when evaluated as a whole," it "is in substantial compliance" with applicable requirements and "results in a CERCLA-quality cleanup." 40 C.F.R. § 300.700(c)(3)(i). The applicable requirements include the NCP's critical provisions relating directly to the selection and implementation of protective response actions. They also include NCP requirements for worker safety and public participation, which private parties independently performing response actions have sometimes neglected—to their regret when they sought cost recovery.

3. Natural Resource Damages

Section 107(a)(4)(C) of CERCLA makes responsible parties liable for "damages for injury to, destruction of, or loss of natural resources, including the reasonable costs of assessing such injury, destruction, or loss resulting from such a release" of hazardous substances—usually referred to by the shorthand phrase "natural resource damages" or "NRD." NRD claims are distinct from claims for response costs.

What is the difference? "Customarily, natural resource damages are viewed as the difference between the natural resource in its pristine condition and the natural resource after the cleanup [i.e., the response action], together with the lost use value and the costs of assessment [of the damages to natural resources]." *In re Acushnet River & New Bedford Harbor*, 712 F. Supp. 1019, 1035 (D. Mass. 1989).

A homely analogy, adapted from a presentation by Interior Department attorney Mark Barash, makes this abstract concept more understandable. Suppose you own a fabulous white jacket, made of an exotic material, that you wear on formal occasions. Someone spills ink on your jacket. You have the jacket cleaned at a shop that specializes in removing difficult stains from fragile fabrics. Several weeks go by before your jacket is ready to pick up. In the meantime, you attend an awards banquet wearing a different outfit that you rented or bought. When you retrieve your jacket, the ink stain is gone but the fabric is visibly thinned where the cleaner had to rub especially hard to get the ink out. The jacket is still wearable, but you realize that it's no longer appropriate for the most elegant occasions, at least without adding some sort of scarf to cover up the thinned fabric. The resale value of the jacket is also lower than it would have been had it never been stained. Every time you see the jacket in your closet, you remember with regret that it's not quite the jacket it once was.

The bill from the dry cleaner is analogous to response costs. The lost use of the jacket while it was being cleaned, the cost of the replacement outfit, the reduction in the usefulness of the jacket because of the thinned fabric, the reduced resale value of the jacket, and your distress about the jacket's compromised condition are all analogous to types of natural resource damages.

Just like a claim for response costs, an NRD claim begins with proof of the common elements of CERCLA liability and proof that the defendant is in one of the four classes of liable parties. Then the plaintiff must prove "injury to, destruction of, or loss of natural resources . . . resulting from such a release." "Natural resources" are:

> land, fish, wildlife, biota, air, water, ground water, drinking water supplies, and other such resources belonging to, managed by, held in trust by, appertaining to, or otherwise controlled by the United States . . . , any State or local government, any foreign government, any Indian tribe, or, if such resources are subject to a trust restriction on alienation, any member of an Indian tribe.

42 U.S.C. § 9601(16) (CERCLA § 101(16). Thus, a release of hazardous substances into an estuary, for example, might require remedial action to eliminate the source of the hazardous substances, but might also cause substantial injury to natural resources if, for example, it rendered the river unsuitable for swimming, the fish in the river unsafe to eat, and the groundwater associated with the river unfit to drink — and if it diminished the reproductive success of eagles that ate the river's fish.

CERCLA limits the ability to bring NRD claims to government "natural resource trustees" — agencies of the sovereign that own, manage, regulate, or otherwise control the natural resources that have been injured, lost, or destroyed. *Id.* § 9607(f) (CERCLA § 107(f)) (stating that liability for NRD shall be to the United States Government, a State, or an Indian tribe); *see Ohio v. U.S. Dept. of the Interior*, 880 F.2d 432, 460 (D.C. Cir. 1989) (stating that purely private property is excluded from CERCLA's definition of "natural resources"); *see also Alaska Sport Fishing Ass'n v. Exxon Corp.*, 34 F.3d 769 (9th Cir. 1994) (holding that settlement of NRD claims by federal and state trustees precluded private action for loss of use of resources).

What is the appropriate measure of damages in an NRD case? It can be difficult to determine the extent of the injury to, loss of, or destruction of natural resources that resulted from a release of hazardous substances, and then to convert those harms into a dollar figure of damages. For example, what does it mean to injure water? If a release of hazardous substances kills some ducks but a few years later there are just as many ducks as ever, was a natural resource destroyed? How can we measure the dollar value of the destroyed ducks?

The issue is complicated by the fact that natural resources may have different types of values. For resources with market uses — say, a commercial fishery — market prices may make valuing a loss relatively straightforward. Even non-market "use values" — for example, a recreational fishery or a private drinking water well — may be amenable to relatively straightforward evaluation using proxy values such as the amount of money spent by recreational fishers or the cost of obtaining a substitute water source. "Nonuse values" — such as the "existence value" a person may place on knowing that an unspoiled beach or a heron colony exists, even if the person will never visit them — are more challenging to quantify. Economists accept that nonuse values exist as a theoretical matter, but turning them into damage amounts that real defendants have to pay has been controversial. In NRD cases, defendants and plaintiff trustees often engage in vigorous disputes about the extent of harm to natural resources, the extent of lost use and nonuse values, and the quantification of damages.

Anticipating such disputes, Congress required the government, within two years after CERCLA's enactment, to "promulgate regulations for the assessment of damages for injury to, destruction of, or loss of natural resources resulting from a release of oil or a hazardous substance for the purposes of" CERCLA and §311 of the Clean Water Act (which at the time of CERCLA's enactment was the sole liability provision with respect to oil spills). 42 U.S.C. §9651(c)(1) (CERCLA §301(c)(1)). Specifically, Congress required promulgation of two types of regulations: "standard procedures for simplified assessments requiring minimal field observation," *id.* §9651(c)(2)(A), and "alternative protocols for conducting assessments in individual cases" — presumably cases in which greater harm justified greater individualized assessment effort, *id.* §9651(c)(2)(B).

President Reagan delegated this task to the Department of the Interior, which responded in a manner that "was, to put it charitably, relaxed." *Ohio v. U.S. Dept. of the Interior, supra,* 880 F.2d at 440. But eventually the Interior Department promulgated rules for both standard (Type A) and alternative (Type B) Natural Resource Damages Assessment (NRDA). The rules were promptly challenged and, although upheld in large measure, remanded to correct certain deficiencies. *Ohio v. U.S. Dept. of the Interior, supra; Colorado v. U.S. Dept. of the Interior,* 880 F.2d 481 (D.C. Cir. 1989). When the Interior Department tried again, its new rules were again challenged. The court upheld the revised Type A rules, *National Ass'n of Manufacturers v. U.S. Dept. of the Interior,* 134 F.3d 1095 (D.C. Cir. 1998), and almost all of the revised Type B rules, *Kennecott Copper Corp. v. U.S. Dept. of the Interior,* 88 F.3d 1191 (D.C. Cir. 1996).

The NRDA regulations, codified at 43 C.F.R. Part 11, set forth in great technical detail the methods a trustee may use to accomplish two tasks: first, to estimate the extent of injury to, loss of, or destruction of natural resources resulting from a release of hazardous substances, and second, to monetize the damages. The described methods "are not mandatory." 43 C.F.R. § 11.10. They come with a strong incentive for their use, however: an "assessment of damages to natural resources . . . made by a Federal or State trustee in accordance with the regulations . . . shall have the force and effect of a rebuttable presumption on behalf of the trustee in any administrative or judicial proceeding . . . ." 42 U.S.C. § 9607(f)(2)(C). How does this statutory rebuttable presumption compare with the judicially recognized presumption that government response costs are consistent with the NCP?

Liability for NRD under § 107(A)(4)(C) includes not only the amount of damages but also the "reasonable costs" of assessing the damages. How does this compare with the recoverability of government costs for assessing the appropriate response action?

Just as EPA is allowed to retain cost recoveries in the Superfund for future use, a trustee that recovers natural resource damages is entitled to retain and use them rather than remitting them to the general Treasury. But CERCLA limits a trustee's use of the funds. The money recovered as damages must be used "only to restore, replace, or acquire the equivalent of" the natural resources that were injured, lost, or destroyed. 42 U.S.C. § 9607(f)(1) (CERCLA § 107(f)(1)).

In principle, almost every release of hazardous substances that justifies a response action also entails some harm to natural resources. In practice, however, cost recovery claims have dominated CERCLA litigation and CERCLA case law. Still, the federal, state, and tribal natural resources trustees have brought many NRD claims under CERCLA. NRD claims may also become more numerous as remedial actions are completed at more and more Superfund sites and the residual injury to natural resources becomes clear.

"NRD" = Natural Resource Damage

Some NRD claims have involved significant environmental damage and large dollar amounts. To take two examples in cases that settled: several defendants allegedly liable for releases of PCBs in the mudflats, sediments, and waters of New Bedford Harbor in Massachusetts agreed to pay more than $20 million to settle NRD claims (in addition to a much larger payment to settle response cost claims), 56 Fed. Reg. 535 (Jan. 7, 1991), *id.* 51238 (Oct. 10, 1991), 57 Fed. Reg. 43024 (Sept. 17, 1992); another group of defendants allegedly liable for the release of numerous hazardous substances into the Grand Calumet River in Indiana agreed to pay more than $55 million in damages and assessment costs to the federal and state trustees, as well as to convey to the state for protection 233 acres of sand dune habitat. 69 Fed. Reg. 53736 (Sept. 2, 2004). Perhaps the most well-known NRD claim—although brought by the United States under the Oil Pollution Act rather than under CERCLA—resulted from the blowout at the Deepwater Horizon offshore oil well drilling platform in 2010. To settle NRD claims brought by the federal government and several Gulf Coast states, BP Exploration & Production Inc. agreed to pay $8.1 billion. *In re Oil Spill by the Oil Rig "Deepwater Horizon" in the Gulf of Mexico*, 2016 WL 1394949 (Apr. 4, 2016) (approving consent decree).

4. Health Assessment Costs

Section 104(i) of CERCLA created a new federal agency, the Agency for Toxic Substances and Disease Registry (ATSDR). *See* 42 U.S.C. § 9604(i)(1). ATSDR is required to conduct a health assessment for each facility on the NPL, and may conduct a health assessment for other releases of hazardous substances. *Id.* § 9604(i)(6)(A), (B). A health assessment is a study that assesses the potential risk to human health posed by a facility, to help determine whether monitoring or other steps should be taken to protect the health of people exposed to hazardous substances. *Id.* § 9604(i)(6)(F), (G). ATSDR is also authorized to conduct, if warranted by the health assessment results, a "full scale epidemiological" study of the health effects of a release of hazardous substances on the exposed population. Section 107(a)(4)(D) of CERCLA makes responsible parties liable for "the costs of any health assessment or health effects study carried out under" § 104(i). ATSDR, in cooperation with EPA, frequently attempts to recover these costs. CERCLA defendants have occasionally contested ATSDR's claimed costs, but these costs are usually much smaller than EPA response costs and therefore rarely become a focus in cost recovery litigation.

E. Liability of Multiple Responsible Parties

We have seen that it is quite typical for CERCLA cases to involve more than one responsible party. At the very least, because the statute makes four different classes of persons liable, a facility might involve current and past owners and operators, arrangers, and transporters. And many facilities accepted waste from dozens or hundreds of arrangers and transporters.

As you know from your study of other areas of law, the existence of multiple parties who are liable for the same claim immediately raises the question of the scope of liability. Will all liable defendants be jointly and severally liable, allowing the plaintiff (at least in principle) to recover the full amount of the liability from any one defendant? Or will liability be several only, so each defendant is responsible for only a share of the claim? CERCLA does not explicitly say, and the choice has tremendous legal and practical consequences.

In the earliest CERCLA cost recovery complaints, government attorneys alleged that defendants were jointly and severally liable. The allegedly liable parties, of course, argued the opposite. It was not long before a federal district judge decided the issue in an opinion that proved to be extremely influential.

United States v. Chem-Dyne Corp.
572 F. Supp. 802 (S.D. Ohio 1983)

Judge RUBIN:

[In the late 1970's, Chem-Dyne Corporation operated a chemical waste storage, transfer, and disposal facility in Hamilton, Ohio. Chem-Dyne received many different types of chemical waste, from many different sources, and recycled some of it to produce antifreeze. The company ceased operations, leaving behind some 300,000 gallons of chemical waste in tanks, 30,000 drums of waste, and contaminated soil, groundwater, sediments, and structures. EPA listed the site on the NPL. When a state-supervised cleanup faltered because the court-appointed receiver lacked the funds to complete the job, EPA in 1982 began to undertake costly response actions.]

National Priorities List

. . . Plaintiff United States has sued 24 defendants, who allegedly generated or transported the hazardous substances located at the Chem-Dyne treatment facility, for reimbursement of the superfund money expended to institute remedial action at the site. In order to expedite discovery and trial preparation, the defendants have moved for an early determination that they are not jointly and severally liable for the clean-up costs at Chem-Dyne.

means two parties are equally bound and liable

A. Statutory Construction

. . . .

. . . In contrast to plaintiff's assertion that joint and several liability is clear from the express statutory language, the Court finds the language ambiguous with regard to the scope of liability. Consequently, in an attempt to discern the Congressional intent, the Court will review and weigh the legislative history of the Act.

. . . .

As background, two different superfund bills proceeded simultaneously through the House and Senate. On November 24, 1980, the Senate made its final amendment to its bill, . . . eliminating the term strict, joint and several liability from its provisions. Subsequently, on December 3, 1980, the House struck the language in its bill and substituted the language of the Senate bill, which was later enacted. The defendants quote at length from Senator Helms' speech:

> Retention of joint and several liability in S. 1480 received intense and well-deserved criticism from a number of sources, since it could impose financial responsibility for massive costs and damages awards on persons who contributed only minimally (if at all) to a release or injury. Joint and several liability for costs and damages was especially pernicious in S. 1480, not only because of the exceedingly broad categories of persons subject to liability and the wide array of damages available, but also because it was coupled with an industry-based fund. Those contributing to the fund will frequently be paying for conditions they had no responsibility in creating or even contributing to. To adopt a joint and several liability scheme on top of this would have been grossly unfair.

> The drafters of the Stafford-Randolph substitute have recognized this unfairness, and the lack of wisdom in eliminating any meaningful link between culpable conduct and financial responsibility. Consequently, all references to joint and several liability in the bill have been deleted. . . .

> It is very clear [. . .] that now the Stafford-Randolph bill does not in and of itself create joint and several liability.

This view of statutory construction is at odds with the guidelines provided by the Supreme Court. Senator Helms was an opponent of the bill. Accordingly, his statements are entitled to little weight in construing the statute.

... Senator Randolph, [a] sponsor [of the bill], explained ...:

> We have kept strict liability in the compromise, specifying the standard of liability under section 311 of the Clean Water Act, but we have deleted any reference to joint and several liability, relying on common law principles to determine when parties should be severally liable.... The changes were made in recognition of the difficulty in prescribing in statutory terms liability standards which will be applicable in individual cases. The changes do not reflect a rejection of the standards in the earlier bill.
>
> . . . .
>
> It is intended that issues of liability not resolved by this act, if any, shall be governed by traditional and evolving principles of common law. An example is joint and several liability. Any reference to these terms has been deleted, and the liability of joint tortfeasors will be determined under common or previous statutory law.

Turning to the House proceedings, Representative Florio, sponsor, commented at length:

> [...] Issues of joint and several liability not resolved by this shall be governed by traditional and evolving principles of common law. The terms joint and several have been deleted with the intent that the liability of joint tortfeasors be determined under common or previous statutory law ... [....] this bill refers to section 311 of the Clean Water Act and to traditional and evolving principles of common law in determining the liability of such joint tortfeasors. To insure the development of a uniform rule of law, and to discourage business dealing in hazardous substances from locating primarily in States with more lenient laws, the bill will encourage the further development of a Federal common law in this area.
>
> I might point out that section 311 has been interpreted by the Coast Guard, the Government body responsible for administering the section 311(k) revolving fund, as imposing joint and several liability under appropriate circumstances ... This established policy seems particularly applicable in cases of hazardous waste sites, where several persons have often contributed to an indivisible harm.
>
> . . . .

Statements of the legislation's sponsors are properly accorded substantial weight in interpreting the statute, although the remarks of a single legislator are not controlling. The fact that the term joint and several liability was deleted from a prior draft of the bill ... , in and of itself, is not dispositive of the scope of liability under CERCLA. Perhaps in other contexts, when Congress deletes certain language it "strongly militates against a judgment that Congress intended a result that it expressly declined to enact."

This case, however, presents an exceptional situation. A reading of the entire legislative history in context reveals that the scope of liability and term joint and several liability were deleted to avoid a mandatory legislative standard applicable in all situations which might produce inequitable results in some cases. The deletion was not intended as a rejection of joint and several liability. Rather, the term was omitted in order to have the scope of liability determined under common law principles, where a court performing a case by case evaluation of the complex factual scenarios associated with multiple-generator waste sites will assess the propriety of applying joint and several liability on an individual basis.

B. Scope of Liability

... [T]he next issue becomes whether state or federal common law should be applied. In situations where, as here, there is a lack of an express statutory provision selecting state or federal law, the inevitable incompleteness presented by all legislation means that interstitial federal lawmaking is a basic responsibility of the federal courts....

State law as a rule of decision is not mandated under the *Erie* doctrine in this case because it falls within the exception provided for federal laws. 28 U.S.C. § 1652; *Erie v. Thompson*, 304 U.S. 64 (1938). Although *Erie* eliminated the power of federal courts to create federal general common law, the power to fashion federal specialized common law remains untouched when it is "necessary to protect uniquely federal interests."

The improper disposal or release of hazardous substances is an enormous and complex problem of national magnitude involving uniquely federal interests. Typically, an abandoned waste site will consist of waste produced by companies in several states within the area or region. The pollution of land, groundwater, surface water and air as a consequence of this dumping presents potentially interstate problems.... Additionally, the superfund monies expended, for which the United States seeks reimbursement, are funded by general revenues and excise taxes. The degree to which the United States will be able to protect its financial interest in the trust fund is directly related to the scope of liability under CERCLA and is in no way dependent upon the laws of any state .... In conclusion, the rights, liabilities and responsibilities of the United States under 42 U.S.C. § 9607 are governed by a federal rule of decision.

The question now becomes whether the scope of liability should be interpreted according to the incorporated state law of the forum state or a federally created uniform law. This determination is a matter of judicial policy dependent upon a variety of considerations relevant to the nature of the specific governmental interests and to the effects upon them of applying state law. Federal programs that by their nature are and must be uniform in character throughout the nation necessitate the formulation of federal rules of decision. CERCLA is such a federal program.... A liability standard which varies in the different forum states would undermine the policies of the statute by encouraging illegal dumping in states with lax liability laws. There is no good reason why the United States' right to reimbursement should be subjected to the needless uncertainty and subsequent delay occasioned by diversified local disposition when this matter is appropriate for uniform national treatment.

. . . [D]etermination of the content of the federal rule is the final step in the analysis . . . .

    . . . .

Typically, as in this case, there will be numerous hazardous substance generators or transporters who have disposed of wastes at a particular site . . . . An examination of the common law reveals that when two or more persons acting independently caused a distinct or single harm for which there is a reasonable basis for division according to the contribution of each, each is subject to liability only for the portion of the total harm that he has himself caused. Restatement (Second) of Torts, §§ 433A, 881 (1976). But where two or more persons cause a single and indivisible harm, each is subject to liability for the entire harm. Restatement (Second) of Torts, § 875. Furthermore, where the conduct of two or more persons liable under § 9607 has combined to violate the statute, and one or more of the defendants seeks to limit his liability on the ground that the entire harm is capable of apportionment, the burden of proof as to apportionment is upon each defendant. These rules clearly enumerate the analysis to be undertaken when applying 42 U.S.C. § 9607 and are most likely to advance the legislative policies and objectives of the Act.

C. Summary Judgment

. . . The proposition of the defendants is that because joint and severally liability is not expressly provided for in CERCLA, there is no basis for its imposition. . . . The Motion of defendants is essentially a Motion for a Partial Summary Judgment on the issue of joint and several liability.

    . . . .

The question of whether the defendants are jointly or severally liable for the clean-up costs turns on a fairly complex factual determination. Read in the light most favorable to the plaintiff, the following facts illustrate the nature of the problem. The Chem-Dyne facility contains a variety of hazardous waste from 289 generators or transporters, consisting of about 608,000 pounds of material. Some of the wastes have commingled but the identities of the sources of these wastes remain unascertained. The fact of the mixing of the wastes raises an issue as to the divisibility of the harm. Further, a dispute exists over which of the wastes have contaminated the ground water, the degree of their migration and concomitant health hazard. Finally, the volume of waste of a particular generator is not an accurate predictor of the risk associated with waste because the toxicity or migratory potential of a particular hazardous substance generally varies independently with the volume of the waste.

This case, as do most pollution cases, turns on the issue of whether the harm caused at Chem-Dyne is "divisible" or "indivisible." If the harm is divisible and if there is a reasonable basis for apportionment of damages, each defendant is liable only for the portion of harm he himself caused. In this situation, the burden of proof as to apportionment is upon each defendant. On the other hand, if the defendants caused an indivisible harm, each is subject to liability for the entire harm. The defendants have not carried their burden of demonstrating the divisibility of the harm and the degrees to which each defendant is responsible.

. . . Because there are genuine issues of material fact concerning the divisibility of the harm and any potential apportionment, the defendants are not entitled to judgment as a matter of law.

. . . .

Notes and Questions

1. Why was the scope of liability so important to both the government (and other plaintiffs) and the defendants in CERCLA cases? You probably know from previous law school courses that plaintiffs generally prefer joint and several liability and that defendants generally prefer several liability. Is there anything about CERCLA claims that makes these preferences even stronger than in other types of cases? How would the outcome of CERCLA litigation be different if the courts had decided that liability would be several only?

2. The *Chem-Dyne* court might have decided that CERCLA liability would always be joint and several or that CERCLA liability would always be several only. Instead, the court took a middle ground, defining the circumstances in which joint and several liability would or would not be appropriate. The court had to decide which party bears the burden of proving that those circumstances exist. As a practical matter, how important is the allocation of this burden of proof? How would the outcome of CERCLA litigation be different if the courts had assigned the burden of proof differently?

3. The opinion states that waste from 289 generators or transporters was brought to Chem-Dyne. The United States sued only 24 of them. Why do you suppose the government sued such a small percentage of the possible defendants?

4. Most CERCLA cases, like most civil litigation, settle before being litigated to final judgment. What effect do you think the possibility of joint and several liability has had on settlement negotiations in CERCLA matters between alleged responsible parties and government entities?

5. The *Chem-Dyne* court acknowledged that during debate and amendment of the bill that became CERCLA, language requiring imposition of joint and several liability was removed. The court concluded that this change did not indicate a congressional intent to preclude joint and several liability, but left courts free to use "evolving principles of common law" to decide the issue. Are you persuaded by the court's analysis?

6. To find "evolving principles of common law," Judge Rubin looked to the then-current RESTATEMENT (SECOND) OF TORTS. Did the court consider any other potential sources of applicable common law principles? Did the legislative history compel analogy to tort law? Is tort law the best analogy?

As we have seen, many doctrines of CERCLA liability are quite different from comparable tort liability doctrines. Causation and strict, status-based liability are especially important examples, but others exist. For example, courts have virtually uniformly rejected a right to jury trial in CERCLA cost recovery cases, concluding that recovery of response costs is more like an equitable restitution remedy than an award of tort damages. *See, e.g., United States v. Northeastern Pharm. & Chem. Co.*, 810 F.2d 726, 749 (8th Cir. 1986). If not by analogy to tort law, how else might the court have developed "evolving principles of common law" under CERCLA?

7. Judge Rubin also concluded that developing "common law" in this context required establishing a uniform federal rule of decision, rather than borrowing substantive rules from state law. Do you agree with this conclusion? What problems would the use of state law have caused?

In fashioning the standard for scope of liability under CERCLA, did Judge Rubin engage in statutory interpretation or did he create a rule of federal common law? Does the distinction matter?

In other contexts, the Supreme Court has sometimes held that state substantive law should apply, rather than a uniform federal rule, even in cases that involved federal programs or interstitial gaps in federal statutes. *E.g. United States v. Kimbell Foods, Inc.*, 440 U.S. 715 (1979). Which approach did the Supreme Court take in *United States v. Bestfoods*, p. 786 above, or *Burlington Northern and Santa Fe Ry. Co. v. United States*, p. 833 below? For a careful discussion of the choice between uniform federal rules and state law rules in the CERCLA context, see *United States v. General Battery Corp., Inc.*, 423 F.3d 294, 298–305 (3d Cir. 2005).

8. The court described the defendants' motion as "essentially" a motion for partial summary judgment. On what basis did the court decide whether to grant summary judgment?

9. *Chem-Dyne* held that "the burden of proof as to apportionment is upon each defendant." What, exactly, must a defendant prove in order to avoid joint and several liability? What evidence might satisfy the defendant's burden? The opinion stated that 608,000 pounds of material from 289 generators (arrangers) or transporters had been deposited in the Chem-Dyne facility. Suppose an arranger defendant could prove that it had contributed, say, 3,040 pounds, or one-half of one percent of the total. Should that defendant be jointly and severally liable for the entire cost of response, or severally liable for only one-half of one percent of the cost?

10. Federal district courts all over the country, and every court of appeals that considered the issue, agreed with or expressly adopted Judge Rubin's *Chem-Dyne* analysis. *See, e.g., United States v. Monsanto Co.*, 858 F.2d 160, 171–73 (4th Cir. 1988); *United States v. R.W. Meyer, Inc.* 889 F.2d 1497, 1507 (6th Cir. 1989). With the legal issue resolved, the question posed above—how a defendant could satisfy its burden of proof on apportionment—became paramount. The government typically argued that any commingled mixture of diverse hazardous substances constituted, by its nature, a single indivisible harm. Defendants typically argued that regardless of commingling, liability should be apportioned in proportion to the amount of waste or hazardous substances for which each defendant was responsible, which—although hard to prove—could sometimes be estimated. Most courts rejected both of these extreme positions. *See, e.g., United States v. Alcan Aluminum Co.*, 964 F.2d 252, 270 n.29 (3d Cir. 1992) ("'commingled' waste is not synonymous with 'indivisible' harm"); *Monsanto*, 858 F.2d at 172–73 (holding that where hazardous substances were commingled, to prove a reasonable basis for apportionment required evidence of the mobility, toxicity, and interactive properties, as well as volume, of hazardous substances contributed by each defendant). Even when courts acknowledged that a harm might reasonably be apportioned, they insisted on "concrete and specific" evidence supporting the requested apportionment. *United States v. Hercules, Inc.*, 247 F.3d 706, 718 (8th Cir. 2001).

In most cases, defendants could not meet these daunting evidentiary requirements. The one notable exception, *United States v. Bell Petroleum Servs.*, 3 F.3d 889 (5th Cir. 1993), seemed to prove the rule. The defendants in that case were three businesses that successively operated a facility in substantially the same way for different periods, each releasing the same single hazardous substance to the same contaminated environmental medium. The court held, over a dissent, that each defendant was only severally liable, in proportion to its share of the total years of operation of the facility. *Bell Petroleum* notwithstanding, after nearly 30 years of litigation it became something of an article of faith among CERCLA practitioners that "[t]he practical effect of placing the burden on defendants has been that responsible parties rarely escape joint and several liability." *O'Neil v. Picillo,* 883 F.2d 176, 179 (1st Cir. 1989). Then the Supreme Court, after denying certiorari in several cases that presented the issue, finally weighed in.

Burlington Northern and Santa Fe Railway Co. v. United States

556 U.S. 599 (2009)

Justice STEVENS:

. . . .

In 1960, Brown & Bryant, Inc. (B&B), began operating an agricultural chemical distribution business . . . . on a 3.8 acre parcel of former farmland in Arvin, California, and in 1975, expanded operations onto an adjacent .9 acre parcel of land owned jointly by . . . [companies] now known respectively as the Burlington Northern and Santa Fe Railway Company and Union Pacific Railroad Company . . . (Railroads). Both parcels . . . were graded toward a sump and drainage pond located on the southeast corner of the primary parcel . . . .

During its years of operation, B&B stored and distributed various hazardous chemicals on its property. Among these were the herbicide dinoseb . . . and the pesticides D-D and Nemagon . . . . Dinoseb was stored in 55-gallon drums and 5-gallon containers on a concrete slab outside B&B's warehouse. Nemagon was stored in 30-gallon drums and 5-gallon containers inside the warehouse. [The map appended to the Court's opinion shows the warehouse on B&B's parcel and the concrete slab on the Railroads' parcel.] Originally, B&B purchased D-D in 55-gallon drums; beginning in the mid-1960's, however, . . . B&B purchased D-D in bulk . . . . [and] . . . transferred [it] from tanker trucks to a bulk storage tank located on B&B's primary parcel . . . .

. . . .

Over the course of B&B's 28 years of operation, delivery spills, equipment failures, and the rinsing of tanks and trucks allowed Nemagon, D-D and dinoseb to seep into the soil and upper levels of ground water of the Arvin facility. [As described in the earlier excerpt from this opinion, p. 797 above, the California Department of Toxic Substances Control (DTSC) and U.S. EPA incurred more than $8 million in response costs for the Arvin facility. By 1989 B&B was insolvent.]

. . . .

In 1991, EPA issued an administrative order to the Railroads directing them, as owners of a portion of the property on which the Arvin facility was located, to perform certain remedial tasks in connection with the site. The Railroads did so, incurring expenses of more than $3 million in the process. Seeking to recover at least a portion of their response costs, in 1992 the Railroads brought suit against B&B in the United States District Court for the Eastern District of California. In 1996, that lawsuit was consolidated with two [cost] recovery actions brought by DTSC and EPA against . . . the Railroads.

[After a bench trial, the district court held that the Railroads were liable under CERCLA] because they were owners of a portion of the facility . . . .

Although the court found the parties liable, it did not impose joint and several liability on . . . the Railroads for the entire response cost incurred by the Governments. The court found that the site contamination created a single harm but concluded that the harm was divisible and therefore capable of apportionment. Based on three figures—the percentage of the total area of the facility that was owned by the Railroads, the duration of B&B's business divided by the term of the Railroads' lease, and the Court's determination that only two of three polluting chemicals spilled on the leased parcel required remediation and that those two chemicals were responsible for roughly two-thirds of the overall site contamination requiring remediation—the court apportioned the Railroads' liability as 9% of the Governments' total response cost.[4] . . .

The Governments appealed the District Court's apportionment . . . .

. . . .

On the subject of apportionment, the Court of Appeals found "no dispute" on the question whether the harm caused by . . . the Railroads was capable of apportionment.

---

4. Although the Railroads did not produce precise figures regarding the exact quantity of chemical spills on each parcel in each year of the facility's operation, the District Court found it "indisputable that the overwhelming majority of hazardous substances were released from the B&B parcel." The court explained that "the predominant activities conducted on the Railroad parcel through the years were storage and some washing and rinsing of tanks, other receptacles, and chemical application vehicles. Mixing, formulating, loading, and unloading of ag-chemical hazardous substances, which contributed most of the liability causing releases, were predominantly carried out by B&B on the B&B parcel."

The court observed that a portion of the site contamination occurred before the Railroad parcel became part of the facility, only some of the hazardous substances were stored on the Railroad parcel, and "only some of the water on the facility washed over the Railroads' site." . . . Given those facts, the court readily concluded that "the contamination traceable to the Railroads . . . , with adequate information, would be allocable, as would be the cost of cleaning up that contamination." Nevertheless, the Court of Appeals held that the District Court erred in finding that the record established a reasonable basis for apportionment. Because the burden of proof on the question of apportionment rested with . . . the Railroads, the Court of Appeals reversed the District Court's apportionment of liability and held . . . the Railroads jointly and severally liable for the Governments' cost of responding to the contamination of the Arvin facility.

. . . . [W]e now reverse.

. . . .

The seminal opinion on the subject of apportionment in CERCLA actions was written in 1983 by Chief Judge Carl Rubin of the United States District Court for the Southern District of Ohio . . . .

Following *Chem-Dyne*, the courts of appeals have acknowledged that "[t]he universal starting point for divisibility of harm analyses in CERCLA cases" is §433A of the Restatement (Second) of Torts. Under the Restatement,

> "when two or more persons acting independently caus[e] a distinct or single harm for which there is a reasonable basis for division according to the contribution of each, each is subject to liability only for the portion of the total harm that he has himself caused. . . . But where two or more persons cause a single and indivisible harm, each is subject to liability for the entire harm."

In other words, apportionment is proper when "there is a reasonable basis for determining the contribution of each cause to a single harm." Restatement (Second) of Torts §433A(1)(b). . . .

Not all harms are capable of apportionment, however, and CERCLA defendants seeking to avoid joint and several liability bear the burden of proving that a reasonable basis for apportionment exists. When two or more causes produce a single, indivisible harm, "courts have refused to make an arbitrary apportionment for its own sake, and each of the causes is charged with responsibility for the entire harm." [*Id.*] Comment *i* . . . .

Neither the parties nor the lower courts dispute the principles that govern apportionment in CERCLA cases, and both the District Court and Court of Appeals agreed that the harm created by the contamination of the Arvin site, although singular, was theoretically capable of apportionment. The question then is whether the record provided a reasonable basis for the District Court's conclusion that the Railroads were liable for only 9% of the harm caused by contamination at the Arvin facility.

The District Court criticized the Railroads for taking a "'scorched earth,' all-or-nothing approach to liability," failing to acknowledge any responsibility for the release of hazardous substances that occurred on their parcel throughout the 13-year period of B&B's lease. According to the District Court, the Railroads' position on liability, combined with the Governments' refusal to acknowledge the potential divisibility of the harm, complicated the apportioning of liability. ("All parties . . . effectively abdicated providing any helpful arguments to the court and have left the court to independently perform the equitable apportionment analysis demanded by the circumstances of the case").[9] Yet despite the parties' failure to assist the court in linking the evidence supporting apportionment to the proper allocation of liability, the District Court ultimately concluded that this was "a classic 'divisible in terms of degree' case, both as to the time period in which defendants' conduct occurred, and ownership existed, and as to the estimated maximum contribution of each party's activities that released hazardous substances that caused Site contamination." Consequently, the District Court apportioned liability, assigning the Railroads 9% of the total remediation costs.

The District Court calculated the Railroads' liability based on three figures. First, the court noted that the Railroad parcel constituted only 19% of the surface area of the Arvin site. Second, the court observed that the Railroads had leased their parcel to B&B for 13 years, which was only 45% of the time B&B operated the Arvin facility. Finally, the court found that the volume of hazardous-substance-releasing activities on the B&B property was at least 10 times greater than the releases that occurred on the Railroad parcel, and it concluded that only spills of two chemicals, Nemagon and dinoseb (not D-D), substantially contributed to the contamination that had originated on the Railroad parcel and that those two chemicals had contributed to two-thirds of the overall site contamination requiring remediation. The court then multiplied .19 by .45 by .66 (two-thirds) and rounded up to determine that the Railroads were responsible for approximately 6% of the remediation costs. "Allowing for calculation errors up to 50%," the court concluded that the Railroads could be held responsible for 9% of the total CERCLA response cost for the Arvin site.

The Court of Appeals criticized the evidence on which the District Court's conclusions rested, finding a lack of sufficient data to establish the precise proportion of contamination that occurred on the relative portions of the Arvin facility and the rate of contamination in the years prior to B&B's addition of the Railroad parcel. The court noted that neither the duration of the lease nor the size of the leased area alone was a reliable measure of the harm caused by activities on the property owned by the

9. As the Governments point out, insofar as the District Court made reference to equitable considerations favoring apportionment, it erred. Equitable considerations play no role in the apportionment analysis; rather, apportionment is proper only when the evidence supports the divisibility of the damages jointly caused by the PRPs. As the Court of Appeals explained, "[a]pportionment . . . looks to whether defendants may avoid joint and several liability by establishing a fixed amount of damage for which they are liable," while contribution actions allow jointly and severally liable PRPs to recover from each other on the basis of equitable considerations. The error is of no consequence, however, because despite the District Court's reference to equity, its actual apportionment decision was properly rooted in evidence that provided a reasonable basis for identifying the portion of the harm attributable to the Railroads.

Railroads, and — as the court's upward adjustment confirmed — the court had relied on estimates rather than specific and detailed records as a basis for its conclusions.

Despite these criticisms, we conclude that the facts contained in the record reasonably supported the apportionment of liability. The District Court's detailed findings make it abundantly clear that the primary pollution at the Arvin facility was contained in an unlined sump and an unlined pond in the southeastern portion of the facility most distant from the Railroads' parcel and that the spills of hazardous chemicals that occurred on the Railroad parcel contributed to no more than 10% of the total site contamination, some of which did not require remediation. With those background facts in mind, we are persuaded that it was reasonable for the court to use the size of the leased parcel and the duration of the lease as the starting point for its analysis. Although the Court of Appeals faulted the District Court for relying on the "simplest of considerations: percentages of land area, time of ownership, and types of hazardous products," these were the same factors the court had earlier acknowledged were *relevant* to the apportionment analysis. ("We of course agree with our sister circuits that, if adequate information is available, divisibility may be established by 'volumetric, chronological, or other types of evidence,' including appropriate geographic considerations").

The Court of Appeals also criticized the District Court's assumption that spills of Nemagon and dinoseb were responsible for only two-thirds of the chemical spills requiring remediation, observing that each PRP's share of the total harm was not necessarily equal to the quantity of pollutants that were deposited on its portion of the total facility. Although the evidence adduced by the parties did not allow the court to calculate precisely the amount of hazardous chemicals contributed by the Railroad parcel to the total site contamination or the exact percentage of harm caused by each chemical, the evidence did show that fewer spills occurred on the Railroad parcel and that of those spills that occurred, not all were carried across the Railroad parcel to the B&B sump and pond from which most of the contamination originated. The fact that no D-D spills on the Railroad parcel required remediation lends strength to the District Court's conclusion that the Railroad parcel contributed only Nemagon and dinoseb in quantities requiring remediation.

The District Court's conclusion that those two chemicals accounted for only two-thirds of the contamination requiring remediation finds less support in the record; however, any miscalculation on that point is harmless in light of the District Court's ultimate allocation of liability, which included a 50% margin of error equal to the 3% reduction in liability the District Court provided based on its assessment of the effect of the Nemagon and dinoseb spills. Had the District Court limited its apportionment calculations to the amount of time the Railroad parcel was in use and the percentage of the facility located on that parcel, it would have assigned the Railroads 9% of the response cost. By including a two-thirds reduction in liability for the Nemagon and dinoseb with a 50% "margin of error," the District Court reached the same result. Because the District Court's ultimate allocation of liability is supported by the evidence and comports with the apportionment principles outlined above, we reverse the Court of Appeals' conclusion that the Railroads are subject to joint and several liability for all response costs arising out of the contamination of the Arvin facility.

... [W]e conclude that the District Court reasonably apportioned the Railroads' share of the site remediation costs at 9%. The judgment is reversed ....

Justice GINSBURG, dissenting:

. . . .

As to apportioning costs, the District Court undertook an heroic labor. The Railroads ..., the court noted, had pursued a "'scorched earth,' all-or-nothing approach to liability. Neither acknowledged an iota of responsibility. ... Neither party offered helpful arguments to apportion liability." Consequently, the court strived "independently [to] perform [an] equitable apportionment analysis." Given the party presentation principle basic to our procedural system, it is questionable whether the court should have pursued the matter *sua sponte*.

The trial court's mode of procedure, the United States urged before this Court, "deprived the government of a fair opportunity to respond to the court's theories of apportionment and to rebut their factual underpinnings—an opportunity the governmen[t] would have had if those theories had been advanced by petitioners themselves."[3] I would return these cases to the District Court to give all parties a fair opportunity to address that court's endeavor to allocate costs. Because the Court's disposition precludes that opportunity, I dissent from the Court's judgment.

Notes and Questions

1. Did the Supreme Court change the legal standard that the lower courts had established for imposition of joint and several liability in CERCLA cases?

2. The Railroads made no effort to satisfy their burden of proof with respect to divisibility and did not argue for imposition of apportioned, several liability. In light of the Railroads' litigation strategy, would it have been appropriate for the district judge to hold the Railroads jointly and severally liable? If so, why did the district court *sua sponte* peruse the record for evidence that would support a reasonable apportionment? Do you agree with the Supreme Court majority that it was appropriate for the district judge to do so? Are you persuaded, instead, by the dissent, that the case should be remanded for adversary development of the record on this issue? Or do you believe, as the dissent hints, that the district judge should not have pursued the issue in the first place?

---

3. For example, on brief, the United States observed: "[P]etitioners identify no record support for the district court's assumption that each party's contribution to the overall harm is proportional to the relative volume of hazardous substances attributable to it." And at oral argument, counsel for the United States stressed that the District Court "framed the relevant inquiry as what percentage of the contamination was attributable to the railroad parcel ... and to the B&B parcel. But it made no finding ... as to what the cost of [remediation] would have been ... if the only source of contamination had been the railroad parcel."

3. The Supreme Court, like many courts before it, concluded that courts must ask two questions before deciding whether joint and several liability is appropriate. The first is whether the harm is "theoretically capable of apportionment." Is this a legal issue or a factual question? If it is a legal issue, what standard should a trial court apply in order to decide it? If it is a factual question, what evidence would be relevant? How did the Supreme Court decide whether the harm at the Arvin site was theoretically capable of apportionment? The second question is whether "there is a reasonable basis for determining the contribution of each cause" to the harm. Is this a legal issue or a factual question? How did the Supreme Court resolve it? What is the "harm" being apportioned in *Burlington Northern*?

4. Is each of the three figures on which the district court based its apportionment appropriate to that purpose? Why or why not? Do you agree with the Supreme Court's analysis? If not, what other figures might have provided a reasonable basis for apportionment?

5. The district court calculated its initial apportionment by multiplying together the three figures on which it relied. What assumption is implicit in this methodology?

6. Did the record in *Burlington Northern* provide sufficient evidence of the value of each of the three figures on which the district court relied? The number of years during which B&B operated on each parcel was not in serious dispute; the acreage of each parcel could readily be measured; and the number of chemicals involved could easily be counted. What if the relevant figures were more uncertain, as is often the case when litigants try to reconstruct the volume and nature of hazardous substances shipped to a landfill years earlier by many arrangers and transporters? How precise must the figures used to apportion liability be, in order to provide a "reasonable basis"?

7. The district court accounted for uncertainty by increasing its calculated apportionment by 50 percent, from six percent to nine percent. What was the basis for that adjustment? How did the Supreme Court treat the adjustment the district court made? How, if at all, should district courts in future cases account for uncertainties in the values used to apportion CERCLA liability?

8. At the trial, the state and federal governments proved that through July 1, 1997, they had incurred more than $8 million in response costs associated with the Arvin facility. How much of that money will the plaintiffs recover?

9. Response actions continued at Arvin after 1997 and are still ongoing (as of 2017). EPA spent more than $23 million in additional response costs between 1997 and 2011. How much of that money will the United States recover?

10. For the United States, the total amount of money at stake in *Burlington Northern* was even higher. As the Supreme Court described, the Railroads had complied with an EPA administrative order directing them to perform response actions on their property. The Railroads tried to recover at least some of the costs of those actions by suing B&B, but they also filed an administrative petition seeking reimbursement from EPA (see p. 764 above), on the grounds that the Railroads were not liable for any response costs in connection with the Arvin facility. After the Railroads were held liable only for an apportioned share, they argued that EPA must reimburse 91 percent of their costs (100 percent minus the Railroads' nine percent share of liability), plus interest. The Railroads and EPA eventually settled the Railroads' claim for reimbursement as well as EPA's claim for additional recoverable response costs incurred after the district court's original judgment. The net result was that EPA paid the Railroads more than $3.7 million.

11. Could a liable party ever prove that its apportioned share of a divisible harm is zero? The Third Circuit thought so. Recall that in *Alcan*, p. 774 above, the court held that Alcan could be liable despite the low concentration of hazardous substances in Alcan's waste emulsion and without proof that Alcan's waste itself caused the government to incur response costs. In a portion of the opinion omitted from the excerpt you read, the court also held that Alcan's liability would be joint and several unless Alcan could "prove that the harm is divisible and that the damages are capable of some reasonable apportionment." 964 F.2d at 270. Furthermore,

> if Alcan proves that the emulsion did not or could not, *when mixed with other hazardous wastes*, contribute to the release and the resultant response costs, then Alcan should not be responsible for any response costs. In this sense, our result thus injects causation into the equation but ... places the burden of proof on the defendant instead of the plaintiff .... Of course, if Alcan cannot prove that it should not be liable for any response costs or cannot prove that the harm is divisible and that the damages are capable of some reasonable apportionment, it will be liable for the full claim ....

Id. (emphasis in original). On remand, the district court found that Alcan failed to meet its burden of proof and held Alcan jointly and severally liable for nearly half a million dollars in response costs the United States incurred that had not been recouped through settlements with other liable parties. *United States v. Alcan Aluminum Corp.*, 892 F. Supp. 648 (M.D. Pa. 1995), *aff'd without opinion*, 96 F.3d 1434 (3d Cir. 1996).

12. The "starting point" for divisibility analysis under CERCLA, for Judge Rubin in 1983 and the Supreme Court in 2009, was the SECOND RESTATEMENT OF TORTS, adopted by the American Law Institute in 1963–1964. But, beginning in the 1980s, many states changed the application of joint and several liability in tort cases, usually through "tort reform" legislation. The most recent torts RESTATEMENT recognizes the existence of five different approaches to indivisible harms caused by independent tortfeasors. Some of these approaches abolish joint and several liability or impose joint and several liability only in limited circumstances. RESTATEMENT (THIRD) OF TORTS: APPORTIONMENT OF LIABILITY §§ 17, A18–A19, B18–B19, C18–C21, D18–D19, E18–E19 (2000). Should the Supreme Court have considered these statutory changes to state common law rules in considering the "evolving principles of common law" governing the scope of CERCLA liability? Why or why not?

13. How much did *Burlington Northern* alter the landscape of CERCLA litigation? Predictably, attorneys for responsible parties argued that by upholding the district court's apportionment, the Supreme Court had upended the established pattern of routine imposition of joint and several liability. Equally predictably, government

attorneys argued that, by embracing *Chem-Dyne,* the Supreme Court had cemented into place the legal framework that routinely led to imposition of joint and several liability. So far, the lower federal courts for the most part have seemed more inclined to distinguish *Burlington Northern* than to follow it. *See, e.g., United States v. NCR Corp.,* 688 F.3d 833, 838–42 (7th Cir. 2012) (defendant failed to establish reasonable basis for apportionment despite proving the percentage of PCBs in river sediments attributable to defendant's discharge); *see also* Steve C. Gold, *Dis-Jointed? Several Approaches to Divisibility After* Burlington Northern, 11 Vᴛ. J. Eɴᴠᴛʟ. L. 307 (2009) (arguing that even under *Burlington Northern,* joint and several liability remains appropriate in many typical CERCLA fact patterns).

Practice Problem:
Apportionment or Joint and Several Liability for the Overflowing Industrial Landfill

Part I: Fact Pattern

A. Hazardous Substance Release and EPA Response Action

Routine testing of a rural homeowner's drinking water well disclosed several CERCLA hazardous substances at concentrations exceeding drinking water standards. These included the metals lead, copper, and manganese, as well as the organic chemicals benzene, toluene, hexane, trichloroethane, trichloroethylene, tetrachloroethylene, and methyl ethyl ketone. A preliminary assessment and site inspection traced the contamination to its source: a nearby closed landfill called the Overflowing Industrial Landfill (OIL). EPA placed the OIL site on the National Priorities List and performed a remedial investigation and feasibility study (RI/FS).

In the remedial investigation, EPA used visual observation and remote sensing to estimate that the landfill has a surface area of about 30 acres with an average depth of approximately 41 feet, meaning that a total of two million cubic yards of waste is buried at OIL. EPA drilled numerous sampling wells in and around the landfill, removing and analyzing samples of soil, waste, and groundwater. The samples showed that the metals and organic chemicals listed above were present in the landfilled waste and also in a plume of groundwater contamination that had migrated nearly half a mile beyond the landfill's western edge. The groundwater contamination had reached 20 residential wells and was close to several others. EPA immediately provided an alternate water supply to the residents whose wells had been or would soon be contaminated, by building pipes connecting their homes to the municipal water supply of a nearby town. But EPA understood this was only an interim solution, because the nearby town's main municipal water supply well, although a mile more distant, was also in the path of the groundwater contamination plume.

In the feasibility study, EPA considered several possible approaches to remediation of the release of hazardous substances at and from OIL, including the "no action" alternative. After public notice and comment, EPA issued a Record of Decision selecting a two-part remedial action involving "source control" and "management of migration."

To control the source of contamination, EPA decided to construct a multilayer, impermeable engineered cap atop the landfill. The cap would intercept rainfall that otherwise would land on and seep through the layers of stored waste. Thus the cap would prevent, or at least greatly slow, the leaching of hazardous substances from the landfill into the groundwater. The cap would need long-term maintenance to ensure continued integrity of the rainfall barrier.

To manage the migration of contaminants in the groundwater plume, EPA decided to build a "pump-and-treat" system. The system would pump contaminated water out of an extraction well and through a treatment plant that would remove the contaminants. An injection well would return clean water to the aquifer. The extracted contaminants would be shipped for disposal off-site. The wells, pumps, and treatment plant would require an estimated 30 years of operation and maintenance in order to remove enough contamination for the groundwater to meet drinking water standards.

B. Identification of Potentially Responsible Parties

EPA investigated the site's history and searched for potentially responsible parties (PRPs). The investigators learned that decades ago, a mining company extracted sand and gravel from the site, creating a large, deep pit. After mining operations ceased, Carl Dirtwiler purchased the site and took title to the property in his own name.

Dirtwiler owned a dump truck and earned his living hauling loads of fill dirt and other materials. When Dirtwiler bought the gravel pit, he had just signed a contract with the ABC Corporation, a major manufacturing company. Under the contract, ABC agreed to pay Dirtwiler to haul fly ash, a combustion by-product, away from the coal-burning furnace at ABC's nearby factory. Dirtwiler hoped to sell the fly ash to companies that could use it in construction or landscaping projects. He knew he would need to store the fly ash somewhere before selling it, so he bought the gravel pit for that purpose.

Dirtwiler soon discovered that there was essentially no market for the fly ash. As fly ash accumulated at the gravel pit, Dirtwiler decided to start a landfill business there. He accepted industrial waste and bulky residential waste (such as large appliances) that municipal trash trucks would not pick up. Dirtwiler charged his customers a fee for each load of waste dumped.

Most of Dirtwiler's customers brought solid waste to the site in pickup trucks or dump trucks and dumped it into the main 25-acre pit. But Dirtwiler also constructed a five-acre lagoon adjacent to the main pit. Customers who hauled liquid waste to the site, in tanker trucks or in drums carried on flatbed trucks, dumped the liquid waste into this lagoon. Dirtwiler used the accumulated fly ash to cover successive layers of waste deposited in the pit and to soak up liquids in the lagoon.

At first Dirtwiler operated the landfill business as a sole proprietorship. Then Dirtwiler and a local investor, Christopher Porelli, created a new corporation: Overflowing Industrial Landfill, Inc. (OILI). Dirtwiler and Porelli each owned 50 percent of the stock of OILI. Dirtwiler was OILI's President and CEO; Porelli was Vice-President and Chairman of the Board. At the end of the landfill's second year of operation, Dirt-wiler sold both the business and the property to OILI. At Porelli's insistence, after OILI was formed, the landfill refused to accept any more liquid wastes but continued to accept solid waste. The business grew rapidly, and so did the amount of waste material buried in the landfill. After eight more years of operation, Dirtwiler and Porelli realized that the landfill had reached its capacity. OILI stopped accepting waste shipments of any kind, covered the landfill with a thin layer of dirt, and hung a chain with a "CLOSED" sign across the entrance. Experts who analyzed historic aerial photographs later estimated that about 95 percent of the total waste volume at the landfill was deposited during the eight years in which OILI operated the landfill. Even after the business stopped operating, OILI continued to hold title to the site, which is OILI's only remaining asset.

One of the landfill's customers was Highflower Corporation, a waste hauling company. Highflower contracted with many industrial customers to haul general garbage—broken-down cardboard boxes, plastic bags, other packaging material, cafeteria food waste, and the like, but not industrial process waste. Highflower placed a large container at each customer's plant, into which the customer's employees deposited trash collected from office and factory buildings around the plant. When a container filled up, Highflower sent a truck to remove the full container and leave an empty container in its stead. The truck driver then brought the full container to a landfill, paid the required fee, and dumped the contents. The driver brought the newly emptied container to the next Highflower customer who needed service and repeated the process. Until OILI was formed, Highflower dumped these loads at any of several landfills, including Dirtwiler's, depending on which landfill allowed for the most efficient truck routing. But after OILI was formed, Highflower used OIL exclusively, in exchange for a discount on dump fees.

QQX Industries, Inc., contracted with Highflower for trash removal. Like Highflower's other customers, QQX put ordinary trash in the Highflower containers. But QQX also placed in the containers spent activated charcoal filters from one of QQX's industrial processes. The filters consisted of 99 percent carbon and one percent metals, including lead, copper, and manganese.

ABC Corp., the same company that generated the fly ash Dirtwiler brought to the OIL site, also generated spent organic solvents in its manufacturing processes. When Dirtwiler owned the landfill, ABC disposed of these spent solvents in the lagoon. Three other companies in the same industry also used the OIL site to dispose of similar spent solvents during that period: Bonans Corporation, Pontroche Corporation, and Admiracorp, Inc.

C. EPA Cost Recovery Action

EPA asked the United States Department of Justice (DOJ) to file a civil action seeking cost recovery against the potentially responsible parties EPA had identified. DOJ filed a complaint in the name of the United States, on behalf of EPA, against: Carl Dirtwiler; Christopher Porelli; Overflowing Industrial Landfill, Inc.; Highflower Corp.; ABC Corp.; QQX Industries, Inc.; Bonans Corp.; Pontroche Corp.; and Admiracorp, Inc.

The United States' complaint alleges that each defendant is jointly and severally liable under CERCLA for all costs of removal and remedial action in response to the release of hazardous substances at the OIL site. The complaint alleges that the United States has incurred response costs: $8 million for the preliminary assessment, site inspection, remedial investigation, and feasibility study; $1.75 million for installation of the alternate water supply; and $0.25 million for enforcement activities. The complaint further alleges that to design, build, operate, and maintain the remedial action, the United States will incur an estimated $40 million (present value) in additional response costs: $20 million for the source control cap and $20 million for the pump-and-treat management of migration. The complaint seeks a declaratory judgment that each defendant will be jointly and severally liable for these anticipated future response costs as well.

D. Additional Facts Disclosed During EPA Investigation and Discovery

During EPA's investigation, EPA served on all of the PRPs information requests under § 104(e) of CERCLA. In response, the PRPs provided written answers and documents from their records. After the United States filed suit, the parties obtained additional evidence through mandatory disclosures, answers to interrogatories, documents requested and produced, and deposition testimony. This information, summarized below, relates to the 10-year period of waste dumping at the OIL site unless otherwise stated.

ABC Corp. stated that "Dirtwiler removed all of the fly ash generated at our furnace. We did not measure the amount of fly ash Dirtwiler removed. But we have records showing the total amount of coal we burned during that time. Standard industrial reference works state the approximate amount of fly ash generated per ton of coal burned. We can therefore estimate that Dirtwiler picked up between 250,000 and 300,000 tons of fly ash in the relevant period. The density of fly ash is variable, but standard industrial reference works state that a ton of fly ash occupies approximately 1 to 1.33 cubic yards. Therefore we estimate that Dirtwiler picked up between 250,000 and 500,000 cubic yards of fly ash from our factory."

At a deposition, Dirtwiler testified: "Fly ash pickups from ABC? I don't have any records of that. I know it was a lot. And I know I didn't sell much of it, either."

Neither Dirtwiler nor ABC performed any chemical tests on the fly ash Dirtwiler picked up. That fly ash, buried in the landfill and mixed with other waste, is not available for analysis. An EPA chemist relied on published, peer-reviewed articles to prepare a report on the composition of fly ash. The report concluded: "Coal fly ash consists mainly of harmless mineral oxides and some unburned carbon. Most fly ash contains trace amounts—between one and 1,000 parts per million—of metal hazardous substances, including copper and lead. The exact chemical composition of fly ash is highly variable. It depends on the combustion process and the source of the coal. The amount of metal that leaches out of fly ash in the ground is also highly variable, depending on the fly ash composition and environmental conditions at the disposal site."

Dirtwiler did not keep detailed records of who brought what to the landfill when he ran it as a sole proprietorship, and he long ago discarded any records he did have.

OIL, Inc., by contrast, created and kept a "dump ticket" every time a customer discarded a load of waste at the landfill. OILI produced many thousands of these dump tickets during discovery. Dirtwiler and Porelli both testified that each dump ticket identifies the customer and states the price paid, but does not describe the waste that was dumped or the type or size of vehicle that brought it.

Approximately 60 percent of the OILI dump tickets listed "Highflower" as the customer dumping at the landfill. But these tickets did not say which of Highflower's many customers was the actual source of the waste. Highflower did not retain records of the number of containers it hauled from each of its customers to the OIL Site. But Highflower's bank records show that QQX Industries was a Highflower customer throughout the 10 years of the landfill's operation.

Porelli testified at his deposition: "I think we hauled about two or three containers a week out of QQX. Before I founded OILI, we only took some of those to Dirtwiler's. I don't know how many. Afterward it all went to OILI."

QQX produced two internal memos. The first memo was from the factory manager to shift supervisors. The memo stated: "This is to remind you that the Highflower waste container is to be used for packaging materials and ordinary waste only. No filters or other process waste." The second memo, from a mid-level manager to a corporate vice-president, stated: "You asked me to assess the cost of our waste disposal contract with Highflower. Over the last twelve months Highflower has hauled away 100 full 40-cubic-yard waste containers. The other waste haulers I have contacted cannot beat Highflower's price for 100 loads." QQX stated that it has no other records of the amount of waste Highflower hauled from QQX's plant.

A former shift supervisor at QQX's factory testified: "We used to sometimes throw filters in the Highflower trash container. We knew we weren't supposed to, but it was easier than taking them to the hazardous waste collection point on the other side of the plant. I would say we probably put them in the container most of the time." In response to an interrogatory, QQX stated: "Filters were disposed and replaced at the end of their useful life, about every two weeks. Each used filter occupied a volume of about one cubic yard and weighed about 2,000 pounds."

In response to requests for admission, ABC Corp., Bonans Corp., Pontroche Corp., and Admiracorp, Inc., each admitted that it shipped to the OIL site, using its own trucks, organic solvent liquid waste "consisting of a mixture of benzene, toluene, methyl ethyl ketone, hexane, trichloroethane, trichloroethylene, and tetrachloroethylene." Each company also answered interrogatories and EPA information requests asking how much organic solvent waste the company sent to OIL.

ABC Corp. stated: "During the two years in which Dirtwiler accepted liquid waste at OIL, ABC shipped one flatbed truck of drummed solvent waste per week to OIL. The average shipment was 25 55-gallon drums, for a total of 143,000 gallons or approximately 700 cubic yards. In addition, ABC shipped a total of 75 tanker trucks of bulk solvent waste to OIL. A high-end estimate is that each tanker truck may have contained up to 3,500 gallons, which means the volume of bulk solvent waste shipped from ABC to OIL could have been as high as 262,500 gallons or approximately 1,300 cubic yards."

Bonans Corp. stated: "Bonans collected all of its solvent waste in drums and brought some of those drums to OIL for disposal. Our records do not indicate the exact number of drums taken to OIL. The best estimate Bonans can make at this time is 7,400 to 14,750 drums." At 55 gallons per drum, this estimate works out to 407,000 to 811,250 gallons or approximately 2,000 to 4,000 cubic yards.

Pontroche Corp. stated: "Pontroche sent drums of liquid solvent waste to OIL from its main manufacturing facility. The facility kept records of these shipments but the official files were destroyed in a fire three years ago. We were able to locate duplicate copies of a few records in an employee's personal files. These records show shipments totaling 4,590 drums (252,000 gallons or 1,250 cubic yards) during a three-month period."

Admiracorp, Inc. stated: "Admiracorp, Inc. has no documents that state the amount of liquid solvent waste sent to Dirtwiler's landfill. During the relevant time period, Admiracorp collected solvent waste in a concrete sump. At the end of each day, the contents of the sump were pumped into a 5,000-gallon tank truck. Every few days an employee drove that truck to Dirtwiler's landfill." At depositions, former Admiracorp employees stated different recollections of the frequency and size of these shipments. Some testified that the truck went to OIL about three times every four weeks; others testified that there were about three shipments every two weeks. Some testified that the trucks were typically half full; others testified that the trucks were almost always full. Two years of shipments of three half-full trucks every four weeks works out to about 407,000 gallons or 6,000 cubic yards of liquid waste. Three full trucks every two weeks for two years works out to about 811,250 gallons or 24,000 cubic yards of liquid waste.

Part II: Questions

Based on the evidence described above, the parties cross-move for partial summary judgment on the issue of scope of liability. The United States seeks a judgment that each defendant's liability is joint and several. Each defendant seeks a judgment that: (1) it is only severally liable for (2) a specific percentage of EPA's response costs. What are the best arguments in support of the position of the United States? What are the best arguments in support of the position of each defendant?

———

F. Contribution and Private Cost Recovery Actions

By definition, joint and several liability means that a defendant is liable for the full amount of a plaintiff's judgment—and that a plaintiff may compel any one defendant to satisfy the entire judgment. Thus, in a case like *Chem-Dyne*, if a court imposed joint and several liability on all of the nearly 300 potentially responsible parties, the government could in principle recover all of its response costs from a single arranger with deep pockets, even if that arranger contributed only a small percentage of the hazardous substances disposed of at the site. This result would serve CERCLA's goals of facilitating cleanup, conserving government cleanup resources, and imposing costs on responsible parties. But would it be a fair allocation of the liable parties' responsibility?

Just as the common law of torts developed the doctrine of joint and several liability to protect the interests of an innocent plaintiff vis-à-vis multiple liable defendants, it developed the doctrine of contribution to protect the interests of a jointly and severally liable defendant vis-à-vis other liable co-defendants. This doctrine allows a jointly and severally liable party that paid more than its "share" of a common liability to reduce its overpayment by recovering appropriate shares from other liable parties. Thus, a defendant in a tort action could become the plaintiff in a contribution claim. In the contribution claim, the paramount issue would be determining the appropriate share of liability to allocate to each party.

As *Chem-Dyne* illustrated, courts were quick to hold that applying evolving common law principles to CERCLA cases would, in appropriate cases (which turned out to mean most cases) result in the imposition of joint and several liability. Would a right of contribution follow? The Supreme Court described what happened:

> As originally enacted in 1980, CERCLA contained no provision expressly providing for a right of action for contribution. A number of District Courts nonetheless held that, although CERCLA did not mention the word "contribution," such a right arose either impliedly from provisions of the statute, or as a matter of federal common law. That conclusion was debatable in light of two decisions of this Court that refused to recognize implied or common-law rights to contribution in other federal statutes.

> Congress subsequently amended CERCLA in the Superfund Amendments and Reauthorization Act of 1986 (SARA), to provide an express cause of action for contribution, codified as CERCLA § 113(f)(1).

Cooper Inds., Inc. v. Aviall Servs., Inc., 542 U.S. 157, 162 (2004) (excerpted below, p. 855). Section 113(f)(1) provides:

> Any person may seek contribution from any other person who is liable or potentially liable under [section 107(a)], during or following any civil action under [section 106] or under [section 107(a)]. Such claims shall be brought in accordance with this section and the Federal Rules of Civil Procedure, and shall be governed by Federal law. In resolving contribution claims, the court may allocate response costs among liable parties using such equitable factors as the court determines are appropriate. Nothing in this subsection shall diminish the right of any person to bring an action for contribution in the absence of a civil action under [section 106] or [section 107].

42 U.S.C. § 9613(f)(1). How should a court determine a liable party's share in a CERCLA contribution case? The following opinion illustrates CERCLA's contribution provision in action.

United States v. Consolidation Coal Co.

345 F.3d 409 (6th Cir. 2003)

Judge DAUGHTREY:

Third-party defendant Neville Chemical Company appeals a district court decision holding it liable for a portion of the past and future costs of cleanup at the Buckeye Reclamation Landfill in Belmont County, Ohio. . . . Third-party plaintiffs Consolidation Coal Company ["Consol"] and Triangle Wire & Cable, Inc., brought an action under § 113 of [CERCLA], seeking a declaration of liability and equitable allocation of response costs to Neville Chemical. Although the chemical company stipulated that it had deposited 472,000 gallons of wastewater sludge from its Pennsylvania treatment plant in the landfill between December 1978 and February 1979, Neville Chemical claims that the district court was unreasonable in imposing any of the cleanup costs on it because the wastewater caused no harm. The district court found Neville Chemical liable under CERCLA and determined its equitable share of past and future response costs for cleanup of the landfill to be 6%.

. . . .

The record indicates that three different kinds of waste were deposited at the Buckeye Reclamation Landfill over the last seven decades. First, the landfill contains "gob," material left over from coal mining operations in the area from 1934 to 1954 and composed of coal, rock, clay, and other geological materials. The "gob" was left on the property before the area was a landfill. Second, the landfill contains industrial waste, which was disposed of primarily in a small area known as the "waste pit." The parties have stipulated the weight, type, and relative amount of the 45,000 tons of industrial waste that various entities deposited at the landfill from 1972 to 1980. Neville Chemical's share was calculated to be 4.78%. Third, the landfill contains municipal waste, between 755,000 and 955,000 tons of which were disposed of at the landfill from 1970 to 1991. All three types of waste contain hazardous substances and contribute to the current need for cleanup.

. . . [T]he USEPA placed the landfill on the list of Superfund sites in September 1983. In December 1984, the USEPA notified a number of companies that it considered them potentially responsible parties (PRPs) and requested that the companies conduct a remedial investigation and feasibility study. Neville Chemical declined to participate, but the other companies worked with the USEPA to develop an administrative consent order that required a remedial investigation and feasibility study, as well as an endangerment assessment. After evaluating the results of the remedial investigation and feasibility study, the USEPA selected construction of a solid waste landfill cap as the appropriate remedy, at a cost of $48 million to $52 million. When the USEPA notified non-participating PRPs of their potential liability, a number of them began to participate in the remediation process that resulted in a second administrative consent order. Neville Chemical again declined to participate.

In 1994, Consol filed a complaint for declaratory judgment, in part to determine liability and allocation of costs under CERCLA, and the United States filed a complaint for the recovery of costs . . . . Ten of the defendant PRPs filed a third-party complaint for contribution against 64 third-party defendants, including Neville Chemical. During this time, the USEPA and the cooperating PRPs, including Consol and Triangle Wire, continued to negotiate modifications to the remediation plan. Although invited to do so by the court, Neville Chemical once again declined to participate.

As a result of the negotiations, the USEPA modified its decision as to the chosen remediation for the site. The cost of the revised plan was estimated at $25 million, about one-half of the cost of the original plan. In March 1998, the court entered a consent decree between the United States and the cooperating PRPs providing for performance of the selected remediation at the landfill site. Consol, acting individually and on behalf of a number of other cooperating PRPs, and Triangle Wire continued to pursue their third-party action against Neville, seeking contribution under CERCLA's § 113.

After a long and detailed analysis, the district court ultimately ruled for Consol and Triangle Wire, determining that Neville Chemical was responsible for 6% of the past and future response cost of the Buckeye Reclamation Landfill. Neville appeals both the finding of liability and the allocation of a 6% equitable share.

A district court's allocation of response costs in a CERCLA contribution [action] will not be set aside in the absence of a finding that the district court abused its discretion . . . .

In addition, we set aside factual findings underlying the district court's allocation of response costs only if such findings are clearly erroneous . . . .

. . . [A] party is liable in a contribution claim under § 113(f)(1) if it was liable or potentially liable under § 107(a). The court found Neville Chemical liable to Consol and Triangle Wire under the § 113 claim because all four elements necessary for § 107(a) liability were met . . . . The district court did not abuse its discretion in finding Neville Chemical liable and, in fact, nowhere in its briefs does the chemical company contest the district court's conclusion of law that it meets all four elements of liability . . . .

The district court next recognized the broad discretion it had in making CERCLA contribution allocations using "such equitable factors as the court determines are appropriate." 42 U.S.C. § 9613(f)(1). It discussed commonly used equitable factors, including the six so-called "Gore factors" considered by Congress in enacting the law and the four "critical factors" identified . . . in *United States v. Davis*, 31 F.Supp.2d 45, 63 (D.R.I.1998), *aff'd*, 261 F.3d 1 (1st Cir.2001). Neither of these lists is intended to be exhaustive or exclusive, and "in any given case, a court may consider several factors, a few factors, or only one determining factor . . . depending on the totality of the circumstances presented to the court."

Although both Consol and Neville Chemical argued that the district court had to determine only Neville Chemical's equitable share, and not the share of any other PRP, the district court rejected that argument, reasoning that a fair and equitable allocation could only be achieved by comparing Neville's role as a PRP to other PRPs. The district court then divided the PRPs into four categories: generators and transporters of industrial waste; owners and operators of the landfill; Consol as the generator of the gob; and generators and transporters of the municipal solid waste. In allocating response costs, the district court focused primarily on the second "critical factor" from *Davis*, the PRP's varying levels of culpability, and two of the "Gore factors," the amount of waste and cooperation with the government, after carefully explaining why other factors were not helpful in deciding this particular case.

The court determined the equitable allocation across the four groups in the following way. First, the court assigned the industrial generators and transporters, including Neville Chemical, an equitable share of 60% of past and future costs, finding they were the most culpable. Their culpability arose from the fact that they knew or should have known, of the hazardous substances present in their waste, yet they disposed of their waste without seeking the permission required by the Belmont County Board of Commissioners. Second, the court assigned the owners and operators of the landfill a 25% equitable share of the response costs based on their lesser culpability, but also on their irresponsibility in not doing more to prevent the disposal of industrial wastes. Third, the court assigned Consol as generator of the "gob" a 10% equitable share, finding that Consol had knowledge that it contained hazardous substances, but recognizing at the same time that the material was deposited at the site between 1934 and 1952, at a time when there was nothing to prohibit such disposal. Finally, the court assigned the generators and transporters of municipal solid waste a 5% equitable share, because the group had little or no knowledge that the waste contained hazardous substances and because they were required to dispose of the waste at the landfill by rule of the Belmont County Board of Commissioners.

Within the 60% equitable share assigned to the industrial generators and transporters, the court used percentage weight of the waste as a fair and equitable way of determining individual shares. The parties stipulated that Neville Chemical was responsible for 4.78% of the industrial waste by percentage weight. The court rounded Neville's 4.78% share up to 5% based on the fact that Neville did not seek prior written approval of the Belmont County Board of Commissioners, as the county regulations required it to do. Triangle Wire is the only industrial generator which did seek prior approval, and the court found that this fact made that company marginally less culpable than its percentage weight would reflect. By rounding up Neville Chemical's individual share and decreasing Triangle Wire's share, the district court adjusted for Neville Chemical's violation of applicable local regulation and Triangle Wire's compliance. Thus, at this point in the court's analysis, Neville Chemical had an individual share of 5% of 60%, or 3%, of the past and future response costs.

The court considered one additional equitable factor in its analysis: cooperation with the government. The court concluded that Neville Chemical did not cooperate with the [Ohio Environmental Protection Agency] or the USEPA and that it did not participate in any efforts of the other PRPs to work with the government to investigate the site, design a remedy, abide by the remedy. In sum, the district court found that "Neville did not meaningfully cooperate in any phase of the CERCLA process in this case, although it was given ample opportunity to do so." Because of this "persistent, pervasive, and unjustified" lack of cooperation when Neville Chemical knew or should have known that its sludge had been deposited at the site, the court doubled the company's share of response costs from 3% to 6%. The court also noted that because the cooperating PRPs had negotiated a remedy that was half the cost of the originally approved remedy, doubling Neville Chemical's individual share would avoid the possibility of a windfall to that company, based on the successful efforts of the cooperating PRPs to find a less costly solution.

Neville Chemical argues on appeal that the district court abused its discretion in this allocation of chemical costs, given the opinion of Neville Chemical's expert that the company's waste caused no harm. However, the district court found the opinion of the expert unreliable because it was not based on conditions similar to those that existed in the waste pit.

Neville Chemical also argues that the district court abused its direction in allocating 60% of the response costs to the industrial generators and 5% of that share to Neville Chemical. Finally, the company argues that the district court abused its discretion in doubling Neville Chemical's share from 3% to 6%. However, all these arguments boil down to a disagreement with the particular equitable factors the district court chose to use and how the court applied them. After an independent review, we conclude that nothing in Neville's arguments leads us to a "definite and firm conviction that the trial court committed a clear error of judgment."

For the foregoing reasons, we AFFIRM the judgment of the district court as to Neville Chemical Company's liability and its individual share of pasts and future response costs . . . .

Notes and Questions

1. What is the relation between CERCLA's liability provision, § 107(a), and its contribution provision, § 113(f)(1)?

2. What factors did the district court use to determine the parties' appropriate shares of liability for the Buckeye Reclamation Landfill? The "Gore factors" mentioned in the opinion are so called because during the legislative process that resulted in CERCLA, then-Representative Al Gore proposed including them in the statute as factors that a court "may" consider in apportioning liability. Although the factors were not included in CERCLA as enacted, many courts have found it appropriate to consider them when deciding CERCLA contribution claims. The Gore factors are:

(1) the ability of the parties to demonstrate that their contribution to a discharge[,] release[,] or disposal of a hazardous waste can be distinguished;

(2) the amount of the hazardous waste involved;

(3) the degree of toxicity of the hazardous waste involved;

(4) the degree of involvement by the parties in the generation, transportation, treatment, storage, or disposal of the hazardous waste;

(5) the degree of care exercised by the parties with respect to the hazardous waste concerned, taking into account the characteristics of such hazardous waste; and

(6) the degree of cooperation by the parties with Federal, State, or local officials to prevent any harm to the public health or the environment.

United States v. R.W. Meyer, Inc., 932 F.2d 568, 571 (6th Cir. 1991). The four "critical factors" listed in the *Davis* case cited in the excerpt are:

1. The extent to which cleanup costs are attributable to wastes for which a party is responsible.

2. The party's level of culpability.

3. The degree to which the party benefited from disposal of the waste.

4. The party's ability to pay its share of the cost.

Davis, 31 F. Supp. 2d at 63. How do these two lists of equitable considerations differ? If, as the *Consolidation Coal* court stated, these lists are not exhaustive, what other factors might a court appropriately consider?

3. Think about what a complicated task the district court faced. The releases of hazardous substances resulted from the disposal of three different types of material. The claims involved at least 74 PRPs, including both owners/operators (Consol, whose mining operations produced the "gob" left at the site, as well as the subsequent owners who operated the landfill) and arrangers/transporters (the many parties who brought waste to, or whose waste was dumped at, the landfill). The district court decided that Neville's share could not be calculated in isolation. Do you agree? Did the court actually decide the share of liability to be allocated to each liable party? If not, should it have?

4. How did the district court allocate liability to the owners and operators of the landfill relative to the parties that arranged for or transported waste to the landfill for disposal? Do you agree with the court's allocation? Why or why not?

5. The district court began its analysis of Neville's share with the undisputed fact that Neville contributed 4.78 percent of the industrial waste deposited at the landfill between 1972 and 1980. That this figure was undisputed suggests that the parties had access to uncommonly good information about both the total amount of waste and the amount that came from Neville. Often such information is fragmentary, as in the Overflowing Industrial Landfill practice problem (p. 841 above), and the extrapolations that may be drawn from available information are hotly disputed.

But given that Neville's share of the industrial waste was undisputed, why shouldn't the court simply hold Neville liable for 4.78 percent of the response costs? How did the court reach its conclusion that Neville was liable for a six percent share? What factors did the court apply? Did the court apply the correct factors in the correct way?

First, was the court correct to "round up" from 4.78 percent to five percent based on Neville's non-compliance with county regulations? If compliance with county regulations matters, shouldn't the contribution plaintiff, Triangle Wire, get even *more* benefit for having been "the only industrial generator which did" comply?

Second, was the court correct to multiply Neville's rounded five percent share by the 60 percent share assigned to the group of parties responsible for placing industrial waste in the landfill? By doing this, the court computed that a five percent share of the "industrial generator" parties' liability worked out to a three percent share of the total liability. How did the court justify assigning the "industrial generator" group a 60 percent share?

Third, was the court correct to double Neville's computed three percent share because of Neville's lack of cooperation with the environmental agencies? The "degree of cooperation . . . with Federal, State, or local officials" is one of the Gore factors. Is it fair to penalize Neville for denying liability and insisting on its due process rights instead of joining, first, the AOC for the RI/FS and, second, the consent decree for the remedial action? What if the group of settling parties demanded that Neville pay 10 percent or 20 percent of the total costs as a condition for becoming part of the group?

6. How did the district court decide what share to assign to Consol for generating "gob" disposed of at the site? Why didn't the court compare the amount of "gob" to the amount of industrial waste at the site?

7. How is the exercise that the district court undertook in *Consolidation Coal* similar to what the district court did in *Burlington Northern*? How is it different?

8. What statutory standard must a trial judge apply when apportioning liability in a CERCLA contribution action? If the judge's decision is appealed, what is the appellate standard of review? How likely is it that a trial court's apportionment will be reversed?

9. In *Consolidation Coal*, the trial court assigned a five percent equitable share of liability to "generators and transporters of municipal solid waste." As you might imagine, given the breadth of CERCLA's list of hazardous substances, much household waste contains at least small amounts of hazardous substances, such as (to take just one obvious example) residues of chemicals used around the home. Under *Alcan*, p. 774, could arranging for disposal of such small quantities of hazardous substances make a person liable?

Recall (p. 693 above) that EPA excludes household waste from regulation as "hazardous waste" under Subtitle C of RCRA. In a 2002 amendment to CERCLA, Congress generally exempted residential, small business, and nonprofit generators of municipal solid waste from CERCLA liability under § 107 or 113 with respect to NPL sites. The provision defines municipal solid waste for purposes of the exemption, excludes certain wastes from the exempted category, and makes exceptions for, among other things, municipal solid waste that "has contributed significantly or could contribute significantly" to response costs or natural resource damages. 42 U.S.C. § 9607(p).

10. Liability allocations in CERCLA contribution cases are heavily fact-dependent. The situation in *Consolidation Coal*, a landfill with numerous arrangers, is a common pattern, but courts face a wide range of allocation scenarios.

A court in Michigan, for example, had to apportion liability between the operators of an electroplating business that became "a true environmental disaster area" and the owner that leased the property to the business. *United States v. R.W. Meyer, Inc.*, 932 F.2d 568, 570 (6th Cir. 1991). After holding all parties jointly and severally liable to the United States, the district court apportioned one-third of the liability to the electroplating company, one-third to the company's shareholder and officer who was personally liable as an operator, and one-third to the owner. The owner appealed. The Sixth Circuit affirmed, holding that "the trial court quite properly considered here not only the appellant's contribution to the toxic slough described above in a technical causative sense, but also its moral contribution as the owner of the site." *Id.* at 573.

In *Control Data Corp. v. S.C.S.C. Corp.*, 53 F.3d 930 (8th Cir. 1995), Control Data discovered a leak in its sewer line that released a hazardous substance, TCA, into groundwater. Control Data voluntarily analyzed the groundwater contamination, reported the release to state authorities, signed a consent decree agreeing to perform the cleanup, and built the required treatment plant. But the contaminated groundwater also contained another hazardous substance, PERC, which Control Data had never used or disposed of. The PERC was traced to a dry cleaner across the street from Control Data's plant. The plume of PERC from the dry cleaner had merged with the plume of TCA from Control Data; as a practical necessity Control Data treated the groundwater for both chemicals. Control Data sued the owners and operators of the dry cleaning property in contribution. The trial court found that the PERC constituted only 10 percent of the contamination. But the trial court also found that PERC is more toxic than TCA and more difficult to remove from groundwater. Based on these findings, the court allocated one-third of the liability to the dry cleaner parties. The court of appeals affirmed.

11. The plaintiff in a CERCLA contribution action must allege that it has been obligated to pay more than its fair share of liability for a release—either by paying to perform a response action or by paying to reimburse another party's (e.g., the government's) response costs. In *Consolidation Coal*, how did Consol become obligated to pay? Notice that the United States sued Consol and other parties for cost recovery, and then settled that lawsuit in a consent decree that resolved the cost recovery claim and also obligated the settling parties to perform a remedial action at the site. But Consol filed its contribution claim even *before* the government sued Consol, based in part on the fact that Consol had, along with other PRPs, agreed to perform the RI/FS under an administrative order on consent (AOC).

With an express right to contribution ensconced in CERCLA via SARA, parties that became obligated to pay for response actions brought contribution claims whenever it was convenient to do so. *How* a party became obligated to pay did not seem to matter: contribution plaintiffs sued because they had been adjudged jointly and severally liable, because they had settled a case brought by the government, because they had performed response actions under an AOC, or because they had performed response actions under a unilateral administrative order (UAO). Then a surprising ruling by a court of appeals caught the attention of the Supreme Court.

Cooper Industries, Inc. v. Aviall Services, Inc.

543 U.S. 157 (2004)

Justice THOMAS:

Section 113(f)(1) of [CERCLA] . . . specifies that a party may obtain contribution "during or following any civil action" under CERCLA § 106 or § 107(a). The issue we must decide is whether a private party who has not been sued under § 106 or § 107(a) may nevertheless obtain contribution under § 113(f)(1) from other liable parties. We hold that it may not.

I

Under CERCLA, the Federal Government . . . may recover its response costs under § 107, the "cost recovery" section of CERCLA . . . . Section 107(a) further provides that PRPs shall be liable for "any other necessary costs of response incurred by any other person consistent with the national contingency plan." § 107(a)(4)(B).

After CERCLA's enactment in 1980, litigation arose over whether . . . a private party [PRP] that had incurred response costs, but that had done so voluntarily and was not itself subject to suit, had a cause of action for cost recovery against other PRPs . . . .

. . . [L]itigation also ensued over the separate question whether a private entity that had been sued in a cost recovery action (by the Government or by another PRP) could obtain contribution from other PRPs . . . .

Congress subsequently amended CERCLA in the Superfund Amendments and Reauthorization Act of 1986 (SARA), to provide an express cause of action for contribution, . . . CERCLA § 113(f)(1) . . . . SARA also created a separate express right of contribution, § 113(f)(3)(B), for "[a] person who has resolved its liability to the United States or a State for some or all of a response action or for some or all of the costs of such action in an administrative or judicially approved settlement." In short, after SARA, CERCLA provided for a right to cost recovery in certain circumstances, § 107(a), and separate rights to contribution in other circumstances, §§ 113(f)(1), 113(f)(3)(B).

II

This case concerns four contaminated aircraft engine maintenance sites in Texas. Cooper Industries, Inc., owned and operated those sites until 1981, when it sold them to Aviall Services, Inc. Aviall operated the four sites for a number of years. Ultimately, Aviall discovered that both it and Cooper had contaminated the facilities when petroleum and other hazardous substances leaked into the ground and ground water through underground storage tanks and spills.

Aviall notified the Texas Natural Resource Conservation Commission (Commission) of the contamination. The Commission informed Aviall that it was violating state environmental laws, directed Aviall to clean up the site, and threatened to pursue an enforcement action if Aviall failed to undertake remediation. Neither the Commission nor the EPA, however, took judicial or administrative measures to compel cleanup.

Aviall cleaned up the properties under the State's supervision . . . . Aviall has incurred approximately $5 million in cleanup costs; the total costs may be even greater. In August 1997, Aviall filed this action against Cooper . . . . The original complaint asserted a claim for cost recovery under CERCLA § 107(a) [and] a separate claim for contribution under CERCLA § 113(f)(1) . . . . Aviall later amended the complaint, combining its two CERCLA claims into a single, joint CERCLA claim. That claim alleged that, pursuant to § 113(f)(1), Aviall was entitled to seek contribution from Cooper, as a PRP under § 107(a), for response costs and other liability Aviall incurred in connection with the Texas facilities.[4] . . .

Both parties moved for summary judgment, and the District Court granted Cooper's motion. The court held that Aviall, having abandoned its § 107 claim, sought contribution only under § 113(f)(1). The court held that § 113(f)(1) relief was unavailable to Aviall because it had not been sued under CERCLA § 106 or § 107. . . .

A divided panel of the Court of Appeals for the Fifth Circuit affirmed [but] . . . [o]n rehearing en banc, the Fifth Circuit reversed by a divided vote, holding that § 113(f)(1) allows a PRP to obtain contribution from other PRPs regardless of whether the PRP has been sued under § 106 or § 107. The court held that "[s]ection 113(f)(1) authorizes suits against PRPs in both its first and last sentence[,] which states without qualification that 'nothing' in the section shall 'diminish' any person's right to bring a contribution action in the absence of a section 106 or section 107(a) action." The court reasoned in part that "may" in § 113(f)(1) did not mean "may only." . . . We granted certiorari, and now reverse.

III

A

Section 113(f)(1) does not authorize Aviall's suit. The first sentence, the enabling clause that establishes the right of contribution, provides: "Any person *may* seek contribution . . . *during or following* any civil action under section 9606 of this title or under section 9607(a) of this title," 42 U.S.C. § 9613(f)(1) (emphasis added). The natural meaning of this sentence is that contribution may only be sought subject to the specified conditions, namely, "during or following" a specified civil action.

Aviall answers that "may" should be read permissively, such that "during or following" a civil action is one, but not the exclusive, instance in which a person may seek contribution. We disagree. First, as just noted, the natural meaning of "may" in the context of the enabling clause is that it authorizes certain contribution actions—ones that satisfy the subsequent specified condition and—no others.

Second, and relatedly, if § 113(f)(1) were read to authorize contribution actions at any time, regardless of the existence of a § 106 or § 107(a) civil action, then Congress need not have included the explicit "during or following" condition. In other words, Aviall's reading would render part of the statute entirely superfluous, something we

---

4. Aviall asserts that it framed its claim in the manner compelled by Fifth Circuit precedent holding that a § 113 claim is a type of § 107 claim.

are loath to do. Likewise, if § 113(f)(1) authorizes contribution actions at any time, § 113(f)(3)(B), which permits contribution actions after settlement, is equally super-fluous. There is no reason why Congress would bother to specify conditions under which a person may bring a contribution claim, and at the same time allow contribution actions absent those conditions.

The last sentence of § 113(f)(1), the saving clause, does not change our conclusion. That sentence provides: "Nothing in this subsection shall diminish the right of any person to bring an action for contribution in the absence of a civil action under section 9606 of this title or section 9607 of this title." The sole function of the sentence is to clarify that § 113(f)(1) does nothing to "diminish" any cause(s) of action for contribution that may exist independently of § 113(f)(1). In other words, the sentence rebuts any presumption that the express right of contribution provided by the enabling clause is the exclusive cause of action for contribution available to a PRP. The sentence, however, does not itself establish a cause of action; nor does it expand § 113(f)(1) to authorize contribution actions not brought "during or following" a § 106 or § 107(a) civil action; nor does it specify what causes of action for contribution, if any, exist outside § 113(f)(1) . . . .

Our conclusion follows not simply from § 113(f)(1) itself, but also from the whole of § 113. As noted above, § 113 provides two express avenues for contribution: § 113(f)(1) ("during or following" specified civil actions) and § 113(f)(3)(B) (after an administrative or judicially approved settlement that resolves liability to the United States or a State). Section 113(g)(3) then provides two corresponding 3-year limitations periods for contribution actions[. One begins at the date of judgment, § 113(g)(3)(A); the other begins] at the date of settlement, § 113(g)(3)(B). Notably absent from § 113(g)(3) is any provision for starting the limitations period if a judgment or settlement never occurs, as is the case with a purely voluntary cleanup. The lack of such a provision supports the conclusion that, to assert a contribution claim under § 113(f), a party must satisfy the conditions of either § 113(f)(1) or § 113(f)(3)(B).

Each side insists that the purpose of CERCLA bolsters its reading of § 113(f)(1). Given the clear meaning of the text, there is no need to resolve this dispute or to consult the purpose of CERCLA at all . . . . Section 113(f)(1) authorizes contribution claims only "during or following" a civil action under § 106 or § 107(a), and it is undisputed that Aviall has never been subject to such an action.[5] Aviall therefore has no § 113(f)(1) claim.

B

Aviall . . . contend[s] that, in the alternative to an action for contribution under § 113(f)(1), Aviall may recover costs under § 107(a)(4)(B) even though it is a PRP. The dissent would have us so hold. We decline to address the issue. Neither the District Court, nor the Fifth Circuit panel, nor the Fifth Circuit sitting en banc considered Aviall's § 107 claim . . . .

---

5. Neither has Aviall been subject to an administrative order under § 106; thus, we need not decide whether such an order would qualify as a "civil action under [section 106 or 107]."

. . . .

C

In addition to leaving open whether Aviall may seek cost recovery under § 107, we decline to decide whether Aviall has an implied right to contribution under § 107 . . . . [W]e need not and do not decide today whether any judicially implied right of contribution survived the passage of SARA.

We hold only that § 113(f)(1) does not support Aviall's suit. We therefore reverse the judgment of the Fifth Circuit and remand the case for further proceedings consistent with this opinion.

[The dissenting opinion of Justice Ginsburg is omitted.]

Notes and Questions

1. Do you agree that § 113(f)(1) is as clear as the Court held? If it is, then why did many federal courts, in the years between SARA's enactment and the *Cooper Industries* decision, allow contribution claims by PRPs that had not been sued under § 106 or 107?

2. Each party in *Cooper Industries* argued that its construction of § 113(f)(1) better advanced the objectives of CERCLA. Can you make such an argument in support of each side? Which statutory objectives are best supported by each interpretation? Was it appropriate for the Supreme Court to refuse even to consider whether its decision would advance or hinder CERCLA's goals? Why or why not?

3. According to *Cooper Industries*, a responsible party that incurs response costs is allowed to sue other potentially responsible parties for contribution only if the would-be contribution plaintiff has: (1) per § 113(f)(1), been sued under § 106 (by whom? for what?); or (2) per § 113(f)(1), been sued under § 107 (by whom? for what?); or (3) per § 113(f)(3)(B), "resolved its liability to the United States or a State for some or all of a response action or for some or all of the costs of such action in an administrative or judicially approved settlement." 42 U.S.C. § 9613(f)(3)(B). How could a responsible party resolve its liability to the government without being sued? Conversely, if a responsible party had neither been sued nor settled, how would it become obligated to pay response costs in the first place? How did Aviall end up incurring response costs without being sued? Are there any other circumstances under which a responsible party might perform response actions without either a lawsuit or a settlement?

4. Many CERCLA practitioners predicted that *Cooper Industries* would discourage responsible parties from voluntarily undertaking Superfund cleanups. *See, e.g.,* Michael Mazzone et al., *New Supreme Court Decision Discourages Voluntary Cleanup Under CERCLA*, 42 Houston Law. 52 (Jan./Feb. 2005). Moreover, by the time of the *Cooper Industries* decision, a goodly number of parties already had incurred response costs voluntarily, assuming that they would be able to get part of their money back through contribution suits. After the Court's decision, what recourse did these parties have? If you were counsel to one of these parties, what would you have advised?

5. EPA and the Department of Justice responded to *Cooper Industries* by issuing a joint guidance memo and revising certain model documents used as templates for agreements with responsible parties. In particular, EPA's former model "Administrative Order on Consent" was renamed the model "Administrative Settlement Agreement and Order on Consent." Why do you think the agencies made this change?

6. In *Cooper Industries*, the Court, over the dissent of two Justices, declined to decide whether a responsible party unable to bring suit for contribution under § 113(f) could instead seek cost recovery under § 107. The Court put the issue off only for a short while.

United States v. Atlantic Research Corp.
551 U.S. 128 (2007)

JUSTICE THOMAS:

. . . In this case, we must decide a question left open in [*Cooper Industries*]: whether [CERCLA] § 107(a) provides so-called potentially responsible parties (PRPs) with a cause of action to recover costs from other PRPs. We hold that it does.

Courts have frequently grappled with whether and how PRPs may recoup CERCLA-related costs from other PRPs. The questions lie at the intersection of two statutory provisions—CERCLA §§ 107(a) and 113(f). Section 107(a) defines four categories of PRPs, and makes them liable for, among other things:

"(A) all costs of removal or remedial action incurred by the United States Government or a State or an Indian tribe not inconsistent with the national contingency plan; [and]

"(B) any other necessary costs of response incurred by any other person consistent with the national contingency plan."

Enacted as part of [SARA], § 113(f) authorizes one PRP to sue another for contribution in certain circumstances.

Prior to the advent of § 113(f)'s express contribution right, some courts held that § 107(a)(4)(B) provided a cause of action for a private party to recover voluntarily incurred response costs and to seek contribution after having been sued. After SARA's enactment, however, some Courts of Appeals believed it necessary to "direc[t] traffic between" § 107(a) and § 113(f). As a result, many Courts of Appeals held that § 113(f) was the exclusive remedy for PRPs. But as courts prevented PRPs from suing under § 107(a), they expanded § 113(f) to allow PRPs to seek "contribution" even in the absence of a suit under § 106 or § 107(a).

In *Cooper Industries,* we held that a private party could seek contribution from other liable parties only after having been sued under § 106 or § 107(a). This narrower interpretation of § 113(f) caused several Courts of Appeals to reconsider whether PRPs have rights under § 107(a)(4)(B), an issue we declined to address in *Cooper Industries*. After revisiting the issue, some courts have permitted § 107(a) actions by PRPs. However, at least one court continues to hold that § 113(f) provides the exclusive cause of action available to PRPs . . . .

In this case, respondent Atlantic Research leased property at the Shumaker Naval Ammunition Depot, a facility operated by the Department of Defense. At the site, Atlantic Research retrofitted rocket motors for petitioner United States. Using a high-pressure water spray, Atlantic Research removed pieces of propellant from the motors. It then burned the propellant pieces. Some of the resultant wastewater and burned fuel contaminated soil and ground water at the site.

Atlantic Research cleaned the site at its own expense and then sought to recover some of its costs by suing the United States under both §§ 107(a) and 113(f). After our decision in *Cooper Industries* foreclosed relief under § 113(f), Atlantic Research amended its complaint to seek relief under § 107(a) and federal common law. The United States moved to dismiss, arguing that § 107(a) does not allow PRPs (such as Atlantic Research) to recover costs. The District Court granted the motion to dismiss, relying on a case decided prior to our decision in *Cooper Industries.*

The Court of Appeals for the Eighth Circuit reversed. Recognizing that *Cooper Industries* undermined the reasoning of its prior precedent, the Court of Appeals joined the Second and Seventh Circuits in holding that § 113(f) does not provide "the exclusive route by which [PRPs] may recover cleanup costs." The court reasoned that § 107(a)(4)(B) authorized suit by any person other than the persons permitted to sue under § 107(a)(4)(A). Accordingly, it held that § 107(a)(4)(B) provides a cause of action to Atlantic Research. To prevent perceived conflict between §§ 107(a)(4)(B) and 113(f)(1), the Court of Appeals reasoned that PRPs that "have been subject to §§ 106 or 107 enforcement actions are still required to use § 113, thereby ensuring its continued vitality." We granted certiorari, and now affirm.

The parties' dispute centers on what "other person[s]" may sue under § 107(a)(4)(B). The Government argues that "any other person" refers to any person not identified as a PRP in §§ 107(a)(1)-(4). In other words, subparagraph (B) permits suit only by non-PRPs and thus bars Atlantic Research's claim. Atlantic Research counters that subparagraph (B) takes its cue from subparagraph (A), not the earlier paragraphs (1)-(4). In accord with the Court of Appeals, Atlantic Research believes that subparagraph (B) provides a cause of action to anyone except the United States, a State, or an Indian tribe—the persons listed in subparagraph (A). We agree with Atlantic Research.

Statutes must "be read as a whole." Applying that maxim, the language of subparagraph (B) can be understood only with reference to subparagraph (A). The provisions are adjacent and have remarkably similar structures. Each concerns certain costs that have been incurred by certain entities and that bear a specified relationship to the national contingency plan. Bolstering the structural link, the text also denotes a relationship between the two provisions. By using the phrase "other necessary costs," subparagraph (B) refers to and differentiates the relevant costs from those listed in subparagraph (A).

In light of the relationship between the subparagraphs, it is natural to read the phrase "any other person" by referring to the immediately preceding subparagraph (A), which permits suit only by the United States, a State, or an Indian tribe. The phrase "any other person" therefore means any person other than those three. Consequently, the plain language of subparagraph (B) authorizes cost-recovery actions by any private party, including PRPs.

The Government's interpretation makes little textual sense. In subparagraph (B), the phrase "any other necessary costs" and the phrase "any other person" both refer to antecedents—"costs" and "person[s]"—located in some previous statutory provision. Although "any other necessary costs" clearly references the costs in subparagraph (A), the Government would inexplicably interpret "any other person" to refer not to the persons listed in subparagraph (A) but to the persons listed as PRPs in paragraphs (1)-(4). Nothing in the text of § 107(a)(4)(B) suggests an intent to refer to antecedents located in two different statutory provisions. Reading the statute in the manner suggested by the Government would destroy the symmetry of §§ 107(a)(4)(A) and (B) and render subparagraph (B) internally confusing.

Moreover, the statute defines PRPs so broadly as to sweep in virtually all persons likely to incur cleanup costs. Hence, if PRPs do not qualify as "any other person" for purposes of § 107(a)(4)(B), it is unclear what private party would. The Government posits that § 107(a)(4)(B) authorizes relief for "innocent" private parties—for instance, a landowner whose land has been contaminated by another. But even parties not responsible for contamination may fall within the broad definitions of PRPs in §§ 107(a)(1)-(4). The Government's reading of the text logically precludes all PRPs, innocent or not, from recovering cleanup costs. Accordingly, accepting the Government's interpretation would reduce the number of potential plaintiffs to almost zero, rendering § 107(a)(4)(B) a dead letter.

. . . .

The Government also argues that our interpretation will create friction between §§ 107(a) and 113(f), the very harm courts of appeals have previously tried to avoid. In particular, the Government maintains that our interpretation, by offering PRPs a choice between §§ 107(a) and 113(f), effectively allows PRPs to circumvent § 113(f)'s shorter statute of limitations. See 42 U.S.C. §§ 9613(g)(2)-(3). Furthermore, the Government argues, PRPs will eschew equitable apportionment under § 113(f) in favor of joint and several liability under § 107(a). Finally, the Government contends that our interpretation eviscerates the settlement bar set forth in § 113(f)(2).

. . . .

Section 113(f) explicitly grants PRPs a right to contribution. Contribution is defined as the "tortfeasor's right to collect from others responsible for the same tort after the tortfeasor has paid more than his or her proportionate share, the shares being determined as a percentage of fault." Black's Law Dictionary 353 (8th ed.2004). Nothing in § 113(f) suggests that Congress used the term "contribution" in anything other than this traditional sense. The statute authorizes a PRP to seek contribution "during or following" a suit under § 106 or § 107(a). Thus, § 113(f)(1) permits suit before or after the establishment of common liability. In either case, a PRP's right to contribution under § 113(f)(1) is contingent upon an inequitable distribution of common liability among liable parties.

By contrast, § 107(a) permits recovery of cleanup costs but does not create a right to contribution. A private party may recover under § 107(a) without any establishment of liability to a third party. Moreover, § 107(a) permits a PRP to recover only the costs it has "incurred" in cleaning up a site. When a party pays to satisfy a settlement agreement or a court judgment, it does not incur its own costs of response. Rather, it reimburses other parties for costs that those parties incurred.

Accordingly, the remedies available in §§ 107(a) and 113(f) complement each other by providing causes of action "to persons in different procedural circumstances." Section 113(f)(1) authorizes a contribution action to PRPs with common liability stemming from an action instituted under § 106 or § 107(a). And § 107(a) permits cost recovery (as distinct from contribution) by a private party that has itself incurred cleanup costs. Hence, a PRP that pays money to satisfy a settlement agreement or a court judgment may pursue § 113(f) contribution. But by reimbursing response costs paid by other parties, the PRP has not incurred its own costs of response and therefore cannot recover under § 107(a). As a result, though eligible to seek contribution under § 113(f)(1), the PRP cannot simultaneously seek to recover the same expenses under § 107(a). Thus, at least in the case of reimbursement, the PRP cannot choose the 6-year statute of limitations for cost-recovery actions over the shorter limitations period for § 113(f) contribution claims.[6]

For similar reasons, a PRP could not avoid § 113(f)'s equitable distribution of reimbursement costs among PRPs by instead choosing to impose joint and several liability on another PRP in an action under § 107(a). The choice of remedies simply does not exist. In any event, a defendant PRP in such a § 107(a) suit could blunt any inequitable distribution of costs by filing a § 113(f) counterclaim. Resolution of a § 113(f) counterclaim would necessitate the equitable apportionment of costs among the liable parties, including the PRP that filed the § 107(a) action.

Finally, permitting PRPs to seek recovery under § 107(a) will not eviscerate the settlement bar set forth in § 113(f)(2). That provision prohibits § 113(f) contribution claims against "[a] person who has resolved its liability to the United States or a State in an administrative or judicially approved settlement. . . ." The settlement bar does not by its terms protect against cost-recovery liability under § 107(a). For several reasons, we doubt this supposed loophole would discourage settlement. First, as stated above, a defendant PRP may trigger equitable apportionment by filing a § 113(f) counterclaim. A district court applying traditional rules of equity would undoubtedly consider any prior settlement as part of the liability calculus. Second, the settlement

---

6. We do not suggest that §§ 107(a)(4)(B) and 113(f) have no overlap at all. For instance, we recognize that a PRP may sustain expenses pursuant to a consent decree following a suit under § 106 or § 107(a). In such a case, the PRP does not incur costs voluntarily but does not reimburse the costs of another party. We do not decide whether these compelled costs of response are recoverable under § 113(f), § 107(a), or both. For our purposes, it suffices to demonstrate that costs incurred voluntarily are recoverable only by way of § 107(a)(4)(B), and costs of reimbursement to another person pursuant to a legal judgment or settlement are recoverable only under § 113(f). Thus, at a minimum, neither remedy swallows the other, contrary to the Government's argument.

bar continues to provide significant protection from contribution suits by PRPs that have inequitably reimbursed the costs incurred by another party. Third, settlement carries the inherent benefit of finally resolving liability as to the United States or a State.

Because the plain terms of § 107(a)(4)(B) allow a PRP to recover costs from other PRPs, the statute provides Atlantic Research with a cause of action. We therefore affirm the judgment of the Court of Appeals.

Notes and Questions

1. The Supreme Court noted that after SARA's enactment and before the *Cooper Industries* decision, "many Courts of Appeals held that § 113(f) was the exclusive remedy for PRPs." Why would many courts of appeals have reached this conclusion, which the Supreme Court eventually held was incorrect? Are there any policy objectives of CERCLA that would be served by refusing to allow responsible parties to bring cost recovery claims under § 107(a)?

2. In *Atlantic Research*, the United States government was the defendant. In many other CERCLA cases, of course, the United States government is the plaintiff. Sometimes, as we have seen, the United States government may play both roles in the same case: EPA, exercising its response and enforcement authorities, might sue nonfederal PRPs, who in turn might seek contribution from a federal agency (such as the Defense Department) alleged to be liable as an owner, operator, or arranger. How do you think the government's varied roles affected the position the United States took in *Atlantic Research* (or, as *amicus curiae*, in *Cooper Industries*)? Does the *Atlantic Research* decision allow EPA to relegate a private party to a contribution claim (instead of a cost recovery claim) simply by asking the Department of Justice to sue the private party? How do you think such issues are, or should be, handled within the Executive Branch?

3. The *Atlantic Research* decision rescued the claim that Aviall had lost in *Cooper Industries*. On remand in *Cooper Industries*, the district court held that Aviall could not sue under § 107(a) and entered judgment for Cooper. Aviall appealed. While the appeal was pending, the Supreme Court decided *Atlantic Research*, so the court of appeals vacated and remanded. Finally confronting the merits, the district court decided cross-motions for summary judgment with respect to whether the response costs Aviall incurred were consistent with the NCP. The court held that some were, some were not, and some involved disputed material issues of fact to be decided at trial. *See Aviall Servs., Inc. v. Cooper Inds., Inc.*, 2006 WL 2263305 (N.D. Tex. Aug. 8, 2006), *vacated*, 235 Fed. Appx. 222 (5th Cir. 2007); 572 F. Supp. 2d 676 (N.D. Tex. 2008) (granting summary judgment in part); 2009 WL 498133 (N.D. Tex. Feb. 27, 2009) (same).

4. Suppose the Supreme Court had ruled differently, and had held that responsible parties were limited to contribution claims and could not sue for cost recovery. Would such a ruling have rendered § 107(a)(4)(B) superfluous? To put it differently, can you think of any private parties that would *not* be PRPs but might nevertheless incur response costs for which they might seek cost recovery?

Continuing our thought experiment, if the Court had ruled differently in *Atlantic Research*, would responsible parties that voluntarily incurred response costs have had any remaining option for obtaining relief from other responsible parties? Recall that in *Cooper Industries*—and again in *Atlantic Research*, 552 U.S. at 141 n.8—the Court explicitly declined to decide whether § 107(a), by imposing joint and several liability, also created an implied right of contribution. What explains the Court's reluctance to decide this issue?

5. In *Atlantic Research* the government argued that allowing responsible parties to sue for cost recovery would make § 113 redundant as a practical matter. A § 107 cost recovery claim, the government observed, has advantages over a contribution claim: the ability to hold defendants jointly and severally liable and a long limitations period in which to sue.

The Court's first response was to deny that the responsible party would have a choice. A responsible party that voluntarily incurred response costs (that is, without being sued or settling with the government) could sue *only* under § 107(a), and a responsible party that reimbursed another party's response costs could sue *only* under § 113(f). Do you find persuasive the court's explanation that a party does not "incur" response costs by paying a cost recovery claim? Even if persuasive, is the Court's analysis complete? The Court acknowledged a gap in its analysis regarding "compelled costs," such as those incurred by an allegedly liable party that agrees to perform response actions "pursuant to a consent decree following a suit under § 106 or § 107(a)."

The "compelled costs" scenario is very common. For example, EPA frequently sues to recover costs incurred for one or more removal actions, a PA/SI, and an RI/FS, even before beginning to perform the remedial action. Such cases often settle via a consent decree under which one or more defendants agrees to pay some fraction of the government's costs and to design, construct, and operate the remedial action. Consider whether each of these potentially responsible parties would be able to bring a § 113(f) claim under *Cooper Industries* and/or a § 107(a) claim under *Atlantic Research*:

- A party that agreed in a consent decree to reimburse some fraction of the government's response costs and to perform a remedial action.

- A party that agreed in a consent decree to pay for some fraction of the cost of a remedial action that another party would perform, but that did not itself agree to perform a remedial action.

- A party that agreed in an administrative settlement agreement and order on consent to perform a removal action.

- A party that received a unilateral administrative order directing the party to perform a remedial action, complied with the order, and performed the remedial action as required by the order.

Did the Supreme Court give answers for these scenarios? For an award-winning student essay on "compelled costs," see Luis Inaraja Vera, *Compelled Costs Under CERCLA: Incompatible Remedies, Joint and Several Liability, and Tort Law*, 17 Vt. J. Envtl. L. 394 (2016).

6. The Court also questioned whether responsible parties would ever really be able to hold other responsible parties jointly and severally liable for response costs. To limit its liability to an allocated share, the court reasoned, a defendant would simply file a § 113(f) counterclaim against the "volunteer" responsible party plaintiff. (Could a defendant do that under *Cooper Industries*)?

If a responsible party that voluntarily incurred response costs brings a cost recovery action and the defendant counterclaims for contribution, is the situation really the same as it would have been had the plaintiff brought a contribution claim in the first instance? Would the burden of proof be the same in both situations? Would the situations be different from each other if (as was not the case in *Atlantic Research*) the plaintiff sued multiple defendants? What if some of the defendants were insolvent?

7. The government also argued that allowing responsible parties to bring cost recovery claims would "eviscerate the settlement bar set forth in § 113(f)(2)," which provides that a "person who has resolved its liability to the United States or a State in an administrative or judicially approved settlement shall not be liable for claims for contribution regarding matters addressed in the settlement." Why would Congress, in the very provision that expressly granted a right to contribution, protect certain parties from contribution claims?

The Court gave three reasons why its holding would not discourage settlement. How persuasive were these reasons? Imagine that you represent a responsible party in a case in which the EPA has incurred $1 million in response costs and a private party is performing a response action estimated at $4 million. You estimate that in a contribution action, a court would hold your client liable for a 25 percent equitable share. If EPA offers to settle its claims against your client in exchange for paying EPA's $1 million of response costs, would you recommend the settlement: (a) if the private party has no right to sue your client for cost recovery or (b) if the private party has a right to sue your client for cost recovery? Would your answer change if EPA were offering to settle a $2 million claim for $1 million? If the private party response action were estimated to cost $10 million? If you knew that absent a settlement, EPA would sue your client, but not the other private party, for response costs? If you thought the court would probably allocate to your client a 50 percent share of liability? A 10 percent share?

8. It takes two to settle, of course. In CERCLA litigation, settlement may require the agreement of many parties—multiple PRPs and sometimes multiple plaintiffs (such as the United States and a state). Think about the CERCLA court opinions you have read. What incentives does the case law interpreting CERCLA, considered as a whole, provide to plaintiffs and defendants with respect to settlement?

Although the court decisions in this chapter have involved judicial resolution of disputed factual or legal issues, most CERCLA litigation—like most civil litigation generally—is resolved, sooner or later, by settlement. Indeed, even in the majority of the cases you have studied in this chapter, settlement was the predominant method of resolution, with only one or a few defendants litigating to the bitter end.

Congress anticipated and desired that CERCLA plaintiffs and defendants would negotiate settlement agreements. Thus, the statute includes provisions granting a settling party the right to bring its own contribution action and protecting a settling party from contribution claims by others. What else does CERCLA say about settlements? That is the subject of the next section.

G. Settlements

CERCLA says little about purely private settlements of CERCLA claims. If, for example, Consol and Neville, p. 848 above, had been able to agree on an allocation of costs for cleanup of the Buckeye Reclamation Landfill, they could have done so on any terms and in any form that they wished. For settlements involving the government, however, CERCLA requires some procedural formalities, imposes some substantive limitations, and specifies some consequences.

Most, but not all, of CERCLA's important provisions regulating settlements are in § 122, 42 U.S.C. § 9622, which Congress enacted as part of the SARA amendments, partly in response to concerns about "sweetheart deals" offered to defendants during the Reagan Administration. Section 122's provisions distinguish between the government's basic enforcement choices under CERCLA: to perform a response action at its own expense and seek cost recovery from responsible parties, or to induce responsible parties to perform a response action at their expense.

CERCLA imposes few requirements on cost recovery settlements. EPA (or another government agency that incurred response costs) may settle cost recovery claims by an administrative order on consent, subject to two limitations: first, a cost recovery claim may not be settled administratively by EPA (or other agency) if the claim has been referred to the Department of Justice for litigation; second, even if the claim has not been referred for litigation, the Attorney General must approve the settlement if the total response costs for the facility exceed $500,000. *See* 42 U.S.C. § 9622(h). The settling agency must provide public notice of the proposed settlement and must accept and consider public comments before the settlement may become final. *Id.* § 9622(i). Cost recovery claims that have been referred to the Department of Justice are typically resolved in a consent decree; we describe the consent decree process below, p. 867.

When an EPA settlement requires a responsible party to undertake a response action, the requirements depend on the type of response action to be performed. In general, EPA may negotiate agreements under which a responsible party will perform removal actions. *See* 42 U.S.C. §§ 9604(a)(1), (a)(2), 9622(a) (CERCLA §§ 104(a)(1), (a)(2), 122(a)). Congress was a little more cautious with respect to responsible party performance of an RI/FS. Because of that study's critical importance to EPA's choice of remedial action, Congress explicitly required EPA to determine "that the party is qualified to conduct the RI/FS" and to ensure that a "qualified person" assists in overseeing and reviewing the conduct of the RI/FS. *Id.* § 9604(a)(1).

CERCLA's strictest requirements apply to settlements under which a responsible party agrees to perform a remedial action. Substantively, CERCLA prohibits such settlements from containing general releases of liability, requiring instead that the resolution of settling defendants' liability take the form of a covenant not to sue that takes effect only upon completion of the remedial action, that is conditioned on satisfactory performance, and that includes a "reopener" in the event the new information or unknown conditions demonstrate that the originally selected remedial action is not protective of human health or the environment. 42 U.S.C. § 9622(f). Moreover, the settlement must provide stipulated penalties for a settling defendant's failure to perform. *Id.* § 9621(e)(2). Procedurally, CERCLA authorizes EPA to invoke a special negotiation process, including a 120-day enforcement moratorium, if EPA determines that doing so will facilitate a settlement and expedite remedial action. *Id.* § 9622(e). Further, CERCLA specifies the procedural mechanism to be used for any settlement under which a responsible party will perform remedial action: the settlement agreement must be set forth in a judicial consent decree, subjected to public notice and comment, and thereafter approved not just by the parties but also by the court. *Id.* § 9622(d). Why do you think Congress imposed such elaborate substantive and procedural requirements on remedial action settlements?

The structure of CERCLA's liability scheme gives the government substantial leverage in settlement negotiations. It is not particularly unusual for a government plaintiff to obtain complete or nearly complete relief in a CERCLA settlement. Often the terms of settlement between the government and a group of responsible parties are easier to work out than the agreement among the responsible parties about how to share the costs.

The government does sometimes compromise its CERCLA claims based on various litigation risks or a desire to save time and litigation effort. In addition, government plaintiffs in settlement negotiations sometimes offer incentives for desired outcomes. Thus the government may reward parties that agree to undertake response actions by accepting only partial recovery of costs the government already incurred, or may reward parties that settle quickly by accepting payments smaller than those parties' estimated "share" of response costs. In such circumstances, the government usually pursues nonsettling parties to make up the difference—a strategy made possible by other provisions of CERCLA that specify how a settlement agreed to by some defendants affects the rights of other defendants that did not settle.

We have already seen two of these provisions in *Atlantic Research*, p. 859 above: a party that resolves its liability to the United States or a State in an administrative or judicially approved settlement obtains a right to seek contribution from other potentially responsible parties under § 113(f)(3)(B), and is itself protected from claims for contribution "with respect to matters addressed in the settlement" under § 113(f)(2). What is the purpose of protecting settling defendants from contribution claims by non-settling defendants?

Section 113(f)(2) continues: "Such settlement does not discharge any of the other potentially liable persons unless its terms so provide, but it reduces the potential liability of the others by the amount of the settlement." How does that sentence affect non-settling defendants? Suppose that the United States incurred $1 million in response costs for a particular release, and the liable parties are the facility owner as well as three arrangers (A, B, and C) who each arranged for disposal of the same amount of the same hazardous substance. Assume that early in the litigation the court rules that joint and several liability is appropriate under *Chem-Dyne* and *Burlington Northern*. If the United States then settles with the site owner for $250,000, what would be the liability of A, B, and C to the United States? Next, suppose that A offers to settle with the United States for $150,000, and the United States accepts the offer because A was highly cooperative with EPA when the site was first discovered. What would be the liability of B and C to the United States? Now suppose the owner files a contribution claim against B and C, and the court concludes that the owner is more culpable than the arrangers for the conditions at the site, so the appropriate shares of liability are 70 percent for the owner and 10 percent each for A, B, and C. What would be B and C's liability to the United States? To the owner? What would be the owner's liability to B and C?

As you can tell, § 113(f)(2) means that a CERCLA settlement by some defendants has powerful effects on nonsettling defendants. And settlements that include only some of the potentially responsible parties, either because of EPA's negotiating strategy or some defendants' unwillingness to agree to the terms that other defendants will accept, have been a recurring phenomenon: think about *United States v. Monsanto*, p. 766 above, *United States v. Alcan*, p. 774 above, *United States v. American Cyanamid*, p. 815 above, and *United States v. Consolidation Coal*, p. 848, above. As a result, although CERCLA's requirement that certain settlements be embodied in a consent decree approved by a court after public notice and comment was perhaps intended partly or mainly to protect the public from the risk of poorly negotiated deals, opposition to proposed consent decrees had most often come from nonsettling defendants.

When the government and some or all defendants have agreed to a settlement, how does a court decide whether to approve the consent decree? The principles announced in leading cases decided by the First Circuit have gained widespread acceptance. A court must conclude that the settlement is procedurally and substantively fair, reasonable, and faithful to the objectives of CERCLA. *United States v. Cannons Engineering Corp.*, 899 F.2d 79 (1st Cir. 1990). But the court is highly deferential to the government's assessments of litigation risk, settlement strategy, the appropriate classifications of PRPs into groups for settlement purposes, and the timing and sequence of settlement offers. *United States v. Charles George Trucking, Inc.*, 34 F.3d 1081 (1st Cir. 1994). And the standard for appellate review of a trial judge's decision — affirming absent a "manifest abuse of discretion" — is deferential in turn. *Id.* As a result of these legal standards, CERCLA consent decrees almost always have won judicial approval, even if they have had quite harsh effects on nonsettling defendants.

Practice Problems

Problem 1: Settling OILI

Review the facts of the Overflowing Industrial Landfill hypothetical, p. 841, above. Assume that the trial court held that all the defendants are jointly and severally liable to the government for all costs of responding to the release of hazardous substances at OIL. Every defendant sued every other defendant. In the next phase of the case, the court will decide the share of liability to be apportioned to each defendant. Taking one of the defendants as your client, prepare a written or oral argument, as assigned by your instructor, describing your client's claim and advocating for an appropriate share for your client.

Problem 2: The Dorsay Mining District

The 250-square-mile Dorsay Mining District lies in the heart of the homeland of the Shotonee Tribe; the western third of the Mining District is within the Shotonee Indian Reservation. Beginning in the 1880s, the MALARCO Mining Company, along with a number of other mining companies, owned and operated dozens of mines and mills in the Dorsay Mining District. Over more than a century, these companies produced prodigious quantities of lead, zinc, silver, and gold, creating many fortunes for the families who controlled these companies. The mining operations were served by the Orange Pacific Railroad (OPRR). OPRR transported ore from the mines to the mills in the District and transported concentrated metals from the mills to metal smelters out of state. OPRR built a large railyard in the District, where it stored diesel fuels and maintained engines and rail cars.

As a result of the mining and railroad operations, soils, groundwater, surface waters, and sediments in the Dorsay Mining District are severely polluted. In the groundwater, the major contaminant is diesel fuel from OPRR's railyard. In the soil, surface waters, and sediments, the major contaminants are metals, including arsenic, lead, and zinc from MALARCO's mining and milling activities. The zinc contamination has virtually extirpated the native trout that used to inhabit the Dorsay River, which runs east to west through the Mining District. Lead contamination in the wetlands adjacent to the Dorsay River kills hundreds of tundra swans every year during spring migration. In towns within the Dorsay Mining District, cases of lead poisoning in children have been traced to lead contamination in residential yards, schools, parks, and commercial properties.

A. In response to the documented cases of lead poisoning in children, MALARCO agrees to remove lead contamination from all residential yards in the Dorsay Mining District. But MALARCO refuses to do anything more, and the Shotonee Tribe remains concerned about other contamination by metals in soils, surface waters, and sediments throughout the Mining District. What are the Tribe's options for proceeding under CERCLA?

B. If MALARCO agrees to address the metals contamination throughout the Dorsay Mining District, can it compel any other parties, including other mining companies that operated in the mining district, to participate in the cleanup as well? Would MALARCO have any other rights against other parties?

C. If the OPRR refuses to address the plume of diesel fuel contaminating groundwater beneath its railyard, can EPA or the Tribe compel Orange Pacific to act under CERCLA?

D. Should the Dorsay Mining District be added to the National Priorities List? What would be the advantages or disadvantages of doing so?

Chapter 10

The Regulation of Toxic Products: The Federal Insecticide, Fungicide and Rodenticide Act and the Toxic Substances Control Act

In this chapter we shift our focus from the oversight of various sources of byproducts and wastes to the oversight of the useful products themselves. Many of the same health and environmental concerns arise, only it is the design of the products that serve as the target of regulatory oversight.

As a result of this shifted focus, the first challenge in understanding the regulation of toxic products is to isolate some of the justifications for public regulation. Unlike the familiar negative externalities that result from hazardous wastes and pollution, why should the government intervene at all in the sale of toxic products? One clue arises from RCRA itself. All products at some point become wastes. Thus, regulating products earlier in their life cycle—perhaps by restricting or even taxing the most hazardous and least useful products that cannot be disposed of permanently, safely, or in a cost-effective way—provides one reason for some type of regulatory oversight of useful products. Congress articulated precisely this rationale in passing the chemical regulatory statute, the Toxic Substances Control Act (TSCA), in 1976: "While air and water laws authorize limitations on discharges and emissions, . . . there are no existing statutes which authorize the direct control of industrial chemicals themselves for their health or environmental effects. . . . [T]hese other authorities will in many cases be sufficient to adequately protect health and the environment, [but . . .] preventing or regulating the use of the chemical in the first instance may be a far more effective way of dealing with the hazard." S. Rep. No. 698, 94th Cong., 2d Sess. 1–2 (1976).

In addition, some products—pesticides being the most obvious—present risks to bystanders and not just to purchasers. When a pesticide is used for agricultural purposes, it is technically exempt from being classified as either a "hazardous waste" under RCRA, 40 C.F.R. § 261.2 (clarifying that materials that are being used are not discarded), or a "hazardous substance" that triggers remedial costs under CERCLA, 42 U.S.C. § 9607(i), but it can still behave like a waste in the environment. Rachel Carson's famous SILENT SPRING, published in 1962, documented the deadly effects of unregulated pesticides on health and the environment. In presaging a future "where no birds sing," Carson documented how chemical pesticides "occur everywhere" and "have immense power not merely to poison but to enter into the most vital processes of the body and change them in sinister and often deadly ways." RACHEL CARSON, SILENT SPRING 15 (1962). As Carson explains, pesticides "have been recovered from most of the major river systems and even from streams of groundwater flowing unseen through the earth. Residues of these chemicals linger in soil to which they may have been applied a dozen years before. They have entered and lodged in the bodies of fish, birds, reptiles, and domestic and wild animals so universally that scientists carrying on animal experiments find it almost impossible to locate subjects free from such contamination." *Id.*

Other toxic products—chemicals that have specific uses within industrial processes—present far fewer external harms. Yet even here, there is yet a third reason for government intervention in the hazardous product market arising from the asymmetries in information that can cause consumers to be underinformed about the risks of products. Unless consumers test the chemicals themselves, they may lack reliable information about the chemical's risks or benefits. If consumers cannot gauge these critical features of the products, then the market cannot accurately account for the costs associated with the risks of using these products. The manufacturers who sell the least expensive—and often the most hazardous—chemicals will generate the largest sales, even from consumers who ordinarily might discriminate and opt for safer products. The result is a problem of adverse selection or a market for "lemons"; the very worst products with the lowest sales prices drive out other products. For an excellent discussion of these problems that still describes the regulatory challenges today, see Mary L. Lyndon, *Information Economics and Chemical Toxicity: Designing Laws to Produce and Use Data*, 87 MICH. L. REV. 1795, 1813–17 (1989).

All of these reasons and more justify some government oversight of the market in toxic products. But, as the materials here will reveal, these regulatory programs vary dramatically in how they operate and how vigorously they have been implemented.

I. The History and Justification for Regulation of Toxic Products

Unlike the pollution control statutes, which have a more recent origin, the laws regulating the sale of potentially dangerous products date back to the turn of the last century in the Insecticide Act of 1910 and the 1906 Pure Food and Drugs Act. This early legislation focused primarily on addressing problems of fraud; sellers and manufacturers might exaggerate the effectiveness of their products, much like the infamous "snake oil" salesmen who defrauded consumers. Farmers would sometimes invest considerable money in pesticides that proved to be essentially worthless, losing both out of pocket costs and their crops as a result. The consumer market for drugs raises the same worries, with opportunity costs associated with substituting unproven or ineffective drugs for effective treatments, to the detriment of a person's health.

Nevertheless, many decades passed before Congress took a more active interest in overseeing the untested and undisclosed risks associated with toxic products. Even when products are effective and accomplish what the manufacturers advertise, some products are extremely hazardous in ways that are neither justified nor explained to consumers. In addition, and particularly for pesticides, bystanders and environmental harms are external to the user's concerns and deserve additional protection.

On the other hand, government intervention in the market carries its own risks; regulatory programs can go too far, leading to the removal of some useful products and chilling innovation on the development of new ones. This is particularly worrisome because some dangerous products may save more lives than are lost as a result of the hazards. Consider the short excerpt below that emphasizes these important benefits of pesticides:

Angela Logomasini and Jennifer Zambone, *Pesticides and Agriculture*

COMPETITIVE ENTERPRISE INSTITUTE, THE ENVIRONMENTAL SOURCE, SECOND EDITION 175

(Angela Logomasini ed., 2008)

Pesticide levels rarely, if ever, approach unsafe levels. Even when activists cry wolf because residues exceed federal limits that does not mean the products are not safe. In fact, residues can be hundreds of times above regulatory limits and still be safe. . . .

To promote public health, policy should work to ensure that families—particularly lower income families—are able to afford fresh produce. Pesticides play a key role in increasing supply and thereby keeping these products affordable.

- Use of modern agricultural technology and chemicals has reduced the cost of food, improving nutrition, particularly for lower-income families. In fact, at the turn of the 20th century before the use of modern agricultural practices, Americans spent 20 percent of their income on food. Now, the average American family spends approximately 10 percent of its disposable income on food.

- Affordability is a key concern for most Americans. Consumers that say they would pay for residue-free foods are only willing to pay a small increase. In one survey, 46 percent said they would pay more for such products, but only 15 percent of those respondents would pay more than 10 percent extra.

- Without pesticides, the price of raising a crop could increase five to 200 times, and these costs would be transferred to consumers in the price of the goods, according to one estimate. Scientist Philip Ableson warned that continued banning of pesticides and fungicides could lead to food scarcities.

"Carcinogens" in Perspective

Environmentalists have long claimed that we should avoid all pesticides because these chemicals give cancer to rodents and, hence, must be dangerous to us. But even if pesticides weren't used, every time we opened our mouths to eat we would shovel in these "rodent carcinogens." People consume such natural rodent carcinogens without ill effects, and the same is true for low-level pesticide exposures. Consider these facts:

- Bruce Ames and Lois Swirsky Gold of the University of California at Berkeley estimate that the amount of residual carcinogenic pesticides in food is 1,800 times less than the amount of carcinogens derived from 54 natural plants chemicals that are found in food.

- Cooking food produces 2,000 milligrams of burnt material per person per day. Burnt material contains many rodent carcinogens and mutagens.

- On the other hand, a person consumes only 0.09 milligrams per day of the residues of 200 synthetic chemicals that the FDA measures.

- As Ames and Gold point out, 99.99 percent of the chemicals that we eat are natural. Plants produce such chemicals to defend themselves against insects, fungi, and other predators. Ames and gold estimate that "on average Americans ingest roughly 5,000 to 190,000 different natural pesticides and their breakdown products." Hence, we consume far more naturally occurring pesticides on plants than we do manmade ones — without ill effect. This reality underscores the fact that current exposure to manmade chemicals is not significant and poses a very low-level risk. Ames and Gold specifically note: "The possible carcinogenic hazards from synthetic pesticides (at average exposures) are minimal compared to the background of nature's pesticides, though neither may present a hazard at the low doses consumed."

Notes and Questions

1. If the risks of synthetic, toxic pesticides are concentrated most heavily on poor communities, is that fact significant when assessing the desirability of pesticide regulation? Pesticide use records in fact reveal that more pesticides are used in urban areas than agricultural areas and that, in these urban areas, the toxic burden of pesticides appears to fall heaviest on the poor. In one scientific study, researchers report:

> Heavy applications of pesticides have been required in inner-city neighborhoods because of the age and poor maintenance of the urban housing stock. The resulting heavy exposure of inner-city children to pesticides is therefore a direct consequence of poverty, overcrowding, and poor housing and must therefore be viewed as yet another manifestation of the environmental injustice that these children suffer.

Philip J. Landrigan et al., *Pesticides and Inner-City Children: Exposures, Risks, and Prevention*, 107 ENVTL. HEALTH PERSP. SUPP. 431, 435–36 (1999). These same researchers found that "[t]he number of gallons of chlorpyrifos [used to control fleas, termites, and roaches] applied in Manhattan exceeded the total number of gallons of all pesticides applied in any other single county." *Id.* at 432. Pesticide use in Harlem not only included high quantities of these two lethal pesticides (chlorpyrifos and organochlorine pesticides), but also illegal "street" pesticides. *Id.* In another study of poor minority women living in or near New York City, "85% of the women report that pest control measures were used in the home during pregnancy" and "at least four pesticides [were detected] in the personal air samples of all women monitored during the third trimester." Robin Whyatt et al., *Residential Pesticide Use During Pregnancy Among a Cohort of Urban Minority Women*, 110 ENVTL. HEALTH PERSP. SUPP. 507, 512 (2002). In fact, the poorer the household, the greater the pest risks and the greater the use of pest control measures. *Id.*

2. Does the ingestion of naturally occurring pesticides necessarily suggest that additional, synthetic pesticides should be tolerated without regulatory oversight? What scientific and policy assumptions are implicit in this conclusion? Might chemical pesticides that are designed to be reactive and toxic to pests pose greater health and environmental risks than pesticides that are produced naturally? Does the fact that manufacturers produce and profit from the production of synthetic pesticides introduce additional considerations regarding whether the risks of synthetic pesticides can or ought to be minimized?

3. The environmental literature is replete with references to numbers, statistics, and technical facts. Re-read the excerpt with a critical eye and consider whether more precision would have been helpful in communicating certain key facts. For example, what does it mean to suggest that "the price of raising a crop could increase five to 200 times" without the use of pesticides? Does that mean the price of all produce is likely to increase by five to 200 times? Or do the authors mean that this projection lies at the high end of increased price projections for specific crops and serves as a worst-case scenario? Along these same lines, the authors report that survey participants are reluctant to spend more than 10 percent more on residue-free foods, but perhaps some residue-free foods are not more expensive and may even fall comfortably within the consumers' mean price point? Although there is considerable variability in the market and among produce, residue-free produce is not always exorbitantly more expensive (although sometimes it is). See Consumer Reports, *The Cost of Organic Food* (March 19, 2015), available at http://www.consumerreports.org/cro/news/2015/03/cost-of-organic-food/index.htm

II. Regulatory Design Challenges Governing Toxic Products

A. Identifying an End Point for Regulation

In light of the health and environmental benefits of some toxic products, the regulator must proceed carefully to ensure that government oversight marks a net improvement for the public health and welfare. The first and most difficult challenge arises in identifying the correct end-goal for regulation. In the search for this regulatory end goal, the mandates of the pollution control statutes prove most unhelpful. Consider, for example, what would happen if we regulated pesticides at levels that ensured the "protection of public health" and allowed "an adequate margin of safety" as required by the Clean Air Act for NAAQS. 42 U.S.C. at §7409(b)(1). This type of regulatory goal raises more questions than it answers in determining how to balance the benefits of a product against the costs.

The triggers used in CERCLA and RCRA to justify regulation are similarly unhelpful in imagining how to regulate useful, but toxic, products. As CERCLA itself notes, the normal use of pesticides is exempted from the statute's reach; without this exemption the use of most pesticides (many of which contain at least one hazardous substance) would constitute a "release or a threatened release of a hazardous substance." 42 U.S.C. 9607(a)(1). Similarly, under RCRA, if pesticides were categorized as Subtitle C wastes because they are ultimately disposed on land, the sale and use of pesticides would come to an abrupt end.

Instead, some other end-point is needed to determine the appropriate trigger for regulatory intervention. In virtually all of the statutes passed to regulate toxic products, Congress adopted an "unreasonable risk" test. See, e.g., Toxic Substances Control Act (TSCA), 15 U.S.C. §§ 2604(f)(1), 2605(a) (chemical substances); Federal Hazardous Substances Act, 15 U.S.C. § 1261 and the Consumer Product Safety Act (CPSA), 15 U.S.C. § 2082 (consumer products).

"Unreasonable risk" is generally interpreted to require that the risks of a product or substance outweigh its benefits before the product can be restricted by regulation. As a result, products that have significant health benefits (e.g., pesticides that help prevent malaria) will be tolerated with more toxic side effects than substances that provide little social or economic benefit.

Despite its conceptual simplicity, when put into practice this simple cost-benefit test raises a number of difficult issues for regulators. For starters, consider the different approaches available to conduct a cost-benefit assessment. Congress might only intend the agency to tally up the evidence pro and con in an informal, qualitative way to assess risks and benefits. Alternatively, Congress might demand a full-blown, quantitative risk assessment in which all of the benefits and costs are fully quantified and then monetized.

In addition, the statute must necessarily place the burden of proof of justifying the "reasonableness" of a product on either the manufacturer or the regulator. Under some regulatory programs, the product may enjoy the benefit of the doubt. In other regulatory programs, the manufacturer will be expected to defend its product before EPA to keep the product on the market.

Finally, given the information-intensive features of cost-benefit analyses, Congress will need to identify the parties that are responsible for conducting research. Producers of the product could be required to prepare a dossier of research in support of the product's safety as a condition to approval or, conversely, the burden could fall on the regulatory agency to amass the relevant evidence to determine whether some products are unreasonably risky. Once a product is on the market and adverse effects are discovered, moreover, there will need to be some provision for requiring manufacturers or regulators to factor the new information back into their existing cost-benefit analysis.

As we will see from the examples drawn from pesticide and chemical regulation, Congress adopted a wide range of approaches to implement the "unreasonable risk" test. But in all of its incarnations, at bottom is Congress' realization that most (but not all) products produce some benefits that must be compared against their aggregate social costs.

It is also worth noting that despite its prevalence in legislation governing toxic products, the "unreasonable risk" standard is not the only approach Congress has used to regulate toxic products. One striking exception is the Delaney Clause, passed in 1958 to restrict color and food additives. For these additives, Congress mandated the elimination of the additive altogether "if [the additive] is found to induce cancer when ingested by man or animal." 21 U.S.C. 348(b)(3)(A); see also 21 U.S.C. 376 (imposing the same requirement for color additives). The courts interpret the Delaney Clause to require a complete ban of an additive if there is any evidence that it is even slightly carcinogenic to animals. *Public Citizen v. Young*, 831 F.2d. 1108 (D.C. Cir. 1987). In understanding the basis for such a protective standard for food and color additives, consider the utility or benefits side of the equation. At some level, Congress considered the benefits of food additives to approach zero, making it easy to ban additives that cause cancer in animals. As Representative King stated in support of the bill: "The colors which go into our feeds and cosmetics are in no way essential to the public interest or the national security . . . . [C]onsumers will easily get along without [carcinogenic colors]." Cited in *Public Citizen v. Young*, 831 F.2d. at 1117.

B. Implementing a Licensing Program

A second design challenge in the regulation of products, as opposed to wastes and pollutants, arises in determining the appropriate mechanism for government intervention. Should hazardous products be cleared through a regulatory agency like EPA before they can be sold? And if this is the best approach, how shall EPA assess all of the products that are already on the market at the time a statute is passed? If we "grandfather" them in (i.e., the products do not go through an initial clearance before being sold), then we will face the old versus new dichotomy, in which the regulatory program ultimately tips in favor of potentially less safe, existing formulations over new innovations that must surmount regulatory obstacles before they can be sold. *See* Peter Huber, *The Old-New Division in Risk Regulation*, 69 Va. L. Rev. 1025, 1073–75 (1983). Alternatively, if all products must be approved by the regulator before they can be sold, the agency will face an enormous backlog that threatens to delay and restrict commerce in useful toxic products.

An alternate regulatory tack is to provide the agency with the motivation and authority to pull the worst of the existing products off the market, while overseeing new products slightly more rigorously by requiring some regulatory clearance before they can be marketed. This second approach tends to be the more common approach in product regulation statutes.

When the agency is tasked with culling out the worst products, however, the agency must have enough information about the products to make this judgment, as well as sufficient staff to investigate all of the products on the market. In some statutes, Congress gives the regulators tools to mandate specific tests to be conducted by the manufacturers when there is some reason to suspect a hazard. But for a number of reasons—politics, legality, and resources—the EPA has used these tools cautiously. In the regulation of chemicals, in particular, out of more than 80,000 chemicals in commerce, EPA has required manufacturers to test for fewer than two percent of the chemicals in its inventory. Wendy Wagner, *Using Competition-Based Regulation to Bridge the Toxics Data Gap*, 83 INDIANA L. J. 629, 634 (2008). Even these efforts to require testing have been stunningly protracted and have produced less data than EPA initially sought. The record for testing in pesticides is far better primarily because the agency enjoys stronger legal authority to require testing. Yet even here, there have been disappointments in the quality and quantity of data as discussed later in this chapter.

C. Summary

In the product regulation statutes, legal analysts must be attuned to several key decision points that prove critical to the design of the regulatory program. First and foremost, what is the regulatory end goal set for the governments' oversight of products sold on the market? Should products not present "an unreasonable risk," or is the utility of the product so high (e.g., drugs) or so low (e.g., color additives) that other statutory goals or burdens of proof should be used? Second, how does the system operate to help the regulator apply this end-goal to the products on the market? Do manufacturers need to develop a rigorous body of evidence to convince the regulator that their products do not present "an unreasonable risk" before the products can be sold? Or do regulators carry the burden of figuring this out with whatever evidence they can access or, in some cases, mandate through testing authorities? Third, in all cases, where does the scientific information come from? How do we know it is reliable?

Although we will consider these design issues only as they apply to the regulatory oversight of chemicals and pesticides, you should be aware that similar variations on this theme are used to regulate drugs, dietary supplements, and consumer products (including hazardous consumer products).

FIFRA

III. The Regulation of Pesticides

Although Congress' regulation of pesticides dates back to 1910, the program in place today was enacted more recently, in 1972. (Congress did pass a regulatory act that required more rigorous information labels for pesticides in 1947, but this was a small move compared to the 1972 legislation). Like other landmark environmental statutes (e.g., CAA, CWA, and CERCLA), the Federal Insecticide, Fungicide, and Rodenticide Act (FIFRA) was passed in response to public pressure for stronger government oversight of the safety of pesticides. As mentioned, Rachel Carson's SILENT SPRING, which was a best-seller in the mid 1960s and was even read by John F. Kennedy during his presidency, made the potential risks of pesticides salient to the public. This public awareness provided the impetus that later triggered the passage of FIFRA.

FIFRA has been amended many times since its initial passage in 1972—in some instances weakening and in some instances strengthening EPA's powers; but the basic structure remains the same. At a general level, FIFRA requires new pesticides to be licensed before they can be sold on the market and requires EPA to review existing pesticides at regular intervals.

FIFRA's jurisdictional reach encompasses a broad range of agents (both biological and chemical) that control "pests." 7 U.S.C. § 136(s). "Pests" are defined to include: "(1) any insect, rodent, nematode, fungus, weed, or (2) any other form of terrestrial or aquatic plant or animal life or virus, bacteria, or other micro-organism (except viruses, bacteria, or other micro-organisms on or in living man or other living animals) which the Administrator declares to be a pest." 7 U.S.C. § 136(t). EPA interprets FIFRA broadly to encompass not only conventional chemical pesticides but even the genetically modified strains of plants that involve biological forms of pest controls (e.g., the release of enzymes by plants that resist pests). In pesticide law today, it is also well-settled that the manufacturer must establish that these new pesticides do not present an "unreasonable risk" and must produce a substantial body of scientific information to support this conclusion.

In the early years of FIFRA, EPA was intimately involved in interpreting the statute in the course of building up its program. EPA tended to be aggressive in those early years—producing clear, streamlined interpretations of its authority that placed as much of the burden of proof as possible on manufacturers and that afforded EPA broad discretion.

Particularly in the first decade of FIFRA, pesticide manufacturers and the agricultural community were sometimes dramatically impacted by EPA's decisions (e.g., banning a widely used pesticide like DDT). Not surprisingly, manufacturers and agricultural interests participated vigorously in the administrative decision-making process. Indeed, not only private entities, but also the United States Department of Agriculture (USDA)—which typically advocated for the farming community—played a major role in many of these proceedings.

Because Congress recognized that eliminating a pesticide product could affect various industries and commercial activities, FIFRA required EPA to provide the manufacturers with the opportunity for a hearing to contest proposed restrictions before the restrictions could take effect. FIFRA § 6(b), 7 U.S.C. § 136d(b). And in amendments to FIFRA passed in 1975, Congress required EPA to formally consult with the Secretary of Agriculture before taking regulatory action. FIFRA §§ 6(b), 21(a), 7 U.S.C. §§ 136d(b), 136s(a). Additionally, due to the due process implications of product restrictions, Congress placed a heavier evidentiary burden on the agency— one that required "substantial evidence" for a proposed restriction on a pesticide as opposed to the more familiar "arbitrary and capricious standard" in the Administrative Procedure Act. FIFRA § 6(d), 7 U.S.C. § 136d(d).

A. The Regulation of Existing Pesticides

One of the first projects for EPA in implementing FIFRA was to establish a way to identify and restrict the most dangerous pesticides swiftly. The case excerpted below is a classic case that set the regulatory framework for the EPA's regulation of existing pesticides in the decades that followed. The key sections of the statute at issue are provided for reference in the text box below.

6(c) Suspension

(1) Order

If the Administrator determines that action is necessary to prevent an imminent hazard during the time required for cancellation or change in classification proceedings, the Administrator may, by order, suspend the registration of the pesticide immediately. Except as provided in paragraph (3), no order of suspension may be issued under this subsection unless the Administrator has issued, or at the same time issues, a notice of intention to cancel the registration or change the classification of the pesticide under subsection (b) of this section. . . .

FROM THE DEFINITIONS SECTION OF FIFRA:

2(l) Imminent hazard

The term "imminent hazard" means a situation which exists when the continued use of a pesticide during the time required for cancellation proceeding would be likely to result in unreasonable adverse effects on the environment or will involve unreasonable hazard to the survival of a species declared endangered or threatened by the Secretary pursuant to the Endangered Species Act of 1973 [16 U.S.C. §§ 1531 et seq.].

2(bb) Unreasonable adverse effects on the environment

The term "unreasonable adverse effects on the environment" means

(1) any unreasonable risk to man or the environment, taking into account the economic, social, and environmental costs and benefits of the use of any pesticide, or

(2) a human dietary risk from residues that result from a use of a pesticide in or on any food inconsistent with the standard under section 346a of title 21. The Administrator shall consider the risks and benefits of public health pesticides separate from the risks and benefits of other pesticides. In weighing any regulatory action concerning a public health pesticide under this subchapter, the Administrator shall weigh any risks of the pesticide against the health risks such as the diseases transmitted by the vector to be controlled by the pesticide.

Environmental Defense Fund, Inc. v. Environmental Protection Agency

548 F.2d 998 (D.C. Cir. 1977)

Judge LEVENTHAL:

This case involves the pesticides heptachlor and chlordane. Consolidated petitions seek review of an order of the Environmental Protection Agency (EPA) suspending the registration of those pesticides under the Federal Insecticide, Fungicide and Rodenticide Act (FIFRA) for certain uses. The Administrator of EPA issued an order on December 24, 1975. The order prohibited further production of these pesticides for the suspended uses, but permitted the pesticides' continued production and sale for limited minor uses. Even as to the suspended uses, the Order tempered its impact in certain respects: It delayed until August 1, 1976, the effective date of the prohibition of production for use on corn pests; and it permitted the continued sale and use of existing stocks of registered products formulated prior to July 29, 1975.

One petition to review was filed by Earl L. Butz, Secretary of Agriculture of the United States (U.S.D.A.). Secretary Butz and intervener Velsicol Chemical Corporation, the sole manufacturer of heptachlor and chlordane, urge that the EPA order as to chlordane be set aside on both substantive and procedural grounds. They contend that substantial evidence does not support the Administrator's conclusion that continued use of chlordane poses an "imminent hazard" to human health, and that the Administrator made critical errors in assessing the burden of proof and in weighing the benefits against the risks of continued use of chlordane.

The other petition, filed by Environmental Defense Fund [EDF], urges that the Order did not go far enough to protect against the hazards of heptachlor and chlordane use. EDF sought an injunction against the provisions permitting continued production and use of the pesticides on corn pests until August 1, 1976. EDF also challenges the Administrator's decision to allow continued use of the stocks of the two pesticides existing as of July 29, 1975, contending that EPA should have provided for retrieval and controlled disposal of such stocks. EDF also contends that the Administrator erred in failing to suspend certain "minor uses" of chlordane and heptachlor.

On the issue of retrieval of existing stocks, we remand for further consideration. In all other respects, we affirm the Administrator's Order. In view of our conclusion, we denied EDF's request for a stay pending appeal of the provision delaying the effective date for use on corn pests. In effect, we approved the delay of effective date (as to corn) until August 1, 1976, and in this opinion we set forth our reasons for that conclusion. (Part II, B, 1)

I. Statutory Framework and Standard of Review

The issues posed by administrative action pursuant to FIFRA are not new to this court, and we have previously extensively described the statutory framework for such actions. What is involved here is a suspension of registration of two pesticides during the pendency of the more elaborate cancellation of registration proceeding, initiated in this case by a November 18, 1974, notice of intent to cancel. This 1974 notice stated that there existed "substantial questions of safety amounting to an unreasonable risk to man and the environment" from continued use of heptachlor and chlordane. Public cancellation hearings pursuant to that notice were not expected to commence for some time. On July 29, 1975, the Administrator issued a Notice of Intent to Suspend the registrations of most uses of the two pesticides. The Administrator then commented on that expected delay in completing the cancellation hearings, and cited "new evidence . . . which confirms and heightens the human cancer hazard posed by these pesticides." On August 4, 1975, registrant Velsicol Chemical Corporation requested an expedited adversary hearing on the suspension question pursuant to § 6 of FIFRA, 7 U.S.C. § 136d(c). Administrative Law Judge Herbert L. Perlman presided over the cancellation hearings beginning August 12. Evidence was limited to human health issues and the benefits of continued use of heptachlor and chlordane. The record was closed December 4, 1975, and on December 12, the ALJ recommended against suspension, stating that he was unable to find that "heptachlor and chlordane are conclusively carcinogens in laboratory animals." The Administrator reversed that decision on December 24, 1975, and suspended most uses of chlordane and heptachlor.

The Administrator is authorized to suspend the registration of a pesticide where he determines that an "imminent hazard" is posed by continued use during the time required for cancellation. Section 6(c) of FIFRA, 7 U.S.C. § 136d(c)(1). An "imminent hazard" exists where continued use during the time required for the cancellation proceeding would be likely to result in "unreasonable adverse effects on the environment." Section 2(l) of FIFRA, 7 U.S.C. § 136(l). The term "unreasonable adverse effects on the environment" is, in turn, defined as "any unreasonable risk to man or the environment, taking into account the economic, social, and environmental costs and benefits of the use of any pesticide." Section 2(bb) of FIFRA, 7 U.S.C. § 136(bb).

As in our previous suspension case involving aldrin/dieldrin, the primary challenge raised by Velsicol and USDA goes to the adequacy of the evidentiary basis of EPA's finding that the suspended pesticides present an imminent hazard during the time required for cancellation. The standard against which we test that challenge is defined in § 16(b) of FIFRA:

The court shall consider all evidence of record. The order of the Administrator shall be sustained if it is supported by substantial evidence when considered on the record as a whole.

The standard of substantial evidence has been defined as:

something less than the weight of the evidence . . . (T)he possibility of drawing two inconsistent conclusions from the evidence does not prevent an administrative agency's finding from being supported by substantial evidence.

In applying this principle of review in the specific context of a suspension of pesticides, this court has reiterated that "the function of the suspension decision is to make a preliminary assessment of evidence, and probabilities, not an ultimate resolution of difficult issues. We cannot accept the proposition . . . that the Administrator's findings . . . (are) insufficient because controverted by respectable scientific authority. It (is) enough at this stage that the administrative record contain(s) respectable scientific authority supporting the Administrator." Environmental Defense Fund v. EPA (Shell Chemical Co., et al.), 167 U.S.App.D.C. 71, 77, 510 F.2d 1292, 1298 (1975) quoting Environmental Defense Fund v. EPA, 150 U.S.App.D.C. 348, 357, 465 F.2d 528, 537 (1972).

These decisions of our court also point out that the Administrator is not required to establish that the product is unsafe in order to suspend registration, since FIFRA places "(t)he burden of establishing the safety of a product requisite for compliance with the labeling requirements . . . at all times on the applicant and registrant." Velsicol and USDA urge that this allocation of burden of proof relied on by the Administrator is inconsistent with the explicit terms of FIFRA. They rely on FIFRA's specific incorporation of subchapter II of the Administrative Procedure Act, which provides in relevant part that "Except as otherwise provided by statute, the proponent of a rule or order shall have the burden of proof." 5 U.S.C. § 556(d).

The EPA regulation governing the burden of proof in suspension proceedings provides:

> At the hearing, the proponent of suspension shall have the burden of going forward to present an affirmative case for the suspension. However, the ultimate burden of persuasion shall rest with the proponent of the registration. 40 C.F.R. § 164.121(g) (1975).

Assuming that the Administrator is the "proponent" of a suspension order and is governed by § 556(d), the legislative history of that provision indicates that it allocates the burden of going forward rather than the burden of ultimate persuasion and is consistent with the EPA's apportionment of burden:

> That the proponent of a rule or order has the burden of proof means not only that the party initiating the proceeding has the general burden of coming forward with a prima facie case but that other parties, who are proponents of some different result, also for that purpose have a burden to maintain. S.Doc. No.248, 79th Cong., 2d Sess. 208, 270 (1946).

This allocation of the burden of going forward structures evaluation of the factual evidence adduced for both the Administrator and the reviewing court, and is consistent with the traditional approach that this burden normally falls on the party having knowledge of the facts involved.

In urging that the ultimate burden of proof in a suspension proceeding rests on the Administrator, Velsicol and USDA assert that the suspension decision is a drastic step differing fundamentally from both the registration and cancellation decisions made under FIFRA. But we have already cautioned that the "imminent hazard" requisite for suspension is not limited to a concept of crisis: "It is enough if there is substantial likelihood that serious harm will be experienced during the year or two required in any realistic projection of the administrative process." "FIFRA confers broad discretion" on the Administrator to find facts and "to set policy in the public interest." . . . This broad discretion was conferred on the implicit assumption that interim action may be necessary to protect against the risk of harm to the environment and public health while a fuller factual record is developed in the cancellation proceeding. This avenue of protective relief would be effectively foreclosed if we accepted Velsicol's argument that the Administrator must prove imminent hazard apparently in some sense of weight of the evidence, going beyond substantial likelihood. But as we have already pointed out, the basic statutory directive requires affirmance of the Administrator's decision if supported by substantial evidence, and this requires "something less than the weight of the evidence." We reject that renewed invitation to exercise increased substantive control over the agency decision process, and turn to a consideration of whether the Administrator's decision to suspend most uses of heptachlor and chlordane is supported by substantial evidence.

II. Substantial Evidence Support for the Administrator's Decision

To evaluate whether use of a pesticide poses an "unreasonable risk to man or the environment," the Administrator engages in a cost-benefit analysis that takes "into account the economic, social, and environmental costs and benefits of the use of any pesticide." 7 U.S.C. § 136(bb). We have previously recognized that in the "preliminary assessment of probabilities" involved in a suspension proceeding, "it is not necessary to have evidence on . . . a specific use or area in order to be able to conclude on the basis of substantial evidence that the use of (a pesticide) in general is hazardous." . . . "Reliance on general data, consideration of laboratory experiments on animals, etc." has been held a sufficient basis for an order cancelling or suspending the registration of a pesticide. *Id.* Once risk is shown, the responsibility to demonstrate that the benefits outweigh the risks is upon the proponents of continued registration. Conversely, the statute places a "heavy burden" of explanation on an Administrator who decides to permit the continued use of a chemical known to produce cancer in experimental animals. Applying these principles to the evidence adduced in this case, we conclude that the Administrator's decision to suspend most uses of heptachlor and chlordane and not to suspend others is supported by substantial evidence and is a rational exercise of his authority under FIFRA.

A. Risk Analysis — Carcinogenicity of Heptachlor and Chlordane

Velsicol and USDA contend that the laboratory tests on mice and rats do not "conclusively" demonstrate that chlordane is carcinogenic to those animals; that mice are too prone to tumors to be used in carcinogenicity testing in any case; and that human exposure to chlordane is insufficient to create a cancer risk. They place strong reliance on the Administrative Law Judge's refusal to recommend suspension because he was "hesitantly unwilling at this time to find that heptachlor and chlordane are conclusively carcinogens in laboratory animals." . . . The ALJ recognized however, that on the basis of the record made the Administrator "could determine that the pesticides involved pose potential or possible carcinogenic risk to man" and that he could "find that heptachlor and chlordane are conclusively carcinogenic in laboratory animals." While adopting the ALJ's factual findings, the Administrator concluded that the ALJ had applied an erroneous legal standard in requiring a conclusive rather than probable showing that the pesticides were animal carcinogens, and concluded in any case that the evidence showed heptachlor and chlordane to be animal carcinogens. We affirm.

1. Mice and Rat Studies

An ultimate finding in a suspension proceeding that continued use of challenged pesticides poses a "substantial likelihood of serious harm" must be supported by substantial, but not conclusive, evidence. In evaluating laboratory animal studies on heptachlor and chlordane there was sufficient "respectable scientific authority" upon which the Administrator could rely in determining that heptachlor and chlordane were carcinogenic in laboratory animals.

We start by rejecting Velsicol's argument that the "cancer principles" EPA relied on in structuring its analysis of the mice and rat studies improperly biased the agency's open-minded consideration of the evidence. In brief form, the principles accept the use of animal test data to evaluate human cancer risks; consider a positive oncogenic effect in test animals as sufficient to characterize a pesticide as posing a cancer risk to man; recognize that negative results may be explained by the limited number and sensitivity of the test animals as compared to the general human population; note that there is no scientific basis for establishing a no-effect level for carcinogens; and view the finding of benign and malignant tumors as equally significant in determining cancer hazard to man given the increasing evidence that many "benign" tumors can develop into cancers. The Agency's reliance on these principles did not come as a surprise to Velsicol; they were included in the Administrator's Notice of Intent to Suspend; and as recognized in EDF v. EPA, 167 U.S.App.D.C. at 77–78, 510 F.2d at 1298–99, form part of the Agency's "scientific expertise." Velsicol was properly given an opportunity to put in evidence contesting those principles, but failed to demonstrate anything more than some scientific disagreement with respect to them. Velsicol's principal complaint that mice are inappropriate test animals was specifically rejected by the Administrator, citing statements by the National Academy of Sciences' Food Protection Committee, the World Health Organization, HEW's Commission on Pesticides and their Relationship to Environmental Health, FDA Advisory Panel on Carcinogenesis, International Agency for Research on Cancer, and Director of the National Cancer Institute's Carcinogenesis Program. . . . EPA's specific enunciation of its underlying analytic principles, derived from its experience in the area, yields meaningful notice and dialogue, enhances the administrative process and furthers reasoned agency decisionmaking. . . .

In reviewing and evaluating the studies relied on by the Administrator, five EPA witnesses and five Velsicol consultants agreed that animals fed chlordane and animals fed heptachlor/heptachlor epoxide in fact underwent cellular changes indicating malignancy. . . . The Administrator has adequately explained his reliance on these test results which show significant carcinoma development in treated animals. None of the tests yielded negative results; chlordane was shown to be independently carcinogenic, as well as to contain a carcinogenic component (heptachlor/heptachlor epoxide). We think it plain that the foregoing establishes substantial evidence supporting the Administrator's result, and that Velsicol cannot be said to have met its burden of overcoming EPA's prima facie case by showing that chlordane and heptachlor are not carcinogenic in laboratory animals.

2. Extrapolation of Animal Data to Man

Human epidemiology studies so far attempted on chlordane and heptachlor gave no basis for concluding that the two pesticides are safe with respect to the issue of cancer. To conclude that they pose a carcinogenic risk to humans on the basis of such a finding of risk to laboratory animals, the Administrator must show a causal connection between the uses of the pesticides challenged and resultant exposure of humans to those pesticides. He made that link by showing that widespread residues of heptachlor and chlordane are present in the human diet and in human tissues. Their widespread occurrence in the environment and accumulation in the food chain is explained by their chemical properties of persistence, mobility and high solubility in lipids (the fats contained in all organic substances). Residues of chlordane and heptachlor remain in soils and in air and aquatic ecosystems for long periods of time. They are readily transported by means of vaporization, aerial drift, and runoff of eroding soil particles. The residues have been consistently found in meat, fish, poultry and dairy products monitored in the FDA Market Basket Survey and are also frequent in components of animal feeds. This evidence supports a finding that a major route of human exposure is ingestion of contaminated foodstuffs. EPA's National Human Monitoring Survey data shows that heptachlor epoxide and oxychlordane, the principal metabolites of heptachlor and chlordane respectively, are present in the adipose tissue of over 90% of the U.S. population.

The population's exposure to these pesticides, in large part involuntary, can be divided into agricultural and nonagricultural related routes. Seven million pounds of heptachlor and chlordane were used as corn soil insecticide in 1975, producing residues which persist in the soil for several years after application. These residues are taken up by such food, feed, and forage crops as soybeans, barley, oats, and hays typically rotated with corn. By volatilization the pesticides contaminate corn and other plant leaves. And root crops like potatoes, carrots and beets directly absorb the pesticides from the soil. Other sources of agricultural-related residues include exposure to contaminated dust particles and agricultural runoff containing eroded soil particles.

Velsicol urges that the dietary exposure resulting from agricultural uses of the pesticides is insignificant, and that current exposure is well below "safe" dose levels as calculated by the Mantel-Bryan formula, or by the World Health Organization's Acceptable Daily Intake figures. Mantel himself criticized the use of the formula for a persistent pesticide, and the Administrator rejected the concept of a "safe" dose level defined by mathematical modeling because of "the incomplete assumptions made by the registrant's witnesses about the sources of human exposure in the environment, the natural variation in human susceptibility to cancer, the lack of any evidence relating the level of human susceptibility to cancer from heptachlor and chlordane as opposed to that of the mouse, and the absence of precise knowledge as to the minimum exposure to a carcinogen necessary to cause cancer." That explanation is within the reasonable bounds of the agency's expertise in evaluating evidence. And it is confirmed by the common sense recognition that reliance on average "safe" dietary levels fail to protect people with dietary patterns based on high proportional consumption of residue-contaminated foods (e.g., children who ingest greater quantities of milk than the general population).

There are several non-agricultural uses which involve a large volume of heptachlor and chlordane as well as significant human exposures. For example, the record shows that approximately six million pounds of chlordane are used annually on home lawns and gardens. The Administrator found that these uses involve high risks of human intake "due to the many avenues which exist for direct exposure, through improper handling and misuse, inhalation, and absorption through the skin from direct contact." Velsicol asserts that the mice studies showing carcinogenic effects after ingestion of chlordane do not warrant an inference about the carcinogenic effects of inhaling it or absorbing it through the skin, and that consequently nonagricultural routes of exposure cannot be considered to present a cancer risk. . . . [T]he FIFRA statutory scheme mandates explicit relief—the suspension of registration—when an unreasonable risk to health is made out. We have previously held that it is not necessary to have evidence on a specific use to be able to conclude that the use of a pesticide in general is hazardous. Once the initial showing of hazard is made for one mode of exposure in a suspension proceeding, and the pesticide is shown to be present in human tissues, the burden shifts to the registrant to rebut the inference that other modes of exposure may also pose a carcinogenic hazard for humans. Velsicol has totally failed to meet that burden here. . . .

. . . .

B. Benefits

Velsicol and USDA challenge the Administrator's finding that the benefits derived from the suspended uses of chlordane do not outweigh the harms done. EDF urges that the Administrator's decision to continue some uses was not justified by evidence that the risk of harm was outweighed by benefits from the continued uses.

1. Use on Corn

Heptachlor and chlordane were used on an estimated 3.5% of the total corn acreage in the United States in 1975, largely in an effort to control black cutworm. Cutworms sporadically infest 2 to 8% of total U.S. corn farms, and occur most often in lowland, river bottom areas. Chlordane and heptachlor are used as preplant treatments to insure against possible infestations. The Administrator found, with record support, that no macro-economic impact will occur as a result of suspending those pesticides. He also found that crop surveillance or "scouting" for infestations during the early weeks of plant growth, together with application of post-emergence baits or sprays where necessary, provide an effective alternative to the more indiscriminate prophylactic use of chlordane and heptachlor. Velsicol urges that this approach is not as effective as the persistent protection provided by chlordane. Especially in the absence of proof of a serious threat to the nation's corn, there is no requirement that a pesticide can be suspended only if alternatives to its use are absolutely equivalent in effectiveness. The Administrator reasonably took into account that a transition period would be necessary to implement post-emergent techniques of control and concluded that the challenged pesticides could continue in use for corn protection until August 1, 1976. This evaluation of alternatives and the time required to implement them is supported by substantial evidence, and we find no basis to disturb the Administrator's balancing of costs and benefits.

2. Miscellaneous Agricultural Uses

The Administrator suspended a number of agricultural uses where the record was insufficient to support any finding that benefits outweigh costs of continued use of heptachlor or chlordane on these crops. Possibly the lack of benefits evidence reflected readily available alternatives, possibly a relative lack of interest in lesser-volume uses. In any event, the registrant's failure to carry its burden of adducing sufficient evidence on benefits in effect leaves the Administrator nothing to weigh in his cost-benefit analysis except the evidence that the use of the challenged pesticides in general is hazardous. That evidence of general hazard is sufficient to support a suspension of uses.

3. Non-Agricultural Uses Suspended by the Administrator

Chlordane is a common household, lawn, garden, and ornamental turf insecticide, with over 7.5 million pounds (36% of total use) so employed in 1974. The ALJ and Administrator found on the basis of substantial evidence that the "efficaciousness of the substitutes for control of household and lawn insects is not really at issue" and that when lack of evidence of substantial benefits from continued use is weighed against the special hazards of exposure presented by the possibilities of inhalation, dermal absorption, and the increased dangers associated with improper handling, suspension of those uses was justified. Similarly, on the basis of evidence in the record, the Administrator could reasonably find that the residual capacity of chlordane was not necessary to control either structural pests or ticks and chiggers, given the existence of effective alternatives to each of those uses. . . .

C. Continued Sale and Use of Existing Stocks of Chlordane and Heptachlor for Suspended Uses

Although we have no doubt that the Administrator has the power under FIFRA to exempt from a suspension order the use of existing stocks (in this case stocks existing as of July 29, 1975), the Administrator acted arbitrarily when he failed to even inquire into the amount of stocks left, and the problem of returning and disposing of them. Some evidence must be adduced before an exemption decision is made, and it is the responsibility of the registrant to provide it. It may be that the lapse of time has lessened the current significance of this issue but we are in no position to do other than remand for further consideration.

We affirm the Agency's suspension order of December 24, 1975, as clarified by the order of January 19, 1976, except for the exemption of the sale and use of existing stocks. The record is remanded for further consideration of that issue.

So ordered.

Notes and Questions

1. Who has the burden of proving that a pesticide presents an "unreasonable risk to man or the environment" under §6 of FIFRA? Velsicol objected strenuously to the courts' holding on this issue and petitioned for a rehearing (which it lost). But from Velsicol's perspective, is the court's reading of FIFRA the only, or even the best, reading of the statute? Why is the placement of the burden of proof so important in a case like this?   *EPA has unbiased approach; if its put in commerce, the corp who put it there should prove it's safe.*

2. What does the court interpret "substantial evidence" to mean in this case? Does EPA have the burden of essentially establishing a "more likely than not" causal link between the pesticide and harm as is required under tort law?

3. From the manufacturer's perspective, what types of arguments are likely to be the most successful in a case like this? What kinds of benefits are the most important to tip the balance back in favor of chlordane and heptachlor?   *What they're preventing & the cost of food production*

4. There are several aspects of this case (and other FIFRA cases) that are likely to be unfamiliar. The first, as mentioned earlier, is the hearing process before an administrative law judge. Because EPA's decision raises due process types of concerns — the elimination of a particular pesticide made by specific manufacturers — manufacturers are allowed to request an adjudicatory hearing, known as a formal rulemaking, in which EPA and the manufacturers engage in a trial-like process. In these formal rulemakings, administrative rules of evidence and rights to cross examination apply, and an administrative law judge presides over the dispute. Moreover, both sides — the agency and the manufacturer — can appeal adverse findings to the EPA Administrator and then to the D.C. Court of Appeals. Notice the history of the dispute in *EDF*. The Administrative Law Judge ruled in favor of the manufacturers and the Administrator (appointed by President Nixon) reversed. The manufacturers then appealed EPA's decision to the D.C. Circuit.

5. In this case, you also see the U.S. Department of Agriculture (USDA) opposing the EPA's decision and joining the manufacturers in the litigation. Subsequent amendments to FIFRA gave the USDA even greater power to negotiate in advance with EPA over pesticide restrictions. If the farming industry is the motivating force, does USDA's formal role give them too much power? Or is there still a concern that their role may not be large enough?

6. In light of this case, if you were the Assistant Administrator in charge of the pesticide program, how might you set up EPA's regulatory program for existing pesticide re-registrations? (Recall that the statute required EPA, over time, to review existing pesticides to determine whether they should stay on the market). In the wake of cases like *EDF*, EPA ultimately established a re-registration method called RPAR (rebuttable presumption against registration) in which the burden was placed on manufacturers to establish why their pesticides should *not* be restricted or banned. In fact, "[i]f a pesticide ingredient was found to be oncogenic in test animals, it automatically triggered a RPAR process under which the burden of proof formally shifted to manufacturers to submit data rebutting the presumption." Donald T. Hornstein,

Lessons from Federal Pesticide Regulation on the Paradigms and Politics of Environmental Law Reform, 10 YALE J. ON REG. 369, 433 (1993).

EPA's broad regulatory powers embodied in the RPAR process quickly met with opposition from industry and agricultural interests. In the decade that followed, Congress amended FIFRA several times to impose added speedbumps on EPA's authority. For example, EPA's streamlined registration approach (RPAR) was later limited by Congress in the 1978 Amendments because of the evidentiary burden that approach placed on industry to rebut the presumption. Another important legislative speedbump on EPA's authority involved an amendment to FIFRA requiring peer review of EPA's major scientific decisions and also requiring EPA to consult with a permanent Science Advisory Panel on all suspension and cancellation decisions.

7. While the issue in *EDF v. EPA* involved EPA's proposed suspension of two pesticides, with the ultimate goal of banning the pesticides entirely, EPA enjoys many other powers to restrict pesticides. For example, EPA also has regulatory authority to require labeling, limiting uses (e.g., only to address certain pests in specified environmental conditions), and restricting those who can apply the pesticides (i.e., a restricted rather than a general pesticide).

8. Throughout the first two decades of FIFRA implementation, EPA struggled to review and re-register tens of thousands of "grandfathered" pesticides that had been on the market at the time the statute was passed in 1972. The delays and unequal treatment of these old pesticides as compared to new pesticides not only sparked harsh criticism of EPA's pesticide program, but it prompted a series of congressional amendments intended to rectify the delay. Congress now requires EPA to review all the registrations of existing pesticides every 15 years. Section 3(g) of FIFRA, 7 U.S.C. § 136a(g). This statutorily mandated time frame is intended to ensure that pesticide registrations will not fall too far behind scientific and technological developments. Since the late 1990s, EPA has worked steadily to clear through its backlog of existing pesticides and has successfully completed the review and re-registration of the entire universe of existing pesticides. Because it must re-register more than 1,000 active ingredients and related products every 15 years, EPA conducts reviews and re-registrations on approximately 60 to 70 pesticide products annually. Each pesticide product takes EPA about five to six years to review.

9. The court identified a number of scientific uncertainties that justified EPA's precautionary approach to the suspension of chlordane and heptachlor. Scientific research continually tries to reduce such uncertainties, of course. For example, at the time of the D.C. Circuit's opinion some 40 years ago, "the natural variation in human susceptibility to cancer" was known to exist but completely mysterious. Today, genomic techniques are finding more and more genetic variations that appear associated with susceptibility to the toxic effects of carcinogens. *See* Steve C. Gold, *The More We Know, the Less Intelligent We Are? How Genomic Information Should, and Should Not, Change Toxic Tort Causation Doctrine*, 34 HARV. ENVTL. L. REV. 369, 389–392 (2010). How should these findings affect risk assessments for hazardous products? For conflicting views, *compare* Jamie A. Grodsky, *Genetics and Environmental Law: Redefining Public*

Health, 93 Calif. L. Rev. 171 (2005) *with* David E. Adelman, *The False Promise of the Genomics Revolution for Environmental Law*, 29 Harv. Envtl. L. Rev. 117 (2005).

B. Scientific Challenges in Assessing Pesticide Risks

One of the most difficult challenges in pesticide registration is generating reliable research on health and environmental risks associated with their use. Toxicity testing is expensive and manufacturers will be reluctant to produce it on their own.

To that end, EPA has mandated a number of tests that must be performed by a manufacturer as a condition to registering or re-registering a pesticide. EPA has also specified the methods and protocols for these tests in considerable detail. In its review of the manufacturers' research results, however, EPA sometimes identifies other risks not adequately captured by these mandated tests. In such cases, EPA has the authority to require the manufacturer to conduct additional tests, including tests in the field, to assess specific risks on various biota and/or to examine the risks with respect to certain end points, like cancer, developmental abnormalities, endocrine disruption, etc. FIFRA § 3(c)(2)(B), 7 U.S.C. § 136a(c)(2)(B). In these more open-ended research projects required by EPA staff—called "data call-ins"—the protocols for conducting the tests are not defined in advance. As a result, manufacturers generally have more discretion to develop their own scientific methods to address EPA's request for more research.

One particularly striking example of the science-intensive conflicts that can result, particularly for high-stakes pesticides, is highlighted in the journalistic account below. EPA required Syngenta, the manufacturer of Atrazine, to conduct additional research on the potential effects of their herbicide on endocrine systems. Yet assessing the reliability of the resulting research has been fraught with difficulty. As you read, consider whether there is a better way to generate toxicity research on pesticides, while still tasking the manufacturer with responsibility for financing the research.

Goldie Blumenstyk, *The Price of Research*
Chron. Higher Educ., Oct. 31, 2003

Tyrone Hayes wasn't all that concerned about who was signing the checks when he agreed to do some consulting on one of the most widely used pesticides in the country.

And when the early studies from his laboratory at the University of California at Berkeley began producing hints that the product, the herbicide atrazine, might be inhibiting the sexual development of male frogs, he was excited. Maybe, he thought, his research would lead to some breakthrough findings. He never imagined just how unenthusiastic his research sponsors—and others with a financial stake in atrazine— would be about his discovery.

Six frustrating years later, Mr. Hayes and his defenders say they know only too well the lengths to which those companies will go to undermine his findings that atrazine may be harmful. This week the U.S. Environmental Protection Agency is expected to make its final ruling on the reapproval of atrazine. Mr. Hayes and some other scientists believe that the campaign to discredit him will have played a part in helping the herbicide's primary manufacturer, a company called Syngenta, win that approval.

His colleagues here at Berkeley and around the country say the story is a classic example of the subtle and not-so-subtle tactics that companies sometimes use to influence the outcome of university research that they pay for.

Mr. Hayes maintains that Ecorisk Inc., the consulting company that hired him and several other academic scientists to study atrazine on behalf of Syngenta, stalled and delayed his research progress once he began finding that the substance had damaging effects on frogs. It turned out that in the contracts covering Mr. Hayes's work and that of many of the other researchers, Syngenta and Ecorisk retained final say over what and whether the scientists could publish.

Even after he quit working as an Ecorisk consultant, in November 2000, he asserts, the company tried to buy his silence: He says the Ecorisk consultant in charge of the atrazine studies told him that it would arrange with Syngenta to provide him with as much as $2-million in lab support if he would continue his research "in a private setting," unencumbered by the academic ethos that promotes publication of results.

The Ecorisk consultant, Ronald J. Kendall, of Texas Tech University, says the charge is "absolutely" untrue.

Whatever the truth of that allegation, what happened next is undisputed: Freed from the contractual constraints on publication and confidentiality, Mr. Hayes repeated and expanded upon the original frog studies. He continued to find damaging effects of atrazine at low levels.

His work, which has appeared in Nature and other journals, has been attacked by Syngenta and a host of other critics — including the Kansas Corn Growers Association, a Fox News commentator known for minimizing the potential threat of global warming, and the Center for Regulatory Effectiveness, an organization based in Washington that is challenging the use of academic studies in federal rule making.

As part of its rebuttal of Mr. Hayes's work, Syngenta cited studies by three other teams of university scientists, working for the company through Ecorisk, who could not replicate his findings showing the same effects at low doses. Several of those academics, contacted by The Chronicle, said that Syngenta did not influence the outcome of their work. They also take pains to describe their differences with Mr. Hayes as an example of the kind of scientific disagreement that is typical of academe. If the debate is heated, they say, that is largely because the stakes are so high. Atrazine, an important product for Syngenta, is widely used by farmers to kill weeds.

Mr. Hayes says some of those studies are flawed, and he has gone public with allegations that Ecorisk was interested only in bending its panel of scientists to benefit Syngenta.

> "It's very directly involved with the hubris of corporations that think, 'We can fund the research we want,'" says Sheldon Krimsky, a professor at Tufts University who studies conflicts of interest in academe. "Corporations think they can

fund academic science in their own interests. Hayes is a case where they made a miscalculation. For every miscalculation, how many accurate ones are out there?"...

Mr. Hayes has his defenders, too, most notably on a Web site called Our Stolen Future. John Peterson Myers, the former director of the foundation that provided $5,000 to Mr. Hayes in 2001, helps run the site. After an EPA scientific advisory panel met in June 2003 to consider the studies by Mr. Hayes, Ecorisk, and others, the Web site took the company to task, saying it had used misleading news releases against Mr. Hayes.

Hiring academic scientists and portraying them as an independent panel is the kind of tactic that "creates this aura of scientific respectability," says Mr. Myers. The site also raised questions about Mr. Kendall's role, noting that he had served as a member of the EPA's main scientific advisory board until 2002, a period that overlapped with the time he was coordinating the atrazine panel for Syngenta as it sought reapproval for atrazine.... (The journal's chief editor says Mr. Kendall took no part in publication decisions related to atrazine. Mr. Kendall says he recused himself from discussions on atrazine while serving on the agency panel.)

Rena Steinzor, a professor of law and director of the Environmental Law Clinic at the University of Maryland School of Law, says the Data Quality Act challenge against Mr. Hayes's studies is part of a broader assault on academic freedom, amounting to harassment. "It's the innuendo that surrounds a data-quality petition," she says. "This is a very well-funded campaign that serves not the quality of science but serves industry self-interest."

Ultimately, the EPA did consider Mr. Hayes's studies, along with 15 others. Twelve of them were produced by Ecorisk, including the one by Mr. Carr's group that has been published. (Mr. Kendall says other Ecorisk studies will be published soon.)

Based on what it found, the EPA preliminarily recommended further studies on the effects of atrazine on amphibians. In June, the agency's scientific advisory panel concurred. "Sufficient data were available to establish the hypothesis" that atrazine interferes with the sexual development of frogs," it concluded. But the panel also found that many of the studies had serious flaws of design or methodology.

In its final ruling, scheduled to be released this week, the EPA is expected to reapprove atrazine, while also requiring Syngenta to conduct further studies on its effects on amphibians. The Natural Resources Defense Council says such a ruling would be inadequate because it includes no trigger for further restricting atrazine's use, even if the new research finds negative effects. Syngenta says it will involve Ecorisk to help with the additional studies....

Notes and Questions

1. Is it right for scientists to be portrayed as "independent" if the corporation funding their research has the ability to suppress publication of the research results through contractual nondisclosure clauses? Why would scientists agree to such restrictions?

2. Much of the research that feeds into regulation is — out of financial necessity — produced by regulated parties. Yet this raises a number of challenges with respect to how to ensure the reliability of this research. Indeed, in biomedical studies, there is a phenomenon known as the "funding effect" that reveals strong correlations between the funding of a study by an interested party and results that favor that sponsor. See, e.g., Justin E. Bekelman, Yan Li & Cary P. Gross, *Scope and Impact of Financial Conflicts of Interest in Biomedical Research: A Systemic Review*, 289 JAMA 454, 463 (2003) ("By combining data from articles examining 1140 studies, we found that industry-sponsored studies were significantly more likely to reach conclusions that were favorable to the sponsor than were nonindustry studies.").

3. Today, and in recognition of the funding effect, the biomedical journals require all authors to disclose any private financial support for their research that might create conflicts of interest as a condition of publication. Should conflict of interest disclosures be similarly required for all regulation-related research submitted to federal agencies? Additionally, would it help to distinguish those studies that are sponsored by companies who retain the right to influence or control publication from studies that are funded by companies with no strings attached? Currently, most agencies do not require any conflict or funding disclosures for regulation that affects research. For arguments in favor of a mandatory conflicts disclosure for regulatory research, see David Michaels & Wendy Wagner, *Disclosure in Regulatory Science*, 302 Sci. 2073 (2003).

C. The Inaccessibility of Some Scientific Research Used for Pesticide Regulation

Ensuring the scientific integrity of manufacturer-produced research is made still more difficult because of the limited public availability of unpublished studies. Although the Atrazine study by Hayes was published (as were several others refuting that study), most pesticide research used in registration and re-registration decisions is not published. This means that the research has not been peer reviewed or subjected to the scrutiny of a larger body of skeptical scientists. Moreover, a requirement in FIFRA § 10(g) further limits general public access to these unpublished studies based on concerns that manufacturers in other countries might gain unfair competitive advantages by accessing the testing. 7 U.S.C § 136h(g)(1). To obtain access to this information under § 10(g), a person must certify that he or she does "not seek access to the data for purposes of delivering it or offering it for sale to any such business or entity or its agents or employees and will not purposefully deliver or negligently cause the data to be delivered to such business or entity or its agents or employees." *Id.* FIFRA also requires EPA to keep a record of the "names of persons to whom data are disclosed" and must "inform the applicant or registrant of the names and affiliations of such persons." The data must be viewed in EPA offices. Perhaps most problematic from the standpoint of those concerned about pesticide safety, the unpublished studies cannot be publicly accessed in this way until *after* a registration decision has concluded.

Despite limited public access, EPA staff do review all of the submitted data carefully. Members of an interdisciplinary team within EPA's pesticide unit work together to conduct a risk assessment of the pesticide. This includes assessing the risks of the pesticide through various exposure pathways, from drinking water to worker exposure to food. The guidelines and models used to prepare the assessment have been peer reviewed by the Science Advisory Panel (SAP), an external EPA science advisory group, although the individual assessments pertaining to each registration decision are not peer reviewed. After proposing a decision with regard to re-registering the pesticide (e.g., restricting certain uses; label changes) and soliciting notice and comment, the EPA will ultimately issue a final decision on the registration of the pesticide.

D. The Broader Context of EPA's Pesticide Program: FIFRA and Other Statutes

We have seen the very important, but limited, slice of FIFRA that involves restricting or banning the existing use of pesticides. FIFRA intersects with many other statutes and addresses pesticide risks in a variety of other, fascinating ways. We here provide a preliminary introduction to some of these other provisions, powers, and points of intersection of FIFRA with other regulatory programs.

Pesticide tolerances in food. Spurred by inconsistencies in the regulation of pesticide residues on food—and concerns that in some cases the pesticide tolerances allowed on foods were far too high, particularly for children—Congress passed the Food Quality Protection Act (FQPA) in 1996. FQPA is a protective statute that requires EPA to set pesticide tolerances for food that ensure "a reasonable certainty of no harm," 21 U.S.C. §§ 321(s), (q), 346a(b)(2), rather than using an "unreasonable risk" test. EPA must also make an explicit determination that the tolerances are safe for children by adding in a tenfold safety factor where necessary. Beyond setting more protective levels for pesticides in some foods, FQPA has also generated a great deal of additional research on pesticide toxicity, which has been a boon to expedite EPA's FIFRA registration decisions. It is worth considering, however, why FIFRA's regulatory process itself would not be adequate to provide the needed protection for residues on food. Why might residues be excessively hazardous on foods, even with rigorous pesticide licensing decisions under FIFRA?

Pesticides and endangered species. EPA's "unreasonable risk" approach to registering pesticides allows dangerous pesticides on the market as long as their benefits outweigh their risks. We are learning, however, that some pesticides—both in nature and in use—are particularly detrimental to certain endangered species. One example is the use of the pesticide strychnine to poison pocket gophers who inflict damage on conifer seedlings. Yet strychnine also poisons endangered species, such as the grizzly bear. *See, e.g.,* Mary Jane Angelo, *The Killing Fields: Reducing the Casualties in the Battle between U.S. Species Protection Law and U.S. Pesticide Law,* 32 HARV. ENVTL. L. REV. 95 (2008). As a result, there are occasional conflicts between EPA's pesticide approvals and the Fish and Wildlife Service's (FWS's) protection of listed species.

As you read in Chapter 4, under the Endangered Species Act, federal agencies are required to ensure that their actions do not jeopardize the continued existence of a threatened or endangered species or adversely affect its critical habitat. Thus, when a species may be adversely affected by a federal activity, the Endangered Species Act requires the FWS to use the best available evidence in a way that gives the endangered species the benefit of the doubt. 16 U.S.C. § 1533(b). By contrast, in its regulatory assessment of a pesticide registration, the EPA is required to balance the benefits of a pesticide against its costs to human health and environment. 7 U.S.C. § 136a(a). This net balancing produces a much more open-ended framework that does not afford species the benefit of the doubt. Instead, an endangered species' risks are compared against the benefits of the pesticide. At the behest of these two agencies who face conflicting goals and missions, the National Academies of Science issued a report to help resolve the differences as they apply to pesticide re-registration that has the potential to impact endangered species. See NATIONAL RESEARCH COUNCIL, ASSESSING RISKS TO ENDANGERED AND THREATENED SPECIES FROM PESTICIDES (2013).

Pesticides and farmworkers. Agricultural workers in the field have historically received the highest exposures to pesticides. They have suffered both acute effects (death) and more long-term effects (cancer and birth defects) that become evident over time:

> The death of José Antonio Casillas is a disquieting example of the workplace hazards pesticides pose to farmworkers. The fifteen-year-old migrant worker was in prime health. At the end of each workday, while other farmworkers sat exhausted, Casillas had the energy to bicycle, lift weights, and play soccer. In 1999, Casillas left his hometown of Guanajuato, Mexico for the orchards of central Utah, intending to make enough money to support his mother and younger siblings back home. But two months after arriving in Utah, Casillas's journey ended abruptly. On June 26, 1999, an applicator-tractor doused Casillas with Guthion Solupak, a pesticide similar in formulation to Sarin, the nerve gas used in chemical warfare. This was the second time in a week Casillas had been sprayed with pesticides while working in the fields. Unaware that a highly toxic pesticide covered his body, Casillas thought he had been sprayed only with water. After his first exposure, Casillas experienced intense head pain. After his second exposure, the teenager was vomiting, sweating, and suffering from diarrhea. That night, Casillas slept in the same clothes he had worn during the exposure. While riding his bicycle to work the next morning, Casillas lost consciousness and collapsed. By the time paramedics arrived, Casillas was dead, with white foam streaming from his nose.

> A legal framework exists to protect farmworkers from tragedies like Casillas's. Pesticides are not supposed to be sprayed while workers are in the fields. Farmworkers are supposed to be informed of the dangers of field chemicals and the steps to take in the event of a poisoning. But for Casillas, none of those regulatory "guarantees" took place. A Utah Department of Agriculture investigation found that Casillas's employer had violated federal and state laws by failing to: (1) train employees on pesticide use; (2) supply

workers with protective gear; and (3) properly monitor pesticide applicators. Further, the grower allowed workers to enter recently sprayed fields during prohibited reentry intervals and had not posted mandatory safety information. The grower was fined $10,000 for these violations, the maximum allowed by state law. However, no tort suit was ever filed against the applicator or chemical manufacturer on behalf of Casillas, probably because of the difficulty of establishing a causal link between the pesticide exposure and Casillas's death.

Keith Cunningham-Parmeter, *A Poisoned Field: Farmworkers, Pesticide Exposure, and Tort Recovery in an Era of Regulatory Failure*, 28 N.Y.U. REV. L. & SOCIAL CHANGE 431, 433–44 (2004).

To provide stronger protection for workers, EPA interpreted FIFRA § 12(a)(2)(G), 7 U.S.C. § 136j(a)(2)(G), to provide the agency with the authority to set Worker Protection Standards for the use of pesticides in agricultural settings. EPA's standards, found at 40 C.F.R. Part 170, impose a number of restrictions on farm operators, including reentry restrictions after spraying, posting signs, and mandated education and training for farmworkers. Despite its importance, EPA's implementation and enforcement of its worker protection program has been disappointing, as Prof. Cunningham-Parmeter describes above. What problems can you imagine with these standards in implementation and enforcement? Both non-profit organizations and tort litigators have proved critical in providing added protections to farmworkers from pesticide risks.

Pesticide Exports. What happens to pesticides banned in the United States? Are they removed from the market? As it turns out, manufacturers may sell banned pesticides, like DDT, to other countries provided the manufacturers comply with limited restrictions (governing the label, notices to the importing country, signed statements from the purchaser acknowledging the risks). *See* FIFRA § 17, 7 U.S.C. § 136o. International treaties generally reinforce the U.S. requirements, but in some cases go still further with regard to ensuring that countries importing the pesticides give "prior informed consent." *See, e.g.,* The International Code of Conduct on the Distribution and Use of Pesticides, 23 FAO Con. Res. 10/85 (1985).

What justifications are there for allowing the export of canceled pesticides to other countries, including developing countries? Those supporting a free market in pesticides note that different countries face very different risks and benefits (e.g., malaria from mosquitoes) and also are entitled to make their own decisions based on these different risk-benefit calculations. In addition, if other countries intend to buy banned pesticides, U.S. manufacturers, who may make cleaner products, should not be excluded from this market. There are problems with this free market approach, however. "Most developing countries have neither the technical capability nor the regulatory infrastructure to ensure safe handling and destruction of toxic wastes ... [This fact makes U.S. exports to these countries] economically, environmentally, morally, and technically indefensible." M.D. Uva & J. Bloom, *Exporting Pollution: The International Waste Trade*, 31 ENVIRONMENT 4 (June 1989).

Pesticides and the Preemption of State Tort Law. Under FIFRA, EPA not only controls the sale of pesticides, but also oversees the labeling of the products. Indeed, this labeling authority provides an important way for EPA to regulate risks—both by ensuring safe application and by requiring the disclosure of risk and emergency information to users. Once a pesticide is approved, the manufacturer is required to use an EPA-approved label on their product, although the manufacturer typically provides the initial proposal for the label in its registration packets FIFRA § 12(a)(1) (G), 7 U.S.C. § 136j(a)(1).

Since the label is federally approved and is mandatory, what happens if the manufacturer is later sued by an injured user for inadequate warning? Is the claim preempted? After several decades of vacillating opinions by lower courts, the Supreme Court weighed in on this issue in *Bates v. Dow Agrosciences*, 544 U.S. 431 (2005), and held that tort warning claims would not be preempted in situations in which it appeared that the manufacturer withheld important and relevant information related to use or risk or in settings where the state demanded more specific warnings of foreseeable risks. Otherwise, EPA's labels generally will preempt defective and negligent warning claims under § 24(b), 7 U.S.C. § 136v(b), of FIFRA since these state tort claims effectively "impose . . . requirements for labeling or packaging in addition to or different from those required" under FIFRA and conflict with federal law.

Section 24(a) of FIFRA, 7 U.S.C. § 136v(a), nevertheless explicitly reserves for the states the ability to restrict the "sale and use" of pesticides. "Sale and use" has been interpreted as providing the state with authority to restrict or totally prohibit the use of a licensed pesticide. See, e.g., *New York State Pesticide Coalition, Inc. v. Jorling*, 874 F.2d 115 (2d Cir. 1989).

The Excessive Use of Pesticides. FIFRA allows EPA to regulate the quality of all of the pesticides sold in the United States, but the basic design of the statute leaves out federal oversight of the *quantity* of pesticide use. As Prof. Donald Hornstein discusses:

> For all its complexity, . . . it is important to underscore what pesticide regulation is not: it is not a body of law that addressed in any strategic way the underlying prevalence of pesticides in American agriculture, nor is it a body of law designed to minimize pesticide use. On reflection, this characteristic is especially striking because the impetus for modern pesticide regulation, if not for the modern environmental movement in general, was the argument made in 1962 by Rachel Carson in Silent Spring for developing just such a strategic environmental law. . . . Although EPA still chooses occasionally to boast that the Agency exists as "the extended shadow of Silent Sprint," in truth the defining features of modern pesticide regulation languish far too much in the "shadow" of Rachel Carson's vision of what an enlightened strategy for crop protection should be—a fact perhaps demonstrated most succinctly by an increase in pesticide usage between 1964 and 1982 of 170%. . . .

Donald T. Hornstein, *Lessons from Federal Pesticide Regulation*, *supra*, at 392. Professor Hornstein makes innovative suggestions for how we might do a better job of encouraging the reduction of pesticides through familiar tools such as taxes or even reporting requirements modeled after the Emergency Planning and Community Right-to-Know Act (EPCRA), 42 U.S.C. §§ 11001–11050, which requires companies to report publicly the amounts of specified toxic chemicals that they manufacture, process, or release. Who are the constituencies to lobby for a reduced use of all pesticides? Would the organic farm industry be supportive of this move?

Practice Problem

As a recap of our whirlwind study of FIFRA, imagine that you are working as a city attorney when city maintenance workers discover seven sacks of powdery material in an old shed near the municipal golf course. The sacks are obviously very old. Other than the bold "DDT," the labels are no longer legible. The city workers have heard that DDT was a very effective substance for controlling pests "in the good old days," but the product was canceled by EPA in 1972. As city attorney, advise the city workers of any legal concerns you may have with this use of DDT today. If you conclude that the DDT should not be used in the City's insect control program, must it be treated as a hazardous waste under RCRA, or is there some other way to get rid of it? What aspect of FIFRA deserves further research in that regard?

IV. The Regulation of Chemicals

The regulation of chemical products—codified in the Toxic Substances Control Act (TSCA)—was passed in 1976, only four years after FIFRA. Yet we will see that TSCA has taken a very different course with regard to the oversight of the chemical market.

TSCA governs the sale of toxic chemicals and, except for amendments on individual substances, the statute was essentially unaltered for 40 years. In 2016, Congress passed a long-overdue set of amendments that promises to improve some features of the statute, although there are doubts about the extent of the net improvements. These new provisions are summarized at the end of this chapter.

Unlike the regulation of pesticides, there were no crises and public catastrophes that motivated the passage of TSCA. Instead, TSCA arose as a gap-filling statute. The downstream risks of indiscriminate chemical use and disposal led Congress to look upstream, regulating the most dangerous chemicals at their source. But this more dispassionate orientation—after all, there were no widows, orphans or charismatic mammals in immediate danger—also meant that there was less public outrage to counterbalance efforts by the chemical industry to limit EPA's authority to regulate chemicals. See Joel Reynolds, *The Toxic Substances Control Act of 1976: An Introductory Background and Analysis*, 4 Colum. J. Envt'l L. 35 (1977). As a result, the statute is filled with contradictions—gesturing toward meaningful regulatory oversight on the one hand, but then imposing numerous legal restraints on EPA in the course of fulfilling its legislative commands on the other. Even the statutory goals in the first section of the statute reflect a lukewarm commitment to chemical regulation. For example, compare the goals articulated in subsections (1) and (2) of Section 1(b) of TSCA with those listed in subsection (3):

§ 2601. Findings, policy, and intent

. . . .

(b) **Policy** It is the policy of the United States that—

(1) adequate information should be developed with respect to the effect of chemical substances and mixtures on health and the environment and that the development of such information should be the responsibility of those who manufacture and those who process such chemical substances and mixtures;

(2) adequate authority should exist to regulate chemical substances and mixtures which present an unreasonable risk of injury to health or the environment, and to take action with respect to chemical substances and mixtures which are imminent hazards; and

(3) authority over chemical substances and mixtures should be exercised in such a manner as not to impede unduly or create unnecessary economic barriers to technological innovation while fulfilling the primary purpose of this chapter to assure that such innovation and commerce in such chemical substances and mixtures do not present an unreasonable risk of injury to health or the environment.

Before examining the challenges EPA faces in restricting chemicals—authorities that contrast sharply with EPA's analogous authorities governing pesticides that are detailed in *EDF*—it is worth first considering the jurisdictional reach of this chemicals program. By design, TSCA extends only to chemical products. Under TSCA, moreover, "chemicals" do not include mixtures, nor do chemicals include consumer products, pesticides, or drugs, or other regulated products enumerated in the definition section. TSCA, § 2(2), 15 U.S.C. § 2601(2). As a result, much of EPA's oversight applies only to basic chemicals sold in commerce, many of which are used exclusively in-house in manufacturing processes or serve as feedstocks for more complicated products that ultimately make it onto the market for consumers.

Much like FIFRA, however, EPA oversees new chemicals differently from existing chemicals. Under TSCA and the recent amendments, EPA is provided authority to oversee new chemicals before they enter the market. However, in contrast to pesticide regulation, under TSCA manufacturers need only share the scientific information available to them at the time of the application, unless EPA requires added information. TSCA §§ 5(b) and (d)(1), 15 U.S.C. § 2604(b) and (d)(1). EPA must then make a final determination whether the chemical substance presents "an unreasonable risk of injury to health or the environment." TSCA as amended, § 5(a)(3)(A), 15 U.S.C. § 2604(a)(3)(A).

A. EPA's Regulation of Existing Chemicals

The differences between chemical and pesticide licensing become most apparent when one compares EPA's authority to cancel or otherwise restrict existing chemicals with EPA's more vigorous authority to oversee existing pesticides under FIFRA. We begin our study of existing chemical regulation with the original statute and a landmark case that set the course for EPA's regulatory future. Indeed, the 2016 amendments are not expected to significantly alter EPA's powers to regulate existing chemicals; we will return to these amendments at the end of this chapter.

EPA's first major effort to regulate an existing chemical took aim at one of the most well-known hazardous products—asbestos. Because of its resistance to heat and flame, asbestos was used in a vast array of products. Yet asbestos had been recognized as a toxicant for more than 1,000 years, and in the 1960s, research linked asbestos to lung cancers and other harms. The scientific research, in turn, triggered a spate of toxic tort litigation that continues to this day.

It was not until the mid-1980s that EPA attempted to ban asbestos from use in numerous products. Since TSCA required documentation of "unreasonable risk" as a precursor to regulation, EPA spent more than a decade reviewing the uses of asbestos that appeared to meet that unreasonable risk standard. The underlying administrative record of EPA's ultimate decision "consist[ed] of over 45,000 pages of analyses, comments, testimony, correspondence, and other materials." 54 Fed. Reg. at 2946. In 1989, EPA published its final rule banning a number of uses of asbestos. Excerpts from the preamble to the rule are provided below:

ENVIRONMENTAL PROTECTION AGENCY, ASBESTOS: MANUFACTURE, IMPORTATION, PROCESSING, AND DISTRIBUTION IN COMMERCE PROHIBITIONS
54 Fed. Reg. 29460 (July 12, 1989)

Section 6 of TSCA authorizes EPA to promulgate a rule prohibiting or limiting the amount of a chemical substance that may be manufactured, processed, or distributed in commerce in the U.S. if EPA finds that there is a reasonable basis to conclude that the manufacturer, processing, distribution in commerce, use, or disposal of the chemical substance, or any combination of these activities, presents or will present an unreasonable risk of injury to human health or the environment.

Section 6(c)(1) of TSCA requires EPA to consider the following factors when determining whether a chemical substance presents an unreasonable risk:

1. The effects of such substance on human health and the magnitude of the exposure of human beings to such substance.

2. The effects of such substance on the environment and the magnitude of the exposure of the environment to such substance or mixture.

3. The benefits of such substance for various uses and the availability of substitutes for such uses.

4. The reasonably ascertainable economic consequences of the rule, after consideration of the effect on the national economy, small businesses, technological innovation, the environment, and public health.

To determine whether a risk from activities involving asbestos-containing products presents an unreasonable risk, EPA must balance the probability that harm will occur from the activities against the effects of the proposed regulatory action on the availability to society of the benefits of asbestos. EPA has considered these factors in conjunction with the extensive record gathered in the development of this rule. EPA has concluded that the continued manufacture, importation, processing, and distribution in commerce of most asbestos-containing products poses an unreasonable risk to human health. This conclusion is based on information summarized in the following paragraphs and discussed in the units that follow.

EPA has concluded that exposure to asbestos during the life cycles of many asbestos-containing products poses an unreasonable risk of injury to human health. EPA has also concluded that section 6 of TSCA is the ideal statutory authority to regulate the risks posed by asbestos exposure. This rule's pollution prevention actions under TSCA are both the preferable and the least burdensome means of controlling the exposure risks posed throughout the life cycle of asbestos-containing products. Findings supporting this conclusion include the following:

1. Exposure to asbestos causes many painful, premature deaths due to mesothelioma and lung, gastrointestinal, and other cancers, as well as asbestosis and other diseases. Risks attributable to asbestos exposure and addressed by this rule are serious and are calculated for this rule using direct evidence from numerous human epidemiological studies. Studies show that asbestos is a highly potent carcinogen and that severe health effects occur after even short-term, high-level or longer-term, low-level exposures to asbestos. Asbestos exposure is compatible with a linear, no-threshold dose-response model for lung cancer. In addition, there is no undisputed evidence of quantitative differences in potency based on fiber size or type.

For the quantitative risk assessment performed as part of this rulemaking, EPA used dose-response constants for lung cancer and mesothelioma that were the geometric means of the "best estimates" from a number of epidemiological studies. If EPA had instead used an upper bound estimate, as is normally done by the scientific community and in EPA regulatory risk assessment when only data from animal studies is available to extrapolate human health risk, predicted lung cancer deaths could increase by a factor of 10 and mesothelioma deaths could increase by a factor of 20 (Ref. 1).

2. People are frequently unknowingly exposed to asbestos and are rarely in a position to protect themselves. Asbestos is generally invisible, odorless, very durable, and highly aerodynamic. It can travel long distances and exist in the environment for extended periods. Therefore, exposure can take place long after the release of asbestos and at a distant location from the source of release.

3. Additions to the current stock of asbestos-containing products would contribute to the environmental loading of asbestos. This poses the potential for an increased risk to the general population of asbestos-related disease and an increased risk to future generations because of asbestos' longevity.

4. Asbestos fibers are released to the air at many stages of the commercial life of the products that are subject to this rule. Activities that might lead to the release of asbestos include mining of the substance, processing asbestos fibers into products, and transport, installation, use, maintenance, repair, removal, and disposal of asbestos-containing products. EPA has found that the occupational and non-occupational exposure existing over the entire life cycles of each of the banned asbestos-containing products poses a high level of individual risk. EPA has determined that thousands of persons involved in the manufacture, processing, transport, installation, use, repair, removal, and disposal of the asbestos-containing products affected by this rule are exposed to a serious lifetime asbestos exposure risk, despite OSHA's relatively low workplace PEL [Permissible Exposure Limit set by the Occupational Safety and Health Administration pursuant to the Occupational Safety and Health Act]. In addition, according to the EPA Asbestos Modeling Study, millions of members of the general U.S. population are exposed to elevated levels of lifetime risk due to asbestos released throughout the life cycle of asbestos-containing products. EPA believes that the exposure quantified for the analyses supporting this rule represent an understatement of actual exposure.

5. Release of asbestos fibers from many products during life cycle activities can be substantial. OSHA stated in setting its PEL of 0.2 f/cc [fibers per cubic centimeter of air] that remaining exposures pose a serious risk because of limitations on available exposure control technologies. Even with OSHA's controls, thousands of workers involved in the manufacture and processing of asbestos-containing products are exposed to a lifetime risk of 1 in 1,000 of developing cancer. Many other exposures addressed by this rule are not affected by engineering controls required by OSHA's PEL or by other government regulation. Because asbestos is a highly potent carcinogen, the uncontrolled high peak episodic exposures that are faced by large populations pose a significant risk.

6. Because of the life cycle or "cradle-to-grave" nature of the risk posed by asbestos, attempts by OSHA, the Consumer Product Safety Commission (CPSC), and other EPA offices to regulate the continued commercial use of asbestos still leave many persons unprotected from the hazards of asbestos exposure. Technological limitations inhibit the effectiveness of existing or possible exposure control actions under non-TSCA authorities. Many routes of asbestos exposure posed by the products subject to this rule are outside the jurisdictions of regulatory authorities other than TSCA. EPA has determined that the residual exposure to asbestos that exists despite the actions taken under other authorities poses a serious health risk throughout the life cycle of many asbestos-containing products. This residual exposure can only be adequately controlled by the exposure prevention actions taken in this rule.

7. Despite the proven risks of asbestos exposure and the current or imminent existence of suitable substitutes for most uses of asbestos, asbestos continues to be used in large quantities in the U.S. in the manufacture or processing of a wide variety of commercial products. Total annual U.S. consumption of asbestos dropped from a 1984 total of about 240,000 metric tons to less than 85,000 metric tons in 1987, according to the U.S. Department of Interior, Bureau of Mines data. This change suggests that the use of substitutes has increased markedly since the proposal. However, the 1987 consumption total indicates that significant exposure due to the commercial use of asbestos and the resultant risks would continue for the foreseeable future absent the actions taken in this rule.

Evidence supports the conclusion that substitutes already exist or will soon exist for each of the products that are subject to the rule's bans. In scheduling products for the different stages of the bans, EPA has analyzed the probable availability of non-asbestos substitutes. In the rule, the various asbestos products are scheduled to be banned at times when it is likely that suitable non-asbestos substitutes will be available. However, the rule also includes an exemption provision to account for instances in which technology might not have advanced sufficiently by the time of a ban to produce substitutes for certain specialized or limited uses of asbestos.

8. EPA has calculated that the product bans in this rule will result in the avoidance of 202 quantifiable cancer cases, if benefits are not discounted, and 148 cases, if benefits are discounted at 3 percent. The figures decrease to 164 cases, if benefits are not discounted, and 120 cases, if benefits are discounted at 3 percent, if analogous exposures are not included in the analysis. In all likelihood, the rule will result in the avoidance of a large number of other cancer cases that cannot be quantified, as well as many cases of asbestos-related diseases. Estimates of benefits resulting from the action taken in this rule are limited to mesothelioma and lung and gastrointestinal cancer-cases-avoided, and do not include cases of asbestosis and other diseases avoided and avoided costs from treating asbestos diseases, lost productivity, or other factors. EPA has estimated that the cost of this rule, for the 13-year period of the analyses performed, will be approximately $458.89 million, or $806.51 million if a 1 percent annual decline in the price of substitutes is not assumed. This cost will be spread over time and a large population so that the cost to any person is likely to be negligible. In addition, the rule's exemption provision is a qualitative factor that supports the actions taken in this rule. EPA has concluded that the quantifiable and unquantifiable benefits of the rule's staged-ban of the identified asbestos-containing products will outweigh the resultant economic consequences to consumers, producers, and users of the products.

9. EPA has determined that, within the findings required by section 6 of TSCA, only the staged-ban approach employed in this final rule will adequately control the asbestos exposure risk posed by the product categories affected by this rule. Other options either fail to address significant portions of the life cycle risk posed by products subject to the rule or are unreasonably burdensome. EPA has, therefore, concluded that the actions taken in this rule represent the least burdensome means of reducing the

risk posed by exposure to asbestos during the life cycles of the products that are subject to the bans.

10. Based on the reasons summarized in this preamble, this rule bans most asbestos-containing products in the U.S. because they pose an unreasonable risk to human health. These banned products account for approximately 94 percent of U.S. asbestos consumption, based on 1985 consumption figures. The actions taken will result in a substantial reduction in the unreasonable risk caused by asbestos exposure in the U.S.

A few minor uses of asbestos and asbestos products are not included in the ban. These uses, which account for less than 6 percent of U.S. asbestos consumption based on 1985 data, do not pose an unreasonable risk, based on current knowledge. For some product categories, EPA was unable to find that the products pose an unreasonable risk because asbestos exposure is minimal over the product's life cycle relative to the exposures posed by other products. In other instances EPA currently has insufficient information about either asbestos exposure attributable to the products or the future availability of suitable substitutes to make a finding of unreasonable risk . . . .

The asbestos industry appealed EPA's final rule to the Fifth Circuit, the home of most of the chemical manufacturing industry in the US.

Corrosion Proof Fittings v. Environmental Protection Agency
947 F.2d 1201 (5th Cir. 1991)

Judge SMITH:

The Environmental Protection Agency (EPA) issued a final rule under section 6 of the Toxic Substances Control Act (TSCA) to prohibit the future manufacture, importation, processing, and distribution of asbestos in almost all products. Petitioners claim that the EPA's rulemaking procedure was flawed and that the rule was not promulgated on the basis of substantial evidence. Certain petitioners and amici curiae contend that the EPA rule is invalid because it conflicts with international trade agreements and may have adverse economic effects on Canada and other foreign countries. Because the EPA failed to muster substantial evidence to support its rule, we remand this matter to the EPA for further consideration in light of this opinion.

I. Facts and Procedural History.

Asbestos is a naturally occurring fibrous material that resists fire and most solvents. Its major uses include heat-resistant insulators, cements, building materials, fireproof gloves and clothing, and motor vehicle brake linings. Asbestos is a toxic material, and occupational exposure to asbestos dust can result in mesothelioma, asbestosis, and lung cancer.

The EPA began these proceedings in 1979, when it issued an Advanced Notice of Proposed Rulemaking announcing its intent to explore the use of TSCA "to reduce the risk to human health posed by exposure to asbestos." *See* 54 Fed. Reg. 29,460 (1989).

While these proceedings were pending, other agencies continued their regulation of asbestos uses, in particular the Occupational Safety and Health Administration (OSHA), which in 1983 and 1984 involved itself with lowering standards for workplace asbestos exposure.

An EPA-appointed panel reviewed over one hundred studies of asbestos and conducted several public meetings. Based upon its studies and the public comments, the EPA concluded that asbestos is a potential carcinogen at all levels of exposure, regardless of the type of asbestos or the size of the fiber. The EPA concluded in 1986 that exposure to asbestos "poses an unreasonable risk to human health" and thus proposed at least four regulatory options for prohibiting or restricting the use of asbestos, including a mixed ban and phase-out of asbestos over ten years; a two-stage ban of asbestos, depending upon product usage; a three-stage ban on all asbestos products leading to a total ban in ten years; and labeling of all products containing asbestos. *Id.* at 29,460–61.

Over the next two years, the EPA updated its data, received further comments, and allowed cross-examination on the updated documents. In 1989, the EPA issued a final rule prohibiting the manufacture, importation, processing, and distribution in commerce of most asbestos-containing products. Finding that asbestos constituted an unreasonable risk to health and the environment, the EPA promulgated a staged ban of most commercial uses of asbestos. The EPA estimates that this rule will save either 202 or 148 lives, depending upon whether the benefits are discounted, at a cost of approximately $450–800 million, depending upon the price of substitutes. *Id.* at 29,468.

. . . . [P]etitioners challenge the EPA's final rule, claiming that the EPA's rulemaking procedure was flawed and that the rule was not promulgated based upon substantial evidence.

. . . .

IV. The Language of TSCA.

A. Standard of Review.

Our inquiry into the legitimacy of the EPA rulemaking begins with a discussion of the standard of review governing this case. EPA's phase-out ban of most commercial uses of asbestos is a TSCA § 6(a) rulemaking. TSCA provides that a reviewing court "shall hold unlawful and set aside" a final rule promulgated under § 6(a) "if the court finds that the rule is not supported by substantial evidence in the rulemaking record . . . taken as a whole." 15 U.S.C. § 2618(c)(1)(B)(i).

Substantial evidence requires "something less than the weight of the evidence, and the possibility of drawing two inconsistent conclusions from the evidence does not prevent an administrative agency's finding from being supported by substantial evidence." ... This standard requires (1) that the agency's decision be based upon the entire record, taking into account whatever in the record detracts from the weight of the agency's decision; and (2) that the agency's decision be what "'a reasonable mind might accept as adequate to support [its] conclusion.'" *American Textile Mfrs. Inst. v. Donovan,* 452 U.S. 490, 522, 101 S. Ct. 2478, 2497, 69 L.Ed.2d 185 (1981) (quoting

Universal Camera Corp. v. NLRB, 340 U.S. 474, 477, 71 S. Ct. 456, 459, 95 L.Ed. 456 (1951)). Thus, even if there is enough evidence in the record to support the petitioners' assertions, we will not reverse if there is substantial evidence to support the agency's decision. . . .

> "Under the substantial evidence standard, a reviewing court must give careful scrutiny to agency findings and, at the same time, accord appropriate deference to administrative decisions that are based on agency experience and expertise." *Environmental Defense Fund,* 636 F.2d at 1277. As with consumer product legislation, "Congress put the substantial evidence test in the statute because it wanted the courts to scrutinize the Commission's actions more closely than an 'arbitrary and capricious' standard would allow." *Aqua Slide,* 569 F.2d at 837. . . .

We note that in undertaking our review, we give all agency rules a presumption of validity, and it is up to the challenger to any rule to show that the agency action is invalid. The burden remains on the EPA, however, to justify that the products it bans present an unreasonable risk, no matter how regulated . . . .. Finally, as we discuss in detail *infra,* because TSCA instructs the EPA to undertake the least burdensome regulation sufficient to regulate the substance at issue, the agency bears a heavier burden when it seeks a partial or total ban of a substance than when it merely seeks to regulate that product. *See* 15 U.S.C. § 2605(a).

B. The EPA's Burden Under TSCA.

TSCA provides, in pertinent part, as follows:

> (a) Scope of regulation.—If the Administrator finds that there is a *reasonable basis* to conclude that the manufacture, processing, distribution in commerce, use, or disposal of a chemical substance or mixture, or that any combination of such activities, presents or will present an *unreasonable risk of injury* to health or the environment, the Administrator shall by rule apply one or more of the following requirements to such substance or mixture to the extent necessary *to protect adequately* against such risk using the *least burdensome* requirements.

Id. (emphasis added). As the highlighted language shows, Congress did not enact TSCA as a zero-risk statute. The EPA, rather, was required to consider both alternatives to a ban and the costs of any proposed actions and to "carry out this chapter in a reasonable and prudent manner [after considering] the environmental, economic, and social impact of any action." 15 U.S.C. § 2601(c).

We conclude that the EPA has presented insufficient evidence to justify its asbestos ban. We base this conclusion upon two grounds: the failure of the EPA to consider all necessary evidence and its failure to give adequate weight to statutory language requiring it to promulgate the least burdensome, reasonable regulation required to protect the environment adequately. Because the EPA failed to address these concerns, and because the EPA is required to articulate a "reasoned basis" for its rules, we are compelled to return the regulation to the agency for reconsideration.

1. Least Burdensome and Reasonable.

TSCA requires that the EPA use the least burdensome regulation to achieve its goal of minimum reasonable risk. This statutory requirement can create problems in evaluating just what is a "reasonable risk." Congress's rejection of a no-risk policy, however, also means that in certain cases, the least burdensome yet still adequate solution may entail somewhat more risk than would other, known regulations that are far more burdensome on the industry and the economy. The very language of TSCA requires that the EPA, once it has determined what an acceptable level of non-zero risk is, choose the least burdensome method of reaching that level.

In this case, the EPA banned, for all practical purposes, all present and future uses of asbestos—a position the petitioners characterize as the "death penalty alternative," as this is the *most* burdensome of all possible alternatives listed as open to the EPA under TSCA. TSCA not only provides the EPA with a list of alternative actions, but also provides those alternatives in order of how burdensome they are. The regulations thus provide for EPA regulation ranging from labeling the least toxic chemicals to limiting the total amount of chemicals an industry may use. Total bans head the list as the most burdensome regulatory option.

By choosing the harshest remedy given to it under TSCA, the EPA assigned to itself the toughest burden in satisfying TSCA's requirement that its alternative be the least burdensome of all those offered to it. Since, both by definition and by the terms of TSCA, the complete ban of manufacturing is the most burdensome alternative—for even stringent regulation at least allows a manufacturer the chance to invest and meet the new, higher standard—the EPA's regulation cannot stand if there is any other regulation that would achieve an acceptable level of risk as mandated by TSCA.

We reserve until a later part of the opinion a product-by-product review of the regulation. Before reaching this analysis, however, we lay down the inquiry that the EPA should undertake whenever it seeks total ban of a product.

The EPA considered, and rejected, such options as labeling asbestos products, thereby warning users and workers involved in the manufacture of asbestos-containing products of the chemical's dangers, and stricter workplace rules. EPA also rejected controlled use of asbestos in the workplace and deferral to other government agencies charged with worker and consumer exposure to industrial and product hazards, such as OSHA, the CPSC, and the MSHA. The EPA determined that deferral to these other agencies was inappropriate because no one other authority could address all the risks posed "throughout the life cycle" by asbestos, and any action by one or more of the other agencies still would leave an unacceptable residual risk.

Much of the EPA's analysis is correct, and the EPA's basic decision to use TSCA as a comprehensive statute designed to fight a multi-industry problem was a proper one that we uphold today on review. What concerns us, however, is the manner in which the EPA conducted some of its analysis. TSCA requires the EPA to consider, along with the effects of toxic substances on human health and the environment, "the benefits of such substance[s] or mixture[s] for various uses and the availability of substitutes for such uses," as well as "the reasonably ascertainable economic consequences of the rule, after consideration for the effect on the national economy, small business, technological innovation, the environment, and public health." *Id.* § 2605(c)(1)(C–D).

The EPA presented two comparisons in the record: a world with no further regulation under TSCA, and a world in which no manufacture of asbestos takes place. The EPA rejected calculating how many lives a less burdensome regulation would save, and at what cost. Furthermore the EPA, when calculating the benefits of its ban, explicitly refused to compare it to an improved workplace in which currently available control technology is utilized. *See* 54 Fed. Reg. at 29,474. This decision artificially inflated the purported benefits of the rule by using a baseline comparison substantially lower than what currently available technology could yield.

Under TSCA, the EPA was required to evaluate, rather than ignore, less burdensome regulatory alternatives. TSCA imposes a least-to-most-burdensome hierarchy. In order to impose a regulation at the top of the hierarchy — a total ban of asbestos — the EPA must show not only that its proposed action reduces the risk of the product to an adequate level, but also that the actions Congress identified as less burdensome also would not do the job. The failure of the EPA to do this constitutes a failure to meet its burden of showing that its actions not only reduce the risk but do so in the congressionally mandated *least burdensome* fashion.

Thus it was not enough for the EPA to show, as it did in this case, that banning some asbestos products might reduce the harm that could occur from the use of these products. If that were the standard, it would be no standard at all, for few indeed are the products that are so safe that a complete ban of them would not make the world still safer.

This comparison of two static worlds is insufficient to satisfy the dictates of TSCA. While the EPA may have shown that a world with a complete ban of asbestos might be preferable to one in which there is only the current amount of regulation, the EPA has failed to show that there is not some intermediate state of regulation that would be superior to both the currently-regulated and the completely-banned world. Without showing that asbestos regulation would be ineffective, the EPA cannot discharge its TSCA burden of showing that its regulation is the least burdensome available to it.

Upon an initial showing of product danger, the proper course for the EPA to follow is to consider each regulatory option, beginning with the least burdensome, and the costs and benefits of regulation under each option. The EPA cannot simply skip several rungs, as it did in this case, for in doing so, it may skip a less-burdensome alternative mandated by TSCA. Here, although the EPA mentions the problems posed by intermediate levels of regulation, it takes no steps to calculate the costs and benefits of these intermediate levels. *See* 54 Fed. Reg. at 29,462, 29,474. Without doing this it is impossible, both for the EPA and for this court on review, to know that none of these alternatives was less burdensome than the ban in fact chosen by the agency.

The EPA's offhand rejection of these intermediate regulatory steps is "not the stuff of which substantial evidence is made." *Aqua Slide,* 569 F.2d at 843. While it is true that the EPA considered five different ban options, these differed solely with respect to their effective dates. The EPA did not calculate the risk levels for intermediate levels of regulation, as it believed that there was no asbestos exposure level for which the risk of injury or death was zero. Reducing risk to zero, however, was not the task that Congress set for the EPA in enacting TSCA. The EPA thus has failed "cogently [to] explain why it has exercised its discretion in a given manner," *Chemical Mfrs. Ass'n,* 899 F.2d at 349, by failing to explore in more than a cursory way the less burdensome alternatives to a total ban.

2. The EPA's Calculations.

[The Court expressed concerns regarding the methodology employed by EPA. In particular, it criticized the agency's failure to discount the benefits of an asbestos ban, its failure to compute the costs and benefits of its proposed rule beyond the year 2000, and its calculation of "unquantified benefits" to inflate the costs of continued asbestos use.]

3. Reasonable Basis.

In addition to showing that its regulation is the least burdensome one necessary to protect the environment adequately, the EPA also must show that it has a reasonable basis for the regulation. 15 U.S.C. § 2605(a). To some extent, our inquiry in this area mirrors that used above, for many of the methodological problems we have noted also indicate that the EPA did not have a reasonable basis. We here take the opportunity to highlight some areas of additional concern.

Most problematical to us is the EPA's ban of products for which no substitutes presently are available. In these cases, the EPA bears a tough burden indeed to show that under TSCA a ban is the least burdensome alternative, as TSCA explicitly instructs the EPA to consider "the benefits of such substance or mixture for various uses and the availability of substitutes for such uses." *Id.* § 2605(c)(1)(C). These words are particularly appropriate where the EPA actually has decided to ban a product, rather than simply restrict its use, for it is in these cases that the lack of an adequate substitute is most troubling under TSCA.

As the EPA itself states, "[w]hen no information is available for a product indicating that cost-effective substitutes exist, the estimated cost of a product ban is very high." 54 Fed. Reg. at 29,468. Because of this, the EPA did not ban certain uses of asbestos, such as its use in rocket engines and battery separators. The EPA, however, in several other instances, ignores its own arguments and attempts to justify its ban by stating that the ban itself will cause the development of low-cost, adequate substitute products.

As a general matter, we agree with the EPA that a product ban can lead to great innovation, and it is true that an agency under TSCA, as under other regulatory statutes, "is empowered to issue safety standards which require improvements in existing technology or which require the development of new technology." . . . As even the EPA acknowledges, however, when no adequate substitutes currently exist, the EPA cannot fail to consider this lack when formulating its own guidelines. Under TSCA, therefore, the EPA must present a stronger case to justify the ban, as opposed to regulation, of products with no substitutes.

We note that the EPA does provide a waiver provision for industries where the hoped-for substitutes fail to materialize in time. *See* 54 Fed. Reg. at 29,464. Under this provision, if no adequate substitutes develop, the EPA temporarily may extend the planned phase-out. . . .

By its own terms, the exemption shifts the burden onto the waiver proponent to convince the EPA that the waiver is justified. *See id.* As even the EPA acknowledges, the waiver only "may be granted by [the] EPA in very limited circumstances." *Id.* at 29,460.

The EPA thus cannot use the waiver provision to lessen its burden when justifying banning products without existing substitutes. While TSCA gives the EPA the power to ban such products, the EPA must bear its heavier burden of justifying its total ban in the face of inadequate substitutes. Thus, the agency cannot use its waiver provision to argue that the ban of products with no substitutes should be treated the same as the ban of those for which adequate substitutes are available now.

We also are concerned with the EPA's evaluation of substitutes even in those instances in which the record shows that they are available. . . .

This presents two problems. First, TSCA instructs the EPA to consider the relative merits of its ban, as compared to the economic effects of its actions. The EPA cannot make this calculation if it fails to consider the effects that alternate substitutes will pose after a ban.

Second, the EPA cannot say with any assurance that its regulation will increase workplace safety when it refuses to evaluate the harm that will result from the increased use of substitute products. While the EPA may be correct in its conclusion that the alternate materials pose less risk than asbestos, we cannot say with any more assurance than that flowing from an educated guess that this conclusion is true. . . .

In short, a death is a death, whether occasioned by asbestos or by a toxic substitute product, and the EPA's decision not to evaluate the toxicity of known carcinogenic substitutes is not a reasonable action under TSCA. Once an interested party brings forth credible evidence suggesting the toxicity of the probable or only alternatives to a substance, the EPA must consider the comparative toxic costs of each. Its failure to do so in this case thus deprived its regulation of a reasonable basis, at least in regard to those products as to which petitioners introduced credible evidence of the dangers of the likely substitutes.

4. Unreasonable Risk of Injury.

The final requirement the EPA must satisfy before engaging in any TSCA rulemaking is that it only take steps designed to prevent "unreasonable" risks. In evaluating what is "unreasonable," the EPA is required to consider the costs of any proposed actions and to "carry out this chapter in a reasonable and prudent manner [after considering] the environmental, economic, and social impact of any action." 15 U.S.C. § 2601(c).

As the District of Columbia Circuit stated when evaluating similar language governing the Federal Hazardous Substances Act, "[t]he requirement that the risk be 'unreasonable' necessarily involves a balancing test like that familiar in tort law: The regulation may issue if the severity of the injury that may result from the product, factored by the likelihood of the injury, offsets the harm the regulation itself imposes upon manufacturers and consumers." *Forester v. CPSC*, 559 F.2d 774, 789 (D.C.Cir.1977). We have quoted this language approvingly when evaluating other statutes using similar language. *See, e.g., Aqua Slide*, 569 F.2d at 839.

That the EPA must balance the costs of its regulations against their benefits further is reinforced by the requirement that it seek the least burdensome regulation. While Congress did not dictate that the EPA engage in an exhaustive, full-scale cost-benefit analysis, it did require the EPA to consider both sides of the regulatory equation, and it rejected the notion that the EPA should pursue the reduction of workplace risk at any cost. *See American Textile Mfrs. Inst.*, 452 U.S. at 510 n. 30, 101 S. Ct. at 2491 n. 30 ("unreasonable risk" statutes require "a generalized balancing of costs and benefits" (citing *Aqua Slide*, 569 F.2d at 839)). Thus, "Congress also plainly intended the EPA to consider the economic impact of *any* actions taken by it under . . . TSCA." *Chemical Mfrs. Ass'n*, 899 F.2d at 348.

Even taking all of the EPA's figures as true, and evaluating them in the light most favorable to the agency's decision (non-discounted benefits, discounted costs, analogous exposure estimates included), the agency's analysis results in figures as high as $74 million per life saved. . . .

While we do not sit as a regulatory agency that must make the difficult decision as to what an appropriate expenditure is to prevent someone from incurring the risk of an asbestos-related death, we do note that the EPA, in its zeal to ban any and all asbestos products, basically ignored the cost side of the TSCA equation. The EPA would have this court believe that Congress, when it enacted its requirement that the EPA consider the economic impacts of its regulations, thought that spending $200—300 million to save approximately seven lives (approximately $30—40 million per life) over thirteen years is reasonable.

As we stated in the OSHA context, until an agency "can provide substantial evidence that the benefits to be achieved by [a regulation] bear a reasonable relationship to the costs imposed by the reduction, it cannot show that the standard is reasonably necessary to provide safe or healthful workplaces." *American Petroleum Inst.*, 581 F.2d at 504. Although the OSHA statute differs in major respects from TSCA, the statute does require substantial evidence to support the EPA's contentions that its regulations both have a reasonable basis and are the least burdensome means to a reasonably safe workplace.

The EPA's willingness to argue that spending $23.7 million to save less than one-third of a life reveals that its economic review of its regulations, as required by TSCA, was meaningless. As the petitioners' brief and our review of EPA caselaw reveals, such high costs are rarely, if ever, used to support a safety regulation. If we were to allow such cavalier treatment of the EPA's duty to consider the economic effects of its decisions, we would have to excise entire sections and phrases from the language of TSCA. Because we are judges, not surgeons, we decline to do so. . . .

VI. Conclusion.

In summary, of most concern to us is that the EPA has failed to implement the dictates of TSCA and the prior decisions of this and other courts that, before it imposes a ban on a product, it first evaluate and then reject the less burdensome alternatives laid out for it by Congress. While the EPA spent much time and care crafting its asbestos regulation, its explicit failure to consider the alternatives required of it by Congress deprived its final rule of the reasonable basis it needed to survive judicial scrutiny.

Furthermore, the EPA's adoption of the analogous exposure estimates during the final weeks of its rulemaking process, after public comment was concluded, rather than during the ten years during which it was considering the asbestos ban, was unreasonable and deprived the petitioners of the notice that they required in order to present their own evidence on the validity of the estimates and its data bases. By depriving the petitioners of their right to cross-examine EPA witnesses on methodology and data used to support as much as eighty percent of the proposed benefits in some areas, the EPA also violated the dictates of TSCA.

Finally, the EPA failed to provide a reasonable basis for the purported benefits of its proposed rule by refusing to evaluate the toxicity of likely substitute products that will be used to replace asbestos goods. While the EPA does not have the duty under TSCA of affirmatively seeking out and testing all possible substitutes, when an interested party comes forward with credible evidence that the planned substitutes present a significant, or even greater, toxic risk than the substance in question, the agency must make a formal finding on the record that its proposed action still is both reasonable and warranted under TSCA.

We regret that this matter must continue to take up the valuable time of the agency, parties and, undoubtedly, future courts. The requirements of TSCA, however, are plain, and the EPA cannot deviate from them to reach its desired result. We therefore GRANT the petition for review, VACATE the EPA's proposed regulation, and REMAND to the EPA for further proceedings in light of this opinion.

Notes and Questions

1. What exactly does the Fifth Circuit require EPA to do in order to ban a product? And in what ways did EPA fall short of conducting a sufficient analysis? Is it relevant to this question that Congress itself did not seem to expect EPA to conduct a rigorous quantitative risk assessment in regulating products under § 6? For example, the House Committee report stated that § 6 "does not require a formal benefit-cost analysis" given the difficulties of quantification and monetization. H.R. Rep. 94-1341, 94th Cong. 2d Sess. 14 (1976). The Senate Committee report went still further in emphasizing the difficulties of comparing incommensurables in a quantitative analysis and emphasized the importance of ensuring that EPA gave "full consideration" to the health costs, such as the "burdens of human suffering and premature death." Toxic Substances Control Act, Report of the Senate Comm. on Commerce, S. Rep. 94-698, 94th Cong., 2d Sess. 13 (1976).

2. EPA amassed considerable evidence in support of its asbestos rule and made a number of specific findings based on the scientific evidence. Given this seemingly detailed work, why did the court find EPA's evidence insufficient? What additional evidence would EPA need to proceed with a ban or even a partial restriction? Must it develop quantitative estimates of lives saved well into the future, for example?

3. On what basis did EPA find there was no less burdensome alternative? If EPA did not make this finding, why do you believe it skipped this step when the statute lists it explicitly as a prerequisite? What kind of evidence might be required for such a showing—e.g., that other protective approaches like the use of respirators are not feasible and are more expensive?

4. What kind of analysis does the court have in mind to meet its demands for the added assessment of substitutes? In RISK VERSUS RISK: TRADEOFFS IN PROTECTING HEALTH AND THE ENVIRONMENT, a book published in 1995, John Graham and Jonathan Weiner discuss the importance of ensuring that substitutes are not worse than the problems they seek to cure. But in investigating the risks posed by substitutes, is there any clear stopping point, or must EPA also investigate the costs and benefits of substitute products and perhaps the substitutes for substitutes? Oliver Houck has suggested that regulatory demands like these threaten to "eat up heroic amounts of money, remain information-starved, feature shameless manipulation of the data, face crippling political pressure, and produce little abatement." Oliver A. Houck, *Tales from a Troubled Marriage: Science and Law in Environmental Policy,* 17 TUL. ENVL. L. J. 163, 169–170 (2003). Is there a better way to marry rigorous science-based assessments with practical regulatory programs?

5. Is the court's interpretation of §6 of TSCA the only plausible reading of the statute? What did Congress mean in inserting the phrase "to the extent necessary" in §6(a)? If there are other plausible readings of the EPA's burdens under §6(a), should EPA be entitled to any deference in its interpretation? What might EPA argue under *Chevron,* for example?

6. Compare the court's analysis with the approach the D.C. Circuit took in *EDF v. EPA* above. The two judicial panels were looking at very different statutes, of course, but are the operative sections that different? Consider in the excerpts below whether the two statutes are clearly distinguishable in the way they treat the burden of proof of establishing unreasonable risk.

> **TSCA 6(a) Scope of regulation** If the Administrator finds that there is a *reasonable basis* to conclude that the manufacture, processing, distribution in commerce, use, or disposal of a chemical substance or mixture, or that any combination of such activities, *presents or will present an unreasonable risk of injury to health or the environment,* the Administrator shall by rule apply one or more of the following

requirements to such substance or mixture to the extent necessary to protect adequately against such risk using the least burdensome requirements . . .

FIFRA 6(b) If it *appears* to the Administrator that a pesticide or its labeling or other material required to be submitted does not comply with the provisions of this subchapter or, when used in accordance with widespread and commonly recognized practice, *generally causes unreasonable adverse effects on the environment,* the Administrator may issue a notice of the Administrator's intent either . . . . (emphasis added)

---

7. The fact that at least one of EPA's rules appeared to cost about $74 million per life struck the court as problematic. Indeed, even though life is priceless, $74 million does seem like a high price tag. On the other hand, does this estimate also showcase the malleability of cost-benefit estimates? Can't one slice the analysis in ways that alter the cost-benefit ratio dramatically, for example by averaging across many firms on one hand or selecting out the worst case costs imposed on an outlier firm, on the other hand? If both approaches are fair for purposes of cost-benefit analysis, is there a way to discipline these analyses so that this lumping versus segregation cannot be used to distort the ultimate findings?

8. After the *Corrosion Proof* decision, EPA effectively halted all of its activities under § 6, and EPA's existing chemical oversight program under TSCA withered away. Was this regulatory inactivity prudent in light of *Corrosion Proof,* or did EPA back down too soon?

On the twenty-fifth anniversary of *Corrosion Proof,* and prompted by a mandate in the 2016 reauthorization of TSCA, EPA listed asbestos as one of the 10 chemicals it will consider first in evaluating risks to human health and the environment. EPA, *EPA Names First Chemicals for Review Under New TSCA Legislation* (Nov. 29, 2016), at https://www.epa.gov/newsreleases/epa-names-first-chemicals-review-under-new-tsca-legislation. Nine other chemicals, including Trichloroethylene (a common degreasing agent) and Perchloroethylene (commonly used in dry cleaning operations), were also identified for priority evaluation. All 10 chemicals will undergo complete risk assessments over the next three years. If there is a "significant risk" posed by one or more of these chemicals, EPA is then required to develop a mitigation plan for the chemical within two years.

9. In reversing and remanding the Consumer Product Safety Commission's (CPSC's) ban of urea-foam insulation used in homes (because it emitted a human carcinogen, formaldehyde, and appeared to cause acute health effects), the Fifth Circuit reiterated the heavy burden placed on an agency attempting to ban a product under the "unreasonable risk" standard. The Fifth Circuit panel criticized the Commission for its incomplete scientific evidence — for example, there was only one large rat study supporting estimates of carcinogenicity and limited evidence on the offgassing of formaldehyde from the insulation. *Gulf South Insulation v. CPSC,* 701 F.2d 1137 (5th Cir. 1983). Even though the court concluded that "the truth appears to lie

somewhere between the positions taken by the Commission and the industry," it held that CPSC had not met its burden: "To make precise estimates, precise data are required." *Id.* at 1146. The effect on the agency was much like the effect of *Corrosion Proof* on EPA's § 6 regulation: CPSC effectively shut down its efforts to ban latent hazards in consumer products due to the heavy burden placed on establishing an "unreasonable risk." In both cases, the courts required a substantial body of evidence from the agency to support a restriction, a burden that stands in stark contrast to the burden placed on EPA under FIFRA.

B. TSCA Regulation in Context

As a result of *Corrosion Proof* and the procedural requirements imposed on EPA through TSCA, the regulation and oversight of the safety of chemicals has been considered a failure. Only a few hundred chemicals have been subjected to EPA's "test rules" requiring added testing for safety. Fewer than a dozen chemicals have been formally restricted.

Perhaps the most worrisome result of these cumulative weaknesses of TSCA, however, arose with respect to the statute's perverse effect on manufacturers' incentives to conduct toxicity testing. Under the provisions in place up until 2016, manufacturers of dangerous chemicals were at risk of a test rule or use restriction only if EPA could establish either that the chemical "may present an unreasonable risk of injury to health or the environment" or that the chemical was manufactured in high quantities and lacked sufficient data to assess the safety of the chemical. TSCA § 4(a), 15 U.S.C. § 2603(a). Given the burden on EPA to justify additional safety testing, why would manufacturers investigate the toxicity of their chemicals voluntarily? In fact, TSCA also requires manufacturers to submit all information regarding adverse effects to EPA. Thus, bad news about product risks must be shared immediately, making willful ignorance regarding long-term toxicity only that much more rational from the standpoint of manufacturers. Section 8(c) and (e), 15 U.S.C. § 2607(c) and (e).

Rather than counteract these perverse incentives for ignorance, tort liability generally serves to exacerbate them. Consider again basic tort causation requirements. The plaintiff has the burden of proof to establish causation. If little to nothing is known about a toxic chemical, does that burden help absolve the manufacturers? Indeed, is the safer course for manufacturers to do as little as possible with regard to learning about long-term risks of their products? See, e.g., Margaret A. Berger, *Eliminating General Causation: Notes Towards a New Theory of Justice and Toxic Torts*, 97 Colum. L. Rev. 2117, 2135–40 (1997). If you follow these questions, you will see that even tort claims alleging a negligent or even reckless failure to test by the manufacturer still can only succeed if the plaintiffs can prove that their damages were caused by the under-testing.

It is thus not very surprising that we know alarmingly little about the long-term safety of most chemicals sold in commerce. In a study done in the mid-1980s, the National Academies of Science found that for more than 80 percent of the chemicals in commerce (60,000 or so) there was not a single test or study on the long-term toxicity (acute toxicity is different in part because of the higher risk of tort liability and the relative ease in proving causation). See Figure 10.1, below, which is reproduced from the STEERING COMM. ON IDENTIFICATION OF TOXIC AND POTENTIALLY TOXIC CHEMICALS FOR CONSIDERATION BY THE NAT'L TOXICOLOGY PROGRAM, NAT'L RESEARCH COUNCIL, TOXICITY TESTING: STRATEGIES TO DETERMINE NEEDS AND PRIORITIES at 118 fig.2 (1984).

Figure 10-1.

TOXICITY TESTING INFORMATION AVAILABLE ON SEVEN CATEGORIES OF CHEMICALS

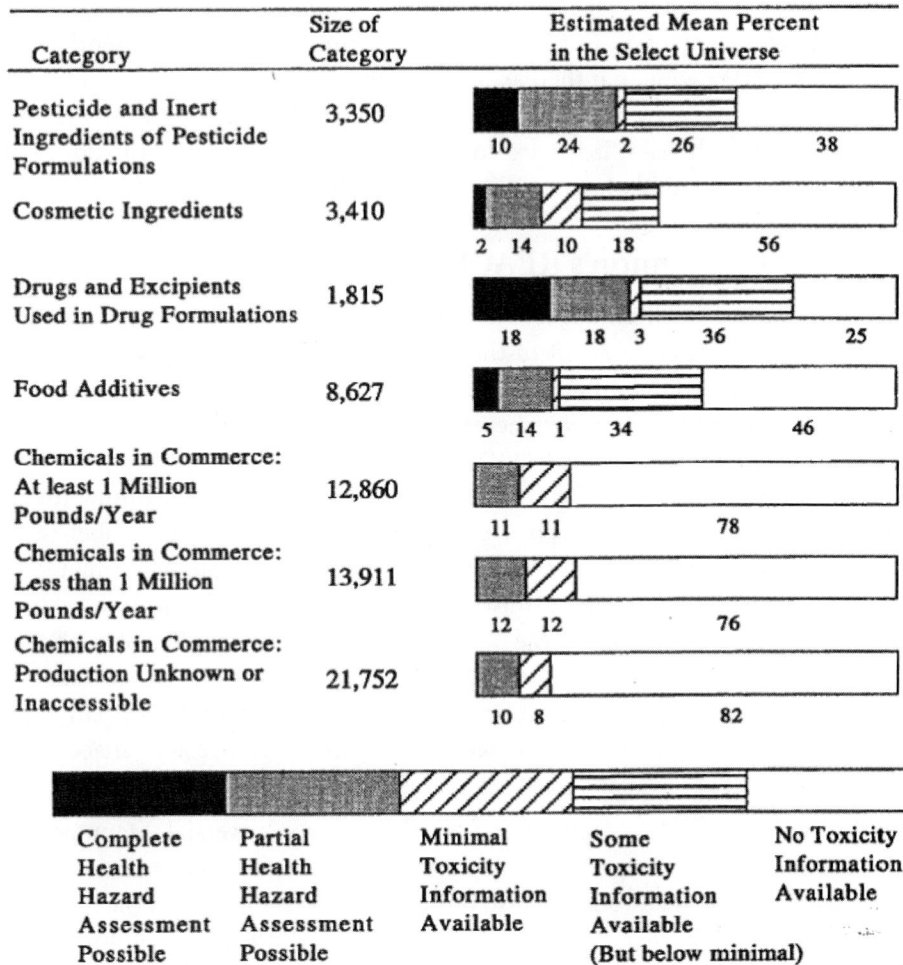

Twenty years later, the National Academies study was repeated only with respect to chemicals produced in the highest volume. The testing record was slightly better for these high-volume chemicals, but the results were hardly reassuring: there was only limited toxicity data available on about two-thirds of all chemicals in commerce, and the remaining chemicals were supported by almost no data. *See, e.g.*, ENVTL. HEALTH PROGRAM, ENVTL. DEFENSE FUND, TOXIC IGNORANCE (1997); *Testing: CMA More*

Optimistic than EDF on Lack of Data for 100 Chemicals, 230 DAILY ENV'T REP. (BNA), at A-4, (Dec. 1, 1997); OFFICE OF POLLUTION PREVENTION & TOXICS, ENVTL. PROT. AGENCY, WHAT DO WE REALLY KNOW ABOUT THE SAFETY OF HIGH PRODUCTION VOLUME CHEMICALS? (1998).

Thus, TSCA and tort law combined may unwittingly encourage manufacturers to learn nothing about the long-term safety of the chemicals they manufacture. Given this dearth of information about risk, how can the legislative process find momentum to reverse these incentives for ignorance? Here the law encounters an added challenge: without some mass public support for a more vigorous chemical testing program, the resistance of industry to costly testing and regulation is likely to prevail. In the abstract, generating public support for more comprehensive safety testing on chemicals would seem easy. But in practice, gaining the public's attention and resources requires showing that there is some credible threat or risk that results from the lack of testing. Here again ignorance produces complacency. Without a crisis or at least tangible health risks, it is hard to move the political process to address the enormous gaps in scientific understanding of most chemicals in use.

C. The European Union's REACH

Interestingly, however, a shift in constituency support for some basic testing is arising in the United States as a result of the European Union's activities. In 2006, the European Union passed an ambitious directive, REACH, that required a prescribed list of tests to be conducted on any chemical sold above threshold quantities in the European Union. See Regulation 1907/2006, concerning the Registration, Evaluation, Authorisation and Restriction of Chemicals (REACH). This incoming toxicity data is also evaluated by a European Agency that may, in turn, impose labeling and other market restrictions on individual chemicals. *Id*. at Art. 56. More dangerous chemicals ("chemicals of concern") must also obtain agency "authorization" to be on the market, which in turn requires the manufacturer to make an affirmative showing that there are not more effective substitutes available at a reasonable price. *Id*. at Art. 56 and 57. Under the REACH legislation, there is even the possibility of banning or significantly restricting particularly dangerous chemicals if there are "unacceptable risks," even without the availability of safer substitutes. *Id*. at Art. 58(1).

The European Union's REACH legislation has been controversial. Manufacturers worry that the costs of testing will produce few public benefits since most laboratory tests are generally designed to favor false positives over false negatives (i.e., to err on the side of predicting harm). Positive results will thus be indecisive and may trigger more and more testing only to show — after considerable financial investments — that the chemicals are not hazardous after all. On the other side, public health and environmental advocates worry about the implementation and enforcement of such an ambitious program. Can manufacturers skimp on the testing requirements under REACH? And if they can, what are the enforcement consequences?

Perhaps one of the most clearly beneficial features of REACH has been the effect it has had on United States chemicals policy. Manufacturers participating in the

European chemicals market must conduct basic tests in order to sell their products. Thus, these manufacturers are more supportive of identical requirements in the United States that impose the requirements on their U.S. competitors who may be avoiding the European market. Interest in stronger amendments to TSCA thus came from a portion of industry itself that is eager to capitalize on the costs they invest in testing in order to participate in the European market.

In addition, with the chemicals of concern designation, the European Union, through REACH, is beginning to triage testing and analysis on the worst chemicals in a way that EPA was not able to accomplish under TSCA. The resulting increased public awareness of risks of certain chemicals has also led to more public pressure in the United States.

In the wake of the European Union's REACH legislation, some states in the United States have become still more active in the chemical regulation game. A flurry of state laws regulating chemicals were passed after REACH that parallel the European model in a number of important respects. See Figure 10-2 below. At an aggregate level, since 2006, 919 state and local laws regulating chemicals have been passed or proposed. Prior to 2006 and going back to 1957, 325 laws were passed. In the years after REACH was passed, more than 190 state and local laws regulating chemicals were proposed or passed each year. The comparable average before REACH was about 6.5 per year. These data were collected with simple searches of a legislative database found at http://www.newmoa.org/prevention/ic2/projects/chempolicy/index.php. State statutes passed in California, Massachusetts, and Maine in particular impose considerably greater oversight and testing requirements on chemicals sold within the state as compared to federal law.

Figure 10-2. The Number of State and Local Laws Regulating Chemicals Passed in the United States by Year

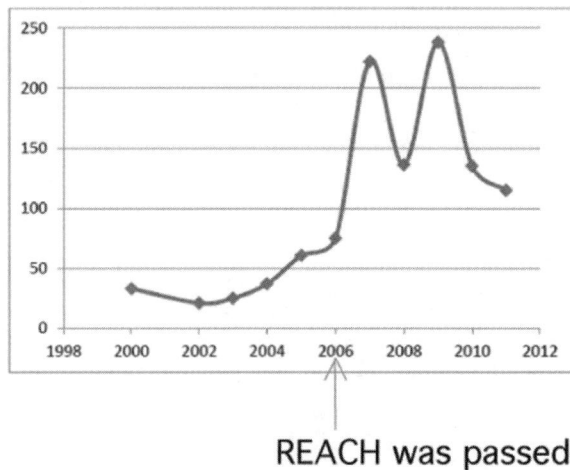

REACH was passed

The increased activity from the states (bottom up) and from Europe (abroad) ultimately heightened public awareness while also raising the benefits to manufacturers of a more unified federal solution. This created the right climate for federal reform legislation.

D. The 2016 Amendments to TSCA

After years of debate, legislation was finally passed and consolidated in the Frank R. Lautenberg Chemical Safety Act, Pub. L. 114-182 (June 22, 2016). A redlined version of the Act and the changes it made to the previous TSCA is available at http://blogs .edf.org/health/files/2016/06/TSCA-as-amended-by-final-bill-6-22-16.pdf. The developments leading up to the Lautenberg Act are grist for a novel, with intrigue and inside battles. Ultimately and perhaps in part in response to these internal struggles, the amendments only serve to exacerbate TSCA's convoluted approach to chemical regulation. As a result, much remains to be learned about how the complicated Lautenberg Act will play out in the future.

Several clear changes wrought by the Lautenberg Act do stand out, however. The first is the stronger authority EPA enjoys to require testing and to ensure that added testing occurs. In the course of conducting this mandated research, moreover, industry will face greater restrictions in classifying information as trade secret protected. The second set of changes creates mechanisms for preemption of state laws (defined as new statutes, criminal penalties, or administrative actions) in cases in which EPA is taking action with respect to a particular chemical substance. This will presumably include some, and perhaps much, of the state and local legislation just described. Finally, the 2016 amendments set deadlines for EPA in its review of the most worrisome chemicals.

The amendments also made dozens and perhaps hundreds of adjustments to other features of TSCA as well. Foremost among them is the different trigger for banning or restricting existing chemicals under §6. Rather than leave in place the failed cost-benefit approach to determine unreasonable risk, Congress amended TSCA so that costs are no longer a relevant consideration. The redlined §§6(a), 6(b)(4)(A), and 6(c)(2)(A) are shown below. As a visual overview, you can also review the flow chart prepared by the Environmental Defense Fund that traces the new approach to existing chemical regulation ushered in by the Frank Lautenberg Act (from http://blogs.edf.org/health/files/2016/06/FRL21-TSCA-flowcharts-6-28-16 -Slide2.jpg).

SEC. 6. PRIORITIZATION, RISK EVALUATION, AND REGULATION OF HAZARDOUS CHEMICAL SUBSTANCES AND MIXTURES.

(a) SCOPE OF REGULATION.—If the Administrator finds that there is a reasonable basis to conclude determines in accordance with subsection (b)(4)(A) that the manufacture, processing, distribution in commerce, use, or disposal of a chemical substance or mixture, or that any combination of such activities, presents, or will present an unreasonable risk of injury to health or the environment, the Administrator shall by rule, and subject to section 18, and in accordance with subsection (c)(2), apply one or more of the following requirements to such substance or mixture to the extent necessary so that the chemical substance no longer presents such risk~~to protect adequately against such risk using the least burdensome requirements~~:

(1) A requirement (A) prohibiting <u>or otherwise restricting</u> the manufacturing, processing, or distribution in commerce of such substance or mixture, or (B) limiting the amount of such substance or mixture which may be manufactured, processed, or distributed in commerce.

(2) A requirement—

(A) prohibiting<u> or otherwise restricting</u> the manufacture, processing, or distribution in commerce of such substance or mixture for (i) a particular use or (ii) a particular use in a concentration in excess of a level specified by the Administrator in the rule imposing the requirement, or

(B) limiting the amount of such substance or mixture which may be manufactured, processed, or distributed in commerce for (i) a particular use or (ii) a particular use in a concentration in excess of a level specified by the Administrator in the rule imposing the requirement.

(3) A requirement that such substance or mixture or any article containing such substance or mixture be marked with or accompanied by clear and adequate <u>minimum</u> warnings and instructions with respect to its use, distribution in commerce, or disposal or with respect to any combination of such activities. The form and content of such <u>minimum</u> warnings and instructions shall be prescribed by the Administrator.

(4) A requirement that manufacturers and processors of such substance or mixture make and retain records of the processes used to manufacture or process such substance or mixture <u>or</u> ~~and~~ monitor or conduct tests which are reasonable and necessary to assure compliance with the requirements of any rule applicable under this subsection.

(5) A requirement prohibiting or otherwise regulating any manner or method of commercial use of such substance or mixture.

(6)(A) A requirement prohibiting or otherwise regulating any manner or method of disposal of such substance or mixture, or of any article containing such substance or mixture, by its manufacturer or processor or by any other person who uses, or disposes of, it for commercial purposes.

(B) A requirement under subparagraph (A) may not require any person to take any action which would be in violation of any law or requirement of, or in effect for, a State or political subdivision, and shall require each person subject to it to notify each State and political subdivision in which a required disposal may occur of such disposal.

(7) A requirement directing manufacturers or processors of such substance or mixture (A) to give notice of such <u>determination</u> ~~unreasonable risk of injury~~ to distributors in commerce of such substance or mixture and, to the extent reasonably ascertainable, to other persons in possession of such substance or mixture or exposed to such substance or mixture, (B) to give public notice of such <u>determination</u>~~risk of injury~~, and (C) to replace or repurchase such substance or mixture as elected by the person to which the requirement is directed.

Any requirement (or combination of requirements) imposed under this subsection may be limited in application to specified geographic areas.

(4) RISK EVALUATION PROCESS AND DEADLINES.—
     (A) IN GENERAL.—The Administrator shall conduct risk evaluations pursuant to this paragraph to determine whether a chemical substance presents an unreasonable risk of injury to health or the environment, without consideration of costs or other nonrisk factors, including an unreasonable risk to a potentially exposed or susceptible subpopulation identified as relevant to the risk evaluation by the Administrator, under the conditions of use.

Section 6(c)(2)(A)

(2~~1~~) REQUIREMENTS FOR RULE.—
     (A) STATEMENT OF EFFECTS.—In proposing and promulgating a ~~any~~ rule under subsection (a) with respect to a chemical substance or mixture, the Administrator shall consider

and publish a statement based on reasonably available information with respect to—
     (i~~A~~) the effects of ~~such~~ the chemical substance or mixture on health and the magnitude of the exposure of human beings to ~~such~~ the chemical substance or mixture;~~,~~
     (ii~~B~~) the effects of ~~such~~ the chemical substance or mixture on the environment and the magnitude of the exposure of the environment to such substance or mixture;~~,~~
     (iii~~C~~) the benefits of ~~such~~ the chemical substance or mixture for various uses ~~and the availability of substitutes for such uses~~;~~,~~ and
     (iv~~D~~) the reasonably ascertainable economic consequences of the rule, ~~after~~ including consideration of—
          (I) the likely effect of the rule on the national economy, small business, technological innovation, the environment, and public health;
          (II) the costs and benefits of the proposed regulatory action and of the 1 or more primary alternative regulatory actions considered by the Administrator; and
          (III) the cost effectiveness of the proposed regulatory action and of the 1 or more primary alternative regulatory actions considered by the Administrator.

Figure 10-3. How the Lautenberg Act Works

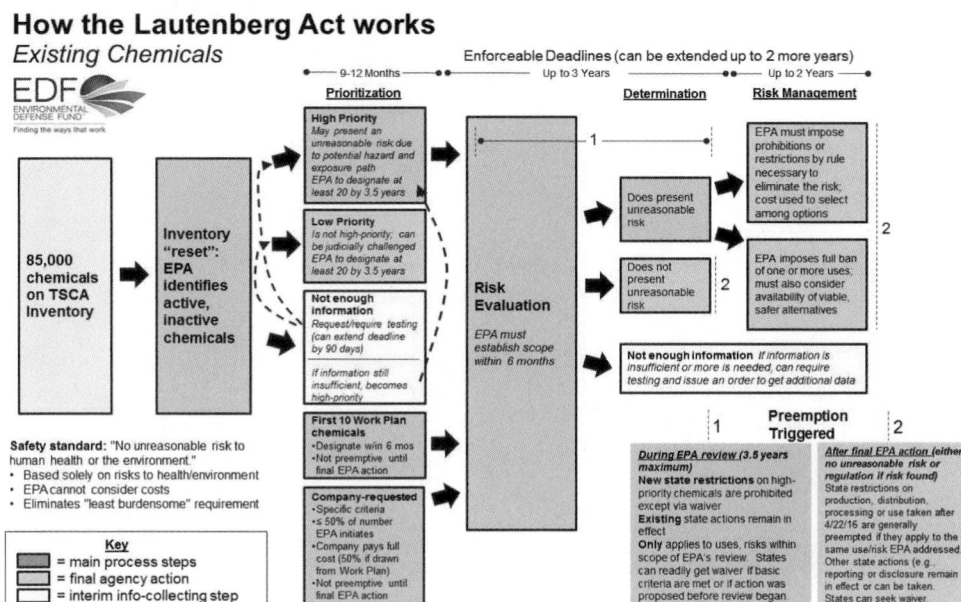

How the Lautenberg Act works

Existing Chemicals

EDF ENVIRONMENTAL DEFENSE FUND — Finding the ways that work

Enforceable Deadlines (can be extended up to 2 more years)

9-12 Months — Up to 3 Years — Up to 2 Years

Prioritization | **Determination** | **Risk Management**

85,000 chemicals on TSCA Inventory

Inventory "reset": EPA identifies active, inactive chemicals

High Priority — May present an unreasonable risk due to potential hazard and exposure path. EPA to designate at least 20 by 3.5 years

Low Priority — Is not high-priority; can be judicially challenged. EPA to designate at least 20 by 3.5 years

Not enough information — Request/require testing (can extend deadline by 90 days). If information still insufficient, becomes high-priority

First 10 Work Plan chemicals — •Designate w/in 6 mos •Not preemptive until final EPA action

Company-requested — •Specific criteria •≤ 50% of number EPA initiates •Company pays full cost (50% if drawn from Work Plan) •Not preemptive until final EPA action

Risk Evaluation — EPA must establish scope within 6 months

Does present unreasonable risk

Does not present unreasonable risk — 2

EPA must impose prohibitions or restrictions by rule necessary to eliminate the risk; cost used to select among options

EPA imposes full ban of one or more uses; must also consider availability of viable, safer alternatives — 2

Not enough information — If information is insufficient or more is needed, can require testing and issue an order to get additional data

Safety standard: "No unreasonable risk to human health or the environment."
• Based solely on risks to health/environment
• EPA cannot consider costs
• Eliminates "least burdensome" requirement

Key
■ = main process steps
▨ = final agency action
□ = interim info-collecting step

Preemption Triggered — 1 | 2

During EPA review (3.5 years maximum) — New state restrictions on high-priority chemicals are prohibited except via waiver. Existing state actions remain in effect. Only applies to uses, risks within scope of EPA's review. States can readily get waiver if basic criteria are met or if action was proposed before review began.

After final EPA action (either no unreasonable risk or regulation if risk found) — State restrictions on production, distribution, processing or use taken after 4/22/16 are generally preempted if they apply to the same use/risk EPA addressed. Other state actions (e.g., reporting or disclosure remain in effect or can be taken. States can seek waiver.

Source: Environmental Defense Fund.

Practice Problem

To gain still more insight into the implications of the 2016 amendments for the regulation of existing chemicals, imagine yourself now as the lucky attorney in EPA's Office of General Counsel asked to assist some of EPA's scientific staff in their effort to regulate one of the first existing chemicals under the 2016 amendments—MCHM (4-methylcyclohexane methanol), the chemical that spilled into the Elk River in West Virginia in 2014, shutting down the water supply to nine counties and leading to a federal state of emergency. (MCHM is a chemical foaming agent used to clean coal.) The staff believes that the lack of scientific information on the chemical, coupled with the environmental risks of its release, justify added restrictions on the chemical's use and manufacture, potentially including a ban. There is very little scientific knowledge about the risks of MCHM, other than that the chemical is lethal when ingested at relatively high doses and that it causes nausea, vomiting, and headaches. There is virtual no research on the long-term toxicity and there are reasons to believe that these risks might be high. For that reason, EPA wishes to bypass the testing stage and proceed straight to restrictions on this chemical that has been on the market for at least 50 years.

In light of the redlined amendments to the original §6 of TSCA, which is provided above and summarized in the flow chart, what can you advise the EPA scientific staff with respect to the nature of the evidence and other considerations EPA must make to proceed with some type of manufacture and use restriction on this chemical? What interpretative questions remain after reading the amended TSCA section? In advising the staff on how best to proceed, you should also be aware that EPA's §6 actions are still subject to judicial review under the substantial evidence standard.

Chapter 11

Enforcement: Ensuring Compliance with Environmental Laws

I. Introduction

On August 26, 1996, Allen Elias, the owner of a fertilizer company located near Soda Springs, Idaho, ordered four workers to enter a large, 25,000-gallon tank in order to clean out sludge from the bottom of the tank. On this hot summer day, the workers entered the tank through a 22-inch manhole at the top, but had difficulty washing out the sludge through a small hole at the end of tank. The workers also reported experiencing sore throats and other health effects from the air inside the tank. Despite repeated requests from one of the workers, Elias failed to provide the workers with any safety equipment or training for the work inside the tank. The next morning, August 27, 1996, the workers attempted to resume the work inside the tank. Two workers entered the tank and began to empty the sludge through the small hole onto the ground. After about 45 minutes, one of the workers, Scott Dominguez, collapsed inside the tank. The second worker got out. Dominguez's colleagues tried but were unable to remove Dominguez from the tank. The fire department eventually had to cut a hole in the side of the tank to remove Dominguez and rush him to the hospital.

Unknown to the workers, the sludge inside the tank was the byproduct of a cyanide leaching process that Elias had patented. After extricating Dominguez from the tank, the fire chief asked Elias whether cyanide could be in the tank. Elias denied knowledge of anything in the tank other than water and sludge. After Dominguez arrived at the hospital, the treating physician suspected Dominguez was suffering from cyanide poisoning and called Elias to ask him if there was a possibility of cyanide in the tank. Elias again replied no. Nevertheless, the physician ordered and administered a cyanide antidote kit, and Dominguez responded positively. Blood tests in the hospital confirmed that Dominguez had extremely toxic levels of cyanide in his body.

A grand jury later charged Elias with a four-count indictment. Count I charged Elias with storage or disposal of hazardous waste without a permit, thereby placing another person in imminent danger of death or seriously bodily injury, in violation of RCRA § 3008(e), 42 U.S.C. § 6928(e). Counts II and III charged Elias with improper disposal of hazardous waste without a permit, in violation of RCRA § 3008(d), 42 U.S.C. § 6928(d). Count IV charged Elias with making material misstatements to federal officers, in violation of 18 U.S.C. § 1001. On May 7, 1999, the jury convicted Elias on all four counts. Allen Elias was sentenced to prison for 17 years, with the prison sentence sustained after years of appeals. *U.S. v. Elias*, 269 F.3d 1003 (9th Cir. 2001).

925

Most matters of environmental enforcement are not quite as extreme as the case of *U.S. v. Elias*. Indeed, it was the first-ever conviction for the crime of "knowing endangerment" under RCRA after the provision had been added to the statute in 1980. But the case does illustrate a few common points about environmental enforcement. For example, as clearly demonstrated by the tragic impact on Mr. Dominguez, violations of environmental laws sometimes result in very serious harm to human health as well as the broader "environment." Second, violations of environmental laws sometimes lead to substantial penalties, up to and including incarceration. Third, violations of environmental statutes sometimes raise implications for other areas of law, such as the federal criminal code, Title 18 U.S.C.

Whether the violation is big or small, environmental laws — including all the statutes discussed in earlier chapters of this book — would lose meaning if they could not be enforced. As Justice Brennan once observed, "Ultimately, enforcement of the law is what really counts." *Evans v. Jeff D.*, 475 U.S. 717, 743 (1986) (Brennan, J., dissenting).

Enforcement is widely recognized as a crucial component of effective environmental protection. It is frequently a complex task, carried out every day by thousands of actors — at federal, state, tribal, and local levels of government and, in many instances, by private citizens. When done effectively, environmental enforcement may serve three major functions: (1) fixing existing environmental problems; (2) promoting future compliance; and (3) ensuring fairness and a level playing field among regulated entities. As you read this chapter, consider which of the various mechanisms of environmental enforcement may be best suited for addressing the needs of each individual case.

Federal environmental statutes provide regulators with a number of enforcement tools. While environmental statutes vary, most federal environmental legislation authorizes EPA to inspect facilities and to compel regulated entities to self-monitor and to report on their discharges and emissions. Where violations are detected, EPA is generally empowered to respond with enforcement actions. States and Tribes, too, may have an important role to play in pursuing environmental violators. In addition, citizens may bring suit against parties that are not in compliance with an environmental standard, permit condition, or order.

As we will see in this chapter, most violations of environmental law can be addressed through administrative tools, such as the issuance of violation notices, administrative orders, and administrative penalties. For more significant cases, environmental agencies may file civil claims with a court of competent jurisdiction, seeking remedies that may include damages, injunctive relief, and declaratory judgments. In the most serious of cases, such as the case of *U.S. v. Elias*, environmental agencies may work with prosecutors to seek criminal penalties, including incarceration of individual defendants. We can picture these enforcement tools as a pyramid:

Figure 11-1. Schematic of Government Enforcement Options

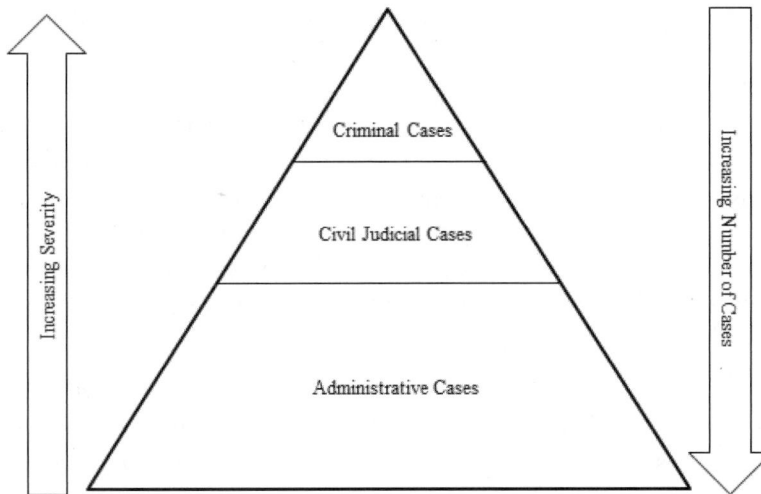

Increasing Severity

Increasing Number of Cases

Criminal Cases

Civil Judicial Cases

Administrative Cases

This chapter includes a selection of materials that pertain to various categories of environmental enforcement activities and the sometimes challenging legal questions that environmental enforcement raises.

II. Information Gathering

In most environmental enforcement programs, self-monitoring and self-reporting play important roles. Regulated pollution sources are very often required to sample and analyze their own effluents and discharges for the presence and concentration of pollutants, measure how well their pollution control equipment is functioning, and monitor groundwater quality.

Self-reported data may form the basis for an administrative order or a civil judicial enforcement action by governmental officials or citizens. (Due to constitutional prohibitions on self-incrimination, however, source-reported data may not be introduced as evidence in an environmental criminal prosecution.) Beyond this, agencies sometimes use the self-monitoring reports submitted by sources as a tool for allocating limited government resources to on-site inspections. Additionally, self-monitoring reports may lead to increased attention by source managers to preventing pollution and achieving compliance.

One question that has arisen in environmental enforcement cases is whether a permittee that has self-reported an environmental violation may defend itself by contending that its reports were unreliable as a result of its own flawed sampling and analysis. The following case considers that issue.

Sierra Club v. Union Oil Co.

813 F.2d 1480 (9th Cir. 1987)

Judge PREGERSON:

The Sierra Club brought a citizen enforcement action against Union Oil Company of California ("Union Oil") alleging that Union Oil violated the terms of its National Pollutant Discharge Elimination System ("NPDES") permit on seventy-six occasions. After a five-day trial, the district court found no violations of the permit. The court excused some of the reported exceedances of permit limitations . . . on the ground that reports of exceedances were mistakes caused by sampling error . . . .

Union Oil argued that seven of the alleged violations were excusable because, while the Discharge Monitoring Reports ostensibly indicated that Union Oil has exceeded limitations contained in the permit, these reports were invalid due to sampling error. We hold that the district court should not have excused these exceedances on the basis of sampling error.

The NPDES program fundamentally relies on self-monitoring. The Code of Federal Regulations contains several provisions that are obviously designed to ensure utmost accuracy in the reports submitted by permittees. For instance, 40 C.F.R. § 122.22 requires that a person signing a self-monitoring report shall make the following certification:

> I certify under penalty of law that this document and all attachments were prepared under my direction or supervision in accordance with a system designed to assure that qualified personnel properly gather and evaluate the information submitted. Based on my inquiry of the person or persons who manage the system, or those persons directly responsible for gathering the information, the information submitted is, to the best of my knowledge and belief, true, accurate, and complete. I am aware that there are significant penalties for submitting false information, including the possibility of fine and imprisonment for knowing violations.

The regulations at 40 C.F.R. §§ 122.4(j) and (k) establish numerous requirements for self-monitoring and reporting. These sections provide for heavy criminal penalties for anyone who knowingly falsifies reports or knowingly makes any false statement.

These and other EPA regulations demonstrate the agency's concern that reports be accurate. The legislative history surrounding the 1972 amendments to the Act supports the conclusion that accurate reports are critical to effective operation of the Act:

> The bill . . . establishes and makes precise new requirements imposed on persons and subject to enforcement. One purpose of these new requirements is to avoid the necessity of lengthy fact finding, investigations, and negotiations at the time of enforcement. Enforcement of violations of requirements under this Act should be based on relatively narrow fact situations requiring a minimum of discretionary decision making or delay.

S. Rep. No. 414, 92nd Cong., 1st Sess. 64, *reprinted in* 1972 U.S. Code Conf. & Ad. News 34668, 3730.

Were we to accept Union Oil's argument regarding the use of sampling errors to excuse reported permit exceedances, we would be sanctioning countless additional hours of NPDES litigation and creating new, complicated factual questions for district courts to resolve. As indicated by the legislative history, Congress hoped to limit such situations. In addition, if each self-monitoring report is to be considered only prima facie rather than conclusive evidence of an exceedance of a permit limitation, citizen groups like the Sierra Club would be taking a considerable risk whenever they initiated a citizen enforcement action pursuant to 33 U.S.C. § 1365. While a permittee's publicly filed report might clearly indicate that illegal pollution was taking place, the permittee might have additional information unavailable to citizen groups indicating that sampling error rendered the reports meaningless. Finally and most importantly, allowing permittees to excuse their reported exceedances by showing sampling error would create the perverse result of rewarding permittees for sloppy laboratory practices. Such an approach would surely undermine the efficacy of the self-monitoring program.

We conclude that when a permittee's reports indicate that the permittee has exceeded permit limitations, the permittee may not impeach its own reports by showing sampling error.

Notes and Questions

1. Beyond the EPA regulations and the legislative history cited in this excerpt from the Ninth Circuit's decision in *Union Oil*, accurate reporting may be required directly by environmental statutes themselves. For example, under the Clean Water Act § 309(c)(1)-(2), any person who "negligently violates" requirements, including reporting and recordkeeping obligations, may be punished by imprisonment for up to one year, while "knowing violations" of the same may be punishable by up to three years. Does this mean that if a regulated party submits inaccurate information to an agency, but the error is neither knowing nor negligent, the regulated party is not in violation of reporting requirements? For example, what if there was a technical "glitch" in the transmission of the reported data, or it contained a typographical error? How would that conclusion differ from the result in *Union Oil*?

2. As demonstrated by *Sierra Club v. Union Oil Co.*, one of the most common sources of information about a particular facility is the facility itself, which may be required regularly to submit environmental information to regulators pursuant to a permit or regulation. Regulators may also have statutory authority to require a facility to submit information upon a specific request. *See, e.g.,* Clean Water Act § 308(a), 33 U.S.C. § 1318(a); CERCLA § 104(e), 42 U.S.C. § 9604(e). Failure by a facility to respond fully and properly to such an information request may result in the assessment of penalties and further enforcement actions. Of course, regulators can and often do request that information be provided voluntarily. Can you see why members of the regulated community would provide information to regulators voluntarily?

Environmental statutes typically authorize representatives of environmental agencies to conduct on-site inspections at private facilities. These inspections may be routine and random — where there is no reason to suspect that a facility is out of compliance — or for cause, i.e., based on a suspicion that a facility is violating applicable standards. Owners and operators of facilities that are inspected are sometimes notified prior to the inspection, as a way of ensuring that knowledgeable plant personnel will be present when an inspector arrives. In other instances, however, inspectors may show up at a targeted facility with absolutely no advance warning.

One question that has arisen with regard to on-site inspections is whether representatives of government agencies must obtain a search warrant in instances where a facility owner refuses to consent to an inspection. The United States Supreme Court addressed that question in the following decision.

Marshall v. Barlow's, Inc.

436 U.S. 307 (1978)

Justice WHITE:

Section 8(a) of the Occupational Safety and Health Act of 1970 (OSHA or the Act) empowers agents of the Secretary of Labor (Secretary) to search the work area of any employment facility within the Act's jurisdiction. The purpose of the search is to inspect for safety hazards and violations of OSHA regulations. No search warrant or other process is expressly required under the Act.

On the morning of September 11, 1975, an OSHA inspector entered the customer service area of Barlow's, Inc., an electrical and plumbing installation business located in Pocatello, Idaho. The president and general manager, Ferrol G. "Bill" Barlow, was on hand; and the OSHA inspector, after showing his credentials, informed Mr. Barlow that he wished to conduct a search of the working areas of the business. Mr. Barlow inquired whether any complaint had been received about his company. The inspector answered no, but that Barlow's, Inc. had simply turned up in the agency's selection process. The inspector again asked to enter the nonpublic area of the business; Mr. Barlow's response was to inquire whether the inspector had a search warrant. The inspector had none. Thereupon, Mr. Barlow refused the inspector admission to the employee area of his business. He said he was relying on his rights as guaranteed by the Fourth Amendment of the United States Constitution.

Three months later, the Secretary petitioned the United States District Court for the District of Idaho to issue an order compelling Mr. Barlow to admit the inspector. The requested order was issued on December 30, 1975, and was presented to Mr. Barlow on January 5, 1976. Mr. Barlow again refused admission, and he sought his own injunctive relief against the warrantless searches assertedly permitted by OSHA. A three-judge court was convened. On December 30, 1976, it ruled in Mr. Barlow's favor. Concluding that *Camara v. Municipal Court*, 387 U.S. 523, 528–529 (1967), and *See v.*

Seattle, 387 U.S. 541, 543 (1967), controlled this case, the court held that the Fourth Amendment required a warrant for the type of search involved here and that the statutory authorization for warrantless inspections was unconstitutional.

[T]he Fourth Amendment prohibition against unreasonable searches protects against warrantless intrusions during civil as well as criminal investigations. The reason is found in the "basic purpose of this Amendment . . . [which] is to safeguard the privacy and security of individuals against arbitrary invasions by government officials." If the government intrudes on a person's property, the private interest suffers whether the government's motivation is to investigate violations of criminal laws or breaches of other statutory or regulatory standards. It therefore appears that unless some recognized exception to the warrant requirement applies, *See v. Seattle* would require a warrant to conduct the inspection sought in this case. . . .

The critical fact of this case is that entry over Mr. Barlow's objection is being sought by a Government agent. Employees are not being prohibited from reporting OSHA violations. What they observe in their daily functions is undoubtedly beyond the employer's reasonable expectations of privacy. The Government inspector, however, is not an employee. Without a warrant he stands in no better position than a member of the public. What is observable by the public is observable, without a warrant, by the Government inspector as well. The owner of a business has not, by the necessary utilization of employees in his operation, thrown open the areas where employees alone are permitted to the warrantless scrutiny of Government agents. That an employee is free to report, and the Government is free to use, any evidence of non-compliance with OSHA that the employee observes furnishes no justification for federal agents to enter a place of business from which the public is restricted and to conduct their own warrantless search. . . .

The Secretary submits that warrantless inspections are essential to the proper enforcement of OSHA because they afford the opportunity to inspect without prior notice and hence to preserve the advantages of surprise. While the dangerous conditions outlawed by the Act include structural defects that cannot be quickly hidden or remedied, the Act also regulates a myriad of safety details that may be amenable to speedy alteration or disguise. The risk is that during the interval between an inspector's initial request to search a plant and his procuring a warrant following the owner's refusal of permission, violations of this latter type could be corrected and thus escape the inspector's notice. To the suggestion that warrants may be issued *ex parte* and executed without delay and without prior notice, the Secretary expresses concern for the administrative strain that would be experienced by the inspection system, and by the courts should *ex parte* warrants issued in advance become standard practice.

We are unconvinced, however, that requiring warrants to inspect will impose serious burdens on the inspection system or the courts, will prevent inspections necessary to enforce the statute, or will make them less effective. . . .

Whether the Secretary proceeds to secure a warrant or other process, with or without prior notice, his entitlement to inspect will not depend on his demonstrating probable cause to believe that conditions in violation of OSHA exist on the premises. Probable cause in the criminal law sense is not required. For purposes of an administrative search such as this, probable cause justifying the issuance of a warrant may be based not only on specific evidence of an existing violation but also on a showing that "reasonable legislative or administrative standards for conducting an . . . inspection are satisfied with respect to a particular [establishment]." *Camara v. Municipal Court.* A warrant showing that a specific business has been chosen for an OSHA search on the basis of a general administrative plan for the enforcement of the Act derived from neutral sources such as, for example, dispersion of employees in various types of industries across a given area, and the desired frequency of searches in any of the lesser divisions of the area, would protect an employer's Fourth Amendment rights. We doubt that the consumption of enforcement energies in the obtaining of such warrants will exceed manageable proportions. . . .

Nor do we agree that the incremental protections afforded the employer's privacy by a warrant are so marginal that they fail to justify the administrative burdens that may be entailed. The authority to make warrantless searches devolves almost unbridled discretion upon executive and administrative offices, particularly those in the field, as to when to search and whom to search. A warrant, by contrast, would provide assurances from a neutral officer that the inspection is reasonable under the Constitution, is authorized by statute, and is pursuant to an administrative plan containing specific neutral criteria. Also, a warrant would then and there advise the owner of the scope and objects of the search, beyond which limits the inspector is not expected to proceed. These are important functions for a warrant to perform, functions which underlie the Court's prior decisions that the Warrant Clause applied to inspections for compliance with regulatory statutes. We conclude that the concerns expressed by the Secretary do not suffice to justify warrantless inspections under OSHA or vitiate the general constitutional requirement that for a search to be reasonable a warrant must be obtained.

Notes and Questions

1. The Clean Water Act, § 308(a)(B)(i), provides as follows: "[T]he [EPA] Administrator or his authorized representative . . . upon presentation of his credentials— (i) shall have a right of entry to, upon, or through any premises in which an effluent source is located . . . ." 33 U.S.C. § 1318(a)(B)(i). No mention is made here about the need to obtain a warrant before exercising this authority to enter a facility. Does this statutory language authorize EPA inspectors to conduct warrantless searches of facilities subject to regulation under the Clean Water Act? How would that be consistent with the Fourth Amendment, as interpreted by the Supreme Court in *Marshall v. Barlow's*? Should this statutory language be considered unconstitutional, or can it be exercised in a manner consistent with the U.S. Constitution?

In reality, EPA and state inspectors almost always gain access to facilities by the consent of the facility owner or operator. Such consent, of course, would implicate no violation of the Fourth Amendment, so long as it was given freely and lawfully (e.g., not from a minor child or other individual with no authority to consent). In the rare cases where consent to enter is withheld by the facility owner or operator, EPA and state inspectors may seek and obtain a warrant to compel access to a facility while ensuring compliance with the Fourth Amendment. Note that a failure to comply with the Fourth Amendment and other constitutional requirements may lead to adverse consequences for the environmental agencies, such as the exclusion of evidence obtained during an inspection. A violation of constitutional rights may also lead to the potential for *Bivens* actions asserting personal liability against inspectors and other government employees. *See Bivens v. Six Unknown Named Agents*, 403 U.S. 388 (1971).

2. In *Marshall v. Barlow's*, the Court acknowledges the complaints of the Secretary of Labor about the "administrative burdens" that the necessity of seeking a warrant may entail. How great are these burdens? In practice, it may take an experienced agency attorney a few days or more to seek and obtain a warrant, as such warrants are usually issued by judges through *ex parte* procedures. *See, e.g., National-Standard Co. v. Adamkus*, 881 F.2d 352 (7th Cir. 1989) (upholding *ex parte* procedures for administrative warrant obtained by EPA to search two industrial facilities in Michigan). The requirements for obtaining a warrant are laid out explicitly in the Fourth Amendment Warrant Clause, which provides, "[N]o warrants shall issue, but upon probable cause, supported by Oath or affirmation, and particularly describing the place to be searched, and the persons or things to be seized." Note that the Warrant Clause makes no distinction between searches to support criminal and civil or administrative actions; among other things, all searches require a showing of probable cause. However, in *Marshall v. Barlow's*, the Court establishes a different standard for "probable cause," stating in this administrative context that "Probable cause in the criminal law sense is not required." So what is the standard for probable cause in order to obtain an administrative warrant? Review the Court's answer to this question in *Marshall v. Barlow's*. Do you see two independent bases for a finding of probable cause, one with perhaps a lesser burden of proof than required for a criminal warrant? How would you articulate these two independent bases?

3. Is a warrantless search ever permissible for purposes of environmental enforcement? The short answer is yes. Over time, courts recognized have various legal doctrines to allow entry onto private property without either consent or a warrant. Perhaps the most familiar doctrine may be "exigent circumstances," the general principle that allows law enforcement officers, for example, to enter private property while engaged in "hot pursuit" of a suspect. Exigent circumstances in the environmental context may apply, for example, during an emergency response to the rupture of an oil pipeline. Another doctrine that may allow a warrantless entry in the environmental context is that of the "pervasively regulated industry." Under this theory, many industries that are heavily regulated by the government should have an expectation of inspections of their property, and thus no warrant for entry may be needed. *See, e.g., In re Mullins & Prichard, Inc.*, 549 So. 2d 872 (La. Ct. App. 1989) ("obvious that the oil and gas production facilities subject to the warrantless searches fall under the 'pervasively regulated industry' exception to the warrant requirement"); *New York v. Burger*, 388 U.S. 41 (1987) (junkyards); *Donovan v. Dewey*, 452 U.S. 594 (1981) (underground mines); *U.S. v. Biswell*, 406 U.S. 311

(1972) (gun dealers). Following this line of cases, would hazardous waste landfills or wastewater treatment facilities also be considered "pervasively regulated" for purposes of authorizing warrantless searches?

4. In addition to facility inspections, environmental regulators may collect information from or about facilities in a number of other ways. Under the doctrine of "open fields," regulators may collect information on a facility by making observations from a public sidewalk or nearby hill, by making use of Google Earth and other mapping programs, or by flying overhead in commercial aircraft. *See Dow Chemical v. United States*, 476 U.S. 227 (1986) (approving EPA's use of aerial photography of a Dow facility in Michigan, and observing more broadly, "When Congress invests an agency with enforcement and investigatory authority, it is not necessary to identify explicitly each and every technique that may be used in the course of executing the statutory mission"). Would this also allow the use of drones or remote sensing equipment to collect information on private facilities? The Court in *Dow Chemical* appeared to anticipate the question, noting "It may well be . . . that surveillance of private property by using highly sophisticated surveillance equipment not generally available to the public . . . might be constitutionally proscribed absent a warrant." *Id.* at 238. Consistent with this admonition, the Court 15 years later drew a line on the use of thermal-imaging technology by drug enforcement agencies to detect grow operations in private homes. *See Kyllo v. U.S.*, 533 U.S. 27 (2001).

III. Administrative Enforcement

Administrative enforcement includes a variety of mechanisms that environmental agencies are authorized to implement, on their own, to compel environmental compliance or to assess monetary penalties against violators of environmental laws. In many environmental agencies, administrative enforcement represents a substantial proportion of all of the agency's enforcement activities. It requires less expenditure of scarce government resources, and it seems especially well-suited to remedying less egregious environmental regulations.

The mildest administrative enforcement mechanism is the Notice of Violation (NOV), sometimes referred to as a Notice of Noncompliance. This document is analogous to a traffic warning issued by a police officer to a speeding motorist. It simply informs the party to whom it is issued that that party is in violation of pertinent environmental requirements, and it requests compliance. Through the issuance of an NOV, bringing an environmental violation to the attention of the violator, an environmental agency may help fix a problem with a minimum expenditure of enforcement resources. The NOV may also help document a violation or history of violations should further enforcement action prove necessary. Under the federal environmental laws, NOVs may be discretionary with the agency, *see, e.g.,* Clean Water Act § 309(a)(1), or may be compulsory before bringing any other enforcement action, *see, e.g.,* Clean Air Act § 113(a)(1).

For an interesting example of an NOV under the Clean Air Act, see the following:

UNITED STATES ENVIRONMENTAL PROTECTION AGENCY
REGION 6

IN THE MATTER OF:)	
)	
Luminant Generating Company, LLC)	
)	**Proceedings Pursuant to**
and)	**Section 113(a)(1) of the**
)	**Clean Air Act,**
Big Brown Power Company, LLC)	
)	
)	**42 U.S.C. § 7413(a)(1)**
)	
)	
)	
_____)	

AMENDED NOTICE OF VIOLATION

The U.S. Environmental Protection Agency ("EPA") is issuing this amended Notice of Violation ("Amended Notice") to Luminant Generation Company, LLC ("Luminant") and Big Brown Power Company, LLC ("Big Brown Power") under Section 113(a)(1) of the Clean Air Act (the "Act"), 42 U.S.C. § 7413(a)(1). EPA finds that Luminant and Big Brown Power are violating the Clear Air Act, 42 U.S.C. §§ 7401 *et. seq.,* at the Big Brown Power Plant in Firestone County, Texas and at the Martin Lake Power Plant in Rusk County, Texas. Specifically, Luminant and the Big Brown Power have violated the federally-approved Prevention of Significant Deterioration ("PSD") regulations of the Texas State Implementation Plan ("SIP"). The authority to issue this Amended Notice has been delegated to the Regional Administrator of EPA, Region 6, and re-delegated to the Director, Compliance Assurance and Enforcement Division, EPA, Region 6.

STATUTORY AND REGULATORY BACKGROUND

1. The Clean Air Act is designed to "protect and enhance the quality of the Nation's air resources so as to promote the public health and welfare and the productive capacity of its population." Section 101(b)(1) of the Act, 42 U.S.C. § 7401(b)(1).

The National Ambient Air Quality Standards

2. Section 108(a) of the Act, 42 U.S.C. § 7408(a), requires the Administrator of EPA to identify and prepare air quality criteria for each air pollutant, emissions of which may endanger public health or welfare, and the presence of which results from numerous or diverse mobile or stationary sources. For each such "criteria" pollutant, Section 109 of the Act, 42 U.S.C. § 7409, requires EPA to promulgate national ambient air quality standards ("NAAQS") requisite to protect the public health and welfare.

3. Pursuant to Sections 108 and 109 of the Act, 42 U.S.C. §§ 7408 and 7409, EPA has identified nitrogen oxides ("NO_x") and sulfur dioxide ("SO_2") as criteria pollutants, and has promulgated NAAQS for NO_x and SO_2. *See* 40 C.F.R. §§ 50.4, 50.5, and 50.11. SO_2 and NO_x interact in the atmosphere to form particulate matter smaller than 2.5 microns ("$PM_{2.5}$"). NO_x reacts in the atmosphere in the presence of sunlight to form ground level ozone ("ozone"). Effective July 15, 2008, SO_2 is also regulated as a precursor to $PM_{2.5}$. 73 Fed. Reg. 28,321, 28,327–28 (May 16, 2008).

4. Under Section 107(d) of the Act, 42 U.S.C. § 7407(d), each state is required to designate those areas within its boundaries where the air quality is better or worse than the NAAQS for each criteria pollutant, or where the air quality cannot be classified due to insufficient data. An area that meets the NAAQS for a particular pollutant is termed an "attainment" area with respect to that pollutant. An area that does not meet the NAAQS for a particular pollutant is termed a "nonattainment" area with respect to that pollutant.

5. An area that cannot be classified as either "attainment" or nonattainment" with respect to a particular pollutant due to insufficient data is termed "unclassifiable" with respect to that pollutant.

Prevention of Significant Deterioration

6. Part C of Title I of the Act, 42 U.S.C. §§ 7470–92, establishes the federal PSD permitting program and requires each state to include a PSD program as part of its SIP.

7. Section 165(a) of the Act, 42 U.S.C. § 7475(a), prohibits the construction and operation of a "major emitting facility" in an area designated as attainment or unclassifiable for the applicable NAAQS without first obtaining a PSD permit and installing Best Available Control Technology ("BACT").

8. Section 169(1) of the Act, 42 U.S.C. § 7479(1), defines fossil-fuel fired steam electric plants of more than two hundred and fifty million British thermal units per hour heat input, which emit or have the potential to emit one hundred tons per year or more of any pollutant, to be "major emitting facilities."

9. Section 169(2)(C) of the Act, 42 U.S.C. § 7479(2)(C), defines "construction" to include "modification" (as defined in Section 111(a) of the Act). "Modification"

is defined in Section 111(a) of the Act, 42 U.S.C. § 7411(a), to be "any physical change in, or change in the method of operation of, a stationary source which increases the amount of any air pollutant emitted by such source or which results in the emission of nay air pollutant not previously emitted."

10. On June 19, 1978, EPA issued regulations implementing the federal PSD program at 40 C.F.R. § 52.21 and the requirements for SIP-approved PSD programs at 40 C.F.R. § 51.166. *See* 43 Fed. Reg. 26,388, 26,403 (June 19, 1978) (federal PSD program) and 43 Fed. Reg. 26,380, 26,382 (June 19, 1978) (requirements for SIP-approved PSD programs (originally codified at 40 C.F.R. § 51.24)). Since that time, the federal PSD regulations have been revised, with subsequent revisions incorporated under 40 C.F.R. §§ 52.21 and 51.166.

11. On June 24, 1992, EPA approved Texas's PSD program. *See* 57 Fed. Reg. 28,093 and 40 C.F.R. §§ 52.2299(c) and 52.2303. Pursuant to its PSD program, that State of Texas issues permits governing the operation and construction of regulated facilities.

12. In 2001, Texas revised its PSD program to incorporate certain sections of the 1996 federal PSD rules. EPA approved these revisions in 2004. *See* 69 Fed. Reg. 43,752 (July 22, 2004).

13. Under the federal PSD regulations, "major stationary source" is defined to include fossil fuel-fired steam electric plants of more than 250 million British thermal units per hour heat input which emit or have the potential to emit one hundred tons per year or more of any regulated air pollutant. *See* 40 C.F.R. § 52.21(b)(1)(i)(a) (1996) and 30 Tex. Admin. Code § 116.160(a) (2001) (incorporating the federal PSD definition of "major stationary source").

14. Under the federal PSD regulations, "major modification" is defined as any physical change in or change in the method of operation of a major stationary source that would result in a significant net emissions increase of any pollutant subject to regulation under the Act. *See* 40 C.F.R. § 52.21(b)(2)(i) (1996) and 30 Tex. Admin. Code § 116.160(a) (2001) (incorporating the federal PSD definition of "major modification").

15. Under the federal PSD regulations, "net emissions increase" means the amount by which the sum of the following exceeds zero: "any increase in actual emissions from a particular physical change or change in the method of operation at a source" and "any other increases and decreases in actual emissions at the source that are contemporaneous with the particular change and are otherwise creditable." *See* 40 C.F.R. § 52.21(b)(3)(i) (1996) and 30 Tex. Admin. Code § 116.160(a)(2001) (incorporating the federal PSD definition of "net emissions increase").

16. Under the federal PSD regulation, a "significant" net emissions increase means an increase in the rate of emissions that would equal or exceed a rate of 40 tons per year of NOx or SO_2. *See* 40 C.F.R. § 52.21(b)(23)(i) (1996) and 30 Tex. Admin. Code § 116.160(a)(2001) (incorporating the federal PSD definition of "significant").

17. The federal PSD regulations define "actual emissions" as the average rate, in tons per year, at which the unit actually emitted the pollutant during a two-year period which precedes the particular date and which is representative of normal source operation. *See* 40 C.F. R. § 52.21(b)(21)(ii) (1996) and 30 Tex. Admin. Code § 116.160(a) (2001) (incorporating the federal PSD definition of "actual emissions").

18. Under the federal PSD regulations, "construction" means any physical change or change in the method of operation (including fabrication, erection, installation, demolition, or modification of an emissions unit) that would result in a change in actual emissions. *See* 40 C.F.R. § 52.21(b)(8)(1996) and 30 Tex. Admin. Code § 116.16-(a) (2001) (incorporating the federal PSD definition of "construction").

19. Under the federal PSD regulations, "best available control technology" ("BACT") means an emissions limitation (including a visible emission standard) based on the maximum degree of reduction for each pollutant subject to regulation under the Act which would be emitted from any proposed major stationary source or major modification which the Administrator, on a case-by-basis, taking into account energy, environmental, and economic impacts and other costs, determines is achievable for such source or modification through application of production processes or available methods, systems and techniques, including fuel cleaning or treatment or innovative fuel combustion techniques for control of such pollutant. *See* 40 C.F. R. § 52.21(b)(12) (1996) and 30 Tex. Admin. Code § 116.160(a) (2001) (incorporating the federal PSD definition of "best available control technology").

20. According to 40 C.F.R. § 52.21(i)(1), incorporated by reference into 30 Tex. Admin. Code § 116.160(a), no stationary source or modification ... shall begin actual construction without a permit which states that the stationary source or modifications would meet the requirements of [40 C.F.R. § 52.21 (j)-(r)]. *See* 40 C.F.R. § 52.21(i)(l) (1996) and 30 Tex. Admin. Code § 116.160(a) (2001).

21. The owner or operator of the proposed modification must, among other things, perform a source impact analysis and an air quality analysis. *See* 40 C.F.R. § 52.21(k) and (m) (1996).

22. Further, the owner or operator of the proposed modification must demonstrate that the proposed major emitting facility will utilize the best available control technology [BACT]. *See* 30 Tex. Admin. Code § 116.111(a)(2)(C) (2001); *see also* 54 Fed. Reg. 52,823 (Dec. 22, 1989), 57 Fed. Reg. 28,093 (June 24, 1992), 75 Fed. Reg. 55,978 (Sept. 15, 2010).

23. Violations of the federally-approved Texas PSD program are federally enforceable pursuant to Section 113(a) of the Act, 42 U.S.C. § 7413(a).

General Texas SIP Permitting Requirements

24. Under 30 Tex. Admin. Code § 116.110(a) of the Texas SIP, before any actual work is begun on a major emitting facility, any person who plans to construct

any new major emitting facility or to engage in the modification of any existing major emitting facility which may emit air contaminants into the air of this state shall obtain a permit under § 116.111. 30 Tex. Admin. Code § 116.110(a) (2001).

25. Section 116.111(a) set forth the requirements for permits. 30 Tex. Admin. Code § 116.111(a) (2001). Section 116.111(a) provides that the application must contain, among other things, information showing that the facility will utilize BACT and comply with all applicable requirements concerning PSD review in 30 Tex. Admin. Code Chapter 116, including the requirements of 40 C.F.R. § 52.21 (1996) that are incorporated by reference into the Texas SIP.

FACTUAL BACKGROUND

26. The Big Brown and Martin Lake Power Plants (collectively, the "Plants") are owned by Big Brown Power and Luminant, respectively. The Plants are operated by Luminant. Luminant and Big Brown Power are engaged in the generation of energy, mining operations and wholesale marketing and trading. The Plants were owned and/or operated by Luminant and Big Brown Power at all times relevant to this Amended Notice. Prior to 2007, Luminant operated under the name of TXU Energy Corporation and Big Brown Power operated under the name of TXU Big Brown Company, LP.

27. Luminant and Big Brown Power were created under the laws of the State of Texas and is each a "person," as that term is defined in Section 302(e) of the Act, 42 U.S.C. § 7602(e).

28. The Plants were located in areas classified as attainment for NO_x, SO_2, $PM_{2.5}$ and ozone for all relevant periods of this Amended Notice.

29. The Big Brown Power Plant is a fossil fuel-fired electric utility steam generating station located in Freestone County, Texas and has the potential to emit more than 100 tons per year each of NO_x and SO_2. The Big Brown Poser Plant consists of two operating coal-fired units. Units 1 and 2 are tangentially-fired boilers which began operations in 1971 and 1972, respectively. Each unit is connected to an approximately 575 megawatt (MW) turbine generator.

30. The Martin Lake Power Plant is a fossil fuel-fired electric utility steam generating station located in Rusk County, Texas and has the potential to emit more than 100 tons per year each of NO_x and SO_2. The Martin Lake Power Plant consists of three operating coal-fired units. Units 1, 2, and 3 are tangentially-fired boilers which began operation in 1977, 1978, and 1979, respectively. Each unit is connected to an approximately 750 MW turbine generator.

31. The Big Brown and Martin Lake Power Plants are each "fossil fuel-fired steam electric plants of more than 250 million British thermal units per hour." Therefore, each of these plants constitutes a "major stationary source" within the meaning of 40 C.F.R. § 52.21(b))(1)(i)(a) and a "major emitting facility" within the meaning of Section 169(1) of the Act, 42 U.S.C. § 7479(1).

32. On multiple occasions between 2005 and 2010, Luminant and/or Big Brown Power completed physical changes and/or changes in the method of operation at the Big Brown Unit 2 and Martin Lake Units 1, 2, and 3 as described in the attached Appendix.

VIOLATIONS

Prevention of Significant Deterioration and the Texas SIP

33. The physical changes and/or changes in the method of operation performed in or near in time to each of the seven (7) outages referenced in the attached Appendix resulted in a "significant" net emissions increase of SO_2 and/or NO_x under 40 C.F.R. § 52.21 (b)(23)(i) (as incorporated by 30 Tex. Admin. Code § 116.160).

34. The physical changes and/or changes in the method of operation performed in or near in time to each of the seven (7) outages references in the attached Appendix constitute a "major modification(s)" under 40 C.F.R. § 52.21(b)(2)(i) (as incorporated by 30 Tex. Admin. Code § 116.160).

35. For each of the major modifications referenced herein, Luminant and/or Big Brown Power failed to obtain a PSD permit as required by 40 C.F.R. § 52.21(i)(l) (as incorporated by 30 Tex. Admin. Code § 116.160). Luminant continues to operate the modified plants without the required PSD permits.

36. For each of the modifications referenced herein, Luminant and/or Big Brown Power failed to utilize BACT as required by 30 Tex. Admin. Code § 116.111(a)(2)(C) and defined in 40 C.F.R. § 52.21(b)(12) (as incorporated by 30 Tex. Admin. Code § 116.160). Luminant continues to operate the modified plants without utilizing BACT.

37. Luminant and/or Big Brown Power are in violation of 40 C.F.R. § 52.21 (as incorporated by 30 Tex. Admin. Code § 116.160) and 30 Tex. Admin. Code § 116.111(a)(2)(C) for constructing major modifications at the Big Brown and Martin Lake Power Plants and continuing to operate the plants without applying for and obtaining PSD permits and utilizing BACT.

General Texas SIP Permitting Requirements

38. The physical changes and/or changes in the method of operation referenced in the attached Appendix were modifications to the plants that resulted in the emission of air contaminants into the air of the State of Texas. Therefore, Luminant and/or Big Brown Power were required to obtain a permit to construct under 30 Tex. Admin. Code §§ 116.110, 116.111 and 116.160, and 40 C.F.R. § 52.21, as incorporated by reference.

39. Luminant and/or Big Brown Power failed and continue to fail to submit an application for, and obtain, a permit containing information demonstrating that

the plants will utilize BACT and comply with all applicable requirements concerning PSD review.

40. Luminant and/or Big Brown Power are in violation of 30 Tex. Admin. Code §§ 116.110 and 116.111 by failing to submit an application for a permit demonstrating that the plants will utilize BACT and comply with all applicable requirements concerning PSD review.

ENFORCEMENT AUTHORITY

41. Section 113(a)(1) of the Act, 42 U.SC. § 7413(a)(1), provides that at any time after the expiration of 30 days following the date of the issuance of a Notice of Violation, the Administrator may, without regard to the period of violation, issue an order requiring compliance with the requirements of the state implementation plan or permit, issue an administrative penalty order in accordance with Section 113(d), or bring a civil action in accordance with Section 113(b) for injunctive relief and /or civil penalties.

Dated <u>7-11-13</u>   [signature]

John Blevins

Director

Compliance Assurance and Enforcement Division

Notes and Questions

1. Does an NOV, such as the one above, have any independent legal effect? Can it be challenged in court? In fact, the NOV above was subject to vigorous challenge by one of the recipients. In the end, the Fifth Circuit Court of Appeals dismissed the challenge, finding, consistent with every other circuit that has considered the question, that NOVs are not "final agency action" and thus not subject to judicial review. *Luminant Generation Co., LLC v. U.S. EPA*, 757 F.3d 439 (5th Cir. 2014). Among other things, the Fifth Circuit found that no legal consequences flow from issuance of the notice because all rights and obligations are determined by the statute itself, not a notice of violation of the statute.

2. If no legal consequences flow from issuance of an NOV, can they just be ignored? Why might you advise a client who just received an NOV to respond attentively?

3. According to the NOV above, what actions must the recipients take in order to come into compliance with the Clean Air Act? Are these actions defined by federal regulations, state regulations, or both?

———

Beyond issuance of an NOV, enforcement agencies may have the statutory authority to issue an administrative compliance order (ACO) — sometimes called an abatement order, cease and desist order, or Unilateral Administrative Order (UAO) — to compel compliance with environmental regulations or require actions deemed necessary by the agency. *See, e.g.,* Clean Water Act § 309(a); RCRA § 3008(a); CERCLA § 106(a). The ACO may be a potent enforcement tool. It allows environmental agencies to require regulated parties to take specific steps to achieve final compliance, consistent with a detailed, enforceable timetable. ACOs may be issued unilaterally or upon consent, following negotiations between agency personnel and representatives of the regulated party. Violation of an ACO may trigger substantial liability for penalties, including the potential for treble damages under some statutes. *See, e.g.,* CERCLA § 107(c)(3). Accordingly, most recipients of an ACO or UAO will choose to comply with them. However, whether they are unilateral or consented to, if the recipient of an ACO or UAO chooses not comply, violation of an order must be redressed in a civil action in the courts.

The following is an example of a Unilateral Administrative Order (UAO) that, as usual, prompted the recipient to respond appropriately and did not require enforcement through the courts.

UNITED STATES

ENVIRONMENTAL PROTECTION AGENCY

REGION 10

IN THE MATTER OF:	DOCKET NO. CWA-10-2011-0035
Trans-Alaska Pipeline System	UNILATERAL ADMINISTRATIVE
Pump Station 1, Prudhoe Bay,	ORDER FOR REMOVAL
Deadhorse, Alaska	ACTIVITIES
	Proceeding Under Section 311(c) and
Alyeska Pipeline Service Company,	(e) of the Federal Water Pollution
	Control Act, as amended, 33 U.S.C. §
Respondent.	1321(c) and (e).

I. JURISDICTION AND GENERAL PROVISIONS

1. This Order is issued pursuant to the authority vested in the President of the United States by Section 311(c) and (e) of the Federal Water Pollution Control Act, 33 U.S.C. § 1321(c) and (e), as amended ("CWA"). This authority has been delegated to the Administrator of the United States Environmental Protection Agency ("EPA") by Executive Order No. 12777, 58 FR 54757 (Oct. 22, 1991); and further delegated to the Regional Administrators by EPA Delegation Nos. 2-85 (May 11, 1994) and 2-89 (Jan. 19, 1993); and to Region 10's Director, Office of Environmental Cleanup, by Regional Redelegations R10 2-85 (Aug. 24, 2005) and R10 2-89 (Aug. 8, 2005).

2. This Order pertains to a discharge or a substantial threat of a discharge of oil, that occurred and is occurring at a facility ("Facility") located at Trans-Alaska Pipeline System Booster Pump Station 1, Prudhoe Bay, Alaska. This Order requires Respondent to conduct removal actions described herein to abate or mitigate an imminent and substantial threat to the public health or welfare of the United States that may be presented by the actual or substantial threat of a discharge of oil from the Facility into navigable waters.

3. EPA has notified the State of Alaska of this action pursuant to CWA Section 311(e)(1)(B), 33 U.S.C. § 1321(e)(1)(B). This Order is also based on OPA Section 1002, 33 U.S.C. § 2702, for reimbursement of costs.

II. PARTIES BOUND

4. This Order applies to and is binding upon Respondent, any persons acting on behalf of Respondent, and Respondent's directors, officers, employees, agents, successors and assigns. Any change in ownership or corporate status of Respondent including, but not limited to, any transfer of assets or real or personal property shall in no way alter Respondent's responsibilities under this Order.

5. Respondent shall ensure that its contractors, subcontractors, and representatives receive a copy of this Order and comply with this Order. Respondent shall be responsible for any noncompliance with this Order.

III. DEFINITIONS

6. Unless otherwise expressly provided herein, terms used in this Order which are defined in CWA Section 311, or in the Oil Pollution Act (OPA) shall have the meaning assigned to them in CWA or OPA. Whenever terms listed below are used in this Order or in the appendices attached hereto and incorporated hereunder, the following definitions shall apply:

7. "Discharge" shall have the meaning set forth in CWA Section 311(a)(2), 33 U.S.C. § 1321(a)(2), and 40 CFR Part 110.1 for purposes of the work to be performed under this Order, and shall have the meaning set forth in OPA Section 1001(7), 33 U.S.C. § 2701(7), for purposes of reimbursement of cost[s].

8. "EPA" shall mean the United States Environmental Protection Agency and any successor departments or successor agencies of the United States

9. "Facility" shall mean the Trans-Alaska Pipeline System Pump Station 1, located approximately 4.5 miles south of Prudhoe Bay near Deadhorse, Alaska, and depicted generally on the figure attached as Appendix 1. "Facility" shall also have the meaning set forth in CWA Section 311(a)(10), 33 U.S.C. § 1321(a)(10), and by OPA Section 1001(24), 33 U.S.C. § 2701(24).

10. "National Contingency Plan" or "NCP" shall mean the National Oil and Hazardous Substances Pollution Contingency Plan, codified at 40 CFR Part 300, including, but not limited to, any amendments thereto.

11. "Navigable waters" shall have the meaning set forth in CWA Section 502(7), 33 U.S.C. § 1362(7) and OPA Section 1001(21), 33 U.S.C. § 2701(21), and 40 CFR part 110.

12. "Order" shall mean this Unilateral Administrative Order and all appendices attached hereto. In the event of conflict between this order and any Appendix, this Order shall control.

13. "OPA" shall mean the Oil Pollution Act of 1990, 33 U.S.C. § 2701 et. seq.

14. "Oil" shall have the meaning set forth in the CWA Section 311(a)(1), 33 U.S.C. § 1321(a)(1), for the purposes of the work to be performed under this Order, and OPA Section 1001(23), 33 U.S.C. § 2701(23), of reimbursement of costs.

15. "Paragraph" shall mean a portion of the Order identified by an Arabic numeral.

16. "Section" shall mean a portion of this Order identified by a roman numeral.

17. "Work" shall mean all activities Respondent is required to perform under this Order, except those required by Paragraph 48 (Record Retention).

IV. <u>FINDINGS OF FACT</u>

18. The Facility includes a pumping station of the Trans-Alaska Pipeline System (TAPS), located approximately 4.5 miles south of Prudhoe Bay near Deadhorse, Alaska and depicted generally on the figure attached as Appendix 1. The Facility receives and meters crude oil from producers on the Alaska North Slope and pumps this oil to TAPS, which delivers the oil south across Alaska to the Valdez Marine Terminal.

19. On January 8, 2011, employees of Respondent discovered crude oil leaking inside the Booster Pump Building at the Facility. Within an hour of that discovery, Respondent cut the flow of oil to TAPS. Respondent later estimated that approximately 378 to 420 gallons of oil had been recovered from the Booster Pump Building.

20. The oil appeared to have originated from an underground concrete encasement outside the Booster Pump Building. It is suspected that the oil leaked from one of the encased pipes and then flowed along the encasement through a wall into the basement of the building. The oil is suspected to have originated from one of several pipes within the encasement. As of January 10, 2011, the leaking pipe had not been definitively identified.

21. The geographic area immediately underlying and surrounding the Facility is coastal arctic tundra and includes wetlands and tributaries adjacent to the Putuligayuk River, which flows into Prudhoe Bay and the Beaufort Sea.

22. The Putuligayuk River is classified as an anadromous fish stream at its lower end, approximately two miles from the Facility, and may contain fish during the open-water season. Caribou may be found in the area throughout the year and water-fowl nesting may occur on nearby ponds and lakes. The spectacled eider, a threatened species under the Endangered Species Act, is found in the marine and estuarine areas along the coast. Musk ox may occasionally be seen in the area.

23. Respondent is the owner and/or operator of the Facility from which the discharge or substantial threat of a discharge took place.

V. CONCLUSIONS OF LAW AND DETERMINATIONS

24. Based on the Findings of Fact set forth above, EPA has determined that TAPS Pump Station 1 is an "onshore facility" as defined in CWA sections 311(a)(10), 33 U.S.C. § 1321(a)(10), and by OPA Section 1001(24), 33 U.S.C. § 2701(24).

25. The Putuligayuk River, its tributaries, and its adjacent wetlands, are "navigable waters" as defined in CWA Section 502(7), 33 U.S.C. § 1362(7), and OPA Section 1001(21), 33 U.S.C. § 2701(21), 40 CFR part 110 and "navigable waters of the United States" as that term is used in CWA Section 311(b), 33 U.S.C. § 1321(b).

26. Respondent is an "owner or operator" of the Facility as defined by CWA Section 311(a)(6), 33 U.S.C. § 1321(a)(6), OPA Section 1001(26)[, 33 U.S.C. § 2701(26)]. Respondent is also a "responsible party" as defined by OPA § 1001(32), 33 U.S.C. § 2701(32).

27. Respondent is a "person" as defined by CWA Section 311(a)(7), 33 U.S.C. § 1321(a)(7), and by OPA Section 1001(27), 33 U.S.C. § 2701(27).

28. The incident described in the Statement of Facts presents a discharge or a substantial threat of a "discharge" as defined in CWA Section 311(a)(2), 33 U.S.C. § 1321[(a)(2)], and 40 CFR Part 110.1 and OPA Section 1001(7), 33 U.S.C. § 2701(7).

29. The substantial threat of a discharge is: (i) into or on the navigable water; (ii) on the adjoining shorelines to a navigable water; or (iii) may affect natural resources belonging to, appertaining to, or under the exclusive management authority of the United States.

30. The quantity of oil or hazardous substances which may be discharged from the Facility is a quantity that may be harmful within the meaning of CWA Section 311(b)(3), 33 U.S.C. § 1321(b)(3), and 40 CFR § 110.3(b), because the substantial threat of a discharge may cause a violation of applicable water quality standards or may cause a film or sheen upon or a discoloration of the surface of the water or adjoining shorelines.

31. The threat of discharge is a violation of CWA Section 311(b), 33 U.S.C. § 1321(b) because a harmful quantity of oil may be discharged from the facility:

(i) into or upon the navigable waters of the United States; or, (ii) which may affect natural resources belonging to, or appertaining to, the United States.

32. The substantial threat of a discharge may cause an imminent and substantial threat to the public health or welfare of the United States, including fish, wildlife, public and private property, shorelines, beaches, habitat, and/or other living and nonliving natural resources under the jurisdiction or control of the United States.

33. The removal actions required by this Order are necessary to protect the public health and welfare of the United States of America, including fish, wildlife, public and private property, shorelines, beaches, habitat, and other living and/or nonliving natural resources under the jurisdiction or control of the United States. Further, these measures are necessary to ensure effective and immediate removal or prevention of a substantial threat of a discharge of oil into or on the navigable waters, on the adjoining shorelines to the navigable waters, or that may affect natural resources belonging to, appertaining to, or under the exclusive management authority of the United States.

34. The removal actions required by this Order are in accordance with the NCP and are authorized by EPA pursuant to the authority granted in CWA Section 311(c)and 311(e), 33 U.S.C. § 1321(c) and 1321(e), as delegated by the President in Executive Order 12777, Section 2(b)(1), 56 FR 54757 (Oct. 22, 1991).

35. Under OPA Section 1002(b)(1), 33 U.S.C. § 2702(b)(1), and CWA Section 311(f), 33 U.S.C. § 1321(f), Respondent is liable to the United States for all removal costs incurred by the United States in connection with the discharge or the threatened discharge of oil from the Facility.

36. A "removal," as defined in CWA Section 311(a)(8), 33 U.S.C. § 1321(a)(8) and OPA Section 1001(30), 33 U.S.C. § 2701(30), is necessary at the Facility to minimize and mitigate damage to the public health or welfare.

VI. <u>ORDER</u>

Based upon the Findings of Fact and Conclusions of Law and Determination set forth above, EPA hereby orders that Respondent shall comply with all requirements of this Order and shall perform the following actions:

<u>Work To Be Performed</u>

37. Respondent must perform the work necessary to complete the tasks described below within the dates specified and in accordance with the NCP, 40 CFR Part 300.

38. Respondent must identify a contact person responsible for the removal within one day of the Effective Date of this Order.

39. <u>Facility Re-Start and Operation</u>. Respondent shall, when re-starting or operating the Facility, take measures to ensure that there is no discharge or threat of discharge of oil, as defined in CWA Section 311(a)(2), 33 U.S.C. § 1321. Respondent shall carry out all Facility re-start and operations consistent with the Restart Plan for Interim Operation, including all amendments and updates thereto.

40. Respondent must take the following removal actions:

    a. Immediately take all necessary steps to prevent and mitigate the discharge of oil to the environment.

    b. Within one day of the Effective Date of this Order, deploy all appropriate oil recovery resources to recover, record, and track the volume of crude oil recovered from the Pump Station 1 Booster Pump Building basement, including but not limited to oil, oily water, and other oily materials (e.g., absorbent materials, solvents).

    c. By January 28, 2011, complete a preliminary assessment to identify and delineate any crude oil contamination present in the gravel pad associated with the Pump Station 1 piping incident, consistent with the approved Work Plan.

    d. Consistent with the schedule and other requirements in an approved Petroleum Cleanup Plan, remediate all crude oil impacted areas at the Facility discovered by the preliminary assessment.

    e. Dispose of all incident-generated wastes at EPA approved disposal facilities.

    f. By May 31, 2011, submit a final report to EPA detailing all work completed including analytical and monitoring data, disposal records, and all documentation related to the response.

41. Within two days from the Effective Date of this Order, Respondent must develop and submit to EPA for approval, a Preliminary Assessment work plan (PA Work Plan) that includes a schedule for completing the tasks described in the preceding Paragraph. Respondent must begin work within one day of EPA approval of the PA Work Plan. The PA Work Plan must also include, at a minimum, the following elements:

    a. Health and Safety Plan

    b. Sampling and Analysis Plan

    c. Quality Assurance Project Plan

42. If, in carrying out the work under the PA Work Plan, oil contamination associated with the Pump Station 1 Booster Pump Building piping is found outside of any buildings or pipes at the Facility, Respondent shall provide immediate notice to the EPA On-Scene Coordinator (OSC). Within two days of such notice, Respondent shall submit an Oil Cleanup Plan for the OSC's review and approval. Respondent shall promptly carry out the work under the Oil Cleanup Plan as approved or modified by the OSC. The Oil Cleanup Plan shall include a schedule for the completion of all work and shall include, at a minimum, the following elements:

a. Health and Safety Plan

b. Sampling and Analysis Plan

c. Quality Assurance Project Plan

43. Respondent shall submit all work plans and other submittals required under this Order to the EPA OSC. Unless otherwise notified by EPA in writing, the EPA OSC shall be the following individual:

Matt Carr
Federal On-Scene Coordinator
U.S. EPA Region 10
Alaska Operations Office
222 W. 7th Ave., #19
Anchorage, AK 99513
[Mr. Carr's email address and telephone number have been omitted]

44. The OSC will approve, disapprove and require modifications, or modify all work plans under the Order. Once approved or approved with modifications, all work plans and schedules become an enforceable part of this Order.

45. **Reporting Requirements.** Respondent must submit a written progress report to the OSC concerning actions undertaken pursuant to this Order every seven days after the Effective Date of this Order, unless otherwise directed in writing by the OSC. These reports must describe all significant developments during the preceding period, including work performed and any problems encountered, analytical data received during the reporting period, and developments anticipated during the next reporting period, including a schedule of work to be performed, anticipated problems, and planned resolutions of past or anticipated problems.

46. Respondent may assert a business confidentiality claim pursuant to 40 CFR § 2.203(b) with respect to part or all of any information submitted to EPA pursuant to this Order, provided such claim is allowed by CWA Section 308(b) (2), 33 U.S.C. § 1318(b)(2). EPA shall only disclose information covered by a business confidentiality claim to the extent permitted by, and by means of the procedures set forth at 40 CFR Part 2, Subpart B. If no such claim accompanies the information when it is received by EPA, EPA may make it available to the public without further notice to Respondent. Respondent must not assert confidentiality claims with respect to any data or documents related to site conditions, sampling, or monitoring.

47. **Access to Property and Information.** Respondent must provide access to the Facility, to off-site areas where access is necessary to implement this Order, and to all documents related to conditions at the Facility and work conducted under the Order. Respondent must provide this access to EPA and its contractors and authorized representatives.

48. **Record Retention.** Respondent shall preserve all documents and information relating to work performed under this Order, or relating to the oil found on or discharged from the Facility, for **six** years following completion of the removal

actions required by this Order. At the end of this six-year period and 60 days before any document or information is destroyed, Respondent shall notify EPA that such documents and information are available to EPA for inspection, and upon request, shall provide the originals or copies of such documents and information to EPA. In addition, Respondent shall provide documents and information retained under this Section at any time before expiration of the six-year period upon the written request of EPA.

49. **Compliance With Other Laws.** Respondent shall perform all actions required pursuant to this Order in accordance with all applicable Federal, state, and local laws and regulations. Where any portion of the work requires a Federal or state permit or approval, Respondent shall submit timely applications and take all other actions necessary to obtain and to comply with all such permits or approvals. This Order is not, and shall not be construed to be, a permit issued pursuant to any Federal or state law or regulation.

VII. ENFORCEMENT: PENALTIES FOR NONCOMPLIANCE

50. Violation of any provision of this Order may subject Respondent to civil penalties of up to thirty-seven thousand five hundred dollars ($37,500) per day of violation, or an amount up to three times the cost incurred by the United States, as provided in CWA Section 311(b)(7)(B), 33 U.S.C. § 1321(b)(7)(B), as adjusted by Civil Monetary Penalty Inflation Adjustment Rule, 40 CFR § 19.4.

VIII. RESERVATION OF RIGHTS

51. Except as specifically provided in this Order, nothing herein shall limit the power and authority of EPA or the United States to take, direct, or order all actions necessary to protect public health or welfare of the United States, or to prevent, abate, or minimize an actual or substantial threat of a discharge of oil, hazardous substances, pollutants or contaminants, or hazardous or solid waste on, at, from or outside of the Facility. Further, nothing herein shall prevent EPA from seeking legal or equitable relief to enforce the terms of this Order, from taking other legal or equitable action as it deems appropriate and necessary, or from requiring Respondent in the future to perform additional activities pursuant to CWA or any other applicable law. The United States reserves the right to bring an action against Respondent under any applicable authority, including but not limited to, CWA Section 311(f), 33 U.S.C. § 1321(f), and/or OPA Sections 1002 and 1015, 33 U.S.C. §§ 2702 and 2715, for penalties, injunctive relief, and/or recovery of any costs incurred by the United States related to this Order and not reimbursed by Respondent. Response costs shall include, but are not limited to, past costs, direct costs, indirect costs, costs of monitoring, and accrued interest as provided in CWA Section 311(f), 33 U.S.C. § 1321(f), and OPA § 1005, 33 U.S.C. § 2705.

52. Notwithstanding any other provision of this Order, at any time during the response action, EPA reserves the right to perform its own studies, complete the removal action, and seek reimbursement from Respondent for its costs, or seek any other appropriate relief. Nothing in this Order shall limit the authorities of the OSC as outlined in the NCP.

53. Notwithstanding any other provision of this Order, EPA and the United States reserve all rights against Respondent with respect to liability, including criminal liability, for violations of federal or state law arising from any past, present, or future discharges or substantial threat of discharge of oil or any hazardous substance at or from the Facility.

54. Nothing in this Order shall preclude EPA from taking any additional enforcement actions, including modification of this Order or issuance of additional orders, and/or additional response actions as EPA may deem necessary, or from requiring Respondent in the future to perform additional activities pursuant to the Resource Conservation and Recovery Act (RCRA), the Comprehensive Environmental Response, Compensation, and Liability Act (CERCLA), the Clean Water Act, the Oil Pollution Act, or any other applicable law.

55. Nothing in this Order shall constitute a satisfaction of or discharge from any claim or cause of action against Respondent or any person, for any liability such person may have under CWA, OPA, other statutes, or the common law, including but not limited to any claims of the United States for penalties, costs, damages, and interest.

56. If a court issues an order that invalidates any provision of this Order or finds that Respondent has sufficient cause not to comply with one or more provisions of this Order, Respondent shall remain bound to comply with all provisions of this Order not invalidated by such court's order.

IX. <u>OTHER CLAIMS</u>

57. By issuance of this Order, the United States and EPA assume no liability for injuries or damages to persons or property resulting from any acts or omissions of Respondent. Neither EPA nor the United States shall be deemed a party to any contract entered into by the Respondent's directors, officers, employees, agents, successors, representatives, assigns, contractors, or consultants in carrying out actions pursuant to this Order.

X. <u>MODIFICATIONS</u>

58. Modifications to any plan or schedule required by this Order may be made in writing by the OSC or at the OSC's oral direction. If the OSC makes an oral modification, it will be memorialized in writing within two days, provided,

however, that the effective date of the modification shall be the date of the OSC's oral direction. Modifications to any portion of the Order, other than plans or schedules, may only be made in writing under signature of EPA signatory below.

59. No informal advice, guidance, suggestion, or comment by EPA regarding reports, plans, specifications, schedules, or any other writing submitted by the Respondent shall relieve Respondent of obligation to obtain such formal approval as may be required by this Order, and to comply with all requirements of this Order unless it is formally modified.

XI. NOTICE OF COMPLETION

60. When EPA determines, after EPA's review of Respondent's Final Report, that all removal actions have been fully performed in accordance with this Order, with the exception of any continuing obligations required by this Order, EPA will (i) notify Respondent in writing or (ii) provide a list of the deficiencies and require that Respondent modify the Work Plan to correct such deficiencies. Respondent shall implement the modified and approved Work Plan and shall submit a modified Final Report in accordance with the EPA notice. Failure by Respondent to implement the approved modified Work Plan shall be a violation of this Order.

XII. EFFECTIVE DATE

61. The Effective Date of this Order shall be the date of the receipt of this Order by the Respondent.

62. Respondent may request a conference with EPA regarding the terms and requirements of this Order.

IT IS SO ORDERED.

BY: [signature]   DATE: 1/11/11
     Dennis McLerran
     Regional Administrator
     U.S. EPA Region 10

Received by: [space for a representative of respondent to sign to acknowledge receipt, and date]

[Appendix 1, an annotated aerial photograph / map showing the location of Pump Station 1, is omitted]

Notes and Questions

1. In form and legal effect, how does this Unilateral Administrative Order differ from the Notice of Violation we saw earlier? How are the two documents alike?

2. What is the violation underlying issuance of this Unilateral Administrative Order? What exactly does the order require the respondent to do? Might the respondent have private incentives to perform some or all of this work even without an order? If so, what value might this order bring to these private incentives?

3. Note that this order, to address an oil spill from the Trans-Alaska Pipeline System on the North Slope of Alaska, was issued by the EPA in the January 2011, following the unprecedented oil spill from the Deepwater Horizon in the Gulf of Mexico in April 2010. In the latter case, because the oil spill involved the marine environment, the U.S. Coast Guard was the lead regulator and the Coast Guard declined to issue any order to BP or other responsible parties. What might explain these two different responses to oil spills affecting waters of the United States?

4. As we will see later in this chapter with the case of *Sackett v. Environmental Protection Agency*, some administrative orders — unlike NOVs — may be subject to immediate judicial review. In the case of an environmental emergency, such as the Deepwater Horizon spill in the Gulf of Mexico and the Trans-Alaska Pipeline System spill on the North Slope, is there any way to distinguish these urgent cases so that the orders are not tied up in litigation while the underlying problems go unabated?

––––––––––

In addition to administrative orders, which compel or prohibit specific actions, environmental agencies are sometimes also authorized to issue administrative penalty orders. Upon the receipt of such an order, a recipient may choose to pay the proposed penalty, ignore the proposed penalty, seek to negotiate a lower penalty, or contest the penalty assessment entirely. The rights of a regulated party vary according to agency, statute, and jurisdiction. Parties that have received penalty orders are frequently afforded an opportunity to negotiate lower penalties than those that were proposed by the agency. If those conversations do not result in an agreement, the regulated party is then often entitled to a hearing before an administrative law judge or a hearing board. In other jurisdictions, the regulated party may have the right to obtain immediate and direct judicial review of the amount of penalties the government is proposing to extract.

Parties that receive administrative orders from regional enforcement officials at EPA that seek to assess civil monetary penalties have a right to an adjudicatory hearing before an EPA administrative law judge (ALJ).

EPA has also established an internal appeals system for regulated parties and regional office officials who are dissatisfied with the opinions of the Agency's ALJs. Particular ALJ decisions may be appealed to the EPA's Environmental Appeals Board (EAB), a part of the Office of the EPA Administrator that operates as a permanent, impartial body that is the final EPA decision-maker regarding administrative proceedings. The following case illustrates how the EAB relates to EPA's ALJs in deciding cases brought before it.

M.A. Bruder and Sons, Inc.

10 E.A.D. 599 (EAB 2002)

(Administrative Law) Judge REICH:

The matter before the Environmental Appeals Board (the "Board") involves the penalty assessment for a violation of the Resource Conservation and Recovery Act of 1976 ("RCRA"), as amended, 42 U.S.C. §§ 6901–6992k, and its implementing regulations. Specifically, the Administrative Law Judge ("ALJ") assessed a civil penalty under § 3008(a) of RCRA, 42 U.S.C. § 6928(a), in the amount of $8,950 against M.A. Bruder & Sons, Inc. (hereinafter "Bruder" or "Respondent") for illegally operating a treatment, storage, or disposal facility ("TSDF" or "TSD facility") without interim status or a RCRA permit. On December 17, 2001, U.S. EPA, Region V (the "Region") filed its notice of appeal with the Board. The only issues raised in the Region's appeal involve the civil penalty assessed in the Initial Decision.

In the Initial Decision, the ALJ reviewed the Region's use of the RCRA Civil Penalty Policy (October 1990) ("Penalty Policy"), as well as Bruder's arguments regarding the application of the Penalty Policy to the violation. The ALJ, for reasons more fully discussed later in this decision, disagreed with the Region's proposed penalty of $64,900. Instead the ALJ, after finding that the Region's application of the applicable penalty policy was "technically accurate," disregarded the Penalty Policy and used the statutory factors (seriousness of the violation and good faith efforts of the Respondent to comply with the applicable requirements) to assess a civil penalty of $8,950 against Bruder.

In the present case, the ALJ considered the Region's penalty analysis under the Penalty Policy. Although he rejected the Region's proposed penalty as too harsh, the ALJ found that the Region applied the Penalty Policy correctly. He then set out two reasons why he disagreed with the Region's proposed penalty of $64,900. First, the ALJ explained that in his view, the Region's proposed penalty "loses sight of the fact that, but for the failure of [Bruder to timely install] ... the valve, MAB [Bruder] would have continued to be exempt from the permit requirements entirely." The ALJ explained that, even if the Region's minor/major gravity designation was correct, the Region's adoption of the midpoint range within the minor/major cell of the gravity matrix did not accurately reflect the status of Bruder's violation in comparison to other cases where respondents have failed to obtain a RCRA permit. Second, the ALJ found that the Region's minor/major gravity designation resulted in the Region's assessment of a multi-day component in the proposed penalty, which he did not believe appropriately reflected the "case specific facts" in this matter. The ALJ concluded that the Penalty Policy was "wanting:' because he found that even though the Region's application was correct, the Region's proposed penalty was myopic. Therefore, he departed from the Penalty Policy.

After explaining why he did not agree with the Region's use of the Penalty Policy, the ALJ turned to the statutory criteria of seriousness and good faith to assess a penalty in this matter. From here, the ALJ determined that the seriousness of the violation was "manifestly minimal" and that Bruder's good faith required a reduction in the penalty. The ALJ cited Bruder's responses to the Region's information requests as evidence of its "good faith:' as well as Bruder's "overall good faith." He assessed a civil penalty of $8,950 against Bruder — $50 per day for each of the 179 days of violation alleged in the complaint.

On appeal, the Region contends that the ALJ abused his discretion or committed clear error when he departed from the relevant Penalty Policy in this instance. The Region argues chiefly that the Region's proposed penalty was appropriate for this case. . . .

The Region, furthermore, takes issue with the ALJ's penalty assessment, arguing that the ALJ did not reasonably apply the statutory criteria when arriving at a penalty. Here, the Region discusses what it identifies as "the central disagreement between the parties." The Region attacks the ALJ's framing of the violation for penalty purposes. In this case, the ALJ granted the Region's motion for accelerated decision on liability finding Bruder liable for the illegal storage of hazardous waste without a permit, but when determining a penalty, the ALJ framed the violation as a failure to install the requisite pressure relief valve on the tank in a timely manner and found that the "seriousness" of this violation was significantly less than the Region suggested in its proposed penalty calculation. The Region argues that this application of the statutory criterion for seriousness was unreasonable. . . .

The regulations that govern a presiding officer's assessment of a civil penalty provide:

> *Amount of civil penalty.* If the Presiding Officer determines that a violation has occurred and the complaint seeks a civil penalty, the Presiding Officer shall determine the amount of the recommended civil penalty based on the evidence in the record and in accordance with any penalty criteria set forth in the Act. Th Presiding Officer shall consider any civil penalty guidelines issued under the Act. The Presiding Officer shall explain in detail in the initial decision how the penalty to be assessed corresponds to any penalty criteria set forth in the Act. If the Presiding Officer decides to assess a penalty different in amount from the penalty proposed by complainant, the Presiding Officer shall set forth in the initial decision specific reasons for the increase or decrease. 40 C.F.R. § 22.27(b).

The Board has explained that this regulatory equipment does not necessitate the use of a penalty policy in determining a particular penalty amount, but rather a "Presiding Officer, having considered any applicable civil penalty guidelines issued by the Agency, is nonetheless free not to apply them to the case at hand." *In re Employers Ins. of Wausau,* 6 E.A.D. 735, 758 (EAB 1997). The penalty policies do not bind either the ALJ or the Board since these policies, not having been subjected to the rulemaking procedures of the Administrative Procedure Act, lack the force of law. Moreover, while an ALJ must consider the applicable penalty policy, he or she has the "discretion either to adopt the rationale of an applicable penalty policy where appropriate or to deviate from it where the circumstances warrant. . . ."

As previously noted, although an ALJ is not required to use an applicable penalty policy, the Agency designs penalty policies to be used as valuable tools for assessing penalties . . . . Furthermore, we have in past cases held that penalty policies serve to facilitate the application of statutory penalty criteria, and that ALJs and the Board may utilize applicable penalty policies in determining civil penalty amounts. . . .

Given the very limited nature of Bruder's noncompliance with the generator regulations and the minimal potential environmental impact, the Region's framing of the penalty analysis in terms of a failure to obtain a permit rather than a failure to install a pressure relief valve, the effect of which was to greatly increase the penalty, is unreasonable. . . .

The ALJ found that the Penalty Policy did not render an appropriate result, and therefore he departed from the Penalty Policy. . . . Since the ALJ disagreed with the pro- posed penalty produced by the Region's use of the Penalty Policy, the ALJ concluded that the Penalty Policy itself was inappropriate to use in this matter, and instead directly used the statutory factors to determine a civil penalty. . . .

In this instance, we do not find the ALJ's rationale for departing from the Penalty Policy to be compelling and, as such, find that it does not in this case warrant our deference. The ALJ's decision to depart from the Penalty Policy flowed directly from his mistaken belief that the Region's analysis under the Penalty Policy was correct, a premise we reject. Since we reject this fundamental premise of the ALJ's reasoning, we find that his decision does not perform our own penalty assessment in this matter.

While we agree with the ALJ that the Region's proposed penalty produces an unduly harsh result, we believe that the Penalty Policy can be applied in a way that would ensure an appropriate penalty, and choose to use it in determining the penalty we assess. . . .

[We] reverse the ALI's penalty assessment in this matter. We assess a total civil penalty of $17,510.22 against Bruder. Bruder shall pay the full amount of the civil penalty within thirty (30) days of the date of service of this order, unless another time frame is mutually agreed upon by the parties.

Notes and Questions

1. EPA's Policy on Civil Penalties establishes a standard approach to the Agency's assessment of civil penalties, both in administrative enforcement matters and in the settlement of civil judicial enforcement actions. It includes an "economic benefit component" that is designed to recover any money that the violator saved by failing to comply with environmental requirements. It also includes a "gravity component" intended to penalize violators for the seriousness of their violations and to deter others from failing to comply. EPA's regulations also include several statute-specific penalty policies.

2. Should the EAB permit ALJs to deviate from the Agency's penalty policies? What do you see as the advantages and disadvantages of allowing ALJs the discretion not to apply those policies in particular cases?

————

Because administrative compliance orders often reflect the product of negotiations, parties may seek to use such orders for relief from environmental requirements that would otherwise be applicable. One issue that has arisen in some enforcement cases is whether an administrative compliance order — or an application for a waiver of one or more limitations in an environmental permit — can legally shield a permittee from liability for violating the discharge limitations contained in its permit. That question is addressed in the following case.

United States v. Metropolitan District Commission

23 ERC (BNA) 1350 (D. Mass. 1985)

Judge MAZZONE:

At the heart of this case lies a fifty square mile expense of water known as Boston Harbor. It is the largest harbor serving a major city on the East Coast, and is of unique historical, natural, and recreational significance. It was the site of the Boston Tea Party shortly before the birth of this Nation; it was the home for much of the fledgling Nation's merchant marine; it has always been the home port for what is now the oldest ship still commissioned in the United States Navy whose copper fittings were hammered by Paul Revere. Today, it serves millions of citizens who swim, sail, and fish in and around the Harbor. It boasts 15 virtually undeveloped islands; thousands of acres of marshes, tidelands, and fishbed; and many beaches, rivers, and inlets. The Harbor is used by the largest tankers and containers ships as well as the smallest pleasure boats. . . .

On August 12, 1976, the EPA issued NPDES permit number MA0102351 (the Permit) to "the Commonwealth of Massachusetts Metropolitan District Commission." Although the Permit states that it expires on May 1, 1981, it remains in effect and enforceable until a new permit is issued. The Permit limits the volume of pollutants that the defendant may discharge at Deer and Nut Islands (the sites of two principal treatment facilities for Boston Harbor).

On August 8, 1980, the EPA issued an administrative order (the 1980 AO) finding that the MDC had violated the construction requirements of the Permit by failing to complete secondary treatment and sludge management facilities. The order specifically noted the pendency of the secondary treatment waiver application, but nonetheless ordered the permittee to comply with a detailed implementation schedule designed "to bring all discharges of wastewater and combined wastewater/stormwater into compliance with the Act, [and] with the interim effluent [?] limitations set forth [in the 1980 AO]." The 1980 AO set an interim "implementation schedule" for construction projects and set out various effluent limitations for Deer and Nut Islands. Section VI of the 1980 AO, entitled "General Provisions," specifically notes that "[v]iolations of any of the terms of this Order shall subject the permittee to further enforcement action under . . . 33 U.S.C. § 1319 . . ." and that "this Administrative Order does not preclude the initiation of any action, pursuant to Section 505 of this Act, by a third person other than the Agency to enforce the Permit's requirements to achieve the limitations by July 1, 1977."

In June, 1983, the EPA tentatively denied the MDC's waiver application . . . . The MDC was entitled to file an amended application for a waiver, which it did in October, 1984.

Another administrative order was issued in July 1984 (the 1984 AO), citing violations of the sludge limits set by the permit, of the sludge management schedule set by the 1980 AO, and of the effluent levels of the Permit. The 1984 AO ordered the MDC to comply with the 1980 AO effluent limits until construction of facilities capable of complying with the Permit Limits. The 1984 AO also set out an interim schedule for pre-construction facilities planning. It noted, however, that "[c]ompliance with such interim requirements, however, does not amount to compliance with the MDC's permit or the Clean Water Act and shall not preclude additional enforcement action by EPA. Any language in the August 9, 1980 Administrative Order which could be read as an authorization for the MDC to violate its permit or the Clean Water Act is rescinded."

On March 29, 1985, the EPA tentatively re-denied the waiver application. Until the EPA issues a new NPDES permit, the MDC cannot administratively appeal the tentative denial of the waiver. The procedure for issuing a new NPDES permit is governed by 40 C.F.R. § 122.15 *et seq.*, and is both complex and time consuming. . . .

The United States has moved for partial summary judgment as to liability, claiming that the defendants' own self-monitoring reports indicate repeated and serious violations of the Permit, the 1980 AO, and the Act's sludge discharge prohibitions in both the Dear and Nut Island facilities. Its claim is simple: the MDC is a person within the meaning of the Act; the MDC has discharged pollutants into navigable waters from a point source; and those discharges were not authorized.

The first legal question is thus to determine what effluent standard currently governs discharges made into Boston Harbor. The United States argues that the Permit controls; the defendants argue that the 1980 AO controls. For the following reasons, I find that the Permit sets the enforceable effluent levels.

First, it is undisputed that the Permit remains in effect until revoked, modified, or reissued. The Permit has not been revoked or reissued, so the question becomes whether it has been modified. The Code of Federal Regulations sets out extensive regulatory procedures that must be followed before a permit can be modified. 40 C.F.R. § 122.15 *et seq.* For example, the EPA must prepare a fact sheet and draft permit and allow for a period of public comment. There is no dispute that none of these steps were followed in this case. The 1980 AO, then, could not properly modify the Permit limits since the proper regulatory steps were not taken to effect a modification.

Second, the 1980 AO itself is explicitly issued as "Findings of Violation and Orders for Compliance." While noting the pending waiver application, the AO reads as follows:

> Based on the above findings, I further find that because of [the defendants']
> failure to achieve secondary treatment, the permittee's discharge of pollut-
> ants from its POTW's [sic] is in violation of § 301(a) of the Act.

The 1980 AO thereafter lists various interim effluent levels with which the Permittee must comply on pain of "further enforcement action . . . [including] . . . a civil
action for injunctive relief and penalties or, in appropriate cases, criminal prosecution." The language of the AO and the section of the Act pursuant to which it was
issued make clear that the AO was intended to enforce existing limits, not to modify
those limits. The AO does not and could not alter the permittee's duty to comply with
the Act. As counsel for the United States argued at the hearing, it simply makes no
sense to interpret this order, which was clearly issued to compel the defendants to comply with the Permit's limits, as granting the right to indefinitely violate the limits set
by that Permit. The defendants would remake what was patently a sword to compel
compliance into a shield to protect themselves from liability. I will not accept such an
argument.

Third, the 1980 AO specifically notes that it "does not preclude the initiation of an
action, pursuant to § 505 of the Act, by a third person other than the Agency to enforce
the Permit's requirements to achieve the limitations by July 1, 1977." Had the AO legally
modified the Permit's requirements, it would have barred third parties from instituting citizen lawsuits.

The defendants, however, raise a final argument concerning the applicable effluent limits which requires somewhat more extended discussion. Briefly stated, they
claim that the pendency of their waiver application relieves them of the obligation to
comply with the Permit's secondary treatment requirements until that application is
permanently denied. They claim that this view of the effect of a pending section 1311(h)
waiver application is supported by the legislative history of the Act and the "leading
case" construing section 1311(h).

The United States argues that the legislative history of the Act and the same "leading case" support exactly the opposite view, namely that the pendency of a waiver
application does not excuse noncompliance with the Act . . . .

[I]t is well established as a general principle of environmental law that waiver
requests and appeals from decisions on those requests are "on the polluter's time." I
therefore hold that the pendency of a section 1311(h) waiver application does not
shield the defendants from liability for violations of the Act's otherwise applicable secondary treatment standards.

Notes and Questions

1. By some estimates, administrative enforcement (i.e., enforcement actions taken
without judicial action) accounts for more than 90 percent of all environmental
enforcement. Do you see why that might be? First, of course, consider the relative
administrative ease of writing and sending a Notice of Violation letter as compared to
drafting and filing a civil complaint. An NOV might take one agency attorney and

one agency inspector an afternoon to prepare and send. An administrative compliance order, such as the one in the preceding case, may take one very long day or perhaps a week to prepare and send. By contrast, drafting a civil complaint to seek injunctive relief may take weeks, if not months or longer; involve multiple agencies (including, in the federal government, the United States Department of Justice); require a ruling from the court; and potentially allow for appeals.

2. Where the government is seeking the assessment of administrative penalties, there may be more extensive procedures, though still less than in the civil judicial context. Administrative penalties under federal environmental statutes are generally subject to the EPA's Consolidated Rules of Practice (CROP), 40 C.F.R. Part 22, a set of procedural rules for administrative adjudications. Discovery under the CROP is considerably more limited than discovery under the Federal Rules of Civil Procedure. Parties to a hearing under the CROP are entitled only to the following three categories of "pre-hearing exchange": (1) documents each party will rely upon at hearing; (2) a list of witnesses each party proposes to call at hearing; and (3) a brief summary of the expected testimony of each witness. 40 C.F.R. § 22.19. Beyond those three categories, discovery is denied unless specifically approved by the hearing officer. What is the likely effect of such limitations on discovery? Would the limits on discovery help you, as an enforcement attorney, choose between administrative and civil judicial enforcement? If so, how?

3. Administrative enforcement actions, particularly actions seeking assessment of a penalty, may — if no settlement is reached first — lead to a hearing before an Administrative Law Judge (ALJ). In form and substance, the hearing may resemble a bench trial in federal court, including informal use of the Federal Rules of Evidence and the examination of lay and expert witnesses. Following the conclusion of the hearing, the ALJ may issue a decision that could be subject to appeal to another administrative court — in the EPA system, the Environmental Appeals Board (EAB). From there, a decision by the EAB, together with a fully developed hearings record, may be subject to appeal directly to the relevant federal circuit court of appeals. In theory, one advantage of administrative hearings is the availability of ALJs with expertise in environmental law to hear cases involving highly technical matters of environmental regulation. However, judicial courts, up to and including the United States Supreme Court, have also proven adept at mastering complexities of environmental regulation as the needs of an individual case may demand. *See, e.g., Alaska Dept. of Environmental Conservation v. EPA*, 540 U.S. 461 (2004) (detailed analysis of the PSD program under the Clean Air Act).

————

As noted above, if the recipient of an order refuses to comply with the order, there may be penalties for violation of the order in addition to penalties for the underlying statutory or regulation violation. However, agencies are usually powerless to compel compliance or collect such penalties without going to court. In part because the agencies would have to go to court to enforce violations of the orders, many agencies and courts traditionally held that administrative orders were not subject to "pre-enforcement review"—that is, judicial review of administrative orders would be denied until such time as the agency may seek judicial assistance in enforcing the order. In some cases, this could leave the recipient of an order in a quandary if they believe the order was invalid: should they incur the expense of complying with the order and then challenge the order later, or should they refuse to comply with the order and risk penalties for noncompliance if or when the agency later decided to seek judicial enforcement? In 2012, the traditional denial of pre-enforcement review was put to the test in the following case before the U.S. Supreme Court, which resulted in a reversal of the law that had prevailed for many decades.

Sackett v. Environmental Protection Agency
132 S. Ct. 1367 (2012)

Justice SCALIA:

We consider whether Michael and Chantell Sackett may bring a civil action under the Administrative Procedure Act, 5 U.S.C. § 500 et seq., to challenge the issuance by the Environmental Protection Agency (EPA) of an administrative compliance order under § 309 of the Clean Water Act, 33 U.S.C. § 1319. The order asserts that the Sacketts' property is subject to the Act, and that they have violated its provisions by placing fill material on the property; and on this basis it directs them immediately to restore the property pursuant to an EPA work plan.

The Clean Water Act prohibits, among other things, "the discharge of any pollutant by any person," § 1311, without a permit, into the "navigable waters,"—which the Act defines as "the waters of the United States." If the EPA determines that any person is in violation of this restriction, the Act directs the agency either to issue a compliance order or to initiate a civil enforcement action. § 1319(a)(3). When the EPA prevails in a civil action, the Act provides for "a civil penalty not to exceed [$37,500] per day for each violation." And according to the Government, when the EPA prevails against any person who has been issued a compliance order but has failed to comply, that amount is increased to $75,000—up to $37,500 for the statutory violation and up to an additional $37,500 for violating the compliance order.

The particulars of this case flow from a dispute about the scope of "the navigable waters" subject to this enforcement regime. Today we consider only whether the dispute may be brought to court by challenging the compliance order—we do not resolve the dispute on the merits. . . .

The Sacketts . . . own a ⅔-acre residential lot in Bonner County, Idaho. Their property lies just north of Priest Lake, but is separated from the lake by several lots containing permanent structures. In preparation for constructing a house, the Sacketts filled in part of their lot with dirt and rock. Some months later, they received from the EPA a compliance order. [The order found, among other things, that the Sacketts' property contained jurisdictional wetlands subject to regulation under the Clean Water Act, and that by discharging fill material into navigable waters without a permit, the Sacketts were in violation of section 301 of the Act.]

The order directs the Sacketts, among other things, "immediately [to] undertake activities to restore the Site in accordance with [an EPA-created] Restoration Work Plan" and to "provide and/or obtain access to the Site . . . [and] access to all records and documentation related to the conditions at the Site . . . to EPA employees and/or their designated representatives.

The Sacketts, who do not believe that their property is subject to the Act, asked the EPA for a hearing, but that request was denied. They then brought this action in the United States District Court for the District of Idaho, seeking declaratory and injunctive relief. . . . The District Court dismissed the claims for want of subject matter jurisdiction, and the United States Court of Appeals for the Ninth Circuit affirmed . . . . We granted certiorari.

The Sacketts brought suit under Chapter 7 of the APA, which provides for judicial review of "final agency action for which there is no other adequate remedy in a court." 5 U.S.C. § 704. We consider first whether the compliance order is final agency action. . . . By reason of the order, the Sacketts have the legal obligation to "restore" their property according to an agency-approved Restoration Work Plan, and must give the EPA access to their property and to "records and documentation related to the conditions at the Site." Also, "'legal consequences . . . flow'" from issuance of the order. For one, according to the Government's current litigating position, the order exposes the Sacketts to double penalties in a future enforcement proceeding. . . . The issuance of the compliance order also marks the "'consummation' of the agency's decisionmaking process". . . . As the Sacketts learned when they unsuccessfully sought a hearing, the "Findings and Conclusions" that the compliance order contained were not subject to further agency review . . . .

The APA's judicial review provision also requires that the person seeking APA review of final agency action have "no other adequate remedy in a court," 5 U.S.C. § 704. In Clean Water Act enforcement cases, judicial review ordinarily comes by way of a civil action brought by the EPA under 33 U.S.C. § 1319. But the Sacketts cannot initiate that process, and each day they wait for the agency to drop the hammer, they accrue, by the Government's telling, an additional $75,000 in potential liability. . . . The Government relies on § 701(a) (1) of the APA, which excludes APA review "to the extent that [other] statutes preclude judicial review." The Clean Water Act, it says, is such a statute.

Nothing in the Clean Water Act expressly precludes judicial review under the APA or otherwise . . . . The APA, we have said, creates a "presumption favoring judicial review of administrative action," but as with most presumptions, this one "may be overcome by inferences of intent drawn from the statutory scheme as a whole." The Government offers several reasons why the statutory scheme of the Clean Water Act precludes review. . . ."

The Government argues that, because Congress gave the EPA the choice between a judicial proceeding and an administrative action, it would undermine the Act to allow judicial review of the latter. But that argument rests on the question-begging premise that the relevant difference between a compliance order and an enforcement proceeding is that only the latter is subject to judicial review. There are eminently sound reasons other than insulation from judicial review why compliance orders are useful. The Government itself suggests that they "provid[e] a means of notifying recipients of potential violations and quickly resolving the issues through voluntary compliance." It is entirely consistent with this function to allow judicial review when the recipient does not choose "voluntary compliance." The Act does not guarantee the EPA that issuing a compliance order will always be the most effective choice.

The Government also notes that compliance orders are not self-executing, but must be enforced by the agency in a plenary judicial action. It suggests that Congress therefore viewed a compliance order "as a step in the deliberative process . . . rather than as a coercive sanction that itself must be subject to judicial review." But the APA provides for judicial review of all final agency actions, not just those that impose a self-executing sanction. And it is hard for the Government to defend its claim that the issuance of the compliance order was just "a step in the deliberative process" when the agency rejected the Sacketts' attempt to obtain a hearing and when the next step will either be taken by the Sacketts (if they comply with the order) or will involve judicial, not administrative, deliberation (if the EPA brings an enforcement action). As the text (and indeed the very name) of the compliance order makes clear, the EPA's "deliberation" over whether the Sacketts are in violation of the Act is at an end; the agency may still have to deliberate over whether it is confident enough about this conclusion to initiate litigation, but that is a separate subject.

The Government further urges us to consider that Congress expressly provided for prompt judicial review, on the administrative record, when the EPA assesses administrative penalties after a hearing, but did not expressly provide for review of compliance orders. But if the express provision of judicial review in one section of a long and complicated statute were alone enough to overcome the APA's presumption of reviewability for all final agency action, it would not be much of a presumption at all. . . .

Finally, the Government notes that Congress passed the Clean Water Act in large part to respond to the inefficiency of then-existing remedies for water pollution. Compliance orders, as noted above, can obtain quick remediation through voluntary compliance. The Government warns that the EPA is less likely to use the orders if they are subject to judicial review. That may be true — but it will be true for all agency actions subjected to judicial review. The APA's presumption of judicial review is a repudiation of the principle that efficiency of regulation conquers all. And there is no reason to think that the Clean Water Act was uniquely designed to enable the strong-arming of regulated parties into "voluntary compliance" without the opportunity for judicial review — even judicial review of the question whether the regulated party is within the EPA's jurisdiction. Compliance orders will remain an effective means of securing prompt voluntary compliance in those many cases where there is no substantial basis to question their validity.

We conclude that the compliance order in this case is final agency action for which there is no adequate remedy other than APA review, and that the Clean Water Act does not preclude that review. We therefore reverse the judgment of the Court of Appeals and remand the case for further proceedings consistent with this opinion.

Notes and Questions

1. With its decision in *Sackett*, reversing decades of precedent in the circuit courts, the Supreme Court determined that administrative orders issued under § 309 of the Clean Water Act are subject to judicial review whether or not EPA moves to enforce the order through judicial proceedings. In part, the Court reached this conclusion through a combination of the APA's presumption of reviewability and a finding that "Nothing in the Clean Water Act explicitly precludes judicial review under the APA . . . ." If other environmental statutes are equally silent on the reviewability of administrative orders, does this mean that *Sackett* should apply equally to all other statutes? What about emergency orders to address oil spills or hazardous materials that pose immediate threats to human health or the environment? Is it realistic to believe that true emergencies can be addressed through judicial review? The EPA, at least, does not appear to believe so. For one thing, orders to address hazardous substances under the federal Superfund statute are subject to a statutory ban on pre-enforcement review. See CERCLA § 113(h), 42 U.S.C. § 9613(h). For another, following *Sackett*, EPA issued a new policy that explicitly anticipates the possibility of judicial review for administrative orders issued under most federal environmental statutes, with two notable exceptions for orders to address releases of hazardous substances subject to CERCLA and oil spills subject to the Clean Water Act § 311. U.S. EPA, *Language Regarding Judicial Review of Certain Administrative Enforcement Orders Following the Supreme Court Decision in* Sackett v. EPA (Mar. 21, 2013).

2. The Court's relatively brief and unanimous opinion in *Sackett* may reflect the relative paucity of facts before the Court in this case. In line with prevailing case law until that time, the trial court summarily dismissed the Sacketts' petition for pre-enforcement judicial review of the compliance order, and the Ninth Circuit Court of Appeals affirmed the dismissal. *Sackett v. U.S. EPA*, 622 F.3d 1139 (9th Cir. 2010). At the same time, perhaps because EPA had not itself sought to enforce the compliance order, it had not developed an administrative record for that purpose. As a result, this may have left the government with having to defend the compliance order before the U.S. Supreme Court on a weak record. During the oral argument before the U.S. Supreme Court, Deputy Solicitor General Malcolm Stewart attempted to introduce facts that were not in the record before the Court, prompting a swift rebuke from Chief Justice Roberts: "If they weren't in the record, I don't want to hear about them. You appreciate the rule, that we don't consider things that aren't in the record." Tr. at 36.

Given the outcome of this case, if you were an EPA attorney, would you do anything differently before issuing a compliance order if you knew that every compliance order could now be subject to pre-enforcement review? Would the prospect of pre-enforcement review discourage you from issuing a compliance order, or would it rather encourage you to develop a solid administrative record to support the order? If you were the attorney for a party that received a compliance order, how would you advise your client to proceed? What factors would you consider before giving that advice?

IV. Civil Enforcement

The civil judicial action is an enforcement mechanism that tends to be used against serious or recalcitrant environmental violators, or in cases where discovery tools or a legal precedent is needed, or where authoritative action is necessary to stop an environmentally damaging activity. The elements that the government must prove in civil enforcement cases vary from statute to statute. Typically, though, violations must be proven by a preponderance of the evidence, through a demonstration of noncompliance with an applicable environmental requirement, under a strict liability regime. Generally, environmental harm need not be alleged or proven for the government to obtain injunctive relief or civil penalties. Moreover, once the fact of a violation has been established, affirmative defenses tend to be quite limited and difficult to establish.

The case below illustrates what the government must prove to establish liability in an action alleging noncompliance with a Clean Water Act discharge permit. It also refers to some of the more frequently raised affirmative defenses asserted in these matters.

United States v. Sharon Steel Corporation

30 ERC (BNA) 1778 (N.D. Ohio 1989)

Judge MASON:

On March 30, 1987, the United States of America filed the above-captioned case against Sharon Steel Corporation ("Sharon"), alleging that Sharon discharged pollutants without authorization, in violation of § 301(a) of the Clean Water Act ("CWA"). On January 10, 1989, the United States filed a supplemental complaint alleging that Sharon, after receiving authorization, continued to violate § 301(a) by discharging pollutants in excess of authorized levels. The United States has moved for partial summary judgment on the issue of Sharon's liability. For the following reasons, the motion is granted in part and denied in part.

"[T[he objective of the [CWA] . . . is to 'restore and maintain the chemical, physical, and biological integrity of the Nation's waters.'" This objective is implemented through § 301(a) of the CWA which prohibits all discharges of pollutants except as authorized pursuant to § 402. The § 402 exception established the National Pollutant Discharge Elimination System ("NPDES"), 33 U.S.C. § 134. Under the NPDES, the Environmental Protection Agency ("EPA") issues permits to individual dischargers. The permits make the generally applicable effluent limitations and other water quality standards the individual obligation of the discharger. The [CWA] . . . provides that each discharger holding a NPDES permit shall monitor and report on its compliance with its permit. Each discharger must install, use, and maintain monitoring equipment and must sample its effluents. The discharger must report the results of its self-monitoring to the EPA. Compliance with a NPDES permit is deemed compliance with § 301(a). . . .

Sharon owns and operates the Brainard Strapping Division, a steel producing plant in Warren, Ohio. In conjunction with its manufacturing processes, the plant discharges waste water into two outfalls, 001 and 002. The waste water flows from the outfalls through a drainage pipe into the Red Run tributary of the Mahoning River.

On November 24, 1982, Sharon filed a NPDES permit application with the Ohio Environmental Protection Agency ("OEPA"). On August 31, 1987, OEPA issued a permit to Sharon. The following day, September 1, 1987, OEPA issued the Director's Final Findings and Orders ("DFFO"). On September 30, 1987, Sharon appealed both the permit and the DFFO to the Ohio Environmental Board of Review.

Summary judgment is appropriate when "there is no genuine issue as to any material fact and . . . the moving party is entitled to a judgment as a matter of law." Fed. R. Civ. P. 56(c). It "is [particularly] appropriate on the issue of liability for violations of the [CWA] . . . since NPDES enforcement actions are based on strict liability thus making intent and good faith irrelevant . . . ." To establish a § 301(a) violation, the United States must prove two elements: (1) that a person discharged pollutants from a point source into navigable waters of the United States (2) without a NPDES permit or in violation of a permit.

It is undisputed that from April 16, 1973 until August 31, 1987, Sharon discharged pollutants from a point source into navigable waters of the United States without a NPDES permit. Hence the United States seeks a judgment that Sharon violated the CWA during that period. Sharon raises four arguments in opposition to the United States' motion.

First, Sharon argues that it cannot be held liable for violations that occurred more than five years before the commencement of this action. It is well established that actions for civil penalties under the CWA are governed by the five-year federal statute of limitations, 28 U.S.C. § 2462. Accordingly, the United States' motion for partial summary judgment with respect to violations that occurred prior to March 30, 1982 is denied.

Second, Sharon argues that it is not liable for discharges which occurred during the pendency of its permit application—November 24, 1982 to August 31, 1987. Under § 309 of the CWA, EPA is authorized to bring an enforcement action and to recover civil penalties when a polluter is in violation of § 301(a). Sharon argues that its filing of a permit application amounts to compliance with § 301(a), thus shielding it from liability under § 309. This argument is predicated upon a portion of the legislative history of § 309 [excerpt omitted].

The plain language of § 309 and § 301(a) is clear and unambiguous: "[a]ny discharge except pursuant to a permit is illegal." In *United States v. Tom-Kat Dev.* the court reached the same conclusion. There, the polluter, citing the same legislative history, argued that EPA lacked standing to sue it because it had applied for a permit. The court rejected this argument, stating . . ."After December 31, 1974, Congress intended that liability attach to all dischargers without a permit, regardless of whether the polluter had applied for one." Thus Sharon's argument is without merit.

Finally, Sharon argues that equitable considerations preclude liability for the period March 31, 1982 through November 23, 1982. It argues that any violation of the CWA prior to October 27, 1982 was unintentional because it had no knowledge that it was discharging pollutants into navigable waters. It also argues that laches may bar or mitigate the United States' claim for penalties.

Neither argument has merit. Strict liability is imposed for violations of the CWA; intent is irrelevant, "except in connection with the amount of the penalty imposed." Further, "[t]he Supreme Court has consistently adhered to the principle that laches is not a defense against the sovereign."

Additionally, the United States seeks a judgment that Sharon violated the CWA by discharging in excess of the levels authorized by its NPDES permit which was issued on August 31, 1987. To establish these violations, the United States relies on monthly operating reports (MORs) submitted by Sharon to OEPA. The MORs indicate that Sharon's discharges exceeded permit limitations from October 1987 through January 1988. Since the MORs "are reports or records which are required to be kept by law, [they] . . . may be used as admissions to establish [Sharon's] . . . liability for that period.

Nevertheless, in one sentence in its brief, Sharon argues that summary judgment is improper because the DFFO, issued by OEPA on September 1, 1987, "did not require [it] . . . to adhere to the final discharge limitations set forth in the . . . [p]ermit." The DFFO is a three page document which states that Sharon "is not yet in compliance with its NPDES permit" and orders it to attain compliance, pursuant to a construction schedule, by September 1, 1988. The United States argues that the terms of the DFFO suggest that no permit modification was intended and that for modification to occur, the DFFO must be issued under different statutory authority. In the absence of evidence that the DFFO suspended Sharon's obligation to comply with the permit under the CWA, Sharon's argument is without merit.

Alternatively, Sharon argues that under the doctrine of primary jurisdiction, the court should refrain from ruling until the Ohio Board of Environmental Review acts on its appeal of the permit and the DFFO.

Primary jurisdiction . . . comes into play whenever enforcement of the claim requires the resolution of issues which, under a regulatory scheme, have been placed within the special competence of an administrative body; in such a case the judicial process is suspended pending referral of such issues of the administrative body for its views. Here, the court is not faced with complex technical issues, but rather "is asked to enforce the standards [OEPA] . . . has already determined are appropriate." Since the court is able to determine whether Sharon has violated those standards, the doctrine of primary jurisdiction is inapplicable.

Accordingly the United States' motion for partial summary judgment is granted with respect to all CWA violations that occurred from October 1987 through January 1988.

Notes and Questions

1. Statute of Limitations. In the absence of a statute of limitations in the Clean Water Act, the court in *Sharon Steel* invokes the federal statute of limitations established by 28 U.S.C. § 2462. The statute provides: "Except as otherwise provided by Act of Congress, an action, suit or proceeding for enforcement of any civil fine, penalty, or forfeiture, pecuniary or otherwise, shall not be entertained unless commenced within five years from the date when the claim first accrued . . . ." As indicated in *Sharon Steel*, this statute of limitations clearly applies to civil penalties for environmental violations. Does it also apply to administrative penalties? *See 3M Co. v. Browner,* 17 F.3d 1453 (D.C. Cir. 1994). Does it apply to actions for injunctive relief? *See U.S. v. Telluride Co.,* 146 F.3d 1241 (10th Cir. 1998) (concluding that "we do not consider the Government's request for injunctive relief an action for 'civil penalty' barred by § 2462").

What if an environmental violation occurred more than five years ago, but was only discovered recently? Would an enforcement action today necessarily be denied? As explicitly provided in 28 U.S.C. § 2462 ("Except as otherwise provided by Act of Congress"), another federal statute may establish a different statute of limitations period. *See, e.g.,* CERCLA § 113(g)(2) (for CERCLA removal actions, cost recovery actions must be brought within three years of *completion* of cleanup). Another theory that may effectively extend the statute of limitations period is the doctrine of "continuing violations," where an act in the past represents a violation continuing today. *See, e.g., Sierra Club v. Johnson,* 69 ERC (BNA) 1919 (N.D. Cal. 2009) (EPA failure to promulgate financial assurance regulations constitutes continuing violation years after rule was due by law); *United States v. Reaves,* 923 F. Supp. 1530 (M.D. Fla. 1996) (illegal filling of wetlands in 1981 constitutes continuing violation in 1994 where illegal fill material remained in place). A final, and perhaps most common, means of effectively extending a statute of limitations period is by consent of the parties, through a mechanism often know as a "tolling agreement." In practice, attorneys representing parties facing the prospect of environmental enforcement often readily agree to entry of tolling agreements. Can you imagine why?

2. The court in *Sharon Steel* recognizes that the standard for liability under the Clean Water Act (in line with other environmental statutes) is strict liability. However, the court also suggests that intent may be relevant in the limited context of determining "the amount of the penalty imposed." Why and how may intent be relevant in this particular context? One answer may be found directly within the environmental statutes, which often provide explicit factors for consideration in determining the amount of penalties. *See, e.g.,* Clean Water Act § 311(b)(8); Clean Air Act § 113(e)(2); CERCLA § 109(a)(3). Factors to consider in determining appropriate penalties often include a violator's degree of culpability; any economic benefit to the violator from the violation; the gravity of the harm caused or threatened by the violation; any good faith efforts to comply with requirements or to mitigate damages; any prior history of violations; and the ability or inability of a violator to pay a penalty. Among these factors, EPA policy almost always requires a penalty to recover at least the economic benefit of the violation.

This requirement creates a "level playing field" with other regulated parties that incurred costs for added labor, capital expenditures, and other costs necessary to comply with a regulation. Penalties are also commonly reduced if a violator agrees to undertake a Supplemental Environmental Project (SEP), which EPA defines as "environmental beneficial projects, which a defendant agrees to undertake in settlement of an enforcement action, but which the defendant is not otherwise legally required to perform." For the latest (2015) EPA policy concerning SEPs, see the following link: https://www.epa.gov/sites/production/files/2015-04/documents/sepupdatedpolicy15.pdf In many cases, the cost of conducting an SEP may exceed the amount that a violator would otherwise pay in cash for an environmental penalty. In such cases, why would any violator agree to incur such greater expenses?

———

As noted previously, only a limited number of affirmative defenses may be raised in civil judicial enforcement actions. However, one defense that has succeeded in some such cases is the "fair notice defense," a defense premised on the notion that an environmental agency's regulations did not provide regulated parties with fair notice of the conduct that was expected of them. The case below arose from a dispute between EPA and a regulated company over how to interpret an Agency regulation regarding the disposal of toxic PCBs used in electrical transformers. It provides an illustration of how courts sometimes apply the fair notice doctrine in an enforcement context.

General Electric Co. v. U.S. Environmental Protection Agency
53 F.3d 1324 (D.C. Cir. 1995)

Judge TATEL:

The Environmental Protection Agency fined the General Electric Company $25,000 after concluding that it had processed polychlorinated biphenyls in a manner not authorized under EPA's interpretation of its regulations. We conclude that EPA's interpretation of those regulations is permissible, but because the regulations did not provide GE with fair warning of the agency's interpretation, we vacate the finding of liability and set aside the fine.

GE's Apparatus Service Shop in Chamblee, Georgia decommissioned large electric transformers. Inside these transformers was a "dielectric fluid" that contained high concentrations of polychlorinated biphenyls ("PCBs"), which are good conductors of electricity. PCBs are also dangerous pollutants. Recognizing the danger of PCBs, Congress has required their regulation under the Toxic Substances Control Act ("TSCA"). Pursuant to TSCA, the EPA promulgated detailed regulations governing the manufacture, use, and disposal of PCBs.

Because GE's transformers were contaminated with PCBs, the company had to comply with the disposal requirements of 40 C.F.R. § 761.60. Section 761.60 (b) (1) requires the disposal of transformers by either incinerating the transformers, or by placing it into a chemical waste landfill after the PCB-laced dielectric fluid has been drained and the transformer rinsed with a PCB solvent. GE chose the "drain-and-land-fill" option . . . .

The drain-and-landfill alternative required GE to dispose of the liquid drained from the transformer "in accordance with" the terms of section 761.60(a). Since the dielectric fluid contained extremely high concentrations of PCBs, the relevant provision of section 761.60(a) was section (1), a catch-all section applicable to liquids contaminated with more than 500 parts per million ("ppm") of PCBs. This section required those disposing of these particularly dangerous materials to do so solely by incineration in an approved facility. In accord with that requirement, GE incinerated the dielectric fluid after draining it from the transformers. It then soaked the transformers in a PCB solvent—in this case, freon—for 18 hours, drained the contaminated solvent, and immediately incinerated it as well.

In March, 1987, GE changed these procedures, beginning a process that ultimately led to the EPA complaint in this case. While GE continued to incinerate the dielectric fluid, it began a recycling process that recovered a portion of the dirty solvent through distillation. . . .

GE and EPA agree that the regulations require the incineration of the solvent. They disagree about whether the intervening distillation and recycling process violated the regulations. EPA argues that section 761.60(b)-(1)-(B)-(i) required GE to dispose of all the dirty solvent . . . by immediate incineration. GE did not think that section prohibited it from taking intermediate steps like distillation prior to incinerating the PCBs. To GE, distillation was permitted by section 761.20(c) (2), which allows the processing and distribution of PCBs "for purposes of disposal in accordance with the requirements of § 761.60." GE believed that this section authorized intermediate processing "for purposes of disposal"—processing such as distillation—as long as it complied with the other requirements of the PCB regulations like those relating to the management of spills, storage, and labeling of PCB materials. EPA has not alleged that GE's distillation process failed to comply with those requirements. In fact, as the ALJ later concluded, distillation reduced the amount of contaminated materials, thus producing environmental benefits.

Despite those benefits, EPA charged the company with violating the PCB disposal regulations. After a hearing, an ALJ agreed and assessed a $25,000 fine. On appeal, the Environmental Appeals Board modified the ALJ's reasoning, but agreed with the disposition of the complaint and upheld the $25,000 penalty. In other proceedings, the agency found the company liable for distillation it performed in six other locations, but suspended the fines for those violations pending the outcome of this appeal.

GE argues that EPA's complaint is based on an arbitrary, capricious, and otherwise impermissible interpretation of its regulation. To prevail on this claim, GE faces an uphill battle. We accord an agency's interpretation of its own regulations a "high level of deference," accepting it "unless it is plainly wrong."

GE argues that EPA's reading of the regulation is impermissible because all the solvent was eventually incinerated, because distillation is not a means of disposal but merely pre-disposal proceeding, and because the regulations explicitly allow pre-disposal processing to occur prior to the ultimate incineration. While GE's claims have merit, they do not demonstrate that the agency's interpretation of this highly complex regulatory scheme is impermissible.

Particularly in the context of this comprehensive and technically complex regulatory scheme, EPA's interpretation of the regulations is permissible. Although GE's interpretation may also be reasonable, at stake here is the proper disposal of a highly toxic substance. We defer to the reasonable judgment of the agency to which Congress has entrusted the development of rules and regulations to ensure its safe disposal.

Had EPA merely required GE to comply with its interpretation, this case would be over. But EPA also found a violation and imposed a fine. Even if EPA's regulatory interpretation is permissible, the company argues, the violation and fine cannot be sustained consistent with fundamental principles of due process because GE was never on notice of the agency interpretation it was fined for violating. It is to this issue that we now turn.

Due process requires that parties receive fair notice before being deprived of property. The due process clause thus "prevents . . . deference from validating the application of a regulation that fails to give fair warning of the conduct it prohibits or requires." In the absence of notice — for example, where the regulation is not sufficiently clear to warn a party about what is expected of it — an agency may not deprive a party of property by imposing civil or criminal liability.

Although the agency must always provide "fair notice" of its regulatory interpretations to the regulated public, in many cases the agency's pre-enforcement efforts to bring about compliance will provide adequate notice. If, for example, an agency informs a regulated party that it must seek a permit for a particular process, but the party begins processing without seeking a permit, the agency's pre-violation contact with the regulated party has provided notice, and we will enforce a finding of liability as long as the agency's interpretation was permissible. In some cases, however, the agency will provide no pre-enforcement warning, effectively deciding "to use a citation [or other punishment] as the initial means for announcing a particular interpretation" — or for making its interpretation clear. This, GE claims, is what happened here. In such cases, we might ask whether the regulated party received, or should have received, notice of the agency's interpretation in the most obvious way of all: by reading the regulation. If, by reviewing the regulation and other public sentiments issued by the agency, a regulated party acting in good faith would be able to identify, with "ascertainable certainty," the standards with which the agency expects parties to conform, then the agency has fairly notified a petitioner of the agency's interpretation.

Although we defer to EPA's interpretation regarding distillation because it is "logically consistent with the language of the regulation," we must, because the agency imposed a fine, nonetheless determine whether that interpretation is "ascertainably certain" from the regulations. [W]e conclude that the interpretation is so far from a reasonable person's understanding of the regulations that they could not have fairly informed GE of the agency's perspective. We therefore reverse the agency's finding of liability and the related fine.

On their face, the regulations reveal no rule or combination of rules providing for notice that they prohibit pre-disposal processes such as distillation. To begin with, such notice would be provided only if it was "reasonably comprehensible to people of good faith" that distillation is indeed a means of "disposal." While EPA can permissibly conclude, given the sweeping regulatory definition of "disposal," that distillation is a means of disposal, such a characterization nonetheless strays far from the common understanding of the word's meaning. A person of "good faith" would not reasonably expect distillation—a process which did not and was not intended to prevent the ultimate destruction of PCBs—to be barred as an unapproved means of disposal.

Not only do the regulations fail clearly to bar distillation, they apparently permit it. § 761.20(c)(2) permits processing and distribution of PCBs "for purposes of disposal." This language would seem to allow parties to conduct certain pre-disposal processes without authorization as long as they facilitate the ultimate disposal of PCBs and are done "in compliance with the requirements of this Part"—i.e. in accordance with other relevant regulations governing the handling, labeling, and transportation of PCBs. § 761.20(c)(2). EPA argues—permissibly, as we concluded above—that the section allows parties to "use" PCBs in the described manner, but that those uses must still comply with the disposal requirements of section 761.60, including the requirement that unauthorized methods of disposal receive a disposal permit from the agency. This permissible interpretation, however, is by no means the most obvious interpretation of the regulation, particularly since, under EPA's view, § 761.20(c)(2) would not need to exist at all. If every process "for purposes of disposal" also requires a disposal permit, § 761.20(c)(2) does nothing but lull regulated parties into a false sense of security by hinting that their processing "for purposes of disposal" is authorized. While the mere presence of such a regulatory trap does not reflect an irrational agency interpretation, it obscures the agency's interpretation of the regulations sufficiently to convince us that GE did not have fair notice that distillation was prohibited. . . .

Our concern about the regulations' lack of clarity is heightened by several additional factors. First, GE and EPA have had considerable difficulty even identifying which portion of § 761.60(a) applied to the disposal of the dirty solvent.

Second, it is unlikely that regulations provide adequate notice when different divisions of the enforcing agency disagree about their meaning. Such is the case here. In 1984, one EPA regional office concluded that companies could distill PCB materials without seeking additional authorization from the EPA. Although GE never proved it, the company asserted in its initial replies to the agency that a second regional office had told it the same thing. While we accept EPA's argument that the regional office interpretation was wrong, confusion at the regional level is yet more evidence that the agency's interpretation of its own regulation could not possibly have provided fair notice . . . .

We thus conclude that EPA did not provide GE with fair warning of its interpretation of the regulations. Where, as here, the regulations and other policy elements are unclear, where the petitioner's interpretation is reasonable, and where the Agency itself struggles to provide a definitive reading of the regulatory requirements, a regulated party is not "on notice" of the agency's ultimate interpretation of the regulations, and may not be punished. EPA thus may not hold GE responsible in any way — either financially or in future enforcement proceedings — for the actions charged in this case.

Notes and Questions

1. In determining the penalty liability for violations of PCB disposal requirements under TSCA, the D.C. Circuit Court of Appeals finds significant "the confusion at the regional level." To what extent should such "confusion" or other inconsistent interpretation of regulations among EPA regional offices or other large environmental agencies affect legal obligations or liabilities? In general, reliance on misinformation provided by one government employee may not provide a violator with the basis for an estoppel defense. *See, e.g., EPA v. Environmental Waste Control*, 917 F.2d 327, 324 (7th Cir. 1990) ("Information provided by a government hot line cannot be enough to estop the government from enforcing violations of [RCRA]"). Moreover, there may be good reasons for a single environmental agency to hold differing interpretations of the same regulatory requirements. The U.S. EPA, for example, is organized into 10 regional offices, administering federal environmental statutes in all 50 states, hundreds of Indian nations and reservations, plus U.S. territories. Within this broad and diverse expanse, environmental requirements may differ as a consequence of variations in state, tribal, and local codes; precedent established by U.S. district and appellate courts; and the unique demands of geography, economy, culture, and community concerns. Given the potential for such regional or local variations, when entering unfamiliar territories, savvy practitioners of environmental law may do well to research local interpretations and practices, and/or to seek the assistance of local counsel.

V. Criminal Enforcement

Criminal enforcement provisions may be found in nearly all federal pollution control statutes as well as in many natural resources laws. Over the past three decades, federal and state environmental officials have relied on them with increased frequency to redress environmental crimes. Most environmental criminal prosecutions are reserved for cases that involve intentional wrongful conduct. Individual corporate officials, as well as corporate entities, are often made defendants in these cases — a prosecutorial practice that seems to have a significant deterrent effect.

Environmental crimes are frequently drafted to require the government to prove, beyond a reasonable doubt, that the defendant "knowingly" violated the law. As the following case illuminates, courts generally hold that the word "knowingly" connotes an awareness on the defendant's part of the actions that violate the law rather than specific knowledge that the defendant's conduct was prohibited by law.

United States v. Sinskey

119 F.3d 712 (8th Cir. 1997)

Judge ARNOLD:

[Timothy Sinskey was the plant manager at the Morrell meat-packing plant in Sioux Falls, South Dakota. Plant operations included the slaughtering of hogs, which created a large amount of wastewater with pollutants including ammonia nitrogen. The plant's wastewater was treated in part by its own wastewater treatment plant (WWTP). From the WWTP, Morrell discharged treated water to the Big Sioux River, subject to conditions in an NPDES permit. Among other conditions, the permit set discharge limits for pollutants and required Morrell to perform weekly tests of its effluent. In 1991, Morrell doubled the number of hogs it slaughtered and processed at the plant, which resulted in pollutant discharges exceeding its permit limits. Plant employees manipulated the testing process so that the plant would discharge the highest levels of pollutants after the tests had been conducted each week, so that it would appear the plant was still in compliance with its permit conditions. Sinskey signed and submitted the manipulated test results to the EPA every month. Sinskey and the plant engineer, Wayne Kumm, were subsequently charged with various CWA violations. After a three-week trial, the jury found both Sinskey and Kumm guilty of knowingly rendering inaccurate a required monitoring method. Sinskey was also found guilty of knowingly discharging a pollutant into waters of the United States in amounts exceeding permit conditions.]

The defendants appeal their convictions for criminal violations of the Clean Water Act. We affirm the judgments of the trial court.

The trial court gave an instruction, which it incorporated into several substantive charges, that in order for the jury to find Sinskey guilty of acting "knowingly," the proof had to show that he was "aware of the nature of his acts, perform[ed] them intentionally, and [did] not act or fail to act through ignorance, mistake, or accident." The instructions also told the jury that the government was not required to prove that Sinskey knew that his acts violated the CWA or permits issued under that act. Sinskey contests these instructions as applied to 33 U.S.C. § 1319(c)(2)(A), arguing that because the adverb "knowingly" immediately precedes the verb "violates," the government must prove that he knew that his conduct violated either the CWA or the NPDES permit. We disagree.

Although our court has not yet decided whether 33 U.S.C. § 1319(c) (2) (A) requires the government to prove that a defendant knew that he or she was violating either the CWA or the relevant NPDES permit when he or she acted, we are guided in answering this question by the generally accepted construction of the word "knowingly" in criminal statutes, by the CWA's legislative history, and by the decisions of the other courts of appeals that have addressed this issue. In construing other statutes with similar language and structure, that is, statutes in which one provision punishes the "knowing violation" of another provision that defines the illegal conduct, we have repeatedly held that the word "knowingly" modifies the acts constituting the underlying conduct. . . .

We see no reason to depart from that commonly accepted construction in this case, and we therefore believe that in 33 U.S.C. § 1319(c) (2)(A), the word "knowingly" applies to the underlying conduct prohibited by the statute. Untangling the statutory provisions discussed above in order to define precisely the relevant underlying conduct, however, is not a little difficult. At first glance, the conduct in question might appear to be violating a permit limitation, which would imply that § 1319(c) (2)(A) requires proof that the defendant knew of the permit limitation and knew that he or she was violating it. To violate a permit limitation, however, one must engage in the conduct prohibited by that limitation. The permit is, in essence, another layer of regulation in the nature of a law, in this case, a law that applies only to Morrell [the owner of the facility]. We therefore believe that the underlying conduct of which Sinskey must have had knowledge is the conduct that is prohibited by the permit, for example, that Morrell's discharges of ammonia nitrates were higher than one part per million in the summer of 1992. Given this interpretation of the statute, the government was not required to prove that Sinskey knew that his acts violated either the CWA or the NPDES permit, but merely that he was aware of the conduct that resulted in the permit's violation.

This interpretation comports not only with our legal system's general recognition that ignorance of the law is no excuse, but also with Supreme Court interpretations of statutes containing similar language and structure. In *United States v. International Minerals & Chemical Corp.*, for example, the Court analyzed a statute that punished anyone who "knowingly violate[d]" certain regulations pertaining to the interstate shipment of hazardous materials. In holding that a conviction under the statute at issue did not require knowledge of the pertinent law, the Court reasoned that the statute's language was merely a shorthand designation for punishing anyone who knowingly committed the specific acts or omissions contemplated by the regulations at issue, and that the statute therefore required knowledge of the material facts but not the relevant law. The Court also focused on the nature of the regulatory scheme at issue, noting that where "dangerous or . . . obnoxious waste materials" are involved, anyone dealing with such materials "must be presumed" to be aware of the existence of the regulations. Requiring knowledge only of the underlying actions, and not of the law, would therefore raise no substantial due process concerns. Such reasoning applies with equal force, we believe, to the CWA, which regulates the discharge into the public's water of such "obnoxious waste materials" as the byproducts of slaughtered animals. . . .

Contrary to the defendants' assertions, moreover, *United States v. Ahmad* is inapposite. In *Ahmad*, a convenience store owner pumped out an underground gasoline storage tank into which some water had leaked, discharging gasoline into city sewer systems and nearby creeks in violation of 33 U.S.C. § 1319(c) (2) (A). At trial, the defendant asserted that he thought that he was discharging water, and that the statute's requirement that he act knowingly required that the government prove not only that he knew that he was discharging something, but also that he knew that he was discharging gasoline. The Fifth Circuit agreed, holding that a defendant does not violate the statute unless he or she acts knowingly with regard to each element of an offense. *Ahmad*, however, involved a classic mistake-of-fact defense, and is not applicable to a mistake-of-law defense such as that asserted by Sinskey . . . .

Notes and Questions

1. Environmental Crimes. Were you aware that people could go to prison for violation of environmental laws? The concept that violation of an environmental law could constitute a crime is about as old as federal environmental law itself. Rivers and Harbors Act of 1899, 33 U.S.C. §403, 403a (establishing misdemeanor for "The creation of any obstruction . . . to the navigable capacity of any waters, in respect of which the United States has jurisdiction"). Originally, the Clean Air Act, Clean Water Act, RCRA, CERCLA, and other environmental statutes established criminal penalties as misdemeanors only; i.e., with a maximum prison sentence of only up to 12 months. In the 1980s, the federal environmental statutes were amended to add felony counts for certain violations; i.e., potential for imprisonment greater than 12 months. For example, under Clean Water Act §309(c), while a negligent discharge without a permit carries a maximum penalty of 12 months, a knowing discharge without a permit carries the possibility of a fine and/or prison up to three years. Similarly, under CERCLA §103(a), to fail to report a release of a hazardous substance above reportable quantities carries a maximum penalty of three years in prison. Under RCRA, to knowingly treat, store, or dispose of hazardous waste without a permit carries a maximum penalty of up to two years in prison. Under the Clean Air Act, to knowingly violate any requirement of an SIP, preconstruction review, or administrative order carries a maximum penalty of five years in prison. For the worst environmental crimes, potential penalties may be much higher. For example, where the environmental violation constitutes "knowing endangerment," defined generally as placing another person in imminent danger of death or serious bodily injury, RCRA, the Clean Air Act, and the Clean Water Act all establish maximum penalties of 15 years in prison. As we have seen from the Introduction to the chapter, the first conviction for knowing endangerment under RCRA involved the owner of a fertilizer company in Idaho who knowingly sent workers into a tank without personal protection in order to remove cyanide sludge. For an inside look at this extraordinary and tragic case, coauthored by one of the investigating agents, see JOSEPH HILLDORFER AND ROBERT DUGONI, THE CYANIDE CANARY (2004).

In addition to crimes involving pollution, more than half of all federal environmental crimes charged actually arise in response to offenses involving wildlife. More than half of wildlife offenses arise specifically under the Lacey Act, 16 U.S.C. §3373(d). Passed originally in 1900, the Lacey Act generally prohibits trafficking in fish, wildlife, or plants taken in violation of federal, state, or tribal law. Penalties for violation of the Lacey Act are generally a misdemeanor; however, penalties involving illegal import, export, or commercial conduct may result in a maximum penalty of five years in prison, plus forfeiture of vehicles, vessels, and other property. Violations of the

Migratory Bird Treaty Act, 16 U.S.C. § 703, which generally prohibits the unlawful hunting, taking, capturing, or killing of a bird, or the unlawful transport of any part, is punishable as a misdemeanor; however, violations involving commercial conduct may be punishable by up to two years in prison. Finally, violations of the Endangered Species Act are generally punishable only as misdemeanors; however, convictions may also result in forfeitures of property, cancellation of grazing permits, and other serious consequences.

2. Mens Rea. Consistent with the Supreme Court's decision in *United States v. International Minerals & Chemicals Corp.*, 402 U.S. 558 (1971), the Clean Water Act, RCRA, and other environmental statutes have been recognized by courts as "public welfare" statutes, for which a conviction may be sustained with only proof of general intent; i.e., proof the defendant understood the nature of his conduct, not necessarily proof the defendant understood that his conduct violated a law. *See, e.g., United States v. Weitzenhoff*, 35 F.3d 1275 (9th Cir. 1993) (CWA convictions sustained); *United States v. Hoflin*, 880 F.2d 1033 (9th Cir. 1989) (RCRA conviction sustained). Given that violations of environmental statutes may result in substantial jail time, what do you think of felony convictions supported by nothing more than general intent? In *Weitzenhoff*, as in *Sinskey*, two plant managers, Weitzenhoff and Mariani, were convicted of felony counts under the Clean Water Act, based largely upon acts carried out by plant employees. If the plant employees understood the "nature of their conduct" (i.e., understood that they discharged pollutants into waters), could they also be subject to felony convictions? In a vigorous dissent in *Weitzenhoff*, Ninth Circuit Judge Kleinfeld warned, "We have now made felons of a large number of innocent people doing socially valuable work." Following *Sinskey* and *Weitzenhoff*, should "innocent" blue-collar workers fear felony convictions for doing their "socially valuable work" of slaughtering animals (*Sinskey*) or treating municipal wastewater (*Weitzenhoff*)? Why or why not?

3. Case Selection Criteria. One answer to the fears expressed by the *Weitzenhoff* dissent is the government's use of *case selection criteria* to identify appropriate cases for criminal enforcement. Quite simply, while environmental laws may define as crimes a very broad range of conduct, there is neither public interest nor sufficient prosecutorial resources for bringing criminal charges in every case that the law may allow. As such, government agencies typically reserve criminal enforcement for only the most egregious cases. Traditionally, for purposes of federal prosecution, these cases were distinguished by meeting both of the following selection criteria: (1) significant environmental harm, to include actual or threatened harm to human health or the environment; and (2) culpable conduct, as demonstrated by deliberate misconduct, a history of violations, or other considerations. Do you imagine these criteria were satisfied in the *Sinskey* and *Weitzenhoff* cases? Do these criteria also help explain not just which cases receive prosecutorial interest, but which individuals may become targets for prosecution?

4. Sentencing. Like the calculation of penalties in the civil judicial context, the determination of prison sentences in the criminal context rarely reflects the maximum authorized by statute. For generations, in fact, many courts (and prosecutors) failed to recognize that criminal convictions for environmental violations ever merited any prison time at all. That has changed since the 1980s, with many significant prison sentences levied for the worst environmental offenders as seen in the opening vignette from *United States v. Elias*, 269 F.3d 1003 (9th Cir. 2001). Today, federal courts may be guided in their calculations of prison sentences for environmental crimes by the United States Sentencing Guidelines, which generally divide convictions into two broad categories: pollution crimes (2.Q.1) and wildlife/conservation crimes (2.Q.2). Consistent with the structure of pollution statutes, the highest base offense levels are usually reserved for "knowing endangerment" convictions, with lesser base offenses for regulatory violations involving toxic or non-toxic substances. From the base offense level, sentences may be enhanced or reduced for factors including ongoing or single releases to the environment, offenses requiring substantial cleanup, and offenses resulting in "substantial likelihood of death or serious bodily injury." *See, e.g., United States v. Pearson*, 274 F.3d 1225 (9th Cir. 2001) (sentencing of Navy contractor convicted of Asbestos NESHAPs violations).

Practice Problem

You are a senior Assistant Regional Counsel in the EPA Office of Regional Counsel for Region 12. Lucy Lacey, an attorney who began working in your office recently, comes to you for some informal assistance and advice.

Lucy tells you that an environmental engineer working for the State of Skilonia Department of Environmental Quality (SDEQ) recently informed EPA personnel that that there is a major problem of particulate matter emissions from a large grain elevator and storage unit in Westfalls, Skilonia. The facility is owned and operated by Three T, Inc., a wealthy corporation that also runs a number of other industrial operations throughout the United States and Canada.

SDEQ has learned that Jim Fosdick, the plant manager at the Westfalls grain elevator, has ordered employees at the facility to turn off the elevator's electrostatic precipitator—an effective air pollution control device—every night, as a way to lower the plant's energy bills. As a result, the Westfalls grain elevator is in gross violation of the Skilonia State Implementation Plan (SIP) requirements regarding particulate emissions from grain elevator and storage operations.

Lucy has drafted a Clean Air Act Notice of Violation for Three T's facility in Westfalls that has not yet been sent out. In addition, adhering to the routine procedures followed in your office before Notices of Violation are issued, she placed a courtesy phone call to the CEO of Three T, Inc., Marvin Biggs, to inform him that a Notice of Violation would be issued to his corporation shortly.

In their phone conversation, Lucy mentioned to Mr. Biggs that she had been told that Jim Fosdick was intentionally shutting down the ESP at the Westfalls facility each night, and that she and the SDEQ believed that this was the cause of Three T's SIP violations. Biggs responded that this was the first he had heard of this problem and that he wanted to look into it immediately himself in order to "make it right," and to preserve Three T's reputation as a clean, law-abiding corporate citizen. He asked Lucy if she could arrange to send an EPA inspector out to the plant within 48 hours to measure the particulate emission levels there. Lucy told Biggs that she might be able to make that happen, but that she would need to check with other folks in the Regional Counsel's Office to find out how requests of this kind are generally handled.

Lucy tells you that she thinks Three T's CEO told her the truth. However, she wants your advice about whether she should promptly send an EPA inspector out to Westfalls, as Mr. Biggs had requested. She also wants your informal advice about whether to recommend criminal prosecution of Jim Fosdick and/or Three T, Inc., What will you tell her? In your opinion, what policy approach should EPA follow in situations of this sort?

––––––––––

Cases that involve criminal violations of federal environmental laws sometimes also involve violations of some of the general federal criminal laws set out in Title 18 of the United States Code. As a result, in addition to alleging environmental crimes, indictments of alleged environmental criminals frequently also contain counts of conspiracy, mail fraud, wire fraud, false claims, perjury, obstruction of justice, or another general crime. The following case provides an example of the use of the federal aiding and abetting statute to prosecute an environmental offender, and the potential criminal liability of a defendant who turns a blind eye to how its waste is being disposed of.

United States v. Wasserson
418 F.3d 225 (3d Cir. 2005)

Judge McKEE:

Gary Wasserson was the president and chief executive officer of Sterling Supply Company, located in Philadelphia, Pennsylvania. . . . Sterling had a warehouse in Philadelphia where it stored cleaning products consisting of cleaners, soaps and detergents, as well as equipment and business records. When Sterling went out of business in 1991, the warehouse contained hundreds of containers of chemicals, including napthene, acetone, and perchloroethylene.

Charles Hughes was a Sterling employee from 1980 through 1994. According to the government, in August of 1999, Wasserson asked Hughes to hire someone to remove the remaining materials at Sterling's warehouse . . . [but] . . . neither Wasserson nor Hughes, his representative, provided Davis or Will-Haul [the companies hired to dispose of the materials] with the required hazardous waste manifest identifying the items for disposal. Similarly, no one informed Davis or Will-Haul that the drums and containers contained hazardous waste and therefore had to be transported to, and disposed of at, a permitted facility pursuant to the RCRA.

Wasserson was indicted by a federal grand jury and charged with three counts of violating the RCRA: causing, and aiding and abetting, the transportation of hazardous waste without a manifest, in violation of 42 U.S.C. § 6928(d)(5) and 18 U.S.C. § 2 (Count One); causing, and aiding and abetting, the transportation of hazardous waste to facilities which were not authorized to store or dispose of hazardous waste, in violation of 42 U.S.C. § 6928(d)(1) and 18 U.S.C. § 2 (Count Two); and causing and aiding and abetting, the disposal of hazardous waste without a permit, in violation of 42 U.S.C. § 6928(d)(2) and 18 U.S.C. § 2 (Count Three)

A jury convicted Wasserson of all three counts at the end of a three-day trial. Thereafter, Wasserson filed a motion for new trial . . . arguing that 42 U.S.C. § 6928(d)(2)(A) only applied to owners and operators of disposal facilities, and that he could therefore not be convicted of violating that statute.

The district court granted Wasserson's motion in part . . . on the court's conclusion that "one who merely generates but does not carry out the disposal of hazardous waste cannot be convicted under subsection (d)(2)(A)."

The government moved for reconsideration of the judgment of acquittal on Count Three arguing that it had charged Wasserson with aiding and abetting disposal of hazardous waste in violation of 42 U.S.C. § 6928(d)(2)(A) and 18 U.S.C. § 2. The district court disagreed, and this appeal followed. . . .

The government bottomed its aiding and abetting theory on the premise of Wasserson's willful blindness in handling the disposal of the hazardous waste. "A willful blindness instruction is often described as sounding in deliberate ignorance." "Such instructions must be tailored . . . to avoid the implication that a defendant may be convicted simply because he or she should have known of facts of which he or she was unaware." "Willful blindness is not to be equated with negligence or lack of due care, for willful blindness is a subjective state of mind that is deemed to satisfy a scienter requirement of knowledge." "The instruction must make clear that the defendant himself was subjectively aware of the high probability of the fact in question, and not merely that a reasonable man would have been aware of the probability."

Our review of the evidence in the light most favorable to the government leads us to conclude that there was clearly sufficient evidence for a reasonable jury to find that Wasserson was willfully blind to the ultimate destination of his hazardous waste.

Wasserson had owned Sterling since about 1980, and was actively involved in running the business. Although Sterling ceased operations around 1993 or 1994, Wasserson kept the warehouse. Wasserson knew the warehouse contained dry cleaning products, and Wasserson concedes that he knew the products constituted hazardous waste.

Wasserson also knew the requirements for handling hazardous waste and particularly for handling hazardous dry cleaning chemicals. From about mid-1989 through 1990, Wasserson employed an environmental consultant, Michael Tatch, to advise him on a number of regulatory matters, including transporting hazardous waste. At one point, Wasserson was interested in expanding his business into hauling hazardous waste from dry cleaners. At another point, Wasserson asked Tatch about becoming a disposal facility, and Tatch reviewed the requirements for generators, haulers and disposers of hazardous waste with Wasserson.

Tatch also instructed Wasserson about the importance of manifests and their relevance to the regulatory framework governing hazardous waste. He told Wasserson that generators were required to manifest their waste, and that transporters had to sign those manifests and pass them along to those who took possession as well as to state agencies. Tatch described the information that a manifest must contain. He specifically covered the obligation of a generator of waste to provide a manifest if it generates more than 230 pounds of waste, and he advised Wasserson that it is the generator's responsibility to ensure that any waste leaving the generator's control has a properly completed and signed manifest.

Thus, as Wasserson stipulated, he knew that a completed manifest must accompany any hazardous waste shipped for disposal; that hazardous waste may only be transported to a facility that has a proper permit; and that a facility that disposes of hazardous waste must also have a proper permit to do so. Significantly for our purposes, Wasserson also knew that the proper disposal of hazardous waste was expensive.

Wasserson asked Hughes, his intermediary and employee, to find someone to clean out the trash in the warehouse. When Hughes reported back to Wasserson that Davis would clear everything out, including the hazardous wastes, Wasserson told Hughes to get it in writing because he did not want any problems.

In contrast to Wasserson's knowledge about the requirements for handling hazardous waste, Hughes knew nothing about hazardous waste disposal. Hughes had worked for Wasserson at Sterling from about 1980 as a truck or tractor-trailer driver making deliveries of dry cleaning supplies. Before Wasserson hired him, Hughes had also been a truck driver. After Sterling closed in 1993 or 1994, Hughes was Wasserson's chauffeur for a few years. He also undertook various assignments for Wasserson, such as general clean-up of the warehouse, and helping load trucks for people interested in any of the goods at the warehouse. One of these assignments included hiring someone to get rid of the trash in the warehouse.

Before he hired Davis, Hughes had never been involved in disposing of Sterling's supply of hazardous waste. He knew nothing about the legal and technical requirements for a manifest. All that he did know was that if a manifest was needed on a job he drove, it was provided by "the office upstairs." Hughes did not participate in preparing any manifests. It was only after Davis disposed of the hazardous waste that Hughes first saw a manifest, which had been provided by a company called "Only" that was eventually hired to perform a proper clean-up of the warehouse.

Given this evidence, Wasserson's level of knowledge about the legal requirements for handling hazardous waste, and Hughes's lack of knowledge; a jury could reasonably infer that Wasserson's failure to make proper inquiry and to provide a proper manifest were tantamount to willful blindness to the ultimate destination and disposal of the waste. Wasserson did not ask Davis, and Hughes did not even know to ask Davis, about the essential requirements for the proper transport and disposal of Sterling's hazardous waste. Wasserson did communicate directly with Davis's company, but only to ensure that Davis agreed to assume responsibility for the waste. Wasserson spoke to Davis's secretary, dictated those terms to her, and had her read them back to him and fax him the signed agreement. Thus, the jury could have believed that for the $13,000 he paid to Davis, Wasserson thought he could wash his hands of the trash, debris, and hazardous waste in his warehouse, and leave Davis "holding the bag."

As Wasserson knew, the warehouse that Davis agreed to clean was quite large, and the amount of debris and waste was significant. The areas to be cleaned included about 125 multi-drawer filing cabinets full of old papers and trash, plastic pipe, long crates, old machinery, old safes, about 500 multiple tier racks and three "huge" filters; and then there was the hazardous waste. A reasonable jury could conclude from this evidence that Wasserson's only concern regarding the hazardous waste was shifting legal responsibility to Davis.

Accordingly, it was reasonable for the jury to conclude that Wasserson knew that the hazardous wastes might well be disposed of at an unpermitted facility, or at least that he was willfully blind to that eventuality. *See United States v. Hayes International Corp.* ("It is common knowledge that properly disposing of wastes in an expensive task, and if someone is willing to take away wastes at an unusual price or under unusual circumstances, then a juror can infer that the transporter knows the wastes are not being taken to a permit facility.").

For all of these reasons, we find that there is more than sufficient evidence to support the unlawful disposal conviction. Accordingly, we will reverse the district court's order granting judgment of acquittal on Count Three and reinstate the jury's verdict of guilty. . . .

Notes and Questions

1. Willful Blindness. If "ignorance of the law is no excuse," then why is "blindness" ever a concern? The concern here is blindness not to applicable law but to operative *facts.* In limited circumstances, genuine ignorance may provide an effective defense to charges requiring some "knowing" conduct under environmental law. The case of *United States v. Pacific Hide & Fur Depot*, 768 F.2d 1096 (9th Cir. 1985) involved a defendant, William Knick, who managed a salvage yard in Pocatello, Idaho. During an inspection of the salvage yard, EPA investigators observed hundreds of "black boxes" on the property. The "black boxes" were capacitors containing PCBs, and Knick was eventually tried and convicted under TSCA for charges relating to illegal disposal of PCBs. On appeal, the conviction was reversed, as there appeared no evidence that Knick understood the capacitors contained PCBs nor evidence that Knick engaged in "deliberate avoidance" of information concerning the content of the capacitors. Confirming Knick's genuine ignorance respecting the "black boxes," the court observed evidence that Knick had attempted to hide certain drums that he believed (wrongly) to contain hazardous materials, but Knick indicated no concern with the inspectors observing the "black boxes" lying around the property. Should Knick's apparent intent to hide hazardous materials from the inspectors (even though he hid the wrong thing), be enough to sustain his conviction for illegal disposal of hazardous materials? Do you agree with the appellate court's ruling in this case?

The common law doctrine of "willful blindness," or "deliberate avoidance," has been codified in various environmental provisions as a consideration expressly authorized to prove a mental state necessary for certain environmental crimes. *See, e.g.*, Clean Air Act § 113(c)(5)(B) ("in proving a defendant's possession of actual knowledge" necessary to sustain a conviction for knowing endangerment, "circumstantial evidence may be used, including evidence that the defendant took affirmative steps to be shielded from relevant information"). *See also* CWA § 309(c)(3)(B) (same); RCRA § 3008(f)(2) (same).

2. Vagueness. As we have seen, environmental regulations may be very complex and subject to differing interpretations. This has led many criminal defendants in environmental cases to challenge environmental requirements as unconstitutionally vague. So far, no criminal provision of a federal environmental statute has been held on its face to be void for vagueness. However, courts have considered challenges for vagueness as applied. Such a challenge was raised, for example, in the case of *United States v. Iverson*, 162 F.3d 1015 (9th Cir. 1998), in which the president of a chemical company personally emptied drums of chemical waste through sewer drains at his business, home, and an apartment complex. The defendant was convicted of four counts under the Clean Water Act, state water pollution statute, and municipal code. In sustaining the defendant's conviction against a challenge of vagueness, the appellate court observed:

> A criminal statute is not vague if a "reasonable person of ordinary intelligence" would understand what conduct the statute prohibits. Moreover, where, as here, a criminal statute regulates economic activity, it generally "is subject to a less strict vagueness test, because its subject matter is more often narrow and because businesses can be expected to consult relevant legislation in advance of action."

In this case, what does it mean "to consult relevant legislation" in advance of action? What if the defendant truly could not understand the requirements applicable to his business, or perceived an actual conflict in the requirements between federal, state, and local code? Before proceeding to empty the drums down the drains unlawfully, what options did the defendant have available to ensure his lawful conduct?

3. Double Jeopardy. The Fifth Amendment to the U.S. Constitution provides that, "[N]or shall any person be subject for the same offense to be twice put in jeopardy of life and limb . . . ." Over time, the Double Jeopardy Clause, like many other provisions in the Bill of Rights, has been interpreted by courts in various and perhaps surprising ways. One such interpretation has given rise to the "Dual Sovereignty Doctrine," which holds that the Double Jeopardy Clause does not bar prosecutions by federal and state actors for the same offense. *See generally*, Thomas White, *Limitations Imposed on the Dual Sovereignty Doctrine by Federal and State Governments*, 38 N. Ky. L. Rev. 173 (2001). Another doctrine recognized by courts is that the Double Jeopardy Clause "protects only against imposition of multiple *criminal* punishments for the same offense," *Hudson v. U.S.*, 522 U.S. 93, 99 (1997) (emphasis in original), thus posing no bar to both civil and criminal penalties for violations arising from the same set of facts. Nevertheless, EPA policy provides that where both civil and criminal enforcement may be appropriate in a certain circumstance, in general, the criminal case should go first. See EPA Parallel Proceedings Policy (Sept. 24, 2007), available at: https://www.epa.gov/enforcement/parallel-proceedings-policy. Can you think of any legal or prudential concerns underlying this policy? What about any exceptional circumstances where "parallel proceedings" (civil and criminal actions proceeding simultaneously) may be appropriate or legally required?

4. Statutory Defenses. In addition to defenses based upon constitutional requirements, the federal environmental statutes provide a number of specific defenses to civil and criminal charges. Included among these are the following affirmative defenses:

- Consent: whereby a charge of knowing endangerment, for example, may be defeated by proof that "the conduct charged was consented to by the person endangered and that the danger and conduct charged were reasonably foreseeable hazards of —

  (A) an occupation, a business, or a profession; or (B) medical treatment . . . ." RCRA § 3008(f)(3), 42 U.S.C. § 6928(f)(3).

- Self-defense: whereby a charge under the Endangered Species Act, for example, may be defeated based upon a "good faith belief" in the need to "protect himself or herself, a member of his or her family, or any other individual, from bodily harm from any endangered or threatened species." ESA § 11(b)(3), 16 U.S.C. § 1540(b)(3).

- Permit: whereby liability under CERCLA, for example, may be defeated by proof that the release of a hazardous substance was subject to, and in compliance with, the provisions of an applicable permit. CERCLA § 107(j), 42 U.S.C. § 9607(j).

Practice Problem

The Friendly Forest Products Company operated a timber mill and wood treatment facility in the Ozark Mountains of Markansas for almost a century. Among other things, the Friendly facility produced wooden railroad ties and telephone poles that used the chemical pentachlorophenol (PCP) in the wood treatment process. Unfortunately, PCP proved to be highly toxic, and the use of PCP at the Friendly facility resulted in substantial contamination of soils at and around the facility. Contamination of the soils was so substantial that the soils constitute hazardous waste and must be disposed properly in a hazardous waste disposal facility. The nearest disposal facility permitted to accept hazardous waste is 75 miles away from the Friendly wood treatment facility. Based on the estimated volume of contaminated soils for disposal, Friendly will have to make more than 900 round-trips to the disposal facility. After the first few such trips, Mr. Frederick Friendly, the CEO of the Friendly Forest Products Company, decides that instead of hauling the contaminated soils to the hazardous waste disposal facility 75 miles away, they will simply dump the contaminated soils into an old quarry five miles from the Friendly wood treatment facility. The quarry, on property owned by Mr. Friendly, is not permitted to accept hazardous waste such as the contaminated soils. However, Mr. Friendly reasons that using his own private property for this purpose will save money on fuel and labor, will accelerate the cleanup schedule, and will reduce the carbon footprint of the cleanup operation—all of which should please the U.S. Environmental Protection Agency (EPA), should they ever learn of this change in plans.

You are an attorney for EPA Region 12, which has jurisdiction in the State of Markansas. As an EPA attorney, you just received a tip from one of the truck drivers hired to haul the contaminated soils to the hazardous waste disposal facility 75 miles away from the Friendly facility. The truck driver is concerned about the new direction from Friendly to haul the contaminated soils to the old quarry on Friendly's property.

1. Without entering the old quarry or any other property owned by Friendly, what means are available to EPA to gather information in order to confirm the truck driver's report?

2. If your information confirms the illegal disposal of hazardous waste at the old quarry, evaluate your options between administrative and civil enforcement: which track is likely to stop the illegal disposal the soonest?

3. EPA investigators suspect that Mr. Frederick Friendly, the CEO of the Friendly Forest Products Company, was personally involved in the decision to engage in the illegal disposal. Among other things, several truck drivers tell EPA investigators that they heard the decision to reroute the contaminated soils from the hazardous waste disposal facility to the old quarry "came from the top." What theory or theories of criminal law may help you build a case for prosecution of Mr. Friendly?

VI. Citizen Enforcement

In addition to enforcement by government agencies, most environmental laws are also subject to enforcement by concerned citizens and organizations. Beginning with the Clean Air Act of 1970, Congress included specific provisions for citizen enforcement in most federal environmental statutes. *See, e.g.,* Clean Air Act § 304, 42 U.S.C. § 7604; Clean Water Act § 505, 33 U.S.C. § 1365; RCRA § 7002, 42 U.S.C. § 6972; CERCLA § 310, 42 U.S.C. § 9659; Safe Drinking Water Act § 1449, 42 U.S.C. § 300j-8; Endangered Species Act § 11(g), 16 U.S.C. § 1540(g). Moreover, for environmental statutes such as NEPA and FIFRA, which do not include specific provisions for citizen suits, citizen enforcement may often be pursued through claims brought under the APA.

Beyond doubt, citizen enforcers have been very effective in compelling compliance with environmental law. Citizen suits have included some of the most momentous cases in environmental law, including *TVA v. Hill*, 437 U.S. 153 (1978), and many of the principal cases excerpted in this book. As one commentator reflected upon the first 30 years of citizen suit enforcement:

> Citizen suits work; they have transformed the environmental movement, and
> with it, society. Citizen suits have secured compliance by myriad agencies and

thousands of polluting facilities, diminished pounds of pollution produced by the billions, and protected hundreds of rare species and thousands of acres of ecologically important land. The foregone monetary value of citizen enforcement has conserved innumerable agency resources and saved taxpayers billions."

James May, *Now More Than Ever: Trends in Environmental Citizen Suits at 30*, 10 WIDENER L. REV. 1 (2003).

A logical parallel to the success of citizen suits has been the popularity of citizen suits. According to one study, three-fourths of all reported judicial decisions in environmental law over a certain period involved citizen suits. *Id*. at 4. This extraordinary percentage may be a bit deceiving, however, for in the same time period more environmental lawsuits were actually filed by governmental regulators. What might explain the disparity between citizen suits' share of lawsuits filed and their share of the reported opinions? One reason citizen suits may be less likely to settle is that defendants may have more opportunities for challenging citizen suits and preventing cases from reaching the merits. You have likely already seen one of those special opportunities for challenging citizen suits: standing to sue, as seen in such cases as *Lujan v. Defenders of Wildlife*, 504 U.S. 555 (1992). In addition to standing requirements grounded in Article III of the U.S. Constitution, citizen plaintiffs may face additional hurdles established by environmental statutes. One of the most fundamental statutory requirements involves the provision of proper notice before a citizen suit can be filed, as examined in the following case.

Hallstrom v. Tillamook County

493 U.S. 1037 (1989)

Justice O'CONNOR:

The citizen suit provision of the Resource Conservation and Recovery Act of 1976 (RCRA) permits individuals to commence an action in district court to enforce waste disposal regulations promulgated under the Act. At least 60 days before commencing suit, plaintiffs must notify the alleged violator, the State, and the Environmental Protection Agency (EPA) of their intent to sue. This 60-day notice provision was modeled upon § 304 of the Clean Air Amendments of 1970. Since 1970, a number of other federal statutes have incorporated notice provisions patterned after § 304. In this case, we must decide whether compliance with the 60-day notice provision is a mandatory precondition to suit or can be disregarded by the district court at its discretion.

Petitioners own a commercial dairy farm located next to respondent's sanitary landfill. In April 1981, believing that the landfill operation violated standards established under RCRA, petitioners sent respondent written notice of their intention to file suit. A year later, petitioners commenced this action. On March 1, 1983, respondent moved for summary judgment on the ground that petitioners had failed to notify Oregon's Department of Environmental Quality (DEQ) and the EPA of their intent to sue, as required by § 6972(b)(1). Respondent claimed that this failure to comply with the notice requirement deprived the District Court of jurisdiction. On March 2, 1983, petitioners notified the agencies of the suit.

The District Court denied respondent's motion. It reasoned that petitioners had cured any defect in notice by formally notifying the state and federal agencies on March 2, 1983. The agencies would then have 60 days to take appropriate steps to cure any violation at respondent's landfill. The court noted that the purpose of the notice requirement was to give administrative agencies an opportunity to enforce environmental regulations. In this case, neither the state nor the federal agency expressed any interest in taking action against respondent. Therefore, the court concluded that dismissing the action at this stage would waste judicial resources.

After the action proceeded to trial, the District Court held that respondent had violated RCRA. The court ordered respondent to remedy the violation but refused to grant petitioners' motion for injunctive relief. In a later order, the District Court denied petitioners' request for attorney's fees. Petitioners appealed both rulings; respondent cross-appealed from the denial of its summary judgment motion.

The Court of Appeals for the Ninth Circuit concluded that petitioners' failure to comply with the 60-day notice requirement deprived the District Court of subject matter jurisdiction. Relying on the plain language of §6972(b)(1), the Court of Appeals determined that permitting the plaintiff to proceed without giving notice would constitute "'judicial amendment'" of a clear statutory command. The Court of Appeals also determined that strict construction of the notice requirement would best further the goal of giving environmental agencies, rather than courts, the primary responsibility for enforcing RCRA. Therefore, the Court of Appeals remanded the action to the District Court with instructions to dismiss. We granted certiorari to resolve the conflict among the Courts of Appeals regarding the correct interpretation of the notice provision.

As we have repeatedly noted, "the starting point for interpreting a statute is the language of the statute itself." Section 6972(a)(1) permits any person to commence a civil action against an alleged violator of regulations established under RCRA "[except] as provided in subsection (b)." Subsection (b)(1) states:

"(b) Actions prohibited. No action may be commenced under paragraph (a)(1) of this section—

"(1) prior to sixty days after the plaintiff has given notice of the violation (A) to the Administrator [of the EPA]; (B) to the State in which the alleged violation occurs; and (C) to any alleged violator of such permit, standard, regulation, condition, requirement, or order. . . ."

The language of this provision could not be clearer. A citizen may not commence an action under RCRA until 60 days after the citizen has notified the EPA, the State in which the alleged violation occurred, and the alleged violator. Actions commenced prior to 60 days after notice are "prohibited." Because this language is expressly incorporated by reference into §6972(a), it acts as a specific limitation on a citizen's right to bring suit. Under a literal reading of the statute, compliance with the 60-day notice provision is a mandatory, not optional, condition precedent for suit.

Petitioners do not contend that the language of this provision is ambiguous; rather, they assert that it should be given a flexible or pragmatic construction. Thus, petitioners argue that if a suit commenced without proper notice is stayed until 60 days after notice had been given, the District Court should deem the notice requirement to be satisfied. According to petitioners, a 60-day stay would serve the same function as delaying commencement of the suit: it would give the Government an opportunity to take action against the alleged violator and it would give the violator the opportunity to bring itself into compliance.

Whether or not a stay is in fact the functional equivalent of a pre-commencement delay, such an interpretation of § 6972(b) flatly contradicts the language of the statute. Under Rule 3 of the Federal Rules of Civil Procedure, "[a] civil action is commenced by filing a complaint with the court." Reading § 6972(b)(1) in light of this Rule, a plaintiff may not file suit before fulfilling the 60-day notice requirement. Staying judicial action once the suit has been filed does not honor this prohibition. Congress could have excepted parties from complying with the notice or delay requirement; indeed, it carved out such an exception in its 1984 amendments to RCRA. See, *e.g.,* 42 U.S.C. § 6972(b)(1)(A) (abrogating the 60-day delay requirement when there is a danger that hazardous waste will be discharged). RCRA, however, contains no exception applicable to petitioners' situation; we are not at liberty to create an exception where Congress has declined to do so.

Petitioners further argue that under our decision in *Zipes v. Trans World Airlines, Inc.,* 455 U.S. 385, 393 (1982), RCRA's 60-day notice provision should be subject to equitable modification and cure. In *Zipes,* we held that the timely filing of a charge of discrimination with the Equal Employment Opportunity Commission, as required under Title VII of the Civil Rights Act of 1964 ("[a] charge under this section shall be filed within one hundred and eighty days after the alleged unlawful employment practice occurred . . ."), was not a jurisdictional prerequisite to suit but was subject to waiver, estoppel, and equitable tolling. This decision does not help petitioners. First, as we noted in *Zipes,* both the language and legislative history of § 2000e-5(e) indicate that the filing period operated as a statute of limitations. The running of such statutes is traditionally subject to equitable tolling. Unlike a statute of limitations, RCRA's 60-day notice provision is not triggered by the violation giving rise to the action. Rather, petitioners have full control over the timing of their suit: they need only give notice to the appropriate parties and refrain from commencing their action for at least 60 days. The equities do not weigh in favor of modifying statutory requirements when the procedural default is caused by petitioners' "failure to take the minimal steps necessary" to preserve their claims.

Nor can we excuse petitioners' failure on the ground that "a technical reading [of § 6972] would be 'particularly inappropriate in a statutory scheme in which laymen, unassisted by trained lawyers, initiate the process.'" While the initial charge in a Title VII proceeding is normally filed by an aggrieved individual, see § 2000e-5(b), citizen suits under RCRA are like any other lawsuit, generally filed by trained lawyers who are presumed to be aware of statutory requirements. (Indeed, counsel for petitioners in this case admitted at oral argument that he knew of the notice provisions but inadvertently neglected to notify the state and federal agencies.) Under these circumstances, it is not unfair to require strict compliance with statutory conditions precedent to suit.

Petitioners next contend that a literal interpretation of the notice provision would defeat Congress' intent in enacting RCRA; to support this argument, they cite passages from the legislative history of the first citizen suit statute, § 304 of the Clean Air Amendments of 1970, indicating that citizen suits should be encouraged. This reliance on legislative history is misplaced. We have held that "[a]bsent a clearly expressed legislative intention to the contrary," the words of the statute are conclusive. Nothing in the legislative history of the citizen suit provision militates against honoring the plain language of the notice requirement. Nor is this one of the "'rare cases [in which] the literal application of a statute will produce a result demonstrably at odds with the intentions of its drafters.'" Rather, the legislative history indicates an intent to strike a balance between encouraging citizen enforcement of environmental regulations and avoiding burdening the federal courts with excessive numbers of citizen suits. Requiring citizens to comply with the notice and delay requirements serves this congressional goal in two ways. First, notice allows Government agencies to take responsibility for enforcing environmental regulations, thus obviating the need for citizen suits. In many cases, an agency may be able to compel compliance through administrative action, thus eliminating the need for any access to the courts. Second, notice gives the alleged violator "an opportunity to bring itself into complete compliance with the Act and thus likewise render unnecessary a citizen suit." This policy would be frustrated if citizens could immediately bring suit without involving federal or state enforcement agencies. Giving full effect to the words of the statute preserves the compromise struck by Congress.

Petitioners next assert that giving effect to the literal meaning of the notice provisions would compel "absurd or futile results." In essence, petitioners make two arguments. First, petitioners, with *amici,* contend that strictly enforcing the 60-day delay provision would give violators an opportunity to cause further damage or actually accomplish the objective that the citizen was attempting to stop. Similarly, they assert that courts would be precluded from giving essential temporary injunctive relief until 60 days had elapsed. Although we do not underestimate the potential damage to the environment that could ensue during the 60-day waiting period, this problem arises as a result of the balance struck by Congress in developing the citizen suit provisions. Congress has addressed the dangers of delay in certain circumstances and made exceptions to the required notice periods accordingly. See, *e.g.,* the Clean Water Act, 33 U.S.C. §§ 1365(b) and 1317(a) (citizen suits may be brought immediately in cases involving violations of toxic pollutant effluent limitations); the Clean Air Amendments of 1970, 42 U.S.C. § 7604(b) (citizen suits may be brought immediately in cases involving stationary-source emissions standards and other specified compliance orders). Moreover, it is likely that compliance with the notice requirement will trigger appropriate federal or state enforcement actions to prevent serious damage.

Second, petitioners argue that a strict construction of the notice provision would cause procedural anomalies. For example, petitioners contend that if a citizen notified

Government agencies of a violation, and the agencies explicitly declined to act, it would be pointless to require the citizen to wait 60 days to commence suit. While such a result may be frustrating to the plaintiff, it is not irrational: as the Court of Appeals for the First Circuit noted, "[p]ermitting immediate suit ignores the possibility that a violator or agency may change its mind as the threat of suit becomes more imminent."

In sum, we conclude that none of petitioners' arguments requires us to disregard the plain language of §6972(b). "[I]n the long run, experience teaches that strict adherence to the procedural requirements specified by the legislature is the best guarantee of evenhanded administration of the law." Therefore, we hold that the notice and 60-day delay requirements are mandatory conditions precedent to commencing suit under the RCRA citizen suit provision; a district court may not disregard these requirements at its discretion. The parties have framed the question presented in this case as whether the notice provision is jurisdictional or procedural. In light of our literal interpretation of the statutory requirement, we need not determine whether §6972(b) is jurisdictional in the strict sense of the term.

As a general rule, if an action is barred by the terms of a statute, it must be dismissed. . . . As we have noted, dismissal of an RCRA suit serves important federal goals. Indeed, the EPA, the federal agency charged with enforcement of RCRA, interprets the notice provision as requiring dismissal for non-compliance. Such a remedy for actions filed in violation of §6972(b)(1) will further judicial efficiency; courts will have no need to make case-by-case determinations of when or whether failure to fulfill the notice requirement is fatal to a party's suit.

Petitioners urge us not to require dismissal of this action after years of litigation and a determination on the merits. They contend that such a dismissal would unnecessarily waste judicial resources. We are sympathetic to this argument. The complex environmental and legal issues involved in this litigation have consumed the time and energy of a District Court and the parties for nearly four years. Nevertheless, the factors which have led us to apply decisions nonretroactively are not present in this case. Our decision here does not establish a new rule of law; nor does it overrule clear past precedent on which litigants may have relied. Moreover, the statute itself put petitioners on notice of the requirements for bringing suit. Retroactive operation of our decision will further the congressional purpose of giving agencies and alleged violators a 60-day nonadversarial period to achieve compliance with RCRA regulations. Nor will the dismissal of this action have the inequitable result of depriving petitioners of their "right to a day in court." Petitioners remain free to give notice and file their suit in compliance with the statute to enforce pertinent environmental standards.

Accordingly, we hold that where a party suing under the citizen suit provisions of RCRA fails to meet the notice and 60-day delay requirements of §6972(b), the district court must dismiss the action as barred by the terms of the statute.

The judgment of the Court of Appeals is affirmed.

Justice MARSHALL, with whom Justice BRENNAN joins, filed a dissenting opinion [omitted].

Notes and Questions

1. According to Justice O'Connor in *Hallstrom,* what are the purposes of the statutory requirement for citizens to provide advance notice of intent to sue? Would a stay of the litigation, after it was filed, satisfy these purposes? If so, why doesn't O'Connor find a stay sufficient to allow the petitioner's case to continue?

2. As Justice O'Connor notes in *Hallstrom,* advance notice is not always required before citizens may file a citizen suit under federal environmental statutes. O'Connor cites the exception in RCRA § 7002(b)(1) ("except that such action may be brought immediately . . . in the case of an action . . . respecting a violation of [RCRA hazardous waste requirements]"). Other exceptions may allow for immediate filings under the Clean Water Act, Clean Air Act, and other statutes. *See, e.g.,* CWA § 505(b) (exceptions including for discharges of toxic pollutants); CAA 304(b) (exceptions including for preconstruction permits and enforcement of administrative orders). Given the purposes of providing notice of intent to sue, what is the policy supporting such exceptions?

3. Notice the year when the original notice of intent to sue was filed in *Hallstrom* and the year of the Court's decision. In light of the passage of time, what value would you place upon Justice O'Connor's observation that, "Petitioners remain free to give notice and file their suit" eight years later? Will the petitioner's case be barred now by concerns such as stale facts or the statute of limitations?

4. Content. While the Court in *Hallstrom* addressed the timing of required notices, it did not focus on the requisite *content* of such notices. Under the Clean Water Act, for example, what does it mean to provide "notice of the alleged violation"? For the Clean Water Act and other statutes, the question may be answered to some degree by implementing regulations. Among other things, the implementing regulations for the Clean Water Act specifically require the following:

> Notice regarding an alleged violation . . . shall include sufficient information to permit the recipient to identify the specific standard, limitation, or order alleged to have been violated, the activity alleged to constitute a violation, the location of the alleged violation, the date or dates of such violation, and the full name, address, and telephone number of the person giving notice.

40 C.F.R. § 135.3. Given these regulatory requirements, how would you draft a notice of intent to sue to address illegal discharges of pollutants into a river? What if you didn't know the exact "date or dates" when the discharge occurred? What if you didn't know exactly which of several possible outfalls to the river had contributed the discharge? What if you didn't know the full extent of the discharge and all the specific chemical pollutants contained in the discharge? The courts interpreting the Clean Water Act regulations and other rules have differed on the level of detail required to allow the citizen suit to proceed. In one case, citizen claims were dismissed because the would-be plaintiff failed to identify each specific pollutant contained within an allegedly unlawful discharge. *See Catskill Mountains Chapter of Trout Unlimited v. City of New York,* 273 F.3d 481 (2d Cir. 2001). Other courts, however, have taken a more

flexible approach, given that notice is to provide "sufficient information to permit the *recipient*" (emphasis added) to identify the nature of the alleged violation, recognizing that the recipient may be better positioned to understand the violation than members of the general public or a reviewing court. *See San Francisco Baykeeper v. Tosco Corp.*, 309 F.3d 1153 (9th Cir. 2002).

Note that some statutes, such as the Endangered Species Act, have no implementing regulations to guide the content of notices of intent to sue. Nevertheless, practice with citizen suits over four decades now has resulted in the development of many good examples of notice letters for almost every occasion under federal environmental law. Savvy practitioners use their organizations and networks to obtain copies of good examples, but must always exercise independent judgment to make sure the letter satisfies all legal requirements in order to allow the claim to proceed.

———

In addition to complying with statutory notice requirements, plaintiffs in environmental citizen suits must establish that the court has subject matter jurisdiction to hear their case. Some statutes are drafted to authorize citizen suits against any person who is "alleged to be in violation" of a relevant environmental requirement. In some lawsuits based on those provisions, the defendants raised the issue of whether the "alleged to be in violation" language—as written in the presence tense—authorizes the courts to hear citizen suits instituted to redress environmental violations that took place wholly in the past. The United States Supreme Court resolved that question in the case below.

Gwaltney of Smithfield v. Chesapeake Bay Foundation
484 U.S. 49 (1987)

Justice MARSHALL:

In this case, we must decide whether § 505(a) of the Clean Water Act . . . confers federal jurisdiction over citizen suits for wholly past violations . . . .

The Commonwealth of Virginia established a federally approved state NPDES program administered by the Virginia State Water Control Board (Board). Va. Code § 62.1-44.2 *et seq.* (1950). In 1974, the Board issued a NPDES permit to ITT-Gwaltney authorizing the discharge of seven pollutants from the company's meat-packing plant on the Pagan River in Smithfield, Virginia. The permit, which was reissued in 1979 and modified in 1980, established effluent limitations, monitoring requirements, and other conditions of discharge. In 1981, petitioner Gwaltney of Smithfield acquired the assets of ITT-Gwaltney and assumed obligations under the permit.

Between 1981 and 1984, petitioner repeatedly violated the conditions of the permit by exceeding effluent limitations on five of the seven pollutants covered. These violations are chronicled in the Discharge Monitoring Reports that the permit required petitioner to maintain . . . . Between October 27, 1981, and August 30, 1984, petitioner violated its TKN [total Kjeldhal nitrogen] limitation 87 times, its chlorine limitation

34 times, and its fecal coliform limitation 31 times. Petitioner installed new equipment to improve its chlorination system in March 1982, and its last reported chlorine violation occurred in October 1982. The new chlorination system also helped to control the discharge of fecal coliform, and the last recorded fecal coliform violation occurred in February 1984. Petitioner installed an upgraded wastewater treatment system in October 1983, and its last reported TKN violation occurred on May 15, 1984.

Respondents Chesapeake Bay Foundation and Natural Resources Defense Council, two nonprofit corporations dedicated to the protection of natural resources, sent notice in February 1984 to Gwaltney, the Administrator of EPA, and the Virginia State Water Control Board, indicating respondents' intention to commence a citizen suit under the Act based on petitioner's violations of its permit conditions. Respondents proceeded to file this suit in June 1984, alleging that petitioner "has violated . . . [and] will continue to violate its NPDES permit." Respondents requested that the District Court provide declaratory and injunctive relief, impose civil penalties, and award attorney's fees and costs. The District Court granted partial summary judgment for respondents in August 1984, declaring Gwaltney "to have violated and to be in violation" of the Act. The District Court then held a trial to determine the appropriate remedy.

Before the District Court reached a decision, Gwaltney moved in May 1985 for a dismissal of the action for want of subject-matter jurisdiction under the Act. Gwaltney argued that the language of § 505(a), which permits private citizens to bring suit against any person "alleged to be in violation" of the Act, requires that a defendant be violating the Act at the time of suit. Gwaltney urged the District Court to adopt the analysis of the Fifth Circuit in *Hamker v. Diamond Shamrock Chemical Co.*, 756 F.2d 392 (1985), which held that "a complaint brought under [§ 505] must allege a violation occurring at the time the complaint is filed." *Id.* at 395, Gwaltney contended that because its last recorded violation occurred several weeks before respondents filed their complaint, the District Court lacked subject-matter jurisdiction over respondents' action.

The District Court rejected Gwaltney's argument . . . [and] [t]he Court of Appeals affirmed . . . . Subsequent to the issuance of the Fourth Circuit's opinion, the First Circuit also had occasion to construe § 505 . . . . The First Circuit's approach precludes suit based on wholly past violations, but permits suit when there is a pattern of intermittent violations, even if there is no violation at the moment suit is filed. We granted certiorari to resolve this three-way conflict in the Circuits. We now vacate the Fourth Circuit's opinion and remand the case . . . .

The Court of Appeals concluded that the "to be in violation" language of § 505 is ambiguous, whereas petitioner asserts that it plainly precludes the construction adopted below. We must agree with the Court of Appeals that § 505 is not a provision in which Congress' limpid prose puts an end to all dispute. But to acknowledge ambiguity is not to conclude that all interpretations are equally plausible. The most natural reading of "to be in violation" is a requirement that citizen-plaintiffs allege a state of either continuous or intermittent violation—that is, a reasonable likelihood that a past polluter will continue to pollute in the future. Congress could have phrased its requirement in language that looked to the past ("to have violated"), but it did not choose this readily available option.

Respondents urge that the choice of the phrase "to be in violation," rather than phrasing more clearly directed to the past, is a "careless accident," the result of a "debatable lapse of syntactical precision." But the prospective orientation of that phrase could not have escaped Congress' attention. Congress used identical language in the citizen suit provisions of several other environmental statutes that authorize only prospective relief. *See, e.g.*, Clean Air Act, 42 U.S.C. § 7604; Resource Conservation and Recovery Act of 1976, 42 U.S.C. § 6972; Toxic Substances Control Act, 15 U.S.C. § 2619. Moreover, Congress has demonstrated in yet other statutory provisions that it knows how to avoid this prospective implication by using language that explicitly targets wholly past violations . . . .

Our reading of the "to be in violation" language of § 505(a) is bolstered by the language and structure of the rest of the citizen suit provisions in § 505 of the Act. These provisions together make plain that the interest of the citizen-plaintiff is primarily forward-looking.

One of the most striking indicia of the prospective orientation of the citizen suit is the pervasive use of the present tense throughout § 505. A citizen suit may be brought only for violation of a permit limitation "which is in effect" under the Act. 33 U.S.C. § 1365(f). Citizen-plaintiffs must give notice to the alleged violator, the Administrator of EPA, and the State in which the alleged violation "occurs." § 1365(b)(1)(A). A governor of a State may sue as a citizen when the Administrator fails to enforce an effluent limitation "the violation of which is occurring in another State and is causing an adverse effect on the public health or welfare in his State." § 1365(h). The most telling use of the present tense is in the definition of "citizen" as "a person . . . having an interest which is or may be adversely affected" by the defendant's violations of the Act. § 1365(g). This definition makes plain what the undeviating use of the present tense strongly suggests: the harm sought to be addressed by the citizen suit lies in the present or the future, not in the past.

Any other conclusion would render incomprehensible § 505's notice provision, which requires citizens to give 60 days' notice of their intent to sue to the alleged violator as well as to the Administrator and the State. § 1365(b)(1)(A). If the Administrator or the State commences enforcement action within that 60-day period, the citizen suit is barred, presumably because governmental action has rendered it unnecessary. § 1365(b)(1)(B). It follows logically that the purpose of notice to the alleged violator is to give it an opportunity to bring itself into complete compliance with the Act and thus likewise render unnecessary a citizen suit. If we assume, as respondents urge, that citizen suits may target wholly past violations, the requirement of notice to the alleged violator becomes gratuitous. Indeed, respondents, in propounding their interpretation of the Act, can think of no reason for Congress to require such notice other than that "it seemed right" to inform an alleged violator that it was about to be sued.

Adopting respondents' interpretation of § 505's jurisdictional grant would create a second and even more disturbing anomaly. The bar on citizen suits when governmental enforcement action is under way suggests that the citizen suit is meant to supplement rather than to supplant governmental action . . . . Permitting citizen suits for wholly past violation so the Act could undermine the supplementary role envisioned for the citizen suit. This danger is best illustrated by an example. Suppose that the Administrator identified a violator of the Act and issued a compliance order under § 309(a). Suppose further that the Administrator agreed not to assess or otherwise seek civil penalties on the condition that the violator take some extreme corrective action, such as to install particularly effective but expensive machinery, that it otherwise would not be obliged to take. If citizens could file suit, months or years later, in order to seek the civil penalties that the Administrator chose to forgo, then the Administrator's discretion to enforce the Act in the public interest would be curtailed considerably. The same might be said of the discretion of state enforcement authorities. Respondents' interpretation of the scope of the citizen suit would change the nature of the citizens' role from interstitial to potentially intrusive. We cannot agree that Congress intended such a result . . . .

Our conclusion that § 505 does not permit citizen suits for wholly past violations does not necessarily dispose of this lawsuit, as both lower courts recognized. The District Court found persuasive the fact that "[respondents'] allegation in the complaint, that Gwaltney was continuing to violate its NPDES permit when plaintiffs filed suit[,] appears to have been made fully in good faith." On this basis, the District Court explicitly held, albeit in a footnote, that "even if Gwaltney were correct that a district court has no jurisdiction over citizen suits based entirely on unlawful conduct that occurred entirely in the past, the Court would still have jurisdiction here." The Court of Appeals acknowledged, also in a footnote, that "[a] very sound argument can be made that [respondents'] allegations of continuing violations were made in good faith," but expressly declined to rule on this alternative holding. Because we agree that § 505 confers jurisdiction over citizen suits when the citizen-plaintiffs make a good-faith allegation of continuous or intermittent violation, we remand the case to the Court of Appeals for further consideration.

Petitioner argues that citizen-plaintiffs must prove their allegations of ongoing noncompliance before jurisdiction attaches under § 505. We cannot agree. The statute does not require that a defendant "be in violation" of the Act at the commencement of suit; rather, the statute requires that a defendant be "*alleged* to be in violation." Petitioner's construction of the Act reads the word "alleged" out of § 505. As petitioner itself is quick to note in other contexts, there is no reason to believe that Congress' drafting of § 505 was sloppy or haphazard. We agree with the Solicitor General that "Congress's use of the phrase 'alleged to be in violation' reflects a conscious sensitivity to the practical difficulties of detecting and proving chronic episodic violations of environmental standards." Our acknowledgment that Congress intended a good-faith allegation to suffice for jurisdictional purposes, however, does not give litigants license to flood the courts with suits premised on baseless allegations. Rule 11 of the Federal

Rules of Civil Procedure, which requires pleadings to be based on a good-faith belief, formed after reasonable inquiry, that they are "well grounded in fact," adequately protects defendants from frivolous allegations.

Petitioner contends that failure to require proof of allegations under § 505 would permit plaintiffs whose allegations of ongoing violation are reasonable but untrue to maintain suit in federal court even though they lack constitutional standing. Petitioner reasons that if a defendant is in complete compliance with the Act at the time of suit, plaintiffs have suffered no injury remediable by the citizen suit provisions of the Act. Petitioner, however, fails to recognize that our standing cases uniformly recognize that allegations of injury are sufficient to invoke the jurisdiction of a court . . . . This is not to say, however, that such allegations may not be challenged. In *United States v. SCRAP*, 412 U.S. 669, 689 (1973), we noted that if the plaintiffs' "allegations [of standing] were in fact untrue, then the [defendants] should have moved for summary judgment on the standing issue and demonstrated to the District Court that the allegations were sham and raised no genuine issue of fact." If the defendant fails to make such a showing after the plaintiff offers evidence to support the allegation, the case proceeds to trial on the merits, where the plaintiff must prove the allegations in order to prevail. But the Constitution does not require that the plaintiff offer this proof as a threshold matter in order to invoke the District Court's jurisdiction . . . .

Because the court below erroneously concluded that respondents could maintain an action based on wholly past violations of the Act, it declined to decide whether respondents' complaint contained a good-faith allegation of ongoing violation by petitioner. We therefore remand the case of consideration of this question.

Notes and Questions

1. "The *Gwaltney* Problem." The problem in *Gwaltney* arises because of the text of the Clean Water Act citizen suit provision in § 505(a), requiring the identification of a person "alleged to be in violation" of any CWA requirement. Following the Court's decision in *Gwaltney*, analogous language in the Clean Air Act was amended to "fix" the *Gwaltney* problem, allowing citizen suits to proceed based upon identification of a person "alleged to have violated [past tense] (if there is evidence that the alleged violation has been repeated) or to be in violation" of certain requirements of the CAA. CAA § 304(a), 42 U.S.C. § 7604. Similarly, RCRA authorizes citizen suits "against any person . . . who has contributed [past tense] or who is contributing to the past or present handling, storage, treatment, transportation, or disposal of any solid or hazardous waste . . . ." RCRA § 7002(a)(1)(B), 42 U.S.C. § 6972(a)(1)(B). *Gwaltney* cannot be a problem under CERCLA because CERCLA only seeks to remedy present concerns with hazardous substances, regardless of when the release occurred. If the *Gwaltney* problem today arises only under the Clean Water Act, should students still care? Consider this: according to one study, the Clean Water Act accounted for almost half of all citizen suits between 1999 and 2003: 1,428 CWA cases out of 3,077 cases total. May, *supra*, at 23. Why do you think this is so?

2. "To Be [or Not To Be] in Violation." According to Justice Marshall in *Gwaltney*, a would-be CWA plaintiff need not establish that an alleged violator "is" in violation on the very day the notice or complaint is filed. But what must the would-be plaintiff show? What exactly does a "continuous or intermittent violation" look like? Could it include violations spaced apart by months or seasons? What if we needed to wait to see whether a water treatment system worked properly during spring floods or throughout the year? For one answer, see *Gwaltney of Smithfield v. Chesapeake Bay Foundation* ("*Gwaltney II*"), 890 F.2d 690 (4th Cir. 1989) (holding, on remand from Supreme Court, that trial court reasonably found continuing likelihood of TKN violations where expert testimony indicated uncertainty whether treatment system would work properly through upcoming winter).

3. Mootness. If it is "absolutely clear" that a violation in the past will not recur in the future, a case may be dismissed under the doctrine of mootness. However, a defendant asserting mootness must meet a "heavy burden" of proof and cannot rely solely upon "voluntary cessation" of the offending conduct. *See Friends of the Earth v. Laidlaw Environmental Services*, 528 U.S. 167 (2000) (denying dismissal for mootness where industrial facility was closed, but company retained its NPDES permit). If violations are indeed "wholly past," is there any point to continuing litigation? For the majority in *Laidlaw*, Justice Ginsburg suggested one answer: "[C]ivil penalties in Clean Water Act cases do more than promote immediate compliance by limiting the defendant's economic incentive to delay its attainment of permit limits; they also deter future violations." *Id.* at 185. Is Justice Ginsburg's observation here consistent with the purposes of environmental enforcement discussed at the beginning of this chapter?

VII. Federal Facilities Enforcement

Some of the largest, costliest, and most hazardous contamination problems in the United States are on properties currently or formerly owned or operated by the federal government. This includes almost every current or former military base and every facility within our nation's industrial complex that was devoted to the production of nuclear weapons during the Cold War. For a general introduction to the multi-billion-dollar problems with contamination at federal facilities across the country, see SETH SHULMAN, THE THREAT AT HOME: CONFRONTING THE TOXIC LEGACY OF THE U.S. MILITARY (1992).

In general, federal facilities are required to comply with federal environmental statutes "in the same manner, and to the same extent as any nongovernmental entity . . . ." CWA § 313(a), 33 U.S.C. § 1323(a). *See also* CAA § 118(a) (same); RCRA § 6001(a) (same); CERCLA § 120(a) (same); SDWA § 1447 (same). However, despite this general proposition, two legal theories or doctrines work to limit enforcement actions against federal facilities. One of these is known as the Unitary Executive Theory. Drawing from the Article III jurisdiction of federal courts, which is premised upon the existence of a "case or controversy," the Unitary Executive Theory forbids one federal agency from suing another federal agency in federal court, as the so-called "Unitary Executive" is unable to sue itself. Accordingly, while the U.S. EPA may be able to bring a civil action to address many environmental violations, the U.S. EPA may not bring a civil action against the U.S. Navy for an environmental violation at a U.S. Navy base. For a thorough discussion and analysis of the Unitary Executive Theory, albeit challenging some of the underlying precepts for the doctrine, see Michael W. Steinberg, *Can EPA Sue Other Federal Agencies?*, 17 ECOLOGY L.Q. 317 (1990).

In addition to the Unitary Executive Theory, a second — and more significant — limitation on federal facilities enforcement is the legal doctrine of sovereign immunity. That doctrine, and its particular application in the context of environmental law, was most notably explored by the U.S. Supreme Court in the following decision.

Department of Energy v. Ohio
503 U.S. 607 (1992)

Justice SOUTER:

The question in these cases is whether Congress has waived the National Government's sovereign immunity from liability for civil fines imposed by a State for past violations of the Clean Water Act (CWA), 86 Stat. 816, as amended, 33 U.S.C. § 1251 et seq., or the Resource Conservation and Recovery Act of 1976 (RCRA), 90 Stat. 2795, 2796, as amended, 42 U.S.C. § 6901 et seq. We hold it has not done so in either instance.

The CWA prohibits the discharge of pollutants into navigable waters without a permit. Section 402, codified at 33 U.S.C. § 1342, gives primary authority to issue such permits to the United States Environmental Protection Agency (EPA), but allows EPA to authorize a State to supplant the federal permit program with one of its own, if the state scheme would include, among other features, sufficiently stringent regulatory standards and adequate provisions for penalties to enforce them. RCRA regulates the disposal of hazardous waste in much the same way, with a permit program run by EPA but subject to displacement by an adequate state counterpart.

This litigation began in 1986 when respondent State of Ohio sued petitioner Department of Energy (DOE) in Federal District Court for violations of state and federal pollution laws, including the CWA and RCRA, in operating its uranium-processing plant in Fernald, Ohio. Ohio sought, among other forms of relief, both state and federal civil penalties for past violations of the CWA and RCRA and of state laws enacted to supplant those federal statutes. Before the District Court ruled on DOE's motion for dismissal, the parties proposed a consent decree to settle all but one substantive claim, and Ohio withdrew all outstanding claims for relief except its request for civil penalties for DOE's alleged past violations. By a contemporaneous stipulation, DOE and Ohio agreed on the amount of civil penalties DOE will owe if it is found liable for them. The parties thus left for determination under the motion to dismiss only the issue we consider today: whether Congress has waived the National Government's sovereign immunity from liability for civil fines imposed for past failure to comply with the CWA, RCRA, or state law supplanting the federal regulation.

DOE admits that the CWA and RCRA obligate a federal polluter, like any other, to obtain permits from EPA or the state permitting agency.

DOE also concedes that the CWA and RCRA render federal agencies liable for fines imposed to induce them to comply with injunctions or other judicial orders designed to modify behavior prospectively, which we will speak of hereafter as "coercive fines." The parties disagree only on whether the CWA and RCRA, in either their "federal-facilities" or "citizen-suit" sections, waive federal sovereign immunity from liability for fines, which we will refer to as "punitive," imposed to punish past violations of those statutes or state laws supplanting them.

The United States District Court for the Southern District of Ohio held that both statutes waived federal sovereign immunity from punitive fines, by both their federal-facilities and citizen-suit sections. A divided panel of the United States Court of Appeals for the Sixth Circuit affirmed in part, holding that Congress had waived immunity from punitive fines in the CWA's federal-facilities section and RCRA's citizen-suit section, but not in RCRA's federal-facilities section.

In No. 90-1341, DOE petitioned for review insofar as the Sixth Circuit found any waiver of immunity from punitive fines, while in No. 90-1517, Ohio cross-petitioned on the holding that RCRA's federal-facilities section failed to effect such a waiver. We consolidated the two petitions and granted certiorari.

We start with a common rule, with which we presume congressional familiarity, that any waiver of the National Government's sovereign immunity must be unequivocal. "Waivers of immunity must be 'construed strictly in favor of the sovereign,' and not 'enlarge[d] ... beyond what the language requires.' By these lights we examine first the two statutes' citizen-suit sections, which can be treated together because their relevant provisions are similar, then the CWA's federal-facilities section, and, finally, the corresponding section of RCRA.

So far as it concerns us, the CWA's citizen-suit section reads that

"any citizen may commence a civil action on his own behalf—

"(1) against any person (including ... the United States ...) who is alleged to be in violation of (A) an effluent standard or limitation under this chapter or (B) an order issued by the Administrator or a State with respect to such a standard or limitation. . . .

. . . . .

"The district courts shall have jurisdiction ... to enforce such an effluent standard or limitation, or such an order ... as the case may be, and to apply any appropriate civil penalties under [33 U.S.C. § 1319(d)]." 33 U.S.C. § 1365(a).

The relevant part of the corresponding section of RCRA is similar:

"[A]ny person may commence a civil action on his own behalf—

"(1)(A) against any person (including ... the United States) ... who is alleged to be in violation of any permit, standard, regulation, condition, requirement, prohibition, or order which has become effective pursuant to this chapter ...

"(B) against any person, including the United States . . . who has contributed or who is contributing to the past or present handling, storage, treatment, transportation, or disposal of any solid or hazardous waste which may present an imminent and substantial endangerment to health or the environment. . . .

. . . . .

". . . The district court shall have jurisdiction . . . to enforce the permit, standard, regulation, condition, requirement, prohibition, or order, referred to in paragraph (1)(A), to restrain any person who has contributed or who is contributing to the past or present handling, storage, treatment, transportation, or disposal of any solid or hazardous waste referred to in paragraph (1)(B), to order such person to take such other action as may be necessary, or both, . . . and to apply any appropriate civil penalties under [42 U.S.C. §§ 6928(a) and (g)]." 42 U.S.C. § 6972(a).

A State is a "citizen" under the CWA and a "person" under RCRA, and is thus entitled to sue under these provisions.

Ohio and its amici argue that by specifying the United States as an entity subject to suit and incorporating the civil-penalties sections of the CWA and RCRA into their respective citizen-suit sections, "Congress could not avoid noticing that its literal language subject[ed] federal entities to penalties." It is undisputed that each civil-penalties provision authorizes fines of the punitive sort.

The effect of incorporating each statute's civil-penalties section into its respective citizen-suit section is not, however, as clear as Ohio claims. The incorporations must be read as encompassing all the terms of the penalty provisions, including their limitations, and significant limitations for present purposes result from restricting the applicability of the civil-penalties sections to "person[s]." While both the CWA and RCRA define "person" to cover States, subdivisions of States, municipalities, and interstate bodies (and RCRA even extends the term to cover governmental corporations), neither statute defines "person" to include the United States. Its omission has to be seen as a pointed one when so many other governmental entities are specified, see 2A Singer, supra, § 47.23, a fact that renders the civil-penalties sections inapplicable to the United States.

Against this reasoning, Ohio argues that the incorporated penalty provisions' exclusion of the United States is overridden by the National Government's express inclusion as a "person" by each of the citizen-suit sections. There is, of course, a plausibility to the argument. Whether that plausibility suffices for the clarity required to waive sovereign immunity is, nonetheless, an issue we need not decide, for the force of Ohio's argument wanes when we look beyond the citizen-suit sections to the full texts of the respective statutes.

What we find elsewhere in each statute are various provisions specially defining "person" and doing so expressly for purposes of the entire section in which the term occurs. Thus, for example, "[f]or the purpose of this [CWA] section," 33 U.S.C.

§ 1321(a)(7) defines "person" in such a way as to exclude the various governmental entities included in the general definition of "person" in 33 U.S.C. § 1362(5). Again, "[f]or the purpose of this section," § 1322(a)(8) defines "person" so as to exclude "an individual on board a public vessel" as well as the governmental entities falling within the general definition. Similarly in RCRA, "[f]or the purpose of . . . subchapter [IX]" the general definition of "person" is expanded to include "the United States Government," among other entities. 42 U.S.C. § 6991(6). Within each statute, then, there is a contrast between drafting that merely redefines "person" when it occurs within a particular clause or sentence and drafting that expressly alters the definition for any and all purposes of the entire section in which the special definition occurs. Such differences in treatment within a given statutory text are reasonably understood to reflect differences in meaning intended, see 2A Singer, supra, § 46.06, and the inference can only be that a special definition not described as being for purposes of the "section" or "subchapter" in which it occurs was intended to have the more limited application to its own clause or sentence alone. Thus, in the instances before us here, the inclusion of the United States as a "person" must go to the clauses subjecting the United States to suit, but no further.

This textual analysis passes the test of giving effect to all the language of the citizen-suit sections. Those sections' incorporations of their respective statutes' civil-penalties sections will have the effect of authorizing punitive fines when a polluter other than the United States is brought to court by a citizen, while the sections' explicit authorizations for suits against the United States will likewise be effective, since those sections concededly authorize coercive sanctions against the National Government.

A clear and unequivocal waiver of anything more cannot be found; a broader waiver may not be inferred. Ohio's reading is therefore to be rejected.

The relevant portion of the CWA's federal-facilities section provides that

> "[e]ach department, agency, or instrumentality of the . . . Federal Government . . . shall be subject to, and comply with, all Federal, State, interstate, and local requirements, administrative authority, and process and sanctions respecting the control and abatement of water pollution in the same manner . . . as any nongovernmental entity. . . . The preceding sentence shall apply (A) to any requirement whether substantive or procedural (including any recordkeeping or reporting requirement, any requirement respecting permits and any other requirement, whatsoever), (B) to the exercise of any Federal, State or local administrative authority, and (C) to any process and sanction, whether enforced in Federal, State, or local courts or in any other manner. . . . [T]he United States shall be liable only for those civil penalties arising under Federal law or imposed by a State or local court to enforce an order or the process of such court." 33 U.S.C. § 1323(a).

Ohio rests its argument for waiver as to punitive fines on two propositions: first, that the statute's use of the word "sanction" must be understood to encompass such fines; and, second, with respect to the fines authorized under a state permit program approved by EPA, that they "aris[e] under Federal law" despite their genesis in state statutes, and are thus within the scope of the "civil penalties" covered by the congressional.

Ohio's first proposition is mistaken. As a general matter, the meaning of "sanction" is spacious enough to cover not only what we have called punitive fines, but coercive ones as well, and use of the term carries no necessary implication that a reference to punitive fines is intended. One of the two dictionaries Ohio itself cites reflects this breadth. See Black's Law Dictionary 1341 (6th ed. 1990) (defining "sanction" as a "[p]enalty or other mechanism of enforcement used to provide incentives for obedience with the law or with rules and regulations. That part of a law which is designed to secure enforcement by imposing a penalty for its violation or offering a reward for its observance"). Ohio's other such source explicitly adopts the coercive sense of the term. See Ballentine's Law Dictionary 1137 (3d ed. 1969) (defining sanction in part as "[a] coercive measure").

Beyond the dictionaries, examples of usage in the coercive sense abound. See, e.g., Penfield Co. of Cal. v. SEC, 330 U.S. 585, 590 (1947) (fines and imprisonment imposed as "coercive sanctions" when imposed to compel target "to do what the law made it his duty to do"); Hicks v. Feiock, 485 U.S. 624, 633–634, n. 6 (1988) ("sanction" in Penfield was civil because it was conditional; contemnor could avoid "sanction" by agreeing to comply with discovery order); Fed.Rule Civ.Proc. 37(b) (describing as "sanctions" various steps district court may take in response to noncompliance with discovery orders, including holding recalcitrant deponent in contempt); Latrobe Steel Co. v. United Steelworkers of America, Local 1537, 545 F.2d 1336, 1344 (CA3 1976) ("Coercive sanctions . . . look to the future and are designed to aid the plaintiff by bringing a defiant party into compliance with the court order or by assuring that a potentially contumacious party adheres to an injunction by setting forth in advance the penalties the court will impose if the party deviates from the path of obedience".) Thus, resort to a "sanction" carries no necessary implication of the punitive as against the coercive.

The term's context, of course, may supply a clarity that the term lacks in isolation. It tends to do so here, but once again the clarity so found cuts against Ohio's position. The word "sanction" appears twice in § 1323(a), each time within the phrase "process and sanction[s]." The first sentence subjects Government agencies to "process and sanctions," while the second explains that the Government's corresponding liability extends to "any process and sanction, whether enforced in Federal, State, or local courts or in any other manner."

Three features of this context are significant. The first is the separate statutory recognition of three manifestations of governmental power to which the United States is subjected: substantive and procedural requirements; administrative authority; and "process and sanctions," whether "enforced" in courts or otherwise. Substantive requirements are thus distinguished from judicial process, even though each might require the same conduct, as when a statute requires and a court orders a polluter to refrain from discharging without a permit. The second noteworthy feature is the conjunction of "sanction[s]" not with the substantive "requirements," but with "process," in each of the two instances in which "sanction" appears. "Process" normally refers to the procedure and mechanics of adjudication and the enforcement of decrees or orders that the adjudicatory process finally provides. The third feature to note is the statute's reference to "process and sanctions" as "enforced" in courts or otherwise. Whereas we commonly understand that "requirements" may be enforced either by backward-looking penalties for past violations or by the "process" of forward-looking orders enjoining future violations, such forward-looking orders themselves are characteristically given teeth by equity's traditional coercive sanctions for contempt: fines and bodily commitment imposed pending compliance or agreement to comply. The very fact, then, that the text speaks of sanctions in the context of enforcing "process" as distinct from substantive "requirements" is a good reason to infer that Congress was using "sanction" in its coercive sense, to the exclusion of punitive fines.

The last relevant passage of § 1323(a), which provides that "the United States shall be liable only for those civil penalties arising under Federal law or imposed by a State or local court to enforce an order or the process of such court," is not to the contrary. While this proviso is unlike the preceding text in that it speaks of "civil penalties," not "sanctions," it is obviously phrased to clarify or limit the waiver preceding it. Here our concern is with its clarifying function (leaving its limiting effect until later), and it must be said that as a clarifier the proviso speaks with an uncertain voice. To be sure, the second modifier of "civil penalties" at least makes it plain that the term (like "sanction," to which it relates) must include a coercive penalty, since "civil penalties" are exemplified by those "imposed by a State or local court to enforce an order or the process of such court." To this extent, then, the proviso serves to confirm the reading we reached above.

The role of the first modifier is problematical, however. On the one hand, it tugs toward a more expansive reading of "civil penalties." If by using the phrase "civil penalties arising under Federal law" Congress meant nothing more than coercive fines arising under federal law, it would have been simpler to describe all such penalties as imposed to enforce an order or process, whether of a local, state, or federal court. Thus, the first modifier suggests that the civil penalties arising under federal law may indeed include the punitive along with the coercive. Nevertheless, a reading expansive enough to reflect a waiver as to punitive fines would raise a new and troublesome question about the source of legal authority to impose such a fine. As far as federal law is concerned, the only available source of authority to impose punitive fines is the civil-penalties section, § 1319(d). But, as we have already seen, that section does not authorize liability against the United States, since it applies only against "persons," from whom the United States is excluded.

Ohio urges us to find a source of authority good against the United States by reading "arising under Federal law" to include penalties prescribed by state statutes approved by EPA and supplanting the CWA. Ohio argues for treating a state statute as providing penalties "arising under Federal law" by stressing the complementary relationship between the relevant state and federal statutes and the role of such state statutes in accomplishing the purpose of the CWA. This purpose, as Ohio states it, is "to encourage compliance with comprehensive, federally approved water pollution programs while shielding federal agencies from unauthorized penalties." Ohio asserts that "federal facility compliance . . . cannot be . . . accomplished without the [punitive] penalty deterrent."

The case for such pessimism is not, however, self-evident. To be sure, an agency of the Government may break the law where it might have complied voluntarily if it had faced the prospect of punitive fines for past violations. But to say that its "compliance cannot be . . . accomplished" without such fines is to assume that without sanctions for past conduct a federal polluter can never be brought into future compliance, that an agency of the National Government would defy an injunction backed by coercive fines and even a threat of personal commitment. The position seems also to ignore the fact that once such fines start running they can be every dollar as onerous as their punitive counterparts; it could be a very expensive mistake to plan on ignoring the law indefinitely on the assumption that contumacy would be cheap.

Nor does the complementary relationship between state and federal law support Ohio's claim that state-law fines thereby "arise under Federal law." Plain language aside, the far more compelling interpretative case rests on the best known statutory use of the phrase "arising under federal law," appearing in the grant of federal-question jurisdiction to the courts of the United States. See 28 U.S.C. § 1331. There, we have read the phrase "arising under" federal law to exclude cases in which the plaintiff relies on state law, even when the State's exercise of power in the particular circumstances is expressly permitted by federal law. The probability is enough to answer Ohio's argument that "arising under Federal law" in § 1323(a) is broad enough to cover provisions of state statutes approved by a federal agency but nevertheless applicable *ex proprio vigore*.

Since Ohio's argument for treating state-penalty provisions as arising under federal law thus fails, our reading of the last-quoted sentence from § 1323(a) leaves us with an unanswered question and an unresolved tension between closely related statutory provisions. The question is still what Congress could have meant in using a seemingly expansive phrase like "civil penalties arising under Federal law." Perhaps it used it just in case some later amendment might waive the Government's immunity from punitive sanctions. Perhaps a drafter mistakenly thought that liability for such sanctions had somehow been waived already. Perhaps someone was careless. The question has no satisfactory answer.

We do, however, have a response satisfactory for sovereign immunity purposes to the tension between a proviso suggesting an apparently expansive but uncertain waiver and its antecedent text that evinces a narrower waiver with greater clarity. For under our rules that tension is resolved by the requirement that any statement of waiver be unequivocal: as against the clear waiver for coercive fines the indication of a waiver as to those that are punitive is less certain. The rule of narrow construction therefore takes the waiver no further than the coercive variety.

We consider, finally, the federal-facilities section of RCRA, which provides, in relevant part, that the National Government

> "shall be subject to, and comply with, all Federal, State, interstate, and local requirements, both substantive and procedural (including any requirement for permits or reporting or any provisions for injunctive relief and such sanctions as may be imposed by a court to enforce such relief) . . . in the same manner, and to the same extent, as any person is subject to such requirements. . . . Neither the United States, nor any agent, employee, or officer thereof, shall be immune or exempt from any process or sanction of any State or Federal Court with respect to the enforcement of any such injunctive relief." 42 U.S.C. § 6961.

Ohio and its amici stress the statutory subjection of federal facilities to "all . . . requirements," which they would have us read as an explicit and unambiguous waiver of federal sovereign immunity from punitive fines. We, however, agree with the Tenth Circuit that "all . . . requirements" "can reasonably be interpreted as including substantive standards and the means for implementing those standards, but excluding punitive measures."

We have already observed that substantive requirements can be enforced either punitively or coercively, and the Tenth Circuit's understanding that Congress intended the latter finds strong support in the textual indications of the kinds of requirements meant to bind the Government. Significantly, all of them refer either to mechanisms requiring review for substantive compliance (permit and reporting requirements) or to mechanisms for enforcing substantive compliance in the future (injunctive relief and sanctions to enforce it). In stark contrast, the statute makes no mention of any mechanism for penalizing past violations, and this absence of any example of punitive fines is powerful evidence that Congress had no intent to subject the United States to an enforcement mechanism that could deplete the federal fisc regardless of a responsible officer's willingness and capacity to comply in the future.

The drafters' silence on the subject of punitive sanctions becomes virtually audible after one reads the provision's final sentence, waiving immunity "from any process or sanction of any State or Federal Court with respect to the enforcement of any such injunctive relief." The fact that the drafters' only specific reference to an enforcement mechanism described "sanction" as a coercive means of injunctive enforcement bars any inference that a waiver of immunity from "requirements" somehow unquestionably extends to punitive fines that are never so much as mentioned.

The judgment of the Court of Appeals is reversed, and the cases are remanded for further proceedings consistent with this opinion.

It is so ordered.

Justice WHITE, concurring in part and dissenting in part [omitted].

Notes and Questions

1. Notice the caption in this case. While the Unitary Executive Theory may forbid the U.S. Environmental Protection Agency from suing the U.S. Department of

Energy for environmental violations, it obviously does not forbid the State of Ohio from suing the U.S. DOE. Nor does it forbid other states, tribes, and private parties from suing the federal government. Outside the context of civil litigation, do you imagine that the Unitary Executive Theory has any relevance to administrative actions or criminal prosecutions? For answers, *see, e.g., In re U.S. Army, Fort Wainwright Central Heating & Power Plant*, 33 ELR 41264 (June 5, 2003) (EPA Environmental Appeals Board upholding ALJ finding that Army is liable for administrative penalty, including economic benefit, in action brought by EPA for CAA violations at Fort Wainwright, Alaska); *United States v. Dee*, 912 F.2d 741 (4th Cir. 1990) (upholding convictions of Army officials for RCRA violations at Aberdeen Proving Ground, Maryland).

2. Notice that Ohio seeks punitive penalties against DOE under four distinct statutory authorities: the CWA citizen suit provision (§ 505); the CWA federal facilities provision (§ 313); the RCRA citizen suit provision (§ 7002); and the RCRA federal facilities provision (§ 6001). While the Court denies punitive penalties under each of these four provisions, one of them appears to be the closest call. Which provision is that, and why?

3. Who exactly is the "sovereign" for purposes of sovereign immunity? As civilian employees of the U.S. Army at Aberdeen Proving Ground, defendants Dee, Lentz, and Gepp argued that they should be entitled to sovereign immunity from criminal charges brought against them under RCRA. In response to this argument, the Fourth Circuit observed dryly, "The defendants, of course, were indicted, tried, and convicted as individuals, not as agents of the government. Suffice it to say that sovereign immunity does not attach to individual government employees so as to immunize them from prosecution for their criminal acts." *United States v. Dee*, 912 F.2d 741, at 744. Of course, as government employees are not the "sovereign" for purposes of sovereign immunity, government contractors may be even less so, providing yet another avenue for addressing environmental violations at many federal facilities.

4. What does it mean for a waiver of sovereign immunity to be "unequivocal"? One answer may be found in the way *DOE v. Ohio* provoked a swift and scathing response from Congress in the very same year. Among other things, the Federal Facility Compliance Act of 1992, Pub. L. No. 102-386 (1992), amended RCRA § 6001(a) to provide that —

> The Federal, State, interstate, and local substantive and procedural requirements [enforceable against federal facilities] include, but are not limited to, all administrative penalties and fines, regardless of whether such penalties or fines are punitive or coercive in nature or are imposed for isolated, intermittent, or continuing violations.

And in case you still didn't get the point, Congress continued:

> The United States hereby expressly waives any immunity otherwise applicable to the United States with respect to any such substantive or procedural

requirement (including, but not limited to, any injunctive relief, administrative order or civil or administrative penalty or fine . . . or reasonable service charge).

Subsequent amendments to the Safe Drinking Water Act in 1996 mirrored these amendments to RCRA. See SDWA § 1447(a), 42 U.S.C. § 300j-6(a). The Clean Air Act and CERCLA were never so amended, but have proven unequivocal enough to support substantial enforcement actions against federal facilities. The Clean Water Act, however—one of the two statutes at issue in *DOE v. Ohio*—was never amended, so that punitive penalties, at least, remain unenforceable against federal facilities. Injunctive relief remains available against federal facilities for violations of the Clean Water Act. However, as we saw in Chapter 2 with the Supreme Court's decision in *Weinberger v. Romero-Barcelo*, affirming that injunctive relief is an equitable remedy, courts will not always provide injunctive relief for Clean Water Act violations, even where the violations are clear and continuing for decades.

5. Disputes between federal agencies. In the inevitable event of legal disputes between federal agencies, where the Unitary Executive Theory bars access to the federal courts, agency attorneys may consider a number of alternative mechanisms in order to resolve their disputes. The first and most common mechanism is a system of informal or formal dispute resolution, where issues are elevated to successive levels of management in both agencies until the matter is resolved in some way. In some cases, if no agreement between the agencies is reached through dispute resolution, Congress has identified a specific agency to provide a final decision on the matter. *See, e.g.,* CERCLA § 120(e), 42 U.S.C. § 9620(e)(4)(A) (if EPA and another federal agency are "unable to reach agreement on selection of a remedial action, selection [of the remedy will be] by the [EPA] Administrator"). Absent such statutory specificity, who would make the ultimate decision for the Executive Branch? A second means may be through resort to formal administrative proceedings before an Administrative Law Judge or other hearings officer. *See, e.g., In the matter of Department of Energy, Rocky Flats Field Office*, Docket No. CERCLA-VIII-98-11, 2000 WL (968320 (EPA ALJ), June 28, 2000 (ALJ decision finding U.S. Dept. of Energy not liable for alleged violations of CERCLA cleanup agreement).

A third mechanism for dispute resolution between federal agencies may be through submission of a legal dispute to the U.S. Department of Justice Office of Legal Counsel (OLC). *See* Exec. Order 12,146, § 1-4 (July 19, 1979). While rare, at least in the context of environmental law, submission of legal disputes to OLC has proven a useful mechanism in exceptional circumstances. *See, e.g.,* Letter from Steven G. Bradbury, Principal Deputy Asst. Attorney General, DOJ Office of Legal Counsel, to Daniel J. Dell'Orto, Principal Deputy General Counsel, Dept. of Defense (Dec. 1, 2008) (upholding EPA authority to issue administrative orders to federal agencies under authorities of RCRA § 7003 and Safe Drinking Water Act § 1431 to address groundwater contamination at federal NPL sites).

VIII. International Enforcement

A final consideration in this chapter's introduction to environmental enforcement is whether and to what extent enforcement tools may be used to address environmental problems of international scale. We have already seen in this casebook how some international environmental concerns may be addressed through treaties and other diplomatic measures. In Chapter 4, for example, we saw how international concerns for protecting endangered species may be addressed through implementation of the Convention on International Trade in Endangered Species (CITES). Likewise, in Chapter 6, we saw how the world community came together in 2015 to address the problem of global climate change through development of the Paris Agreement. The concluding section of this chapter will focus on another potential means for addressing international environmental problems: the direct application of domestic law. Through this mechanism, many of the enforcement tools discussed already in this chapter may become available to help solve environmental problems with international dimensions. As you read the excerpt below from an influential article on this subject, compare the famous diplomatic efforts to address air pollution from Canada's Trail Smelter with the domestic enforcement actions to address modern problems of water pollution from that same Canadian source.

Michael Robinson-Dorn, *The Trail Smelter: Is What's Past Prologue? EPA Blazes a New Trail for CERCLA*
14 NYU Envtl. L.J. (2006)

. . .

III. What's Past Is Prologue

. . .

A. The Trail Smelter Arbitration

1. The Factual and Procedural Background

The Trail Smelter is located in Trail, British Columbia, approximately ten miles from the U.S.-Canada border. Now one of the largest integrated lead and zinc smelting and refining complexes in the world, its beginnings were much more humble. The Trail Smelter began as one of two small smelters that competing American interests built in the late 1890's just miles apart alongside the banks of the Columbia River: one in the U.S. at Northport, Washington, and one in Canada, at Trail, British Columbia. Though their starts were temporally coincidental and their pursuits intertwined, their destinies were quite different. Founded by F. Augustus Heinze in 1896, the Trail Smelter started as a processing station for gold and copper ores from the nearby Rossland mines. Heinze soon built a railway connection to the mines supplying the smelter with ore, which in turn attracted the interest of the Canadian Pacific Railway ("CPR") . . . .

As the Trail Smelter grew, so too did its emissions. The smelter emitted thousands of tons a month of sulfur dioxide fumes that harmed crops and animals in Trail Consolidated Mining and Smelting Co., the Trail Smelter's owner, was well aware that lawsuits against other smelters were not uncommon in the United States, and as early as 1916, Consolidated considered a strategy of purchasing covenants and easements (so called "smoke easements") on timber stands in Trail to preempt litigation. Invariably, as emissions continued and damages mounted, land owners on the Canadian side of the border near Trail sought redress. While Consolidated was able to settle about half of the Canadian land owners' claims, the remaining half went through an extended arbitration process under British Columbian law. In 1924, Judge John A. Forin, a respected Canadian jurist, ruled against Consolidated. As a result, Consolidated wound up both paying Canadian plaintiffs economic damages and purchasing smoke easements in order to avoid future damages.

The Trail Smelter's emissions were also carried by prevailing winds into the Columbia Valley in Washington State. Improvements to the smelter's infrastructure in 1925 and 1927 led to significantly increased outputs of zinc and lead ores and consequent emissions of sulfur dioxide fumes. Additionally, and in part related to the settlements of the lawsuits in Trail, the smelter also raised its stacks to just over 400 feet. Whether as the result of the increased smoke stack height and increased production, the fact that Trail was growing while Northport was declining, the fact that Canadian farmers' claims against the Trail Smelter had succeeded where American land owners' claims against the Le Roi Smelter largely failed, or some combination of all of the above, the residents of Stevens County, Washington, including Northport, found the smell and taste of the increasingly polluted air less palatable. Before long, the first American farmer's claim against the Trail Smelter was filed. Soon, additional claims were filed, and the seeds of the Trail Smelter Arbitration had been sown.

. . .

Frustrated and facing hard times, many of the American farmers organized themselves into an association, the Citizens Protective Association ("CPA"). Members of the CPA eschewed individual settlements, enlisted the help of their Congressional delegation, and ultimately received the assistance of the U.S. State Department. In June 1927, the U.S. State Department forwarded an official complaint to the Government of Canada. In turn, Consolidated requested that the Canadian government intercede on its behalf. What essentially started out as a private nuisance suit by private parties against a private company had been transformed into an international dispute.

Later in 1927, the United States proposed that the dispute be referred to the International Joint Commission ("IJC"). The IJC, made up of three members from each nation, had been created in 1909 under the Boundary Waters Treaty to address issues relating to transboundary waters between the U.S. and Canada. Pursuant to Article IX of the Treaty, either nation could refer any matter involving "the rights, obligations, or interests of either in relation to the other or to the inhabitants of the other, along the common frontier," to the Commission for investigation and report.

At first, Canada was understandably hesitant to agree to such a referral. The Canadian government had been working closely with Consolidated who, as the Canadian External Affairs Undersecretary at the time described, saw the whole dispute as little more than "an attempt at holdup by farmers in a nearly hopeless section who have come to think that they can get much more out of farming this rich corporation across the boundary than from farming their farms . . . ." Moreover, Canada was also concerned, of course, that a decision reached outside of diplomatic circles would have the potential to require the Trail Smelter to curtail its operations, or even shut down; an outcome simply unacceptable to Canadian interests. With American pressure for a diplomatic solution strengthening, the Canadian Prime Minister ultimately concluded that "Canada as the smaller country st[ood] in the long run to gain more than the United States." Even still, it was not until August 7, 1928, some two years after the first claims had been made, that the two nations agreed to submit the matter to the IJC.

2. The International Joint Commission's 1931 Report

Hundreds of claims were submitted to the IJC totaling several million dollars. As John Read has explained in his seminal work on the Trail Smelter Arbitration, "[t]he Commission made an exhaustive investigation." The Commission appointed scientists, heard from interested parties, accepted evidence in multiple locations, and heard witnesses and arguments from counsel. In 1931, three years after the matter had been referred to the IJC and seven years after the first U.S. claims had been made, the IJC Tribunal found that the Trail Smelter had caused serious harm, and recommended an award in the amount of $350,000. The IJC's recommendation was expressly premised on the expectation that Consolidated would be employing and continuing to operate technology that by 1931 would cut the emissions of sulfur from the stacks by approximately one third.

3. The Trail Smelter Arbitration Decision

Despite being in the depths of the Great Depression, the United States (at the behest of the claimants) rejected the $350,000 award, and for the next two years the two nations engaged in often less than diplomatic discussions regarding the case. Finally, in 1935, the countries agreed to submit the dispute to a three member arbitration panel under an agreed upon, or compromise, Convention. The Convention required the Canadian Government to pay the $350,000 for damages from emissions from the Trail Smelter prior to 1932, and established a three person tribunal to determine post-1932 damages to come to a result that was "just to all parties concerned." Of particular importance to the United States, the Convention provided the Tribunal with the authority to set emissions levels.

The Tribunal then embarked on a multi-year journey. It conducted site investigations of the Trail Smelter and the allegedly damaged agricultural and timber lands in Washington state, and heard evidence (including extensive scientific expert testimony) from the countries, the smelter and the claimants in Ottawa, Washington, D.C., and Spokane, Washington. The U.S submitted claims totaling more than $2 million for damages. Bound as it was by the compromis Convention, the Tribunal found that an additional $78,000 was owed for damages accruing between 1932 and 1937, a "decided victory" for Consolidated. The Tribunal did so by applying "the law and practice" followed in the U.S. as well as international law and practice, while taking into account the desire of the parties to reach a solution "just to all parties concerned" and concluded, in a now famous passage:

> [U]nder principles of international law, as well as the law of the United States, no State has the right to use or permit the use of its territory in such a manner as to cause injury by fumes in or to the territory of another or the properties or persons therein, when the case is of serious consequence and the injury is established by clear and convincing evidence.

The Tribunal also found, owing in large measure to the scientific evidence presented, (including evidence relating to new control technologies that Consolidated had developed and employed) that there was no damage for the years 1937–1940, and ruled that "if any damage . . . shall occur in the future, whether through failure on the part of the Smelter to comply with regulations herein prescribed or notwithstanding the maintenance of the regime, an indemnity shall be paid for such damage." Thus, the Trail Smelter would be permitted to operate under a new, stricter regime, and if landowners in Washington State experienced material damage in the future, they could be compensated up to a maximum of $7,500 per annum.

. . .

IV. Plus Ça Change, Plus C'est la Même Chose

Given the result and the seminal importance of the Trail Smelter Arbitration to the development of international environmental law, it may be somewhat stunning to the uninitiated to learn that for the next half-century following the Arbitration, the Trail Smelter continued to dump vast quantities of slag, metals, and mercury into the Columbia River, where they were transported downstream and ultimately came to rest on the beaches, and in the sediments, of Lake Roosevelt, Washington.

A. Lake Roosevelt: Geography, History, and Uses

The Trail Smelter is located along the banks of the Columbia River approximately 10 miles upstream of the Canada-U.S. border. In 1940, the year before the end of the Trail Smelter Arbitration, the U.S. completed construction of the Grand Coulee Dam. A federal reclamation project sometimes referred to as the eighth wonder of the world, the Grand Coulee is the largest hydroelectric facility in North America. The Grand Coulee blocks the free flow of the Columbia River as it flows downstream from Canada and across into Washington State. The resulting lake, Lake Roosevelt, stretches some 135 miles behind the Grand Coulee Dam to within approximately fifteen miles of the international border with Canada.

Though originally constructed primarily to provide irrigation water, the Grand Coulee Dam is now operated for several purposes: hydro-electric power generation, irrigation, flood control, recreation, and supporting downstream fisheries. To meet these competing demands, in an average year, water levels in Lake Roosevelt fluctuate up to eighty feet, with the Lake remaining filled during summer.

Lake Roosevelt is also designated a National Recreation Area and is one of the most popular recreation areas in Washington state. Drawing up to 1.5 million visitors a year, the Lake is a center for recreational use, including camping, boating, fishing, and swimming. Along its shores, visitors enjoy many beautiful areas and encounter surprisingly and deceptively enchanting black sand (mining slag) beaches.

The Lake Roosevelt National Recreation Area also lies within the ancestral homelands of the Colville and Spokane Tribes. The current Colville Indian Reservation borders Lake Roosevelt on the North and West for approximately 93 river miles. The Spokane Indian Reservation borders the Lake to the East for about 8 miles north of the confluence of the Spokane River with the Columbia River. Because the area taken for the Grand Coulee Project included traditional tribal lands, Congress required approximately one quarter of the reservoir area above the Dam to be reserved for the paramount use of the Colville Confederated Tribes and the Spokane Tribe for hunting, fishing, and boating purposes.

B. Historical Discharges to the Columbia from the Trail Smelter

By any measure, the quantity of hazardous substances discharged from the Trail Smelter is staggering. It has been reported, for example, that the smelter discharged well over 100,000 tons of slag annually into the Columbia River. EPA has estimated that the smelter discharged more than 13 million tons of heavy metals-tainted slag into the Columbia. Further, a 1996 Report from Teck Cominco indicates that its discharges into the Columbia River from 1980–1996 averaged as high as 18 kg/day of arsenic, 62 kg/day of cadmium, 200 kg/day of lead, 4 kg/day mercury, and 7400 kg/day of zinc into the Columbia. Additionally, Teck Cominco's related fertilizer plant operations contributed up to an additional 4 kg/day of mercury. By way of context, as late as 1994 and 1995, the Trail Smelter was discharging more copper and zinc into the Columbia River than the cumulative totals of all permitted U.S. discharges for those materials.

Environmental studies have demonstrated elevated levels of arsenic, cadmium, lead, zinc, and organochlorines in sediments and fish in Lake Roosevelt. The United States Geological Survey ("USGS") has reported that the Trail Smelter is the source of most of the contaminants found, and that slag from the smelter is weathering and breaking down and metals in slag are contaminating the river both on the surface, and deeper into bed sediments. Materials released in this weathering and decaying process include arsenic, cadmium, copper, zinc and lead. Characteristics of liquid metal wastes and mercury are also present in sediments.

Studies further show that these contaminants pose a risk to aquatic life including benthic organisms. Once in the food chain, these contaminants biomagnify as they work their way up the food chain, posing risks to fish species, and humans. In fact, the Washington State Department Health issued an advisory against consumption of walleye from the Upper Columbia River Basin due to elevated levels of mercury. In addition to human exposure pathways from deposition in sediments, bio-uptake by fish, plants, and other organisms and direct ingestion of water from the Columbia River and Lake Roosevelt, scientific reports indicate that when the sediments become exposed to air (as they often do as a result of the Grand Coulee Dam's operations) they threaten human health via fugitive air emissions.

C. Pakootas: Procedural Background

Following up on earlier studies that demonstrated elevated levels of certain metals in Lake Roosevelt sediments, on August 2, 1999, the Colville Tribes petitioned the EPA to conduct a preliminary assessment to investigate the human health and environmental risks associated with the presence of hazardous substances in the Upper Columbia River south of the Canadian border to the Grand Coulee Dam (the UCR Site). In early 2000, EPA granted the Colville Tribes' Petition, and began multiple preliminary assessments.

In early 2003, EPA completed its assessments of the UCR Site, and pursuant to CERCLA's Hazard Ranking System found that the Site was eligible for listing on the National Priorities List—as one of the nation's most contaminated sites. At the same time, EPA initiated informal settlement discussions with Teck Cominco in an effort to enter an Administrative Order on Consent ("AOC") whereby Teck Cominco's American subsidiary would conduct a Remedial Investigation and Feasibility Study.

Within six months, EPA concluded that informal negotiations were not progressing as hoped, and it issued a Special Notice triggering formal negotiations. In response, Teck Cominco offered to pay up to $13 million for independent studies, but refused to submit itself to the Superfund process. Following the break-down of these formal negotiations, on Dec. 11, 2003, EPA issued a Unilateral Administrative Order under section 106 of CERCLA directing that Teck Cominco investigate the extent of contamination throughout the site and develop alternatives to remediate the contamination.

Consistent with its early position that it was not subject to CERCLA liability that resulted from its activities in Canada, Teck Cominco soon enlisted the assistance of the Canadian Government. On January 8, 2004, Canada sent a diplomatic note to the U.S. State Department, in which the Canadian Embassy requested that EPA rescind the UAO and instead work with Teck Cominco toward a "mutually acceptable cleanup plan." The diplomatic note also made clear Canada's position that the U.S. had overstepped its authority, stating: "Canada does not believe that CERCLA applies to Teck Cominco Metals." While Teck Cominco continued to reiterate its offer to have its wholly owned, U.S.-based corporate affiliate address potential risks and investigate and fund appropriate cleanup related to the company's operations, it refused to comply with the UAO. At the same time, Teck Cominco remained engaged in the war for hearts and minds, asserting that its discharges of slag presented no real problem and that EPA and others have misrepresented the risks.

D. The Battle is Joined: The Pakootas Citizen Suit

Faced with Teck Cominco's refusal to comply with the UAO, two individual members of the Colville Tribes, Joseph Pakootas and D.R. Michel, initiated a citizen's suit under section 310(a)(1) of CERCLA to enforce the UAO. Teck's response was predictably hostile, and after diplomatic and lobbying efforts failed to convince EPA to rescind the UAO, Teck moved to dismiss the case. Arguing that that EPA's actions were "extraterritorial," "unsupported by [CERCLA's] language, and inconsistent with its provisions," Teck argued that the court lacked subject matter and personal jurisdiction, and in the alternative, that the plaintiffs had failed to state a claim for relief under CERCLA. In sum, Teck Cominco argued that CERCLA has no reach to parties whose conduct took place outside of the U.S., even if the effects of those actions created a Superfund site in the United States. The State of Washington subsequently intervened in support the citizen's suit enforcement of the UAO, and to defend against Teck Cominco's motion to dismiss.

VI. A Border Shield? Does the Trail Smelter's Location in Canada Bar the Application of CERCLA to Teck Cominco?

Teck Cominco and several of its amici supporters argue that even if CERCLA would apply were the smelter located just ten miles downstream, on the American side of the border, the presumption against extraterritorial operation of United States' law precludes its application in Pakootas . . . .

A. Is the Presumption Against Extraterritoriality Even Triggered In Pakootas?

CERCLA is a remedial statute, and its focus is "decidedly domestic." Congress's unmistakable goals were to facilitate the cleanup of the most hazardous waste sites in the United States, and to hold those who contributed to the problem responsible for the costs of cleanup. As explained above, the President's authority to issue a section 106 unilateral order, and CERCLA's corresponding liability provisions of section 107, are triggered by the "release" or "threatened release" of hazardous substances from a facility. "Release" is broadly defined to mean any "spilling, leaking, pumping, pouring . . . or disposing into the environment," and includes passive migration of hazardous substances. Tellingly, Congress defined "environment" as the waters, land and air under the management authority of the United States, within the United States, or under the jurisdiction of the United States. In other words, Congress specifically conditioned CERCLA liability on "releases" of hazardous substances into the environment of the United States.

As the facts of Pakootas make clear, CERCLA is being applied to the Lake Roosevelt Upper Columbia River Site—a site which is located entirely within the United States. The EPA concluded that releases from that site "may present an imminent and substantial endangerment to public health or welfare or the environment." Those releases are, by definition, located entirely within the United States. The UAO is likewise directed at remedial activities that will take place wholly in the United States. Teck's liability under CERCLA is connected solely to the releases of hazardous substances that are occurring currently within the United States, not its discharges into the Columbia River in Canada . . . .

Interestingly, Canadian courts have agreed. On at least two separate occasions, Canadian courts have enforced judgments obtained against Canadian companies under CERCLA. The Canadian court in United States v. Ivey, for example, made clear that it did not view CERCLA enforcement against a Canadian PRP as the extraterritorial application of U.S. law. Adopting the reasoning of the lower court, the Court of Appeals added that in applying CERCLA to the Canadian company, the United States was not trying to regulate in Canada:

[t]he United States did not seek to enforce any laws against extraterritorial conduct. It simply sought financial compensation for actual costs incurred in the United States in remedying environmental damage inflicted in the United States on property in the United States. It is no extension of U.S. sovereign jurisdiction to enforce its domestic judgments against those legally accountable for an environmental mess in the United States by reason of their ownership or operation of American waste disposal sites.

As in *Ivey*, in Pakootas, there is no enforcement against extraterritorial conduct, and therefore the presumption shouldn't even be triggered . . . .

. . .

Notes and Comments

1. Did you find the author's argument persuasive that EPA's issuance of the CERCLA UAO to Teck Cominco was *not* an extraterritorial application of domestic law? It is important to note that the Ninth Circuit Court of Appeals apparently found the argument persuasive, specifically citing the article and adopting its analysis in concluding that "applying CERCLA here to the release of hazardous substances at the Site is a domestic, rather than an extraterritorial application of CERCLA, even though the original source of the hazardous substances is located in a foreign country." *Pakootas v. Teck Cominco Metals, Ltd.*, 452 F.3d 1066, 1079 & no.5 (9th Cir. 2006), *cert denied*, 128 S. Ct. 858 (2008).

2. Why isn't EPA the plaintiff in this litigation? Note that after issuing the UAO to Teck Cominco, EPA declined to seek enforcement of the UAO in federal court, as CERCLA would allow, despite Teck's refusal to comply with the UAO. Why do you suppose EPA declined to seek judicial enforcement, even after the Ninth Circuit affirmed the validity of the UAO?

3. Who is Joseph Pakootas, the lead plaintiff in this case? How do you imagine he was able to establish standing to sue in this case, based upon the facts provided in the article excerpt and the principles of standing established in Chapter 2?

4. Following the Ninth Circuit's reasoning and decision in *Pakootas*, how else might the domestic application of U.S. environmental law help address international problems? Consider in this regard, for example, ESA § 9, 16 U.S.C. § 1538(a) (restricting trade of endangered species "in interstate or foreign commerce"); RCRA § 3017, 42 U.S.C. § 6938 (banning export of hazardous wastes except under specified conditions); TSCA § 13(a), 15 U.S.C. § 2612 (a) (banning import of "any chemical substance, mixture, or article" that "fails to comply with any rule in effect" under TSCA).

Chapter 12

Implementing Environmental Requirements: The Fundamentals of Environmental Permitting

Permitting is at or near the center of environmental law. The seemingly abstract requirements of environmental law have real-world consequences when a facility or activity regulated by a particular environmental statute requires a permit (often called a license) in order to be operated or conducted. In fact, statutory requirements to obtain a permit for many facilities or activities represent a key change brought by modern environmental law. In a 1974 Oregon case, for example, a court held that a hazardous waste disposal facility in a remote area was not a common law public nuisance, but lacked the statutorily required permit. *See Oregon Dep't of Envtl. Quality v. Chemical Waste Storage and Disposition, Inc.,* 528 P.2d 1076 (Or. App. 1974). Over and over, permitting is where environmental law meets the real world.

A majority of the most important federal environmental statutes require that a person obtain a permit to engage in an activity regulated by that statute. For example, permits are required for:

- the treatment, storage, and disposal of hazardous waste under the Resource Conservation and Recovery Act (RCRA), 42 U.S.C. § 6925,

- the discharge of a pollutant under the Clean Water Act's National Pollutant Discharge Elimination System (NPDES), 33 U.S.C. §§ 1311(a), 1342(a), 1262(12); *Dubois v. U.S. Department of* Agriculture, 102 F.3d 1273, 1294 (1st Cir. 1996) ("The most important component of the Act is the requirement than an NPDES permit be obtained.");

- the discharge of a pollutant because of "dredge and fill" activities under the Clean Water Act, 33 U.S.C. §§ 1311(a), 1344(a), 1362(12);

- the construction of any "major emitting facility" of air pollutants in any attainment or unclassifiable area under the Clean Air Act, 42 U.S.C. § 7475(a)(1);

- the construction and operation of new or modified major stationary sources of air pollution in nonattainment areas under the Clean Air Act, 42 U.S.C. §§ 7502(b)(5), 7503; and even

- the "incidental taking" of endangered species under the Endangered Species Act, 16 U.S.C. § 1539.

To be sure, permits are not required under all federal environmental laws. The two most prominent exceptions are the National Environmental Policy Act (NEPA), which requires preparation of an environmental impact statement prior to any major federal action significantly affecting the quality of the human environment, and the Comprehensive Environmental Response, Compensation, and Liability Act (CERCLA), which imposes liability on persons for certain releases or threatened releases of hazardous substances that cause the incurrence of response costs. Still, these statutes are in the minority of major federal environmental laws.

Good state permitting programs are an essential feature of the cooperative federalism model on which most of these federal environmental laws are based. Under the Clean Air Act, the Clean Water Act, and RCRA, states are allowed to continue to administer their own regulatory programs if they can demonstrate that these programs will conform to federal law. The federal government does not categorically require states to do so, but it rewards them with substantial federal funding and regulatory discretion if they do. Among the most important things a state needs to demonstrate is the adequacy of its permitting program. In order for a state to run its own NPDES program under the Clean Water Act, for example, the state must demonstrate to EPA that it meets nine different requirements. Nearly every one of these requirements pertains to permitting. The state must demonstrate that it has the authority and ability to do all of the following:

- "issue permits" that "apply, and ensure compliance with," requirements of the Clean Water Act;

- ensure "that the public (and any other state the waters of which may be affected) receive notice of each application for a permit and ... provide an opportunity for public hearing before a ruling on each application";

- ensure that EPA gets notice and a copy of each permit application;

- ensure that any state "whose waters may be affected by the issuance of a permit may submit written recommendations to the permitting State";

- ensure that "no permit will be issued" if the U.S. Army Corps of Engineers determines that such permit would substantially impair anchorage or navigation in navigable waters;

- "abate violations of the permit or the permit program"; and

- ensure that any permit for a publicly owned treatment works has an effective pretreatment program for any significant industrial or other source introducing pollutants into the system. 33 U.S.C. § 1342(b).

Similarly, if states seek to run their own permitting programs under the Clean Air Act, they must demonstrate to EPA that their programs meet detailed requirements for, among other things, permit applications, monitoring and reporting, payment of an annual fee, adequate personnel and funding, and "[a]dequate, streamlined, and reasonable" permit application and public notice procedures. 42 U.S.C. § 7661a(b).

Many of the most important cases in environmental law involve attempts to enforce a permit requirement for a specific activity, particularly the deposit of dredge-and-fill material in wetlands. Nearly all of the major cases testing the boundaries of the federal government's authority to regulate the deposit of dredge and fill materials in wetlands, for example, involve landowners who did not get permits under the Clean Water Act prior to conducting their activities. These involve "sidecasting"—piling excavated dirt on either side of a ditch that was being used to drain a wetland, *United States v. Deaton*, 209 F.3d 331 (4th Cir. 2000); "deep ripping" of wetlands, *Borden Ranch Partnership v. U.S. Army Corps of Engineers*, 261 F.3d 810 (9th Cir. 2001); wetlands adjacent to navigable waters, *United States v. Riverside Bayview Homes, Inc.*, 474 U.S. 121 (1985); wetlands in isolated gravel pits, *Solid Waste Agency of Northern Cook County v. U.S. Army Corps of Engineers*, 531 U.S. 159 (2001); and wetlands where the nearest navigable waters were 11 or more miles away, *Rapanos v. United States*, 547 U.S. 715 (2006).

Permitting also plays a major role in the enforcement of environmental law. As will be seen, governmental agencies use the permitting process to ensure that proposed facilities and activities are willing and able to comply with the applicable statutes and regulations. Many of these facilities and activities, moreover, will never be subject to any significant enforcement action because they will operate in compliance with their permit. For those facilities and activities, in particular, the permitting process itself has a larger impact on their compliance with environmental law than any formal enforcement action.

Permit requirements make a regulatory program more transparent, effective, and enforceable. Prior to the 1990 Clean Air Act amendments, the statute had been enforced largely through state implementation plans (SIPs). The 1990 amendments, however, require permits for all major stationary sources of air pollution. The Senate Environment and Public Works Committee, which played a major role in drafting these amendments, explained the change as follows:

> Title V of the bill adds a new Part B to Title III of the Act. The Clean Air Act currently contains no explicit Federal requirement for sources of air pollution to obtain an operating permit. This is a serious gap in the current Act. Operating permits are needed to (1) better enforce the requirements of the law by applying them more clearly to individual sources and allowing better tracking of compliance, and (2) provide an expedited process for implementing new control requirements.

> The failure of the current Act to require operating permits puts it at odds with the other major environmental statutes . . . .

S. Rep. No. 101-228, 101st Cong., 1st.Sess. 346 (1989).

The Committee identified several benefits of adding a permitting program, including the following:

> The first benefit of the Title V permit program is that, like the CWA program, it will clarify and make more readily enforceable a source's pollution control requirements. Currently, in many cases, the source's pollution control

obligations—ranging from emissions controls and monitoring requirements to recordkeeping and reporting requirements—are scattered throughout numerous, often hard-to-find provisions of the SIP or other federal regulations . . . .

The air permit program will ensure that all of a source's obligations with respect to each of the air pollutants it is required to control will be contained in one permit document . . . .

This system will enable the State, EPA, and the public to better determine the requirements to which the source is subject, and whether the source is meeting those requirements. Better enforcement will result for all air pollution requirements, including SIP limits, new source performance standards, hazardous air pollution control requirements, and acid deposition limits. In addition, this system will benefit stationary sources by providing greater certainty as to what their pollution control obligations are. Permits will also clearly identify baseline requirements for each source, facilitating emissions trading.

Another benefit of the permit program—which will accrue to regulated sources—is the simplification and expediting of procedures for modifying a source's pollution control obligations. In general, under the current Act, for sources subject to a SIP, the vast majority of changes in the source's pollution control obligations, no matter how minor, must be developed by the State and then approved or disapproved by EPA through informal, notice-and-comment rulemaking . . . This "double-key" system has long been recognized as being laborious and resource-intensive, and has led to unacceptably long delays in EPA action on even relatively minor SIP revisions . . . .

Id. at 347–48; *See also* U.S. EPA, 1990 Clean Air Act Amendment Summary: Title V, https://www.epa.gov/clean-air-act-overview/1990-clean-air-act-amendment-summary-title-v (last visited July 14, 2016) (similar explanation of benefits of Title V permitting program).

In spite of its importance, permitting is not well understood by law students as a conceptual system. Professors Eric Biber and J.B. Ruhl lament that "the law school curriculum is virtually devoid of *permitting* as a topic of study," and that even a law student who focuses his or her curriculum choices on administrative law and a regulated field such as environmental law could easily graduate with very little exposure to regulatory permitting systems and the design of permits. Eric Biber & J.B. Ruhl, *The Permit Power Revisited: The Theory and Practice of Regulatory Permits in the Administrative State*, 64 Duke L.J. 133, 152–53 (2014) (emphasis in original).

This chapter, which is intended to help correct that omission, provides an overview of the permitting process in environmental law. It has two parts. The first part explains what a permit is, distinguishing between specific permits and general permits. It also provides an overview of the permitting process and explains the role of lawyers in that process for several different types of clients. The second part explains six permitting processes in greater detail—the Clean Air Act's prevention of significant deterioration

(PSD) permitting program for attainment areas or unclassifiable areas; the Clean Air Act's program permitting process for nonattainment areas; RCRA's permitting process for treatment, storage, and disposal facilities; the Clean Water Act's NPDES permitting process; the Clean Water Act's permitting process for dredge-and-fill activities; and the Endangered Species Act permitting process for incidental take permits.

I. A Conceptual Overview of Environmental Permitting

A. What Is a Permit?

In broad terms, a permit can be understood is "an administrative agency's statutorily authorized, discretionary, judicially reviewable granting of permission to do that which would otherwise be statutorily prohibited." *Id.* at 146. The permit must be statutorily authorized; the authority to provide or withhold this approval is too important to be left to administrative regulation or agency authority alone. The approval or denial of a permit application must involve some discretion or judgment on the part of the reviewing agency; otherwise there is nothing to decide, and no need for a permitting process. In accordance with basic administrative law, the approval or denial of a permit application is subject to judicial review. Finally, statutes requiring permits all forbid the facility or activity in question unless the person operating the facility or conducting the activity has first obtained a permit from the appropriate governmental agency. It does not matter if there has been compliance with all other relevant statutes and regulations. Operating without a permit is a separate violation of law. *Id.* at 146–49.

If you have a driver's license, you already have some experience with a permitting process. Under each state's statutes, you cannot lawfully drive unless you have a license from the state Department of Transportation, the state Bureau of Motor Vehicles, or a similar agency. You had to apply for the license and pass both a written test and a driving or road test in order to get the license. On the written test, the examining agency makes a judgment about what questions to ask, and what counts as a passing grade. On the driving or road test, the examiner makes a judgment about whether, based on what he or she experienced of your actual driving, you should be given a license. There is also an appeals process for unsuccessful applicants.

In your Property class, there is a very good chance that you learned about special exceptions or conditional uses as part of your coursework on land use and zoning. A special exception, as you may recall, is a use permitted by a municipality's zoning ordinance if certain specified criteria are met. To obtain a special exception, "the owner must apply for a special permit to obtain authorization for the use." JOSEPH WILLIAM SINGER, PROPERTY § 13.3.3 (3d ed. 2010). For the zoning hearing board or zoning board of adjustment to approve the special exception, the owner's application must demonstrate that the owner will meet the specified criteria. A special exception differs from other uses that are simply authorized in a zoning ordinance, and that do not require specific prior approval. Special exceptions are ordinarily reserved for uses, such as schools or apartment buildings in an area zoned for single-family residences, where the municipality believes that a permitting process will better enable it to limit any adverse effects. *Id. See, e.g., Cope v. Inhabitants of Town of Brunswick*, 464 A.2d 223 (Me. 1983) (multi-unit apartment buildings in "suburban A residential" zone).

Permitting and regulation are different concepts. Some activities are regulated but do not require a permit. Under RCRA, for example, there are recordkeeping, labeling and other requirements for the generation and transportation of hazardous waste. 42 U.S.C. §§ 6922 & 6923. But neither the generation nor the transportation of hazardous waste requires a RCRA permit. While an entity must follow the applicable requirements for such activities, it does not need to get prior approval from a government agency to do so. On the other hand, the treatment, storage, or disposal of hazardous waste does require a permit under RCRA. 42 U.S.C. §§ 6925. It is not enough to comply with the applicable requirements.

It is helpful to understand two contrasting types of permits—specific permits and general permits. Biber and Ruhl, *The Permit Power Revisited*, at 140 & 229. A specific permit is based on an application setting out the facts and circumstances of a particular person and its proposed facility or activity, and is issued for that specific person, facility, or activity. The driver's license and special exception (or conditional use permit) are examples of specific permits. Most of this chapter is about specific permits in environmental law, which involve individualized determinations by regulatory agencies and are intended to prevent significant adverse environmental impacts. The agency decision is ordinarily delivered through approval or denial of a permit application.

The second type of permit, the general permit, is issued by an administrative agency for specific classes of facilities or activities, and allows persons to operate such facilities or engage in such activities so long as they comply with the requirements of the general permit. General permits tend to cover activities where the potential for environmental harm is relatively small, and are intended to reduce the administrative burden of a specific permit for both the regulated entities and the government. Depending on the general permit, these persons may or may not need to even notify the agency in advance. When prior notice is required, the agency ordinarily has some ability to require additional information or modify or even prohibit the proposed activity. (When prior notice to the regulatory agency is not required, a general permit is difficult to distinguish from ordinary regulation.) General permits are ordinarily issued through an administrative regulation that applies to the entire class of affected persons and activities.

A basic question, for specific and general permits, is determining which agency or agencies has (or have) authority over the permitting process. The "Ghostbusters" question ("Who you gonna call?"), while not a model of good grammar, captures the point precisely. There may be one permit involving only a single agency, one permit involving two or more agencies, or several permits involving several different agencies; for example, a permit from the U.S. Army Corps of Engineers, and two permits from a state environmental agency. For each permit process, you need to know not only the agency involved, but also, if possible, the specific individuals in the agency who have responsibility for that process, and their geographic location.

B. Specific Permits

Specific permitting has important consequences for all of the major players in the world of environmental law. For the government, the permit application process provides an opportunity to review the proposed activity before it has even occurred, determining whether it will comply with applicable statutes and regulations, requiring corrections or changes before the application can be approved, or denying the application if does not demonstrate that the proposed activity will comply with applicable law. For regulated parties, the permit application process must be built into the timing of any proposed project, and presents an enormous hurdle that must be passed in order for the project to even be constructed. For affected citizens and the public, the permit application process is an opportunity to understand what is being proposed, to suggest changes to the permit application, and/or marshal support for or opposition to the proposed activity.

Specific permitting involves a determination of whether the proposed facility or activity requires any permits, and an understanding of the applicable operating requirements. It also requires an understanding of the permit application process, public notice and opportunity to comment, and approval or denial criteria for the application. Permit decisions are subject to judicial review, as already noted. Formal enforcement by the government (and in some cases through citizen suits) is an available option for permitted facilities that are not complying with their permit or other applicable laws.

1. Applicability Determination

Before a permit application is even prepared or filed, the person proposing the facility or activity must first make a determination of whether the facility or activity requires one or more permits in order to proceed lawfully. This determination is particularly important for a new facility or activity for which no previous permits have been issued. But it is also important for modifications of ongoing facilities or activities. If there is already a permit, does the permit need to be modified? If there is not already a permit, does the modification trigger a requirement to first obtain a permit?

As you have seen elsewhere in this book, lawyers typically make determinations about the applicability of specific statutory permitting programs by looking carefully at statutory and regulatory language about what constitutes an activity requiring a permit, including definitions. For example: Does the facility or activity involve a point source discharge of pollutants into waters of the United States from a point source? If so, is this facility or activity covered by any exceptions?

This determination has significant consequences. If a permit is required, the proposal cannot go forward without it, and the permit application process involves time, money, and uncertainty. On the other hand, operating without a permit is unlawful, and subjects a proposed activity to the risk of an administrative or judicial order enjoining the activity, civil penalties, and even criminal penalties.

2. Operating Requirements

If a permit is required, the next important step is to determine the operating requirements or performance standards for the facility or activity. The operating requirements are the rules that must be followed when the facility is actually operating or the activity is being conducted. The major focus of the permit application process is to ensure that the proposed facility or activity will operate in accordance with these requirements. The requirements for each permitting program are somewhat different, and are covered in greater detail elsewhere in this text. Under the Clean Air Act, a stationary source cannot emit more air pollution than is allowed by the relevant emission standards and other requirements. Under the Clean Water Act, a point source cannot discharge effluent in concentrations that exceed the applicable effluent limitations and other requirements. Under RCRA, a hazardous waste treatment, storage, or disposal facility must be operated in accordance with a series of strict design requirements.

3. Permit Application Requirements

The permitting process typically begins with a permit application, which essentially is a formal written request that an agency issue a permit, and the applicant's justification for the issuance of a permit. (Many agencies require or encourage a pre-application conference, which can clarify and resolve major issues in advance.) Application requirements are often expressly stated in the agency's authorizing statute or regulations. It is not enough for the applicant to assert that the facility will comply with applicable statutes and regulations, including operating requirements. The applicant must explain how the facility or activity has been planned and designed, and explain in detail how that particular plan and design will comply with the applicable operating requirements. Under many federal and state laws, the applicant must also pay a specified fee as part of the application.

Thus, permit application requirements typically include information about the applicant itself, the location and operation of the facility or activity, and the specific technologies or techniques that the applicant will employ to comply with the relevant law if the permit application is approved. Permit applications also tend to include a great deal of scientific and technical information, including information about the site (such as maps and drawings), engineering design specifications and calculations, plans for installation and construction of various pollution control and prevention facilities, and biological information about the habitat and characteristics of relevant species. The quality of the scientific and technical information submitted in a permit application has a considerable effect on the environmental protectiveness of the decisions made by that agency; more and better information tends to produce better decisions. *See, e.g.,* John C. Dernbach, *Pennsylvania's Implementation of the Surface Mining Control and Reclamation Act: An Assessment of How "Cooperative Federalism" Can Make State Regulatory Programs More Effective,* 19 U. Mich. J.L. Ref. 903, 920–27 (1986) (explaining how new federally required permit application review process improved Pennsylvania regulatory agency's ability to make technically sound decision because it increased the quality and quantity of the information required of a permit applicant to show that it is entitled to a permit).

A properly functioning permit application process will identify and resolve real and potential violations before they even occur. The subsequently permitted facility or activity will thus be designed to comply with the applicable statutes and regulations, and will more likely operate in compliance with those laws. It is much cheaper, easier, and less environmentally damaging to correct a problem that exists only in a permit application than it is to fix the same problem once a facility has been constructed or an activity is occurring. Sometimes problems exist in a permit application because the application has been prepared in a way that is rushed, careless, or is intentionally cutting corners. Sometimes the applicant does not fully understand the relevant legal rules. But even the best and most careful permit applications can benefit from an impartial governmental review, just as the best writers can benefit from a good editor. In any event, the permit application process plays a considerable role in ensuring compliance.

A critical issue in the permit application process is the completeness of the application. To allow for a proper review of the proposal, the application should include all required documentation, maps, forms, drawings, and other information. In the real world, for a variety of reasons, this often does not happen. For that reason, many permitting programs contain statutory or regulatory provisions that require the agency to determine that the application is complete — that it contains all of the required information — before formal review can begin. Formal review of an incomplete application puts an agency in the awkward position of reviewing something it cannot approve anyway and reviewing a proposal without fully understanding it. It is also likely to prolong review of the permit application. A complete application can be fully reviewed, and approved or denied, based on a full understanding of the proposal.

EPA has adopted consolidated permit application process regulations for a variety of the permitting programs it administers, including PSD, NPDES, and RCRA. 40 C.F.R. Part 124. (Use of the same permit application process requirements under several statutes means that a proposed facility that requires several permits can have the applications for those permits consolidated into a single process, and reviewed in the same manner and at the same time. 40 C.F.R. § 124.4.) Under these regulations, EPA must notify the applicant within 30 or 60 days (depending on the permit sought) whether the application is complete or not, and identify any deficiencies in the application. If the applicant fails to correct the deficiencies, EPA may deny the application. 40 C.F.R. §§ 124.3(c), (d).

4. Public Notice and Opportunity to Comment

A nearly universal feature of permitting programs in environmental law is a require-ment to provide the public with notice of a pending permit application as well as an opportunity to comment. Why does public participation matter? Professor Kenneth Kristl explains that public involvement in environmental decision-making makes the resulting decisions better in three ways:

1. Public Participation=More Knowledgeable Decisions. Public involvement can expand the knowledge base upon which decisions are made. Sometimes, the "public" (perhaps in the form of nongovernmental organizations (NGOs)) can provide expertise and "hidden" legal, environmental, financial, govern-mental, and other information that can be, and invariably is, used in govern-mental decision processes — the "knowledge and practices" of indigenous persons and local communities . . . .The members of the general public are often better suited to evaluate the on-the-ground effects of laws, policies, and actions affecting the environment where they live. When these additional sources of information are tapped, the decision maker can draw upon this wider array of information as the decision is made. Problems not known or readily apparent to a decision maker can be identified and rectified before the decision is made. In effect, allowing for public participation means that decisions can be more informed, and therefore better able to achieve sustainable results.

2. Public Participation=More Credible Decisions. Public involvement can also build support for the decisions made, thereby increasing their credibility and thereby strengthening their implementation. Public participation can help educate and inform the public. It allows the public to express its needs and concerns. When the public believes it has input into the decision-making pro-cess, and that its needs and concerns can be addressed, they will more likely support the ultimate decision made. This is especially true when the even-tual decision reflects, at least in part, suggestions and recommendations from the public; the public is more likely to respect a decision if it feels that its concerns have been taken seriously than if those concerns were ignored.

3. Public Participation=More Transparent Decisions. A decisionmaking process in which the public can offer information and critique of proposed govern-mental action helps to expose the decision-making process to the light of day, fostering transparency. Decision makers who understand that their deci-sions are subject to public review may make those decisions more carefully, utilizing all the information available, if for no other reason than to insulate those decisions from criticism. Whatever the motive, a transparent decision-making process fostered by public participation means that the resulting deci-sions are more likely to be sustainable.

Kenneth T. Kristl, *Public Participation and Sustainability: How Pennsylvania's Shale Gas Program Thwarts Sustainable Outcomes, in* Shale Gas and the Future of Energy: Law and Policy for Sustainability 125, 129–30 (John C. Dernbach & James R. May eds., Edward Elgar, 2016) (citations omitted).

EPA's consolidated permitting regulations for PSD, NPDES, and RCRA permit applications provide one example of the workings of public notice and an opportunity to comment. Once a permit application is determined to be complete, EPA or the state or tribal permitting authority must make a tentative decision to either deny the application or prepare a draft permit. All draft permits must contain relevant permit conditions, compliance schedules, and monitoring requirements. Additional requirements pertain to certain types of permits. Draft RCRA permits also must contain standards for treatment, storage, and disposal; draft NPDES permits must contain effluent limitations as well as other standards and prohibitions. 40 C.F.R. § 124.6. A separate fact sheet providing basic information about the proposed facility or activity must also be prepared. 40 C.F.R. § 124.7.

EPA or the state or tribal permitting authority must provide public notice of a tentative decision to deny an application or prepare a draft permit. The public must be given 30 days to comment on a tentative denial of a permit application or a draft permit for most permit applications, but 45 days for RCRA permit applications. Public notice must also be given at least 30 days prior to any public hearing on a permit application. 40 C.F.R. § 124.10(a), (b).

Public notice is to be given by mailing a copy of the notice to the applicant, other agencies with jurisdiction over the subject matter affected by the permit application, persons who asked to be on mailing lists for such applications, local governments with jurisdiction over the area where the proposed facility or activity would be located, and state agencies with authority over the proposed facility or activity, among others. 40 C.F.R. § 124.10(c)(1). For certain permits, notice must also be given by "publication of a notice in a daily or weekly newspaper within the area affected by the facility or activity." 40 C.F.R. § 124.10(c)(2)(i). In addition, the regulations require that notice be provided by "[a]ny other method reasonably calculated to give actual notice of the action in question to the persons potentially affected by it, including press releases or any other forum or medium to elicit public participation." 40 C.F.R. § 124.10(c)(4).

At a minimum, all public notices must contain this information:

(i) Name and address of the office processing the permit action for which notice is being given;

(ii) Name and address of the permittee or permit applicant and, if different, of the facility or activity regulated by the permit . . . .;

(iii) A brief description of the business conducted at the facility or activity described in the permit application or the draft permit . . . .;

(iv) Name, address and telephone number of a person from whom interested persons may obtain further information, including copies of the draft permit . . . ,fact sheet, and the application; and

(v) A brief description of the comment procedures . . . and the time and place of any hearing that will be held, including a statement of procedures to request a hearing (unless a hearing has already been scheduled) and other procedures by which the public may participate in the final permit decision . . . .

40 C.F.R. § 124.10(d).

The regulations emphasize the importance of raising all relevant comments during the comment period:

> All persons, including applicants, who believe any condition of a draft permit is inappropriate or that the . . . tentative decision to deny an application, terminate a permit, or prepare a draft permit is inappropriate, must raise all reasonably ascertainable issues and submit all reasonably available arguments supporting their position by the close of the public comment period.

40 C.F.R. § 124.13. After the close of the comment period, the application is to be either approved or denied. Notice is to be given to the applicant and any person who submitted written comments or requested notice of the final decision. 40 C.F.R. § 124.15(a). EPA or the state or tribal authority, whichever made the final decision, must also issue a response to the public comments that were made, specifying "which provisions, if any, of the draft permit have been changed in the final permit decision, and the reasons for the change; and" briefly describing and responding to "all significant comments" on the draft permit or tentative decision to deny the application. 40 C.F.R. § 124.17(a). When EPA is the permitting authority, the administrative record of a final permit decision for judicial review purposes includes not only the permit application, the draft permit, the fact sheet, and the final permit, but also all public comments received, the transcript of any public hearing, and the agency's response to public comments. 40 C.F.R. § 124.18(b).

This consolidated permit application process is but one of many approaches to public notice and opportunity to comment, particularly when state environmental permitting programs are included. In some permit processes, the permitting authority receives a permit application and takes public comment without issuing a draft permit or a fact sheet; the public simply comments on the application itself. There is also considerable variation in which members of the public receive notice and what types of comments are considered appropriate by the permitting agency.

Public notice requirements are often amplified in permitting situations where environmental justice issues are raised. As you recall, one of the objectives of Executive Order No. 12898, the 1994 Executive Order on environmental justice described in the Introduction, is "greater public participation." In areas where the population of low-income or minority persons exceeds a certain percentage, for example, an agency may require additional public meetings and hearings, a longer public comment period, and explicit encouragement of public participation. Where substantial segments of the affected population do not speak English, public notice should be provided in the language that this population speaks and reads. These are issues that a sensitive agency will understand and address without prompting, but they also provide lawyers and others with advocacy opportunities against agency processes that ignore them.

Professor Kristl compares and contrasts who can comment, how much time they have to comment, and limitations on the topics of comments for five separate environmental permitting programs in Pennsylvania. He examines permitting programs under state laws implementing the federal Clean Air Act, the federal Clean Water Act, the federal Surface Mining Control and Reclamation Act, as well as the program for municipal waste management facilities under the state Solid Waste Management Act. He then contrasts these with the relevant provisions of the state Oil and Gas Act as it applies to unconventional shale gas development, which involves hydrofracturing (or fracking). In the first four programs, any person is allowed to provide comments on a permit application. There is no limit on the kinds of comments they can make. The comment period is ordinarily 30 days. Kristl, at 138–39. The rules for permitting of shale gas wells, however, are different:

> *1. Limitations on Who Can Comment:* The Act recognizes surface owners of the tract on which the well will be located, owners and operators of coal mines within 1,000 feet of the well, municipalities where the well is located, storage operators, and those parties entitled to notification of the application as parties who can comment. At least implicitly, this limits who can comment to the categories of persons listed.

> *2. Limitations on Time to Comment:* Surface tract owners, coal mine owners and operators, municipalities, and storage operators have 15 days to submit comments. Parties entitled to notification of the application have only 10 days to submit their written responses to comments submitted by the others.

> *3. Limitations on Topics of Comments:* Surface owners of the tract on which the well is to be located can file written objections based on the claim that the well location violates the restrictions on well locations set forth in the statute or that material in the application is untrue is some material respect. Coal mine owners or operators can object if the owner/operator believes the well will unduly interfere with or endanger the mine. Municipalities and storage operators do not appear to have content limits on their comments, but parties entitled to notification of the application appear to be limited to those topics raised in other comments (given that they are only allowed to "submit a written response" to the comments).

Id. at 134–35 (citations omitted).

5. Approval or Denial Criteria

Approval or denial criteria are essential to any effective permitting system. These are the rules, of course, that define when a permit application can be approved or denied. Without these rules, a government agency would not likely have any rational or legally defensible basis for making a decision about the application. If a permit application process is to have any integrity or public credibility, there must be clear legal rules providing a basis for an agency to say yes or no. These rules are of enormous importance for the permitting process. The entire process—for the government, the applicant, affected citizens, nongovernmental organizations, and the public—is about whether these criteria have been satisfied.

Perhaps the two most basic approval or denial criteria are:

- The permit application is complete and accurate
- The application demonstrates that the proposed facility or activity will be conducted in accordance with applicable laws.

There may be other criteria as well. In some permitting programs, for example, agencies are required to deny applications if the applicant, or any person related to the applicant (partners, officers, parent corporations, subsidiary corporations, and affiliates), has shown a lack of willingness or ability to comply with the law. This lack of willingness or ability can be shown by current violations, past violations, or both. The premise of such requirements is straightforward: why issue a new permit to a person that is violating the same law at this or other sites, or that has demonstrated that it cannot or will not comply with the law? Where such a requirement exists, it has considerable value in fostering an attitude of continuing compliance with the law, and is often regarded as one of an agency's most important enforcement tools. Dernbach, *Pennsylvania's Implementation of the Surface Mining Control and Reclamation Act*, at 943–45.

6. Permit Terms and Conditions

Permit conditions are permit-specific requirements that are imposed to assure compliance with the applicable law and to ensure that the proposed activity is protective of public health and the environment. Some of these permit conditions are specific to the circumstances of an individual facility or activity, and others tend to apply to all relevant facilities or activities.

The driver licensing process illustrates the first category of permit condition. Some of us have a condition in our driver's license that corrective lenses are required to be worn while driving. This condition is only imposed in the licenses of people who require glasses or contact lenses, and not to all those with a drivers license. The first category of permit conditions in environmental permitting is like that.

To ensure compliance with the relevant law, a permit ordinarily contains terms and conditions that are often tailored to the specific circumstances of that facility or activity, and that may not be precisely reflected in the relevant statutes and regulations. Perhaps the most basic permit conditions require that the permittee comply with facility-specific emission limitations, effluent limitations, or other environmental requirements imposed in the permit. These performance standards continue to be applicable after the facility or activity is permitted. Thus, a permit, once issued, does more than simply require compliance with applicable statutes and regulations. It is the culmination of a decision-making process about how the relevant laws apply to, and will govern, the facility or activity in question.

Government agencies are also required to insert a variety of terms into every permit they issue. This is the second category of permit conditions. These include requirements for environmental monitoring: emissions or effluent from the facility, groundwater quality beneath or adjacent to the facility, or the condition of endangered species affected by an activity. Thus, Title V of the Clean Air Act (which applies to both PSD and nonattainment permits) provides:

> Each permit issued under this subchapter shall include . . . a requirement that the permittee submit to the permitting authority, no less often than every 6 months, the results of any required monitoring, and such other conditions as are necessary to assure compliance with applicable requirements of this chapter, including the requirements of the applicable [state] implementation plan.

Clean Air Act § 504(a); 42 U.S. C. § 7661c(a).

They also include requirements to allow agency officials to enter the property to conduct inspections; consent to enter the property is ordinarily requested in the permit application. Consent is needed to avoid Fourth Amendment search and seizure issues. The requirement to allow access is needed for agency inspectors to determine whether the facility or activity is in compliance. Other permit terms may pertain to record keeping and reporting. Section 504(c) of the Clean Air Act, for example, provides: "Each permit issued under this subchapter shall set forth inspection, entry, monitoring, compliance certification, and reporting requirements to assure compliance with the permit terms and conditions." 42 U.S. C. § 7661c(c).

Permittees may also be obliged to pay an annual fee. Under Title V of the Clean Air Act, for example, the annual fee must be "sufficient to cover all reasonable (direct and indirect) costs required to develop and administer the permit program requirements of this subchapter." Clean Air Act § 502(b)(3)(A), 42 U.S.C. § 7661a(b)(3)(A). These include:

> . . . the reasonable costs of—
>
> (i) reviewing and acting upon any application for such a permit,
>
> (ii) if the owner or operator receives a permit for such source, whether before or after November 15, 1990, implementing and enforcing the terms and conditions of any such permit (not including any court costs or other costs associated with any enforcement action),
>
> (iii) emissions and ambient monitoring,
>
> (iv) preparing generally applicable regulations, or guidance,
>
> (v) modeling, analyses, and demonstrations, and
>
> (vi) preparing inventories and tracking emissions.

Id. Such fees, of course, are intended to shift some of the costs of administering the permitting program from taxpayers to permittees. Because of budgetary constraints at the federal and state level, such fees are an increasingly used by regulatory agencies to supplement general fund revenues. The amount of the fee, of course, is often controversial.

Many permits also contain an expiration date or permit term, which means that the operator must seek reissuance of the permit to continue operating after that date. NPDES permits, for example, have a term of five years. 40 C.F.R. § 122.46(a).

7. Judicial Review

A government agency's decision to approve or deny a permit application does not end the story. Decisions to approve or deny permit applications are ordinarily appealable. A variety of legal challenges can be raised in an appeal—including failure by the applicant or the government to conform to particular performance standards or other substantive legal requirements, and failure by the agency to provide proper public notice. Some statutes require that these appeals first be brought before administrative law judges who specialize in environmental law (e.g., EPA's Environmental Appeals Board for RCRA, NPDES, and PSD and certain other permits, 40 C.F.R. § 124.19; Pennsylvania's Environmental Hearing Board for permit decisions by the Department of Environmental Protection). An unsuccessful party before one of these boards may then appeal to a specific court. Appellants who did not first raise their specific concerns during the public notice and comment period, however, are likely to find that they are foreclosed from raising those issues on appeal. The jurisdiction of the Environmental Appeals Board, for example, is generally limited to "[a]ny person who filed comments on the draft permit or participated in a public hearing on the draft permit . . . ." 40 C.F.R. § 124.19(a).

8. Enforcement

As explained above, the permit application and review process plays a significant enforcement role—ensuring that the proposed facility or activity, if approved, will actually comply with the applicable laws. But permits raise a number of unique issues for traditional or formal enforcement. First, as also explained above, operating without a required permit is a violation independent of any other possible violation of law. The failure to obtain a permit is also a relatively easy violation for the government to prove. Second, the terms and conditions of permits are fully enforceable. Any requirement that is contained in any approved permit—including any permit condition—is ordinarily subject to the full range of enforcement actions.

Third, a permit, once approved, can be revoked. Permit revocation is one more enforcement option that the government has. The Endangered Species Act, for example, authorizes the Secretary of the Department of the Interior (acting through the Fish and Wildlife Service) to revoke an incidental taking permit "if he finds that the permittee is not complying with the terms and conditions of the permit." 16 U.S.C. § 1539(a)(2)(C). If a permit is revoked, the person no longer has governmental permission to operate the facility or conduct the activity in question, and is subject to the same types of enforcement action to which it would be subject had it not obtained a permit at all.

Fourth, under many statutes, compliance with a permit is deemed to be compliance with the statute under which the permit was issued. Under the Clean Air Act, this "permit shield" covers any applicable provision of the Act if the permit "includes the applicable requirements of such provisions" or if the permit contains or summarizes the agency's determination that these provisions are not applicable. 42 U.S.C. § 7661a(f). Permit shields are often invoked by permittees in enforcement litigation, and frequently succeed.

These enforcement issues are not only relevant to actions by the government. They are also relevant to citizen suits against those operating facilities or conducting activities that are subject to permit requirements. In addition, they are relevant to citizen suits against the government for failing to carry out nondiscretionary duties. *See, e.g.,* 33 U.S.C. § 1365 (citizen suit provision of Clean Water Act).

C. General Permits

While general permits are authorized under many environmental laws, perhaps the most well-known examples of general permits are those for dredge-and-fill activities under the Clean Water Act. Section 404(e)(1) of that Act, 33 U.S.C. § 1344(e)(1), authorizes the U.S. Army Corps of Engineers to issue general permits for certain dredge-and-fill activities:

> In carrying out his functions relating to the discharge of dredged or fill material under this section, the Secretary may, after notice and opportunity for public hearing, issue general permits on a State, regional, or nationwide basis for any category of activities involving discharges of dredged or fill material if the Secretary determines that the activities in such category are similar in nature, will cause only minimal adverse environmental effects when performed separately, and will have only minimal cumulative adverse effect on the environment.

These general permits, which have a term of five years, 33 U.S.C. § 1344(e)(2), are issued through a notice-and-comment rulemaking process.

Fifty nationwide permits (NWPs) have been issued. They cover a wide range of activities that involve dredge and fill: aids to navigation; fish and wildlife harvesting, enhancement, and attraction devices and activities; oil and gas structures in the Outer Continental Shelf; hydropower projects; minor discharges; minor dredging; aquatic habitat restoration, establishment, enhancement activities; residential developments; temporary construction, access, and dewatering; cranberry production activities; maintenance dredging of existing basins; boat ramps; commercial and institutional developments, agricultural activities, stormwater management facilities; and discharges in ditches. Proposal To Reissue and Modify Nationwide Permits; Proposed Rule, 85 Fed. Reg. 35,185, 35,217 (proposed June 1, 2016) (to be codified at 33 C.F.R. Ch. 11) (the proposal to reissue and modify these permits is based on the expiration of their five-year term).

These general permits authorize more than 90 percent of the activities covered by the § 404 program. Claudia Copeland, Cong. Research Serv., The Army Corps of Engineers' Nationwide Permits Program: Issues and Regulatory Developments 2 (2012), https://www.fas.org/sgp/crs/natsec/97-223.pdf (explaining that, in 2003, "[a]pproximately 74,000 activities per year (representing 92% of the Corps' regulatory workload) were authorized by nationwide and other general permits.").

General permits, as indicated earlier, work in a very different way from specific permits. *See, The Permit Power Revisited*. The U.S. Army Corps of Engineers explains that the level of notice to the Corps as well as Corps review varies from some to none:

> For some NWPs [nationwide permits], the project proponent may proceed with the NWP activity as long as he or she complies with all terms and conditions of the applicable NWP(s), including regional conditions. When required, water quality certification and/or Coastal Zone Management Act consistency concurrence must be obtained or waived . . . .Other NWPs require project proponents to notify district engineers of their proposed activities prior to conducting regulated activities, so that district engineers can make case specific determinations of NWP eligibility. The notification takes the form of a pre-construction notification (PCN). The purpose of a PCN is to give the district engineer an opportunity to review a proposed NWP activity (generally 45 days after receipt of a complete PCN) to ensure that the proposed activity (i.e., discharges of dredged or fill material into waters of the United States and/or structures or work in navigable waters of the United States) is authorized by NWP. The PCN requirements for the NWPs are stated in the terms of those NWPs . . . .

Id. at 35,187.

D. Role of Lawyers in the Permitting Process

Permitting plays a major role in the real-world practice of environmental law. For all participants in the permit application process, lawyers help their clients understand the basic rules that govern the process, including application requirements, public notice requirements, and approval or denial criteria. They are often essential to the question of whether a permit is required at all. And they are, of course, involved in any subsequent litigation. Litigation is particularly likely for larger or more controversial proposals.

For the government, lawyers also help ensure that the relevant statutes and regulations are actually followed. They respond to questions by the applicant and the public about what particular statutory and regulatory provisions actually mean and how they are ordinarily applied. They flag legal issues that must be addressed satisfactorily for the application to be approved or denied.

For the applicant, lawyers also help clients understand what must be in a permit application to maximize the likelihood that it will be approved. They help clients understand which comments by the public or the governmental agency reviewing the application most likely require changes in the application itself in order for the application to be approved. They help clients negotiate permit conditions. In many cases, lawyers guide their clients to decisions that do not require permits at all—for example, by not building in a wetland or by limiting the facility's capacity to emit air pollutants to amounts that are below regulatory thresholds for permitting.

For affected citizens, nongovernmental organizations, and the public, lawyers are particularly important in understanding what the permit application process is about, and the limits of the government's authority. Unlike the government and the applicant, which are familiar with permit application processes based on considerable experience, affected citizens and the public often come into the permit application process for a facility or activity with no background. They simply live or work near the location of a proposed facility or activity, and their first concern understandably is what effect it could have on them. Lawyers for affected citizens and the public often look for legal flaws in the permit application to stop a proposal. When a proposal cannot be stopped, they help their clients find legal ways to make the project more acceptable, or at least less unacceptable.

Notes and Questions

1. Why do you think a permit is required under RCRA for hazardous waste treatment, storage, and disposal facilities, but not for generation and transportation of hazardous waste? When should a permit, as opposed to "mere" regulation, be required?

2. In Professor Kristl's commentary, the contrast in public notice and ability to provide comment is not between federal laws and a state law. The municipal waste management regulations in Pennsylvania are based primarily on state law, not federal law, and yet have many of the same characteristics for public notice and comment as the Clean Air Act and the Clean Water Act. Why do you think the public receives more limited notice of proposed shale gas wells in Pennsylvania, and more limited opportunity to comment, than for other proposed facilities? Do shale gas wells present fewer public health and environmental risks than municipal waste landfills?

3. General permits are authorized under § 404(e) of the Clean Water Act for certain categories of activity "when activities in such category are similar in nature, will cause only minimal adverse environmental effects when performed separately, and will have only minimal cumulative adverse effects on the environment." Yet these activities are responsible for 90 percent of the activities authorized under § 404.

   A.   What explains the prevalence of general permits?

   B.   In comparison to specific permits, what are the strengths and weaknesses of general permits?

II. Specific Permitting Programs

This section shows how the conceptual framework described above actually works for each of six major permitting programs. For each program, this section also identifies some key issues.

A. Endangered Species Act Incidental Take Permits

The Endangered Species Act prohibits any person from "taking" an endangered species, 16 U.S.C. § 1538(a)(1)(B) and (C), but § 10(a)(1)(B) authorizes the Fish and Wildlife Service to issue permits for certain takings "if such taking is incidental to, and not otherwise the purpose of, the carrying out of an otherwise lawful activity." 16 U.S.C. § 1539(a)(1)(B). The Act sets forth the requirements for what must be contained in the permit application:

> No permit may be issued by the Secretary authorizing any taking referred to in [Section 10(a)(1)(B)] unless the applicant therefor submits to the Secretary a conservation plan that specifies—
>
> (i) the impact which will likely result from such taking;
>
> (ii) what steps the applicant will take to minimize and mitigate such impacts, and the funding that will be available to implement such steps;
>
> (iii) what alternative actions to such taking the applicant considered and the reasons why such alternatives are not being utilized; and
>
> (iv) such other measures that the Secretary may require as being necessary or appropriate for purposes of the plan.

16 U.S.C. § 1539(a)(2)(A).

The approval or denial criteria for an incidental-taking permit under the Endangered Species Act are as follows:

> If the Secretary finds, after opportunity for public comment, with respect to a permit application and the related conservation plan that—
>
> (i) the taking will be incidental;
>
> (ii) the applicant will, to the maximum extent practicable, minimize and mitigate the impacts of such taking;
>
> (iii) the applicant will ensure that adequate funding for the plan will be provided;
>
> (iv) the taking will not appreciably reduce the likelihood of the survival and recovery of the species in the wild; and
>
> (v) the measures, if any, required under subparagraph (A)(iv) will be met; and he has received such other assurances as he may require that the plan will be implemented, the Secretary shall issue the permit. The permit shall contain such terms and conditions as the Secretary deems necessary or appropriate to carry out the purposes of this paragraph, including, but not limited to, such reporting requirements as the Secretary deems necessary for determining whether such terms and conditions are being complied with.

16 U.S.C. § 1539(a)(1)(B).

Notes

1. The statutory language for permit applications and approval or denial criteria provides a good opportunity to see the conceptual differences between the two kinds of rules. Compare the approval/denial language to the permit application requirement language. Notice that the permit application language describes what information must be contained in the application, and what issues must be addressed. By contrast, the approval or denial criteria set out rules for evaluating the adequacy of the application. Applicants for an incidental taking permit, for example, must specify what steps the applicant will take to "minimize and mitigate" the impact of an incidental taking, and must describe "the funding that will be available to" do so. But FWS may not lawfully approve the application unless, among other things, the applicant "will, to the maximum extent practicable, minimize and mitigate the impacts of such taking, and "ensure that adequate funding for the plan will be provided." It is not enough to describe mitigation activities and say something about how funding for those activities will be provided; the applicant must also demonstrate the adequacy of its conservation plan under these approval or denial criteria.

2. Not surprisingly, failure by the government to explain and document compliance with criteria for approval of the permit can result in the judicial invalidation of an incidental take permit. In *Sierra Club v. Babbitt*, for example, a court remanded to the Fish and Wildlife Service (FWS) the issuance of incidental take permits for high-density housing in the habitat of the Alabama beach mouse. 15 F. Supp. 1274 (S.D. Ala. 1998). Although the Endangered Species Act requires, as a condition of issuance of an incidental take permit, that the applicant "ensure that adequate funding for the [habitat conservation] plan will be provided," 16 U.S.C. § 1539(a)(2)(B)(iii), the FWS did not explain why the funding levels in the permits were adequate, had not determined what levels of funding were actually needed, and relied on speculative and unnamed sources to provide additional funding.

B. Clean Air Act Prevention of Significant Deterioration (PSD) Program for Attainment or Unclassifiable Areas

Title V of the Clean Air Act requires all major stationary sources of air pollution and certain other sources to have a Title V operating permit. Title V generally does not impose new substantive requirements, but, as noted above, it does require permit holders to conduct recordkeeping, monitoring, and reporting. *See* 40 C.F.R. Part 70 (Title V requirements for programs implemented by state or local agencies and tribes) and 40 C.F.R. Part 71 (Title V requirements for programs generally implemented by the EPA). It also, as indicated above, consolidates into one document all of the Clean Air Act requirements applicable to a particular facility. One Clean Air Act program implemented through Title V is the Prevention of Significant Deterioration (PSD) permitting program for "major emitting facilities" in attainment or unclassifiable areas.

While these areas are by definition in compliance with national ambient air quality standards, this permitting program is intended to prevent significant deterioration of the air quality in these areas. A "major emitting facility" includes stationary sources "which emit, or have the potential to emit" at least 100 tons per year of any air pollutant from a list of 28 types of stationary sources that include iron and steel mill plants, petroleum refineries, and large fossil-fuel-fired steam electric plants. It also includes "any other source with the potential to emit" at least 250 tons per year of any air pollutant. 42 U.S.C. § 7479(1).

The PSD program applies not only to new facilities, but also to major modifications of existing facilities. Construction of a major emitting facility is prohibited without a PSD permit, and construction is defined to include modification. 42 U.S.C. § 7479(2)(C). By regulation, EPA has limited application of PSD review to "major modifications." *Environmental Defense v. Duke Energy Corp.*, 549 U.S. 561 (2007) (explaining relationship between modification and major modification in EPA regulations). EPA has defined major modification of an existing major stationary source to mean "any physical change in or change in the method of operation of a major stationary source that would result in: a significant emissions increase . . . and a significant net emissions increase of that pollutant from the major stationary source." 40 C.F.R. § 52.21(b)(2)(i). A significant emissions increase, in turn, means that the modification has the potential to emit specified pollutants at a rate that is equal to or greater than a specified figure (e.g., 40 tons per year for nitrogen oxides and sulfur dioxide, 25 tons per year for particulate emissions, and 0.6 tons per year of lead). 40 C.F.R. § 52.21(b)(2)(i). A net emissions increase that exceeds these figures means that the increase in that pollutant from the modification exceeds any decrease in that pollutant from the modification by the stated amount (e.g., 40 tons per year for nitrogen oxides).

EPA has adopted detailed regulations specifying the requirements for a permit application. 40 C.F.R. § 52.21. These regulations are directed toward ensuring that the application can meet the requirements of § 165(a) of the Clean Air Act, 42 U.S.C. § 7475(a), which sets out the approval or denial criteria for a PSD permit application:

> No major emitting facility on which construction is commenced after August 7, 1977, may be constructed in any area to which this part applies unless—
>
> (1) a permit has been issued for such proposed facility in accordance with this part setting forth emission limitations for such facility which conform to the requirements of this part;
>
> (2) the proposed permit has been subject to a review in accordance with this section, the required analysis has been conducted in accordance with regulations promulgated by the Administrator, and a public hearing has been held with opportunity for interested persons including representatives of the Administrator to appear and submit written or oral presentations on the air quality impact of such source, alternatives thereto, control technology requirements, and other appropriate considerations;

(3) the owner or operator of such facility demonstrates, as required pursuant to section 7410(j) of this title [42 U.S.C. § 7410(j)], that emissions from construction or operation of such facility will not cause, or contribute to, air pollution in excess of any

(A) maximum allowable increase or maximum allowable concentration for any pollutant in any area to which this part applies more than one time per year,

(B) national ambient air quality standard in any air quality control region, or

(C) any other applicable emission standard or standard of performance under this chapter;

(4) the proposed facility is subject to the best available control technology for each pollutant subject to regulation under this chapter emitted from, or which results from, such facility;

(5) the provisions of subsection (d) of this section with respect to protection of class I areas have been complied with for such facility;

(6) there has been an analysis of any air quality impacts projected for the area as a result of growth associated with such facility;

(7) the person who owns or operates, or proposes to own or operate, a major emitting facility for which a permit is required under this part agrees to conduct such monitoring as may be necessary to determine the effect which emissions from any such facility may have, or is having, on air quality in any area which may be affected by emissions from such source; and

(8) in the case of a source which proposes to construct in a class III area, emissions from which would cause or contribute to exceeding the maximum allowable increments applicable in a class II area and where no standard under section 7411 of this title has been promulgated subsequent to August 7, 1977, for such source category, the Administrator has approved the determination of best available technology as set forth in the permit.

Key issues in PSD permitting include the following:

Maximum Allowable Increment in Air Pollution. As § 165(a) says, the application must demonstrate that "operation of such facility will not cause, or contribute to, air pollution in excess of any . . . national ambient air quality standard in any air quality control region." But in addition, operation of the facility must "not cause, or contribute to, air pollution in excess of the "maximum allowable increase or maximum allowable concentration for any pollutant in any area to which this part applies more than one time per year." As a result, any given PSD permit only gets to "use" part of the available gap between existing ambient air quality concentrations of a pollutant in a region and the air quality concentrations of that pollutant represented by the national ambient air quality standard.

For purposes of determining the maximum allowable increment (increase or concentration), the Act divides the country into three areas—Class I, Class II, and Class III. Class I areas include international parks and certain national wilderness areas, national memorial parks, and national parks. 42 U.S.C. § 7472(a). In general, areas designed by the state as attainment or unclassifiable, but that are not in Class I, are designated as Class II. 42 U.S.C. § 7472(b). To a limited degree, EPA may redesignate some areas in Class I to Class II, and some areas in Class II to Class I. 42 U.S.C. § 7474(a). EPA may also redesignate some areas as Class III areas if, among other things, it is "specifically approved by the Governor of the State," representatives of the state legislature, and municipalities representing a majority of the area so redesignated. 42 U.S.C. § 7474(a)(2)(A). In general, the lowest maximum allowable increment is in Class I areas and the highest is in Class III areas. 42 U.S.C. § 7473(b).

Best Available Control Technology (BACT). Unlike many of the technology forcing requirements of the Clean Air Act and the Clean Water Act, which are based on national determinations, the BACT determination for a PSD permit is based on a case-by-case determination. According to the Act:

> The term "best available control technology" means an emission limitation based on the maximum degree of reduction of each pollutant subject to regulation under this chapter emitted from or which results from any major emitting facility, which the permitting authority, on a case-by-case basis, taking into account energy, environmental, and economic impacts and other costs, determines is achievable for such facility through application of production processes and available methods, systems, and techniques, including fuel cleaning, clean fuels, or treatment or innovative fuel combustion techniques for control of each such pollutant. In no event shall application of "best available control technology" result in emissions of any pollutants which will exceed the emissions allowed by any applicable standard established pursuant to section 7411 or 7412 of this title.

42 U.S.C. § 7479(c).

As you saw in Chapter 5, the BACT determination is made on a facility-by-facility basis, and needs to be based on adequate equipment performance, financial, and other data. If not, the BACT determination can be remanded back to the permitting authority. *Alaska Department of Conservation v. Environmental Protection Agency,* 540 U.S. 461 (2004).

Notes and Questions

1. For another case reaching a similar result, see *In re Northern Michigan University Ripley Heating Plant,* Environmental Appeals Board, U.S. EPA, PSD Appeal No. 08-02 (2009) (remanding PSD permit for failure to comply with BACT requirements). See also John-Mark Stensvaag, *Preventing Significant Deterioration Under the Clean Air Act: The BACT Requirement and BACT Definition,* 41 Envtl. L. Rep. (Envtl. Law Inst.) 10902 (2011); John-Mark Stensvaag, *Preventing Significant Deterioration*

Under the Clean Air Act: The BACT Determination—Part II, 42 Envtl. L. Rep. (Envtl. Law Inst.) 10024 (2012) (explaining BACT determination in greater detail.

2. The other issue in *Alaska Department of Environmental Conservation v. EPA* was EPA's authority to veto a state-issued PSD permit because the state had not demonstrated that its BACT determination complied with federal law. Indeed, the case was seen primarily by the Court and outside commentators as a federalism case, not as a case about the niceties of BACT permitting. The majority drew its conclusions about EPA's authority from § 113(a)(5), 42 U.S.C. § 7413(a)(5) (authorizing EPA to issue an order prohibiting construction or modification of any major stationary source when "a State is not acting in compliance with any requirement or prohibition" relating to such sources) and § 167, 42 U.S.C. § 7477 (requiring EPA to "take such measures, including issuance of an order . . . as necessary to prevent the construction or modification of a major emitting facility which does not conform" to the specific statutory requirements for such facilities). EPA nonetheless took care to assure the Court that, on remand, it "was open to ADEC to prepare 'an appropriate record' supporting its selection of Low NOx as BACT." 124 S. Ct. at 1009. EPA's authority, in other words, was not to enforce its desired choice of BACT, but to make sure that the state adequately justified its BACT choice.

3. While the Supreme Court's decision in *Utility Air Regulatory Group v. Environmental Protection Agency*, 134 S. Ct. 2427 (2014), struck down significant parts of the "tailoring rule," it upheld EPA's authority to require BACT for greenhouse gases emitted by sources otherwise subject to PSD review in quantities of at least 75,000 tons per year of carbon dioxide equivalent. *Prevention of Significant Deterioration and Title V Permitting for Greenhouse Gases: Removal of Certain Vacated Elements*, 80 Fed. Reg. 50,199 (Aug. 19, 2015).

4. Why do you think the Clean Air Act prohibits the *construction* of any major emitting facility without a permit? Why should it not state instead that the *emission of any air pollutants* from such a facility is prohibited without a permit?

C. Clean Air Act Program for Nonattainment Areas

Like the PSD program, the Clean Air Act permit requirements for nonattainment areas are covered by Title V of the Clean Air Act. Unlike the PSD program, which is designed to minimize the increase in regulated pollutants in attainment areas or unclassifiable areas, the Clean Air permitting program for nonattainment areas is actually designed to reduce emissions of regulated pollutants. As Chapter 5 explains, the basic idea is to allow economic growth in nonattainment areas through the construction of new facilities, but only if the result is reductions in the specific pollutants for which the area is not in attainment. These facilities must do so by offsetting their additional pollution through reduced emissions—theirs or those of another person.

The Clean Air Act provides that the state implementation plan for nonattainment areas is to "require permits for the construction and operation of new and modified major stationary sources anywhere in the nonattainment area . . . ." 42 U.S.C. § 7502(c)(5). A major stationary source is "any stationary facility or source of air pollutants which directly emits, or has the potential to emit, one hundred tons per year or more of any air pollutant . . . ." 42 U.S.C. § 7602(j). A modification is "any physical change in, or change in the method of operation of, a stationary source which increases the amount of any air pollutant emitted by such source or which results in the emission of any air pollutant not previously emitted." 42 U.S.C. § 7501(4) (employing definition of modification in 42 U.S.C. § 7411(a)(4)).

Section 173(a) of the Clean Air Act, 42 U.S.C. § 7503(a), sets out the basic approval or denial criteria for Title V permit in a nonattainment area:

> The permit program required by section 7502(b)(6) of this title shall provide that permits to construct and operate may be issued if—
>
> (1) in accordance with regulations issued by the Administrator for the determination of baseline emissions in a manner consistent with the assumptions underlying the applicable implementation plan approved under section 7410 of this title and this part, the permitting agency determines that—
>
> (A) by the time the source is to commence operation, sufficient offsetting emissions reductions have been obtained, such that total allowable emissions from existing sources in the region, from new or modified sources which are not major emitting facilities, and from the proposed source will be sufficiently less than total emissions from existing sources (as determined in accordance with the regulations under this paragraph) prior to the application for such permit to construct or modify so as to represent (when considered together with the plan provisions required under section 7502 of this title) reasonable further progress (as defined in section 7501 of this title); or
>
> (B) in the case of a new or modified major stationary source which is located in a zone (within the nonattainment area) identified by the Administrator, in consultation with the Secretary of Housing and Urban Development, as a zone to which economic development should be targeted, that emissions of such pollutant resulting from the proposed new or modified major stationary source will not cause or contribute to emissions levels which exceed the allowance permitted for such pollutant for such area from new or modified major stationary sources under section 7502(c) of this title;
>
> (2) the proposed source is required to comply with the lowest achievable emission rate;
>
> (3) the owner or operator of the proposed new or modified source has demonstrated that all major stationary sources owned or operated by such person (or by any entity controlling, controlled by, or under common

control with such person) in such State are subject to emission limitations and are in compliance, or on a schedule for compliance, with all applicable emission limitations and standards under this chapter; and

(4) the Administrator has not determined that the applicable implementation plan is not being adequately implemented for the nonattainment area in which the proposed source is to be constructed or modified in accordance with the requirements of this part; and

(5) an analysis of alternative sites, sizes, production processes, and environmental control techniques for such proposed source demonstrates that benefits of the proposed source significantly outweigh the environmental and social costs imposed as a result of its location, construction, or modification.

Any emission reductions required as a precondition of the issuance of a permit under paragraph (1) shall be federally enforceable before such permit may be issued.

Where do offsets come from? Section 173(c)(1), 42 U.S.C. § 7503(c)(1), states:

The owner or operator of a new or modified major stationary source may comply with any offset requirement in effect under this part for increased emissions of any air pollutant only by obtaining emission reductions of such air pollutant from the same source or other sources in the same nonattainment area, except that the State may allow the owner or operator of a source to obtain such emission reductions in another nonattainment area if (A) the other area has an equal or higher nonattainment classification than the area in which the source is located and (B) emissions from such other area contribute to a violation of the national ambient air quality standard in the nonattainment area in which the source is located. Such emission reductions shall be, by the time a new or modified source commences operation, in effect and enforceable and shall assure that the total tonnage of increased emissions of the air pollutant from the new or modified source shall be offset by an equal or greater reduction, as applicable, in the actual emissions of such air pollutant from the same or other sources in the area.

Notes and Questions

1. Defining key terms:

The term "reasonable further progress" means such annual incremental reductions in emissions of the relevant air pollutant as are required by this part or may reasonably be required by the Administrator for the purpose of ensuring attainment of the applicable national ambient air quality standard by the applicable date. 42 U.S.C. § 7501(1).

The term "lowest achievable emission rate" means for any source, that rate of emissions which reflects —

(A) the most stringent emission limitation which is contained in the implementation plan of any State for such class or category of source, unless the owner or operator of the proposed source demonstrates that such limitations are not achievable, or

(B) the most stringent emission limitation which is achieved in practice by such class or category of source, whichever is more stringent.

In no event shall the application of this term permit a proposed new or modified source to emit any pollutant in excess of the amount allowable under applicable new source standards of performance. 42 U.S.C. § 7501(3).

2. Of all the technology-based emission limits in the Clean Air Act, the lowest achievable emission rate (LAER) is the most stringent. Why do you think this is so?

3. How would you know from an area's air quality whether a nonattainment permit is needed? A PSD permit? Could the same facility be required to obtain both a PSD and a nonattainment permit?

D. Clean Water Act NPDES Program

Section 301(a) of the Clean Water Act prohibits "the discharge of any pollutant by any person" unless that person meets one of several stated exceptions. 33 U.S.C. § 1311(a). One of those exceptions is a National Pollutant Discharge Elimination System (NPDES) permit issued under § 402 of that Act. 33 U.S.C. § 1342.

Section 402(a), 33 U.S.C. § 1342(a), provides in part:

(1) ... [T]he Administrator may, after opportunity for public hearing issue a permit for the discharge of any pollutant, or combination of pollutants, notwithstanding section 1311(a) of this title, upon condition that such discharge will meet either (A) all applicable requirements under sections 1311, 1312, 1316, 1317, 1318, and 1343 of this title, or (B) prior to the taking of necessary implementing actions relating to all such requirements, such conditions as the Administrator determines are necessary to carry out the provisions of this chapter.

(2) The Administrator shall prescribe conditions for such permits to assure compliance with the requirements of paragraph (1) of this subsection, including conditions on data and information collection, reporting, and such other requirements as he deems appropriate.

(3) The permit program of the Administrator under paragraph (1) of this subsection, and permits issued thereunder, shall be subject to the same terms, conditions, and requirements as apply to a State permit program and permits issued thereunder under subsection (b) of this section [which relates to state permit programs].

As § 402(a)(1)(A) and (B) indicate, the object of the permit application is to demonstrate that the facility will be operated in accordance with applicable technology-based effluent limitations and water quality standards described in Chapter 7. To that end, the permit application must include an explanation of the activities to be conducted that require a NPDES permit; the name, address, and location of the facility; "the principle products or services provided by the facility;" a list of other state and federal permits it has received or for which it has submitted an application; and a topographic map "depicting the facility and each of its intake and discharge structures." 40 C.F.R. § 122.21(f). If the application is for a new source or a new discharge, it must also include the expected outfall location, the "expected date of commencement of discharge," a "[d]escription of the treatment that the wastewater will receive," and "estimated daily maximum" and "daily average" discharge of conventional pollutants, nonconventional pollutants, and toxic pollutants (metals and organics) from each outfall. 40 C.F.R. § 122.21(k). The permit application requirements are somewhat different for particular types of point source discharges, including concentrated animal feeding operations, 40 C.F.R. § 122.23, stormwater discharges, 40 C.F.R. § 122.26, and silvicultural activities. 40 C.F.R. § 122.27.

The permit application process requires the reviewing authority (EPA, state, or tribe) to calculate appropriate effluent limitations for a draft and final permit. Based on the flow, volume, and concentration of pollutants in the receiving water body as well as the flow, volume, and concentration of pollutants from the discharge outfall(s), the permit application reviewer must decide if the technology-based effluent limitations applicable to a particular facility will allow the facility to meet the applicable water quality standards. A relatively small discharge into a relatively large water body may have a very different impact on compliance with water quality standards than a relatively large discharge into a relatively small water body. If the water quality standard will not be met, as Chapter 7 explains, the permitting authority will need to impose a more stringent effluent limitation as a permit condition.

If EPA, a state, or tribe issues a NPDES permit, its most important permit conditions are arguably its effluent limitations. 40 C.F.R. § 125.3. EPA regulations establish a general rule that "[a]ll permit effluent limitations, standards and prohibitions shall be established for each outfall or discharge point of the permitted facility . . . ." 40 C.F.R. § 122.45(a). Another general rule is that the "calculation of any permit limitations, standards, or prohibitions which are based on production (or other measure of operation) shall be based not upon the designed production capacity but rather upon a reasonable measure of actual production of the facility." 40 C.F.R. § 122.45(b)(2)(i). For continuous discharges, "all permit effluent limitations, standards, and prohibitions, including those necessary to achieve water quality standards, shall unless impracticable be stated" in terms of "[m]aximum daily and average monthly discharge limitations for all dischargers." 40 C.F.R. § 122.45(d)(1).

Neither the Clean Water Act nor its implementing regulations contain explicit permit application denial criteria, although the regulations recognize that EPA or a state may deny an NPDES permit application. *See, e.g.,* 40 C.F.R. § 124.6(a) and (b) (explaining procedure for tentative denial of NPDES permit application). Permit denial criteria can nonetheless be inferred from the applicant's failure to meet either of the requirements stated in § 402(a)(1)(A) and (B).

Notes and Questions

1. The permit writer has a fair amount of discretion in determining effluent limitations and other permit conditions. This discretion exists, for example, when water quality standards are not expressed in numerical terms ("20 milligrams per liter for total suspended solids") but rather in narrative terms ("Surface waters of the state must be free from deleterious materials in concentrations that impair designated beneficial uses."). In *American Paper Institute v. U.S. EPA*, 996 F.2d 346, 350 (D.C. Cir. 1993), the D.C. Circuit explained the problem that narrative criteria created for the permit writer:

> On its face, section 301 imposes this strict requirement as to all standards — i.e., permits must incorporate limitations necessary to meet [water quality] standards that rely on narrative criteria to protect a designated use as well as standards that contain specific numeric criteria for particular chemicals. The distinctive nature of each kind of criteria, however, inevitably leads to significant distinctions in how the two types of criteria are applied to derive effluent limitations in individual permits. When the standard includes numeric criteria, the process is fairly straightforward: the permit merely adopts a limitation on a point source's effluent discharge necessary to keep the concentration of a pollutant in a waterway at or below the numeric benchmark. Narrative criteria, however, present more difficult problems: How is a state or federal NPDES permit writer to divine what limitations on effluent discharges are necessary to assure that the waterway contains, for example, "no toxics in toxic amounts"? Faced with this conundrum, some permit writers threw up their hands and, contrary to the Act, simply ignored water quality standards including narrative criteria altogether when deciding upon permit limitations.

In response, EPA adopted a regulation requiring permit writers to calculate a numerical water quality criterion for the pollutant based on various sources, to establish an effluent limitation for the pollutant based on various sources, or to establish an effluent limitation for an indicator parameter for that pollutant. 40 C.F.R. § 122.44(d)(1) (vi). The court in *American Paper Institute* upheld the regulation.

2. Does it matter that there are no explicit denial criteria?

E. Clean Water Act Dredge-and-Fill Permitting Program

As previously noted, the Clean Water Act prohibits "the discharge of any pollutant by any person" unless that person meets one of several stated exceptions. 33 U.S.C. § 1311(a). Another of those exceptions is a dredge-and-fill permit issued by the U.S. Army Corps of Engineers under § 404 of the Act. 33 U.S.C. § 1344.

The Corps of Engineers regulations require the following information to be contained in a permit application:

(1) The application must include a complete description of the proposed activity including necessary drawings, sketches, or plans sufficient for public notice (detailed engineering plans and specifications are not required); the location, purpose and need for the proposed activity; scheduling of the activity; the names and addresses of adjoining property owners; the location and dimensions of adjacent structures; and a list of authorizations required by other federal, interstate, state, or local agencies for the work, including all approvals received or denials already made . . . .

(2) All activities which the applicant plans to undertake which are reasonably related to the same project and for which a DA [Department of the Army] permit would be required should be included in the same permit application. District engineers should reject, as incomplete, any permit application which fails to comply with this requirement. For example, a permit application for a marina will include dredging required for access as well as any fill associated with construction of the marina.

(3) If the activity would involve dredging in navigable waters of the United States, the application must include a description of the type, composition and quantity of the material to be dredged, the method of dredging, and the site and plans for disposal of the dredged material.

(4) If the activity would include the discharge of dredged or fill material into the waters of the United States or the transportation of dredged material for the purpose of disposing of it in ocean waters the application must include the source of the material; the purpose of the discharge, a description of the type, composition and quantity of the material; the method of transportation and disposal of the material; and the location of the disposal site. Certification under section 401 of the Clean Water Act is required for such discharges into waters of the United States . . . .

(7) For activities involving discharges of dredged or fill material into waters of the United States, the application must include a statement describing how impacts to waters of the United States are to be avoided and minimized. The application must also include either a statement describing how impacts to waters of the United States are to be compensated for or a statement explaining why compensatory mitigation should not be required for the proposed impacts . . . .

(8) Signature on application. The application must be signed by the person who desires to undertake the proposed activity (i.e., the applicant) or by a duly authorized agent . . . . The signature of the applicant or the agent will be an affirmation that the applicant possesses or will possess the requisite property interest to undertake the activity proposed in the application . . . .

33 C.F.R. § 325.1(d).

There are essentially two sets of permit approval or denial criteria. In 40 C.F.R. § 230.10(b)-(d), there is an extensive set of categorical rules. These rules work by simply prohibiting the issuance of a permit if certain standards cannot be met:

(b) No discharge of dredged or fill material shall be permitted if it:

(1) Causes or contributes, after consideration of disposal site dilution and dispersion, to violations of any applicable State water quality standard;

(2) Violates any applicable toxic effluent standard or prohibition under section 307 of the Act;

(3) Jeopardizes the continued existence of species listed as endangered or threatened under the Endangered Species Act of 1973, as amended, or results in likelihood of the destruction or adverse modification of a habitat which is determined by the Secretary of Interior or Commerce, as appropriate, to be a critical habitat under the Endangered Species Act of 1973, as amended. If an exemption has been granted by the Endangered Species Committee, the terms of such exemption shall apply in lieu of this subparagraph;

(4) Violates any requirement imposed by the Secretary of Commerce to protect any marine sanctuary designated under title III of the Marine Protection, Research, and Sanctuaries Act of 1972.

(c) Except as provided under section 404(b)(2) [33 U.S.C. § 1344(b)], no discharge of dredged or fill material shall be permitted which will cause or contribute to significant degradation of the waters of the United States . . . .

(d) Except as provided under section 404(b)(2), no discharge of dredged or fill material shall be permitted unless appropriate and practicable steps have been taken which will minimize potential adverse impacts of the discharge on the aquatic ecosystem . . . .

In addition to these categorical rules, there are also rules that require the Corps to make some decisions based on the availability of alternatives:

(a) Except as provided under section 404(b)(2), no discharge of dredged or fill material shall be permitted if there is a practicable alternative to the proposed discharge which would have less adverse impact on the aquatic ecosystem, so long as the alternative does not have other significant adverse environmental consequences.

(1) For the purpose of this requirement, practicable alternatives include, but are not limited to:

(i) Activities which do not involve a discharge of dredged or fill material into the waters of the United States or ocean waters;

(ii) Discharges of dredged or fill material at other locations in waters of the United States or ocean waters;

(2) An alternative is practicable if it is available and capable of being done after taking into consideration cost, existing technology, and logistics in light

of overall project purposes. If it is otherwise a practicable alternative, an area not presently owned by the applicant which could reasonably be obtained, utilized, expanded or managed in order to fulfill the basic purpose of the proposed activity may be considered.

(3) Where the activity associated with a discharge which is proposed for a special aquatic site (as defined in subpart E) does not require access or proximity to or siting within the special aquatic site in question to fulfill its basic purpose (i.e., is not "water dependent"), practicable alternatives that do not involve special aquatic sites are presumed to be available, unless clearly demonstrated otherwise. In addition, where a discharge is proposed for a special aquatic site, all practicable alternatives to the proposed discharge which do not involve a discharge into a special aquatic site are presumed to have less adverse impact on the aquatic ecosystem, unless clearly demonstrated otherwise. *See* 40 C.F.R. § 230.10(a); *see also,* 40 C.F.R. § 230.10(d) (containing a somewhat similar rule, prohibiting the issuance of a permit "unless appropriate and practicable steps have been taken which will minimize potential adverse impacts of the discharge on the aquatic ecosystem . . . .").

40 C.F.R. § 230.10(a).

Notes and Questions

1. The term "special aquatic site" includes not only wetlands, but also wildlife sanctuaries and refuges, mud flats, vegetated shallows, coral reefs, and riffle and pool complexes. 40 C.F.R. §§ 230.3(q-1), 230.41-.45.

2. The decision of the Corps of Engineers to issue a § 404 permit does not necessarily end the matter. Section 404(c), 33 U.S.C. § 1344(c), provides:

The [EPA] Administrator is authorized to prohibit the specification (including the withdrawal of specification) of any defined area as a disposal site, and he is authorized to deny or restrict the use of any defined area for specification (including the withdrawal of specification) as a disposal site, whenever he determines, after notice and opportunity for public hearings, that the discharge of such materials into such area will have an unacceptable adverse effect on municipal water supplies, shellfish beds and fishery areas (including spawning and breeding areas), wildlife, or recreational areas. Before making such determination, the Administrator shall consult with the Secretary. The Administrator shall set forth in writing and make public his findings and his reasons for making any determination under this subsection.

3. A key issue concerning the alternatives analysis arose in *Bersani v. U.S. Environmental Protection Agency*, 850 F.2d 36 (2d Cir. 1988). A developer (Pyramid) applied for a § 404 permit to build a mall in a 49.5-acre wetland, and the Corps approved the application. EPA vetoed the permit under § 404(c), stating that another site was "available" at the time that the developer began its search for a suitable property. The developer argued that the date of the § 404 permit application is the correct date for determining when an alternative site is "available," not the date on which it first began its search for a suitable site. In upholding EPA's decision, the Court stated:

> With regard to the language of the regulations, Pyramid reasons that the 404(b)(1) guidelines are framed in the present tense, while the market entry approach focuses on the past by considering whether a practicable alternative was available at the time the applicant entered the market to search for a site. To support its argument that the 404(b)(1) guidelines are framed in the present tense, Pyramid quotes the following language:

> "An alternative is practicable if it is available. . . . If it is otherwise a practicable alternative, an area not presently owned by the applicant which could reasonably be obtained, utilized, expanded or managed in order to fulfill the basic purpose of the proposed activity may be considered."

> 40 C.F.R. § 230.10(a)(2) (emphasis added). It then argues that EPA says "is" means "was." It cites *Gwaltney of Smithfield v. Chesapeake Bay Foundation*, 108 S.Ct. 376, 381 (1987), to indicate that the Supreme Court believes that the "most natural" reading of present tense language in § 505(a) of the Act refers only to the present and future.

> While this argument has a certain surface appeal, we are persuaded that it is contrary to a common sense reading of the regulations; that it entails an overly literal and narrow interpretation of the language; and that it creates requirements not intended by Congress.

> First, while it is true that the language is in the present tense, it does not follow that the "most natural" reading of the regulations would create a time-of-application rule. As EPA points out, "the regulations do not indicate when it is to be determined whether an alternative 'is' available," (emphasis in original), i.e., the "present" of the regulations might be the time the application is submitted; the time it is reviewed; or any number of other times. Based upon a reading of the language in the context of the controlling statute and the regulations as a whole, moreover, we conclude that when the agencies drafted the language in question they simply were not thinking of the specific issues raised by the instant case, in which an applicant had available alternatives at the time it was selecting its site but these alternatives had evaporated by the time it applied for a permit. We therefore agree with the district court that the regulations are essentially silent on the issue of timing and that it would be appropriate to consider the objectives of the Act and the intent underlying the promulgation of the regulations.

> Second, as EPA has pointed out, the preamble to the 404(b)(1) guidelines states that the purpose of the "practicable alternatives" analysis is "to recognize the special value of wetlands and to avoid their unnecessary destruction, particularly where practicable alternatives were available in non-aquatic areas to achieve the basic purpose of the proposal." 45 Fed.Reg. 85,338 (1980) (emphasis added). In other words, the purpose is to create an incentive for

developers to avoid choosing wetlands when they could choose an alternative upland site. Pyramid's reading of the regulations would thwart this purpose because it would remove the incentive for a developer to search for an alternative site at the time such an incentive is needed, i.e., at the time it is making the decision to select a particular site. If the practicable alternatives analysis were applied to the time of the application for a permit, the developer would have little incentive to search for alternatives, especially if it were confident that alternatives soon would disappear. Conversely, in a case in which alternatives were not available at the time the developer made its selection, but became available by the time of application, the developer's application would be denied even though it could not have explored the alternative site at the time of its decision.

4. The alternatives analysis under the § 230.10(a) is different from the approval or denial criteria that exist in other permitting programs, and even different from that in §§ 230.12(b)-(d). Why do you think the regulation is drafted in this way, and not in categorical terms (say, a prohibition against placing dredge-and-fill material in wetlands, regardless of whether an alternative is available)?

F. RCRA Permitting Program for Treatment, Storage, and Disposal (TSD) Facilities

Section 3005(a) of the Resource Conservation and Recovery Act, 42 U.S.C. § 6925(a), requires EPA to adopt regulations "requiring each person owning or operating an existing facility or planning to construct a new facility for the treatment, storage, or disposal of hazardous waste identified or listed under this subchapter to have a permit issued pursuant to this section."

With respect to permit applications, § 3005(b), 42 U.S.C. 6925(b), states:

Each application for a permit under this section shall contain such information as may be required under regulations promulgated by the Administrator, including information respecting—

(1) estimates with respect to the composition, quantities, and concentrations of any hazardous waste identified or listed under this subchapter, or combinations of any such hazardous waste and any other solid waste, proposed to be disposed of, treated, transported, or stored, and the time, frequency, or rate of which such waste is proposed to be disposed of, treated, transported, or stored; and

(2) the site at which such hazardous waste or the products of treatment of such hazardous waste will be disposed of, treated, transported to, or stored.

Not surprisingly, EPA's regulations for TSD permit applications are considerably more detailed. The TSD permit application must describe "activities conducted by the applicant which require it to obtain a permit under RCRA," and describe "the processes to be used for treating, storing, and disposing of hazardous waste, and the design capacity of these items." It must also include a map showing, among other things, "each of its hazardous waste treatment, storage, or disposal facilities," and "those wells, springs, other surface water bodies, and drinking water wells listed in public records or otherwise known to the applicant within ¼ mile of the facility property boundary." 40 C.F.R. § 270.13.

Other application requirements include "[c]hemical and physical analyses of the hazardous waste and hazardous debris to be handled at the facility," security procedures, a contingency plan, and a description of "procedures, structures, or equipment" that will be used to prevent contamination of water supplies, atmospheric releases, and "undue exposure of personnel to hazardous waste." The application also needs to include the closure plan for the facility, a post-closure cost estimate for the facility, and a copy of the insurance policy or other documentation providing assurance that post-closure costs (e.g., ground water monitoring, maintenance of security, and water pollution treatment) will be paid. 40 C.F.R. § 270.14. Such plans, and such information, are all needed to show that the proposed TSD facility will comply with detailed standards for operation of the facility. 40 C.F.R. ch. 264.

EPA's regulations make clear that EPA and states are authorized to deny TSD permit applications. 40 C.F.R. § 270.29. As was the case with NPDES permits, EPA or the state can deny an application that is not complete or that fails to show that the applicable statutory and regulatory requirements can be achieved.

Notes and Questions

1. Notice that much of the TSD permit application is organized around the idea of containing the wastes managed at the facility, preventing their release into the environment, and preventing adverse effects on public health and safety.

2. Many, if not most, of the TSD permits now issued are for treatment, not disposal, thanks in no small part to the land ban on the disposal of untreated hazardous waste.

3. Given the technical complexity of a TSD permit application, how can a neighborhood organization or other nongovernmental organization comment effectively?

Problems

All of the following problems occur in the (hypothetical) state of Chesapeake.

1. Eco-Car Supply is a company that makes parts and equipment for motor vehicles that get low gas mileage. The company is planning to build a new manufacturing facility in Chesapeake. This will be Eco-Car Supply's first plant of any kind in Chesapeake.

The company plans to produce its own electricity from a 75-megawatt natural gas-fired power plant. The national ambient air quality standard for carbon monoxide for an eight-hour period is nine parts per million. No more than one exceedance per year is allowed. In this region, the average concentration of carbon monoxide is 11 parts per million. The power plant would produce 2,000 tons per year of carbon monoxide and 7,000 tons per year of carbon dioxide. The company would like to advertise that it is offsetting these increased emissions by having most of its 300 employees walk to work, ride bicycles, or ride in carpools. The company has data indicating that this program would annually prevent emissions of 3,000 tons per year of carbon monoxide emissions and 4,500 tons of carbon dioxide. Chesapeake has never regulated this particular type of natural gas plant. Only one plant in the world in this class achieves lower emissions of carbon monoxide: it emits 1,000 tons and is located in Germany. EPA recently sent Chesapeake a letter expressing satisfaction with Chesapeake's progress in implementing its SIP.

What permit(s) or approval(s), if any, does the company need to obtain? What is the likelihood of obtaining these permits or approvals?

2. Zapp Batteries, Inc., is planning to build its first manufacturing plant in the state of Chesapeake. The plant would make batteries for wind turbines and solar collectors, enabling these facilities to provide electricity to the grid even when the wind is not blowing and the sun is not shining. These batteries are significantly less expensive and more durable than anything else that is now being employed outside of demonstration facilities. As a result, Zapp is working on a fast track to get this particular plant constructed. Each additional month required to build the plant could cost the company millions of dollars.

Using the air pollution control technology proposed in its current plan, the plant would emit 425 tons of nitrogen dioxide per year. The national ambient air quality standards for nitrogen dioxide are 53 parts per billion (annual) and 100 parts per billion (one hour). Chesapeake has a single air quality region, and monitoring data for the region show a concentration of nitrogen dioxide that ranges between 25 and 40 parts per billion. In selecting the 425-ton option, Zapp says it did not choose more commonly used air pollution control technologies that would reduce emissions to 900–1,000 tons of nitrogen dioxide. Zapp also says it rejected two other air pollution control options. Option 1 would reduce emissions to 325 tons per year, but is manufactured by an Iranian company (Zapp management strongly prefers not to do business with Iranian companies), is slightly more expensive, and is less reliable than the current proposal. Option 2 would reduce emissions to 75 tons per year, but is about three times as expensive as the option that Zapp prefers. Another company, Delta Corporation, is planning to shut down its existing facility, which would eliminate its current annual emissions of 300 tons of nitrogen dioxide and 200 tons of fine particulate.

What permit(s) or approval(s), if any, does the company need to obtain? What is the likelihood of obtaining these permits or approvals?

3. Save Our Community ("SOC") is an unincorporated association of approximately 200 individuals organized to oppose expansion of the 73-acre Skyline Landfill located near Ferris, Chesapeake. One purpose of SOC is to promote the protection of the wetlands in and around its members' communities. Global Waste Management ("Global") is the owner and operator of the landfill. The Skyline Landfill receives municipal waste and some industrial solid waste. Global is preparing to file an

application with the Chesapeake Department of Environmental Quality (DEQ) to expand the Skyline Landfill from 73 to 180 acres.

Some months ago, Global solicited an opinion from the U.S. Army Corps of Engineers as to whether any portion of the proposed expansion area constituted "waters of the United States" subject to the Corps' jurisdiction. The Corps made a jurisdictional determination that six or seven "ponds" located on the proposed expansion area were waters of the United States. The EPA concurred in this determination. The ponds were artificially created and formed in part through a prior owner's construction of levees to catch runoff water. Approximately 10 acres of surface water remain from the original 21 acres. Global intends to fill the 10 acres as part of its landfill expansion. Migratory birds such as ducks, herons and storks have been occasionally sighted at or near the ponds. The ponds are located about one-quarter mile from the Leopold River in the state of Chesapeake, a navigable waterway. During severe storm events, the ponds overflow and some of the overflow reaches the Leopold River, even though there are no channels to convey the water. Because of residual dampness from storm water between the ponds and the river, there are fewer trees in the area and more insects, frogs, and turtles. There are no other nearby bodies of surface water.

What permit(s) or approval(s), if any, does Global need to obtain under the Clean Water Act? What is the likelihood of obtaining these permits or approvals? Global proposes a mitigation plan that would create an alternative wetland site as part of its landfill expansion.

Assume SOC wants to stop the facility, or at least minimize any adverse environmental effects. What legal strategies should SOC pursue?

4. New Age Motors, a Chesapeake auto manufacturer, has just about completed the developmental work necessary to mass-produce a new line of solar-powered cars.

To manufacture the cars, the company is considering the purchase of an 85-acre tract near Chesapeake State Highway 3. The tract is rectangular in shape. It is bounded on the east by Highway 3, which runs north and south at that point. It is bounded on the west by the Leopold River, which also runs from north to south there.

The tract includes a large wooded area that is home to the Chesapeake box turtle, which is listed as endangered under federal law. To transport parts and materials to the factory, and to ship manufactured automobiles out, the company will have to construct a half-mile of railroad track from the main railroad line to the factory building. The main railroad line is owned and operated by Chesapeake and Western Ry. Co. The new track will cross through habitat of about eight percent of the known population of box turtles, including areas where these turtles eat and lay eggs. New Age Motors considered expansion of the existing private roads on the tract as an alternative. That alternative would require transportation of raw materials and finished cars on trucks, however; the company prefers rail transport to reduce pollution and conserve energy.

The company plans to spend $35,000 over the next three years to study the effect of the rail line on the turtle population. Chesapeake Steel, whose trustee in bankruptcy currently owns the property, had an eight-acre parking lot that New Age Motors does not plan to use; SOS has suggested that New Age Motors convert the old lot into additional habitat for the turtle. New Age Motors believes such extra efforts are not necessary. The U.S. Fish and Wildlife Service, which is part of the U.S. Department of the Interior, says the existing turtle population may be too small to withstand any additional pressure.

What permit(s) or approval(s) are required for the Chesapeake project? For each permit or approval, explain why it is required under the relevant statute(s), the likelihood that the company will be able to obtain the permit or approval under its current plans, and any conditions or other requirements that are likely to be imposed.

Index

enjoin — prohibit via injunction

effluent — liquid waste/sewage discharged
into a river or sea.

manifest system: RCRA   641